VIETNAM
AIR LOSSES

UNITED STATES AIR FORCE, NAVY AND MARINE CORPS
FIXED-WING AIRCRAFT LOSSES IN SOUTHEAST ASIA 1961-1973

CHRIS HOBSON

Midland Publishing

Contents

Vietnam Air Losses
© 2001 Christopher Michael Hobson
ISBN 1 85780 115 6

Published by Midland Publishing
4 Watling Drive, Hinckley
LE10 3EY, England
Tel: 01455 254 490   Fax: 01455 254 495
E-mail: midlandbooks@compuserve.com

Midland Publishing is an imprint of
Ian Allan Publishing Ltd

Worldwide distribution (except North America):
Midland Counties Publications
4 Watling Drive, Hinckley, LE10 3EY, England
Telephone: 01455 254 450   Fax: 01455 233 737
E-mail: midlandbooks@compuserve.com
www.midlandcountiessuperstore.com

North American trade distribution:
Specialty Press Publishers & Wholesalers Inc.
11605 Kost Dam Road, North Branch, MN 55056
Tel: 651 583 3239   Fax: 651 583 2023
Toll free telephone: 800 895 4585

Design concept and layout
© 2001 Midland Publishing

Printed in England by
Ian Allan Printing Ltd
Riverdene Business Park, Molesey Road,
Hersham, Surrey, KT12 4RG

All rights reserved. No part of this
publication may be reproduced,
stored in a retrieval system, transmitted
in any form or by any means, electronic,
mechanical or photo-copied, recorded
or otherwise, without the written
permission of the publishers.

Photograph on the title page: **Ten US Navy squadrons used the A-1H and A-1J in the light attack role during the war. This aircraft is about to be launched on an air strike from the USS *Intrepid* in May 1966. The *Intrepid* lost three Skyraiders during its 1966 war cruise.** USN

Photograph on this page: **An RF-4C Phantom of the 12th TRS has its precious film unloaded at Tan Son Nhut after a reconnaissance sortie. The scarred radome of the aircraft illustrates the wear and tear suffered by aircraft in combat.** USAF

Introduction

The Vietnam War is far enough in the past to be considered history yet recent enough to still have a deeply personal affect on millions of Americans, whether they be veterans, relatives of the dead and missing or simply US citizens. There is a growing wealth of literature on the war, especially in recent years as the pain of the war recedes and the development of the Internet has given an added impetus to publishing.

As an aviation enthusiast and historian the Vietnam War and its place in the development of air power technology, tactics and doctrine has always fascinated me. Virtually every available aircraft type and every weapon in the US arsenal, with the notable exception of nuclear weapons, was used during the war. The variety of aircraft and the multitude of roles, tactics and operations makes the Vietnam air war well worth studying. Yet perhaps because of its very specific nature, fought over mountainous or jungle terrain in a little known country against a shadowy enemy, the military lessons of the air war are sometimes intangible and difficult to relate to present day air power. Hopefully this book may, in some small way, make the air war over Southeast Asia less intangible and may point the way to further research to ensure that the lessons of the air war are not forgotten.

In reporting the facts of the war I have tried to steer clear of the politics of Vietnam, unless they have a direct effect on the air war.

Being neither an American nor a serviceman I do not feel qualified to comment on the political issues or higher strategy involved and nor is any such comment necessary in a work of this nature. This history is about men, aircraft and air operations. The more strategic aspects of the war have already been covered by many excellent authors in a host of publications. I have culled the information presented in this book from a variety of sources, both official and unofficial. Some of the sources disagree on minor points and certain information, such as that relating to many of the men listed as missing in action, may be regarded as speculative. However, I take full responsibility for any errors or inaccuracies contained in the book.

I am very aware of the sensitivity of writing about events that are so recent and in particular about the people mentioned, the memory of whom is still fresh in the minds of loved ones, friends and colleagues. It is not my intention to characterise or criticise any individual in any way and it is certainly not my intention to cause pain to relatives and friends of the deceased listed in these pages.

A number of people have assisted in the research and production of this book. My wife Alison has helped greatly by compiling the index of personnel and by providing support when needed and my son Jonathan has helped with my numerous IT and Internet-related queries and problems. Sincere thanks are also

The Helio U-10 was a rugged light aircraft with an amazing STOL performance. It was used by the USAF in the psychological warfare role and by Air America for the resupply of remote camps, operating into some of the most dangerous airstrips in the world. Twelve U-10s were destroyed in the war but only four of these were lost in action. USAF

due to Robert Daley and Peter Bird for their assistance in providing information on the C-130 Hercules and C-7 Caribou respectively. It is thanks to dedicated men such as these that superb websites on a whole variety of subjects are now available on the Internet.

This book was inspired, at least in part, by one of the men mentioned in the text, Lieutenant Colonel Harold Eugene Johnson. I knew Harry Johnson when he was a USAF exchange officer at the Royal Air Force Staff College in the late 1970s. His experience as a Wild Weasel electronic warfare officer made him a valuable asset as a military instructor but his experience as a prisoner of war made him something even more special. This book is dedicated to the dignity, bravery and sacrifice of the thousands of men like Harry Johnson who fought the war in the skies over Southeast Asia.

Chris Hobson, July 2001

Background to the Wars in Southeast Asia

The wars in Southeast Asia had their origins in the ethnic, colonial and nationalist tensions that came to a head after the end of the Second World War. Having cooperated with the Allies in the war against the Japanese, Vietnamese communists turned against their French colonial rulers in 1945. A guerilla campaign by Viet Minh communist forces against the French expanded into open warfare in September 1950 with an initial victory against the French at Dong Khe. The final crushing defeat of French forces at Dien Bien Phu in May 1954 spelled the end of French colonial rule in Indo-China and resulted in the partition of Vietnam, pending elections of a national government, under the terms of an agreement signed in Geneva. However, the elections failed to materialise and two separate states evolved; the northern Democratic Republic of Vietnam and the southern State of Vietnam. A 12-mile deep Demilitarised Zone (DMZ) at the 17th parallel separated the two states and an International Control Commission was formed to monitor the compliance of the Geneva Accords. The Superpowers gave their support to the opposing factions, the USA supporting President Ngo Dinh Diem's government in the South while China and the Soviet Union supported Ho Chi Minh's communist government in the North. In September 1954 the Southeast Asia Treaty Organisation (SEATO) was formed with the encouragement of the USA to guarantee the security of Laos, Cambodia and South Vietnam from communist aggression. The US took over military training of the armed forces in South Vietnam from the French in 1957 and provided arms and equipment to build up the Army of the Republic of Vietnam and the Vietnamese Air Force.

However, the nation-building process in South Vietnam suffered numerous setbacks, mostly caused by sectarian rivalry, ethnic conflict and corruption. The problems were made worse by the influx of over 900,000 refugees who fled from the communist-dominated North. When the two Vietnams were created many Viet Minh soldiers stayed behind in South Vietnam and later formed the National Liberation Front of South Vietnam, popularly known as the Viet Cong. To the Americans the Viet Cong, often shortened to VC or Charlie, became synonymous with the North Vietnamese Army but there were many differences in terms of organisation and equipment. Ho Chi Minh spent the first three years after the partition consolidating his authority over North Vietnam but in late 1957 guerrilla action against the government in the South commenced with assistance from the North. Guerrilla attacks and terrorist incidents increased rapidly as the Viet Cong forces in the South were supplied with arms and reinforcements from North Vietnam. Arms and men flowed into

South Vietnam along a series of roads and tracks that connected the two Vietnams through southern Laos and Cambodia and which became known as the Ho Chi Minh Trail.

As a result of the 1954 Geneva agreement Laos became an independent state with a pro-Western government but the communist Pathet Lao movement had popular support in much of the country. In 1957 the Laotian government negotiated with the Pathet Lao and declared Laos to be neutral and independent of foreign interference. Soon after an election confirmed the neutralist government in power in May 1958 it was toppled in a coup by right wing forces and the neutralists and Pathet Lao joined forces against the new government. In December 1959 the Laotian government was again showing signs of an accommodation with the Pathet Lao but a military coup removed the government and planned new elections in April 1960. The military junta won what was regarded as a rigged election and received covert military support from the USA. In August 1960 the political instability in Laos finally boiled over into outright civil war when yet another coup ousted the pro-Western government. The neutralists were once more in power in Vientiane and requested assistance from the Pathet Lao and the Soviet Union. However, in December 1960, right wing forces once more took the capital and the neutralists joined the Pathet Lao in their stronghold in the Plain of Jars, close to the border with North Vietnam.

As in Vietnam the Superpowers predictably took sides. The communist Pathet Lao were supported by the Soviet Union and North Vietnam while the right wing Royalist forces and Meo guerrillas were supported by the USA. North Vietnam in particular needed Laotian assistance in developing and keeping open the system of roads and trails that the North needed to infiltrate into South Vietnam. A Soviet airlift of arms and supplies to rebel forces in the Plain of Jars commenced in December 1960. The US reacted to the crisis in Laos by activating Joint Task Force 116 in March 1961 while the 315th Air Division's transport aircraft started to deploy to a forward base at Clark AB in the Philippines. Contingency plans were about to be put into practice to deploy thousands of American troops to Laos but the situation improved as peace talks were commenced and the Task Force was stood down.

Between May and December 1961 a 14-nation conference held in Geneva devised an accord that assured the neutrality of Laos and established a coalition government under Prime Minister Souvanna Phouma. However, the Pathet Lao and their neutralist allies took little heed of the peace accord. Having regrouped, they started a new offensive early in 1962 and by the end of March

had swept aside the Laotian government forces, surrounded Luang Prabang and were threatening Vientiane itself. JTF 116 was reactivated and US transport aircraft began flying military equipment into Thailand for stockpiling as a Marine Corps assault force sailed towards the South China Sea. On 18 May 1962 the USAF deployed the F-100-equipped 428th TFS from Cannon AFB, New Mexico to Takhli RTAB as the first of several temporary duty rotations. On the same day A-4C Skyhawks of Marine Corps squadron VMA-332 and UH-34Ds of HMM-261 arrived at Udorn. Two weeks later USAF C-130s and C-124s began flying arms and supplies directly from Clark to Vientiane airport. For several days the situation was very tense while President Kennedy took counsel on whether or not to deploy combat forces into Laos and make his stand against communism there. In the event the fighting in Laos subsided as the warring factions came towards a negotiated agreement and US forces in Southeast Asia began a gradual stand down from a war footing. The conference at Geneva made slow progress but eventually, on 23 July 1962, a Declaration on the Neutrality of Laos was signed requiring the removal of foreign troops from Laos and the monitoring of the agreement by the International Control Commission.

When President Kennedy took office in January 1961 the most pressing problems in Southeast Asia appeared to be in Laos and he soon became aware of the need to make a firm stand against communist aggression but decided that South Vietnam stood the best chance of success. However, President Diem refused to institute the political and military reforms that the USA recommended and his position as president deteriorated. In September 1961 Diem finally asked the USA for a bilateral defence treaty which opened the way for the gradual influx of American military units into South Vietnam. The first American unit, the Farm Gate air commando detachment, arrived in South Vietnam in early November followed the next month by two companies of US Army H-21C helicopters. Deployed under the guise of 'advisors' or 'trainers', these units and those that followed fought the war while attempting to train and encourage the South Vietnamese military. There were noticable improvements in the organisation and performance of the ARVN and VNAF soon after the Americans started their work. There was also a willingness to adopt new strategies and tactics including the concept of creating fortified hamlets that formed a network of bases from which operations could be mounted and protection of the local populace could be afforded.

However, despite improvements in the South Vietnamese military performance President Diem remained alienated from his people and his military. A major government defeat at the hands of the Viet Cong at Ap Bac in January 1963 and the growing repression of Buddhists throughout South Vietnam brought matters to a head later in the year. Several ARVN generals planned a coup against Diem in August but were unsure of American support at that time. However, in September the Americans announced restrictions in military and economic assistance as a consequence of Diem's actions against the Buddists and on 1 November the generals finally acted and Diem was removed from office and shot dead. Three weeks later President Kennedy was also assassinated leaving the quagmire that was to become the Vietnam War to his successors.

The first American fixed-wing aircraft lost in South Vietnam was a Ranch Hand C-123 Provider spray aircraft that crashed on 2 February 1962. Eight Ranch Hand C-123s were lost during the war as they pursued a highly controversial defoliation programme. USAF

Chapter One

1961 to 1964

Civil War in Laos and Early Operations in South Vietnam

23 March 1961

C-47B 44-76330 315 AD Detachment on TDY from Osan,
USAF, Vientiane
1Lt Ralph Wayne Magee (KIA)
1Lt Oscar Branch Weston (KIA)
2Lt Glenn Matteson (KIA)
SSgt Alfons Aloyze Bankowski (KIA)
SSgt Frederick Thomas Garside (KIA)
SSgt Leslie Verne Sampson (KIA)
Maj Lawrence Robert Bailey,
US Army (POW)
WO1 Edgar Wilken Weitkamp, US Army (KIA)

During the increasingly tense situation in Laos in 1960 the USAF had detached a small number of aircraft from the 315th AD to monitor the Soviet airlift and locate airfields that were being constructed with Soviet and North Vietnamese assistance. On 23 March 1961 a C-47 took off from Vientiane for a flight to Saigon via the Plain of Jars region where it was intended to gather radio intelligence from several Soviet-built airstrips in the Xieng Khouangville area. The aircraft was hit by Pathet Lao AAA or small arms fire and lost a wing and crashed about 4 miles north-west of Phon Savan airfield, Xiangkhoang province. Maj Bailey and WO1 Weitkamp were assigned to the Army Attaché Office at Vientiane. Maj. Bailey, who always wore a parachute when he flew, jumped from the falling aircraft and was captured. He was flown in an An-2 Colt biplane to Sam Neua, the Pathet Lao head-quarters near the border with North Vietnam, and spent 17 months as a POW until released on 15 August 1962 following the signing of the Geneva Accords on Laos. This was the first US aircraft lost in action and the first US casualties in Southeast Asia since the Second World War. In July 1991 a joint US-Lao investigation team located the graves of the seven airmen who died and recovered identifiable remains of Garside, Magee, Matteson and Sampson.

This was not the first hostile act commited by the Pathet Lao against a US aircraft in Laos. The US Ambassador in Laos had a VC-47, which was sometimes used for surveillance flights and it was shot at and damaged on one such flight on 23 December 1960.

Jungle Jim, Farm Gate, Ranch Hand and Mule Train

In response to communist support for nationalist insurgent movements in the 1950s and early 1960s, the US set about creating specialist counter-insurgent forces. The US Army formed its Green Beret Special Forces units and the USAF responded by recreating the Air Commandos, an organisation that had achieved considerable success in the China-Burma-India theatre during the Second World War. The 4400th CCTS was formed at Hurlburt Field, Florida on 14 April 1961 tasked with developing air operations against guerrillas and insurgents using either overt or covert military action. Code named Jungle Jim, the Squadron formed several detachments that were deployed to various trouble spots in Africa and Central America to provide training to national forces supported by the USA. Detachment 2A, code named Farm Gate, was formed in November and arrived in South Vietnam on the 14th on what was originally intended to be a six month temporary duty detachment.

Detachment 2A consisted of 151 officers and men, eight T-28s, four SC-47s and four B-26s and set up bases at Bien Hoa and Tan Son Nhut. Ostensibly the detachment was in South Vietnam to train the VNAF in counter-insurgency techniques and the aircraft flew in VNAF markings (which was a simple modification

of the US stars and bars) and had to carry a Vietnamese observer on all flights. However, within a short time of arriving in South Vietnam American airmen were flying operational missions against the Viet Cong and although training of the VNAF was undoubtedly being conducted, it was the USAF aircrew who were flying many of the operational missions. Farm Gate flew it first offensive sorties on 26 December when T-28s from Bien Hoa took part in a close air support mission.

The Farm Gate detachment was joined on 7 January 1962 by another unit, the Special Aerial Spray Flight, which consisted of six C-123B Providers converted to spray herbicide chemicals as part of a defoliation programme. The dense jungles and mangrove swamps that cover much of Southeast Asia provided ideal conditions for Viet Cong operations in that they masked their movement from the air and enabled them to move their forces with relative impunity. The modified Providers, usually flying in a tight formation to concentrate coverage, sprayed large tracts of jungle with a variety of herbicides in an attempt to reduce the foliage thereby denying its cover to the Viet Cong. Known as Ranch Hand, the Special Aerial Spray Flight flew its first mission on 10 January 1962 and the unit, which changed its designation several times over the next 10 years, became notorious due to the use of the chemical known as Agent Orange, controversy over which still rages today.

The last of the early deployments to Southeast Asia was a transport squadron of C-123 Providers that supplemented the C-47s of the VNAF. The 464th TCW deployed the 346th TCS under the code name Mule Train from Pope AFB, North Carolina to South Vietnam in January 1962. The squadron was later replaced by the 776th TCS and consisted of 12 aircraft at Tan Son Nhut and two at Da Nang.

2 February 1962

C-123B 56-4370 Special Aerial Spray Flight, attached to
464 TCW, USAF, Tan Son Nhut
Capt Fergus Coleman Groves (KIA)
Capt Robert Darrel Larson (KIA)
SSgt Milo Bruce Coghill (KIA)

The first US aircraft lost in South Vietnam was a C-123 Provider of the Ranch Hand defoliation unit. The aircraft was on a training flight when it crashed into dense forest during a practice spray run in an inaccessible area near Route 15 between Bien Hoa and Vung Tau killing all on board. The Viet Cong were thought to have removed items of equipment from the wreckage before a search party could be flown into the area. As the wreckage was largely destroyed by a post-impact fire it was not possible to find evidence of sabotage or engine failure or hits from ground fire. However, after this crash all Ranch Hand aircraft were escorted by fighters during their spray missions.

11 February 1962

SC-47A 43-15732 Detachment 2A, 4400 CCTS, USAF, Bien Hoa
Capt Edward Knell Kissam (KIA)
Capt Joseph Michael Fahey (KIA)
1Lt Stanley Gerald Hartson (KIA)
1Lt Jack Date Le Tourneau (KIA)
TSgt Floyd Milton Frazier (KIA)
A1C Robert Lee Westfall (KIA)
2Lt Lewis Metcalfe Walling, US Army (KIA)
SP4 Glen Frederick Merrihew, US Army (KIA)
1 VNAF observer, name unknown (KIA)

In the early phase of American involvement the US military was supposed to be in South Vietnam on an advisory or training basis. Consequently each aircraft had to have a Vietnamese on board, ostensibly for training but often merely to 'legalise' the operation. This was especially true with regard to aircraft like the B-26, which the US had no intention of providing to the South Vietnamese. Nevertheless, the USAF did train thousands of VNAF air and ground crew over the next 10 years and valuable combat experience was gained during these early operations. An SC-47A was on an early morning leaflet dropping sortie along the main route from Saigon to Da Nang when it crashed in the mountains near Bao Loc with the loss of all on board. It was unconfirmed whether the crash was due to enemy action or an accidental cause. This aircraft had been based at RAF Bovingdon in England in 1961.

20 April 1962

C-123B 56-4368 Special Aerial Spray Flight, attached to
464 TCW, USAF, Tan Son Nhut
Capt Harry Overman (survived)
2 crew, names unknown (survived)

The Ranch Hand defoliation programme had got off to a slow start and the aircraft and crews were under utilised as the initial set of defoliation trials drew to an end. Four of the C-123s had their spray equipment removed and the crews flew cargo missions within South Vietnam under the control of the Mule Train squadron of the 464th TCW. On 20 April during a cargo flight from Da Nang a pilot landed in error at a small strip near the DMZ called Hipp Khanh instead of his intended destination of Dong Ha. During the landing roll the pilot saw what he mistook to be hostile Vietnamese and thought he had landed in North Vietnam. He tried to take off again but the runway was not long enough and the aircraft force landed heavily and was so badly damaged that it had to be scrapped.

15 July 1962

C-123B 56-4366 777 TCS, 464 TCW on TDY, USAF, Da Nang
4 crew, names unknown (survived)

A second C-123 transport squadron arrived from Pope AFB in mid-June and was based at Da Nang and, like the original Mule Train squadron, flew transport missions throughout South Vietnam. Twelve aircraft were based at Da Nang and four were detached to Don Muang RTAB, Thailand. On 15 July during a flight from Tan Son Nhut to Ban Me Thuot, the pilot descended through cloud over high ground but was forced to climb due to the low cloud ceiling. During the climb out the aircraft crashed into a hillside but the impact was cushioned by trees and the crew survived with minor injuries. The men were rescued three days later by helicopter.

28 August 1962

T-28D 53-8376 Detachment 2A, 1 ACG, USAF, Bien Hoa
Capt Robert Lewis Simpson (KIA)
Lt Hoa, VNAF (KIA)

In April the Farm Gate detachment previously known as Detachment 2A of the 4400th CCTS became Detachment 2A of the 1st ACG that had formed at Hurlburt Field as part of the USAF's Special Air Warfare Centre. The T-28 Trojan was originally built as a basic trainer and was used as such by both the USAF and US Navy. The T-28D was an armed and strengthened

5

The second aircraft lost by the USAF in Vietnam was an SC-47 that crashed near Bao Loc during a leaflet dropping mission. The dropping of propaganda leaflets continued virtually throughout the entire war. USAF

conversion of the T-28A or T-28B that could carry gun pods and up to 4,000lbs of ordnance. The T-28B designation was often used in contemporary records rather than the more correct T-28D. In addition to being used by the USAF in Southeast Asia, the T-28D was also supplied in quantity to the VNAF. On the aircraft the serial was painted as '38376' and was written in USAF records as '53-8376' indicating an aircraft from a batch ordered in 1953 but in fact no such USAF serial was allocated. Neither does it appear to be a genuine US Navy Bureau of Aeronautics serial, as the batch of T-28s for the Navy ended at 138367 and was then followed by a batch commencing 138368 reserved for 50 Vought A2U Cutlasses that were never built. It is possible that as the T-28D was a remanufactured aircraft rather than a new one, the aircraft were reserialled with the unused numbers of the Cutlass order.

Capt Simpson was leading a flight of two T-28Ds escorting an assault on a VC stronghold by ARVN troops carried in UH-34s of HMM-163, USMC. As they neared the enemy position about 17 miles south of Soc Trang a forward air controller asked for suppressive fire along a mangrove swamp where guerillas had been spotted. Capt Simpson led the attack but his aircraft was shot down by small arms fire on his second pass. This was the first US aircraft to be confirmed as being shot down in South Vietnam and the first offensive aircraft lost in the war in Southeast Asia. A Viet Cong propaganda pamphlet printed soon after the event credits the destruction of the aircraft to the 'VC Army of Lac-Hoa village at My Thanh in Soc Trang Province'. An extensive search found small remains of the aircraft in the swamp but no trace of either crewman. Capt Simpson had joined the USAF in 1951 and had flown 67 missions in the F-80 during the Korean War. He later flew the F-89 Scorpion and the F-102 Delta Dagger before joining the Air Commandos. He had been in Vietnam for just over a month when he was killed.

15 October 1962

U-10A 62-5909   Detachment 2A, 1 ACG, USAF, Bien Hoa
       Capt Herbert W Booth (KIA)
       TSgt Richard L Foxx (KIA)

The Helio Courier was a rugged four/five-seat light aircraft with an excellent STOL capability that suited it to the kind of airstrips carved out of the jungle and high ground in Southeast Asia. A small number had been bought by the USAF for evaluation in the late 1950s and the type was used by the Air Commandos for psychological warfare, especially leaflet dropping and aerial broadcasting of propaganda to the enemy. The U-10 was also used by Air America in Laos where many of the airstrips required the Courier's ruggedness and STOL capability. Capt Booth's aircraft was probably involved in a leaflet drop and was thought to have been shot down in Darlac province in the Central Highlands. However, as the names of the crew of this U-10 appear on the FAC Memorial at Hurlburt they may have been flying an FAC mission.

16 October 1962

T-28D 53-8365   Detachment 2A, 1 ACG, USAF, Bien Hoa
       Capt B L Chambers (survived)

Capt Chambers's aircraft was shot down while acting as an escort for a rescue mission. The mission was probably connected to the loss of the U-10 the previous day. Chambers was recovered with only minor injuries.

29 October 1962

C-123B 56-4364   464 TCW, USAF, Da Nang or Tan Son Nhut
       Capt Richard S Dowell (survived)
       5 crew, names unknown (survived)

When landing at a newly constructed airfield at Dak To in the Central Highlands a Provider's landing gear hit a rocky ridge and the aircraft was damaged beyond repair. The pilot should have landed at an older dirt strip at Dak To but was incorrectly briefed and his map showed the new airfield as ready for use when it was not.

5 November 1962

B-26B 44-35530   Detachment 2A, 1 ACG, USAF, Bien Hoa
       Capt Robert David Bennett (KIA)
       1Lt William Boyd Tully (KIA)
       1 VNAF observer, name unknown (KIA)

The B-26 Invaders, which equipped a flight of the Farm Gate detachment, were known locally as RB-26Bs to disguise the fact that these 'reconnaissance' aircraft were actually bombers which were not officially permitted in Vietnam under the terms of the Geneva Accords signed earlier in July. Captain Bennet and his crew (including the obligatory VNAF observer) were shot down in An Xuyen province in the southern tip of South Vietnam during a napalm attack on a VC position in the early hours of the morning. The aircraft was working with a C-47 flare ship in response to a VC attack during the night and a VNAF A-1 Skyraider was also shot down during the night.

3 February 1963

B-26B 44-35692   Detachment 2A, 1 ACG, USAF, Bien Hoa
       Capt John F Shaughnessy (KIA)
       Capt John Peter Bartley (KIA)
       1 VNAF observer, name unknown (KIA)

By February 1963 Farm Gate was operating 10 B-26s, five T-28s and two C-47s. The unit lost two of its B-26s within the space of four days in February. The first was shot down by small arms fire during a strafing run on a Viet Cong concentration in the Mekong Delta. All the crew were killed. This B-26, along with at least a dozen others used by the Farm Gate unit, was thought to have been deployed to Takhli RTAB in 1961 for use during the Laotian civil war by a clandestine USAF unit known as Mill Pond. In the event, apart from a few reconnaissance flights, the B-26s were not used in action and were ferried to Okinawa in August 1961.

6 February 1963

B-26B 44-35507   Detachment 2A, 1 ACG, USAF, Bien Hoa
       Maj James Raymond O'Neill (KIA)
       1 Lt J E Johnson (survived)
       1 VNAF observer, name unknown (survived)

Another Farm Gate B-26 was shot down during a close air suport mission, this time near Pleiku when small arms or AAA knocked out an engine. Two of the crew escaped by parachute but the pilot, Maj O'Neill, stayed with the aircraft which hit a mountainside before he could escape. Following the loss of two B-26s within the space of three days, it became common to despatch the bombers in pairs, one of the aircraft providing defence suppression while the other made the attack. This also applied to T-28s from around this time.

8 April 1963

B-26B 44-35525   Detachment 2A, 1 ACG, USAF, Bien Hoa
       Capt Andrew C Mitchell (KIA)
       Capt Jerry Alan Campaigne (KIA)
       1 VNAF observer, name unknown (KIA)

A fourth Farm Gate B-26 was lost when it was shot down during a strafing run on a target 20 miles west of Kontum. Observers reported that part of the aircraft's wing might have broken off prior to the crash.

12 April 1963

C-123B 56-4380   777 TCS, 464 TCW on TDY, USAF, Don Muang
       1Lt Raymond E Doyle (KIA)
       1Lt Richard L Hatlestad (KIA)
       SSgt Stanley E Truesdale (KIA)

After taking off from the airfield at Nakhon Phanom the pilot of a Provider attempted to snare a red flag on top of a flag pole. Apparently, this trick had been attempted before by other C-123 crews based in Thailand. During the second attempt the left wing hit a house and the aircraft crashed killing all three crew and two Thai civilians on the ground. Nakhon Phanom airfield in north-eastern Thailand, close to the border with Laos, was still under construction when this accident happened. It is possible that the C-123s were bringing in construction equipment or supplies.

5 May 1963

T-28D 53-8370   Detachment 2A, 1 ACG, USAF, Bien Hoa
       2 crew, names unknown (survived)

A Farm Gate T-28 struck a parked aircraft tug while landing and was burnt out on the runway.

27 June 1963

T-28D 53-8375   Detachment 2A, 1 ACG, USAF, Bien Hoa
       Capt Condon Hunter Terry (KIA)
       1 VNAF observer, name unknown (KIA)

The Farm Gate detachment lost its fourth T-28 when it crashed during a close air support mission in Military Region 4.

The FACs

The nature of the enemy and the terrain, together with the peculiar political circumstances in which the wars in Southeast Asia were fought, soon highlighted the need for precise control of air attacks. During the Korean War the USAF had developed a system of airborne forward air control using specially trained pilots and observers who controlled air and artillery strikes in T-6 Texans, often in close proximity to friendly troops. By the early 1960s the aircraft of choice for the forward air control mission was the little Cessna O-1 Bird Dog. Several O-1s were supplied to the VNAF even before the US forces began to take over the air war. The first USAF FACs were brought in with the Jungle Jim detachment and flew T-28s and borrowed O-1s from the VNAF to perform FAC

duties. The US Army also employed FACs in their own Bird Dogs in the early years but after 1965 the FAC mission was turned over to the USAF and the Army's O-1s specialised primarily in artillery observation. The USAF's first FAC squadron, the 19th TASS, was formed at Bien Hoa in June as part of the 34th TG and became operational in September. The Squadron was equipped with the O-1F model of the Bird Dog and was only intended to spend six months in Vietnam after which it would pass on its aircraft to the South Vietnamese and deactivate. The O-1F was an FAC conversion of the Army's O-1D light liaison aircraft. Later a variety of Bird Dog versions would be used by the US forces in Southeast Asia. Supposedly the Squadron's prime mission was to train the VNAF in forward air control and visual reconnaissance techniques but it also provided operational forward air control for the Farm Gate strike aircraft. Four O-1s had arrived by the end of July and a further 18 arrived in August on board the USS Card*. Six aircraft were later deployed to Can Tho. Eventually four Tactical Air Support Squadrons were activated in South Vietnam, each one attached to a Corps which covered a geographical region of the country. The 19th TASS based at Bien Hoa was attached to III Corps; the 20th at Da Nang was attached to I Corps; the 21st at Pleiku was attached to II Corps; and the 22nd at Binh Thuy was attached to IV Corps. By August 1965 the four Squadrons had a total of about 120 O-1Fs on charge. In 1966 a fifth squadron, the 23rd TASS, was formed at Nakhon Phanom for FAC duties over Laos.*

1 August 1963

O-1F serial ..? 19 TASS, 34 TG, USAF, Bien Hoa
1Lt W B Meiggs (survived)

Details of the first USAF FAC loss are not known except that it was one of the 19th's original four aircraft and the pilot survived with injuries. The Squadron became fully operational in September.

16 August 1963

B-26B 44-34681 1 ACS, 34 TG, USAF, Bien Hoa
Capt John Howard McClean (KIA)
Capt Arthur Eugene Bedal (KIA)
1 VNAF observer, name unknown (KIA)

On 1 June the 1st Air Commando Group at Hurlburt Field was redesignated as the 1st Air Commando Wing to form the nucleus of USAF special forces activity. On 8 July, with any pretext of being in South Vietnam simply in a training and advisory role long since gone, the Farm Gate detachment was officially redesignated as the 1st Air Commando Squadron and was attached to the 34th TG. It was now a regular USAF combat squadron and could go about its business in a more open manner than circumstances had previously allowed, however, its code name of Farm Gate still stuck with it for some years. At this time the squadron consisted of 6 C-47s, 4 U-10s, 13 T-28s and 13 B-26s. Capt McClean's aircraft was lost when one of its wings broke off during a dive on a target in Quang Ngai province. Although enemy gunfire was reported during the mission it was thought that the wing may have failed through metal fatigue. The B-26s in use in Southeast Asia were originally built in 1944 and, although having been refurbished since then, they were now operating with heavy underwing loads from some very rough runways which imposed huge strain on the wing structure. The aircraft were also used as dive bombers, a role for which they were not designed nor were they stressed to take the G forces encountered when pulling out of the dive. After McClean's crash and another B-26 accident in the USA on 11 February 1964 when a wing separated during an air power demonstration, severe limitations were imposed on the Farm Gate aircraft that would eventually halt their use in combat as soon as a replacement could be found.

Identification of Remains and the POW-MIA Issue

The wars in Southeast Asia ended for the USA in August 1973 by which time over 58,000 Americans had been killed of which around 2,580 were listed as missing in action. In 1981 President Reagan assigned the highest priority to accounting for Americans missing from the war in Southeast Asia. Although relations between the USA and Vietnam remained strained for many years after the US withdrawal from Southeast Asia, the Vietnamese had repatriated some remains even before the US government's renewed efforts. Improving diplomatic relations between the USA and Vietnam from the late 1980s eventually permitted the return of more remains and joint investigations within Vietnam itself. In 1987 President Reagan appointed Gen John Vessey as a special POW-MIA emmisary who did much to improve relations with the Vietnamese. In 1991 the Senate created a Select Committee on POW-MIA affairs further highlighting the growing concern for those who had not yet returned. In January 1992 the Joint Task Force-Full Accounting office was set up under CINCPAC and based at Hawaii. This organisation was to undertake field investigations within Southeast Asia in conjuction with Vietnamese and Laotian representatives. In July 1993 the Defense Prisoner of War Missing Personnel Office was established to consolidate the various government agencies involved in POW and MIA personnel issues. It is the DPMO that today drives the POW-MIA recovery effort while the JTF-FA does much of the investigative work. Remains returned from Vietnam normally go first to the US Army Central Identification Laboratory in Hawaii for a series of forensic examinations and tests in an effort to ascertain identity. The state of preservation and the amount of remains recovered is extremely variable and successful identification, even for remains discovered in known circumstances, is by no means assured. However, developments in mitochondrial DNA testing throughout the 1980s has had a major impact on this branch of forensic science. Mitochondrial DNA is extracted from the remains and amplified using a polymerase chain reaction. The results of DNA sequencing are then matched with those obtained from maternal family members of the deceased and if the sequences match then a relationship can be proved. In many cases the identity of the remains are already suspected and DNA testing serves to provide positive proof. The Armed Forces DNA Identification Laboratory at Rockville, Maryland made the first identification of remains from Southeast Asia using DNA testing in 1991 and is building a database of DNA from family members which will aid future investigations. In the last few years the application of DNA testing has been extended to investigating remains from the Korean War, the Cold War and, most recently, the Second World War.

2 September 1963

B-26B 44-34682 1 ACS, 34 TG, USAF, Bien Hoa
detached to Da Nang
Capt Howard Philip Purcell (KIA)
1Lt Neil Bernard McKinney (KIA)
SSgt Raphael Cruz (KIA)
1 VNAF observer, name unknown (KIA)

An aircraft was lost during an escort mission over Kontum province and may have been shot down as it was seen by the relief aircraft but never returned to Da Nang. No wreckage was found at the time despite an extensive SAR effort that included the dropping of half a million leaflets offering a reward for information on the crew or the aircraft. However, in 1992 the Socialist Republic of Vietnam repatriated to the United States human remains that were subsequently identified as being the crew of this aircraft. Mitochondrial DNA testing was used to confirm the three identifications.

10 September 1963

T-28D 53-8367 1 ACS, 34 TG, USAF, Bien Hoa
Capt E C Meek (survived)
1 VNAF observer, name unknown (survived)

On 10 September strong Viet Cong forces attacked Soc Trang airfield and towns in the Ca Mau Peninsula. Two 1st ACS T-28s detached to Soc Trang reacted quickly and were soon joined by other USAF and VNAF aircraft. One of the T-28s was shot down by ground fire on its third pass over a machine gun position near Dam Doi. The crew were rescued by an Army UH-1 gunship but the T-28 had to be destroyed to prevent its ordnance being recovered by the VC. This battle lasted five days and involved heli-borne assaults by USMC and Army troops and a parachute assault by 498 Vietnamese paratroopers dropped from C-47s and C-123s.

28 September 1963

C-123B 55-4513 311 TCS, 315 TCG, USAF, Da Nang
detached to Don Muang
4 crew, names unknown (survived)

On 8 December 1962 the 315th TCG had been activated at Tan Son Nhut to take control of the C-123 Providers that were deployed to Vietnam. In July the 777th TCS, which had a detachment of four aircraft in Thailand, was redesignated as the 311th TCS and became part of the 315th TCG. The Group's first casualty was an aircraft that crashed in Thailand during an airlift support mission.

8 October 1963

T-28D 53-8373 1 ACS, 34 TG, USAF, Bien Hoa
Capt Dean Amick Wadsworth (KIA)
1 VNAF observer, name unknown (KIA)

A T-28, radio call sign Grad OK 02, went out of control and crashed when it was diving on a target near the Laotian border about 40 miles southwest of Da Nang. The wreckage fell in a swollen stream which fed into the Buong River in mountainous jungle terrain. The USAF mounted a major SAR mission led by Maj A W Saunders. In the first attempt to reach the wreck two USMC UH-34s of HMM-361 were shot down with the loss of 10 crew in an area known as 'VC Valley'. Later, against considerable enemy opposition, two ARVN infantry companies supported by Farm Gate strike aircraft were flown into the area by USMC helicopters. The search party reached the wreck site on 11 October but was soon forced to withdraw due to enemy fire. Another USMC UH-34 was lost during the recovery of the SAR party in the evening, fortunately without further loss of life. Three days later Maj Saunders led another mission to the wreck, again encountering much enemy opposition. The party, escorted by a strong force of US Green Berets and South Vietnamese Rangers, found no sign of the crew and little to indicate the cause of the crash. In 1993 a Vietnamese villager handed in remains he claimed were from the T-28 wreck site. This was followed up by three digs at the site in 1994 and 1995 and during the latter excavation human remains and identification tags were found identifying Capt Wadsworth.

24 October 1963

C-123B 56-4385 315 TCG, USAF, Tan Son Nhut
Capt Woodrow Melvin Fitzgerald (KIA)
Capt Gordon Richard Brown (KIA)
SSgt Charles Bernard Lankford (KIA)
SSgt Walter Kenneth Morris (KIA)
4 crew, probably VNAF observers,
names unknown (KIA)

Along with transport and defoliation duties the C-123 Provider was also used as a flare ship during the war in Southeast Asia. Parachute flares were dropped over villages and outposts that were either under attack or under threat to deter the VC and allow the defenders to see. Flares were also used to illuminate targets at night for attack aircraft. It was during a flare drop just south of Saigon that this C-123 was thought to have been shot down by ground fire.

24 November 1963

B-26B 44-35703 1 ACS, 34 TG, USAF, Bien Hoa
Capt Howard Rudolph Cody (KIA)
1Lt Atis Karlis Lielmanis (KIA)

On 24 November a major battle developed between Viet Cong forces and the ARVN's 21st Division at Cha La on the Ca Mau Peninsula. US Army helicopters brought in more troops during which an H-21 was shot down and 10 other helicopters damaged. USAF and VNAF strike aircraft attacked throughout the day in what was the largest air operation flown during a single day up to that time. A B-26 was shot down while attacking entrenched machine gun positions. Capt Cody's aircraft was damaged in the first pass over the target but he continued to make another attack forcing the VC gunners to reveal their positions. Cody's aircraft was shot down but other aircraft destroyed

the machine gun positions. Capt Cody was posthumously awarded the AFC and an academic building at Keesler AFB, the USAF's largest technical training base, is named in his honour.

6 December 1963

RB-26L 44-35782   1 ACS, 34 TG, USAF, Bien Hoa
                   Capt Gary W Bitton (KIA)
                   Capt Thomas Frederick Gorton (KIA)
                   Capt Norman Ray Davison (KIA)
                   A2C Richard Dale Hill (KIA)
RB-26L 44-35782 was one of Farm Gate's four special camera-equipped B-26s and one of only two that had any real night capability. The main task was low-level photographic reconnaissance for target acquisition and bomb damage assessment. The aircraft were also used to make photographic surveys of poorly mapped parts of South Vietnam especially with regard to the planning of new airfields. The aircraft crashed in shallow water near Binh Dai, in the mouth of the Mekong River, 40 miles south of Saigon. A2C Hill was an aerial photographer from the 21st Armament & Electronics Maintenance Squadron and was presumably operating the on-board cameras. Unusually, there appears to have been no VNAF crewmember on this flight. This particular aircraft was thought to have been used by the CIA-sponsored Cuban Liberation Air Force during the abortive Bay of Pigs invasion in April 1961 before being converted to RB-26L standard.

20 December 1963

O-1F   57-2831   19 TASS, 34 TG, USAF, Bien Hoa
                   1Lt Billy John Coley (KIA)
                   1Lt Donald Allan Mollicone (KIA)
An O-1 FAC aircraft crashed in the Mekong Delta region due to pilot error killing both the crew.

7 January 1964

B-26B   44-35207   1 ACS, 34 TG, USAF, Bien Hoa
                     Maj Hughie Darell Adams (KWF)
                     Maj Cleveland William Gordon (KWF)
A B-26 crashed 10 miles south of Bien Hoa due to a technical problem during a test flight.

14 January 1964

B-26B   44-35566   1 ACS, 34 TG, USAF, Bien Hoa
                     Maj Carl Berg Mitchell (KIA)
                     Capt Vincent Joseph Hickman (KIA)
                     1 VNAF observer, name unknown (KIA)
A B-26 was lost during a close air support mission 17 miles northeast of Bien Hoa. The aircraft made a napalm run on a Viet Cong position but was then shot down by machine gun fire before it could make a second attack. Ground troops fought their way to the crash site five days later but found no sign that anyone had survived the crash. This aircraft was the tenth and last B-26 lost in Southeast Asia until the reintroduction of the type in much-

modified form in June 1966. The 13 remaining B-26s of the 1st ACS were retired on 11 February and flown to Clark AFB in the Philippines in April where most were scrapped. Capt Mitchell, who had previously flown B-29s and B-47s with SAC, has been the subject of several live sighting reports but neither he nor his navigator returned from Southeast Asia despite a JTF-FA investigation into the case in 1995.

T-28D   53-8372   1 ACS, 34 TG, USAF, Bien Hoa
                    Capt E M Adkins (survived)
                    1 VNAF observer, name unknown (survived)
A T-28 was hit and caught fire as it was diving at a target during a close air support mission. The aircraft crash-landed and was damaged beyond repair.

21 January 1964

T-28D   53-8374   1 ACS, 34 TG, USAF, Bien Hoa
                    1 pilot, name unknown (survived)
A T-28 crashed, this time due to engine failure.

18 February 1964

T-28D   53-8369   1 ACS, 34 TG, USAF, Bien Hoa
                    2 crew, names unknown (survived)
Another T-28 was hit and caught fire when attacking dug-in VC troops and crashed.

19 February 1964

T-28D   53-8855   1 ACS, 34 TG, USAF, Bien Hoa
                    Capt Bernard Francis Lukasik (KIA)
                    1 VNAF observer, name unknown (KIA)
Yet another T-28 (the 10th so far) was shot down while strafing VC forces. This occurred when supporting ARVN ground troops in Phuong Dinh province inland from the Mekong Delta.

8 March 1964

A-1H   serial ..?   1 ACS, 34 TG, USAF, Bien Hoa
                      Col Thomas Malcolm Hergert (KIA)
With the withdrawal of the B-26 in February the 1st ACS was running short of strike aircraft. Twenty-five ex-US Navy A-1E Skyraiders were being converted for USAF use but would not be ready before May. In the meantime the 1st ACS borrowed T-28s and A-1s from the VNAF to continue operations. This A-1H, lost during an armed reconnaissance mission near Tay Ninh, was almost certainly one of those on loan from the VNAF. Col Hergert was the highest ranking USAF officer to lose his life in the war up to this time.

24 March 1964

T-28D   53-8362   1 ACS, 34 TG, USAF, Bien Hoa
                    Capt Edwin Gerald Shank (KIA)
                    1 VNAF observer, name unknown (KIA)
Having suffered structural fatigue problems with the B-26 leading to its early withdrawal, the USAF was now faced with a sim-

ilar problem with the T-28. Capt Shank's aircraft lost a wing and crashed on its third dive bombing run against a target near Soc Trang. For the moment there was no move to ground the T-28, however, a similar incident on 9 April brought the matter to a head.

26 March 1964

O-1F   55-4695   19 TASS, 34 TG, USAF, Bien Hoa
                   detached to Khe Sanh
                   Capt Richard Lebrou Whitesides (KIA)
                   Capt Floyd James Thompson, US Army
                   (POW)
An O-1 FAC aircraft was flown by Capt Whitesides with Capt Thompson of the US Army Special Forces as observer on a visual reconnaissance of the Khe Sanh region. Capt Thompson was based at the Special Forces camp at Khe Sanh close to the DMZ and the aircraft was brought down by small arms fire about 15 miles to the west near Lang Kat. Capt Whitesides was killed in the crash but Thompson survived although badly injured with burns and a broken back. Capt Thompson was taken prisoner by the Viet Cong and spent the next nine years as a prisoner of war, being kept initially in South Vietnam by the VC until moved to Hanoi in March 1970. After much suffering and deprivation he was released on 16 March 1973 in Operation Homecoming. Although not as widely known as the early aircrew POWs, Capt Thompson was the longest held American POW of the Vietnam war.

9 April 1964

T-28D   53-8361   1 ACS, 34 TG, USAF, Bien Hoa
                    Capt Robert Newton Brumet (KIA)
                    1 VNAF observer, name unknown (KIA)
The accident of 24 March was repeated as Capt Brumet's T-28 lost both its wings during a strafing attack in Military Region 4. There was now no doubt that the T-28s in South Vietnam were being stressed beyond safe limits and that the aircraft would need replacing as soon as possible. Fortunately, the first six of the Air Commando's 'new' A-1E Skyraiders were delivered on 30 May as replacements for the B-26s. However, as it would be some time before more A-1s could be made available the T-28 continued in use but with flight restrictions that reduced its operational capability. In the meantime the five remaining T-28s that had been flying combat for nearly three years were supplemented by 15 more T-28s borrowed from the VNAF's 516th FS and which were in better condition, having seen less use. The older aircraft were retired later in the month.

1 May 1964

T-28D   53-8368   1 ACS, 34 TG, USAF, Bien Hoa
                    1 pilot, name unknown (survived)
Another T-28 crashed on take off on a non-operational flight due to engine failure. This was probably one of the T-28s the Air Commandos had borrowed from the VNAF. Towards the end of the month six aircraft were transferred to Udorn leaving eight in service with the 1st ACS at Bien Hoa.

Escalation in Laos

The Geneva Accords of 1962 made little difference to the fighting in Laos and in the spring of 1964 a major offensive by the Pathet Lao and NVA drove Laotian government troops out of the Plain of Jars. The government situation became critical and US assistance was requested to halt a complete collapse. The Royal Lao government under Prime Minister Souvanna Phouma received T-28Ds and allowed US reconnaissance aircraft to provide intelligence on the movement of the communist forces. In April Detachment 6 of the 1st ACW (code named Water Pump) was established at Udorn RTAB with four T-28Ds to train Laotian

A large number of T-28 Trojans were modified to T-28D standard and supplied to the air forces of South Vietnam, Thailand, Laos and Cambodia. The USAF lost 23 T-28s during the war, mostly prior to 1965. USAF

and Thai airmen on the type. Air America pilots were also trained on the T-28 as they flew the aircraft for close air support and helicopter escort. In addition to training, the aircraft also took part in operations against the Pathet Lao. Under the code name Yankee Team, the reconnaissance flights over the Plain of Jars were flown by USAF RF-101s from Tan Son Nhut and Navy RF-8s from TF 77 aircraft carriers. After an aircraft was shot down on 6 June the reconnaissance aircraft were escorted by fighters. Detachments of F-100s deployed to Takhli and to Da Nang in South Vietnam to provide escorts for the reconnaissance missions. On 9 June, following the loss of a second Crusader in Laos, President Johnson authorised the first US retaliatory strike by F-100s against AAA sites in Laos. Thus started US offensive operations in the northern provinces of Laos that would develop into the Barrel Roll campaign. Later, in April 1965, US forces started flying missions (under the code name Steel Tiger) in the southern panhandle of Laos specifically against the movement of North Vietnamese traffic along the series of roads and tracks known as the Ho Chi Minh Trail towards South Vietnam. There were, in effect, two separate wars fought in Laos although both campaigns often used the same resources based in Thailand and at sea.

6 June 1964

RF-8A 146823   Detachment C, VFP-63, USN,
                 USS *Kitty Hawk*
                 Lt Charles Frederic Klusmann
                 (POW - escaped)

When the US decided to increase air support to the Royal Laotian forces the USAF was already fully stretched in their 'advisory' role in South Vietnam so initially it fell to the US Navy to provide air support over Laos. The Navy had deployed ships to the South China Sea and Gulf of Tonkin earlier in the year and by the spring of 1964 four attack carriers, the USS *Bon Homme Richard*, *Constellation*, *Kitty Hawk* and *Ticonderoga* were deployed to the western Pacific for potential use in Southeast Asia. The reconnaissance flights were code named Yankee Team and the USS *Kitty Hawk* became the first US aircraft carrier to launch operational missions during the war in Southeast Asia. The RF-8A Crusaders of Detachment C, VFP-63 flew the first Yankee Team mission over Laos on 19 May and two days later Lt Klusmann's aircraft was damaged by AAA but returned safely to the *Kitty Hawk*. On 6 June Lt Klusmann's aircraft was hit again on a reconnaissance mission to Khang Khay but this time his hydraulics were so badly damaged by ground fire that the aircraft became uncontrollable and he was forced to eject near Ban Ban to the east of the Plain of Jars. An Air America C-123 arrived on the scene to co-ordinate a rescue attempt. An Air America U-10 joined in the search and soon spotted Lt Klusmann but when two Air America UH-34 helicopters approached to pick up the pilot they were met with a hail of fire and had to withdraw. The Pathet Lao and North Vietnamese frequently employed a flak trap by allowing a downed airman to call in the rescue helicopters which were then shot at by the waiting enemy gunners. The Crusader was the first US Navy loss of the war and was also the first jet aircraft lost during the conflict. Klusmann was soon captured by the Pathet Lao and taken to a camp nearby. On 30 August, after three months of captivity, Klusmann managed to escape with five Laotian political prisoners and four days later he arrived in a friendly village from where he was picked up by an Air America helicopter. He is one of only a handful of men who successfully escaped from captivity during the war in Southeast Asia. Charles Klusmann retired from the Navy with the rank of Captain in 1980.

7 June 1964

F-8D 147064   VF-111, USN, USS *Kitty Hawk*
                Cdr Doyle Wilmer Lynn (survived)

The day after Klusmann was shot down the Navy flew two more reconnaissance missions to the Plain of Jars. On the second mission an RF-8A was escorted by three Crusader fighters of VF-111 (one of them flown by the squadron commander, Cdr Doyle Lynn) which would attack AAA sites during the photo runs.

Cdr Lynn's aircraft was hit by ground fire which damaged the hydraulic system and he was forced to eject in the same area where Klusmann had been lost. A large-scale rescue mission was launched but the original loss position as reported was about 40 miles out. However, an Air America Caribou picked up Cdr Lynn's homing beacon and on the following day an Air America UH-34 picked up Cdr Lynn from his hiding place in the jungle. Unfortunately, Cdr Lynn was later killed on 27 May 1965 during a strike on North Vietnam. With two aircraft lost within the space of two days the US Navy's introduction to the air war in Southeast Asia got off to a bad start. Soon after the second Crusader was shot down USAF F-100s refuelled by KC-135 tankers from Clark AFB flew a strike against known AAA sites on the Plain of Jars. However, the gun sites were difficult to spot let alone destroy and the Pathet Lao gunners would, like their North Vietnamese counterparts, exact an increasingly heavy toll on US aircraft in the future.

26 June 1964

T-28D 51-7871   1 ACS, 34 TG, USAF, Bien Hoa
                  Capt E S Johnson (survived)
                  1 crew, name unknown (survived)

A T-28 was shot down while on its second pass dropping napalm on a target. The two crewmen baled out and were rescued by helicopter. As the refurbished A-1Es were now being delivered the 1st ACS started to retire their T-28s and this was fourteenth and last T-28 lost on operations as the type was largely phased out of USAF service during the first week of July (although two more were lost in November on their way to Thailand).

23 July 1964

C-123B 56-4383   315 TCG, USAF, Tan Son Nhut
                   4 crew, names unknown (survived)

Upon landing at Gia Vuc when returning from a flare-dropping mission a Provider's propeller reverse pitch mechanism failed on one engine with the result that the aircraft swerved off the runway and smashed into a barracks building. Although the aircraft and the barracks were completely burnt out there were no casualties.

The Gulf of Tonkin Incident and Task Force 77 Operations

On 2 August, against the background of open warfare in Laos and increasing infiltration across the North/South Vietnamese border, North Vietnamese torpedo boats attacked the destroyer USS Maddox in international waters in the Gulf of Tonkin. The destroyer was cruising along a patrol line in the northern region of the Gulf in order to gather intelligence as part of Operation Plan 34A. This was a covert campaign that started in February 1964 and intended to deter the North Vietnamese from interfering with the South. One of the torpedo boats that attacked the Maddox was sunk by a flight of F-8s led by Cdr James Stockdale of VF-51 from USS Ticonderoga. During the night of 4/5 August USS Maddox, now reinforced by USS Turner Joy, returned to its station off the North Vietnamese coast to listen for radio traffic and monitor communist naval activity. Shortly after a covert South Vietnamese attack on a coastal radar station near Cua Ron, the two destroyers tracked on radar what they took to be enemy torpedo boats. Debate still rages whether there really was any North Vietnamese boats in the vicinity of the two destroyers. Apparently no attack developed and no boats were seen by the pilots of the aircraft launched to provide air cover. However, the incident was enough to goad President Johnson into ordering Operation Pierce Arrow, a limited retaliatory raid on military facilities in North Vietnam. On 10 August the US Congress passed what came to be known as the Gulf of Tonkin Resolution which was as close as the US ever came to declaring war on North Vietnam but which actually fell far short of that. The Gulf of Tonkin Incident also resulted in a major increase in US air strength in the Southeast Asian theatre and saw US involvement change from an advisory role to a more operational role, even though US aircraft and airmen had been participating in operations ever since they first arrived in the region.

The political and physical restrictions on the basing of US aircraft in South Vietnam was to some extent solved by the permanent stationing of aircraft carriers in the South China Sea. By the end of August four aircraft carriers, the USS Bon Homme Richard, Constellation, Kearsarge and Ticonderoga, had arrived in position in the Gulf and started a pattern of line duty that continued until August 1973. The carriers and their protecting forces constituted the US 7th Fleet's Task Force 77 which in March 1965 developed a pattern of positioning carriers at Yankee Station in the South China Sea off Da Nang from which to launch attacks against North Vietnam. On 20 May TF 77 established Dixie Station 100 miles southeast of Cam Ranh Bay from where close air support missions could be mounted against South Vietnam. The carriers developed a system that normally kept each ship on line duty for a period of between 25 and 35 days after which the carrier would visit a port in either the Philippines, Japan or Hong Kong for rest and replenishment of supplies. Each carrier would normally complete four spells of duty on the line before returning to its homeport for refitting and re-equipping. However, the period spent on line duty could vary considerably and some ships spent well over the average number of days on duty. The establishment of Dixie Station required the assignment of a fifth carrier to the Western Pacific to maintain the constant presence of at least two carriers at Yankee Station and one at Dixie Station. By the summer of 1966 there were enough aircraft based in South Vietnam to provide the required air power and Dixie Station was discontinued from 4 August.

The USAF also increased its forces in Southeast Asia following the Gulf of Tonkin Incident. Immediate reinforcements consisted of six F-102 interceptors (from the 509th FIS at Clark) to Da Nang and a further six (from the 16th FIS at Naha AB, Okinawa) to Tan Son Nhut; eight F-100s (from the 615th TFS temporarily deployed to Clark) to Da Nang and another 10 (from the 405th FW at Clark) to Takhli; 36 B-57Bs (also from the 405th) to Bien Hoa, six RF-101Cs to Tan Son Nhut; eight KB-50s (421st ARS) split equally between Tan Son Nhut and Takhli; and eight F-105Ds (36th TFS) to Korat. Other aircraft, including a large number of F-100s, deployed to Clark to form a composite task force that would move to South Vietnam or Thailand as required.

5 August 1964

A-1H 139760   VA-145, USN, USS *Constellation*
                Lt(jg) Richard Christian Sather (KIA)

A-4C 149578   VA-144, USN, USS *Constellation*
                Lt(jg) Everett Alvarez (POW)

Operation Pierce Arrow commenced in the early afternoon of 5 August with 20 aircraft from USS *Constellation* (10 Skyraiders, eight Skyhawks and two Phantoms) attacking the torpedo boat base at Hon Gay while 12 more (five Skyhawks, four Skyraiders and three Phantoms) from the same carrier struck the Loc Chao base. Simultaneously, the USS *Ticonderoga* sent six F-8s to the torpedo boat bases at Quang Khe and Ben Thuy and 26 other aircraft to bomb an oil storage depot at Vinh. Unfortunately, President Johnson's premature television announcement that the raids were to take place may have warned the North Vietnamese who put up a fierce barrage of anti-aircraft fire at all the targets resulting in the loss of two aircraft. Lt Sather's Skyraider (or Spad as it was nicknamed by both Navy and Air Force pilots) was hit by AAA while on its third dive bomb attack and crashed just offshore from Thanh Hoa. No parachute was seen or radio emergency beeper heard and it was assumed that Sather died in the crash, the first naval airman to be killed in the war. The North Vietnamese eventually repatriated his body in August 1985.

Having taken part in the abortive hunt for North Vietnamese torpedo boats during the night, Lt Alvarez also took part in the Pierce Arrow attack on torpedo boats at Hon Gay. He was forced to eject at low level when his Skyhawk flew into a barrage of AAA during the attack. Alvarez was captured and became the first airman to become a prisoner of the North Vietnamese (as opposed to Capt F J Thompson captured on 26 March who was a US Army observer shot down in a USAF aircraft). Everett Alvarez, who was on his first tour since graduating as a pilot in 1961, spent eight and a half years in various North Vietnamese prisons before being released in

Operation Homecoming on 12 February 1973. He was known to other POWs as the Old Man of the North due to his longevity in the POW camps. Alvarez retired as a Commander in 1980 and went to law school and later became the Deputy Administrator of the Veterans Administration under the Reagan presidency. Results claimed for Operation Pierce Arrow included the destruction of 90 per cent of the petroleum storage facility at Vinh together with the destruction or damage of an estimated 25 torpedo boats, representing two-thirds of the North Vietnamese force.

F-8E 150319 VF-191, USN, USS *Bon Homme Richard*
Lt W D Storey (survived)

In an incident unrelated to Operation Pierce Arrow, a Crusader was lost through engine failure during a training flight in the South China Sea

B-57B 53-3884 405 FW, USAF, Clark AFB, Philippines
2 crew, names unknown (uninjured)

On the evening of 4 August, 20 B-57Bs from the 7th and 13th TBSs took off from Clark AFB in the Philippines to fly to Bien Hoa. The deployment had been expected to be in daylight as few of the aircrew were qualified in night formation flying, but it was dark before permission to deploy was received. The weather was very bad with low cloud and heavy rain making the approach to Bien Hoa extremely difficult. During landing two aircraft collided on the runway at Bien Hoa causing 53-3884 to be subsequently scrapped and 53-3877 to be badly damaged.

5/6 August 1964

B-57B 53-3870 405 FW, USAF, Clark AFB, Philippines
Capt Fred Clay Cutrer (KIA)
1Lt Leonard Lee Kaster (KIA)

The second wave of B-57s also run into trouble on their deployment flight to South Vietnam. One aircraft crashed into the Song Dong Nai River in Long Khan province (about 25 miles northeast of Bien Hoa) either as a result of enemy ground fire or accidentally flying into the ground while on a TACAN approach. It was normal procedure for airmen posted missing in action and who could possibly have been captured by the enemy to be promoted during their absence. Capt Cutrer was promoted to the rank of Major before it was discovered that he had died in this incident. In these cases the rank is retained and is the rank that is inscribed on the Vietnam Memorial Wall in Washington, DC. Upon arrival at Bien Hoa the B-57 unit became known as the 405th FW ADVON 1 and crews rotated from Clark AFB on a regular basis. The mere presence of the B-57s in South Vietnam was intended to send a strong message to the Viet Cong and North Vietnam. However, for the time being the US had no intention of using the aircraft in action. For the next seven months the B-57 squadrons were restricted to flying unarmed reconnaissance missions which had a detrimental effect on the morale of the aircrew who could barely fly enough hours to keep current.

The US Marines Corps in Vietnam

It was aviation units that led the US Marine Corps' contribution to the war in Southeast Asia. The leading elements of Marine Task Unit 79.3.5 (more commonly known as SHUFLY) arrived at Soc Trang on 9 April 1962. This unit was would provide the headquarters and command function for a Marine medium lift helicopter squadron that would be based in South Vietnam on a rotational basis. The first squadron, HMM-362, arrived on 15 April and consisted of 24 UH-34s, three O-1B Bird Dogs (on detachment from VMO-2), and one C-117D transport. In September 1962 the Marines left Soc Trang for Da Nang which would become their main base in South Vietnam as the Corps was allocated responsibility for the northern provinces closest to the DMZ. The US Marines would eventually take on responsibility for most US ground operations in I Corps. The first Marine aircraft lost during the war was a UH-34 of HMM-163 which crashed on 6 October 1962 killing the pilot. The Bird Dogs were used for a variety of tasks including visual reconnaissance for the helicopters, obtaining intelligence on potential landing sites, providing information on weather prior to a mission, and acting as a battlefield command post and radio relay vehicle.

12 August 1964

O-1B 136905 VMO-2 Detachment, MTU 79.3.5, USMC, Da Nang
2 crew, names unknown (survived)

As an O-1B was performing a visual reconnaissance mission in the northwest region of Quang Ngai province on 12 August its engine failed and the aircraft force landed. Bad weather delayed rescue for over an hour until a Marine UH-34 could reach the injured crew and evacuate them to Da Nang for treatment. The VMO-2 detachment was attached to HMM-162, the resident UH-34D SHUFLY squadron, at the time of the accident.

13 August 1964

A-4E 150018 VA-56, USN, USS *Ticonderoga*
1 pilot, name unknown (survived)

During a catapult launch on a training flight a Skyhawk's engine failed and the aircraft fell into the sea.

The F-105 Thunderchief

Probably more than any other aircraft the Republic F-105 Thunderchief epitomises the air war against North Vietnam. From 1965 to the bombing halt in 1968 the F-105 bore the brunt of the air war in the north flying more missions than any other aircraft type with the result that more F-105s were lost than any other aircraft type with the exception of the F-4 Phantom.

The Thunderchief was designed in the early 1950s as a single-seat, single-engined fighter bomber with the primary role of nuclear attack. The entire design was optimised for this role which, when the aircraft came to be used for tactical strike using conventional weapons, had both advantages and disadvantages. On the plus side the aircraft had been designed to be very fast and stable at low level to perform its nuclear attack mission. Like most Republic-built aircraft it was heavy but sturdy and could carry a total of 16x750lb bombs on racks under the fuselage and wings, although the normal load in Southeast Asia's hot and humid climate was usually only six or eight 750lb bombs. However, it had not been designed with a high degree of survivability in mind and had very little systems redundancy for the flight controls, fuel or hydraulic systems. Although there were no fuel tanks in the wings, fuel tanks were built into the internal bomb bay prior to use in Vietnam. While the structure of the Thunderchief was very sturdy and aircraft came back with large sections of wing or tail missing, the aircraft appears to have been susceptible to catching fire when hit in the fuselage, even from small arms fire. Twin-engined fighters like the F-4 Phantom and RF-101 Voodoo also had the edge over the single-engined F-105 as far as battle damage was concerned. With one engine out an F-4 or RF-101 could still make it home!

When the conflict in Vietnam escalated in late 1964 the USAF had a total of 24 Thunderchief squadrons operational in the USA, Europe and Japan having largely replaced the F-100 Super Sabre as the Air Force's primary front-line fighter-bomber. The first F-105s to arrive in Thailand were eight aircraft of the 36th TFS that departed Yokota AB, Japan on 9 August for a spell of temporary duty. The Thai bases of Takhli and Korat were to become the eventual homes of the F-105 wings that were later deployed to Southeast Asia. Although destined to become the USAF's primary tactical bomber in the war against North Vietnam, in 1964 it was restricted to supporting the CIA's secret war in Laos. The US refused to acknowledge that F-105s were based in Thailand for some considerable time.

14 August 1964

F-105D 62-4371 36 TFS, 41 AD on TDY, USAF, Takhli
Lt David Graben (survived)

Three days after the 36th TFS arrived at Korat the first F-105 to be lost in Southeast Asia was hit by ground fire when flying on a RESCAP mission for an Air America T-28 over Laos. The Thunderchief was attacking an anti-aircraft gun position when it was hit in the engine and stabiliser causing a small fire. The pilot climbed the aircraft to 39,000 feet to starve the fire of oxygen. He then descended slowly and made an emergency landing at Korat.

The aircraft was too badly damaged to be repaired and was struck off and scrapped.

18 August 1964

F-100D 56-3085 428 TFS, 474 TFW on TDY, USAF, Takhli
1Lt Colin Arnie Clark (survived)

Since May 1962 onwards F-100 squadrons had been deploying to Thailand and South Vietnam on temporary tours of duty lasting from a few months to over a year. The F-100s had been flying air operations over Laos and South Vietnam for more than two years before the first Super Sabre was shot down.

On 18 August a Royal Lao Air Force T-28 was shot down during a close air support mission in the northwest sector of the Plain of Jars. An Air America UH-34 was sent in to rescue the T-28 crew and a flight of four F-100s was scrambled from Takhli to provide top cover and defence suppression for the helicopter. The UH-34 was shot down by Pathet Lao gunners as it approached the area where the T-28 was lost. The F-100s then commenced strafing the enemy gun emplacements but one aircraft was hit. The pilot managed to gain altitude and head south towards safety. He crossed the Mekong River and, as the aircraft became harder to handle, he ejected near the Thai town of Nong Khai and was rescued by another Air America helicopter. Arnie Clark was later shot down again on 22 January 1969. One of the crew of the Air America helicopter that had been shot down was rescued later in the day when the Pathet Lao defences had been subdued by further attacks from USAF and Royal Lao aircraft. Two more Laotian T-28s were shot down during further rescue attempts over the next two days. None of the T-28 crews were ever found.

19 August 1964

A-4E 150033 VA-55, USN, USS *Ticonderoga*
1 pilot, name unknown (survived)

A Skyhawk was lost due to a catapult launch error on board the USS *Ticonderoga*.

29 August 1964

A-1E 52-132465 1 ACS, 34 TG, USAF, Bien Hoa
Capt Richard Dean Goss (KIA)
1 VNAF observer, name unknown (KIA)

After the fatigue problems suffered by the T-28 and B-26 the 1st ACS was re-equipped with 25 A-1E Skyraiders from ex-Navy stocks in May and June. The Skyraider was selected because the aircraft had an excellent load-carrying capability and a good endurance as well as being sturdy and relatively simple to maintain. As the Skyraider had already been delivered to the VNAF there was also benefits from the USAF operating the same type. The model selected by the USAF was the two-seat A-1E, originally designed as a submarine hunter-killer. The two-seat Skyraider was needed by the USAF so that they could train Vietnamese pilots to fly the aircraft and also so that they could carry a VNAF observer in order to comply with Washington's rules regarding US air operations in South Vietnam. Eventually about 150 A-1Es were refurbished for use by the USAF, many of them seeing service in Southeast Asia. In USAF documents the aircraft serial number was recorded by prefixing the Navy's Bureau of Aeronautics serial with the year of manufacture. The first USAF A-1E to be lost in the war was shot down by AAA during a night training flight near Bien Hoa.

6 September 1964

A-4E 150024 VA-56, USN, USS *Ticonderoga*
Lt Donald Vol Hester (KWF)

Another Skyhawk crashed during a catapult launch on a training flight from USS *Ticonderoga*. The pilot could not be rescued.

7 September 1964

U-10A 62-5911 1 ACS, 34 TG, USAF, Bien Hoa
2 crew, names unknown (survived)

An Air Commando U-10 Courier crashed during a psychological warfare mission in South Vietnam due to engine failure.

Four squadrons deployed the SP-2 Neptune to Southeast Asia to take part in the Market Time surveillance campaign to reduce infiltration in to South Vietnam by sea. VP-1 sent four detachments to Tan Son Nhut and Cam Ranh Bay between October 1964 and February 1969 but the only Neptune lost during the war was a VP-42 aircraft. USN

8 September 1964

SP-2E 131513 VP-42, USN, Iwakuni NAS, Japan
Lt Cdr John Clarence Thomas (KIA)
ADR1 Deloss William Anderson (KIA)
AO1 Donald Frank Marit (KIA)
AE1 Weslie David Newborn (KIA)
AMS1 Michael John Ulicsni (KIA)
8 crew, names unknown (survived)

US Navy maritime patrol aircraft were tasked with surveillance of Vietnamese coastal waters and the South China Sea on the lookout for enemy boats. Although anti-submarine warfare was the primary role of the squadrons involved, they also had an anti-surface vessel capability. At first the patrol aircraft were based in Japan and the Philippines but later detachments would be based in South Vietnam and Thailand. This SP-2E Neptune flew into the South China Sea 75 miles off the coast of South Vietnam and 340 miles northeast of Saigon killing five of its crew. The other eight crewmen were rescued by the USS *Maddox*. VP-42 had only recently moved into its new base at Iwakuni from North Island NAS, California on 6 July.

23 September 1964

A-1E 52-132441 1 ACS, 34 TG, USAF, Bien Hoa
1Lt George Edward Flynn (KIA)
1 VNAF observer, name unknown (POW)

A-1E 52-132656 1 ACS, 34 TG, USAF, Bien Hoa
Capt W H May (survived)
1 VNAF observer, name unknown (POW)

Two Skyraider aircraft were shot down by .50 calibre gunfire as they were defending a government outpost at night near Ap Vinh Tho, south of the Mekong Delta. The aircraft were silhouetted by flares when making low-level napalm attacks on Viet Cong forces. US Army helicopters from the 57th Medical Detachment arrived at the scene and rescued Capt May but the other two survivors were captured. Following this incident the use of napalm in night support missions was discontinued for some time.

26 September 1964

A-1E 52-132450 1 ACS, 34 TG, USAF, Bien Hoa
Maj W G Harris (survived)
1 VNAF observer, name unknown (survived)

A Skyraider was shot down near Ap An Dien in the Mekong Delta during a close air support mission. The crew bailed out and were rescued by helicopter.

2 October 1964

A-1E 52-132654 1 ACS, 34 TG, USAF, Bien Hoa
Capt Kenneth Earl Walker (KIA)
2Lt B F Fi, probably VNAF (KIA)

Yet another 1st ACS A-1E was lost while conducting a napalm attack on a close air support mission near Giong Dua at the mouth of the Mekong River.

14 October 1964

KB-50J 48-0065 Detachment 1, 421 ARS, 41 AD on TDY,
USAF, Takhli
6 crew, names unknown (survived)

The ageing KB-50, a modified variant of the wartime B-29 Superfortress, was used in the early stage of the war in Southeast Asia as a tanker aircraft. Only about 20 KB-50s were still in use in PACAF in 1964 and these were due to be withdrawn in 1966 to be replaced by the KC-135 Stratotanker. In June 1964 four KB-50s of Detachment 1, 421st ARS deployed from Yokota AB, Japan to Takhli to support Yankee Team missions over Laos.

Another four aircraft formed Detachment 2 at Tan Son Nhut. A KB-50 crashed in Thailand after an engine failed shortly after taking off on an air-to-air refuelling training mission. The amount of corrosion discovered when the wreckage of this aircraft was examined forced the immediate early retirement on the KB-50 fleet and its replacement by SAC KC-135 Stratotankers.

24 October 1964

C-123B 55-4549 315 TCG, USAF, Tan Son Nhut
Capt Edward Stephen Krukowski (KIA)
1Lt Valmore William Bourque (KIA)
1Lt Robert George Armstrong (KIA)
SSgt Ernest Joseph Halvorson (KIA)
SSgt Theodore Bert Phillips (KIA)
A1C Eugene Richardson (KIA)
SSgt Lawrence Woods, US Army,
5th Special Forces Group (KIA)
PFC Charles Pierce Sparks, US Army (KIA)

A Provider took off from Nha Trang to drop ammunition to an isolated Special Forces camp at Bu Prang close to the Cambodian border. During the mission it wandered over the border and was hit in the starboard engine by AAA from within Cambodia itself. The aircraft crashed with the loss of all on board a few miles from Phum Dak Dam just inside Cambodia. A second C-123 was damaged by ground fire on the same mission.

26 October 1964

A-1E 52-132411 1 ACS, 34 TG, USAF, Bien Hoa
1Lt Glenn Charles Dyer (KIA)
1 VNAF observer, name unknown (KIA)

A Skyraider on an airborne alert for possible Viet Cong activity was shot down five miles west of Tan Son Nhut airfield.

29 October 1964

A-1E 52-132476 1 ACS, 34 TG, USAF, Bien Hoa
Capt Edward Aloysius Blake (KWF)
Capt John Christopher Knaggs (KWF)

Another A-1E, the seventh lost since August, crashed during a training flight near Bien Hoa killing both the crew.

1 November 1964

B-57Bs 52-1555, 53-3892, 53-3894, 53-3914, 53-3924
8/13 TBS, 405 FW, USAF, Bien Hoa

At 25 minutes past midnight as October became November Bien Hoa air base was rocked by the explosion of mortar rounds. The Viet Cong had set up six 81mm mortars less than a quarter of a mile from the northern perimeter of the base and fired 83 rounds before withdrawing without loss to themselves. Twenty B-57s of the 7th and 13th TBSs were parked in four neat rows in the

centre of the base and five were destroyed with 13 others damaged to some degree. In addition an HH-43B Huskie rescue helicopter was destroyed and two more damaged and the VNAF had three A-1s destroyed, three more damaged and two C-47s damaged. Four American soldiers were killed and 72 others wounded. This was a devastating and highly embarrassing attack for the American forces and was only the first of many such attacks. Air base defence in South Vietnam was a constant problem that was never really solved. Defensive perimeters were pushed out further and further (in some cases several miles) but it was a costly task in that it tied down considerable numbers of combat troops and the very nature of the enemy made them difficult to stop entirely.

F-8E 149141 VF-53, USN, USS *Ticonderoga*
1 pilot, name unknown (KIA)

A Crusader accidentally crashed into the sea soon after launch and the pilot was killed.

7 November 1964

O-1F 57-2828 1 ACS, 34 TG, USAF, Bien Hoa
Lt Col A H Holman (survived)
SSgt P L Battle (survived)

Although normally operated by the 19th TASS, this Bird Dog appears to have belonged to 1st ACS when it was shot down during a visual reconnaissance mission. Both crew survived a crash landing and were recovered.

The Phantom in Southeast Asia

The F-4 Phantom was probably the most ubiquitous and the most successful combat aircraft in the Southeast Asian theatre. Originally designed for the US Navy the aircraft was also used extensively by the Air Force and the Marine Corps. The Phantom was a truly multi-role aircraft being equally capable of air-to-air and air-to-ground missions. Its sturdy airframe enabled it to carry up to 22,500lbs of stores including just about every bomb in the US inventory together with AIM-7 Sparrow and AIM-9 Sidewinder air-to-air-missiles. One of its few limitations was the lack of an internal gun. The Phantom was designed when the advent of the air-to-air missile was thought to be the complete answer to air combat. As a fighter the aircraft's intended role was as a bomber destroyer and the target could be more easily killed with a missile than a gun. Any thought of the return to dogfighting as in the Second World War or Korea was dismissed. However, the value of a gun soon became apparent in Vietnam and the Phantom could be fitted with externally mounted gun pods but these were heavy and caused drag that slowed the aircraft down considerably. Only when the F-4E version of the Phantom entered service in Southeast Asia in November 1968 was this deficiency remedied. However, despite the omission of a gun the Phantom proved to be one of the truly great aircraft of the 1960s and 1970s and it played

a major role in the air war in Southeast Asia. The first Phantoms to enter action were Navy F-4Bs operating on board the USS Constellation, Ranger and Coral Sea in 1964.

13 November 1964

F-4B 151402 VF-142, USN, USS *Constellation*
Lt W R Moore (survived)
Lt(jg) W M Myers (survived)

The first US Navy F-4 Phantom lost in Southeast Asia stalled and spun during practice air combat manoeuvring. Both the crew ejected safely and were picked up by a Navy helicopter.

A-4C 149570 VA-146, USN, USS *Constellation*
1 pilot, name unknown (survived)

RF-8A 146879 Detachment F, VFP-63, USN,
USS *Constellation*
Capt Darl Russell Bloom, USMC (KWF)

The USS *Constellation* did not have a very good day on Friday 13 November. Following the loss of a Phantom, a Skyhawk then collided with an RF-8A during a training flight just off the coast about 15 miles north of Da Nang. The Crusader was being flown by a USMC pilot on detachment to the *Constellation* from VMCJ-1, the Marines' own photo-reconnaissance squadron. The Skyhawk pilot ejected safely but Capt Bloom was not seen to eject and probably died in his aircraft.

Search and Rescue - I

As the war in Southeast Asia escalated, so the need for search and rescue became more important. Following the loss of the first two USAF aircraft in South Vietnam Detachment 3 of the Pacific Air Rescue Center was established at Tan Son Nhut on 1 April 1962. Initially the rescue coordinator used whatever aircraft and helicopters were available if SAR was required but in May 1964 the Joint Chiefs of Staff directed that the SAR mission in Southeast Asia be assigned to the USAF and that sufficient aircraft be assigned to fulfil the mission. Two HH-43B Huskie helicopters

were sent to Nakon Phanom in June while two HU-16B Albatross amphibians were sent to Korat and another three to Da Nang. The need for search and rescue was highlighted by the loss of the two Yankee Team F-8s over Laos in June 1964. After the Gulf of Tonkin Incident in August further HH-43s were deployed on temporary duty to Takhli and Korat. The HH-43B was particularly unsuitable for operations in the Southeast Asian environment. Its low power, limited radius of action, and small capacity severely limited its usefulness. The improved HH-43F, introduced late in 1964, was a little better but the rescue forces often had to rely on helicopters operated by the Army, Marine Corps, VNAF or, in the case of Laos, Air America. By the end of 1964 USAF HH-43s were based at Bien Hoa, Da Nang, Nakon Phanom, Takhli, Korat and Pleiku. However, the first major SAR effort of the war in Southeast Asia that took place on 18/19 November relied heavily on Air America aircraft and it was obvious that the USAF needed to enhance its capability in this critical area.

18 November 1964

F-100D serial ..? 613 TFS, 401 TFW on TDY, USAF, Da Nang
Capt William Reynolds Martin (KIA)

The 613th TFS arrived at Da Nang from England AFB, Louisiana early in November. Before the month was out the Squadron had lost an aircraft and its pilot. Capt Martin was flying one of two F-100s escorting a Yankee Team reconnaissance mission over southern Laos when he was shot down. The aircraft was hit by AAA near Ban Senphan as Capt Martin was attacking a gun emplacement. His loss triggered what turned out to be the largest SAR effort so far mounted in the war. Martin's wingman called to the Air America Air Operations Centre in Vientiane that ran the SAR system in Laos. The F-100 came down close to the border with North Vietnam. An Air America C-123 was first on the scene and acted as airborne controller until handing over to a USAF HU-16 Albatross from Korat. The HU-16 called for US Navy Skyraiders, which were already airborne, to fly to the area to pro-

vide defence suppression for the rescue forces. The Skyraiders duly arrived and attacked gun emplacements but were themselves slightly damaged during the action. One of the Navy pilots spotted what he thought was burning wreckage in the jungle and the airborne controller called in two HH-43 Huskie rescue helicopters from Nakhon Phanom. The Navy aircraft escorted the helicopters to the fire but no wreckage was seen and the helicopters returned to base. By the end of the first day the search had involved a C-123, two Air America H-34s, 13 F-105s, eight F-100s, six Navy A-1Es and two HH-43s, all controlled by the HU-16 airborne controller. The next morning another HU-16 and four F-105s returned to Ban Senphan and the Albatross pilot eventually spotted the F-100's wreckage and Capt Martin's parachute very close to an AAA site. The gun emplacement was destroyed by the F-105s and two H-34s escorted by four T-28s from Udorn arrived to attempt a pick up. After the site was cleared the co-pilot from one of the helicopters was lowered to the crash site but found that Capt Martin had died of injuries when he hit the rocky ground. Although the outcome was negative, this SAR attempt was indicative of the many hundreds of such missions that would be flown over the next eight years, many of them successful in returning aircrew to safety from seemingly hopeless positions.

19 November 1964

T-28D 51-7870 Detachment 6, 1 ACW attached to
35 TACG, USAF, Udorn
Capt George Henry Albrecht (KIA)
1Lt Leonard Paul Hudson (KIA)

T-28D serial ..? Detachment 6, 1 ACW attached to 35 TACG,
USAF, Udorn
Maj Otis Gordon (KIA)
Capt Edwin Raymond Eason (KIA)

In April 1964 Detachment 6 of the 1st ACW was set up at Udorn RTAB in northern Thailand with four T-28Ds. This small unit, operating under the code name Water Pump, was tasked with training pilots of the Royal Laotian Air Force. However, it also played a full part in the war against the Pathet Lao in the Plain of Jars and the supply routes of what came to be known as the Ho Chi Minh Trail in the Laotian panhandle. The unit was absorbed into the 606th ACS in 1966. These aircraft, however, were shot down by AAA in South Vietnam and were said to be on a fact-finding mission to Da Nang to investigate the possibility of replacing the T-28s at Udorn with A-1Es.

The RF-101 in Southeast Asia

The RF-101C was a single-seat photographic reconnaissance version of the Voodoo interceptor that had first entered service with the USAF in 1958. The RF-101C was one of the first US jet aircraft to be based in Southeast Asia. On 18 October 1961 four aircraft from the 15th TRS based at Kadena AB, Japan deployed to Tan Son Nhut under the code name Pipe Stem to photograph suspected Viet Cong strongholds. Three weeks later, on 6 November, they were replaced by another detachment of four RF-101Cs from the 45th TRS (code name Able Mable) that deployed from Misawa AB, Japan to Don Muang airport in Thailand. The two detachments made reconnaissance flights over South Vietnam and Laos until the Geneva talks brought a temporary cessation of flights over Laos in July 1962. The Able Mable detachment moved to Tan Son Nhut in December 1962 as the concentration of effort shifted from Laos to South Vietnam. In the early years of the war four Voodoo squadrons (the 15th from Kadena AB, the 45th from Misawa AB, and the 20th and 29th from Shaw AFB, South Carolina) provided air and ground crews for the detachments based in South Vietnam and Thailand. Two more aircraft were added to the

The Kaman HH-43 Huskie was the first USAF helicopter deployed to Southeast Asia to provide SAR coverage for downed airmen. The type was responsible for more rescues than any other helicopter and at least two Huskies were normally assigned to each US airbase throughout the war. USAF

The RF-101C Voodoo was one of the first aircraft to be camouflaged in Southeast Asia as this example at Tan Son Nhut in December 1965 illustrates. A total of 38 RF-101Cs were lost during the war, 28 of them while on reconnaissance missions over North Vietnam. USAF

Able Mable detachment on 1 April 1963 and by August 1964 a total of 16 RF-101Cs were based at Tan Son Nhut. The 20th TRS was the only RF-101C unit assigned to Southeast Asia in full strength and was based at Tan Son Nhut before moving to Udorn in September 1966.

In the spring of 1964 the situation in Laos became more serious and the US decided to resume reconnaissance flights over the country. This time the flights were of a more tactical nature, supplying targeting information on Pathet Lao troop movements to Royalist forces. Under the code name Yankee Team the joint US Air Force and Navy operation commenced on 19 May when four Able Mable aircraft flew sorties over Laos. In March 1965 the RF-101s started reconnaissance flights (code named Blue Tree) over North Vietnam, a development facilitated by moving four aircraft of the 15th TRS from Tan Son Nhut to Udorn to start a detachment code named Green Python.

The role of the RF-101C evolved into four types of reconnaissance mission: surveillance, concentrating on lines of communications; pre-strike reconnaissance for targeting purposes; post-strike reconnaissance for battle damage assessment; and (from mid-1965) searching for SAM sites. The very early missions were escorted by F-100s, later replaced by F-105s and F-4s. However, the reconnaissance aircraft often flew unescorted singly or in pairs, often preferring this to flying with escorts. Unencumbered by large amounts of ordnance, the Voodoo was actually faster than its escorts and recce pilots relied primarily on speed, tactics and terrain masking for survival. In April 1966 a study showed that many of the Voodoos shot down by AAA were the wingmen who were following their leaders and were hit by AAA aimed at the lead aircraft which usually escaped unscathed. The result was that from this date most reconnaissance missions were flown by single aircraft. However, this caused problems in determining the cause of attrition when aircraft did not return nor did it give the redundancy of a second aircraft to complete the mission if the first aircraft was shot down or had to abort.

Probably because the Voodoos spent much of their time at low level, the aircraft was one of the first USAF types to receive the three tone tactical camouflage in mid-1965. Curiously, the Voodoo squadrons were among the last to adopt squadron tail codes when they came into use later in the war.

21 November 1964

RF-101C 56-0230   15 TRS, 18 TFW on TDY, USAF,
Tan Son Nhut
Capt B L Waltz (survived)

Capt Waltz was flying a Yankee Team photo-reconnaissance mission near Ban Senphan in southern Laos at 3,000 feet when his aircraft was hit by 37mm anti-aircraft fire. The Voodoo caught fire and Capt Waltz ejected near Ban Kouantan but was picked up, albeit badly injured, within an hour by an Air America UH-34 helicopter that happened to be in the vicinity. This particular aircraft was the penultimate RF-101C of 166 built between 1958 and March 1959. Following the loss of this aircraft and the F-100 three days earlier, the theatre commanders wanted to make a major strike on targets in the Mu Gia Pass in the hope that it would force the North Vietnamese to stop using the area for the movement of supplies to South Vietnam. However, permission was denied by Washington as it did not wish to escalate the war further at this stage.

23 November 1964

A-4E   151037   VA-55, USN, USS Ticonderoga
1 pilot, name unknown (survived)

The fifth and final loss of USS Ticonderoga's first tour of the war involved a Skyhawk that suffered engine failure thought to have been caused by salt water contamination of the fuel.

27 November 1964

F-102A 56-1189   Detachment 5, 509 FIS, 405 FW, USAF,
Tan Son Nhut
1 pilot, name unknown (survived)

F-102 Delta Dagger interceptors had been deployed in small detachments to bases in Southeast Asia since April 1961. The detachments became larger and more frequent from August 1964 after the Gulf of Tonkin Incident. The first F-102 to be lost in Southeast Asia crashed on 27 November after suffering engine failure, forcing the pilot to eject.

1 December 1964

A-1E   52-132640   1 ACS, 34 TG, USAF, Bien Hoa
1Lt K P Roedeman (survived)
WO D S Tan, VNAF (KIA)

A Skyraider was on a training flight when it was hit in the starboard wing by ground fire and crashed near Phuoc Vinh. Although both the crew bailed out of the stricken Spad only 1Lt Roedeman survived to be rescued by helicopter.

7 December 1964

A-4C   serial ..?   Detachment T, VMA-223, USMC, USS Yorktown
1 pilot, name unknown (survived)

The USS Yorktown was one of the US Navy's oldest carriers at this time. It had been commissioned on 15 April 1943 and was redesignated as an ASW support carrier in September 1957. As such its normal complement consisted primarily of S-2 Trackers and SH-3A Sea King helicopters. However, occasional detachments from USMC attack squadrons deployed on board the Navy's ASW carriers to enable the attack pilots to keep current in carrier qualifications. The Skyhawks also gave the carriers a small measure of fast jet offensive capability while ensuring a degree of air defence protection. On 7 December an A-4 from the VMA-223 detachment was about to launch when a missile motor ignited and set the aircraft on fire resulting in its destruction.

9 December 1964

RA-5C   149306   RVAH-5, USN, USS Ranger
Lt Cdr Donald Wayne Beard (KIA)
Lt(jg) Brian John Cronin (KIA)

The first RA-5C Vigilante lost during the war was also the first aircraft lost by USS Ranger, although it had been on the line in the Gulf of Tonkin since 18 September. The Vigilante was a large aircraft, originally designed as a nuclear attack bomber but by the time the war in Vietnam became 'hot' the only version in service with TF 77 was the RA-5C reconnaissance aircraft. The Vigilantes provided a long range, high speed photographic reconnaissance capability for TF 77 under the operation code name Blue Tree. Lt Cdr Beard's aircraft was thought to have been lost at sea off the coast of South Vietnam due to a navigational error. Vigilante 149306 was the first of 55 production RA-5Cs to be built although a further 59 aircraft were converted from earlier models.

27 December 1964

A-3B   142250   Detachment L, VAH-4, USN, USS Hancock
3 crew, names unknown (survived)
1 crew, name unknown (KWF)

The USS Hancock first took up station in the Gulf of Tonkin on 28 December, but the day before she lost one of her A-3B Skywarrior attack bombers. During a training mission the aircraft apparently suffered a control system failure and caught fire. All the crew except one managed to escape and were rescued. Most carriers had a detachment of A-3 Skywarriors on board during the war although they were only used in their primary role of heavy attack bombers in the early years. Later, Skywarriors, or Whales as they were nicknamed, were used mainly as tankers, electronic warfare and reconnaissance aircraft.

30 December 1964

A-4C   149625   VA-216, USN, USS Hancock
Lt Frank Scot Crismon (KWF)

Three days after her first loss, the Hancock suffered another tragedy on the 30th when an A-4 Skyhawk hit the ramp and exploded when landing back on the carrier after a training flight.

31 December 1964

O-1F   57-2823   366 TFS, USAF, Da Nang
Capt Kurt Casey McDonald (KIA)
SFC Edward Ray Dodge, US Army,
Detachment C-1, 5th Special Forces
Group (KIA)

As well as its use as an FAC aircraft, the O-1 was also used as a liaison aircraft for short flights between airfields or airstrips. SFC Dodge was based at Da Nang with Detachment C-1 of the 5th Special Forces Group. On New Year's eve he accompanied Capt McDonald in an O-1F on a flight to the Special Forces camp at A Shau. The aircraft took off in poor weather in company with another O-1F flown by WO G B Mundis. As the two aircraft made a turn in a valley about 20 miles northwest of Da Nang, McDonald and Dodge's aircraft disappeared as it entered low cloud and Mundis pressed on to A Shau alone. Neither the aircraft nor its crew were ever found and despite uncorroborated information regarding their capture, their loss remains a mystery.

Chapter Two

1965

Escalation of the War and the Start of Rolling Thunder

2 January 1965

F-100D 56-2908   probably 428 TFS, 474 TFW on TDY,
USAF, Takhli
1 pilot, name unknown (survived)

A Super Sabre on temporary deployment from Cannon AFB, New Mexico, crashed in Thailand due to engine failure.

12 January 1965

O-1F 55-4712   19 TASS, 34 TG, USAF, Bien Hoa
Capt T L Craig (survived)
1 other, probably VNAF observer (survived)

An O-1 FAC was hit in the wing by AAA and was forced to crash-land, fortunately without injury.

13 January 1965

F-105D 62-4296   44 or 67 TFS, 18 TFW attached to 6234
TFW, USAF, Korat
Capt Albert C Vollmer (survived)

F-100D serial ..?   probably 613 TFS, 401 TFW on TDY,
USAF, Da Nang
Capt C L Ferguson (survived)

On 14 December F-105s and F-100s flew the first mission of what was intended to be a limited bombing campaign against targets in Laos. The campaign was code named Barrel Roll and was aimed specifically at infiltration routes through Laos into South Vietnam through which the North Vietnamese were keeping the Viet Cong supplied. Just one month after the start of the Barrel Roll missions the USAF suffered its first casualties in the campaign. Targets on Route 7 and Route 8 were attacked in the early weeks of the campaign and on the 13th a major strike was planned on the Ban Ken Bridge on Route 7 at the northern end of the Laotian panhandle. The strike involved 16 F-105s from the 44th and 67th TFSs led by an RF-101 acting as a pathfinder. Eight F-100s armed with cluster bombs would attack the 34 known AAA positions around the bridge, and another RF-101 would follow up to obtain photographs of the expected damage. The F-105s dropped 64 x 750lb bombs and fired 16 Bullpup missiles at the bridge, destroying it early on in the raid. Unexpended ordnance was then used against the AAA sites but the aircraft had to make several passes at low level with the result that one F-105 and one F-100 were shot down and four other aircraft damaged. The Thunderchief pilot was shot down on his third pass as he fired a Bullpup missile while the Super Sabre pilot was shot down on his fifth pass. Capt Vollmer ejected about four miles from the target after his aircraft caught fire and he lost control. Fortunately, both pilots were soon rescued by an Air America UH-34 helicopter directed by an Air America C-123 that had been standing by to act as airborne controller in the eventuality of a rescue being required. The mission was criticised for continuing once the bridge had been dropped and loss of the two aircraft prompted charges by a US senator that the strike violated the Geneva Accords.

Albert Vollmer was one of several pilots who were shot down twice during the war. He had enlisted in the USAF in 1950 and had served as a B-29 gunner during the Korean War before commissioning as a pilot and flying the F-86, F-94 and F-100 before converting to the F-105. He was shot down on his third mission but was then shot down again on 17 August 1967 receiving injuries serious enough to curtail his flying career for over two years.

F-8C 147011   VF-24, USN, USS *Hancock*
Lt(jg) Tom Irwin (survived)

Upon landing back from an air intercept training flight a Crusader suffered a tail hook failure as it snagged the *Hancock's* No 4 wire and went over the side. The aircraft was not flying fast enough for a safe ejection so the pilot stayed with the F-8 as it ditched. The afterburner cut in just as the aircraft hit the water and the engine exploded. The canopy was jettisoned and Lt Irwin swam away from the aircraft before it sank. He was rescued by one of the carrier's SH-2 Seasprites and was back on the deck of the *Hancock* within two minutes of ditching.

15 January 1965

O-1F 57-2806   19 TASS, 34 TG, USAF, Bien Hoa
Capt H L Brown (survived)
1 VNAF observer, name unknown
(survived)

A Bird Dog FAC aircraft was hit by ground fire in the port wing and had to make a crash landing.

27 January 1965

A-1E 52-132666   1 ACS, 34 TG, USAF, Bien Hoa
Maj George Frederick Vlisides (KIA)
1 VNAF observer, name unknown (KIA)

A Skyraider crashed due to pilot error during a close air support mission in Bien Hoa province killing both the crew.

7 February 1965

A-4E 150075   VA-155, USN, USS *Coral Sea*
Lt Edward Andrew Dickson (KIA)

Following the establishment of TF 77 aircraft carriers in the South China Sea in August 1964 it was six months before the US Navy was again in action although 13 naval aircraft had been lost in accidents over Southeast Asian waters during this time. Although air strikes against North Vietnam were part of President Johnson's 2 December plan they were not immediately instigated. However, VC attacks on US facilities at Saigon on 24 December and Pleiku and Camp Holloway on 7 February caused President Johnson to order the first air strike against North Vietnam since Pierce Arrow in August 1964. The new strike, code named Flaming Dart I, was due to be flown by the US Navy from the carriers *Coral Sea*, *Hancock* and *Ranger*. The targets were at Dong Hoi and Vit Thu Lu while other targets were hit by VNAF A-1s. The raid was led by Cdr Warren H Sells, Commander of *Hancock's* Air Wing 21. In the event monsoon weather forced the 34 aircraft of USS *Ranger's* strike force to abort their mission against Vit Thu Lu but Dong Hoi's barracks and port facilities were attacked by 20 aircraft from the *Coral Sea* and 29 from the *Hancock*. The strike was carried out at low level under a 700 feet cloud base in rain and poor visibility. Only one naval aircraft was lost during the strike, a Skyhawk flown by Lt Dickson of VA-155. Lt Dickson was a section leader of a flight of four aircraft. About five miles south of the target he reported that he had been hit by AAA and requested his wingman to check his aircraft over as they commenced their run in to the target. Just as the flight was about release its bombs Lt Dickson's aircraft was seen to burst into flames, but despite a warning from his wingman, he continued with his bomb run and released his Snakeye bombs on target. Lt Dickson headed out towards the sea but his aircraft became engulfed in flames and he ejected. Although he was seen to eject

his parachute was not seen to deploy and the aircraft crashed into the sea about half a mile offshore. There was no sign of Lt Dickson in the water despite a SAR effort that continued for two days. However, in March 1968 a Vietnamese newspaper printed a photograph of a grave on a beach which was claimed to be that of Lt Dickson and in August 1985 the Vietnamese handed over the Lieutenant's Geneva Convention and ID Card which would seem to confirm the beach burial.

Edward Dickson had had a miraculous escape from death just one year earlier when he was forced to eject from his Skyhawk over the Sierra Nevada mountains in California during a training exercise. His parachute failed to deploy properly but he landed in a deep snowdrift that broke his fall causing only minor injuries. However, on 7 February 1965 his luck ran out and he became the second US aviator to die while attacking North Vietnam. Edward Dickson was posthumously awarded the Navy Cross for his determination to complete the mission despite crippling combat damage.

10 February 1965

A-1E 52-132401   1 ACS, 34 TG, USAF, Bien Hoa
Capt William Young Duggan (survived)
1 VNAF observer, name unknown (KIA)

During a close air support mission an A-1 was hit by ground fire and the starboard wing burst into flames. The aircraft crashed into the sea just off the Mekong Delta and only the USAF pilot survived to be rescued by helicopter. Capt Duggan later returned to Southeast Asia as a Phantom pilot and was killed during a mission over southern Laos on New Year's Eve 1971.

11 February 1965

F-8D 148633   VF-154, USN, USS *Coral Sea*
Lt Cdr Robert Harper Shumaker (POW)

A-4C 149572   VA-153, USN, USS *Coral Sea*
Lt W T Majors (survived)

The Flaming Dart 1 mission of 7 February did not appear to have the salutary effect on the North Vietnamese that Washington had hoped for. On 10 February the Viet Cong struck at an American camp at Qui Nhon causing serious casualties. The immediate response to this was Flaming Dart 2, flown the following day. A more far-reaching response was a plan agreed by President Johnson to send four tactical squadrons to Southeast Asia and 30 B-52 strategic bombers to Anderson AFB, Guam. On 13 February the President authorised the start of operation Rolling Thunder, a sustained bombing campaign against military targets in North Vietnam, the first mission being flown on 2 March.

For Flaming Dart 2 a total of 99 naval aircraft from the *Coral Sea*, *Hancock* and *Ranger* were sent against NVA barracks at Chanh Hoa near Dong Hoi. The target was attacked in poor visibility with low cloud and the *Coral Sea* suffered two aircraft and one pilot lost on this raid. The first to be brought down was Lt Cdr Shumaker's Crusader which was hit in the tail (possibly by debris from his own rockets) when he was pulling out from an attack on an anti-aircraft gun position. The aircraft's afterburner blew out and the hydraulic system must have been damaged as the F-8 soon became uncontrollable forcing Shumaker to eject over land although his aircraft crashed a few miles offshore from Dong Hoi. Shumaker's parachute opened about 30 feet above the ground and he broke his back on landing for which he received no medical treatment. Shumaker became the second naval avi-

ator to be taken prisoner in North Vietnam and spent the next eight years in various POW camps including the infamous Hoa Lo prison dubbed the Hanoi Hilton by Shumaker as one of its first inmates. Robert Shumaker continued his naval career following his release from North Vietnam on 12 February 1973 and retired as a Rear Admiral.

A few minutes after Lt Cdr Shumaker's Crusader was shot down another wave of aircraft hit the Chanh Hoa barracks and another aircraft was lost. Lt Majors was also attacking enemy AAA, using CBU-24 cluster bombs. After delivering his bombs he climbed the Skyhawk to 4,000 feet and set course for the carrier. However, his engine suddenly seized and could not be relit. Faced with no alternative Majors ejected over the sea but was picked up almost immediately by a USAF rescue helicopter. It could not be known for sure whether the engine seized due to battle damage or a technical malfunction.

Bomb damage assessments at Chanh Hoa showed that 23 of the 76 buildings in the camp were either damaged or destroyed during the raid but the loss of two aircraft (and almost a third as another Skyhawk flown by Lt E G Hiebert of VA-155 was badly damaged when it made a wheels up landing at Da Nang with hung ordnance) was a high cost to pay.

19 February 1965

F-100D 55-3783   613 TFS, 401 TFW on TDY, USAF, Da Nang
Maj Robert Francis Ronca (KIA)
A Super Sabre was lost during an enemy air defence suppression mission near the Ban Ken Bridge in northern Laos, site of the first major air strike on 13 January.

21 February 1965

F-8E 150897   VF-211, USN, USS *Hancock*
Lt(jg) R N Smith (survived)
A Crusader crashed when the engine failed during a launch from the *Hancock* on a test flight.

24 February 1965

A-3B 147664   VAH-2, USN, USS *Coral Sea*
RMC Dwight Glenn Frakes (KIA)
3 crew, names unknown (survived)
During a tanker sortie, a Skywarrior suffered a fuel transfer problem and the crew of four were forced to abandon the aircraft eight miles from the *Coral Sea*. Only three of the crew were found and rescued by helicopters from the *Coral Sea* and the *Yorktown*. The aircraft was the fifth to last Skywarrior built and had been delivered to the Navy in November 1960.

A-1E 52-132471   1 ACS, 34 TG, USAF, Bien Hoa
Capt Kurt William Gareiss (KIA)
Capt Thomas C McEwen (KIA)
Little is known about this crash of an Air Commando Skyraider except that it occurred in Bien Hoa province and was attributed to pilot error.

Rolling Thunder

The retaliatory Flaming Dart raids appeared to have had no effect on Viet Cong activity in the South nor on the North's open support. Frustration at the lack of response led President Johnson to order a more sustained air campaign against North Vietnam to be put into operation. The campaign was named Rolling Thunder and was intended to be a graduated and measured response to North Vietnamese support for the VC in the South. As early as April 1964 the Joint Chiefs of Staff had drawn up a list of 94 potential targets in North Vietnam that would form the basis of a 12-week sustained air offensive. In the event, this intensive

campaign was not pursued and many of these lucrative targets were not released for attack until years after the start of Rolling Thunder thereby blunting the impact that American air power could have had. The targeting policy and the hesitant way in which the war was fought also had a direct detrimental affect on US aircraft losses.

Instead of an all-out air offensive the intention was for air strikes to start in the southern provinces of North Vietnam and gradually move north, slowly approaching the major cities of Hanoi and Haiphong by which time it was hoped that the North Vietnamese would have capitulated. However, the North Vietnamese showed no such signs of giving up and the US, not wishing to fight an all-out war, imposed restrictions on its air operations. Limitations during the whole of 1965 included no-go areas of 30-mile radius around Hanoi and 10-mile radius around Haiphong and a 30-mile buffer zone along the Chinese border.

It soon became apparent that the many operational restrictions imposed on US airmen limited the types of lucrative targets that could be hit. Industry, ports and, perhaps most surprising of all, airfields were not allowed to be attacked. The range of worthwhile targets that could be struck fell mainly in the category of lines of communications: railways; roads (particularly junctions); rail and road bridges; and, most difficult of all, moving traffic.

The USAF flew the first Rolling Thunder mission on 2 March with the Navy's TF 77 joining in on the second mission on 15 March. By late August 1965 an average of 65 aircraft were operating daily against North Vietnam, rising to 120 the following month.

2 March 1965

F-105D 61-0214   67 TFS, 18 TFW attached to 6234 TFW, USAF, Korat
Capt Robert V Baird (survived)

F-100D 55-2857   613 TFS, 401 TFW on TDY, USAF, Da Nang
1Lt Hayden James Lockhart (POW)

F-105D 62-4325   67 TFS, 18 TFW attached to 6234 TFW, USAF, Korat
Capt K L Spagnola (survived)

F-105D 62-4260   67 TFS, 18 TFW attached to 6234 TFW, USAF, Korat
Maj George W Panas (survived)

F-100D 56-3150   428 TFS, 474 TFW on TDY, USAF, Takhli
Lt J A Cullen (survived)

The first Rolling Thunder strike mission against North Vietnam proved to be a very costly affair with the loss of five USAF aircraft in action within the space of two-and-half hours. The targets were an ammunition depot at Xom Biang just 17 miles north of the DMZ and the Quang Khe naval base at the mouth of the Sou Giang River. The mission was originally planned for 20 February but was postponed twice due firstly to an attempted coup in Saigon and secondly due to bad weather and Soviet attempts to revive the Geneva Accords. Early in the morning of 2 March a strike force of 44 F-105s, 40 F-100s, seven RF-101s, 20 B-57s and 19 VNAF A-1s took off to strike their targets. It appears that the lessons learned during the Ban Ken strike of 13 January had not been heeded as all five aircraft lost on 2 March were hit while attacking enemy AAA sites, three of them while making their second pass at the target. However, the suppression of AAA sites was vital and proved to be effective as none of the strike aircraft which followed the suppression flights were shot down. Lt Cullen's F-100 was shot down on the Quang Khe strike and he came down in the sea just offshore from the target to be rescued by an HU-16 but the other four were all involved in the Xom Bang raid. Capt Baird's Thunderchief was hit by ground fire at extremely low level and crashed moments after he ejected. He was picked up by a USAF HH-43 rescue helicopter, the first combat rescue in North Vietnam. Capt Spagnola managed to fly his badly damaged Thunderchief across the border into Thailand before he eventually had to eject near the town of Roi Et. Maj Panas made it into Laos before he had to part company with his F-105 and he too was soon rescued by a USAF HH-43 helicopter. Unfortunately, 1Lt Lockhart was not so lucky. After ejecting from his Super Sabre he evaded for a week until he was eventually captured on 9 March. Hayden Lockhart gained the dubious distinction of becoming the first member of the USAF to be captured in North Vietnam and joined Lt Alvarez and Lt Cdr Shumaker in captivity until his release on 12 February 1973.

The apparently insignificant little Cessna O-1 Bird Dog was one of the most important aircraft in South Vietnam. Forward air controllers flying the O-1, and later the O-2 and OV-10, controlled practically all air strikes in South Vietnam. O-1F 55-4719 of the 19th TASS crashed on 9 March 1965 during a training flight. USAF

3 March 1965

A-4C 149612 VA-216, USN, USS *Hancock*
1 pilot, name unknown (KWF)

A Skyhawk crashed on the USS *Hancock* when landing from a training flight killing the pilot.

6 March 1965

A-1E 52-135005 1 ACS, 34 TG, USAF, Bien Hoa
1 pilot, name unknown (survived)

An Air Commando Skyraider crashed during a training flight.

9 March 1965

O-1F 55-4719 19 TASS, 34 TG, USAF, Bien Hoa
2 crew, names unknown (survived)

A Bird Dog FAC aircraft crashed during a training flight due to pilot error.

From this date the JCS directed that the US units based in South Vietnam have a greater degree of autonomy. Although restrictions remained on the employment of US aircraft when VNAF air power was available, the necessity to carry VNAF 'observers' was relaxed and the USAF and Army aircraft based in South Vietnam could now fly in US markings rather than VNAF markings.

11 March 1965

B-57B 53-3890 8 TBS, 405 FW attached to 34 TG, USAF, Bien Hoa
Capt William Carroll Mattis (KIA)
1Lt Richard Dean Smith (KIA)

The B-57 squadrons at Bien Hoa had seen little action since their arrival in South Vietnam in August 1964. However, on 18 February restrictions on their use in the offensive role were lifted and the Canberras began air strikes in South Vietnam and took part in some of the early Rolling Thunder operations in North Vietnam. On 11 March two Canberras were attacking a target about 30 miles northeast of Kontum when one of the aircraft suddenly burst into flames and crashed. It was thought that the aircraft had probably been destroyed by the explosions from its own 500lb bombs as the B-57 had dropped them from a very low altitude. The body of Capt Mattis was recovered soon after the incident but it was not until 1994 that the remains of Richard Smith, since promoted to Lt Col in absentia, were recovered and identified during a JTF-FA investigation.

15 March 1965

A-1H 135375 VA-95, USN, USS *Ranger*
Lt(jg) Charles Frederick Clydesdale (KIA)

The US Navy was to play a major part in the Rolling Thunder campaign and flew most its strikes against targets to the east of Hanoi or close to the coast. The first Rolling Thunder strike flown by the Navy was against an ammunition dump at Phu Qui. Lt Clydesdale was killed when his Skyraider flew into the sea while returning to his carrier.

21 March 1965

A-1E 52-132649 1 ACS, 34 TG, USAF, Bien Hoa
Capt William Henry Campbell (KIA)
Capt Jerry Pavey Hawkins (KIA)

During an interdiction sortie near Can Tho a Skyraider was seen to catch fire and crash-land. Although both pilots were found to be dead the aircraft itself was deemed salvageable so an Army CH-54 Skycrane helicopter airlifted it to Tan Son Nhut. The Skyraider was indeed repaired and re-assigned to the 1st ACS. On 10 March 1966 this Skyraider was flown by Maj Bernard Fisher when he performed a daring rescue of a fellow pilot at the A Shau Special Forces Camp, a feat for which Maj Fisher was awarded the Medal of Honour.

22 March 1965

F-105D 62-4233 67 TFS, 18 TFW attached to 6234 TFW, USAF, Korat
Lt Col Robinson Risner (survived)

Lt Col Robinson Risner became a well known POW when he was shot down on 16 September 1965 but that was the second time that the CO of the 67th TFS had parted company with a Thunderchief during a raid on North Vietnam. The first occasion occurred during an early Rolling Thunder mission on 22 March against the Vinh Son radar site when his aircraft was hit by ground fire as he was attacking an AAA site. He managed to fly his aircraft out over the sea where he ejected about a mile offshore and was picked up by a USAF HU-16B Albatross. Risner appeared on the front cover of Time magazine after this incident, a fact that did not serve him well when he became a POW later in the year.

26 March 1965

A-1H 139790 VA-215, USN, USS *Hancock*
Lt(jg) C E Gudmunson (survived)

A-4E 150130 VA-212, USN, USS *Hancock*
Cdr K L Shugart (survived)

F-8D 148644 VF-154, USN, US *Coral Sea*
Lt C E Wangeman (survived)

The US Navy's second Rolling Thunder mission proved very costly with the loss of three aircraft out of 70 despatched, although all three pilots were rescued. The ability of the North Vietnamese air defence system to monitor US raids was a concern even in the early days of the war and the targets for this mission were radar sites at Bach Long Vi, Cap Mui Ron, Ha Tinh and Vinh Son. Bach Long Vi is a small island situated strategically in the Gulf of Tonkin, 70 miles southeast of Haiphong and midway between the mouth of the Red River and the Chinese island of Hainan. It was an obvious choice for the North Vietnamese to position a radar warning station. Lt Gudmunson's Skyraider was hit on his sixth pass over the target at Ha Tinh but he managed to fly to Da Nang where he crash-landed about 5 miles west of the airfield. Cdr Shugart's Skyhawk was hit on his second run as he dropped his Snakeye bombs on the radar site at Vinh Son. Cdr Shugart headed out to sea as the aircraft caught fire but the electrical system failed forcing him to eject about 10 miles offshore. He was picked up by a USAF helicopter. Lt Wangeman did not realise that his Crusader had been hit as he was attacking an AAA site at Bach Long Vi. However, after leaving the target area his aircraft began to lose oil pressure and his wingman observed an oil leak. Wangeman climbed to high altitude and managed to fly the aircraft for over 200 miles before the engine seized and he was forced to eject 20 miles north of Da Nang. He was flying the *Coral Sea* Air Wing Commander's aircraft at the time and he was rescued by a USAF rescue helicopter.

28 March 1965

C-123B 57-6292 unit ..?, USAF, base ..?
4 crew, names unknown (survived)

A C-123 was destroyed in a ground collision with a VNAF A-1H. This particular C-123 was the third to last Provider built having been delivered to the USAF in July 1958 and was the 10th Provider lost in Southeast Asia.

29 March 1965

A-4E 150078 VA-155, USN, USS *Coral Sea*
Cdr Jack H Harris (survived)

F-8D 148642 VF-154, USN, USS *Coral Sea*
Cdr William N Donnelly (survived)

F-8D 148668 VF-154, USN, USS *Coral Sea*
Lt Cdr Kenneth Edward Hume (KIA)

One of the worst features of the Rolling Thunder campaign was Washington's insistence of sending aircraft to the same target again and again until either the target was assessed as being destroyed or the losses sustained outweighed the benefits gained.

On 29 March the *Coral Sea's* air wing returned to Bach Long Vi island which it had visited three days earlier. Again, 70 aircraft were despatched on the mission including six A-3B bombers from VAH-2. Three aircraft were lost in the first wave as they were attacking AAA sites around the target. Coincidentally, two of the airmen shot down and recovered on the 29th were squadron commanders whose loss at this stage would have been a major blow for the *Coral Sea*. Cdr Harris's Skyhawk was hit during his low level bomb run causing his engine to wind down. Despite attempts to restart the engine the Cdr had to eject over the sea close to the target but was picked up by a Navy ship. Cdr Donnelly's Crusader was hit during his first attack and his controls froze as he was making his second pass. He ejected at 450 knots at about 1,000 feet with the aircraft in an inverted dive and was extremely lucky to survive the ejection with only a fractured neck vertebra and dislocated shoulder. He came down in the shark-infested waters four miles north of Bach Long Vi and for 45 hours he drifted in his liferaft which sprung a leak and needed blowing up every 20 minutes. Twice during the first night he had to slip into the water to evade North Vietnamese patrol boats that were searching for him. Fortunately he was spotted by an F-8 pilot on 31 March and was picked up by a USAF HU-16 Albatross amphibian. Another squadron commander, Cdr Pete Mongilardi of VA-153, was almost lost when his A-4 was hit and had to be 'towed' back to a safe landing on the *Coral Sea* by a tanker as the Skyhawk leaked fuel as fast as it was being pumped in. Lt Cdr Hume's aircraft was hit by ground fire as he was firing his Zuni unguided rockets at an AAA site on the island. A small fire was seen coming from the engine and Lt Cdr Hume attempted to make for Da Nang but after a few minutes the aircraft suddenly dived into the sea and although the canopy was seen to separate there was no sign of an ejection.

31 March 1965

A-1H 137584 VA-215, USN, USS *Hancock*
Lt(jg) Gerald Wayne McKinley (KIA)

The battle against the North Vietnamese radar system continued with further raids on the Vinh Son and Cap Mui Ron radar sites involving 60 aircraft from the *Hancock* and *Coral Sea*. Lt McKinley's A-1H was hit by ground fire during its second low level bomb run and the aircraft crashed immediately.

F-100D 55-2906 613 TFS, 401 TFW on TDY, USAF, Da Nang
Capt Ron A Bigoness (survived)

A Super Sabre was hit by ground fire near Ha Tinh in North Vietnam during an early morning weather reconnaissance sortie. Capt Bigoness realised he would not be able to reach Da Nang so instead flew due south towards Laos. He was about 20 miles into Laos before he was forced to eject and was picked up by a USAF HH-43 helicopter from Nakhon Phanom.

The Ho Chi Minh Trail

The Ho Chi Minh Trail was actually a labyrinth of roads, tracks and trails that stretched from North Vietnam via some strategic points, such as the Mu Gia and Ban Karai passes, into Laos and Cambodia and down into South Vietnam. The system, known to the North Vietnamese as the Trung Son Road, was to become the subject of a massive but ultimately futile air interdiction campaign. The trail was divided into a number of sections by the Americans in order to coordinate air operations. The area of the Laotian panhandle that bordered North Vietnam was designated Steel Tiger and this is where the majority of missions on the Trail took place. There were three main roads into Laos from North Vietnam and these roads twisted through mountain passes that straddled the border. The northernmost road was designated Route 8 and came through the Keo Neua Pass; further south was Route 23 which snaked through the Mu Gia Pass; and further south still, just 20 miles northwest of the DMZ, was Route 912 which came through the Ban Karai Pass. All these passes were very heavily defended as not only were they natural truck 'killing zones' for the tactical aircraft but they were also low-level routes for aircraft entering or exiting North Vietnam from the west. The first Barrel Roll mission over the Ho Chi Minh Trail was on 14 December 1964 when four F-105s bombed a bridge near

Nape. The first Steel Tiger mission was flown on the night of 3 April by two B-57s with the assistance of a Blind Bat C-130 flareship. Later the Steel Tiger area was split into two sectors close to the DMZ with the northern half known as Cricket and the southern half called Tiger Hound. The first Tiger Hound mission was flown on 6 December 1965 and the first Cricket mission on 21 January 1966. All air strikes in the Steel Tiger area were flown under the control of an Air America, Raven or USAF FAC.

2 April 1965

A-1H   139721   VA-215, USN, USS *Hancock*
            Lt Cdr James Joseph Evans (KIA)

By this time both the US Navy and the USAF were flying regular missions over the Ho Chi Minh Trail in Laos in an attempt to staunch the flow of arms and other supplies from North Vietnam to the Viet Cong in the South. A Navy A-1H was shot down by AAA north of Ban Muong Sen during an armed reconnaissance mission while in the process of attacking another AAA site. In November 1971 skeletal remains were handed over to the US government by the North Vietnamese and on 22 April 1974 these remains were identified by the Armed Services Graves Registration Office Board of Review as being those of Lt Cdr Evans.

3 April 1965

F-100D   55-3625   613 TFS, 401 TFW on TDY, USAF, Da Nang
            1Lt George Craig Smith (KIA)

A-4C   148557   VA-216, USN, USS *Hancock*
            Lt Cdr Raymond Arthur Vohden (POW)

The Rolling Thunder raids of 3 and 4 April were significant for a number of reasons. Firstly, the loss of seven aircraft and pilots in these two days represented the most serious casualties suffered by the Americans in the war up to this point. Secondly, the target for the raids was an important railway and road bridge at Thanh Hoa which crossed the Song Ma River and was a major line of communication from Hanoi and Haiphong to the southern provinces of North Vietnam and from there to the DMZ and South Vietnam. Thirdly, the raids were only 70 miles south of Hanoi, representing the furthest location north at that time. Lastly, the raids were the first occasion when the Vietnamese People's Air Force employed its MiG-17 fighters, thus marking a significant escalation of the air war in Southeast Asia.

The Ham Rong or Dragon's Jaw railway and road bridge three miles north of Thanh Hoa had only been completed in 1964 and, compared to most other bridges in North Vietnam, was a massive structure of concrete and steel. Its 540 feet span was supported by nine concrete piers and 40 feet-thick concrete abutments anchored the bridge at either end. The bridge was heavily defended by a ring of 37mm AAA sites that were supplemented by several 57mm sites following these initial raids. The bridge became a legend in US and Vietnamese history and it became a point of honour for the USAF and US Navy to destroy the structure. Whether the effort and sacrifice expended in ultimately achieving this aim was worthwhile is debatable as the North Vietnamese developed by-passes and alternative routes that greatly reduced the strategic importance of the bridge as the war progressed.

The raid on 3 April was planned and led by Lt Col Robinson Risner, a Korean War ace, well known throughout the Air Force. The strike force consisted of 31 F-105 bombers that would be supported by 15 F-105s and seven F-100s tasked with flak suppression. Ten KC-135 tankers refuelled the aircraft before they crossed the Thai border and eight more F-100s were launched for RESCAP duties with a further two F-100s for weather reconnaissance. As it was known that the North Vietnamese had MiGs in service, although they had not been used up to that point, four more F-100s were assigned for combat air patrol. Lastly two RF-101Cs were tasked with pre and post-strike photographic reconnaissance runs over the target.

Prior to the arrival of the strike force the defence suppression aircraft attacked the several AAA sites around the target and one of the Super Sabres was hit on its second attack and crashed before the pilot, 1Lt George Smith, could eject. The bridge was

hit by several 750lb bombs and Bullpup missiles but was scarcely damaged. The missiles, which were carried by 16 of the F-105s, proved particularly ineffective against the bridge's sturdy structure. Several aircraft received minor damage during the raid including Risner's F-105, which sprang a fuel leak forcing him to divert to Da Nang.

The US Navy also mounted two raids against bridges near Thanh Hoa on the 3rd. A total of 35 A-4s, 16 F-8s and four F-4s were launched from the *Hancock* and *Coral Sea*. Lt Cdr Vohden was lost during an attack on a bridge at Dong Phuong Thong about 10 miles north of the Dragon's Jaw. His Skyhawk was hit by small arms fire during his first bombing run and his wingman saw the aircraft streaming fluid and the arrester hook drop down. Soon afterwards, Vohden ejected and was captured to become the Navy's third POW in North Vietnam. During this raid three MiG-17s attacked and damaged an F-8 forcing it to divert to Da Nang. This was the first time a MiG had attacked a US aircraft during the war in Southeast Asia.

RF-101C 56-0075   45 TRS, 39 AD on TDY, USAF, Tan Son Nhut
            Capt Herschel Scott Morgan (POW)

While the Thanh Hoa raid was taking place, some 70 miles to the southwest an RF-101C was attempting to obtain photographs of a radar site near Phu Van on the Song Ca River to the east of Vinh. The aircraft was hit by AAA from the Tam Dao and Vinkh Quang AAA Regiments and the pilot ejected and was taken prisoner. Capt Morgan had flown his first sortie in Southeast Asia in October 1963 and was flying his 94th combat sortie when he was shot down. Like Vohden, he was released by the North Vietnamese on 12 February 1973 having spent seven years, 10 months and nine days in prison.

North Vietnamese MiGs

North Vietnam's air force dates back to March 1956 when the first group of airmen were sent to China and the Soviet Union for training. A number of small airfields were constructed in North Vietnam and transport aircraft and trainers were acquired from communist sources. In 1960 a total of 52 pilots were sent to China to learn to fly the MiG-15/17. Progress was slow and it was not until 3 February 1964 that the 921st Fighter Regiment of the Vietnamese People's Air Force was formed at Mong Tu air base in China. The Regiment was equipped initially with 36 MiG-17s donated by the Soviet Union. Meanwhile construction of the first jet-capable airfield was progressing at Yen Bai northwest of Hanoi. The base was substantially complete by mid-1964 but the Regiment remained in China where it continued to train until the Gulf of Tonkin Incident. On 6 August 1964 the first group of MiGs flew from China to Yen Bai where they commenced preparations to defend their homeland. The training was methodical and thorough and concentrated on the use of a network of ground controlled interception radars that was being built in North Vietnam. The tactics adopted recognised the strengths and weaknesses of the MiG-17 compared to its American adversaries and these tactics were later modified with experience. The MiG force was held back until the Rolling Thunder strikes began to reach the 20th parallel. On 3 April the 921st Fighter Regiment made its first operational sorties against the US Navy strike force which attacked the Thanh Hoa bridges. The North Vietnamese claimed two F-8 Crusaders destroyed during this engagement although, in fact, only one F-8 was damaged. The following day saw the VPAF's first real victories when two F-105s were shot down although this was achieved for the loss of three of the MiGs and their pilots. Five more MiGs were shot down in June and July and others lost in accidents with the result that the MiGs were virtually stood down for nine months of retraining, not being seen in numbers again until April 1966. Meanwhile the 921st had been joined by the 923rd Fighter Regiment which was formed at Kep airfield northeast of Hanoi on 7 September 1965. In November of the same year the MiG-17s were joined by the first of the more capable MiG-21s. The MiG-21 was equipped with two K-13 air-to-air missiles, designated the AA-2 Atoll by NATO. The first reported sighting of a MiG-21 took place on 15 January 1966 and the aircraft often operated in conjunction with the MiG-17s. By the end of 1965 the VPAF had about 75 MiGs together with eight

Il-28 jet bombers in service. To counter the MiG threat the USAF introduced Big Eye (later College Eye) EC-121D detachments from the 552nd AEW&C Wing based at various airfields from 17 April 1965. Ships of TF 77 also provided radar coverage and MiG warnings for US aircraft operating over North Vietnam.

4 April 1965

A-1H   serial ..?   unit ..?, USAF
            Capt Walter Frank Draeger (KIA)

Yet another victim of the 3 April raid was Capt Walter Draeger who was lost near the Dragon's Jaw Bridge on 4 April while flying RESCAP on a search and rescue mission for the two airmen downed near Thanh Hoa the previous day. Draeger's Skyraider, an A-1H probably borrowed from the VNAF, was seen to crash in flames near the bridge and no parachute was seen nor beeper heard.

F-105D 62-4217   44 TFS, 18 TFW on TDY, USAF, Korat
            Capt Carlyle Smith Harris (POW)

F-105D 59-1754   354 TFS, 355 TFW attached to 2 AD,
            USAF, Korat
            Maj Frank Everett Bennett (KIA)

F-105D 59-1764   354 TFS, 355 TFW attached to 2 AD,
            USAF, Korat
            Capt James A Magnusson (KIA)

As the BDA photographs of the Dragon's Jaw showed very little structural damage to the bridge from the raid on the 3rd, it was decided to mount another strike the following day. This time the ineffectual Bullpups were left behind and only 750lb bombs carried. The strike force consisted of 48 F-105s supported by eight F-100s for flak suppression and two more for weather reconnaissance. Lt Col Risner led the mission again but from the very beginning things started to go wrong. Problems with the initial refuelling rendezvous and hazy conditions at the target disrupted the plan and caused the strike aircraft to bunch up close to the target zone. Several flights of F-105s were forced to orbit south of Thanh Hoa to await their turn. At the bridge Capt 'Smitty' Harris flying as Steel 3 was shot down although he ejected safely and was captured. Harris is credited with instituting a 'tap code' while in prison which enabled the POWs to communicate to each other secretively, as the penalties for being caught attempting to talk or pass messages were severe. 'Smitty' Harris was released from prison on 12 February 1973. The cause of Harris's loss was probably ground fire although this was not confirmed, however, there was no doubt as to the cause of the next two Thunderchiefs to be brought down.

Four MiG-17s had been vectored to the bomb-laden F-105s orbiting near Thanh Hoa and dived through the clouds to attack the US aircraft. Maj Frank Bennett's Zinc flight became the centre of attention for the MiGs and the North Vietnamese flight leader, Capt Tran Hanh, fired at Capt Magnusson's aircraft which immediately caught fire and crashed to the south of Thanh Hoa. Meanwhile Hanh's wingman, Le Minh Huan, fired at Maj Bennett's Thunderchief scoring several hits in the fuselage. The MiGs then disengaged from their attack and dived away to the north before any of the US aircraft could react. This 'hit and run' method would become a favourite tactic of the MiGs as it limited their exposure to the missiles and guns of the US aircraft and usually enabled them to escape to fight another day at a time and place of their choosing. Maj Bennett's fatally damaged aircraft headed out to sea but eventually crashed some 30 miles from Thanh Hoa near the island of Hon Me. Maj Bennett was seen to eject from his aircraft but he drowned before help could reach him. These two F-105s were the first US aircraft to be shot down in air-to-air combat in the war in Southeast Asia. Curiously, three of the MiGs that attacked Zinc flight were lost with their pilots (Pham Giay, Le Minh Huan and Tran Nguyen Nam) during the mission. An F-100D pilot (Capt D Kilgus) from the 416th TFS claimed one MiG but was only allowed a probable by the USAF and no one claimed the other two. It is likely that North Vietnamese AAA brought down the other MiGs in error. Ground fire was usually very intense and the North Vietnamese gunners' aircraft recognition was probably not too good at this

early stage of the war so friendly fire incidents such as this may have been a fairly common occurrence until a more integrated air defence system was developed.

In addition to the tragic losses incurred, the results of this raid were disappointing. Over 300 hits were thought to have been scored on the bridge but it still appeared to be functional and would have to be struck yet again.

5 April 1965

F-105D 59-1742   354 TFS, 355 TFW attached to 6234 TFW,
USAF, Korat
Capt T Gay (survived)

Following their mauling at Thanh Hoa the F-105s from Korat returned to armed reconnaissance but now this mission had extended from Laos into North Vietnam itself. Capt Gay's aircraft was shot down by ground fire while hunting for trucks on Route 9 in the mountainous region near Ban Pang. He was fortunate to be rescued by a USAF HH-43 helicopter.

7 April 1965

A-4C   148317   VA-153, USN, USS Coral Sea
Lt William Marshall Roark (KIA)

During an armed reconnaissance mission near Dong Cao just a few miles north of the DMZ, a flight of A-4s from the Coral Sea spotted and attacked an AAA site with cluster bombs. During his third pass Lt Roark's Skyhawk was hit by ground fire and he ejected half a mile offshore. A helicopter eventually reached him two hours later but he was found floating face down and appeared to have been shot. On 24 April 1967 the Knox-class destroyer escort USS Roark was launched and named in honour of Lt William Roark. This was the first of several US Navy ships to be named after American servicemen killed in Vietnam.

B-57B   53-3880   8 TBS, 405 FW attached to 34 TG, USAF,
Bien Hoa
Capt James Wimberley Lewis (KIA)
Capt Arthur Dale Baker (KIA)

The B-57s from Bien Hoa were by this time taking part in Barrel Roll operations in northern Laos, a task suited to their long range and endurance. A flight of four aircraft was tasked with an interdiction mission in Xieng Khouang province. One of the aircraft failed to recover from a dive bombing attack on a target on Route 7 a few miles east of Ban Ban and was probably hit by ground

fire. No sign of the aircraft or its crew was found during a five-day search. A week later the New China News Agency reported the shooting down of a B-57 about three miles northeast of Khang Khay.

9 April 1965

F-4B   151425   VF-96, USN, USS Ranger
Lt Cdr William E Greer (survived)
Lt(jg) R Bruning (survived)

F-4B   151403   VF-96, USN, USS Ranger
Lt(jg) Terence Meredith Murphy (KIA)
Ens Ronald James Fegan (KIA)

The threat of MiG activity over Southeast Asia resulted in increased efforts to provide combat air patrols and airborne early warning. The versatile F-4 Phantom, along with the F-8 Crusader, was tasked with air defence of the fleet and protection of strike forces. On 9 April two Phantoms were launched to relieve two other aircraft flying a BARCAP racetrack pattern in the northern Gulf of Tonkin. However, the first aircraft to launch crashed as it was being catapulted from the carrier. The aircraft's starboard engine failed during the catapult shot and the aircraft ditched into the sea but both Lt Cdr Greer and Lt Bruning ejected just as the aircraft impacted the water and were rescued.

Lt Murphy and Ens Fegan were then launched and took over as section leader with a replacement aircraft flown by Lt Watkins and Lt(jg) Mueller as their wingman. As the two Phantoms flew north they were intercepted by four MiG-17s that were identified as belonging to the air force of the Chinese People's Liberation Army. The two Phantoms that were waiting to be relieved on BARCAP heard Lt Murphy's radio calls and flew south to engage the MiGs. The air battle took place at high altitude near the Chinese island of Hainan and Lt Murphy's Phantom was not seen after the MiGs disengaged. The aircraft was thought to have been shot down by the MiGs but a Chinese newspaper claimed that Lt Murphy had been shot down in error by an AIM-7 Sparrow missile fired by another Phantom. One of the MiG-17s was seen to explode and was thought to have been shot down by Lt Murphy during the dogfight but it was never officially credited due to the sensitivity of US aircraft engaging Chinese aircraft. Lt Murphy's last radio call was to the effect that he was out of missiles and was returning to base. Despite an extensive two-day SAR effort no sign of the Phantom or its crew was ever found.

A-4C   148481   VA-153, USN, USS Coral Sea
Lt Cdr C H McNeil (survived)

During an attack on the Tam Da Bridge on the coast north of Vinh, Lt Cdr McNeil's Skyhawk was hit by 37mm flak and the aircraft caught fire. The fire quickly burned through the fuselage and the tail section separated causing the aircraft to pitch down and enter a flat spin. Lt Cdr McNeil had difficulty ejecting from the aircraft but eventually got out safely and was picked up by a USAF HU-16 Albatross amphibian.

10 April 1965

F-100D 56-3151   401 TFW attached to 23 ABG, USAF, Da Nang
1 pilot, name unknown (survived)

One of the Super Sabres on detachment from the 401st TFW from England AFB, Louisiana crashed following engine failure.

11 April 1965

A-1H   135226   VA-95, USN, USS Ranger
Lt(jg) William Edward Swanson (KIA)

In addition to Rolling Thunder attacks, the Navy was also participating in the Steel Tiger interdiction campaign in southern Laos. Lt Swanson was flying one of two Skyraiders on an armed reconnaissance mission east of Ban Senphan when they encountered heavy AAA fire. Swanson's aircraft was hit and began to trail smoke as it made a slow descent into the jungle canopy. Swanson may have been wounded as he never acknowledged his wingman's calls nor made any apparent attempt to escape.

15 April 1965

EA-1E   139603   Detachment T, VAW-11, USN,
USS Yorktown
3 crew, names unknown (survived)

The EA-1F was a 4-seat electronic countermeasures version of the versatile Skyraider. The type could also be used for AEW and was used in small numbers on some of the older carriers. One of the 'electric Spads' crashed due to engine failure during a training flight, the three crewmen being rescued.

When the conflict in Southeast Asia was escalating in 1965 the F-4B Phantom was in the process of replacing earlier US Navy fighters with Fleet squadrons. A total of 128 F-4Bs and F-4Js were lost by the Navy during the war. USN

17 April 1965

F-105D 61-0171   563 TFS, 23 TFW on TDY, USAF, Takhli
Capt Samuel Alexander Woodworth (KIA)

The Mu Gia Pass on the mountainous North Vietnamese-Laotian border was one of a small number of strategically important choke points where supplies from North Vietnam had to pass through on their way south. Capt Woodworth was the first American to die at the Mu Gia Pass when his aircraft dived into the ground during an attack. Capt Woodworth probably misjudged his attack and crashed before he could pull out. The 563rd TFS was one of two F-105 squadrons to deploy on temporary duty from the 23rd TFW, McConnell AFB, Kansas and had arrived in Thailand on 8 April.

A-1E   52-133886   1 ACS, 34 TG, USAF, Bien Hoa
Capt L D Haight (survived)

Although the war in North Vietnam and Laos had escalated rapidly in March and April the war in South Vietnam still continued to claim aircraft. Capt Haight was shot down while making a strafing pass during an air interdiction mission in South Vietnam.

18 April 1965

A-1E   52-132601   1 ACS, 34 TG, USAF, Bien Hoa
Capt James Atlee Wheeler (KIA)

During an interdiction mission about 10 miles south of Tinh Bien near the Cambodian border a Skyraider was damaged by one of its own bombs which exploded soon after release. The aircraft dived into the ground trailing smoke and streaming fuel and Capt Wheeler had no chance to escape.

19/20 April 1965

A-1H   139818   VA-215, USN, USS Hancock
Lt(jg) James Patrick Shea (KIA)

In addition to pre-planned bombing raids the Rolling Thunder campaign also included armed reconnaissance missions, although the type and location of targets that could be hit was strictly controlled. During a night armed reconnaissance by a flight of Skyraiders from the Hancock a number of trucks were spotted and attacked west of Phu Qui, about 30 miles north of the DMZ. Lt Shea's aircraft was lost during the attack and probably dived into the ground in the dark.

20 April 1965

A-4C   149507   VA-22, USN, USS Midway
Lt Philip Neal Butler (POW)

The USS Midway departed Alameda on 6 March and arrived in the South China Sea for assignment to TF 77 on 22 March. The Midway first assumed line duty at Yankee Station on 10 April and suffered her first aircraft loss just 10 days later. Lt Butler was taking part in a night armed reconnaissance hunt for trucks between Thanh Hoa and Vinh. The flight attacked some trucks near Nghia Hung but when Lt Butler released his six Mk81 bombs they detonated immediately and blew off the Skyhawk's wings and tail. The bombs were fitted with variable-time fuses that enabled ordnance men to set the bombs to detonate at set times after dropping. Evidently the setting of these fuses or the fuses themselves were causing problems as this was not the only incident of this type. Butler was lucky to be able to eject from the remains of his aircraft and he evaded for four days and nights until his luck finally ran out when he was tracked down by North Vietnamese using tracker dogs. He spent the rest of the war as a POW and was released on 12 February 1973.

24 April 1965

C-130A 57-0475   817 TCS, 6315 OG on TDY from Naha,
USAF, Da Nang
Maj Theodore R Loeschner (KIA)
Capt Robert A Butterfield (KIA)
Capt Charles M Dansby (KIA)
SSgt Peter R Coyman (KIA)
SSgt Donnie D Ezell (KIA)
Sgt James T Gray (KIA)

The first C-130 tactical transports were introduced in the Southeast Asia theatre in 1961 during the crisis in Laos. From early 1965 C-130s from the PACAF and MATS wings were regularly rotated into South Vietnam. Based mainly at the major airfields of Da Nang, Tuy Hoa, Cam Ranh Bay and Tan Son Nhut, the C-130s were deployed to South Vietnam on a temporary duty basis. The only Hercules based permanently in Southeast Asia were the special mission aircraft such as flareships, SAR aircraft, special operations aircraft and, later, gunships. The first C-130 to be lost during the war was actually a Blind Bat flareship that crashed into high ground during a go-around in bad weather at Korat. The Blind Bat detachment had deployed to Da Nang in January 1965 and operated mainly over the Ho Chi Minh Trail and the Barrel Roll area of northern Laos. The Blind Bat's function was to drop flares over the Trail at night to illuminate trucks for accompanying strike aircraft to attack.

27 April 1965

A-1H   137545   VA-215, USN, USS Hancock
Lt(jg) S B Wilkes (survived)

Following the loss of an F-105 at the Mu Gia Pass 10 days earlier, the US Navy also lost an aircraft on a strike mission in this increasingly important area. Lt Wilkes's Skyraider was hit by ground fire just a few miles south of the pass on his way to the target. The aircraft's port wing caught fire but Lt Wilkes managed to fly the aircraft across Laos into Thailand and was within two miles of the airfield at Nakhon Phanom when he was forced to bail out.

29 April 1965

RF-101C 56-0190   15 TRS, 18 TFW on TDY, USAF, Udorn
Capt Charles Ervin Shelton (POW-died)

Capt Shelton was flying a BDA photographic reconnaissance mission over northern Laos with a wingman, when he was shot down. The first target was obscured by low cloud so Capt Shelton went on to the next target near Sam Neua, the headquarters of the Pathet Lao forces. As the two aircraft approached Sam Neua at 3,000 feet Capt Shelton's Voodoo was hit by ground fire and burst into flames. The Captain ejected safely and about two hours later he was seen by two rescue aircraft and contacted by radio. An attempted rescue by helicopter before dark had to be postponed because of bad weather. Shelton told his rescuers that he would hide from the Pathet Lao and await a break in the weather when a rescue could take place. Unfortunately, it was not until 2 May that the weather again became suitable for rescue aircraft to try again. Despite a total of 148 sorties by a variety of USAF and Air America aircraft and the insertion of a team of Hmong guerillas, no sign of Shelton was ever seen.

Capt Shelton had been captured by the Pathet Lao after three days in hiding. According to intelligence sources he was thought to have been kept prisoner in caves in the Sam Neua area for the next three and a half years. He is also said to have made several escape attempts and to have killed three of his captors in the process. Later, Shelton was thought to have been kept with another American POW, Capt D L Hrdlicka. Apparently, at least four rescue attempts took place in which ground teams were inserted into the Sam Neua area but without success. One of the rescue attempts is said to have involved Hmong tribesmen and actually succeeded in freeing Shelton and Hrdlicka only to have to return them to captivity when the rescue force encountered a force of NVA soldiers. Stories about Shelton's continued captivity continued to circulate long after the war in Southeast Asia came to an end. Allegedly, Shelton was held in a POW camp near Tchepone, Laos from 1981 to 1985 and was then taken to North Vietnam. For many years he remained the only American POW who had not been declared dead by the US Government, despite the length of his absence. As late as August 1987 a news story claimed that Shelton was still alive in captivity. Sadly, it was all too much for his wife, Marian, who for 25 years had steadfastly campaigned for her husband's release. On 4 October 1990 Marian Shelton took her own life, as much a victim of the war in Southeast Asia as was her husband. Charles Shelton was officially declared killed in action in September 1994.

---

6 May 1965

RF-101C 56-0045   45 TRS, 39 AD on TDY, USAF, Tan Son Nhut
Capt Robert Austin Stubberfield (KIA)

Low level photographic reconnaissance was a dangerous business and a week after Shelton was lost in Laos another RF-101 was shot down with the loss of its pilot. Capt Stubberfield was flying a BDA reconnaissance mission over Vinh Linh barracks near the coast and just a couple of miles north of the DMZ when his aircraft crashed. Stubberfield was most probably shot down by ground fire in this heavily defended area and his emergency beeper was heard by other aircraft in the vicinity. A SAR mission was mounted that included attacks on anti-aircraft sites by USAF F-105s and USMC F-4Bs. Unfortunately the SAR effort failed to find any trace of Capt Stubberfield but his remains were eventually discovered after the war and returned to the USA in June 1989.

7 May 1965

F-105D 59-1718   354 TFS, 355 TFW attached to 6234 TFW,
USAF, Korat
Maj R E Lambert (survived)

On 7 May the USAF made another attempt to destroy the Thanh Hoa railway and road bridge. Twenty-eight F-105s bombed the bridge with 750lb bombs and the eastern approach road and the railway line was badly damaged. This time only one aircraft was lost, an F-105 flown by Maj Lambert who managed to fly out over the Gulf of Tonkin before having to eject from his burning aircraft. He was subsequently picked up by a USAF HU-16 Albatross amphibian.

8 May 1965

F-8D   148637   VF-111, USN, USS Midway
Cdr James David La Haye (KIA)

On 8 May the US Navy mounted its first raid against a North Vietnamese airfield when Vinh air base was attacked by a strike force. Cdr La Haye, the CO of VF-111, was attacking the airfield's AAA defences with Zuni unguided rockets and 20mm cannon fire when his aircraft was hit by ground fire. The Crusader was seen to turn towards the coast with its wings level but streaming fuel until it crashed into the sea a few miles offshore near the island of Hon Nieu. No attempt at ejection was seen although the pilot had radioed that his aircraft had been hit.

RF-8A   145620   Detachment A, VFP-63, USN, USS Midway
Lt(jg) W B Wilson (survived)

About six hours after the strike on Vinh airfield Midway's photographic reconnaissance detachment flew a BDA mission to assess the damage done to the target. During the run over the airfield Lt Wilson's Crusader was hit by ground fire and sustained damage to the fuel tanks, hydraulic system and tail fin. Despite the damage and loss of fuel Lt Wilson managed to make for the coast and fly south towards a tanker where he took on enough fuel to reach the carrier or Da Nang. Unfortunately, soon after taking on fuel two explosions were heard from the rear of the aircraft as either fuel or hydraulic fluid ignited. The aircraft's controls froze and Lt Wilson ejected over the sea about 30 miles off Dong Hoi from where he was rescued by a USAF Albatross.

9 May 1965

F-8D   148673   VF-154, USN, USS Coral Sea
Lt David Allen Kardell (KIA)

Lt Kardell and Lt J Terhune were flying their F-8s as escorts for a flight of attack aircraft on a road reconnaissance about 20 miles west of Thanh Hoa when the flight spotted trucks on the road. As the truck were near a populated area the flight leader did not want to use bombs but instead asked the F-8 escorts to strafe the vehicle. Kardell made a strafing run on a truck but the F-8 flew into the ground, apparently accidentally as there was no ground fire reported during the attack. Target fixation is a common problem in low level ground attack missions and the judgement to achieve a safe pull up following an attack, especially when using guns that requires the aircraft to get very close to the

target, is an acquired skill. It was obvious that Lt Kardell had not survived the crash and his remains were eventually handed over by the Vietnamese on 31 July 1989.

F-105D 62-4408   563 TFS, 23 TFW on TDY, USAF, Takhli
Capt Robert Carl Wistrand (KIA)

During an armed reconnaissance mission over the Steel Tiger area of Laos the AAA defences surrounding the Mu Gia Pass were attacked. The ever-increasing number of anti-aircraft gun sites protecting the pass was causing concern and resulted in missions flown specifically to knock them out. When diving on a gun position Capt Wistrand's aircraft was hit and crashed immediately, no ejection being seen or SAR beeper heard. Like many US aircrew posted missing in action in Southeast Asia, Capt Wistrand was promoted (to the rank of Colonel) before his death was officially accepted.

O-1F   57-2896   19 TASS, 34 TG, USAF, Bien Hoa
Capt L L Reed (survived)
Capt J A Hodges (survived)

During a dusk FAC sortie in South Vietnam Capt Reed's Bird Dog was hit in the engine by small arms fire. Capt Reed made a forced landing that resulted in the destruction of the aircraft but the crew walked away with minor injuries and was quickly rescued. During May three more USAF tactical air support squadrons were deployed to South Vietnam to satisfy the ever-increasing demand for forward air control. The 20th TASS formed at Da Nang; the 21st at Pleiku; and the 22nd at Binh Thuy. Each squadron was equipped with about 30 Bird Dogs and by the end of the year the four FAC squadrons were operating detachments from 65 locations throughout South Vietnam. Although largely unsung, the FACs were the crucial element of the air support system in South Vietnam as no targets could be attacked unless under the control of an FAC.

11 May 1965

A-4C   148489   VA-22, USN, USS *Midway*
1 pilot, name unknown (survived)

During a training flight, a Skyhawk collided in mid-air with another aircraft and crashed into the sea. The pilot was recovered safely.

12 May 1965

O-1F   57-2781   19 TASS, 34 TG, USAF, Bien Hoa
1 pilot, name unknown (survived)

A Bird Dog crashed due to engine failure during an FAC mission.

F-105D   61-0125   563 TFS, 23 TFW on TDY, USAF, Takhli
1 pilot, name unknown (survived)

The second victim of engine failure on the 12th was an F-105D that crashed in Thailand on its way to a strike.

C-123B   55-4516   315 ACG, USAF, Tan Son Nhut
5 crew, names unknown (survived)

The last of three accidental losses on this day was a C-123 that crashed due to pilot error during a flight in South Vietnam. On 8 March the 315th TCG was redesignated as an Air Commando Group and consisted at that time of four C-123 squadrons, the 19th, 309th and 310th at Tan Son Nhut and the 311th ACS at Da Nang.

15 May 1965

F-105D   62-4374   probably 563 TFS, 23 TFW on TDY, USAF, Takhli
Capt Robert Greskowiak (KIA)

When taking off from Takhli on a strike mission a Thunderchief suffered engine failure and crashed near the end of the runway killing the pilot and five Thai civilians. The crash also badly damaged a Buddhist temple hall that was later rebuilt by the USAF.

16 May 1965

A-1E   52-133901   34 TG, USAF, Bien Hoa

B-57B   52-1568, 53-3867, 53-3871, 53-3873, 53-3893,
53-3904, 53-3913, 53-3915, 53-3930, 53-3937
8/13 TBS, 405 FW attached to 34 TG,
USAF, Bien Hoa

F-8E   150931   VF-162, USN, USS *Oriskany*

At 08:15 on Sunday morning, 16 May, Capt C N Fox and his navigator, Capt V L Haynes, were sitting in their B-57B at Bien Hoa about to start engines to lead a flight of four aircraft on a strike. Fox's Canberra was loaded with four 750lb bombs under the wings and nine 500lb bombs in the bomb bay. Without warning Fox's aircraft exploded and debris hit other aircraft on the flight line causing further explosions in what seemed to be a chain reaction. When the smoke cleared the scene was one of utter devastation with dead, dying and wounded airmen and wrecked aircraft everywhere. A complete J65 engine was hurled half a mile and smaller fragments were found at twice that distance from the flight line. The only man from Capt Fox's flight of four aircraft to survive was navigator Lt Barry Knowles. He and his pilot, Capt Kea, had had to abort the sortie due to a malfunction and were walking away from the aircraft when the explosion occured. Kea was killed by flying shrapnel but Knowles was knocked over and injured by the blast and was rescued by SMSgt L E Adamson, the maintenance line chief. In addition to Fox,

Haynes and Kea, the other Canberra crewmen killed were Maj Underwood, Capt Shannon, Capt Jepson and 1Lt Wagner. As well as the 10 B-57s that were destroyed, a US Navy F-8E, a USAF A-1E and two VNAF A-1Hs were also completely wrecked. The F-8E had diverted to Bien Hoa just minutes before the explosion after it developed a fuel leak while on a close air support mission over South Vietnam. The Crusader pilot was Maj R G Bell, a USAF exchange officer with the *Oriskany's* VF-162, who was also killed in the explosion. A total of 30 VNAF A-1s received some degree of damage as did a USAF HH-43 helicopter. The remnants of the 8th and 13th TBSs immediately set up shop at Tan Son Nhut and continued operations as best they could but it was some time before the squadrons could function normally again.

The 27 USAF men who died were: SSgt Jesse Rodriquez Acosta, SSgt Jose Ruben Aragon, TSgt Secundino Baldonado, Maj Robert Graham Bell, SSgt Brian Dale Brown, TSgt Claude Marvin Bunch, SSgt James Martin Cale, SSgt Robert Lewis Clark, A1C William Thomas Crawford, SSgt Edgar Stoms Donaghy, A1C Terence Dean Engel, TSgt Aaron Gregor Fidiam, Capt Charles Nathan Fox, Capt Vernon Lee Haynes, SMS William Donald Hicks, SSgt David Lee Hubbard, Capt Arthur C Jepson, Capt Andrew Millard Kea, Capt Ernest McFeron, TSgt Charles William Rachal, A1C Clifford H Raulerson, TSgt Donald Joseph Seaman, Capt Billy Eugene Shannon, TSgt Gerald Allison Snyder, Maj James Edward Underwood, 1Lt Lee Celin Wagner, and A1C Hayden Edward Weaver.

This was the worst single incident suffered by the USAF on the ground during the entire war and was only eclipsed by the terrible fires on board the USS *Oriskany* and *Forrestal*. Twice as many aircraft were lost in the accidental explosion at Bien Hoa than had been destroyed by Viet Cong attacks on aircraft on the ground in the war up to that date. The cause of the explosion was thought to have been a malfunction on a time-delay fuse on one of the bombs carried by Capt Fox's aircraft.

17 May 1965

F-105D   62-4222   44 or 67 TFS, 18 TFW attached to 6234
TFW, USAF, Korat
Capt J U Taliaferro (survived)

A Thunderchief was shot down by 37mm AAA while flying on an armed reconnaissance mission along Route 7 near Ban Kia Na in North Vietnam close to the Laotian border. Capt Taliaferro ejected near the Song Ba River and landed on a hillside in dense jungle close to a village. Two USAF HH-43s soon arrived and one helicopter made the pick up as the other stood by and fighter aircraft pounded enemy positions. The helicopter flew over 200 miles across enemy territory, a feat made possible by the installation of extra drums of fuel in the cabin.

18 May 1965

F-105D   59-1753   563 TFS, 23 TFW on TDY, USAF, Takhli
Capt David Louis Hrdlicka (POW-died)

Capt Hrdlicka was leading a flight of four aircraft to attack road traffic to the east of the Pathet Lao stronghold of Sam Neua in northern Laos when his aircraft was hit by ground fire. The aircraft was seen to be on fire and Hrdlicka ejected and landed in a small valley where he was seen being led away by Laotian villagers. Capt Hrdlicka was used for propaganda purposes by both the Laotians and the North Vietnamese. Photographs of Hrdlicka in captivity were also published in Soviet and Chinese newspapers in 1966. US intelligence sources indicate that Capt Hrdlicka was kept in caves near Sam Neua and he is thought to have been kept with Capt Charles Shelton and was allegedly rescued by a Hmong rescue team but then recaptured. Capt Hrdlicka was said to have been photographed in captivity as late as 1968 or 1969 but one Laotian source claims that he died in captivity in 1968.

The A-4B variant of the Skyhawk was used only briefly by some of the smaller aircraft carriers during the war and had been completely replaced by the A-4C and A-4E versions by the end of 1967. USN

Whatever the truth, like the majority of airmen who were captured in Laos, he was never released and his fate remains a mystery. His wife became a prominent figure in fighting for legislation to highlight the POW/MIA issue.

21 May 1965

A-4B   144938   Detachment Q, VA-113, USN,
                  USS *Bennington*
                  1 pilot, name unknown (survived)

One the USS *Bennington's* Skyhawks from VA-113 was blown overboard when landing back from a training flight. The *Bennington* had only arrived in the South China Sea a few weeks before and this accident was the only loss from the ASW carrier's tour, which ended on 9 September 1965. Much of the flying performed by the attack squadron detachments on the ASW carriers was mundane and the *Bennington* only spent 34 days of its first tour of duty actually on the line. The USS *Bennington* returned for two more tours of duty between 1966 and 1968 but no further fixed-wing aircraft were destroyed although three SH-3As were lost along with five crewmen. The *Bennington* was decommissioned on 15 January 1970 and was stricken for disposal on 20 September 1989. It was finally towed to India for scrapping in 1994.

23 May 1965

F-105D   61-0054   354 TFS, 355 TFW attached to 6234 TFW,
                     USAF, Korat
                     Maj Robert F Herman (survived)

Another victim of an armed reconnaissance operation was Maj Herman whose Thud was hit by ground fire when flying along Route 74 about 20 miles east of Vinh. Maj Herman managed to make it to the coast and ejected a few miles offshore where he was picked up by a USAF Albatross amphibian.

25 May 1965

A-3B   138947   Detachment G, VAH-4, USN, USS *Oriskany*
                  4 crew, names unknown (survived)

The *Oriskany* was assigned to TF 77 on 27 April and started her first line duty on 8 May. She suffered her first aircraft loss on 25 May when an A-3B crashed due to a structural failure during a catapult launch for a tanker mission. Each major strike was accompanied by an A-3 tanker to extend the strike force's range and provide emergency air-to-air refuelling in case of battle damage.

27 May 1965

F-8D   148706   VF-111, USN, USS *Midway*
                  Cdr Doyle Wilmer Lynn (KIA)

One of the most frequently hit targets in the southern part of North Vietnam was the city of Vinh and on 27 May the Navy flew a strike against the railway yards at Vinh. Cdr Doyle Lynn, CO of VF-111, was attacking an AAA site near the target when his aircraft was hit by ground fire. Lynn radioed that the aircraft had been hit and the F-8 was seen to go out of control and hit the ground before an ejection could take place. Cdr Doyle Lynn had been one of the first Navy pilots shot down in Southeast Asia when his Crusader was shot down on 7 June 1964 over the Plain of Jars. He was rescued on that occasion by an Air America helicopter but on 27 May Cdr Lynn's luck finally ran out.

31 May 1965

F-105D   62-4381   probably 563 TFS, 23 TFW attached to
                     6441 TFW(P), USAF, Takhli
                     1Lt Robert D Peel (POW)

The USAF made another strike against the Thanh Hoa Bridge on the last day of May. Only one aircraft was lost during this raid, an F-105 that was shot down at 14,000 feet a few miles south of the target. 1Lt Peel, whose English father had been a Royal Air Force pilot in the First World War, ejected and was taken prisoner. He was released on 12 February 1973 and resumed his Air Force career. 62-4381 was painted as 'Give 'em L'.

1 June 1965

RF-8A   146881   Detachment A, VFP-63, USN, USS *Midway*
                   Lt(jg) M R Fields (survived)

In preparation for further attacks on the railway yards at Vinh, the *Midway* sent one of its photographic reconnaissance Crusaders to check the state of damage and to see which areas needed to be attacked again. At 500 feet over the target the aircraft was hit by ground fire which damaged its hydraulic system. Lt Fields felt the controls gradually stiffening as he for raced the sea. He was fortunate to be able to get over 30 miles from the coastline before the controls eventually froze solid and he was forced to eject. He was soon rescued by a USAF Albatross amphibian.

RF-8A   146852   Detachment E, VFP-63, USN,
                   USS *Bon Homme Richard*
                   Lt Cdr Frederick Peter Crosby (KIA)

The *Bon Homme Richard* arrived in the South China Sea on 12 May for its second tour of duty off Vietnam having spent nine months in 1964 with TF 77. The *Bon Homme Richard's* first loss of its second tour was another RF-8A, the second that day. About six hours after Lt Fields's incident, Lt Cdr Crosby was flying a BDA sortie over the Dong Phong Thuong Bridge about 10 miles north of Thanh Hoa. He approached the bridge at low level doing 550 knots but the aircraft flew into a hail of fire and was hit in the wing. The aircraft slowly rolled inverted and dived into the ground. Lt Cdr Crosby may have been hit as he made no apparent attempt to eject.

2 June 1965

A-4E   151144   VA-23, USN, USS *Midway*
                  Lt(jg) David Marion Christian (KIA)

EA-1F   132540   Detachment A, VAW-13, USN, USS *Midway*
                   Lt(jg) M D McMican (KIA)
                   Lt(jg) Gerald Michael Romano (KIA)
                   PO3 William Harry Amspacher (KIA)
                   ATN3 Thomas Lee Plants (KIA)

During a raid on a radar site a few miles south of Thanh Hoa, an A-4E flown by Lt Christian was hit by AAA when pulling up from its second attack with Zuni rockets. The aircraft caught fire immediately and Lt Christian radioed that his engine had flamed out. It could not be confirmed if Christian ejected from the stricken Skyhawk before it hit the ground. Thirty minutes after the aircraft was lost an EA-1F arrived from the *Midway* to coordinate a SAR effort for Lt Christian. As the Skyraider was about to cross the coast at low level near Sam Son, east of Thanh Hoa, it was hit by ground fire and crashed. One crewmember is reported as having bailed out while the aircraft was still over the sea but his parachute did not open. An intelligence report suggested that his body was washed ashore a week later. It is possible that this was Thomas Plant, as the remains of the other three occupants were returned to US control in July 1988 and that of Lt Christian was returned in 1986. ATN3 Plant's remains are also listed by the Department of Defense as having been returned at some date prior to December 1996.

A-4E   151161   VA-23, USN, USS *Midway*
                  Lt John Bryan McKamey (POW)

Five hours after the two aircraft were lost near Thanh Hoa, the *Midway* suffered another loss during an armed reconnaissance mission northwest of Vinh. A flight of Skyhawks was looking for a ferry known to be in use across the Song Ca River near Cam Ngoc. As Lt McKamey was pulling up from a low level search for the ferry his aircraft was hit, possibly by small arms fire, and the engine flamed out and the aircraft caught fire. He ejected and was quickly captured and spent the next eight years as a POW until his release on 12 February 1973. He resumed his naval career and retired with the rank of Captain.

O-1B   133810   VMO-2, MAG-16, USMC, Da Nang
                  1Lt Richard Eugene Heister (KIA)
                  Capt Werner Erhard Lutz (KIA)

On 9 March, in conjunction with the landings the previous day at Da Nang of the 9th Marine Expeditionary Brigade, Marine

Aircraft Group 16 was formed to control the helicopter squadrons at Da Nang. When more Marine aviation units arrived at both Da Nang and Chu Lai the 1st Marine Aircraft Wing was established at Da Nang to control all Marine Corps aviation units in South Vietnam. On 3 May the VMO-2 detachment at Da Nang was joined by the rest of the squadron which also included UH-1E helicopters as well as the Bird Dogs. A month later one of its O-1s stalled and spun into the ground while on a visual reconnaissance mission near the Hai Van Pass in Quang Nam province. Both crew were killed in the crash. A HH-43F Huskie (63-9713) was scrambled from Da Nang but was hit by ground fire and crashed. All three crewmen survived and were themselves rescued.

3 June 1965

A-4C   148577   VA-22, USN, USS *Midway*
                  Lt Raymond P Ilg (survived)

The *Midway* lost its fifth aircraft in three days on 3 June during an armed reconnaissance mission in the Barrel Roll area of Laos. Lt Ilg's Skyhawk was hit by AAA over Route 65 near Ban Nakay Neua, 10 miles east of Sam Neua. The aircraft caught fire and Lt Ilg ejected immediately. He evaded for two days until he was picked up by an Air America helicopter. Considering that he came down in the heart of Pathet Lao country he was very fortunate to be rescued and only just made it as the helicopter's rescue cable was too short to reach the ground through the tall trees. The quick thinking Filipino flight mechanic, Luis Moser, fastened a cargo strap weighted by a tool box onto the cable and Lt Ilg was able to reach up and hang on. The helicopter pilot, Capt Julian Kanach, held the helicopter rock steady among tall trees as the makeshift rescue hoist was lowered and raised with the survivor. An F-105D taking part in the search for Lt Ilg was lost on the 5th but luckily its pilot also survived. Lt Ilg retired from the US Navy as an Admiral.

5 June 1965

F-105D   61-0133   563 TFS, 23 TFW attached to 6441
                     TFW(P), USAF, Takhli
                     Capt Walter B Kosko (survived)

Several flights of F-105s took part in the search for Lt Ilg who ejected from his A-4 on 3 June. The F-105s escorted SAR aircraft and helicopters and also took part in the visual search for the downed pilot. Capt Kosko's aircraft was hit and damaged somewhere over Laos but he just managed to make it back across the Thai border before being forced to eject about 20 miles east of Vientiane. Unfortunately, Capt Kosko was shot down and killed a few weeks later on 27 July 1965.

8 June 1965

F-105D   62-4290   354 TFS, 355 TFW attached to 6234 TFW,
                     USAF, Korat
                     Capt Harold Rademacher (survived)

During an armed reconnaissance mission a flight of F-105s spotted a wooden bridge near Co Dien, about 40 miles south of Vinh and rolled into the attack. Lt Rademacher's aircraft was hit by ground fire as he pulled up off the target. The pilot flew about 10 miles to the south before he was forced to eject. He was rescued by a USAF helicopter, despite being nearly 80 miles north of the DMZ. This was the last aircraft lost by the 354th TFS during its three-month temporary deployment to Korat. During that time the Squadron had flown 1,271 sorties, including 637 Rolling Thunder sorties, and had lost six aircraft and two pilots.

B-57B   53-3882   13 TBS, 405 FW attached to 33 TG, USAF,
                    Tan Son Nhut
                    Capt Gordon F Nelson (survived)
                    Capt James R Carnes (survived)

Four B-57s were flying a close air support mission in the Mekong Delta west of Can Tho when the last aircraft of the flight was hit by ground fire while on its third attack. The aircraft's wing caught fire and both crew ejected. Before they even hit the ground, Nelson and Carnes were being protected by Army helicopter gunships that were laying down suppressive fire as the

remaining Canberras circled overhead. One of the Army helicopters landed and rescued the two downed airmen. The .50 calibre machine gun that was probably responsible for the loss of the aircraft was later destroyed by the other three B-57s.

9 June 1965

F-4C 64-0674 45 TFS, 15 TFW on TDY, USAF, Ubon
Capt C D Keeter (survived)
Capt G L Getman (survived)

The first USAF F-4 Phantom unit to arrive in Southeast Asia was the 45th TFS, which deployed to Ubon in April when elements of the 15th TFW arrived from MacDill AFB, Florida. This was not only the first aircraft lost from Ubon but it was also the first USAF Phantom lost in the war. The aircraft had to be abandoned when it ran out of fuel after a strike in South Vietnam.

10 June 1965

A-1H 137521 VA-25, USN, USS *Midway*
Lt(jg) Carl Louis Doughtie (KIA)

During a Rolling Thunder strike on the Co Dinh power plant about 10 miles southwest of Thanh Hoa Lt Doughtie's Skyraider failed to pull out of its second dive bombing attack and crashed. It is probable that the pilot had been hit by ground fire and was incapacitated. Lt Doughtie had only joined the *Midway* two weeks earlier and was on his 10th mission of his tour when he was lost. In 1997 a JTF-FA investigation team excavated a crash site and recovered human remains that were later identified through DNA testing as those of Carl Doughtie. He was buried at Arlington National Cemetery on 26 February 1999.

11 June 1965

C-123B 56-4379 310 ACS, 315 ACG, USAF, Tan Son Nhut
Maj Samuel Joseph Ganci (KIA)
Capt Alvin James Dimond (KIA)
Capt Terrence Richard Titus (KIA)
SSgt Paul Glen Dawson (KIA)
SSgt Merle Edward Estes (KIA)
SSgt Norman Columbus Williams (KIA)
A1C James Anthony Coy (KIA)

A Provider crashed into a mountain while attempting an airdrop in marginal weather south of Pleiku during a resupply operation. Enemy action was not thought to have been a factor.

12 June 1965

F-100D 55-3702 615 TFS, 401 TFW on TDY, USAF, Da Nang
Capt Lawrence Thomas Holland (KIA)

The 615th TFS from England AFB, Louisiana spent several brief periods in 1964 and 1965 at Da Nang on temporary duty rotation from Clark AFB in the Philippines. The Squadron suffered its first combat loss of the war on 12 June. Capt Holland was lead pilot of a two-aircraft flight on a close air support mission near Don Luan, 10 miles northeast of Bien Hoa. The two Super Sabres made a rocket attack on VC gun positions and buildings but Capt Holland's aircraft was hit and he was forced to eject. His parachute was seen to land in tall trees near the target and a US Army helicopter landed nearby to attempt a rescue. Members of the helicopter crew were fired on as they proceeded into the jungle on foot and they saw Capt Holland's body being dragged into a ditch by several VC before they were forced to retire to the helicopter and take off. Information was later received indicating that Capt Holland was killed when he opened fire on the VC as they closed in on his position.

13 June 1965

F-100D 55-3600 416 TFS, 3 TFW on TDY, USAF, Da Nang
Capt E F Gallarco (survived)

The day after Capt Holland was lost another Super Sabre from Da Nang went down during a close air support mission in South Vietnam. Capt Gallarco was more fortunate as he was rescued with only slight injuries. The 416th TFS was also at Da Nang on temporary duty rotation from the 3rd TFW, England AFB.

14 June 1965

F-105D 62-4220 44 TFS, 18 TFW attached to 6234 TFW, USAF, Korat
Maj Lawrence Nicholas Guarino (POW)

During a Rolling Thunder strike against army barracks at Ban Xom, an F-105D was shot down about 30 miles northeast of Sam Neua, just inside North Vietnam itself. Maj Guarino ejected and landed in a village where he was captured. He was released in Operation Homecoming on 12 February 1973

Maj Guarino was commissioned in 1943 and had seen service in North Africa and Italy during the Second World War and had also flown with the American Volunteer Group (the Flying Tigers) in China. He was recalled for the Korean War and was the oldest pilot to be captured during the war in Southeast Asia. His son, Allan Guarino, also flew with the USAF during the war in Southeast Asia.

16 June 1965

A-1E 52-135040 34 TG, USAF, Bien Hoa
Capt Robert Daryl Gallup (KIA)

A-1E 52-133889 34 TG, USAF, Bien Hoa
1 pilot, name unknown (survived)

Two Skyraiders collided in mid-air during a combat air patrol or escort mission over Pleiku province.

The B-52 in Southeast Asia – Deployment and Early Operations

In 1965 the B-52 Stratofortresses of Strategic Air Command represented (along with intercontinental ballistic missiles housed in underground silos or in submarines) the United States major strategic nuclear deterrent. A number of B-52s, like the B-47s before them, sat on nuclear alert 24 hours a day, 365 days a year in the event of an all-out nuclear war. Their use in the growing conflict in Southeast Asia was resisted by SAC but the aircraft's huge bomb-carrying capability and long range that enabled them to be based well out of harm's way, made them an attractive proposition for commanders in Vietnam. The US reaction to Viet Cong raids on Pleiku and Camp Holloway included the rapid deployment of B-52s to Guam, although at the time very little thought had been given as to the best way to use these valuable aircraft.

A total of 30 B-52Fs were drawn from the 20th BS, 2nd BW at Barksdale AFB, Louisiana and the 441st BS, 320th BW from Mather AFB, California. The aircraft took off from their bases on 11 February accompanied by 30 KC-135 tankers and two C-135 transport aircraft. The B-52s arrived at Andersen on the island of Guam after a non-stop flight while the tankers landed at Kadena AFB on Okinawa. The choice of the older B-52F model was dictated by the fact that 28 of them had been modified in 1964 to increase their conventional bomb carrying capacity. The modified aircraft could carry 27 x 750lb bombs internally and a further 24 under the wings on the pylons originally fitted to carry the Hound Dog missile. The aircraft's bomb load was almost doubled from 20,250lb to 38,250lb. Following the deployment of the modified aircraft to Vietnam in February a further 46 B-52Fs were modified in June and July.

For four months after their arrival on Guam the B-52s flew only training flights until a role for them in the war could be found. In May 1965 the 20th BS was replaced by the 9th BS, 7th BW from Carswell AFB, Texas, thus starting the pattern for rotational deployments among the B-52 squadrons. Each squadron would typically spend about six months at Guam before the personnel were sent back to the USA. Aircraft were usually passed on to replacement squadrons as they arrived.

As the B-52s sat idle at Andersen arguments raged as to their role in Southeast Asia. SAC did not want them involved in the war at all as the aircraft were no longer under their sole control once deployed to Guam. If they were to be involved then SAC wanted the aircraft to used in a strategic bombing campaign against the industry and cities of North Vietnam. Most commanders in South Vietnam, including General Westmoreland himself, wanted the B-52s to add their enormous firepower to the tactical

air campaign against the Viet Cong in the South. Eventually Westmoreland won the arguement although with hindsight it is difficult to see the logic in such a decision.

Under the generic code name Arc Light, the first B-52 raid on South Vietnam was planned for 25 May but was cancelled when it became apparent that the VC had moved out of the area to be bombed. The first raid was eventually flown on 18 June with disastrous results. In addition to the loss of two valuable aircraft and eight crewmen, the bombing accuracy had been less than outstanding and in any case there was evidence following the strike that the area had been vacated shortly before the bombers arrived. It was an inauspicious start to the B-52's Arc Light missions over South Vietnam. However, the campaign continued, the B-52s flying 140 sorties in July, 165 in August and 322 in September. The B-52 raids would continue over South Vietnam for seven years and would be extended into North Vietnam, Laos and Cambodia. Most B-52 raids were flown in multiples of cells, each cell consisting of three aircraft and each cell given a colour as a radio call sign. The early raids were flown by all 30 aircraft but later it was realised that a smaller number of aircraft assigned to each target gave greater flexibility and enabled more targets to be struck. On 15 November 1965 B-52s were used in direct support of ground troops for the first time. The 4133rd BW (Provisional) was formed at Andersen on 1 February 1966 to control all squadrons on rotation to the base. In March 1966 the first Big Belly modified B-52Ds arrived on Guam. These aircraft could carry a total of 108 bombs (84 x Mk82 500lb bombs internally and 24 x 750lb bombs externally) giving a total bomb load of 60,000lb. On 11 April 1966 the B-52s made their first bombing raid over North Vietnam starting a series of small scale raids on the Ho Chi Minh Trail and on 30 July 1966 the first raid on targets in the DMZ itself took place. In April 1967 a second B-52 base was opened at U-Tapao in Thailand which in September 1970 took over responsibility for all Arc Light missions in Southeast Asia. However, more would be heard of Andersen in 1972 when the revitalised air war over North Vietnam brought the war to a temporary conclusion.

18 June 1965

B-52F 57-0047 441 BS, 7 BW attached to 3960 SW, USAF, Anderson
5 crew (KIA) - see below
1 crew, name unknown (survived)

B-52F 57-0179 441 BS, 7 BW attached to 3960 SW, USAF, Anderson
3 crew (KIA) - see below
3 crew, name unknown (survived)

It is not known which crewmember was in which aircraft, but those who died were:
Capt Robert Laurence Armond (KIA)
1Lt James Alfred Marshall (KIA)
Capt Frank Peter Watson (KIA)
MSgt Harold James Roberts (KIA)
TSgt William Edward Neville (KIA)
Capt Tyrrell Gordon Lowry (KIA)
Capt Joe Carrol Robertson (KIA)
Maj James Monroe Gehrig (KIA)

The first Arc Light raid on South Vietnam was targeted on a VC stronghold at Ben Cat, 40 miles north of Saigon. Thirty B-52s from the 9th BS and the 441st BS took off from Andersen just after midnight on the 17th for the raid. Twenty-four aircraft each carried a full internal and external bomb load of 51 x 750lb bombs while six carried 1,000lb armour-piercing bombs. Thirty KC-135 tankers took off from Kadena to rendezvous with the bombers over the South China Sea between South Vietnam and the island of Luzon in the Philippines. However, when the first wave of bombers arrived at the rendezvous point they were several minutes early due to a strong tailwind and they started manoeuvring to remain near the planned refuelling point. Green cell in the lead began a 360-degree turn that took it across the path of Blue cell and directly towards the oncoming Yellow cell. In the darkness two aircraft in the opposing cells collided at a position of 17 degrees 30 minutes North, 118 degrees east, about

250 miles from the coast of Vietnam. Eight airmen were killed while four survived. The survivors were located and taken on board an HU-16 Albatross amphibian (51-4287) but on attempting to take off in a heavy swell the aircraft was damaged and the survivors had to be transferred to a Norwegian freighter. The Albatross sank minutes after the crew were taken off by a Navy vessel.

The 28 remaining B-52s were further reduced when an aircraft suffered a hydraulic pump failure and lost its radar. Unable to refuel, the aircraft diverted to Kadena. The remaining 27 aircraft aimed 1,300 bombs from between 19,000 and 22,000 feet at a target box one mile wide by two miles long. The formation used a helicopter-borne radar beacon to assist their navigation and bombing. After the target had been hit another B-52 left the formation and diverted to Clark AFB with an electrical problem. The remaining 26 aircraft landed back at Andersen after this inaugural 13-hour mission. A post-raid assessment by ground forces found that only just over half of the bombs had landed in the target box and that the Viet Cong had left the area before the raid took place. This was undoubtedly a bad start to the more than 125,000 B-52 sorties that would be flown over the next eight years.

19 June 1965

B-57B 53-3910 8 TBS, 405 FW attached to 33 TG, USAF,
Tan Son Nhut
Capt Charles Kennedy Lovelace (KIA)
Capt William Edward Cordero (KIA)

Occasionally the Canberras of the 8th and 13th TBSs were used as pathfinders for other strike aircraft. During one such mission over the southernmost province of North Vietnam Capt Lovelace's aircraft was lost, whether as result of enemy action or otherwise was unknown. The remains of the crew were recovered post-war and buried at Arlington National Cemetery in Washington, DC.

20 June 1965

F-4C 64-0685 45 TFS, 15 TFW on TDY, USAF, Ubon
Capt Paul Anthony Kari (POW)
Capt Curt H Briggs (survived)

During a raid on the Son La NVA barracks one of the newly-arrived Ubon Phantoms was shot down by a MiG-17 near Ta Chan in northwest North Vietnam. Capt Kari had been on the first USAF F-4 mission of the war and had the bad luck to be flying the first F-4C to be lost in combat. Capt Kari was eventually released from prison on 12 February 1973. His WSO, Capt Briggs, was more fortunate as he evaded and hid until he was rescued the following day, probably by a USAF or Air America helicopter.

22 June 1965

F-100D 56-3340 615 TFS, 401 TFW on TDY, USAF, Da Nang
1 pilot, name unknown (survived)

During a close air support mission in South Vietnam a Super Sabre pilot had to eject when his aircraft ran out of fuel.

23 June 1965

F-105D 62-4319 357 TFS, 355 TFW attached to 6234 TFW,
USAF, Korat
Maj Robert W Wilson (survived)

During an armed reconnaissance mission over North Vietnam, a formation of F-105s attacked a substantial bridge near Cha Noi about 40 miles north of the DMZ. During the attack one of the aircraft was hit in the rear fuselage by AAA. Maj Wilson flew northwest for about 20 miles but could not get the aircraft to climb over a ridgeline and as the aircraft was on fire, he ejected. The pilot landed in dense jungle and found himself hanging upside down in a tall tree about 150 feet above the ground. He managed to swing towards the tree trunk and found a secure resting place where he unstrapped from his parachute and called for a rescue on his survival radio. An HC-54D Crown SAR airborne command and control aircraft heard the call and directed a flight of four USAF Skyraiders to Wilson's position. The Skyraider pilots spotted Wilson's parachute and called in an HH-43 that had taken off from a forward base in Laos. The helicopter lowered a jungle penetrator down through the foliage and Maj Wilson strapped himself on and was winched up into the helicopter. Some 90 minutes after his ejection, Maj Wilson was rescued safely without ever having set foot on North Vietnamese soil.

24 June 1965

A-1H 137523 VA-25, USN, USS *Midway*
1 pilot, name unknown (survived)

Following a strike mission, one of *Midway's* Skyraiders developed a technical fault that required an emergency landing during which the aircraft crashed.

25 June 1965

A-4C 149574 VA-153, USN, USS *Coral Sea*
Cdr Peter Mongilardi (KIA)

Cdr Mongilardi was the CO of VA-153 until May 1965 when he was appointed CAG or Air Wing Commander of *Coral Sea's* Carrier Air Wing 15. The carrier had left the line on 27 May and was on its way back to the USA when it was recalled for further duty as the tempo of the war increased. Cdr Mongilardi was leading two other Skyhawks on an armed reconnaissance mission when he spotted a small bridge over the Song Cho River about 10 miles

northwest of Thanh Hoa. As the formation rolled into the attack Cdr Mongilardi's aircraft was struck by 37mm flak. The wingmen lost sight of the lead aircraft but they heard the Commander key his radio microphone although he was having difficulty speaking and may have been wounded. No crash site was ever discovered either at the time or by the subsequent SAR operation. Cdr Mongilardi was the first CAG to be lost in the war and had been lucky to survive damage to his Skyhawk during the 29 March raid on Bach Long Vi when he had to be 'towed' back to the carrier by a tanker as his aircraft was leaking fuel almost as fast as it was receiving it. Cdr Mongilardi's place as CO of VA-153 was taken by Cdr H E Thomas who was himself lost on 13 August 1965.

27 June 1965

C-123B serial ..? 310 ACS, 315 ACG, USAF, Tan Son Nhut
detached to Nha Trang
Capt Carl Edwin Jackson (KIA)
SSgt Billie Leroy Roth (KIA)

Considerable mystery surrounds the loss of this Provider. The aircraft was supposedly assigned to the 37th Consolidated Aircraft Maintenance Squadron. The Provider is thought to have exploded in mid-air near Saigon, either while evacuating civilians, or on a 'bombing' raid or a flare drop. It is likely that the aircraft was involved in some kind of Special Forces mission, especially as one source claims that Capt Jackson was attached to the 1131st Special Activities Squadron of the Military Assistance Command Vietnam Studies and Observation Group. It has been claimed that Capt Jackson survived the crash and was held prisoner in the Soc Trang area. According to the unofficial MACVSOG website the Group mounted an attempted rescue mission on 13 October 1966, code named Operation Crimson Tide, to locate and free Capt Jackson. The mission went badly wrong and two US Army Special Forces and a platoon of Nung commandos were killed in the attempt. The exact fate of Capt Jackson and SSgt Roth remains unkown.

29 June 1965

RF-101C '56-0401' 15 TRS, 18 TFW on TDY, USAF, Udorn
Capt Marvin Nelson Lindsey (KIA)

The unarmed photographic reconnaissance RF-101s continued to suffer in their dangerous mission. Capt Lindsey was flying a BDA sortie at 1,000 feet over Son La in northwestern North Vietnam when his aircraft was hit by ground fire. He was not seen to eject and was listed as missing in action. Post-war Vietnamese reports suggests that Capt Lindsey may have been captured alive or was shot while still in his parachute. The serial number is listed as '56-0401' but this number does not belong to an RF-101C.

The deployment of the F-104C Starfighter to Southeast Asia was not a great success. Its short range and poor manoeuvrability suited it to neither the combat air patrols nor close air support missions that it performed. This photograph shows 56-0883, which was the first F-104C to be built and which was shot down by Chinese MiGs over Hainan island on 20 September 1965. USAF

B-57B 53-3895   8 TBS, 405 FW attached to 2 AD, USAF,
                 Da Nang
                 Capt Samuel P Chambers (KIA)
                 1Lt Robert George Landringham (KIA)

Late in June the B-57 force moved from Tan Son Nhut to the growing air base at Da Nang. With the move came a new basing policy whereby the two Canberra squadrons alternated 60-day rotations at Da Nang with periods spent in training at Clark. 'Bud' Chambers and his navigator were flying an air strike in support of Vietnamese Rangers and their aircraft was hit and damaged on its last strafing run. During the return to the airfield the wingman saw several holes in the aircraft's port wing and engine and the aircraft was streaming fuel. As the aircraft approached the runway Capt Chambers lowered the flaps which unfortunately disturbed the airflow over the wings causing the streaming fuel to be sucked through some of the holes near the engine. The port engine exploded and the wing separated and although both crew ejected immediately they were too low and neither survived. A new officers' accommodation block at Clark AFB was named Chambers Hall later in the year in the pilot's honour.

F-104C 56-0937   476 TFS, 479 TFW attached to 6252 TFW,
                  USAF, Da Nang
                  Capt R Cole (survived)

The first F-104 squadron arrived at Da Nang on temporary deployment from George AFB in California on 20 April. A total of 15 F-104Cs were based at Da Nang until the end of the year when the deployment ceased. The primary mission of the Starfighter in Southeast Asia was intended to be as an escort fighter, however, the aircraft did not have the range for this role. Although not really suited to the task, the F-104 was often used for close air support and it was during such a mission near Tri Dao, 15 miles northwest of Kontum, that Capt Cole's aircraft was hit forcing him to eject. Luckily, he was rescued by an Army helicopter although he had suffered injuries during the ejection.

30 June 1965

A-1H 139708   VA-152, USN, USS Oriskany
               1 pilot, name unknown (survived)

VA-152 lost a Skyraider when its engine failed as it was launching from Oriskany on a strike mission.

B-57B 52-1589   8 TBS, 405 FW attached to 2 AD, USAF,
                 Da Nang
                 2 crew, names unknown (survived)

A Canberra was damaged beyond repair during an aborted take off on a close air support sortie. This B-57 had previously been flown by the Kentucky ANG's 165th TRS from Louisville.

F-8E 150657   VF-194, USN, USS Bon Homme Richard
               Lt Cdr R E Weedon (survived)

On 30 June the US Navy suffered its first combat loss in South Vietnam. A flight of F-8s from the Bon Homme Richard was strafing VC positions north of the Mekong Delta when Lt Cdr Weedon's aircraft was rocked by an explosion that damaged the engine causing compressor stalls and rough running. A couple of minutes later the Crusader's engine eventually flamed out. Two attempts to relight failed and Weedon parted company with his aircraft, landing near Ap Bac. It was thought that either the aircraft had been hit by ground fire or that the Crusader's cannon had exploded resulting in foreign object damage to the engine. The Crusader had suffered problems with its 20mm cannon for many years. Although TF 77 aircraft had made their first strike on a Viet Cong target in South Vietnam on 15 April, this was the first Navy aircraft lost in action from Dixie Station.

O-1F 55-4649   19 TASS, 34 TG, USAF, Bien Hoa
                Capt Paul Ralph Windle (KIA)
                Maj Joseph E Parker, US Army (KIA)

Capt Windle and his observer, artilleryman Maj Parker, were flying an FAC mission near the village of Cheo Reo in Darlac province in South Vietnam in support of the Vietnamese Airborne Brigade. Windle was directing an attack by an F-100

when his Bird Dog was hit by ground fire and crashed on a rocky hillside. Capt Windle was one of the original members of the Jungle Jim squadron and flew two tours in Vietnam as pilot in the B-26 before converting to the A-1E for his third tour. However, on arriving back in South Vietnam Capt Windle was reassigned to fly the O-1 as an FAC. He had flown just over 100 FAC missions when he was shot down. After his death, the small airport at Greensburg, Kansas was named in his honour as it was at this airfield that Paul Windle learned to fly in the early 1950s before joining the Air Force.

1 July 1965

C-130A 55-0039, 55-0042 817 TCS, 6315 OG, USAF, Da Nang
                         (TDY from Naha)

F-102A 55-3371, 56-1161, 56-1182 Detachment 3, 509 FIS,
                         405 FW, USAF, Da Nang

Da Nang had grown into the major centre for air operations in the northern provinces of South Vietnam. On 8 March 1,600 US Marines had landed at the base and from then on Da Nang developed to become the main base for Marine Corps activity during the war. The Marines also took over responsibility for the security of the airfield in March 1965. In the early hours of 1 July a mortar attack at one end of Da Nang airfield provided a diversion for a group of VC sappers who killed a USAF guard, SSgt T K Jensen, and gained entry to the flight line. They then placed satchel charges and hand grenades among several aircraft. Two C-130A flareships from Naha's 6315th Operations Group were destroyed along with three of Da Nang's F-102 interceptors from the 509th FIS detachment. The F-102s were sitting on alert status and the enemy sappers simply threw hand grenades into the open cockpits and fired machine guns into the tailpipes. The flareships, which had only recently arrived at Da Nang, flew missions over the Ho Chi Minh Trail at night dropping flares for accompanying strike aircraft, usually B-57s at this stage of the war. Two VNAF C-47s were also destroyed in the attack on Da Nang and three more F-102s, three C-123s, and 18 VNAF C-47s were damaged. A C-130A 56-0475 from the 817th TCS of the 6315th OG was also badly damaged but later repaired and flew with the Air Force Reserve until it was retired to become a battle damage training airframe.

This was the second major VC attack on a US airfield and was even more successful than their first attempt at Bien Hoa on 1 November 1964. Following this attack on Da Nang, the base's Marine Corps commander adopted a more aggressive airfield defence posture and pushed offensive patrols far out from the base.

3 July 1965

F-105D 62-4398   563 TFS, 23 TFW attached to 6441
                  TFW(P), USAF, Takhli
                  1 pilot, name unknown (survived)

During a strike mission an F-105 crashed due to fuel exhaustion after the pilot ejected to safety.

6 July 1965

F-105D 62-4232   12 TFS, 18 TFW attached to 6234 TFW,
                  USAF, Korat
                  Capt Don Ira Williamson (KIA)

The 12th TFS arrived at Korat from Kadena on 15 June following a six-week deployment earlier in the year. A formation of F-105s was on an armed reconnaissance mission when the lead pilot spotted a bridge just east of Ha Tinh near Vinh. As Capt Williamson's aircraft was pulling up from its attack it was hit by ground fire and he was seen to eject and land safely, his SAR beeper being activated after he reached the ground. A SAR operation failed to find any trace of Capt Williamson and a Hanoi press report indicated that he had been killed in the action. Nothing further was heard until remains were returned to the US in June 1989 and were later identified as being those of Capt Williamson. It is not known how, or when, he died.

7 July 1965

O-1F 57-2944   19 TASS, 34 TG, USAF, Bien Hoa
                1Lt Thomas Andrew Sanders (KWF)
                1 crew, name unknown (survived)

A Bird Dog crashed as it was taking off on a non-operational flight killing one crewman and injuring the other. This was the 10th Bird Dog lost by the 19th TASS in two years of operations in South Vietnam.

The Grumman A-6 Intruder

When the USS Independence sailed into the South China Sea on 5 June it introduced a new aircraft to the conflict in the shape of the Grumman A-6A Intruder, a two-seat all-weather attack bomber. The aircraft was equipped with advanced avionics and radar and had a useful bomb load of some 15,000lb. Its specialist role was low level interdiction, often at night and as a single ship operation without escort. However, when the first Intruders deployed to Southeast Asia the DIANE (digital, integrated attack and navigation equipment) suite of avionics was not yet fully functional nor totally reliable. VA-75 flew its first operational mission into North Vietnam on 1 July but by the end of the month the squadron had lost three aircraft. While the vagaries of the DIANE system were not responsible for the losses, the complicated avionics caused a much greater degree of aircraft unserviceability than was normal for an attack squadron. The problems with the avionics and radar were still not solved when the second Intruder squadron, VA-85, arrived on the USS Kitty Hawk in November.

14 July 1965

A-6A 151584   VA-75, USN, USS Independence
               Lt Donald V Boecker (survived)
               Lt Donald R Eaton (survived)

On 27 June the USS Independence took up station off South Vietnam for its first and only tour of duty in the war in Southeast Asia. The Independence was the first Atlantic Fleet carrier to be deployed to Vietnam and increased the strength of carriers available to TF 77 to five. The first Intruder to be lost in the war was on a daylight armed reconnaissance mission over the Barrel Roll area of Laos. About 10 miles north of Sam Neua the aircraft commenced a dive on a road choke point but as the aircraft released its Mk82 bombs the crew saw one of the bombs explode under the starboard wing. The starboard engine was damaged, the aircraft caught fire and the hydraulics failed. When the port engine also failed and the controls froze the crew had to eject and were rescued 18 hours later by an Air America UH-34. Premature detonation of ordnance is a problem that airmen have faced ever since aircraft started to carry bombs. Lt Boecker went on to fly 69 missions in Southeast Asia in the A-6A and progressed through the Navy, commanding VA-85 in 1973-75 and eventually retired as a Rear Admiral.

15 July 1965

A-4C 149576   VA-153, USN, USS Coral Sea
               Lt A J Bennett (survived)

During a night-time reconnaissance mission over a coastal road near Mu Ron Ma, an A-4 from Coral Sea was hit by AAA as it was about to attack a convoy of military vehicles with CBUs. Lt Bennett climbed the aircraft as a fire warning light came on and the hydraulics began to seize. Bennett disconnected the hydraulic boost and coaxed the stricken Skyhawk out over the sea until, about 20 miles from the North Vietnamese coast, the controls eventually froze solid. Lt Bennett ejected and was picked up by a US warship.

18 July 1965

A-6A 151577   VA-75, USN, USS Independence
               Cdr Jeremiah Andrew Denton (POW)
               Lt(jg) William Michael Tschudy (POW)

Just four days after the loss of the first Intruder in combat, the Independence suffered another loss, this time with its crew. The aircraft was part of a formation attacking the Ham Rong port

facilities near the Dragon's Jaw Bridge at Thanh Hoa. The loss of 151577 was almost a carbon copy of the loss of the first aircraft. Just after releasing the Mk82 bombs the crew felt a detonation and the aircraft began to lose hydraulic and electrical power. Throttle control was also lost and the crew were forced to eject near the target to face the next eight years as POWs.

Denton and Tschudy had flown 12 and 13 missions respectively over Vietnam before they were shot down. Cdr Denton was the Air Wing's operations officer and had been due to assume command of VA-75 on 20 July. They were both released on 12 February 1973. Jeremiah Denton eventually retired from the Navy as a Rear Admiral and went on to be elected to the US Senate as a Democrat for Alabama in 1980. He wrote an account of his POW experiences titled *When Hell was in Session* which was published in 1976 and which served as the basis for a television film.

A-4E 151089 VA-163, USN, USS *Oriskany*
Lt Malcolm Arthur Avore (KIA)

On its last day of line duty at Dixie Station before a three week break from operations, the *Oriskany* lost one its Skyhawk pilots in tragic circumstances 180 miles southeast of Saigon. As Lt Avore's Skyhawk was catapulted for a strike mission over South Vietnam the engine faltered and the aircraft failed to gather speed. It ditched in front of the carrier and sank within seconds. Unfortunately Lt Avore was unable to escape.

20 July 1965

F-100D 56-3170 429 TFS, 474 TFW attached to 6251 TFW, USAF, Bien Hoa
1 pilot, name unknown (survived)

During a close air support mission a Super Sabre struck a tree causing damage which forced the pilot to eject.

RA-5C 151619 RVAH-1, USN, USS *Independence*
Cdr Valentin George Matula (KIA)
Lt Carl Eugene Gronquist (KIA)

Following VA-75's experience with its Intruders, the *Independence* continued to be dogged by bad luck. After a photographic reconnaissance mission over North Vietnam, an RA-5C landed back on board but the No.1 arrester cable snapped and the aircraft went overboard at low speed and crashed into the sea. RVAH-1's commanding officer, Cdr Matula, and his NFO perished in the accident.

The 481st TFS and the Nature of Temporary Duty

The 481st TFS was typical of the many USAF squadrons that temporarily deployed to Southeast Asia during 1964 and 1965 before squadrons and wings were assigned on a more permanent basis. The 481st was one of four F-100 squadrons belonging to the 27th TFW based at Cannon AFB, New Mexico. In the spring of 1965 the Squadron was alerted that it would be sent to South Vietnam on temporary duty in June of that year. The deployment was brought forward at short notice and 18 F-100s took off on 12 June under the deployment code name Operation Two Buck 16. The aircraft staged through Hickam AFB, Hawaii and arrived at Clark in the Philippines on the 14th. The F-100s were refuelled across the Pacific by KC-135s, which also provided navigational support. The ground element of the Squadron flew over in C-130 transports. The Squadron was held at Clark for a week until the 21st when it flew to Tan Son Nhut, which would be its temporary home for the next six months. The Squadron flew its first combat mission over South Vietnam on the very day it arrived.

Although still nominally a 27th TFW squadron, on arrival at Tan Son Nhut the 481st was attached to the 33rd TG that was renamed the 6250th CSG on 1 July. Thirty pilots were assigned to the 481st including several reinforcements from the 522nd and the 524th TFSs, also from the 27th TFW. Only four of the Squadron's pilots had any combat experience when they first arrived in Vietnam. The CO, Lt Col Harold E Comstock, was a Second World War fighter ace with seven victories to his credit and three of the Squadron's pilots had already served tours in Vietnam in a variety of aircraft types. In the first two months of its stay at Tan Son Nhut the Squadron flew an average of 30 sorties

each day. Most of the sorties were pre-planned close air support missions but these were interspersed with alert missions that were flown in response to VC attacks. Missions were flown day and night, even though some pilots had done very little night flying until they reached Vietnam. Almost every mission was flown under the control of a ground-based or airborne FAC and permission was required from Vietnamese district chiefs before pre-planned targets could be struck.

The 481st was due to return to the USA in August but this was postponed and eventually the tour was extended to November. Unknown to the Squadron at the time the delay was caused by the need to prepare replacement squadrons to deploy to Southeast Asia on a Permanent Change of Station basis rather than on temporary duty. From November 1965 onwards most of the USAF TDY squadrons in South Vietnam and Thailand were replaced by PCS squadrons permanently assigned to PACAF. The change in status had many implications for personnel including the requirement to fly 100 combat missions before an individual could return home to the USA.

The last of the 481st TFS personnel were flown out of Vietnam on 27 November, having left their aircraft at Tan Son Nhut for assignment to other squadrons. The Squadron had been in Vietnam for six months, which was two to three months longer than most TDY rotations. During this time the 481st had flown around 3,600 combat missions in a total of 5,025 hours. Twenty-one of the Squadron's pilots had each flown over 100 missions. The hardworking ground crews had enabled the Squadron to achieve an amazing 98 per cent in-commission rate for the Squadron's aircraft and not one combat mission was aborted because of a technical problem. The ordnance expended by the 481st included 3,829 x 750lb bombs, 1,681 x 500lb bombs, 155 x Mk82 Snakeye bombs, 3,952 x 750lb napalm cannisters, 18,961 LAU-3 rockets, 25 x AGM-12B Bullpups, 640 CBUs and 1.6 million rounds of 20mm cannon shells. During its tour the Squadron lost six Super Sabres with two pilots killed in action.

21 July 1965

A-1H 139636 VA-152, USN, USS *Oriskany*
1 pilot, name unknown (survived)

During a test flight one of VA-152's Skyraiders suffered engine failure and the pilot was forced to abandon the aircraft.

F-100D 56-3334 481 TFS, 27 TFW attached to 6250 CSG, USAF, Tan Son Nhut
Capt John T Parker (survived)

The first aircraft lost by the 481st TFS was shot down during a close air support mission. A US Army helicopter rescued Capt Parker.

22 July 1965

A-1E 52-132414 6251 TFW, USAF, Bien Hoa
Capt Oliver C Chase (KIA)

In July the 34th TG was replaced at Bien Hoa by the 6251st TFW which controlled two Air Commando Skyraider squadrons and two F-100 squadrons on TDY. One of the Skyraiders from Bien Hoa was shot down during a napalm attack on a VC target in Binh Dinh province, South Vietnam. A US helicopter arrived at the scene soon after the incident but Capt Chase had died in the crash.

F-104C 56-0908 436 TFS, 479 TFW attached to 6252 TFW, USAF, Da Nang
Capt Roy James Blakeley (KIA)

The second Starfighter to be lost during the war in Southeast Asia was shot down during a close air support mission in Quang Tin province south of Da Nang. Little else is known about the circumstances of the loss.

O-1F 56-4218 6253 CSG, USAF, Nha Trang
Capt Francis Edward Geiger (KIA)
Lt Heip, probably VNAF (KIA)

Forward air control missions were as dangerous as close air support or interdiction. Capt Geiger's aircraft was probably hit by small arms fire causing it to crash. Both Capt Geiger and his

observer, Lt Heip, were killed in the crash, which occurred in Kontum province. This aircraft is listed as belonging to the 6253rd CSG that had been formed at Nha Trang earlier in the month to provide support for the 310th ACS which moved in from Tan Son Nhut the same month. However, it is possible that the Bird Dog actually belonged to the 21st TASS that had been activated at Pleiku on 8 May.

The SA-2 SAM

On 5 April 1965 a reconnaissance aircraft brought back the first photographs of a new construction site in North Vietnam. The characteristic six-pointed star shape around a central hub was well known to USAF intelligence and indicated that the North Vietnamese were building their first surface-to-air missile sites. A second site was found in May and by July several sites formed an irregular ring around Hanoi and Haiphong. It was assumed that Soviet or Chinese engineers were assisting in the construction of these sites and for this reason Washington decided not to attack the SAM sites during the construction phase. However, RF-101C reconnaissance aircraft kept a close eye on the construction programme.

The SA-2 surface-to-air missile was revealed by the Soviets in 1957 and was actually designated the S-75 Dvina by the Russians while NATO gave it the code name Guideline. The US already had first hand experience of the SA-2 when a missile brought down a U-2 flown by Gary Powers over the Soviet Union on 1 May 1960 and another U-2 was shot down over Cuba on 27 October 1962 during the Cuban Missile Crisis. The SA-2 missile is 35 feet in length and is powered by a solid fuel booster rocket that falls away five seconds after lift off when a liquid fuel rocket motor cuts in for 22 seconds. The warhead contains 130 kg of high explosives and detonates in a fan-shaped pattern ahead of the line of flight with a kill radius of about 200 feet. Guidance is by radar homing controlled by operators in a control van situated near the missile battery. The Fan Song missile guidance radar sends signals to the missile's receiver guiding it towards its target. The SA-2 weighs about 5,000lb at launch and accelerates to Mach 3.5 although its speed in the early stages of flight is much slower and allowed US aircraft to avoid it if spotted early enough. The missile has an effective range of 25 miles and its effective ceiling of 82,000 feet gives it a virtually unlimited high altitude performance. However, it is relatively ineffective below 1,000 feet as the guidance system does not have enough time to work at such low altitude and the missile has a limited manoeuvring ability. The North Vietnamese SA-2 batteries were very mobile and could be moved from one location to another in a matter of hours, sometimes being moved in the space between a reconnaissance flight and a strike. However, the batteries were very distinctive and, unless well camouflaged, were not too difficult to spot from the air being shaped like a six-pointed star with a launcher at each of the points and a control van near the centre with an Fan Song radar close by.

In mid-July an RB-66C ELINT aircraft picked up signals from an SA-2's Spoon Rest target acquisition radar. On 23 July another ELINT aircraft detected signals from the missile's Fan Song target-tracking radar for the first time. The following day three SAMs were fired minutes after signals were picked up and the North Vietnamese scored their first SAM kill and ushered in a new phase of the air war. A flight by a Ryan 147E Firebee drone over North Vietnam on 13 February 1966 gained much valuable information about the SA-2's proximity fusing system, its terminal phase guidance signals and its warhead explosive characteristics at detonation. This and further flights by Firebee drones obtained enough information for effective countermeasures to be built into tactical aircraft and B-52s to give a higher chance of survival against the SAM.

24 July 1965

A-6A 151585 VA-75, USN, USS *Independence*
Lt Cdr R P Bordone (survived)
Lt(jg) P F Moffett (survived)

Following the loss of two of its Intruders in the last 10 days due to premature detonation of their Mk82 bombs (although the

The USAF search and rescue capability was greatly enhanced by the arrival of the first CH-3C helicopters on loan from TAC in July 1965. The 3rd ARRG's own HH-3Es arrived soon after and were responsible for many saves, often deep into enemy territory. Fourteen CH/HH-3s were lost while on SAR missions during the war. *USAF*

Navy could not have known for sure that this was the cause of Denton/Tschudy's loss as they were POWs), VA-75 was stunned when they lost yet another aircraft to the same cause on the 24th. Lt Cdr Bordone was flying an armed reconnaissance mission over the Steel Tiger area of southern Laos when he spotted what he took to be military buildings. The aircraft dropped bombs successfully on its first two passes at the target but on the third dive the aircraft was rocked by a premature detonation just as two Mk82s were released at 2,000 feet and 400 knots. The aircraft went into a violent corkscrew manoeuvre that Lt Cdr Bordone was powerless to control. The crew ejected as the aircraft was inverted at about 1,000 feet above the ground. They were lucky to escape from the aircraft and even luckier to be rescued by a USAF helicopter. They were soon back on the *Independence* where they told their story although Lt Moffett was invalided home due to his injuries. Lt Cdr Bordone later returned to Southeast Asia as an F-4 pilot and was shot down on 8 September 1972.

The problem was traced to the bomb fuses and the bomb racks used by the Intruder and several other aircraft types at the time. The bombs were armed by a mechanical fuse fitted into the bomb's nose which armed the bomb 0.7 seconds after release. The A-6As of VA-75 were fitted with bomb racks which simply released the weapons rather than propelled them away from the aircraft like the more modern ejector racks. Therefore when the bombs armed they were still very close to the aircraft and probably tumbling in close proximity until two or more collided right underneath the aircraft. This problem was not unique to the A-6 and it was easily remedied by retrofitting ejector racks as quickly as they could be delivered, but it was a problem that the Intruder could well have done without as it marred its combat debut. Premature detonation was not, however, the only problem which VA-75 had to contend with. The aircraft's advanced avionics were causing severe problems as the aircraft had been rushed into combat before it had been thoroughly tested. Systems reliability only reached 35 per cent on the first deployment and was a constant worry for engineers, mission planners and air-

crew alike. In addition, the maps of North Vietnam that the Navy relied upon to programme the Intruder's navigation equipment were found to be inaccurate. Coordinates were sometimes found to be 3-4 miles out in some instances. In between their BDA reconnaissance sorties, the Navy's RA-5Cs surveyed large areas of North Vietnam in an effort to bring the maps up to date.

**F-105D 62-4373   80 TFS, 6441 TFW on TDY, USAF, Takhli
                               Maj W J McClelland (survived)**
As part of the growing SAR organisation in Southeast Asia the USAF and US Navy provided escorts and combat air patrols for rescue forces for each other whenever possible. A flight of F-105 was sent from Takhli to cover the USAF helicopter that eventually rescued Lt Cdr Bordone and Lt Moffett. When the F-105s were within a few miles of the downed Navy fliers Maj McClelland's aircraft was hit by AAA and immediately caught fire. The Major headed eastwards to make for Da Nang but after about 30 miles he was forced to eject just inside the Laotian border with North Vietnam. Fortunately, a USAF helicopter had been alerted and picked up Maj McClelland.

**F-4C   63-7599   47 TFS, 15 TFW on TDY, USAF, Ubon
                           Capt Roscoe Henry Fobair (KIA)
                           Capt Richard Paul Keirn (POW)**
The third US aircraft loss of the day was a highly significant event in the history of the air war over Vietnam. Captains Fobair and Keirn were flying one of four Phantoms providing a CAP for an F-105 strike mission on a munitions factory at Lang Chi. While at 23,000 feet about 40 miles west of Hanoi the crew spotted a smoke trail tracking towards their aircraft and had just realised what they were seeing when their Phantom suddenly exploded. Fobair and Keirn had become the first US airmen to be shot down by a North Vietnamese SA-2 surface-to-air-missile. The crew had just heard a warning from an RB-66C that a SAM radar was on the air when three missiles were launched at the Phantoms. One missile scored a direct hit on Fobair's aircraft and the other two exploded behind the flight causing slight damage to the other three Phantoms.

Both men ejected from the stricken Phantom and it is thought that both were captured by the North Vietnamese. However, on 12 February 1973 only Capt Keirn was released from captivity. The North Vietnamese stated that Capt Fobair had died but refused to say how or when.

Remarkably, Richard 'Pop' Keirn had flown 14 missions as a B-17 Flying Fortress co-pilot with the 100th Bomb Group in the US Eighth Air Force. In September 1944 his aircraft was shot

down near Leipzig and Keirn spent the next nine months as a POW in a Stalag Luft. Following demobilisation, he was recalled to active service in 1956 and flew F-86s and F-100s before converting to the F-4C. He had been at Ubon for two weeks and was on his 11th mission over North Vietnam when he was shot down. After release 'Pop' Keirn flew O-2s and was appointed Assistant Director of Operations, 9th Air Force before retiring in 1976.

Search and Rescue - II
At the beginning of 1965 the USAF search and rescue forces in Southeast Asia amounted to just 12 HH-43s and five HU-16s. However, in 1965 search and rescue recieved a new impetus and the SAR task force was born which evolved throughout the war to become one the most successful operations of the war. In June 1965 three HC-54D Rescuemasters were deployed to Udorn to replace the HU-16 in the rescue command post role. The HC-54s carried airborne mission controllers who coordinated major SARs. The aircraft had a greater endurance than the Albatross but its communications fit proved inadequate. Escort for SAR helicopters was provided over South Vietnam and Laos mainly by A-1s and T-28s and tactical fighters could be called upon if needed. SAR missions into North Vietnam sometime had a MiGCAP flight of fighters to protect the task force from enemy MiGs. On 1 July Detachment 3 of the Pacific Air Rescue Center was redesignated as the 38th ARS with its headquarters at Tan Son Nhut.

On 6 July the SAR capability in Southeast Asia increased dramatically when two Sikorsky CH-3Cs on loan from Tactical Air Command arrived at Nakon Phanom. The twin-turbine CH-3 had a greatly increased performance over the little HH-43 but the CH-3C was a transport version and was being used only until a new SAR model, the HH-3E, became available. The CH-3C was one of the first aircraft in Southeast Asia to be painted in the three-tone green and tan camouflage scheme and the type was nicknamed the Jolly Green Giant, a name that was adopted for their call signs. One of the CH-3Cs was lost on 6 November but the other aircraft was joined by the first two HH-3Es on 10 November when all three helicopters moved to Udorn. Four more of the new helicopters arrived the following month. Capt Lilly's aircraft was the first of 13 Jolly Green Giants that would be lost on SAR missions in Southeast Asia. In December 1965 the HC-54s were replaced by two new HC-130Hs, specially modified versions of the Hercules transport. These aircraft represented a quantum jump over the capabilities of the HC-54 and HU-16 and became the airborne command posts for the SAR task force. Three more aircraft

arrived in June 1966 and the HC-130H detachment became the 39th ARRS on 16 January 1967.

By the end of the year the 38th ARS had replaced the various temporary duty detachments with nine numbered detachments at Nakhon Phanom (No1), Takhli (2), Ubon (3), Korat (4), Udorn (5), Bien Hoa (6), Da Nang (7), Pleiku (9), and Binh Thuy (10) and flew six HH-3Es, one CH-3C and 25 HH-43B/Fs. In addition the rescue forces had two HC-130Hs and five HU-16 amphibians available in Southeast Asia. On 8 January 1966 the USAF Air Rescue Service became the Aerospace Rescue and Recovery Service and the 3rd Aerospace Rescue and Recovery Group was formed at Tan Son Nhut to coordinate all SAR activity in Southeast Asia. Rescue control centres were set up at Da Nang and Udorn and the 37th ARS was formed at Da Nang with a detachment at Udorn. This squadron was given responsibility for SAR over North Vietnam, Laos and the Gulf of Tonkin (notwithstanding the US Navy's contribution) while the 38th ARS concentrated on SAR in South Vietnam together with local base rescue.

27 July 1965

F-105D 62-4257 563 TFS, 23 TFW attached to 6235 TFW, USAF, Takhli
Capt Walter B Kosko (KIA)

F-105D 61-0113 563 TFS, 23 TFW attached to 6235 TFW, USAF, Takhli
Capt Kile Dag Berg (POW)

F-105D 61-0177 357 TFS, 355 TFW attached to 6234 TFW, USAF, Korat
Capt William J Barthelmas (KIA)

F-105D 62-4298 357 TFS, 355 TFW attached to 6234 TFW, USAF, Korat
Maj Jack Graham Farr (KIA)

F-105D 62-4407 12 TFS, 18 TFW attached to 6234 TFW, USAF, Korat
Capt Frank J Tullo (survived)

F-105D 62-4252 12 TFS, 18 TFW attached to 6234 TFW, USAF, Korat
Capt Robert Baldwin Purcell (POW)

27 July 1965 turned out to be one of the blackest days of the war for the USAF, particularly for the close knit F-105 community. Following the shooting down of the USAF Phantom on 24 July by an SA-2 missile, the SAM sites at last came off the restricted list. The first attack on the North Vietnamese SAM system took place three days later, on the 27th, and involved a force of 48 F-105s attacking two confirmed sites near Hanoi. A SAM site on the banks of the Song Hac Giang (Black River) about 30 miles west of Hanoi and only 10 miles from Hoa Lac airfield was designated as SAM Site No7 by the USAF. In the initial stage of the battle against the SAM sites the F-105s used conventional bombs, unguided rockets or napalm and all these weapons were used on this raid. Two raids were made against SAM Site No7 and two of the F-105s were lost at or near the target. Both aircraft were thought to have been shot down by AAA. Capt Kosko was flying one of four F-105s in the first wave and radioed that his aircraft had been hit and that there was smoke in the cockpit. He ejected and his parachute was seen by other members of the flight as it floated down towards the Black River. A search later revealed an inflated life raft but no sign of Capt Kosko. After the war investigations indicated that Capt Kosko had drowned in the river and that his life raft had been recovered and used as a fishing boat by a local man for a number of years until it deteriorated. Walter Kosko had survived being shot down a few weeks earlier on 5 June when his aircraft was damaged over Laos forcing him to eject over Thailand.

One hour after Capt Kosko was shot down another flight of F-105s attacked SAM Site No7 and another aircraft was lost. This F-105 was flown by Capt Kile Berg and was shot down by ground fire near the target after dropping napalm. Capt Berg ejected and was taken prisoner. He survived his years of captivity and was released on 12 February 1973.

Two more F-105s were lost in a raid on SAM Site No6, close to Site No7. Capt Barthelmas's aircraft was damaged by ground fire soon after leaving the target area. The Captain flew his damaged aircraft back across North Vietnam and Laos into Thailand but was killed when the aircraft crashed near Ban Kut Du. The other aircraft lost on this mission was flown by Maj Farr and is thought to have crashed after a mid-air collision 15 miles southeast of Ubon following combat damage over the North.

As the main F-105 strike force left the area of the SAM sites, a last flight of Thuds (Dogwood flight) arrived with the intention of destroying anything that had been left by the main force. As Dogwood flight approached a SAM site at low level a volley of missiles was fired at the aircraft. The flight manoeuvred to avoid the SAMs but in doing so flew right over an AAA position and Capt Tullo's aircraft was hit. The F-105 burst into flames and Capt Tullo jettisoned his ordnance and fuel tanks to obtain the last ounce of performance in the hope of getting as far away from the target as possible. A short while later the aircraft started to nose down and Tullo had to eject. He landed in tall elephant grass near Hoang Trung, about 5 miles west of the Black River.

Miraculously he was rescued by a CH-3C flown by Capt George Martin in what was the deepest penetration by a SAR mission so far in the war. The helicopter staged through Lima Site 36 in northern Laos where it refuelled for the long flight into the heart of North Vietnam. RESCAP was provided by flights of B-57s and Navy A-1s and two B-57s were slightly damaged by ground fire and had to recover to Udorn where they landed with minimum fuel. As Tullo was being hoisted into the aircraft the hoist snagged and Capt Martin had to land in a nearby field so that Tullo could be set down and climb aboard the helicopter. This was one of the very first rescues performed by the recently-arrived Jolly Green Giant helicopters and was so far into North Vietnam that the helicopter crew did not even have a map of the area on board.

Five miles to the south of Capt Tullo's location, Capt Purcell was shot down while bombing barracks at Can Doi. He, however, was not so fortunate and was captured to spend the next seven years as a POW until his release on 12 February 1973. He had flown 25 missions up to the time of his capture. Capt Purcell's aircraft was painted as 'Viet Nam Ang'.

The loss of six F-105s and five pilots in 55 sorties was a bitter blow to the USAF and although the SAM sites were thought to have been destroyed the trade off was very much in favour of the North Vietnamese. It was also becoming obvious that the greatest danger posed by the SA-2 was not the kill capability of the missile itself but the fact that its mere presence forced US aircraft to fly at lower altitudes where AAA and small arms fire became more deadly.

28 July 1965

A-4E 149962 VA-23, USN, USS *Midway*
Lt(jg) G R Townsend (survived)

The problem of premature detonation was not confined to the USS *Independence*, nor to the A-6. Four days after the third Intruder was lost, VA-23 lost a Skyhawk to the same cause. Lt Townsend was part of a flak suppression formation that was attacking an AAA site in a karst region 50 miles south of Vinh. As two Mk82 bombs were released there was an explosion which caused the aircraft to burst into flames and disintegrate. Lt Townsend ejected despite having received injuries from the explosion. He was rescued by a USAF helicopter that had flown from a forward base in Laos. The Mk82 bombs were armed by an electrical fuse and could be fitted with a variable timing fuse to delay detonation after impact. It was suspected that either the electrical fuse was arming itself prematurely or that the sensor in the variable timing fuse was reacting to the proximity of the aircraft or the other bombs.

F-4B 150646 VF-21, USN, USS *Midway*
Lt Cdr W Fitzsimmons (survived)
Lt(jg)R L Griffiths (survived)

VF-21's first loss of the war occurred during a combat air patrol when one its Phantoms suffered engine and electrical power failure. Both crewmen were subsequently rescued after their ejection.

29 July 1965

A-1E 52-132670 6251 TFW, USAF, Bien Hoa
1 pilot, name unknown (survived)

A Skyraider crashed during a close air support mission due to pilot error.

F-8E 150337 VF-191, USN, USS *Bon Homme Richard*
Lt(jg) Edward Dean Brown (KIA)

VF-191 suffered its first fatality in the war on 29 July when a flight of Crusaders was attacking a VC position in woods near Tra Vinh in the Mekong Delta. Lt Brown was making his first strafing pass when his aircraft was seen to plough into the ground at 450 knots. There was light small arms fire in the vicinity at the time and Lt Brown may have been hit. It was also thought likely that he may have been concentrating on the target and did not realise his predicament until too late to attempt an ejection.

RF-101C 56-0067 45 TRS, 39 AD on TDY, USAF, Tan Son Nhut
Capt Jack Wilton Weatherby (KIA)

Two days after the initial strikes against the North Vietnamese SAM sites, two RF-101s were despatched from Tan Son Nhut to photograph SAM sites west of Hanoi. Jack Weatherby had obtained photographs of another SAM site two days earlier and on the 29th he and Maj Jerry Lents were returning from a mission over South Vietnam when they learned of the plan to fly another SAM mission. Weatherby and Lents immediately volunteered to fly the afternoon mission. Weatherby lost his UHF radio shortly after take off and Maj Lents led the way to a tanker over northern Thailand. After taking on fuel Weatherby indicated that he wanted to resume the lead and the pair set course for North Vietnam. Thunderstorms impeded their progress but they finally broke clear near the target. Dropping to 200 feet the aircraft accelerated to 600 knots as reconnaissance pilots reckoned that the best way to survive their missions was to fly as fast and as low as possible. As they were approaching the target Capt Weatherby's aircraft was hit by an anti-aircraft shell that did not explode but which left a gaping hole in the mid-fuselage section. Maj Lents then saw flames issue from the damaged Voodoo and told Weatherby to eject. Instead of escaping Capt Weatherby maintained his course for the target and had passed over it and had turned for home when his aircraft suddenly exploded. Jack Weatherby was awarded a posthumous AFC for his courage and determination to obtain photographs of a target of great importance to the USAF.

31 July 1965

F-100D 55-2837 481 TFS, 27 TFW attached to 6250 CSG, USAF, Tan Son Nhut
1Lt Donald David Watson (KIA)

The last USAF aircraft lost in what was the costliest month of the war so far was an F-100 that crashed as it was dropping napalm on a VC headquarters north of Saigon. On 19/20 July 1Lt Watson had taken part in a dangerous night attack in poor weather on enemy forces that were storming the Bu Dop Special Forces Camp. He was awarded the DFC for this mission but never lived to collect it.

EF-10B 125806 VMCJ-1, MAG-11, USMC, Da Nang
1Lt Milton Keith McNulty (KIA)
CWO Vernard Jay Small (KIA)

In March 1965 the US Marines began to build up their base at Da Nang and brought in the first of its jet squadrons. Marine Aircraft Group 16 was formed on 9 March and an advanced command post of the 1st Marine Air Wing was established on 11 May to control the Marine squadrons at Da Nang as they arrived. The first fixed wing unit to deploy was VMFA-531 which arrived on 10 April with 15 F-4B Phantoms to provide close air support for Marine operations in I Corps. The Phantoms would also be available for operations in North Vietnam when required. The second jet unit to arrive was VMCJ-1, a composite squadron equipped with six ancient EF-10B Skynights and a few RF-8A Crusaders. The EF-10Bs arrived on 10 April to be followed by the rest of the Squadron later in the month. The Crusaders provided photographic reconnaissance but the Skynights, a Korean War-vin-

tage aircraft, were specially modified to provide electronic countermeasures support and electronic intelligence gathering. VMCJ-1 flew its first ECM mission from Da Nang on 21 April. The Skynights operated in both North and South Vietnam and were particularly useful for locating and jamming enemy fire control radars used by AAA and SAM units. MAG-11 arrived at Da Nang on 7 July and the fixed-wing squadrons on the airfield were assigned to it a few days later.

VMCJ-1 lost its first EF-10B during a night ECM mission when one of the aircraft flew into the sea off Da Nang. The crash was thought to have been accidental, rather than caused by hostile action.

2 August 1965

F-105D 62-4249   12 TFS, 18 TFW attached to 6234 TFW, USAF, Korat
Capt Robert Norlan Daughtrey (POW)

On 2 August the USAF made another attempt to destroy the Thanh Hoa Bridge. As Capt Daughtrey dived on the bridge his aircraft was hit by AAA and he was forced to eject. Both his arms were broken during the ejection but he received little medical attention from his North Vietnamese captors. He was released on 12 February 1973 and had to undergo medical attention to reset the bones in his arms. This was the fourth and final F-105 lost by the 12th TFS before its return to Kadena on 25 August. The Squadron did not return to Thailand although some of its aircraft and pilots were loaned to other squadrons at Korat or Takhli from time to time.

A-1G 132625   '1131 SAS, Advance Group', USAF, Da Nang
Maj William Warren Hail (KIA)

Minutes after taking off from Da Nang Maj Hail's Skyraider disappeared. Despite an extensive search no sign of the aircraft or its pilot was ever found. William Hail had flown a total of 180 missions in South Vietnam, most of them either in support of South Vietnamese ground troops or training VNAF pilots. The 1131st SAS is presumably the 1131st Special Activities Squadron of MACVSOG, so Maj Hail may have been on some sort of special operation.

An A-4E Skyhawk of VA-23 from the USS *Midway* attacks Viet Cong positions in October 1965. VA-23 lost four aircraft and three pilots during its 1965 cruise on board the *Midway*. USN

3 August 1965

A-1E 52-132607   6251 TFW, USAF, Bien Hoa
1 pilot, name unknown (survived)

Another Skyraider crashed in South Vietnam due to pilot error during a close air support mission.

F-105D 61-0098   355 TFW attached to 6234 TFW, USAF, Korat
Maj Joseph Edward Bower (KIA)

During an armed reconnaissance mission about 20 miles north of Vinh, Maj Bower's Thud was hit by AAA. He turned south and followed the coast until his aircraft became uncontrollable about five miles south of Vinh where he ejected. Bower's wingman saw the ejection and reported that the parachute had barely deployed when the Major hit the water a mile or so offshore. His body was never found. Maj Bower was on temporary duty from the 421st TFS based at McConnell AFB, Kansas.

5 August 1965

RB-57E 55-4243   Detachment 1, 6250 CSG, USAF, Tan Son Nhut
Capt Richard E Damon (survived)
Capt Richard C Crist (survived)

Although the B-57s of the 8th and 13th TBSs were the first offensive jet aircraft to be based in South Vietnam, they had been preceded by over a year by another B-57 unit. On 6 May 1963 two specially-modified RB-57Es arrived at Tan Son Nhut and flew their first mission the next day. Each aircraft was equipped with a total of five cameras added to which was a highly secret infra-red scanner, the first of its type to be used in the conflict. Tasked with photographic and infra-red reconnaissance, the RB-57Es roamed throughout Southeast Asia using their special radio call sign 'Moonglow'. Many of the unit's missions were flown over the Ho Chi Minh trail in Laos, usually at night and often in co-operation with a C-130 flareship and a B-57 strike aircraft. The Patricia Lynn Project was only intended to last a matter of months to evaluate the new sensor, but the aircraft remained in Vietnam for eight years, the longest deployment of any aircraft or unit of the entire war. The unit became known as Detachment 1 of the 33rd TG and received two more aircraft in December 1964. On 8 July the unit became attached to the 6250th CSG and almost a month later it lost its first aircraft. RB-57E 55-4243 had flown the very first Patricia Lynn sortie in May 1963 and was hit by small arms fire during a night infra-red mission over South

Vietnam on the 5th. Capt Damon turned towards Tan Son Nhut and almost made it there safely but the aircraft caught fire and both crew ejected a mile and a half short of the runway.

O-1F 57-2801   19 TASS, 6250 TASG, USAF, Bien Hoa
2 crewmembers, names unknown (survived)

On taking off on a forward air control mission, an O-1F suffered an engine failure and was damaged beyond repair in a crash landing.

6 August 1965

B-57B 53-3919   8/13 TBS, 405 FW attached to 6252 TFW, USAF, Da Nang
Capt Larry J Horacek (survived)
1Lt F William Johnson (survived)

During a daytime strike near the coastal city of Nha Trang Capt Horacek's B-57 sustained severe damage from ground fire. The aircraft was barely controllable but was still carrying its bombs so Capt Horacek pointed it out to sea and he and 1Lt Johnson ejected as the aircraft crossed the shore line. The crew were picked up from the sea by helicopter but the B-57 then started to make a gentle turn to the left. Realising that the aircraft was turning towards Nha Trang, Capt Horacek's wingman positioned himself behind the stricken Canberra and attempted to shoot it down before it could reach land. Unfortunately, the guns on the B-57 were calibrated for ground strafing and not for air-to-air attack and the attempt failed. As the wingman broke away for fear of his rounds hitting Nha Trang, the pilotless B-57 continued its descent and crashed in the heart of the city killing 14 Vietnamese and injuring 75 others. The death toll could have been even higher but for the fact that only four of the aircraft's 16 bombs exploded on impact. Capt Horacek was shot down again on 17 April 1966.

7 August 1965

A-1H 135329   VA-25, USN, USS *Midway*
Lt Cdr Harold Edwin Gray (KIA)

During a US Navy attack on army barracks at Dong Hoi one of VA-25's Skyraiders was shot down by 37mm AAA near the target. It was thought that the pilot may have been hit and incapacitated.

9 August 1965

F-100D 56-3185   429 TFS, 474 TFW attached to 6251 TFW, USAF, Bien Hoa
1Lt Richard Lee Goudy (KIA)

On a close air support mission an F-100 was lost and the pilot killed about five miles south of Thank Duc on the South Vietnam/Cambodian border.

10 August 1965

A-1J 142012   VA-152, USN, USS *Oriskany*
Lt(jg) Lawrence Scott Mailhes (KIA)

One of the *Oriskany's* Skyraiders failed to return from a RESCAP mission over the Gulf of Tonkin. The cause of the loss was never discovered.

F-105D 61-0184   18 TFW attached to 6234 TFW, USAF, Korat
Capt M J Kelch (survived)

On one of the deepest penetration raids of the war so far an F-105 was hit by 37mm anti-aircraft fire near its target, the Vinh Tuy road bridge, 90 miles northwest of Hanoi. Despite his aircraft being on fire, Capt Kelch managed to fly almost 100 miles across the border into Laos before he was forced to eject. He was picked up safely by a waiting USAF helicopter.

11 August 1965

F-105D 61-0172   563 TFS, 23 TFW attached to 6235 TFW, USAF, Takhli
Capt L E Wilson (survived)

During a Rolling Thunder strike on a radar site near Cam Ngoc on the Song Ca River, 30 miles northwest of Vinh, an F-105 was

hit by 37mm AAA as it completed its strafing run. Capt Wilson coaxed his stricken aircraft towards the coast and ejected a few miles offshore just north of Vinh from where he was rescued by a USAF HU-16 amphibian. This was the eleventh and last F-105 lost by the 563rd TFS during its five-month deployment to Takhli.

A-4E 151185 VA-23, USN, USS *Midway*
Lt(jg) Donald Hubert Brown (KIA)

Following the loss of the first US aircraft to the SA-2 on 24 July and the subsequent disastrous raid on the SAM sites three days later, there had been no further SAM activity apart from new construction of sites. On the night of 11/12 August two A-4s flown by Lt(jg) D H Brown and Lt Cdr F D Roberge were flying at 9,000 feet on a road reconnaissance mission about 30 miles northwest of Thanh Hoa when they spotted what they initially thought were two flares glowing beneath a cloud layer below them. Too late they realized that the 'flares' were in fact the exhaust plumes from two SA-2 missiles. Lt Brown's aircraft was hit and exploded and Lt Cdr Roberge's aircraft was badly damaged but managed to limp back to the *Midway* where it was discovered to have more than 50 shrapnel holes from the missile's explosion. The day after this incident, the US Navy mounted the first sorties of its SAM suppression campaign. Almost exactly 20 years to the day after his death, the remains of Donald Brown were handed over to the US authorities on 14 August 1985.

O-1E 56-2494 19 TASS, 6250 TASG, USAF, Bien Hoa
2 crew, names unknown (survived)

Bad weather (a constant companion to airmen in Southeast Asia) caused the accidental loss of an O-1 aircraft as it took off on an FAC mission.

12 August 1965

A-4E 150067 VA-155, USN, USS *Coral Sea*
Lt W T Fidelibus (survived)

Following the death of Lt Brown the previous day, TF 77 was given permission to seek out and destroy the North Vietnamese SAM sites. Like the USAF, the Navy had no aircraft or weapons specialized for this new role so it had to use any available strike aircraft and had to find the SAMs by low level visual reconnaissance. The Navy's first anti-SAM operation was code named Iron Hand, a name that stuck to both Navy and the Air Force enemy air defence suppression missions. From 20 September all major naval air strikes were accompanied by an Iron Hand flight which targeted SAM and AAA along the route of the strike force. Concentrating on the area where Lt Brown was shot down, Navy aircraft from the *Coral Sea* and *Midway* flew 76 sorties on the 12th and 13th searching for the distinctive star-shaped plan of the SAM sites. The Navy fliers did not find a single SAM on their first attempt but they found plenty of trouble in the shape of intense AAA and small arms fire and by the end of the second day of the SAM search six Navy aircraft had been lost over North Vietnam.

The first aircraft lost on the SAM hunt was an A-4 flown by Lt Fidelibus. He was searching along Route Lima 20 miles west of Thanh Hoa and 15 miles south of where Lt Brown was shot down. His aircraft was hit on the starboard side by 37mm AAA blowing off the starboard wing flap, most of the aileron, the starboard wing tip, two-thirds of the starboard tail plane and the elevator. Miraculously the aircraft remained controllable so Lt Fidelibus dropped all external stores and climbed to 15,000 feet for the flight back to the *Coral Sea*. The Skyhawk kept flying for 250 miles despite a small fire, a tricky in-flight refuelling and no hydraulics. Unfortunately, when the Lieutenant selected the undercarriage down he discovered that there was not enough elevator control to make a safe landing and he ejected alongside the *Coral Sea*.

F-8D 147911 VF-111, USN, USS *Midway*
Lt(jg) Gene Raymond Gollahon (KIA)

As part of the search for the SAM sites the *Midway* despatched several Crusaders from VF-111 to search the area north of Thanh Hoa. About 20 miles almost due north of the city while en route to the search area, Lt Gollahon's aircraft was hit by AAA and he radioed that his hydraulics were failing. His wingman saw Gollahon's aircraft with its canopy missing and then saw flames or explosions from the rear of the aircraft after which it plunged into the ground out of control.

13 August 1965

A-4C 148564 VA-22, USN, USS *Midway*
Lt W E Newman (survived)

A-4C 148475 VA-153, USN, USS *Coral Sea*
Cdr Harry Eugene Thomas (KIA)

RF-8A 146849 Detachment D, VFP-63, USN, USS *Coral Sea*
Maj P A Manning, USMC (survived)

The Navy's search for SAM sites in North Vietnam continued into its second day but with little success and 13 August entered US Navy lore as 'Black Friday'. The first aircraft to be lost was a Skyhawk from the *Midway*. As it was flying north of Vinh Lt Newman's Skyhawk had its nose cone blown off by a direct hit from a large calibre anti-aircraft shell. Parts of the aircraft structure was ingested by the engine causing damage and a loss of power. Lt Newman managed to fly his crippled aircraft to a point about five miles off the coast near Sam Son where he ejected near a waiting US Navy destroyer on SAR watch. A couple of hours later Cdr Thomas, the CO of VA-153 and a Korean War veteran, was shot down 30 miles north of Thanh Hoa while searching for the SAM site that had shot down Lt Brown's aircraft. Cdr Thomas's Skyhawk was hit by AAA at very low level and he was killed instantly as the aircraft slow rolled and hit the ground inverted. It was obvious to his wingmen that the Commander had died in the crash but his family had to wait nearly 30 years before his remains were returned to the USA for burial. Joint field investigations by US and Vietnamese teams in 1994, 1995 and 1996 eventually recovered parts of the wreckage of the Skyhawk along with Cdr Thomas's remains which were identified in October 1996.

At almost the same time as Cdr Thomas was shot down an RF-8A photographic reconnaissance aircraft, also from the *Coral Sea,* was attempting to photograph a radar site at Ninh Binh some 35 miles to the northeast of Thanh Hoa. Maj Manning's Crusader was hit in the starboard wing by either a 57mm or 85mm anti-aircraft shell. The Crusader's wing tank exploded but miraculously, despite the loss of the starboard wing flap, a five foot-hole and a twisted leading edge, the aircraft kept on flying. The loss of fuel made it impossible for Maj Manning to reach his carrier or to divert to Dan Nang but he did manage to rendezvous with a SAR destroyer that picked him up safely after his ejection.

RF-101C 56-0186 20 TRS, 363 TRW on TDY, USAF, Udorn
Capt Fredric Moore Mellor (KIA)

The USAF was also busy hunting for SAM sites at this time but while the Navy searched the area north of Thanh Hoa the USAF concentrated on the region to the west of Hanoi, around where Fobair and Keirn had been shot down on 24 July. Capt Mellor was heading back to base with his wingman at low level when his Voodoo was hit by ground fire near Van Yen, about 50 miles due west of Hanoi. The aircraft caught fire and he ejected and later radioed that he was on the ground and OK. The other RF-101 pilot made contact with Capt Mellor but as the North Vietnamese might be able to locate him by radio direction finding, he was advised to stay off the air until a SAR task force could be put together. However, when a USAF rescue helicopter arrived at the area there was no sign or radio contact with Capt Mellor and a search over the next few days also proved negative. In February 1991 US investigators in Vietnam interviewed witnesses to an incident that they believed related to Capt Mellor. The Vietnamese said that the pilot evaded capture for several hours but was then discovered by members of the local militia. The pilot opened fire on the militia who returned fire causing wounds from which he later died.

The experience of the past 48 hours proved two points. Firstly, low level searching for SAM sites was extremely dangerous and was best performed by specialist aircraft and crews which were not then available. Secondly, the greatest threat from the SA-2 was that it forced aircraft to fly at low level where they became extremely vulnerable to AAA and small arms fire. Unfortunately, it took a little while for these two valuable lessons to really hit home.

A-1H 139772 VA-165, USN, USS *Coral Sea*
Lt R J Hyland (survived)

Unconnected with the SAM hunt near Thanh Hoa, the *Coral Sea* sent a formation of Skyraiders to the more southerly provinces of North Vietnam on an armed reconnaissance mission. One flight found a group of parked trucks about 10 miles south of Vinh and attacked it but Lt Hyland's aircraft was hit by ground fire and was badly damaged. Lt Hyland managed to get five miles offshore before parting company with his A-1 and he was picked up by a USAF HU-16.

O-1F 57-6274 6253 CSG, USAF, Nha Trang
Capt George Harold Norton (KIA)
A2C Jerry Wayne Toon (KIA)

Two airmen were killed when the ordnance fell off their Bird Dog and exploded as the aircraft took off on an FAC mission over Quang Tri province.

22 August 1965

F-105D 62-4235 36 TFS, 6441 TFW on TDY, USAF, Takhli
Maj Dean Andrew Pogreba (survived)

During an armed reconnaissance mission an F-105 was shot down while attacking a target about 25 miles west of Thanh Hoa. The pilot was eventually rescued by a USAF helicopter. Sadly, Maj Pogreba was shot down and killed on 5 October during a raid northeast of Hanoi.

RF-8A 146884 VMCJ-1, MAG-11, USMC, Da Nang
1Lt J Dodson (survived)

VMCJ-1 lost one of its photographic reconnaissance Crusaders when its undercarriage malfunctioned after taking off from Da Nang. The problem proved serious enough for the pilot not to attempt a landing and he ejected just off the coast and was picked up.

24 August 1965

A-4C 149490 VA-22, USN, USS *Midway*
Lt(jg) Richard Marvin Brunhaver (POW)

Lt Brunhaver was flying one of three Skyhawks from VA-22 on an armed reconnaissance mission when the formation attacked a road bridge near Phong Bai, 30 miles south of Thanh Hoa. The attack was at very low level using Snakeye retarded bombs which have large fins that open as soon as the bombs are released and slow the bomb's fall allowing the aircraft to escape the blast. Lt Brunhaver put his Skyhawk into a 20-degree dive to deliver his bombs but when he attempted to pull out he felt a restriction in aft movement of the control column. The aircraft struck a karst ridge a glancing blow but then began to climb away. However, the impact had caused structural damage and the aircraft started to burn forcing Lt Brunhaver to eject. A rescue was attempted but had to be curtailed because of approaching darkness. Lt Brunhaver was captured and spent the rest of the war in captivity. He had flown more than 100 missions in Southeast Asia and was released on 12 February 1973.

F-4B 152215 VF-21, USN, USS *Midway*
Cdr Frederick Augustus Franke (POW)
Lt Cdr Robert Hartch Doremus (POW)

On 24 August the Navy mounted another strike against the Dragon's Jaw Bridge at Thanh Hoa. Although none of the aircraft attacking the bridge were lost, one of the Phantoms providing MiGCAP was shot down. Cdr Franke was the CO of VF-21 and he and Lt Cdr Doremus had the dubious distinction of being the first naval officers to survive being shot down by a SAM. The Phantom was at about 11,000 feet when the SA-2 missile struck, blowing off a large part of the port wing and causing both engines to fail. The incident took place near the village of Phu Ban, north of Thanh Hoa and less than 10 miles from where Lt Brown had been killed by a SAM on 11 August. Franke and Doremus ejected safely but were both captured soon after landing in rice fields. Both men were released on 12 February 1973 and both

resumed their naval careers before finally retiring as Captains. Fred Franke had been an instructor at the Naval Test Pilot School at Patuxent River and commander of VX-4 before his tour in Southeast Asia. Lt Cdr Doremus was credited with a MiG kill on 17 June when he was flying as back seater with Lt Jack Batson.

KC-130F 149802 VMGR-152, MAG-15, USMC, Futenma
6 crew and 65 passengers, names
unknown (59 KWF)

A Marine Corps Hercules crashed into Kowloon Bay moments after taking off from Kai Tak Airport, Hong Kong on a flight to Da Nang. The aircraft was carrying 65 passengers and six crew, only 12 of whom survived the accident. Two crewmembers, Sgt Gordon Harry Blexrude and Cpl Jerry L Gerry, were amongst the dead. The Hercules took off with No1 engine delivering partial power and the aircraft veered off the runway and lifted off in a semi-stalled condition. After a short distance its port wing struck a low sea wall and the aircraft burst into flames before it crashed into the sea. The cause of the accident was attributed to poor judgement on the part of the aircraft commander and non-adherence to standard operating procedures. The aircraft was returning Marine Corps personnel to Vietnam after a period of leave in Hong Kong.

26 August 1965

A-1H 139720 VA-152, USN, USS *Oriskany*
Lt(jg) Edward Anthony Davis (POW)

A flight of Skyraiders was sent out on a night armed reconnaissance mission to look for trucks along coastal roads in the southern province of North Vietnam. Near Xuan Noa, 15 miles north of the DMZ and only about two miles from the sea, the flight leader spotted what looked like a hiding place for trucks and led the flight into a dive bombing attack. Lt Davis's aircraft was hit in the fuselage by AAA and he was forced to bail out when he realised he could not make it back to the relative safety of the sea. Shot down on his 57th mission, Davis was eventually released on 12 February 1973 in Operation Homecoming.

27 August 1965

O-1E 57-6271 6253 CSG, USAF, Nha Trang
1Lt Jerome Elkins (KIA)
1 crew, name unknown (KIA)

An O-1 Bird Dog failed to return from a visual reconnaissance mission just south of the DMZ. The observer may have been either a South Vietnamese or a member of the US Army. This was the third Bird Dog lost from Nha Trang in a little over a month, all six crewmen being killed

28 August 1965

F-105F 63-8282 67 TFS, 18 TFW attached to 6234 TFW,
USAF, Korat
Capt Wesley Duane Schierman (POW)

A flight of four F-105s was sent into the western region of North Vietnam on an armed reconnaissance mission and attacked a barracks near Son La, 105 miles west of Hanoi and 25 miles north of the Laotian border. On his second strafing run, Capt Schierman's aircraft was hit by small arms fire and he was forced to eject. Schierman, who had been a pilot on F-89s and F-94s with the Washington ANG and had flown DC-4s for Northwest Airlines before being assigned to active duty, was captured on his 37th combat mission and spent the next seven and a half years in prison. He was released from captivity on 12 February 1973. After leaving the Air Force following his release, Wesley Schierman resumed his career with Northwest Airlines and became a Boeing 747 captain.

29 August 1965

A-1H 134619 VA-152, USN, USS *Oriskany*
Lt Edd David Taylor (KIA)

Following the loss of Capt Schierman's aircraft near Son La, a SAR operation was mounted which involved the US Navy as well as the Air Force. At almost exactly the same spot that Capt Schierman had been shot down, Lt Taylor's Skyraider was hit by intense anti-aircraft fire. The North Vietnamese often allowed downed airmen to remain free long enough to bring in rescue forces which could then be shot down when they were at their most vulnerable. Lt Taylor's sacrifice in an attempt to rescue a fellow airman is illustrative of the emphasis that was put on returning downed aircrew whenever possible during the war in Southeast Asia. Even by this relatively early stage of the war, it was known that treatment of American prisoners in North Vietnam and Laos was harsh, to say the least. All the US Services contributed unstintingly to SAR operations. The Navy stationed ships and aircraft off the coast of North and South Vietnam and participated in long range efforts like that mounted for Capt Schierman. The USAF stationed helicopters at forward bases in Laos ready to dart forward into the heart of North Vietnam to rescue downed aircrew. South Vietnam was awash with helicopters from the US Army, Air Force, Marines Corps and the VNAF and rescue by air or ground forces could often be relied upon. Throughout the war the rescue effort was substantial but was worthwhile not only from the point of view of returning valuable aircrew who lived to fight another day but also for raising morale throughout the forces engaged. Airmen flying over Southeast Asia knew that if they were shot down and survived then they had at least a fighting chance of being rescued and this knowledge was important in a war where morale was not always at its highest.

RF-8A 146828 Detachment G, VFP-63, USN, USS *Oriskany*
Lt Henry Sterling McWhorter (KIA)

Oriskany's second loss of the day involved one of her photographic reconnaissance Crusaders. In company with a wingman, Lt McWhorter was flying at 8,000 feet about 25 miles northwest of Vinh when the pair encountered heavy ground fire. The wingman warned Lt McWhorter and then took evasive action himself. When he last saw McWhorter's aircraft it was flying wings level but with the canopy and the ejection seat missing. Damage to the cockpit area indicated that the aircraft might have been hit by an anti-aircraft round that could have fired the ejection seat and most likely killed the pilot. The aircraft's wheels came down (probably as a result of damage to the hydraulic system) and the aircraft entered a gentle glide until it hit the ground. In February 1987 the Vietnamese returned human remains that were later identified as being those of Henry McWhorter.

F-105D 61-0193 67 TFS, 18 TFW attached to 6234 TFW,
USAF, Korat
Maj Ronald Edward Byrne (POW)

The third loss over North Vietnam on the 29th took place during an attack on an arsenal at Yen Bai on the banks of the Red River, some 70 miles northwest of Hanoi. Maj Byrne's Thunderchief was hit by AAA and the ammunition from its 20mm cannon began to explode as the aircraft caught fire. Byrne ejected and was quickly captured, spending the rest of the war in the Hanoi Hilton until release on 12 February 1973. The 36-year old Major had flown 75 missions in the F-86 during the Korean War and was on his second tour of duty in Southeast Asia when he was shot down on his 27th combat mission of the war. Maj Byrne had been a Project Officer in the Titan ICBM Program Office at Air Force Systems Command in the early 1960s.

O-1F 56-2539 19 TASS, 6250 TASG, USAF, Bien Hoa
1Lt Robert Marion Carn (KIA)

August 1965 was a bad month for the O-1 FAC community. A Bird Dog collided with another aircraft during a visual reconnaissance mission in Khanh Hoa province in South Vietnam, bringing the number of O-1s lost during the month to five.

30 August 1965

C-1A 146047 USN, USS *Independence*
7 crew, names unknown (survived)

The C-1A Trader Carrier On-board Delivery (COD) aircraft was a development of the S-2 Tracker and was used primarily for transporting passengers and cargo to and from aircraft carriers. This Trader may have been assigned to the *Independence* or it may have belonged to VR-21 based at Cubi Point in the Philippines. On 30 August the aircraft crashed while attempting an emergency landing at Da Nang. All seven passengers and crew survived.

F-105D 62-4355 36 TFS, 6441 TFW on TDY, USAF, Takhli
Lt Col Hendricks (survived)

During the take off roll one of a pair of F-105s suffered engine failure and the pilot called that he was aborting take off and would engage the runway barrier. However, his drag chute failed to deploy and his arrester hook missed the wire so the aircraft ran off the end of the runway at speed, slid through mud and slammed into trees and bushes. The aircraft caught fire immediately but the pilot was rescued from the flames by the base HH-43B rescue helicopter which was usually airborne during the start of each mission for such eventualities. The Thud's 20mm ammunition began to explode and threatened the fire crew and a line of parked F-105s that had to be moved to the other end of the airfield. More serious was the two 750lb bombs which were cooking slowly in the smouldering remains of the aircraft. Operations at Takhli were severely restricted until the bombs could be made safe. One was defused the following day but the other exploded early in the morning of 1 September.

31 August 1965

F-105D 61-0185 67 TFS, 18 TFW attached to 6234 TFW,
USAF, Korat
Maj W H Bollinger (survived)

The 67th TFS was not having a very good month. On the last day of August a flight of F-105s spotted a bridge near Piu-Tho, 40 miles northwest of Hanoi while on an armed reconnaissance mission. Maj Bollinger's aircraft was hit by AAA during the attack but he flew over 50 miles to the southwest, before he was forced to eject close to the Laotian border. He was picked up by a USAF SAR helicopter.

2 September 1965

F-105D 62-4389 36 TFS, 6441 TFW on TDY, USAF, Takhli
Capt James Quincy Collins (POW)

The first loss of September was an F-105D on an armed reconnaissance mission over North Vietnam. Capt Collins was shot down by ground fire while attacking a bridge near Xung Lung just north of the Laotian border, about 80 miles west of Hanoi. Capt Collins was the Wing Weapons Officer at Yokota AB, Japan and had volunteered for duty at Takhli. He was seriously injured during his low level ejection breaking his left leg in three places above the knee. He was released from captivity on 12 February 1973.

4 September 1965

F-4C 63-7700 47 TFS, 15 TFW on TDY, USAF, Ubon
Capt James Alvin Branch (KIA)
1Lt Eugene Millard Jewell (KIA)

Another F-4 loss occurred during a Rolling Thunder strike against barracks in the My Hoa area, 50 miles south of Thanh Hoa. Capt Branch's Phantom crashed during a strafing run with no parachutes being seen or SAR beepers heard. The aircraft was either hit by ground fire or it may have hit the ground before it could pull up from its dive. In 1994 the remains of Capt Branch were returned and identified and his status changed from missing to killed in action.

A-1H 139693 VA-165, USN, USS *Coral Sea*
Lt(jg) Edward Brendan Shaw (KIA)

During an armed reconnaissance mission a flight of Skyraiders from the *Coral Sea* spotted several barges in the mouth of the Song Gia Hoi River, 35 miles south of Vinh. Barges were often used by the North Vietnamese to move supplies down the coast and along the navigable rivers and were an important part of the country's transport system. Lt Shaw's Skyraider was shot down by AAA on his first pass and he was not seen to escape from his aircraft.

5 September 1965

A-1E   52-132562   6251 TFW, USAF, Bien Hoa
Capt Richard Carlton Marshall (KWF)
CWO2 William John LaGrand, US Army (KWF)

Soon after taking off for a training flight from Bien Hoa an A-1E was seen to crash and explode 10 miles northeast of the airfield. Along with the pilot, Capt Marshall, was Army CWO LaGrand, a helicopter pilot of the 197th Aviation Company, 145th Aviation Battalion. Both were killed outright but their bodies were not recovered as the area was held by the VC at the time and was considered too dangerous to force an entry.

6 September 1965

F-105D   62-4337   67 TFS, 18 TFW attached to 6234 TFW, USAF, Korat
Capt J T Clark (survived)

The armed reconnaissance missions continued to take their toll in North Vietnam. During one such mission a flight of Thuds saw a radio mast near Phu Qui, 30 miles north of the DMZ. As the aircraft dived to attack the site Capt Clark's aircraft received a hit in the tail and the aircraft became difficult to control. Capt Clark flew out to sea where he ejected safely and was picked up.

F-105D   62-4400   562 TFS, 23 TFW attached to 6235 TFW, USAF, Takhli
Capt Gary D Barnhill (survived)

The 562nd TFS arrived at Takhli in mid-August to replace its sister squadron from McConnell, the 563rd. The Squadron lost its first aircraft in Southeast Asia during in-flight refuelling from a KC-135 tanker on a Rolling Thunder strike mission. The F-105s had taken off from Takhli and, as was normal, were topping up with fuel over northern Thailand before heading towards the target. During refuelling a wingman saw fuel pouring out of the bomb bay of Capt Barnhill's aircraft. The Captain quickly disconnected from the tanker and ejected as the F-105 caught fire. The aircraft exploded seconds later and the pilot was picked up by helicopter. As an F-100 pilot Gary Barnhill had been a member of USAFE's Skyblazers aerobatic team in 1961. He was awarded the DFC for his part in an attack on a SAM site in October 1965 but in February 1966 he left the Air Force to fly for TWA. He flew with the airline for 21 years until he joined McDonnell Douglas as Manager of their Military Flight Crew Training Division for the C-17 and T-45.

B-57B   52-1544   8/13 TBS, 405 FW attached to 6252 TFW, USAF, Da Nang
Capt W C Hamann (survived)
Capt R J Lane (survived)

The crew of a Canberra received indications of an engine fire during a close air support mission and abandoned the aircraft. The engine failure was not thought to have been due to hostile action. The aircraft was one of nine B-57s that arrived in Vietnam in late May 1965 as replacements for the aircraft lost in the Bien Hoa explosion. 52-1544 had previously been flown by the Nevada ANG from their base at Reno.

A-4E   152042   VA-164, USN, USS Oriskany
Lt J L Burton (survived)

During a strike on the Hai Yen naval base near Thanh Hoa, Lt Burton's Skyhawk was hit by 37mm anti-aircraft fire. The fire warning light came on immediately and Burton climbed the aircraft so that he would be able to reach the sea if the engine failed. Fuel was seen to be streaming from a hole in the fuselage and the hydraulics failed. Ninety seconds after being hit Lt Burton lost control and was forced to eject less than a mile offshore. He was picked up by a USAF HU-16 amphibian although he had sustained injuries during his ejection.

7 September 1965

RF-8A   146826   Detachment D, VFP-63, USN, USS Coral Sea
Lt(jg) Charles Bernard Goodwin (KIA)

Good, timely intelligence was crucial to the running of the air war in Southeast Asia and the unarmed photographic recon-naissance aircraft had a vital role to play, even if the cost was high. Lt Goodwin disappeared on a night reconnaissance mission over North Vietnam. His last reported position was over the Gulf of Tonkin just north of Dong Hoi and he radioed that he was in the middle of a thunderstorm. No trace of Lt Goodwin or his Crusader was ever found but a North Vietnamese militia unit claimed to have shot his aircraft down just off the coast.

8 September 1965

RF-8A   146825   Detachment G, VFP-63, USN, USS Oriskany
Lt(jg) Robert David Rudolph (KIA)

As if to underline the vulnerability of the US photographic recon-naissance aircraft, another RF-8A failed to return from a mission the day after Lt Goodwin was lost. Lt Rudolph was heading into North Vietnam to take part in a search for SAM sites near Thanh Hoa when his aircraft was hit by AAA soon after crossing the coastline. The wingman saw Rudolph's Crusader roll inverted and the canopy fall away. However, as he was trying to avoid being hit himself he was unable to see if Lt Rudolph ejected before his aircraft hit the ground 15 miles northeast of Thanh Hoa. A SAR effort yielded no results and the Navy reluctantly declared Lt Rudolph dead three weeks later. On 15 December 1988 the remains of Robert Rudolph were handed over by the Vietnamese.

9 September 1965

A-4E   151134   VA-163, USN, USS Oriskany
Cdr James Bond Stockdale (POW)

Cdr James Stockdale, the Commander of Oriskany's Carrier Air Wing 16, was on his second tour in Southeast Asia and had led the search for North Vietnamese patrol boats during the attack on the USS Maddox on 2 August 1964. Using VA-163's appropriate call sign Old Salt 353, 42-year old Cdr Stockdale had flown over 175 missions when he set out on 9 September to lead a major raid on the Thanh Hoa Bridge. Unfortunately, the weather closed in over Thanh Hoa half way through the launch cycle and Stockdale had to send his aircraft to secondary targets. After an abortive search for a SAM site Cdr Stockdale decided to attack railway sidings about 15 miles south of Thanh Hoa. Stockdale approached the target at 150 feet, released his Snakeye bombs and pulled up for another pass. As the aircraft reached about 700 feet it was hit by 57mm ground fire and immediately pitched nose down. With the aircraft diving at great speed, the hydraulic system inoperative and the gyro toppled, Cdr Stockdale had no option but to eject. He landed in the village of Tin Gia near the target and was attacked by several villagers and badly beaten. Primarily a Crusader pilot (he was the first man to reach 1,000 hours in the F-8), Jim Stockdale was the Navy's second CAG to be shot down in the war. He was temporarily replaced as CAG by Lt Col Charles H Ludden, CO of VMF(AW)-212. This was the first time since the Second World War that a Marine had commanded a Navy air wing.

Cdr Stockdale spent the next seven and a half years in prison in Hanoi where, as the most senior naval officer captured, he was singled out for the most brutal treatment imaginable. James Stockdale adhered to the Code of Conduct for POWs and provided a superb example for his fellow prisoners thereby bringing him further retribution from his captors. His refusal to co-operate in the propaganda efforts of the North Vietnamese and the discovery of the prisoners' secret communication system brought more torture and beatings from the guards. Cdr Stockdale, realising that the punishment was about to be meted out to the other prisoners, made himself a symbol of their collective resistance and on 4 September 1969 he deliberately inflicted a near fatal wound to convince his captors of his willingness to die rather than capitulate. He was revived by the North Vietnamese who seemed to realise that they could not break his spirit and from that time on, the treatment in the prison camp improved. In recognition of James Stockdale's courageous leadership in the most terrible conditions, he was awarded the Medal of Honor in 1976. He was released on 12 February 1973 and resumed his naval career. James Stockdale retired from the US Navy in 1979 with the rank of Vice Admiral and is currently a senior research fellow with the Hoover Institution.

10 September 1965

A-4E   149991   VA-155, USN, USS Coral Sea
Lt Cdr Wendell Burke Rivers (POW)

Power plants were to become a popular target for Rolling Thunder strikes and the power station at Vinh was one of the first to be struck. As Lt Cdr Rivers dived his Skyhawk to 45 degrees and dropped his bombs he felt his aircraft take a hit in the rear fuselage. Unsure whether the hit was from AAA or from one of his own bombs exploding prematurely, he climbed and turned towards the sea with his aircraft on fire. However, before he reached the sea the Skyhawk suddenly pitched nose down and the fire burnt through the tail and the engine surged wildly.

Wendell Rivers had been in theatre since the Coral Sea arrived on 7 December 1964 and had taken part in the Flaming Dart 2 mission of 11 February. He was on his 96th combat mission when he ejected and was taken prisoner. He was released on 12 February 1973 and eventually retired from the Navy as a Captain.

A-1E   52-132669   602 ACS, 6251 TFW, USAF, Bien Hoa detached to Udorn
Capt Graybill (survived)

The 602nd ACS was formed at Bien Hoa on 12 October 1964 as the USAF's second A-1E squadron. The Squadron was also referred to as the 602nd Fighter Commando Squadron. In August the Squadron started regular detachments of aircraft to Udorn to provide escorts for the USAF rescue helicopters that operated with increasing regularity over southern Laos. Capt Graybill was involved in a RESCAP mission (probably for Lt Cdr Rivers although Graybill came down over 80 mile to the southeast of Rivers's positions) when his A-1E crashed in the sea off Dong Hoi, a few miles north of the DMZ. Graybill bailed out and was picked up by a USAF HU-16.

12 September 1965

F-8E   150331   VF-191, USN, USS Bon Homme Richard
Lt(jg) Gerald Green (KIA)

Following a successful attack mission in North Vietnam, a Crusader impacted the water during an attempted landing back on the carrier. Lt Green had only just arrived on the Squadron and was killed in the crash. The cause of the accident was not determined.

C-1A   136784   VR-21, USN, USS Independence
AE3 William A Mitchell (KWF)
9 crew, names unknown (survived)

Following the loss of a C-1A Trader from the Independence on 30 August, the ship lost another Trader (attached from VR-21) less than two weeks later. This time the aircraft crashed into the sea during a catapult launch and although nine of the passengers and crew escaped and were rescued, one man was drowned.

13 September 1965

F-100D   55-3631   probably 429 TFS, 474 TFW attached to 6251 TFW, USAF, Bien Hoa
Capt P E Orf (survived)

During a close air support mission an F-100 crashed in the sea near Hon Tre island just off the coast at Nha Trang, probably due to damage from ground fire. The pilot was rescued by a US Navy helicopter.

A-4E   149999   VA-72, USN, USS Independence
Lt(jg) Joe Russell Mossman (KIA)

Lt Mossman was flying one of four Skyhawks that were on an armed reconnaissance mission just north of the DMZ. As the formation was about to attack a wooden bridge about 12 miles west of Dong Hoi, Lt Mossman's aircraft was hit by small arms fire and crashed. Mossman's wingman spotted what he thought was a parachute near the Skyhawk's wreckage and a SAR beeper was heard briefly. A SAR and surveillance mission was mounted but there was no sign of Lt Mossman. In October 1982 the Vietnamese turned over Mossman's Navy ID card but, as yet, his remains have not been located.

14 September 1965

A-1J   142057   VA-196, USN, USS *Bon Homme Richard*
                       Lt Cdr James Thomas Kearns (KIA)

On 14 September the *Bon Homme Richard* was at Dixie Station flying several combat missions over South Vietnam. Spells at Dixie Station were seen as 'breathers' between operations over North Vietnam from Yankee Station. However, operations over the South could still be dangerous as Carrier Air Wing 19 was about to find to its cost.

The first aircraft lost on this day was a Skyraider being flown by Lt Cdr Kearns against VC targets five miles southwest of Soc Trang, just south of the Mekong Delta. There was obviously little opposition as the aircraft made no less than eight passes but on the ninth pass one of the Skyraider's bombs detonated upon release and the aircraft was destroyed.

A-4C   147682   VA-192, USN, USS *Bon Homme Richard*
                       Lt(jg) Neil Brooks Taylor (KIA)

Later in the day a formation of Skyhawks from the *Bon Homme Richard* was despatched to bomb a village at Ap So Hai, 15 miles northeast of Quang Long in South Vietnam. Lt Taylor had made six passes and was at 4,000 feet preparing to make his seventh run. The aircraft was then seen to make a descending spiral into the ground with no attempt to eject. It was thought that Lt Taylor was incapacitated in some way, possibly by ground fire.

16 September 1965

F-105D   61-0217   67 TFS, 18 TFW attached to 6234 TFW,
                       USAF, Korat
                       Lt Col James Robinson Risner (POW)

F-105D   61-0189   67 TFS, 18 TFW attached to 6234 TFW,
                       USAF, Korat
                       Maj Raymond James Merritt (POW)

It was ironic that Lt Col Robinson Risner should be shot down close to the Dragon's Jaw Bridge as he had been instrumental in plotting its destruction. In the early morning of 16 September his formation of F-105s was not after the bridge but was going for a SAM site that had been reported north of Thanh Hoa. AAA hit his aircraft at low level and he made for the coast but had to eject over the village of Tuong Loc, 10 miles northeast of the Thanh Hoa Bridge. He was on his 55th combat mission over Southeast Asia. He was captured and spent the rest of the war in various prison camps where he was singled out for severe punishment suffering solitary confinement, torture, malnutrition and disease.

'Robbie' Risner had joined the Air Force in 1943 and flew 110 missions with the F-86-equipped 4th FW during the Korean War and shot down eight MiG-15s during that conflict. He later commanded a number of fighter squadrons and became the CO of the 67th TFS at Kadena in August 1964. He had been shot down on 22 March 1965 during a strike on a radar site at Vinh Son but had made it to the coast and was rescued. The day before his second shoot down his aircraft had its canopy shattered but he was able to return safely to base. He was not so lucky on the 16th and was eventually released in Operation Homecoming on 12 February 1973. It was largely thanks to the leadership and courage of Risner and his Navy counterpart, Cdr Jim Stockdale, that the POWs organized themselves to present maximum resistance. The first living recipient of the AFC, Risner resumed his career flying both the F-4 and the F-111 and commanded the 832nd AD before retiring from the USAF in August 1976 with the rank of Brigadier General. 'Robbie' Risner wrote about his experiences in *The Passing of the Night: My Seven Years as a Prisoner of the North Vietnamese*, which was published in 1973.

Ray Merritt was another Korean War veteran who was shot down on the same raid as Lt Col Risner. Merritt's aircraft was hit by AAA and he was forced to eject a few miles northeast of Risner's position. He was captured immediately by armed villagers (practically all villagers in North Vietnam were armed!) and accompanied Risner to prison and was also released on 12 February 1973. Merritt had flown 100 missions in the F-84 in the Korean War and was on his 40th mission over North Vietnam when he was brought down.

17 September 1965

F-105D   62-4247   67 TFS, 18 TFW attached to 6234 TFW,
                       USAF, Korat
                       1Lt Dean Albert Klenda (KIA)

The seventh F-105 lost by the 67th TFS in three weeks was shot down when attacking barracks 10 miles east of Na San, 90 miles west of Hanoi. The aircraft was seen to be hit in the rear fuselage by AAA and crashed before 1Lt Klenda could eject.

A-6A   151588   VA-75, USN, USS *Independence*
                       Cdr Leonard Frederick Vogt (KIA)
                       Lt Robert Franklin Barber (KIA)

Four Intruders from VA-75 made a night attack on North Vietnamese Navy Swatow torpedo boats that were known to be based near Bach Long Island, 70 miles southeast of Haiphong. The formation was led by Cdr Vogt, CO of VA-75. They found two boats just south of the island and one of the Intruders dropped flares to illuminate the water's surface. Cdr Vogt approached to drop his bombs just as the last of the flares burnt out. After he dropped his bombs the other aircraft in the flight reported seeing a huge fireball on the surface. It was thought that Cdr Vogt's aircraft had flown into the sea due either to disorientation or instrument failure. This was the last of four A-6s lost by VA-75 on what must have been a very unhappy cruise for the Squadron, especially as it involved the death of the squadron commander and his NFO.

18 September 1965

C-130A   55-0038   35 TCS, 6315 OG, USAF, Naha
                       Capt Fred Rost Tice (KIA)
                       1Lt Edsel Deville (survived)
                       Capt Richard Daigle (survived)
                       SSgt Walter Otho Tramel (KIA)
                       SSgt Edward F Kirby (survived)

A Hercules crashed into the sea during the approach to the airfield at Qui Nhon killing four airmen. The crew was attempting to fly a VFR approach in low cloud and rain but the aircraft hit the water as it rolled out of a turn. Qui Nhon airfield became notorious for its tricky crosswind that could catch out an unwary pilot. Two passengers, Capt David Eugene Benson and Capt Thomas James Tolliver were also killed in the accident.

O-1E   56-4167   unit ..?, USAF, base ..?
                       1Lt G E Walters (survived)
                       1 crew, probably US Army (survived)

Very little seems to be known about this incident except that it occurred in South Vitenam and that both crew were safely recovered from a forced landing.

20 September 1965

F-105D   62-4238   67 TFS, 18 TFW attached to 6234 TFW,
                       USAF, Korat
                       Capt Edgar Lee Hawkins (KIA)

The twentieth day of September turned out to be a bad day for US airmen. Early in the day an F-105 was lost just 10 miles over the Laotian border near Sop Cap. The aircraft was one of flight of F-105s sent on an armed reconnaissance mission over northwestern North Vietnam. The aircraft spotted and attacked a bridge 30 miles southwest of Son La but as Capt Hawkins made his first dive his aircraft was hit by ground fire and crashed. The pilot may have been hit, as there appeared to be no attempt to eject.

F-104C   56-0883   436 TFS, 479 TFW attached to 6252 TFW,
                       USAF, Da Nang
                       Capt Phillip Eldon Smith (POW)

Capt Smith was the pilot of one of several Starfighters flying a CAP mission in poor weather over the Gulf of Tonkin. Apparently his navigation system failed and although he came down below the cloud base to try to regain his bearings he became lost. He had flown too far to the east and was shot down by a pair of Chinese Navy Shenyang J-6s (MiG-19s) over the centre of Hainan island. Capt Smith was interrogated at Canton before being transferred to Peking for several years of solitary confinement.

Capt Smith was the only USAF pilot known to have been held captive by the Chinese and was finally released from China on 15 March 1973. Before his shoot down he had graduated from the Fighter Weapons Instructors School at Nellis AFB and was the Squadron and Wing Weapons Officer. During his tour at Da Nang he had flown 80 missions, 24 of them over North Vietnam. He resumed his Air Force career flying the F-4 with the 49th TFW and later commanded the USAF bases at Hellenikon, Greece and Bergstrom AFB, Texas. He retired from the USAF as a Colonel in July 1987. The Starfighter that Capt Smith was flying on 20 September was the first of 77 F-104Cs constructed by Lockheed and had made its maiden flight on 24 July 1958.

F-104C   56-0911   436 TFS, 479 TFW attached to 6252 TFW,
                       USAF, Da Nang
                       1 pilot, name unknown (survived)

F-104C   57-0921   436 TFS, 479 TFW attached to 6252 TFW,
                       USAF, Da Nang
                       1 pilot, name unknown (survived)

Two Starfighters from the 436th TFS collided and crashed as they were returning from an unsuccessful attempt to locate Capt Smith. Both pilots ejected safely. The three Starfighters lost on the 20th were the last of the type to be lost before the Squadron redeployed back to the USA on 20 November at the end of its temporary duty. Although the F-104s flew a total of 2,937 sorties in 8,820 flying hours during their seven-month deployment, the aircraft's limitations in terms of load-carrying capability and range were noticeable compared to the F-4 and F-105.

F-105D   61-0082   334 TFS, 4 TFW attached to 6235 TFW,
                       USAF, Takhli
                       Capt Willis Ellis Forby (POW)

On an armed reconnaissance mission over the southern provinces of North Vietnam a formation of F-105s attacked a railway bridge near Ha Tinh, 35 miles south of Vinh and close to the Laotian border. During the attack Capt Forby's aircraft was hit by AAA and caught fire forcing him to eject close to the target. When Forby's wingman heard his SAR beeper signal he radioed for assistance. Two HH-43 SAR helicopters of the 38th ARS based at Nakhon Phanom took off from a forward Lima Site in Laos and made their way towards Ha Tinh. As the lead helicopter arrived and commenced its run in Capt Forby released a smoke cannister to help mark his position. However, Capt Forby was unaware that the North Vietnamese were hidden all around him waiting for such a rescue attempt to take place so that they could shoot down one of the rescue choppers. Capt Thomas J Curtis was the pilot of Dutchy 41, the lead HH-43B (62-4510), and his crew consisted of 1Lt Duane Martin, co-pilot, A1C William A Robinson, flight engineer; and A3C Arthur N Black, pararescueman. The HH-43 came to a hover over Capt Forby but just as they prepared to hoist him up into the helicopter it was shot down and crashed into tall trees close to Willis Forby and he and the four helicopter crew were quickly captured. The second helicopter was also damaged by ground fire and forced to retire. Duane Martin evaded capture briefly but was eventually caught and imprisoned by the Pathet Lao. He was held in the same camp as Dieter Dengler who was shot down on 1 February 1966 and together with several Air America crewmen the pair attempted to escape in June 1966. Unfortunately Duane Martin was hacked to death by a Lao native during the escape and only Dengler survived the attempt, thereby becoming one of the very few men to escape from Laos. Forby, Curtis, Robinson and Black were eventually transferred to Hanoi and released on 12 February 1973. Robinson and Black were the first USAF enlisted men to become POWs and both received the AFC on their return from captivity.

F-100D   56-3177   481 TFS, 27 TFW attached to 6250 CSG,
                       USAF, Tan Son Nhut
                       Capt Joseph Reynes (survived)

Not all the activity on the 20th was confined to the North. In South Vietnam an F-100 was shot down during a close air support mission. The aircraft was one of four F-100s attacking a target near the 'Seven Sisters', a group of hills near the Mekong Delta. One aircraft was hit and started to vent fuel. Capt Reynes

In mid-1964 the USAF began to receive the first batch of two-seat ex-Navy A-1E Skyraiders to replace its B-26s and T-28s. The Skyraider proved to be one of the most successful close air support aircraft of the war. 132593 was a 602nd ACS aircraft that collided with another Skyraider during a close air support mission on 2 October 1965. USAF

and his wingman climbed rapidly to 20,000 feet leaving the other two aircraft to finish their mission. The aircraft continued to lose fuel and then lost oil pressure causing the engine to seize. Capt Reynes ejected and was soon picked up by a helicopter and returned to Tan Son Nhut.

A-4E   151115   VA-72, USN, USS *Independence*
                  Lt(jg) John R Harris (survived)

Carrier Air Wing 7 made a major strike on a bridge at Dao Nung which carried the railway line from China into Hanoi. This rail link was vital to North Vietnam's military effort as much of its war supplies came from China. At 45 miles northeast of Hanoi this was one of the deepest penetrations into North Vietnam flown up to this date. The Navy was lucky in that only one aircraft was lost on the strike. Lt Harris was on his run to the target at 500 feet when his Skyhawk was hit by ground fire. The aircraft caught fire and large holes were seen around the speed brake in the rear fuselage. Heading south towards the coast as fast as he dare, Lt Harris was forced to abandon his aircraft as the controls froze and the aircraft banked violently to starboard. The fire in the rear fuselage had burnt through the aircraft's structure and the entire tailplane and fin broke away as Harris ejected. He came down in a hilly area 25 miles southwest of the target and still some 35 miles away from the sea. Fortunately he was picked up in a daring rescue by a US Navy UH-2B Seasprite helicopter flown by Lt Cdr W Wetzel and Lt(jg) K Vendevelde of Detachment A, HC-1 from the cruiser USS *Galveston*. The helicopter was escorted by two Skyraiders from VA-25 from the *Midway*. This was the first overland rescue by a US Navy helicopter in North Vietnam and the first anywhere in the Southeast Asian theatre by a ship-based Navy helicopter. Lt Harris was the first American pilot to be shot down to the east of Hanoi, an area that had been largely out of bounds up to this point.

21 September 1965

F-105D 61-0200   562 TFS, 23 TFW attached to 6235 TFW,
                  USAF, Takhli
                  Capt Frederick R Greenwood (survived)

Steel Tiger operations in Southern Laos were still being flown although the escalating air war over North Vietnam was very much the focus of operations. On 21 September a flight of F-105s was on an armed reconnaissance mission when they bombed barracks five miles east of Ban Senphan near the Mu Gia Pass. Capt Greenwood's aircraft was hit by 57mm AAA as he was pulling up from the attack and he headed northwest towards the mountains

where he ejected as his aircraft started to burn. He sprained both ankles during his landing but was rescued two hours later by a USAF HH-43 helicopter, the crew of which exchanged fire with enemy troops who were attempting to reach Capt Greenwood. This was the fiftieth Thunderchief lost by the USAF in Southeast Asia since the first aircraft was lost on 14 August 1964.

22 September 1965

E-1B   148918   Detachment 62, VAW-12, USN,
                  USS *Independence*
                  4 crew, names unknown (survived)

The *Independence* seemed to be an unlucky ship for its multi-engined commuity. Having lost two C-1As recently it also lost one of its E-1B Tracer AEW aircraft when it ran out of fuel on a training flight. The crew were picked up safely by an HU-16 Albatross from the 31st ARS. The Tracer carried the huge AN/APS-82 search radar in a massive aerofoil-section radome above the fuselage and provided the ship with early warning information. Small detachments of Tracers were carried by most aircraft carriers throughout the war although the aircraft was supplemented and gradually replaced by the E-2 Hawkeye from the end of 1965. The Tracer was also used to keep an eye on MiG activity during Rolling Thunder missions.

23 September 1965

F-100D 55-3738   429 TFS, 474 TFW attached to 6251 TFW,
                  USAF, Bien Hoa
                  1Lt G W Marlowe (survived)

The second Super Sabre lost in South Vietnam within the space of four days was brought down as the aircraft was making its sixth strafing pass against Viet Cong troops. Again, its pilot was rescued by helicopter.

24 September 1965

A-1H   135274   VA-196, USN, USS *Bon Homme Richard*
                  Cdr J Gallager (survived)

Cdr Gallager was returning from an administrative visit to the Marine base at Chu Lai when his aircraft was hit by small arms fire 10 miles north of Tam Ky, just a few minutes flying time from Chu Lai. The Commander bailed out of his stricken Skyraider and was rescued by a Marine Corps helicopter.

F-8E   150668   VF-194, USN, USS *Bon Homme Richard*
                  Lt(jg) Geoffrey Holmes Osborn (KIA)

As the *Bon Homme Richard* was cruising at Yankee Station just below the 19th Parallel, it lost one of its aircraft on take off. Soon after a catapult launch for a combat air patrol, a Crusader flew into the water killing the pilot.

F-4C   64-0700   47 TFS, 15 TFW on TDY, USAF, Ubon
                  Capt Jack D Gravis (survived)
                  1Lt Wylie E Nolen (survived)

Missions in the heavily defended region just north of the DMZ took a toll on US aircraft throughout the war. The North Vietnamese used the region as a staging area for men and supplies travelling down the Ho Chin Minh Trail or through the DMZ into the South. Capt Gravis's Phantom was shot down by intense AAA while he was leading his flight in an attack on army barracks at the village of Vinh Linh near the coast, less than five miles north of the DMZ. Capt Gravis headed out towards the coast with both engines failing and the hydraulic system operating erratically. By the time it reached the sea the aircraft was a mass of flames and the hydraulics seized. The crew ejected about five miles off the coast and the three remaining F-4s from the flight set up an orbit over the downed crew along with a pair of A-1Es and a pair of Navy F-8s. A HU-16 Albatross, piloted by Maj D C Hollenfeld, landed to pick up the survivors amid heavy shelling from coastal artillery.

F-100D 56-2923   probably 6251 TFW, USAF, Bien Hoa
                  Maj Martin W Barbena (survived)

Yet another Super Sabre was shot down while on a close air support mission over South Vietnam and once again, the pilot was saved, this time by a USAF helicopter. Maj Barbena later became the CO of the 1st SOS and had the misfortune to have to crash-land a burning Skyraider at Nakon Phanom in March 1972.

25 September 1965

F-8E   149168   VF-194, USN, USS *Bon Homme Richard*
                  Lt(jg) D C Duffy (survived)

VF-194 was unfortunate enough to lose another Crusader the very next day after Lt Osborn's death. After returning from a CAP mission a Crusader crashed when landing back on the carrier. The cause was put down to pilot fatigue and a badly pitching deck. Carrier landings are among the most demanding procedures in military aviation short of actual air combat. The aircraft has to be flown positively and precisely onto the deck and the pilot then has to go to full power in case the aircraft's arrester hook should miss the wires. In poor visibility with a rolling and pitching deck even the most experienced naval aviator is put to the test.

27 September 1965

RF-101C 56-0204   15 TRS, 18 TFW on TDY, USAF, Udorn
                    Capt George Robert Hall (POW)

One of the many critical railway bridges on the JCS target list was the Ninh Binh road and railway bridge, 15 miles southwest of Nam Dinh, which carries the main line from Haiphong over the Nam Dinh River. Capt Hall was tasked with obtaining pre-strike photographic coverage of the target but as he made his run over the bridge at 500 feet and 540 knots his aircraft was hit by AAA and caught fire. He turned southeast to try to make for the sea but after about 10 miles he was forced to eject over a heavily populated area and was quickly captured. He became a resident of the Hanoi prison system for the next seven years and was released on 12 February 1973. He was on his 196th mission over Southeast Asia when he was shot down.

28 September 1965

A-1H   134482   VA-196, USN, USS *Bon Homme Richard*
                    Lt Cdr Carl Julius Woods (KIA)

A flight of Skyraiders on an armed reconnaissance mission were flying over a main railway line en route to a bridge at Qui Vinh, 70 miles north of the DMZ, when one of the aircraft was hit by AAA. Lt Cdr Woods turned the aircraft towards the coast and flew his burning Skyraider for over 40 miles to a position about 10 miles offshore near Mu Ron Ma where he was forced to abandon his aircraft. Tragically, although a USAF helicopter was soon on the scene, the pilot was found to be dead, probably due to drowning. This was the fourth aircraft lost from the *Bon Homme Richard* in the past five days.

F-105D 62-4404   562 TFS, 23 TFW attached to 6235 TFW,
                    USAF, Takhli
                    1 pilot, name unknown (survived)

A Thunderchief returned from a combat mission with the starboard wing drop tank missing and a large hole in the wing that the tank made on leaving the aircraft. Following repairs the aircraft was taken on a test flight but crashed following engine failure. The pilot ejected safely.

29 September 1965

F-100D 55-3613   481 TFS, 27 TFW attached to 6250 CSG,
                    USAF, Tan Son Nhut
                    Capt Samuel H Holmes (survived)

During a close air support mission an F-100 was hit in the starboard wing by ground fire and burst into flames. The aircraft crashed five miles south of Can Tho in the Mekong Delta but the pilot was safely recovered with only minor injuries.

30 September 1965

F-4C   64-0660   47 TFS, 15 TFW on TDY, USAF, Ubon
                    Capt Chambless M Chesnutt (KIA)
                    1Lt Michael Daniel Chwan (KIA)

F-105D 61-0117   334 TFS, 4 TFW attached to 6235 TFW,
                    USAF, Takhli
                    Lt Col Melvin Joseph Killian (KIA)

Despite the loss of Capt Hall's Voodoo over the Ninh Binh Bridge on the 27th, photographs were obtained to plan a major strike on the bridge. A mixed force of F-105s and F-4s struck the target on the last day of the month. Two aircraft were lost on the raid, the first was an F-4C that was shot down by intense large calibre AAA. The aircraft caught fire and crashed immediately, neither of the crew escaping. The second aircraft lost was an F-105 flown by Lt Col Killian, the CO of the 334th TFS on detachment to Takhli from Seymour-Johnson AFB. The aircraft was orbiting above the target at 18,000 feet when it was hit by an SA-2 SAM causing major damage. The aircraft flew on burning furiously for a few minutes before it exploded killing the pilot. This was the only fourth US aircraft to be lost to a SAM since the first aircraft was shot down by an SA-2 on 24 July.

1 October 1965

F-4C   63-7712   47 TFS, 15 TFW on TDY, USAF, Ubon
                    Capt Charles Joseph Scharf (KIA)
                    1Lt Martin John Massucci (KIA)

The first US loss in October took place near Ban Chan, 65 miles west of Hanoi. A flight of four F-4s was on an armed reconnaissance mission when the leader, Capt Scharf, spotted an NVA staging area near Ban Chan, just 25 miles north of the Laotian border. As he dived to attack the target from about 2,500 feet, Capt Scharf's aircraft was hit by small arms fire and immediately burst into flames. One parachute was seen to deploy before the aircraft crashed but neither men appeared in the North Vietnamese prison camp system and were probably killed in the incident. The men were officially declared dead in January 1978.

F-100D 55-3543   429 TFS, 474 TFW attached to 6251 TFW,
                    USAF, Bien Hoa
                    1Lt Gary Phelps Offutt (KIA)

The F-100 continued to bear the brunt of the air war in South Vietnam and losses began to mount as opposition increased. 1Lt Gary Offutt was on his fourth strafing pass during a close air support mission near Sa Dec in the Mekong Delta when his Super Sabre was struck by ground fire. The aircraft went into a vertical dive and crashed before Offutt could escape. Joint US-Vietnamese investigation teams visited the site of the crash several times between 1993 and 1995 and eventually found the remains of the pilot along with his wrist watch. Gary Offutt's remains were returned to his home town of Stewartsville, Missouri for burial in March 1997 to the usual accompanyment of a 21-gun salute and a flypast.

2 October 1965

A-1E   52-132593   602 ACS, 6251 TFW, USAF, Bien Hoa
A-1E   52-133880   602 ACS, 6251 TFW, USAF, Bien Hoa
It is not known which crewmember was in which aircraft, but those who died were:

               Capt Don Richard Hood (KIA)
               Capt Donald Charles Patch (KIA)

Two Skyraiders collided in mid-air while on a close air support mission in Binh Dinh province, South Vietnam, killing the pilots. These were the twenty-fourth and twenty-fifth A-1Es lost by the USAF since the first aircraft arrived in South Vietnam in May 1964. However, by this time the first 25 aircraft had been reinforced by further deliveries from the USA and eventually about 150 A-1Es were used by the USAF in Vietnam.

4 October 1965

A-1E   52-133915   6251 TFW, USAF, Bien Hoa
                    Capt Charles Franklin Allen (KIA)

During a direct air support mission, a Skyraider was shot down on its second pass over a target in South Vietnam.

5 October 1965

F-8E   150848   VF-162, USN, USS *Oriskany*
                    Lt(jg) Richard F Adams (survived)

Lt Adams was Cdr Dick Bellinger's wingman on a BARCAP mission during a strike on a bridge at Kep. Just as Lt Adams was crossing the coast at 30,000 feet a few miles east of Haiphong while en route to the target, Bellinger saw two SAMs streaking towards him off his port side. He radioed a warning to Adams but the transmission was not heard and Adams saw the missiles too late to avoid them. One of the SA-2s exploded just behind the Crusader causing damage to the tail surfaces and a fire in the aft fuselage. Lt Adams managed to fly his burning aircraft 40 miles out to sea towards two destroyers he had seen on the inbound journey. Eventually the Crusader exploded and Adams ejected through the fireball. He was picked up by a Navy rescue helicopter and taken to the cruiser USS *Galveston* for medical attention. Lt Adams was shot down again, this time by flak, during a mission on 12 July 1966.

F-100D 56-3074   481 TFS, 27 TFW attached to 6250 CSG,
                    USAF, Tan Son Nhut
                    1Lt John Charles Hauschildt (KIA)

The second Super Sabre lost in October was hit by small arms fire during a direct air support mission and crashed a mile offshore and 15 miles northeast of Phu Cat in central South Vietnam. Like many aircraft lost to small arms fire over the South, the aircraft had made several passes allowing the VC gunners to track the aircraft accurately and eventually shoot it down. The intensity of the opposition may have been nothing like that encountered in the war in the North, but the principles of air warfare still applied. Making multiple passes on the same target greatly increases the risk of being hit by ground fire.

F-105D 62-4295   36 TFS, 6441 TFW on TDY, USAF, Takhli
                    Maj Dean Andrew Pogreba (KIA)

F-105D 62-4376   36 TFS, 6441 TFW on TDY, USAF, Takhli
                    Capt Bruce Gibson Seeber (POW)

F-4C   63-7563   43 or 47 TFS, 15 TFW on TDY, USAF, Ubon
                    Capt James Otis Hivner (POW)
                    1Lt Thomas Joseph Barrett (POW)

A Rolling Thunder raid on a road bridge at Lang Met, 40 miles northeast of Hanoi and just nine miles northeast of Kep met with disaster on the 5th. Maj Dean Pogreba was leading four other F-105s with Capt Bruce Seeber on his wing. During the attack on the target, which was intermittently obscured by rain showers, first Pogreba's and then Seeber's aircraft was hit by AAA. Seeber ejected and was captured immediately but none of the other American pilots in the flight knew exactly what happened to Pogreba although he was seen heading north towards China after hitting the target. A report claims that an announcement was made on Peking radio on the 5th that Pogreba had been captured by the Chinese and even gave his service serial number. However, there was never any independent confirmation of Pogreba being in Chinese hands. Dean Pogreba had been shot down once before, on 22 August, during a mission west of Thanh Hoa and was rescued and returned to duty. Three other F-105s on this raid were forced to divert to Da Nang due to battle damage. Several of the aircraft were carrying the 3,000lb M-118 bomb, which was the largest conventional bomb that could be carried by the F-105.

Half an hour after Pogreba and Seeber had been shot down the Lang Met Bridge was attacked again, this time by a flight of Phantoms from Ubon. One of the aircraft was hit by AAA and caught fire near the target and tried to escape by flying east. Capt Hivner and 1Lt Barrett were forced to eject 15 miles northeast of Lang Met and only 20 miles from the Chinese border. On 12 February 1973 Seeber, Hivner and Barrett were released from Hanoi in Operation Homecoming but there was no sign of Maj Pogreba. Post-war rumours of him being seen in captivity in North Vietnam were unsubstantiated and simply served to increase the anguish felt by his family. It is most probable that Dean Pogreba died in his Thunderchief but the Peking Radio report, if true, is very curious and as yet his remains have not been returned. According to Col Jack Broughton in his book *Going Downtown*, Dean Pogreba would have faced a courts-martial had he returned from this mission. The previous day he had attacked a SAM site that was under construction near Hanoi when he came under fire from the site's protective anti-aircraft guns. Under the ludicrous rules of engagement at that time new SAM sites could not be attacked until they had been completed and actually fired a missile!

RF-101C 56-0178   15 TRS, 18 TFW on TDY, USAF, Udorn
                    Capt R W Pitts (survived)

The sixth and last US aircraft lost on 5 October was a Voodoo which was hit by AAA a couple of miles south of Kep and was almost certainly on a BDA mission connected to the Lang Met raid. The aircraft caught fire but it remained controllable and the fire quickly went out. Capt Pitts headed south hoping to make it either to South Vietnam or to a SAR destroyer in the Gulf of Tonkin. His luck held out and he managed to reach Da Nang but the aircraft was damaged beyond repair in a crash landing at the airfield.

7 October 1965

A-4E   151192   VMA-311, MAG-12, USMC, Chu Lai
1 pilot, name unknown (survived)

Overcrowding at Da Nang prompted the US Marines to search for a new location for the attack squadrons that were needed to support their operations in South Vietnam. The Marines chose to build a completely new base and selected a sandy stretch of land near a beach, 57 miles south of Da Nang. The airfield was called Chu Lai and was built to a Marine Corps concept known as SATS (Short Airfield for Tactical Support) which relied on the use of sections of steel planking for runways and taxiways. The concept was designed to satisfy Marine requirements for the rapid construction of short, temporary expeditionary airfields. The first troops and construction personnel arrived on 7 May and by 1 June 3,600 feet of airstrip was ready for the first residents. On the latter date the first eight Skyhawks from VMA-225 and VMA-311 landed at the airfield and flew their first combat missions later the same day. Chu Lai thus became the fourth airfield in South Vietnam capable of operating jet aircraft. However, the runway was intended to be 8,000 feet long and while work continued to extend it to its full length, arrester gear was used for shortening the landing runs and the A-4s were fitted with JATO equipment to achieve short take off runs. The work took some considerable time to complete as the surface on which the runway was built, either sand or mud depending on how much it rained, was very unstable and the steel planking suffered from buckling and other damage. In April 1966 a catapult was also installed but was not used on a regular basis. The SATS runway was still in use in 1970 when the Marines left Chu Lai although it had been largely superseded by a 10,000 feet conventional runway by the end of 1966.

On 7 October an A-4 commenced its take off run using its JATO system. Heavy rain had made much of the runway at Chu Lai unusable and JATO take offs were required until the runway could be repaired. Normally only one bottle fired, although two were fitted, but on this occasion both bottles fired simultaneously and were ripped from the aircraft causing it irrepairable damage.

8 October 1965

RF-8A   145617   Detachment D, VFP-63, USN,
USS *Coral Sea*
Lt M E Dunne (survived)

When launching from the *Coral Sea* on a photographic reconnaissance mission, an RF-8A suffered a control systems failure and the pilot was forced to eject. This was the last of three photo Crusaders lost from the *Coral Sea* during her first tour in Southeast Asia.

11 October 1965

A-4E   152016   VA-155, USN, USS *Coral Sea*
Lt Cdr P M Moore (survived)

The *Coral Sea* suffered another aircraft loss during a strike on barracks near Lien Qui, 20 miles northeast of Thanh Hoa during an armed reconnaissance mission. A section of Skyhawks from VA-155 was assigned to Iron Hand defence suppression and Lt Cdr Moore was pulling out from his second attack with Zuni rockets when his aircraft was hit by ground fire. The aircraft had been hit in the port side of the fuselage and the engine flamed out at 300 feet. Lt Cdr Moore quickly got his engine to relight but there was obviously some damage to the fuel system as it would not achieve anything like full power. He managed to limp south to a rendezvous with a KA-3B tanker which passed him some fuel but the engine continued to lose power. Realising that he could not reach the carrier, Lt Cdr Moore headed for the SAR destroyer and ejected close by.

12 October 1965

A-1E   52-133910   6251 TFW, USAF, Bien Hoa
Capt D W Rice (survived)

During a close air support mission over South Vietnam, an A-1E was hit by ground fire. Knowing that it was unsafe to come down in the vicinity of the target, the pilot chose to ditch just off Tuy Hoa where he was picked up by a helicopter.

13 October 1965

F-105D   61-0180   562 TFS, 23 TFW attached to 6235 TFW,
USAF, Takhli
Maj James Edward Prestle Randall
(survived)

A Rolling Thunder strike on a bridge near Ban Bung in a mountainous area of western North Vietnam just 20 miles over the border from Laos accounted for another Thud. Maj Randall was the Squadron operations officer and his aircraft was hit by ground fire on his second pass resulting in his ejection a few miles from the target. He was slightly injured on landing and was fortunate to be rescued as he was pursued by villagers with rifles. A USAF CH-3C rescue helicopter that refuelled at Lima Site 36, a forward site in Laos, dashed into North Vietnam for the pick up. Piloted by Capt J W Jennings this was one of the earliest rescues accomplished by 38th ARS with its new Jolly Green Giant helicopters.

14 October 1965

F-105D   62-4333   36 TFS, 6441 TFW on TDY, USAF, Takhli
Capt Thomas William Sima (POW)

F-105D   62-4305   36 TFS, 6441 TFW on TDY, USAF, Takhli
Capt Robert Harry Schuler (KIA)

Takhli lost another two Thunderchiefs during a Rolling Thunder strike on a barracks and military storage area in the hills 55 miles east of Hanoi. Capt Sima ejected over the target when his aircraft was hit by 37mm AAA and caught fire. As soon as it was known that Sima was down the rest of the strike force was diverted to support the rescue mission that was mounted, albeit in vain in this instance. While orbiting Sima's suspected position near the target, Capt Schuler's aircraft crashed, either as a result of ground fire or by flying into the ground, although in at least one reference this F-105 is listed as a MiG victim. Whatever the cause, Capt Schuler did not survive his crash and Capt Sima was captured and spent the next seven years in the North Vietnamese prison system until his release on 12 February 1973. Thomas Sima was on his third two-monthly rotation to Takhli when he was shot down.

F-8D   147899   VF-154, USN, USS *Coral Sea*
Lt Jack A Terhune (survived)

The *Coral Sea* mounted a strike on military buildings at Dong Hoi near the DMZ. Lt Terhune was assigned flak suppression using the Crusader's 20mm cannon and was making his second strafing run when his aircraft was hit. Small arms fire struck the aircraft just behind the nose wheel bay and the F-8 began to lose hydraulic and engine oil pressure. Lt Terhune headed back out to sea towards his carrier but after flying just over 100 miles the aircraft's landing gear suddenly lowered by itself and a few minutes later the engine seized. The pilot ejected safely and was quickly picked up by *Coral Sea's* plane guard helicopter. Several photographs of this Crusader were taken as Lt Terhune ejected and have appeared in print in numerous publications.

16 October 1965

RA-5C   151615   RVAH-1, USN, USS *Independence*
Lt Cdr James Franklin Bell (POW)
Lt Cdr James Leo Hutton (POW)

Although two Vigilantes had already been lost on operations in Southeast Asia, this was the first of the large reconnaissance aircraft to be shot down while on a Blue Tree mission. The aircraft had been flying over the region east of Hanoi looking for SAM sites and other potential targets and was just crossing the coast at 1,500 feet and 620 knots near Hon Gay, 35 miles east of Haiphong, when it was hit in the tail. The pilot thought that the aircraft had been hit by AAA but the navigator thought that the aircraft had been damaged by one of two SA2s which exploded behind the aircraft. Whatever the cause, the result was that the aircraft's tail was soon enveloped in flames and after about a minute the hydraulics failed resulting in loss of control. By this time the Vigilante had flown about 10 miles further east but was still among the many small islands that ring the coast of North Vietnam between Haiphiong and the Chinese border. Bell and

Hutton ejected over the sea and got into their survival dinghys. Lt Cdr Hutton attempted to activate his SAR beeper but after 30 seconds the battery went dead. After about 30 minutes they were picked up by local fishermen in their sampans and tied to the boat's mast. Having watched the 1946 feature film 'Two Years Before The Mast' on board the *Coral Sea* the previous evening which told of one man's crusade to expose mistreatment of men at sea, Lt Cdr Bell saw the funny side of this incident.

James Bell flew the F4D Skyray for four years before converting to the attack and then reconnaissance version of the Vigilante. James Hutton had been an air electronics operator and bombardier/navigator in the A-3 Skywarrior before he also flew in the attack and reconnaissance versions of the Vigilante. Bell and Hutton were on their 35th and 28th missions respectively when they were shot down and they were both released on 12 February 1973 and both later retired from the Navy as Captains.

A-1E   52-132541   6251 TFW, USAF, Bien Hoa
2 crew, names unknown (survived)

An A-1E from either the 1st or 602nd ACS crashed during take off, probably from Bien Hoa.

17 October 1965

F-4B   151515   VF-84, USN, USS *Independence*
Lt Cdr Stanley Edward Olmstead (KIA)
Lt(jg) Porter Alexander Halyburton (POW)

F-4B   151494   VF-84, USN, USS *Independence*
Ens Ralph Ellis Gaither (POW)
Lt(jg) Rodney Allen Knutson (POW)

F-4B   150631   VF-41, USN, USS *Independence*
Lt Roderick Lewis Mayer (KIA)
Lt(jg) David Robert Wheat (POW)

On 17 October the Navy flew an Alpha Strike or major mission against the Thai Nguyen road bridge, 30 miles due north of Hanoi. The mission proved costly for the *Independence's* air wing although, curiously, the losses occured not at the bridge itself but on the way to and from the target. The strike force of 15 aircraft crossed the coast well to the east of Haiphong and approached Thai Nguyen from due east. The first aircraft to go down was a Phantom assigned to the flak suppression force and was hit by AAA at 2,000 feet while still 40 miles short of the target. An anti-aircraft shell burst in the cockpit and the NFO, Lt Halyburton could not make contact with his pilot who was either killed or knocked unconscious by the blast. With the aircraft out of control, Lt Halyburton had no alternative but to eject.

After the raid at Thai Nguyen the strike force headed back towards the east to avoid the heavier flak concentrations around Hanoi and Haiphong. Another VF-84 Phantom crewed by Ens Gaither and Lt Knutson strayed too far east and was shot down within a couple of miles of the Chinese border and 65 miles northeast of Thai Nguyen. Although US aircraft were not permitted by the Pentagon's rules of engagement to enter a 15-mile buffer zone west of the Chinese border, it was easy for an aircraft to stray into the zone by accident considering the confined airspace of the region to the east of Hanoi. At 450 knots it would have taken less than 10 minutes for the Phantom to reach the Chinese border from Thai Nguyen. Gaither and Knutson ejected from their Phantom when it was hit by AAA causing an engine fire followed quickly by total loss of control. Knutson was badly injured during the ejection suffering fractures to his neck and backbone. As he landed he was fired upon by North Vietnamese soldiers and Knutson drew his service revolver and killed two of his attackers before he was knocked unconscious by a shot at point blank range which fortunately only grazed his forhead and nose. He was lucky not be killed and was taken to Hanoi along with his pilot. Rodney Knutson's injuries had still not healed when he and Ralph Gaither were released over seven years later. He eventually retired from the Navy as a Captain.

The last Phantom to be lost on this raid was from VF-41, the other F-4 squadron resident on the *Independence*. Lts Mayer and Wheat were assigned to CAP duties to protect the strike force from MiGs. The Phantom was orbiting at low level covering the strike aircraft as they left the target when it was hit by small arms

fire. Lt Mayer soon lost control of the aircraft and it crashed less than 10 miles from where Lt Cdr Olmstead's Phantom had been lost earlier in the mission. Two parachutes were seen but it appears that Lt Mayer was killed either during the ejection or upon landing. On 12 February 1973 Halyburton, Gaither, Knutson and Wheat emerged from the North Vietnam prison system. Ralph Gaither later wrote of his experience as a POW in a 1973 book titled *With God in a POW Camp*.

F-8E 149198 VMF(AW)-212, USMC, USS *Oriskany*
1 pilot, name unknown (survived)

In addition to deploying several fighter and attack squadrons to South Vietnam, the US Marine Corps also occasionally deployed squadrons on board some of the Navy's carriers during the war. VMF(AW)-212 lost four Crusaders on *Oriskany's* first tour of duty. The first aircraft to be lost hit the carrier's ramp during a night approach in rough weather. The pilot was returning from a CAP mission and the stormy seas heaved the deck up and down making a safe landing extremely difficult.

On this day the US Navy claimed its first destruction of a SAM site when an Iron Hand flight of four A-4Es led by an A-6 from the *Independence* struck a site near Kep. Cdr H B Southworth, CO of VA-72, leading the A-4s saw the radar vans on fire and one missile lying on the ground broken and burnt and another hurtling along at ground level.

18 October 1965

F-4C 64-0730 68 TFS, 8 TFW attached to 6234 TFW,
USAF, Korat
Capt Thomas Edward Collins (POW)
1Lt Edward Alan Brudno (POW)

A USAF raid on a railway bridge near Ha Tinh, 35 miles south of Vinh, resulted in the loss of one of the raiders. Capt Collins had just put his Phantom into a dive at 7,000 feet when it was hit by AAA. The aircraft immediately became uncontrollable and Collins and Brudno ejected. Capt Collins suffered compression fractures to several vertebrae (a common result of ejection even with today's more sophisticated ejection seats). The crew were captured by local militia and taken to Hanoi to begin more than seven years of brutal treatment in the North Vietnamese prison system. Collins was incarcerated in no less than 12 camps during his time as a POW and contracted beri-beri amongst other diseases and ailments in the unsanitary conditions found in these camps. Both men were released from their imprisonment on 12 February 1973. Brudno had been able to send coded messages in his letters from prison in Hanoi which greatly assisted the Department of Defense's knowledge of the POW camps. However, Brudno suffered greatly both physically and psychologically and on 3 June 1973, just four months after his release, he committed suicide, unable to cope with the return to 'normality'.

O-1E 56-2600 20 TASS, 6250 TASG, USAF, Da Nang
Maj Harley Boyd Pyles (KIA)
Capt Winfield Wade Sisson, USMC (KIA)

Although Maj Pyles was based at Da Nang he was actually operating from Kham Duc Special Forces Camp on 18 October. He took off with Capt Sisson as an observer to lead a flight of helicopters carrying ARVN troops to a landing zone in enemy territory and then to mark a target for an air strike. Following the air strike the Bird Dog crew checked the target to provide BDA and then started back to base. The aircraft was last known to be flying in bad weather above a low cloud base and was about 10 minutes from Da Nang when it disappeared. Capt Sissons was the Marine Corps liaison officer with MACVSOG. Although Capt Sissons was allegedly reported as being a POW, neither he nor Maj Pyles ever returned from their last flight. A recent report claims that the Bird Dog's mission was in support of a Shining Brass reconnaissance force that had been inserted into enemy-held territory.

19 October 1965

A-4C 148584 VA-195, USN, USS *Bon Homme Richard*
Lt(jg) John Bowers Worcester (KIA)

A section of two A-4s from the *Bon Homme Richard* was sent out on an armed reconnaissance mission to attack targets of opportunity between Thanh Hoa and Vinh. Soon after attacking a bridge Lt Worcester failed to check in with his leader. Lt 'Smiley' Worcester was last seen 35 miles southeast of Thanh Hoa 20 miles from the coast. The section leader retraced the route three times and was joined by other aircraft in the search for Lt Worcester. A SAR mission the following day also found no trace of wreckage. John Worcester joined the growing ranks of aircrew who disappeared, apparently without trace, while flying over Southeast Asia. He had only been in theatre for six weeks and was on his 14th mission when he was lost.

20 October 1965

B-57B 53-3920 8 TBS, 405 FW attached to 6252 TFW,
USAF, Da Nang
Maj Gerald T Hamilton (survived)
Maj Harold E Holzapple (survived)

The Special Forces camps in South Vietnam were particularly vulnerable to Viet Cong attack and air power was often called upon to assist the defenders. The attacks usually started at night when air support was at its least effective and one such attack commenced at the Plei Mei Special Forces Camp 80 miles west of Qui Nhon and close to the Laotian border. The attack was more intensive and prolonged than any previous such attack and it was later established that the attackers included NVA soldiers as well as local VC forces. In the early hours of 20 October two Canberras were scrambled from Da Nang and, despite the darkness and low cloud, dropped a total of four 500lb general purpose bombs and 42 x 260lb fragmentation bombs which halted the attack. The bombing had to be very accurate to avoid casualties to friendly forces and damage to the dirt airstrip at the camp. This in turn meant the aircraft had to bomb straight and level at a low altitude. However, the attack renewed soon after daybreak and two more Canberras were diverted from a strike mission north of Da Nang to assist in the fight for Plei Mei. By the time the Canberras arrived over the camp, a US Army helicopter and a U-6 Beaver had been shot down and the O-1 FAC reported heavy fighting around the camp perimeter. Again the Canberras were forced by low cloud and the proximity of friendly forces to bomb low and slow in level flight. On his seventh pass having expended all his bombs and having now resorted to strafing the enemy troops, Maj Hamilton's aircraft was hit by .50 calibre machine gun fire which exploded the starboard wing tip tank and took with it a large section of wing. The other Canberra attacked the gun site that had damaged Hamilton's aircraft but was also damaged by several rounds. Maj Hamilton turned north towards Pleiku where a rescue helicopter had been alerted but the aircraft soon became uncontrollable and Hamilton and Holzapple ejected just before the aircraft crashed into the jungle. The remaining Canberra, despite its own damage, stayed over the crew's positions until they were rescued by the helicopter and the aircraft then landed safely at Pleiku for much needed repairs.

21/22 October 1965

A-1E 52-133897 1 ACS, 6251 TFW, USAF, Bien Hoa
Capt Melvin C Elliott (survived)

The battle for the Special Forces Camp at Plei Mei continued unabated. Flights of F-100s and A-1s were over the camp almost continuously in an attempt to assist the defenders on the ground. On the night of the 21st an A-1E from Bien Hoa was hit by ground fire and crashed five miles east of the Camp after the pilot bailed out. A flight of Skyraiders was waiting for an Army Caribou for which they were going to provide cover as it dropped supplies to the camp's defenders. However, the Caribou never turned up so the Skyraiders made one final strafing pass before they had to return to base. It was during this last pass that Capt Elliott's aircraft was hit in the port wing and caught fire. Capt Elliott became snagged on the cockpit canopy as he tried to bail out of the aircraft. His helmet came off in the slipstream but he eventually freed himself and parachuted into a tree close to the camp. He tried to reach the camp but had to hide from Viet Cong during

the night and in the evening of the following day he was almost rescued by an Army UH-1 but it was driven away by ground fire. He spent another night in hiding but was eventually rescued the next morning (23rd) by a USAF HH-43 helicopter that was guided by two Bird Dog FACs and protected by Army UH-1 gunships. Capt Elliott had spent 36 hours on the ground and had evaded Viet Cong troops and American bombs on several occasions.

The B-66 variants in Southeast Asia

The improvement in North Vietnam's air defence system, and particularly the potential of the SA-2 missile, led to the introduction of the RB-66 Destroyer to the conflict. Two versions of the aircraft were deployed commencing in May 1965. The RB-66B was originally designed for the night photographic reconnaissance role but a small number of aircraft were fitted with a package of electronic warfare equipment known as Brown Cradle. These aircraft were limited to jamming the frequencies used by the North Vietnamese air defence radars while the RB-66C not only performed jamming but collected electronic signal information that could be analysed for information on types and location of enemy radars. The 363rd TRW deployed six RB-66Cs to Takhli in May 1965, followed by three more aircraft in September. The first RB-66Bs arrived in October 1965 and the 41st TRS was activated at Takhli on the 20th of the month. The two types were often used in combination during Rolling Thunder strikes with the RB-66C standing off at a distance to locate and identify radars for the RB-66B to move in and jam their transmissions. The big aircraft were vulnerable to MiG attack and this factor limited their usefulness in that they had to stay out of areas of known MiG activity and often flew with fighter escorts. In 1966 the aircraft was redesignated as the EB-66 and the EB-66B and EB-66C were later joined by the more capable EB-66E. With the widespread availability of the QRC-160 self-protection jamming pod from 1967 the role of the EB-66 changed from standoff jamming and ECM escort for USAF strike aircraft to the protection of B-52s and Navy tactical aircraft.

22 October 1965

F-105D 62-4350 36 TFS, 6441 TFW on TDY, USAF, Takhli
Maj Fred Vann Cherry (POW)

The hunt for SAM sites in North Vietnam continued but still proved costly as the wily North Vietnamese surrounded their sites, both real and dummy, with rings of AAA positions which took a greater toll of US aircraft than did the missiles themselves. Maj Cherry was looking for a SAM site just south of Kep when his aircraft was hit by a barrage of ground fire. His F-105 burst into flames and although he managed to fly southeast for 15 miles in an attempt to make the coast he was forced to eject when the aircraft became uncontrollable. Maj Cherry was captured and joined the growing number of US aircrew in North Vietnamese prisons until his release on 12 February 1973. As one of the first black American airmen to be captured, the North Vietnamese attempted to exploit Fred Cherry and cause dissension among the POWs. In all instances these attempts at racial exploitation failed.

RB-66B 53-0452 Detachment 1, 41 TRS, 6250 CSG, USAF,
Tan Son Nhut
Capt Robert Lee Mann (KIA)
1Lt John Weger (KIA)
1Lt James Arthur McEwen (KIA)

The first of the RB-66 fleet to be lost in Southeast Asia crashed during a night mission near the village of Plei Toun Breng, 25 miles west of Pleiku and less than 10 miles from the border with Laos. The cause of the crash was not ascertained.

A-1E 52-132442 602 ACS, 6251 TFW, USAF, Bien Hoa
Capt M W Burr (survived)

The Plei Mei Camp siege claimed yet another aircraft. A Skyraider was lost over the Camp during a mission on the 22nd. The aircraft was struck by ground fire and Capt Burr made a crash landing on the airstrip. The aircraft was damaged beyond repair and the Captain was slightly injured.

23 October 1965

O-1E 56-2624   19 TASS, 6250 TASG, USAF, Bien Hoa
2 crew, names unknown (survived)

During take off on a visual reconnaissance mission, a Bird Dog's engine failed causing it to crash. Both crew were recovered safely.

26 October 1965

F-4B 151505   VF-84, USN, USS *Independence*
Lt Grover G Erickson (survived)
Lt(jg) John H Perry (survived)

The radar on the island of Bach Long Vi, 70 miles offshore from Haiphong, was vital in providing early warning to the North Vietnamese of raids by TF 77 aircraft. The Navy carried out numerous strikes on the installation to try to keep it off the air. During a strike on the radar and a torpedo boat anchorage in the early hours of the 26th a Phantom from VF-84 was lost. Lt Erickson's aircraft was just pulling out from a rocket attack when the crew felt a dull thud followed by a muffled explosion. The undercarriage dropped down and the starboard engine fire warning light came on. The engine was closed down but the aircraft then began to lose electrical power followed by indications of a fire from the port engine. After smoke began to fill the cockpit and the controls went slack the crew abandoned the aircraft about 10 miles south of the island. They were both later picked up, the pilot by a US Navy vessel and the NFO by a Seasprite helicopter.

F-4B 149410   VMFA-115, MAG-11, USMC, Da Nang
F-4B 150998   VMFA-115, MAG-11, USMC, Da Nang

It is not known which crewmember was in which aircraft, but those who died were:

Capt William Jennings Tebow (KIA)
1Lt William Raymond Gendebien (KIA)
1Lt John Bunce McHale (KIA)
CWO John Robert Petty (KIA)

VMFA-531, the first USMC Phantom squadron to serve in Southeast Asia, arrived at Da Nang on 10 April 1965 and was replaced by other Phantom squadrons on brief rotations. VMFA-115 was the fourth Phantom squadron to rotate into South Vietnam and arrived at Da Nang on 15 October from MCAS Cherry Point, North Carolina. The first Marine Phantom casualties were caused by bad weather rather than by enemy action. A pair of Phantoms was returning from a strike mission in poor visibility when they both flew into the side of Monkey Mountain, a promontory of high ground five miles northeast of Da Nang. One of the Phantom pilots had reported engine trouble and it is possible that this problem distracted the crews during the final critical stages of the approach to Da Nang. These were the only aircraft lost by VMFA-115 during its initial combat tour in Southeast Asia.

27 October 1965

F-8E 150655   VF-191, USN, *USS Bon Homme Richard*
Lt Dennis Anthony Moore (POW)

Lt Moore was flying a BARCAP mission about 40 miles southwest of Hanoi when he became the sixth victim of a SAM. The Crusader was flying straight and level at about 33,000 feet over an overcast when the rear end of the aircraft suddenly exploded. The SA-2 blew the tail off and Lt Moore ejected and landed near the village of Man Luong. He was quickly captured and spent the rest of the war as a POW until released on 12 February 1973. Following his retirement from the Navy, Dennis Moore emigrated to Britain and lived in London.

27/28 October 1965

A-4C 148550, 148595   VMA-311, MAG-12, USMC, Chu Lai

During the night of 27/28 October VC sappers attacked the Marine bases at Chu Lai and Marble Mountain. About 20 Vietnamese infiltrated the flight line at Chu Lai and threw satchel charges into the tail pipes of the parked Skyhawks destroying two and damaging six more of VMA-311's aircraft. Fortunately,

several charges failed to detonate. Aviation fuel was leaking from aircraft that had been riddled with machine gun fire and armourers braved bullets and flames to unload ordnance from the aircraft to reduce the danger of further damage. Fifteen of the VC attackers were killed in the attack. The destruction at Marble Mountain was much greater than that at Chu Lai. Just across the Da Nang River from the Marine's main base, Marble Mountain was a newly constructed base that was home to several Marine helicopter squadrons. A total of 19 helicopters, including 13 of VMO-2's UH-1Es, were destroyed and 11 badly damaged during the attack. Three Americans were killed at Marble Mountain and 91 wounded.

28 October 1965

F-4B 150626   VF-41, USN, USS *Independence*
Lt Cdr A M Lindsey (survived)
Lt(jg) Robert W Cooper (survived)

Although the war over North Vietnam was taking the lion's share of the Navy's war effort it also participated in operations in the Steel Tiger area of southern Laos. Lt Cdr Lindsey was pulling up from his second bombing run on a bridge about 25 miles west of the DMZ when his aircraft was hit by ground fire. He climbed to 3,500 feet but the oxygen system failed followed by the radio. Dense smoke filled the rear cockpit forcing Lt Cooper to eject. With the loss of hydraulic power the pilot also ejected although his seat failed to fire at first and only left the aircraft at 1,500 feet. A SAR task force consisting of an HC-54, two A-1Es, a Navy A-1H and two HH-43s arrived at the scene and the two helicopters each picked up a survivor.

A-4C 148596   VA-22, USN, USS *Midway*
1 pilot, name unknown (KIA)

Following an interdiction mission over North Vietnam, a Skyhawk crashed while attempting to land on the *Midway*. Hostile action was not suspected as the cause.

30 October 1965

C-123B 56-4381   315 ACG, USAF, Tan Son Nhut
4 crew, names unknown (survived)

During an aborted take off a Provider from the 315th ACG was damaged beyond repair.

31 October 1965

A-4E 151173   VA-164, USN, USS *Oriskany* TDY to Korat
Lt Cdr Trent Richard Powers (KIA)

The SAM threat caused the Air Force and the Navy to cooperate to seek an effective solution. The Navy detached a number of Skyhawks to Korat to fly as pathfinders for the F-105 Iron Hand aircraft. On the last day of the month Lt Cdr Powers led eight Thunderchiefs on a mission to attack a SAM site five miles southeast of Kep during a combined Air Force-Navy 65-aircraft strike on a road bridge at Kep. A total of 27 SAMs were launched during this attack and another strike later in the day. None of the missiles caused any damage to US aircraft. Lt Cdr Powers was seen to commence a run at about 150 feet to release its Snakeye bombs and mark the site for the F-105s. During the run over the target the aircraft was hit by AAA and burst into flames. The aircraft climbed but then banked suddenly and Lt Cdr Powers ejected at about 200 feet. His parachute was seen to develop and he was seen to wave to his wingman to indicate he was OK. His SAR beeper was heard briefly but he never responded to any of the radio calls made to him and a SAR mission was not possible due to the degree of enemy opposition in the area. Nothing more was heard about Trent Powers until May 1987 when his remains were identified in a package of bones and teeth returned by the North Vietnamese. Further remains were handed over in November 1987 which also proved to be those of Lt Cdr Powers. There was no indication as to the cause of death. His remains were buried at Chan Hassen, Minnesota on 15 April 1988. Trent Powers, who was the operations officer of VA-164, was posthumously awarded the Navy Cross for his sacrifice on his last mission.

1 November 1965

RF-101C 56-0174   15 TRS, 18 TFW on TDY, USAF, Udorn
Capt Norman T Huggins (survived)

The month started badly with three aircraft lost on the first day. The first to fall was a reconnaissance Voodoo that failed to return from a SAM site search mission. Capt Huggins was flying low over the island of Dao Cat Ba, the largest of the islands off the coast near Haiphong, when his aircraft was hit by ground fire. The Voodoo caught fire but Capt Huggins managed to fly over 25 miles in an easterly direction before he was forced to eject. He came down close to a small island and swam ashore only to return to the sea when villagers shot at him. A flight of four F-105s arrived and fired at the boats that had set out to capture the pilot. An Albatross amphibian piloted by Capt David Westenbarger landed on the choppy seas and taxied up to Capt Huggins. The Albatross crew shot at North Vietnamese swimmers who were approaching the Voodoo pilot and the parajumper, A1C J E Pleiman, dived in and brought Capt Huggins safely in.

A-4E 151142   VA-86, USN, USS *Independence*
Lt Cdr Billy V Wheat (survived)

Three hours after Capt Huggins had been shot down, a flight of Skyhawks from the *Independence* was flying an armed reconnaissance mission between Vinh and Dong Ha. The flight had already attacked two targets and was about to attack a bridge in hills seven miles south of Ha Tinh when one of the aircraft was hit by 37mm AAA as it rolled into its dive. The engine immediately flamed out and could not be restarted so the pilot ejected. He was later picked up by a USAF CH-3C operating from one of the forward sites in Laos. This was the last aircraft lost by the *Independence* before the conclusion of her one and only tour of duty off Vietnam. The carrier was finally decommissioned to the reserve on 30 Sep 1998.

O-1E 56-2508   21 TASS, 6250 TASG, USAF, Pleiku
2 crew, names unknown (survived)

During a forward air control mission a Bird Dog suffered engine failure and crashed. Fortunately, both pilot and observer were rescued.

2 November 1965

O-1F 57-2964   19 TASS, 6250 TASG, USAF, Bien Hoa
Capt G H Moore (survived)
Sgt Kluck (survived)

On another FAC mission a Bird Dog was hit by small arms fire 10 miles east of Xuan Loc and 35 miles east of Bien Hoa. The aircraft crash-landed and the crew was recovered with only minor injuries.

3 November 1965

F-8D 148635   VF-111, USN, USS *Midway*
1 pilot, name unknown (survived)

During an attack mission a VF-111 Crusader suffered a control systems failure and the pilot was forced to eject as he lost control of the aircraft. This was the last aircraft lost by the *Midway* as it came to the end of its first tour of duty off Vietnam on 4 November. The ship had been assigned to TF 77 on 22 March and took up its position on the line on 10 April. It had spent a total of 144 days on the line during five periods. During its tour the *Midway* had lost 17 aircraft in combat and another five aircraft in accidents. These losses were made up of 10 Skyhawks, six Crusaders (including two reconnaissance models), four Skyraiders (including an EA-1F), and two Phantoms. A total of 12 airmen had been killed during the tour and another five became POWs. The ship had therefore lost the equivalent of one of its six squadrons in terms of aircrew and aircraft.

F-105D 61-0163   562 TFS, 23 TFW attached to 6235 TFW, USAF, Takhli
Capt Dwight Pollard Bowles (KIA)

A flight of F-105s on an armed reconnaissance mission had just crossed the Laotian border into North Vietnam when the leader spotted a bridge near Ban Heo in mountainous terrain about 100 miles west of Hanoi. Capt Bowles dived to attack the target but his

aircraft failed to pull out of the dive and hit the ground. It is possible that Capt Bowles was hit and killed or at least incapacitated. Another account suggests that only one of his two 3,000lb bombs released and the imbalance caused the aircraft to roll uncontrollably. The aircraft was painted as 'Tommy's Hawk' while at Takhli.

5 November 1965

F-8E   150665   VMF(AW)-212, USMC, USS *Oriskany*
Capt Harlan P Chapman (POW)

VMF(AW)-212 lost its second aircraft (and its first pilot) during a strike on the road and rail bridge at Hai Duong, 30 miles east of Hanoi, which connected the capital city with the port of Haiphong. Although primarily a fighter squadron, VMF(AW)-212 was used mainly in the ground attack role during its tour on the *Oriskany*. Capt Chapman was making his dive on the target and was just about to release his two 2,000lb Mk84 bombs when his Crusader received a direct hit by a 57mm shell and exploded. Chapman was very fortunate to be able to eject but he was quickly captured and became the first Marine Corps aviator to become a POW in North Vietnam. He was released on 12 February 1973 having been awarded the DFC and promoted to the rank of Lt Col while in prison. He later commanded VMFA-314 before retiring from the Corps.

F-105D   62-4342   357 TFS, 355 TFW attached to 6234 TFW, USAF, Korat
Lt Col George Carlton McCleary (KIA)

Lt Col McCleary was leading his flight of four Iron Hand aircraft back from a mission near Hanoi when the aircraft flew into a layer of cloud near Phu Ban, 25 miles southwest of Nam Dinh. Without warning, a SAM shot up through the clouds and exploded right in front of McCleary's aircraft. A wingman saw the canopy jettison before losing sight of the F-105 as it entered cloud. Lt Col McCleary was the third F-105 squadron commander to be lost up to this point in the war. George McCleary was declared dead (body not recovered) in November 1973 based on a presumptive finding of death. In July 1988 the Vietnamese handed over remains that were claimed to be those of Lt Col McCleary although they were not positively identified as such until May 1991.

Search and Rescue - III

The US Navy, like the USAF, was not well equipped for combat SAR at the start of the war in Southeast Asia. The UH-2 Seasprite was used as a plane guard aircraft for local rescue near the aircraft carriers on which it was based and the SH-3A Sea King was used for ASW duties. Both helicopters were used for SAR and both were modified to incorporate armour plate, door guns, extra fuel and other features essential for the role. The UH-2 was limited in range and endurance but was fast and presented a smaller target and served well in the SAR role. There was little requirement for the SH-3 to perform its primary role of submarine detection in the Gulf of Tonkin, so many of them were stripped of ASW equipment, fitted with armour and door guns and transferred to the SAR role. The UH-2 and the SH-3 were also based on the destroyers and other vessels that fulfilled the function of mobile SAR bases in the Gulf of Tonkin. Two operating stations were established, the northern station and the southern station, and when air operations were mounted, helicopters were deployed to these destroyers to be prepared for a rescue attempt. Helicopters were airborne just offshore as raids were in progress and much of the Navy's SAR success was due to the short reaction time that this forward basing permitted. The Navy helicopters were originally operated by detachments of existing squadrons and it was not until 1 September 1967 that a dedicated SAR squadron, HC-7, was formed to replace the UH-2 detachments. A system known as High Drink was devised that allowed a helicopter to lower a hose to a ship that was not fitted with a flight deck so the helicopter could take on fuel. The helicopters came to be known by their radio call signs, Clementine for the UH-2s and Big Mother for the SH-3s. The Navy SAR effort was rather piecemeal and low-key compared to that of the Air Force. This is reflected in the survival rate of airmen shot down

over North Vietnam. Thirty-one percent of USAF airmen were rescued by SAR forces during the war compared to just 16 per cent of US Navy airmen.

6 November 1965

A-1E   52-132469   602 ACS, 6251 TFW, USAF, Bien Hoa
detached to Udorn
Capt Richard Eugene Bolstad (POW)

A-1E   52-132439   602 ACS, 6251 TFW, USAF, Bien Hoa
detached to Udorn
Capt George Grigsby McKnight (POW)

When a SAM had shot down Lt Col McCleary on the 5th it was thought that he might have ejected safely so a large-scale SAR effort was mounted to try to rescue him. The search was to be led by the Skyraiders of the 602nd ACS detachment at Udorn. Bad weather and approaching darkness postponed any rescue attempt until the following day and at dawn two A-1Es, with the call signs Sandy 11 and Sandy 12, took off from Udorn and headed to McCleary's last known position. The Sandy call sign would soon become a familiar part of the air war over North Vietnam and the word became synonymous with the A-1s assigned to the RESCAP mission. The Sandys began searching the area for signs of wreckage and in the hope that Lt Col McCleary would contact them on his survival radio. About 35 miles west of Nam Dinh (and 20 miles northwest of where McCleary was actually lost) Sandy 12 flown, by Capt Richard Bolstad, was shot down by a barrage of AAA. Bolstad bailed out and was quickly spotted by Capt McKnight flying Sandy 11. At the news of this incident two more A-1Es took off from Udorn to join the SAR task force and a CH-3C (63-9685) of Detachment 5 of the 38th ARS, which was already on its way to the scene, was diverted to Capt Bolstad's position. As the helicopter, using the call sign Jolly Green 85, approached Capt Bolstad it was hit by small arms fire. The helicopter pilot, Capt Warren R Lilly, managed to gain enough height for his crew (consisting of Lt J Singleton, Sgt B E Naugle and Sgt A Cormier) to bail out and after engaging the autopilot he quickly followed suit. Sgt Naugle was hung up briefly by his safety harness but freed himself and landed in dense jungle some distance from the rest of his crew. Although SAR helicopters normally flew combat missions in pairs, it just happened that on this day the second helicopter had to turn back with an engine malfunction. Jolly Green 85 was operating from a forward location known as Lima Site 36 deep in the Barrel Roll area of northern Laos and close to the border with North Vietnam.

A Navy SH-3 Sea King SAR helicopter (148993 call sign Nimble 62) flown by Lt(jg) T Campbell and Lt(jg) M Howell of HS-2 from USS *Independence* radioed that it was inbound from the sea and would attempt a rescue. The two Sandys from Udorn, Sandy 13 and Sandy 14, rendezvoused with the Sea King and escorted it over the coast just north of Thanh Hoa. About seven miles northwest of the infamous Dragon's Jaw Bridge, Capt McKnight, the pilot of Sandy 14 radioed that he was receiving ground fire and then disappeared into cloud. Capt McKnight could not be raised on the radio so Nimble 62 and Sandy 13 searched the area for as long as their fuel would allow but to no avail. After refuelling on board the *Independence*, Nimble 62 flew back to Thanh Hoa to search for Capt McKnight, this time escorted by two Navy Skyraiders. After an hour of fruitless searching Nimble 62 flew on to the crash site of Jolly Green 85, some 40 miles to the northwest. Just as the SAR task force was about to give up and return to the carrier due to approaching darkness, a SAR beeper was heard and a low level search revealed a light from a cigarette lighter. The Sea King dropped a jungle penetrator on a long cable and Sgt Naugle, the flight engineer from the USAF helicopter, was hauled up to safety. The helicopter had to refuel from a destroyer at sea in order to reach the *Independence* safely. Sgt Naugle wrote an excellent account of his rescue that was published on the Internet under the Jolly Green Association's website.

The following morning Nimble 62 took off again to continue the search for survivors. As the task force crossed the coast the helicopter was hit by small arms fire and the pilot was forced to crash-land on the top of a 4,000 feet mountain. The accompa-

nying Navy Skyraiders strafed and bombed enemy troops as they attempted to close with the stricken helicopter. On hearing of the loss of Nimble 62, another Sea King was launched from the *Independence* and an HH-3E took off from a forward operating base in Laos. The North Vietnamese brought in a mobile anti-aircraft gun to supplement the machine gun and small arms fire and eventually both Navy Skyraiders were hit and had to make belly landings at Da Nang. In the meantime a USAF HH-3 and a Navy UH-2 arrived and safely extracted the crew of Nimble 62. The escorting Skyraiders then destroyed the downed Sea King to prevent it falling into enemy hands.

On the 8th another SAR mission was mounted to try to reach any survivors from Jolly Green 85. Skyraiders from both the Air Force and the Navy converged on the area where Jolly Green 85 was shot down. A beeper was heard but two Air Force A-1Es were hit by ground fire and damaged and had to return to Udorn. Other Skyraiders strafed the anti-aircraft guns and enemy troops but by this time the rescue commanders realised that they would only lose more aircraft if they continued the SAR mission and reluctantly recalled the task force. The Jolly Green 85 crew (minus Sgt Naugle) had in fact been captured very soon after their helicopter had been shot down and they joined the two Sandy pilots in a North Vietnamese prison camp. All three helicopter crewmen remained incarcerated until their release on 12 February 1973.

The events of the 6-8 November had little tangible results for the loss of two helicopters and two Skyraiders and damage to four others, together with the loss (although fortunately all eventually survived) of five airmen. The incident shows the remarkable lengths to which the US forces were willing to go to attempt a rescue. However, this was not the end of the story as in October 1967 George McKnight together with Navy Lt George Coker escaped from a prison camp in North Vietnam. Unfortunately, they were recaptured the next day after travelling 15 miles and were severely tortured for the attempt. They are among a very small number of Americans who escaped, albeit briefly, from captivity in North Vietnam. Capt Bolstad and Capt McKnight were both released from captivity on 12 February 1973.

7 November 1965

A-4E   150071   VA-163, USN, USS *Oriskany*
Lt Cdr Charles G Wack (survived)

The Air Force and Navy continued their campaign against the SAM sites as more were being constructed and made operational. A formation of Skyhawks from the *Oriskany* was despatched to attack a SAM site 10 miles southwest of Nam Dinh. Lt Cdr Wack took over as leader of the raid when the squadron commander's aircraft developed a mechanical problem before launch. Wack's aircraft was hit and badly damaged by ground fire as he rolled in on the target but he continued his bomb run before pointing the stricken aircraft out to sea and managed to get about 12 miles off the coast before he was forced to eject. This happened on the second day of the major SAR effort to recover the two Skyraider pilots and the crew of Jolly Green 85 and it was a measure of the cooperation between the services that Lt Cdr Wack was picked up by a USAF HU-16 piloted by 1Lt J Kirby. Charlie Wack was awarded the Silver Star for his leadership and determination during this mission.

9 November 1965

A-1H   137566   VA-152, USN, USS *Oriskany*
Lt Cdr Paul G Merchant (survived)

Although the Navy's and the Air Force's Skyraiders were increasingly being used as SAR escorts, the aircraft was still used for offensive operations, especially in the southern provinces of North Vietnam where enemy opposition was supposed to be less intense. A flight of Skyraiders from the *Oriskany* was sent on a night armed reconnaissance mission and found a number of trucks about 35 miles southeast of Vinh. During the attack one of the aircraft was hit by ground fire damaging the engine. Lt Cdr Merchant jettisoned his ordnance and turned east with his engine gradually losing power. When his hydraulics and his engine failed he managed to glide out over the sea and make a

successful ditching in the dark a few miles off the coast and was rescued by a Navy helicopter just as two North Vietnamese boats were approaching him.

12 November 1965

F-105D 62-4218   562 TFS, 23 TFW attached to 355 TFW, USAF, Takhli
                                  Capt William N Miller (KIA)

As a formation of Thunderchiefs was about to refuel from a KC-135 tanker one of the Thuds exploded without warning. Capt Miller ejected, probably involuntarily, from the aircraft but he was found to be dead in his parachute. The accident was thought to be due to either a catastrophic engine failure or the detonation of one of the aircraft's bombs. Capt Miller had narrowly escaped having to eject from his F-105 during the 5 October raid on Lang Met when four aircraft were lost. Miller's aircraft took a hit in an engine burner chamber but he nursed it for 40 minutes until he reached Da Nang. Known as 'Nasty Ned', William Miller was a very popular and experienced member of the F-105 fraternity. He enlisted in the Air Force in 1950 as an airborne electrical specialist and then applied for Cadet training and graduated as a navigator in 1954. He completed a course with the University of Maryland and took pilot training in 1959. He flew F-100s before transitioning to F-105s and joining the 562nd TFS at McConnell AFB. Miller's rise through the ranks and his progression through ground, academic and flight training typifies the way the USAF strongly encourages professional military education and training. This was the sixth and final F-105 and the second pilot lost by the 562nd TFS during its deployment to Takhli.

13 November 1965

A-4E   151067   VA-163, USN, USS Oriskany
                                  Cdr Harry Tarleton Jenkins (POW)

An armed reconnaissance mission claimed another Oriskany aircraft on the 13th, this time a Skyhawk flown by Cdr Harry Jenkins, CO of VA-163. Flying a Skyhawk with the call sign Old Salt 340, the 17-year Navy veteran Cdr Jenkins was looking for signs that a river near Dong Hoi was being used for transport of supplies. As the river appeared not to be navigable Cdr Jenkins and his wingman decided to bomb a road junction which he knew of to the south of Dong Hoi. As the pair flew over the village of Xuan Noa, just 15 miles north of the DMZ Cdr Jenkins spotted what appeared to be signs of recent vehicle activity. He flew very low and slow to make a positive identification and saw tracer from a 37mm anti-aircraft gun curving towards his Skyhawk. He pulled up into a shallow climb to try to reach cloud cover but his aircraft was hit. He immediately lost all aileron control and electrical power and the aircraft started to roll uncontrollably. Cdr Jenkins ejected from the wildly gyrating Skyhawk just short of the coast. The Commander's wingman, Lt(jg) Vance Schufeldt, was soon joined by nine other Navy aircraft that began searching for their downed leader but he had been captured by armed Vietnamese. He was driven to Hanoi over several nights and was amazed to see a large quantity of trucks on the road with dimmed lights following reflective strips set along the road at short distances. He was taken to the Hoa Loa Prison (the infamous Hanoi Hilton) in Hanoi and was interrogated and tortured like so many of the men who had preceded him. As a senior officer Harry Jenkins became an example for the other POWs to follow and, like Jim Stockdale, he was often singled out for harsh punishment, spending almost four years in solitary confinement. He fought back against his captors whenever he could and several times he fused the camp's lights by shorting out the wires that run through his cell. Cdr Harry Jenkins had been shot down on his 133rd combat mission and was released on 12 February 1973 with the rank of Captain. He later retired from the Navy and joined a defence contractor. Sadly, Harry Jenkins died in the crash of a homebuilt aircraft on 2 August 1995.

F-100D 55-2795   481 TFS, 27 TFW attached to 6250 CSG, USAF, Tan Son Nhut
                                  Capt Charles M Summers (survived)

The war continued in the South and the Super Sabre squadrons still bore the brunt of the 'hot' missions. Capt Summers' aircraft was hit by small arms fire during a strafing attack on a VC concentration south of the Mekong Delta. Although barely able to control his damaged aircraft, Summers headed towards a friendly village but overshot it and ejected at very low altitude. He came down in some small trees in the middle of a swamp and was unable to stand. He crawled away from his parachute as he heard shots being fired and could not contact the circling F-100s as his survival radio had malfunctioned. An Army helicopter swooped in for the rescue but as it neared the ground it sucked up Capt Summers' parachute which became entangled in the rotor blades causing the helicopter to crash. A second helicopter was then summoned which picked up Capt Summers and the crew from the first helicopter.

Charlie Summers had deployed to Clark AFB with the 27th TFW from Cannon AFB the day after the Gulf of Tonkin Incident and flew some of the first F-100 combat missions over South Vietnam. Following his ejection on the 13th (during his 124th mission) he was evacuated from Southeast Asia for medical treatment but returned in 1967 and flew a further 102 missions as a Misty FAC. Altogether, Charlie Summers flew over 350 combat missions during his tours in Southeast Asia. Post-war he became base commander at Osan, South Korea and commander of the 8th TFW in 1978/79. After retiring from the Air Force in December 1981 he formed his own aviation company in Montgomery, Alabama, not far from the Air University where he had been Dean of Curriculum in 1980.

14 November 1965

A-1E   52-132898   1 ACS, 6251 TFW, USAF, Bien Hoa
                                  Capt Paul Truman McClellan (KIA)

On 12 November troops from the US 1st Cavalry Division (Airmobile) had been deployed to an area in western Pleiku province to start search and destroy missions in the Ia Drang Valley near the border with Cambodia. Four companies of troops were lifted by helicopter to a site designated as Landing Zone X-Ray but ran into two NVA regiments. Heavy fighting ensued and one of the companies became cut off from the rest. The Army called for air support and Capt McClellan took off from Pleiku to assist in the defence of LZ X-Ray. He was making his eighth pass against the North Vietnamese troops when he was shot down. His aircraft was hit at low level by heavy automatic weapons and crashed before McClellan could escape. More US troops were flown in and helped to extricate the survivors in a battle that lasted a total of six days.

16 November 1965

A-1H   137590   VA-52, USN, USS Ticonderoga
                                  1 pilot, name unknown (survived)

With the departure of the Midway, the Independence and, later, the Oriskany in November, the Ticonderoga took up its position on the line on 5 November for its second tour. Eleven days after combat operations commenced it lost its first aircraft of the tour when the pilot of a Skyraider had to abandon his aircraft after the hydraulics failed. The failure was due to the loss of oil during a combat mission but it was not thought to have been caused by hostile action.

F-105D 62-4332   469 TFS, 6234 TFW, USAF, Korat
                                  Capt Donald George Green (KIA)

The 355th TFW moved permanently to Takhli on 8 November having previously been resident at McConnell AFB in Kansas. However, one of its squadron, the 469th TFS, was reassigned to Korat and eventually became part of the 388th TFW. The last elements of the Squadron arrived at Korat on 15 November and the Squadron flew its first combat missions the following day. An armed reconnaissance mission by an Iron Hand flight of F-105s in northeast North Vietnam resulted in the loss of the third Thunderchief to be shot down by a SAM. Capt Green was flying at 4,000 feet over a road near Uong Bi, 12 miles northeast of Haiphong, looking for SAM sites. Unfortunately the missile operators saw Capt Green's aircraft first and fired an SA-2 that

exploded near the aircraft causing major damage. The Captain managed to fly 40 miles out to sea heading south and hoped to make it either to Da Nang or to eject near a US warship. Sadly, he was killed when his aircraft crashed in the sea.

17 November 1965

F-8E   150675   VMF(AW)-212, USMC, USS Oriskany
                                  Capt Ross C Chaimson (survived)

A-4E   151083   VA-163, USN, USS Oriskany
                                  Lt Cdr Roy Howard H Bowling (KIA)

A-1H   135244   VA-152, USN, USS Oriskany
                                  Lt Cdr Jesse Junior Taylor (KIA)

F-8E   150308   VF-194, USN, USS Bon Homme Richard
                                  Cdr Robert S Chew (survived)

On 17 November the Navy returned to the Hai Duong Bridge east of Hanoi. The Oriskany had lost a VMF(AW)-212 Crusader there on 5 November during the first raid but this second raid proved more disastrous for Air Wing 16. Within the space of about 30 minutes four aircraft were shot down, three of them from the Oriskany, and the bridge still remained operational.

The first aircraft hit during the attack was another Crusader from the Marine squadron on board the carrier. Capt Chaimson had just started his dive to release his bombs when his Crusader was struck by 37mm AAA. The aircraft's electical power died immediately and the bombs failed to release. Chaimson deployed the aircraft's ram air turbine, which should have generated some electrical power, but nothing happened. Capt Chaimson flew back towards the carrier alone and descended through the clouds to find the Bon Homme Richard but his fuel was exhausted as he had been unable to radio for a tanker and could not deploy his refuelling probe in any case. Chaimson ejected about 100 miles east of Dong Hoi and was picked up safely by a Navy helicopter.

The first aircraft to be shot down at the bridge was a Skyhawk flown by Lt Cdr 'Hap' Bowling, the operations officer of VA-163 under the new leadership of Cdr Wynn Foster. The Skyhawk had just dropped its Snakeye bombs on the bridge and was making a low-level, high-speed egress from the target area when it was hit by AAA. The wingman saw the starboard horizontal tailplane blown off and the aircraft roll to the right and impact the ground. Although the aircraft had been flying at less than 150 feet at very high speed the pilot had managed to eject. Another pilot reported seeing a parachute but saw that the occupant was inert and without his helmet. The parachute was later seen on the ground but there was no sign of 'Hap' Bowling. About 25 minutes later a section of Skyraiders, which had been launched for RESCAP, flew into the area to search for Lt Cdr Bowling. The aircraft came down to low level to try to obtain a sighting of the downed pilot and Lt Cdr Taylor's aircraft was hit by ground fire in the port wing, which burst into flames. Lt Cdr Taylor, who was the Air Wing's operation officer, had volunteered for the mission. He tried to return to the carrier but the aircraft crashed into coastal marshes about 15 miles southwest of Haiphong.

A few minutes after the Skyraider went down another wave of strike aircraft attacked the bridge, this time from the Bon Homme Richard's Air Wing 19. Although the Marine Corps Crusader squadrons were often used as bombers in close air support missions, it was less usual for the Navy to use its Crusaders in this role. However, this raid was a maximum effort and Cdr Chew, the CO of VF-194, led his squadron in the attack. The Commander started his dive at 3,500 feet, released his two large Mk84 bombs and pulled out at 1,900 feet and 500 knots jinking to avoid the intense ground fire. As the wingman closed up after his attack he noticed fuel streaming from underneath his CO's aircraft. The formation flew south towards the carrier and Cdr Chew refuelled three times to replace the fuel that was constantly pumping out of the aircraft. Eventually, the fuel was exhausted and Cdr Chew was forced to eject about 120 miles southeast of Haiphong where he was rescued by a USAF HU-16 amphibian piloted by Capt D Richardson.

Although it was suspected that Lt Cdr Bowling had been killed in the high-speed ejection, it could not be proved and he was

promoted to the rank of Captain during the time the Navy maintained him as missing. In March 1977 the remains of Captain Bowling were handed over to a US Presidential commission which was visiting Hanoi. Two years earlier, in December 1975, the remains of Jesse Taylor had been handed over by the Vietnamese as a goodwill gesture. Jesse Taylor had been awarded a posthumous Navy Cross and in December 1984 an *Oliver Hazard Perry*-class guided missile frigate was launched with the name USS *Taylor* in honour of the dead Skyraider pilot.

F-8E   150875   VMF(AW)-212, USMC, USS *Oriskany*
              1Lt G E Peil (survived)
In addition to the four aircraft lost over North Vietnam, the *Oriskany* also lost another Crusader when the aircraft hit the carrier's ramp as it was landing back from the strike. Luckily the pilot survived the accident. The four aircraft lost by the *Oriskany* on the 17th were the last on its first tour of duty. The ship had launched over 12,000 sorties and had lost 15 aircraft in combat and another 7 in accidents during its tour. The carrier flew its last mission with TF 77 on 25 November but was to return to the South China Sea in June the following year.

18 November 1965

F-8E   150332   VF-191, USN, USS *Bon Homme Richard*
              Lt(jg) W D Sharp (survived)
Following the disastrous raid on Hai Duong, the Navy had a better day on the 18th, losing only one aircraft. Lt Sharp was flying one of a number of Crusaders tasked with bombing AAA sites which were dug in around a railway bridge near Phong Bai, 35 miles north of Vinh. On his second pass over the target, Lt Sharp heard a thump and his wingman reported that the aircraft had been hit and the port undercarriage well and was on fire. Lt Sharp turned east and crossed the coast hoping to make it to the carrier. However, the hydraulic pressure faded and the fire continued unabated forcing the pilot to eject 40 miles from the coast. He was picked up safely by a Navy rescue chopper.

F-105D   61-0062   469 TFS, 6234 TFW, USAF, Korat
              Capt Larry C Mahaffey (survived)
A flight of F-105s was flying an armed reconnaissance mission over the southern provinces of North Vietnam looking for SAM sites, AAA concentrations and other possible targets, when one of the aircraft was brought down. Capt Mahaffey's Thud was hit by ground fire 35 miles southwest of Vinh, close to the border with Laos. He ejected over mountainous terrain and was hung up in a tree about 100 feet above the ground. He was later rescued from the tree by a USAF HH-43 from the 38th ARS using a jungle penetrator to break through the foliage.

O-1E   56-2544, 56-2585, 56-2587, 56-2675, 56-4228
              505 TACG, USAF, Ben Trang
Five O-1 FAC aircraft were destroyed during a Viet Cong mortar attack on an airstrip at Ben Trang.

19 November 1965

F-100D   56-3125   unit ..?, USAF, base ..?
While parked in its revetment an F-100 caught fire and burnt out when a fuel leak ignited.

21 November 1965

C-123B   55-4530   315 ACG, USAF, Tan Son Nhut
              A1C Michael Kelly (survived)
              A1C Kirby R Whellern (survived)
              5 crew, names unknown (survived)
A Provider crashed about one mile short of Da Nang's runway in heavy rain, high winds and darkness when it suffered an engine failure. Although none of the crew were killed in the crash several were badly injured and two had to be airlifted to hospital by one of the base HH-43s flown by Capt A Graham who had to land in a minefield to pick up the injured. This was the fifteenth Provider lost in Southeast Asia since the start of the war.

O-1E   56-2535   21 TASS, 505 TACG, USAF, Pleiku
              Maj R E Poestel (survived)
              MSgt C R Jones (survived)

Following the end of the six-day firefight in the Ia Drang Valley the situation in the Central Highlands was still far from quite. During a visual reconnaissance mission near Pleiku, a Bird Dog was hit by small arms fire and forced to crash-land. The crew received only minor injuries and were eventually recovered.

Route Packages
In December an Air Force/Navy Armed Reconnaissance Coordinating Committee established a system to assist the command and control of air operations over North Vietnam by dividing the country into geographical regions and assigning them to one or other of the air services. Prior to this time air operations over North Vietnam during the Rolling Thunder campaign were conducted by the Air Force and the Navy in alternate three-hour intervals which led to some chaotic situations. In the early days there was not even much coordination between individual units and it was not unheard of for aircraft from two different Navy aircraft carriers to attack targets in the same area without knowing of each other's operations until they arrived over the target. The system devised in November 1965 divided North Vietnam into seven Route Packages or Route Packs. Immediately north of the DMZ was Route Pack I and the other packs extended northwards in sequence. Route Package VI was subdivided in VIA to the north and west of Hanoi and VIB to the south and east of the city, the dividing line running along the main railway line to China. Initially, the Air Force and Navy operated in all Route Packages at assigned times, alternating Packages every six weeks. However, in April 1966 operations within the Route Packages were more strictly divided with the Air Force being assigned to operations in Route Packages 1, 5 and 6A and the Navy being assigned to Route Packages 2, 3, 4 and 6B. Although the Route Packages were allocated at CINCPAC level, in actual operations the Services frequently crossed boundaries if necessary.

28 November 1965

F-8E   150327   VF-191, USN, USS *Bon Homme Richard*
              Cdr Howard Elmer Rutledge (POW)

F-8E   150854   VF-194, USN, USS *Bon Homme Richard*
              Lt Frank H Harrington (survived)
A raid on the Phuong Dinh Bridge close to the Dragon's Jaw at Thanh Hoa resulted in the loss of two aircraft and the making of another chapter in the saga of the Vietnam POW story. Cdr 'Howie' Rutledge, the CO of VF-191, was making his second run against the bridge and had just pulled up after releasing his ordnance when his Crusader was hit by anti-aircraft fire. Still able to control his aircraft Cdr Rutledge attempted to egress from the target area but his aircraft was hit again, this time destroying the flying control systems. With the aircraft now totally out of control and losing altitude rapidly, Rutledge ejected just seconds before his Crusader exploded.

Later in the morning another raid struck the Phuong Dinh Bridge and another Crusader was lost. Lt Harrington was also making his second pass over the bridge when his aircraft was hit in the tail area by ground fire. The aircraft caught fire but Harrington managed to turn east and reach a position about 10 miles out to sea before the aircraft became uncontrollable and he was forced to eject. He was rescued by a USAF HU-16 that was standing by during the raid.

'Howie' Rutledge was a veteran of the Korean War having flown 200 missions with VF-52 from the USS *Valley Forge*. He was on his 75th mission over Vietnam when he was shot down. During his capture he shot and killed one of his assailants and was almost killed by a mob but was saved by the intercession of a village commisar. Rutledge was taken to Hanoi to begin seven years of hell in the North Vietnamese prison system. He wrote a fascinating and moving account of his experiences in his book *In the Presence of Mine Enemies* published in 1973 and which was illustrated with line drawings by a fellow POW, Gerald Coffee who was shot down on 3 February 1966. Rutledge was a deeply spiritual man and he became the unofficial prison chaplain, encouraging and supporting the other prisoners and holding religious ceremonies whenever it was possible. After release on 12 February 1973 he retired from the Navy as a Captain and

made two unsuccessful bids to be elected to Congress. Sadly, 'Howie' Rutledge died of cancer at the age of 55 on 11 June 1983.

F-105D   62-4285   334 or 335 TFS, 4 TFW attached to 355
              TFW, USAF, Takhli
              Capt John Anzuena Reynolds (POW)
During a raid on army barracks near Van Yen, 60 miles west of Hanoi, an F-105 was hit by ground fire during its strafing run. Capt Reynolds only managed to fly about 10 miles south towards the Laotian border before being forced to eject. He was captured immediately and was imprisoned in several of the North Vietnamese POW camps including Heartbreak Hotel, The Zoo, Briarpatch, Little Vegas, Dirty Bird, Son Tay, Camp Faith, Camp Unity, and Dogpatch. It was not unusual for prisoners to be moved from camp to camp on a regular basis. The North Vietnamese did this in order to break up the secret communications systems the prisoners built up at each camp and to further disorient the POWs. John Reynolds had served a tour as an FAC pilot in Vietnam in 1963 and had previously flown F-100s before converting to F-105s. He was released on 12 February 1973 and eventually retired from the USAF in 1990 as a Brigadier General following a long career that included a tour as the US defence attaché to China. He became the first westerner to be allowed to fly Chinese fighter aircraft during his four years in Peking.

F-4C   64-0729   557 TFS, 12 TFW, USAF, Cam Ranh Bay
              Capt R D Street (survived)
              1Lt H J Knoch (survived)
Work on a new airfield at Cam Ranh Bay started in June 1965. A temporary runway was started early in September and finished 50 days later. The 12th TFW moved from MacDill AFB, Florida to the new base at Cam Ranh Bay on 8 November with two of its four Phantom squadrons, the 557th and 558th TFSs. A temporarily assigned squadron (the 43rd TFS detached from the 15th TFW) had arrived a week earlier. On 1 January 1966 the 43rd returned to MacDill and was replaced by the 12th TFW's own 559th TFS. On the last day of fighting in the Ia Drang Valley one of the Phantoms despatched to provide air support for the defenders of Pleiku was hit by ground fire less than two miles north of the airfield. The crew ejected safely and were plucked out of hostile territory by a USAF helicopter.

29 November 1965

C-123B   54-0651   309 ACS, 315 ACG, USAF, Tan Son Nhut
              Capt J T Rutledge (survived)
              1Lt T O Norris (survived)
No details are known of this incident except that the aircraft was brought down by ground fire in South Vietnam with no serious casualties.

30 November 1965

F-8E   149176   VF-53, USN, USS *Ticonderoga*
              Lt(jg) Stephen Gould Richardson (KIA)
Tragedy struck the *Ticonderoga* on the 30th when it was conducting operations at Yankee Station about 60 miles northeast of Da Nang. The arrester hook of a VF-53 Crusader failed as it caught one of the ship's wires when returning from a CAP mission. The aircraft went over the side and the pilot was killed. Another F-8 pilot from VF-53, Lt Richard W Hastings, was standing on the LSO platform at the time and was hit by flying debris from the aircraft and later died of his injuries.

1 December 1965

A-4C   149560   VA-144, USN, USS *Ticonderoga*
              Lt(jg) John Vern McCormick (KIA)
The first day of December saw the Navy make another attempt to drop the Hai Duong Bridge near Thanh Hoa. During the raid the *Ticonderoga* suffered its first combat loss of the war, which was remarkable considering that the ship had spent a total of 86 days on the line in two cruises up to this date. Lt McCormick's aircraft exploded instantly when it was hit by 57mm flak at about 6,000 feet on its dive into the target. He had no chance to escape and the wreckage fell about half a mile from the bridge.

F-105D 61-0182   334 TFS, 4 TFW attached to 355 TFW,
                 USAF, Takhli
                 Capt Thomas Edward Reitmann (KIA)
A few hours after the Navy strike on the Hai Duong Bridge, a
flight of F-105s hit the Cao Nung railway bridge on the main rail
line from China and 50 miles northeast from Hanoi. At 8,000 feet,
as Capt Reitmann commenced his dive, AAA hit the aircraft and
severely damaged the tail. The aircraft immediately became
uncontrollable and crashed about two miles south of the bridge
killing the pilot.

A-1H   137621   VA-52, USN, USS *Ticonderoga*
                1 pilot, name unknown (survived)
One of the *Ticonderoga's* Skyraiders, probably one that had
been launched for RESCAP for the Hai Duong raid, suffered an
engine failure forcing the pilot to part company with his aircraft.
Fortunately he was rescued by a Navy helicopter.

2 December 1965

A-1H   139755   VA-196, USN, USS *Bon Homme Richard*
                Lt Cdr Gerald Ray Roberts (KIA)
During an armed reconnaissance mission a flight of Skyraiders
spotted a small bridge a few miles inland from Mu Ron Ma and
35 miles north of Dong Hoi. On his third pass Lt Cdr Roberts
crashed near the target, either as a result of ground fire or by flying into the ground. Intense ground fire precluded a close
inspection of the crash site and there was no attempt at a SAR
operation as their was no evidence that Lt Cdr Roberts had survived the crash. Joint US-Vietnamese excacations of the crash
site in 1993 and 1994 yielded human remains that were later
positively identified as being those of Lt Cdr Roberts.

F-4B   151409   VF-92, USN, USS *Enterprise*
                Lt T J Potter (survived)
                Lt(jg) C W Schmidt (survived)
In 1965 the USS *Enterprise* was the US Navy's pride and joy. The
$451 million ship was launched on 24 September 1960, being not
only the world's largest ship at the time but also the world's first
nuclear-powered aircraft carrier. The USS *Enterprise* is 1,123ft
long and weighs 89,600 tons fully loaded including a complement of 84 aircraft and 5,500 men. Accompanied by the nuclear
powered guided-missile cruiser USS *Bainbridge*, the *Enterprise* sailed into the South China Sea and was assigned to TF 77
on 21 November. It took up position at Dixie Station on 2 December to fly missions over South Vietnam before moving to Yankee
Station for operations over North Vietnam. Although Navy aircrew always regarded air operations over the South merely as a
prelude to the 'real' air war in the North, things could, and did,
go wrong, especially with a new carrier on its first war cruise. On
its first day of operations the *Enterprise* launched 118 sorties
against Viet Cong targets in South Vietnam, however, only 116
aircraft returned to the carrier's deck.
    Two Phantoms from VF-92 were tasked to provide close air
support to US troops about 5 miles north of An Loc, which is 55
miles north of Saigon and only 10 miles from the border with
Cambodia. Lt Potter put his Phantom into a 30-degree dive and
released six Mk82 bombs at 5,000 feet. As soon as the bomb
released the crew felt an explosion and the wingman reported
that the Phantom was trailing fuel which had ignited. Within
seconds most of the fuel had been lost and the aircraft was still
on fire leaving no alternative for the crew but to eject. They were
picked up after some anxious minutes by a USAF HH-43 helicopter that was directed to the scene by a C-123 that happened
to be in the area. The Mk82 bombs were fitted with a tail fuse that
had a 4.5 second arming delay but for some reason the bombs
had armed instantly upon release and then one bomb may have
touched another causing a detonation. This incident was remi-
niscent of the Intruder's introduction to combat in July.

**The C-123 Provider was the most widely-used tactical
transport aircraft in Southeast Asia in the early years of the
war. A total of 54 aircraft were lost between February 1962
and March 1971. USAF**

F-4B   152220   VF-114, USN, USS *Kitty Hawk*
                Cdr Carl Benjamin Austin (KIA)
                Lt(jg) Jacob Drummond Logan (KIA)
Another new addition to TF 77 was the carrier USS *Kitty Hawk*.
The lead ship of a class of four, the *Kitty Hawk* had been
launched on 21 May 1960. It was assigned to the Task Force on
26 November but quickly took up line duty at Yankee Station for
operations over North Vietnam. The ship brought the Navy's
second Intruder squadron (VA-85) to Southeast Asia and also
introduced another new Grumman aircraft to the conflict, the
E-2A Hawkeye AEW aircraft. Like the *Enterprise*, the *Kitty
Hawk* also suffered its first combat loss on the 2nd. Cdr Austin,
the CO of VF-114 was following about one and a half miles
behind a flight of Skyhawks with the intention of providing flak
suppression if required. The formation crossed the coast 10 miles
south of Mu Ron Ma but the cloud was so low that it enveloped
the hills near the coastline. The Skyhawks entered cloud and
reversed their course back out to sea to attempt a penetration on
instruments. However, when the formation broke through the
cloud a few miles from the beach there was no sign of the accompanying Phantom. The next day searchers spotted a freshly
burned patch of ground on a hillside in the location where Cdr
Austin and Lt Logan disappeared and it was presumed that the
aircraft had flown into the hill soon after it entered cloud.

F-4B   149468   VF-96, USN, USS *Enterprise*
                Lt(jg) Robert J Miller (survived)
                Lt(jg) G F Martin (survived)
Another Phantom from the *Enterprise* was lost on its first day of
operations, this one from VF-96. Returning from a strike over
South Vietnam, the aircraft was running short of fuel and the
weather was deteriorating. The seas were rough causing the carrier's deck to pitch violently and the Phantom made several
approaches. The crew had difficulty refuelling from a Skyhawk
tanker and ejected from the Phantom just before the fuel ran out.
A Seasprite helicopter from the carrier's HC-1 detachment rescued the crew.

7 December 1965

F-4B   152261   VMFA-323, MAG-11, USMC, Da Nang
                Maj John Howard Dunn (POW)
                CWO John William Frederick (POW - Died)
VMFA-323 was the fifth Marine Corps Phantom squadron to
rotate into Da Nang, having arrived on 1 December. A week
later Maj Dunn, the executive officer of VMFA-323, and CWO
Frederick were escorting an EF-10B Skynight on a night ECM

mission over North Vietnam when they were shot down about 45
miles west of Thanh Hoa. The loss was attributed to either an
SA-2 missile or possibly a MiG, however MiG activity was mini-
mal at this time and there is no evidence that the North
Vietnamese had the all-weather MiG-17PF version in service in
1965. Maj Dunn ejected safely and evaded capture for six days
before he was found. He was imprisoned in seven different camps
until release on 12 February 1973. CWO John Frederick was also
captured and survived torture and mistreatment for seven years
only to die of typhoid on 19 July 1972. On 13 March 1974 the
North Vietnamese handed over the remains of several individ-
uals which upon investigation were found to include those of
CWO Frederick.

F-4C   64-0723   557 TFS, 12 TFW, USAF, Cam Ranh Bay
                 Capt James Donald Sala (KIA)
                 Capt Robert Wayne Wranosky (KIA)
A Phantom on a close air support mission from Cam Ranh Bay
was shot down by ground fire in the Central Highlands 20 miles
east of Dak Seang and 50 miles due north of Pleiku. The aircraft
was hit by ground fire and crashed into a hill before the crew
could eject.

O-1E   55-4675   19 TASS, 505 TACG, USAF, Bien Hoa
                 1 pilot, name unknown (survived)
A Bird Dog crashed in South Vietnam due to engine failure.

8 December 1965

A-1E   52-133987   602 ACS, 3 TFW, USAF, Bien Hoa
                   detached to Udorn
                   Capt Ronald M Canter (KIA)
The 3rd TFW was moved to Bien Hoa from England AFB,
Louisiana on 8 November and replaced the 6251st TFW which
had been in existence for less than four months. Although no aircraft were lost in combat on the 8th, the USAF lost three aircraft
and one pilot in accidents. During a SAR mission a Skyraider
from the Udorn detachment accidentally crashed in Thailand
killing the pilot. On 21 November the two Skyraider squadrons
were attached to the 3rd TFW.

F-105D   62-4302   6234 TFW, USAF, Korat
                   1 pilot, name unknown (survived)
The pilot of a Thunderchief ejected safely in Thailand when the
engine failed while on a strike mission.

C-130A   56-0502   817 TCS, 6315 OG, USAF, Naha
                   Capt Frank Delzangaro (survived)
                   4 crew, names unknown (survived)

A Hercules on a resupply mission crashed in bad weather at Chu Lai without any fatalities. The accident was attributed to pilot error in that Capt Delzangaro attempted a take off with a known engine malfunction.

9 December 1965

A-4E   151992   VMA-224, MAG-12, USMC, Chu Lai
                         1 pilot, name unknown (survived)

The Marine Skyhawk pilots at Chu Lai still had to use JATO at the end of the year as the full length of the SATS runway was not yet available. On take off, a Skyhawk pilot accidentally over-rotated the aircraft causing major damage to the Skyhawk that was deemed beyond repair.

11 December 1965

C-123B 56-4376   315 ACG, USAF, Tan Son Nhut
                          Maj Robert Milvoy Horsky (KIA)
                          Capt George Parker McKnight (KIA)
                          SSgt Mercedes Perez Salinas (KIA)
                          SSgt Donald David Stewart (KIA)
                          81 ARVN troops (KIA)

The USAF was going through a bad patch for aircraft accidents in the second week in December but the worst was yet to come. A Provider took off from Pleiku in poor visibility for a flight to Tuy Hoa. The aircraft carried 81 ARVN paratroopers in addition to its flight crew of four. The flight should have taken less than an hour and no navigator was carried but the aircraft crashed in low cloud about 20 miles west of Tuy Hoa killing all on board. The aircraft apparently hit a tree on a mountain ridge as it was descending and then spun down a thousand feet in a flat spin. The wreckage was not found for two weeks and even then a ground party was unable to reach the site due to heavy Viet Cong resistance. This was the worst accidental air crash in terms of loss of life to take place during the war in Southeast Asia. However, on 4 April 1975, two years after the American withdrawal, a C-5A Galaxy crashed near Saigon as it was evacuating civilians and 155 people were killed, many of them orphaned children.

14 December 1965

B-57B 52-1565   8 TBS, 405 FW attached to 6252 TFW,
                         USAF, Da Nang
                         Capt Robert Jerome Moroney (KIA)
                         Capt Jere P Joyner (survived)

The Canberras from the 8th and 13th TBSs at Da Nang roamed the length and breadth of South Vietnam to provide heavy close air support whenever needed. In December the squadrons were engaged in operations near Pleiku nearly 150 miles to the south of Da Nang. An aircraft was shot down by ground fire near the Chu Prong mountain, a well-known stronghold used by the NVA, 30 miles southwest of Pleiku and close to the border with Cam-

bodia. The aircraft was making its second dive attack when it was hit and the navigator, Capt Jere Joyner, managed to eject and was subsequently rescued by a US Army helicopter. It was thought that the pilot, Capt Moroney, did not eject from the aircraft and was killed in the crash.

Capt Joyner's luck held for on 15 March 1966 he was badly wounded by an anti-aircraft shell that exploded in his cockpit during a mission near Tchepone, Laos. His pilot, Capt Larry Mason, saved Joyner's life by flying the badly damaged aircraft to Da Nang where he made an emergency landing. Mason was subsequently awarded the AFC for his achievement.

O-1E   56-4191   21 TASS, 505 TACG, USAF, Pleiku
                          Capt James Carl Kindel (KIA)
                          Capt Paul Joseph Simon (KIA)

The forward air controllers were acknowledged as having one of the most enjoyable but one of the most dangerous flying jobs in the in-country war in South Vietnam. The small, low-powered, slow and low-flying aircraft were frequent targets for ground fire. One of the FACs, from a detachment at Dalat, was shot down by ground fire during a mission in support of ground forces in Tuyen Duc province and both the crew were killed.

15 December 1965

RA-5C 151633   RVAH-7, USN, USS *Enterprise*
                         Lt J K Sutor (survived)
                         Lt(jg) G B Dresser (survived)

The *Enterprise* was still operating at Dixie Station and flying missions over South Vietnam. It was operating at a high level of activity as on 12 December it launched a record 165 combat sorties in one day. Three days later one of its Vigilantes was tasked with photographing sampans in a swampy area on the west coast of South Vietnam near the border with Cambodia. The aircraft was flying at 3,800 feet over the bay of Vinh Cay Duong, 17 miles southeast of Ha Tien, when the crew felt and heard a loud thump followed by an ominous rumbling noise. Smoke and fumes began to fill the cockpit as they headed south out to sea but about 10 miles from the coast the aircraft began to pitch nose down and then started to roll uncontrollably. The crew ejected when it became obvious that they could not regain control and were rescued by an Army helicopter. It could not be confirmed whether the problem was caused by an engine fire or damage to the hydraulics but a Skyhawk pilot reported that the aircraft was on fire and trailing a long plume of grey smoke. If the aircraft had been hit by ground fire rather than suffered an accidental explosion it is ironic that such a large, powerful and sophisticated aircraft like the RA-5C could be brought down by small arms fire while looking for sampans which were of dubious military value anyway. Ironic it may have been, but unfortunately it was an irony that was repeated many times during the air war in Southeast Asia where the results did not always justify the expenditure in lives and equipment.

F-102A 55-3373   Detachment 5, 509 FIS, 405 FW, USAF,
                           Tan Son Nhut
                           1Lt R D Scheu (survived)

The F-102 detachment at Tan Son Nhut was tasked with air defence as its main duty in case the VPAF should ever threaten Saigon. This eventuality never arose during the war and the F-102s were under utilised. Occasionally, the Delta Daggers were used on offensive air support missions although neither the aircraft nor its weapons were suited for air-to-ground work and its pilots had not been trained in the role. During one such mission an aircraft was hit in the fuselage by ground fire as it was making a rocket run on an enemy target and the pilot forced to eject. This particular aircraft first entered USAF service with the 318th FIS at McChord AFB, Washington in 1957.

F-105D 62-4363   334 TFS, 4 TFW attached to 355 TFW,
                           USAF, Takhli
                           Capt Harry D Dewitt (survived)

On 15 December the USAF bombed the Uong Bi thermal power plant, 12 miles northeast of Haiphong. This was the largest power plant to be bombed so far and was the first major industrial target to be bombed in North Vietnam. During the raid Capt Dewitt's aircraft was hit by 37mm flak and a few minutes later the controls froze forcing him to eject over the sea. He was picked up safely by an HU-16 amphibian that was fired at continuously by shore batteries as it made the pick up. Capt Dewitt suffered a broken his leg during his ejection and was medevaced to the USA for recovery. He had previously flown the RF-101 with a reconnaissance squadron in France.

Skoshi Tiger

By 1965 the Northrop F-5 Freedom Fighter light fighter-bomber had already been successfully exported, being used by or on order for over a dozen air forces. However, some critics claimed that although the Department of Defense was eager to promote the aircraft for overseas sales, the USAF had not ordered any F-5s. To answer these critics and further prove the capabilities of the aircraft, Secretary of Defense Robert McNamara ordered an operational evaluation of the F-5 in Southeast Asia under a project named Skoshi Tiger. On 22 July 1965 the 4503rd TFS (Provisional) was formed at Williams AFB with 12 F-5Cs. This variant was simply an F-5A with a few modifications, the most obvious of which were an in-flight refuelling capability, the addition of armour plating and some changes in avionics and ordnance fits. The Squadron left Williams on 22 October and arrived at Bien Hoa four days later, flying its first combat missions later the same day. The combat evaluation was planned to last just over four months, after which the aircraft would then return home.

The evaluation included a deployment to Da Nang from 1 January 1966 for experience in forward operating base operations and missions over North Vietnam. The Skoshi Tiger evaluation

Under Operation Skoshi Tiger, the 4503rd TFS introduced the F-5 to combat as a possible replacement for the F-100. Despite a successful combat trial the F-5 was not adopted by the USAF although a large number were supplied to the VNAF. USAF

came to an end on 9 March 1966, the Squadron having flown 2,093 sorties from Bien Hoa and 571 from Da Nang in a total of 3,116 combat flying hours. Only one aircraft was lost during the evaluation period and another 16 aircraft were damaged and 42 sorties aborted due to technical problems. The evaluation was deemed a success and, as a recent increase in US strength had just been authorised, it was decided that the F-5 unit (renamed the 10th FCS in April 1966) would stay on in South Vietnam. The F-5's main disadvantage in combat in Vietnam was found to be its relatively short range and endurance. However, its good load-carrying capability, survivability and cheapness eventually persuaded the US to supply the type to the VNAF in large numbers and the aircraft became the VNAF's most potent weapon from 1967 onwards.

16 December 1965

F-5C   63-8425   4503 TFS(P), 3 TFW, USAF, Bien Hoa
Maj Joseph Bradshaw Baggett (KIA)

The Skoshi Tiger evaluation had been running for nearly two months before the Squadron suffered its first casualty. Maj Baggett was one of the Squadron's flight commanders and his aircraft was hit by automatic weapons fire during a strafing run near Duc Hoa, just 10 miles west of Tan Son Nhut airfield. The aircraft caught fire and the wingman advised Maj Baggett to eject. Joe Baggett initiated the ejection but as the seat fired the rocket motor broke away and hit the pilot's helmet. The Major was recovered by a rescue helicopter but died later in the day from his injuries.

AC-47 Gunship I

Coincidental with the increased US involvement in Southeast Asia, the USAF had been experimenting with the concept of side-firing fixed-wing gunships as a means of providing heavy fire support in low-threat environments. Following successful trials at Eglin AFB with a modified Convair C-131 in 1963 and 1964 the USAF modified two of the 1st ACS's C-47s at Bien Hoa in December 1964 to gunship standard as an operational trial. The fixed-wing gunship concept involved the aircraft maintaining a constant banked turn about 3,000 feet above the target. Firepower was provided by three 7.62mm Gatling-type guns firing through the side windows. As it was envisaged that the C-47's size and performance would limit its use primarily to night operations, each aircraft carried an ample supply of flares with which to illuminate the target. The system was ideal for the protection of isolated outposts and camps that were increasingly coming under Viet Cong attack at night.

The trial in South Vietnam proved the potential of the gunship concept and further aircraft were modified in the USA. The 4th ACS arrived at Tan Son Nhut on 14 November 1965 with 20 gunships and had flown 277 operational sorties by the end of the year. Initially designated the FC-47, the gunships were soon redesignated as the AC-47D and were quickly nicknamed Puff the Magic Dragon or simply Dragonship due to their apparent fire-breathing capability as they spat out thousands of rounds of tracer. To the crews who flew them, the aircraft also became known as Spooky, after the Squadron's radio call sign. Once established at Tan Son Nhut the Squadron deployed flights of four aircraft to Da Nang, Pleiku, Nha Trang and Bin Thuy to provide gunship support throughout the country. Twelve of the 47 AC-47s sent to Southeast Asia would be lost during the war.

17 December 1965

AC-47D   43-49492   4 ACS, 6250 CSG, USAF, Tan Son Nhut
Maj Robert William Abbot (KIA)
Maj Robert Lloyd Abernathy (KIA)
1Lt Francis Richard Buckley (KIA)
MSgt Joseph Anthony Cestaric (KIA)
TSgt John Monroe Chappell (KIA)
TSgt Thomas Newton Sloan (KIA)
SSgt Ralph Leon Hinson (KIA)
A1C Claude Wesley Mathews (KIA)
A1C Johnson Ashley Meade (KIA)

Although the first AC-47 gunships arrived on 14 November, their

guns had been removed before leaving the USA in order to reduce the weight for the long trans-Pacific flight. The guns did not arrive in Vietnam for another month and in the meantime the Squadron was put to work flying courier and cargo missions. It was on one of the last courier missions flown that the 4th ACS lost its first aircraft and crew. The aircraft went missing during a night cross country courier flight between Tan Son Nhut and Phan Rang. The wreckage was found on 23 December and the indications were that the aircraft had been shot down by ground fire. By the end of the year about 20 AC-47s had reached South Vietnam.

O-1E   57-2873   19 TASS, 505 TACG, USAF, Bien Hoa
Capt Donald Rey Hawley (KIA)

During a forward air control mission a Bird Dog was shot down by ground fire 10 miles northwest of its base at Bien Hoa, killing the pilot. Despite heavy ground fire in the area necessitating many suppressive air strikes, an HH-43 landed to retrieve Capt Hawley's body.

A-4C   148510   VA-113, USN, USS *Kitty Hawk*
Lt David Wallace Wickham (KIA)

When returning from an armed reconnaissance mission a Skyhawk encountered air turbulence on the approach to the *Kitty Hawk* and crashed on the carrier's deck.

19 December 1965

F-4C   63-7527   433 TFS, 8 TFW, USAF, Ubon
Capt R S Kan (survived)
1Lt J L Moran (survived)

The 8th TFW transferred from George AFB, California to Ubon on 8 December with two squadrons of Phantoms, the 433rd and 497th. The Wing was known as the Wolfpack and its main task was to provide fighter escorts for the F-105 bombers during Rolling Thunder raids. It later became involved in day and night interdiction missions over the Ho Chi Minh Trail.

On the return journey from escorting a strike on a road bridge at Bac Can, one of the 8th TFW's Phantoms was damaged by a near miss from an SA-2 missile 35 miles due west of Hanoi. The Phantom was at 20,000 feet when the missile detonated on the aircraft's starboard side causing major damage. Capt Kan nursed his crippled aircraft 250 miles across North Vietnam, over Laos and into Thailand but unfortunately the aircraft became uncontrollable and the crew had to eject at a point about 15 miles east of Nakhon Phanom. The crew was on their first mission of their tour of duty.

Wild Weasel I

Although only nine US aircraft had been destroyed by SAMs up to the end of November 1965, the growing threat posed by the SA-2 was taken very seriously. Soon after the first SAM was fired in North Vietnam, the USAF formed a task force to devise a way to counter the new threat. It was quickly established that the weakest point of the SA-2 system was the missile's reliance on its Fan Song target-tracking radar that was usually situated within or very close to the star-shaped missile battery site. One way to counter the SAM threat was to jam the target acquisition and tracking radar using modified RB-66 aircraft. However, it was also realised that a more aggressive approach was needed and the USAF task force put forward another solution.

The result of the investigation was a program that became known as Wild Weasel I and involved the use of two-seat F-100Fs modified to carry newly-developed avionics. The system consisted primarily of the AN/APR-25 radar homing and warning receiver which gave a warning and the bearing of an active enemy radar; the AN/APR-26 tuned crystal receiver which detected a missile launch as the strength of the SA-2's guidance signal increased just before lift off; and the IR-133 panoramic receiver which gave a longer range indication of the type of threat by signal analysis. The receivers could also detect whether the radar was either SAM, AAA or early warning but none of the equipment could give an indication of range from the enemy radar.

The first four of a total of seven F-100Fs were modified and delivered to Eglin AFB where the system was to be tested in early

September 1965. The original five Weasel crews consisted of F-100 pilots together with electronic warfare officers (who were usually known simply as 'EWOs' or 'Bears') from the B-52 and B-66 communities. As the Weasel mission depended very much on teamwork the crews were allowed to team up and usually flew together. After several weeks of testing and training the four aircraft left Eglin for Korat on 21 November, arriving there four days later. The unit was still regarded as being a test unit and was attached to the 6234th TFW at Korat.

The Wild Weasels flew their first operational mission on 1 December when two F-100Fs led a flight of F-105s to a target in North Vietnam. The Weasels flew either as part of a Rolling Thunder strike force or, usually accompanied by a small number of strike aircraft, on search and destroy missions not necessarily connected to any ongoing strike. The Weasels usually flew some minutes ahead of the strike force with the EWO listening for any indication that their aircraft had been illuminated by a SAM radar. When a radar was heard the EWO vectored the pilot towards it. If the Weasel could get close enough to see it before a missile was launched, it would attack the site (aiming, if possible, for the radar antenna or control van) thereby marking it for the accompanying flight of F-105s to complete the destruction with bombs and napalm. If, however, a missile was launched before the site could be attacked, the Weasel pilot used a manoeuvre that was developed early on and usually worked. If the pilot could see the missile tracking towards him, he waited until he judged that it was close enough and then broke hard towards it in a diving turn. This manoeuvre was usually sufficient to break the missile radar's lock on the target which could not then be re-acquired in time before the SA-2 passed the aircraft and exploded way beyond it or on the ground. In the early Weasel missions the F-100Fs carried LAU-3 rockets and napalm but later it was found that 500lb or 750lb bombs or CBUs were the most effective weapons.

The Wild Weasels got their first confirmed kill against a SAM site hidden in a village near the Red River on 22 December during a Rolling Thunder strike on a railway yard at Yen Bai. Three more F-100Fs arrived at Korat in February 1966 and two months later the first AGM-45A Shrike anti-radiation missiles were received. The Navy-developed Shrike used a passive homing receiver to ride the SAM's radar beam back to its source, the Fan Song radar, which it then destroyed. The first Shrike was fired by the USAF on 18 April 1966 but its effective range of 10-12 miles limited its effectiveness and it was eventually replaced by the Standard ARM. The US Navy had been fitting some of its Iron Hand Skyhawks with Shrikes for about year by this time. VA-23 was the first Navy squadron to fire the Shrike on 23 April 1965 but the A-4 lacked the specialist avionics that the Weasels carried.

20 December 1965

F-105D   61-0090   354 TFS, 355 TFW, USAF, Takhli
Capt John S Ruffo (survived)

On the 20th the USAF flew a strike against the Vu Chua railway bridge, seven miles northeast of Kep, on the main railway line from China and just a few miles from the Lang Met Bridge. During the raid an F-105 was hit by AAA but the pilot was able to head southeast and cross the coast before he had to part company with his aircraft. He came under fire from the shore and from a number of small boats that made towards him but he was rescued by one of the ever-present USAF HU-16s piloted by Maj W Dewitt.

F-4C   64-0678   433 TFS, 8 TFW, USAF, Ubon
1Lt George Ivison Mims (KIA)
Capt Robert Duncan Jeffrey (POW)

Minutes after Capt Russo's aircraft had been hit one of four Ubon Phantoms which had been escorting the bombers was hit by an 85mm shell about 10 miles to the east of the bridge. The aircraft was seen to explode and it was thought by other pilots who saw the incident that neither of the crew could have survived. However, on 12 February 1973 during the initial release as part of Operation Homecoming, Bob Jeffrey emerged from a North Vietnamese prison. Miraculously, Capt Jeffrey had ejected through the fireball of his exploding Phantom and was captured soon

after landing. The pilot's fate was unknown but most probably he died when the aircraft exploded.

Bob Jeffrey was actually a rated F-102 and F-4 pilot and had been in theatre for three days when he was shot down. He was on his first mission and was probably taking a back seat with an experienced pilot before flying his own aircraft. Early in the war Phantoms were crewed by two pilots but this practice later changed as it meant the unnecessary loss of two pilots when a crew was lost. Trained navigators or weapons systems officers were also better able to assist a pilot than another pilot who may not have been proficient in the aircraft's navigation or weapon systems. Bob Jeffrey's wife was told unofficially that there was very little hope that Bob was alive. His son was 10 months old when Bob was shot down: he was eight years old when Bob was released. This is indicative of the problem faced by many POWs. In some cases the years of incarceration caused permanent marital rifts, although the majority of wives and families just waited and hoped and suffered until the men returned home.

F-100F 58-1231   Wild Weasel Detachment, 6234 TFW,
                  USAF, Korat
                  Capt John Joseph Pitchford (POW)
                  Capt Robert Douglas Trier (KIA)

Capt Pitchford and his EWO, Capt Trier, were one of the original Wild Weasel crews. John Pitchford had flown the Super Sabre with the 27th TFW at Cannon AFB and had just completed a course at the Fighter Weapons School at Nellis AFB when he was posted to the Wild Weasel project at Eglin. On their third mission over North Vietnam Pitchford and Trier led a flight of 12 F-105s on a Rolling Thunder strike near Kep airfield. About 20 miles northeast of Haiphong, as the aircraft was flying over a cloud layer, it was hit in the rear fuselage by a large calibre anti-aircraft shell. Pitchford fired his rockets in the general area of a radar that was tracking him, and the F-105s dropped their bombs on the site and then followed the stricken F-100F to assist. With the aircraft on fire John Pitchford tried to reach the safety of the Gulf of Tonkin but when the hydraulics failed the aircraft pitched into an uncontrollable dive and the crew were forced to eject. The two men landed about 800 yards from each other and John Pitchford was quickly captured after being shot three times in the right arm. The North Vietnamese told Pitchford that Robert Trier was killed in a shoot out while resisting capture. His remains were returned to the USA on 3 November 1982. After his release on 12 February 1973 John Pitchford resumed his Air Force career and retired as a Colonel.

C-130E 62-1843   345 TCS, 314 TCW, USAF, Sewart
                  1Lt Donald Clayton Smith (KIA)
                  1Lt David J Wax (KIA)
                  Capt Terry Fisher Katterhenry (KIA)
                  TSgt William Henry Crisp (KIA)
                  A1C Willie Mitchell (KIA)

One of the losses on this day was the first Hercules assumed to be lost in the air to enemy action. The aircraft was attempting to land at Tuy Hoa under a very low cloud base when it was hit by ground fire five miles south of the air base and crashed killing all the crew. The Hercules (the first C-130E model lost in the war) was temporarily based at Nha Trang and was bringing in a load of 13 tons of aviation fuel and it was 1Lt Smith's first mission as aircraft commander. Enemy action was never actually confirmed to have caused the loss of this aircraft which may simply have flown into high ground in poor visibility. For some reason the remains of 1Lt Wax were not recovered and identified until December 1996. The serial 62-1843 is still carried today by an MC-130E of the 711th SOS.

RA-5C 151624   RVAH-13, USN, USS Kitty Hawk
                Lt Cdr Guy David Johnson (KIA)
                Lt(jg) Lee Edward Nordahl (KIA)

Following recent raids on the Uong Bi thermal power plant two Vigilantes, together with an escort, set off to obtain BDA photographs of the site. Radio contact with one of the Vigilantes was lost at about the time it should have been over the target. Nothing was heard from the aircraft and there was no sign of any wreckage but it was strongly suspected that the aircraft had been

shot down near the coast in the vicinity of Hon Gay. On 18 March 1977 the mortal remains of Guy Johnson, who had been promoted to Captain during the time he was regarded as missing in action, were handed over to US authorities by the Vietnamese. Post-war evidence indicates that Lee Nordahl was captured but probably died of wounds soon afterwards.

21 December 1965

A-6A 151781   VA-85, USN, USS Kitty Hawk
                Cdr Billie Jack Cartwright (KIA)
                Lt Edward Frank Gold (KIA)

On board the Kitty Hawk when it arrived off Vietnam in late November was VA-85, the Navy's second Intruder squadron. The Intruder's introduction to combat with the Independence in July had been something of a disaster with four aircraft lost, three of them destroyed by their own bombs. It was confidently expected that VA-85 would perform better, although not all the aircraft's advanced electronic systems were yet operating satisfactorily. However, VA-85's Intruders did have a radar warning receiver fitted which would alert the crew when their aircraft was being tracked by enemy radar.

The squadron lost its first aircraft during a night attack on a road bridge on the outskirts of Haiphong. Several Intruders were making coordinated runs over the bridge but one aircraft failed to call in over the target. The radar operator in an orbiting E-2 Hawkeye over the Gulf of Tonkin reported that the aircraft's radar return disappeared from his screen about 20 miles north of Haiphong on the way to the target. Two other aircraft noted SAM firings in the area but no hits were reported. The approach to the target was over mountainous terrain and the penetration altitude was 4,000 feet. The standard procedure at that time to counter a SAM was to dive towards the ground to attempt to break the missile's radar lock. It was surmised that the Intruder attempted this manoeuvre at night over the mountains and flew into the ground. VA-85 had got off to a bad start but the loss was made even worse as the aircraft was flown by Cdr Cartwright, the Squadron's CO. The Squadron never really recovered from this disaster and went on to lose a further six aircraft during the cruise. Lt Gold's remains were handed over and identified in January 1995.

F-105D 59-1823   421 TFS, 6234 TFW, USAF, Korat
                  Capt James V Sullivan (survived)

A flight of F-105s was sent to bomb a small bridge near Ha Tinh, 20 miles south of Vinh, and one of the aircraft was hit by 57mm AAA in the rear fuselage. Despite a fire fed by aviation fuel, the pilot flew the Thud nearly 30 miles to the south near the border with Laos before having to eject. A HC-54 co-ordinated a rescue force of HH-3s and A-1E escorts. The rescue was made more difficult by low cloud, and the helicopter pilot, Capt Butera, had to be guided through cloud to the survivor's position by one of the Skyraider pilots who had arrived on the scene earlier. Capt Sullivan was picked up by the helicopter and taken to Udorn for the customary celebrations that took place after each successful rescue.

22 December 1965

A-4C 149521   VA-76, USN, USS Enterprise
                Lt John Douglas Prudhomme (KIA)

A-4C 148305   VA-36, USN, USS Enterprise
                Lt(jg) Wendell Reed Alcorn (POW)

The Uong Bi power plant was the target of yet another raid on the 22nd. Around 100 aircraft from the Enterprise, Kitty Hawk and Ticonderoga took part in the strike and the power plant was reported to be left in a shambles. The Enterprise group approached the target from the north and lost an aircraft from two its four Skyhawk squadrons. John Prudhomme was No2 in a 4-plane section that approached at low level to drop Snakeye retarded bombs. As the section made a left turn over the target, Prudhomme's aircraft was seen to level its wings and fly into the ground. There was a lot of flak in the sky around the target and the other members of the flight suspected that the pilot had been hit and incapacitated, causing the aircraft to crash.

A few minutes after Prudhomme was shot down a flight of Skyhawks from VA-36 approached the target at 150 feet and 450 knots. Just after releasing its bombs, 'Ray' Alcorn's aircraft was hit in the cockpit by small arms fire. Alcorn was wounded in the neck and shoulder but his biggest problem was his oxygen mask which caught fire forcing him to eject. Badly wounded, Alcorn was captured and spent the next seven years in prison. He was shot down on his 29th mission and was released from captivity on 12 February 1973. After recovering from his ordeal Wendell Alcorn completed jet refresher training and joined VA-174 flying the A-7E Corsair. He later commanded VT-25, a training squadron, then took a number of staff jobs and finally commanded NAS Fallon before retiring as a Captain. Uong Bi power station was severely damaged during this raid and produced little power for the next few weeks.

RA-5C 151632   RVAH-13, USN, USS Kitty Hawk
                Lt Cdr Max Duane Lukenbach (KIA)
                Lt(jg) Glenn Henri Daigle (POW)

About one hour after the Uong Bi strike a Navy Vigilante approached the Hai Duong railway bridge to obtain reconnaissance photographs for a raid planned for the next day. The aircraft was flying at 3,000 feet between two layers of cloud close to the target when the NFO saw puffs of smoke from AAA bursts and then heard the aircraft being hit several times. He thought that the pilot was incapacitated as there was no response from him when the aircraft became uncontrollable. Daigle ejected but Lukenbach died in the crash and was reported to have been buried close to the wreckage. This loss is reported in some sources as being caused by an SA-2 SAM but there is no direct evidence of this. Glenn Daigle was released from captivity on 12 February 1973.

23 December 1965

A-4C 149562   VA-94, USN, USS Enterprise
                Lt(jg) William Leonard Shankel (POW)

Despite the loss of the Vigilante the previous day, the raid on the Hai Duong Bridge went ahead as planned. Bill Shankel was in the second section of Skyhawks to attack the bridge and was some distance behind the others as his aircraft was not performing as well as it should. He pulled up and dived on the target and just as he released his Mk83 bombs the Skyhawk was hit in the undersides by ground fire. The aircraft caught fire and smoke filled the cockpit and entered Shankel's oxygen mask. After less than a minute the controls went limp and the aircraft rolled inverted as Shankel ejected a few miles south of Hai Duong town. He was quickly captured and joined Alcorn and Daigle who had been shot down the previous day. The three were all released in Operation Homecoming on 12 February 1973 and Bill Shankel became a surgeon in Nevada.

A-1H serial ..?   unit ..?, USAF, base ..?
                    Capt James Carl Wise (KIA)

Little is known about this incident except that Capt Wise was killed during an armed reconnaissance mission in Hua Nghia province northwest of Saigon in a single-seat Skyraider, probably an aircraft belonging to the VNAF.

U-10B 63-13093   5 ACS, 6253 CSG, USAF, Nha Trang
                  2 crew, names unknown (survived)

The 5th ACS was formed at Nha Trang in August 1965 to specialise in psychological warfare operations. Initially its equipment consisted of four C-47s but, on 20 November, 17 brand new Helio U-10Bs arrived from the USA on board the USS Breton. The Squadron's primary role was the dissemination of propaganda and other forms of psychological warfare. Its aircraft were fitted with loudspeakers for broadcasting to Viet Cong (or potential Viet

The strategic transport aircraft of Military Airlift Command were frequent visitors to South Vietnam hauling troops and supplies to and from the USA. This C-124C Globemaster is pictured taking off from Pleiku in December 1965 having brought in troops of the 25th Infantry Division from Hawaii.
USAF

Cong) and the aircraft were also used to drop leaflets encouraging Viet Cong to surrender or to warn friendly villagers of air strikes or defoliation missions in their area. This was the first of the new batch of U-10Bs to be destroyed when it crashed on landing.

The First Bombing Halt
President Johnson announced a cessation of the bombing campaign in North Vietnam from Christmas Eve. This was done in the hope that the damage that the US assumed it was inflicting on the North would encourage Ho Chi Minh to start peace negotiations. The first bombing halt lasted for just over a month but with little sign of any reciprocal gesture from the North Vietnamese the Rolling Thunder campaign was resumed on 31 January 1966.

24 December 1965

F-8E   150891   VF-211, USN, USS *Hancock*
                    Cdr P H Spear (survived)
The USS *Hancock* returned to Vietnamese waters for re-assignment to TF 77 on 6 December following a seven-month break. It assumed duties at Dixie Station on the 17th and had its first aircraft loss on Christmas Eve. When returning from a CAP mission, a Crusader pilot misjudged his approach and landing and crashed onto the deck, destroying the aircraft.

AC-47D   45-1120   4 ACS, 6250 CSG, USAF, Tan Son Nhut
                     Maj Derrell Blackburn Jeffords (KIA)
                     1Lt Dennis Lee Eilers (KIA)
                     Maj Joseph Christiano (KIA)
                     MSgt Larry C Thornton (KIA)
                     TSgt William Kevin Colwell (KIA)
                     SSgt Arden Keith Hassenger (KIA)
A few hours before the Christmas bombing halt was due to come into effect, an AC-47 gunship took off from Da Nang for a daylight mission over southern Laos looking for targets of opportunity. When the aircraft was a few miles south of Ban Bac, a mayday call from Spooky 21 was heard by other aircraft in the area but there was no further radio contact with the gunship.

No trace of the wreckage or crew was ever found although unconfirmed reports suggest that Christiano and Hassenger were captured by the Pathet Lao after escaping from the aircraft. If these reports are true then the men disappeared in Laos and have not yet been accounted for.

O-1E   56-4166   21 TASS, 505 TACG, USAF, Pleiku
                     1Lt C W Hastings (survived)
                     Capt R L Kuiper (survived)
During a visual reconnaissance sortie over South Vietnam a Bird Dog pilot was requested to mark the position of friendly troops. During the mission the aircraft crash-landed (probably due to ground fire) injuring both the crew.

26 December 1965

F-8E   150843   VF-53, USN, USS *Ticonderoga*
                    Lt(jg) W S Brougher (survived)
A repeat of the Crusader landing accident on Christmas Eve happened on board the *Ticonderoga* on Boxing Day with the same results, a broken aircraft and a chastened pilot.

A-1E   52-132637   602 ACS, 3 TFW, USAF, Bien Hoa
                     Maj Louis Raymond Raleigh (KWF)
During a test flight a Skyraider crashed near Bien Hoa due to a technical malfunction and the pilot was killed.

28 December 1965

F-4B   151412   VF-92, USN, USS *Enterprise*
                    Cdr Edgar Arthur Rawsthorne (KIA)
                    Lt Arthur Sinclair Hill (KIA)
After several tough missions over North Vietnam the *Enterprise* was tasked with a spell of armed reconnaissance in the Steel Tiger area of southern Laos, a supposedly 'easy' mission. Cdr Rawsthorne, the CO of VF-92, and his NFO, Lt Hill, were flying a night road reconnaissance along the Mu Gia Pass on the border of North Vietnam and Laos on the lookout for trucks. The wingman saw his leader drop flares and then attack a target with LAU-10 unguided rockets. He then saw the Commander's Phan-

tom crash into the side of a ridge near Ban Pondong, five miles west of the Pass. There was no ground fire seen at the time and it was thought that the aircraft flew into the ground while trying to pull out of its dive.

F-4B   151438   VF-96, USN, USS *Enterprise*
                    Lt Dean H Forsgren (survived)
                    Lt(jg) Robert M Jewell (survived)
Atrocious weather caused one of the *Enterprise's* Phantoms to run short of fuel when attempting to land back on the ship from an armed reconnaissance mission. It is not known if this occurred on the same mission as that described above. With eight aircraft lost during its first month of operations, the *Enterprise* was suffering from appallingly bad luck which must have affected morale on board the Navy's 'Supercarrier'.

29 December 1965

F-100D   55-3719   416 TFS, 3 TFW, USAF, Tan Son Nhut
                     Capt C M Schlick (survived)
During a direct air support mission a Super Sabre was shot down by ground fire but the pilot ejected and was rescued by an Army helicopter.

A-4E   150019   VMA-211, MAG-12, USMC, Chu Lai
                    1Lt Thomas Farrell Eldridge (KIA)
VMA-211 arrived at Chu Lai on 11 October bringing MAG-12 up to full strength as its fourth Skyhawk squadron. VMA-211's first loss and the Marine's first Skyhawk combat loss in Vietnam took place near Minh Long, 30 miles south of Chu Lai. A flight of Skyhawks was escorting a formation of Marine Corps helicopters in an attempt to resupply a besieged South Vietnamese district headquarters. As the helicopters approached their objective they came under fire from three heavy machine guns. 1Lt Eldridge rolled in on the target and dropped his napalm but his aircraft was hit by .50 calibre machine gun fire. Thomas Eldridge was wounded in the leg during the attack and although he managed to fly 20 miles north towards his airfield the Skyhawk crashed near An Cuong and Eldridge was killed.

Chapter Three

1966
Rolling Thunder Gets into its Stride

2 January 1966

O-1F   57-2889   19 TASS, 505 TACG, USAF, Bien Hoa
Capt Harlow Kenneth Halbower (KIA)
The first USAF casualty of the new year was an FAC pilot whose Bird Dog was shot down in flames by ground fire near Duc Hoa, 18 miles west of Tan Son Nhut. Capt Halbower was a graduate of the very first class at the Air Force Academy in 1959 and was the first member of his class to die in Southeast Asia.

A-4C   147704   VA-76, USN, USS *Enterprise*
Lt(jg) Donald Clay MacLaughlin (KIA)
With the bombing halt on operations over North Vietnam being extended into January, the US Navy turned its attention to operations over South Vietnam and Laos. The *Enterprise* sent two Skyhawks on a mission to bomb a suspected VC storage area near Duc Pho, not far from the coast south of Quang Ngai. The weather over the target consisted of low cloud and fog on the ground as the leader made a pass over the target and called Lt MacLaughlin to commence his attack. However, MacLaughlin reported that he had lost sight of the target and was then told to pull up and hold clear of the clouds. After the leader completed his second pass he tried to contact MacLaughlin but without success. Later the wreckage of the aircraft was spotted on the slopes of a hill near the target and although a SAR helicopter managed to land near the site the following day and its crew spotted MacLaughlin's body, they were unable to retrieve it due to enemy fire.

3 January 1966

A-1J   142081   VA-52, USN, USS *Ticonderoga*
Lt J W Donahue (survived)
A VC troop concentration near Phu Cuong, 10 miles north of Saigon, was the target for a section of Skyraiders from the *Ticonderoga*. On his ninth strafing pass, Lt Donahue's aircraft was hit in the fuselage by automatic weapon fire setting his aircraft alight. He coaxed the aircraft about 10 miles away from the enemy concentration before having to crash-land. Luckily, he

was rescued unharmed by a US Army helicopter before the VC could reach him. This aircraft was the last of 72 AD-7s (later redesignated A-1Js) built and therefore the final Skyraider to be constructed.

4 January 1966

C-123B   56-4369   315 ACG, USAF, Tan Son Nhut
5 crew, names unknown (survived)
A Provider suffered engine failure and crash-landed in South Vietnam without fatalities. The aircraft may have been on a flare-dropping mission.

5 January 1966

O-1E   56-4171   probably 20 TASS, 505 TACG, USAF,
Da Nang detached to Khe Sanh
A mortar attack at the Khe Sanh Special Forces Camp destroyed a USAF Bird Dog. The strategic location of Khe Sanh close to the DMZ and the Laotian border became even more important as North Vietnamese forces started to infiltrate into the area in large numbers at this time. Khe Sanh was also an important forward operating base for the FAC aircraft that controlled strikes in the Tiger Hound region of southern Laos and around the DMZ.

6 January 1966

C-130B   61-0972   774 TCS, 463 TCW, USAF, Mactan
Capt Richard Joseph Callanan (KIA)
Capt Lee Christopher Dixon (KIA)
1Lt Jon Alfred Greenley (KIA)
SSgt James Robert Lute (KIA)
A2C Lowell Franklin White (KIA)
The second Hercules to be brought down by ground fire in South Vietnam during the war was hit during a dawn resupply mission just east of Pleiku. The aircraft was from the 463rd TCW at Mactan AB in the Philippines and was temporarily based at Tan Son Nhut during the unit's rotation in Vietnam.

9 January 1966

F-100D   56-3166   3 TFW, USAF, Bien Hoa
Capt Louis Kenneth Kanaar (KIA)
A flight of Super Sabres was attacking an enemy strongpoint just south of Xa Thanh Binh, 35 miles north of Bien Hoa, when one of the aircraft was shot down. Capt Kanaar was on his third pass over the target dropping napalm in an attempt to silence a gun position when his aircraft was hit by 12.7mm AAA. He climbed his aircraft, with his starboard wing on fire, and headed away from the area but a short while later the aircraft crashed and, although Capt Kanaar ejected, he was killed.

C-123B   54-0676   315 ACG, USAF, Tan Son Nhut
Capt Coulter (survived)
Capt Bagnant (survived)
During a dusk resupply flight a fire started in the fuselage of a Provider. The aircraft crash-landed, fortunately without serious injury, but the aircraft was destroyed. The cause was suspected to be sabotage, probably involving the cargo carried in the aircraft. This was a constant worry in South Vietnam where many Vietnamese worked at American airfields. The political persuasion of some workers was not always apparent.

C-130B   61-0970   774 TCS, 463 TCW, USAF, Mactan
5 crew, names unknown (survived)
During a resupply mission another Hercules on temporary duty at Tan Son Nhut from Mactan was accidentally damaged beyond repair during a landing at the airstrip at An Khe in the Central Highlands.

10 January 1966

F-4B   152218   VMFA-323, MAG-11, USMC, Da Nang
1Lt G E Perry (survived)
1Lt R T Morrissey (survived)
The first Marine Corps aircraft lost in 1966 fell victim to its own weapons. As a Phantom was attacking a VC target near Phuoc Binh, 20 miles south of Da Nang, one of its bombs exploded prematurely. The crew ejected and were picked up by helicopter but the pilot, 1Lt Perry, suffered major injuries. After flying 1,567 combat sorties in three months VMFA-323 was redeployed to Tainan AB, Taiwan on 1 March for air defence alert duties but returned to Vietnam later in the year.

11 January 1966

F-105D   59-1736   334 TFS, 4 TFW attached to 355 TFW,
USAF, Takhli
Capt J R Stell (survived)
Although the bombing halt prevented strikes on North Vietnam the F-105s from Takhli and Korat were still kept busy flying armed reconnaissance and strikes in Laos. During one such mission a flight of Thuds attacked a bridge five miles east of Ban Ban in northern Laos. As one of the aircraft pulled up from its dive it was hit in the fuselage by ground fire and started to burn. Capt Stell ejected a few miles from the bridge but was picked up safely by a USAF HH-3.

The importance of the O-1 Bird Dog to the war in South Vietnam and Laos is shown by the fact that 469 were lost by the Army, Marines and the Air Force during the war, more than any other fixed-wing type other than the F-4 Phantom. USAF

Although little used in their primary anti-submarine warfare role, the S-2 Tracker squadrons played their part by flying SAR, sea surveillance and radar coverage missions. This S-2E is landing on board the USS *Bennington*, one of the four ASW carriers deployed to Southeast Asia during the war. USN

A-1H   serial ..?   unit ..?, USAF, base ..?
                    Capt Johnny Howard Godfrey (KIA)
Capt Godfrey was killed when strafing a target in Ba Xuyen province in South Vietnam. As the USAF was not yet using any single-seat versions of the Skyraider, it is assumed that he was flying with the VNAF, possibly as an instructor, at the time of his death.

12 January 1966

A-1E   52-132468   1 ACS, 3 TFW, USAF, Pleiku
                    2 crew, names unknown (survived)
The 1st ACS moved from Bien Hoa to Pleiku in November 1965 due to the worsening military situation in the Central Highlands. The Squadron remained attached to the 3rd TFW for the time being. The first Skyraider lost by the Squadron following its move was destroyed in a landing accident.

B-57B   53-3876   13 TBS, 405 FW attached to 6252 TFW,
                    USAF, Da Nang
                    Maj Elijah Goar Tollett (KIA)
                    Capt Leon Boyd Smith (KIA)
During its take off from Da Nang for an armed reconnaissance mission, a Canberra crashed and exploded killing both the crew. The aircraft's nosewheel collapsed but the pilot managed to lift the nose and the aircraft staggered into the air. The pilot raised the undercarriage in an attempt to climb away but the aircraft settled back onto the runway and slid off onto soft earth. It eventually came to a halt several hundred feet from the runway and the crew jumped out. Tragically, before they could make their escape, one of the aircraft's 500lb bombs exploded killing both men and destroying the aircraft. The rest of the aircraft's ordnance detonated and it was over an hour before fire crews could get close to the wreck.

13 January 1966

A-1E   52-133989   1 ACS, 3 TFW, USAF, Pleiku
                    Capt Robert Neal Middlebrooks (KIA)

C-123B   55-4519   310 ACS, 315 ACG, USAF, Nha Trang
                    Capt Warren Lester Anderson (KIA)
                    Capt Herman Hiram Ritchie (KIA)
                    TSgt Thomas Anthony Fodaro (KIA)
                    TSgt Irwin Lewis Hoffman (KIA)
                    SSgt Byron Hugh Crotwell (KIA)
                    SSgt Edward Joseph Hincewicz (KIA)
Night operations in aircraft with limited avionics and with poor ground radar coverage is always risky. During a night mission near An Khe a Skyraider from Pleiku was attacking VC positions under the light provided by a C-123 flareship. The Skyraider made its pass but then pulled up into the path of the Provider,

the two aircraft colliding at about 1,200 feet, too low for any of the occupants to escape.

14 January 1966

A-4C   147753   VA-36, USN, USS *Enterprise*
                    Lt(jg) S B Jordan (survived)
The US Navy flew many air strikes in the Steel Tiger region of southern Laos during the bombing halt. A section of Skyhawks from the *Enterprise* was sent to bomb a bridge 35 miles northwest of Saravan using Snakeye retarded bombs. On his fifth pass Lt Jordan came too low and hit trees just after releasing a bomb. The aircraft began to stream fuel and a close inspection revealed extensive damage. Both wings had lost about a foot off each wingtip, the slats were partially torn off, the ailerons damaged (one of them was bent vertical), and the main landing gear doors were badly damaged. Miraculously, the aircraft remained controllable and Lt Jordan made it back to the *Enterprise* but he was unable to jettison his last bomb and had to eject near the carrier.

16 January 1966

F-4C   63-7469   559 TFS, 12 TFW, USAF, Cam Ranh Bay
                    Capt J A Gagan (survived)
                    1Lt F M Malagarie (survived)
The 559th TFS had been in South Vietnam for a little over two weeks before it lost its first aircraft. A flight of Phantoms was sent to attack a supply area near Ban Ralao in southern Laos. Capt Gagan was strafing on his sixth run over the target when his aircraft was hit by small arms fire. Although strafing with the Phantom's SUU-16 or SUU-23 gun pod was devastating, it required the aircraft to come down low where it was vulnerable to rifle and machine gun bullets as well as heavier calibre weapons. Even at 400 mph and 500 feet a single bullet in the wrong place can bring down a 20-ton fighter. The crew ejected soon after the aircraft caught fire and they were rescued by a USAF HH-43 helicopter.

F-105D   59-1719   354 TFS, 355 TFW, USAF, Takhli
                    Capt Don Charles Wood (POW-died)
Five Thunderchiefs flew a combat mission over the communist-held Plain of Jars in northern Laos. Capt Wood had commenced his third strafing run against an anti-aircraft gun position near Ban Xal when a 37mm shell hit his aircraft. The F-105 crashed soon after being hit and it was not known if Capt Wood had ejected despite an extensive aerial search of the area. However, it was later reported that he had been identified in a Pathet Lao film showing several Americans POWs and may have been held in the caves near Sam Neua with Shelton and Hrdlicka. In addition, his ID card was later found in a Hanoi museum. Whatever his fate, Don Wood has not yet returned from Southeast Asia.

B-57B   53-3903   13 TBS, 405 FW attached to 6252 TFW,
                    USAF, Da Nang
                    Capt Hugh M Davidson (survived)
                    Capt Edward J Cook (survived)
A second Canberra was lost within the space of four days when an aircraft suffered an engine failure as it was returning from an armed reconnaissance mission. The aircraft crashed into the sea off Da Nang after the crew ejected safely.

F-8C   147012   VF-24, USN, USS *Hancock*
                    Lt Cdr Frederick Albert Neth (KWF)
During a training flight a Crusader from VF-24 was practising carrier landings on the *Hancock* off the coast of South Vietnam when its tail hook sheared as it caught a wire. The aircraft continued over the side and the pilot was drowned when the aircraft sank.

RA-5C   149312   RVAH-9, USN, USS *Ranger*
                    Lt Cdr Charles David Schoonover (KIA)
                    Ensign Hal T Hollingsworth (KIA)
A Vigilante was lost the day after the *Ranger* returned to line duty on its second tour of the war. The aircraft returned from a reconnaissance flight over South Vietnam and was making a bolter or touch and go landing when its starboard engine exploded as full power was applied. The aircraft crashed and both crew were killed. The ship was about 60 miles from the mouth of the Mekong Delta at the time of the accident.

20 January 1966

F-105D   59-1717   333 TFS, 355 TFW, USAF, Takhli
                    1 pilot, name unknown (survived)

F-105D   62-4324   333 TFS, 355 TFW, USAF, Takhli
                    1 pilot, name unknown (survived)
On two separate missions during the same day two Thunderchiefs from Takhli suffered engine failures and crashed. Fortunately, both pilots ejected and were picked up safely. Thunderchief 59-1717 was the first aircraft from the second production batch of F-105s and was delivered to the USAF in 1961.

21/22 January 1966

S-2D   149252   VS-35, USN, USS *Hornet*
                    Lt William Stannard Forman (KIA)
                    Lt(jg) Erwin Bernard Templin (KIA)
                    SN Edmund Henry Frenyea (KIA)
                    SA Robert Russell Sennett (KIA)
Four anti-submarine carriers saw service in the South China Sea and the Gulf of Tonkin during the war: the USS *Bennington*, *Hornet*, *Kearsarge* and *Yorktown*. Their role in the war was unspectacular compared to the larger attack carriers but they

nevertheless performed important functions including anti-submarine patrols, search and rescue, sea surveillance, radar coverage and airborne early warning. The main fixed-wing aircraft flown by the ASW carriers was the S-2 Tracker.

On the night of 21/22 January a Tracker was launched from the *Hornet* to provide surveillance cover for the SAR destroyers that operated close to the North Vietnamese coastline and which were occasionally challenged by enemy patrol boats and small craft. Under the control of a guided missile destroyer, the USS *Berkeley*, the Tracker was investigating an unidentified radar contact when it suddenly disappeared from the *Berkeley's* radar screen. Within a few hours of the aircraft's disappearance Hanoi Radio reported that a US aircraft had been shot down in the Gulf of Tonkin to the south of Bach Long Vi island. The weather was good at the time of the loss and the sea was very calm, which might have made depth perception difficult for the crew. An extensive search was conducted in the Gulf for days afterwards and on 1 February a four-man liferaft from the Tracker was picked up some 150 miles from the aircraft's last known position. On 14 March Lt Templin's flying helmet was found in the same area as the raft. However, no trace of the crew was ever found and they were all declared dead in 1975.

24 January 1966

F-4B 152265 VMFA-314, MAG-11, USMC, Da Nang
Capt Albert Pitt (KIA)
2Lt Lawrence Neal Helber (KIA)

F-4B 152276 VMFA-314, MAG-11, USMC, Da Nang
Capt Doyle Robert Sprick (KIA)
2Lt Delmar George Booze (KIA)

Two Marine Corps Phantoms failed to return from a mission to bomb a landing zone in preparation for a Marine helicopter assault about 15 miles south of Hué. It was suspected that the aircraft may have collided somewhere between Da Nang and the target. VMFA-314 had only arrived at Da Nang on 15 January and these were the Squadron's first casualties of the war.

25 January 1966

C-123B 54-0702 probably 311 ACS, 315 ACG, USAF,
Da Nang
Capt Harry Richard Crumley (KIA)
Capt Edward Clarence Handly (KIA)
SSgt Leonard Williams (KIA)
SSgt Richard Duane Youtsey (KIA)
42 US Army troops (KIA)

January was a costly month for the USAF's transport fleet in Southeast Asia. The seventh transport to be lost during January was a Provider that crashed soon after taking off from An Khe on the short flight to Bong Son near the coast. In addition to the crew of four the aircraft was carrying 42 troops of the 1st Air Cavalry Division who were being taken to Bong Son to take part in Operation Masher, the first division-size search and destroy mission of the war. Ten minutes after taking off the aircraft climbed into low cloud and then crashed near Binh Khe killing all on board. A mechanical failure of No2 engine was thought to have been the cause of the accident. By the time Masher (renamed White Wing) had concluded on 4 March the USAF had flown 1,100 airlift sorties in support of the operation.

A-4E 152021 VA-55, USN, USS *Ranger*
1 pilot, name unknown (survived)

As it was launched for an armed reconnaissance sortie a Skyhawk settled into the sea. The catapult had not been set correctly and so could not provide sufficient power to allow the aircraft to achieve a safe flying speed.

26 January 1966

RF-101C 56-0084 20 TRS, 6250 CSG, USAF, Tan Son Nhut
Capt Wilber Newlin Grubb (POW - died)

Although President Johnson had temporarily stopped the bombing of North Vietnam, reconnaissance flights over the country were still permitted. Capt 'Newk' Grubb was sent on a lone mis-

sion to obtain photographs of barracks at Xuan Son, about 20 miles northwest of Dong Hoi. The aircraft may have suffered an engine problem as it was unable to gain altitude and Capt Grubb ejected moments before it crashed into a hillside near his target. 'Newk' Grubb was taken prisoner and was forced by the North Vietnamese to make a radio broadcast accusing the US of breaking the cease-fire. Photographs of Capt Grubb showed him to be in good condition but with a leg wound. Nothing more was heard about him until 1970 when the North Vietnamese announced that he had died of his wounds nine days after his crash (and before his photographs had been published by any newspaper). His remains were returned to the USA on 13 March 1974.

27 January 1966

A-4E 151998 VMA-211, MAG-12, USMC, Chu Lai
1 pilot, name unknown (survived)

Chu Lai's permanent runway was still not finished and MAG-12's Skyhawks had to use JATO to achieve a safe take off, especially with fully loaded aircraft in the hot and humid climate of South Vietnam. Unfortunately a pilot from VMA-211 omitted to ignite his JATO and he failed to take off and ran off the end of the runway. Operating problems continued to plague Chu Lai until the 10,000 feet runway was finally completed in September 1966.

A-4E 150034 VMA-224, MAG-12, USMC, Chu Lai
1 pilot, name unknown (survived)

As if one accident on the runway at Chu Lai was not bad enough, another Skyhawk, this time from VMA-224, was damaged beyond repair when the aircraft attempted to make an arrested landing. The pilot had lost all radio communications so the arrester gear was not properly rigged and pulled out when the aircraft's hook caught the wire.

28 January 1966

A-1E 52-132412 602 ACS, 3 TFW, USAF, Bien Hoa
Maj Fred Lawer McPherson (KIA)

The 602nd ACS lost two aircraft on the 28th. The first Skyraider went down 10 miles southeast of Tay Ninh during a close air support mission, its pilot being killed.

A-1E 52-133907 602 ACS, 3 TFW, USAF, Bien Hoa
1 pilot, name unknown (survived)

Another 602nd Skyraider suffered engine failure to become the ninth USAF aircraft lost accidentally during January. The following month the 602nd moved from Bien Hoa to Nha Trang on the coast.

31 January 1966

A-1E 52-132464 1 ACS, 3 TFW, USAF, Pleiku
Capt J R Gearheart (survived)

From its new base at Pleiku the 1st ACS could operate in the Steel Tiger area of southern Laos as well the Central Highlands of South Vietnam. During one of the Squadron's early missions in Laos a Skyraider was hit by AAA forcing the pilot crash-land his aircraft. He was subsequently recovered safely.

F-105D 61-0210 469 TFS, 6234 TFW, USAF, Korat
Capt Eugene David Hamilton (KIA)

The bombing halt that had commenced on Christmas Eve came to an end on the last day of January with no signs that the North Vietnamese were willing to negotiate a settlement. The Rolling Thunder bombing campaign resumed on the 31st. Although the weather was poor with low cloud and poor visibility a series of raids was planned to mark the end of the bombing halt. On one of the first raids of the new offensive, a formation of F-105s was returning from an armed reconnaissance mission during which several barges had been seen and attacked. As the formation was flying under the low cloud base one of the aircraft was hit by anti-aircraft fire and crashed 10 miles south of Vinh, killing the pilot.

A-4E 152066 VA-55, USN, USS *Ranger*
Lt Cdr S G Chumley (survived)

The Navy also resumed its air operations over North Vietnam on the 31st. A flight of Skyhawks from the *Ranger* was assigned to

bomb a ferry crossing on the Kien Giang River south of Dong Hoi. Again, there was a low cloud base at the time and the aircraft had to make several low passes over the heavily defended area. Lt Cdr Chumley was just pulling up from his third pass, having dropped CBU-2 cluster bombs on the target, when his aircraft was hit by AAA. A few moments later the aircraft became uncontrollable and Chumley ejected just offshore and was subsequently rescued by a US Navy helicopter.

F-4B 152233 VF-114, USN, USS *Kitty Hawk*
Lt W Fritz Klumpp (survived)
Lt(jg) J N Stineman (survived)

A Navy F-4 was hit by ground fire while attacking a bridge near Ban Soppeng, south of the Mu Gia Pass in Laos. The aircraft's hydraulic system was badly damaged but Lt Klumpp maintained control and flew back to his carrier. As the flaps were extended during the approach to land the aircraft began to roll uncontrollably and the crew ejected. They were both picked up safely by the carrier's plane guard helicopter, a UH-2 Seasprite of HC-1 Detachment 1, Unit C. Fritz Klumpp was on his 30th mission and went on to complete 106 more by the end of May.

1 February 1966

A-1J 142038 VA-115, USN, USS *Kitty Hawk*
Lt(jg) B S Eakin (survived)

During an armed reconnaissance mission a flight of Skyraiders attacked an anti-aircraft gun site near Ban Senphan in southern Laos. On his second pass Lt Eakin's aircraft was hit in the fuselage and caught fire. He flew a short distance away before he abandoned the aircraft and was later rescued by a USAF helicopter.

A-1J 142031 VA-145, USN, USS *Ranger*
Lt(jg) Dieter Dengler (POW - escaped)

About an hour after Lt Eakin was shot down, another flight of four Skyraiders attacked a target deeper into Laos, near Ban Phathoung. Lt Dengler was the last to dive on the target when his aircraft was hit by ground fire. He crash-landed the aircraft a few miles from the target but both wings were ripped off when the aircraft struck some trees. Despite a SAR attempt in which a USAF helicopter crew spotted and photographed his wrecked aircraft, Dengler was nowhere to be seen. He had moved away from the wreck and evaded for several hours but was then captured by Pathet Lao troops. He escaped eight days after his capture but he was soon recaptured and tortured for his attempt. He was marched to a new camp at Houei Het and imprisoned with Eugene De Bruin and other members of an Air America C-46 crew who had been shot down on 5 September 1963. Also imprisoned with them was 1Lt Duane Martin who had been shot down in an HH-43 during a SAR mission on 20 September 1965. Fearing that they were about to be killed, the prisoners decided to make an all-out escape attempt. On 29 June Dengler and the others escaped from their hut and broke into the camp's armoury and a firefight broke out during which several guards were killed. Most of the prisoners escaped and Dengler and Martin stayed together as they travelled through the jungle. Eighteen days after the escape Martin was killed by a Laotian villager leaving Dieter Dengler to travel on alone. After an epic struggle for survival Dieter Dengler was eventually spotted and rescued by an HH-3E on 20 July, one of the few Americans ever to escape from Laos. He was on the verge of death from starvation and exhaustion when he was found and weighed just 98lbs compared to the 157lbs he had weighed before he was shot down. Dieter Dengler, who was a German who had emigrated to the USA in his teens, was awarded the Navy Cross for his actions during captivity. In 1979 he wrote a classic book, *Escape from Laos*, about his experiences and he has also been the subject of a television documentary.

A-4C 149527 VA-146, USN, USS *Ranger*
Cdr Hubert Bradford Loheed (KIA)

Cdr Loheed, the CO of VA-146, led a four-aircraft section on a raid against barges on the coast 20 miles north of Vinh. With a layer of cloud at about 1,000 feet, the first two aircraft released their ordnance and pulled up into a nose high wingover and then

The A-6 Intruder built up an enviable reputation for its superb capability in all-weather, low-level strike missions. The aircraft's bomb-carrying capacity was most impressive but its advanced avionics were unreliable in the early days. USN

dived down back into cloud to make another run. Cdr Loheed was seen to enter the cloud but his wingman then lost sight of him and he was not seen or heard from again. It was surmised that he may have been incapacitated by ground fire or he failed to pull out of the dive before hitting the ground. Hubert Loheed was posted as missing in action until his remains were handed over and identified in August 1994, having been promoted to the rank of Captain during the time for which he was unaccounted.

KC-130F 149809   VMGR-152, MAG-15, USMC, Da Nang
1Lt Albert Michael Prevost (KIA)
Maj Richard Andrew Alm (KIA)
SSgt Russell Burr Luker (KIA)
SSgt Donald Leroy Coates (KIA)
GSgt Galen Francis Humphrey (KIA)
Sgt Peter George Vlahakos (KIA)

Throughout much of the war the Marines based a detachment of KC-130Fs at Da Nang to provide both air transport and air refuelling for Marine forces. The aircraft and crews were provided by VMGR-152 from Futema but were occasionally supplemented by aircraft from VMGR-352. When Marine aircraft operated over the southern provinces of North Vietnam the tankers sometimes had to go with them. 1Lt Prevost's Hercules was returning from a mission when it exploded about 15 miles offshore between Dong Hoi and the DMZ. If it was shot down then it must have been fired at by a vessel as it was too far from land to be reached by AAA and there were no SAM sites in the region at this time. Another possible explanation for the explosion was some kind of technical malfunction during refuelling operations or an on-board fire. Whatever the cause, the aircraft and its six crew were lost without trace.

2 February 1966

F-8E   149142   VMF(AW)-235, MAG-11, USMC, Da Nang
Capt R I Harris (survived)

VMF(AW)-235 arrived at Da Nang from Iwakuni on 1 February to replace VMF(AW)-312 as the resident Crusader squadron. The day after the Squadron arrived in Vietnam it lost its first aircraft. The Squadron was tasked with preparing a landing zone about 15 miles south of Quang Ngai on the southern edge of the Marines' area of operations. Capt Harris was pulling up from his fourth pass over the target when his aircraft was hit in the tail by small arms fire. He made for the sea and ejected over the beach near An Tho and was picked up by a Navy helicopter.

O-1E   56-2493   probably 19 TASS, 505 TACG, USAF,
Bien Hoa detached to Tan Son Nhut
Capt Craig Slade Blackner (KIA)
A1C John Irwin Cameron (KIA)

A Bird Dog crashed during a visual reconnaissance flight in Long An province, South Vietnam killing both crewmembers. Enemy action was not thought to have been the cause of the crash.

3 February 1966

RA-5C   151625   RVAH-13, USN, USS *Kitty Hawk*
Lt Gerald Leonard Coffee (POW)
Lt(jg) Robert Taft Hanson (POW- died)

A Vigilante was hit by AAA soon after crossing the coast near the island of Hon Me, midway between Thanh Hoa and Vinh, while on a road reconnaissance mission. The pilot headed back towards the coast where the escort rejoined him. Just as the aircraft crossed the beach its hydraulics failed completely and it exploded. Both crew ejected from the disintegrating aircraft and both landed in the water about a mile offshore. North Vietnamese boats soon appeared on the scene and Lt Coffee was hauled aboard one of the boats. He had seen his NFO in the water and thought he had also been rescued. He was later told that

Lt Hanson had died and had been buried on the beach. In November 1988 the North Vietnamese handed over remains that were identified as those of Lt Robert Hanson.

Gerald Coffee had flown reconnaissance Crusaders over Cuba during the missile crisis of 1962 and was an instructor pilot on the Vigilante before deploying on board the *Kitty Hawk*. He was incarcerated in the Hanoi Hilton with Cdr Howard Rutledge and Coffee provided illustrations for Rutledge's book *In the Presence of Mine Enemies*. Lt Coffee was repatriated on 12 February 1973. RVAH-13 was one of the *Kitty Hawk* squadrons to paint its aircraft in camouflage for the 1966 tour.

C-123B 55-4537   311 ACS, 315 ACG, USAF, Da Nang
Maj James Louis Carter (KIA)
Capt Wilbur Ronald Brown (KIA)
A1C Edward Milton Parsley (KIA)
A1C Therman Morris Waller (KIA)

Hostile action was suspected when a Provider disappeared on a short resupply flight between Khe Sanh and Dong Ha close to the DMZ. It is thought that four South Vietnamese troops were also on board the aircraft for the flight. Radio contact with the aircraft was lost and it was suspected to have come down about 10 miles from Khe Sanh, close to the border with Laos. An extensive search over the next three days failed to produce any sign of the aircraft or its crew.

7 February 1966

A-4E   152027   VA-56, USN, USS *Ticonderoga*
Lt Cdr Render Crayton (POW)

During an armed reconnaissance mission between Vinh and Thanh Hoa, a flight of Skyhawks attacked a number of railway trucks on the coastal railway near Phu Dien Chau. Lt Cdr Crayton's aircraft was hit by 37mm AAA as it dived to attack the target. His wingman reported seeing an explosion on the starboard side of the fuselage and the aircraft quickly became uncontrollable. Crayton was forced to eject before he could reach the coast. He made contact with the rest of his flight on his survival radio and two Skyhawks made several passes to keep the North Vietnamese at bay until Crayton could be rescued. Unfortunately, the Skyhawks began to run out of fuel and had to depart before the SAR force arrived. The helicopter and its escorts were damaged by ground fire and spotted only an empty parachute. Render Crayton was released from captivity in North Vietnam on 12 February 1973. Lt Cdr Crayton had flown in the first retaliatory strikes following the Gulf of Tonkin incident in August 1964 and for 18 months was senior POW in the Son Tay prison camp. He was awarded the Silver Star for his actions during his last mission.

8 February 1966

O-1E   56-2621   22 TASS, 505 TACG, USAF, Binh Thuy
1 pilot, name unknown (survived)

Engine failure caused the crash of a Bird Dog during a visual reconnaissance flight in South Vietnam.

9 February 1966

A-4C   149557   VA-144, USN, USS *Ticonderoga*
Cdr Jack L Snyder (survived)

Cdr Snyder, the commander of the *Ticonderoga's* Air Wing 5, was leading a flight of Skyhawks on a road reconnaissance mission about 20 miles southwest of Thanh Hoa when his aircraft was rocked by a huge explosion. An SA-2 missile had exploded close to his aircraft even though he was only flying at 500 feet and the missile could not have had time to guide properly. The Skyhawk was riddled with shrapnel from the explosion and a hydraulic fire started but later went out. Cdr Snyder disconnected the hydraulic flying control system and flew the aircraft manually for about 60 miles at 200 knots. The fire restarted and Cdr Snyder felt the controls go slack. Seconds after he ejected the aircraft broke in two just behind the wing trailing edge where the fire had burnt through the aircraft's structure. Cdr Snyder was picked up about 50 miles from the North Vietnamese coast by a Navy SAR helicopter operating from the destroyer USS *England*. This was the first aircraft lost to a SAM since 22 December 1965.

10 February 1966

A-1H   137627   VA-145, USN, USS *Ranger*
Lt Gary Douglas Hopps (KIA)

Armed reconnaissance missions over the southern provinces of North Vietnam were proving dangerous. A Skyraider from VA-145 dived into the ground while attacking a road bridge midway between Dong Hoi and the DMZ. It was thought likely that the pilot had been hit by ground fire and was wounded and therefore did not bail out.

B-57B 52-1575   13 TBS, 405 FW attached to 6252 TFW,
USAF, Da Nang
Capt Russell Palmer Hunter (KIA)
Capt Ernest Philip Kiefel (KIA)

The Canberra squadron at Da Nang was now spending much of its time on night missions over the Ho Chi Minh Trail in the Steel Tiger area of southern Laos. The aircraft's good endurance, weapons capacity and stability made it suitable for this particular mission although it lacked the advanced avionics necessary for night work. Capt Hunter was working with a C-130 flareship and reported attacking a target near Ban Vangthon.

After making a second pass he reported problems with the aircraft and that he and his navigator were ejecting. A flash was seen on the ground and later the wreckage was found but there was no trace of the crew.

14 February 1966

A-1E   52-132665   1 ACS, 3 TFW, USAF, Pleiku
Maj John Russell Hills (KIA)

A flight of Skyraiders was conducting an armed reconnaissance mission in the southern provinces of Laos near the town of Chavane, 110 miles northwest of Pleiku, when one of the aircraft crashed on the top of a hill and exploded. The site of this crash was much further south than most US crash sites in southern Laos at this time.

A-4C   149552   VA-144, USN, USS *Ticonderoga*
Lt(jg) J C Durham (survived)

Lt Durham was attacking a target in southern Laos and pulled up to 25,000 feet for the return flight to his carrier when he noticed that his engine's temperature was climbing. He tried reducing and increasing the power but the engine just got hotter without developing any extra thrust. Having also lost electrical power Lt Durham tried to make an engine-out landing at Da Nang but bad weather prevented this and he ejected about 20 miles off the coast and was picked up by a Marine Corps helicopter.

15 February 1966

A-1E   52-133885   602 ACS, 3 TFW, USAF, Bien Hoa
detached to Nakhon Phanom
Maj Oscar Mauterer (POW - Died)

During an escort mission for an O-1E FAC near Ban Senphan, south of the Mu Gia Pass, a USAF Skyraider was hit by ground fire and burst into flames. Maj Mauterer was seen to bail out and, once on the ground, spoke to other pilots but was then thought to have been captured either by the North Vietnamese or the Pathet Lao. A SAR helicopter arrived but found no sign of the downed pilot. Maj Mauterer's name was mentioned by a Laotian official in a September 1968 statement as being a POW along with several other US airmen. Oscar Mauterer was not released alive from Laos but on 30 April 1994 the symbol on the Vietnam Memorial Wall in Washington was changed from a cross to a star indicating that information or remains had been received that proved his death.

18 February 1966

F-4B   152297   VF-92, USN, USS *Enterprise*
Lt(jg) James Thomas Ruffin (KIA)
Lt(jg) Larry Howard Spencer (POW)

Towards the middle of February US raids began to reach further north as part of Washington's tactics of gradually increasing the pressure on North Vietnam. On 18 February a section of Phantoms from VF-92 flew escort for an EC-121 Big Look aircraft of VQ-1 on a surveillance mission just off the coast near Thanh Hoa. At 25,000 feet and the relatively slow speed of 280 knots one of the Phantoms was rocked by a massive explosion. Lt Spencer, the NFO, believed it was an SA-2 as no AAA or MiGs were reported. The aircraft immediately pitched over into a steep dive towards the North Vietnamese coast and, following standard operating procedure, Lt Spencer ejected first followed by his pilot. Two parachutes were seen but only Larry Spencer entered the North Vietnamese POW system. Lt Ruffin probably died at the time and may have been killed by the North Vietnamese or he may have drowned when he came down in the sea. Whatever the cause, his remains were handed over on 3 June 1983 while Lt Spencer had been released from seven years of captivity on 12 February 1973.

A-6A   151797   VA-85, USN, USS *Kitty Hawk*
Lt(jg) Joseph Vaughn Murray (KIA)
Lt(jg) Thomas Anthony Schroeffel (KIA)

VA-85 lost its second Intruder on its initial deployment during a daylight armed reconnaissance mission over the northwestern provinces of North Vietnam about 70 miles west of Hanoi. Lt Murray spotted a truck on a mountain road and dived to attack it with Snakeye bombs. Moments after the flight leader cautioned Lt Murray about not leaving his pull out too late in the difficult terrain, the Intruder slammed into the ground 500 yards beyond its target. The inexperienced pilot had probably fallen victim to target fixation whereby intense concentration on the target leaves the pilot oblivious to all other circumstances. Many pilots will admit to having been affected by it, but for some the experience proves fatal. It is surprising that the highly capable Intruder should be used on daylight armed reconnaissance when it was better suited to its primary role of night and all-weather attack.

19 February 1966

F-105D   62-4251   354 TFS, 355 TFW, USAF, Takhli
Capt R O Green (survived)

Capt Green was acting as a pathfinder for a formation of F-105s on a raid in the Mu Gia Pass region of Laos. His aircraft was hit by 37mm AAA and he ejected after struggling for some time to keep his aircraft airborne. He was rescued by a USAF SAR helicopter.

21 February 1966

B-57B   52-1523   8 TBS, 405 FW attached to 6252 TFW, USAF, Da Nang
Capt J T Stanley (survived)
Capt H E Sjogren (survived)

Although spending much of their time at night over the Ho Chi Minh Trail, the Da Nang Canberras were also available for daytime close air support and strikes. An aircraft was strafing a target near the Song Bo River five miles west of Hué when it was hit by ground fire and burst into flames. The crew ejected safely and were picked up by an Army helicopter. This B-57 originally served with the 461st TBG at Blytheville AFB, Arkansas.

F-4C   64-0728   8 TFW, USAF, Ubon
Capt J L Moore (survived)
1Lt M J Peters (survived)

At dusk a flight of Phantoms from Ubon was flying an armed reconnaissance mission over the Barrel Roll area of northern Laos on the lookout for traffic on the Trail. The flight spotted several trucks near Ban Muangphan on the eastern edge of the Plain of Jars and rolled into the attack. Capt Moore's aircraft was hit by ground fire and burst into flames. The crew ejected and were lucky to evade capture and be rescued by a USAF HH-3.

22 February 1966

F-105D   62-4388   357 TFS, 355 TFW, USAF, Takhli
1 pilot, name unknown (survived)

An F-105 was accidentally lost near Takhli during an armed reconnaissance mission. Having spent five months on temporary deployment to Takhli in 1965, the 357th TFS had arrived back from McConnell AFB, Kansas when the 355th TFW was assigned permanently to Takhli on 29 January 1966.

24 February 1966

F-4B   151411   VMFA-314, MAG-11, USMC, Da Nang
1Lt J W Pierce (survived)
2Lt B R Ellis (survived)

In addition to providing close air support to the Marine Division, the USMC Phantoms at Da Nang were also used for strikes in North Vietnam and Laos, especially against the Ho Chi Minh Trail which fed troops and supplies into the Marines' area in I Corps. On 24 February a flight of Phantoms was attacking a river crossing near Ban Vangthon in southern Laos when one of the aircraft was lost. On his fifth pass over the target the aircraft was hit by AAA, which started a fire in the fuselage. Both crew ejected and were rescued by a USAF helicopter from Nakhon Phanom.

A-1E   52-133908   1 ACS, 2 AD, USAF, Pleiku
Capt Raymond Harry Hetrick (KIA)

Capt Hetrick was flying one of the Skyraiders that escorted the SAR helicopter searching for Lts Pierce and Ellis. As the SAR task force approached the location of the downed Marines it encountered heavy ground fire. Capt Hetrick dived on a gun position but his aircraft was hit and caught fire. The Skyraider crashed close to the two Marines but Capt Hetrick did not bail out and was killed in the crash.

25 February 1966

F-4B   152308   VMFA-314, MAG-11, USMC, Da Nang
1Lt R L Pappas (survived)
1Lt J R Coleman (survived)

VMFA-314 was unfortunate enough to lose two aircraft in two consecutive days. During a close air support mission on the coast 15 miles northwest of Hué, a Phantom was hit by ground fire as it was dropping napalm on a VC concentration. The pilot immediately turned the burning aircraft out to sea and the crew ejected five miles from the shore. A US Navy vessel rescued both airmen.

RB-66C   54-0457   41 TRS, 460 TRW attached to 355 TFW, USAF, Takhli
Maj R P Walker (survived)
Capt John Bernard Causey (KIA)
4 crew, names unknown (survived)

In the early days of the war the RB-66 crews had little to worry about in pursuing their mission of locating and identifying the North Vietnamese air defence radars. However, although the aircraft usually flew above the reach of most AAA, the ever-growing number of SAM sites in North Vietnam was proving to be a danger for the large aircraft. On 25 February an RB-66 was damaged by an SA-2 while flying at 30,000 feet some five miles north of Vinh. The aircraft was badly damaged but remained flyable and Maj Walker headed out to sea to find a SAR destroyer. After flying 130 miles in a southeasterly direction Maj Walker ordered the crew to abandon the aircraft. Maj Walker and the others were rescued by a US Navy helicopter but Capt Causey was not found and may not have been able to eject for some reason.

26 February 1966

F-105D   61-0215   421 TFS, 6234 TFW, USAF, Korat
Capt Charles Graham Boyd (survived)

During a strafing run on a target near Ban Dang in southern Laos a Thud was hit by ground fire and began to burn. Capt Boyd ejected near Nam Theun and was rescued by a USAF HH-3 from Nakhon Phanom. Capt Boyd was shot down again two months later on 22 April but on that occasion he was taken prisoner.

27 February 1966

F-4C   64-0742   433 TFS, 8 TFW, USAF, Ubon
Capt J C Kahl (survived)
1Lt G H Hall (survived)

The Steel Tiger region of southern Laos was becoming a more dangerous area than ever before. A Ubon Phantom was flying a night mission over the Trail when the pilot spotted a vehicle 10 miles northwest of Muang Nong. As the aircraft was making its bombing run it was hit in the port wing by ground fire and started to burn. The fire went out and Capt Kahl nursed his aircraft back towards Ubon but about 10 miles short of the airfield the aircraft became uncontrollable and the crew had to eject.

F-105D   62-4362   355 TFW, USAF, Takhli
1 pilot, name unknown (survived)

An F-105 crashed near Takhli due to engine failure during an armed reconnaissance mission.

1 March 1966

F-4B   150443   VF-143, USN, USS *Ranger*
Lt William David Frawley (KIA)
Lt(jg) William Murrey Christensen (KIA)

A flight of three Phantoms was on a coastal reconnaissance mission about 40 miles south of Haiphong in deteriorating weather when they received a SAM warning (probably from an EC-121). Flying under a 500 feet cloud base with less than one mile visibility the flight leader ordered a level 180-degree turn to head back out to sea. Half way through the turn the leader lost sight of

Lt Frawley who reported that he had lost contact with the formation. It was thought that the aircraft flew into the water in the poor visibility while the pilot was trying to relocate the formation. A search revealed a small amount of wreckage but no survivors.

A-4E   152057   VA-55, USN, USS *Ranger*
Lt(jg) David Joseph Woloszyk (KIA)

The *Ranger* lost another aircraft at almost the same time as the VF-143 Phantom crashed in the Gulf of Tonkin. Two Skyhawks were despatched on a road reconnaissance over southern North Vietnam. Soon after crossing the coast at a position about 40 miles southeast of Vinh Lt Woloszyk reported that he had lost contact with his leader in the poor visibility and that he was climbing above the cloud base. He also stated that he had sighted another section of Skyhawks and was going to join them. The leader also climbed through the cloud as soon as he heard Woloszyk's call but he could not see his wingman. The other Skyhawk formation had not seen Woloszyk's aircraft and despite an extensive three-day search no sign was ever found of Lt Woloszyk or his aircraft. In a cruel twist of fate Kenneth Woloszyk, David's brother who was also in the Navy, was assigned to post names of the missing pilots that day and saw his brother's name on the list.

2 March 1966

O-1E   56-2529   21 TASS, 505 TACG, USAF, Pleiku
Capt Paul Albert Meiners (KIA)
Capt Marshall Myron Holt (KIA)

A Bird Dog observation aircraft was shot down during a visual reconnaissance mission 12 miles south of Bong Son near the South Vietnamese coast. Both crewmen died in the crash.

O-1F   57-2902   Det 3, 505 TACG, USAF, Nakhon Phanom
Capt Karl Edward Worst (KIA)

F-105D   59-1724   355 TFW, USAF, Takhli
1 pilot, name unknown (survived)

An F-105 collided with a Bird Dog FAC aircraft over Thailand resulting in the death of the FAC pilot. This O-1, like many of its type at this stage of the war, was camouflaged and may have been difficult to see by the fast moving F-105. Later in the year most of the Thailand-based O-1s were repainted in a light grey colour scheme to make them more visible from above.

3 March 1966

F-4B   151453   VMFA-314, MAG-11, USMC, Da Nang
1Lt T P Keenan (survived)
Capt C R Fairchild (survived)

The risk of making multiple runs over the same target, even in a relatively 'safe' area, was illustrated once more on 3 March. A Marine Corps Phantom was on its seventh run dropping napalm on enemy trenches 10 miles west of Quang Ngai when it was hit by ground fire from automatic weapons. 1Lt Keenan headed north to Chu Lai where he and his navigator ejected just off the coast and were picked up by a Marine UH-34.

4 March 1966

O-1E   56-2499   21 TASS, 505 TACG, USAF, Pleiku
Maj Stuart Merrill Andrews (KIA)
1Lt John Francis Conlon (KIA)

Following the loss of an O-1 on the 2nd, the 21st TASS lost another aircraft and crew two days later. Maj Andrews was flying with an observer who was still undergoing training in the art of visual reconnaissance and forward air control. The aircraft took off from Qui Nhon airfield on the coast and made radio contact with a nearby Special Forces Camp and was asked to check on campfires that had been sighted in the area. The aircraft

failed to arrive at its destination and no further radio messages were received. Andrews and Conlon simply disappeared over the South Vietnamese jungle.

5 March 1966

F-4B   152224   VF-114, USN, USS *Kitty Hawk*
Lt Cdr M N Guess (survived)
Lt R E Pile (survived)

During one of its periodic spells at Dixie Station, the *Kitty Hawk* lost a Phantom during an operation over the Mekong Delta region of South Vietnam. A flight of aircraft was attacking a VC storage area near the town of Cai Lay, 15 miles west of My Tho, when Lt Cdr Guess felt two distinct thuds as he pulled up from his second dive on the target. The Phantom began streaming fuel and the controls froze as the hydraulic system failed. The aircraft rolled inverted at 1,500 feet and both crew ejected and were picked up by an Army helicopter. It was thought that the aircraft had been damaged by debris from the target as it blew up.

A-1H   137589   VA-215, USN, USS *Hancock*
Cdr Robert Charles Hessom (KIA)

The squadron commander of VA-215 led a section of Skyraiders on a Rolling Thunder strike about 35 miles south of Vinh. Cdr Hesson's aircraft was hit by AAA but he managed to fly some 15 miles to the south before crashing in hilly terrain. Cdr Hessom did not escape from his aircraft and it was thought that he may have been wounded. Hessom had taken command of the Squadron almost exactly a year previous. In 1994 the remains of Cdr Hessom were discovered during a joint US/Vietnamese excavation of a crash site near Ha Tinh.

F-100D   55-3780   416 TFS, 3 TFW, USAF, Tan Son Nhut
Capt P V McCallum (survived)

During a close air support mission a Super Sabre was lost near Ben Cat, 20 miles north of Tan Son Nhut. The pilot ejected safely and was recovered.

7 March 1966

F-105D   62-4219   357 TFS, 355 TFW, USAF, Takhli
Capt Harold Victor Smith (KIA)

Monday 7 March proved to be a costly day for the USAF units based in Thailand with two F-105s and two RF-101s lost before the day was done. Capt Smith was assigned to lead three other F-105s on an attack on a SAM site near Xom Gia, 20 miles west of Thanh Hoa. During a strafing run Capt Smith's Thunderchief was hit by ground fire, burst into flames and crashed near the target. Capt Smith was not seen to eject. In August and September 1998, following several abortive attempts, a burial site was

found and human remains were recovered. In May 2000 the Central Identification Laboratory in Hawaii positively identified the remains as being those of Capt (now Colonel) Smith.

RF-101C   56-0043   45 TRS, 39 AD on TDY, USAF, Udorn
Capt Jerdy Albert Wright (KIA)

RF-101C   56-0220   45 TRS, 39 AD on TDY, USAF, Udorn
Capt Gordon Lee Page (KIA)

About one hour after Capt Smith was shot down two RF-101 Voodoos were flying about 10 miles east of the position where Smith had crashed. The aircraft were on a photographic reconnaissance mission to the Vinh area and it may have been mere coincidence that they were in the same area as Capt Smith. The Voodoos are thought to have either collided or fallen victim to SAMs. Either a single SA-2 destroyed both aircraft or, more likely as they would be flying tactical formation rather than close formation, more than one missile was fired at the aircraft. Both pilots were killed and Capt Wright's remains were among 28 sets of remains handed over to US authorities on 21 June 1989 and the formal identification announced in the following September. It was only in 1998 that the unidentified sets of remains left from those handed over in 1989 were re-examined using more modern forensic techniques and one set was determined to be those of Capt Page.

F-105D   62-4410   469 TFS, 6234 TFW, USAF, Korat
Maj J L Hutto (survived)

The Korat Wing also sent a formation of Thuds out on an armed reconnaissance mission on the 7th but this formation flew well to the south of the Takhli aircraft. Maj Hutto's aircraft was hit by 57mm AAA over the Annamite Mountains some 45 miles south of Vinh in a sparsely-populated area. It was this latter fact which accounted for Maj Hutto being successfully rescued by a USAF HH-3 from Nakhon Phanom rather than spending the next seven years as a POW. Thunderchief 62-4410 was the 609th and penultimate F-105D model to be built for the Air Force.

9 March 1966

AC-47D   44-76290   4 ACS, 14 ACW, USAF, Tan Son Nhut
detached to Da Nang
Capt Willard Marion Collins (KIA)
1Lt Delbert Ray Peterson (KIA)
1Lt J L Meek (survived)
SSgt J G Brown (survived)
Sgt Robert Eugene Foster (KIA)
Sgt J Turner (survived)

The Special Forces Camp in the A Shau Valley was in a particularly vulnerable position nestled in a narrow valley 25 miles

The RF-101C Voodoo was the USAF's prime photographic reconnaissance aircraft in Southeast Asia until the introduction of the RF-4C. This RF-101C 56-0176, 'Little Miss Beth Ann' of the 45th TRS, is about to have its cameras loaded at Tan Son Nhut for yet another mission. USAF

southwest of Hué and less than three miles from the border with Laos. The Camp was situated close to an important enemy infiltration route and had a 2,300 feet airstrip which was used to keep the base supplied. At 0200 on 9 March the Camp, manned by 20 US and 375 ARVN troops, came under heavy attack from around 2,000 NVA troops. Low cloud precluded air strikes but a C-123 Candlestick aircraft dropped flares throughout the night to illuminate the area outside the wire so the defenders could see the enemy. By mid-morning the Camp reported it was in immediate danger of being overrun and was in desparate need of air support. Despite a cloud base in the valley of around 400 feet Capt Collins took off from Da Nang, where the 4th ACS kept a detachment, and headed for the A Shau Valley. After three attempts Capt Collins, using the call sign Spooky 70, penetrated the cloud and made a firing pass at the enemy forces massing at the outer perimeter. On the second pass ground fire hit the starboard engine, which fell away from the aircraft, and the port engine was also hit and caught fire. The aircraft crash-landed on a mountain slope about five miles north of the camp and although all the crew survived the crash they were soon under attack from enemy troops. Capt Collins and Sgt Foster were shot and killed and another crewman wounded. A USAF HH-43 helicopter soon appeared overhead and rescued three of the airmen but this was only possible through the heroic efforts of 1Lt Peterson who charged at an enemy machine gun position as the last three survivors were being evacuated. Delbert Peterson was listed as missing until February 1978 when he was declared dead. Both he and Capt Collins were posthumously awarded the AFC.

The 4th ACS was assigned to the 14th ACW that had been formed at Nha Trang on 8 March to control most Air Commando units in Southeast Asia. The 4th ACS's reassignment from the 6250th CSG took place on the day before this aircraft was shot down and the squadron remained based at Tan Son Nhut until 1 June. The exceptions to the 14th ACW's control were the C-123 squadrons, which were controlled by the 315th ACW that had been formed on the same day. By the end of 1966 the Air Commando Wings controlled a total of 10 squadrons in Vietnam and Thailand.

A-4C　148518　　VMA-311, MAG-12, USMC, Chu Lai
　　　　　　　　　　1Lt Augusto Maria Xavier (KIA)
The Marines were also involved in the fierce defence of the A Shau Special Forces Camp. 1Lt 'Gus' Xavier was assigned to lead another Skyhawk on a pre-dawn close air support mission. Under a parachute flare dropped by a C-123 he descended through clouds and flew around mountains to drop his bombs on NVA positions. On his second pass he strafed the enemy troops but crashed into the side of a mountain as he was leaving the target area. Augusto Xavier was awarded a posthumous Silver Star for his determination in pressing home his attack in foul weather in an attempt to support the defenders on the ground.

10 March 1966

A-1E　52-133867　602 ACS, 14 ACW, USAF, Nha Trang
　　　　　　　　　　detached to Qui Nhon
　　　　　　　　　　Maj Dafford W Myers (survived)
On the second day of the siege of the Special Forces Camp in the A Shau Valley the situation became even more desperate with the few remaining defenders being driven into a single bunker. Following a slight improvement in the weather as the cloud base lifted to 800 feet, Skyraiders from the 602nd ACS arrived overhead and proceeded to strafe the enemy troops who were on the very perimeter of the camp. On his third pass Maj Myers's aircraft was hit by ground fire stopping the engine and forcing him to crash-land on the camp's runway, which was littered with rubble and debris and holed by mortar rounds. Maj Myers's wingman, Maj Hubert G King, was also hit and almost blinded forcing him to return to Qui Nhon. Maj Myers was in grave danger of being captured by the North Vietnamese troops who were by now inside the wire and just across the runway from the downed pilot. Maj Bernard F Fisher, who had been leading the attack in another Skyraider, had watched the events unfold and saw the predicament of the downed pilot. Realising that a rescue helicopter could not possibly arrive before the enemy troops would reach Maj Myers, Fisher carefully picked out a length of the runway that was not too obstructed, landed safely on his second attempt and taxied up close to Myers who sprinted towards the aircraft. Myers leaped into the seat next to Fisher who then opened up full throttle and took off in a hail of bullets. When the aircraft landed back at Pleiku it was found to have 19 bullet holes in it. Later on the 10th the Camp fell to enemy forces. For his daring and courage Maj Fisher was awarded the Medal of Honor, the first of America's highest award for bravery to be awarded to a USAF officer during the war. Bernie Fisher finished his tour in Vietnam in June with 200 combat missions and was awarded his Medal by President Johnson at the White House on 19 January 1967.

The Skyraider, 52-132649, flown by Maj Fisher on this historic flight had a most eventful career. It had crashed at Can Tho on 21 March 1965 killing the two crew but had been repaired and returned to the 1st ACS. The aircraft crashed again in 1967 when it force landed wheels up at Qui Nhon with the centreline fuel tank still attached. The aircraft was once more repaired but this time it was shipped to Hurlburt Field where it spent its last days training new Spad pilots. Later the aircraft was donated to the USAF Museum at Wright-Patterson AFB, Ohio where it remains today, the first Medal of Honour aircraft to be preserved.

The 602nd ACS had moved from Bien Hoa to Nha Trang during February and transferred from the 3rd TFW to the 14th ACW on the Wing's activation on 8 March. The Squadron continued to maintain a regular detachment of aircraft at Nakhon Phanom.

11 March 1966

A-1J　142071　　VA-115, USN, USS *Kitty Hawk*
　　　　　　　　　　1 pilot, name unknown (survived)
During the catapult launch of a Skyraider from the *Kitty Hawk* the catapult bridle separated before the launch sequence was completed and the aircraft fell into the sea.

12 March 1966

A-1E　52-133864　1 ACS, 14 ACW, USAF, Pleiku
　　　　　　　　　　Maj M E Blaylock (survived)
Like the 602nd, the 1st ACS transferred to the new 14th ACW on 8 March. A Skyraider was shot down while strafing an anti-aircraft gun position 45 miles west of Da Nang and only five miles from the border with Laos. The area was one of many entry points into South Vietnam on the extensive Ho Chi Minh Trail system. Maj Blaylock bailed out from his aircraft and was subsequently rescued by helicopter.

13 March 1966

AC-47D　43-49268　4 ACS, 14 ACW, USAF, Tan Son Nhut
　　　　　　　　　　detached to Da Nang
　　　　　　　　　　Capt Howard William Henninger (KIA)
　　　　　　　　　　Capt Robert Edward Pasekoff (KIA)
　　　　　　　　　　Capt Gerald Everett Olson (KIA)
　　　　　　　　　　SSgt Marshall Irvin Pauley (KIA)
　　　　　　　　　　SSgt Gene Edmond Davis (KIA)
　　　　　　　　　　TSgt Edwin Everton Morgan (KIA)
　　　　　　　　　　Sgt Dean Arnold Duvall (KIA)
Four days after the loss of the 4th ACS gunship at A Shau, the Da Nang detachment lost another aircraft with its entire crew. Capt Henninger and his crew was tasked with armed reconnaissance along Route 92 west of Da Nang. Radio contact with the AC-47 was lost soon after take off but it was thought that the aircraft came down near A Ro, about 45 miles southwest of Da Nang and only 10 miles from the border with Laos. A search failed to reveal the exact location of the aircraft's wreckage and the crew was posted as missing in action.

F-100F　58-1221　Wild Weasel Detachment, 6234 TFW,
　　　　　　　　　　USAF, Korat
　　　　　　　　　　2 crew, names unknown (survived)
The Wild Weasel Detachment lost its second Super Sabre during a training sortie when the aircraft suffered an engine failure. The final three F-100F Wild Weasels had arrived at Korat from the USA on 27 February leaving five aircraft in service after the loss on 13 March.

14 March 1966

F-4B　152274　　VMFA-314, MAG-11, USMC, Da Nang
　　　　　　　　　　Maj E C Paige (survived)
　　　　　　　　　　WO D D Redmond (survived)
During a Steel Tiger strike in southern Laos 70 miles west of Hué, a Marine Phantom was hit when pulling up from the target and the crew was forced to eject. Both airmen were injured but were rescued by a USAF helicopter. This was the sixth and last VMFA-314 Phantom to be lost during the Squadron's eventful three month tour of duty at Da Nang. VMFA-314 returned to Iwakuni on 14 April and was replaced by VMFA-115 on its second tour at Da Nang.

The HU-16B Albatross amphibian was an important part of the SAR operation in Southeast Asia and was responsible for many saves during the early years of the war. Often in great danger, two of the aircraft were lost; one disappeared in a storm and the other was blown out of the water by enemy coastal artillery. USAF

F-4C 64-0740 480 TFS, 35 TFW, USAF, Da Nang
Maj James M Peerson (survived)
Capt Lynwood C Bryant (survived)

On 14 March the 35th TFW was activated at Da Nang to replace the 6252nd TFW. The new Wing would control three squadrons of Phantoms, one of which, the 480th, had arrived from Holloman AFB in mid-February. Although it was activated on 14 March the Wing was not fully organized until 8 April and the 480th may still have been under the operational control of the 6252nd TFW when it lost its first aircraft on a Rolling Thunder armed reconnaissance mission. Maj Peerson's aircraft was hit by AAA and caught fire a mile offshore from the island of Hon Nghi Son, 30 miles south of Thanh Hoa. The crew ejected and, despite their proximity to the North Vietnamese coast, were eventually picked up by Navy SAR helicopters following the loss of a USAF HU-16B.

HU-16B 51-0071 33 ARRS on TDY, 3 ARRG, USAF, Da Nang
Capt David P Westenbarger (survived)
Lt Walter Hall (survived)
Captain Donald Price (survived)
SSgt Clyde Jackson (survived)
A1C Robert Larie Hilton (KIA)
A1C James Edward Pleiman (KIA)

When Maj Peerson and Capt Bryant ejected from their Phantom near Hon Nghi Son island a SAR operation was immediately set in motion. An HU-16B Albatross was usually on station in the Gulf of Tonkin whenever strikes on North Vietnam were scheduled. It took 20 minutes for the Albatross to reach the spot where the Phantom crew was waiting to be rescued, just over a mile from the shore. Capt Westenbarger landed on the choppy sea and brought the the aircraft close to the shoreline to attempt a rescue. A large group of North Vietnamese boats converged on the aircraft as it sat on the water. The parajumper, A1C James Pleiman, jumped into the sea and brought one of the survivors close to the aircraft. The navigator, Capt Price and the radio operator, A1C Hilton, fired at the approaching boats with their rifles as Pleiman tried to get the survivor aboard the aircraft. Hilton was killed by machine gun fire and then the Albatross was struck by a mortar shell and burst into flames. Capt Price dived into the sea and towed Maj Peerson away from the burning aircraft and almost certainly saved the Phantom pilot's life. Capt Westenbarger, Lt Hall and SSgt Jackson and the two Phantom crew were then rescued by two Navy SH-3s from HS-4 while a UH-2 from HC-1 rescued Capt Price after almost leaving him behind. Airmen Hilton and Pleiman went down in the burning wreck of the Albatross. In December 1988 James Pleiman's remains were returned by the Vietnamese. Donald Price was awarded the AFC for his heroism in saving the F-4 survivor's life.

F-100D 55-3793 90 TFS, 3 TFW, USAF, Bien Hoa
Capt Karl Edwin Klute (KIA)

A Super Sabre crashed during its third strafing run on a target near the village of Ap Long Pho in the mouth of the Mekong Delta, some 65 miles south of Saigon. It was unclear whether the aircraft had been shot down or had simply flown into the ground. This was the first aircraft lost by the 90th TFS since its arrival at Bien Hoa on 3 February from the 401st TFW at England AFB, Louisiana.

15 March 1966

O-1E 56-2530 22 TASS, 505 TACG, USAF, Binh Thuy
detached to Khe Sanh
Capt David Hugh Holmes (KIA)

The increasing intensity of air operations in the Steel Tiger sector of the Ho Chi Minh Trail resulted in several 'friendly fire' incidents that strained US relations with friendly Laotian forces. As a result the use of forward air controllers became more common in order to control air strikes more effectively. However, the war in Laos was not supposed to involve US forces and was highly secret, and FAC operations were even more dangerous than over South Vietnam as very few airmen survived captivity in Laos. A Bird Dog FAC was flying over Route 9 on a Tiger Hound mission on 15 March when the pilot spotted a large concentration of North Vietnamese troops at a concealed truck park in the Xe Namkok river valley on the Trail, 11 miles northwest of Sepone. The truck park was protected by at least six gun emplacements and the Bird Dog was shot down on the eastern slopes of the valley near the village of Ban Keng Khan Kao. Another O-1E was sent to search the area and the pilot spotted Capt Holmes slumped in his cockpit, apparently unconscious or dead. A few minutes later a US Army OV-1A Mohawk flew up the valley and was also shot down although one parachute was seen. The loss of two aircraft and the discovery of large numbers of North Vietnamese troops prompted a five-hour attack on the area by tactical aircraft. A SAR force reached the downed Bird Dog the next day but there was no sign of Capt Holmes.

F-4C 64-0732 497 TFS, 8 TFW, USAF, Ubon
Capt Martin Ronald Scott (KIA)
Lt Col Peter Joseph Stewart (KIA)

Two Phantoms were flying along Route 19 in the extreme west of North Vietnam when one of the aircraft was shot down. The flight leader had spotted two trucks on a road one mile south of Dien Bien Phu airport and directed his wingman to make the first bombing run. The leader then saw a fireball, which he assumed was the aircraft exploding as it hit the ground, possibly as a result of ground fire. It was not possible to conduct a thorough search of the area due to intense ground fire. Dien Bien Phu figures prominently in Vietnamese history as the site of the defeat of French forces, which brought the colonial war in Indo-China to a conclusion in 1954.

16 March 1966

F-105D 60-0411 333 TFS, 355 TFW, USAF, Takhli
Maj Paul Gerard Underwood (KIA)

The day after the Ubon Phantom was shot down near Dien Bien Phu the Takhli Wing sent several F-105s to fly armed reconnaissance in the area. One of the aircraft, flown by Maj Underwood, was hit by 37mm AAA two miles east of the town just after releasing its bombs on a target. The aircraft caught fire and eventually crashed about 5 miles northwest of Dien Bien Phu. In 1996, acting upon information provided by local villagers, a joint US-Vietnamese investigation team excavated a crash site and discovered human remains, identification tags and personal effects. The remains were later identified as those of Maj (since promoted to Col) Underwood and returned to the USA for burial.

17 March 1966

A-4C 147740 VA-94, USN, USS *Enterprise*
Lt(jg) Frederick Charles Baldock (POW)

A section of Skyhawks was assigned to a Rolling Thunder strike against a pontoon bridge about 25 miles south of Vinh. As the aircraft were en route to the target they received a SAM warning and began to take evasive action. Lt Baldock put his aircraft into a vertical dive but at 6,000 feet an SA-2 hit the aircraft and blew its tail off. Lt Baldock ejected immediately and was captured. Frederick Baldock had flown over 80 missions during the war and had a narrow escape in 1965 when flying from the *Ranger* with VA-94 when he landed his badly damaged Skyhawk at Da Nang with an eight-inch hole in the tailpipe. He was released from captivity on 12 February 1973.

18 March 1966

EF-10B 127041 VMCJ-1, MAG-11, USMC, Da Nang
1Lt Everett Alvin McPherson (KIA)
1Lt Brent Eden Davis (KIA)

The Marine Corps EF-10B Skynights of VMCJ-1 were a much sought after asset in Southeast Asia. Although obsolescent by the mid-1960s the aircraft was one of the few types equipped for electronic counter-measures. The Skynights spent much of their time jamming enemy radar during USAF and US Navy Rolling Thunder raids in North Vietnam. Two EF-10s were orbiting southwest of Thanh Hoa to provide jamming support for a USAF raid that was taking place about 10 miles west of the city. Flying at 26,000 feet one of the Skynights suddenly exploded and was assumed to have been the victim of an SA-2 missile although the crew of the other aircraft also saw some 85mm flak bursts in the area. The aircraft wreckage fell to earth near Ban Tang Luong, 45 miles southwest of Thanh Hoa, and a SAR effort failed to find any sign of the crew who were presumed to have been killed in the incident. A joint US-Vietnamese investigation into this case in 1993 found local villagers who claimed that one of the crew had ejected but his parachute failed to open and that the other crewmember was found in the aircraft wreck. The crash site was excavated in 1995 and 1997 and bone fragments were recovered that were proved by mitochondrial DNA testing to be those of 1Lt Davis. The remains were buried at Arlington National Cemetery on 8 December 1997.

20 March 1966

A-4C 148313 VA-36, USN, USS *Enterprise*
Cdr James Alfred Mulligan (POW)

Cdr Mulligan led three Skyhawks on a Rolling Thunder strike against a road bridge near Lang Dong, 15 miles southwest of Vinh. As he was pulling up from dropping the first of his Mk83 Snakeye bombs from 100 feet he felt several hits. He climbed the aircraft to 10,000 feet although it was on fire and streaming fuel from the rear fuselage. Three miles short of the coast there was an explosion in the forward engine compartment and Cdr Mulligan was forced to eject. He broke a shoulder and cracked several ribs on ejection and was captured and spent the next seven years as a POW until released on 12 February 1973. Like many prisoners he was moved about frequently and spent time in five different POW camps. He was in solitary confinement for a total of 42 months and spent more than 30 months in leg irons. Cdr Mulligan was the executive officer of VA-36 and was due to become the squadron commander on 1 April 1966. He had flown over 80 missions over North Vietnam during the war and in 1981 wrote a book titled *The Hanoi Commitment* about his experiences as a POW.

A-4C 145081 VA-144, USN, USS *Ticonderoga*
Lt(jg) Jerald Lee Pinneker (KIA)

Another Skyhawk was lost this day at the opposite end of Vietnam. A section of aircraft from the *Ticonderoga* was called upon to attack a VC troop concentration in the Mekong Delta near Vinh Binh, 25 miles south of Saigon. Like the vast majority of strikes in South Vietnam, the Navy aircraft operated under the watchful eye of a forward air controller. Lt Pinneker's aircraft was seen to start its second run, drop napalm canisters and then fly on until it hit several trees and disintegrated. It was thought that the pilot may have been hit by ground fire or the aircraft's elevator may have been damaged.

F-4B 151410 VF-92, USN, USS *Enterprise*
Lt(jg) James S Greenwood (survived)
Lt(jg) Richard Raymond Ratzlaff (POW)

During a strike on a bridge 10 miles southwest of Vinh, a Phantom was damaged, probably by shrapnel from its own Snakeye bombs. The aircraft started to burn and Lt Greenwood immediately turned east toward the coast. Several minutes later and just a short distance out to sea north of Mu Ron Ma, the aircraft became uncontrollable as the fire burnt through flight control cables and both crew ejected. The crew came down a few hundred yards from the beach where Lt Ratzlaff was quickly captured by a North Vietnamese fishing junk. Lt Greenwood was a little further from the beach and decided to swim for open water. A USAF HU-16 arrived and dropped flares under a thick overcast in preparation for a water landing. However, the aircraft was hit by AAA and the hull damaged so badly that it could not land on the sea. The Albatross continued to circle Lt Greenwood until a Seasprite, flown by Lt Cdr D J McCracken from the USS *Worden*, arrived on the scene. The helicopter door gunner fired at a North Vietnamese junk that was within 150 yards of Lt Greenwood. A flight of four A-4s from the *Enterprise* made strafing runs over the junks as Lt Cdr McCracken hovered over the survivor to complete the rescue as mortar rounds started falling all around. Lt Ratzlaff spent the next seven years as a POW until released on 12 February 1973.

21 March 1966

A-4C 149515 VA-94, USN, USS *Enterprise*
Lt Frank Ray Compton (KIA)

A-4C 148499 VA-94, USN, USS *Enterprise*
Lt Cdr John Mark Tiderman (KIA)

A flight of three Skyhawks was letting down to 1,000 feet over the sea for their run in across the North Vietnamese coast on a Rolling Thunder strike mission. The leader saw a flash in his rear view mirror and neither of his wingmen responded to his radio calls. It was assumed that the two aircraft had collided at a point about 15 miles off the coast and 30 miles due north of Dong Hoi. A SAM had been seen in flight in the general area and it was just possible that the two pilots, if they saw it, were distracted by it thereby causing the collision. It was thought very unlikely that the Skyhawks had actually been hit by a SAM.

RF-101C 56-0066 45 TRS, 39 AD on TDY, USAF, Udorn
Capt Arthur William Burer (POW)

A Voodoo on a photographic reconnaissance sortie was flying along the coast of North Vietnam at 2,000 feet near Hon Me island when it was hit by ground fire and burst into flames. The aircraft crashed on the coast about five miles south of Hon Nghi Son and Capt Burer ejected and was quickly captured. Arthur Burer had risen through the ranks, enlisting in the USAF in 1951 as an aircraft technician. In 1957 Burer was commissioned and attended flight school. He had flown around 40 missions over North Vietnam when he was shot down. He was released on 12 February 1973 and resumed his Air Force career.

O-1E 56-2617 unit ..?, USAF, base ..?
Maj Joseph Barnett Fearno (KIA)
1 crew, name unknown (survived)

A Bird Dog from an unknown unit crashed in Lam Dong province, South Vietnam during a visual reconnaissance mission when its engine failed. One of the crew was killed in the resulting force landing.

23 March 1966

F-100F 58-1212 Wild Weasel Detachment, 6234 TFW, USAF, Korat
Maj Clyde Duane Dawson (KIA)
Capt Donald E Clark (KIA)

The second Wild Weasel lost in combat was shot down during an Iron Hand mission over North Vietnam on 23 March. The aircraft was attacking a SAM site 20 miles northwest of Vinh when it was hit by AAA and crashed about five miles away killing both the crew. This was the last F-100F lost by the Wild Weasel detachment. The F-100F was soon to be replaced by the F-105F

in the Wild Weasel role but the Super Sabre did not fly its last Iron Hand mission until 11 July. The initial Weasel detachment destroyed nine SAM sites and forced a large number of batteries off the air at a critical time thereby protecting many hundreds of strike aircraft. This record had been achieved for the loss of three aircraft and four crewmen, one of whom was a prisoner. The Wild Weasel I detachment had pioneered the Air Force's anti-SAM mission and had developed many of the tactics and procedures that their successors use to this day.

F-105D 61-0178 357 TFS, 355 TFW, USAF, Takhli
Maj R A Hill (survived)

F-105D 60-0473 469 TFS, 6234 TFW, USAF, Korat
1Lt Kenneth Deane Thomas (survived)

Both F-105 wings sent aircraft on armed reconnaissance missions over the southern provinces of North Vietnam on the afternoon of 23 March. Maj Hill's aircraft was hit by 37mm flak as he was strafing vehicles in the Annamite Mountains near the Laotian border close to the village of Don Bai Dinh. As the aircraft remained controllable Maj Hill headed west to try to reach Takhli but he was forced to eject 10 miles west of Nakhon Phanom. About 10 minutes after Maj Hill's aircraft was hit, 1Lt Thomas attacked several vehicles about five miles north of Don Bai Dinh. His aircraft was also hit by 37mm fire during a strafing run and he tried to head west but he only got about 15 miles before he was forced to eject over Laos. 1Lt Thomas was rescued by helicopter having suffered minor injuries.

A-4C 147738 VA-93, USN, USS *Enterprise*
Lt Cdr John Bethel Tapp (KIA)

Following a successful night mission over South Vietnam two Skyhawks from the *Enterprise* regrouped off the coast and checked each other over for damage using the illumination of their aircraft lights. As the aircraft approached the carrier some 70 miles offshore the pilots were vectored for an instrument approach to the ship. Lt Cdr Tapp's approach appeared to going well until his aircraft disappeared from the radar screen eight miles from touch down. Two helicopters and two destroyers searched the sea thoroughly but found no sign of the pilot although an oil slick and scattered wreckage was seen in the area in the morning. It was thought that Lt Cdr Tapp inadvertently flew into the water and that hostile action was not thought to have caused the crash.

24 March 1966

F-105D 61-0095 421 TFS, 6234 TFW, USAF, Korat
Capt Robert Edward Bush (KIA)

Armed reconnaissance missions were proving just as costly as major Rolling Thunder strikes as another F-105 loss on the 24th

illustrates. Capt Bush's aircraft was hit by ground fire in the starboard wing and crashed in the mouth of the Sou Giang River 15 miles north of Dong Hoi. Nothing more was heard of the fate of Capt Bush until 15 December 1988 when the Vietnamese handed over human remains that were identified in September the following year as being those of Robert Bush.

25 March 1966

A-4C 148444 VA-76, USN, USS *Enterprise*
Lt(jg) Bradley Edsel Smith (POW)

A section of three Skyhawks was sent to attack a road ferry and ford across the Sou Giang River near the villages of Bau Khe and Tho Ngoa, 15 miles up the coast from Dong Hoi. The ford, nicknamed the 'Sandpile' by American pilots, was an important river crossing point on Road 1A and the target was bombed so often that the course of the river was changed. At 5,000 feet Lt Smith put his aircraft into a shallow dive to deliver his Snakeye bombs but the aircraft was hit by AAA and burst into flames. As the hydraulic system was knocked out Lt Smith ejected at 1,000 feet with the aircraft still in a dive. No one in the flight saw Lt Smith's aircraft go down and it was not until Radio Hanoi reported that a US pilot had been captured that it was discovered that he was still alive. Lt Smith was on his 77th mission when he was shot down. He was released in Operation Homecoming on 12 February 1973 and eventually retired from the Naval Reserve as a Commander.

The *Enterprise* was going through a very bad spell in late March. Between the 17th and the 25th the ship lost six A-4s and an F-4 with the loss of seven aircrew killed or missing.

F-8E 150673 VMF(AW)-235, MAG-11, USMC, Da Nang
1Lt John Brooks Sherman (KIA)

A section of Crusaders was assigned to fly a close air support mission against Viet Cong troops under the control of an FAC south of Tam Ky. 1Lt Sherman was making his second run at the target when his aircraft was shot down by ground fire five miles southeast of Phuoc An. A JTF-FA investigation team visited the crash site in 1993 and discovered that local villagers had buried the pilot's body near the wreckage. The site was excavated and remains and personal items recovered. However, it was not until July 1998 that a positive identification could be announced.

U-10B 63-13091 5 ACS, 14 ACW, USAF, Nha Trang
3 crew, names unknown (survived)

The 5th ACS lost its second U-10 Courier when an aircraft accidentally crashed as it took off for a mission in South Vietnam.

26 March 1966

C-130A 56-0506 41 TCS, 6315 OG, USAF, Naha
Capt John Butterfield (survived)
Several other crew, names unknown
(survived)

When a Hercules was landing on the runway at Tuy Hoa the aircraft suffered a malfunction of the propeller pitch mechanism and the pilot could not obtain reverse thrust from one of the engines. As the aircraft approached the end of the runway Capt Butterfield saw that a truck was blocking the runway and was forced to swerve off to one side. Unfortunately the aircraft ran into a drainage ditch and ended up on its belly. Although the damage was assessed as repairable the aircraft was later damaged beyond repair by an Army unit that tried to move the aircraft by passing a steel cable through the crew door and out of the pilot's side wind. When a tank tried to tow the aircraft away the cable simply sliced through the thin metal fuselage skin causing major damage. Ironically, the fuselage was later adapted by the Army at Tuy Hoa as an Officers' Club building.

The ubiquitous A-3 Skywarrior was used in a variety of roles during the war including attack, reconnaissance, electronic warfare and as a tanker. Only 20 A-3s were lost during the war, most of them in accidents. USN

27 March 1966

F-4C   63-7681   433 TFS, 8 TFW, USAF, Ubon
Capt D G Rokes (survived)
1Lt J Q Ozbolt (survived)

The Wolfpack lost a Phantom during a night mission over the Trail on the 27th. Capt Rokes and 1Lt Ozbolt ejected after their aircraft struck trees during an attack on a target near Ban Nampakhon, 30 miles west of the DMZ. Both the crew were rescued by helicopter.

A-4E   150128   VA-212, USN, USS *Hancock*
1 pilot, name unknown (survived)

While on a combat mission a Skyhawk suffered engine failure, probably due to a technical malfunction, forcing the pilot to eject.

29 March 1966

C-130B 61-0953   29 TCS, 463 TCW, USAF, Clark
Lt Col Lee Bernard Tate (KIA)
1Lt John Lawrence Banks (KIA)
A1C Ronald Charles Logan (KIA)
2 crew, names unknown (survived)

Three crew of a Philippines-based Hercules on rotation to South Vietnam were killed when their aircraft undershot the runway on a night flight into Pleiku. The 29th TCS was a newly-formed Hercules squadron and many of its aircrew had very little experience of either the Hercules or the airlift role. Due to its inexperience and initially poor safety record, the Squadron earned the unenviable nickname 'F-Troop' after a US television programme of that name. However, it later acquitted itself very well in Southeast Asia and ended the war with an excellent combat record.

30 March 1966

F-100D 55-3534   416 TFS, 3 TFW, USAF, Tan Son Nhut
Capt R C Oaks (survived)

The last aircraft loss of the month was a Super Sabre that was on a close air support mission in South Vietnam. Capt Oaks was making a strafing run against a building 12 miles west of Khanh Hung, just south of the Mekong Delta, when his aircraft was hit by small arms fire forcing him to eject.

1 April 1966

A-3B   142665   Detachment M, VAH-4, USN, USS *Enterprise*
Cdr William Ronald Grayson (KIA)
Lt(jg) William Frederick Kohlrusch (KIA)
ADJ2 Melvin Thomas Krech (KIA)

The *Enterprise's* bad luck continued into April. On the morning of the 1st the carrier was in the Gulf of Tonkin about 45 miles southwest of the Chinese island of Hainan. As a Skywarrior was being launched from the ship's catapult on a tanker sortie the aircraft's nose wheel collapsed causing the aircraft to crash into the sea. Lt Kohlrusch, the electronics flight officer, was picked up by the plane guard helicopter, a UH-2 Seasprite of HC-1, but died soon after. Niether the pilot, Cdr Grayson, nor the navigator, ADJ2 Krech, surfaced from the wreckage.

On this day the 2nd Air Division was redesignated as the Seventh Air Force and became responsible for all USAF units based or temporarily deployed to Southeast Asia with the exception of SAC's B-52 and KC-135 units.

2 April 1966

A-1H   serial ..?   unit ..?, USAF, probably Bien Hoa
Maj William L Richardson (KIA)

Maj Richardson was shot down in a single-seat Skyraider in Vinh Long province southwest of Saigon on a strafing run during an air strike. He was probably flying a VNAF Skyraider at the time.

RF-101C 56-0172   45 TRS, 39 AD on TDY, USAF, Tan Son Nhut
Capt Daniel James Doughty (POW)

During a photographic reconnaissance mission a Voodoo was shot down by ground fire near Xom Duong Quan in the Annamite Mountains, about 50 miles south of Vinh. Capt Doughty was

flying his 169th combat mission when he was shot down and taken prisoner. He was released on 12 February 1973.

3 April 1966

F-8C   146919   VF-24, USN, USS *Hancock*
Lt Richard Lee Laws (KIA)

During an air strike on a POL site at Bai Thuong, 20 miles northwest of Thanh Hoa, one of the Crusaders tasked with defence suppression was hit by AAA as it pulled up from its bombing run. Lt Laws reported that the aircraft had been hit and that he had a fire warning light in the cockpit. Twenty seconds later the leader saw the Crusader hit the side of a hill and explode. There was no evidence that the pilot had ejected.

4 April 1966

O-1F   57-2787   19 TASS, 505 TACG, USAF, Bien Hoa

A Bird Dog accidentally crashed in South Vietnam. Casualties, if any, are unknown.

F-100D 55-3573   510 TFS, 3 TFW, USAF, Bien Hoa
1 pilot, name unknown (survived)

Another accident occurred to a Bien Hoa aircraft when a Super Sabre was on a test flight over South Vietnam. A problem with the flight controls forced the pilot to abandon the aircraft.

5 April 1966

O-1E   56-4165   6253 CSG, USAF, Nha Trang
2 crew, names unknown (survived)

A structural failure during a training flight caused a Bird Dog to force land and crash.

6 April 1966

A-4E   152052   VA-212, USN, USS *Hancock*
Lt Dennis Philip Cook (KIA)

A catapult malfunction on board the *Hancock* caused the loss of a Skyhawk and its pilot in the South China Sea as it was being launched on a combat mission.

7 April 1966

B-57B   52-1530   8 TBS, 405 FW attached to 6252 TFW,
USAF, Da Nang
Capt Robert Russell Barnett (KIA)
Capt Thomas Taylor Walker (KIA)

A Canberra was lost during a daylight raid in the Steel Tiger area of Laos about 55 miles west of Hué. The cause was not determined although it was thought probable that the aircraft had been hit by ground fire. This aircraft had previously served with both the Nevada and Kentucky ANG prior to service in Southeast Asia.

8 April 1966

A-1E   52-133882   1 ACS, 14 ACW, USAF, Pleiku
Capt S Knickerbocker (survived)

As a Skyraider was strafing a target five miles west of Da Nang it was hit by small arms fire in the fuselage. The pilot bailed out safely and was rescued by an HH-43 SAR helicopter.

9 April 1966

RF-8A   144611   Detachment L, VFP-63, USN, USS *Hancock*
Lt(jg) Thomas Gavin Walster (KIA)

One of the *Hancock's* reconnaissance Crusaders was hit in the tail section by AAA during a run over Vinh. Although badly damaged the aircraft still remained controllable and Lt Walster flew to Da Nang where he intended to make an emergency landing. The aircraft became uncontrollable as the landing gear was lowered and he realised that a safe landing was impossible. Lt Walster took the aircraft out to sea and ejected about five miles north of Da Nang but unfortunately he was drowned. Apparently his life jacket did not inflate and although a PJ jumped into the water and grabbed the pilot's parachute he was unable to save Lt Walster from being dragged under and drowned.

12 April 1966

KA-3B   142653   Detachment C, VAH-4, USN,
USS *Kitty Hawk*
Lt Cdr William Albert Glasson (KIA)
Lt(jg) Larry Michael Jordan (KIA)
PRCS Kenneth Ward Pugh (KIA)
ATCS Reuben Beaumont Harris (KIA)

On the morning of 12 April a Skywarrior tanker took off from Cubi Point NAS in the Philippines (where it had been undergoing minor repairs) to return to the *Kitty Hawk*. When the aircraft became overdue a search was organised by the *Kitty Hawk* and *Enterprise* together with USAF aircraft but no trace of the aircraft or its crew were ever found. Soon after the aircraft disappeared the Chinese claimed that an American aircraft had entered Chinese territory near Hainan Island and had been shot down by Chinese MiGs. It was later determined that the Skywarrior had indeed been shot down by the Chinese over the Luichow Peninsula in Kuangtung province. Despite protests from the US State Department nothing more was heard until 16 December 1975 when the Chinese handed over ashes said to be those of Kenneth Pugh, one of the crewmen of the Skywarrior.

13 April 1966

C-123B 56-4382   315 ACW, USAF, Tan Son Nhut

In the early hours of the 13th the Viet Cong launched a mortar attack on Tan Son Nhut. This was the heaviest air base attack up to this time with 245 rounds fired from mortars and recoilless rifles, and although only one aircraft was destroyed, about 60 others (including five SP-2H Neptunes of VP-1) received some degree of damage. In addition, 34 vehicles were destroyed or badly damaged and a 420,000-gallon fuel tank was set on fire and destroyed. The damage would have been even worse had not earth revetments been built as a result of earlier experience at Bien Hoa and other bases.

O-1E   serial ..?   22 TASS, 505 TACG, USAF, Binh Thuy
Capt R M Overland (survived)
1 crew, name unknown (survived)

A Bird Dog from the Mekong Delta base of Binh Thuy was flying a visual reconnaissance mission along the coast a few miles south of Ba Dong when it was hit by ground fire and burst into flames. The pilot quickly crash-landed the aircraft and both crewmen were picked up unhurt by an Army helicopter.

A-1H   139692   VA-52, USN, USS *Ticonderoga*
Cdr John Clement Mape (KIA)

A section of Skyraiders from VA-52 on an armed reconnaissance mission was preparing to attack a small wooden bridge that had been spotted during an earlier flight. As the aircraft were flying at 7,500 feet near Giao Phuong 15 miles southwest of Vinh, an SA-2 missile was launched, which destroyed one of the Skyraiders. The aircraft was flown by Cdr Mape, who had been the CO of VA-52 since 10 December 1965. JTF-FA investigators visited the crash site several times in the early 1990s but did not find any remains. However, in 1994 the investigators learned that a number of Vietnamese men had been arrested two years earlier for illegally excavating the crash site and removing human remains. Vietnamese authorities confiscated the remains and handed them over to the JTF-FA team. The remains were later positively identified as being those of Cdr Mape.

RF-101C 56-0086   20 TRS, 460 TRW, USAF, Tan Son Nhut
detached to Udorn
1 pilot, name unknown (survived)

The Voodoo was said to be a tricky aircraft to land due to its highly sensitive longitudinal stability, particularly at low speed. An aircraft was destroyed in a landing accident at Udorn when returning from a sortie over North Vietnam.

14 April 1966

F-8E   149179   VF-51, USN, USS *Ticonderoga*
Ens G W Riese (survived)

Returning from an escort mission a Crusader struck the ramp of the *Ticonderoga* during a night landing. The pilot ejected safely.

B-57B 53-3925 8 TBS, 405 FW attached to 35 TFW, USAF, Da Nang
Maj Robert P Bateman (survived)
Capt Robert H McCaw (survived)

B-57B 53-3926 8 TBS, 405 FW attached to 35 TFW, USAF, Da Nang
Maj James T Greshel (survived)
Capt Vernon G Wittkopp (survived)

Two Canberras collided in mid-air during a practice formation flight over Da Nang. Fortunately, all the crewmembers survived the accident.

15 April 1966

F-105D 58-1158 469 TFS, 388 TFW, USAF, Korat
Capt John A McCurdy (KIA)

The 388th TFW was activated at Korat on 14 March 1966 and organised on 8 April to take over operations from the 6234th TFW, which had controlled the Korat F-105 squadrons since January 1965. The first casualty sustained by the 388th TFW happened just a week after it started operations. A Thunderchief crashed killing its pilot when the aircraft's engine failed over Thailand during an armed reconnaissance mission. This aircraft was the 13th F-105D to be built and had previously served with the 4th TFW at Seymour Johnson AFB.

16 April 1966

F-4C 63-7677 433 TFS, 8 TFW, USAF, Ubon
Maj Samuel Robert Johnson (POW)
1Lt Larry James Chesley (POW)

A Phantom was hit by automatic weapons fire during an armed reconnaissance mission near Ha Loi, 35 miles north of the DMZ. Both crew ejected and were captured. Maj Johnson was on his 25th mission and Lt Chesley on his 76th. During the ejection Maj Johnson suffered a broken back, broken arm and a dislocated shoulder. Later Lt Chesley contracted beri beri, which debilitated him throughout his years of captivity. Both men were released from captivity on 12 February 1973.

Samuel Johnson had flown 62 combat missions in the F-86 during the Korean War and flew tours with the Air Force Fighter Weapons School and the Thunderbirds display team after his release from Vietnam. Highly decorated, Samuel Johnson retired from the USAF as a Colonel in 1979 and became active in politics, culminating in his being elected Congressman for Dallas, Texas in May 1991. Johnson became prominent in his criticism of the Smithsonian Institution's exhibition at the National Air and Space Museum of 'Enola Gay' and its atomic mission. He was later appointed to the Smithsonian's Board of Regents. He wrote a book titled *Captive Warriors* about his POW experience in Vietnam. Larry Chesley also wrote a book about his experiences, titled *Seven Years in Hanoi*, which was published in 1973.

17 April 1966

B-57C 53-3833 8 TBS, 405 FW attached to 35 TFW, USAF, Da Nang
Capt Larry J Horacek (survived)
Capt D N Harnage (survived)

A costly day for the US forces in Southeast Asia commenced with the loss of a Canberra during an attack on an automatic weapons site on the North Vietnamese border with Laos about 25 miles north of the DMZ. The aircraft was on its second strafing run when it was hit and caught fire. Both crew ejected and were rescued by a USAF helicopter. Larry Horacek had been shot down previously on 6 August 1965 during an earlier tour at Da Nang. This Canberra was a B-57C model fitted with dual controls for training and 53-3833 was the only C-model lost during the war.

A-4E 151058 VA-56, USN, USS *Ticonderoga*
Lt Cdr V G Hough (survived)

A section of Skyhawks was searching for a SAM site near the Laotian border 40 miles south of Vinh when one of the aircraft was hit by AAA. The aircraft caught fire which spread rapidly and

as the pilot ejected the aircraft's tail section broke away. Lt Cdr Hough was rescued by a USAF helicopter.

A-6A 151794 VA-85, USN, USS *Kitty Hawk*
Lt Cdr D L Sayers (survived)
Lt Cdr C J Hawkins (survived)

As a section of Intruders was flying an armed reconnaissance mission along the coast of North Vietnam near Mu Ron Ma one of the aircraft was hit in the starboard wing by 37mm anti-aircraft fire. The hydraulics failed and a fire burned continuously as the aircraft limped over 125 miles towards the carrier. As the aircraft was uncontrollable below 250 knots and the fire had almost burnt through the wing the crew ejected over the sea some 35 miles northeast of Hué. Both crewmen were picked up safely by a USAF Albatross amphibian.

A-1H 135398 VA-115, USN, USS *Kitty Hawk*
Lt(jg) William Leslie Tromp (KIA)

Two of *Kitty Hawk's* Skyraiders were flying a night coastal reconnaissance mission between Mu Ron Ma and Vinh when Lt Tromp sighted and attacked a target in the mouth of the Song Gia Hoi River. Following his attack Lt Tromp told his wingman not to make his run as a SAM had been fired at his aircraft. As both aircraft headed out to sea Tromp radioed that he had an emergency and soon after contact with him was lost. No trace was ever found of Lt Tromp although in 1973 US divers located and investigated the wreck of his aircraft without finding any remains.

A-4C 148583 VA-113, USN, USS *Kitty Hawk*
1 pilot, name unknown (survived)

The fifth aircraft lost this day was a Skyhawk that crashed into the Gulf of Tonkin during a catapult launch from the *Kitty Hawk*. It was suspected that an incorrect trim setting caused the aircraft to nose over after it left the catapult.

18 April 1966

A-1J 142032 VA-52, USN, USS *Ticonderoga*
Lt A D Wilson (survived)

During a SAR mission for one of the aircraft lost the previous day (probably the Skyraider flown by Lt Tromp), Lt Wilson overflew Tiger Island, 15 miles off the coast opposite the DMZ. On his fifth pass over the island his aircraft was hit by automatic weapons fire forcing him to ditch two miles off shore. He was picked up by a USAF helicopter.

19 April 1966

F-105D 62-4330 333 TFS, 355 TFW, USAF, Takhli
1Lt Lee Aaron Adams (KIA)

The 19th proved to be another costly day for the Air Force and Navy in Southeast Asia. The first aircraft lost on this day was one of a flight of four F-105s that crashed as it was strafing a truck near Van Loc, 40 miles north of the DMZ. No ejection or parachute was seen and it was assumed that Lt Adams died in the crash, which was caused either by ground fire or by flying into the ground.

O-1F 57-2800 Det 3, 505 TACG, USAF, Nakhon Phanom
Capt Joseph Orville Brown (KIA)
1 crew, name unknown (KIA) - probably not USAF

Capt Brown was flying with an observer of unknown nationality near Ban Pongdong just south of the Mu Gia Pass when his aircraft was hit by ground fire. He reported that part of his starboard tailplane had been blown off and was going to attempt to gain altitude but the aircraft was then seen in a steep dive and rolling out of control. Although it was not known at the time it was later established that both men died in the crash. The crash site was investigated in 1994 and 1995 and Capt Brown's remains were recovered and buried at Arlington National Cemetery on 19 April 1999, 33 years to the day of his death.

A-1E 52-132425 602 ACS, 14 ACW, USAF, Nha Trang
Capt Richard Joseph Robbins (KIA)

As soon as Capt Brown's Bird Dog went down a flight of Skyraiders was despatched to provide escort for a USAF HH-3

helicopter that was to attempt a rescue if either of the crew had survived. As the Skyraiders were orbiting over the Bird Dog's crash site one of the aircraft was hit in the wing by ground fire. Capt Robbins must have estimated that his best chance of rescue was over the sea and he tried to make for the coast. However, the aircraft crashed near the North Vietnamese border and Capt Robbins was killed. In May 1995 a joint US/Lao investigation of a crash site yielded human remains, personal effects and other items. Following positive identification, the remains of Capt Robbins were returned to the USA in September 1996.

RF-8A 146843 Detachment B, VFP-63, USN, USS *Ticonderoga*
Lt Ron F Ball (survived)

Following the Air Force losses in the morning of the 19th, the Navy lost two Crusaders during the afternoon. Lt Ball was flying at 2,000 feet over Cao Ba Island off Haiphong, taking photographs of potential targets, when his aircraft was hit by AAA. The damage caused a fuel fire and a loss of oil pressure. Lt Ball immediately put the Crusader into a climb and reached 12,000 feet before his engine seized through lack of oil. He ejected 15 miles south of the island and was rescued by a Navy SH-3A from HS-4 from the USS *Yorktown*.

F-8E 150853 VF-53, USN, USS *Ticonderoga*
Cdr R A Mohrpardt (survived)

An hour after Lt Ball's incident an air strike took place on a major road bridge five miles north of Haiphong. A section of Crusaders was assigned as escorts to defend the Skyhawk bombers from any potential MiG threat. As the escorts flew over the target one of the Crusaders received hits from AAA in both wings. Wing fuel and hydraulics were lost in quick succession but the aircraft remained flyable and Cdr Mohrpardt set course for his carrier. Unfortunately, the damage to the hydraulics meant that he was unable to deploy the Crusader's refuelling probe and after flying south for about 100 miles Cdr Mohrpardt had to eject over the Gulf of Tonkin as his fuel was exhausted. He was rescued by a Navy helicopter. Five of the bridge's 21 spans were dropped as a result of this raid.

20 April 1966

F-105D 60-0442 421 TFS, 388 TFW, USAF, Korat
Capt J B Abernathy (survived)

A Thunderchief was shot down by 37mm AAA in the Annamite Mountains near Don Bai Dinh, close to the border with Laos, while flying an armed reconnaissance mission along a mountain road. These missions over the Annamites were part of the interdiction effort to reduce the amount of supplies flowing down the Ho Chi Minh Trail into South Vietnam. However, worthwhile targets rarely presented themselves, especially during the daytime. Capt Abernathy was fortunate to be rescued by an HH-3 from Nakhon Phanom.

A-4C 148512 VA-113, USN, USS *Kitty Hawk*
Cdr John Abbott (POW - died)

Cdr Abbott, the CO of VA-113, led a strike of eight Skyhawks against the Vinh Son road bridge over the Song Ca River, 25 miles northwest of Vinh. There was intense anti-aircraft fire over the target and Cdr Abbott's aircraft was hit in the starboard wing causing a fire. As the Commander flew toward the coast the aircraft started to roll uncontrollably and disintegated at about 2,000 feet. It is thought that Cdr Abbott, who had only taken over as acting squadron commander on 11 April, had died shortly after being taken prisoner.

A-4C 149495 VA-113, USN, USS *Kitty Hawk*
Lt(jg) H G Welch (survived)

Soon after Cdr Abbott was shot down a section of Skyhawks was assigned to provide SAR cover for a possible rescue attempt. Just after the aircraft crossed the coast, about 15 miles north of Vinh, one of the Skyhawks was hit by 37mm ground fire. With the aircraft on fire Lt Welch headed back out to sea and flew 80 miles to where the *Kitty Hawk* was waiting for him to make an emergency landing. Unfortunately, as the Skyhawk approached the ship the fire burned through vital controls and

Lt Welch was forced to eject and was picked up by one of the carrier's Seasprite helicopters.

21 April 1966

F-4C 63-7531 559 TFS, 12 TFW, USAF, Cam Ranh Bay
1Lt R E Goodenough (survived)
1Lt P A Bush (survived)

During a Steel Tiger strike a Phantom was hit by ground fire near Tang Hune Nord in southern Laos. The aircraft flew northeast towards South Vietnam but the crew was soon forced to eject and were picked up safely by two Marine Corps UH-34Ds of HMM-161, although one of the helicopters was damaged by ground fire and its pilot wounded.

A-6A 151798 VA-85, USN, USS *Kitty Hawk*
Cdr Jack Elmer Keller (KIA)
Lt Cdr Ellis Ernest Austin (KIA)

Two Intruders from the *Kitty Hawk* took off just before dusk for a night attack on the heavily defended Tan Loc barracks and supply area on the coast 10 miles north of Vinh. On the run in to the coast Cdr Keller's wingman had a problem and broke away to dump his bombs on Hon Mat island, after which he waited for his leader to return. It was Cdr Keller's intention to fly past the target then turn over high ground and bomb the target before heading straight out to sea. The wingman saw a bright flash, which he initially thought might have been a bomb explosion, but at the same time the Intruder disappeared from an E-2 Hawkeye's radar screen. It was thought that the Intruder was either shot down or flew into high ground during the run in to the target. Cdr Keller had taken command of VA-85 on 22 December 1965 following the loss of Cdr Cartwright.

F-4B 151010 VMFA-542, MAG-11, USMC, Da Nang
Capt F A Huey (survived)
2Lt J L Arendale (survived)

To return the favour of the Marine helicopter picking up the USAF Phantom crew earlier in the day, a USAF helicopter rescued a Marine Phantom crew during the night. A flight of Da Nang Phantoms was attacking a group of six trucks on the Ho Chi Minh Trail in Laos about five miles north of where the USAF Phantom was hit. On its second run dropping napalm, Capt Huey's aircraft was hit by 37mm ground fire and the crew ejected immediately. The crew was rescued but 2Lt Arendale was badly injured during the ejection.

22 April 1966

RF-101C 56-0090 20 TRS, 460 TRW, USAF, Tan Son Nhut
detached to Udorn
Maj Alan Leslie Brunstrom (POW)

A Voodoo was lost while photographing the Cao Nung railway bridge, 50 miles northeast of Hanoi, which had been a target in December 1965 before the bombing halt. The aircraft was flying at 4,500 feet when it was hit by ground fire in the port engine. Maj Brunstrom ejected from his blazing aircraft and became a POW for the rest of the war. This was the seventh RF-101 lost in Southeast Asia since beginning of the year. In his Air Force career Alan Brunstrom had instructed on the T-33 and F-86 and had flown the C-119 and C-123 support aircraft for the Thunderbirds display team. He was on his 115th combat mission when he was shot down and was released from captivity on 12 February 1973.

A-6A 151785 VA-85, USN, USS *Kitty Hawk*
Lt Cdr Robert Franklin Weimorts (KIA)
Lt(jg) William Brewster Nickerson (KIA)

The third Intruder lost by VA-85 during April went down during an Iron Hand strike on Vinh. The Intruder's stability and excellent load-carrying capability made it a suitable platform for the anti-SAM mission for which it carried Shrike missiles and bombs. Following the attack on Vinh, Lt Cdr Weimorts rendezvoused with his wingman over the sea before orbiting to identify any radar or SAM signals that could be picked up and analyzed. The wingman saw his leader's aircraft descend smoothly into the water 10 miles off the coast. The conditions were deceptive because although visibility was generally good,

haze made the horizon indistinct and this, together with the crew's possible preoccupation with their operational task, may have caused the aircraft to fly into the sea.

F-105D 62-4409 421 TFS, 388 TFW, USAF, Korat
Capt Charles Graham Boyd (POW)

A Thunderchief was shot down by AAA as it was attacking a SAM site near the Song Lo River near Phu Tho, 35 miles northwest of Hanoi. Capt Boyd ejected and was quickly captured. He had arrived at Korat in November 1965 and was on his 105th combat mission when he was shot down. He had also been shot down on 26 February but was rescued on that occasion. He was released on 12 February 1973 and resumed his Air Force career finally retiring in 1995 as a four-star General as Deputy Commander-in-Chief of US European Command after being vice commander of SAC's Eighth Air Force and commander of the Air University.

A-1E 52-132634, 1 ACS, 14 ACW, USAF, Pleiku
52-135021

An early morning mortar attack on Pleiku resulted in the destruction of two Skyraiders and damage to 11 other aircraft. A total of 79 mortar rounds are thought to have landed on the base and five men were wounded.

23 April 1966

F-105D 61-0157 421 TFS, 388 TFW, USAF, Korat
Capt Robert Raymond Dyczkowski (KIA)

F-105D 61-0048 421 TFS, 388 TFW, USAF, Korat
Maj Bernard Joseph Goss (KIA)

The Thunderchiefs from Korat struck a road bridge at Phu Lang Thuong 30 miles northeast of Hanoi and only 10 miles from Kep. The bridge was one of several on a major supply route from China to Hanoi. Capt Dyczkowski failed to rejoin his flight after dropping his bombs and was thought to have been shot down either at the target or near Thai Nguyen during the flight's egress. Capt Dyczkowski was on his 99th mission over North Vietnam and was due to return home in a few days.

About 15 minutes after the first wave of bombers hit the Phu Lang Thuong Bridge it was struck again by another flight of Thunderchiefs. Maj Goss's aircraft was hit by AAA as he neared the target and he was seen to eject and land on a steep hillside. Neither airmen became POWs and it is assumed that they were both killed. Capt Dyczkowski's aircraft was painted as 'Shirley Ann'.

A-4E 152025 VA-55, USN, USS *Ranger*
Lt Cdr C A Gray (survived)

As a Skyhawk pulled out from a dive bombing run on a VC concentration in the Mekong Delta, the pilot felt a thump and lost control of the aircraft. At 2,000 feet the pilot ejected and was subsequently picked up by an Army helicopter. The cause of the aircraft's loss was never determined.

24 April 1966

F-105D 61-0051 469 TFS, 388 TFW, USAF, Korat
Lt Col William Earl Cooper (KIA)

F-105D 62-4340 469 TFS, 388 TFW, USAF, Korat
1Lt Jerry Donald Driscoll (POW)

Despite the loss of two aircraft on the 23rd the Phu Lang Thuong Bridge was attacked again on the 24th. This time it was the turn of the 469th TFS led by the squadron commander, Lt Col William Cooper. As the first flight of aircraft approached the bridge from the north at 6,000 feet, Lt Col Cooper's Thunderchief was hit by an SA-2 missile. The aircraft broke in half and the forward section fell to earth in a flat spin. No ejection or parachute was seen.

Five minutes later, as another flight started their bombing run on the bridge, 1Lt Driscoll's aircraft was hit by large calibre AAA and caught fire. Trailing flames twice the length of his aircraft, 1Lt Driscoll ejected just as the Thud rolled inverted. The Phu Lang Thuong Bridge had now cost the USAF four aircraft and four pilots, only one of whom survived. Driscoll's parachute had barely had time to open when he hit the ground and was immediately surrounded by about 20 North Vietnamese. Jerry Driscoll spent the next seven years in various POW camps. On 6 July 1966

he was forced to lead one of two groups of POWs as they were paraded through the streets of Hanoi where the prisoners suffered much physical abuse from the gathered mob. He had been on his 112th mission when he was shot down and was released on 12 February 1973. Jerry Driscoll resumed his Air Force career after his release but eventually retired with the rank of Colonel and went to fly for American Airlines.

25 April 1966

RF-4C 64-1045 16 TRS, 460 TRW, USAF, Tan Son Nhut
Capt Warren Leroy Anderson (KIA)
1Lt James Hale Tucker (KIA)

The RF-4C was the USAF's photographic reconnaissance version of the Phantom, similar to the Marine's RF-4B. The 16th TRS was the first RF-4C Phantom squadron to deploy to Southeast Asia and arrived at Tan Son Nhut in October 1965. By the end of 1967 there were four RF-4C squadrons in the theatre, two based at Tan Son Nhut and two at Udorn. In addition to its primary role of photographic reconnaissance, the RF-4C was also used for weather reconnaissance and as part of a fast FAC team with other Phantoms. The RF-4C supplemented and then gradually replaced the older RF-101C Voodoo in the photographic reconnaissance role.

The first RF-4C lost in Southeast Asia was brought down during a night mission over an important road ferry on the Sou Giang River, 20 miles north of Dong Hoi. The aircraft was photographing the intense anti-aircraft defences when it disappeared from radar screens monitoring the flight. The aircraft was descending after crosssing a mountain range and may either have been shot down or flew into the ground. No trace of aircraft or crew has yet been found.

26 April 1966

F-4B 152255 VF-114, USN, USS *Kitty Hawk*
Lt(jg) N W Smith (survived)
Lt(jg) R Blake (survived)

During an attack on junks and sampans on the coast about 25 miles north of Vinh, a Phantom commenced its dive at 5,000 feet, dropped several Mk82 bombs and pulled out at 500 feet. The crew felt a thump and the aircraft's electrical power failed. The wingman reported fuel streaming from the aircraft and a fire warning light prompted the pilot to shut down the starboard engine. The aircraft flew 90 miles back to the vicinity of the *Kitty Hawk* but damage to the hydraulic system meant that neither the flaps nor the undercarriage would come down. A fire warning light on the remaining engine left no option but for the crew to eject and be rescued by one of the ship's helicopters. The damage was probably caused either by shrapnel from the bombs or debris from one of the targets.

27 April 1966

A-6A 151788 VA-85, USN, USS *Kitty Hawk*
Lt William R Westerman (survived)
Lt(jg) Brian E Westin (survived)

Photographic coverage following the attack on the coastal vessels on the 26th prompted the Navy to send a flight of Intruders to the same vicinity the next day. A number of wooden barges had been spotted in a canal just inland from the coast and the Intruders attacked with napalm from low level. As Lt Westerman started his run a small calibre bullet penetrated the cockpit and hit him in the shoulder. With Westerman slipping in and out of consciousness and his left arm incapacitated he ejected just offshore near the mouth of the Song Ca River, just north of Vinh. Lt Westin then realised how close the aircraft was to the coast so he unstrapped and leaned over to steer the Intruder a few more miles out to sea and made a Mayday call before he too ejected. Lt Westin was picked up first and when they found the wounded pilot, Lt Westin insisted on going down on the rescue hoist to ensure his pilot was rescued. Lt Westin then waited in the sea, surrounded by sharks, until he also was rescued, once more, by a second helicopter. Lt Brian Westin was later awarded the Navy Cross for his exploits to save his pilot.

28 April 1966

F-4G   150645   VF-213, USN, USS *Kitty Hawk*
          Lt R A Schiltz (survived)
          Lt(jg) C C Lewis (survived)

The F-4G variant of the Phantom was fitted with the AN/ASW-21 two-way data link equipment in an attempt to automate the air defence process between ships, AEW aircraft and fighters. Only 12 aircraft were built and only VF-213 flew the aircraft in Southeast Asia. The experiment was not a success and neither was an overall dark green camouflage paint scheme on VF-213's aircraft and those of other aircraft on the *Kitty Hawk*'s 1966 cruise. The first and only F-4G lost in Southeast Asia was hit by ground fire as it was making a rocket attack on some cargo-carrying junks about two miles off the North Vietnamese coast, 15 miles northeast of Thanh Hoa. The aircraft caught fire, the port engine was shut down and fuel was seen to be streaming from the aircraft. As the aircraft flew towards the carrier the fire spread and when the starboard engine also had to be shut down the crew ejected and were picked up by a Navy helicopter 60 miles from the coast. After returning to the USA the remaining F-4Gs were remanufactured to F-4B standard. The F-4G designation was re-used in 1978 for the Wild Weasel variant of the F-4E.

29 April 1966

A-4E   151047   VMA-223, MAG-12, USMC, Chu Lai
          Capt William Francis Mullen (KIA)

The 29th was another bad day for the US in Southeast Asia with six aircraft and their pilots lost. Capt Mullen was taking part in a strike against gun emplacements near the Ban Karai Pass in Laos, close to the DMZ, when he was shot down on his first low level pass. His aircraft was last seen on fire entering cloud and heading towards the north. William Mullen, like so many other airmen lost over Laos, disappeared without a trace, despite initial hopes that he may have been captured when a beeper signal was picked up. Capt Mullen's wife, Barbara, later wrote of the attempts to discover the fate of her husband in a book titled *Every Effort*. This was the first aircraft lost by VMA-223 since it arrived at Chu Lai in December 1965 and the 29th of April should have been a day of rejoicing as the Squadron reached its 10,000th accident-free flying hour on that day.

F-8E   150867   VF-211, USN, USS *Hancock*
          Lt(jg) Thomas Edward Brown (KIA)

Lt Brown was the wingman on a two-plane armed reconnaissance along the coast of North Vietnam. The section spotted a motorized junk just east of Dao Cat Ba island near Haiphong and prepared to make shallow, low level strafing runs on the vessel. On Lt Brown's first run his aircraft collided with a karst rock jutting out of the sea about 300 yards from the target. It was considered that the pilot had inadvertently flown into the rock as no ground fire was seen.

A-1H   137576   VA-215, USN, USS *Hancock*
          Lt Cdr William Patrick Egan (KIA)

While on a Steel Tiger road reconnaissance mission in southern Laos Lt Cdr Egan's Skyraider was shot down by small arms fire near Ban Senphan as it was diving on a vehicle. Like Capt Mullen, no trace was ever found of Lt Cdr Egan.

F-105D   62-4304   333 TFS, 355 TFW, USAF, Takhli
          1Lt Donald William Bruch (KIA)

On the 29th the USAF mounted a raid on the railway yards at Thai Nguyen, an important centre for steel production in North Vietnam. Over the target 1Lt Bruch's Thunderchief was hit by 85mm AAA. The aircraft climbed as it sped off towards the northwest but about 20 miles from Thai Nguyen the Thunderchief suddenly went out of control and dived into the ground.

RF-101C   56-0218   20 TRS, 460 TRW, USAF, Tan Son Nhut
          detached to Udorn
          Maj Albert Edward Runyan (POW)

The eighth RF-101 lost in Southeast Asia since the beginning of the year was shot down 15 miles southwest of Yen Bai and 65 miles northwest of Hanoi, possibly while heading towards Thai

Nguyen to take post-strike photographs of the F-105 raid on the railway yards. Maj Runyan was taken prisoner and released during Operation Homecoming on 12 February 1973. Commissioned in 1951, he had flown 100 combat missions during the Korean War and was on his 88th mission in Vietnam when he was shot down. He retired from the USAF as a Colonel in 1974.

A-1E   52-132680   602 ACS, 14 ACW, USAF, Udorn
          Capt Leo Sydney Boston (KIA)

During April the 602nd ACS moved its headquarters to Udorn as more and more of its tasking constituted SAR escort over southern Laos and North Vietnam. Soon after it was known that Maj Runyan's Voodoo had been shot down a SAR task force was organised to attempt a rescue. Just after the two leading Skyraiders crossed the Laotian border into North Vietnam en route to the search area, one of the Sandys became separated from the other aircraft. Capt Boston was then jumped by a MiG-17 that shot down the Skyraider over a mountainous area 10 miles east of Na San. Capt Boston was maintained as missing until 27 April 1978 when his status was changed to 'presumed dead'. During the time he was listed as missing, he was promoted to the rank of Colonel.

30 April 1966

A-4E   151145   VA-55, USN, USS *Ranger*
          Lt J S Buzby (survived)

Lt Buzby had successfully completed an armed reconnaissance mission over southern Laos and was returning to his carrier at high altitude when the Skyhawk's oil pressure started to drop. Lt Buzby commenced a shallow descent towards Da Nang where he hoped to make an emergency landing. However, as he neared Da Nang the engine began to run rough and started to come apart forcing the pilot to eject just off the coast. He was soon picked up by a USAF helicopter. The cause of the damage was not determined but was most likely due to mechanical failure rather than enemy action.

1 May 1966

A-1E   52-133871   602 ACS, 14 ACW, USAF, Udorn
          Capt J M Ingalls (survived)

Barrel Roll strikes still continued although aircraft losses in this campaign remained at a low level. A Skyraider on a Firefly strike mission was hit by ground fire while orbiting near the Ban Nalong storage area in northeastern Laos. Capt Ingalls managed to fly a few miles from the target area before bailing out and was eventually recovered unharmed.

A-4E   151179   VA-212, USN, USS *Hancock*
          Lt R H Mansfield (survived)

A section of Skyhawks from the *Hancock* on an armed reconnaissance mission spotted a truck convoy on a road 10 miles south of Vinh. Convoys on main roads in North Vietnam were rare and valuable targets and the aircraft commenced an attack straight away. As Mansfield fired rockets from his LAU-3 pod he saw one rocket tumble and hit the aircraft's tail and his engine then began to malfunction. He headed towards the coast but two minutes later was forced to eject as the aircraft caught fire and the engine failed. He was picked up safely by a Navy helicopter. It was suspected that parts of a rocket had been ingested into the engine or had penetrated the fuselage and ruptured a fuel line.

2 May 1966

F-8E   149169   VF-211, USN, USS *Hancock*
          Lt Eugene J Chancy (survived)

Hon Me island off the North Vietnamese coast between Thanh Hoa and Vinh was a frequent target as it was the site of an early warning radar facility. On commencement of a strafing run over the radar site Lt Chancy's Crusader suffered complete hydraulic failure and the aircraft was seen to be on fire. The pilot ejected after the aircraft began to roll uncontrollably. He landed close to Hon Me and had to swim away from the island as the current was carrying him towards the shore and his life raft had been punctured. He was picked up by a Navy UH-2 and spent a few hours

on board a radar picket destroyer before returning to the *Hancock* to fly again the next day. Gene Chancy shot down a MiG-17 during a dogfight on 21 June. This was the second time Lt Chancy had ejected from a Crusader, the first time was during a training flight over the Californian desert on Friday 13 December 1963.

A-4E   151034   VA-55, USN, USS *Ranger*
          Lt Cdr Walter Sutton Wood (KIA)

Following the loss of Lt Mansfield's Skyhawk the previous day, another aircraft was lost in similar circumstances on the 2nd. Lt Cdr Wood was returning from an armed reconnaissance mission and made an attack on Hon Ngu island just off the coast near Vinh, as he had one rocket left in his LAU-3 pod. Lt Cdr Wood was seen to eject after firing the rocket and his parachute was observed to come down in the sea near the island. However, he may have been incapacitated during the ejection as he was not seen to move in the water nor separate from his parachute and his body disappeared beneath the surface 10 minutes after ejecting. Rocket disintegration was again suspected as the cause of this tragic loss.

4 May 1966

F-4C   64-0688   557 TFS, 12 TFW, USAF, Cam Ranh Bay
          2 crew, names unknown (survived)

Following a strike mission a Phantom crashed during a GCA landing attempt at Cam Ranh Bay. The aircraft was making its second approach in heavy rain when the engines flamed out from lack of fuel.

5 May 1966

F-105D   61-0147   469 TFS, 388 TFW, USAF, Korat
          1Lt Kenneth Deane Thomas (KIA)

During a Rolling Thunder strike a Thunderchief was shot down by intense AAA near Na Lang, 40 miles north of Haiphong, while en route to the Cao Nung railway bridge. The aircraft was at 5,000 feet when it was hit and the pilot radioed that he was about to eject. His parachute was seen and a beeper was heard but he apparently did not survive. 1Lt Thomas had been shot down over North Vietnam on 23 March 1966 and had been rescued but this time he was not so fortunate.

RF-8A   146831   Detachment L, VFP-63, USN, USS *Hancock*
          Lt John Heilig (POW)

During a medium level photographic reconnaissance run over the Song Ca River 20 miles northwest of Vinh, an RF-8A was hit by 37mm AAA. With his aircraft on fire, Lt Heilig turned towards the Annamite Mountains where he hoped he might stand a better chance of rescue but the aircraft began to roll and he was forced to eject. He was taken prisoner and spent almost seven years in various POW camps. He eventually retired as a Captain following resumption of his naval career upon being released on 12 February 1973.

A-4C   149571   VA-146, USN, USS *Ranger*
          1 pilot, name unknown (survived)

During an armed reconnaissance mission just off the coast of North Vietnam a Skyhawk accidentally hit the water and although it remained airborne, the aircraft caught fire and the pilot ejected.

A-4C   147808   VMA-311, MAG-12, USMC, Chu Lai

The use of heavy lift helicopters like the CH-47, CH-53 and CH-54 to recover downed aircraft from otherwise inaccessible locations saved the US taxpayers millions of dollars. Unfortunately things didn't always go according to plan. A US Army CH-54 was airlifting a Marine Corps Skyhawk back to Chu Lai but was forced to jettison it, probably because the load became unstable or because the helicopter came under fire.

6 May 1966

F-105D   61-0179   421 TFS, 388 TFW, USAF, Korat
          Lt Col James Lasley Lamar (POW)

During a raid on the Yen Bai railway yard 70 miles northwest of Hanoi an F-105 was hit by 57mm AAA as it dived on the target.

Lt Col Lamar ejected and was quickly captured by Vietnamese peasants. Veteran pilot Lamar was commissioned in the USAF 1949 after serving as a rating in the US Naval Reserve. He had flown 100 combat missions in the F-51 and F-80 during the Korean War and had also flown the F-86 and the F-84 series aircraft as well as being an instructor pilot. He arrived in Thailand in November 1965 and was flying his 84th mission over North Vietnam when he was shot down. He was released on 12 February 1973 and retired six years later as a Colonel.

O-1F 57-2856 630 CSG, USAF, Udorn
2 crew, names unknown (survived)

During a forward air control mission a Bird Dog suffered engine failure and crashed.

8 May 1966

F-105D 62-4236 469 TFS, 388 TFW, USAF, Korat
1Lt James Edwin Ray (POW)

The Cao Nung railway bridge was becoming a favourite target for the planners if not for the aircrew who were tasked with its destruction. On 8 May a Thunderchief was hit by ground fire as it pulled up from its attack on the bridge. The aircraft caught fire and 1Lt Ray ejected to start nearly seven years of captivity. Jim Ray had only arrived at Korat the previous month and was shot down on his 13th mission over North Vietnam. Following his release from captivity on 12 February 1973 he resumed flying and converted to the F-4E before promotion to Colonel and appointment as US air attaché to Italy in 1986.

9 May 1966

A-1H 139616 VA-215, USN, USS *Hancock*
Lt Cdr C W Sommers (survived)

When returning from an anti-surface vessel patrol along the South Vietnamese coast a Skyraider ditched in the South China Sea 70 miles south of Cam Ranh Bay. Lt Cdr Sommers was rescued by a US Navy helicopter.

10 May 1966

F-105D 61-0135 333 TFS, 355 TFW, USAF, Takhli
Capt Martin H Mahrt (survived)

Three Thunderchiefs were lost on three different raids within the space of an hour on the 10th. The first aircraft lost was hit by AAA at 8,000 feet as it was pulling up from an attack on an arsenal at Yen Bai on a Rolling Thunder strike. Capt Mahrt succeeded in flying 15 miles to the west of the target before ejecting over hills. After two hours on the ground he was extremely lucky to be rescued by an HH-3E in what may have been the deepest penetration by a helicopter into North Vietnam up to that date. Capt Mahrt had flown 102 combat missions, including 88 over North Vietnam. He was evacuated for hospitalisation but returned twice more to Southeast Asia, first to South Korea during the Pueblo Incident, then to Saigon for the final withdrawal. Once again he was rescued by helicopter when he was airlifted out of Saigon as it fell to communist forces in 1975.

F-105D 62-4255 469 TFS, 388 TFW, USAF, Korat
Capt John Edward Bailey (KIA)

Half an hour later a Korat F-105 was shot down by ground fire on an armed reconnaissance mission as it was pulling up from bombing a bridge near Xuan Hoa, 15 miles north of the DMZ. The pilot may have been hit as the aircraft flew into the ground near Dong Hoi without any apparent attempt to eject. Following several visits to a suspected crash site, an excavation in July 1995 eventually revealed human remains that were identified in March 1999 as being those of Capt Bailey.

F-105D 59-1819 355 TFW, USAF, Takhli
1Lt G L Clouser (survived)

The last F-105 lost on this day was taking part in a Barrel Roll mission in northern Laos. The aircraft was one of several that fired Bullpup guided missiles against weapons positions seven miles northeast of Sam Neua in the heartland of the Pathet Lao. The aircraft was hit by AAA and 1Lt Clouser was rescued by a USAF HH-3E.

F-100D 55-3773 531 TFS, 3 TFW, USAF, Bien Hoa
1 pilot, name unknown (survived)

To round off an expensive day for the USAF, a Super Sabre crashed in South Vietnam due to pilot error while on a direct air support mission.

11 May 1966

F-105D 62-4293 333 TFS, 355 TFW, USAF, Takhli
Capt Francis James Feneley (KIA)

A Thunderchief was strafing a bridge about 20 miles north of Dong Hoi when the aircraft was hit by ground fire. The engine stopped, the F-105 caught fire and was seen to crash into the sea five miles offshore, opposite the mouth of the Ngan Sou Giang River. Capt Feneley was killed while flying what was to have been his last mission in Southeast Asia before reassignment to the USA.

A-4E 151995 VMA-311, MAG-12, USMC, Chu Lai
1Lt James H Villeponteaux (KIA)

During a night-time Steel Tiger strike 1Lt Villeponteaux collided with another aircraft from his squadron and crashed seven miles east of Saravan in southern Laos. 1Lt Villeponteaux was killed but the other pilot, flying 151994, flew his damaged aircraft safely back to Chu Lai.

12 May 1966

A-4C 148535 VMA-214, MAG-12, USMC, Chu Lai
1 pilot, name unknown (survived)

When returning from a combat mission a VMA-214 pilot accidentally landed his Skyhawk short of Chu Lai's runway and then ran off the side, damaging the aircraft beyond repair.

13 May 1966

O-1E 56-2680 20 TASS, 505 TACG, USAF, Da Nang
detached to Nha Trang
Maj David Ashby Farrow (KIA)

Southern Laos was proving to be an increasingly unhealthy place for the slow, unarmed FACs. Maj Farrow's aircraft was hit by ground fire 15 miles west of Khe Sanh and he attempted to reach Nakhon Phanom (where he may have been temporarily based). Unfortunately the aircraft crashed about five miles short of the airfield and Maj Farrow was killed.

F-4C 64-0760 8 TFW, USAF, Ubon
Capt Donald Lewis King (KIA)
1Lt Frank Delzell Ralston (KIA)

During an armed reconnaissance mission north of the DMZ a Ubon Phantom was lost in mysterious circumstances. A garbled radio transmission was heard and a streak of light was seen by the crew of another aircraft, which suggests that the Phantom may have been shot down by a SAM. Whatever the cause the aircraft was last plotted about 15 miles northwest of Dong Hoi. Capt King was a former test pilot and a Russian linguist.

F-105D 60-0427 421 TFS, 388 TFW, USAF, Korat
1 pilot, name unknown (survived)

During an armed reconnaissance mission an F-105 crashed at Korat due to an 'ordnance delivery system malfunction'. The pilot was recovered safely.

14 May 1966

A-1J 142050 VA-215, USN, USS *Hancock*
1 pilot, name unknown (survived)

When a Skyraider was being launched from the *Hancock* for an attack mission the aircraft suffered a control system failure and crashed into the sea. The pilot was picked up by the plane guard helicopter.

15 May 1966

F-105D 61-0174 421 TFS, 388 TFW, USAF, Korat
Capt Ralph Carol Balcom (KIA)

During an armed reconnaissance mission over Quang Binh province just north of the DMZ, a Thunderchief, one of a flight

of three, was lost 10 miles southwest of Dong Hoi. The flight had been unable to bomb their primary target due to low cloud and dropped their bombs on Route 1A instead. Capt Balcom was last heard to say that he had dropped his bombs and and was climbing through cloud heading west for the return flight to Korat. Although it was thought that Capt Balcom had ejected from his aircraft a search of the area proved negative. It appears that Capt Balcom had flown across the border into Laos as Pathet Lao radio later reported shooting down an F-105 on this date.

AC-47D 43-49546 4 ACS, 14 ACW, USAF, Tan Son Nhut
detached to Ubon
Maj George William Jensen (KIA)
Maj Lavern George Reilly (KIA)
Capt Marshall Landis Tapp (KIA)
1Lt George Winton Thompson (KIA)
SSgt James Arthur Preston (KIA)
Sgt James Ellis Williams (KIA)
Sgt William Louis Madison (KIA)
A1C Kenneth Dewey McKenney (KIA)

An AC-47 gunship disappeared while on a mission over southern Laos. The pilot made his last radio call as dusk was approaching and the aircraft's last known position was near Ban Nampakhon in Savannakhet province, 30 miles west of the DMZ. A SAR mission failed to find any trace of the aircraft or any of its crew and Pathet Lao radio later claimed to have shot it down. This particular AC-47 was being used as a trials aircraft to evaluate the use of .50 calibre machine guns instead of 7.62mm Miniguns and Maj Reilly was a Seventh Air Force project officer who was participating in the trials. The trials also involved the use of a starlight scope, which intensified the light reflected from the moon and the stars and greatly enhanced night vision. Between 1994 and 1997 several joint US-Lao investigation teams excavated the wreckage and recovered human remains and personal items resulting in a group identification that was announced in December 1999.

A-6A 151800 VA-85, USN, USS Kitty Hawk
Lt Cdr R G Blackwood (survived)
Lt Cdr John Cooley Ellison (survived)

As an Intruder was returning from an armed reconnaissance mission over North Vietnam the crew discovered that they were unable to receive fuel from the tanker due to a technical malfunction. Unable to make it to the carrier, the crew ejected when the fuel was exhausted. Unfortunately, Lt Cdr Ellison was lost during a raid on Bac Giang on 24 March 1967.

16 May 1966

A-1E 52-132417 602 ACS, 14 ACW, USAF, Udorn
Capt H Lewis Smith (survived)

A Skyraider was hit by anti-aircraft fire on its second dive on a vehicle on one of the many routes that made up the Ho Chi Minh Trail in southern Laos. Capt Smith realised that the Vietnamese coast was closer than his base at Udorn and set off towards the east. However, he was forced to abandon his badly damaged aircraft soon after crossing into North Vietnam and landed about 25 miles southwest of Dong Hoi. He was later rescued by an HH-3.

17 May 1966

F-4C 64-0717 433 TFS, 8 TFW, USAF, Ubon
Capt D G Rokes (survived)
Lt E S S Osbolt (survived)

After returning from an armed reconnaissance mission a Wolfpack Phantom crashed on landing back at Ubon.

17/18 May 1966

C-123B 55-4534 310 ACS, 315 ACW, USAF, Nha Trang
Capt Stanley Gilbert Cox (KIA)
1Lt Albert Richard Wilson (KIA)
MSgt Raymond Charles Jajtner (KIA)
A1C William John Moore (KIA)
A1C Jerry Mack Wall (KIA)

On the night of 17/18 May a C-123 took off from Nha Trang on a Candlestick mission dropping flares over friendly positions in South Vietnam's Central Highlands. As the aircraft was circling at 6,500 feet near Vinh Thanh, about 10 miles northeast of An Khe, it was hit by ground fire and burst into flames. The pilot attempted to reach an airfield but the aircraft crashed before he could land and all on board were killed.

18 May 1966

O-1F   57-2877   23 TASS, 505 TACG, USAF, Nakhon Phanom
Capt Lee Dufford Harley (KIA)
A2C Andre Roland Guillet (KIA)

Two days after Capt Smith's Skyraider was hit near the Ban Karai Pass, a Bird Dog FAC was hit by .50 calibre gunfire at almost the same location and was brought down near a recently-discovered section of the Trail. The aircraft exploded on impact and both crew were killed.

F-4B   152257   VF-213, USN, USS *Kitty Hawk*
Lt Cdr C N Sommers (survived)
Lt Cdr W K Sullivan (survived)

About one hour after the O-1 was shot down a section of Phantoms from the *Kitty Hawk* was reassigned from a Steel Tiger strike to assist in the search for the Bird Dog and its crew. The Phantoms arrived in the vicinity and came down to 500 feet to make a visual identification of the wreckage. During the first pass one of the aircraft was hit by ground fire and began to burn. The crew ejected a few miles from the Bird Dog's crash site and were picked up by a USAF HH-3E. This was one of two F-4Bs that VF-213 used to supplement the 10 F-4Gs flown on this cruise.

19 May 1966

A-1J   142051   VA-115, USN, USS *Kitty Hawk*
1 pilot, name unknown (survived)

A Skyraider suffered engine failure just as it was being catapulted off the bows of the USS *Kitty Hawk*. It was suspected that a cylinder valve had failed.

21 May 1966

A-4C   148473   VA-216, USN, USS *Hancock*
Lt Cdr O F Baldwin (survived)

During an armed reconnaissance mission a section of Skyhawks spotted a cargo barge near Phong Bai, 35 miles north of Vinh. As Lt Cdr Baldwin pulled up from his first strafing run on the barge he felt his aircraft hit by ground fire. His wingman saw fuel streaming from the aircraft and an internal fire started but extinguished itself after a few minutes. Lt Cdr Baldwin flew 90 miles back to the carrier but had to eject when the aircraft's starboard landing gear failed to extend due to fire damage.

22 May 1966

F-105D   58-1164   469 TFS, 388 TFW, USAF, Korat
1Lt R H Hackford (survived)

The Ban Karai area of Laos claimed yet another victim on the 22nd when an F-105 was hit by ground fire as it was attacking a truck park. 1Lt Hackford flew his crippled aircraft 15 miles to the northeast before he was forced to eject. A USAF SAR helicopter eventually picked him up.

23 May 1966

A-4C   147762   VA-36, USN, USS *Enterprise*
Ens K W Leuffen (survived)

As Ens Leuffen was making his run towards the Dong Khe railway bridge, 23 miles north of Vinh, he felt a thump as his Skyhawk was hit by ground fire but he pressed on and bombed the target. After the strike his wingman reported that Leuffen's aircraft was streaming fuel so a hook up with a tanker was made on the 125 mile-return trip to the *Enterprise*. As the aircraft entered the traffic pattern to land on the carrier the engine began to run down (probably from lack of oil) and Ens Leuffen was forced to eject from 350 feet.

F-8E   150901   VF-211, USN, USS *Hancock*
Lt L S Miller (survived)

A Crusader suffered a similar fate later the same day. Lt Miller felt a hit as he flew over the mouth of the Song Kanh Canal on the North Vietnamese coast seven miles north of Ha Tinh. The aircraft's hydraulics failed and it began to lose fuel, which caught fire as the aircraft crossed the coast heading out to sea. Lt Miller stayed with the burning aircraft until he was about a mile from the shore before ejecting. The ever-efficient Navy rescue system swung into action and he was quickly rescued by a SAR helicopter.

24 May 1966

O-1F   57-6028   21 TASS, 505 TACG, USAF, Pleiku
Capt Joseph Anthony Machowski (KIA)

The toll of FAC aircraft continued with the loss of a Bird Dog near the town of Plei Toun Brieng, 20 miles west of Pleiku and only 10 miles from the border with Cambodia. The aircraft was hit by ground fire that was thought to have wounded or killed the pilot.

25 May 1966

F-105D   59-1746   354 TFS, 355 TFW, USAF, Takhli
1Lt Robert Gerald Hunter (KIA)

The USAF lost a second F-105 in May during a strike in the Barrel Roll area of Northen Laos. 1Lt Hunter was shot down by automatic weapons and killed during a raid near Ban Niang, 10 miles east of Ban Ban.

A-1E   52-132447   602 ACS, 14 ACW, USAF, Udorn
Capt Robert Ira Bush (survived)

As soon as 1Lt Hunter's aircraft was reported down the SAR task force at Udorn swung into action. However, as the Sandys orbited a few miles to the southeast of the crash site, one of the aircraft was hit by ground fire and Capt Bush was forced to bail out. He was quickly rescued by the HH-3 which he had been protecting. Capt Bush was killed two weeks later when he collided with another aircraft on a SAR mission.

F-4B   152268   VMFA-115, MAG-11, USMC, Da Nang
1Lt Richard Howard Royer (KIA)
2Lt John David Kramer (KIA)

On returning from an air strike on a VC-held village in South Vietnam, a Marine Corps Phantom crashed into the sea just off the coast near Hoi An, 15 miles south of Da Nang airfield. No enemy fire was observed at the time and the cause of the crash was thought to have been accidental. VMFA-115 had arrived back at Da Nang on 14 April having spent three months at Iwakuni training and regrouping.

26 May 1966

F-4C   64-0722   391 TFS, 12 TFW, USAF, Cam Ranh Bay
1Lt Terrence Hastings Griffey (KIA)
1Lt Gary Alven Glandon (KIA)

The only USAF fast jet lost over South Vietnam during May was a Phantom from Cam Ranh Bay. The aircraft was one of three that were attacking a VC position on the coast 10 miles north of Qui Nhon. As the aircraft pulled up from its low level run over the target it was seen to burst into flames, probably as a result of small arms fire, and crash into the ground and explode.

30 May 1966

F-105D   61-0142   333 TFS, 355 TFW, USAF, Takhli
Capt David Burnett Hatcher (POW)

On 30 May the Takhli Wing flew a strike against a railway bridge near Bao Ha on the main northwest railway from China to Hanoi. Capt Hatcher was making his second strafing run on the target when his aircraft was hit by ground fire forcing him to eject. Capt Hatcher was taken prisoner and eventually repatriated on 12 February 1973. With 83 missions flown during the day, 30th May saw the highest number of missions flown during any one day since the war began.

31 May 1966

F-105D   62-4386   354 TFS, 355 TFW, USAF, Takhli
1Lt Leonard C Ekman (survived)

F-105D   61-0120   469 TFS, 388 TFW, USAF, Korat
Capt Martin William Steen (KIA)

The two Thunderchief wings made a co ordinated raid on military targets at Yen Bai on the northwest railway. The Takhli bombers attacked first followed about half an hour later by the Korat Wing, both groups losing an aircraft during the raid. 1Lt Ekman's aircraft was thought to have been hit by an 85mm AAA shell, which set the aircraft on fire. He ejected over hills about 12 miles southwest of the target and was most fortunate to be rescued by a HH-3E that made one of the deepest penetrations into North Vietnam up to that time. The Korat Wing was less fortunate, for although Capt Steen was shot down close to 1Lt Ekman, he could not be found and does not appear to have been captured. Capt Steen reported being hit and said that he was going to eject and other pilots in his flight saw his parachute land in mountainous terrain. A SAR helicopter reached the area and a PJ was lowered to the ground and found Capt Steen's parachute snagged in a tree about 30 feet above the ground but the harness was empty. In 1990 a JTF-FA investigation found villagers who claimed that Capt Steen's body was found four days after he was shot down and was buried but was later dug up and eaten by animals.

F-4B   152309   VMFA-115, MAG-11, USMC, Da Nang
Lt C Geiger (survived)
Lt M L Crabb (survived)

During one of VMFA-115's rare non-combat flights a Phantom became uncontrollable after the pilot encountered problems with the trim, it was thought due to incorrect rigging by maintenance personnel.

31 May/1 June 1966

F-4C   63-7664   555 TFS, 8 TFW, USAF, Udorn
Maj Dayton William Ragland (KIA)
1Lt Ned Raymond Herrold (KIA)

During a night armed reconnaissance mission over North Vietnam a Phantom was hit by ground fire near the coast near Van Yen, 25 miles south of Thanh Hoa. The aircraft was thought to have come down in the sea just four miles offshore near the island of Hon Me but neither crewman survived. It has been suggested that the aircraft was flying a diversionary raid for the attack on the Thanh Hoa Bridge (see below). However, the Phantom was lost almost three hours before the Hercules was thought to have commenced its run on the bridge. Another report puts the loss of the Phantom only 15 miles south of Thanh Hoa. Maj Ragland had flown during the Korean War and had been shot down and taken prisoner in November 1951. He had already flown 97 missions over Southeast Asia and was about to return to the USA at the end of his tour.

C-130E   64-0511   61 TCS, 64 TCW, USAF, Sewart
Maj Thomas Franklin Case (KIA)
1Lt Harold Jacob Zook (KIA)
Capt Emmett Raymond McDonald (KIA)
Capt Armon D Shingledecker (KIA)
1Lt William Rothroc Edmondson (KIA)
SSgt Bobby Joe Alberton (KIA)
AM1C Philip Joseph Stickney (KIA)
AM1C Elroy Edwin Harworth (KIA)

Despite repeated attempts by both the USAF and the US Navy, the Thanh Hoa Bridge stubbornly resisted to fall. Although undoubtedly an important strategic target, the destruction of which would have a serious impact on the North Vietnamese railway system, it had also become a symbol of resistance, both to the North Vietnamese and to the Americans who plotted its destruction. As conventional bombing appeared to be having little effect on the immense structure of the bridge, thought was given to alternative means to bring it down. One of these avenues of thought resulted in Project Carolina Moon, an attempt to destroy the bridge by dropping a number of 8-feet diameter

saucer-shaped mass-focus bombs. The weapons would have to be dropped at low level in the Song Ma River where the current would carry the floating bombs under the bridge when a sensor would detonate the 5,000lbs of explosives. Due to the size and shape of the weapon, the aircraft chosen to drop it was a C-130 Hercules. Two crews were trained at Eglin AFB, Florida and they deployed to Da Nang two weeks before the attack took place.

The first attempt was made on the night of the 30th when a Hercules captained by Maj Richard T Remers dropped five bombs in the river and escaped unharmed thanks, in part, to a nearby diversionary attack by two Phantoms and jamming of North Vietnamese radar by an RB-66. Although the mission was successfully executed, post-strike reconnaissance revealed that the bridge was undamaged indicating either that the bombs had not detonated or they had not exploded in the right position.

Maj Case flew the second attempt the following night and took 1Lt Edmondson with him as he had successfully navigated the aircraft on the first attempt. At the time the Hercules should have been making its attack a large explosion was seen a few miles north of the bridge and it was assumed that the aircraft had either been shot down or had flown into the ground or the river. No trace of the aircraft or its crew was discovered despite several reconnaissance missions. The remains of 1Lt Zook and AM1C Harworth were amongst 22 boxes of remains handed over by the Vietnamese on 10 April 1986 and those of Maj Case were returned in February 1987. In 1998 the other boxes of remains were re-examined using Mitochondrial DNA testing and the remains of Capt Shingledecker were also positively identified.

1 June 1966

F-105D   62-4393   357 TFS, 355 TFW, USAF, Takhli
                    Capt G H Peacock (survived)

During an armed reconnaissance mission over the southern region of North Vietnam the USAF lost yet another F-105. Capt Peacock's aircraft was hit by small calibre ground fire as he was attacking a target about 20 miles northwest of Dong Hoi. With his aircraft on fire Peacock just managed to cross the border into Laos before he was forced to eject. He was rescued by a USAF helicopter.

F-4C   serial ..?   433 TFS, 8 TFW, USAF, Ubon
                     Capt Armand Jesse Myers (POW)
                     1Lt John Lorin Borling (POW)

A night-time raid on the northeast railway near Kep resulted in the loss of one of Ubon's Phantoms. The aircraft was shot down by ground fire 12 miles northeast of Kep and both the crew were captured. Capt Myers, who had flown 94 missions at the time of his capture, broke his left leg and ankle in several places on landing and ill treatment in the POW camps exacerbated the injuries. Myers retired from the USAF in 1983 still suffering severe pain from his injuries until he tried a newly developed pain killer which worked so well that he became a distributor for the product. 1Lt Borling was flying his 99th mission when he was shot down and had been due to return home in the next few days. Myers and Borling were released on 12 February 1973 and John Borling eventually rose to the rank of Major General as Chief of Staff of NATO's Allied Forces North Europe command until retiring on 1 August 1996.

A-4E   151057   VA-55, USN, USS *Ranger*
                 1 pilot, name unknown (survived)

Pilot error caused the loss of a Skyhawk as it was catapulted from the *Ranger* on an armed reconnaissance mission.

2 June 1966

F-105D   59-1721   333 TFS, 355 TFW, USAF, Takhli
                    Capt J D Whipple (survived)

During an armed reconnaissance mission over the southern provinces of North Vietnam a flight of Thunderchiefs spotted a boat on a small river near Troc, 20 miles northwest of Dong Hoi. On its second strafing run one of the aircraft was hit by small arms fire and burst into flames. Capt Whipple headed towards the Laotian border but was forced to eject near Ban Katoi. He was later rescued by a USAF helicopter.

F-4C   64-0744   558 TFS, 12 TFW, USAF, Cam Ranh Bay
                  Capt Joseph Frank Rosato (KIA)
                  1Lt C R Ogle (survived)

A flight of Phantoms was attacking an enemy weapons position 10 miles northeast of Dak To in the Central Highlands when one of the aircraft was hit by ground fire. The aircraft burst into flames and crashed a few seconds later. The pilot was killed but the back-seater ejected and was eventually recovered with just minor injuries.

O-1F   57-2832   23 TASS, 505 TACG, USAF, Nakhon Phanom
                  Capt B H Witterman (survived)
                  Lt Col M D Marshall (survived)

An FAC was shot down near Ban Namkop in the Steel Tiger area of southern Laos. The pilot skilfully crash-landed the aircraft and a USAF helicopter eventually rescued him and his observer.

F-105D   61-0160   421 TFS, 388 TFW, USAF, Korat
                    1 pilot, name unknown (survived)

Another Thunderchief was lost on 2 June when an aircraft crashed in Thailand following engine failure.

3 June 1966

F-105D   58-1171   469 TFS, 388 TFW, USAF, Korat
                    Capt R D Pielin (survived)

The Korat Wing lost an F-105 during an armed reconnaissance mission over the southern provinces of North Vietnam. The aircraft was hit by AAA as it pulled up from an attack on a bridge over the Song Ron River near Kiem Loong. Within seconds the pilot crossed the coast but was soon forced to eject from his crippled aircraft. He was later picked up by a USAF helicopter.

A-4E   152047   VMA-223, MAG-12, USMC, Chu Lai
                 Capt Ralph Warren Caspole (KIA)

Capt Caspole was leading a two-aircraft section on a strike mission against a VC assembly area two miles south of Gia An, about 55 miles south of Chu Lai. After dropping their napalm the two aircraft made several strafing runs and as Capt Caspole was pulling up from his seventh pass his aircraft was hit by automatic weapons, caught fire and crashed immediately.

AC-47D   43-48925   4 ACS, 14 ACW, USAF, Nha Trang
                     detached to Ubon
                     Maj Harding Eugene Smith (KIA)
                     Capt Theodore Eugene Kryszak (KIA)
                     1Lt Russell Dean Martin (KIA)
                     TSgt Harold Eugene Mullins (KIA)
                     TSgt Luther Lee Rose (KIA)
                     SSgt Ervin Warren (KIA)

Three weeks after the loss of Maj Jensen's gunship over the Ho Chi Minh Trail, the 4th ACS lost another aircraft and crew while searching for convoys at night. Maj Smith's aircraft was part of a detachment at Ubon and was operating over Khammouane province in the Laotian panhandle. Other aircraft in the vicinity saw the aircraft as it burst into flames and plunge into the ground near Ban Phakat. A subsequent search located the aircraft's wreckage but trace of the crew was seen. Following the loss of this Spooky, the AC-47 was withdrawn from operations over the Trail as it was proving too vulnerable to ground fire. However, the aircraft continued to perform sterling work in the defence of hamlets and camps within South Vietnam.

5 June 1966

O-1E   56-2647   14 ACW, USAF, Nha Trang
                  Maj Frederick Earl Bailey (KIA)

A Bird Dog crashed during an escort mission in Binh Dinh province in South Vietnam killing the pilot.

7 June 1966

A-1E   52-132449   1 ACS, 14 ACW, USAF, Pleiku
                    Capt Robert Louis Sandner (KIA)

A Skyraider was hit by groundfire and crashed during an attack on enemy positions 10 miles west of Pleiku. The pilot was unable to escape from the aircraft before it hit the ground.

O-1E   55-4736   19 TASS, 505 TACG, USAF, Bien Hoa
                  Capt John Charles Jacobs (KIA)
                  1Lt Charles Stephen Franco (KIA)

During a visual reconnaissance mission a Bird Dog from Bien Hoa crashed seven miles north of Vung Tau. Enemy action was thought possible but not confirmed as being the cause of the crash, which killed both crewmen. This was the 50th USAF Bird Dog lost in South Vietnam since the war began.

F-105D   61-0168   333 TFS, 355 TFW, USAF, Takhli
                    Capt J F Bayles (survived)

A Thunderchief was hit by AAA as it was pulling up from an attack on a boat in a river mouth about 5 miles north of Bo Trach, north of the DMZ. Capt Bayles managed to get well out to sea before he ejected and was picked up by a USAF rescue helicopter.

F-4C   64-0671   389 TFS, 366 TFW, USAF, Phan Rang
                  Maj C F Frost (survived)
                  Maj R M Keith (survived)

The fourth USAF aircraft lost on this day was a Phantom that caught fire on take off from Phan Rang and had to be abandoned by its crew. The 366th TFW had arrived at Phan Rang from Holloman AFB on 20 March with three squadrons and added a fourth Phantom squadron later in the month.

8 June 1966

F-105D   62-4273   334 TFS, 4 TFW attached to 355 TFW,
                    USAF, Takhli
                    Maj J C Holley (survived)

The Takhli Wing lost another aircraft on an armed reconnaissance mission over the southern provinces of North Vietnam. Maj Holley's aircraft was hit by groundfire as it was strafing a target about 10 miles south of Dong Hoi. Once again, the sturdy Thunderchief held together long enough for the pilot to fly out to sea and eject and from there to be rescued by a USAF helicopter.

O-1E   56-2614   14 ACW, USAF, Nha Trang
                  1 pilot, name unknown (survived)

A Bird Dog FAC crashed in South Vietnam due to engine failure.

9 June 1966

A-1E   52-132400   602 ACS, 14 ACW, USAF, Udorn
                    Capt J L Caskey (survived)

During an armed reconnaissance mission near Ban Ban in the Barrel Roll region of Laos, a Skyraider was hit by automatic weapons fire and burst into flames. Capt Caskey flew about 30 miles to the west before abandoning the aircraft near Muong Soui from where he was eventually recovered with only minor injuries.

A-1E   52-133899   602 ACS, 14 ACW, USAF, Udorn
                    Capt Robert Ira Bush (KIA)

During an escort for a SAR mission a 602nd ACS Skyraider collided in mid-air with another aircraft and crashed in North Vietnam. Capt Bush had survived being shot down over Laos during a SAR mission on 25 May only to be killed in this accident.

10 June 1966

O-1E   56-4178   20 TASS, 505 TACG, USAF, Da Nang
                  Capt Dan Bruen Packard (KIA)

An FAC was lost near Ban Vangthon in Laos a few miles west of the DMZ. The pilot was thought to have been hit by ground fire and the aircraft crashed.

12 June 1966

B-57E   55-4268   13 TBS, 405 FW attached to 35 TFW,
                   USAF, Da Nang
                   Capt Charles William Burkart (KIA)
                   Capt Everett Oscar Kerr (KIA)

The Da Nang Canberras with their long endurance and large ordnance loads played a major role in the growing interdiction campaign over the Ho Chi Minh Trail. Three Canberras were flying a strike mission at night in the Steel Tiger area of southern Laos when they became separated from each other in bad

weather. Burkart and Kerr's aircraft failed to return and was thought to have crashed near Ban Thapathon, probably due to enemy action. It was not until 1979 that the two crewmen were officially declared to be dead during which time Capt Burkart had been promoted to Colonel and Capt Kerr to Lieutenant Colonel. This Canberra was one of 12 B-57Es that had been refurbished late in 1965 by Martin as combat replacements for Southeast Asia. The B-57E was originally designed to tow aerial targets but the refurbished aircraft had the same offensive capability as the B-57B model.

13 June 1966

F-4C   63-7697   480 TFS, 35 TFW, USAF, Da Nang
                   Capt Alan Pierce Lurie (POW)
                   1Lt Darrell Edwin Pyle (POW)
The southern provinces of North Vietnam were becoming almost as dangerous as the Hanoi/Haiphong region. Anti-aircraft fire hit a Phantom as it was attacking a target about 10 miles northwest of Dong Hoi. Both crew ejected at low level but Capt Lurie suffered a compression fracture of his spine. Both men were quickly captured and spent the next seven years in various POW camps until they were released on 12 February 1973. Darrel Pyle was killed in an light aircraft accident in Alaska the year after his release. Alan Lurie reached the rank of Brigadier General before his retirement from the USAF.

RA-3B   144842   VAP-61, USN, NAS Cubi Point
                  Lt Cdr John Turner Glanville (KIA)
                  Lt(jg) George Gregory Gierak (KIA)
                  CPO Bennie Richard Lambton (KIA)
The RA-3Bs and EA-3Bs of VAP-61 made regular deployments to South Vietnam or to one of the TF 77 carriers. These Skywarrior variants were used to gather photographic or electronic intelligence on the enemy. The RA-3B was used particularly for night reconnaissance work over the Ho Chi Minh Trail using both conventional and infra-red cameras. Some of the aircraft were camouflaged to reduce their visibility at night. On 13 June an RA-3B, temporarily operating from the USS *Hancock*, was shot down on a low level night photographic sortie over North Vietnam. The crew of an escorting aircraft saw a bright flash over the mouth of the Gia Hoi River 20 miles up the coast from Mu Ron Ma. It was assumed that the aircraft had been shot down by ground fire. No trace of the aircraft or crew was ever found.

14 June 1966

F-105D   60-0429   421 TFS, 388 TFW, USAF, Korat
                    1 pilot, name unknown (survived)
A Thunderchief crashed at Korat following a flame out at too low an altitude to restart the engine.

15 June 1966

F-4B   152251   VF-143, USN, USS *Ranger*
                  Lt C W Bennett (survived)
                  Ens D W Vermilyea (survived)
During a coastal reconnaissance mission on the lookout for North Vietnamese patrol boats a Phantom was hit by AAA as it was climbing through 1,000 feet over Da Cat Ba island near Haiphong. The port engine was hit and had to be shut down and the starboard wing was holed and began to stream fuel. Lt Bennett attempted to rendezvous with a tanker but the starboard engine failed as the damage to the fuel system would not allow fuel to transfer to the live engine. Both crew ejected and were picked up by a helicopter from the northern SAR destroyer, about 45 miles south of Haiphong.

F-105D   62-4377   333 TFS, 355 TFW, USAF, Takhli
                    1Lt P J Kelly (survived)
A Thunderchief was hit by large calibre AAA near a river mouth about 5 miles north of Bo Trach, north of the DMZ, the same location where Capt Bayles's aircraft had been hit a week earlier. The starboard wing of 1Lt Kelly's aircraft caught fire but he managed to fly about 20 miles to the south before ejecting over hilly terrain. He was rescued by a USAF helicopter.

A-4E   152063   VA-55, USN, USS *Ranger*
                  Lt Cdr Theodore Frank Kopfman (POW)
SA-2 sites continued to proliferate throughout North Vietnam and posed an ever-increasing threat to US air strikes. Many missions up North were now preceded by Iron Hand flights that struck SAM sites in the path of the attacking aircraft. During an attack on a SAM site 10 miles southwest of Nam Dinh a Skyhawk fired its Shrike anti-radiation missile and was just pulling up from another pass, having expended several Zuni rockets, when it was hit in the rear fuselage by AAA. Within minutes the aircraft caught fire and Lt Cdr Kopfman was forced to eject before he could reach the coast. He was captured and spent the next seven years as a POW until released on 12 February 1973. He was flying his 198th mission when he was shot down and was awarded the Silver Star for his actions on this mission.

17 June 1966

A-4C   149528   VA-216, USN, USS *Hancock*
                  Lt(jg) Paul Edward Galanti (POW)
During a strike on a railway yard at Qui Vinh, 30 miles south of Thanh Hoa, a Skyhawk was hit by small arms fire. The aircraft caught fire immediately and the hydraulics failed as the engine wound down. Lt Galanti almost made it to the coast and the waiting SAR destroyer but had to eject when the aircraft became uncontrollable. Lt Galanti was captured on his 97th mission and was paraded through the streets of Hanoi with other prisoners as a propaganda stunt. He was released on 12 February 1973 and resumed his naval career, returning to flying and touring the USA giving presentations on behalf of naval recruiting.

C-130E   63-7785   VR-7, USN, Moffett Field
                    Lt Cdr Ralph Burton Cobbs (KIA)
                    Lt(jg) Donald Edwin Siegwarth (KIA)
                    Lt(jg) Clement Olin Stevenson (KIA)
                    Lt(jg) Edward Leon Romig (KIA)
                    AN M J Savoy (KIA)
                    YN2 Jack Ishum Dempsey (KIA)
                    ADJ2 Curtis David Collette (KIA)
                    ADR2 Stanley Jon Freng (KIA)
VR-7 was one of four C-130 squadrons formed in 1963 under Navy ownership as part of the joint Air Force-Navy MATS. Thirty minutes after taking off from Cam Ranh Bay on a routine transport flight to Kadena AB on the island of Okinawa, a Hercules from VR-7 exploded and crashed into the South China Sea killing all on board. The aircraft came down about 45 miles northeast of Nha Trang and about five miles off a small spit of land south of Phu Hiep. Although very little of the aircraft was ever found it was strongly suspected that the aircraft had been a victim of sabotage by Vietnamese communist sympathisers who worked at the base. Only one body was recovered from the sea soon after the crash. Six USAF airmen killed on board the aircraft were Capt Connie Mack Gravitte, 1Lt Claiborne Parks McCall, SSgt Oley Neal Adams, SSgt Robert Alexander Cairns, SSgt Gene Karl Hess and A2C Larry Eugene Washburn. All the Navy MATS squadrons were inactivated in 1967 and the aircraft handed over to the USAF. The serial number usually quoted for this aircraft is currently carried by an MC-130E still serving with the 711th SOS.

U-10B   63-13104   5 ACS, 14 ACW, USAF, Nha Trang
                    A Courier was accidentally dropped from a heavy lift helicopter as it was being recovered from a forced landing.

20 June 1966

UC-123B   56-4378   Special Aerial Spray Flight, 309 ACS,
                     315 ACW, USAF, Bien Hoa detached to
                     Tan Son Nhut
                     1Lt Paul L Clanton (survived)
                     1Lt Steven A Aigner (survived)
                     SSgt Elijah R Winstead (survived)
The Ranch Hand unit had not lost an aircraft since April 1962. However on 20th June the unit's luck ran out and an aircraft was hit by small arms fire about three miles north of Tam Ky near the

---

coast between Chu Lai and Da Nang. Two aircraft were spraying defoliant on an area known as the Pineapple Forest when one of the Providers was hit in the engine while on its fifth pass. Fortunately the pilot was able to make a successful crash landing in a rice paddy, although the aircraft caught fire, all the crew escaped. The pilot had been seriously injured in the crash and was pulled free of the burning wreckage by the other two members of the crew who had suffered only minor injuries. Approaching VC were kept at bay by the C-123's fighter escort that strafed a tree line where the enemy troops had assembled. A flight of six Marine Corps helicopters heard the pilot's distress call and two of the helicopters landed at the crash site to rescue the crew while under fire from enemy forces. The aircraft's wreckage was later destroyed by a flight of B-57s to prevent it being scavenged by the Viet Cong.

A-1H   139806   VA-145, USN, USS *Ranger*
                  Lt Cdr John Wallace Tunnell (KIA)
One of the *Ranger*'s Skyraiders crashed into the sea following a catapult launch for an attack mission. It was suspected that the pilot either suffered vertigo or had an instrument failure.

EA-1F   135010   VAW-13, USN, USS *Hancock*
                  Lt John Richard McDonough (KIA)
                  2 crew, names unknown (survived)
During a night launch of an EA-1F Skyraider from the USS *Hancock* off the coast of North Vietnam the catapult bridle failed and the aircraft ditched in the sea just ahead of the carrier. Unfortunately, the aircraft sank quickly and only two of the three crew survived the ditching. The aircraft was setting out on a jamming mission in support of a naval air strike.

A-4E   151201   MAG-12, USMC, Chu Lai
                  A Marine Corps Skyhawk was destroyed by fire on the ground when the hose from a refuelling vehicle ruptured and the fuel ignited.

21 June 1966

F-105D   62-4358   388 TFW, USAF, Korat
                    1Lt John Bernard Sullivan (KIA)
As a result of a change in US policy, the USAF mounted its first raid on major POL targets in North Vietnam on the 21st. Oil and petroleum plants and depots would be frequent targets for the next few weeks and although much damage would be done, there is little evidence that supplies fell to a critical level. The North Vietnamese eventually countered these raids by constructing underground fuel storage tanks or by storing fuel in caves and other dispersed positions.

One of the first raids as a result of the new policy was on the Dao Quan POL storage site about five miles northwest of Kep airfield. As 1Lt Sullivan's aircraft commenced its dive from 10,000 feet, it was hit twice by 85mm AAA and crashed near the target. Nothing more was known of the fate of John Sullivan until his remains were handed over by the Vietnamese on 13 September 1990.

RF-8A   146830   Detachment L, VFP-63, USN, USS *Hancock*
                  Lt Leonard Corbett Eastman (POW)
The *Hancock* lost two Crusaders on the 21st, the first being a photographic reconnaissance aircraft from the carrier's VFP-63 detachment. Lt Eastman was flying along the main railway line about 20 miles northeast of Kep at 3,500 feet and 500 knots when the aircraft was hit in the tail by AAA. The aircraft caught fire forcing Lt Eastman to eject and fall into the hands of the North Vietnamese although not before four Crusaders set up a RESCAP over the pilot in the vain hope of a rescue. Eastman had flown about 45 reconnaissance missions before being shot down. He was released on 12 February 1973 and resumed his naval career. This was the third photo Crusader lost by the *Hancock* within the space of three months and was the last RF-8A model lost in action during the war.

F-8E   149152   VF-211, USN, USS *Hancock*
                  Lt Cdr Cole Black (POW)
The second of *Hancock*'s Crusaders to be lost this day was one of four flying escort for a six-aircraft A-4 strike when they were

diverted to cover the rescue forces attempting to rescue Lt Eastman. Lt Cdr Black, VF-211's executive officer, sent two of the Crusaders to refuel from a tanker while he and Lt Chancy orbited Lt Eastman's position at 2,000 feet. Lt Cdr Black's aircraft was hit by AAA in the rear fuselage damaging the hydraulic system. The two Crusaders were then jumped by four MiG-17s from the 923rd Fighter Regiment and a dogfight ensued during which Cole Black's aircraft was shot down by cannon fire from one of the MiG-17s. Lt Cdr Black was forced to eject and he joined his colleagues in the North Vietnamese prison system until he was released on 12 February 1973. However, the balance was redressed somewhat on 21 June by Lt Gene Chancy and Lt Phil Vampatella who each shot down one of the MiG-17s during the engagement.

22 June 1966

O-1F   55-4653   23 TASS, 505 TACG, USAF, Nakhon Phanom
Capt Warren Parker Smith (KIA)

A Nail FAC and its pilot, known as 'Willie Pete' Smith, was lost when it was shot down by automatic weapons fire near Ban Muong Sen in Savannakhet province in southern Laos. Another pilot in the vicinity saw the O-1 make what appeared to be a controlled landing near Route 911 but thought that the pilot was slumped over in the cockpit. He did not answer any of the radio calls made to him and when a rescue helicopter arrived about an hour later, the cockpit was found to be empty. A more intensive search had to be abandoned due to intense ground fire in the vicinity of the wreck.

F-100D   56-2925   90 TFS, 3 TFW, USAF, Bien Hoa
Capt D K Anderson (survived)

A Super Sabre was shot down by ground fire as it was making its third napalm pass on VC troops five miles northeast of Can Tho in the Mekong Delta. The aircraft caught fire immediately forcing Capt Anderson to eject close to the enemy troops. Fortunately, he was quickly rescued by a US Army helicopter.

23 June 1966

F-4B   152324   VF-151, USN, USS Constellation
Lt(jg) Lawrence Frederick Nyman (KIA)
Ens Harry John Belknap (KIA)

The USS Constellation arrived back off Vietnam on 29 May for its second tour of duty. It commenced operations on 14 June and lost its first aircraft nine days later. During a BARCAP mission a Phantom pilot is thought to have become disorientated and allowed the aircraft to fly into the water.

25 June 1966

A-6A   151816   VA-65, USN, USS Constellation
Lt Richard M Weber (survived)
Lt(jg) Charles Weldon Marik (KIA)

VA-65 was the third Intruder squadron to deploy to Southeast Asia and was probably hoping that it had not inherited the bad luck of it predecessors. The Squadron lost its first aircraft during a daylight raid on barracks at Hoi Thuong on the coast near Vinh. As the A-6 was pulling out of its dive on the target the aircraft was hit by AAA and failed to respond to the pilot's attempts to turn towards the coast. Despite almost complete hydraulic failure the pilot climbed the aircraft to 12,000 feet and both crew ejected. Lt Weber spoke to Lt Marik over their survival radios while they were descending in their parachutes. Lt Weber landed in the sea a few miles offshore and was rescued by a Navy helicopter but despite a four hour search Lt Marik could not be found and he was presumed to have drowned.

A-4C   149567   VA-146, USN, USS Ranger
Lt F H Magee (survived)

As soon as the Intruder was shot down aircraft from the Constellation and Ranger mounted a rescue attempt. One of the RESCAP aircraft, a Skyhawk of VA-146, was climbing through 5,500 feet about three miles northeast of Vinh when it was hit by a 57mm shell under the cockpit. A fire started in the forward fuselage, the controls stiffened and the engine failed. However, by the time the aircraft became unflyable it was over the sea and Lt Magee ejected and was picked up by a Navy helicopter.

27 June 1966

A-4E   152073   VA-155, USN, USS Constellation
Lt Cdr Gene Albert Smith (KIA)

As four Skyhawks were bombing transport barges in a canal near Van Yen, 30 miles south of Thanh Hoa, the leader saw a large fireball on the ground about half a mile west of the canal. Lt Cdr Smith's aircraft could not be seen and he could not be raised on radio. The three remaining aircraft circled the site of the explosion and saw a large crater with pieces of metal scattered around. RESCAP aircraft combed the area for two hours but found no trace of the pilot. It was assumed that the aircraft had been hit by 37mm ground fire on its run in and had crashed and exploded. The remains of Lt Cdr Smith were eventually handed over by the Vietnamese in December 1988.

A-4E   150000   VA-212, USN, USS Hancock
1 pilot, name unknown (survived)

While on its way to a target in South Vietnam, a Skyhawk caught fire and the pilot had to eject. The cause of the fire could not be determined. This was the last Navy aircraft lost on a combat mission over South Vietnam before the Navy flew its final mission from Dixie Station on 4 August. By that time enough USAF and Marine Corps aircraft had arrived at South Vietnamese bases to relieve the Navy of assistance in the in-country war. However, later in the war the Navy participated in further combat operations over the South but from this date onwards its main area of operations would be North Vietnam.

Return of the Invader

Even before the B-26 began to suffer from fatigue problems in early 1964 the USAF had made plans to upgrade the aircraft. In October 1962 a B-26 was delivered to On Mark Engineering of Van Nuys, California for a major upgrade that involved almost rebuilding the entire aircraft. The result was the B-26K which featured a completely re-manufactured fuselage, wing and tail, more powerful engines, wing-tip fuel tanks, eight wing pylons for ordnance and updated cockpit instrumentation and avionics. The first of 40 aircraft (sporting new 1964 serial numbers) was delivered to the USAF in June 1964 but by then the B-26 had been withdrawn from Vietnam and the need for replacement aircraft did not appear to be a high priority as it had been replaced successfully by the A-1 Skyraider. The 603rd ACS worked up the aircraft at England AFB, Louisiana and after two years of testing and training including small scale deployments to the Congo and Panama, it was decided to deploy the aircraft to Southeast Asia. Initially eight aircraft were sent to Nakhon Phanom in June 1966 on a six-month combat evaluation under the code name Big Eagle where, as Detachment 1 of the 603rd ACS, they were attached to the 606th ACS. The aircraft's designation was changed from B-26K to A-26A due to the sensitivity of basing bomber aircraft in Thailand at that time. So successful was the A-26A in the night interdiction role over the Ho Chi Minh Trail that it was decided to keep the aircraft in Southeast Asia on a permanent basis. The unit ceased to be a detachment of the 603rd on 21 December 1966 but was absorbed into the 606th ACS and was assigned to the 634th CSG. On 15 September 1967 the 609th ACS was formed at Nakhon Phanom to operate the A-26A. The aircraft's main roles were night interdiction of the Trail in the Steel Tiger area of southern Laos and close air support and air strikes in the Barrel Roll area in the north of the country. The aircraft was only intended as a stop gap until fixed-wing gunships became available, however, this did not happen until late in 1968. The A-26A was usually known as Nimrod after its radio call sign.

Despite its age, the much-modified A-26A version of the Invader became one of the most successful weapons in the night interdiction war against truck traffic on the Ho Chi Minh Trail. Twelve of the 30 A-26As used in Southeast Asia were lost. USAF

28 June 1966

A-26A 64-17650   Detachment 1, 603 ACS attached to
                   606 ACS, 634 CSG, USAF, Nakhon Phanom
                   Capt Charles Glendon Dudley (KIA)
                   1Lt Anthony Frank Cavalli (KIA)
                   Maj Roger William Carroll (KIA)
                   Capt Thomas Hubert Wolfe (KIA)

The first Invader to be lost was on a daylight Steel Tiger mission 10 miles north of Ban Phakat when it was hit by ground fire and crashed killing all onboard. In addition to the normal crew complement the aircraft was also carrying an O-1 Bird Dog FAC pilot from the 23rd TASS, Capt Wolfe, who was giving the crew an orientation of the area.

29 June 1966

F-105D 60-0460   333 TFS, 355 TFW, USAF, Takhli
                   Capt Murphy Neal Jones (POW)

POL storage had become a regular target by the end of the month and on the 29th the heaviest raid so far on a POL target was made in two simultaneous strikes by 46 USAF and Navy aircraft. Navy aircraft from the *Constellation* and the *Ranger* hit a storage site on the outskirts of Haiphong while the USAF struck at storage sites close to Hanoi. This was the closest that raids had come to North Vietnam's two major cities. Maj James H Kasler, the operations officer of the 354th TFS, planned and led the USAF strike force that consisted of F-105s from both wings. Some of the Thunderchiefs made more than one pass at the target and it was on Capt Jones's second 'pop up' to attack that his aircraft was hit by 85mm AAA. The aircraft quickly became uncontrollable and the pilot ejected just one mile north of Hanoi's Gia Lam airport. Capt Jones was wounded in the leg by shrapnel from the flak burst. He also sustained a compression fracture of his spine and a severely broken left arm when he ejected at a very low altitude and was not able to assume the correct ejection posture before his seat fired. Despite his injuries he was paraded through the streets of Hanoi in the back of a truck and, like most of his fellow prisoners, was tortured by the North Vietnamese. He was on his third tour of duty when he was shot down and was released on 12 February 1973. Three other F-105s suffered battle damage during the first Hanoi POL strike.

A-1E 52-133918   602 ACS, 14 ACW, USAF, Udorn
                   Capt N J Baker (survived)

When not being used for RESCAP duties the 14th ACW's Skyraiders were also used for armed reconnaissance in Laos and the southern provinces of North Vietnam. On one such mission Capt Baker's aircraft was hit by AAA near Ban Katoi, 25 miles west of Dong Hoi and just across the North Vietnamese border with Laos. He bailed out over hilly terrain and was rescued by a USAF HH-3.

30 June 1966

F-105D 62-4224   388 TFW, USAF, Korat
                   Capt R K Nierste (survived)

Another strike on a POL site resulted in the loss of another Thunderchief on the last day of the month. The raid was on the Nguyen Khe POL site seven miles north of Hanoi, and Capt Nierste's aircraft was hit and damaged by AAA as he dived on the target. The aircraft held together and Capt Nierste was able to fly almost 200 miles before he was forced to abandon the Thunderchief near Moung Cha in Laos where he was picked up by a USAF rescue helicopter.

C-123B '55-4644'   310 ACS, 315 ACW, USAF, Nha Trang
                     4 crew, names unknown (survived)

A Provider crashed due to pilot error during a cargo flight in South Vietnam. All the crew survived the accident. The serial number of the C-123 as listed in an official document is incorrect.

1 July 1966

F-105D 59-1722   354 TFS, 355 TFW, USAF, Takhli
                   Capt Lewis Wiley Shattuck (survived)

The area around the mouth of the Sou Giang River 20 miles north of Dong Hoi was proving to be a graveyard for USAF aircraft. The Nam Lamh road bridge, which spanned the river, was the target for a raid by a flight of Thunderchiefs on the first day of the month. Capt Shattuck's aircraft was hit by groundfire and burst into flames forcing him to eject just offshore. He was rescued by a USAF HU-16B Albatross amphibian but 10 days later was shot down again and captured.

A-4E 150017   VA-155, USN, USS *Constellation*
                Cdr Charles Henry Peters (KIA)

Strikes against POL targets in North Vietnam continued into July. During a raid on a POL site at Dong Nham near Dong San, 20 miles northeast of Haiphong, the Skyhawk of the CO of VA-155 was hit in the starboard wing by 37mm AAA as it exited the target area. The aircraft began to stream fuel and caught fire but Cdr Peters radioed that as he could still maintain control he would try to reach the coast. Just as it crossed the beach near the island of Dao Ma Mun the fire suddenly worsened and the aircraft snap rolled. Cdr Peters ejected at low level and landed in the sea but was not seen to surface. It was assumed that he had been injured during the ejection and had drowned. At Dong Nham seven fuel tanks and four support buildings were destroyed during this raid.

F-105D 62-4354   13 TFS, 388 TFW, USAF, Korat
                   1Lt Burton Wayne Campbell (POW)

The 13th TFS transferred from the 18th TFW at Kadena on 15 May to bring the 388th up to full strength. On 1 July the Squadron

sent a flight of aircraft to attack a railway and road bridge near Xam Quyen, 40 miles northwest of Dong Hoi. As 1Lt Campbell's aircraft dived on the target it was struck by anti-aircraft fire and burst into flames. He attempted to head back towards the Laotian border but was forced to abandon the aircraft about five miles from the target. Burton Campbell had flown 13 missions during his tour in Southeast Asia and was held in captivity in North Vietnam until 12 February 1973.

A-1E 52-133890   602 ACS, 14 ACW, USAF, Udorn
                   Maj Robert Cyril Williams (KIA)

As soon as 1Lt Campbell's aircraft went down a SAR force swung into action to attempt a rescue. One of the Skyraiders was orbiting over the position of the downed pilot when it was hit by AAA, possibly incapacitating the pilot. The aircraft crashed soon after it was hit and no ejection was seen. On 2 August 1994 a joint US-Vietnamese investigation team recovered human remains from the crash site, which were positively identified as being those of Maj Williams in May 1995. On 1 July 1995, the 29th anniversary of his death, the mortal remains of Robert Williams were laid to rest in a small cemetery at McLeansboro, Illinois

2 July 1966

O-1E 56-2521   23 TASS, 505 TACG, USAF, Nakhon Phanom
                 Maj Lawrence John Frahman (KIA)

A Bird Dog crashed on an FAC mission in Quang Nam province, South Vietnam, killing the pilot. Enemy action was not thought to have been the cause.

3 July 1966

F-5C 64-13319   10 FCS, 3 TFW, USAF, Bien Hoa
                  Capt David Joseph Phillips (KIA)

The Skoshi Tiger detachment had completed its combat evaluation in March with the loss of only one aircraft. Redesignated the 10th Fighter Commando Squadron, the unit stayed on at Bien Hoa and supplemented the F-100s and VNAF aircraft in providing close air support for ground forces throughout South Vietnam. The unit lost its second aircraft and pilot on 3 July when Capt Phillips was shot down by small arms fire as he was about to drop napalm on a VC position five miles west of Ben Cat, 20 miles north of Saigon.

4 July 1966

F-105D 60-0486   355 TFW, USAF, Takhli
                   1Lt B L Minton (survived)

Air operations did not stop even for America's national holiday. As a flight of Thunderchiefs was flying at 12,000 feet off the coast of North Vietnam east of the DMZ en route to an armed reconnaissance mission, one of the aircraft was hit by AAA and caught fire. The pilot flew a further 15 miles out to sea before ejecting and was rescued.

A-4C 149616   VA-216, USN, USS *Hancock*
                Lt Cdr C F Baldwin (survived)

A Skyhawk from the *Hancock* was hit by AAA as it pulled up from an attack on a bridge five miles south of Mu Ron Ma. The cockpit began to fill with smoke and the aircraft's systems began to fail progressively culminating in the engine disintegrating with a loud bang. Lt Cdr Baldwin ejected safely over the Gulf of Tonkin 25 miles northeast of Mu Ron Ma and was picked up by a US Navy helicopter.

A-4E 151026   VA-155, USN, USS *Constellation*
                Lt N E Holben (survived)

During a night armed reconnaissance mission Lt Holben was making his third pass over what were assumed to be patrol boats 15 miles east of Dao Cat Ba island when his aircraft was struck

The F-105F Wild Weasels normally led a flight of single-seat F-105Ds, some of which carried the Shrike anti-radar missile, the Weasels' weapon of choice in the early years. USAF

by ground fire in the tail. Holben heard an explosion from the engine compartment and attempted to head south but the controls froze and he was forced to eject as the Skyhawk started a shallow dive into the sea. Luckily, he was rescued by a US Navy helicopter before the North Vietnamese boats could reach him.

Wild Weasel III

As successful as the F-100F undoubtedly was in the defence suppression role, the aircraft had a number of deficiencies and was only ever regarded as an interim platform to prove the Wild Weasel concept. The F-100F had a poorer performance than the aircraft it was supposed to be protecting, the F-105D. The strike aircraft had to weave from side to side in order not to overtake the Super Sabre. The F-100F also had a more limited range and load carrying capability than the F-105. In January 1966 it was decided to develop the F-4C and the F-105F for the Wild Weasel role. Work on the F-105 was rapid and on the 15th of that month the first modified F-105F was flown. The project was designated as Wild Weasel III and the aircraft was known as either the EF-105F or simply and more commonly as the F-105F Wild Weasel. The F-105F carried the same electronic equipment as the F-100F plus the AZ-EL system that gave the azimuth and elevation bearing, and the SEE-SAMS(B) passive warning system (later replaced by the ALR-31) that gave an indication of an imminent SAM launch.

The first of 10 initial F-105F Wild Weasels arrived at Korat on 28 May but the F-100F flew on in the role until 11 July. The F-105F Wild Weasel detachment was incorporated into the 13th TFS in July and gradually took over the Wild Weasel mission from the F-100F detachment, having achieved its first kill on 7 June. On 5 July an Iron Hand flight led by an F-105F attacked and damaged four SAM sites but the very next day the first F-105F was lost along with its crew. A month later another F-105F detachment was formed, this time at Takhli under the 354th TFS. Initially at least, the 388th TFW concentrated all its Weasels under the 13th TFS while the 355th TFW spread the aircraft around its three squadrons.

6 July 1966

F-105D 62-4254 388 TFW, USAF, Korat
Capt E L Stanford (survived)

An armed reconnaissance mission in the southern provinces of North Vietnam proved fruitful as a formation of Thunderchiefs found a number of railway wagons on a line 25 miles north of Dong Hoi. Unfortunately as one of the aircraft pulled up from its attack it was hit by AAA. The aircraft held together but was too badly damaged to reach Korat so Capt Stanford flew some 35 miles out to sea before ejecting and being rescued.

F-105F 63-8286 13 TFS, 388 TFW, USAF, Korat
Maj Roosevelt Hestle (KIA)
Capt Charles Elzy Morgan (KIA)

The first Thunderchief Wild Weasel to be lost during the war was shot down during an Iron Hand strike against a SAM site six miles west of Thai Nguyen. As the flight approached the target it came under heavy fire from anti-aircraft guns and SAMs. The leader of Pepper flight was seen to burst into flames, probably having been hit by 57mm AAA, and then crashed into the side of a hill close to the target. No parachutes were seen or SAR beepers heard and it was assumed that both crew had died instantly. However, some time later a press conference held in Hanoi was shown on US television and Charles Morgan's wife recognised her husband on the screen. He was one of the few negro airmen to be shot down over North Vietnam and had distictive facial scars from a childhood attack of chicken pox. However, when the prisoners were released in 1973 Charles Morgan was not among them even though some other POWs told Mrs Morgan they had seen her husband in a camp. The Department of Defense could throw no light on the apparent sighting of Charles Morgan but speculation ended when remains were handed over on 31 July 1989 that were later proved to be those of Capt Morgan, although how or when he had died could not be determined. As a Wild Weasel EWO he would certainly have been very valuable to the North Vietnamese had his identity been known to them.

A-1E 52-132423 602 ACS, 14 ACW, USAF, Udorn
Capt J R Crane (survived)

While on a RESCAP mission over northern Laos a Skyraider from Udorn was hit and badly damaged by small arms fire about 25 miles northwest of Sam Neua. Capt Crane headed south and coaxed his aircraft across the Mekong River, which forms the border with Thailand. However, about 20 miles north of Udorn he was forced to part company with his aircraft but was quickly picked up by a USAF helicopter.

RF-101C 56-0051 20 TRS, 460 TRW, USAF, Tan Son Nhut
detached to Udorn
Maj James Faulds Young (POW)

A Voodoo was lost during a reconnaissance mission along Route 50 in North Vietnam. Little is known about the cause or exact location of the incident but the pilot was captured and survived almost seven years of captivity to be released on 12 February 1973.

7 July 1966

A-4C 148456 VA-216, USN, USS *Hancock*
Lt Cdr William J Isenhour (survived)

The campaign against North Vietnam's POL storage system continued and on 7 July it was Haiphong's turn. As a Navy strike force was flying low over the outskirts of Haiphong, one of the Skyhawks was hit in the cockpit and engine by AAA. The aircraft began to trail smoke and the hydraulic system failed. Lt Cdr Isenhour disconnected the powered flight control system and reverted to manual as he flew the aircraft out of the target area and headed south. However, 25 miles southeast of Haiphong the aircraft's electrical system also failed and the aircraft began to roll out of control forcing the pilot to eject. He was picked up safely off the coast by a US Navy helicopter.

F-105D 59-1741 354 TFS, 355 TFW, USAF, Takhli
Capt Jack Harvey Tomes (POW)

In addition to the POL campaign, North Vietnam's rail system was also a major target for the USAF and Navy bombers. During a raid on a railway bridge 10 miles northwest of Yen Bai one of the attacking Thunderchiefs was shot down by 85mm AAA. Capt Tomes ejected close to the target and was quickly captured joining many of his colleagues in the POW system. He was released on 12 February 1973.

8 July 1966

F-105D 61-0158 333 TFS, 355 TFW, USAF, Takhli
1Lt Ralph Thomas Browning (POW)

The following day the Takhli Wing sent a raid to strike a truck park that had been discovered close to Thai Nguyen. One of the aircraft was hit by a 85mm shell and immediately burst into flames. Within seconds the Thunderchief became uncontrollable and 1Lt Browning ejected. Ralph Browning spent nearly seven years in various prison camps until his release on 12 February 1973. This was an ironic case of history repeating itself as his father, an Eighth Air Force B-17 navigator/ bombardier during the Second World War, had also been shot down and spent 19 months in a German POW camp. After release Ralph Browning resumed his Air Force career and became an instructor in an Aggressor Squadron. He later commanded an F-15 squadron and eventually rose to the rank of Brigadier General in 1988 when he took command of the 58th Wing at Luke AFB, Arizona. Ralph Browning retired from the USAF in September 1992.

A-4C 149494 VA-216, USN, USS *Hancock*
1 pilot, name unknown (survived)

As a Skyhawk was catapulted off the USS *Hancock* on a RESCAP mission a bomb fell off and ricocheted off the deck damaging the aircraft and forcing the pilot to eject.

10 July 1966

F-4C 63-7546 480 TFS, 35 TFW, USAF, Da Nang
Capt T P Weeks (survived)
Capt F J Lennon (survived)

The Air Force and Marine Corps Phantoms based at Da Nang made regular raids across the DMZ as well as providing close air support to US and allied troops in South Vietnam. As a Phantom was dropping napalm on a target two miles north of the DMZ near Thom Cam Son it was hit in the starboard engine by AAA. The aircraft burst into flames but remained airborne just long enough to cross the beach where the crew ejected less than a mile offshore. They were subsequently rescued by a USAF helicopter.

A-4C 147732 VA-153, USN, USS *Constellation*
Lt Cdr George Henry Wilkins (KIA)

A section of Skyhawks from the *Constellation* taking part in the night interdiction offensive against North Vietnamese road traffic spotted what looked like a convoy north of Vinh. Lt Cdr Wilkins dropped two flares and radioed that he was going to make a pass under the flares in order to positively identify the potentially lucrative target. Soon afterwards his wingman observed a long trail of fire on the ground and lost radio contact with his leader. Anti-aircraft fire was seen in the area and may have been the cause of the crash or Lt Cdr Wilkins may have flown into the ground under the light of the flares. Lt Cdr Wilkins was officially declared dead by the Navy on 28 June 1974. In 1989 the remains of a number of unidentified US airmen together with crash debris were handed over to the US by the Vietnamese. However, it was not until 1996 that mitochondrial DNA testing confirmed that one set of remains belonged to George Wilkins.

11 July 1966

F-105D 62-4282 354 TFS, 355 TFW, USAF, Takhli
Capt Lewis Wiley Shattuck (POW)

F-105D 61-0112 355 TFW, USAF, Takhli
Capt R H Laney (survived)

F-105D 61-0121 355 TFW, USAF, Takhli
Maj W L McClelland (survived)

Capt Shattuck had had a lucky escape on 1 July when he was shot down near Dong Hoi and was rescued from the Gulf of Tonkin by an HU-16. However, he was not so lucky 10 days later during a raid on the Vu Chua railway bridge five miles north of Kep. His aircraft was hit and badly damaged by 85mm AAA over the target. Unable to control the aircraft Capt Shattuck ejected 25 miles north of Vu Chua. This time he could not cheat capture and he spent the next seven years as a POW. He was released on 12 February 1973 and retired from the Air Force as a Colonel.

The next flight to hit the Vu Chua Bridge also met with intense anti-aircraft fire resulting in the loss of another Thunderchief. Capt Laney's aircraft was hit as it popped up to dive on the bridge. The damage did not at first seem too severe and Capt Laney started the long flight home. However, after flying for 125 miles the pilot had to eject and came down near Ban Thin in Laos. His good luck held and he was rescued by a USAF helicopter.

The Takhli Wing lost a third aircraft on this day when Maj McLelland's Thunderchief was damaged near Thai Nguyen. The cause was not the ever-present North Vietnamese anti-aircraft fire but a fight with a MiG that left Maj McLelland short of fuel. McLelland tried to make it back to Thailand but he was forced to eject over Laos when he ran out of fuel.

F-4B 152262 VF-143, USN, USS *Ranger*
Lt(jg) M McCarthy (survived)
Lt(jg) D F Granitto (survived)

During a training flight a Phantom developed a technical problem and was unable to take on fuel from a tanker. The aircraft's fuel was exhausted before it could reach the carrier and the crew were forced to eject.

12 July 1966

F-8E 150902 VF-162, USN, USS *Oriskany*
Lt(jg) Richard F Adams (survived)

On 30 June the *Oriskany* took up her position on the line for her second tour of duty off Vietnam. The ship would spend a total of 87 days on the line and in the process would suffer 16 aircraft losses in combat, extreme bad luck from a spell of accidents and the tragic early termination of its cruise on 26 October.

By mid-1966 most USAF tactical aircraft had been painted in the three-tone camouflage colours as dictated by TO 1-1-4. This freshly-painted F-4C is seen over South Vietnam in December 1965. USAF

The *Oriskany* joined in the POL campaign with a raid on Dong Nham near Dong San, 20 miles northeast of Haiphong. Four Crusaders were assigned to protect the strike force from possible MiG attack in the target area. A SAM launch was called and the strike force dived into a small valley. One of the Crusaders was hit in the tailpipe by small arms fire and started to burn. The fire rapidly spread forward into the fuselage and the aircraft became uncontrollable. Lt Adams ejected near the target and was picked up 45 minutes later in a daring rescue by a US Navy helicopter escorted by four A-1s. This was the second time that Lt Adams had been shot down during a mission over North Vietnam. His Crusader had been hit by a SAM on 5 October the previous year and he had to be rescued from the Gulf of Tonkin. He was posted back to the US after his second shoot down and his exploits were related in an article in Time magazine. Two years later he flew with the Blue Angels aerobatic team.

14 July 1966

F-8E   150908   VF-162, USN, USS *Oriskany*
Cdr Richard M Bellinger (survived)

A Navy strike on a storage depot in the Nam Dinh area was escorted by a trio of Crusaders from the *Oriskany* flown by Lt Cdr C Tinker, Lt Dick Wyman and Cdr Dick Bellinger, VF-162's flamboyant commander. The Crusaders orbited the target and were engaged by two MiG-17s. Cdr Bellinger's aircraft was hit by cannon fire during a dogfight about 25 miles southeast of Hanoi. With the starboard wing badly damaged and the port spoiler stuck in the full up position Cdr Bellinger broke away into cloud and headed south. When the hydraulics failed the pilot decided to divert to Da Nang rather than risk a landing back on the carrier. Unfortunately when Cdr Bellinger attempted to take on fuel he found that the in-flight refuelling probe would not extend due to the damage to the hydraulics. The aircraft ran out of fuel just 16 miles short of Da Nang and Bellinger was obliged to eject and be picked up by a USAF helicopter. Three months later Dick Bellinger had his revenge on the VPAF when he shot down a MiG-21 on 9 October. Dick Bellinger had flown bombers with the USAAF during the Second World War and later transferred to the Navy to fly combat missions during the Korean War. Dick Bellinger died of Alzheimer's disease in 1978. His adversary on 14 July was Ngo Duc Mai of Kep's 923rd Fighter Regiment.

15 July 1966

A-4E   151024   VA-55, USN, USS *Ranger*
Lt James Joseph Connell (POW-died)

An Iron Hand flight of four Skyhawks encountered heavy anti-aircraft fire as they were about to attack a SAM site near the Red River, 12 miles south of Hanoi. Four SA-2s were fired at the aircraft but all the missiles missed their mark. However, as the flight left the

target area one of the pilots saw a parachute on the ground and moments later Lt Connell called his flight to let them know he was OK. It was assumed that his aircraft had been shot down by AAA rather than by a missile. It was also assumed that Lt Connell had been taken prisoner and would eventually be released along with his colleagues, however, this was not to be. Although he had only received minor injuries on being shot down, Lt Connell's physical and mental health deteriorated in prison and the North Vietnamese stated that he died of natural causes on 14 January 1971.

F-105D 59-1761   388 TFW, USAF, Korat
Capt C L Hamby (survived)

Rolling Thunder claimed yet another Thunderchief when Capt Hamby's aircraft was hit by AAA over the coast near Cam Pha east of Haiphong. Capt Hamby turned out to sea and flew for almost 90 miles before being forced to eject. He was rescued soon after by a Navy helicopter.

F-4B   150470   VMFA-323, MAG-11, USMC, Da Nang
Maj B O Fritsch (survived)
1Lt C D Smith (survived)

Operation Hastings was a large scale search and destroy mission undertaken by the Marines just south of the DMZ. The operation was aimed at countering the movements of the NVA's 324B Division, which had become increasingly aggressive in this area in recent weeks and had made numerous large-scale incursions through the DMZ into the Marine's I Corps area. The ground operations were heavily supported by Marine Corps aircraft from Da Nang and Chu Lai and included a heliborne landing in the Ngan Valley on 15 July. It was during this operation that a Phantom was lost 15 miles northwest of Dong Ha. The aircraft was making its second pass dropping napalm on several small buildings near a site known as the Rockpile when it was observed by a USAF FAC to be on fire, probably as a result of ground fire. Both crew ejected safely as the aircraft flew through the tops of some tall trees and were recovered 30 minutes later by a USAF helicopter. This was the only Marine fixed-wing aircraft lost from the 1,677 tactical sorties flown in support of Operation Hastings. VMFA-323 had only just returned to Da Nang on 5 July.

17 July 1966

F-4C   63-7690   390 TFS, 35 TFW, USAF, Da Nang
Capt F D Moruzzi (survived)
1Lt J F Preston (survived)

The area north of the DMZ was still proving to be dangerous. A Da Nang Phantom on an armed reconnaissance sortie was attacking a target near Vinh Linh when it was hit in the engine bay by AAA. Capt Moruzzi coaxed the burning aircraft out to sea where he and his WSO ejected just a mile offshore. They were both picked up safely by a rescue helicopter.

F-105D 58-1165   388 TFW, USAF, Korat
1Lt W C Spelius (survived)

Seventh Air Force planners had still not taken to heart the folly of sending sophisticated and expensive Thunderchief strike aircraft on road reconnaissance missions. Flying at 10,000 feet a few miles north of Dong Hoi, 1Lt Spelius's aircraft was hit by ground fire and started to burn. He was forced to eject but was eventually picked up with only minor injuries by a USAF helicopter.

18 July 1966

F-105D 62-4312   421 TFS, 388 TFW, USAF, Korat
1 pilot, name unknown (survived)

A Thunderchief suffered an engine failure while flying over Thailand and crashed after the pilot ejected safely.

19 July 1966

F-8E   150919   VF-162, USN, USS *Oriskany*
Lt Terry Arden Dennison (KIA)

Although several aircraft had been hit and two brought down by ground fire while attacking SAM sites, no US aircraft had been confirmed lost to an SA-2 since 24 April. However, on 19 July this run of good luck came to an end during a Navy strike on the Co Trai Bridge. The bridge was an important crossing point south of Hanoi and was well defended by AAA and SAM sites. As the strike force was leaving the target area one of the Crusaders providing CAP was seen to be hit by one of the 13 SA-2s that were fired during the raid. The aircraft was flying at around 12,000 feet and burst into flames and broke up immediately. No parachute was observed or SAR beeper heard. The aircraft crashed near Hoang Xa, 18 miles south of Hanoi.

F-100F 58-1217   90 TFS, 3 TFW, USAF, Bien Hoa
Capt John Richard Bottesch (KIA)
A1C Darryl Gordon Winters (KIA)

Occasionally official USAF photographers flew on combat missions to take photographs for publicity or operational purposes. A1C Darryl Winters was a member of the 600th Photo Squadron and on 19 July he was assigned to photograph a combat mission and flew in a two-seat F-100F that took part in a close air support mission. The aircraft was making a strafing pass on a VC concentration near Tan An, 17 miles southwest of Tan Son Nhut, when it was either hit by groundfire or flew into the ground killing both crew.

F-105D 59-1755   354 TFS, 355 TFW, USAF, Takhli
1Lt Stephen Whitman Diamond (KIA)

North Vietnamese MiGs were becoming more aggressive throughout the summer of 1966 and scored a Thunderchief kill on 19 July. A formation of Thuds was on its way to strike a POL target when MiG-17s attacked over Phuc Yen, 15 miles north of Hanoi. One of the Thunderchiefs was attacked by Vo Van Man of the 923rd Fighter Regiment and immediately burst into flames. It was thought that the F-105 pilot had ejected but he was posted as missing in action and does not appear to have been seen in any of the POW camps.

F-105D 60-5382   354 TFS, 355 TFW, USAF, Takhli
Capt R E Steere (survived)

Half an hour after 1Lt Diamond was shot down another force of Thunderchiefs attacked a target seven miles north of Hanoi. As Capt Steere put the aircraft into a dive at 6,000 feet it was hit in the fuselage by AAA. Escorted by the rest of his flight Capt Steere flew back across North Vietnam and Laos and just made it into Thailand before having to abandon his aircraft.

20 July 1966

F-105D 62-4308   34 TFS, 388 TFW, USAF, Korat
                      Capt Merrill Raymond Lewis (KIA)

The Vu Chua railway bridge, a favourite target for both Air Force and Navy bombers, claimed another victim on the 20th. As a flight of four Thunderchiefs started to pull up to their bombing height 15 miles northeast of the target, the lead aircraft was hit by an 85mm anti-aircraft shell. Capt Lewis radioed that his cockpit was full of smoke and his wingman saw the aircraft on fire and diving out of control. Like 1Lt Diamond, Capt Lewis was thought to have ejected from his aircraft and to have come down about 25 miles northeast of Kep but was never seen or heard of again. In September 1989, twenty-three years after his death, the remains of Capt Lewis were handed over by the Vietnamese and positively identified by the USAF.

RB-66C 54-0464   41 TRS, 460 TRW attached to 355 TFW,
                      USAF, Takhli
                      Capt William Harley Means (POW)
                      1Lt Edward Lee Hubbard (POW)
                      Capt Lawrence Barbay (POW)
                      Capt Norman Alexander McDaniel (POW)
                      Capt Glendon William Perkins (POW)
                      1Lt Craig Roland Norbert (KIA)

At exactly the same time that Capt Lewis was being shot down an RB-66C was orbiting 25 miles north of Thai Nguyen on an ELINT mission, probably in support of the Thunderchief attack on the Vu Chua Bridge. The aircraft was in a gentle turn at 29,000 feet when it was suddenly rocked by an explosion as it was hit by one or two SA-2 missiles. The crew fought hard to save the aircraft and managed to fly some 55 miles to the southwest but were then forced to abandon the aircraft near Phu An near the confluence of the Red River and the Black River. All the crew, with the exception of 1Lt Norbert, were captured and eventually released in the second group release of Operation Homecoming on 4 March 1973 (for some reason Capt Perkins was released on 12 February 1973). Craig Norbert, an electronic warfare officer, did not accompany his fellow crewmen into captivity. A North Vietnamese interrogator told one of the prisoners that Norbert had died of burns soon after his capture. He was officially declared dead by the USAF on 18 January 1978. Capt Means was on his 89th mission over North Vietnam when he was shot down. Sadly, he died in 1986 from complications arising from his years in captivity. In 1975 Norman McDaniel wrote a book titled *Another Voice* about his experiences as a POW.

F-105D 61-0116   355 TFW, USAF, Takhli
                      Col William Humphrey Nelson (KIA)

A flight of Thunderchiefs on an armed reconnaissance mission spotted a truck on a road 10 miles south of Hoa Binh and 35 miles southwest of Hanoi. As Col Nelson was making his second strafing run his aircraft crashed and exploded. It was thought that the pilot may have been hit by ground fire. Col Nelson was on the headquarters staff of the 355th TFW and was the highest ranking USAF officer to be lost in the war since the death of Col Hergert on 8 March 1964.

F-4C 63-7695   555 TFS, 8 TFW, USAF, Ubon
                      Capt R A Walmsley (survived)
                      1Lt S W George (KIA)

The 8th TFW built up a reputation for night operations during its career in Southeast Asia. Its Phantoms ranged along the Ho Chi Minh Trail and well into North Vietnam on the lookout for targets of opportunity. One of the Wolfpack's aircraft was hit by groundfire and damaged on a night mission near Vinh Linh just north of the DMZ. The aircraft limped back across Laos and attempted to make an emergency landing at Udorn, the nearest airfield with a runway long enough to take the crippled Phantom. Unfortunately, the aircraft crashed during the landing killing the WSO, 1Lt George, and seriously injuring the pilot.

21 July 1966

A-4E 150101   VMA-224, MAG-12, USMC, Chu Lai
                      Maj H N Levin (survived)

Even though Operation Hastings took up a large proportion of the Marine Corps' air effort until the operation concluded on 3 August, the units from Da Nang and Chu Lai also flew armed reconnaissance and strike missions into the southern region of North Vietnam. On 20 July the area north of the DMZ up to Dong Hoi was designated by the Seventh Air Force as the Tally Ho area for a concerted interdiction campaign. As troops in the DMZ could not be attacked at this stage of the war, the Tally Ho campaign was intended to restrict movement into the zone from the north and west. The missions were monitored by a C-47 airborne command post and the strikes were controlled by O-1 FACs. The first aircraft lost on a Tally Ho mission was a Skyhawk that was hit in the fuselage by 37mm AAA as it was attacking a bridge near Xuan Noa, 12 miles north of the DMZ. The pilot headed out to sea and ejected some 10 miles offshore where he was picked up by a Marine Corps helicopter.

F-105D 62-4227   388 TFW, USAF, Korat
                      Capt Rainford Tiffin (KIA)

A strrike on the La Banh POL storage site 10 miles north of Yen Bai resulted in the loss of another Thunderchief and its pilot. Capt Tiffin's aircraft was hit by AAA in level flight at 3,500 feet and crashed without any ejection being observed.

23 July 1966

A-4E 152100   VA-163, USN, USS *Oriskany*
                      Cdr Wynn F Foster (survived)

On the 23rd the *Oriskany* flew a major strike on a POL storage site seven miles north of Vinh. The raid was led by Cdr Wynn Foster, CO of VA-163, who was flying his 238th combat sortie. Soon after the formation crossed the coast north of Vinh at 12,000 feet en route to the target Cdr Foster's aircraft was shaken by the close detonation of a 57mm AAA shell. Shrapnel from the shell smashed the cockpit and severed the pilot's right arm just below the shoulder. Cdr Foster was stunned by the impact and looked down to see his right hand resting on the aircraft's radio console. The aircraft's wing was also damaged resulting in a slow fuel leak. Bleeding profusely and in danger of losing consciousness completely, Cdr Foster managed to fly out to sea using his knees to hold the control column as his left arm held the shattered remains of his right arm and tried to stem the flow of blood. He realised he would probably not be able to make it back to the carrier even if the aircraft could reach it, so he flew to the nearest ship (the SAR destroyer USS *Reeves*) and ejected about 20 miles offshore. He was picked up by a boat from the destroyer, which fortuitously had a doctor on board at the time, and was rapidly evacuated to the *Oriskany*. Once on board the carrier the doctors further stabilised his condition until he was transferred to hospital at Cubi Point in the Philippines a week later for onward transfer to the USA. Following a long convalescence, Cdr Foster was fitted with a prosthetic right arm in March 1967 but then spent a frustrating year fighting a legal battle to stay in the Navy rather than be retired on medical grounds. He eventually won his case and even returned to sea duty as an operations officer before retiring from the Navy on 1 August 1972. He later wrote an excellent account of his career that was published with the title *Captain Hook*, the nickname he acquired during the latter stage of his long naval career.

F-105F 63-8338   354 TFS, 355 TFW, USAF, Takhli
                      Maj Gene Thomas Pemberton (KIA)
                      Maj Benjamin Byrd Newsom (KIA)

The second Wild Weasel F-105F to be lost (and the first from Takhli) went down on an Iron Hand strike seven miles west of Phuc Yen. It was thought that the aircraft was flying at high altitude and may have been hit by an SA-2 missile. The Thunderchief crashed just north of Hoa Lac and the fate of the crew is unknown although there appears to be some indications that they were captured and killed or died in captivity.

O-1E 57-6268   20 TASS, 505 TACG, USAF, Da Nang
                      Capt William Ward Smith (KIA)

During Operation Hastings the Marines did not have enough FACs themselves to deal with the many requests for air support and so requested assistance from the USAF. One of the Bird Dogs

---

assisting the Marines collided with a Marine UH-34D helicopter during a visual reconnaissance flight close to the DMZ and crashed, killing the O-1 pilot. The helicopter crash-landed but all the crew were rescued. The Bird Dog crashed near a hill known to the Marines as the Rockpile.

24 July 1966

A-4E 150040   VA-55, USN, USS *Ranger*
                      Lt E L Foss (survived)

A flight of Skyhawks was despatched from the *Ranger* to attack a truck convoy that had been reported by another flight. En route to this lucrative target one of the aircraft was hit by ground fire about 10 miles west of Mu Ron Ma in southern North Vietnam. Lt Foss saw fire warning and hydraulic failure lights come on and immediately reversed his course to take him out to sea. The wingman reported the aircraft was burning in the port wing root area. As the fire burnt through more of the aircraft and the controls began to freeze solid, Lt Foss put the aircraft into a climb and ejected as the Skyhawk commenced a slow roll to the left. Foss came down in the sea three miles offshore and was rescued by a Navy helicopter.

F-100D 56-3343   510 TFS, 3 TFW, USAF, Bien Hoa
                      1 pilot, name unknown (survived)

While on a close air support mission a Super Sabre suffered an accidental engine failure and crashed after the pilot ejected safely.

O-1E 56-4193   probably 19 TASS, 505 TACG, USAF,
                      Bien Hoa
                      Capt Ronald Ethridge Tinsley (KIA)
                      1 crew, name unknown (survived)

During an escort mission over Gia Dinh province in South Vietnam a Bird Dog crashed killing the pilot and injuring the observer.

A-26A 64-17643   Detachment 1, 603 ACS attached to
                      606 ACS, 634 CSG, USAF, Nakhon Phanom
                      Maj George G Duke (KIA)
                      Capt Miles T Tanimoto (KIA)

An Invader crashed on its approach to land at Nakhom Phanom as it returned from a strike over Laos. The crash was probably the result of fuel starvation due to a miscalculation of the fuel reserves remaining after a long patrol.

25 July 1966

F-105D 62-4271   469 TFS, 388 TFW, USAF, Korat
                      Maj F C Hiebert (survived)

During a raid on Thai Nguyen a Thunderchief was hit in the fuselage by AAA as it pulled up from its bombing run. Maj Hiebert flew back to base but the aircraft was destroyed in the subsequent crash landing.

F-100D 55-3739   615 TFS, 366 TFW, USAF, Phan Rang
                      Capt G J Farrell (survived)

The 615th TFS arrived at Phan Rang on 16 July as the first of the 366th TFW's three squadrons. One of the Squadron's early missions was a strike on VC structures in the Mekong Delta near Ba Tri, 45 miles south of Saigon. As Capt Farrell was making his second strafing run his aircraft was hit in the fuselage by small arms fire. He headed towards Bien Hoa but was forced to eject near Long Thanh, 10 miles southeast of the airfield, from where he was recovered by helicopter.

C-117D 17211   H&MS-11, MAG-11, USMC, Da Nang
                      Lt Col David Cleeland (KWF)
                      Maj Clifton Bishop Andrews (KWF)
                      Maj Gerard Martin Kieswetter (KWF)
                      Capt Jerome Cordell Winters (KWF)
                      Sgt Robert Clayton Morre (KWF)
                      GSgt Willis Shepherd Bowman (KWF)
                      Cpl Mickey Ray Grable (KWF)
                      23 passengers (survived)

Although it was not an operational squadron, Headquarters and Maintenance Squadron 11 was the Marines' longest continuous

serving aviation squadron in Southeast Asia. Established on 7 July 1965 when MAG-11 formed at Da Nang, the Squadron served at the base until 1 June 1971. Each MAG had a Head-quarters and Maintenance Squadron that had a small number of aircraft for liaison and transport duties. Usually the squadrons were equipped with a single C-117 for transport and logistics although the type was also used on occasions as a flare ship. Some of these squadrons also had UH-34s and TF-9Js and later some had O-1 Bird Dogs and two-seat TA-4 Skyhawks.

On 25 July MAG-11's C-117D commenced its take off from Da Nang on a routine transport flight carrying 31 passengers and crew. Soon after lift off the aircraft stalled and crashed killing seven of those on board and injuring most of the survivors. This aircraft was originally built as a C-47A but was first delivered to the Navy's VR-1 squadron in August 1944 designated as an R4D-5. It was converted to the much-modified C-117D version of the Skytrain in 1950.

26 July 1966

RF-4C 64-1040   16 TRS, 460 TRW, USAF, Tan Son Nhut
     Capt M G Mayfield (survived)
     1Lt R D Clark (survived)

The second USAF RF-4C to be lost in Southeast Asia was shot down by AAA over the coast of North Vietnam about 10 miles north of the DMZ. Both crew ejected safely, the pilot being rescued by a Navy helicopter and the navigator by a Marine Corps helicopter exemplifying inter-service cooperation in the SAR mission.

RF-101C 56-0201   20 TRS, 460 TRW, USAF, Tan Son Nhut
     detached to Udorn
     1 pilot, name unknown (survived)

A Voodoo crashed out of control as it returned to Udorn from a reconnaissance mission. The aircraft pitched up as the pilot attempted an overshoot when the runway became obstructed. The Voodoo had little longitudinal stability at low speeds and the aircraft crashed at the side of the runway, severely injuring the pilot.

27 July 1966

F-105D 61-0045   421 TFS, 388 TFW, USAF, Korat
     Capt James R Mitchell (survived)

The twentieth Thunderchief lost in combat during the month of July was hit by small arms fire while it was strafing a river ferry 20 miles northwest of Dong Hoi. Capt Mitchell immediately

headed east for the relative safety of the sea but was forced to eject 10 miles from the coastline and was lucky to be rescued by a USAF SAR helicopter.

28 July 1966

A-4E 152077   VA-164, USN, USS *Oriskany*
     Ens George Palmer McSwain (POW)

The increasing success of the North Vietnamese SAM batteries resulted in more intensive Iron Hand strikes. A missile site had been reported near the mouth of the Song Ca River near Vinh and a flight of Skyhawks from the *Oriskany* was despatched to deal with it. After firing a Shrike missile Ens McSwain put his aircraft into a climb, which by the time he had reached 12,000 feet had brought the aircraft's speed back to around 200 knots. At this point an SA-2 exploded nearby and, although Ens McSwain could see no damage, the aircraft fell out of control, possibly as a result of it stalling. After spending six and a half years as a POW McSwain was released on 4 March 1973.

29 July 1966

A-4E 152045   VA-155, USN, USS Constellation
     Lt(jg) Virgil King Cameron (KIA)

Lt Cameron was on an armed reconnaissance mission over the coastal waterways and was firing Zuni rockets at barges at Phu Dien Chau, 20 miles north of Vinh, when his aircraft was hit by AAA. The Skyhawk was diving at 480 knots and passing 2,000 feet when it was hit in the starboard wing root causing fuel to stream out. The aircraft rapidly rolled to the left and crashed before Lt Cameron had a chance to eject. In 1990 the Vietnamese handed over to the US several boxes of human remains with indications as to where the remains were found. However, some of the infor-mation was incorrect and it was not until 1998 that the mistake was discovered and the remains of Lt Cameron were found to be amongst those returned in 1990.

F-100D 56-2956   615 TFS, 366 TFW, USAF, Phan Rang
     Capt William Ray Gower (KIA)

The 615th TFS lost its second aircraft within the space of five days but this time the pilot was also also lost. Capt Gower was making his fifth strafing run against a Viet Cong target 25 miles west of Saigon when his aircraft was either hit by small arms fire or simply flew into the ground.

RC-47D 43-48388   606 ACS, 634 CSG, USAF, Nakhon Phanom
     Capt Bernard Conklin (KIA)
     Capt Robert Eugene Hoskinson (KIA)

     1Lt Vincent Augustus Chiarello (KIA)
     1Lt Robert Joseph Di Tommaso (KIA)
     Maj Galileo Fred Bossio (KIA)
     TSgt John Micheo Mamiya (KIA)
     TSgt Herbert Eugene Smith (KIA)
     SSgt James Shreve Hall (KIA)

On 19 July an RC-47D (call sign Dogpatch 2) set off for a sur-veillance mission around the Pathet Lao stronghold of Sam Neua. During the mission the aircraft flew close to (and may even have crossed) the border into North Vietnam. MiGs had occasionally been seen operating close to the Laotian border but it was thought that they posed little threat to aircraft operating in the Sam Neua area. However, a MiG-17 made a high speed dash to the border and shot down the RC-47D before making off deep into North Vietnam. This was undoubtedly a major success for the VPAF, which had succeeded in shooting down an important aircraft in a daring and skilful attack. Despite an unconfirmed report that one or two parachutes had been seen, none of the crew of the aircraft appears to have survived. In March 1988 the remains of Conklin, Chiarello, Hall, Mamiya and Smith were returned and identified. A witness reported seeing a badly burned survivor who was said to have died in a hospital the day after being shot down.

A-4E 152095   VA-164, USN, USS *Oriskany*
     Lt(jg) Donovan Ewoldt (KWF)

Having just spent 20 days on the line, the *Oriskany* sailed south for a week's break. During this period it lost a Skyhawk in tragic circumstances. During a practice in-flight refuelling the Sky-hawk pilot either became disoriented or was concentrating only on the tanker as he apparently flew into the water and was killed.

31 July 1966

A-1E 52-132421   probably 602 ACS, 14 ACW, USAF, Udorn
     Capt D W Lester (survived)

During an armed reconnaissance sortie a Skyraider was hit by small arms fire near Ban Kato, 25 miles west of Dong Hoi in a mountainous region of southern North Vietnam. Capt Lester bailed out and was picked up by a USAF HH-3.

RF-101C 56-0226   20 TRS, 460 TRW, USAF, Tan Son Nhut
     detached to Udorn
     Maj William David Burroughs (POW)

On his 99th combat mission over North Vietnam (just one before he could complete his tour and return home), Maj Burroughs was shot down by AAA as he was about to photograph a railway

and road bridge at Bac Ninh, 15 miles northeast of Hanoi. Maj Burroughs was actually on detachment from the 15th TRS and was released on 4 March 1973 and eventually retired from the USAF as a Colonel.

A-4C   147677   VA-172, USN, USS *Franklin D Roosevelt*
1 pilot, name unknown (survived)

The USS *Franklin D Roosevelt* arrived off Southeast Asia to replace the USS *Ranger* and was assigned to TF 77 on 25 July for its first, and as it transpired, only cruise of the war. The fourth Atlantic Fleet carrier to serve in the war, the *Franklin D Roosevelt* carried two Phantom and three Skyhawk squadrons along with detachments of Skywarriors, Tracers and reconnaissance Crusaders. The first aircraft loss occured as the carrier was working up off the Philippines before heading north to take position off the coast of Vietnam. One of VA-172's Skyhawk suffered an engine failure during a training flight forcing the pilot to eject. This was the first of 15 aircraft that would be lost by the carrier during its 95 days of operations off Vietnam.

1 August 1966

F-104C   56-0928   435 TFS, 8 TFW, USAF, Udorn
Capt John Charles Kwortnik (KIA)

The F-104 Starfighter returned to Southeast Asia in June 1966 when the 435th TFS deployed to Udorn to be attached to the Wolfpack. The aircraft brought to Udorn by the 435th had been modified to carry four, rather than two, AIM-9 Sidewinders as well as bombs and rockets for air-to-ground attack. However, the Starfighter was still not proving to be a great success as a strike or ground attack aircraft, which was hardly surprising considering it was designed primarily for high speed interception and nuclear strike. However, it was thought that it could serve as an escort fighter despite its short endurance and limited missile load.

Activity over North Vietnam was centred around the iron and steel producing town of Thai Nguyen on the first day of August. To protect the strike force the Iron Hand aircraft were sent after known SAM sites in the area. To allow the Iron Hand aircraft to get on with their task unhindered by the threat of MiGs they often had their own escort fighters covering them from higher altitude. A flight of four Starfighters were orbiting near a SAM site 30 miles northwest of Thai Nguyen at 4,000 feet as an Iron Hand flight made an attack. A SAM was launched at the aircraft and Capt Kwortnik's aircraft was seen to be hit by the missile. The aircraft immediately burst into flames and broke up. It was reported that a parachute had been seen but intense ground fire precluded any further investigation. If Capt Kwortnik did eject safely then he did not survive as he never appeared in the North Vietnamese POW system although a Hanoi newspaper is said to have reported the capture of a pilot on this date.

F-105D   62-4380   13 TFS, 388 TFW, USAF, Korat
Capt Kenneth Walter North (POW)

Nearly two hours after Capt Kwortnik's Starfighter had been shot down a flight of Thunderchiefs from the Korat Wing was en route to attack the Thai Nguyen railway yard. About 7 miles north of Yen Bai and some 55 miles west of his target Capt North's aircraft was hit by AAA and caught fire. The pilot ejected at 10,000 feet and was quickly captured, spending the rest of the war as a POW until his release on 4 March 1973. Capt North was on his 33rd combat mission over North Vietnam when he was shot down. He resumed his career after release and eventually rejoined the 388th TFW becoming the Wing's vice commander. He later commanded the 401st TFW at Torrejon in Spain and retired from the USAF as a Brigadier General on 1 October 1985 after commanding NORAD's 24th Air Division

The College Eye task force of EC-121s started operations in Southeast Asia in April 1965 and kept watch on air activity over North Vietnam for the duration of the war. The aircraft were initially based at Tan Son Nhut, where this aircraft is seen, but moved to Korat in 1967. USAF

F-104C   57-0925   435 TFS, 8 TFW, USAF, Udorn
Lt Col Arthur Thomas Finney (KIA)

As Capt North's flight was being engaged by AAA near Yen Bai another Iron Hand strike force was approaching the Thai Nguyen area. When the Wild Weasels and their Starfighter escorts were about 10 miles southwest of the city one of the Starfighters suddenly turned into a ball of flame. The aircraft was assumed to have been yet another SA-2 SAM victim and, like Capt Kwortnik earlier in the day, Lt Col Finney was posted missing, later changed to killed in action.

O-1E   56-2550   20 TASS, 505 TACG, USAF, Da Nang
detached to Tan Son Nhut
Lt Col E Abersold (survived)

The fourth USAF aircraft lost on this day was a Bird Dog FAC that crash-landed due to damage to its port wing from ground fire. The aircraft landed close to Dong Ha just south of the DMZ and the pilot was recovered with only minor injuries.

3 August 1966

F-100D   56-3375   308 TFS, 3 TFW, USAF, Bien Hoa
1Lt T L Hodges (survived)

During a direct air support mission in South Vietnam a Super Sabre was shot down and its pilot rescued by a USAF helicopter.

A-1H   134586   VA-145, USN, USS *Ranger*
Lt O Franz (survived)

Two days before the *Ranger* was due to be withdrawn from Yankee Station at the conclusion of its second tour of duty in Southeast Asia, the ship lost one of its Skyraiders. Lt Franz's aircraft was damaged by small arms fire during a road reconnaissance over the southern provinces of North Vietnam. He flew out to sea to a position about 65 miles northeast of Hué where he successfully ditched the aircraft and was rescued by a Navy helicopter. On 5 August the *Ranger* steamed south after spending 137 days on the line and losing 21 aircraft and 11 men in the process.

F-4B   152330   VMFA-323, MAG-11, USMC, Da Nang
Capt R C Johnson (survived)
1Lt J C Lesieur (survived)

Six of VMFA-323's Phantoms had been detached from Da Nang to Chu Lai at the end of July to provide increased air support to the southern area of Military Region I until MAG-13 was established at Chu Lai in September. As a Phantom was being catapulted from Chu Lai's SATS runway it suffered foreign object damage to an engine and failed to maintain flying speed. Both crew escaped before the aircraft crashed.

4 August 1966

A-1E   52-133872   602 ACS, 14 ACW, USAF, Udorn
Capt John Robert Burns (KIA)

Two Skyraiders were assigned to attack a military complex in the hills near Kang Mong, about 20 miles east of Sam Neua and close to the Laotian border with North Vietnam. The attack took place under low cloud and his wingman saw Capt Burns's aircraft dive into the ground, possibly as a result of a hit by AAA. No parachute was seen or SAR beeper heard and it was assumed that Capt Burns had died in the crash. Further information may have been recieved as the USAF changed Capt Burns's status from missing to killed in action on 10 October 1966. His name also appears on an official December 1996 list of remains returned.

F-105D   61-0119   357 TFS, 355 TFW, USAF, Takhli
1Lt Allen V Rogers (survived)

Even though his wingman saw no parachute it was just possible that Capt Burns had escaped from his aircraft so a rescue mission was mounted. A flight of Thunderchiefs flew RESCAP for the SAR task force but the mission proved unsuccessful and the task force prepared to return home. As the Thunderchiefs made a final strafing pass on a target a few miles from the wreck of the Skyraider, one of the aircraft was hit by AAA and caught fire. The aircraft remained controllable and 1Lt Rogers nursed it back across Laos and into Thailand only to have to eject 40 miles northwest of Udorn.

6 August 1966

F-105D   62-4315   421 TFS, 388 TFW, USAF, Korat
Capt Allen K Rutherford (survived)

A flight of Thunderchiefs was sent on an attack mission against known AAA positions in North Vietnam. While en route to the target one of the aircraft was hit by AAA near Dao Cai Bau island 25 miles northwest of Hon Gay. Capt Rutherford turned out to sea with the aircraft on fire and managed to fly over 160 miles to the south before ejecting and being picked up by a USAF Albatross amphibian.

F-4C   63-7587   557 TFS, 12 TFW, USAF, Cam Ranh Bay
Lt Tarre (survived)
Capt Bavousett (survived)

During a combat air patrol over South Vietnam a Phantom suffered an engine failure serious enough to force the crew to eject. They were both picked up safely.

7 August 1966

F-105D   60-0499   333 TFS, 355 TFW, USAF, Takhli
Capt John Henry Wendell (POW)

F-105D   61-0140   333 TFS, 355 TFW, USAF, Takhli
Maj Willard Selleck Gideon (POW)

Sunday 7 August turned out to be one of the most expensive days for the US air services so far during the war with a total of eight aircraft destroyed and seven airmen lost. 'Black Sunday' saw several major strikes on POL storage facilities throughout North Vietnam. The strikes were to be protected by Iron Hand flights that would tackle any SAM sites that posed a threat to the bombers.

One of the first strikes of the day was against a POL storage site near Hoang Lien, 20 miles north of Hanoi. As Capt Wendell's Thunderchief commenced its dive onto the target from 10,000 feet it was struck by an SA-2 SAM and began to disintegrate. Capt Wendell ejected and was taken prisoner. A few minutes later as the same flight was finishing its attack, Maj Gideon's aircraft was hit in the tail by AAA as it pulled up to 6,000 feet. The aircraft quickly became uncontrollable and Maj Gideon was also forced to eject 12 miles east of Kep joining Capt Wendell in captivity. Both men were released on 4 March 1973. Maj Gideon's aircraft was painted as 'The Lone Star Special'.

F-105F   63-8358   354 TFS, 355 TFW, USAF, Takhli
Capt Edward Larson (survived)
Capt K A Gilroy (survived)

Ten minutes after Maj Gideon was shot down an Iron Hand flight of Thunderchiefs attacked a SAM site in support of a raid on a marshalling yard on the northeast railway when it was engaged by another SAM site about 12 miles north of Haiphong. The F-105F Wild Weasel leading the flight fired a Shrike missile at a SAM radar signal but was then hit and damaged by an SA-2 at 13,000 feet. The cockpit was badly damaged when the 20mm ammunition drum exploded and the aircraft caught fire. Capt Larson jettisoned the canopy to clear the cockpit of smoke and turned the aircraft south to cross the coast. However, a few miles south of Hon Gay the crew were forced to eject as the fire burnt through the aircraft's controls. Both men, who were on their 11th mission, were picked up from the sea by a USAF HU-16B Albatross that came under mortar fire from one of the many islands just off the coast. The Albatross was flown by Maj R H Angstadt who was killed on 18 October. Mike Gilroy completed two combat tours in Southeast Asia and flew a total of 119 missions.

F-105F   63-8361   354 TFS, 355 TFW, USAF, Takhli
Capt Robert James Sandvick (POW)
Capt Thomas Shaw Pyle (POW)

The loss of one of the valuable F-105F Wild Weasel aircraft was bad enough but worse was to follow. A few minutes after Larson and Gilroy had been hit another Iron Hand flight was setting about a SAM site a mile south of Kep. As Capt Sandvick's aircraft was climbing through 4,000 feet it was struck by an 85mm shell and quickly became unflyable forcing the crew to eject about 12 miles southeast of Kep. Sandvick and Pyle had trained and

fought as a crew and had arrived at Takhli on 4 July. Like many 'Bears', the term for Wild Weasel back-seaters, Capt Pyle had previously served as an EWO in B-52s. Sandvick was on his 13th mission when he was shot down and Pyle was on his sixth. Both men became POWs and were eventually released on 4 March 1973. The loss of the two Wild Weasels on the 7th temporarily left just a single F-105F in commission at Takhli until replacements arrived.

A-1H 139701 VA-152, USN, USS *Oriskany*
Lt Charles Wigger Fryer (KIA)
The Navy was also busy on the 7th but was fortunate to lose only one aircraft in combat. During an armed reconnaissance mission near Phong Bai, 35 miles north of Vinh, a section of Skyraiders spotted several trucks and commenced strafing attacks. During the attack Lt Fryer's aircraft was hit in the port wing by small arms fire. The pilot turned out to sea immediately and attempted to ditch the aircraft a couple of miles off the coast. Unfortunately, unlike Lt Franz four days earlier, Lt Fryer did not survive the ditching.

F-105D 62-4370 357 TFS, 355 TFW, USAF, Takhli
1Lt Michael Lee Brazelton (POW)
The final combat loss of the day involved yet another Thunderchief that was lost on a raid on a POL storage site five miles north of Thai Nguyen. As one of the aircraft was pulling up through 3,000 feet from its bombing run it was hit by 100mm AAA and began to burn. After flying about five miles further north 1Lt Brazelton was forced to eject and was quickly taken prisoner. Michael Brazelton had accumulated over 330 hours of combat flying and was shot down on his 111th sortie. He was released from North Vietnam on 4 March 1973 and after recuperation and requalification he was posted to an Aggressor training squadron at Nellis AFB to teach air combat in the F-5 and T-38. He was later sent to Mexico to assist in the introduction of the F-5 into Mexican Air Force service.

A-4B 145040 VA-15, USN, USS *Intrepid*
Lt Cdr Richard Allen Moran (KIA)
The USS *Intrepid* was another Atlantic Fleet carrier that was temporarily redeployed to the Pacific Fleet to ease the burden of operations as the tempo of the war increased during the year. The *Intrepid* had been serving for some years as an anti-submarine carrier but replaced its ASW Air Wing with CVW-10 before sailing for the Pacific. The new Air Wing consisted of just two Skyhawk squadrons and two Skyraider squadrons along with a pair of Seasprite helicopters. The ship had arrived as long ago as 15 May and had lost one of its Seasprites on 19 June but the Skyhawk lost on 7 August was the first fixed-wing aircraft lost during the cruise. The aircraft was about to land back on the carrier after flying a sortie as a tanker but after making a run in and break over the carrier the aircraft was seen to descend with wings level and apparently under control until it struck the sea. The cause of this tragic accident was never established.

RF-101C 56-0064 20 TRS, 460 TRW, USAF, Tan Son Nhut
Maj Don Dyer (survived)
A Voodoo landed back at Tan Son Nhut from a mission to Laos but aquaplaned along the runway, which had patches of standing water from a recent downpour. Neither the brakes nor the brake parachute could stop the aircraft from veering off the runway. Its undercarriage was ripped off as it dug into soft mud and the aircraft broke in two when it hit a drainage ditch. Luckily the pilot escaped major injury.

8 August 1966

F-4C 63-7560 555 TFS, 8 TFW, USAF, Ubon
Capt Lawrence Herbert Golberg (KIA)
1Lt Patrick Edward Wynne (KIA)
The heavy losses of the 7th were compounded by the loss of another six aircraft the next day. The first aircraft to fall was a Wolfpack Phantom that was attacking trucks found near Na Lang, 30 miles northeast of Kep during an armed reconnaissance mission. As the aircraft was retiring from the attack it was hit by AAA and crashed killing both the crew. Larry

Golberg was one of the first USAF F-4 instructor pilots and had shot down a MiG-17 on 30 April during a CAP mission for a downed RF-101 pilot. His remains were returned by the Vietnamese in 1978 and he was buried in his home town of Duluth, Minnesota.

F-105D 62-4327 354 TFS, 355 TFW, USAF, Takhli
1Lt Fredrick R Flom (POW)
A few minutes after the Wolfpack Phantom had gone down, a flight of Thunderchiefs was retiring from a strike against trucks and barrack buildings to the northwest of Hanoi. At a position about 15 miles northwest of Yen Bai one of the aircraft was hit by AAA and crashed about 10 miles to the south. The pilot, 1Lt Flom, was on his 82nd mission and ejected and was captured. He was released on 4 March 1973 and finally retired from the USAF as a Colonel.

F-105D 62-4343 354 TFS, 355 TFW, USAF, Takhli
Maj James Helms Kasler (POW)
A rescue mission was mounted as soon as 1Lt Flom's aircraft went down and the escort for the rescue force included several of Flom's colleagues from the 354th TFS. Maj James Kasler, operations officer of the 354th TFS and one of the most experienced and respected Thud pilots in the USAF, led the F-105s. As the Thunderchiefs were orbiting at 1,000 feet about 10 miles southeast of Yen Bai, Kasler's aircraft was hit by AAA and burst into flames. Kasler turned to the west but only got about 10 miles before he was forced to eject. Like Flom, he was soon captured and spent the next six and a half years as a POW. James Kasler had served as a B-29 Superfortress tailgunner in the Pacific theatre during the Second World War. Kasler underwent pilot training after the war and was one of the USAF's most successful F-86 Sabre pilots during the Korean War flying 100 missions and scoring six MiG kills. He was flying his 91st mission of his third war when he was shot down over North Vietnam. In June 1972 Kasler was involved in Operation Thunderhead, an aborted plan to escape from prison in Hanoi in which the escapees would be picked up by Navy SAR helicopters from the Red River. He was released on 4 March 1973 and after serving as Vice Commander of the 366th TFW at Mountain Home he retired from the USAF as a Colonel in 1975. He achieved the dream of many fighter pilots by retiring and owning his own golf course.

F-4C 64-0687 557 TFS, 12 TFW, USAF, Cam Ranh Bay
Capt Charles Milton Walling (KIA)
1Lt Aado Kommendant (KIA)
A flight of Phantoms from Cam Ranh Bay were vectored to a position about 20 miles north of Bien Hoa to bomb suspected VC positions in support of US ground forces. Soon after Capt Walling completed his fourth run against the target the FAC who was controlling the bombing noticed an explosion on the ground five miles east of Phuoc Vinh. Failing to raise Capt Walling on the radio, the FAC and the other Phantom flew to the position of the explosion but could not see any wreckage due to very dense foliage. Ground troops could not reach the suspected wreck as it was heavily defended by VC troops. No parachutes were seen or SAR beepers heard so it was assumed that the crew had perished in their aircraft, which was either shot down by small arms fire or had simply flown into the ground.

F-105D 61-0155 421 TFS, 388 TFW, USAF, Korat
1Lt J R Casper (survived)
A third Thunderchief was lost on the 8th during an armed reconnaissance of the southern provinces of North Vietnam. A flight of Thunderchiefs was attacking what was thought to be a storage area near Troc, 25 miles northwest of Dong Hoi, when one of the aircraft was hit by ground fire. The pilot ejected close by and was fortunate to be rescued by a USAF SAR helicopter. 1Lt Casper was shot down again in a Thunderchief on 14 September 1966.

F-5C 63-8426 10 FCS, 3 TFW, USAF, Bien Hoa
1 pilot, name unknown (survived)
During a direct air support mission over South Vietnam one of the 10th FCS's F-5s suffered an engine failure and the pilot ejected safely.

10 August 1966

A-4E 151065 VA-155, USN, USS *Constellation*
Lt Cdr Joseph Stephen Henriquez (KIA)
As the *Constellation* was launching several Skyhawks on armed reconnaissance missions, one of the aircraft suffered an engine failure as it left the deck. The pilot ejected but the parachute failed to deploy and he was killed.

11 August 1966

F-8E 150880 VF-111, USN, USS *Oriskany*
Lt(jg) C A Balisteri (survived)
The hundreds of islands along the coast between Haiphong and the Chinese border was an ideal hiding place for sampans, barges and small vessels that were as much a part of North Vietnam's transport system as was the Ho Chi Minh Trail. The islands were frequently the attention of armed reconnaissance flights by carrier aircraft and on one such flight a Crusader was hit by ground fire about 10 miles south of Hon Gay. The aircraft's hydraulic, oil and fire warning lights came on in rapid succession and the pilot ejected as the aircraft started to roll out of control. He was soon picked up by one of the Navy's rescue helicopters.

F-4C 63-7502 497 TFS, 8 TFW, USAF, Ubon
Capt P L Penn (survived)
1Lt Benjamin B Finzer (survived)
The Wolfpack lost its second Phantom of the month during an armed reconnaissance mission near Kep. A flight of F-4s was attacking anti-aircraft gun positions when an 85mm shell hit one of the aircraft. The Phantom did not appear to be on fire but Capt Penn made for the coast and he and his back-seater were later forced to eject over the Gulf of Tonkin from where they were rescued by a Navy helicopter. 1Lt Finzer was killed in an accident at Ubon on 13 September with a different pilot.

12 August 1966

F-105D 62-4326 333 TFS, 355 TFW, USAF, Takhli
1Lt Martin James Neuens (POW)

F-105D 61-0156 333 TFS, 355 TFW, USAF, Takhli
Capt David Jay Allinson (KIA)
The POL campaign may or may not have been having an effect on North Vietnam's transportation and industry but it was certainly resulting in increased losses over the North. The POL storage site at Thai Nguyen was once again the target for a Rolling Thunder strike. One of the aircraft was hit by AAA over the target and caught fire. 1Lt Neuens ejected after a short while and was captured to spend the rest of the war as a POW. He was released on 4 March 1973.

Another flight of four Thunderchiefs from the 333rd TFS was also on the Thai Nguyen raid this day and was looking for targets of opportunity after hitting the POL storage site. The leader's aircraft was hit by AAA as he made a strafing pass on a target. Egressing the area Capt Allinson was soon forced to eject and was seen to parachute into some trees standing along a ridge about 10 miles northwest of Yen Bai. Radio contact was never made with Capt Allinson and he is assumed to have been killed in action.

RF-101C 56-0056 20 TRS, 460 TRW, USAF, Tan Son Nhut
detached to Udorn
Maj Blair Charlton Wrye (KIA)
A Voodoo from Udorn was lost in unknown circumstances north of Hanoi during a Rolling Thunder reconnaissance mission. The aircraft was last reported about five miles east of Nam Dinh in the Red River Delta. The remains of Maj Wrye (promoted to Colonel during the period he was listed as missing) were returned to the US authorities on 13 September 1990.

13 August 1966

F-8E 150866 VF-111, USN, USS *Oriskany*
Lt Cdr N S Levy (survived)

Armed reconnaissance over the islands around Hon Gay claimed another Crusader from VF-111. Lt Cdr Levy found a large barge about 10 miles south of Hon Gay and was pulling up from his second attack using his Zuni rockets when his aircraft was hit by ground fire. Hydraulic pressure was soon lost and the cockpit filled with smoke. The aircraft suddenly pitched nose up and the controls froze, whereupon Lt Cdr Levy ejected about five miles east of Dao Cat Ba from where he was rescued by a Navy helicopter.

14 August 1966

F-105D 61-0197   469 TFS, 388 TFW, USAF, Korat
                  Capt Charles Edward Franklin (KIA)

F-105D 59-1763   333 TFS, 355 TFW, USAF, Takhli
                  Capt Curtis Abbot Eaton (KIA)

F-105D 62-4266   354 TFS, 355 TFW, USAF, Takhli
                  Capt John Warren Brodak (POW)

Once more POL storage around the city of Thai Nguyen was a target for elements of both Thunderchief strike wings. The Korat Wing attacked first but AAA hit one of the 469th TFS aircraft over the target and it eventually crashed about 10 miles to the north. Capt Franklin radioed that his aircraft had been hit and was going to eject. However, nothing more was heard or seen of Capt Franklin until 13 July 1988 when his remains (which were positively identified in the following October) where handed over by the Vietnamese.

About 20 minutes after Capt Franklin was shot down, elements of the Takhli Wing began to bomb POL targets around Thai Nguyen. An aircraft in one of the leading flights was hit by AAA over the target and sped away to the north. The Thunderchief crashed about 20 miles north of Thai Nguyen and the pilot, Capt Eaton, was presumed to have died in the crash. Twenty minutes later another Thunderchief was hit by AAA over Thai Nguyen but the aircraft remained airborne long enough for Capt Brodak to attempt to get home. Unfortunately, he only managed to reach about half way and was forced to eject near Phlen Luong near the Laotian border. Capt Brodak had flown over 60 missions in Southeast Asia but was captured and spent the rest of the war as a POW, being released on 4 March 1973.

F-8E 150322   VMF(AW)-235, MAG-11, USMC, Da Nang
               Capt E S Kowalczyk (survived)

As a Marine Corps Crusader was taking off from Da Nang the aircraft caught fire and crashed, probably due to a failure of the afterburner. A similar accident happened to an aircraft from the same squadron just three days later.

17 August 1966

F-105F 63-8308   354 TFS, 355 TFW, USAF, Takhli
                  Maj Joseph William Brand (KIA)
                  Maj Donald Maurice Singer (KIA)

Maj Brand and Maj Singer were shot down when their Thunderchief was hit by AAA over a target 12 miles north of Van Yen, 65 miles west of Hanoi. The aircraft was leading an Iron Hand flight and was attacking a SAM site when the aircraft was hit and both crew ejected at low level. One parachute was seen to open but the other did not deploy fully before hitting the ground. Maj Brand radioed that he had landed and was OK but despite an attempt by Sandys to locate the airmen they were not recovered. Neither of the men survived their ordeal. The fact that five F-105F Wild Weasels had by now been lost since the first one went down on 6 July illustrates the increasing intensity of the air war over North Vietnam and the highly dangerous nature of the Iron Hand mission. By this date there had only been 11 F-105Fs delivered to Southeast Asia so the loss of five aircraft was devastating. For the time being, until the Wild Weasels could be reinforced, the free roaming 'hunter-killer' missions were curtailed and the Weasels were confined to close escort and suppression. Much of the blame lay with inadequate training and the highly dangerous character of the Weasel mission. Nothing much could be done about the latter but throughout 1966 and 1967 training at the 4537th Fighter Weapons Squadron at Nellis AFB was greatly improved and replacements made good.

F-8E 150321   VMF(AW)-235, MAG-11, USMC, Da Nang
               1 pilot, name unknown (survived)

Having lost an aircraft three days earlier in similar circumstances, VMF(AW)-235 lost another Crusader at Da Nang when its afterburner failed on take off. Unfortunately, after the pilot ejected, the aircraft crashed into a village close to the airfield killing 33 Vietnamese civilians and injuring a further 20.

18 August 1966

F-8E 150300   VF-162, USN, USS Oriskany
               Lt Cdr Demetrio A Verich (survived)

Yet another of the Oriskany's Crusaders was lost during an armed reconnaissance mission although this incident took place inland rather than on the coast. Lt Cdr Verich was pulling up from his third bombing run dropping Mk83 bombs on a bridge and barges on a river 15 miles northwest of Vinh, when his aircraft was hit by small arms fire. He immediately turned east and as he made his way towards the coast the aircraft's controls progressively failed. By the time the Crusader became totally uncontrollable it was nearly five miles offshore and Lt Cdr 'Butch' Verich ejected and was rescued by a Navy helicopter. Verich, like his squadron mate Lt Richard Adams, was shot down twice during the war, the second time on 16 July 1967 when his aircraft was hit by a SAM. This particular Crusader had earlier been used by Lt Phil Vampatella to shoot down a MiG-17 on 21 June.

19 August 1966

RA-5C 149309   RVAH-6, USN, USS Constellation
                Lt Cdr J K Thompson (survived)
                Lt(jg) G L Parten (survived)

A Vigilante was flying about 17 miles northwest of Vinh photographing roads and bridges in the area when it came under fire from small arms and AAA. The aircraft suddenly rolled inverted and despite the pilot's efforts only partial control could be maintained. Lt Cdr Thompson headed the aircraft out to sea and the escort reported that there was a fire in the Vigilante's wheel well. Sections of the port wing began to fall off and the nose pitched down at which point both crew ejected some 10 miles offshore. Lt Cdr Thompson was picked up by a Navy helicopter and his NFO by a Navy vessel.

RF-4C 64-1054   16 TRS, 460 TRW, USAF, Tan Son Nhut
                 Capt E T Hawks (survived)
                 1Lt Richard M Milikin (KIA)

The Air Force also lost a reconnaissance aircraft on this day. Capt Hawks was photographing potential targets near Cao Mai, 30 miles north of Dong Hoi, during a night mission when his aircraft was struck in the rear fuselage by AAA. The aircraft crashed almost immediately and although Capt Hawks ejected and was rescued about six hours later by a Navy helicopter, his navigator was not so fortunate. 1Lt Milikin's body was buried by villagers from Mai Hoa but his body was later exhumed and removed by Vietnamese district officials.

F-102A 56-1110   509 FIS, 405 FW, USAF, base ..?
                  1 pilot, name unknown (survived)

One of the air defence Delta Daggers crashed during a night landing and was destroyed. This F-102 first entered service with the 438th FIS at Kinross AFB, Michigan and transferred to PACAF from Alaskan Air Command's 317th FIS. By this date there were 22 F-102s based in small detachments at various airfields in South Vietnam and Thailand.

21 August 1966

A-4E 151109   VA-72, USN, USS Franklin D Roosevelt
               Lt Allan Russell Carpenter (survived)

The USS Franklin D Roosevelt lost its first aircraft in combat during an armed reconnaissance mission five miles southwest of Thanh Hoa. A section of Skyhawks spotted a number of railway trucks and attacked them with 2.75 inch unguided rockets. Lt Carpenter had just climbed to 8,000 feet to make his second attack when he heard and felt a muffled explosion from the engine. He headed towards the sea with the engine still producing power but further explosions were heard and eventually flames engulfed the tailpipe. Lt Carpenter ejected over the Gulf of Tonkin and was picked up by a Navy helicopter. It was thought that the engine had either been hit by ground fire or had suffered from foreign object damage by pieces of 2.75 inch rocket which had broken up and been ingested into the engine. Lt Carpenter became a POW on 1 November 1966 when he was shot down near Haiphong.

F-105D 59-1770   354 TFS, 355 TFW, USAF, Takhli
                  Capt Norman Louross Wells (survived)

North Vietnam's POL storage once more came under attack and once more cost the USAF a Thunderchief. Capt Wells had pulled up to 7,000 feet from his bombing run on the target five miles northwest of Kep when his aircraft was hit in the fuselage by AAA. He nursed the aircraft out over the Gulf of Tonkin and ejected safely and was picked up by a Navy helicopter to conclude his 75th mission over Southeast Asia. A week later Capt Wells was shot down again and this time was not so lucky.

22 August 1966

A-4E 149992   VA-72, USN, USS Franklin D Roosevelt
               Lt K G Craig (survived)

The Franklin D Roosevelt lost its second aircraft in combat in very similar circumstances to its first only the previous day. Lt Craig's section spotted and attacked a motorised junk five miles offshore from Lien Qui, northeast of Thanh Hoa. Lt Craig set his weapons to fire the contents of three 2.75 inch rocket pods and a Zuni pod simultaneously. As he dived towards the target and fired the ordnance Lt Craig noticed that debris from a 2.75-inch rocket was ingested into an air intake causing the engine to suffer compressor stalls. He coaxed the aircraft out over the sea at reduced power but was forced to eject when the hydraulics failed and the controls froze. He was picked up by a Navy helicopter and reported the problem, which had almost certainly accounted for Lt Carpenter's aircraft the previous day.

F-5C 64-13316   10 FCS, 3 TFW, USAF, Bien Hoa
                 Capt Clyde L Johns (survived)

Four F-5s took off from Bien Hoa on a close air support mission but one aircraft had to land almost immediately after an engine failed and another aircraft escorted him back to Bien Hoa. The two remaining F-5s reached the target, which was the headquarters of a VC unit near Dong Thai on the western coast of South Vietnam, 15 miles south of Rach Gia. This important target was defended by up to 20 Quad-50 anti-aircraft guns. The two F-5s made several passes and destroyed many of the guns until Capt Johns's aircraft was hit and caught fire. Capt Johns ejected just inshore and landed in a rice paddy. Four VNAF A-1s arrived and helped to keep the VC away from the downed pilot but two of the Skyraiders were hit by ground fire and the pilots joined Capt Johns on the ground. All the downed aircrew were subsequently rescued by US Army helicopters. Very few fixed-wing aircraft were lost in this region of South Vietnam although the US Army was active in the sector and lost a number of helicopters in the area.

23 August 1966

F-8E 150907   VF-111, USN, USS Oriskany
               Lt(jg) H J Meadows (survived)

Towards the end of August the Oriskany ran into a spell of bad luck and lost five aircraft due to accidental causes together with two more in combat. The first loss occurred during a BARCAP mission when a Crusader suffered an engine failure. Attempts to increase power met with no success and the pilot ejected and was quickly picked up.

25 August 1966

A-4E 152084   VA-164, USN, USS Oriskany
               Lt(jg) William Henry Bullard (KIA)

Oriskany's second accident during August resulted in the loss of the pilot. The carrier was on duty at Yankee Station in the Gulf of Tonkin 75 miles northeast of Dong Hoi and launched a Skyhawk

for a night combat mission. The aircraft apparently started to climb away normally but then lost altitude and crashed into the sea. No trace of the pilot was ever found.

A-1H   135236   VA-152, USN, USS *Oriskany*
1 pilot, name unknown (survived)

The *Oriskany* lost another aircraft the same night when a faulty catapult shot resulted in a Skyraider having insufficient airspeed to avoid mushing into the water just ahead of the carrier. Luckily the pilot was rescued from his sinking aircraft.

26 August 1966

A-4E   152093   VA-164, USN, USS *Oriskany*
1 pilot, name unknown (survived)

Bad luck continued to dog the *Oriskany* when a Skyhawk suffered an electrical failure during an armed reconnaissance mission which forced the pilot to eject before he could reach the carrier.

27 August 1966

A-6A   151822   VA-65, USN, USS *Constellation*
Lt Cdr John Heaphy Fellowes (POW)
Lt(jg) George Thomas Coker (POW)

VA-65 had been fortunate to lose only one Intruder so far during its cruise on the *Constellation*, however, on 27 August its luck changed. Two aircraft were en route to bomb the Ngoc Son road bridge but just as they started their pop up manoeuvre to commence their bombing run they ran into AAA about 15 miles northwest of Vinh. Part of the starboard wing of the leading aircraft was blown away and the remainder of the wing caught fire. As the controls froze the aircraft snapped into an inverted spin and Lt Cdr Jack Fellowes and Lt(jg) George Coker ejected at about 3,000 feet. Both men were captured and suffered the usual maltreatment in the POW camps. In October 1967 George Coker and USAF Capt George McKnight became two of the few Americans to escape from captivity in North Vietnam. However, they were recaptured the next day after travelling 15 miles and were severely tortured for the attempt. Fellowes and Coker had been on their 55th mission when they were shot down and were both released on 4 March 1973. Lt Cdr Fellowes was badly injured during his ejection and this, combined with the regular torture sessions resulted in him being unable to look after himself for more than four months. His roommate, USAF 1Lt Ron Bliss who was shot down a week later, cared for him during this time and probably saved Jack Fellowes's life, a story of comradeship and courage oft repeated in the North Vietnamese camps.

F-4C   63-7525   497 TFS, 8 TFW, USAF, Ubon
Maj J E Barrow (survived)
1Lt T H Walsh (survived)

At night a flight of USAF Phantoms on an armed reconnaissance mission just north of the DMZ was engaged by AAA about 15 miles west of Dong Hoi and decided to retaliate. Unfortunately, one of the aircraft was hit and caught fire but remained airborne long enough for the crew to eject 10 miles offshore from Dong Hoi from where a Navy helicopter picked up the crew.

A-4E   150079   VA-163, USN, USS *Oriskany*
1 pilot, name unknown (survived)

The last of *Oriskany's* spell of five accidents during four days was a repeat of the previous one. A Skyhawk on an armed reconnaissance sortie suffered an electrical failure and the pilot was forced to eject leaving another Skyhawk on the seabed in the Gulf of Tonkin.

28 August 1966

A-1H   135231   VA-152, USN, USS *Oriskany*
Cdr Gordon H Smith (survived)

The squadron commander of VA-152 was almost lost when his Skyraider was hit by AAA while flying along the coast near Van Yen, 25 miles south of Thanh Hoa during an armed reconnaissance mission. The aircraft was hit in the fuselage centre section, which started to burn, and Cdr Smith bailed out just offshore and was rescued by a Navy helicopter.

F-4C   64-0798   390 TFS, 35 TFW, USAF, Da Nang
2 crew, names unknown (survived)

A Phantom suffered an accident during take off and sheared off its undercarriage legs and then caught fire. Fortunately both crew managed to escape from the wreck

29 August 1966

F-105D   60-0523   354 TFS, 355 TFW, USAF, Takhli
Capt Norman Louross Wells (POW)

The 19th and last Thunderchief lost during August was shot down by small arms fire as it was strafing trucks on a road 12 miles northwest of Dong Hoi. Capt Wells must have had a strong feeling of deja vu as he had been forced to eject from his Thunderchief only eight days earlier when his aircraft was hit near Kep. That time he had been able to reach the sea and was rescued by the Navy but this time he was not so lucky and was captured on his 78th mission. He was released from captivity on 4 March 1973 and eventually retired from the USAF as a Colonel.

F-4C   63-7503   497 TFS, 8 TFW, USAF, Ubon
Capt Kenneth Dale Robinson (KIA)
1Lt Sammie Don Hoff (KIA)

The Wolfpack continued to specialise in night armed reconnaissance throughout North Vietnam and the Ho Chi Minh Trail and gained several notable successes. However, the role also produced its casualties for the Wing. On the 29th a Phantom was dropping napalm on trucks that had been spotted 20 miles northwest of Dong Hoi when it was hit by AAA and crashed immediately. Capt Robinson gave the order to eject and 1Lt Hoff left the aircraft and was briefly in radio contact with other aircraft in the flight. Nothing more was heard of either Capt Robinson or 1Lt Hoff until early in 1989 when it was announced that remains that had been handed over by the Vietnamese had been positively identified as those of the Phantom crew.

31 August 1966

RF-8G   146874   Detachment G, VFP-63, USN, USS *Oriskany*
Lt Cdr Thomas A Tucker (survived)

The *Oriskany* finished a terrible month by losing yet another aircraft but the pilot was recovered in one of the most remarkable rescues of the war. The commander of the *Oriskany's* VFP-63 detachment was tasked with obtaining photographs of a foreign oil tanker and other ships in Haiphong Harbour. As the aircraft was nearing Quang Yen, about five miles northeast of Haiphong, it was hit by 37mm ground fire and the pilot lost all control with the exception of the rudder. The aircraft started to gyrate wildly and Lt Cdr Tucker ejected at 1,500 feet over Haiphong harbour. He came down in Haiphong's secondary ship channel less than 150 yards offshore and a number of junks got under way to capture the pilot. An SH-3A of HS-6 from the USS *Kearsarge* arrived within minutes and went straight in for a rescue attempt with only Lt Cdr Tucker's escorting F-8 flown by Lt Cdr F Teague overhead as escort. Teague strafed the approaching junks as the helicopter door gunner also kept up a steady stream of suppressive fire. The helicopter, piloted by HS-6 CO Cdr Robert S Vermilya, flew for 20 minutes up the channel at 50 feet while under constant fire from shore and vessels. The helicopter rescued Lt Cdr Tucker from right under the noses of the North Vietnamese in one of the most daring and dangerous rescue missions of the war. This was the first RF-8G to be lost in Southeast Asia and was a strenthened and improved conversion of the RF-8A Crusader. Tom Tucker later commanded VF-51 during its transition from the F-8E to the F-4B.

1 September 1966

F-104C   57-0913   435 TFS, 8 TFW, USAF, Udorn
Maj Norman Schmidt (POW-died)

Although known to be unsuited to the armed reconnaissance role the Starfighter was occasionally used for such missions as well as for escort duties and direct air support. Maj Schmidt's aircraft was hit by AAA as it pulled up from an attack on a truck park near Troc, 25 miles northwest of Dong Hoi. The aircraft flew for a further 10 miles towards the northwest before Maj Schmidt was

forced to eject and, despite an intense rescue effort, was captured and held in captivity in the infamous Hoa Lo prison, the so-called Hanoi Hilton. In August 1967 Maj Schmidt was taken from his cell to the interrogation room and never returned. Some of his fellow POWs heard sounds coming from the interrogation room and believe that Norm Schmidt was beaten to death by his guards. In March 1974 Maj Schmidt's remains were returned to the USA, presumably having been buried within the prison precincts since 1967.

A-1E   52-132648   602 ACS, 14 ACW, USAF, Udorn
Maj Hubert Campbell Nichols (KIA)

A-1E   52-132624   602 ACS, 14 ACW, USAF, Udorn
Capt A L Minnick (survived)

As soon as Norm Schmidt's Starfighter went down a SAR task force was readied to attempt a rescue. Two Skyraiders from Udorn, operating temporarily from Nakhon Phanom, arrived on the scene about an hour after Maj Schmidt was shot down. The cloud base was down to 500 feet and the two Skyraiders were ordered to orbit offshore with two helicopters that would attempt the rescue. After more than an hour of waiting Maj Nichols and his wingman, Capt Minnick, were ordered in to replace two Navy Skyraiders that had been searching for Maj Schmidt. As the two USAF aircraft started a search pattern northwest of Dong Hoi they were both hit by AAA. Capt Minnick nursed his badly damaged Skyraider back towards Nakhon Phanom and did not see Maj Nichols's aircraft again. A Navy Skyraider pilot spotted the remains of Maj Nichols's aircraft but there was no sign of the pilot and the search for him and for Maj Schmidt was suspended shortly afterwards. Capt Minnick almost made it home but he had to bail out near Sakhon Nakhon in Thailand when the aircraft became uncontrollable.

2 September 1966

A-1H   137534   VA-165, USN, USS *Intrepid*
Cdr William S Jett (survived)

The *Intrepid* lost the first of three Skyraiders in combat in September when an aircraft was shot down by AAA while on a road reconnaissance mission near Vinh Son, 10 miles west of Mu Ron Ma. With the aircraft's starboard wing on fire Cdr Jett coaxed the aircraft out to sea and bailed out about five miles offshore. He was rescued by a Navy helicopter and in the following December took command of the Squadron.

3 September 1966

F-105D   62-4303   13 TFS, 388 TFW, USAF, Korat
Capt E R Skowron (survived)

The region around Mu Ron Ma was obviously providing plenty of targets as the USAF sent several flights of Thunderchiefs to the area the day after Cdr Jett's incident. Capt Skowron was orbiting at 4,500 feet over the coast waiting his turn to attack road traffic when his aircraft was struck by AAA. He ejected five miles out to sea and he was picked up by a USAF helicopter.

F-4C   64-0771   557 TFS, 12 TFW, USAF, Cam Ranh Bay
Capt Clifford S Heathcote (KIA)
Capt William Prestwood Simmons (KIA)

A Phantom was preparing to land at Cam Ranh Bay in poor visibility using an instrument approach when it suddenly disappeared from the radar screen. It was later discovered to have crashed into a mountain south of the airfield killing both crewmembers.

4 September 1966

F-4C   63-7561   555 TFS, 8 TFW, USAF, Ubon
1Lt Raymond Paul Salzarulo (KIA)
1Lt John Herbert Nasmyth (POW)

Strikes against POL targets once again dominated USAF activity over North Vietnam but resulted in the loss of a further three aircraft. A flight of Phantoms was approaching Thai Nguyen from the west when one of the aircraft was shot down by an SA-2 SAM. 1Lt Nasmyth ejected and was captured but was later told by his captors that his pilot had died in the aircraft. John Nasmyth was

released on 18 February 1973 and the remains of Ray Salzarulo were returned to the USA on 13 September 1990.

F-105D 62-4369   357 TFS, 355 TFW, USAF, Takhli
                   1Lt Ronald Glenn Bliss (POW)

F-105D 61-0085   354 TFS, 355 TFW, USAF, Takhli
                   1Lt Thomas Mitchell McNish (POW)

The Takhli Wing sent its bombers against a large POL storage facility at Nguyen Khe, six miles north of Hanoi. As 1Lt Ron Bliss climbed up to 5,000 feet to start his dive on the target his aircraft was hit by a 57mm shell and was badly damaged. He flew about 40 miles towards the west before ejecting. Ron Bliss was captured and spent the next six and a half years as a POW before being released on 4 March 1973.

Twenty minutes later Nguyen Khe was hit by another wave of Thunderchiefs. The 'pop up' manoeuvre that the bombers performed before the aircraft dived onto the target was a vulnerable point in the flight and another aircraft was lost during this manoeuvre. 1Lt McNish's aircraft was hit by AAA and started to burn. He ejected and was soon captured. He was shot down on his 45th mission and was released on 4 March 1973. Thomas McNish took a medical degree after his return, became a flight surgeon and eventually retired from the Air Force as a Colonel.

5 September 1966

F-8E   150896   VF-111, USN, USS *Oriskany*
                 Capt Wilfred Keese Abbott (POW)

A section of Crusaders from the *Oriskany* was jumped by MiG-17s that suddenly emerged from cloud near Ninh Binh. Both Crusaders were damaged by cannon fire, one of them fatally, as it tried to turn inside the MiG. The North Vietnamese must have been somewhat confused when they captured the Crusader pilot because Capt Abbott was a USAF pilot on exchange with the Navy. Capt Abbott's right leg was broken when he ejected and although the North Vietnamese eventually operated on the injury it took over two years for it to heal properly. Capt Abbott was released from captivity on 4 March 1973.

F-105D 60-0495   354 TFS, 355 TFW, USAF, Takhli
                   Capt T D Dobbs (survived)

In addition to the costly POL strikes the Thunderchiefs were also busy hitting transport system targets. Truck parks were particularly lucrative targets, when they could be found, but they were also well defended from air attack. A flight of Thuds was bombing a truck park seven miles west of Dong Hoi when one of their number was hit by ground fire. Capt Dobbs ejected close by and was very fortunate to be rescued by an HH-3 before the North Vietnamese could find him.

6 September 1966

RF-8G   144624   Detachment 42, VFP-62, USN,
                  USS *Franklin D Roosevelt*
                  Lt(jg) Norman Lee Bundy (KIA)

During a photographic reconnaissance mission a Crusader was seen to be manoeuvring close to the water about 10 miles offshore from Thanh Hoa shortly before it crashed killing the pilot. The crash was thought to have been due to a misjudgement of altitude above the sea.

C-130E 63-7878   314 TCW, USAF, Ching Chuan Kang
                   Capt William Shinn (KWF)
                   1Lt John Bechacek (KWF)
                   1Lt David Scovill (KWF)
                   A1C Wilbur Adkisson (KWF)
                   A1C Lucious Lunnie (KWF)

A Hercules crashed into a mountain on the island of Taiwan when it strayed off course during a logistics flight from Southeast Asia. In addition to the five crewmembers, three passengers were also killed in the accident.

8 September 1966

A-4E   150020   VMA-224, MAG-12, USMC, Chu Lai
                 1Lt John Richard Fischer (KIA)

A Skyhawk went missing during a radar-directed bombing mission at night and was thought to have crashed just seven miles due west of Chu Lai.

A-1E   52-132588   probably 1 ACS, 14 ACW, USAF, Pleiku
                   1 pilot, name unknown (survived)

During a combat mission a Skyraider suffered a sudden engine failure, which distracted the pilot with the result that it collided with another aircraft. The pilot bailed out and the other aircraft landed safely.

9 September 1966

F-105D 62-4275   357 TFS, 355 TFW, USAF, Takhli
                   Capt John Charles Blevins (POW)

A flight of Thunderchiefs en route to bomb a railway bridge encountered heavy flak about 10 miles north of Kep that badly damaged one of the aircraft. Capt Blevins steered southeast but was forced to eject about 24 miles from Kep and could not evade due to a broken leg so was quickly captured. John Blevins, who was on his 85th mission when he was shot down, was given no medical treatment and was nursed back to a reasonable degree of health by his prison roommates. He was released on 4 March 1973.

10 September 1966

F-5C   63-8424   10 FCS, 3 TFW, USAF, Bien Hoa
                  Capt Thomas Charles Walsh (KIA)

The 10th FCS lost its third F-5 within the space of two months during an attack on a VC base camp 15 miles east of Cao Lanh, just north of the Mekong Delta. Capt Walsh was making his fourth run dropping napalm when his aircraft was hit by small arms fire. No ejection attempt was seen and Capt Walsh died in the crash.

A-1E   52-132675   1 ACS, 14 ACW, USAF, Pleiku
                   Maj Lawrence Byron Tatum (KIA)

Maj Tatum was acting as an FAC for a strike on automatic weapons sites within the DMZ buffer zone. As he was making his fifth strafing pass Maj Tatum's aircraft was hit by .30 calibre machine gun fire, burst into flames and crashed near Thon Cam Son. The pilot was seen to bail out of his aircraft and parachute down into a tree among North Vietnamese troops. Maj Tatum's parachute was observed being pulled down from the trees but nothing more was ever seen or heard of him and he is assumed to have been killed by his captors.

O-1E   56-4184   21 TASS, 505 TACG, USAF, Pleiku
                  Capt Edmund Francis Thornell (KIA)

Capt Thornell was flying an FAC mission near the coast close to Phu Hiep when his aircraft was struck by ground fire. The aircraft crashed into the sea just offshore but Capt Thornell did not survive.

F-4C   64-0832   433 TFS, 8 TFW, USAF, Ubon
                  Capt Douglas Brian Peterson (POW)
                  1Lt Bernard Leo Talley (POW)

On the night of the 10th the Wolfpack attacked a bridge and ferry at Dap Cau, 12 miles east of Kep. As the Phantoms were leaving the target one of the aircraft was rocked by a blast from an SA-2 that exploded close by. Within a short time both engines wound down and the rear of the aircraft became engulfed in flames forcing the crew to eject about 20 miles northwest of Hon Gay. Capt Peterson was badly injured during the ejection suffering a broken shoulder, broken arm, dislocated knee, compression fractures of both ankles plus cuts and bruises. 'Pete' Peterson was interrogated and tortured for four days until receiving treatment for his injuries. Both men were released on 4 March 1973. Most of Capt Peterson's 65 missions had been as part of the Night Owl campaign against the North Vietnamese transportation system.

Coincidentally, both men went into politics after retiring from the Air Force. Bernard Talley became active with several POW and veterans support groups, ran for US Senate and served as Chairman of Supervisors of Elections. These activities were in addition to flying for American Airlines and commanding C-141 and KC-10 units in the Air Force Reserve. 'Pete' Peterson, who

had spent three years at Bitburg AB, Germany, flying the F-100, also went into politics and eventually became Democratic Congressman for Florida in 1990. He later played a key role in restoring diplomatic relations with Vietnam and in 1997 Peterson was selected to be the US Ambassador to Vietnam. To some it must have seemed as supremely ironic and to others entirely fitting that the first post-war US ambassador to Vietnam should have been an ex-POW. One of the tasks for the new Ambassador was to facilitate an intensified search programme for the remains of missing Americans. In May 1998 Ambassador Peterson married Vi Le, a Saigon-born Australian diplomat whose family had emigrated to Australia in the 1960s. The marriage took place by special permission of the Vietnamese Government in Hanoi's Grand Cathedral.

EA-1F   132543   VAW-13, USN, USS *Franklin D Roosevelt*
                   4 crew, names unknown (survived)

During a electronic countermeasures patrol over the Gulf of Tonkin, an EA-1F suffered an instrument failure and lost all its navigational aids. In its attempt to return to the carrier it exhausted its fuel and ditched. Fortunately, all the crew escaped and were rescued.

12 September 1966

F-105D 61-0201   469 TFS, 388 TFW, USAF, Korat
                   Capt Robert Frost Waggoner (POW)

A strike on a storage area near Quang Lang, 35 miles northwest of Vinh, resulted in the loss of yet another Thunderchief and its pilot. Capt Waggoner's aircraft was hit at 5,500 feet by an 85mm shell, burst into flames and cartwheeled out of control. The pilot ejected and landed in a rice paddy where he was captured. He spent the rest of the war as a POW and was released on 4 March 1973. On 26 September a Bright Light guerilla team was inserted in the area but found no trace of the pilot who had already been captured. This secret mission was the first to be organised by the recently-created Joint Personnel Recovery Center, which had been set up in an attempt to recover downed aircrew or prisoners that conventional SAR forces were unable to assist.

A-1E   52-133928   602 ACS, 14 ACW, USAF, Udorn
                   Maj Stanley George Sprague (KIA)

When not engaged on SAR missions, the Skyraiders from Udorn also took part in the Barrel Roll campaign over northern Laos. On such a mission Maj Sprague's aircraft was shot down near the Laotian/North Vietnamese border some 30 miles north of Sam Neua. It appears that Maj Sprague was killed in the crash and his remains were returned by the Vietnamese on 13 September 1990 indicating that he either came down in North Vietnam or was buried by North Vietnamese troops operating in Laos.

A-4C   147763   VA-153, USN, USS *Constellation*
                  Lt Cdr William Francis Coakley (KIA)

A section of Skyhawks was on an armed reconnaissance mission at night over the coast near Hoang Xa, 15 miles south of Thanh Hoa. The leader spotted something on the ground and dropped flares and Lt Cdr Coakley commenced a run to fly under them to identify the target. The section leader saw a long streak of flame as Coakley's aircraft impacted the ground ending in a large explosion. No radio transmission was heard and it was assumed that the pilot had perished in the crash. In 1989 it was announced that remains previously returned by the Vietnamese had been identified as those of Lt Cdr Coakley. The North Vietnamese claimed that a SAM had brought down his aircraft but this seems extremely unlikely.

13 September 1966

A-1E   52-132659   1 ACS, 14 ACW, USAF, Pleiku
                   Lt Col E R Deatrick (survived)

A Skyraider from Pleiku was operating about 10 miles north of the DMZ when it was hit by machine gun fire. The aircraft was making its second pass over a ford on a road at Dong Phat when it was hit in the starboard wing, which then caught fire. Lt Col Deatrick crossed back into South Vietnam and made a successful crash landing at Hué.

F-105D 62-4281   421 TFS, 388 TFW, USAF, Korat
    1Lt K V Hallmark (survived)

A flight of Thunderchiefs was flying along Route 15 near Xom Hoa, 25 miles south of Vinh, looking for a SAM site that was thought to be active in the area. As the flight pulled up to 5,000 feet one of the aircraft was hit by AAA and badly damaged. 1Lt Hallmark turned south towards high ground and ejected after flying about 10 miles. He was later rescued by a USAF HH-3.

F-100D 56-3071   615 TFS, 366 TFW, USAF, Phan Rang
    1Lt John Peter Skoro (KIA)

The 615th TFS lost its third Super Sabre during a strike on an automatic weapon position near Phu Xuan, 20 miles north of Phu Cat. The aircraft was hit by ground fire as it pulled up to 4,000 feet and the pilot may have been hit as he apparently made no attempt to eject.

A-1H 134534   VA-165, USN, USS *Intrepid*
    Lt(jg) T J Dwyer (survived)

During an air strike against an air defence site at Cape Falaise, 25 miles north of Vinh, a Skyraider was hit by AAA in the port wing as it dive bombed the target. Lt Dwyer headed out to sea and abandoned his aircraft about 10 miles offshore. He was rescued by a Navy helicopter.

O-1G 55-11918   19 TASS, 505 TACG, USAF, Bien Hoa
    1Lt Howard Walker Kaiser (KIA)

The FACs were often used to search for missing aircraft as well as performing their primary function of controlling air strikes. A US Army helicopter went missing near Katum and a Bird Dog was despatched from Bien Hoa to assist the search for the helicopter. The Bird Dog never returned from the mission and the wreck was found some time later close to the Cambodian border. The cause of the crash was not determined.

F-4C 63-7694   497 TFS, 8 TFW, USAF, Ubon
    Capt John E Stackhouse (KIA)
    1Lt Benjamin B Finzer (KIA)

A Wolfpack Phantom crashed on take off from Ubon killing both crewmen. 1Lt Finzer had survived being shot down during an armed reconnaissance mission over North Vietnam on 11 August with a different pilot.

F-4C 63-7640   497 TFS, 8 TFW, USAF, Ubon
    2 crew, names unknown (survived)

The Wolfpack lost another Phantom on the 13th when it suffered a flight control failure. Happily, both crew ejected near the airfield and survived the incident.

14 September 1966

F-100D 55-3640   510 TFS, 3 TFW, USAF, Bien Hoa
    Capt C W Findlay (survived)

A Super Sabre was shot down during an air strike near Bac Lieu, south of the Mekong Delta. The aircraft had just rolled in on its target when it was hit in the central fuselage by 12.7mm machine gun fire. Capt Findlay ejected immediately and was rescued by a USAF HH-43, having suffered injuries either during the ejection or the landing.

A-1H 139756   VA-25, USN, USS *Coral Sea*
    Cdr Clarence William Stoddard (KIA)

The *Coral Sea* returned to the Gulf of Tonkin to take its place on the line on 12 September for its second cruise of the war. On its third day of operations tragedy struck when the CO of VA-25 was killed just off the coast near Vinh. He had just led his section on a strike against a storage facility on the coast and the two aircraft were descending from 5,000 feet to about 1,000 feet when they came under attack by SAMs. Three SA-2s were fired from a site near Vinh, the first two exploded close to the aircraft but the third missile detonated right in front of Stoddard's Skyraider and blew it to pieces. This was the 30th US aircraft confirmed destroyed by SAMs since the first one was lost in July 1965. Cdr James D Burden, the Squadron's executive officer, took over command of VA-25 on the day that William Stoddard was killed.

F-105D 62-4306   421 TFS, 388 TFW, USAF, Korat
    1Lt J R Casper (survived)

1Lt J R Casper must have been one of the luckiest pilots in the USAF. He had been shot down near Dong Hoi on 8 August and was plucked from the hands of the North Vietnamese by a USAF rescue helicopter. On 14 September he was attacking a road bridge near Bac Ninh, 15 miles northeast of Hanoi, when his aircraft was hit at 6,000 feet by AAA. He flew over 80 miles to the east and ejected close to the island of Dao Cai Bau where he was rescued yet again, this time by a Navy chopper.

F-4C 64-0657   389 TFS, 366 TFW, USAF, Phan Rang
    1Lt Howard Eugene Knudsen (KIA)
    1 crew, name unknown (survived)

A Phantom crashed in Ninh Thuan province, South Vietnam due to a flight control failure. One crewman ejected but 1Lt Knudsen was killed.

16 September 1966

A-4E 152020   VMA-311, MAG-12, USMC, Chu Lai
    1Lt Thomas Howard Hawking (KIA)

Although the Marine Corps A-4 squadrons were primarily in Vietnam to support Marine ground troops, they also supported non-Marine Corps operations when required. Operation Seward was a minor offensive by the Army's 101st Airborne Division against the Viet Cong's 5th Division in Phu Yen province. During a strike in support of Operation Seward a VMA-311 Skyhawk hit trees as it pulled out from its attack on a target about 12 miles southwest of Tuy Hoa. The pilot ejected safely and was spotted by an Army UH-1 Huey, which attempted to rescue him. Tragically, the helicopter was not equipped for rescue work and the pilot slipped out of a makeshift sling and fell 1,000 feet to his death.

F-4C 63-7613   557 TFS, 12 TFW, USAF, Cam Ranh Bay
    1Lt B D Giere (survived)
    1Lt H J Knoch (survived)

It was well known that the North Vietnamese used the DMZ buffer zone as a storage area for military supplies before they were transported into South Vietnam. A storage site near the village of Thon Cam Son was bombed by a flight of Phantoms but one of the aircraft was hit by ground fire. The aircraft crashed within the buffer zone just five miles short of the coast and a USAF helicopter swooped in to rescue the two crew.

F-4C 63-7643   555 TFS, 8 TFW, USAF, Ubon
    Maj John Leighton Robertson (KIA)
    1Lt Hubert Elliot Buchanan (POW)

The Dap Cau railway and road bridge was once more the target for USAF bombers. A flight of four Phantoms from Ubon using the radio call sign Moonglow took part in the raid but en route to the target the flight was jumped by several MiG-17s. Maj Robertson's aircraft was hit by cannon fire and crashed 15 miles southeast of the MiG's base at Kep. The WSO, 1Lt Hubert Buchanan, ejected and was captured but it was thought that Maj Robertson died in the crash. Having been held in seven different prison camps during his years of captivity, Hubert Buchanan was released on 4 March 1973. This was the second USAF Phantom to be lost in air-to-air combat during the war. In 1990 the Vietnamese handed over remains they identified as being those of Maj Robertson but they turned out to be the bones of an animal. A joint US/Vietnamese team later located the wreck site but, as yet, no remains have been recovered.

17 September 1966

F-105D 62-4280   469 TFS, 388 TFW, USAF, Korat
    Capt Darel Dean Leetun (KIA)

F-105D 61-0191   13 TFS, 388 TFW, USAF, Korat
    Capt Allen K Rutherford (survived)

A strike on railway and road bridges near Kep claimed two more Thunderchiefs. As the first flight approached the Cao Nung road bridge, 17 miles northeast of Kep, at 9,000 feet, one of the aircraft was hit in the rear fuselage by AAA and crashed. No parachute was seen or SAR beeper heard and it was assumed that Capt Leetun may have been hit and incapacitated. Another member

of the flight, Capt Mike Lanning, strayed into China due to battle damage to his navigation system and was fired on by Chinese MiG-19s but managed to escape. Thirty minutes later another flight of Thunderchiefs was approaching approximately the same location having already bombed a railway bridge when one of the aircraft was hit by 85mm AAA. Capt Rutherford headed towards the coast where he could eject with a better chance of being picked up. However, once over the coast the aircraft kept flying and Capt Rutherford headed south, probably hoping he might be able to reach Da Nang. Twenty-five miles off the coast near Hué the aircraft finally gave up its struggle to remain airborne and Capt Rutherford ejected and was rescued by a USAF HH-3E. The helicopter landed on the sea to make the first water pick-up by a Jolly Green Giant in combat.

A-4C 148488   VA-22, USN, USS *Coral Sea*
    Lt(jg) R A Hegstrom (survived)

The *Coral Sea* despatched a raid against the Ninh Binh railway yard on the 17th. Several SAMs were fired at a flight of Skyhawks as they crossed the Day Giang River, near Phu Nhac, still 15 miles from the target. As the aircraft jinked to avoid the missiles Lt Hegstrom's Skyhawk was hit in the tail by ground fire. With the hydraulics and electrical system badly damaged Lt Hegstrom controlled the aircraft long enough to fly 10 miles offshore before ejecting and being rescued by a Navy helicopter.

F-4C 63-7509   558 TFS, 12 TFW, USAF, Cam Ranh Bay
    2 crew (KIA)

F-4C 64-0716   558 TFS, 12 TFW, USAF, Cam Ranh Bay
    1 crew (KIA)
    Capt D G Browning (survived)

The crew comprised the following but it is not known who was in which aircraft:

    Capt Edward Dean McCann (KIA)
    Capt Robert Edward Rocky (KIA)
    1Lt Michael Edward Surwald (KIA)

Two Phantoms collided in mid-air at night over the sea two miles north of Cam Ranh Bay resulting in the deaths of three of the crewmen. One of the base HH-43s scrambled and recovered the only survivor from the accident. The two Phantoms were returning to Cam Ranh Bay after their mission had been aborted due to bad weather. The USAF had lost five Phantoms and six aircrew in accidents in South Vietnam and Thailand within the last five days. The accident rate in Southeast Asia was a constant concern for the Air Force for while it was accepted that accidents rates in wartime were going to be higher than those in peacetime, the cost in terms of aircraft and lives sometimes became difficult to bear.

19 September 1966

F-105D 62-4287   13 TFS, 388 TFW, USAF, Korat
    Capt Donald G Waltman (POW)

F-4C 63-7687   555 TFS, 8 TFW, USAF, Ubon
    Capt D J Fitzgerald (survived)
    1Lt P C Bruhn (survived)

The strikes on railway and road bridges around Kep continued but resulted in the loss of another two aircraft. Capt Waltman's aircraft was pulling up from its bombing run over the Cao Nung Bridge when the starboard wing was hit by AAA. He attempted to make for the coast but after less than five miles the aircraft became uncontrollable and Capt Waltman ejected and was captured. He was released on 4 March 1973. Unusually for a Thunderchief pilot, Donald Waltman had been an air defence pilot and had flown F-86D Sabres and F-102 Delta Daggers. He retired from the USAF as a Colonel and died on 5 September 1997.

Just a couple of minutes after Capt Waltman's aircraft was shot down a flight of Phantoms bombed the bridges near Cao Nung and was leaving the target area when one of the aircraft was hit by anti-aircraft fire. The aircraft did not catch fire and Capt Fitzgerald headed to the coast and then towards Da Nang. As the aircraft crossed into South Vietnam Capt Fitzgerald realised it would not make it to Da Nang and pulled off a successful crash landing near Ca Lu, just south of the DMZ.

B-57B 52-1541 13 TBS, 405 FW attached to 35 TFW, USAF, Da Nang
Maj Warren Lee Gould (KIA)
Capt William Sheldon Davis (KIA)

The USAF lost its 10th Canberra of the year as it was returning from a daytime strike against Viet Cong targets. When the aircraft was 10 miles southwest of Chu Lai it sustained several hits from ground fire in the fuselage and crashed near Tra Bang shortly afterwards killing both the crew.

F-4B 152985 VF-154, USN, USS *Coral Sea*
Lt(jg) Don Brown Parsons (KIA)
Lt(jg) Thomas Holt Pilkington (KIA)

Two Phantoms were flying at night along the coast at 4,000 feet near Van Yen, 25 miles south of Thanh Hoa, on a coastal reconnaissance mission on the lookout for coastal and waterway traffic. The leader saw what he thought was a SAM launch a mile or two from his position and radioed his wingman, Lt Parsons, who was some distance behind, to dive and head out to sea. Lt Parsons was not heard to acknowledge the call and his aircraft did not return to the carrier. A Skyhawk flight reported seeing an unexplained flash on the ground in the general area of the missing aircraft and it was assumed that Lt Parson's aircraft had either been hit by an SA-2 or had flown into the ground trying to evade a missile.

F-4B 152315 VF-151, USN, USS *Constellation*
Lt Frank Monroe Brown (KIA)
Lt(jg) David Alan Henry (KIA)

A Phantom crashed into the sea moments after being catapulted off the deck of the *Constellation* during a night-time CAP mission. It was thought that the pilot may have become disoriented during the launch, a commonly reported phenomenon during night launches.

20 September 1966

A-4E 150054 VMA-224, MAG-12, USMC, Chu Lai
1Lt Richard MacAuliffe Bloom (KIA)

A Marine Corps Skyhawk caught fire and crashed as it made its third pass over a truck park near Ha Tan, about 20 miles southwest of Da Nang. The pilot may have been hit as no attempt to eject was seen by his wingman.

F-4B 152973 VF-21, USN, USS *Coral Sea*
Lt Cdr James Reginald Bauder (KIA)
Lt(jg) James Burton Mills (KIA)

The *Coral Sea's* initial run of bad luck continued with its fourth aircraft lost during its first week of operations. A pair of Phantoms was flying a night-time armed reconnaissance along Road 1A midway between Thanh Hoa and Vinh. The plan was for one of the aircraft to drop flares over a suspected target so that the other aircraft could bomb it and then reverse the process. Lt Cdr Bauder dropped his flares for his wingman, Lt Hanley, who then flew on ahead to drop his own flares. A radio call from Lt Cdr Bauder was cut short and his wingman could not regain contact with his leader. No flak or SAMs had been sighted and it was thought likely that Lt Cdr Bauder's aircraft had flown into the ground as it was attacking a target under the light of the flares.

21 September 1966

F-105D 62-4371 357 TFS, 355 TFW, USAF, Takhli
Capt Glendon Lee Ammon (KIA)

A flight of four Thunderchiefs was assigned to bomb a railway and road bridge near Bac Ninh, 15 miles northeast of Hanoi. Capt Ammon's aircraft, leading the flight, was hit by AAA and caught fire just before reaching the bridge. He was heard to say that he was ejecting and other members of the flight saw his parachute descend to the ground and heard a short transmission from Ammon's SAR beeper. Nothing more was heard from or about Capt Ammon during the war. In August 1978 a congressional delegation led by Representative G V Montgomery visited Hanoi to open talks about the POW/MIA issue. As a token of good faith the Vietnamese handed over several sets of remains of US servicemen, one of those sets was later identified as being those of Capt Ammon. It is still not known how or when he had met his death.

F-4C 63-7642 433 TFS, 8 TFW, USAF, Ubon
Capt R G Kellems (survived)
1Lt J W Thomas (survived)

The Wolfpack once more took part in a series of strikes against railway and road bridges on the 21st. When a flight of Phantoms (using the radio call sign Spitfire) was about 15 miles south of Kep en route to the target they were jumped by several MiG-17s. Capt Kellems's aircraft was hit in the fuselage by cannon fire from one of the MiGs but did not catch fire. He flew south out over the sea and was heading towards South Vietnam but the crew had to eject off the coast near the DMZ. Both crewmen were rescued by a USAF helicopter that had been scrambled in case the aircraft could not reach Da Nang. This was one of the largest air battles of the war so far and two MiG-17s were shot down by two F-105s.

22 September 1966

A-1H 135239 VA-176, USN, USS *Intrepid*
Lt Charles Allen Knochel (KIA)

Two Skyraiders came under intense anti-aircraft fire as they were about to recross the North Vietnamese coast at Mu Ron Ma on completion of an armed reconnaissance mission. Lt Knochel's aircraft was hit in the starboard wing, which caught fire and which in turn detonated some of the cannon ammunition in the wing. Lt Knochel abandoned the aircraft over the sea but hit the water hard as his parachute swung wildly. He was not seen to move while in the water and when an Albatross landed some 12 minutes later Lt Knochel had disappeared under the waves, probably having been knocked unconscious during the entry into the water.

25 September 1966

F-105D 62-4341 469 TFS, 388 TFW, USAF, Korat
Capt Clifton Emmet Cushman (KIA)

During a strike on the northeast railway line 10 miles northeast of Kep a flight of three Thunderchiefs was tasked with attacking some of the many anti-aircraft gun positions around the target. Capt Cushman's aircraft was hit in the rear fuselage by AAA and disintegrated and crashed shortly afterwards a few miles to the north. No parachute was seen and it was thought that Capt Cushman either died in the crash or died of his wounds soon after landing. A witness was found in 1992 who claimed that the pilot's body had been buried but that it was later washed away in a flood.

26 September 1966

F-105D 61-0186 13 TFS, 388 TFW, USAF, Korat
Capt Arthur T Ballard (POW)

Returning to POL storage strikes the Korat Wing lost yet another Thunderchief, its ninth and last of the month. Capt Ballard's aircraft was hit by AAA while it was flying at 4,500 feet some 25 miles northwest of Thai Nguyen while still en route to the target. The aircraft caught fire immediately and Capt Ballard ejected, breaking his left leg and spraining his right leg. He was on his 68th mission when he was shot down and he was released from imprisonment on 4 March 1973.

F-5C 65-10519 10 FCS, 3 TFW, USAF, Bien Hoa
Capt J G Paulsen (survived)

One of the 10th FCS's F-5s was lost when it was hit by small arms fire as it pulled up from attacking a target five miles west of Vung Tau. The pilot ejected safely and was rescued by an Army helicopter.

RF-4C 65-0862 16 TRS, 460 TRW, USAF, Tan Son Nhut
Maj Joseph Millard Stine (KIA)
1Lt Dyke Augustus Spilman (KIA)

A Phantom failed to return from a night photographic reconnaissance sortie over North Vietnam. The aircraft probably came down in North Vietnam or Laos close to the DMZ and was thought to have been shot down by AAA.

27 September 1966

O-1E 56-2656 21 TASS, 14 ACW, USAF, Pleiku
2 crew, names unknown (survived)

A Bird Dog was destroyed in a landing accident due to pilot error.

29 September 1966

F-4C 64-0736 497 TFS, 8 TFW, USAF, Ubon
Maj Saul Waxman (KIA)
1Lt J E Glover (survived)

During a Night Owl armed reconnaissance mission a Phantom crew discovered a ferry in use near Phu Son, 35 miles northwest of Dong Hoi. During the attack the aircraft was hit by AAA and Maj Waxman turned the aircraft to the south towards hilly terrain. Both crew ejected but only the WSO was rescued alive by a Bright Light team inserted by USAF helicopters. It was assumed that Maj Waxman, whose body was recovered by the Bright Light team, died during the ejection. This was the second rescue mission organised by the Joint Personnel Recovery Center.

30 September 1966

F-100D 55-3502 531 TFS, 3 TFW, USAF, Bien Hoa
Lt Col W M Fowler (survived)

Nowhere was safe for the US forces in South Vietnam and on the last day of the month a Super Sabre was shot down as it attacked VC troops almost on the outskirts of Saigon itself. Lt Col Fowler was making his third pass when the engine was put out of action by ground fire. With the aircraft on fire, Lt Col Fowler ejected about three miles south of Bien Hoa and was picked up by one of the base HH-43s.

1 October 1966

F-105D 60-0483 421 TFS, 388 TFW, USAF, Korat
Capt Cowan Glenn Nix (POW)

October opened with yet another Thunderchief going down over North Vietnam. Capt Nix was shot down while bombing a ferry across the Sou Giang River near Han Lo, 20 miles northwest of Dong Hoi. The aircraft was hit by AAA as it pulled up from it first attack and crashed soon after near Van Loc, four miles from the sea. Capt Nix became a POW and was released on 4 March 1973.

2 October 1966

F-104C 56-0904 435 TFS, 8 TFW, USAF, Udorn
Capt N R Lockard (survived)

A flight of Starfighters was detailed to fly an armed reconnaissance mission as part of the Barrel Roll campaign in northern Laos. The flight prepared to bomb a truck park eight miles southeast of Sam Neua and Capt Lockard's aircraft had just started its dive at 10,000 feet when it was hit by an SA-2 missile. Capt Lockard ejected immediately and was fortunate to be rescued by a USAF or Air America helicopter. As far as is known this was the first time a US aircraft had been brought down by a SAM over Laos. In September 1966 the first of the new QRC-160 electronic countermeasures pods were delivered to the 355th TFW. This pod was designed to jam the North Vietnamese AAA and SAM fire control radars and proved to be very effective although the Wild Weasels found that they interfered with their specialist equipment. The QRC-160 pod was soon delivered to the other tactical wings in Southeast Asia and became one of the the main weapons against the SA-2, dramatically increasing the survival rate of the F-105 bombers.

F-4C 64-0821 497 TFS, 8 TFW, USAF, Ubon
Capt J W Lacasse (survived)
1Lt A L Workman (survived)

As darkness fell the Night Owl Phantoms started their work over the network of the Ho Chi Minh Trail. A flight of aircraft was sent to attack an enemy base camp and was returning from the raid when one of the F-4s was hit by AAA near Tho Linh Ha, 20 miles northwest of Dong Hoi. Capt Lacasse turned the burning aircraft towards the coast and reached a position about 10 miles off the coast near Hué before he and his WSO ejected. Capt Lacasse was picked up by a USAF helicopter and 1Lt Workman by a Navy ship.

C-130E 62-1840   776 TCS, 314 TCW, USAF,
                   Ching Chuan Kang
                   Capt Jerome Joseph Smith (KIA)
                   1Lt James Howard Graff (KIA)
                   1Lt David Albert Thorpe (KIA)
                   SSgt Raymond Lee Wheeler (KIA)
                   A1C Billy Jack Clayton (KIA)

Hostile action or sabotage was suspected as the cause when a Hercules crashed 16 miles south of Cam Ranh Bay with no survivors. The aircraft was temporarily based at Nha Trang and was returning from an airlift mission within South Vietnam.

A-3B   142633   Detachment A, VAH-2, USN, USS *Coral Sea*
                   Lt Charlie Cellar (survived)
                   Lt Larry Sharpe (survived)
                   ADJ2 Dale V Clark (survived)
                   1 crew, name unknown (survived)

The *Coral Sea* was steaming to Subic Bay for a brief break in operations and, as was normal, some of its aircraft were launched to reach the Philippines ahead of the ship, thereby allowing some extra R and R for the crew. One of the ship's Skywarriors was being launched with three crew and an electrician who had been specially selected for the flight as a reward for excellent work during the line period. As the catapult fired the bridle snapped bursting the aircraft's nosewheel and, despite frantic attempts by the pilot to stop the aircraft, the Skywarrior slowly rolled over the side of the ship. The aircraft was hung up on the ship briefly and then fell inverted into the water. Fortunately, all four crewmen escaped from the aircraft and were picked up by one of the carrier's helicopters.

3 October 1966

F-100D 56-3100   416 TFS, 3 TFW, USAF, Bien Hoa
                   Maj B L Creswell (survived)

A Super Sabre was lost during a strike on VC troops 15 miles southeast of Rach Gia on South Vietnam's western coast. Maj Creswell was flying low and slow to drop his load of napalm accurately when his aircraft was struck by small arms fire. He flew north for about five miles before ejecting. He was rescued later by a USAF helicopter.

4 October 1966

A-4C   147737   VA-22, USN, USS *Coral Sea*
                   Lt Cdr John Douglas Burns (POW)

As a flight of Skyhawks was flying an armed reconnaissance mission along Route 1 some 10 miles north of Thanh Hoa they received a SAM warning and started to jink to break the SAM's

radar lock. As the flight descended through 1,500 feet Lt Cdr Burns felt several hits from AAA on his aircraft's fuselage and wings. Within a few seconds the aircraft was a ball of flame and the controls became ineffective forcing the pilot to eject while still a mile short of the coast. Lt Cdr Burns was captured and spent the rest of the war as a POW, being released on 4 March 1973.

5 October 1966

F-4C   64-0702   433 TFS, 8 TFW, USAF, Ubon
                   1Lt E W Garland (survived)
                   Capt William Richard Andrews (KIA)

A flight of four Phantoms was assigned to provide an escort to two EB-66s during a Rolling Thuunder raid on a bridge 45 miles southwest of Yen Bai. While orbiting the target at 30,000 feet the flight received a MiG warning and at about the same time the flight leader noticed that his No3 was missing. It was assumed that the aircraft had been hit by a MiG although no one saw an actual attack. Both the Phantom crew had in fact ejected safely from their aircraft and Capt Andrews reported that he was uninjured but that North Vietnamese troops were approaching his position. He later radioed that he had been wounded and was losing consciousness. A SAR task force arrived on the scene and an HH-3, piloted by Capt Oliver O'Mara, attempted a pick up but his helicopter was badly damaged by ground fire and he had to withdraw. The second helicopter, 66-13290 piloted by Capt Leland Kennedy of Detachment 5 of the 38th ARRS, was also hit several times as it made five attempts until it eventually located and rescued 1Lt Garland. However, there was no trace of Maj Andrews. Capt Kennedy was awarded the AFC for his actions during this rescue, which was his first combat rescue of his tour. His helicopter, 66-13290, was later selected for preservation by the National Air and Space Museum. On 20 December 1991 the US Government announced that remains previously handed over by the Vietnamese had been identified as those of Capt Andrews. 1Lt Garland reported that his aircraft had been brought down by an Atoll missile fired by a MiG-21. If this was the case, this Phantom was the first US aircraft shot down by an air-to-air missile during the war.

A-1H   137610   VA-152, USN, USS *Oriskany*
                   Lt(jg) James Alvin Beene (KIA)

During an armed reconnaissance mission along the coast between Thanh Hoa and Mu Ron Ma a section of two Skyraiders flew through a thunderstorm from which only one emerged. It was assumed that the aircraft had suffered a gyro failure, which upset the aircraft's artifical horizon. An oil slick was later seen on the water's surface about 15 miles south of Hon Mat island but there was no trace of any wreckage or the pilot.

The C-130 Hercules was, along with the C-123 Provider, the USAF's main tactical transport aircraft of the war. A total of 58 airlift C-130s were lost during the war, including flareships and Special Operations models. Eight USAF C-130s were lost in 1966. USAF

6 October 1966

F-8E   150924   VF-162, USN, USS *Oriskany*
                   Lt R D Leach (survived)

A Crusader from VF-162 was flying as escort to one of *Oriskany's* VFP-63 aircraft on a photographic reconnaissance mission over Hon Gay harbour and the surrounding area. The escort pilot was startled when his low fuel warning light suddenly came on. At this point he should have had plenty of fuel left but the aircraft was obviously leaking badly. The two aircraft immediately headed out to sea towards a waiting tanker but Lt Leach's aircraft ran out of fuel some 70 miles south of Hon Gay before he could refuel. He ejected and was picked up by a Navy helicopter. This Crusader had been flown by Cdr Hal Marr of VF-211 on 12 June 1966 when he shot down two MiG-17s.

B-57B   53-3888   8 TBS, 405 FW attached to 35 TFW, USAF,
                   Da Nang
                   Capt G D Rippey (survived)
                   Capt Louis Frank Makowski (POW)

A Canberra was orbiting over the DMZ near Kinh Mon waiting its turn to bomb a target when it was hit by AAA. With its tail on fire the aircraft crashed within the DMZ buffer zone and although both crew ejected only the pilot was later rescued by an HH-3E. Capt Makowski was captured and held until the Operation Homecoming release on 4 March 1973.

F-4C   63-7486   497 TFS, 8 TFW, USAF, Ubon
                   1Lt Robert Michael Gilchrist (KIA)
                   1Lt Eugene Matthew Pabst (KIA)

The Night Owl mission claimed two more victims on the night of the 6th. A Phantom was hit by ground fire as it pulled up from an attack on a truck park near Tu Loan, 25 miles northwest of Dong Hoi. It crashed almost immediately killing both crewmen.

7 October 1966

RF-4C   65-0885   12 TRS, 460 TRW, USAF, Tan Son Nhut
                   Capt James Allen Treece (KIA)
                   1Lt Larry Dale Knight (KIA)

A Phantom was lost in northern South Vietnam while en route to the North during a night-time photographic reconnaissance sortie. It was thought that the aircraft had either been hit by ground fire or flew into the ground by accident.

Strategic Reconnaissance

In February 1964 SAC deployed a detachment of four U-2s of the 4080th SRW to Bien Hoa to fly high-altitude reconnaissance flights over Southeast Asia. The U-2 had been one of the USA's best kept secrets of the Cold War until the shooting down of Gary Powers over Russia on 1 May 1960. Although difficult to operate and still shrouded in secrecy, its ability to collect intelligence made the U-2 an invaluable asset in Southeast Asia. On 5 April 1965 a U-2 took photographs of SA-2 missile sites under construction near Hanoi and Haiphong. The detachment, initially known as Lucky Dragon then Trojan Horse and then Giant Dragon, was operated by the 4028th SRS but on 11 February 1966 the Wing was redesignated as the 100th SRW and the Bien Hoa detachment later came under the 349th SRS. The aircraft that crashed on 8 October was the only U-2 lost in connection with the wars in Southeast Asia. On 11 July 1970 the U-2 detachment moved to U-Tapao and the detachment was upgraded to become the 99th SRS. The last U-2 did not finally leave Thailand until March 1976.

8 October 1966

A-1H   137629   VA-152, USN, USS *Oriskany*
Lt John Anthony Feldhaus (KIA)

A section of Skyraiders was flying a road reconnaissance mission 25 miles southwest of Thanh Hoa when the aircraft encountered heavy ground fire. Despite jinking in an attempt to throw the gunners off their aim, one of the aircraft was hit in the central fuselage and caught fire, crashing almost immediately.

B-57B   52-1512   8 TBS, 405 FW attached to 35 TFW, USAF,
Da Nang
Capt R W Clark (survived)
1Lt P A Viscasillas (survived)

The 8th TBS lost its second Canberra within three days when an aircraft was hit by ground fire during a daytime interdiction mission. The pilot attempted to return to Da Nang but the aircraft crashed into the sea less than one mile from Da Nang after the crew were forced to eject. Both men were picked up by a USAF HH-43. This B-57 started its Air Force career with the 345th TBG based at Langley AFB, Virginia

RF-8G   146899   Detachment A, VFP-63, USN, USS *Coral Sea*
Lt(jg) F D Litvin (survived)

Two days after the loss of a Crusader while acting as an escort to a photographic mission around Hon Gay, another attempt was made in the same area. The reconnaissance Crusader took its photos of Hon Gay harbour and military installations and was heading south away from the coast when it was hit by a large calibre anti-aircraft shell fired from one of the many small islands off the large island of Dau Cat Ba. The aircraft began to leak fuel and the oil pressure dropped to zero followed quickly by com-

plete engine failure. Lt Litvin ejected just south of Dau Cat Ba and was rescued by a waiting Navy helicopter.

O-1E   56-2610   20 TASS, 505 TACG, USAF, Da Nang
Capt William Lee Schultz (KIA)

A Bird Dog was providing forward air control for an air strike against VC troops about five miles south of Da Nang when it was hit by small arms fire. Capt Schultz made an immediate crash landing but the was severely injured in the process and, although picked up by a USAF helicopter, he later died of his injuries.

U-2C   56-6690   349 SRS, 100 SRW, USAF, Bien Hoa
Maj Leo J Stewart (survived)

During a high altitude reconnaissance flight over North Vietnam a U-2 developed a technical problem and eventually crashed near Bien Hoa. The pilot ejected and was rescued.

9 October 1966

F-4B   152993   VF-154, USN, USS *Coral Sea*
Lt Cdr Charles Neils Tanner (POW)
Lt Ross Randle Terry (POW)

Two Phantoms were assigned flak suppression duties during a major air strike on a railway bridge at Phu Ly, 30 miles south of Hanoi. The lead aircraft was hit in the rear fuselage by a 100mm anti-aircraft shell as it started its roll in to attack the target. Engine warning lights started flashing and the electrical system and hydraulics began to fail as a fire burned through the aircraft's structure. The aircraft quickly became uncontrollable and the crew ejected at a speed of Mach 1.3 with the aircraft inverted in a 60-degree dive. They landed about seven miles northwest of Ninh Binh and were captured. The pair were severely beaten for giving misleading information under torture that was later repeated by the North Vietnamese in a press briefing in Paris. The two fliers claimed to be 'Clark Kent' and 'Ben Casey'!

Lt Cdr Tanner was on his second tour in Southeast Asia and had flown 125 missions, whereas Lt Terry was a relative newcomer and was only on his 20th mission when he was shot down. Both men were released on 4 March 1973 and both eventually retired from the Navy with the rank of Captain. In at least one reference the loss of this Phantom is attributed to an Atoll missile fired by a MiG-21. During the rescue attempt for these two airman a dogfight developed between four A-1H Skyraiders of VA-176 and four MiG-17s with the result that one of the MiGs was shot down.

O-1E   51-12041   21 TASS, 14 ACW, USAF, Nha Trang
2 crew, names unknown (survived)

A Bird Dog FAC aircraft was destroyed in South Vietnam in an accident that was attributed to pilot error.

10 October 1966

A-4E   151150   VA-23, USN, USS *Coral Sea*
Lt(jg) Michael Steele Confer (KIA)

A section of Skyhawks was despatched from the *Coral Sea* to make a night attack on a staging area at Kien An on the coast about 35 miles southeast of Haiphong. After several flares were dropped Lt Confer's aircraft was seen to start a 45-degree dive on the target and fire its 2.75 inch rockets at about 2,500-3,000 feet. The section leader saw the rockets impact followed by a large flash on the ground. No radio call or beeper was heard and it was assumed that the either the aircraft was hit by flak or it flew into the ground by accident.

F-105D   62-4300   469 TFS, 388 TFW, USAF, Korat
1Lt Glen F Bullock (KIA)

The engine of a Thunderchief failed during take off from Korat and the aircraft crashed killing the pilot.

12 October 1966

A-1H   135323   VA-25, USN, USS *Coral Sea*
Lt Robert Deane Woods (POW)

During a road reconnaissance mission a Skyraider was hit by AAA as it flew along Route 15 near Lang Long, some 30 miles southwest of Thanh Hoa. The aircraft's starboard wing was well ablaze as Lt Woods approached the coast but he was forced to abandon the aircraft before he could reach the sea. After being on the run for two days, Lt Woods was captured and spent the rest of the war as a POW. He was released on 4 March 1973 and in the following July married a lady who had worn a POW bracelet with his name on it. These bracelets were produced by a POW support organisation to highlight the continuing fate of America's POWs in North Vietnam. Each bracelet was produced engraved with the name of a POW with the intention that it should be worn until he either returned or was accounted for. Soon after Woods hit the ground a Navy Sea King helicopter made a rescue attempt but it was driven off by intense ground fire. The JPRC arranged for a Shining Brass team in Laos to be flown out to the USS *Intrepid* to attempt a rescue. On the 16th the 12-man team of US Special Forces and Nung commandos was inserted near the Skyraider's crash site by two SH-3s. After about four hours of searching through the jungle the team encountered a patrol of four North Vietnamese soldiers, who they killed. However, the jungle was full of NVA so the team had to call for help and the helicopters returned. The men were winched up into the two helicopters under heavy fire but one of the Sea Kings (150618 of HS-6) was hit by ground fire and two crewmen and two commandos were wounded. The helicopter's engine was badly damaged and the pilot had to ditch near the carrier. All the occupants were rescued by a boat from the destroyer USS *Henley* as the helicopter sank beneath the waves.

The Lockheed U-2 started high-altitude reconnaissance missions as early as February 1964 and continued to provide intelligence to ground and air forces for the duration of the war. Operating initially from Tan Son Nhut, the U-2 detachment moved in July 1970 to U-Tapao, where this photograph was taken. USAF

The *Coral Sea* had made a bad start to its second cruise. In it first 30 days of operations the ship had lost nine aircraft in combat (three Phantoms, three Skyhawks, two Skyraiders and a Crusader) and one more in an accident.

F-100F 56-3869 90 TFS, 3 TFW, USAF, Bien Hoa
Capt J H Bradley (survived)
A1C T Tatnall (survived)
On what may have been a sortie to obtain publicity photographs, a two-seat Super Sabre was shot down by small arms fire as it strafing VC troops on the banks of the Mekong River, 12 miles southeast of Can Tho. Both the pilot and the enlisted man in the back seat ejected and were eventually recovered.

F-100D 55-3809 531 TFS, 3 TFW, USAF, Bien Hoa
Capt W C Hersman (survived)
The 3rd TFW lost another F-100 later in the day when Capt Hersman's aircraft was shot down by ground fire in the Mekong Delta. The aircraft was making its fourth run dropping napalm cannisters when it was hit. Capt Hersman ejected and was later rescued.

A-4E 152075 VA-164, USN, USS *Oriskany*
Lt Frank Callihan Elkins (KIA)
A section of Skyhawks on a night-time road reconnaissance mission was engaged by a SAM site near Tho Trang, about 45 miles south of Thanh Hoa. Lt Elkins saw the missiles being launched at him and is believed to have started evasive manoeuvring. The Skyhawk was either hit by an SA-2 or it may have hit the ground while trying to avoid a missile. There was no indication that Lt Elkins had survived but this was only confirmed in March 1990 when the Vietnamese finally handed over his remains to the US.

13 October 1966

F-4C 64-0654 480 TFS, 366 TFW, USAF, Da Nang
1Lt Murray Lyman Borden (KIA)
1Lt Eugene Thomas Meadows (KIA)
On 10 October the 366th TFW at Phan Rang swapped designations with the 35th TFW at Da Nang. From Da Nang the Phantoms of the 366th began to fly more missions over the North and also took part in the night campaign over the Ho Chi Minh Trail and the southern provinces of North Vietnam. Two Phantoms had just crossed the DMZ and were checking a road for traffic when they spotted several vehicles. The aircraft set up an attack pattern but as 1Lt Borden's aircraft was making its third pass his wingman saw a large explosion on the ground near the road. A SAR beeper was heard briefly by another aircraft but no trace of the Phantom or its crew were found by searching aircraft. In 1994 a joint US-Vietnamese recovery mission discovered human remains at a crash site about 10 miles north of the DMZ and these were positively identified on 21 November 1994 as those of 1Lt Meadows. No trace of the pilot has yet been found.

14 October 1966

F-105D 62-4391 354 TFS, 355 TFW, USAF, Takhli
Maj R P Taylor (survived)
14 October was a very busy day that resulted in a record 175 US sorties flown over North Vietnam. An F-105 was hit by ground fire while flying at 2,000 feet over hilly terrain 50 miles northwest of Vinh, when returning from a Rolling Thunder strike on a road bridge at Khe Bo. The aircraft caught fire and the pilot ejected after a few seconds. He was eventually rescued by a USAF HH-3.

F-100D 55-3559 308 TFS, 3 TFW, USAF, Bien Hoa
Capt Melvin Rupert Ellis (KIA)
A Super Sabre was dropping napalm on a VC target on the banks of the Mekong, seven miles north of Phu Vinh, when it was hit by ground fire. With the aircraft in flames Capt Ellis ejected but was killed when his parachute failed to deploy properly. This aircraft was first brought to Vietnam by the 481st TFS during its deployment in 1965.

A-1H 139731 VA-152, USN, USS *Oriskany*
Ens Darwin Joel Thomas (KIA)
A section of Skyraiders on a night-time armed reconnaissance mission over hills about 25 miles southwest of Thanh Hoa spot-

ted lights on a road. Ens Thomas dived to attack the target with unguided rockets but the aircraft failed to pull out of the dive before it hit the ground and exploded.

18 October 1966

HU-16B 51-7145 37 ARRS, 3 ARRG, USAF, Da Nang
Maj Ralph Harold Angstadt (KIA)
1Lt John Henry Sotheron Long (KIA)
Maj Inzar William Rackley (KIA)
TSgt Robert Laverne Hill (KIA)
SSgt Lawrence Clark (KIA)
SSgt John Reginald Shoneck (KIA)
A2C Steven Harold Adams (KIA)
An Albatross amphibian took off from Da Nang in poor weather for a patrol over the Gulf of Tonkin. Using the call sign Crown Bravo, a name that was assigned to the afternoon patrol of each day, the aircraft encountered worsening weather and failed to make a routine radio report. As soon as the weather cleared enough a second Albatross left Da Nang to search for Maj Angstadt's aircraft. The Albatross was joined by Navy ships and aircraft but no trace of the aircraft or its crew was ever found. The aircraft's last known position was about 40 miles off Dong Hoi and it was suspected that the aircraft was lost due to extreme weather rather than enemy action. SSgt Shoneck was an HH-43 flight mechanic from the 38 ARRS who probably just went along on the patrol for air experience.

20 October 1966

F-4C 63-7518 433 TFS, 8 TFW, USAF, Ubon
Maj L Breckenridge (survived)
1Lt J E Merrick (survived)
During a Steel Tiger armed reconnaissance mission a flight of Phantoms attacked a truck park near Ban Kang in Southern Laos. On its second pass Maj Breckenridge's aircraft was hit by automatic weapons fire. The aircraft flew about 10 miles to the south before the crew were forced to eject. A SAR task force arrived and 'Jolly Green 02', an HH-3E 65-12778 flown by Maj Youngblood of the 38th ARRS, dropped its hoist for one of the survivors. As the survivor was being reeled into the helicopter it was hit repeatedly by ground fire and had to make an emergency landing in a field about a mile away. Capt Leland Kennedy in the second HH-3 landed next to Youngblood's helicopter and took its crew and the Phantom pilot on board before resuming the search for the second Phantom crewman. He was spotted hanging from a tree by an O-1 FAC and Maj Kennedy picked him up under intense small arms fire from enemy troops. The downed HH-3 was destroyed to prevent it from falling into enemy hands. Kennedy was awarded a second AFC for this rescue, having won his first medal for a rescue on 5 October.

A-4C 147775 VA-172, USN, USS *Franklin D Roosevelt*
Lt(jg) Frederick Raymond Purrington (POW)
A section of Skyhawks on an armed reconnaissance mission spotted several barges on a waterway five miles south of Thanh Hoa. As the aircraft popped up to 7,000 feet to roll in to drop their bombs Lt Purrington's aircraft was hit by AAA. The engine ran down and the cockpit filled with smoke. Lt Purrington tried to glide to reach the sea but the stubby-winged Skyhawk was not renowned for its gliding qualities and the pilot was forced to eject over land and was subsequently captured. Lt Purrington was flying his 29th mission when he was shot down. He was released from captivity on 18 February 1973 and eventually retired from the Navy with the rank of Captain.

A-1E 52-132410 602 ACS, 14 ACW, USAF, Udorn
Capt David Raymond Wagener (KIA)
When Maj Breckenridge and 1Lt Merrick ejected from their Phantom over southern Laos a SAR operation was rapidly mounted. Two Skyraiders were assigned as escorts for the mission and arrived over the downed airmen and began orbiting nearby to await the rescue helicopters. As Capt Wagener was orbiting about five miles northwest of Ban Kang his aircraft was hit by small arms fire and the Skyraider dived into the ground. The pilot may have been hit as no attempt to escape was seen by his wingman.

A-4C 148592 VA-153, USN, USS *Constellation*
Lt(jg) Harry Sanford Edwards (KIA)
The *Constellation* mounted a small-scale raid on the Trinh Xuyen railway bridge, five miles southeast of Nam Dinh. Two A-4s commenced a simultaneous 45-degree dive to drop their bombs. The leader saw his wingman's aircraft drop its bombs and continue its dive until it hit the ground a few hundred yards from the bridge. No anti-aircraft fire had been observed during the raid and it was thought likely that Lt Edwards had become fixated on the target and failed to pull out of the dive in time. It was obvious that Lt Edwards had not survived the incident but his remains were not returned to the USA until September 1996.

F-104C 56-0918 435 TFS, 8 TFW, USAF, Udorn
Capt Charles Ehnstrom Tofferi (KIA)
The Starfighter squadron at Udorn lost a second aircraft during the month when an F-104 was shot down during an armed reconnaissance mission over the Plain of Jars in northern Laos. The aircraft was hit in the rear fuselage by ground fire as it pulled up to attack a storage area. Capt Tofferi may have been hit as he was not seen to eject from the aircraft before it crashed.

21 October 1966

F-105D 61-0057 469 TFS, 388 TFW, USAF, Korat
Capt David John Earll (KIA)
The Korat Wing sent two F-105s on a strike against what was judged to be a storage depot 18 miles northwest of Dong Hoi. Capt Earll's aircraft was hit by ground fire as he was making his second pass firing unguided rockets. The aircraft crashed immediately and the pilot did not survive.

22 October 1966

F-4B 151009 VF-161, USN, USS *Constellation*
Lt Cdr Earl Paul McBride (KIA)
Lt(jg) E O Turner (survived)
A strike group of two F-4s and six A-4s were assigned the task of flak suppression for a larger strike force on a raid on railway and road bridges at Mai Xa. Shortly after crossing the coast en route to the target the strike group encountered heavy anti-aircraft fire. Lt Cdr McBride's aircraft was hit by an 85mm shell and he turned back out to sea accompanied by one of the Skyhawks. The Phantom's forward fuselage was on fire, which spread rapidly as the aircraft recrossed the coast. Eventually the fire burnt through the flight controls and the crew ejected although only the NFO, Lt Turner, survived. This aircraft was one of 27 F-4Bs that had been loaned by the Navy to the USAF for use by the 4453rd CCTW in 1963 as the Air Force prepared to introduce the Phantom into service.

RA-5C 150830 RVAH-6, USN, USS *Constellation*
Lt Cdr Thomas Carl Kolstad (KIA)
Lt(jg) William Blue Klenert (KIA)
Less than two hours after the Phantom had been lost the *Constellation* lost another aircraft. One of the ship's Vigilantes was flying a reconnaissance mission with an escort between Hanoi and Hai Duong at 3,000 feet. Five miles southwest of Hai Duong the escorting Phantom was damaged by ground fire and started to turn back. Lt Cdr Kolstad reported a SAM launch as he turned to follow the Phantom. Nothing more was seen or heard from the Vigilante but a Vietnamese report stated that the aircraft had been shot down by an SA-2 and that the crew ejected at a very low altitude and were both killed.

The Phantom and Vigilante lost on the 22nd were the last aircraft lost by the *Constellation* on its second tour. It left the line on 9 November but would return with a new Air Wing the next year.

23 October 1966

A-4E 150072 VA-163, USN, USS *Oriskany*
1 pilot, name unknown (survived)
During an armed reconnaissance mission one of the *Oriskany's* Skyhawks had a mid-air collision with another aircraft and had

to be abandoned. This was the last aircraft lost by the ship before its disastrous fire on 26 October.

T-28D 49-1582 probably 606 ACS, 634 CSG, USAF,
Nakhon Phanom
Lt Col William J Newton (KWF)
Capt Samuel J Baker (KWF)

The USAF had not lost a T-28 since November 1964. An Air Commando T-28 crashed near Nakhon Phanom during a test flight, the cause was not known.

26 October 1966

F-100D 56-3167 614 TFS, 35 TFW, USAF, Phan Rang
Capt Glenn Raymond Morrison (KIA)

The 614th TFS lost its first aircraft of the war during a bombing mission near Minh Thanh, 40 miles north of Saigon. The aircraft was hit by ground fire and crashed. Capt Morrison was not seen to eject and may have been hit and wounded.

A-4E 151075 VA-163, USN, USS *Oriskany*

On 26 October the *Oriskany's* tour of duty off Southeast Asia was cut tragically short by a disastrous fire, the first of two such incidents to plague the carriers on Yankee Station. The fire broke out at 7:15 on the morning of the 26th on the hangar deck of the ship. Six A-1s and seven A-4s were on the deck having been readied for a night strike but bad weather postponed the launch. The ordnance on the aircraft had to be downloaded and stored until morning. The ordnance included several Mk24 Model 3 magnesium parachute flares. The flares were taken down to the forward hangar deck for stowing in a temporary flare storage compartment. The flares were being moved into the store by hand when one of the flares ignited due to mishandling. Flames and toxic fumes rapidly spread to other parts of the ship. The heat set off ordnance on the hangar deck as it was being prepared for an air strike. About 350 bombs had to be thrown overboard to avert further explosions. It was not until noon that the last of the fires had been put out. A total of 36 officers and eight enlisted men died in the fire including 24 aviators. One of the dead airmen was the *Oriskany's* CAG, Cdr Rodney B Carter, who was temporarily replaced by Cdr Dick Bellinger. At least four VA-163 pilots and several from VF-162 also died in the fire. One Skyhawk was destroyed and three others were badly damaged and two Seasprite helicopters were also destroyed. The *Oriskany* fire is well recorded in several books, notably Zalin Grant's *Over the Beach*. The ship sailed back to the USA for a lengthy refit and did not leave her homeport again until 16 June 1967.

27 October 1966

F-105D 62-4396 333 TFS, 355 TFW, USAF, Takhli
Maj Dale Alonzo Johnson (KIA)

A flight of F-105s attacked a road bypass at the mouth of the Sou Giang River, 15 miles north of Dong Hoi. As Maj Johnson started his attack on the target his aircraft was hit by ground fire and burst into flames. The aircraft crashed shortly afterwards but an emergency beeper signal was heard. A SAR task force arrived on the scene but there was no sign of the pilot who was assumed to have been killed in the incident. Maj Johnson was the Wing's standardisation and evaluation officer and was attached to the 333rd TFS for combat missions.

F-105D 60-0431 421 TFS, 388 TFW, USAF, Korat
Maj Robert Earl Kline (survived)

Later in the day a number of Korat Wing F-105s flew armed reconnaissance missions over the Steel Tiger area of southern Laos. A flight of aircraft found a North Vietnamese troop concentration near Muang Fangdeng and commenced an attack. Maj Kline was just pulling out of his dive at about 2,500 feet when his aircraft was hit by automatic weapons fire. He turned north over the Bolovens Plateau and ejected when he was about 10 miles from his target. He was seen to eject by an O-1 pilot who reported his position. As it was getting dark and the USAF SAR helicopters had no night capability at that time it was decided to send in a Bright Light team from Dak To. An Army UH-1D from the 155th

Aviation Helicopter Company flew the team in to rescue Maj Kline and refuelled on the return journey from pre-placed fuel drums at a site deep inside enemy territory. Unfortunately, Maj Kline was lost on a mission over North Vietnam on 2 November.

31 October 1966

UC-123B 54-0597 12 ACS, 315 ACW, USAF, Tan Son Nhut
Capt Thomas E Davie (survived)
Capt Joseph M Dougherty (survived)
SSgt Elijah R Winstead (survived)

The Ranch Hand squadron lost a second aircraft during 1966 when one of the Providers was shot down while on a defoliation mission in the so-called Iron Triangle, eight miles west of Lai Khe. Three aircraft were halfway through their spray run when they were fired on by enemy troops using automatic weapons. All the aircraft were hit by ground fire but Capt Davie's aircraft had its port engine knocked out and he was unable to feather the propeller. The aircraft crashed into the jungle but miraculously all three crew survived with just minor injuries and were rescued 25 minutes later by two HH-43s. For SSgt 'Junior' Winstead this was the second time he had been shot down on a Ranch Hand mission in six months having survived a crash on 20 June.

O-1E 55-4669 19 TASS, 505 TACG, USAF, Bien Hoa
Capt P G Knight (survived)
A1C R E Hemvree (survived)

A Bird Dog on an FAC mission was detached to a strip near Song Be City near the Cambodian border. As it took off from the strip the port wing was hit by small arms fire. The pilot and observer were recovered from the nearby crash site with minor injuries.

1 November 1966

A-4E 151138 VA-72, USN, USS *Franklin D Roosevelt*
Lt Allan Russell Carpenter (POW)

A raid on a SAM site at Uong Bi five miles north of Haiphong was followed up by a reconnaissance mission to obtain BDA photographs. The reconnaissance aircraft was escorted by an Iron Hand flight of three Skyhawks, which were equipped with Shrike anti-radar missiles and rockets. The leader, Lt Carpenter, saw a SAM launch and immediately pulled up to fire a Shrike. He followed this up by diving at the SAM radar and firing his rockets but as the aircraft sped away from the target it was hit in the fuselage by AAA. Lt Carpenter pulled up to 5,000 feet and made for the sea but a fire broke out and burned through the flying controls forcing the pilot to eject three miles east of Haiphong. Lt Carpenter landed in the sea and despite the efforts of his wingmen and a SAR helicopter he was captured and taken into Haiphong in a North Vietnamese junk. Two Skyhawks and the rescue chopper were all hit and damaged by the intense AAA around Haiphong. Carpenter was flying his 107th combat mission (having previously served a tour on the USS *Independence*) and after more than six years as a prisoner he was released on 4 March 1973. Lt Carpenter had been forced to eject from another A-4 on 21 August 1966 when it ingested debris from rockets it was firing. Upon returning to duty he became an instructor with VF-43 at Oceana and retired as a Commander to start his own business building and selling ultralight aircraft.

2 November 1966

F-105D 60-0469 421 TFS, 388 TFW, USAF, Korat
Maj Robert Earl Kline (KIA)

F-105D 62-4379 421 TFS, 388 TFW, USAF, Korat
Capt R F Loken (survived)

A flight of F-105s on an armed reconnaissance mission ran into trouble about 30 miles northwest of Yen Bai. The aircraft were attacking trains and bridges on the northwest railway line along which supplies were brought into North Vietnam from China. Maj Kline was strafing a train when his aircraft crashed either as a result of ground fire or by flying into the ground. Robert Kline had survived being shot down only a week earlier when his aircraft was hit during a mission over Laos. Unfortunately on this occasion his luck deserted him.

Moments later Capt Loken's aircraft was hit by ground fire as he was strafing a railway bridge at Khe Se, 25 miles northwest of Yen Bai. The pilot flew his badly damaged aircraft across North Vietnam and into Laos but was forced to eject 25 miles west of Sam Neua where he was rescued by either a USAF or Air America helicopter.

3 November 1966

F-4B 148433 VF-154, USN, USS *Coral Sea*
Lt R W Schaffer (survived)
Lt(jg) J P Piccoli (survived)

A flight of F-4s from the *Coral Sea* was following Route 1A along the coast south of Vinh on an armed reconnaissance mission when they spotted trucks on the road just inland of the Mu Ron Ma peninsula. As Lt Schaffer's aircraft pulled up from its bombing run it was hit near the starboard wheel well by AAA. The wingman saw a large hole in the wing and a small fire that got larger as the Phantoms flew out to sea. About 20 miles off the coast the fire became so intense that the crew were advised to eject near a SAR helicopter, which then picked them up.

RF-101C 56-0175 Detachment 1, 45 TRS, 460 TRW, USAF,
Tan Son Nhut
Capt D J Haney (survived)

An RF-101C from Tan Son Nhut made a reconnaissance of the DMZ buffer zone, which was becoming more dangerous every day as the North Vietnamese brought in troops, supplies and air defence units. As the aircraft was making a turn over the DMZ at about 7,000 feet it was struck by ground fire. Capt Haney turned east and ejected less than two miles from the coast. He was quickly rescued by a USAF helicopter.

F-4B 151018 VF-14, USN, USS *Franklin D Roosevelt*
Lt W A Wood (survived)
Lt E J Ducharme (survived)

When returning from an armed reconnaissance mission the pilot of a Phantom discovered that a technical malfunction meant that he could not refuel from a tanker aircraft. The aircraft approached the carrier but was waved off and then ran out of fuel, at which point both crew ejected and were rescued.

4 November 1966

F-105D 62-4366 469 TFS, 388 TFW, USAF, Korat
Capt Dean A Elmer (survived)

During an armed reconnaissance mission a flight of Thunderchiefs bombed a road bridge at Xom Ca Trang, 25 miles west of Mu Ron Ma. As Capt Elmer dived at the target his aircraft flew into a hail of anti-aircraft fire and was hit in the fuselage. He turned southwest and crossed into Laos and after flying about 45 miles Capt Elmer ejected near Ban Phonxai. He landed in a tree where he spent an anxious few hours before being rescued by a USAF HH-3. Three F-105s, which were protecting the SAR aircraft, had to refuel from a tanker four times during the rescue attempt. Dean Elmer was evacuated to hospitals in Japan and the USA to recover from his ejection injuries. He resumed his flying career but did not return to Southeast Asia.

F-105F 63-8273 13 TFS, 388 TFS, USAF, Korat
Maj Robert Edwin Brinckmann (KIA)
Capt Vincent Anthony Scungio (KIA)

The Wild Weasels were busy hunting their prey on the 4th during a strike near Kep and came across a SAM site three miles northwest of Kep airfield. During the attack the F-105F leading the flight was shot down and crashed near the target. An SA-2 hit the aircraft head-on and neither of the crew were seen to escape and so became the fifth Wild Weasel crew to be lost since July. Considering the number of trained crews available this was a very high proportion. Fortunately, the introduction of the QRC-160 jamming pod towards the end of 1966 and revised tactics and formations assisted the F-105 force to reduce the SAM threat in the New Year. On 31 July 1989 the Vietnamese returned a set of remains to the USA that were later identified as those of Maj Brinckmann. Capt Scungio's body has not yet been found.

The elderly C-47 Skytrain was used in a number of roles in Southeast Asia including psychological warfare as a leaflet bomber. Millions of leaflets were dropped to VC and NVA troops encouraging them to defect. Only two C-47 leaflet aircraft were lost during the war, one of them on 11 November 1966. USAF

RF-101C 56-0093 20 TRS, 432 TRW, USAF, Udorn
 Capt Vincent John Connolly (KIA)
Half an hour after the F-105F was shot down a SAM site in another province claimed a victim of its own. An RF-101C was en route to photograph a road bridge that had just been attacked when it was hit by an SA-2 near Hoang Xa, 15 miles south of Hanoi. The aircraft was flying at about 3,000 feet and broke up immediately, killing the pilot. In 1984 Capt Connolly's remains were handed over by the Vietnamese and buried at Arlington National Cemetery.

6 November 1966

F-100D 55-3603 416 TFS, 3 TFW, USAF, Bien Hoa
 1Lt G K Bankus (survived)
Tactical fighters were sometimes used in South Vietnam to attack potential landing zones in preparation for a helicopter assault. Sometimes several areas were attacked to keep the VC guessing as to which one would actually be used. An F-100 was strafing a landing zone about 10 miles south of Katum when it was hit by automatic weapons fire. The pilot ejected immediately and was rescued by an Army helicopter, possibly one of those about to land at the prepared zone. Prior to its assignment to Southeast Asia this particular Super Sabre had been used by the Thunderbirds aerobatic team.

F-105D 60-5374 357 TFS, 355 TFW, USAF, Takhli
 Capt W G Carey (survived)
As the ground-based air defences of North Vietnam became more intense and more deadly, they assumed a higher priority for attack during armed reconnaissance missions. A flight of F-105s were attacking anti-aircraft gun positions three miles south of Vinh when one of the aircraft was hit in the forward fuselage causing a small fire, which later went out. Capt Carey flew his damaged aircraft to Da Nang where he made a crash landing during which the aircraft was damaged beyond repair.

F-105D 60-0487 354 TFS, 355 TFW, USAF, Takhli
 Capt Victor Vizcarra (survived)
Most Iron Hand flights consisted of one or two F-105F Wild Weasels and two or three F-105D bombers, which completed the destruction started by the Weasel's Shrike missiles. An F-105D in an Iron Hand flight was hit by AAA near Pho Son, 20 miles southwest of Mu Ron Ma, as the flight was en route to a target. Capt Vizcarra headed south towards the DMZ but after about 20 miles he was forced to eject. He was rescued by a US Navy helicopter after spending two hours on the ground. Capt Vizcarra had served on two previous temporary deployments to Thailand and had taken part in the USAF's first attack on a SAM site on 27 July 1965 when six of his colleagues were shot down. He later returned to Southeast Asia and flew 120 missions in the F-100 with the 35th TFW at Phan Rang and retired in 1984 to join Northrop Corporation.

7 November 1966

O-1E 56-4200 20 TASS, 505 TACG, USAF, Da Nang
 Capt Donald Leroy Jacobsen (KIA)
 1Lt Gardner (survived)
In October and November drier weather in southern Laos resulted in increased enemy movement in the Tiger Hound area requiring an increase in air operations to counter the renewed enemy effort. An O-1E was returning from an FAC mission when it was hit by gunfire five miles south of Kham Duc. The pilot was killed in the ensuing crash but the observer, who was an Army officer and a member of a Shining Brass team, survived with major injuries and was rescued by a SAR helicopter.

O-1G 50-1737 20 TASS, 505 TACG, USAF, Da Nang
 1 pilot, name unknown (survived)
Another Bird Dog was lost during the day but this aircraft crashed following an engine failure and the pilot survived.

9 November 1966

O-1E probably 56-2489 21 TASS, 14 ACW, USAF, Nha Trang
 Capt Charles Frederick Swope (KIA)
 Sgt Arthur Glidden, US Army (KIA)
Yet another Bird Dog was lost when an aircraft from Nha Trang was hit by machine gun fire about 10 miles north of Khe Sanh, on the southern edge of the DMZ buffer zone. The bodies of the crew were later recovered by a USAF helicopter.

10 November 1966

A-1E 52-132633 1 ACS, 14 ACW, USAF, Pleiku
 Capt John Lawrence O'Brien (KIA)
The North Vietnamese used any means available to transport supplies along the Ho Chi Minh trail and even resorted to using oxen and elephants as pack animals. A Skyraider hunting over the Steel Tiger region strafed a team of pack animals near Chanum in southern Laos but was in turn shot down by ground fire.

F-105D 62-4288 469 TFS, 388 TFW, USAF, Korat
 Maj Dain W Milliman (KIA)
A Thunderchief crashed on take off at Korat when its engine failed. The pilot was killed in the accident.

S-2E 152351 VS-21, USN, USS Kearsarge
 Lt Thomas Joseph McAteer (KIA)
 Lt(jg) William Thomas Carter (KIA)
 AX3 John Michael Riordan (KIA)
 AX3 Eric John Schoderer (KIA)
The S-2 Trackers carried by the four ASW carriers (USS Bennington, Hornet, Kearsarge and Yorktown) performed a

variety of duties. There was little need for their primary role of anti-submarine warfare as the North Vietnamese did not possess any submarines. However, ASW missions were flown to keep an eye on Soviet and Chinese submarines in the South China Sea. The Trackers were also used for other duties including maritime patrol, signals intelligence, SAR and anti-surface vessel patrols. The SAR destroyers, which operated close to the North Vietnamese coastline, were likely to encounter enemy gunboats and a constant watch was kept for high speed radar contacts. This radar and visual watch was particularly important at night when the North Vietnamese gunboats were most active. The Trackers flew patrols in the vicinity of the SAR destroyers to provide early warning and an attack capability against enemy gunboats.

On the night of the 10th a Tracker launched from the Kearsarge for a patrol over the Gulf of Tonkin. After about three hours the carrier lost radar contact with the aircraft and at first light other aircraft were launched to search for the Tracker. Wreckage and personal flight gear was spotted in the water about 55 miles northeast of Hué but there was no sign of any of the crew. The cause of the crash could not be determined but it was felt unlikely to have been due to enemy action. This was the only fixed-wing aircraft lost by the Kearsarge during its four tours of duty in Southeast Asia, although two SH-3As of HS-6 were also lost. The ship was decommissioned on 13 February 1970 and was scrapped in 1974.

11 November 1966

F-4C 64-0743 559 TFS, 12 TFW, USAF, Cam Ranh Bay
 Capt Robert Irving Biss (POW)
 2Lt Harold Deloss Monlux (POW)

F-4C 63-7616 559 TFS, 12 TFW, USAF, Cam Ranh Bay
 1Lt Richard Leigh Butt (POW - died)
 1Lt Herbert Benjamin Ringsdorf (POW)
An attack on a gun emplacement near Ba Binh, four miles north of the DMZ, went disastrously wrong when two out of three F-4s were shot down as they were about to drop napalm on their target. All four crewmen ejected from their aircraft and all were eventually captured. However, although Rinsgdorf was released on 18 February 1973 and Biss and Monlux were released on 4 March, 1Lt Richard Butt was not. The Department of Defense received information from intelligence sources that 1Lt Butt had died during captivity but, as yet, no details have been released. On 10 April 1986 the Vietnamese returned remains that were identified as those of Richard Butt. 2Lt Monlux had arrived at Cam Ranh Bay in late October and had only flown 11 missions, whereas his pilot had well over 100 to his credit as he had already completed a tour in Southeast Asia as a WSO with the 431st TFS. Herbert Ringsdorf later obtained a degree in medicine but died in February 1998 and was buried with full military honours at Arlington National Cemetery.

A-1E   52-132392   602 ACS, 14 ACW, USAF, Udorn
Capt R P Rosecrans (survived)

When the two Phantoms were shot down a SAR operation was set in motion and a pair of Skyraiders was flying over the DMZ within 20 minutes. Unfortunately all this particular SAR operation achieved was to add another aircraft to the North Vietnamese list of kills. As the two aircraft approached the position where the Phantoms had gone down, one of the Spads was hit by AAA in the port wing. Capt Rosecrans tried to make it to Laos but had to bail out while still over the DMZ buffer zone. The rescue chopper that had been despatched to rescue the Phantom crew successfully picked up the Skyraider pilot. This aircraft was the first of 212 AD-5s (redesignated as the A-1E in 1962) ordered for the Navy.

F-105D   62-4313   354 TFS, 355 TFW, USAF, Takhli
Maj Arthur Stuart Mearns (KIA)

Not all aerial activity in Southeast Asia was happening around the DMZ on the 11th. The Takhli Wing sent a formation of F-105s to bomb the Bac Le railway yard as part of a series of strikes on the northeast railway to divert the enemy defences from the main target of the day, a large POL site near Phuc Yen airfield. The F-105 strike force approached the target from the Gulf of Tonkin but the weather was poor and the mission was aborted and the aircraft recalled. For some reason one of the flights failed to hear the recall message and pressed on through low cloud and rain. Maj Mearns and his flight pulled up into the clouds, rolled in and dropped their bombs on the target but as the aircraft were leaving the target area his Thunderchief was hit by AAA about 30 miles northeast of Haiphong. The aircraft caught fire and although he climbed to 20,000 feet the aircraft became uncontrollable when the hyrdaulics seized. Maj Mearns is thought to have ejected but did not survive.

F-8E   150858   VMF(AW)-235, MAG-11, USMC, Da Nang
Capt Orson George Swindle (POW)

Just four days before the end of its first tour in Southeast Asia, VMF(AW)-235 lost its fifth Crusader. The aircraft was making its second dive attack against military buildings just two miles north of the DMZ when it was hit by AAA. The pilot tried desperately to make for the Gulf of Tonkin but he was forced to eject near Vinh Linh, about three miles short of the coast. Capt Swindle was flying his 205th and last scheduled mission when he was shot down and captured. He was released by the North Vietnamese on 4 March 1973. After retiring from the Marine Corps, Orson Swindle became the campaign director for Ross Perot's unsuccessful 1992 presidential nomination campaign. Perot was a major benefactor of the POWs and became a personal friend to many of them.

A-4C   147718   VA-22, USN, USS Coral Sea
1 pilot, name unknown (survived)

As two A-4s were flying on an armed reconnaissance mission the wingman overran the leader and the pair collided. The leader's aircraft was so badly damaged that he was forced to eject but the wingman landed safely.

C-47B   43-48961   5 ACS, 14 ACW, USAF, Nha Trang
4 crew, names unknown (survived)

In addition to the U-10, the 5th ACS also used C-47s in the psychological warfare role. The aircraft were fitted with loudspeakers for the delivery of propaganda messages and were also used to drop Chieu Hoi leaflets encouraging members of the VC and NVA to defect. One of the Squadron's aircraft suffered an engine failure that resulted in a crash landing from which all the crew survived.

12 November 1966

A-4E   150088   VMA-311, MAG-12, USMC, Chu Lai
Maj John Henry Gallagher (KIA)

VMA-311 lost a Skyhawk and its pilot in a take off accident at Chu Lai. This was the last of five Skyhawks lost by VMA-311 during its second tour at Chu Lai. VMA-311 flew to Iwakuni MCAS in Japan on 1 March 1967 for a three month break from operations.

A-4E   150048   VA-12, USN, USS Franklin D Roosevelt
Cdr Robert Clarence Frosio (KIA)

A-4E   150051   VA-12, USN, USS Franklin D Roosevelt
Lt(jg) James Gradey Jones (KIA)

Another mid-air collision resulted in the loss of two more Skyhawks, this time with their pilots. A Tacan failure during a section approach following an armed reconnaissance mission caused the two aircraft to collide and crash. Sadly, both pilots, including the Squadron's CO, died as the aircraft crashed into the sea. These were the only casualties suffered by VA-12 during its first tour in Southeast Asia.

15 November 1966

A-1E   52-132454   602 ACS, 14 ACW, USAF, Udorn
Capt G E Fowler (survived)

A Skyraider was on a road reconnaissance mission in southern Laos when it was shot down. The aircraft was near Ban Loupum when it was struck by automatic weapons fire setting the port wing ablaze. Capt Fowler headed northeast and bailed out a few minutes later. He was eventually rescued by a USAF helicopter.

16 November 1966

A-1G   52-132600   602 ACS, 14 ACW, USAF, Udorn
Lt Col C A Smith (survived)
Col G F Bradburn (survived)
A2C Allan D Pittman (KIA)

A Skyraider on an administrative flight from Nha Trang to Udorn was shot down by ground fire near Ban Kagnontanh in southern Laos. There were three occupants on board the Skyraider and all three escaped from the aircraft. Lt Col Smith and Col Bradburn were rescued by a USAF HH-3E helicopter within about 90 minutes but A2C Pittman, although he was seen alive on the ground, could not be rescued. A ground force consisting of Royal Lao Army and US-led irregular troops swept the area on the 17th and 18th but found no trace of Pittman. A few days later a villager who had escaped from the Pathet Lao claimed that a US airman had been captured on the 17th and shot by the North Vietnamese. Allan Pittman was officially declared dead in April 1978.

F-100D   56-3431   614 TFS, 35 TFW, USAF, Phan Rang
Capt D B Moose (survived)

A flight of F-100s was tasked with attacking targets in a region known as Paul Revere IV, close to the South Vietnamese border with Cambodia, 40 miles west of Pleiku. One aircraft was hit by ground fire as it came down to 300 feet for a napalm run. Capt Moose ejected as soon as he cleared the immediate area and was picked up by an Army helicopter.

17 November 1966

A-4C   148496   VA-22, USN, USS Coral Sea
Lt(jg) William Tamm Arnold (KIA)

The seasonal monsoon weather was reducing the tempo of air operations over North Vietnam and many missions had to be scrubbed. A section of A-4s approached the coast of North Vietnam about 15 miles north of Dong Hoi and let down through a dense overcast to see if an armed reconnaissance was feasible. The leader determined that the weather was too bad for the mission and decided that the aircraft should jettison their bombs in a loft manoeuvre and return to the ship. The aircraft pulled up and released their ordnance as they entered cloud. Lt Arnold was heard to say that he was in cloud but coming down to regain visual flight over the sea. The leader saw a flash, which he assumed was his wingman's bombs, but as he could not establish visual or voice contact with Lt Arnold it became obvious that the aircraft had flown into the sea after descending through the cloud layer.

22 November 1966

F-4C   64-0755   480 TFS, 366 TFW, USAF, Da Nang
1Lt Gordon Scott Wilson (KIA)
1Lt Joseph Crecca (POW)

A strike on a POL storage site at Ha Gia in North Vietnam saw yet another US aircraft downed by a SAM. One of a flight of F-4s was hit by an SA-2 while flying at 14,000 feet about 10 miles southwest of Thai Nguyen en route to the target. The rear fuselage caught fire and the crew ejected although the pilot was killed, possibly during the ejection or soon after landing. 1Lt Crecca was captured on his 87th mission and became a POW until his release on 18 February 1973. Joe Crecca later flew F-4Es with the 58th TFS and then flew Boeing 747 freighters for Flying Tigers upon retirement from the Air Force. The POL campaign of 1966 had destroyed most of North Vietnam's above-ground POL storage and pumping sites but the time wasted in deciding whether to hit the POL targets had been put to good use by the North Vietnamese who had dispersed and buried much of its fuel and oil. The costly campaign had succeeded in destroying targets but the observable targets were no longer crucial to the North.

A-1G   52-134997   1 ACS, 14 ACW, USAF, Pleiku
Capt R H Armstrong (survived)
1 crew, name unknown (survived)

A Skyraider was hit in the wing by ground fire 10 miles east of Pleiku. Instead of returning to Pleiku the aircraft flew all the way to Da Nang where the aircraft crash-landed on the runway.

F-105D   58-1161   469 TFS, 388 TFW, USAF, Korat
1 pilot, name unknown (survived)

An F-105 was lost near Korat as the result of an engine failure.

23 November 1966

A-4E   151172   VA-192, USN, USS Ticonderoga
Cdr Allen E Hill (survived)

The USS Ticonderoga had returned to Yankee Station on 13 November for her third tour of duty off Vietnam. Ten days later the ship lost its first aircraft when the CO of VA-192 was shot down off North Vietnam. Cdr Hill was part of an Iron Hand strike force that accompanied a raid on a POL storage site at Can Thon near Hon Gay. As the aircraft pulled up from a dive after firing rockets it was hit twice by AAA. The aircraft was on fire and the engine could only provide partial power but Cdr Hill managed to fly about 40 miles out to sea before having to eject. He was rescued by a Navy helicopter and returned to his ship with minor injuries.

O-1E   56-4188   21 TASS, 14 ACW, USAF, Nha Trang
detached to Tuy Hoa
Capt D E Disbrow (survived)
1Lt Whitesides (survived)

An O-1 flew a visual reconnaissance mission in support of the 101st Airborne Division over hilly terrain 30 miles southwest of Qui Nhon. The aircraft was hit by ground fire and crashed a few minutes later. Both crew were subsequently rescued by a USAF helicopter. Tuy Hoa was the first air base in South Vietnam constructed from scratch under USAF supervision. It was designed to take a fighter-bomber wing, the 31st TFW, which was due to arrive in mid-December. However, the airfield was open for business on 15 November, 45 days ahead of schedule, and a detachment of FAC aircraft from the 21st TASS was among the first occupants.

24/25 November 1966

A-4E   151123   VMA-223, MAG-12, USMC, Chu Lai
Capt Claude Nathaniel Williams (KIA)

During a night TPQ-10 radar-directed bombing mission a Marine Corps Skyhawk was shot down about seven miles northwest of Chu Lai. The TPQ-10 was a mobile radar that was used to guide aircraft to a target in poor visibility or at night. The USAF's Combat Skyspot radar was similar but had a greater range although it was a larger radar system and was less mobile. The aircraft crashed very close to the location of the Marine Skyhawk that went down on 8 September on a similar mission. Ground fire was thought to be responsible for this latest loss. Five days later the Squadron stood down from operations in preparation for its move to Iwakuni for a three-month break from operations.

26 November 1966

C-123B 56-4367   19 ACS, 315 ACW, USAF, Tan Son Nhut
                  Capt R A Nagel (survived)
                  1Lt Anavil (survived)
                  35 ARVN paratroopers (survived)

Just after take off from the airstrip at Dau Tieng, 45 miles north-east of Saigon, a Provider was hit in several places by .50 calibre bullets. Hydraulic lines were ruptured and the fluid caught fire, which panicked many of the Vietnamese paratroopers on board. Some of the paratroopers tried to force the emergency door open to jump out while others forced their way into the cockpit and tried to climb out of the side window. Capt Nagel turned back to the airfield and managed to make a skillful belly landing. He dived the aircraft sharply before touch down so that all the paratroopers were thrown to the floor before the aircraft impacted the ground. All the paratroopers and the crew escaped with only minor injuries.

C-47B 44-76574   388 TFW, USAF, Korat
                  Capt Karl David Sobolik (KWF)
                  Lt Col William Affley Lynch (KWF)
                  Capt Carroll Gene Hogeman (KWF)
                  Capt John Richard Humphrey (KWF)
                  Capt Joe H Trickey (KWF)
                  SSgt Alan Ralph Steffen (KWF)
                  25 passengers (KWF)

Most Wings based in Southeast Asia had a HQ flight, which maintained one or two transport or utility aircraft for administrative flights. The 388th TFW's C-47 crashed while on a flight from Saigon killing all 31 passengers and crew on board, including one civilian. The aircraft had taken off in darkness from Tan Son Nhut for the return flight to Korat but the pilot radioed that he was returning to Tan Son Nhut with an engine problem. The aircraft had to go around from its first approach as the undercarriage would not lower. The aircraft crashed in a rice paddy near the airfield with its port engine propeller in the feathered position.

27 November 1966

A-1H 135341   VA-52, USN, USS *Ticonderoga*
               Lt(jg) W H Natter (survived)

It was not long before the *Ticonderoga* lost its second aircraft of its winter tour. Lt Natter was attacking barges on the coast about 15 miles northeast of Thanh Hoa when his aircraft was hit by automatic weapons fire. With a small fire burning away in the rear fuselage Lt Natter flew the Skyraider some 40 miles out to sea before ditching the aircraft and being rescued by a Navy helicopter.

29 November 1966

A-1E 52-133926   602 ACS, 14 ACW, USAF, Udorn
                  Capt John Morton Roper (KIA)

The Barrel Roll campaign in northern Laos claimed a Skyraider and its pilot on the 29th. Capt Roper was bombing a truck park, which had been discovered near Ban Paka close to the border with North Vietnam. The aircraft was hit in the fuselage, which caught fire, but Capt Roper managed to fly over 70 miles to the west before the aircraft crashed near Ban Nam Tia. Unfortunately, Capt Roper was killed in the crash.

2 December 1966

RF-4C 65-0829   11 TRS, 432 TRW, USAF, Udorn
                 Capt Robert Raymond Gregory (POW - died)
                 1Lt Leroy William Stutz (POW)

An RF-4C on a reconnaissance mission north of Hanoi was hit by ground fire forcing the crew to eject about 40 miles southwest of Yen Bai. After landing the two airmen spoke to each other on their survival radio before they were both captured. Gregory was unconscious when he and Stutz were put into the back of a truck for the ride to the Hanoi Hilton. After arrival at the prison Gregory was never seen again.

Robert Gregory and Leroy Stutz had been together as a crew through advanced training and their first squadron assignement at Shaw AFB. They arrived at Udorn in July 1966 and were on their 65th mission when they were shot down. Leroy Stutz was released from captivity on 4 March 1973. Robert Gregory's remains were eventually returned by the Vietnamese and he was buried at Cape County Memorial Park, Missouri. A missing man formation of four RF-4Cs made a low flypast during the burial service.

F-4B 151014   VF-154, USN, USS *Coral Sea*
               Lt(jg) David Edward McRae (KIA)
               Ens David George Rehmann (POW)

Two F-4Bs were assigned CAP duties during a raid on POL storage at Kep airfield. As the Phantoms were making a last pass over the airfield to get an assessment of the damage done, one of the aircraft was hit by AAA. The entire port wing was blown off and the aircraft became a mass of flames. The NFO ejected to the east of Kep airfield but it seems likely that the pilot did not eject and was killed in the crash. David Rehmann became a POW and his photograph, taken while in captivity, was widely circulated to publicise the plight of the POWs. He was finally released on 12 February 1973. This aircraft was another of the Navy F-4Bs that had been loaned to the USAF for use by the 4453rd CCTW in 1963.

F-105D 59-1820   34 TFS, 388 TFW, USAF, Korat
                  Capt Monte Larue Moorberg (KIA)

F-4C 64-0753   480 TFS, 366 TFW, USAF, Da Nang
                Capt Hubert Kelly Flesher (POW)
                1Lt James Robert Berger (POW)

F-4C 64-0663   389 TFS, 366 TFW, USAF, Da Nang
                Maj Donald Ray Burns (POW)
                1Lt Bruce Chalmers Ducat (POW - died)

A major strike on Phuc Yen airfield's POL storage facility claimed three Air Force aircraft. The first to fall was an F-105 that was hit by 37mm AAA as it dived on the target from about 6,000 feet. The aircraft's rear fuselage was seen to be on fire and the pilot may have been hit as he was not seen to eject before the aircraft crashed about 15 miles west of the airfield.

Next over the target were several flights from the 366th TFW headed by a flight from the 480th TFS, which was providing a CAP at 14,000 feet over the target. As the aircraft were manoeuvring about 10 miles northeast of Phuc Yen to cut off a flight of MiG-21s, Capt Flesher's aircraft was hit by an SA-2 and immediately disintegrated. Both crew ejected but 1Lt Berger suffered a spinal compression, a broken arm and concussion, the latter from an old peasant who beat him over the head. James Berger, like many POWs, was incarcerated in five different prisons during his years of captivity. The longest stay in one place was three years spent in Hanoi's Citadel prison known to the prisoners as the Plantation. Flesher and Berger were both released on 18 February 1973. Hubert Flesher was the first Air Force POW to return to flying following his release, eventually flying F-106s with the 84th FIS at Castle AFB. James Berger also returned to flying after his release and served at the Air Force Survival School where he was able to pass on his experiences as a POW to teach a new generation of USAF aircrew.

A SAM also accounted for a Phantom that was flying as part of the strike force during the Phuc Yen raid. A flight of aircraft were returning from the raid and had headed northwest to the northern edge of Thud Ridge, about 40 miles northwest of Phuc Yen, when they ran into another SAM site. The flight was at about 19,000 feet when an SA-2 struck one of the aircraft. Maj Burns and 1Lt Ducat both ejected but Bruce Ducat died in captivity. His body was returned to the USA on 18 March 1977. Donald Burns was released on 4 March 1973 and eventually retired as a Colonel.

A-4C 145143   VA-172, USN, USS *Franklin D Roosevelt*
               Cdr Bruce August Nystrom (KIA)

A-4C 145116   VA-172, USN, USS *Franklin D Roosevelt*
               Ens Paul Laurance Worrell (KIA)

During a night armed reconnaissance mission a section of two A-4s disappeared near Phuc Nhac, 50 miles down the coast from Haiphong. The wingman had been heard by another flight to warn his leader that he had a SAM warning. The leader, Cdr Nystrom, told the wingman to commence evasive action and then announced a SAM launch. A pilot some distance away saw two flashes on the ground about a minute apart, which were probably SAM launches, followed by two explosions in the air. It was assumed that the two Skyhawks were either hit by the SA-2s or flew into the ground trying to evade the missiles. The SAMs had had a very good day with four American aircraft downed as a result of their efforts. Cdr Bruce Nystrom had been flying with the Navy since 1948 and had flown the F4U Corsair during the Korean War as well as the F8F Bearcat and the F2H Banshee. He joined VA-172 as executive officer in December 1964 and assumed command of the Squadron on 23 December 1965. In July 1985 the Vietnamese returned the remains of Paul Worrell.

3 December 1966

F-4C 63-7608   559 TFS, 12 TFW, USAF, Cam Ranh Bay
                Capt Kenneth William Cordier (POW)
                1Lt Michael Christopher Lane (POW)

The very next day after the SAM's greatest success so far, the SA-2 struck again. A flight of Phantoms was escorting an EB-66 on an electronic warfare mission over North Vietnam. As the aircraft were flying a wide orbit at 24,000 feet about 15 miles southeast of Yen Bai, one of the Phantoms was hit by an SA-2 missile. Both crew ejected and Capt Cordier fell through the fireball of a second SAM that exploded beneath the aircraft. Both men became residents of the Hanoi Hilton until Lane was released on 18 February and Cordier on 4 March 1973. Capt Cordier had been on his second tour in Southeast Asia and had flown a total of 175 missions when he was shot down, whereas 1Lt Lane was only on his 11th mission.

5 December 1966

RF-101C 56-0165   20 TRS, 432 TRW, USAF, Udorn
                   Capt Arthur Leonard Warren (KIA)

A flight of two RF-101Cs was returning from an aborted reconnaissance mission to the Ha Gia POL storage facility when one of the aircraft was shot down two miles north of Yen Bai airfield. Capt Warren had experienced an instrument failure and had handed over the lead to his wingman shortly before his aircraft was hit and caught fire. Capt Warren ejected and was in voice contact with another US aircraft for about two hours. Contact was lost about 20 minutes before a SAR force arrived and nothing more was ever heard of Capt Warren.

F-105D 62-4331   421 TFS, 388 TFW, USAF, Korat
                  Maj Burriss Nelson Begley (KIA)

Maj Begley was flying an F-105D as part of an Iron Hand flight when he became a MiG victim. The F-105 flight was en route to a target at about 10,000 feet when they were attacked by several MiG-17s at the northern edge of Thud Ridge. The Thunderchief was eventually hit in the tail and caught fire, crashing 25 miles southwest of the Ridge. Maj Begley reported that he was losing power and was heading across the Red River in an attempt to reach Laos or Thailand. A few moments later he reported that he was about to eject. The rest of his flight were fighting the MiGs and did not see what happened to Maj Begley but he is not thought to have ejected from the aircraft. In November 1986 the Vietnamese handed over remains they claimed to be of Maj Begley but, as yet, no positive identification had been made.

6 December 1966

RF-4C 65-0819   11 TRS, 432 TRW, USAF, Udorn
                 Lt Col T W Dyke (survived)
                 1Lt W R Fannemel (survived)

Udorn lost its third reconnaissance aircraft in the space of five days on 6 December. A Phantom was en route to a target in the northwest provinces of North Vietnam when it was hit by automatic weapons fire five miles east of Dien Bien Phu. Lt Col Dyke turned the aircraft around and just made it back across the border into Laos before he and his navigator were forced to eject. Both men were eventually rescued by a USAF HH-3.

F-4C   63-7521   559 TFS, 12 TFW, USAF, Cam Ranh Bay
Maj Lee Attilio Greco (KIA)
1Lt John Michael Troyer (KIA)

During a close air support mission over South Vietnam a Phantom was being vectored by a ground control station as it descended through dense cloud when the aircraft hit a mountain in Ninh Thuan province.

7 December 1966

F-5C   65-10520   10 FCS, 3 TFW, USAF, Bien Hoa
Capt Johne Werner Carlson (KIA)

An amazing stroke of bad luck or coincidence saw two F-5s from the 10th FCS shot down within about one hour of each other. Capt Carlson's aircraft was hit by small arms fire as he was bombing VC supply huts and bunkers near Lai Khe, 25 miles north of Saigon. The aircraft dived into the ground and Capt Carlson was not seen to eject.

F-5C   63-8429   10 FCS, 3 TFW, USAF, Bien Hoa
Capt Derald Dean Swift (KIA)

About one hour later and some 20 miles to the west of Lai Khe a second F-5 was shot down. Capt Swift was dropping napalm on a target seven miles southeast of Tay Ninh when his aircraft was hit by small arms fire. He immediately made off towards Bien Hoa but was forced to eject some 10 miles short of the airfield. Unfortunately, his parachute failed to deploy properly and Capt Swift was killed.

8 December 1966

B-57B   52-1590   8 TBS, 405 FW attached to 35 TFW, USAF,
Phan Rang
Maj Leslie R Wilkensen (survived)
Maj W E Schuler (survived)

The B-57 squadrons flew missions the length and breadth of South Vietnam and on the 8th lost an aircraft off the very southern tip of the country. The aircraft was on a close air support mission when it was hit by ground fire near Nam Can. The crew ejected a few miles offshore and was picked up by a Navy ship. This particular B-57B was built in March 1955 and served initially with the 38th TBG at Laon AB in France as part of NATO's 4th Allied Tactical Air Force.

F-100D   56-3063   510 TFS, 3 TFW, USAF, Bien Hoa
Capt Michael Lewis Hyde (KIA)

Another aircraft was lost on a close air support mission in South Vietnam about an hour after the B-57 was shot down. Capt Hyde was dropping napalm on VC troops involved in a firefight 10 miles southeast of Truc Giang in the Mekong Delta when his aircraft was hit by small arms fire. Capt Hyde may have been wounded as he did not eject from the aircraft before it crashed moments later. 56-3063 originally served with the 481st TFS at Cannon AFB.

F-105D   59-1725   354 TFS, 355 TFW, USAF, Takhli
Lt Col Donald Henry Asire (KIA)

A major strike was attempted on the railway and POL store at Phuc Yen on the 8th. Weather precluded a successful attack and the strike was diverted to the secondary target. The lead flight of four F-105s was about 15 miles northwest of Thai Nguyen when it was attacked by several MiG-17s. Lt Col Asire's aircraft was seen to dive into cloud with a MiG in hot pursuit. It was presumed that the MiG shot down the F-105 although Ken Bell in *100 Missions North* claims that Asire was forced down to low-level by the MiGs and lost control of his aircraft and crashed when only one of his wing fuel tanks jettisoned successfully. Don Asire's status was changed from missing to killed in action on 19 September 1973. Lt Col Asire was the CO of the 354th at the time of his loss. His remains were returned to the USA on 21 June 1989.

F-4C   63-7544   480 TFS, 366 TFW, USAF, Da Nang
Maj J K Young (survived)
Capt F H Porter (survived)

The American air bases in South Vietnam may have seemed a safe haven in a largely hostile country but danger was never very far away. This was particularly true of Da Nang, which was a

frequent target for VC activity. A Phantom crew experienced this at first hand on the night of the 8th when their aircraft was hit by small arms fire moments after take off. The aircraft caught fire and the crew ejected just south of the airfield and were picked up by one of the base's HH-43s before the VC could reach them.

O-1C   140081   H&MS-16, MAG-16, USMC, Marble Mountain
2 crew, names unknown (survived)

In addition to the usual transport aircraft, MAG-16's Headquarters and Maintenance Squadron received 10 Bird Dogs in August for visual reconnaissance on behalf of the Group's helicopter squadrons. The O-1 was particularly useful for scouting out potential helicopter landing sites and performing postlanding reconnaissance. During an observation mission one the Squadron's aircraft struck struck trees and crashed.

10 December 1966

F-105D   58-1160   357 TFS, 355 TFW, USAF, Takhli
1 pilot, name unknown (survived)

An F-105 crashed during a test flight near Takhli when its engine failed. The aircraft had a history of engine compressor stalls but the maintenance crews, despite a thorough investigation, could not rectify the fault. As the aircraft took off on its test flight the engine compressor stalled again and the engine fire warning light came on. The pilot ejected and the aircraft crashed just outside the airfield. Apparently, according to Ken Bell, by the time the fire and emergency trucks arrived the crash site had been stripped bare by Thai villagers and the engine, which was urgently needed for investigation, was buried deep in a swamp. For a price, the resourceful Thais were persuaded to dig up the engine and return it to Takhli for investigation.

11 December 1966

F-4C   63-7533   480 TFS, 366 TFW, USAF, Da Nang
Capt Gerald E Woodcock (survived)
1Lt Gerald Oaks Alfred (KIA)

During a night-time road reconnaissance mission near Van Xuan about 15 miles north of the DMZ a Phantom was damaged by ground fire. The aircraft turned east and crossed the coast and the crew ejected 15 miles off the coast near Dong Hoi. The aircraft crashed into the sea close to the destroyer USS *Keppler*, which was on a Sea Dragon patrol on the lookout for North Vietnamese coastal traffic. An aircraft dropped flares in the area as the *Keppler* searched for the crew. Capt Woodcock was rescued by the ship but there was no trace of 1Lt Alfred apart from a brief SAR beeper transmission.

F-100D   55-3787   90 TFS, 3 TFW, USAF, Bien Hoa
Capt A E Belford (survived)

The 3rd TFW lost its fourth aircraft within five days during a close air support mission 35 miles northeast of Bien Hoa. The F-100 was hit by a barrage of automatic weapons fire as it climbed away from a target. Capt Belford flew the aircraft to the west and ejected near Dau Tieng where he was rescued by helicopter.

13 December 1966

F-105D   61-0187   421 TFS, 388 TFW, USAF, Korat
Capt Samuel Edwin Waters (KIA)

An F-105 was returning from a raid on the Yen Vien railway yard and was climbing through about 16,000 feet, 10 miles southwest of Hanoi, when it was badly damaged by an SA-2. Capt Waters managed to fly about 15 miles further east before the aircraft crashed. Capt Waters may have ejected but he apparently did not survive.

A-4C   147776   VA-195, USN, USS *Ticonderoga*
Lt(jg) C O Taylor (survived)

A-4C   147819   VA-195, USN, USS *Ticonderoga*
Lt Cdr Charles Edward Barnett (survived)

Not long after Capt Waters had been shot down a Navy Iron Hand flight of A-4s attacked a SAM site at the Xuan Mai Bridge, 15 miles southwest of Hanoi. This may have been the SAM

battery responsible for the death of Capt Waters. As Lt Taylor fired his rockets and left the target area his aircraft was hit by ground fire. The Skyhawk's fuel consumption increased rapidly indicating a serious fuel leak. Lt Taylor flew out over the Gulf of Tonkin and about 80 miles southeast of Thanh Hoa he rendevouzed with a tanker. Just as he was about to engage the tanker's drogue the Skyhawk's engine flamed out and Lt Taylor had to eject. He was later picked up by a Navy ship.

Another member of the *Ticonderoga*'s Iron Hand flight, Lt Cdr Barnett, attacked the Xuan Mai Bridge SAM site a few minutes after Lt Taylor's aircraft had been hit. An SA-2 exploded directly underneath Lt Cdr Barnett's aircraft and caused damage to the wings, ailerons and the hydraulic system. Reverting to manual back up as the hydraulics failed, Barnett flew the crippled Skyhawk back to the carrier. However, the damage to the ailerons and the low fuel state made it too dangerous to attempt a carrier landing and the pilot ejected and was picked up by one of the ship's helicopters. Sadly, Lt Cdr Barnett was killed on 23 May 1972 when his Corsair was shot down by a SAM over North Vietnam.

14 December 1966

F-8E   149148   VF-194, USN, USS *Ticonderoga*
Lt Michael Thomas Newell (KIA)

A-4E   151068   VA-72, USN, USS *Franklin D Roosevelt*
Lt Claude David Wilson (KIA)

A vehicle depot at Van Dien, five miles west of Hanoi, was the target for a Navy Alpha strike on the 14th. As usual a section of F-8s was assigned to fly a CAP over the target for the duration of the raid. As the Crusaders were flying over the target area at 6,000 feet one of the aircraft was hit by fragments from an SA-2 that exploded nearby. Lt Newell later reported that the aircraft was handling well and headed south, gaining altitude. However, a few minutes later Newell radioed that he had lost his hydraulics and the Crusader was seen to roll and pitch down and dived into the ground 30 miles west of Thanh Hoa from about 17,000 feet. No ejection was seen or radio transmission heard but as Lt Newell had not been injured by the SAM blast it was a mystery why he did not escape.

As part of the Van Diem raid an Iron Hand flight of A-4s were en route to the target area when the leader of the section became separated. After the raid Lt Wilson was seen flying alone at about 5,000 feet when his aircraft was hit by an SA-2, about 10 miles northeast of Thanh Hoa. Despite repeated warnings by his wingman, Wilson's aircraft kept on flying straight and level until it was hit by a second SAM, which blew the aircraft to pieces. Lt Wilson's remains were returned to the USA and positively identified on 23 June 1989.

These two aircraft were the last US aircraft to be shot down by SAMs during 1966. Between July 1965 when the first aircraft was lost, and the end of 1966, 48 US aircraft had been shot down by SAMs. One US report estimated that the North Vietnamese fired approximately 700 missiles during this period. If this figure is accurate then one out of every 14 missiles fired brought down an aircraft. However, the danger from SAMs was not just from the missiles themselves, but also from the fact that aircraft evading SAMs frequently dived from high altitude to low or medium altitudes where they were much more vulnerable to anti-aircraft fire.

F-102A   56-1389   64 FIS, 405 FW on TDY, USAF, Da Nang
Capt D J Seyer (survived)

The threat to aircraft flying from Da Nang was illustrated yet again on the 14th when an F-102, taking off for a routine CAP mission, was hit by small arms fire as it climbed through 1,000 feet. Capt Seyer pointed the burning aircraft out to sea and ejected three miles offshore. He was quickly rescued by a Navy vessel and returned unscathed to Da Nang after a combat mission that had lasted less than a minute of flying time. This was the only F-102 belonging to the 64th FIS to be lost during the war.

F-105D   60-0502   357 TFS, 355 TFW, USAF, Takhli
Capt R B Cooley (survived)

The Takhli Wing returned to the Yen Vien railway yard on the 14th but ran into trouble. As the formation of F-105s was returning and had reached a position about 40 miles southwest of Hanoi, they were intercepted by several MiG-21s. Flying at 7,000 feet Capt Cooley's aircraft was hit by an Atoll air-to-air missile fired by one of the MiGs and started to disintegrate immediately. Cooley ejected as the aircraft literally broke up around him and was surprised to found that he was still holding the aircraft's throttle as he descended by parachute. 'Spade' Cooley had fractured a vertebra and painfully crawled for cover after he had landed on a small hill. Although he was deep in North Vietnam he was very fortunate to be rescued by a USAF HH-3 escorted by four A-1s that put down heavy suppressive fire on groups of North Vietnamese trying to reach the downed pilot. Capt Cooley was flown to the USA for hospitalisation.

A-26A 64-17672 Detachment 1, 603 ACS attached to 606
ACS, 634 CSG, USAF, Nakhon Phanom
Lt Col Albert R Howarth (survived)
1Lt J D Bell (survived)
1 crew, name unknown (survived)

Despite the fact that there were only seven aircraft available by December the A-26 Invader had become well established as a major truck killer on the Ho Chi Minh Trail and its call sign Nimrod was well known in the skies over Laos. Its long endurance, heavy ordnance load and slow speed were useful characteristics for the patient stalking of traffic on the myriad of roads and trails that wound their way through Laos towards South Vietnam. However, its slow speed also made the Invader vulnerable to ground fire, especially as it operated at low level most of the time. Lt Col Howarth's aircraft was hit by automatic weapons fire during a dusk mission near Ban Kapay. One of the aircraft's engines

caught fire but Lt Col Howarth kept the aircraft in the air and managed to fly some 20 miles to the west before the crew were forced to abandon the Invader. All the crew were picked up safely by a USAF helicopter. Lt Col Howarth was awarded the Mackay Trophy for his outstanding airmanship and courage displayed during this mission.

A-1G 52-132605 1 ACS, 14 ACW, USAF, Pleiku
Capt E R Maxson (survived)

The Skyraiders at Pleiku were often called on to provide close air support some distance from their base in the Central Highlands. Capt Maxson was attacking bunkers near Ap Thien, on the coast 50 miles south of Phan Rang, when he was shot down. As he made his fifth pass dropping napalm his aircraft was struck by ground fire and burst into flames. Capt Maxson immediately abandoned the aircraft and was rescued by an Army helicopter.

E-1B 147218 Detachment 42, VAW-12, USN,
USS *Franklin D Roosevelt*
Lt (jg) Gerald Allan Holman (KIA)
Lt Cdr Edwin Lee Koenig (KIA)
Lt (jg) Richard Lynn Mowrey (KIA)
2 crew, names unknown (survived)

The *Franklin D Roosevelt* lost a second aircraft on the 14th when an E-1B Tracer developed engine trouble during an electronic intelligence gathering patrol. Flying on only one engine, the aircraft could not maintain altitude and eventually ditched in the South China Sea. Three of the five crewmen were lost in the incident. The Tracer and the Skyhawk were the final aircraft lost by the *Franklin D Roosevelt* before it left the line on 27 December at the end of its first and only war cruise. The carrier was decommissioned on 1 October 1977 and was scrapped at Kearny, New Jersey, in 1980.

17 December 1966

F-105F 63-8354 354 TFS, 355 TFW , USAF, Takhli
2 crew, names unknown (survived)

During a strike mission a two-seat Thunderchief suffered an engine failure while still over Thailand. The crew ejected and were soon rescued.

20 December 1966

F-4C 64-0698 497 TFS, 8 TFW, USAF, Ubon
1Lt David Anthony Lum (KWF)
1 crew, name unknown (survived)

During a ferry flight a Phantom suffered a control failure and crashed in the sea off Military Region I, killing one of the crew.

21 December 1966

A-4C 148507 VA-144, USN, USS *Kitty Hawk*
Lt(jg) Danny Elloy Glenn (POW)

The USS *Kitty Hawk* returned to Yankee Station on 4 December to start its second tour of the war. On the 20th two of the ship's F-4s shot down a pair of An-2 biplane transport aircraft, the only examples of their type shot down by US aircraft during the entire war. However, on the 21st the *Kitty Hawk* lost its first aircraft of the tour. A Skyhawk was flying a road reconnaissance along Route 1 when it was hit by AAA about 15 miles west of Mu Ron Ma. The undersurface of the fuselage behind the cockpit was engulfed in flames and Lt Glenn ejected when he felt he was losing control of the aircraft. Danny Glenn was captured and spent the next seven years as a POW until released on 4 March 1973.

27 December 1966

A-4C 149641 VA-22, USN, USS *Coral Sea*
1 pilot, name unknown (survived)

A 48-hour Christmas cease fire ended on the morning of the 26th but no more US aircraft were lost in combat during the remainder of the year. However, four aircraft were lost in accidents during this period. As an A-4 was launched from the *Coral Sea* for a test flight, the aircraft's rudder suddenly deflected to the right. The aircraft developed a yaw to starboard that the pilot could not control and the Skyhawk crashed into the sea after the pilot ejected.

F-4C 64-0833 555 TFS, 8 TFW, USAF, Ubon
Lt G D Shepard (survived)
Maj R E Gust (survived)

During a combat air patrol a Phantom had a problem with its fuel transfer system and the aircraft crashed in Thailand when the engines failed through fuel starvation.

28 December 1966

U-6A 51-16565 432 TRW, USAF, Udorn
2 crew, names unknown (survived)

The 432nd TRW lost a Beaver utility aircraft when it suffered an engine failure and crashed in Thailand. There were about 15 Beavers in USAF service in Thailand at this stage of the war and the aircraft was used for liaison and ferry flights.

30 December 1966

O-1G 51-11955 21 TASS, 504 TASG, USAF, Nha Trang
1 pilot, name unknown (survived)

The 504th TASG was activated at Bien Hoa on 8 December to replace the 505th TACG as the supervising organisation for the USAF's FAC squadrons in Southeast Asia. Operational control of the FACs remained vested in the local Army Corps and Divisions. During a visual reconnaissance flight a Bird Dog crashed as a result of pilot error.

An A-4C Skyhawk of VA-144 prepares to be catapulted off the USS *Kitty Hawk* in March 1967. The Skyhawk was the Navy's primary light attack aircraft in the early years of the war and a total of 271 Skyhawks were lost, more than any other Navy type. USN

Chapter Four

1967

Rolling Thunder – The Peak Year

2 January 1967

O-1F   57-2858   23 TASS, 504 TASG, USAF, Nakhon Phanom
1Lt George Bruce Menges (KIA)

The loss of an FAC in southern Laos heralded the start of another year of war. Using the radio call sign Nail, which would become a familiar FAC call sign of the 23rd TASS, 1Lt Menges was shot down by automatic weapons fire near Ban Sappeng and apparently did not survive, although whether he was killed in the crash or on the ground is not known.

On this day the 8th TFW mounted a brilliantly planned and executed fighter sweep near Hanoi, known as Operation Bolo in which seven MiGs were destroyed without loss to the USAF.

4 January 1967

A-4C   150584   VA-22, USN, USS *Coral Sea*
Lt(jg) J M Hays (survived)

F-4B   152974   VF-154, USN, USS *Coral Sea*
Lt Alan M Vanpelt (survived)
Ens R A Morris (survived)

On the 4th, Air Wing 2 from the *Coral Sea* mounted a major strike against a road bridge at Thu Diem on the coast 20 miles south of Haiphong. As one of VA-22's Skyhawks bombed the target it was hit by ground fire causing a fuel leak. A wingman reported to Lt Hays that his aircraft was on fire and soon afterwards the Skyhawk's hydraulic system failed and Lt Hays had to revert to the manual back up system. Soon after crossing the coast the aircraft started to burn furiously, the engine flamed out and the flying controls froze. About 20 miles off the coast Lt Hays ejected and was picked up safely by a Navy SAR helicopter.

About 90 minutes after the first strike another wave of aircraft from the *Coral Sea* attacked the Thu Diem Bridge. This wave included Phantoms dropping Mk82 bombs and just as Lt Vanpelt had dropped six bombs in a shallow dive, his cockpit lit up with fire warning lights and his port engine was seen to be on fire. The fire spread rapidly and a wingman reported pieces of the aircraft falling off. A few miles out to sea both crew ejected and were picked up by a Navy helicopter. As no AAA had been observed during the attack on the bridge it was assumed that these two aircraft were the victims of chance hits by small arms fire or automatic weapons.

C-123B 56-4372   19 ACS, 315 ACW, USAF, Tan Son Nhut
5 crew, names unknown (survived)

A C-123 Provider was destroyed in a landing accident within South Vietnam

5 January 1967

A-4E   151136   VA-192, USN, USS *Ticonderoga*
Lt Cdr Richard Allen Stratton (POW)

A flight of A-4s from the *Ticonderoga* was sent on a mission to destroy a ferry at My Trach, 10 miles south of Thanh Hoa. Unable to spot the ferry the Skyhawks attacked four barges, which were moored nearby. Lt Cdr Stratton fired one LAU-3 pod of rockets and then came round for another attack. As he fired his next pod, debris from one of the rockets was sucked through the aircraft's air intakes and into the engine. The pieces of rocket destroyed the engine, which exploded, blowing the aircraft's tail off. Although he had tried to reach the sea the sequence of events happened too quickly and Dick Stratton ejected over land and parachuted into a tree near a village and was captured. Lt Cdr Stratton was

VA-192's maintenance officer and was flying his 27th mission over North Vietnam when he was brought down. In March 1967 he was severely tortured until he agreed to write a confession for the North Vietnamese. He was released on 4 March 1973 and after retirement from the Navy became a social worker specialising in drug abuse counselling. In 1978 Scott Blakey wrote *Prisoner at War: The Survival of Commander Richard A Stratton*, which is probably the most perceptive of all the books on the POW experience.

6 January 1967

A-4E   150036   VMA-121, MAG-12, USMC, Chu Lai
Capt M F Adams (survived)

A Marine Corps A-4 was lost during an air strike on enemy troops near Ha Tan, 20 miles southwest of Da Nang. Capt Adams was diving on the target when his aircraft was hit in the starboard fuselage by small arms fire. He managed to fly a few miles to the north before ejecting and was picked up by a Marine Corps helicopter.

RF-4C 64-1078   11 TRS, 432 TRW, USAF, Udorn
Capt W J Groves (survived)
1Lt L N Martin (survived)

1967 was the year that saw the balance of the reconnaissance effort over North Vietnam change from the RF-101C to the RF-4C. The Phantom may have been a more capable aircraft than the older Voodoo, but aerial reconnaissance was still a dangerous game and January proved to be an expensive month for the Udorn squadrons. Capt Groves and 1Lt Martin were on a mission to photograph a railway bridge near Bao Ha on the main western line to China, about 40 miles northwest of Yen Bai. As the aircraft was completing its photo run it was struck by AAA and caught fire. The aircraft headed south and actually crossed into Thailand before the fire forced the crew to eject.

F-8E   149184   VF-191, USN, USS *Ticonderoga*
Lt Cdr Richard Dean Mullen (POW)

The North Vietnamese always used their geography to good advantage and many of the country's extensive caves were put to use as storage sites. Occasionally attacks were mounted against caves where it was hoped that they could be sealed by destroying the cave mouth. One such cave was at Ba Lang on the coast near Hoang Xa, 25 miles south of Thanh Hoa. Lt Cdr Mullen was making his second attack with rockets when his F-8 was hit by AAA and caught fire. The aircraft started to disintegrate immediately and the pilot ejected safely. He was seen on the ground waving to aircraft that overflew his position and radioed his wingman that he was unharmed. However, before a rescue helicopter could reach the area, Lt Cdr Mullen was captured and spent the next six years in four different prison camps before being released on 4 March 1973. Known as 'Moon', Lt Cdr Mullen was on his 31st mission over North Vietnam when he was shot down.

8/9 January 1967

AC-47D 43-49124   4 ACS, 14 ACW, USAF, Nha Trang
detached to Da Nang
Capt Charles William Robertson (KIA)
1Lt James Donald Goodman (KIA)
Maj Joseph E Wilkinson (KIA)
SSgt Raymond Medina (KIA)
SSgt Cecil Truman Thompson (KIA)
A1C Dana Richard Kelley (KIA)
A2C Lonny Leroy Mitzel (KIA)

The Spooky gunship was one of the most important assets for defence of friendly troops and villages at night. However, it was slow and relatively easy to track as it left a circular wake of tracer as it orbited the target and so it was vulnerable. On the night of the 8th a gunship was assigned a target near Duc Pho close to the coast, about 20 miles south of Quang Ngai. As it approached the target the AC-47 was hit in the mid-fuselage by automatic weapons fire. Burning furiously, the aircraft quickly became uncontrollable and crashed near the target killing the crew.

10 January 1967

F-105D 62-4265   34 TFS, 388 TFW, USAF, Korat
Capt James Paul Gauley (KIA)

When not occupied over North Vietnam the F-105 squadrons flew strikes in the Barrel Roll campaign in northern Laos. Capt Gauley was flying as part of a formation of aircraft bombing a supply depot 10 miles northwest of Muong Nham. His aircraft was hit by ground fire and he ejected close by. However, when a USAF rescue helicopter arrived and dropped a pararescueman, it was discovered that Capt Gauley's parachute had failed to open properly and he had been killed.

12 January 1967

F-104C 57-0910   435 TFS, 8 TFW, USAF, Udorn
1 pilot, name unknown (survived)

At the end of a CAP mission a Starfighter crashed during landing at Udorn.

13 January 1967

F-100D 56-3448   352 TFS, 35 TFW, USAF, Phan Rang
Capt Morvan Darrell Turley (KIA)

A VC supply area on the coast 25 miles northwest of Vung Tau was the target for a flight of F-100s from Phan Rang on the 13th. Capt Turley dropped his load of napalm just as his aircraft was hit by small arms fire. The aircraft caught fire and crashed a few miles from the target killing Capt Turley.

A-4E   151158   VA-23, USN, USS *Coral Sea*
Lt(jg) Michael Paul Cronin (POW)

A section of two Skyhawks from the *Coral Sea* found several railway wagons on a siding at Vin Loc, 30 miles south of Thanh Hoa. As the aircraft were running in at 4,000 feet to drop their Mk82 bombs, they suddenly ran into a barrage of AAA. Lt Cronin's aircraft was hit in the centre fuselage section and burst into flames. The flames quickly burned through the aircraft's aluminium structure and the Skyhawk broke up into two major sections. Lt Cronin was pinned against the side of the cockpit by G forces as the aircraft broke up but eventually succeeded in ejecting over the sea. However, at this point his good luck deserted him as he was blown back over land by a strong onshore wind. Lt Cronin was soon captured and imprisoned. Released on 4 March 1973 he eventually retired from the Navy as a Captain. Prior to his tour on the *Coral Sea* he had flown his first tour in Southeast Asia in 1965 with VA-23 on board the USS *Midway*.

14 January 1967

A-4E   150106   VMA-121, MAG-12, USMC, Chu Lai
Capt C R Fye (survived)

A second Skyhawk was lost near Ha Tan within eight days when Capt Fye was shot down. As the aircraft was overflying a target at

F-102 Delta Daggers were among the first US jet aircraft to be deployed to Southeast Asia serving primarily in the air defence role from bases in South Vietnam and Thailand. This two-seat TF-102A of the 509th FIS crashed on 15 January 1967 during a ferry flight. USAF

2,500 feet it was hit by ground fire that caused the starboard wing to burn. Capt Fye ejected close to the target and was picked up by a Marine Corps helicopter.

A-4C 145087 VA-56, USN, USS *Enterprise*
Lt Cdr Arthur Kasimi Tyszkiewicz (KIA)

A-4C 147724 VA-56, USN, USS *Enterprise*
1 pilot, name unknown (survived)

The USS *Enterprise* returned off the coast of Vietnam on 18 December 1966 to commence its second cruise of the war. The ship had been conducting operations safely for almost a month before it lost its first aircraft of the cruise. During a night combat mission over Laos the wingman of a section of Skyhawks overran his leader and collided. Both aircraft crashed but only one pilot survived.

15 January 1967

F-105D 60-0440 333 TFS, 355 TFW, USAF, Takhli
Capt G L Hawkins (survived)

The second Thunderchief to be lost on a Barrel Roll mission in Laos in January was damaged during an attack on storage buildings near Na Ham on the Laotian/North Vietnamese border. As Capt Hawkins pulled up from his first run the aircraft was hit in the starboard wing by small arms fire. The F-105 remained controllable as Capt Hawkins flew back across Laos and crossed into Thailand but he had to eject near the village of Ban Tum.

A-4E 151168 VA-23, USN, USS *Coral Sea*
Lt(jg) Daniel Hagan Moran (KIA)

During a strike on railway sidings at Qui Vinh about 10 miles southwest of Van Yen, one of VA-23's A-4s was hit and damaged by AAA. A wingman saw that Lt Moran's aircraft had a large hole in the starboard nose under the cockpit. Lt Moran was seen to move in his cockpit but he made no reply to radio or hand signals. Accompanied by another A-4, Lt Moran flew out to sea on an erratic course with the aircraft rolling and pitching continuously. Lt Moran must have been conscious at this time as he ejected close to a SAR destroyer but he was found to be dead when he was pulled out of the water. He had probably been mortally wounded by the explosion of a 37 or 57mm anti-aircraft shell. This was the last aircraft lost by the *Coral Sea* before it departed at the end of the month at the completion of its second tour. The ship had spent a total of 109 days on the line and had lost 16 aircraft in combat and another three in accidents during that time.

A-4E 151093 VMA-211, MAG-12, USMC, Chu Lai
1 pilot, name unknown (survived)

As a Marine Corps A-4 was taking off from Chu Lai on a combat mission one of its undercarriage legs sheared off and the aircraft slid to a halt. The pilot exited the aircraft safely but the Skyhawk was damaged beyond repair.

TF-102A 55-4036 509 FIS, 405 FW, USAF, Don Muang
2 crew, names unknown (survived)

A Delta Dagger caught fire over Thailand during a ferry flight. The aircraft crashed but the crew escaped and were rescued safely. The cause of the fire was accidental rather than due to enemy action. This was the only two-seat TF-102A variant of the Delta Dagger to be lost in Southeast Asia and had previously been operated by the California ANG.

16 January 1967

RF-4C 65-0818 11 TRS, 432 TRW, USAF, Udorn
Capt Thomas Gordon Storey (POW)
1Lt Ronald Lambert Mastin (POW)

The 16th turned out to be a bad day for the 11th TRS. Several aircraft were despatched on independent missions to various parts of North Vietnam to obtain photographs of past and potential targets. Capt Storey's aircraft was hit by AAA 25 miles north of Kep and the crew had to eject immediately. Both men had flown 34 missions together since their arrival at Udorn in October 1966 and both were captured and eventually released on 4 March 1973.

RF-4C 65-0883 11 TRS, 432 TRW, USAF, Udorn
Capt Robert John Welch (KIA)
1Lt Michael Scott Kerr (POW)

A second Phantom had been sent out to photograph a railway yard at Viet Tri, which had been bombed recently. Suddenly the aircraft was rocked by a nearby explosion from an SA-2 and the Phantom pitched up out of control. 1Lt Kerr blacked out momentarily and could not reach the ejection seat handle above his head due to excessive G forces. He eventually pulled the lower handle and ejected safely and watched the aircraft dive into the side of a mountain near the Song Lo River, 35 miles northwest of Hanoi. He did not see Capt Welch escape and presumed he was injured during the incident and could not eject. Michael Kerr was captured and released on 4 March 1973. The crew were on their 29th mission over North Vietnam when they were lost.

F-104C 57-0914 435 TFS, 8 TFW, USAF, Udorn
1 pilot, name unknown (survived)

The 435th TFS lost a Starfighter during a CAP mission when it suffered engine failure and crashed in Thailand.

17 January 1967

O-1F 57-2789 23 TASS, 504 TASG, USAF, Nakhon Phanom
1Lt Alva Ray Krogman (KIA)

A Nail FAC was lost as it was controlling a strike against a gun site near Ban Muang Angkhan in southern Laos, west of the DMZ. The aircraft was shot down by 37mm AAA and crashed a few miles away near Ban Loumpoum, killing the pilot.

T-28D 49-1604 606 ACS, 634 CSG, USAF, Nakhon Phanom
Capt William Keith Cogdell (KIA)

A SAR mission was launched as soon as Lt Krogman's aircraft went down in the hope that he had survived the crash of his Bird Dog. One of the escorting aircraft was a T-28D from the 606th ACS. As Capt Cogdell approached the crash site near Ban Loumpoum his aircraft was hit in the starboard wing by AAA and rolled into the ground. Two days later the USAF received confirmation of Capt Cogdell's death, probably from either friendly Laotians or from Special Forces that were sometimes used on particularly hazardous rescue missions. William Cogdell's remains were returned to the USA and positively identified on 24 May 1994. The 606th ACS operated a mixed bag of aircraft at this time including A-26As, T-28Ds, U-10s and UH-1 helicopters.

RF-4C 65-0888 11 TRS, 432 TRW, USAF, Udorn
Maj Gary Gene Wright (KIA)
1Lt Frederick Joseph Wozniak (KIA)

For the fourth time in January an RF-4C failed to return to Udorn. Maj Wright and 1Lt Wozniak were tasked with photographing a target about 15 miles southwest of Hanoi and may have been shot down in the target area. The loss of four aircraft and three crews within the space of 11 days must have had a devastating effect on the morale of the Squadron. Maj Wright was a veteran of the Korean War, having flown F-86 Sabres in that conflict.

18 January 1967

A-1H 139748 VA-52, USN, USS *Ticonderoga*
Lt(jg) Marlow Erling Madsen (KIA)

The *Ticonderoga* lost a Skyraider while operating from Yankee Station in the Gulf of Tonkin about 75 miles off Dong Hoi. The aircraft was returning from a combat mission but was unable to slow its approach speed sufficiently for a safe landing and was waved off by the LSO. The aircraft stalled as it attempted to climb away and the Skyraider plunged into the sea killing the pilot.

19 January 1967

A-6A 151590 VA-85, USN, USS *Kitty Hawk*
Cdr Allen Colby Brady (POW)
Lt Cdr William P Yarbrough (KIA)

Instead of employing its excellent night and all-weather capability, the Intruder was still being used in the daylight attack role resulting in the unnecessary loss of expensive aircraft and experienced aircrew. Cdr Brady, VA-85's executive officer, was leading a flight of Intruders against the Dong Phong Thuong bridge complex 10 miles north of Thanh Hoa when he ran into trouble. He had just released 22 Mk82 bombs and was pulling up when the aircraft was struck by AAA. The aircraft exploded immediately and the tail broke away. The remains of the aircraft tumbled end over end as both crew ejected from the wreck. Cdr Brady landed safely but Lt Cdr Yarbrough's parachute did not deploy properly and he fell to his death. Cdr Brady was released on 4 March 1973 but it was not until 14 August 1985 that William Yarbrough's remains were returned to the USA.

F-4C 64-0845 390 TFS, 366 TFW, USAF, Da Nang
Capt Julius Skinner Jayroe (POW)
1Lt Galand Dwight Kramer (POW)

Such were the losses suffered by the unarmed reconnaissance aircraft over North Vietnam that many of their missions were now escorted by flights of fighters. Four Phantoms from Da Nang rendezvoused with two Voodoos from Udorn for a mission to Kep where the pilot of the lead Voodoo, 20th TRS's commander Lt Col John Bull Stirling, would take photographs of the MiG base. The North Vietnamese reacted strongly and Stirling's wingman counted about 18 SAMs fired in the vicinity of the target. As the Voodoos swept over the airfield the Phantoms were orbiting at 14,000 feet about 12 miles to southwest. One of the aircraft, flown by Capt Jayroe and 1Lt Kramer, was hit by either 85mm AAA or

a SAM. Jayroe tried to make for the coast but he did not get very far as his aircraft became uncontrollable and the crew were forced to eject about 5 miles east of Bac Ninh only minutes after being hit. Both men were taken prisoner, a particularly bitter blow for Capt Jayroe as he was on his 100th and final mission before being due to rotate back to the USA. 'Jay' Jayroe had spent the first five years of his Air Force career as an enlisted man before completing flight school and being commissioned in 1955. He had spent several years as an instructor pilot and had flown tours on the F-101 and F-4C at Woodbridge, UK. Lt Kramer was released on 12 February and Capt Jayroe on 4 March 1973.

F-4B   153029   VF-114, USN, USS *Kitty Hawk*
                  Lt Cdr Donald Roberts Ashby (KIA)
                  Lt(jg) Dennis Michael Ehrlich (KIA)
As the *Kitty Hawk* catapulted a Phantom off its deck on a CAP mission, one of the aircraft's engines failed and the aircraft settled into the sea. Tragically both crew were killed in the accident.

20 January 1967

O-1G   51-4851   21 TASS, 504 TASG, USAF, Nha Trang
                   detached to Pleiku
                   1Lt Arthur J Abramoff (KIA)
                   1Lt G D Hull (survived)
An O-1 from Pleiku was shot down during an FAC mission in the Central Highlands with the loss of its pilot. The aircraft was controlling a strike on enemy troops 20 miles north of Dak To when it was hit by small arms fire. 1Lt Abramoff succeeded in flying the Bird Dog out of the target area but the aircraft crashed killing him and injuring the observer.

A-4C   145144   VA-112, USN, USS *Kitty Hawk*
                  Lt(jg) Jerry Franks Hogan (KIA)
During a night armed reconnaissance mission a section of A-4s found several barges on a river near Hoang Xa, 10 miles south of Thanh Hoa. The Skyhawks overflew the barges to drop flares to illuminate the target. Lt Hogan dived at the barges and dropped his bombs but the wingman then saw another flash followed by a fire on the ground. It was assumed that Lt Hogan had struck the ground having misjudged the distance required to pull out of his dive due to the uneven light of the flares.

21 January 1967

F-105D   62-4239   354 TFS, 355 TFW, USAF, Takhli
                     Lt Col Eugene Ogden Conley (KIA)
Lt Col Conley, the CO of the 354th TFS, was the mission commander for a raid on the Thai Nguyen railway yard when he was shot down. He was leading Waco flight, which was the flak suppression flight, and the weather was poor and the defences around Thai Nguyen were always very heavy. As his aircraft approached the target at 11,000 feet and 450 knots it was hit by an SA-2 and dived into the ground without any apparent attempt by the pilot to eject. It is probable that Lt Col Conley had been injured by fragments from the SAM explosion and was unable to escape. Gene Conley, who was on his third flying tour in Southeast Asia, was the second CO of the 354th TFS to be lost in less than two months following Lt Col Don Asire who had been killed on 8 December.

B-57B   52-1557   13 TBS, 405 FW attached to 35 TFW,
                    USAF, Phan Rang
                    Capt George Grady Cooper (KIA)
                    Maj George Lowe (KIA)
The risks involved in making multiple passes on the same target were once more illustrated on the 21st when a B-57 was lost while attacking a bridge 11 miles west of Kontum. Capt Cooper was on his fifth pass dropping napalm on the target when his aircraft was hit by ground fire in the port wing. Neither of the crew was observed to escape from the aircraft before it hit the ground.

F-4C   64-0810   480 TFS, 366 TFW, USAF, Da Nang
                   Capt William Joseph Baugh (POW)
                   1Lt Donald Ray Spoon (POW)

F-105D   58-1156   421 TFS, 388 TFW, USAF, Korat
                     Capt W R Wyatt (survived)
A large raid on railway targets around Kep was protected, as usual, by a flight of F-4s on MiGCAP duties. Capt Baugh's aircraft flying at 10,000 feet was safe from most flak but the North Vietnamese were introducing more 85mm and 100mm guns, which had a higher effective ceiling. The Phantom was hit by one of the large calibre shells about five miles north of Kep and flew on for about 10 miles before the crew were forced to part company with their aircraft. Capt Baugh suffered a compressed vertebra, a broken jaw and cheek bone and was blinded in one eye during the ejection. Both men were captured and both were released on 4 March 1973. Capt Baugh had flown 50 missions (25 in the North and 25 in the South) and 1Lt Spoon had flown 38 missions when they were shot down. Since retirement William Baugh became involved with a Vietnam POW organisation called NAM-POWs.

The strike on the rail targets around Kep also resulted in the loss of one of the F-105 bomber force. Capt Wyatt was approaching the target area at 12,500 feet when his aircraft was also hit by a large calibre anti-aircraft shell. However, the aircraft remained in one piece and Capt Wyatt was able to cross the coast and fly 50 miles out to sea before ejecting. He received major injuries during the ejection but was rescued by a Navy helicopter. This aircraft had been flown by Maj Fred Tracy on 29 June 1966 when he shot down a MiG-17.

23 January 1967

F-4C   64-0773   497 TFS, 8 TFW, USAF, Ubon
                   1Lt Barry Burton Bridger (POW)
                   1Lt David Fletcher Gray (POW)
The SA-2 claimed another victim on the 23rd when a Phantom on a MiGCAP mission was brought down. The F-4 flight was approaching Son Tay, 15 miles northwest of Hanoi, at 14,000 feet when 1Lt Bridger's aircraft was hit by a SAM. The aircraft broke up immediately and the crew were fortunate to escape from the fireball as the aircraft tumbled out of the sky. Both crew were captured and spent the next six years as POWs until their release on 4 March 1973. It was not until 1970 that the airmen's families learned that they had survived being shot down and were POWs. 1Lt Bridger was an experienced combat pilot with 52 previous missions under his belt but 1Lt Gray was a new addition to the Squadron and was only on his second mission over North Vietnam. Since his retirement from the Air Force in 1993, David Gray has been involved in the NAM-POWs organisation and the National League of POW/MIA Families.

25 January 1967

O-1F   55-4730   19 TASS, 504 TASG, USAF, Bien Hoa
                   Maj Wilbur Thomas Stair (KIA)
                   1 crew, name unknown (survived)
During a visual reconnaissance mission in South Vietnam an O-1 collided in mid-air with another aircraft near Bien Hoa and crashed, killing one of the occupants.

26 January 1967

F-100D   55-2911   612 TFS, 35 TFW, USAF, Phan Rang
                     Capt Thomas Raymond Morgan (KIA)
Capt Morgan was taking part in an attack on VC buildings in the hills 30 miles west of Nha Trang when his aircraft was seen to be trailing smoke as it pulled off the target. The aircraft then burst into flames and broke in half before the pilot could escape. Attempts to find Capt Morgan's remains in 1967 and 1968 were unsuccessful but in 1994 a joint US/Vietnamese recovery team excavated the crash site and discovered human remains and recovered personal effects that had been scavenged by a local villager. Mitochondrial testing of the remains was performed at the US Army's Central Identification Laboratory in Hawaii and on 28 July 1997 it was announced that the mortal remains of Thomas Morgan had at last been found and identified. The serial number of this F-100D is also quoted for an aircraft that was shot down on 6 April 1968.

F-100D   55-3541   531 TFS, 3 TFW, USAF, Bien Hoa
                     Maj J C Nabors (KIA)
A second F-100 was lost in South Vietnam on the 26th. A flight of aircraft from Bien Hoa was attacking a VC base camp that had been discovered near Lai Khe, 20 miles north of Saigon. The aircraft was apparently hit by ground fire and dived into the ground close to the target. Maj Nabors may have been wounded, as he did not eject from the aircraft.

A-1E   52-132419   602 ACS, 14 ACW, USAF, Udorn
                     1 pilot, name unknown (survived)
A Skyraider crashed in Thailand due to an accidental control failure.

27 January 1967

F-4C   63-7709   480 TFS, 366 TFW, USAF, Da Nang
                   Maj J A Hargrove (survived)
                   1Lt L D Peterson (survived)
A flight of Phantoms from Da Nang crossed the DMZ on an armed reconnaissance mission and flew along the coast on the look out for North Vietnamese junks and barges that were used to transport supplies to the south. About 12 miles north of the DMZ Maj Hargrove's aircraft was hit in the starboard wing by fire from automatic weapons. He turned the aircraft out to sea and he and his WSO ejected about four miles off the coast and were picked up by a USAF helicopter.

28 January 1967

F-104C   56-0921   435 TFS, 8 TFW, USAF, Udorn
                     1 pilot, name unknown (survived)
The 435th TFS lost its third F-104 during the month when an aircraft suffered an engine failure over Thailand while on a combat air patrol mission.

29 January 1967

F-105F   62-4420   354 TFS, 355 TFW, USAF, Takhli
                     Maj Larry William Biediger (KIA)
                     1Lt Claude Arnold Silva (KIA)
The Wild Weasel community had not lost an aircraft since November but their run of good luck came to an end on 29 January. The Thai Nguyen railway yards were once more the target for a raid by the Takhli Wing. Only one aircraft was lost during the raid, a two-seat F-105F from the Iron Hand flight. According to Ken Bell in his book *100 Missions North*, the aircraft was lost as it jettisoned its fuel tanks, one of which hit the tailplane and knocked it off. The aircraft crashed near the northern extremity of Thud Ridge, about 30 miles northwest of Thai Nguyen and, although two chutes were reported, neither of the crew survived.

30 January 1967

F-105D   59-1768   469 TFS, 388 TFW, USAF, Korat
                     Maj W E Thurman (survived)
Enemy territory in southern Laos extended in some places right up to the border with Thailand. A flight of F-105s was tasked with bombing a choke point on a road near the border, only 10 miles north of Nakhon Phanom. Maj Thurman was pulling up off the target when his aircraft was hit by ground fire. He headed west back towards Korat but was forced to eject about 35 miles southeast of Udorn when the aircraft caught fire.

31 January 1967

UC-123B   54-0611   12 ACS, 315 ACW, USAF, Bien Hoa
                      detached to Da Nang
                      Capt Roy Robert Kubley (KIA)
                      Maj Lloyd Francis Walker (KIA)
                      Capt Harvey Mulhauser (KIA)
                      Lt Howard Leroy Barden (KIA)
                      A1C Ronald Kazuo Miyazaki (KIA)
Although the Ranch Hand defoliation operation was only supposed to be confined to South Vietnam, the unit also flew missions in southern Laos in an attempt to defoliate sections of the

Ho Chi Minh Trail. Three Ranch Hand aircraft based at Da Nang were despatched on a mission to spray in a mountain pass five miles southwest of Sepone. The formation made three spray runs through the shallow pass and were escorted by a flight of A-1s from Pleiku. As the lead aircraft turned for the fourth run it was seen to roll inverted and crash into the jungle, exploding on impact. The aircraft was presumed to have been shot down by ground fire as the last aircraft in the flight had an engine put out of action by a single bullet and was only recovered safely to Khe Sanh by the great skill of its crew as the propeller would not feather. Capt Kubley was on his 500th mission in Southeast Asia when he was killed. These were the first fatalities suffered by the Ranch Hand unit since 1962. In February the Ranch Hand detachment started to fly its first missions over the DMZ.

4 February 1967

EB-66C 55-0387   41 TRS, 432 TRW, USAF, Takhli
                     Capt John Fer (POW)
                     Maj Jack Williamson Bomar (POW)
                     Maj Woodrow Hoover Wilburn (KIA)
                     Capt Herb Doby (KIA)
                     Capt Russell Arden Poor (KIA)
                     1Lt John Owen Davies (POW)

As usual during a Rolling Thunder strike, an EB-66 was orbiting over North Vietnam to identify and jam enemy radars and provide warning of electronic threats to the strike force. As Capt Fer's aircraft was flying at 30,000 feet near Bac Kan, 30 miles north of Thai Nguyen, it was hit in the belly by an SA-2 missile. At least three of the crew ejected from the blazing wreck and were captured. In 1977 the Vietnamese returned remains that were identified on 30 September as being those of Capt Doby. On 3 January 1990 it was announced that the remains of Maj Wilburn had been handed over and identified, leaving only Capt Poor unaccounted for. 1Lt Davies was released from imprisonment on 18 February while Capt Fer and Maj Bomar were released on 4 March 1973.

F-4B 153007   VF-213, USN, USS Kitty Hawk
                     Lt Donald Earl Thompson (KIA)
                     Lt Allan Philip Collamore (KIA)

On a very dark and hazy moonless night a pair of Phantoms were flying a coastal reconnaissance flight when one of the crew spotted truck lights on a road near Long Chau, 30 miles northeast of Thanh Hoa. The leading aircraft dropped flares but they failed to ignite and a minute later the leader saw a huge flash on the ground, which was presumed to be Lt Thompson's aircraft crashing and exploding. There was no sign of any anti-aircraft fire so it was assumed that Lt Thompson had become disorientated over an unlit terrain on a dark night and flew into the ground.

6 February 1967

O-1F 57-2807   23 TASS, 504 TASG, USAF, Nakhon Phanom
                     Capt Lucius Lamar Heiskell (KIA)

The slow and vulnerable little Bird Dog FAC aircraft rarely crossed into North Vietnam except in areas that were thought to be relatively free of AAA. Capt Heiskell took off from Nakhon Phanom with another Bird Dog and flew to the eastern border of Laos on a visual reconnaissance mission. The two aircraft crossed into North Vietnam but came under heavy fire from automatic weapons or 57mm anti-aircraft guns. Capt Heiskell's aircraft was hit in the rear fuselage and crashed near the Mu Gia Pass in the Annamite mountains, some 60 miles east of Nakhon Phanom. The other Bird Dog pilot saw Capt Heiskell bail out of his aircraft and land safely. However, when he reached the ground he radioed that he was surrounded by enemy troops and that a rescue was not feasible at that time. Later in the day an HH-3E (65-12779 flown by Maj P H Wood and his crew from the 37th ARRS from Da Nang) flew two sorties to locate Capt Heiskell. On the second sortie the pararescueman, A2C Duane Hackney, spent some time on the ground searching for Capt Heiskell and eventually located him. Tragically, just as the heli-

copter was leaving the area with the survivor on board it was hit by 37mm ground fire, exploded and crashed on top of a 900 metre karst ridge. Capt Heiskell and all the crew including Maj Wood, Capt R A Kibbey and SSgt D J Hall, with the exception of the pararescueman, A2C Hackney, were killed in the crash. Hackney strapped a parachute onto Capt Heiskell and saw him out of the helicopter and then jumped himself. Unfortunately, Capt Heiskell did not survive the attempted escape but Duane Hackney was more fortunate in that, although he did not have time to buckle his parachute before jumping, he survived and was back in action just days later. Hackney was picked up by another helicopter and was the first living enlisted recipient of the AFC and became one of the most decorated airmen of the war. He retired as a Chief Master Sergeant but died of a heart attack in September 1993.

8 February 1967

RF-101C 56-0203   Detachment 1, 45 TRS, 460 TRW, USAF, Tan Son Nhut
                     Capt J H Rogers (survived)

Capt Rogers was flying a coastal reconnaissance mission and was returning down the coast of North Vietnam. As he reached a point about 10 miles north of Dong Hoi his Voodoo ran into a hail of AAA. With the aircraft burning furiously Capt Rogers pointed it further out to sea and ejected about eight miles from the coast. A Navy ship later rescued him.

11 February 1967

F-8E 149192   VF-51, USN, USS Hancock
                     Lt(jg) T F Carrier (survived)

The Hancock arrived back on the line on 5 February for its third war cruise off Vietnam. For this cruise the ship had embarked Air Wing 5 instead of Air Wing 21, which it usually hosted. The first loss of the new tour took place just six days after operations commenced. During a night landing upon return from a CAP mission a Crusader struck the carrier's ramp and the aircraft's landing gear was sheared off. The pilot was lucky to survive as ramp strikes often had much more serious consequences.

12 February 1967

F-100D 56-3925   510 TFS, 3 TFW, USAF, Bien Hoa
                     1Lt Peter Joel Yeingst (KIA)

Mid-February saw a sudden increase in the attrition of F-100s in Laos and South Vietnam. The first aircraft to be brought down was lost while dropping napalm on a VC base camp about 14 miles north of Vung Tau. 1Lt Yeingst had come in low to make his second pass when his aircraft was hit by ground fire and crashed. The pilot may have been wounded, as he did not eject from the aircraft.

F-100D 56-3451   306 TFS, 31 TFW, USAF, Tuy Hoa
                     Capt Courtney Edward Weissmueller (KIA)

A second F-100 was lost on the same day when a formation of aircraft attacked river traffic near Muang Fangdeng, at the very southern tip of Laos. As Capt Weissmueller prepared to drop napalm, his aircraft was struck by ground fire and crashed. Again the pilot did not escape, possibly due to being wounded. The 31st TFW had arrived at Tuy Hoa from Homestead AFB on 16 December 1966 with the 306th, 308th and 309th Tactical Fighter Squadrons, all equipped with the F-100D. Capt Weissmueller's aircraft was the first lost by the Wing during its service in Southeast Asia.

RA-5C 151623   RVAH-7, USN, USS Enterprise
                     Cdr C H Jarvis (survived)
                     Lt(jg) P M Artlip (survived)

The Enterprise lost two aircraft on the 12th, its first combat losses during its second cruise. An RA-5C and its Phantom escort were flying at 500 feet and 560 knots just off the coast near Long Chau, 30 miles northeast of Thanh Hoa, when they ran into a heavy barrage of anti-aircraft fire. The Vigilante was hit in the starboard wing and soon became uncontrollable forcing the

crew to eject just offshore. A large SAR operation swung into action involving an E-2A, two SH-3s, four F-4Bs, four A-1Hs and a USAF HU-16 Albatross as well a Navy destroyer. Cdr Jarvis was rescued by the Albatross amphibian flown by Lt Col A R Vette, commander of the 37th ARRS, while Lt Artlip was picked up by a Navy SAR helicopter. During the rescue an orbiting F-4B fired a Sparrow air-to-air missile at a North Vietnamese patrol boat that attempted to capture the downed airmen. It was unclear if the missile actually hit the boat but the vessel turned away and made for home.

F-4B 152219   VF-96, USN, USS Enterprise
                     Lt Cdr Martin Joseph Sullivan (KWF)
                     Lt(jg) Paul Victor Carlson (KWF)

During an interception training mission over the Gulf of Tonkin a Phantom flew into the sea. Lt Cdr Sullivan was practising interceptions on his leader but during the third engagement Sullivan's aircraft descended into cloud before it could complete a recovery. The crew did not report any problems and did not eject from the aircraft, which led investigators to suspect that the crash was due to spatial disorientation after entering cloud during a dive. The Enterprise was joined by the USS Bennington and the USS Bauer in the search for the crew but all that was found was an oil slick and a small amount of debris.

14 February 1967

A-1H 139805   VA-115, USN, USS Hancock
                     Lt Robert Clarence Marvin (KIA)

An A-1 from the Hancock was lost in the Gulf of Tonkin soon after it took off on a RESCAP mission. Lt Marvin reported that he was losing oil pressure and he and his wingman turned back towards the carrier. During the return journey the engine failed and the wingman lost sight of Lt Marvin's aircraft. It was assumed that the Skyraider had ditched about 25 miles east of Mu Ron Ma but a search revealed no sign of any wreckage or the pilot. Bob Marvin had flown 111 missions during a previous tour off Vietnam in the USS Kitty Hawk.

15 February 1967

F-100D 55-3714   309 TFS, 31 TFW, USAF, Tuy Hoa
                     1Lt W H Hepler (survived)

Operation Junction City was a major offensive in War Zone C to the northwest of Saigon planned to commence on 22 February. In preparation for the offensive, several smaller-scale operations were mounted to get US troops into position. One of the smaller operations was named Tucson and involved the 1st Infantry Division pressing north towards Katum from the 14th to the 18th. On the second day of Operation Tucson a formation of F-100s attacked a target 10 miles northeast of Dau Tieng. 1Lt Hepler's aircraft was hit by ground fire as it dived on the target but the aircraft did not appear too badly damaged. However, as the aircraft approached Tuy Hoa, 1Lt Hepler was no longer able to maintain control and had to eject near the airfield.

16 February 1967

F-100D 56-2907   309 TFS, 31 TFW, USAF, Tuy Hoa
                     Col F C Buzze (survived)

The 31st TFW's bad luck continued when it lost another aircraft the following day. A flight of aircraft was despatched into southern Laos to attack a truck park that has been spotted near Ban Talan Nua. Col Buzze was making his first strafing run but flew into a barrage of automatic weapons fire that set his aircraft alight. He ejected close to the target and was lucky to escape capture as he was rescued by a USAF HH-3.

17 February 1967

C-130B 60-0307   773 TCS, 463 TCW, USAF, Clark
                     5 crew, names unknown (survived)

A C-130 crash-landed shortly after taking off from Tay Ninh due to a problem with the flaps. Fortunately, all the crew survived the accident.

A total of 12 EC-47 electronic intelligence aircraft were lost during the war. Their role was to detect and locate enemy radio transmissions in an attempt to track enemy movement, particularly along the Ho Chi Minh Trail in Laos and South Vietnam. 43-48947 was later transferred to the VNAF. USAF

The EC-47 and Radio Direction Finding

Radio direction finding was used extensively throughout the wars in Southeast Asia in an attempt to pinpoint the location of enemy radios and to gain real-time intelligence from listening in to the transmissions. The first attempt to provide an RDF capability came in March 1962 when a modified C-54 was deployed to Tan Son Nhut under the project name Hilo Hattie. This was not successful and was soon withdrawn but in February 1964 a modified C-47, under the project name Hawkeye, was sent to Vietnam for a six-month trial. The aircraft returned to Vietnam the following year and flew a number of successful missions. The entire RDF effort was at that time organised by the US Army whose 3rd Radio Research Unit operated modified U-6 Beavers in the role. However, the USAF wanted to take over the role and set about converting additional C-47s with a much better capability than the original aircraft or the Army U-6s. Project Phyllis Ann eventually resulted in a total of 57 C-47s converted to the RDF role for use in Southeast Asia. The first aircraft arrived on 26 May 1966 to join the 360th TRS, which had been activated at Tan Son Nhut on 8 April. Two more squadrons were activated, the 361st at Nha Trang and the 362nd at Pleiku. The 6994th Security Squadron was activated on 15 April and all the security and communications specialists on board the aircraft belonged to this unit. In the last six months of 1966 the RDF RC-47s flew a total of 1,146 missions, mostly in South Vietnam, but some over Laos where intelligence on the Ho Chi Minh Trail was particularly valuable. In an attempt to disguise the highly-classified nature of the aircraft, a leaflet chute was built into one of the RC-47's windows so that the aircraft could pose as leaflet droppers.

18 February 1967

F-105F 63-8262   13 TFS, 388 TFW, USAF, Korat
Capt David Henry Duart (POW)
Capt Jay Robert Jensen (POW)

When the primary mission for the day was scrubbed due to bad weather near Hanoi, an Iron Hand flight was sent to the DMZ area to suppress SAM sites in support of a B-52 raid. As none of the SAM sites challenged the bombers near the DMZ, the Weasel flight headed north to Vinh in the hope that a SAM site would switch on its radar. Eventually a SAM battery launched a missile when the Weasels were poorly placed, flying just 2,000 feet above a 10,000 feet cloud base. An SA-2 hit Capt Duart's aircraft moments after he had launched a Shrike at the site. The explosion blew off one of the aircraft's wings and both the crew ejected immediately. Both men were quickly captured to become POWs. The crew had been shot down on their 13th mission and were released in different batches during Operation Homecoming, Capt Jensen on 18 February and Capt Duart on 4 March 1973. In the following year Jay Jensen wrote a book titled *Six Years in Hell* which describes the horrors of his incarceration and the joys of his return. The F-105F 63-8262 was painted as 'Giddy up go' when it was lost.

AC-47D 44-76542   4 ACS, 14 ACW, USAF, Nha Trang
detached to Tan Son Nhut
7 crew, names unknown (survived)

An AC-47 gunship was destroyed in a landing accident at Binh Thuy. All the crew survived the accident.

RC-47P 43-49679   362 TRS, 460 TRW, USAF, Pleiku
The first of the RC-47 radio intelligence aircraft to be lost in Southeast Asia was destroyed at its parking spot at Tan Son Nhut by a China Airlines Curtiss C-46 that suffered a brake failure when landing and ground looped into a revetment. No one on either aircraft was injured.

19 February 1967

F-100D 56-2927   614 TFS, 35 TFW, USAF, Phan Rang
Capt D B Couch (survived)

Yet another F-100 was lost as it attacked a VC base camp in South Vietnam. A flight of aircraft took off from Phan Rang to attack the target near Xom Moi, which was just 10 miles south of the airfield. Capt Couch's F-100 was hit by small arms fire as he was leaving the target. He turned out to sea and ejected just off the coast from where he was picked up by an HH-43 from Tuy Hoa.

20 February 1967

F-4B 150413   VF-96, USN, USS *Enterprise*
Maj Russell Clemensen Goodman (KIA)
Ens Gary Lynn Thornton (POW)

A section of two F-4s was assigned to attack a railway siding at Thien Lin Dong eight miles southwest of Thanh Hoa. As the aircraft approached the target they popped up to 11,000 feet to commence their dive to drop Mk82 bombs on the railway trucks that were sitting in the siding. As Maj Goodman started to pull out of his dive his aircraft was hit by an anti-aircraft shell, which struck the Phantom's nose and almost certainly injured the pilot. Ens Thornton ejected but there was no sign of Maj Goodman, who probably died in the crash. One report claims the aircraft was hit by a SAM but the official Navy report states the aircraft was hit by AAA. Maj Russell Goodman was a USAF pilot who was serving on board the Enterprise on an exchange posting with the Navy. Gary Thornton was released on 4 March 1973 (the last airman to serve a full six years as a POW) and reported that Maj Goodman had been hit and did not escape from the aircraft.

21 February 1967

A-4E 151042   VMA-211, MAG-12, USMC, Chu Lai
Capt R B Boorer (survived)

A flight of Marine Corps A-4s was attacking a target near Duc Pho near the coast about 35 miles south of Chu Lai, when they encountered small arms and automatic weapons fire. Capt Boorer had pulled up from his second pass when the aircraft's fuselage was hit. It stayed controllable just long enough for him to cross the beach and eject seconds before it plunged into the sea. Capt Boorer was later picked up by a Navy vessel.

A-26A 64-17668   606 ACS, 634 CSG, USAF, Nakhon Phanom
Capt James L McCluskey (survived)
Capt L Michael Scruggs (survived)

A-26A 64-17669   606 ACS, 634 CSG, USAF, Nakhon Phanom
Capt Dwight Stanley Campbell (KIA)
Capt Robert Lee Sholl (KIA)

Two Invaders had found a large truck convoy near the village of Ban Thapachon during a night interdiction mission in southern

Laos. The convoy was well protected by at least two 37mm guns, a ZPU-4 four-barreled 14.5mm gun and a .50 calibre machine gun. The two aircraft made several passes over the convoy and the gun positions until eventually Capt McCluskey's aircraft was hit in the starboard engine by ground fire. The aircraft were about 60 miles from their base at Nakhon Phanom so Capt Campbell escorted Capt McCluskey's aircraft back across Laos. As the two aircraft approached the airfield Capt Campbell flew close to McCluskey's aircraft to check it over for damage before the landing. At that point McCluskey's starboard wing started to burn and Campbell radioed for the crew to bail out immediately. Seconds after McCluskey and Scruggs escaped from their aircraft it blew up in mid-air. Unfortunately, debris from the explosion appears to have hit Capt Campbell's aircraft, which crashed nearby killing him and Capt Scholl.

23 February 1967

O-1E 56-4182   20 TASS, 504 TASG, USAF, Da Nang
detached to Khe Sanh
Capt G L Ziegler (survived)
Capt C Gore (survived)

A Bird Dog had just taken off from the forward base at Khe Sanh just south of the DMZ when it was hit by ground fire. The crew bailed out and were eventually recovered with only minor injuries. This camp was particularly vulnerable and would become the centre of attention in early 1968.

24 February 1967

F-4C 64-0801   391 TFS, 12 TFW, USAF, Cam Ranh Bay
Capt D B Hudson (survived)
Lt H G Floyd (survived)

The danger of multiple passes over the same target was illustrated yet again when a Phantom was shot down near Vinh Binh, five miles north of Kien Long in the southern tip of South Vietnam. A flight of F-4s was attacking sampans and buildings in a suspected VC stronghold but as Capt Hudson came in for his fourth strafing run his aircraft was hit by small arms fire. He managed to fly a few miles away from the target area before he and his WSO ejected. They were both picked up later by a USAF helicopter.

O-1G 51-5078   21 TASS, 504 TASG, USAF, Nha Trang
Capt Hilliard Almond Wilbanks (KIA)

Capt Wilbanks was tasked with patrolling a line between Di Linh and Bao Lac in the Central Highlands of South Vietnam as the 23rd South Vietnamese Ranger battalion and their US 'advisors' swept the area for VC. The South Vietnamese troops were about to walk straight into an ambush but Capt Wilbanks spotted the VC foxholes and trenches and warned the ground troops. Their trap discovered, the VC opened up on the South Vietnamese soldiers

causing heavy casualties. Capt Wilbank fired white phosphorous rockets at the VC positions so that three accompanying Army helicopter gunships could lay down covering fire. However, the gunships retired after one was hit by ground fire. A flight of fighters was on the way but the ARVN troops were taking heavy casualties as the VC advanced, so Wilbanks kept diving at the enemy positions firing marker rockets in an attempt to keep them pinned down. When he was out of rockets he stuck his automatic rifle out of the aircraft's side window and swooped down firing at the VC. On his third pass firing his rifle Capt Wilbanks was hit by enemy ground fire and his Bird Dog crashed a few yards from the South Vietnamese troops he had so skilfully defended. He was pulled unconscious from the wreck and after a flight of F-4s plastered the hillside where the VC were dug in, a helicopter came in to evacuate Capt Wilbanks to Bao Lac. Sadly, Hilliard Wilbanks died in the helicopter en route to hospital but his outstanding bravery and devotion to duty was recognised by his country with the posthumous award of the Medal of Honor. Capt Wilbanks was on his 488th combat mission when he was shot down.

25 February 1967

A-1G   52-132625   1 ACS, 14 ACW, USAF, Pleiku
Lt Col Joseph Leslie Hart (KIA)

Lt Col Hart was flying a road reconnaissance mission just inside Laos, about 45 miles southwest of Hué, when his aircraft came under ground fire. The Skyraider crashed within seconds of being hit and Lt Col Hart does not appear to have escaped from the aircraft.

F-4B   152989   VF-96, USN, USS *Enterprise*
Lt(jg) R C Ewing (survived)
Lt David Wesley Hoffman (survived)

VF-96 lost its third Phantom during February when an aircraft suffered an engine failure during a catapult launch and crashed into the sea. Both crew ejected safely and were rescued. Lt Hoffman was shot down and taken prisoner on 30 December 1971 when serving with VF-111.

27 February 1967

A-4E   152051   VMA-121, MAG-12, USMC, Chu Lai
Maj Harold Joseph Alwan (KIA)

Maj Alwan took off alone from Chu Lai for an air test but having completed that he was then asked to fly as escort for a formation of Marine Corps helicopters. At some stage during the mission Maj Alwan's aircraft disappeared, possibly near Quang Ngai or just off the coast. It has been claimed that a SAR beeper was heard intermittently for the next three days and that Alwan's was the only aircraft that went down in the area. Despite his family's hopes that he had been taken prisoner, Maj Alwan remains missing in action.

A-4C   148607   VA-195, USN, USS *Ticonderoga*
1 pilot, name unknown (survived)

During a strike mission a Skyhawk from the *Ticonderoga* suffered an engine flameout, which forced the pilot to eject. Enemy action was not thought to have been the cause of the engine failure.

28 February 1967

O-1E   56-4195   20 TASS, 504 TASG, USAF, Da Nang
detached to Dong Ha
Capt R C Mays (survived)

The North Vietnamese regarded the DMZ buffer zone as a haven for the storage of ammunition and supplies for their campaigns in the northern provinces of South Vietnam and as such the zone was watched very carefully by the US forces. A Bird Dog operating from a forward airstrip at Dong Ha was flying over the DMZ when it was hit by ground fire. Capt Mays bailed out of his aircraft and landed within the buffer zone but he was rescued by a USAF helicopter.

F-4C   64-0764   558 TFS, 12 TFW, USAF, Cam Ranh Bay
Maj J F Clayton (survived)
Lt K C Simonin (survived)

The Phantoms from Cam Ranh Bay occasionally flew Steel Tiger missions in southern Laos as well as providing close air support for ground forces in South Vietnam and taking part in bombing raids and armed reconnaissance missions against the North. Maj Clayton was bombing a road near Ban Kale and had just started to dive on the target for the second time when ground fire damaged the Phantom's tail. The crew ejected a few miles from their target and were rescued by an HH-3E.

F-105D   59-1766   421 TFS, 388 TFW, USAF, Korat
Capt J S Walbridge (survived)

An F-105 was lost on an armed reconnaissance mission in North Vietnam a few miles north of the Mu Gia Pass. A flight of Thunderchiefs was attacking trucks on a road which led into the Pass but one of the aircraft was hit in the rear fuselage by ground fire. Capt Walbridge's aircraft was well alight when he ejected a few miles to the west. Bearing in mind that the Pass was very well defended, Capt Walbridge was fortunate to be rescued by an HH-3E, possibly the same helicopter that had rescued Maj Clayton who had been shot down only half an hour earlier. 1Lt Karl Richter shot down a MiG-17 on 21 September 1966 while flying Thunderchief 59-1766.

3 March 1967

F-4C   63-7656   497 TFS, 8 TFW, USAF, Ubon
Maj Floyd Whitley Richardson (KIA)
Lt Col Charles Donald Roby (KIA)

The Wolfpack continued their Night Owl role of night interdiction and armed reconnaissance over North Vietnam and Laos. A Phantom crew spotted boats on the Sou Giang River near Ba Don, 20 miles northwest of Dong Hoi, and commenced an attack. On their second pass the aircraft was hit by ground fire and crashed immediately without either pilot or WSO being seen to escape. Their exact fate was uncertain for many years until the Vietnamese handed over the remains of Maj Richardson and Lt Col Roby on 20 November 1989. Charles Roby had flown 100 missions in the F-80 and F-84 during the Korean War and was a graduate of the USAF Test Pilot School at Edwards AFB and had been a test pilot at Eglin AFB.

O-1C   140098   H&MS-16, MAG-16, USMC, Marble Mountain
1 pilot, name unknown (survived)

A Marine Corps Bird Dog crashed due to engine failure during a visual reconnaissance mission.

4 March 1967

F-105D   62-4274   357 TFS, 355 TFW, USAF, Takhli
Maj Ralph Laurence Carlock (KIA)

A flight of F-105s on an armed reconnaissance mission over northeastern Laos spotted a truck on a road near Ban Paka. The flight's leader saw Maj Carlock's aircraft dive towards the truck but then saw the F-105 hit by 37mm anti-aircraft fire and start to burn. Despite radio calls to eject, no one saw Maj Carlock escape from the aircraft as it crashed close to the road near the village of Nong Het, just within Laos. Pathet Lao radio the following day announced the shooting down of the F-105 but also claimed the capture of the pilot. In 1988 a witness told US investigators that he had seen an F-105 shot down and the pilot eject at a very low altitude and was killed. Whatever the actual events, Ralph Carlock remains missing in action to this day.

F-5C   65-10540   10 FCS, 3 TFW, USAF, Bien Hoa
Maj Frank David Wiley (KIA)

During a close air support mission in South Vietnam an F-5 suffered an engine failure and crashed in Bien Hoa province, killing the pilot. This was the last of nine F-5Cs lost by the USAF during the war, seven of them to enemy action, with six pilots being killed. The F-5 had proved to be a reliable and effective close air support aircraft but lacked range and endurance and was no improvement on the F-100s and F-4s used by the USAF. As the Air Force had decided not to adopt the F-5 on a permanent basis the 10th FCS's aircraft were handed over to the VNAF's 522nd Fighter Squadron in April 1967 as the first of over 260 F-5s used by that air force.

7 March 1967

A-4E   152087   VA-192, USN, USS *Ticonderoga*
Lt S N Young (survived)

Lt Young was taking part in a strike on an AAA site near Ban Nathong in southern Laos when he felt a thump shake his aircraft. All instruments gave normal readings and the section set off back to the carrier. On the return flight a wingman spotted a gaping hole in the rear fuselage of Lt Young's aircraft. As the section was approaching the carrier Lt Young's aircraft flamed out and would not restart. The wingman saw a fire near the Skyhawk's tail and Lt Young ejected when it became obvious that he could not reach the *Ticonderoga*.

F-8E   150350   VF-191, USN, USS *Ticonderoga*
Lt Robert Lester Miller (KIA)

Lt Miller was returning from a BARCAP mission over North Vietnam when his aircraft suffered a gyro failure. Without instruments to assist him and flying in thick haze, Lt Miller probably became disorientated and the aircraft crashed into the sea about 55 miles off the coast east of Thanh Hoa.

8 March 1967

A-3B   144627   Detachment C, VAH-4, USN, USS *Kitty Hawk*
Lt Cdr Carroll Owen Crain (KIA)
Lt(jg) George Francis Pawlish (KIA)
AT Ronald Edmond Galvin (KIA)

Mining at sea was a controversial subject during the war. Although mining would have stopped supplies being brought into Haiphong and other ports by sea, it was an indiscriminate weapon that could quite easily have sunk shipping from foreign countries, which were supposedly neutral but which were supplying North Vietnam with arms and other supplies. The risk of sinking a Russian or other Warsaw Pact ship greatly exercised the minds of the Pentagon's planners and so it was not until 1972 that the ports were mined. However, North Vietnam's rivers were a different matter. Foreign shipping was hardly likely to be found in the many smaller rivers of North Vietnam, so in February 1967 the Pentagon eventually decided to allow mining of selected waterways where there was no likelihood of causing an embarrassing international incident. The first mining mission was flown on 26 February when seven A-6As of VA-35 dropped mines in the entrance to the Song Ca and Song Giang rivers.

It was on one of the early mining missions that the *Kitty Hawk* lost one of its A-3s on the night of the 8th. The aircraft's target was the Kien Giang River but the aircraft disappeared en route as it approached the coast near Dong Hoi. No radio transmissions or SAR beepers were heard and no wreckage was seen. It was conjectured that the Skywarrior had either been shot down by AAA near Dong Hoi or had flown into the sea shortly before reaching the coast.

9 March 1967

RA-5C   151627   RVAH-13, USN, USS *Kitty Hawk*
Cdr Charles Lancaster Putnam (KIA)
Lt(jg) F S Prendergast (survived)

An RA-5C and its F-4 escort were tasked with a coastal reconnaissance of a section of North Vietnam's coastline. As the aircraft approached the coast near Long Chau, 30 miles northwest of Thanh Hoa, they started a photo run parallel to the coastline, with the Vigilante flying at only 350 feet. The Phantom pilot saw automatic weapons fire ahead and then saw the Vigilante suddenly pitch up and burst into flames. Two parachutes were seen and the airmen landed in shallow water about 200 yards from the beach. The Phantom called in a SAR helicopter and started to fire at North Vietnamese troops who tried to reach the downed crew. Lt Prendergast waded ashore and was captured by two militiamen on the beach. However, the North Vietnamese were distracted by strafing from Navy aircraft and Lt Prendergast retrieved his concealed .22 automatic pistol and shot both men dead. He then swam back out to sea and a Navy SH-3 came in and picked him up. There was no sign of Cdr Putnam although a Phantom pilot spotted someone on a sandbar. Increased fire from the beach precluded any further rescue attempt. A subse-

quent North Vietnamese report claimed that a dead pilot had been seen on a beach near Long Chau at about this time and it appears that Cdr Putnam was either drowned or shot by enemy troops. Charles Putnam's remains were returned to the USA on 3 November 1988.

RC-47P 43-49201 361 TRS, 460 TRW, USAF, Nha Trang
Maj Ivel Doan Freeman (KIA)
Maj Leroy Preston Bohrer (KIA)
Capt Roger Paul Richardson (KIA)
SSgt Prentice Fay Brenton (KIA)
TSgt Raymond Francis Leftwich (KIA)
A1C Charles Dwayne Land (KIA)
A1C Daniel Cortez Reese (KIA)

Another reconnaissance aircraft was lost on the 9th, one of the RDF aircraft of the 361st TRS. The aircraft, call sign Tide 86, had taken off from Nha Trang in the afternoon on a mission to locate enemy radio transmissions in the Central Highlands. When the aircraft failed to return in the evening a search was initiated but the wreckage of the RC-47 was not found until the 11th. The aircraft had crashed on a hillside about 10 miles south of Duc Pho after it had been hit by ground fire. The VC had removed personal items from the crash site but had not taken the valuable RDF equipment. Following this incident the RC-47s were ordered to operate above 2,000 feet to avoid small arms fire.

O-1E 56-2517 21 TASS, 504 TASG, USAF, Nha Trang
2 crew, names unknown (survived)

A Bird Dog crashed in South Vietnam due to pilot error. Fortunately, both the crew survived the accident.

10 March 1967

F-105F 63-8335 354 TFS, 355 TFW, USAF, Takhli
Maj David Everson (POW)
Capt Jose David Luna (POW)

F-4C 63-7653 433 TFS, 8 TFW, USAF, Ubon
Capt Earl D Aman (survived)
Capt Robert W Houghton (survived)

F-4C 64-0839 433 TFS, 8 TFW, USAF, Ubon
Capt J Robert Pardo (survived)
1Lt Steven A Wayne (survived)

The first American raid on the important Thai Nguyen iron and steel plant took place on the 10th with the loss of three of the USAF participants. Although the target had been released by Washington two weeks earlier, continuing bad weather over North Vietnam delayed the first strike until the 10th, the day on which President Johnson publicly admitted the presence of USAF bases in Thailand. This had probably been one of the worst kept secrets of the war but the President wanted his announcement to coincide with a raid on a major new target to apply further pressure on the North Vietnamese. The raid consisted of some 72 aircraft consisting of F-105s from both Korat and Takhli and F-4s from Ubon to provide MiGCAP. A SAM site that protected the target was attacked by the Takhli Iron Hand flight (Lincoln flight) minutes before the bombers arrived but the lead Wild Weasel aircraft was shot down by 85mm AAA as the flight dived through the intense flak to hit the target. Maj Everson and Capt Luna ejected from their aircraft and were both taken prisoner. Capt Merlyn Hans Dethlefsen, flying the other F-105F, took command of the flight and had to fend off MiGs and cope with AAA damage to his own aircraft. Eventually the MiGs and the flak eased off and allowed Dethlefsen the opportunity to attack the SAM site, which he and his wingman, Maj Ken Bell in a flak-damaged F-105D, destroyed in four passes with bombs and cannon fire. For his conspicuous gallantry on this day Capt Dethlefsen was award the Medal of Honor. Maj Everson and Capt Luna were released from their imprisonment on 4 March 1973.

Ten minutes after the F-105F had been shot down several flights of Phantoms arrived over the target and commenced their bombing runs. Some 20 miles north of Thai Nguyen Capt Aman's aircraft was hit by AAA at 12,000 feet but he dropped his bombs before heading for home, leaking fuel at a high rate. In the last flight over the target Capt Pardo was pulling up from his bomb run when his aircraft was also hit by AAA and damaged. How-

ever, the aircraft did not catch fire and Capt Pardo set off on the long flight home. Soon Aman's and Pardo's aircraft began to fall behind the rest of the Phantoms although the two damaged aircraft were able to climb to 36,000 feet by jettisoning all stores and racks. Capt Aman's aircraft was running out of fuel and would not be able to reach a tanker in time as they were still over North Vietnam. Capt Pardo told Aman to drop his arrester hook, which then hung down at a 45-degree angle. Pardo then slowly moved in behind Aman's aircraft and slid his Phantom up to the arrester hook until it was resting on Pardo's windscreen. Pardo had to tell Aman to shut down his engines as the jet exhaust was making it difficult to maintain formation. In this position Pardo pushed Aman's aircraft across North Vietnam until they were close to the Laotian border. It is probable that they would have reached the tanker had not Pardo's port engine caught fire. Unable to go any further Capt Aman and Capt Houghton ejected safely near Poungthak and Capt Pardo and 1Lt Wayne ejected a few minutes later when they also ran out of fuel. A SAR task force crossed Laos and two HH-3Es rescued the downed airmen. 'Pardo's Push' became one of the epic tales of the war and although the attempt to reach the tanker failed, the push enabled all four men to eject over a relatively unpopulated area where they could be rescued more easily. Perhaps predictably, higher authority was less impressed with 'Pardo's Push' and sent instructions to all flying units in Southeast Asia warning not to emulate the technique. It took over 20 years for the USAF to recognise that this most unorthodox manoeuvre had probably saved the lives of Aman and Houghton and finally awarded Pardo and Wayne their Silver Stars.

Capt Pardo had previously flown tours in the F-84F, F-100D, F-102 and F-106. On 20 May he and Steve Wayne shot down a MiG-17 when they were flying F-4C 63-7623 while 64-0839 had already been credited with a MiG-21 on 6 January when flown by Capt R M Pascoe and 1Lt N E Wells of the 555th TFS. Robert Pardo became the Chief Pilot of the Adolph Coors Company after retirement from the Air Force.

VC-47J 99844 Naval Support Activity Saigon, USN, Tan Son Nhut
Lt Cdr Leo Claude Hester (KWF)
Lt Cdr Robert George Kerr (KWF)
AN Francis Raymond Ferron (KWF)
ADR2 Cecil Leroy Chapman (KWF)
21 passengers (KWF)

In one of the worst aviation accidents to happen to a US Navy aircraft during the war in Southeast Asia, all 25 passengers and crew were killed when a C-47 crashed on an administrative flight. The aircraft was on a flight from Cam Ranh Bay to Saigon and crashed near Phan Rang. The cause of the accident is not known. This aircraft had previously been used for VIP duties by the air attachés in Paris and London.

11 March 1967

A-4E 151108 VA-192, USN, USS *Ticonderoga*
Cdr Ernest Melvin Moore (POW)

The Iron Hand flight of VA-192 was tasked to look for a SAM site near Hanoi. The site was eventually discovered to be a SAM support site, probably where missiles were stored and assembled before distribution to various batteries, and was located at Lang Cam near Hai Duong, 25 miles east of Hanoi. Cdr Moore had flown over 90 missions over Vietnam and had led many Iron Hand missions during his time as executive officer with VA-192. As the flight approached the target at 14,000 feet Cdr Moore was just a few seconds late in starting his evasive manoeuvres and an SA-2 detonated close to his aircraft, peppering it with shrapnel. The aircraft's fuel tanks were holed and the fuel caught fire forcing Cdr Moore to eject near the target. Cdr Moore was captured immediately and joined many of his colleagues as a POW until he was released on 4 March 1973.

F-105D 60-0443 333 TFS, 355 TFW, USAF, Takhli
Capt Charles Edward Greene (POW)

F-105D 62-4261 357 TFS, 355 TFW, USAF, Takhli
Capt Joseph John Karins (KIA)

F-105D 60-0506 354 TFS, 355 TFW, USAF, Takhli
Maj James Edward Hiteshew (POW)

Following the costly raid on the Thai Nguyen iron and steel works on the 10th, the USAF decided to strike the same target the next day, unfortunately with similar results and another three aircraft lost. Crab flight was in the first wave over the target and ran into a hail of flak and SAMs. Capt Greene's aircraft was hit by a 57mm shell as it pulled up through 5,000 feet over Thai Nguyen. With his aircraft badly damaged he flew about 10 miles to the west before ejecting. The aircraft of Tampa flight were jinking to avoid the defences as they approached the target at 7,000 feet but this did not help Capt Karins as his aircraft was hit by an SA-2. Joseph Karins ejected a few miles to the southeast of the city and spoke to other members of his flight on his survival radio. Just two minutes after Capt Karins had been shot down Mumbles flight swept down on Thai Nguyen and began the final stage of their bombing run. Maj Hiteshew's aircraft was hit by AAA in the tail which caught fire forcing him to eject near the target.

Three F-105s had been lost over Thai Nguyen within the space of four minutes, which brought the number of aircraft lost to this particular target over the last two days to six. Majors Greene and Hiteshew were both captured and served their time in the Hanoi Hilton and other prisons until released on 4 March 1973. James Hiteshew was very badly injured with his left arm and both legs broken. However, despite the fact that Capt Karins was known to have survived the ejection and was thought to have been captured, he was not among the prisoners returned in Operation Homecoming. On 6 April 1988 the whereabouts of Capt Joseph Karins was no longer in doubt when his remains were returned by the Vietnamese. However the circumstances of his death remain a mystery.

12 March 1967

RF-4C 65-0877 12 TRS, 460 TRW, USAF, Tan Son Nhut
Capt Edwin Riley Goodrich (KIA)
1Lt John Walter Clark (POW)

A reconnaissance Phantom was lost over hilly terrain seven miles south of Van Yen and about 60 miles west of Hanoi on the 12th. The aircraft was hit by AAA and both the crew ejected but Capt Goodrich, a veteran of over 80 missions in Southeast Asia, was severely injured. He was located by rescue forces and a Fulton extraction kit was dropped to him in the hope that he could use it to escape. Sadly, Edwin Goodrich was killed or died before he could reach the kit. 1Lt Clark became a POW and was eventually released on 18 February 1973 but it was not until 18 April 1985 that Edwin Goodrich's body was handed over by the Vietnamese. John Clark had been based at RAF Alconbury with the 10th TRW until posted to Tan Son Nhut in September 1966.

C-130E 63-7772 345 TCS, 314 TCW, USAF, Ching Chuan Kang
5 crew, names unknown (survived)

A Hercules crashed when the rotor downwash from an Army Chinook obscured visibility as the C-130 was taking off from An Khe on an airlift mission. All the crew escaped from the crash.

RF-101C 56-0063 20 TRS, 432 TRW, USAF, Udorn
1 pilot, name unknown (survived)

A second reconnaissance aircraft was lost on the 12th when a Voodoo crashed at Udorn due to pilot error.

F-100D 55-3611 308 TFS, 31 TFW, USAF, Tuy Hoa
Capt Joseph Daniel Adrian (KIA)

Three F-100s scrambled from Tuy Hoa after dark on a close air support mission. Capt Adrian made a turn to join up with his leader but his aircraft was then seen to continue turning until it disappeared from sight and presumably crashed into the sea about six miles from Tuy Hoa.

14 March 1967

F-105D 62-4325 469 TFS, 388 TFW, USAF, Korat
1 pilot, name unknown (survived)

During a test flight a Thunderchief suffered a control failure forcing the pilot to eject from the aircraft.

1Lt V H Thompson was killed in this F-100D 56-3277 on 15 March 1967 during an attack on a Viet Cong base camp near the mouth of the Cua Soirap River, 20 miles south of Saigon. On average three Super Sabres were lost every month during 1967. USAF

15 March 1967

F-100D 56-3277   3 TFW, USAF, Bien Hoa
1Lt Victor Hugo Thompson (KIA)

An F-100 was lost and its pilot killed on the 15th during an attack on a VC base camp near the mouth of the Cua Soirap River, 20 miles south of Saigon. 1Lt Thompson was making his first strafing run against the camp when his aircraft ran into a hail of ground fire and dived straight into the ground allowing no time for the pilot to escape.

F-105D 59-1825   357 TFS, 355 TFW, USAF, Takhli
Lt Col Peter Joseph Frederick (KIA)

A flight of two F-105s on a road reconnaissance along Route 7 came under fire near the Bartholemy Pass, on the Laotian border with North Vietnam. The leading aircraft dived to attack a target on the road and was followed by Lt Col Frederick. However, after the attack the leader could not see Lt Col Frederick's aircraft and could not raise him on the radio. No beeper was heard and the wreckage could not be found but it was assumed that the aircraft had either been hit by flak or flew into the ground during the attack. At 42, Peter Frederick was one of the older fast jet pilots in Southeast Asia and was actually approaching his retirement point when he volunteered for combat duty.

F-8C 147027   VF-24, USN, USS *Bon Homme Richard*
Lt(jg) Dean Smith (KIA)

The *Bon Homme Richard* arrived back on Yankee Station on 26 February for its third tour of duty off Southeast Asia. The cruise started badly as on the next day after taking up position one of its UH-2B Seasprite SAR helicopters crashed into the sea when it was taking off from the carrier's deck and four crewmen died. The ship's first loss on a combat mission took place during a coastal reconnaissance mission on 15 March. Two Crusaders were flying just off the coast south of Thanh Hoa at 1,500 feet when they flew over several fishing boats. The wingman, Lt Smith, started to turn and descend so the leader warned him to watch his altitude but the Crusader continued to descend until it hit the water near the island of Hon Me. No flak was seen at the time and it was surmised that the pilot may have been fixated on the fishing boats as potential targets and did not realise he was losing altitude despite his leader's warning.

A-4E 151188   VMA-223, MAG-12, USMC, Chu Lai
Capt Stanley P Krueger (survived)

VMA-223 arrived back at Chu Lai on 1 March after a well-earned three-month break at Iwakuni. During a night-time armed reconnaissance mission just north of the DMZ a section of Skyhawks spotted and attacked an automatic weapons site. At 3,000 feet in the dive, Capt Krueger's aircraft was hit in the starboard wing but, although the aircraft caught fire, he was able to reach the sea and fly south before he was forced to eject about 15 miles off the coast. He was picked up safely by a USAF helicopter.

17 March 1967

A-4C 148585   VMA-214, MAG-12, USMC, Chu Lai
Capt Robert Boughton Beale (KIA)

Another A-4 from Chu Lai was lost during a coastal reconnaissance mission. Capt Beale's Skyhawk was hit by automatic weapons fire, which eventually caused it to crash in the sea five miles off Tam Ky and just 15 miles from Chu Lai.

A-1H 135297   VA-115, USN, USS *Hancock*
Lt Cdr A H Henderson (survived)

A-1H 139768   VA-115, USN, USS *Hancock*
Lt R B Moore (survived)

During a night-time armed reconnaissance over the southern provinces of North Vietnam a pair of Skyraiders found a barge in the mouth of the Sou Giang River, 15 miles north of Dong Hoi. The two aircraft dived down to attack the barge in a coordinated attack but as they pulled up they were both hit by automatic weapons fire. Both aircraft flew out to sea in their crippled aircraft. Lt Cdr Henderson ditched his Skyraider 10 miles offshore while Lt Moore almost made it back to the ship before having to ditch. Both pilots were rescued by naval vessels.

A-1H 135225   VA-115, USN, USS *Hancock*
Lt(jg) Gene William Goeden (KIA)

A-1H 134625   VA-115, USN, USS *Hancock*
1 pilot, name unknown (survived)

The 17th proved to be a very black day for VA-115 and the *Hancock*. During a SAR mission, possibly searching for their colleagues, two more Skyraiders collided in mid-air over the Gulf of Tonkin. Both aircraft crashed and one of the pilots was killed in the incident.

18 March 1967

F-4B 152271   VMFA-314, MAG-13, USMC, Chu Lai
Maj David Whittier Morrill (KIA)
2Lt Maxim Charles Parker (KIA)

MAG-13 had been formed at Chu Lai on 25 September 1966 as the Marines' third fixed-wing aviation group in Vietnam. Equipped with the F-4, the Group took over two of MAG-11's Phantom squadrons and added a third squadron in October. MAG-13 lost its first aircraft on 18 March when a flight of F-4s attacked an automatic weapons site near Kinh Mon in the DMZ buffer zone. Maj Morrill's aircraft crashed near the target on its fourth pass either as a result of ground fire or by flying into the ground as a result of target fixation.

A-1E 52-133873   1 ACS, 14 ACW, USAF, Pleiku
Capt Michael J Dugan (survived)

One of the many munitions used to stem the flow of supplies that streamed down the Ho Chi Minh Trail towards South Vietnam was the XM66 anti-personnel mine. The weapon consisted of

small explosive bomblets called 'gravel', which detonated when trodden on. Capt Dugan and his wingman were tasked for a night mission to drop the new ordnance as a trial in the Steel Tiger area of southern Laos. One source suggests that Dugan's wingman dropped his 'gravel' above Dugan's aircraft blowing the wing off, which sounds unlikely. It is more likely that the aircraft was hit by AAA. In any event Dugan's aircraft was damaged and crashed near Ban Nampakhon. As the aircraft became inverted Capt Dugan opened his canopy and released his straps, dropping out of the aircraft. It is claimed that Capt Dugan made the last successful unassisted bail out from an A-1E as shortly after this date the aircraft was fitted with the Yankee Extraction System that used two shotgun charges and a small rocket motor to pull the pilot out of the aircraft. Capt Dugan landed in the jungle and spent the night hiding from the North Vietnamese, who he heard moving all around his position. He was rescued early the next morning by a USAF helicopter.

Capt Michael Dugan eventually flew 1,700 hours in the Skyraider in Southeast Asia and went on to a distinguished career in the USAF that included command of the 23rd and 355th TFWs and command of US Air Forces in Europe. His final appointment was as the USAF's Chief of Staff on 1 July 1990. Unfortunately, he made some unguarded remarks about the forthcoming Desert Storm air campaign against Iraq and was forced to relinquish his appointment on 17 September. He resigned from the USAF on 31 December 1990.

F-8E 149171   VMF(AW)-232, MAG-11, USMC, Da Nang
Lt C W Clarke (survived)

During a mission over South Vietnam a Crusader suffered an electrical generator failure, which eventually caused the aircraft to run out of fuel and crash. VMF(AW)-232 had arrived at Da Nang in September 1966 having just converted to the F-8E model of the Crusader at Kaneohe Bay MCAS in Hawaii.

19 March 1967

F-105D 61-0123   34 TFS, 388 TFW, USAF, Korat
Lt Col Joseph Clair Austin (KIA)

On 19 March the two F-105 Wings flew the first trial missions using a radar bombing technique against a target in North Vietnam. This was part of a Seventh Air Force effort to bomb targets in bad weather, which the Navy could do with their A-6s but the USAF had no realistic all-weather low-level bombing capability. As part of the trial each wing flew a practice mission to Laos on the morning of the 19th before the 'real' mission in the afternoon. The targets chosen were in the passes on the Laos/North Vietnam border. As the three F-105s from Korat made their radar run through thick cloud to bomb a road in the Ban Karai Pass, one of the aircraft hit the top of a hill and exploded. The other two aircraft managed to pull up in time to avoid hitting the ground but Lt Col Austin was killed instantly. The afternoon missions were more successful and completed without loss. The results of the radar bombing trials eventually led to the formation of Ryan's Raiders, a flight of the 13th TFS equipped with F-105Fs. Under the code name Commando Nail, the aircraft were fitted with expanded radar scopes and and an improved radar bombing system for all-weather operations. Joseph Austin was a well-known lacrosse player and captain of the Army national championship lacrosse team.

F-100D 55-2912   614 TFS, 35 TFW, USAF, Phan Rang
Capt Barry Ronald Delphin (KIA)

A Super Sabre was shot down during a close air support mission near Lai Khe north of Saigon. Capt Delphin was making his first pass over the target when his aircraft was struck by automatic weapons fire and crashed in flames before he could eject.

20 March 1967

O-1E   56-2518   21 TASS, 504 TASG, USAF, Nha Trang
                 detached to Qui Nhon
                 Maj P T Jones (survived)

Two FACs were lost on the 20th in different regions of South Vietnam. Maj Jones was shot down five miles northwest of Bong Son, about 45 miles north of his base at Qui Nhon. The aircraft was hit by automatic weapons fire and crashed but Maj Jones escaped with only minor injuries and was later rescued.

O-1G   51-5150   19 TASS, 504 TASG, USAF, Bien Hoa
                 detached to Dau Tieng
                 1Lt Walter Henry Forbes (KIA)
                 Capt Tonie Lee England (KIA)

The Army Fire Support Base at Suoi Tre in the Michelin rubber plantation, 20 miles northeast of Tay Ninh, was an important location in the battle for War Zone C. On 20 March 2,500 troops of the 272nd North Vietnamese Infantry Regiment suddenly attacked the base resulting in frantic calls for air support. One of the first aircraft on the scene was a Bird Dog flown by 1Lt Forbes. The FAC controlled a strike by a flight of F-5s and then 1Lt Forbes came down low to assess the damage caused by the jets. Unfortunately, the aircraft was hit by automatic weapons fire, its port wing disintegrated and the aircraft crashed killing both occupants. Two more FACs arrived as replacements and within two and a half hours had brought in 85 fighters, which turned back the North Vietnamese forces.

21 March 1967

A-1H   137516   VA-215, USN, USS *Bon Homme Richard*
                 Lt Paul Claude Charvet (KIA)

During a Sea Dragon patrol along the coast of North Vietnam an A-1 crashed in the sea in poor weather near Hon Me island, killing the pilot. No flak or other defences were seen and the cause of the crash remains a mystery.

F-4C   64-0788   433 TFS, 8 TFW, USAF, Ubon
                 Lt L R Egea (survived)
                 Maj C W Hetherington (survived)

A Phantom collided in mid-air with another aircraft over Thailand and crashed. Both crew ejected safely.

23 March 1967

AC-47D   43-48356   4 ACS, 14 ACW, USAF, Nha Trang
                     detached to Bien Hoa
                     Capt C A Boatwright (survived)
                     Capt E H Vettergren (survived)
                     5 crew, names unknown (survived)

As pressure on the many outposts north of Saigon continued, the AC-47 gunships were in great demand to provide base defence during the hours of darkness. When a base was thought to be under direct threat of night attack a gunship would be despatched to drop flares throughout the night, which was often enough to prevent an attack taking place. As dusk fell on the 23rd an AC-47 took off from Bien Hoa to drop flares over an outpost but got little further than the airfield perimeter. The aircraft was hit by .30 calibre machine gun fire as it took off and crash-landed close to the airfield. The crew survived the crash but had to be recovered by a strong force of US and South Vietnamese troops.

A-6A   152608   VMA(AW)-242, MAG-11, USMC, Da Nang
                 Capt Frederick Cone (survived)
                 Capt Doug Wilson (survived)

C-141A   65-9407   62 MAW, USAF, McChord AFB
                    Capt Harold Leland Hale (KIA)
                    Capt Leroy Edward Leonard (KIA)
                    Capt Max Paul Starkel (KIA)
                    SSgt Alanson Garland Bynum (KIA)
                    SSgt Alfred Funck (KIA)
                    1 other crew, name unknown (survived)

Some of the bases in South Vietnam were among the world's busiest airfields during the height of the war in Southeast Asia.

The number of aircraft movements at bases like Da Nang and Tan Son Nhut equalled or exceeded those at major US and European airports. With the huge amount of activity involved it is inevitable that accidents should sometimes occur on the ground. The worst such accident happened in the early hours of 23 March and involved a Marine Corps A-6, which was taking off from Da Nang on a strike mission, and a MAC C-141 Starlifter. The air traffic controller had cleared the Intruder to take off but also unwittingly cleared the C-141 to cross the runway. The Intruder pilot saw the Starlifter at the last moment and tried to veer off the runway to avoid it but the Intruder's port wing sliced through the Starlifter's nose. The Intruder sumersalted onto it back and continued down the runway. The pilot and navigator miraculously escaped death and crawled though their smashed canopy. The aircraft was carrying 16x500lb bombs and six rocket packs, some of which later exploded in the fire. The C-141 immediately burst into flames igniting its cargo of 72 acetylene gas cylinders, which resulted in a tremendous explosion. All the Starlifter crew died except the loadmaster who managed to escape from one of the aft doors before the aircraft exploded.

This was the first A-6 Intruder that the Marine Corps had lost in Southeast Asia. Although the US Navy had been flying the A-6 since February 1963 and had deployed them on carriers off Vietnam from May 1965, the first Marine Corps Intruders did not arrive in Vietnam until 1 November 1966 when VMA(AW)-242 took up residence at Da Nang.

24 March 1967

EF-10B   125786   VMCJ-1, MAG-11, USMC, Da Nang
                   Capt Joseph Patrick Murphy (KIA)
                   2Lt Walter Leroy Albright (KIA)

One of VMCJ-1's elderly EF-10B Skynight electronic warfare aircraft disappeared during a test flight from Da Nang. The aircraft was thought to have come down at sea and is regarded as a combat loss, although there was no evidence of enemy action being the cause.

A-6A   151587   VA-85, USN, USS *Kitty Hawk*
                 Lt Cdr John Cooley Ellison (KIA)
                 Lt(jg) James Edwin Plowman (KIA)

An A-6 disappeared during a four-aircraft night strike on a thermal power plant at Bac Giang near Kep. After the crew radioed that they had released their bombs the Intruder was tracked by radar (probably by an E-2 Hawkeye) to be about 10 miles north of their planned course. The radar plot disappeared in Ha Bac province when the aircraft probably fell victim to AAA. One source claims that Lt Cdr Ellison made voice contact with a SAR force but neither crewman was rescued or ever heard from again although rumours persist that at least one of the men was held captive in China. However, after the end of the war when China released the US airmen who had been shot down over Chinese territory, neither Ellison nor Plowman was amongst them. Photographs of POWs taken by the North Vietnamese together with first hand information from a released POW indicate that one or both men may have been captured. In 1980 Ellison and Plowman were declared dead for administrative purposes but the mystery surrounding their disappearance still persists. John Ellison had been forced to abandon an A-6A on 15 May 1966 when the aircraft was unable to take on fuel as it was returning from a mission.

25 March 1967

O-1E   56-2509   21 TASS, 504 TASG, USAF, Nha Trang
                 1Lt John Wayne Mower (KIA)
                 Sgt Albert Clifton Files, US Army (KIA)

The danger to FACs and helicopters that operated from remote strips and bases in enemy-infested territory was definitely on the increase. The pilot and observer of a Bird Dog were killed on the 25th when their aircraft was shot down by small arms fire as it was taking off from a landing ground called Plateau, 20 miles northeast of Kontum in the Central Highlands.

F-8E   149147   VF-53, USN, USS *Hancock*
                 Lt(jg) James Hamilton Hise (KWF)

As an F-8 was landing on the USS *Hancock* off the coast of South Vietnam after a ferry flight the ship's arrester gear failed and the aircraft fell over the side killing the pilot.

26 March 1967

F-105D   60-0516   469 TFS, 388 TFW, USAF, Korat
                    Maj Jack C Spillers (survived)

The deployment of SA-2 batteries in North Vietnam was by now extensive and and not only included the main targets around Hanoi, Haiphong and Thai Nguyen but other locations further south. The search for SAM batteries extended throughout the country, even down to the area around the DMZ. An Iron Hand flight was searching this area on the 26th when one of its F-105 bombers was hit by automatic weapons fire just north of the DMZ. Maj Spillers turned south but had to eject while still over the buffer zone and thereby came down in very unfriendly territory. Luckily, he was able to avoid detection long enough to be rescued by an HH-3. Jack Spillers was shot down on his 46th mission but he flew a total of 114 to complete his tour. He returned to Southeast Asia in 1969 and became commander of the 357th TFS at Takhli and flew another 106 missions including several as strike commander.

F-4C   64-0849   433 TFS, 8 TFW, USAF, Ubon
                 Lt Col Frederick Austin Crow (POW)
                 1Lt Henry Pope Fowler (POW)

Son Tay was a name that was to become very well known in the story of the war in Vietnam as the location of a POW camp and a daring resecue attempt. However, this was in the future, for in 1967 Son Tay was just one of many towns on the banks of the Red River that contained NVA units. The barracks at Son Tay was the target for a raid by the Wolfpack on the 26th but during the attack one of the Phantoms was hit by an SA-2 missile. The badly damaged aircraft headed west but after a few minutes it was obviously going no further and the crew ejected. Both crew were captured and spent the next six years as POWs until 1Lt Fowler was released on 18 February and Lt Col Crow on 4 March 1973. Phantom 64-0849 was credited with a MiG-21 on 6 January 1967 when being flown by Maj T M Hirsch and 1Lt R J Strasswimmer of the 555th TFS.

27 March 1967

A-4C   148519   VA-112, USN, USS *Kitty Hawk*
                 Lt Alexander J Palenscar (KIA)

A flight of four Skyhawks attacked the Dao My road bridge, 20 miles northwest of Vinh. Lt Palenscar was the last to bomb and reported that he was clear of the target. However, he failed to join up over the sea with the rest of the flight and a search of the area revealed no wreckage. It is not known what happened to Lt Palenscar and his aircraft.

F-4C   64-0769   558 TFS, 12 TFW, USAF, Cam Ranh Bay
                 2 crew, names unknown (survived)

The USAF lost a Phantom on the 27th in a take off accident at Cam Ranh Bay. Both crew survived the accident.

28/29 March 1967

AC-47D   44-76534   4 ACS, 14 ACW, USAF, Nha Trang
                     detached to Da Nang
                     Capt William Hadley Hosea (KIA)
                     Capt Herbert Charles Rice (KIA)
                     Capt John Bishop Cabana (KIA)
                     SSgt John Larue Brim (KIA)
                     SSgt James Lewis Fields (KIA)
                     TSgt Guy Joseph Brungard (KIA)
                     A1C Robert Edwin Ruonavaara (KIA)

Night attacks on hamlets and outposts continued to cause great concern, especially as there was never enough AC-47 gunships to provide extensive coverage throughout South Vietnam. The USAF lost its fourth gunship of 1967 during the defence of an outpost near Hoi An, 10 miles south of Da Nang. The aircraft arrived over the outpost and started its orbit but was hit by intense automatic weapons fire and crashed a few miles from the

outpost. Such was the fear and hatred that the VC held for the Spooky gunships that they made every effort to bring them down before they could bring their immense firepower to bear on the attackers.

30 March 1967

F-4B 151512 VMFA-542, MAG-13, USMC, Chu Lai
1Lt J B Geller (survived)
2Lt Edward Joseph Keglovits (KIA)

MAG-13 lost its second Phantom when an aircraft was shot down near Khe Sanh during a close air support mission. The target consisted of mortar positions and caves where units of the North Vietnamese Army had dug themselves in to threaten the Marine Corps base at Khe Sanh. As 1Lt Geller pulled up from his first pass over the target his aircraft was hit by ground fire. The pilot ejected immediately but for some reason the navigator was still in the aircraft when it crashed near the target. 1Lt Geller was rescued by a Marine Corps helicopter having suffered minor injuries from the ejection.

F-100D 56-3027 531 TFS, 3 TFW, USAF, Bien Hoa
Capt David Carl Lindberg (survived)

Although by no means a night and all-weather fighter, the F-100 not only maintained night alert in support of troops and outposts that came under attack, but also flew Combat Skyspot missions. These missions involved aircraft being guided to a target that was usually covered by cloud via a ground-based radar, which also indicated to the pilot exactly when to release the bombs. The mission was not much liked by many pilots as it was not as exciting as low level attack and entailed flying straight and level during the bombing run for an extended period. Capt Lindberg was on his bomb run on a Skyspot target 13 miles northwest of Bien Hoa when his aircraft was hit. Remarkably the aircraft was flying at 15,000 feet and was brought down by automatic weapons fire. Capt Lindberg ejected and was rescued by an HH-43 Huskie helicopter. David Lindberg was killed two months later when he was shot down during a close air support mission on 21 May.

A-4C 147844 VA-94, USN, USS *Hancock*
1 pilot, name unknown (survived)

When returning from an armed reconnaissance mission a Skyhawk ran out of fuel and the pilot had to eject. It is not known why the aircraft was not able to return safely to the carrier.

31 March 1967

F-105D 59-1745 421 TFS, 388 TFW, USAF, Korat
Capt Harry J Hennigar (survived)

The waterways of North Vietnam were navigable by small boats for considerable distances from the coast and were an important part of the country's transport system. Armed reconnaissance missions often included attacks on small craft that could be car-

rying weapons and supplies as part of the war effort. On the last day of March a flight of F-105s from Korat attacked several wooden barges that had been found on the Song Ca River near Ban Moi, 70 miles northwest of Vinh. As Capt Hennigar started his strafing run from an altitude of 6,000 feet, his aircraft was hit in the tail by automatic weapons fire. He flew about 15 miles to the west before ejecting and was fortunate enough to be rescued by a USAF HH-3. Although shot down on his 25th mission, Capt Hennigar went on to complete his tour with 110 missions to his credit, 100 of them over North Vietnam.

F-4C 64-0733 480 TFS, 366 TFW, USAF, Da Nang
Maj Cobb (survived)
Lt L D Peterson (survived)

During a flight over South Vietnam an F-4 suffered a flight control failure that resulted in the loss of the aircraft. Both crew ejected safely and the cause was accidental rather than due to enemy action.

1 April 1967

F-4C 64-0746 557 TFS, 12 TFW, USAF, Cam Ranh Bay
Capt George Henry Jourdenais (KIA)
1Lt Robert William Stanley (KIA)

The VC were masters at hiding their precious weapons and stores and these hiding places, if they could be found, were regarded as prime targets. A flight of F-4s from Cam Ranh Bay was tasked with the destruction of underground storage bunkers that had been discovered near Phuoc Tuy, 15 miles west of Tam Ky. Capt Jourdenais was making his third run over the target when his aircraft plunged straight into the ground, probably the victim of small arms fire that penetrated a vulnerable part of the aircraft.

T-28D 49-1559 606 ACS, 634 CSG, USAF, Nakhon Phanom
Maj David Richard Williams (KIA)
Maj Robert Allen Govan (KIA)

The T-28s of the 606th ACS were used for both day and night missions in the campaigns in Laos. Under their radio call sign of Zorro, the little T-28s performed a useful, if somewhat limited, role in the interdiction campaign. Maj Williams and Maj Govan were on an armed reconnaissance mission at night when they spotted a moving truck on Route 911 near Ban Boung in southern Laos, some 35 miles west of the DMZ. As the aircraft was preparing to attack the truck it was hit by 37mm ground fire and crashed immediately, with no indication that either of the crew had escaped. The following day a SAR mission found no trace of the missing airmen or the aircraft.

2 April 1967

F-105D 60-0426 13 TFS, 388 TFW, USAF, Korat
Capt John Arthur Dramesi (POW)

A flight of F-105s was sent on an armed reconnaissance mission that entailed flying along Route 106 and 107 in Quang Bing province in the southern region of North Vietnam. As the aircraft reached a point about 15 miles northwest of Dong Hoi they came under a hail of anti-aircraft fire. Capt Dramesi's aircraft was hit in the tail and with the aircraft on fire he ejected a few minutes later. He twisted his knee on landing and was immediately surrounded by North Vietnamese militia. He shot at them with his revolver but was shot in the right leg and captured. After eight days in his first prison camp he dismantled part of his cell and escaped but was soon captured and stoned and beaten by a crowd of Vietnamese. The next day he was taken to the Hanoi Hilton and then to the Zoo, another prison camp in Hanoi. On 10 May 1969, after months of planning, he and Capt Edwin Atterberry escaped through the roof of their cell but were recaptured 12 hours later about four miles from the prison. Dramesi and Atterberry were beaten and tortured for their escape, Atterberry did not survive and Dramesi was near death when the brutal treatment stopped after 38 days. Dramesi remained in leg irons for six months and the entire POW population was also systematically beaten and tortured as a punishment for the escape. This incident effectively put an end to any further escape attempts as the repercussions were too serious and in any case it was extremely unlikely that an escape and return to friendly territory would ever be successful. However, in June 1972 Capt Dramesi and Maj Kasler were involved in a planned escape, code-named Operation Thunderhead. Despite much planning and assistance from SAR forces in the Gulf of Tonkin, senior POW officers vetoed the escape at the last minute. John Dramesi was released on 4 March 1973 and told his POW story in *Code of Honor* published in 1975. He was awarded the AFC after his release and later flew the F-111 with the 366th TFW.

F-102A 55-3362 509 FIS, 405 FW, USAF, base ..?
1 pilot, name unknown (survived)

At 45,000 feet during a training flight an F-102 suffered an engine flame out. Despite attempts to restart the engine the aircraft had to make an emergency landing during which the F-102 smashed through the barrier gear and was so badly damaged that it had to be scrapped. One source claims that this aircraft belonged to the 64th FIS when it was lost. It was certainly used by the 64th and the 16th FIS as well as the 509th FIS during its time with PACAF.

4 April 1967

F-4B 152984 VF-92, USN, USS *Enterprise*
Lt Edward Philip Szeyller (KIA)
1 other crew, name unknown (survived)

F-4B 151493 VF-92, USN, USS *Enterprise*
Ens David Earl Martin (KIA)
1 other crew, name unknown (survived)

During a BARCAP mission two Phantoms from VF-92 collided in mid-air with the loss of one man from each of the aircraft. The two survivors were Cdr J L Rough and Lt(jg) C R Jones but it is not known who was in which aircraft.

5 April 1967

F-105D 62-4395 44 TFS, 388 TFW, USAF, Korat
1 pilot, name unknown (survived)

When landing back at base a Thunderchief had a drag chute failure and ran off the end of the runway. The aircraft, which was nicknamed 'Emily', was so badly damaged that it never flew again.

The AC-47D Spooky gunship was greatly feared by the Viet Cong. On many occasions these aircraft saved remote outposts from being overrun during night attacks. However, there was a price to pay and on the night of 28 March 1967 Spooky 44-76534 of the 4th ACS was shot down with the loss of all seven crewmen during the defence of an outpost near Hoi An south of Da Nang. USAF

In a tragic coincidence the only C-141 Starlifter strategic transports to be destroyed in Southeast Asia were lost within three weeks of each other in 1967. Despite problems of air base vulnerability, strategic transports regularly flew into major bases such as Da Nang, Tan Son Nhut, Cam Ranh Bay and Pleiku. USAF

6 April 1967

O-1E 51-5074 20 TASS, 504 TASG, USAF, Da Nang
Capt William George Sipos (KIA)
Capt John Robert Minutoli, US Army (KIA)
A Bird Dog was shot down 15 miles west of Da Nang while flying cover for a special operation. Both crew, including the US Army observer, were killed in the crash.

O-1E 56-2613, 56-2654 504 TASG, USAF, Quang Tri
A VC mortar attack on the airfield at Quang Tri destroyed two O-1 FAC aircraft.

F-4B 152999 VF-114, USN, USS *Kitty Hawk*
Lt(jg) F A Nutting (survived)
Lt(jg) M L Tuft (survived)
During a training flight a VF-114 Phantom entered an accelerated stall and then started to spin. The crew could not stop the spin in the altitude available and ejected safely.

7 April 1967

A-4C 149639 VA-195, USN, USS *Ticonderoga*
Cdr Charles E Hathaway (survived)
During an armed reconnaissance mission the CO of VA-195 and his wingman attacked a truck park 15 miles southwest of Mu Ron Ma. They had dropped their bombs on another target earlier in the mission so strafed the truck park with their 20mm cannon. On the second pass Cdr Hathaway felt the aircraft take a hit and lost his oxygen supply. The wingman warned the Commander that the aircraft was trailing a sheet of flame about 200 feet behind the aircraft. They headed east and crossed the coast but 20 miles short of the carrier Cdr Hathaway ejected as the fire progressively ate its way forward through the aircraft. He was picked up safely, probably by one of the *Ticonderoga's* Seasprites. Cdr Hathaway was on his 281st combat mission when he was shot down and achieved the second highest sortie count of any naval aviator during the war. Cdr Samuel R Chessman, who replaced Cdr Hathaway as the CO of VA-195 on 28 April, became the highest naval scorer with a total of 306 combat sorties during the war.

8 April 1967

F-4B 152978 VF-96, USN, USS *Enterprise*
Lt J R Ritchie (survived)
Ens F A Schumacher (survived)
Two Phantoms on a coastal reconnaissance mission had just started their run along the coast near Cam Pha, 15 miles east of Hon Gay, when they ran into AAA. Although the flak bursts appeared to be some distance away and the aircraft emerged unscathed, Lt Ritchie reported hydraulic failure 15 minutes later. The aircraft flew out to sea but 20 miles south of Hon Gay Lt Ritchie's aircraft suddenly became uncontrollable and the crew ejected. They were both picked up safely by a Navy helicopter.

10 April 1967

F-105D 62-4357 357 TFS, 355 TFW, USAF, Takhli
Maj John Francis O'Grady (KIA)
During an armed reconnaissance mission a flight of four F-105s, led by Maj O'Grady, flew through the Mu Gia Pass on the lookout for targets of opportunity, which were never difficult to find in this well-defended area. A battalion of North Vietnamese troops was seen moving through the pass on their way south. Maj O'Grady aborted his first bomb run as he was not lined up properly and came round behind his wingman to try again. As he pulled up from his attack his aircraft was hit by AAA and O'Grady lost control and ejected. His wingman spotted O'Grady's parachute in the air to the southwest of the target but the wind blew him back towards the target area. There was no beeper and no radio contact after the ejection. A search of the area revealed no trace of Maj O'Grady and it was presumed that he had been captured. However, at the end of the war John O'Grady did not reappear with other POWs and he is now presumed to have been killed on the ground. Vietnamese documents reviewed in 1991 indicate that Maj O'Grady was probably shot down by a unit of the 280th Air Defence Regiment and died of his injuries a few hours after capture.

A-4E 151200 VA-192, USN, USS *Ticonderoga*
Lt Cdr G W Shattuck (survived)
During an armed reconnaissance mission, several barges were seen near a river mouth about 20 miles north of Vinh. As the aircraft were orbiting near the river preparing for a dive attack on the barges, Lt Cdr Shattuck's aircraft was damaged by anti-aircraft fire. He could only get 85 per cent power and that was erratic at best. An attempt to refuel from a tanker failed as the Skyhawk's speed could not be controlled sufficiently and Lt Cdr Shattuck had no option but to eject when the engine flamed out. A Navy helicopter soon picked him up.

12 April 1967

A-4E 151039 VMA-211, MAG-12, USMC, Chu Lai
Capt William Clifton Clay (KIA)
A flight of Marine Corps A-4s was bombing a VC strongpoint 15 miles northwest of Tam Ky when one of the aircraft suddenly crashed near the target. As the aircraft pulled up from its dive one of the bombs it had just released detonated and blew off pieces of the port wing. The pilot may have been injured by the blast as he failed to eject.

13 April 1967

C-141A 66-0127 4 MAS, 62 MAW, USAF, McChord AFB
Maj Harry Milton Brenn (KIA)
Capt Morris Bowdoin Witt (KIA)
SMS Roy Earl Shults (KIA)
MSgt Herman Eugene Miller (KIA)

TSgt Marshall Edward Brown (KIA)
TSgt Harold Eugene Mahy (KIA)
2 other crew, names unknown (survived)
It was a tragic coincidence that MAC should lose another Starlifter in Vietnam so soon after the ground collision on 23 March. Less than three weeks after the first accident a Starlifter crashed soon after take off from Cam Ranh Bay killing six of the eight men on board. The accident was attributed to pilot error. These two were the only strategic transports lost by MAC in Southeast Asia during the Vietnam war although a C-5 crashed near Saigon during the evacuation on 4 April 1975.

14 April 1967

F-105D 60-0447 357 TFS, 355 TFW, USAF, Takhli
Maj Paul R Craw (survived)
The border town of Dien Bien Phu, better known for its role in a previous war in Southeast Asia, was visited infrequently by the USAF. However, like any North Vietnamese town, there was always a hot reception waiting for any aircraft that ventured near. A flight of F-105s was sent to bomb construction equipment that had been seen near the town. Maj Craw's aircraft was hit in the port wing by 37mm anti-aircraft fire as it dived on the target. He flew about 10 miles to the west of Dien Bien Phu before he was forced to eject. Despite being over 170 miles from the Thai border, Maj Craw was rescued by an HH-3 in one of the few rescue missions to this region of North Vietnam.

15 April 1967

C-123K 55-4575 311 ACS, 315 ACW, USAF, Tan Son Nhut
5 crew, names unknown (survived)
The rugged C-123B Provider was a valuable asset to the Air Force and Army in Southeast Asia but its performance in the hot and humid climate left much to be desired. In 1966 and 1967 Fairchild modified a number of Providers to C-123K standard. The aircraft was equipped with two J85 jet engines in pods under the wings to supplement its two piston engines thereby significantly enhancing its performance. The K model also had an improved brake system, new nacelle fuel tanks, a stall-warning system and other minor refinements. The C-123K's improvements not only gave the aircraft a better perfomance, thereby allowing the aircraft to operate at higher gross weights in and out of short up-country airstrips, but the jet engines also increased safety margins in the result of the loss of one of the piston engines. The first C-123K Provider to be destroyed in Southeast Asia was on a resupply flight when its nose undercarriage collapsed during landing. These aircraft operated out of some extremely rough airstrips that, coupled with a high rate of descent necessitated by the threat of ground fire, resulted in a considerable pounding for undercarriages and airframes. Many of these tough transports were literally worn out in Southeast Asia.

16 April 1967

C-130B 58-0722   29 TCS, 463 TCW, USAF, Clark
SSgt David Glover (KIA)
SSgt Donald Kannel (KIA)
A1C David Chaney (KIA)
3 crew, names unknown (survived)

The USAF lost its third transport aircraft in Vietnam during the month of April when a Hercules crashed while landing at Bao Loc during an airlift flight. The aircraft failed to slow down sufficiently after touch down due to a brake problem so the pilot lifted off again to attempt a go around. Unfortunately the aircraft struck a small hill a short way beyond the runway and crashed into a ravine detonating the aircraft's cargo of ammunition and killing three of the six crew.

17 April 1967

A-6A 152609   VMA(AW)-242, MAG-11, USMC, Da Nang
Maj James Maurice McGarvey (KIA)
Capt James Edward Carlton (KIA)

Maj McGarvey's target on the night of the 17th was a transshipment point at Vinh. The aircraft was seen to commence its bombing run over the coast about 15 miles southeast of the target but it must have been hit by AAA as the crew of another A-6 some eight miles behind saw the aircraft on fire and dive into the ground. A major SAR operation was mounted but after 10 days but there was no sign of either wreckage or crew.

18 April 1967

F-4B 151486   VMFA-323, MAG-13, USMC, Chu Lai
Lt Col Gordon H Keller (survived)
Capt Hugh L Julian (survived)

As a pair of Marine Corps F-4s climbed away from Chu Lai on a strike mission one of the aircraft suffered a complete electrical failure at 28,000 feet in heavy rain and clouds. The pilot could only communicate with his navigator by the use of hand signals. Lt Col Keller signaled to Capt Julian to eject but it took Keller three attempts to get his own ejection seat to fire. They both landed in the sea where Keller was soon located and picked up but Capt Julian was not found for nine hours. He had broken his arm, lost his life raft, survival radio and emergency light, but luckily was rescued by a passing shrimp boat. Equally lucky was the fact that the boat was crewed by South Vietnamese who were not sympathetic to the Viet Cong. Lt Cdr Keller was the commanding officer of VMFA-323 and this was the last aircraft lost by the unit before it rotated back to MCAS Iwakuni in Japan on 16 May.

19 April 1967

F-105F 63-8341   357 TFS, 355 TFW, USAF, Takhli
Maj Thomas Mark Madison (POW)
Maj Thomas James Sterling (POW)

An F-105F was lost on an Iron Hand mission, the 10th since the aircraft first deployed to Southeast Asia. Carbine flight was led by an F-105F (63-8301) flown by Maj Leo Thorsness and Capt Harry Johnson with Maj Madison and Maj Sterling flying the other Wild Weasel in the flight. The flight supported a raid on NVA barracks at Xuan Mai, 37 miles southwest of Hanoi. Two SAM sites near the target were attacked but Maj Madison's aircraft was shot down, probably by a MiG-17. The other two aircraft in the flight were also engaged by MiGs and had to return home with battle damage leaving just the leader's aircraft over the target. Thorsness circled the parachutes as Madison and Sterling floated down but then a MiG made a fast pass and Thorsness set off in pursuit and destroyed it with cannon fire. Capt Johnson had called for a SAR task force to attempt a rescue and Thorsness flew south to find a tanker to refuel before returning to where Madison and Sterling had landed. As he briefed the Sandy pilots on the situation Thorsness saw more MiGs and headed towards them. He damaged another of the MiGs with the last of his ammunition and then tried to decoy the remaining MiGs away from the Skyraiders. Eventually another flight of F-105s arrived and the MiGs retired after losing three more to the

Thud drivers. As Thorsness was leaving the area he heard one of the F-105 pilots radio that he was lost and short of fuel. Instead of refuelling himself, Thorsness sent the tanker north to rendezvous with the other F-105. Thorsness and Johnson landed at Udorn with their fuel tanks reading empty. For his actions during this mission Leo Thorsness was awarded the Medal of Honor and Harry Johnson was awarded the AFC although they were unaware of this fact as they were shot down and captured on 30 April. Maj Madison and Maj Sterling were both released from captivity on 4 March 1973.

A-1E 52-133905   602 ACS, 56 ACW, USAF, Udorn
Maj John Smith Hamilton (KIA)

The rescue forces moved into high gear as soon as the Wild Weasel crew went down during the raid on Xuan Mai. Within less than an hour a pair of Skyraiders were approaching the location of the downed crew. However, MiGs were still in the air and the slow, heavily-laden Skyraiders were vulnerable. When the Spads were about 25 miles southwest of Hanoi they were intercepted by four MiG-17s. Despite Maj Thorsness's efforts to draw the MiGs away, Maj Hamilton's aircraft was hit by 37mm cannon fire from a MiG. Maj Hamilton's wingman saw pieces of his leader's outer wing being shot off and the Skyraider roll over and crash into a mountain. No parachute was seen or SAR beeper heard. The MiGs then turned their attention to the remaining Sandy and repeatedly attacked it until a flight of F-105s arrived and shot down three MiGs and drove the rest away after a hard fight. Maj Hamilton was posted missing in action and declared killed in action in March 1979.

22 April 1967

B-57B 53-3859   13 TBS, 405 FW attached to 35 TFW,
USAF, Phan Rang
Maj James Edward Oxley (KIA)
Capt W E Estabrooks (survived)

A Canberra was lost during a close air support mission 15 miles southwest of Tan Son Nhut. Maj Oxley's aircraft was on its fourth run strafing the target in support of friendly troops when it was hit by small arms fire in the port wing and crashed less than a mile from the target. Both crew ejected but only the navigator survived.

23 April 1967

O-1G 50-1393   19 TASS, 504 TASG, USAF, Bien Hoa
1Lt John Wilton Vandeventer (KIA)
1 crew, name unknown (survived)

Forward air controllers frequently operated from small airstrips to be closer to the ground forces they were supporting. This close working relationship was vital to ensure that the FAC knew the ground situation in the area he was flying over and exactly where the friendly troops were. 1Lt Vandeventer was operating from Black Horse airstrip about eight miles south of Xuan Loc and was flying with an Army observer. As the aircraft climbed away from the airstrip it was hit by small arms fire and crashed.

F-4C 64-0756   389 TFS, 366 TFW, USAF, Da Nang
Capt W L Mekkers (survived)
1Lt J B Millhollon (survived)

Despite two disastrous raids in March, it was time for another strike on the Thai Nguyen iron and steel works. When the strike force was about 20 miles west of Yen Bai en route to the target, it encountered flak and one of the Phantom escorts was hit in the tail. The aircraft caught fire but Capt Mekkers turned southwest and flew for about 30 miles before he and his WSO were forced to part company with their aircraft. The pair were eventually picked up by an HH-3 SAR helicopter.

24 April 1967

F-4B 153000   VF-114, USN, USS *Kitty Hawk*
Lt Cdr Charles Everett Southwick (survived)
Ens Jim W Laing (survived)

A-6A 152589   VA-85, USN, USS *Kitty Hawk*
Lt(jg) Lewis Irving Williams (POW)
Lt(jg) Michael Durham Christian (POW)

After two years of political indecision, the first major strike on the MiG bases took place when Kep and Hoa Lac airfields were attacked on the 24th resulting in the loss of two naval aircraft at Kep. The strike force was protected by a TARCAP flight of six Phantoms led by Lt Cdr Southwick. As the Phantoms and the strike force approached Kep they came under heavy and accurate anti-aircraft fire. Lt Cdr Southwick's aircraft was hit by AAA as he escorted the first wave of bombers out of the target area. The aircraft appeared to be little damaged but in any case the crew were faced with a more pressing problem when they were attacked by eight MiGs from the 923rd Fighter Regiment. The Phantoms reversed course and headed towards the MiG-17s, four low down and four at the same altitude as the Phantoms. One of the MiGs passed over the Phantoms and Southwick reversed his course again, caught up with the MiG and shot it down. However, there was little time for celebration as Southwick's wingman warned him of another MiG-17 that was on his tail. A Phantom flown by Lt H D Wisely and Lt(jg) G L Anderson destroyed the MiG before it could do any damage. As the Phantoms retired towards the coast Lt Cdr Southwick discovered that he could not transfer fuel from the wing tank. Unable to reach a tanker in time, Southwick and Laing ejected over the sea about 20 miles south of Hon Gay and were rescued by a Navy helicopter. Lt Cdr Southwick, who had attacked North Vietnamese patrol boats during the original Gulf of Tonkin incident in August 1964, was shot down again on 14 May, but this time he was captured.

Among the bombers attacking Kep that day was an A-6 flown by Lt Williams and Lt Christian. The strike formation approached the target from the north and when they were about 10 miles from the airfield the Intruder's port wing was hit by 85mm flak and burst into flames. Within minutes the aircraft had lost engines, electrics and hydraulics and it started to spin. The crew jettisoned their bombs and ejected through a ball of fire and landed within a few yards of each other. They radioed that they were OK but were quickly captured. While in prison Mike Christian made a small American flag out of bits of cloth he scrounged together but it was discovered by the guards and he was almost beaten to death. The incident did not stop him making another flag as soon as he could move again. Both men were released on 4 March 1973. Irving Williams retired as a Captain in 1992 having commanded the naval air station at Alameda but Mike Christian resigned from the Navy in 1978 as a protest against an amnesty for draft dodgers. Tragically, Christian died in a fire at his home in Virginia Beach, Virginia in September 1983.

F-8C 146915   VF-24, USN, USS *Bon Homme Richard*
Lt Cdr Edwin Byron Tucker (KIA)

Simultaneously with the raid on Kep, another strike force pounded the railway yard at Hon Gay. A section of Crusaders provided flak suppression for eight Skyhawks but Lt Cdr Tucker's aircraft took a direct hit from an 85mm shell and disintegrated. A parachute was seen but it does not appear that Lt Cdr Tucker survived to reach a prison camp. A subsequent intelligence report claims that Tucker was severely injured during the ejection and was taken to a hospital in Hon Gay where he later died of his wounds. According to information provided by several sources, Lt Cdr Tucker's skeleton was used as a teaching aid in the hospital in Hon Gay. The remains were finally handed over to the US in 1987 and in 1988 Edwin Tucker was buried at Arlington National Cemetery with full military honours.

F-4C 63-7641   433 TFS, 8 TFW, USAF, Ubon
Maj Herman Ludwig Knapp (KIA)
1Lt Charles David Austin (KIA)

As the Navy was attacking targets east of Hanoi the Air Force was concentrating on targets to the west of the city. A flight of four Phantoms from Ubon had just bombed their target (either Hoa Lac airfield or a bridge near Hanoi according to different sources) and was heading back to Thailand when one of the aircraft was hit by AAA. The aircraft disintegrated and came down in two large pieces 20 miles west of Hoa Binh. It was felt unlikely that the crew could have escaped from the burning wreck as the aircraft was only flying about 200 feet above the ground when it was hit.

25 April 1967

F-105D 62-4294 354 TFS, 355 TFW, USAF, Takhli
1Lt Robert Larry Weskamp (KIA)

An F-105 was lost en route to a raid on a transformer station on the outskirts of Hanoi. This transformer was a small target situated in a village just north of the city but it supplied much of Hanoi's electricity and was therefore a prime target. The raid consisted of five bomber flights, a Wild Weasel flight and an F-4 MiGCAP flight from the 8th TFW. As Crab flight headed south of Phuc Yen towards the target it came under fire from SAMs and AAA. The flight dived towards the ground and had to pull out sharply. 1Lt Weskamp called that his aircraft was hit but the aircraft crashed and exploded before he could eject. Another pilot saw the 3,000lb bombs from 1Lt Weskamp's aircraft break loose as he pulled up to avoid the ground and this may have caused the F-105 to crash. There is also the possibility that the aircraft was hit by 85mm flak as the flight was passing through an intense barrage at the time. The aircraft came down about 10 miles north of Hanoi. Apparently, Bob Weskamp's brother was flying in one of the KC-135 tankers that supported this raid.

A-4C 147799 VA-76, USN, USS *Bon Homme Richard*
Lt Charles David Stackhouse (POW)

A raid on POL and ammunition storage sites at Haiphong resulted in the loss of two of the attackers. Lt Stackhouse had just released his bombs on a revetted ammunition dump when his section was engaged by several MiG-17s that had taken off from Kien An. He was about to shoot at a MiG that was chasing his wingman when he felt his Skyhawk judder as it was hit in the engine by 37mm cannon shells fired by another MiG. The engine wound down rapidly and the aircraft was seen to be on fire. Stackhouse ejected as he lost control and landed in a rice paddy just south of Haiphong, where he was captured. Charles Stackhouse spent almost six years as a POW and was finally released on 4 March 1973.

A-4E 151116 VA-192, USN, USS *Ticonderoga*
Lt Cdr F J Almberg (survived)

As Lt Stackhouse was being chased south of Haiphong, an Iron Hand flight was tackling a SAM site a few miles to the north of the city. Lt Cdr Almberg had just fired his third Shrike missile when a near miss from an SA-2 rocked his aircraft. No damage was seen so the attack continued but another missile exploded close to the aircraft at which point the hydraulics proceeded to fail. Almberg headed for the coast and disconnected the hydraulics to fly the aircraft on manual. As he approached a SAR destroyer about 40 miles southeast of Haiphong, the controls went slack and the aircraft pitched nose down. Lt Cdr Almberg ejected and was picked up by a Navy helicopter.

A-4E 151102 VA-212, USN, USS *Bon Homme Richard*
Lt(jg) A R Crebo (survived)

Later in the day the *Bon Homme Richard* mounted another raid against an ammunition depot on the southern outskirts of Haiphong. Lt Crebo approached the target and pulled up to 8,000 feet to start his dive. At the top of his manoeuvre an SA-2 exploded near the aircraft but Crebo dived down to drop his bombs. As he pulled out of the dive the aircraft became uncontrollable but Lt Crebo skilfully regained control, disconnected the hydraulic system and flew the aircraft on manual back out to sea and towards the carrier. As he approached the *Bon Homme Richard* only the nose undercarriage would extend and then the engine flamed out and would not restart. Lt Crebo ejected and was picked up by the carrier's escort destroyer. A well-publicised photograph was taken of Crebo's aircraft just before he ejected showing that the rudder and top of the tailfin was missing.

26 April 1967

A-4E 152076 VA-192, USN, USS *Ticonderoga*
Lt(jg) J W Cain (survived)

A-4E 151073 VA-192, USN, USS *Ticonderoga*
Lt Cdr Michael John Estocin (KIA)

A raid on a POL site at Haiphong resulted in the loss of two aircraft and one pilot but saw one of the most outstanding acts of bravery and skill of the entire war. On the run in to the target one of the Skyhawk bombers was hit by AAA but continued to drop its bombs and climb away. Lt Cain saw smoke in the cockpit and lost his electrics and eventually the hydraulic system. When the aircraft started rolling into a dense cloud layer, Cain attempted to disconnect the hydraulics but this had no effect so he ejected. He came down just offshore about 15 miles south of Haiphong and was rescued 20 minutes later by a Navy helicopter assisted by 10 F-8s and two A-1s, which strafed enemy vessels and gun positions that were firing at the survivor and the helicopter.

Lt Cdr Estocin, VA-192's operations officer, specialised in the Iron Hand mission and, despite severe damage to his aircraft, had destroyed three SAM launchers on 20 April during a strike on two thermal power plants near Haiphong. He required in-flight refuelling all the way back to the carrier but landed safely into the barrier with his aircraft still burning. Six days later he and his two wingmen once more flew ahead of a strike force to take on a SAM site during the Haiphong POL strike. He fired a Shrike and then climbed to deliver another attack. At 12,000 feet and less than 10 miles northeast of the city, Lt Cdr Estocin spotted an SA-2 that was heading directly for him. Waiting until it closed on the aircraft, probably with the intention of firing a Shrike at the site, he began a hard turn but he had left it too late and the SAM exploded very close to the aircraft. The Skyhawk burst into flames and completed four or five rolls diving towards the ground before the pilot regained some measure of control. Lt Cdr Estocin turned towards the coast with the rear of his aircraft burning furiously and fuel venting from the wings. He was accompanied by an F-8 flown by Lt Cdr J B Nichols of VF-191 who tried in vain to contact Estocin by radio. After flying in this condition for nearly 20 miles the Skyhawk started rolling again and then crashed inverted into the sea just off the island of Dao Cat Ba. During the final manoeuvre the aircraft's centreline fuel tank was seen to separate from the aircraft and both Shrikes fired, probably as a result of fire damage to the aircraft's electrical system. Lt Cdr Estocin was not seen to eject before the aircraft dived into the sea. An extensive search failed to reveal any evidence of aircraft or pilot. Rumours surfaced after the war that Mike Estocin had survived and been captured but this information has not been substantiated and Lt Cdr Estocin was officially declared dead on 10 November 1977. For his courage and devotion to duty on his final mission and that of 20 April Lt Cdr Michael Estocin was posthumously awarded the Medal of Honour, the only Navy jet pilot so honoured for a combat mission. On 3 November 1979 the Oliver Hazard Perry-class firgate, USS *Estocin*, was launched in honor of Mike Estocin.

F-105F 63-8277 333 TFS, 355 TFW, USAF, Takhli
Maj John Francis Dudash (KIA)
Capt Alton Benno Meyer (POW)

Mike Estocin was not the only Iron Hand loss on the 26th. A Wild Weasel crew was leading a flight of F-105s against a SAM site 30 miles west of Thai Nguyen in support of a raid on a thermal power plant near Hanoi when they also became victims of the SA-2. The aircraft was at 6,000 feet when it was hit by the last of three missiles fired at it. The aircraft exploded moments later. Capt Meyer ejected and was captured but the fate of Maj Dudash was not known for many years. In June 1983 the Vietnamese finally handed over remains that proved to be those of Maj Dudash. It is still not known exactly how he died. Alton Meyer, who broke his leg on ejection, was eventually released on 4 March 1973.

F-105D 58-1153 469 TFS, 388 TFW, USAF, Korat
Capt William Michael Meyer (KIA)

By an incredible coincidence another Capt Meyer was shot down in an F-105 over North Vietnam on the 26th. Maj William Meyer was flying on a raid on the Hanoi railway and road bridge when his aircraft was hit by AAA and crashed near Gia Lam, on the northeastern outskirts of Hanoi. Like Maj Dudash, nothing was known for certain of the fate of Capt Meyer until the Vietnamese returned his remains on 14 August 1985.

AC-47D 43-48921 4 ACS, 14 ACW, USAF, Nha Trang
detached to Tan Son Nhut
Maj Burnett Neal (KIA)
Maj Bruce Reginald Williams (KIA)
1Lt Clifford C Barnett (KIA)
SSgt Frederick Edward Barnette (KIA)
SSgt Robert Wendell Davis (KIA)
SSgt Thomas Alfred Preaux (KIA)
A1C Michael Jeff Stephens (KIA)

A Spooky gunship on a night flare mission was flying a normal orbit off the coast near Cam Ranh Bay when it was observed to crash into the sea and explode. All on board the aircraft were killed in the crash, the cause of which was not ascertained.

28 April 1967

O-1G 51-16950 21 TASS, 504 TASG, USAF, Nha Trang
detached to Tuy Hoa
Maj Morrison Arthur Cotner (KIA)
TSgt Carmen Muscara, US Army (KIA)

During an FAC mission a Bird Dog was lost just off the coast about 20 miles south of Tuy Hoa, probably the victim of small arms fire.

F-105D 58-1151 44 TFS, 388 TFW, USAF, Korat
Capt Franklin Angel Caras (KIA)

Hanoi was once again the focus of attention for the Rolling Thunder bombers. The target was Hanoi's railway repair shops, which were vital to keep North Vietnam's locomotives and rolling stock on the rails. On the return journey after the raid the F-105s of the flak suppression flight were attacked by several MiG-21s about 80 miles west of Hanoi. Capt Caras and his wingman were at 12,000 feet when both their aircraft were hit by cannon fire from the MiGs. The wingman's aircraft was only slightly damaged but Capt Caras's aircraft crashed 15 miles east of Na San and it was presumed that he had died in the crash.

F-4C 64-0720 433 TFS, 8 TFW, USAF, Ubon
2 crew, names unknown (survived)

A Phantom was destroyed as it was taking off from Ubon when one of it bombs exploded as it contacted the runway. Both crew somehow survived. This Phantom had been flown by Capt J B Stone and 1Lt C P Dunnegan of the 433rd TFS during Operation Bolo on 2 January when they shot down a MiG-21

29 April 1967

F-4C 64-0670 389 TFS, 366 TFW, USAF, Da Nang
1Lt Loren Harvey Torkleson (POW)
1Lt George John Pollin (KIA)

Another raid on one of Hanoi's bridges took place on the 29th with two more aircraft lost in the process, neither of them actually involved in bombing the bridge. A flight of four Phantoms from Da Nang was tasked to fly CAPs around Hanoi as the F-105 strike force went in. 1Lt Torkleson's Phantom was about 15 miles west of the city and flying at 4,500 feet when the aircraft was hit by AAA. 1Lt Torkleson ejected from the stricken aircraft but his WSO, 1Lt George Pollin, either did not eject or ejected but was killed. George Pollin volunteered to fly on this mission in place of another WSO who was sick. He had flown over 60 missions and was eager to reach the magic figure of 100 when he could return home. George Pollin did finally return home, his remains being positively identified on 20 December 1990 after repatriation by the Vietnamese. Loren Torkleson was released on 4 March 1973.

RF-4C 65-0872 11 TRS, 432 TRW, USAF, Udorn
Maj Mark Lane Stephensen (KIA)
1Lt Gary Richard Sigler (POW)

As night fell an RF-4C sped across Laos and into North Vietnam to take flash photographs of the damage done to the bridge at Hanoi. Flying at low level en route to the target the crew suddenly recieved a warning that a SAM radar had locked on to them. Maj Stephensen started evasive action but the aircraft flew through the tops of several trees with enough violence to cause the navigator to eject immediately. As he swung in his parachute he saw the aircraft crash into a hill with no indication that the pilot had ejected. 1Lt Sigler was captured after two days on the run and spent nearly six years as a POW before his release on 4 March

A two-seat F-105F Wild Weasel of the 44th TFS takes off for another mission to battle the SAM sites that threatened the strike forces over North Vietnam. The Wild Weasel mission was one of the most dangerous missions of the war and the high loss rate reflected the risks involved. USAF

1973. In April 1988 the Vietnamese handed over remains which they said were those of Maj Stephensen and this was verified in the following August. Gary Sigler was flying his 93rd mission when he was shot down.

30 April 1967

F-105F 62-4447   357 TFS, 355 TFW, USAF, Takhli
                   Maj Leo Keith Thorsness (POW)
                   Capt Harold Eugene Johnson (POW)

F-105D 59-1726   354 TFS, 355 TFW, USAF, Takhli
                   1Lt Robert Archie Abbott (POW)

F-105D 61-0130   333 TFS, 355 TFW, USAF, Takhli
                   Capt Joseph S Abbott (POW)

The last day of the month saw a major raid on an important thermal power plant near Hanoi and, although no aircraft were lost over the target, three F-105s were lost during the raid resulting in the capture of four airmen. The raid was led by Col Jack Broughton, the vice-commander of the 355th TFW, who wrote about this mission in his book *Thud Ridge*. Carbine flight consisted of three Wild Weasel F-105Fs and a single D model and was the Iron Hand flight responsible for tackling any SAM sites that might threaten the strike force. When Carbine flight was inbound to the target but still about 50 miles west of Hanoi it was intercepted by a number of MiG-21s. One of the MiGs fired an Atoll missile that hit and damaged Maj Thorsness's aircraft (Carbine 3). With the aircraft on fire the crew ejected and landed safely in hills about 25 miles south of Yen Bai. The pair contacted their flight leader, Maj Ben Fuller in Carbine 1, who advised them to make their way up a nearby hill to await a possible rescue.

At about the same time that Carbine 3 was being attacked another member of the flight was also in trouble. 1Lt Robert Abbott's aircraft, the single-seat D model flying as Carbine 4, was also hit by a missile and he ejected just a few miles away from his two colleagues. Col Broughton was a couple of minutes behind the Weasel flight and told Maj Ed Dobson leading Tomahawk flight to fly RESCAP over the downed airmen until a SAR force could arrive. Maj Al Lenski, who was flying Tomahawk 3, relates this mission in great detail in his book *Magic 100* and believes that Bob Abbott was actually shot down before Carbine 3 was hit but that most of the strike force failed to see this or hear a warning transmission from Carbine 2.

When Carbine 3 went down the information was passed to Crown, the HC-130 that acted as rescue coordinator, and a SAR force was launched. Tomahawk flight had split so that two aircraft were orbiting low over the downed airmen and two were higher up acting as radio relays to Crown and the SAR aircraft. Meanwhile the other F-105s had aborted the mission to the thermal power plant, which had almost certainly been destroyed in a raid a few days earlier anyway, and set off to find some tankers

to refuel so they could return and take over RESCAP duties if needed. It was only as Carbine flight was heading to the tanker that they realised that Bob Abbott had also been shot down. Maj Al Lenski and Capt Joe Abbott of Tomahawk's high flight set up a racetrack pattern at 15,000 feet about 10 miles south of the survivors' position and orbited for about 30 minutes until the two remaining aircraft of Carbine flight arrived back from the tanker. Almost at the same time the first A-1 Sandies arrived to start searching for the downed airmen but had difficulty seeing where Thorsness and Johnson had come down. Al Lenski and Joe Abbott were just about to turn south to head for the tanker when they were attacked from behind by MiG-21s. Both Tomahawk aircraft were hit by Atoll missiles and Capt Abbott's aircraft burst into flames forcing him to eject. Maj Lenski's aircraft was badly damaged but he managed to escape into a cloud layer and only just made it to a tanker before running out of fuel. Al Lenski landed safely at Udorn despite severe damage to his aircraft including the loss of his Tacan and other navigational aids.

With three aircraft down and four men on the ground Col Broughton's Waco flight arrived back from refuelling and took over the RESCAP. The Sandy flight had to leave the area to return to Udorn for fuel but on their way they heard about Joe Abbott being shot down. They diverted and located Joe Abbott and passed his poistion to Crown before leaving for Udorn. A few minutes later one of the Sandies was hit by ground fire and almost added to the day's toll but the pilot dived the Skyraider to put out the flames and limped back to Thailand. Worse luck followed as one of the two Jolly Greens inbound to the survivors developed a hydraulic problem and had to abort. Standard operating procedures at that time did not normally allow a single helicopter to continue in case it should be shot down with no back up to rescue the crew, so both helicopters turned back. The presence of MiGs in the area must also have had some bearing on the decision not to persist with the rescue attempt until the enemy aircraft had been cleared from the area. A rescue mission was mounted the following day and for several days afterwards F-105s made visual and radio searches of the area for signs of the survivors but none of the airmen who were downed on the 30th were rescued.

The one positive aspect of the mission was that all four airmen survived to become POWs in the Hanoi Hilton. Joseph Abbott, who was a Wing officer attached to the 333rd TFS for this mission, was released on 18 February 1973, slightly earlier than the others. Leo Thorsness, Harry Johnson and Bob Abbott were all released on 4 March 1973 after suffering the usual hardship at the hands of their North Vietnamese captors. The coincidence of two airmen of the same surname being shot down on the same raid that had first occurred on 26 April with the two Meyers, had happened once again with Robert and Joseph Abbott. Another aircraft was almost lost during this incident when an A-1E flown by Capt Bill Thompson of the 602nd ACS ran short of fuel having

jettisoned his drop tanks following a MiG warning. Thompson later assisted in the attempted rescue of Capt Abbott but had to force land in darkness at a forward airstrip in northern Laos.

All four POWs resumed their Air Force careers following release. Robert Abbott returned to flying and retired as a Colonel. Harry Johnson was one of several prisoners who were incarcerated in a prison known as 'Dogpatch' near Cao Bang close to the Chinese border. He later served a tour as an exchange instructor at the Royal Air Force Staff College in Bracknell and retired as a Colonel. Unknown to Leo Thorsness, he had been awarded the Medal of Honor soon after he was taken prisoner. He and Harry Johnson had flown 92 missions before their ill-fated final sortie and they had been successful on many occasions either destroying SAM sites or forcing them to close down at critical periods when the strike force was nearby. However, the Medal of Honor was awarded specifically for his actions on 19 April following the shooting down of his wingman. The award was kept secret at the time in case the North Vietnamese should single Thorsness out for special punishment. As it was the brutal treatment meted out to most prisoners at this period of the war was almost unbearable. After his retirement from the Air Force Leo Thorsness became active in politics and became the Republican Senator for Seattle. He maintained a special interest in POW and veterans affairs and in 1990 sponsored the 'Truth Bill', which forced the US government to release classified information on US prisoners dating back to the Second World War.

1 May 1967

F-8E 150301   VF-51, USN, USS *Hancock*
                Lt(jg) C R Ramskill (survived)

The *Hancock* lost a Crusader on the 1st of the month when its engine seized during an armed reconnaissance mission. The engine failed to relight and the pilot was forced to eject from the aircraft.

2 May 1967

F-100F 56-3980   352 TFS, 35 TFW, USAF, Phan Rang
                   Maj F D Howard (survived)
                   SSgt T P Kulick (survived)

Maj Howard was taking part in a close air support mission near Cam Ranh Bay and was carrying SSgt Kulick who was going to take photographs of a napalm delivery. The mission turned out to be even more spectacular than planned as the two-seat Super Sabre was hit by ground fire as it approached the target at 750 feet. Maj Howard turned the aircraft out over the coast and the two airmen ejected over the sea. They were both picked up safely by an Army helicopter.

F-4C 64-0689   558 TFS, 12 TFW, USAF, Cam Ranh Bay
                 2 crew, names unknown (survived)

A fire developed in a Phantom as it started down the runway at Cam Ranh Bay. The pilot aborted the take off but the aircraft was damaged beyond repair. This aircraft had previously been used by the 555th TFS and was flown by Capt M F Cameron and 1Lt R E Evans when they shot down a MiG-17 on 23 April 1966.

3 May 1967

F-105D 62-4405   333 TFS, 355 TFW, USAF, Takhli
                   Maj Charles C Vasiliadis (survived)

A flight of F-105s on an armed reconnaissance mission near Son La, 100 miles to the west of Hanoi, spotted trucks on a road in the hills. The aircraft went down to strafe the target but one of the F-105s was hit in the port wing by 37mm anti-aircraft fire. With the wing burning Maj Vasiliadis headed away from Son La but was forced to eject after a few minutes. Despite severe injuries to left his leg and hip received during the ejection, he evaded North Vietnamese troops and was rescued by an HH-3E. The injuries

were caused because Maj Vasiliadis was attempting to maintain control of the aircraft by keeping his foot on the rudder when he lost aileron control. As he ejected his leg hit the instrument panel and was badly shattered. Maj Vasiliadis had flown his first tour in Southeast Asia in 1964/65 flying Skyraiders with the 1st and 602nd ACSs. He flew a total of 1,141 combat flying hours during 560 missions in Southeast Asia.

A-1E   52-132638   1 ACS, 14 ACW, USAF, Pleiku
Maj Charles Edward Rogers (KIA)

A truck park had been discovered on Route 111 near Attopeu in southern Laos and was the target for a flight of Skyraiders from Pleiku. Maj Rogers came down to 500 feet to drop napalm but his Skyraider took hits from AAA in the tail and the aircraft dived into the ground. It was apparent that Maj Rogers had not had time to abandon the aircraft and had been killed.

A-4E   152055   VMA-121, MAG-12, USMC, Chu Lai
1 pilot, name unknown (survived)

An accident during in-flight refuelling caused the loss of a Skyhawk during an escort mission over South Vietnam.

4 May 1967

F-8E   150316   VMF(AW)-232, MAG-11, USMC, Da Nang
Maj Edward F Townley (survived)

A Marine Corps F-8 was shot down about 35 miles west of Da Nang on a mission to bomb a ford, which was known to be a crossing point for enemy forces. The aircraft's rear fuselage was engulfed in flames as Maj Townley made for the coast. He ejected safely and was soon rescued by a helicopter.

A-4C   148514   VA-113, USN, USS *Enterprise*
Lt(jg) James Scott Graham (KIA)

A division of four A-4s was assigned to attack a SAM site five miles northeast of Thanh Hoa and close to the village of Sam Son. Lt Graham put his aircraft into a 45-degree dive from 4,500 feet but it must have been hit by AAA as the next time the leader looked in his direction Graham had ejected. The leader flew past the parachute and Lt Graham waved his arm as he descended into the tops of some trees near the village of Kieu Thon. However, Jim Graham apparently never arrived at a North Vietnamese prison camp and was not released during Operation Homecoming. Nothing more was known until the Vietnamese repatriated his remains in August 1985 and the circumstances of his death remain a mystery. Lt Graham had served a tour on the *Kitty Hawk* before returning to Vietnam on the *Enterprise* and had flown 172 missions over Southeast Asia.

5 May 1967

F-105D   61-0198   357 TFS, 355 TFW, USAF, Takhli
1Lt James Richard Shively (POW)

The 5th of May was yet another bad day for the F-105 wings with three aircraft lost within 10 minutes. Aircraft from both wings made simultaneous attacks on various targets around Hanoi. 1Lt Shively was part of the flak suppression flight on a raid on the railway yards at Yen Vien and his aircraft was hit by AAA over Hanoi as it was returning from the raid. Shively ejected from his burning aircraft about 15 miles southwest of Hanoi and was quickly captured. James Shively was released from imprisonment on 18 February 1973.

F-105D   62-4401   469 TFS, 388 TFW, USAF, Korat
Lt Col James Lindberg Hughes (POW)

F-105D   62-4352   469 TFS, 388 TFW, USAF, Korat
Lt Col Gordon Albert Larson (POW)

As aircraft from Takhli were hitting Yen Vien, a squadron from Korat was approaching its target, the army barracks at Ha Dong, a few miles southwest of Hanoi. At 17,000 feet Dagger flight was above the height of most of the flak but the larger calibre guns could reach these altitudes as Lt Col Hughes discovered. His aircraft, nicknamed 'The Flying Dutchman', was hit in the tail by an 85mm shell, which also disrupted the aircraft's electrical and fuel systems. Lt Col Hughes ejected near Hoa Lac, 15 miles west of Hanoi and had his helmet blown off his head during the ejec-

tion sequence and was knocked unconscious. He came to with facial injuries but once on the ground he was stripped and thrown into an animal pen before transfer to the Hanoi Hilton where his injuries did not save him from the usual torture sessions that greeted each new arrival.

When Jim Hughes went down, the 469th's squadron commander and leader of Dagger flight, Lt Col 'Swede' Larson, immediately converted the raid into a SAR mission. He circled the position where Hughes had gone down but less than a couple of minutes later he was also floating down in his parachute, the victim of an SA-2. He ejected at a speed exceeding Mach 1, which resulted in a fractured knee and compression fractures to the vertebrae. Lt Col Larson was captured and tortured as soon as he landed. Hughes and Larson were both released on 4 March 1973, by then promoted in absentia to the rank of full Colonel. 'Swede' Larson had served in the US Navy towards the end of the Second World War and had joined the USAF in 1948. During his long Air Force career he had flown P-47s, P-51s, F-84s, F-86s, B-47s and B-52s before converting to the F-105 and taking command of the 469th in November 1966. He was on his 94th mission when he was shot down and has written a graphic account of his treatment as a POW, which has been published on the Internet. He was medically retired from the Air Force in 1974 due to the injuries suffered during his ejection and the subsequent treatment as a POW. 62-4352 was painted as 'Thunderchief' during its service at Korat.

6 May 1967

A-4E   151082   VA-93, USN, USS *Hancock*
Lt(jg) Robert Earl Wideman (POW)

The *Hancock* lost an A-4 during an armed reconnaissance mission 35 miles south of Thanh Hoa. A section of aircraft was attacking barges on a waterway near the coast when one of the aircraft was hit as it was about to fire rockets at the target. An aileron may have been damaged by anti-aircraft fire as the aircraft began to roll uncontrollably and Lt Wideman ejected. He was captured and imprisoned until his release on 4 March 1973.

8 May 1967

F-105D   61-0105   333 TFS, 355 TFW, USAF, Takhli
Capt Michael K McCuistion (POW)

During an armed reconnaissance in the Mu Gia Pass area a flight of four F-105s spotted a single railway wagon parked in a siding near Xom Hoai. The flight rolled in on the target but the last man, Capt McCustion, was hit by 37mm anti-aircraft fire. With his rear fuselage engulfed in flames he headed west away from the target area but after about a minute he was forced to eject. Two of the F-105s made strafing runs on enemy troops who were approaching the downed pilot while the other aircraft, flown by Maj Al Lenski reprising his role of 30 April, climbed to altitude to provide radio relay to organise the SAR effort. A flight of A-1s arrived and took over the RESCAP from the F-105s, which left to refuel from a tanker. However, before the helicopters could arrive Capt McCustion was captured by North Vietnamese troops. He was taken prisoner and eventually released on 4 March 1973 and retired from the Air Force in 1981 to become a corporate pilot. The aircraft that Capt McCuistion was flying on the 8th was the personal mount of the Wing Commander, Col Bob Scott.

F-4B   152997   VF-114, USN, USS *Kitty Hawk*
Lt(jg) Thomas Jack Steimer (KIA)
Lt(jg) M L Tuft (survived)

During a catapult launch from the *Kitty Hawk* on an armed reconnaissance mission an F-4 overrotated, stalled and crashed into the sea killing one of the crew. Lt Tuft had previously ejected from a Phantom on 6 April.

9 May 1967

F-4C   63-7652   433 TFS, 8 TFW, USAF, Ubon
2 crew, names unknown (survived)

As a Phantom was taking off from Ubon the tyre on its left main undercarriage burst and shredded, which caused the aircraft to slew off the runway.

10 May 1967

F-100D   55-3618   308 TFS, 31 TFW, USAF, Tuy Hoa
Maj Leonard Edward Niski (KIA)

A flight of F-100s was attacking a group of VC buildings near Plei Niang, 35 miles west of Qui Nhon, when one of the aircraft was shot down. Maj Niski was making his second strafing pass when his Super Sabre was hit by small arms fire and crashed immediately. Maj Niski's body was later recovered by a US Army helicopter.

A-4C   149509   VA-94, USN, USS *Hancock*
Cdr Roger Morton Netherland (KIA)

A section of A-4s tasked with flak suppression was approaching Kien An airfield near Haiphong when it encountered SAMs. Two SA-2s were successfully evaded but a third exploded just under Cdr 'Dutch' Netherland's aircraft. The aircraft turned through 180 degress and headed for the sea but was seen to be streaming fuel and on fire. It is possible that the pilot was wounded because the aircraft flew on to a position about 10 miles south of Haiphong before rolling inverted and crashing without any apparent attempt to eject. Cdr Netherland had been the commander of the *Hancock's* CVW-5 since November 1966.

A-4E   151997   VMA-223, MAG-12, USMC, Chu Lai
Maj Robert Lee Snyder (KIA)

Maj Snyder (a MAG-12 staff officer flying with VMA-223) was taking part in a night TPQ-10 radar-directed bombing mission 20 miles south of Dong Hoi and just 15 miles north of the DMZ. His aircraft was flying at 17,000 feet when it was badly damaged by a near miss from an SA-2 missile. Maj Snyder nursed his aircraft back towards South Vietnam but he was killed when the aircraft crashed in the DMZ buffer zone.

11 May 1967

A-4E   150011   VMA-121, MAG-12, USMC, Chu Lai
Capt G R Romano (survived)

Capt Romano was attacking a force of VC with napalm near Tra Bong, 15 miles southwest of Chu Lai when he was shot down. The aircraft was hit by automatic weapons fire and burst into flames. Capt Romano ejected and was fortunate to be picked up by an Army helicopter before the VC could reach him.

12 May 1967

F-4C   63-7614   390 TFS, 366 TFW, USAF, Da Nang
Col Norman Carl Gaddis (POW)
1Lt James Milton Jefferson (KIA)

Another raid on the NVA barracks at Ha Dong took place on the 12th. Col Gaddis was flying wing for Col F C 'Boots' Blesse in a CAP flight of F-4s from Da Nang. Norm Gaddis was the director of operations of the 12th TFW but was flying with the 366th during an exchange programme where the DOs of F-4 and F-100 fighter wings flew with other wings for a short period to exchange views on tactics. As the strike force was retiring from the target a couple of SAMs were fired at it then several MiG-17s appeared on the scene. Col Gaddis's aircraft was damaged by AAA over the target and was lagging behind the others when it was hit by cannon fire from one of the MiGs near Hoa Lac airfield. The WSO, 1Lt Jefferson, ejected first followed by Col Gaddis who was quickly captured. During interrogation in prison the Colonel was shown items of flight clothing belonging to Jefferson but it seems that the young WSO had been killed in the incident. Col Gaddis was on his 73rd mission when he was shot down. He was released on 4 March 1973 but there is still no confirmation as to what happened to his WSO although the Vietnamese claim to have buried him close to the aircraft crash site. Norman Gaddis was commissioned in 1944 and flew P-40s and P-51s in the USA before being demobilised in 1945. He was recalled to active duty in 1949 and flew F-84Gs on ground attack missions during the Korean War. After many appointments including tours with the 81st TFW at Bentwaters in England and the Fighter Weapons School at Nellis AFB, Nevada, he was posted to Cam Ranh Bay in November 1966. He was the first full Colonel to be captured by the North Vietnamese. Following his release he served in a

number of staff appointments and eventually rose to the rank of Brigadier General before retirement on 1 June 1976. At the VPAF Museum in Hanoi MiG-17F serial number 2011 of the 923rd Fighter Regiment is displayed with the information that it was flown by Lt Ngo Duc Mai on 12 May 1967 when he shot down an F-4. It is also claimed that the 923rd Fighter Regiment shot down two other US aircraft on this date which, if true, might account for the two F-105s listed below.

F-105D 59-1728   357 TFS, 355 TFW, USAF, Takhli
                  Capt Earl Wilfred Grenzebach (KIA)
In conjunction with the strike on Ha Dong, a formation of F-105s attacked a storage depot at Nguyen Khe. As the formation climbed for altitude after hitting the target Capt Grenzebach's aircraft was hit in the rear fuselage by ground fire and burst into flames. He apparently ejected about 10 miles south of Yen Bai but he did not survive to reach imprisonment although the exact circumstances of his death are unknown. Col Blesse's CAP flight of three F-4s that had been looking for Col Gaddis returned after in-flight refuelling to look for Capt Grenzebach but found no trace of the downed pilot.

F-105F 63-8269   34 TFS, 388 TFW, USAF, Korat
                  Capt Peter Potter Pitman (KIA)
                  Capt Robert Allen Stewart (KIA)
A two-seat F-105F disappeared during a Rolling Thunder strike on a ferry complex at Ron in the Quang Binh province of North Vietnam. The aircraft was not fitted for the Wild Weasel role and was presumably taking part in the raid as a bomber and may have been a Project Northscope aircraft. These were F-105Fs that were modified with improved radar for all-weather bombing missions. The modified aircraft were normally assigned to the 13th TFS and were nicknamed 'Ryan's Raiders'. Capt Pitman and Capt Stewart were presumably killed during the mission, as they did not survive as POWs.

F-100D 56-2954   3 TFW, USAF, Bien Hoa
F-102A 56-1165   509 FIS, 405 FW, USAF, Bien Hoa
O-1G   51-12825   19 TASS, 504 TASG, USAF, Bien Hoa
                  A VC mortar attack on Bien Hoa destroyed
three USAF aircraft. Two VNAF aircraft were also destroyed during the attack. A total of 189 rounds were fired at the air base and its facilities causing six fatalities.

13 May 1967

A-4E   152060   VMA-223, MAG-12, USMC, Chu Lai
                  Capt George A Kinser (survived)
MAG-12 at Chu Lai was going through a rough patch as their third A-4 was lost within the space of four days. Capt Kinser was attacking North Vietnamese troops five miles west of Dong Ha, just south of the DMZ, when his aircraft was hit by ground fire

while on his second pass. He ejected immediately and was rescued by helicopter before the enemy troops could reach him.

US-2C 133365   VC-5, USN, Cubi Point
                  Lt Cdr Robert Eugene Robinson (KWF)
                  Ens John Wesley Coghill (KWF)
                  1 crew, name unknown (survived)
VC-5 was a Navy utility squadron based at Cubi Point NAS in the Philippines operating a variety of aircraft including US-2 Trackers, A-4 Skyhawks and even the ancient Beech SNB. The Squadron's duties included target towing and logistics and it was while on a logistics flight that a Tracker suffered an engine fire and crashed. The Veteran's Memorial Wall database claims that the aircraft crashed on land in Kien Giang province in the southern tip of South Vietnam but the official Navy account states that the aircraft crashed in the sea.

A total of seven MiG-17s were shot down by USAF F-4s and F-105s in a major air battle during a strike on the Yen Vien railway yard. Five of the MiGs were shot down by Thunderchiefs.

14 May 1967

F-4B   153001   VF-114, USN, USS *Kitty Hawk*
                  Lt Cdr Charles Everett Southwick (POW)
                  Lt David John Rollins (POW)
A strike on the Than Hoa Bridge was accompanied by a flight of F-4s that attacked the densely packed anti-aircraft defences around the target. Lt Cdr Southwick rolled in from 9,000 feet and at 500 knots in a 30-degree dive he fired his Zuni rockets. As the aircraft pulled out of its dive both engines suddenly flamed out, probably as a result of ingesting debris from the Zunis. The crew ejected as they could not restart the engines and both were quickly captured. Both men were eventually released on 4 March 1973. Charles Southwick had previously flown FJ-3s and F-8s before converting to the F-4 whereas David Rollins had spent his entire Navy career in the F-4. Lt Cdr Southwick had earlier ejected from his aircraft and was rescued on 24 April following a dogfight and flak damage. The wreckage of F-4B 153001 is currently on display in Hanoi.

F-105D 60-0421   13 TFS, 388 TFW, USAF, Korat
                  Maj G R Wilson (survived)
Yet another raid on the barracks at Ha Dong resulted in the loss of another Thunderchief although, happily, its pilot lived to fly again. Maj Wilson was at 12,000 feet over Hanoi about to start his dive on the target when his aircraft was rocked by the nearby explosion of an SA-2. The blast damaged the port wing but the aircraft did not seem too badly affected at first and Maj Wilson set course for home. He flew about 70 miles from Hanoi but was forced to eject about five miles short of the Laotion border from where he was rescued by an HH-3. Thunderchief 60-0421 was

painted as 'The Great Pumpkin' when serving with the 469th TFS at Korat.

F-100D 56-3094   3 TFW, USAF, Bien Hoa
                  Capt S R Winborn (survived)
Capt Winborn probably knew he was pushing his luck when he rolled in for his ninth strafing run against a VC target near Ap An Diem on the banks of the Mekong Delta. His F-100 was hit in the central fuselage section by small arms fire and Capt Winborn headed north hoping to reach his base. However, about eight miles south of Bien Hoa the aircraft became uncontrollable and the pilot ejected. He was picked up by an Army helicopter that happened to be in the vicinity.

F-104C 57-0922   435 TFS, 8 TFW, USAF, Udorn
                  1 pilot, name unknown (survived)
During an armed reconnaissance mission the engine of an F-104 failed and the aircraft crashed in Thailand. This was the 14th and final Starfighter to be lost during the war in Southeast Asia. The type had not built up a particularly distinguished war record being deficient in both range and endurance and not able to dogfight with the more agile MiGs. In July the 435th moved to Ubon to begin conversion to the F-4D Phantom while the Starfighters were eventually passed on to the Puerto Rican ANG until final retirement in 1975. In just over a year of operations at Udorn the Starfighters had flown 2,269 combat sorties totaling 8,820 flying hours for the loss of nine aircraft.

15 May 1967

F-105F 62-4429   13 TFS, 388 TFW, USAF, Korat
                  Capt Donald Lester Heiliger (POW)
                  Maj Ben M Pollard (POW)
Although most F-105 missions were flown in daylight the two wings did fly the occasional night mission. A night, low level strike on the railway marshalling yards at Kep was one such mission. Maj Pollard and Capt Heiliger flew their Wild Weasel aircraft ahead of the strike force to keep the SAM sites around Kep busy. The aircraft approached Kep at 17,000 feet from the east but about 12 miles from the target it was hit by AAA. Both crew ejected and Maj Pollard severely injured his back, which resulted in his medical retirement from the Air Force after the war. Donald Heiliger was released on 18 February and Ben Pollard was repatriated on 4 March 1973. The men were on temporary detachment from the 80th TFS at Yokota during their tour in Thailand and Capt Heiliger was on his 42nd mission on 15 May. He later became a US air attaché in Uruguay, Chile and Israel.

16 May 1967

F-4B   152266   VMFA-314, MAG-13, USMC, Chu Lai
                  Capt C E Hay (survived)
                  1Lt M Carson (survived)
A Marine Corps F-4 was lost during a mission close to the DMZ on the 16th. Capt Hay was making his third pass against the target, a .50 calibre gun position near Dong Ha, when his aircraft was hit by return fire from the gun. The crew ejected just within the DMZ buffer zone but were rescued by a USAF HH-3E helicopter from Da Nang.

17 May 1967

F-8E   149138   VF-51, USN, USS *Hancock*
                  Lt Ronald Wayne Dodge (POW - died)
Lt Dodge and his wingman were assigned to a flak suppression mission during a strike on the Dao My road bridge. He was orbiting at 12,000 feet near Yen Lac, about 20 miles northwest of Vinh, when his aircraft was hit by 85mm anti-aircraft fire. He ejected and landed safely and then used his survival radio to tell his wingman that he was surrounded by North Vietnamese and

The 3rd TFW was one of the longest serving USAF wings in Southeast Asia having arrived at Bien Hoa with three F-100 squadrons in November 1965. F-100D 56-2954 was destroyed at Bien Hoa air base during a major Viet Cong attack on 12 May 1967. USAF

VA-35 was the fourth squadron to introduce the A-6A Intruder to combat in Southeast Asia and lost a total of 10 aircraft in four deployments. A total of 84 Intruders were lost by the Navy and Marine Corps during the war. USN

about to be captured. Over the next few years Ronald Dodge was seen in several photographs and an East German film on the subject of POWs in North Vietnam. He was obviously alive and in captivity but he did not return home during Operation Homecoming. No more information surfaced about Lt Dodge until his mortal remains were handed over by the Vietnamese on 8 July 1981. Fellow POWs were of the opinion that he had been tortured to death by his guards.

18 May 1967

A-4C 147816 VA-76, USN, USS *Bon Homme Richard*
Cdr Kenneth Robbins Cameron (POW - died)
The executive officer of VA-76 led an attack on the Thuong Xa transshipment point 10 miles north of Vinh. This was an important facility where supplies could be transferred from the railway, which terminated at Vinh, to the main coastal road that fed other roads heading south. Cdr Cameron rolled in to attack the target from about 10,000 feet but during the dive his aircraft was hit by AAA and Cdr Cameron ejected. He was captured but, according to the Vietnamese, he died on 4 October 1970. Several POWs reported that Cdr Cameron was with them until that month but was in poor physical and mental health, by then having spent most of his time in solitary. When other prisoners were about to be moved from one part of the Hanoi Hilton to another, guards told the POWs that Cameron was in the camp hospital. He was never seen again until his remains were repatriated on 6 March 1974.

A-4C 147842 VA-113, USN, USS *Enterprise*
Lt Robert John Naughton (POW)
Lt Naughton was leading another pilot on an armed reconnaissance mission during which they attacked the Dong Thuong railway bridge, 10 miles northeast of Thanh Hoa. As the aircraft started a 30-degree dive to fire a pod of unguided rockets it was hit by ground fire. The aircraft burst into flames, probably having taken a hit in a fuel line or tank, and within seconds Lt Naughton lost control of the aircraft and ejected. He was captured and spent the rest of the war as a POW until released on 4 March 1973. He was on his second tour in Southeast Asia and flying his 194th mission when he was shot down.

19 May 1967

A-1E 52-133909 602 ACS, 56 ACW, USAF, Udorn
Maj Roy Abner Knight (KIA)
Maj Knight was flying a mission in northern Laos when he was shot down by AAA near the Pathet Lao stronghold of Ban Nakay, about 10 miles to the east of Sam Neua. The pilot may have been hit by the anti-aircraft fire as he was not seen to escape from his aircraft before it dived into the ground from 10,000 feet. He had joined the Air Force in 1948 and was promoted to the rank of Colonel during the time he was maintained on USAF records as missing in action.

F-4B 152264 VF-96, USN, USS *Enterprise*
Cdr Richard Rich (KIA)
Lt Cdr William Robert Stark (POW)

F-4B 153004 VF-114, USN, USS *Kitty Hawk*
Lt(jg) Joseph Charles Plumb (POW)
Lt(jg) Gareth Laverne Anderson (POW)

A-6A 152594 VA-35, USN, USS *Enterprise*
Lt Eugene Baker McDaniel (POW)
Lt James Kelly Patterson (POW - died)
The 19th of May 1967 proved to be one of the blackest days of the war for the US Navy with the loss of six aircraft and 10 aircrew over North Vietnam. The three participating carriers, the *Enterprise*, *Bon Homme Richard* and the *Kitty Hawk*, each lost two aircraft. The reason for the heavy losses on this day lies in the

importance of the targets and the level of air defences that protected those targets. The strikes on the 19th were the first Navy raids on targets in Hanoi itself. However, the 19th of May was also the birthday of Ho Chi Minh and this may have spurred the defences on to new levels of ferocity. The first Alpha strike of the day was on the Van Dien military vehicle and SAM support depot near Hanoi, which had already been bombed on 14 December 1966 when two aircraft were shot down.

Among the first aircraft into the target area was the CAP flight of F-4s from VF-96 led by Cdr Rich, the Squadron's executive officer. Volleys of SAMs were fired at the formation forcing the aircraft down to a lower altitude, which was dangerous due to the intense AAA and small arms fire. Cdr Rich's aircraft was damaged by an SA-2 that detonated close to the F-4. Two minutes later, with the Phantom even lower, a second SAM was seen to explode close to the aircraft at which point a command ejection sequence was initiated by the NFO. Lt Cdr Stark was knocked unconscious by the ejection and suffered compound fractures of the lower vertebrae, a broken arm and a broken knee. He landed about 20 miles southwest of Hanoi but there was no sign of Cdr Rich, who is presumed to have been killed in the crash. William Stark was released on 4 March 1973 and resumed his career until retirement as a Commander after which he worked for a city Police Department in California until his second retirement in 1993.

The *Kitty Hawk's* CAP flight fared no better when it took over about one hour later and it also lost one its F-4s. The SAMs were still being fired in great numbers and despite violent evasive manoeuvres, Lt Plumb's aircraft was hit in the belly by an SA-2. The aircraft became a mass of flames and the engines wound down rapidly. As the tail section began to disintegrate the crew decided that it was time to leave and ejected near Xan La, 12 miles southwest of Hanoi. Lt Plumb recalls being captured by peasants and thrown into a pen where a bull buffalo was goaded by the villages into charging the pilot. Luckily, the animal was less than enthusiastic about the whole affair. The two fliers were incarcerated in the Hanoi Hilton and Lt Plumb was released on 18 February and Lt Anderson on 4 March 1973. Joseph Plumb acted as the POW's chaplain when conditions in the camps allowed such social activity.

One of the waves of bombers that attacked the Van Dien depot consisted of six Intruders from the *Enterprise*. When the formation was 30 miles southwest of Hanoi they began to receive warnings on their APR-27s of Fan Song radar signals, which meant that they were being tracked by a SAM site. Flying at 12,000 feet Lt Cdr McDaniel saw an SA-2 coming towards his aircraft so he rapidly jettisoned his bombs and made a hard right turn but the missile exploded directly in the path of the A-6. The hydraulics must have been hit as the aircraft became uncontrollable after a few seconds and the crew ejected about 20 miles south of Hanoi. Lt Patterson broke his leg on landing but hid for four days as enemy forces searched for him. A Fulton extraction kit was

dropped to him on the morning of the 21st but it was recovered by North Vietnamese troops before he could reach it. The Fulton system consisted of an inflatable balloon and harness that enabled the airborne recovery of a person from the ground. It was used primarily by Special Forces and intelligence agents. One of his last radio messages was to say that he was moving further up a hill to avoid enemy forces. The fate of Jim Patterson has been the subject of much debate and mystery. He was not seen in any of the POW camps in North Vietnam but information suggests that he had been captured. There has even been a suggestion that Lt Patterson was taken to Kazakhstan for interrogation by the Soviets. He would certainly have known information that would have been useful to the Soviet Union but perhaps no more so than any other A-6 crewmember and less than some of the other prisoners that the North Vietnamese held. Another report claims that villagers from Thuong Tien found Patterson, shot him and buried him quickly as there was a standing order for all prisoners to be turned over to the authorities. Patterson's ID card and Geneva Convention card were handed over to the US in 1985. However, an investigation of the supposed grave site near Thuong Tien revealed no clues. Yet another report claims that the aircraft came down near Ky Son. Wherever the location of the crash, Lt James Patterson is still not yet accounted for and his case remains one of the most perplexing and intriguing of the many mysterious incidents relating to the fate of missing US servicemen in Southeast Asia.

'Red' McDaniel was captured almost as soon as he touched down and suffered very badly at the hands of his captors. He was released on 4 March 1973 and after his retirement from the Navy he founded the American Defense Institute, which includes in its aims the recovery of US prisoners thought by some to still be alive in Southeast Asia. The mysterious disappearance of his own navigator no doubt prompted 'Red' McDaniel's quest for full accounting. In 1975 he co-wrote a book with James Johnson titled *Before Honour* which was reprinted as *Scars and Stripes* five years later.

F-8E 149213 VMF(AW)-232, MAG-11, USMC, Da Nang
Capt Harold James Hellbach (KIA)
Interposed in time between the two major naval raids in North Vietnam, the Marines lost a Crusader in an unrelated incident near the DMZ. Capt Hellbach was attacking an ammunition dump about three miles north of Thon Cam Son when his aircraft was hit by automatic weapons fire. The pilot radioed that he had been hit and was making for the coast but the aircraft pitched up, rolled inverted and dived into the ground after the hydraulic system failed. It was presumed at the time that Capt Hellbach had died in the crash, as there was no evidence of a parachute or emergency beeper signal. In August 1997 a JTF-FA investigation of the crash site recovered human remains that were later identified by DNA testing to be those of Capt Hellbach. His remains were buried at Arlington on 16 July 1998.

F-8E 150930 VF-211, USN, USS *Bon Homme Richard*
Lt Cdr Kay Russell (POW)

F-8C 147021 VF-24, USN, USS *Bon Homme Richard*
Lt(jg) William John Metzger (POW)

A special raid on the North was targeted at Hanoi's thermal power plant. The attack was made by just two A-4s equipped with Walleye TV-guided bombs and escorted by four A-4 Iron Hand aircraft and 12 F-8s, six for flak suppression and six for fighter escort. The AGM-62 Walleye weighed about 1,500lbs and had large tailfins and a gyro-stabilised TV camera in the nose which the pilot used to guide the bomb to the target. Being unpowered, the range of the weapon was dependent upon release trajectory, altitude and distance from the target. Despite its limitations the Walleye was a useful first-generation precision-guided munition.

During the raid on the power plant both of the *Bon Homme Richard's* Crusader squadrons provided aircraft for the CAP over this 'hot' target. However, the SAM sites that had wrought such havoc in the morning were still active. Lt Cdr Russell was the leader of a six-plane escort flight that engaged a number of MiG-17s just to the west of Hanoi. As the Crusaders were chasing the MiGs away from the target area Lt Cdr Russell's aircraft was hit first by ground fire and then by an SA-2, which caused the aircraft to burst into flames and the pilot to lose control. Kay Russell ejected and was quickly captured. A total of four MiGs were shot down by the F-8s during the engagement.

Six F-8s of VF-24 were assigned the flak suppression mission during the Hanoi raid. This flight also had to contend with MiGs and SAMs but it was the intense anti-aircraft fire that brought Lt Metzger down. He had chased a MiG-17 away from the target but as the Crusader was climbing through 1,500 feet it was hit twice in the fuselage by AAA. One of the anti-aircraft shells tore a hole in the cockpit and wounded the pilot in the left arm and leg and broke his right leg. Lt Metzger ejected about 10 miles west of Hanoi and was soon captured. He was eventually released along with Lt Cdr Russell on 4 March 1973. The Walleye attack on the power plant failed as the bombs were released at too low an altitude to guide to the target. However, two days later another Walleye attack scored a direct hit on this important target.

RA-5C 150826 RVAH-13, USN, USS *Kitty Hawk*
Lt Cdr James Lloyd Griffin (POW - died)
Lt Jack Walters (POW - died)

The final loss on what came to be known in Navy circles as 'Black Friday' involved an RA-5C reconnaissance aircraft from the *Kitty Hawk*. Lt Cdr Griffin and Lt Walters were tasked with obtaining BDA photographs of the Van Dien depot, which had been attacked about four hours earlier. As the aircraft made its initial turn over Hanoi for its photo run it was at about 3,500 feet and doing around 700 knots. The aircraft was next seen to be engulfed in flames and flying in a northwesterly direction. About 10 miles from the city the Vigilante suddenly pitched up and the forward fuselage started to break up. Both crew ejected from the flaming, disintegrating wreck and apparently both men were taken to the Hanoi Hilton but survived only a few days, whether as a result of their injuries or from torture is not known. This final loss was a most unhappy postscript to a disastrous day for naval aviation.

20 May 1967

A-4E 149652 VA-212, USN, USS *Bon Homme Richard*
Cdr Homer Leroy Smith (POW - died)

Despite the heavy losses of the previous day the Navy was out in force again on the 20th. An Alpha strike on the Bac Giang thermal power plant resulted in only one aircraft lost, it was however, the A-4 of the CO of VA-212. This important power plant was situated near Phu Lang Thuong, about 25 miles northeast of Hanoi. Cdr Smith was leading 17 aircraft from the *Bon Homme Richard* against the target and had just pulled up having launched his Walleye bomb when his Skyhawk was hit by AAA and burst into flames. Accompanied by his wingman, he headed for the coast but was forced to eject about 20 miles north of Haiphong. Like Griffin and Walters, Cdr Smith was apparently

taken to the Hanoi Hilton but survived only a few days and was reported to have been tortured to death. Cdr Smith had been awarded the Silver Star for leading an attack on the Bac Giang POL depot on 30 June 1966 and had dropped the Navy's first Walleye bomb during an attack on the Sam Son Army barracks on 11 March 1967. He was posthumously awarded the Navy Cross for his part in the attack on the Bac Giang thermal power plant. Homer Smith's remains were handed over by the Vietnamese on 16 March 1974.

F-4C 63-7669 433 TFS, 8 TFW, USAF, Ubon
Maj Jack Lee Van Loan (POW)
1Lt Joseph Edward Milligan (POW)

Tampa flight of eight Phantoms led by the Wing Commander, Col Robin Olds, was tasked with the role of MiGCAP for an F-105 strike near Kep on the 20th. When the flight was about 10 miles east of Kep at 7,000 feet it was jumped by two groups of MiG-17s. Maj Van Loan was Col Olds's wingman and was hit in the wing by cannon fire early on in what became an epic air battle. The Phantom became a mass of flames and pitched up rapidly as it began to break up forcing the crew to eject into captivity. Later on in the fight Col Olds shot down one of the MiG-17s while other Phantom crews shot down another five to make it one of the most successful days of the war for the Air Force. Joseph Milligan was released on 18 February but Jack Van Loan had to wait until the next release on 4 March 1973. 1Lt Milligan was on his 113th mission when he was shot down. Following his return to the USA he bought a farm, obtained a degree in veterinary surgery and retired as a Colonel.

RF-101C 56-0120 20 TRS, 432 TRW, USAF, Udorn
Maj Notley Gwynn Maddox (KIA)

Two Voodoos from Udorn were sent on a mission to photograph army barracks at Kep, just a few miles south of the airfield. The aircraft crossed Laos and North Vietnam (dodging thunderstorms just north of the DMZ) to reach the Gulf of Tonkin then turned north to recross the coast near Haiphong and approach Kep from the west. Over the target the flak was intense and the two Voodoos lost sight of each other but Maj Notley called to his wingman that he had been hit. The other Voodoo saw no trace of Maj Notley's aircraft, which was almost certainly hit by flak although Red Crown reported that a MiG was also in the vicinity. The aircraft is reported as having crashed near Tien Yen, some 60 miles east of Kep and within a few miles of the coast and (relative) safety.

21 May 1967

A-1E 52-133855 1 ACS, 14 ACW, USAF, Pleiku
Maj James E Holler (survived)

As Maj Holler took off from Pleiku on a close air support mission his aircraft was hit by small arms fire when it reached about 1,000 feet. Although the aircraft did not catch fire it soon became uncontrollable and Maj Holler was forced to abandon it about six miles northwest of the airfield. He landed on rocky ground and broke both his ankles but survived. He became the first Spad pilot to successfully use the Yankee Extraction System, which was being fitted to the USAF's Skyraiders in the spring of 1967.

F-8E 150348 VF-211, USN, USS *Bon Homme Richard*
Lt Cdr R G Hubbard (survived)

Undeterred by the losses of the 19th, the Navy decided to have another crack at the Hanoi thermal power plant and the Van Dien depot. The raid on the thermal power plant was accompanied by several sections of Crusaders dedicated to flak suppression but one of these aircraft fell victim to the intense anti-aircraft fire around the target. Lt Cdr Hubbard was jinking to avoid the flak when his aircraft took a hit in the afterburner section. The afterburner nozzle was stuck in the open position and fuel was leaking from the aircraft but fortunately did not ignite. Lt Cdr Hubbard was escorted out to sea where he refuelled from a tanker before flying to the *Bon Homme Richard*. However, when the gear was lowered the hydraulic system must have ruptured and the aircraft burst into flames. Lt Cdr Hubbard ejected and was picked up by one of the carrier's Seasprite helicopters.

F-4B 153040 VF-114, USN, USS *Kitty Hawk*
Lt H Dennis Wisely (survived)
Ens Jim H Laing (survived)

A strike on the Van Dien SAM and vehicle support depot also resulted in the loss of a single aircraft and the rescue of its crew. The TARCAP flight was once more provided by the F-4s of VF-114 and one of the Squadron's aircraft was hit as it was retiring from the target at low level. The TARCAP flight had evaded three SAMs but came down low and ran into intense flak. The aircraft was peppered with automatic weapons fire and suffered failures of the hydraulic and pneumatic systems. The pilot decided to make for Thailand rather than risk the gauntlet of the intense air defences between Hanoi and the coast. The decision was a wise one as the aircraft crossed the Laotian border before becoming uncontrollable forcing the crew to eject near Sai Koun, 85 miles southwest of Hanoi. Jim Laing's parachute started to open the instant his ejection seat fired with the result that he broke an arm and sprained his other limbs. Both men were picked up safely by a USAF HH-3 after a Navy SH-3A had to be abandoned in Laos after running out of fuel during the first rescue attempt. Lt Wisely had shot down an An-2 Colt biplane on 20 December 1966 and a MiG-17 on 24 April 1967. This was the second ejection and rescue for Ens Laing who had been shot down with Lt Cdr C Southwick on 24 April.

F-100D 56-3285 531 TFS, 3 TFW, USAF, Bien Hoa
Capt David Carl Lindberg (KIA)

An urgent call for assistance from ground troops resulted in a flight of F-100s scrambling to attack VC troops at Khu Tru Mat, 12 miles north of Bien Hoa. As Capt Lindberg came down to 200 feet to make his fifth pass dropping napalm canisters his aircraft was struck by automatic weapons fire and dived into the ground before he could escape. Capt Lindberg had earlier survived being shot down during a Skyspot mission near Bien Hoa on 30 March 1967.

22 May 1967

O-1E 51-12102 20 TASS, 504 TASG, USAF, Da Nang
Lt Col Lester Evan Holmes (KIA)

It had been suspected for some time that the North Vietnamese were building SAM sites close to the DMZ, which was a worrying development. The suspicions were confirmed in a tragic manner on the 22nd when a Bird Dog was blown to bits five miles northwest of Thon Can So, just outside the northern edge of the DMZ buffer zone. Lt Col Holmes was on a visual reconnaissance sortie at 8,000 feet over the DMZ when the SA-2 exploded. The relatively fragile O-1 stood little chance against a missile that, in this case, was bigger than its target.

F-4C 64-0708 497 TFS, 8 TFW, USAF, Ubon
Capt Elton Lawrence Perrine (KIA)
1Lt Kenneth Frank Backus (KIA)

The Night Owls of the 497th were busy on the night of the 22nd attacking railway yards on the main northeast line from Hanoi to China. One flight was about to bomb the yard at Cao Nung when Capt Perrine's aircraft was hit by anti-aircraft fire 15 miles northeast of Kep. The wingman saw Capt Perrine start his bomb run and a few seconds later saw a large explosion on the ground three miles east of the target. There was 37mm and 57mm flak in the area at the time and there was apparently no time for the crew to escape before the aircraft hit the ground.

F-4C 63-7692 497 TFS, 8 TFW, USAF, Ubon
Maj Richard Dale Vogel (POW)
1Lt David L Baldwin (survived)

About half an hour after the raid on Cao Nung another flight of F-4s was approaching Cao Nung on their way to the marshalling yards at Kep when AAA hit one of the aircraft. Maj Vogel turned towards the coast but the crew was forced to eject about 10 miles north of Cam Pha. Maj Vogel was captured but amazingly, considering the intensity of air defences in this area, a Navy helicopter managed to rescue 1Lt Baldwin. Richard Vogel was released from imprisonment on 4 March 1973.

24 May 1967

A-4E   151076   VA-93, USN, USS *Hancock*
                    Lt(jg) M Alsop (survived)

Lt Alsop was taking part in an attack on a target 10 miles southwest of Ninh Binh when he felt his aircraft hit by an anti-aircraft shell. He headed due south for the coast with the A-4's engine making ominous rumbling and grinding noises. Once out to sea the engine flamed out and Lt Alsop ejected about 15 miles off Thanh Hoa, from where he was picked up by a Navy helicopter.

25 May 1967

A-1H   135366   VA-215, USN, USS *Bon Homme Richard*
                    Ens Richard Campbell Graves (KIA)

Two Skyraiders on an armed reconnaissance mission were flying along the coast about 15 miles north of Vinh when they saw a number of small cargo boats that were used for transporting supplies. Lt O'Rourke, the leader of the section, dived on the boats but as Ens Graves pulled up from the attack his Skyraider suddenly dropped one wing and dived into the sea. Ens Graves did not escape from his stricken aircraft, which probably fell victim to anti-aircraft batteries on the nearby shore.

F-4C   64-0714   557 TFS, 12 TFW, USAF, Cam Ranh Bay
                    Maj C C Rhymes (survived)
                    1Lt R E Randolph (survived)

The first Phantom lost by the 12th TFW on operations over North Vietnam since December 1966 was hit by AAA near Xuan Hoa, about 12 miles north of the DMZ. Maj Rhymes headed out to sea and the crew ejected about 10 miles from the coast. Maj Rhymes was picked up by a USAF helicopter and 1Lt Randolph was rescued by a Navy ship.

26 May 1967

A-4E   152022   VA-93, USN, USS *Hancock*
                    Lt(jg) Read Blaine Mecleary (POW)

The MiG-base at Kep was a target for the *Hancock's* A-4s on the 26th. Lt Mecleary was flying in the flak suppression section and had just reached the target area at 13,000 feet when his aircraft was hit by AAA. With the aircraft performing a series of rolls to the right Lt Mecleary managed to fly about 12 miles to the east before having to give up the unequal struggle and eject. He was badly injured during the ejection and was unable to walk for two months. He was released from prison on 4 March 1973 and had been on his 56th mission on 26 May. He retired from the Navy in 1976 although he remained a member of the Naval Reserve until 1987. He then joined American Airlines to fly the Boeing 767 while his wife was a flight attendant with the rival TWA.

27 May 1967

F-105D   59-1723   333 TFS, 355 TFW, USAF, Takhli
                    Capt Gordon Byron Blackwood (KIA)

The northeast railway was once more a target for the bombers from Takhli. An afternoon strike was mounted by five flights of F-105s against the marshalling yard and the road and rail bridge at Bac Giang and as the first wave swept in they were met by a barrage of AAA and SAMs. Capt 'Buz' Blackwood's aircraft was the last aircraft in the last flight and was damaged by the nearby explosion of an SA-2. He stayed with the aircraft for a few minutes until it crashed near Kep. It is thought probable that he ejected but did not survive. 'Buz' Blackwood had just returned from a spell of compassionate leave in the USA to attend his father's funeral. On 20 November 1989 it was announced that remains recently handed over by the Vietnamese government had been positively identified as being those of Gordon Blackwood.

30 May 1967

A-4E   150032   VMA-121, MAG-12, USMC, Chu Lai
                    1Lt Michael Walter Thoennes (KIA)

Chu Lai lost its fourth A-4 during May on a strike on VC structures near Hiep Duc, 20 miles west of Tam Ky. The aircraft was just pulling out of its dive at about 500 feet when it was hit by automatic weapons fire and crashed into the ground. 1Lt Thoennes had no time to escape and was killed in the crash.

A-4E   151049   VA-93, USN, USS *Hancock*
                    Cdr James Patrick Mehl (POW)

The SAMs claimed their 10th and final victim of the month during a raid on the Do Xa transshipment point 15 miles south of Hanoi. Cdr Mehl, the executive officer of VA-93, was leading an Iron Hand section in support of the raid and started to receive warnings of SAM activity near the target. The section evaded one missile but as Cdr Mehl started to climb through 16,000 feet to fire a Shrike, his aircraft was hit by another SA-2. He tried to make for the sea but was forced to eject near Hung Yen and was immediately captured. After nearly six years as a POW he was released on 4 March 1973. Cdr Mehl had joined the US Navy in 1951 and had flown Panthers, Furies and Cougars as well as Skyhawks.

F-4C   64-0668   480 TFS, 366 TFW, USAF, Da Nang
                    Maj W C Schrupp (survived)
                    Capt T R Macdougall (survived)

A Phantom was lost during an armed reconnaissance mission over the southern provinces of North Vietnam on the 30th. A flight of aircraft was following a road near Tho Ngoa, 20 miles northwest of Dong Hoi, when they ran into ground fire. Maj Schrupp's aircraft was hit in one of the engines and he turned out to sea. The crew ejected 15 miles off Dong Hoi and were soon rescued by a naval vessel.

31 May 1967

A-4E   151113   VA-212, USN, USS *Bon Homme Richard*
                    Lt Cdr Arvin Roy Chauncey (POW)

A-4E   151183   VA-212, USN, USS *Bon Homme Richard*
                    Lt(jg) M T Daniels (survived)

A series of raids by the Air Force and the Navy was flown against targets at Kep on the final day of the month. Four Skyhawks were on their way to Kep airfield when they encountered intense anti-aircraft fire about 20 miles northeast of Kep. Lt Cdr Chauncey's aircraft was hit in the engine and caught fire. He turned towards high ground and jettisoned his stores but the aircraft lost power and he was forced to eject. He was captured and joined the rest of his shipmates in the Hanoi Hilton. Like most of the others, he was released on 4 March 1973.

When Lt Cdr Chauncey's aircraft was hit, his flight called for SAR assistance and stayed in the area to protect their leader and the SAR forces when they arrived. However, Lt Daniels almost suffered the same fate as the Lt Cdr when his aircraft was hit by AAA about eight miles northeast of Kep. He headed out to sea in search of a tanker but with his radio inoperative he was not able to rendezvous and take on fuel. Unable to refuel he found a SAR destroyer and ejected close by when the Skyhawk's engine flamed out. He was picked up by the destroyer's Seasprite SAR helicopter.

F-4C   63-7603   389 TFS, 366 TFW, USAF, Da Nang
                    Maj M C Fulcher (survived)
                    Capt A E Wolff (survived)

The USAF flew a raid on barracks at Kep later in the day. Taking part in the raid were the F-4s from the 366th TFW. As the Phantoms were retiring from the target at 11,000 feet one of the aircraft was hit by an 85mm shell and badly damaged. Maj Fulcher flew the aircraft to the coast and started the long return journey to Da Nang. All went well until the aircraft reached a position about 45 miles off Dong Hoi when the crew were forced to eject. A Navy helicopter rescued Maj Fulcher and a ship, probably one of the Navy's SAR destroyers, picked up Capt Wolff.

2 June 1967

F-105D   61-0190   34 TFS, 388 TFW, USAF, Korat
                    Maj Dewey Lee Smith (POW)

The assault on Kep continued into June with an attack on the railway yards by formations of F-105s. As Flapper flight approached the target at 16,000 feet from the northeast Maj Smith's aircraft was hit by an anti-aircraft shell and started to burn. He ejected almost immediately and was quickly captured. He was repatriated on 4 March 1973.

F-4C   63-7548   390 TFS, 366 TFW, USAF, Da Nang
                    Capt Alton Craig Rockett (KIA)
                    1Lt Daniel Lewis Carrier (KIA)

A flight of Phantoms from the Da Nang Wing made a night attack on targets in the Mu Gia Pass on the 2nd. To return to base the formation headed due east to cross the coast for the flight to Da Nang over the sea. However, as the Phantoms reached the coast one of the aircraft was hit by AAA and brought down near Tu Loan, 25 miles north of Dong Hoi. No ejection was seen and it was thought possible that one or both of the the crew were wounded and could not eject. 1Lt Carrier's remains were returned by the Vietnamese on 20 November 1989.

F-8C   147031   VF-24, USN, USS *Bon Homme Richard*
                    Lt Cdr Rex Stewart Wood (KIA)

After a Crusader launched from the *Bon Homme Richard* for a CAP mission it failed to rendezvous with another aircraft and disappeared from the ship's radar screens. It seems probable that the pilot either became disoriented and crashed or suffered a sudden catastrophic technical malfunction.

3 June 1967

B-57B   53-3862   8 TBS, 405 FW attached to 35 TFW,
                    USAF, Phan Rang
                    Maj Theodore Springston (KIA)
                    Capt Joseph Thomas Kearns (KIA)

A B-57 disappeared on an armed reconnaissance mission over the southern provinces of North Vietnam. To this day nothing appears to be known of the circumstances of this loss. B-57B 53-3862 originally served with the 3rd TBG at Johnson AB in Japan.

4 June 1967

A-1E   52-132681   1 ACS, 14 ACW, USAF, Pleiku
                    Lt Col Lewis Merritt Robinson (KIA)

Lt Col Robinson was taking part in an attack on a large North Vietnamese troop concentration that had been sighted near Tavouac in southern Laos, about 50 miles west of Hué. A B-52 strike preceded a heli-borne insertion by Special Forces and Marines but strong enemy opposition resulted in the loss of several helicopters and caused many casualties. Two Skyraiders then arrived to assist the friendly forces. As Lt Col Robinson came round to drop napalm canisters on his second pass he was hit by .50 calibre gunfire. The aircraft pitched up sharply, hit the wing of another Skyraider and entered an inverted spin, exploding as it hit the ground. No ejection or parachute was seen and it was assumed that the pilot died in the crash. The other Skyraider landed safely at Khe Sanh. In 1988 the Laotian government handed over remains claimed to be from this crash site. In 1993 and again in January 1998, joint US-Lao investigation teams excavated the crash site and recovered further remains of Lt Col Robinson along with items of personal equipment.

F-105D   61-0148   34 TFS, 388 TFW, USAF, Korat
                    Maj C J Kough (survived)

During an armed reconnaissance mission in the region north of the DMZ a flight of F-105s came across several trucks at a ferry crossing about five miles south of Dong Hoi. As Maj Kough dived to drop his bombs he felt his aircraft take a hit from anti-aircraft fire. He turned east immediately, crossed the coast and flew about 20 miles out to sea before ejecting. He was picked up safely by a Navy helicopter.

F-8E   149194   VMF(AW)-235, MAG-11, USMC, Da Nang
                    Lt Col L P Bates (survived)

During a combat mission the throttle of a Crusader suddenly disconnected and caused the engine to flame out. Unable to restart the engine, the pilot ejected and was recovered safely.

5 June 1967

RF-8G 145614   Detachment L, VFP-63, USN,
USS *Bon Homme Richard*
Lt Cdr Collins Henry Haines (POW)

Lt Cdr Haines was tasked with photographing the railway line near Thanh Hoa and had started his run at 3,500 feet and 520 knots when his Crusader was hit by AAA. The hydraulics and electrical systems failed instantly and the pilot ejected as he lost control of the aircraft. During the ejection he broke his right kneecap and his left leg was also injured. As commander of the VFP-63 detachment on board the *Bon Homme Richard*, he had flown 40 missions since the ship started operations in February. Lt Cdr Haines was released on 4 March 1973 and retired from the Navy as a Captain in 1987.

O-1G 50-1640   20 TASS, 504 TASG, USAF, Da Nang
detached to An Khe
Capt Douglas Holman Butterfield (KIA)

The 20th TASS maintained a detachment of aircraft at An Khe which was an important 1st Cavalry Division base. Capt Butterfield was flying a visual reconnaissance mission when he was shot down by ground fire about five miles northeast of the base.

6 June 1967

F-100D 55-3766   416 TFS, 37 TFW, USAF, Phu Cat
Capt Duane Scott Baker (KIA)

Work on the base at Phu Cat was started on 1 May 1966 and by the end of the month a temporary 3,000 feet runway had been built to allow further construction material to be flown in. By March 1967 the base was almost complete and the 37th TFW moved in to join two squadrons of C-7 Caribous that had arrived earlier in the year. The first aircraft lost from Phu Cat was an F-100 from the 416th TFS. On 6 June a flight of F-100s was strafing a number of VC structures about 15 miles northwest of Quang Ngai when one of the aircraft dived into the ground, probably as a result of enemy fire. Capt Baker had no time to eject and was killed.

F-8E 150303   VF-211, USN, USS *Bon Homme Richard*
Lt(jg) Thomas Renwick Hall (survived)

Once more the Hanoi thermal power plant was the target of a naval air attack. A flight of Crusaders assigned to provide combat air patrol crossed the beach 50 miles south of Thanh Hoa with the intention of approaching Hanoi from an unexpected direction. However, Lt Hall's aircraft was hit by ground fire soon after crossing the coast and lost electrical power and hydraulic pressure. The pilot headed out to sea and ejected four miles from the coast when the aircraft became uncontrollable. Lt Hall was rescued by a helicopter from USS *England* but his good luck held out only for another four days as he was shot down again on 10 June and captured.

RF-4C 65-0834   11 TRS, 432 TRW, USAF, Udorn
Maj Joy Leonard Owens (KIA)
1Lt Howard Reeves Sale (KIA)

A reconnaissance Phantom from Udorn was flying a mission over the Plain of Jars in northern Laos when radio contact with it was lost. It was assumed to have been shot down and the crew killed about 10 miles east of Xiangkhoang. Maj Owens had flown B-29s in Korea in the mid-1950s and was on his 34th mission when he was lost.

RF-8G 145608   Det L, VFP-63, USN,
USS *Bon Homme Richard*
1 pilot, name unknown (survived)

A Crusader was hit by 57mm flak during a photographic reconnaissance mission near Vinh. Although the aircraft landed safely back on the carrier it had to scrapped as it was too badly damaged to be repaired.

7 June 1967

U-10B 63-13109   5 ACS, 14 ACW, USAF, Nha Trang
Maj Alvie Wayne Gapp (KIA)

A U-10B Courier crashed as it was taking off from Bien Hoa for a psychological warfare mission. The pilot was killed in the accident.

8 June 1967

F-4C 63-7425   389 TFS, 366 TFW, USAF, Da Nang
Capt Victor Joe Apodaca (KIA)
1Lt Jon Thomas Busch (KIA)

As dusk turned day into night over the southern part of North Vietnam two Phantoms started an armed reconnaissance mission. As the aircraft were following a broad river valley near Khe Phat, 25 miles northwest of Dong Hoi, they encountered heavy ground fire. Capt Apodaca radioed his leader that his Phantom had been hit and was told to climb and head for the sea. A later radio message told of control and hydraulics problems and this was followed soon after by an emergency signal from a SAR beeper, which indicated that at least one of the crew had ejected. The leader had to return to base to refuel but an electronic search was conducted with no success. Nothing more was heard until the spring of 1988 when remains identified as being those of Jon Busch were handed over, along with a charred map and a battered nameplate bearing Victor Apodaca's name. The US Army Central Identification Laboratory in Hawaii forensically identified Busch's remains in October 1988. Victor Apodaca was of mixed Spanish-American and Navajo Indian parentage.

F-4C 64-0667   480 TFS, 366 TFW, USAF, Da Nang
Maj C A Colton (survived)
1Lt R D Franks (survived)

The 366th TFW lost a second Phantom on the same day during an armed reconnaissance mission around Chap Le near the coast and only 10 miles north of the DMZ. Maj Colton's aircraft was hit by 37mm anti-aircraft fire as it was strafing a storage area. The Phantom was pointed out to sea and the crew ejected about 20 miles off the coast where they were picked up by a USAF helicopter.

B-57B 53-3908   8 TBS, 405 FW attached to 35 TFW,
USAF, Phan Rang
Capt Elwin Harry Busch (KIA)
1Lt Peter Whitcomb Morrison (KIA)

In another bizarre coincidence two airmen with the same surname were lost on the same day when Capt Busch and his navigator, 1Lt Morrison, were shot down. They were on a night armed reconnaissance mission when their Canberra was hit by small arms fire near the 4,761 feet Hao Chu Hi mountain, which lay just 10 miles north of their own airfield.

9 June 1967

C-130B 58-0737   29 TCS, 463 TCW, USAF, Clark
Capt Jerome Frank Starkweather (KIA)
Capt Rafael L Rivera-Balaguer (KIA)
Capt Richard W Podell (KIA)
SSgt Ricky Lynn Herndon (KIA)
SSgt Ira Edward Scott (KIA)
SSgt Wiliam Everett Tyree (KIA)
1Lt Richard A Gray, US Army (KIA)
SP5 Andrew Harry Shimp, US Army (KIA)
SP5 Frank Richard Ragusa, US Army (KIA)
SP4 Craig Ray Schoenbaum, US Army (KIA)

A Hercules was nearing the end of a routine day shuttling between its temporary base at Tan Son Nhut and several airfields in South Vietnam. The final shuttle of the day was to Nha Trang where a load including classified maps and the bodies of an American and a Korean soldier along with four Army escorts or couriers was loaded for the return trip to Tan Son Nhut. As the aircraft approached Saigon it was vectored around an artillery firing zone. However, the aircraft crashed 12 miles east of Tan Son Nhut, apparently as the result of structural failure as both wings had detached at altitude. As this type of accidental gross structural failure was extremely unlikely it was conjectured that the aircraft might have been hit by an artillery shell causing its destruction.

10 June 1967

A-4C 145145   VA-56, USN, USS *Enterprise*
Cdr Peter Woodbury Sherman (KIA)

The series of raids on the Van Dien SAM support depot continued. Cdr Sherman was the CO of VA-56 and was leading an Iron Hand flight in support of a raid on the depot. As Cdr Sherman and his wingman reached a point about 10 miles southwest of Hanoi they had to take evasive action to avoid numerous SAMs that had been fired at them. During the manoeuvring the wingman lost sight of his leader. No ejection was seen or SAR beeper heard but it was assumed that Cdr Sherman's aircraft had been the victim of an SA-2 missile and that he had been killed. The remains of Cdr Sherman were eventually handed over by the Vietnamese on 19 January 1991. Pete Sherman had only taken over command of the Squadron on 17 March 1967.

F-8E 150352   VF-211, USN, USS *Bon Home Richard*
Lt(jg) Thomas Renwick Hall (POW)

The Hanoi thermal power plant was also on the target list again on the 10th. Once again it was one of the CAP flight Crusaders that was brought down during the raid and, remarkably, once again it was flown by Lt Thomas Renwick Hall. The Crusader was orbiting at low level near Ha Dong, just a few miles southwest of

This F-4D carries the unique individual aircraft code letters worn by the squadrons of the 366th TFW. The system was soon discarded in favour of standardised squadron code letters. This 389th TFS aircraft survived to fly with the 48th TFW at Lakenheath, Suffolk and the 474th TFW at Nellis AFB, Nevada. USAF

Hanoi, when the aircraft was hit by AAA. The aircraft lost fuel rapidly and the hydraulics began to fail. Within seconds the engine flamed out from lack of fuel and the pilot ejected about five miles southwest of Hanoi. Lt Hall had been shot down and rescued on a similar mission just four days earlier, but this time his luck ran out and he was captured. Lt Hall had over 100 missions to his credit as he had flown a tour with VF-211 on board the USS *Hancock* in 1966. Lt Hall was released from imprisonment on 4 March 1973.

F-4D   66-0236   555 TFS, 8 TFW, USAF, Ubon
                    Maj C Allen (survived)
                    Lt B Becker (survived)

The squadrons of the 8th TFW started converting to the new F-4D towards the end of May. The D model of the Phantom was otpimized for the air-to-ground role while still retaining an impressive air-to-air capability. The major difference from the earlier F-4C was the range of new avionic systems that the aircraft carried. The first F-4Ds were delivered to the USAF in March 1966 and the first aircraft lost in Southeast Asia crashed somewhat ignominiously when it ran out of fuel during a CAP mission. Both the crew were rescued.

11 June 1967

F-8C   147002   VF-24, USN, USS *Bon Homme Richard*
                    Lt(jg) J R Miller (survived)

On the 11th a reconnaissance mission was flown over the Uong Bi thermal power plant about 12 miles northeast of Haiphong. As the reconnaissance aircraft started its run the escorting Crusader was hit in the rear fuselage by AAA. Lt Miller flew his burning aircraft northeast for about 12 miles before the engine flamed out and he was forced to eject. He was fortunate to be rescued from such a 'hot' area by a Navy helicopter accompanied by a strong SAR escort force.

A-1E   52-132408   602 ACS, 56 ACW, USAF, Udorn
                      Maj James F Rausch (survived)
                      Maj Robert L Russell (survived)

On 8 April 1967 the 602nd ACS was transferred to the newly activated 56th ACW. In addition to their RESCAP duties, the Skyraiders based in Thailand still flew armed reconnaissance missions in the less hostile regions of North Vietnam. A Skyraider was hit by ground fire at 5,000 feet when rolling in on a target during a road reconnaissance mission in Route Pack 3, close to the Laotian border about 95 miles west of Thanh Hoa. The crew were pulled out of the aircraft by the rockets of their Yankee Extraction System and were eventually rescued by an HH-3E. The A-1E was normally flown by a single pilot but Maj Russell was flying with Maj Rausch on a routine combat check ride.

F-4C   64-0786   390 TFS, 366 TFW, USAF, Da Nang
                    Lt Col Hervey Studdie Stockman (POW)
                    Capt Ronald John Webb (POW)

F-4C   63-7706   389 TFS, 366 TFW, USAF, Da Nang
                    Maj Donald Martin Klemm (KIA)
                    1Lt Robert Harvey Pearson (KIA)

Tragedy struck the 366th TFW on the 11th. Two Phantoms, including one flown by Lt Col Stockman, the CO of the 390th TFS, collided at 14,000 feet about 10 miles northeast of Kep during a MiGCAP mission. Both aircraft fell in flames but only the crew from one aircraft escaped and were captured. During the Second World War Lt Col Stockman had flown P-51 Mustangs from England with the Eighth Air Force while Capt Webb had been a navigator in KB-50 tankers in the early 1960s. Both men were released from captivity on 4 March 1973. Hervey Stockman wrote an excellent study of command and leadership in the POW camps when he attended the Air War College in 1974.

12 June 1967

F-4C   63-7673   555 TFS, 8 TFW, USAF, Ubon
                    Maj V D Fulgram (survived)
                    Capt W K Harding (survived)

Although the Triple Nickel Squadron was converting to the F-4D it still had some of the older F-4C models on strength well into

June. One of these was lost during an armed reconnaissance mission over the southern provinces of North Vietnam. Maj Fulgram's aircraft was flying at 4,500 feet near Van Loc, 12 miles northwest of Dong Hoi, when it was hit by AAA in the starboard wing. Uncertain that he could reach Ubon safely, Maj Fulgram decided to make for Da Nang and almost made it. However, just a few miles short of the runway the aircraft became uncontrollable and the crew ejected and were rescued by a Marine Corps helicopter.

F-4C   64-0662   558 TFS, 12 TFW, USAF, Cam Ranh Bay
                    Capt Edward Arthur Lapierre (KIA)
                    1Lt Lawrence Jay Silver (KIA)

A flight of Phantoms from Cam Ranh Bay was attacking a VC storage complex near Truc Giang in the Mekong Delta when one the aircraft was shot down. Having expended most of his ordnance Capt Lapierre was making his sixth pass over the target using his 20mm cannon. The aircraft was seen to dive into the ground close to the target without either crewmember ejecting. It was surmised that the Phantom had been hit by ground fire.

F-4C   63-7710   555 TFS, 8 TFW, USAF, Ubon
                    Maj M G Slapikas (survived)
                    Lt T E Bougartz (survived)

A third Phantom went down on the 12th when the Wolfpack lost another of its old F-4C models. The aircraft developed problems with its hydraulic system forcing the crew to eject. This Phantom was flown by Capt E T Raspberry and 1 Lt R W Western of the 555th TFS during Operation Bolo on 2 January when they shot down a MiG-21.

13 June 1967

F-100D   55-3510   308 TFS, 31 TFW, USAF, Tuy Hoa
                      1Lt James Lee Cumiskey (KIA)

Although the Phantom was flying more and more missions in support of ground forces in South Vietnam, the Super Sabre was still the predominant close air support aircraft in the South. 1Lt Cumiskey was killed when his aircraft was shot down by ground fire as it was dropping napalm on a target 20 miles southeast of Pleiku. Napalm delivery was among the most vulnerable types of attack as the aircraft had to fly straight and level at altitudes of less than 300 feet.

14 June 1967

F-4C   64-0778   390 TFS, 366 TFW, USAF, Da Nang
                    1Lt Edward John Mechenbier (POW)
                    1Lt Kevin Joseph McManus (POW)

The 366th lost another aircraft and crew over North Vietnam on the 14th during a raid on the Vu Chua railway yard near Kep. 1Lt Mechenbier's F-4 was struck by an 85mm round at 6,000 feet as it dived on the target. The aircraft burst into flames and the crew ejected a few miles away and were captured. Both airmen were released on 18 February 1973 and resumed their Air Force careers. 1Lt Mechenbier had flown a total of 113 missions, 79 of them over North Vietnam, while 1Lt McManus had flown over 140 missions in two tours of duty. After retiring from the active Air Force, Mechenbier, like many Vietnam veterans, joined the Air National Guard and flew F-100s and A-7s.

15 June 1967

F-105D   61-0213   34 TFS, 388 TFW, USAF, Korat
                      Capt John Willard Swanson (KIA)

An F-105 and its pilot was lost during a raid on railway sidings at Dong Khe on the coastal railway line, about 20 miles north of Vinh. Capt Swanson was rolling in to attack the target from 7,000 feet when his aircraft was hit by 37mm anti-aircraft fire. He turned to the east, crossed the coast and ejected about five miles out to sea. Unfortunately he could not be found when a SAR helicopter arrived on the scene and is presumed to have drowned.

16 June 1967

F-105D   60-0485   355 TFW, USAF, Takhli
                      Lt Col William L Janssen (survived)

A formation of F-105s bombed NVA barracks at Yen Hoi, 12 miles southeast of Vinh on the 16th. As Lt Col Janssen dived his Thunderchief towards the target to release his bombs he felt the aircraft take a hit. The formation headed west towards Takhli but Janssen was forced to eject shortly after he crossed into Thailand.

17 June 1967

C-130B   60-0293   772 TCS, 463 TCW, USAF, Mactan
                      7 crew, names unknown (survived)
                      35 passengers (KIA)
                      14 passengers (survived)

A Hercules was involved in a major accident during a scheduled flight from Tan Son Nhut. The aircraft was due to make seven stops within South Vietnam before returning to Tan Son Nhut. At An Khe the Hercules started its take off roll for the next leg to Qui Nhon. Just before the aircraft was about to lift off it suddenly veered to the left and departed the runway. The pilots steered the aircraft back onto the runway but it overshot the end, ran down an embankment and burst into flames. Of the 56 passengers and crew on board a total of 35 were killed, including US, South Vietnamese and South Korean troops.

19 June 1967

F-4B   150439   VF-142, USN, USS *Constellation*
                    Lt Cdr F L Raines (survived)
                    Ens C L Lownes (survived)

The *Constellation* launched an RA-5C to obtain photographic coverage of Route 1A between Hanoi and Nam Dinh. Flying as escort to the Vigilante was an F-4B piloted by Lt Cdr Raines. The Phantom was hit by anti-aircraft fire just as the Vigilante was finishing the photo run less than two miles south of Hanoi. Everything seemed normal so the pair headed out to sea and rendezvoused with the carrier. However, as Lt Cdr Raines extended the undercarriage and the flaps on the downwind leg of the approach, the Phantom's hydraulics failed completely and both crew ejected but were picked up by one of the ship's Seasprites.

20 June 1967

F-8E   149209   VMF(AW)-232, MAG-11, USMC, Da Nang
                    Maj Charles Ligon Cronkite (KIA)

Maj Cronkite had recently been transferred from VMF(AW)-232 to staff duties at the conclusion of his operational tour. Based at Da Nang he still continued to fly with the Squadron whenever he could. During a combat mission the engine of his Crusader flamed out and Maj Cronkite was forced to eject over the sea. Unfortunately, Charles Cronkite did not survive and was thought to have been knocked unconscious during the ejection sequence. It was surmised that the cause of the flame out was likely to have been due to a fuel pump failure.

21 June 1967

A-1E   52-132548   1 ACS, 14 ACW, USAF, Pleiku
                      Capt Darrell John Spinler (KIA)

Two Skyraiders were tasked with a strike on a storage area on the Xe Kong River near Ban Phon in southern Laos. Capt Spinler was flying the lead aircraft and started his second pass to drop napalm from about 200 feet. As the Skyraider started to climb away from the attack it was hit by ground fire and spun into the ground. Capt Spinler did not eject from his aircraft and was killed in the crash.

RF-101C   56-0085   20 TRS, 432 TRW, USAF, Udorn
                       Capt R E Patterson (survived)

Capt Patterson's mission was to obtain photograph of several targets in North Vietnam but when he was still 25 miles southwest of Yen Bai and at 30,000 feet he came under attack from a SAM site. He started to jink the aircraft to try to break the SA-2's radar lock but the SAM exploded close to the aircraft and badly damaged the Voodoo. For some reason Capt Patterson headed north but had to eject about 20 miles northwest of Yen Bai. This

In mid-1967 the USAF's SAR capability was greatly improved by the introduction of in-flight refuelling for its HH-3E helicopters. The HC-130H was modified to HC-130P tanker configuration so that it could perform the dual roles of tanker and airborne SAR mission controller. USAF

RF-8 showed no sign of the Skyhawk's wreckage and no SAR beeper or radio transmissions were ever heard. Lt Cole was on his second tour on board the *Intrepid* when he was shot down having flown 100 missions from the ship in 1966. In November 1988 the Vietnamese returned remains that were said to be those of Lt (since promoted to Cdr during the time he was missing) Cole. This was verified by the Central Identification Laboratory in Hawaii and on 5 May 1989 LeGrande Ogden Cole was finally laid to rest at Arlington National Cemetery.

A-4C   147712   VA-146, USN, USS *Constellation*
                 Lt John Michael McGrath (POW)

The last Navy aircraft lost during the month of June was a Skyhawk on an armed reconnaissance sortie over North Vietnam. A metal bridge was seen near Thieu Ang, 30 miles southwest of Nam Dinh, and the aircraft rolled in to drop their bombs. As Lt McGrath was pulling up from the target his aircraft was hit in the wing by AAA causing sudden and total loss of control. Lt McGrath ejected immediately but his parachute only just opened as he fell through some tall trees. During the ejection and subsequent landing he broke and dislocated his arm and fractured a vertebra and a knee. Further injuries were suffered during the torture sessions soon after arrival at the Hanoi Hilton. John McGrath was released on 4 March 1973 and eventually became CO of VA-97 and naval attaché to Peru before retiring in 1987. He subsequently wrote and illustrated a moving account of his experiences as a POW in a book titled *Prisoner of War: Six Years in Hanoi*. John McGrath joined United Airlines after retirement from the Navy and flew Boeing 737s on domestic routes. He had flown 157 missions on the *Ranger* during a previous tour and a further 22 on the *Constellation* before he was shot down.

F-105D   62-4316   388 TFW, USAF, Korat
                   Maj Ralph L Kuster (survived)

The USAF once more raided the marshalling yards at Thai Nguyen on the last day of the month. As Maj Kuster's F-105 pulled up from his bombing run through 14,000 feet it was hit twice in the port wing by 85mm shells. The aircraft remained airworthy and Maj Kuster started on the long journey home. After flying 125 miles southwest towards the Laotian border Kuster had to eject over a mountainous region near Ban Ta Pha. The pilot was eventually rescued by an HH-3 SAR helicopter.

1 July 1967

F-100F   56-4002   615 TFS, 35 TFW, USAF, Phan Rang
                   Capt T R Olsen (survived)
                   A2C Robert Arthur Saucier (KIA)

A two-seat F-100F was accompanying a close air support mission with an enlisted man on board either to take photographs of the strike or simply as air experience. It was not unusual for hard working ground crew to be taken on a mission and many were eager for the opportunity. Capt Olsen's flight was attacking a VC target 12 miles north of Vinh Long in the Mekong Delta, but his aircraft was hit by ground fire and started to burn. The aircraft headed north to Bien Hoa, the nearest airfield capable of taking the Super Sabre, but two miles short of the runway Capt Olsen had to make a forced landing in which A2C Saucier was fatally injured.

2 July 1967

A-4B   145002   VSF-3, USN, USS *Intrepid*
                Lt(jg) Frederick Morrison Kasch (KIA)

Classed as an ASW carrier, the *Intrepid* hosted the specialist VSF-3, an ASW fighter squadron, in addition to two 'normal' attack squadrons. The VSF squadrons provided detachments to the anti-submarine carriers for CAP and light attack duties. VSF-3 was equipped with the older A-4B version of the Skyhawk and took a full part in Air Wing 10's strike operations. During a

---

turned out to be a good decision as the Captain was rescued from a mountainous region by an HH-3. Capt Patterson was shot down in a Voodoo again on 16 September 1967. The Jolly Green Giants of the 3rd ARRG were about to extend their capability as the first test air-to-air refuelling from an HC-130P tanker took place in Southeast Asia on this day. This capability extended the helicopter's range and endurance thereby further improving the chances of rescue for downed aircrew. Almost simultaneously with this development was the withdrawal of the ageing HU-16 Albatross from Southeast Asia. The type made its last operational sortie in Southeast Asia on 30 September having saved a total of 47 airmen from the Gulf of Tonkin and was replaced by the HH-3/HC-130 combination.

A-4E   151091   VMA-211, MAG-12, USMC, Chu Lai
                1 pilot, name unknown (survived)

During a combat mission over South Vietnam the engine of a Marine Corps Skyhawk exploded and the pilot ejected. The cause of the engine failure was thought to have been accidental rather than enemy action.

22 June 1967

A-4E   151106   VA-93, USN, USS *Hancock*
                Lt Cdr James Glenn Pirie (POW)

The Hai Duong railway bridge was attacked on the 22nd by a flight of A-4s from the *Hancock*. Like all bridges in North Vietnam, it was well defended with numerous AAA sites of various calibres. Lt Cdr Pirie was pulling up from his attack and jinking violently when his aircraft was struck twice by anti-aircraft fire. With the aircraft on fire and the engine winding down, James Pirie ejected near the bridge and was quickly captured. He was released from his imprisonment on 18 February 1973.

RF-4C   65-0861   12 TRS, 460 TRW, USAF, Tan Son Nhut
                  Capt A T Dardeau (survived)
                  1Lt A J Lundell (survived)

A tragic accident occured on the 22nd when a reconnaissance Phantom collided with Lockheed Constellation N6936C of Airlift International four miles north of Saigon. The Constellation was operating a mail contract flight from Manila to Saigon and collided with the Phantom as it commenced its approach to Tan Son Nhut. Both Phantom crew ejected safely but the seven crew on board the Constellation were killed when it crashed out of control.

23 June 1967

O-1G   51-12060   20 TASS, 504 TASG, USAF, Da Nang
                  1 pilot, name unknown (survived)

A Bird Dog crashed in South Vietnam due to accidental engine failure.

26 June 1967

F-4C   63-7577   390 TFS, 366 TFW, USAF, Da Nang
                 Maj J C Blandford (survived)
                 1Lt J M Jarvis (survived)

Maj Blandford and 1Lt Jarvis were ferrying an F-4C either to or from Clark AFB in the Philippines when they were intercepted by Chinese Air Force Shenyang J-5s (MiG-17) about 25 miles off the southern tip of Hainan island. Why their route between Da Nang and Clark would have taken them so near to Chinese airspace is unclear. Badly damaged by cannon fire from the MiGs, the crew ejected at an altitude of about 25,000 feet and were rescued by a US Navy helicopter before they could be reached by the Chinese Navy, thereby avoiding an embarassing international incident. This Phantom was itself a MiG-killer having been flown by Maj R G Dilger and 1Lt M Thies when they shot down a MiG-17 on 1 May 1967.

28 June 1967

F-4B   152242   VF-143, USN, USS *Constellation*
                Cdr William Porter Lawrence (POW)
                Lt(jg) James William Bailey (POW)

Bill Lawrence, the CO of VF-143, led a flak suppression section during a raid on an important transshipment point 10 miles northwest of Nam Dinh. The Phantoms were at 12,000 feet and were preparing to roll in on the target when Cdr Lawrence's aircraft was hit by 85mm flak. With the aircraft's hydraulics failing, Cdr Lawrence released his CBUs on the target and had difficulty in pulling out of his dive before part of the tail section separated from the Phantom. The crew ejected and were captured and suffered the usual torture and beatings. James Bailey was the veteran of 183 combat missions over Southeast Asia, having flown with VF-143 on board the *Ranger* in 1966. He was released on 18 February and Cdr Lawrence was released on 4 March 1973. Both men resumed their naval careers and Bill Lawrence retired with the rank of Vice Admiral having been Deputy Chief of Naval Operations and James Bailey retired as a Commander.

30 June 1967

A-4C   148466   VA-15, USN, USS *Intrepid*
                Lt LeGrande Ogden Cole (KIA)

Four Skyhawks were launched from the *Intrepid* to hit the Ben Thuy thermal power plant on the Song Ca River just south of Vinh. In the face of intense flak the Skyhawks rolled in one after the other to bomb the target but Lt Cole's aircraft was not seen after the attack started. However, Cole's wingman did report seeing a large explosion and fire to the south of the target which at first he thought was a stray bomb. When Lt Cole failed to rendezvous with the rest of the flight it was surmised that he had been shot down. Photographs of the target area taken by an

raid on the railway yard at Hai Duong Lt Kasch was just pulling up from his bombing run when his aircraft was hit by AAA, causing partial engine failure. He trimmed the aircraft in the hope of reaching the coast and was accompanied by his wingman as he flew 35 miles to the south. However, as they approached the coast near Luc Linh, Lt Kasch was down to 500 feet and he was advised to eject. His wingman lost sight of him as Kasch was flying so slow and when he came round again all he saw was the wreckage of Kasch's aircraft among some houses. There was no sign that Lt Kasch had survived. On 3 November 1988 the Vietnamese handed over remains that they said included those of Lt Kasch and this was confirmed by forensic analysis in February 1989. Frederick Kasch was buried at Fort Rosecrans National Cemetery in San Diego.

F-105D 60-0413 357 TFS, 355 TFW, USAF, Takhli
Maj R E Stone (survived)
A flight of F-105s was bombing a target in the Annamite Mountains, 40 miles southeast of Mu Ron Ma, when one of the aircraft was hit by AAA. Maj Stone flew north away from the 'hot' area and deeper into the mountains and ejected. He was rescued by a Navy SH-3, which made a daring flight over 30 miles inland from the coast.

F-4B 151421 VMFA-542, MAG-13, USMC, Chu Lai
Maj Ray Daniel Pendergraft (KIA)
Capt David Glenn Spearman (KIA)
The Marine Aviation Wing in South Vietnam had not lost a fixed-wing aircraft for over a month but its run of good luck came to a halt on the 2nd. Two companies of Marines were caught by a larger NVA force close to the forward Marine Corps base at Con Thien just south of the DMZ and were taking very heavy casualties. A flight of Phantoms was called in to attack the North Vietnamese troops near Kinh Mon, actually within the DMZ buffer zone. One of the aircraft was hit by ground fire on its fourth pass over the target. Maj Pendergraft flew out to sea and then tried to reach Da Nang but the aircraft crashed just off the coast, about 15 miles north of Hué, and both crew were killed.

F-8E 150286 VMF(AW)-232, MAG-11, USMC, Da Nang
Maj Bruce A Martin (survived)
The second Marine Corps aircraft lost on this day occurred a few minutes later as a Crusader that responded to an emergency call for assistance in support of the Marines on the ground was also hit. Maj Martin saw the Phantom leave the target trailing smoke and then saw it crash in the sea. Flying alone due to his wingman having to abort take off, Maj Martin came in at low level and released all his eight bombs in one salvo on NVA positions near Thon Cam Son within the DMZ buffer zone. His aircraft was also hit by AAA and the hydraulics began to fail. With his aircraft on fire Maj Martin flew out to sea escorted by a pair of A-4s and ejected when the fire became worse. He was rescued within minutes by a USAF HH-3 helicopter that had already been alerted to search for the F-4 crew. VMF(AW)-232 left Da Nang for the USA in September 1967 having flown 5,785 sorties for the loss of five Crusaders and two pilots plus two more aircraft destroyed during a Viet Cong attack on Da Nang on 15 July. Once in the USA the Squadron re-equipped with the F-4J and was redesignated VMFA-232. It returned to Vietnam in March 1969.

F-105D 60-0494 44 TFS, 388 TFW, USAF, Korat
Capt Dale M Pichard (survived)
A flight of F-105s was tasked with the destruction of what was thought to be an unoccupied AAA site near Xom Hoai, 25 miles south of Vinh. Unfortunately, there were several active sites in the area and a 57mm shell blew a large hole in Capt Pichard's aircraft and set it on fire. He headed towards Thailand but was forced to eject about 20 miles northeast of the Mu Gia Pass. Capt Pichard landed in the middle of a busy section of the Ho Chi Minh Trail and had to hide immediately after landing. A SAR task force under the command of Maj Larry Mehr in an A-1 from the 602nd ACS arrived at the scene but could not locate Capt Pichard. The search was called off as darkness approached but resumed at first light the next day. A force of 20 F-105s from Korat was directed onto enemy gun positions by Maj Mehr until he was satisfied that most of the ground fire had been subdued.

An HH-3E (65-12781) flown by Capt G Etzel, who was on his first rescue mission, then dashed into the area and successfully picked up Capt Pichard. Both Mehr and Etzel were awarded the AFC for this daring rescue. F-105D 60-0494 was named 'Mr Pride' when it flew with the 469th TFS.

4 July 1967

A-4C 148544 VA-15, USN, USS *Intrepid*
Lt Phillip Charles Craig (KIA)
An Independence Day raid on the railway at Hai Duong resulted in the loss of an aircraft and its pilot. The raid itself was successful and the aircraft headed back to the coast. However, despite radio calls from Lt Craig indicating that he had reached the coast, he did not rendezvous with the rest of the formation and could not be contacted on the radio. A SAR mission was quickly mounted but found no trace of the pilot or his aircraft. North Vietnamese radio later reported that two aircraft had been shot down during the raid. Although this was inaccurate as only one Skyhawk was missing, it was assumed that Lt Craig had indeed been shot down near the coast to the south of Haiphong. 'P C' Craig had flown 100 missions on a previous tour and his remains were eventually handed over to the US on 26 November 1985.

5 July 1967

F-105D 61-0127 354 TFS, 355 TFW, USAF, Takhli
Maj Dewey Wayne Waddell (POW)

F-105D 60-0454 357 TFS, 355 TFW, USAF, Takhli
Capt William Vandervos Frederick (KIA)
The 5th of July was another bad day for the Takhli Wing with the loss of three pilots. Simultaneous raids on the Cao Nung railway bridge and the nearby Vu Chua railway yard northeast of Kep may have been intended to split the attention of the defences. Wolf flight from the 354th TFS lost the first aircraft. Maj Waddell's aircraft was hit twice by AAA as it was diving on the target at Cao Nung and crashed a few miles to the east. A few minutes later Bear flight from the 357th TFS rolled in to the attack but Capt Frederick's aircraft was hit by anti-aircraft fire as it was pulling out of its dive. He also flew a few miles to the east to eject over high ground where he stood a better chance of being rescued. Although Maj Waddell was captured almost immediately after landing and was eventually released on 4 March 1973, there is no direct evidence that Capt Frederick survived to become a POW, although he was seen on the ground following ejection. His remains were among those handed over by the Vietnamese in the late 1980s and positively identified on 3 January 1990. Wayne Waddell was shot down on his 48th mission. He became active in the NAM-POW organisation, having retired from the Air Force in 1987.

F-105D 61-0042 357 TFS, 355 TFW, USAF, Takhli
Maj Ward Kent Dodge (POW - died)
As one formation of Thuds was hitting the Cao Nung Bridge, another group was bombing the railway yard at Vu Chua a few miles to the southeast. Just as Maj Dodge was about to roll in from 15,000 feet to bomb the target, his aircraft was hit by an 85mm anti-aircraft shell. After a brief struggle to regain control he was forced to eject close to the target. Ward Dodge is known to have been captured but he apparently died of unknown causes in a prison camp about a week after he was shot down. Three aircraft had been shot down within the space of four minutes in a small piece of sky near Kep.

6 July 1967

F-4C 63-7698 480 TFS, 366 TFW, USAF, Da Nang
Maj Kenneth Raymond Hughey (POW)
1Lt Melvin Pollack (POW)
The Huong Vi railway yard, five miles northwest of Kep, was the target for a raid on the 6th. One of the F-4s was hit by AAA as it climbed away from the target and the crew were forced to eject soon afterwards. Both men were captured and imprisoned. 1Lt Pollack was on his first tour in Southeast Asia having come straight from training at Davis-Monthan AFB and had flown 78

missions. Maj Hughey had flown as an FAC pilot and had flown a phenomenal 564 missions in total, 106 of these were over North Vietnam. Both men were released in Operation Homecoming on 4 March 1973.

A-4E 151032 VMA-311, MAG-12, USMC, Chu Lai
Maj Ralph E Brubaker (survived)
The SAM sites that the North Vietnamese had constructed close to the DMZ now threatened Marine Corps air operations in the northern provinces of South Vietnam. It was consequently decided that the Marines would also adopt the Iron Hand SAM suppression mission, which had hitherto been the preserve of the USAF and US Navy. The first Marine Corps aircraft lost during an Iron Hand mission was a Skyhawk that was taking part in a night attack on a SAM site about four miles north of Thon Cam Son, just outside the DMZ buffer zone. Maj Brubaker knew he was under fire from the SAM site and had started a split-S manoeuvre to try to evade the missiles but his aircraft was hit by an SA-2 at about 12,000 feet, which severely damaged the A-4's tail. Maj Brubaker ejected just within the DMZ and landed in a small field, dislocating his knee. He spent the night in a bomb crater and was almost bombed by a Marine A-6 on a TPQ-10 mission. Brubaker contacted the Intruder crew on his emergency radio who called in the SAR forces for a rescue attempt at dawn the following day. The SAR helicopter was hit four times when it landed to pick up the injured pilot.

F-105D 61-0136 354 TFS, 355 TFW, USAF, Takhli
1 pilot, name unknown (survived)
A Thunderchief crashed near Takhli on the 6th following engine failure. The pilot ejected safely.

7 July 1967

RF-101C 56-0096 Detachment 1, 45 TRS, 460 TRW, USAF, Tan Son Nhut
Maj J Ketchum (survived)
Maj Ketchum had just taken off from Tan Son Nhut and was climbing through 5,000 feet at the start of a reconnaissance mission when his aircraft was hit by small arms fire about five miles north of the airfield. He attempted to turn back to land the damaged aircraft but he was forced to eject and had to be rescued by an Army helicopter.

B-52D 56-0595 22 BW attached to 4133 BW(P), USAF, Andersen
Maj Gen William Joseph Crumm (KIA)
Maj Paul Andrew Avolese (KIA)
Capt David Fritz Bittenbender (KIA)
4 crew, names unknown (survived)

B-52D 56-0627 454 BW attached to 4133 BW(P), USAF, Andersen
Capt Charles Herman Blankenship (KIA)
1Lt George Emerson Jones (KIA)
MSgt Olen Burke McLaughlin (KIA)
3 crew, names unknown (survived)
Ever since the Arc Light strikes had started in June 1965, the mighty B-52s had been restricted to bombing targets in South Vietnam. Hitherto, the only B-52s that had been lost on Arc Light missions were the two aircraft that collided on the very first mission. Between then and 7 July 1967 the B-52 force had flown over 10,000 sorties and dropped over 190,000 tons of bombs without serious mishap. However, tragedy struck on the 7th when a formation of B-52s was approaching the coast of South Vietnam en route to a strike in the A Shau Valley near the DMZ. Two B-52Ds collided 20 miles off the mouth of the Mekong Delta, about 65 miles south of Saigon, and both aircraft crashed into the sea. The cell of three aircraft approached their IP and had to make a steep turn to start their lengthy bomb run on the target. The leading aircraft and the number 3 aircraft in the cell collided during the turn. Following this accident the rules were changed allowing B-52s on Arc Light missions to fly a looser formation that increased the margin for error yet still retained cell integrity for mutual ECM protection. On board the lead aircraft was Maj Gen William J Crumm, the commander of SAC's 3rd Air Division based at

Most B-52 Arc Light raids were flown in cells of three aircraft and on 7 July 1967 two aircraft from a cell collided when turning to line up on their target. One of those killed was Major General William Crumm, commander of all SAC forces in Southeast Asia.
USAF

Andersen AFB on Guam and who controlled all SAC units in the theatre. Seven other men, including four from Maj Gen Crumm's B-52, managed to escape from the aircraft and were rescued from the South China Sea. The crew are all listed as belonging to the 2nd BS and were based at Andersen AFB on temporary duty. The B-52s on Guam were deployed from various wings, 56-0595 was detached from the 22nd BW at March AFB, California and 56-0627 was from the 454th BW at Columbus AFB, Mississippi. Maj Gen Crumm (together with Maj Gen Worley who was killed on 23 July 1968) was the highest-ranking airman to lose his life during the war in Southeast Asia and was scheduled to become the Director of Aerospace Programs at the Pentagon in August. He became commander of the 3rd Air Division on 16 July 1965 and had directed the B-52 Arc Light missions for all but the first month of the operation.

In 1993 and 1994 a joint US-Vietnamese investigation team interviewed a Vietnamese fisherman who claimed to have discovered the wreckage of a large aircraft under 100 feet of water. He had also recovered some bones from the wreck and handed these over to the team. In 1995 an extensive underwater search located the wreckage of at least one of the B-52s but found no more human remains. By the use of mitochondrial DNA analysis the bones were positively identified on 2 May 1997 as belonging to Capt Blankenship, 1Lt Jones and MSgt McLaughlin.

8 July 1967

B-52D 56-0601 22 BW attached to 4133 BW(P),
USAF, Andersen
Maj Gene Wesley Brown (KIA)
Capt James Thomas Davis (KIA)
Capt Anthony Kent Johnson (KIA)
Capt William Henry Pritchard (KIA)
Capt Donald J Reynolds (KIA)
1 crew, name unknown (survived)

By a strange quirk of fate another B-52 was lost the very next day after the mid-air collision. An aircraft on an Arc Light mission suffered multiple engine failure that led to electrical failure on some of the aircraft's systems and instruments. The pilot elected to attempt an emergency landing at Da Nang but the aircraft touched down half way down the runway and its drag parachute failed causing the aircraft to overrun and explode at the end of the runway as it ploughed through a minefield. Only the tail gunner survived the crash. The aircraft was detached to the Provisional Bombardment Wing on Guam from the 22nd BW.

9 July 1967

A-4C 149542 VA-146, USN, USS *Constellation*
Lt Charles Richard Lee (KIA)

The *Constellation* mounted a strike on the main Haiphong POL storage site on the 9th. A formation of A-4s was approaching the target at 12,500 feet and was just about to roll in when a volley of

SAMs was launched against them. One of the SA-2s hit Lt Lee's aircraft and blew its tail off . The aircraft entered a slow inverted spin until it hit the ground about 10 miles southwest of Haiphong. Lt Lee was not seen to escape and was probably incapacitated by the SAM detonation.

A-4C 149603 VA-34, USN, USS *Intrepid*
Lt Cdr Edward Holmes Martin (POW)

At almost the exact same moment that Lt Lee was being shot down, a SAM battery scored another hit a few miles away to the northwest. The *Intrepid's* aircraft were targeted at the Army barracks at Ban Yen but before they arrived at the target they also encountered SAMs. Lt Cdr Martin, the executive officer of VA-34, was leading the formation at about 10,000 feet and was taking evasive action but an SA-2 exploded close to his aircraft and peppered the Skyhawk with shrapnel. The aircraft caught fire and quickly became uncontrollable forcing Lt Cdr Martin to eject about 10 miles south of Hai Duong. Lt Cdr Martin was quickly captured and spent the rest of the war in various POW camps until his release on 4 March 1973. He had a most distinguished post-war career having captained the USS *Saratoga*, been Chief of Naval Air Training and commanded the US 6th Fleet as a Vice Admiral. In 1985 he was appointed Deputy Chief of Naval Operations (Air Warfare) and as such was the head of US naval aviation. He later became Commander Eastern Atlantic and Deputy Commander-in-Chief, US Naval Forces Europe and eventually retired from the Navy in 1989. He was on his 19th mission over North Vietnam when he was shot down.

10 July 1967

F-105D 60-0424 34 TFS, 388 TFW, USAF, Korat
Maj M E Seaver (survived)

An Iron Hand flight lost one of its bombers during a SAM hunt on the 10th. Maj Seaver's aircraft was hit by automatic weapons fire as the flight was mid-way between Yen Bai and Thai Nguyen. Seaver turned around and headed southwest. Fortunately the aircraft remained airworthy until Maj Seaver could reach relative safety but he had to eject about 30 miles southwest of Sam Neua. He was later rescued by an HH-3. Maj Seaver's aircraft was painted as 'Mickey Titty Chi'.

O-1E 56-4175 21 TASS, 504 TASG, USAF, Nha Trang
1 pilot, name unknown (survived)

During a flight in South Vietnam a Bird Dog suffered an engine failure and was destroyed in a forced landing.

12 July 1967

F-4C 64-0718 391 TFS, 12 TFW, USAF, Cam Ranh Bay
Maj James Alvin Rainwater (KIA)
1Lt T Plank (survived)

The USAF lost two aircraft near Saigon on the 12th. In the first incident a flight of F-4s was circling near Xom Trum Thap, 13

miles northwest of Bien Hoa, as they were preparing to strafe and rocket a potential landing zone. Maj Rainwater's aircraft suddenly dived into the ground from 1,000 feet, presumably the victim of ground fire. Both the crew ejected but only the WSO survived.

F-100D 55-3549 531 TFS, 3 TFW, USAF, Bien Hoa
Capt Charles Larry Moore (KIA)

The second jet lost near Saigon on this day was a Super Sabre that was shot down about 15 miles south of the city, close to Ap Bac. Capt Moore was making his first run over suspected military buildings and was flying at 150 feet as he was dropping napalm. The aircraft was hit by automatic weapons fire, burst into flames and crashed a few miles away killing the pilot.

A-4E 151181 VA-212, USN, USS *Bon Homme Richard*
Lt Cdr J H Kirkpatrick (survived)

The Navy lost a Skyhawk on its way to a strike on the railway at Mai Truong in North Vietnam. Lt Cdr Kirkpatrick was five miles south of Hai Duong when his aircraft was hit in the port wing and fuselage by ground fire. The aircraft suffered hydraulic failure, fuel pump failure, an unsafe undercarriage indication and a loss of engine power. Soon after crossing the coast about 15 miles south of Haiphong, with the aircraft barely able to stay airborne, Lt Cdr Kirkpatrick ejected. He was rescued by a Navy SAR helicopter.

T-28D 49-1569 606 ACS, 56 ACW, USAF, Nakhon Phanom
Capt Jack Paris Dove (KIA)
Maj Boyd Edwin Squire (KIA)

The 606th was by now well established in its role of night interdiction over the Ho Chi Minh Trail. Occasionally these missions took the T-28s into North Vietnam itself as well as throughout the Barrel Roll and Steel Tiger regions of Laos. Capt Dove and Maj Squire were hunting for trucks during a night armed reconnaissance mission and went missing near Ban Katoi, just within North Vietnam. It was thought that they were hit by anti-aircraft fire and crashed before either of the crew could escape. A SAR aircraft spotted a wing from the aircraft but there was no sign of any survivors. On 1 June 1992 the crash site was excavated and remains recovered that were later identified as being those of the T-28 crew.

A-4E 150102 VA-163, USN, USS *Oriskany*
1 pilot, name unknown (survived)

Two days before the *Oriskany* officially took its place back on the line on its third tour of duty off Southeast Asia, it lost its first aircraft. A Skyhawk was launched for a training flight as part of the pre-combat training programme but the aircraft left the deck with insufficient airspeed and crashed in the sea after the pilot ejected.

13 July 1967

F-105D 60-0450 357 TFS, 355 TFW, USAF, Takhli
Maj C D Osborne (survived)

In the continuing search for SAM sites near the DMZ an Iron Hand flight from Takhli lost an aircraft to AAA. Maj Osborne's flight was trolling the area. This involved deliberately flying through a known threat area at a medium speed and altitude in the hope that a SAM site would try a shot and thereby reveal itself to the Iron Hand flight. Eight miles northwest of Thon Cam Son Maj Osborne's aircraft was hit in the fuselage by anti-aircraft fire. The aircraft did not seem too badly damaged so the pilot decided to make for Takhli. However, Maj Osborne was forced to eject 35 miles northwest of Ubon and was subsequently rescued.

A-1E 52-133913 1 ACS, 14 ACW, USAF, Pleiku
Maj F A Armstrong (survived)

A Steel Tiger mission over southern Laos found North Vietnamese troops out in the open. Maj Armstrong started a bombing run from 9,000 feet but his aircraft was hit by automatic wapons fire and burst into flames. He ejected about 12 miles west of Khe Sanh and was rescued by a VNAF H-34 helicopter.

14 July 1967

A-4E   152049   VA-164, USN, USS Oriskany
          Lt(jg) L J Cunningham (survived)

On its first day on the line the Oriskany suffered its first combat loss. Lt Cunningham's A-4 was hit by AAA as it attacked barges on an inland waterway near Gia La, 15 miles southeast of Vinh. The aircraft was hit in the nose and the engine must have then ingested debris as it started running rough on the way back to the carrier. By the time Lt Cunningham reached the Oriskany flames were coming from the engine exhaust and the aircraft was obviously in no shape for a carrier landing. He ejected at very low level close to the carrier and was rescued by a Seasprite from the Oriskany's HC-1 detachment.

A-4C   147759   VA-76, USN, USS Bon Homme Richard
          Lt J N Donis (survived)

A flight of A-4s was sent on an armed reconnaissance mission in search of PT boats when the aircraft came under fire just off the coast near Van Ly, 25 miles south of Nam Dinh. One of the aircraft was hit in the port wing by an anti-aircraft shell, which caused a fire in a rocket pod carried under the wing. The rockets exploded and the debris caused the engine to fail. Lt Donis ejected about 15 miles off the coast and was picked up 30 minutes later by a Navy helicopter.

A-4C   147709   VA-76, USN, USS Bon Homme Richard
          Cdr Robert Byron Fuller (POW)

The CO of VA-76 led a strike against the Co Trai railway and road bridge near Hung Yen on the Red River, 20 miles southeast of Hanoi. Just as the aircraft commenced its attack it was rocked by the explosion of an SA-2 missile but Cdr Fuller delivered his bombs before he encountered any control problems with his aircraft. The Skyhawk's tail was seen to be on fire and fuel was streaming from a leaking tank. As the aircraft started rolling uncontrollably, the pilot ejected and was soon captured. Cdr Fuller was the second CO that VA-76 had lost within eight months. He had taken command of the Squadron on 6 December 1966 when Cdr A D McFall was accidentally killed during a night launch in the Pacific. Robert Fuller had flown 110 missions in Southeast Asia and was released on 4 March 1973. He had started his flying career in 1952 in the F9F-5 Panther and eventually retired as a Rear Admiral in 1982.

15 July 1967

A-1H   135288   VA-152, USN, USS Oriskany
          Lt(jg) Robin Bern Cassell (KIA)

Lt Cassell was the section leader of two Skyraiders on an armed reconnaissance mission searching for boats and barges along the coast of North Vietnam near Thanh Hoa. A number of small boats were found and Lt Cassell commenced an attack. During the bombing run his aircraft was hit by automatic weapons fire from the boats and Lt Cassell radioed that he had been hit. Soon afterwards the Skyraider crashed into the sea and exploded with Lt Cassell still in the cockpit.

F-100D   56-3275   531 TFS, 3 TFW, USAF, Bien Hoa
          Capt T H Herndon (survived)

Ramrod 8 was a Super Sabre flown by Capt Herndon on a close air support mission about 50 miles north of Bien Hoa. As Capt Herndon made his second pass and pulled up his aircraft was hit by ground fire. He ejected seven miles southeast of Loc Ninh and was rescued by an Army helicopter having sustained minor injuries.

F-8E   149134, 150344   VMF(AW)-232, MAG-11, USMC, Da Nang
F-4C   63-7535, 63-7558, 63-7573, 63-7659, 64-0734, 64-0762   390 TFS, 366 TFW, USAF, Da Nang
C-130A   55-0009   41 TCS, 374 TCW, USAF, Naha
C-130E-II   62-1815   Detachment 1, 314 TCW, USAF, Da Nang

In one of the most devastating and costly VC mortar attacks on a US airfield during the war, 10 US aircraft were destroyed and another 49 damaged to varying degrees in a raid on Da Nang. The attack commenced just after midnight of the 14th and a total of 83 mortar and rocket rounds were fired and eight men were killed with another 195 wounded. The attack almost wiped out the 390th TFS, which had 18 of its Phantoms destroyed or badly damaged. One burning Phantom, loaded with eight M117 bombs, was rapidly unloaded by a courageous maintenance crew organised by Col F C Blesse and Col H O Brennan before the fire reached the bombs. Another of the Phantoms was blown upside down in its revetment. The ammunition dump on the Marine Corps side of the airfield was hit and exploded with terrific force. The runway was cratered in a number of places but was quickly repaired the next day to allow replacement aircraft to be flown in almost immediately. The C-130E-II that was destroyed was an airborne command post aircraft and the 314th TCW detachment was redesignated as the 7th ACCS on 13 February 1968.

16 July 1967

F-8E   150925   VF-162, USN, USS Oriskany
          Lt Cdr Demetrio A Verich (survived)

The Oriskany's Air Wing was having a rough return to combat, losing its third aircraft in as many days. In fact before the month was over, the Oriskany would lose a total of 10 aircraft in combat and three in accidents. Lt Cdr Verich was leading the flak suppression element of three F-8s during a raid by A-4s on the Phu Ly railway yard, 30 miles south of Hanoi. As the formation approached the target it came under attack from a SAM site. Lt Cdr Verich started a split-S manoeuvre to evade two of the missiles but his aircraft was hit by a third SA-2 as the Crusader was diving through 5,000 feet. The aircraft began to disintegrate and Verich ejected immediately. Considering that his position was only about 16 miles south of Hanoi when he landed, Lt Cdr Verich was most fortunate to be rescued by a Navy SH-3 of HS-2 from the Hornet at first light on the 17th after 15 hours on the ground close to an AAA position. The helicopter pilot, Lt Neil Sparks, was awarded the Navy Cross for his courage and skill in rescuing the pilot. The helicopter had spent a total of two hours and 23 minutes over North Vietnam during the rescue, much of that time under fire. 'Butch' Verich had also been shot down on 18 August 1966 during the Oriskany's second war cruise.

F-4B   148387   VMFA-115, MAG-13, USMC, Chu Lai
          Capt H E Pyle (survived)
          Capt J A Gordon (survived)

An F-4B pilot reported a fire shortly after take off on a strike mission. Both crew ejected safely and were rescued. The cause of the fire was attributed to a technical malfunction rather than enemy action.

17 July 1967

F-105D   59-1748   333 TFS, 355 TFW, USAF, Takhli
          Maj H C Copeland (POW)

The defences around Kep were among some of the strongest in the whole of North Vietnam and were singled out for an attack on the 17th. Maj Copeland's target was an 85mm gun position in the Kep railway yard. It is uncertain if it was this gun that hit his aircraft, but the F-105 was indeed hit by an 85mm shell at 12,000 feet. The aircraft burst into flames and quickly became uncontrollable so Maj Copeland ejected near his target. He spent the rest of the war as a POW and was released from captivity on 14 March 1973.

18 July 1967

A-4E   151986   VA-164, USN, USS Oriskany
          Lt Cdr Richard Danner Hartman (POW - died)

A-4E   151175   VA-164, USN, USS Oriskany
          Lt(jg) Larrie J Duthie (survived)

A-4E   152034   VA-164, USN, USS Oriskany
          Lt(jg) Barry T Wood (survived)

The 18th turned out to be another bad day for the Oriskany with the loss of three A-4s and one pilot. VA-164 mounted a raid on the Co Trai railway and road bridge, which had been the target just five days earlier. Lt Cdr Hartman had successfully bombed the target and was leaving the area when his aircraft was hit by AAA. The Skyhawk caught fire and Hartman ejected about 25 miles south of Hanoi. Encouraged by the success in recovering Lt Cdr Verich on the 16th, a SAR mission was quickly organised and aircraft from VA-164 orbited over Hartman's position to provide protection. However, this was an extremely 'hot' location and after about 12 minutes another A-4 was hit by anti-aircraft fire. Lt Duthie was jinking to avoid being hit but there was so much flak in the sky that there was very little chance of avoiding it for long. His flight controls began to fail and his oxygen supply failed, probably as a result of the oxygen tank being hit and burning its way through the aircraft's structure. Lt Duthie came down near Nam Dinh, about 45 miles southeast of Hanoi.

Worse was to follow a little while later as a rescue attempt was made by an SH-3 but was beaten back by strong anti-aircraft fire. One of the escorting A-4s from Duthie's section was hit as it pulled out of a 45-degree dive to launch Zuni rockets against gun positions. Lt Wood noticed his fuel gauge rapidly unwinding indicating a fuel leak so he jettisoned his ordnance and made for the coast. He ejected about eight miles out to sea and was picked up by a boat from a SAR destroyer, the USS Richard B Anderson. Meanwhile both Navy and USAF rescue forces were attempting to reach Lt Duthie. In the face of intense ground fire that damaged several helicopters and escorting aircraft, an HH-3E, piloted by Maj Glen York, made a successful pick up. Maj York was awarded the AFC for this daring rescue.

The next day an SH-3A (151538) from the USS Hornet's HS-2 and piloted by Lt D W Peterson attempted to reach Hartman once again. The helicopter was hit by ground fire and crashed killing all on board including the pilot and Ens D P Frye, AX2 W B Jackson and AX2 D P McGrane. Following this tragedy the SAR mission to rescue Lt Cdr Hartman was reluctantly called off. It had cost the Navy two A-4s and a helicopter with the lives of four men.

Meanwhile, through all the activity overhead, Lt Cdr Hartman was in hiding on a karst hill and in radio contact with his flight. He evaded the North Vietnamese for three days and was resupplied by air during this time. However, he was eventually captured and was either killed at the time of capture or died soon after in a POW camp. His remains were returned by the Vietnamese on 6 March 1974.

F-4D   66-0248   555 TFS, 8 TFW, USAF, Ubon
          Capt R R Headley (survived)
          1Lt G A Kuehner (survived)

Capt Headley was returning from an attack on a 37mm anti-aircraft gun site when his aircraft was hit by AAA near Xom Duong Quan in the Annamite Mountains, 35 miles west of Mu Ron Ma. Capt Headley immediately turned south but after flying less than five miles he and his WSO were forced to eject. They were both picked up by an HH-3, having suffered only minor injuries. This was the first of the new F-4Ds to be lost in combat and the rescue was the first in which a Jolly Green Giant used air-to-air refuelling to extend its range.

19 July 1967

F-105D   60-0441   357 TFS, 355 TFW, USAF, Takhli
          Capt H N Johnson (survived)

A Thunderchief was hit by 37mm anti-aircraft fire during a raid on a railway target at Phu Xuyen, 15 miles north of Cam Pha. Capt Johnson reached the coast and set course for Da Nang but was forced to eject over the Gulf of Tonkin about 65 miles northeast of Dong Hoi. He was rescued by a Navy SAR helicopter.

F-8E   150899   VF-162, USN, USS Oriskany
          Cdr Herbert Perry Hunter (KIA)

The Co Trai railway and road bridge, which had been the scene of the losses on the 18th, was hit again the very next day. Once more the raid resulted in tragedy and for VF-162 this raid was exactly a year from a raid on the same target with similar tragic

An F-4B Phantom of VF-11 flies over the USS *Forrestal* shortly before the disastrous fire that brought an abrupt end to the ship's one and only tour of duty off Vietnam. USN

results. Cdr Hunter, the executive officer of VF-162, was leading the flak suppression element during the raid when his Crusader was hit in the port wing by 57mm anti-aircraft fire. The fuel tanks in the wing were ruptured and the aircraft's hydraulics were partially disabled. Cdr Hunter and his wingman, Lt Lee Fernandez, crossed the coast and headed towards the *Bon Homme Richard*, thinking it was the *Oriskany*. The damage to the aircraft meant that two bombs could not be jettisoned nor could the Crusader take on fuel. The Crusader's wing was unusual in that the entire wing was raised at the leading edge to give more lift during the approach and landing. However, Cdr Hunter could not raise the wing and attempted a landing with the wing in the normal flight position. The aircraft hit the deck hard and fast, missed the arrester wires, wiped off its landing gear and plunged over the side into the water. Cdr Hunter may have been stunned as he hit the deck as he was found floating under water with a partially deployed parachute. Herb Hunter had previously flown as a member of the Blue Angels aerobatic team. This traumatic incident, together with his moral opposition to the war and an eyesight problem, badly affected Lt Fernandez who later turned in his wings and then retired from the Navy.

20 July 1967

A-4E 151119 VA-212, USN, USS *Bon Homme Richard*
Cdr Frederick H Whittemore (survived)

A series of strikes on the My Xa POL storage facility 15 miles northwest of Haiphong resulted in the loss of two Navy Skyhawks on the 20th. The first aircraft was hit in the tail by AAA as it climbed to commence its attack on the target. Cdr Whittemore, the executive officer of VA-212, disconnected the flight controls after experiencing complete hydraulic failure. He was only able to control the aircraft by using the horizontal stabilizer and rudder but nevertheless flew out to sea before ejecting 60 miles east of Hon Gay. As the aircraft meandered 30 degrees either side of the desired heading and its altitude varied involuntarily between 2,000 feet and 6,000 feet, it is a miracle that Cdr Whittemore managed to position himself over the water where he could be rescued by a Navy helicopter. Unfortunately, Cdr Whittemore was lost at sea while serving with VA-93 on 11 April 1968.

UC-123B 54-0630 12 ACS, 315 ACW, USAF, Bien Hoa
detached to Da Nang
Lt Col Everett Edward Foster (KIA)
Maj Allan Julius Stearns (KIA)
Maj Donald Thomas Steinbrunner (KIA)
SSgt Irvin Grant Weyandt (KIA)
Sgt Le Tan Bo, VNAF (KIA)

The Ranch Hand squadron lost its second aircraft and crew of 1967 during a defoliation mission near Gia Vuc, 30 miles southwest of Quang Ngai. The aircraft was on a crop destruction mission and was flying at its normal spraying altitude of about 150 feet when it ran into a hail of small arms fire, burst into flames, crashed and exploded. All the crew were killed including a VNAF observer.

A-4E 150097 VA-163, USN, USS *Oriskany*
Lt R W Kuhl (survived)

Another raid on the My Xa POL storage site later in the day resulted in the loss of another Skyhawk. Approaching the coast about 12 miles east of Hon Gay Lt Kuhl encountered light flak and felt his aircraft hit and his engine start to vibrate. Lt Kuhl lost his radio and the cockpit began to fill with smoke, forcing him to turn back. He continued out to sea but as he approached the northern SAR destroyer, which was positioned about 45 miles south of Hon Gay, the aircraft became uncontrollable and he ejected safely.

F-8E 150916 VF-162, USN, USS *Oriskany*
Lt James W Nunn (survived)

As a Crusader was being catapulted on a RESCAP mission, the pilot thought that the catapult officer had not seen his 'OK for launch' signal and inadvertently let go of the throttle just as the catapult fired. Underpowered, the aircraft settled into the water just in front of the carrier as it failed to achieve flying speed. Fortunately, Lt Nunn ejected underwater and rose to the surface and was rescued with minor injuries.

24 July 1967

F-4C 63-7488 390 TFS, 366 TFS, USAF, Da Nang
Maj Herbert Lamar Lunsford (KIA)
1Lt Jeremy Michael Jarvis (KIA)

During a night armed reconnaissance mission off the coast of North Vietnam a Phantom crew spotted a light on the beach about 10 miles south of Dong Hoi. The aircraft apparently rolled in to investigate or attack the light but the Phantom crashed near the target either as a result of being shot down or flying into the ground due to a misjudgement of altitude. No radio transmissions or SAR beepers were heard and it was assumed that the crew perished in the crash.

A-4E 151054 VMA-211, MAG-12, USMC, Chu Lai
1 pilot, name unknown (survived)

A Marine Corps A-4 was lost when it suffered engine failure as it took off from Chu Lai on a strike mission.

25 July 1967

A-4E 149961 VA-163, USN, USS *Oriskany*
Lt Cdr Donald Vance Davis (KIA)

A truck convoy was spotted near Ha Tinh, 20 miles south of Vinh, by a section of two A-4s from the *Oriskany* during a night armed reconnaissance mission. Under the light of flares dropped by one of the A-4s, Lt Cdr Davis started his strafing run but was either shot down or flew into the ground by accident. It was apparent that the pilot had not survived the crash. In 1997, following two earlier unsuccessful attempts, a joint US/Vietnamese team excavated the wreckage of this aircraft and recovered human remains that were later positively identified as those of Lt Cdr Davis.

26 July 1967

O-1E 57-6270 20 TASS, 504 TASG, USAF, Da Nang
Lt Col R M Cassell (survived)

During a visual reconnaissance mission a Bird Dog was hit in the engine by small arms fire near Gong Nai, 10 miles south of Kham Duc. Lt Col Cassell crash-landed the aircraft a few miles to the north and was eventually recovered with only minor injuries. The aircraft was probably operating from one of the 20th TASS's many forward operating locations at the time of its loss.

F-4C 64-0848 433 TFS, 8 TFW, USAF, Ubon
Capt Richard Ames Claflin (KIA)
1Lt Richard Brazik (KIA)

A flight of Phantoms came upon a truck convoy consisting of up to 10 vehicles during a night armed reconnaissance mission near Xom Duong Quan in the mountains 35 miles west of Mu Ron Ma. As Capt Clafin was making his second bombing run over the convoy the aircraft suddenly exploded in mid-air. It was thought that the aircraft had been destroyed by the premature detonation of one its own bombs as it was released from the aircraft.

RF-4C 64-1042 16 TRS, 460 TRW, USAF, Tan Son Nhut
Maj Gilland Wales Corbitt (KIA)
1Lt William Orlan Bare (KIA)

Another Phantom was lost in the Annamites during the night of the 26th. Maj Corbitt and 1Lt Bare took off from Tan Son Nhut for a photographic reconnaissance mission over the southern provinces of North Vietnam, which would include taking photographs of a ferry at Laut Son. Apparently the crew had finished their task and was returning when their aircraft disappeared in the mountains about 25 miles west of Dong Hoi. Their was no evidence to suggest that the crew had survived the crash of their aircraft.

28 July 1967

F-105D 62-4334 34 TFS, 388 TFW, USAF, Korat
1Lt Karl Wendell Richter (KIA)

It was usual in the F-105 squadrons to assign a pilot who was nearing the end of his tour to the relatively 'easy' targets in the southern provinces rather than the 'hot' targets around Hanoi and Haiphong in the north. Karl Richter was approaching his 200th mission at the end of his second tour and had already signed up for yet another tour in Southeast Asia, this time in the F-100. 1Lt Richter and his wingman were on an armed reconnaissance mission when they spotted a bridge in the mountains 35 miles west of Dong Hoi. Richter rolled in on the target but his aircraft was hit by AAA as it pulled up from its dive. The burning aircraft headed northwest but after about 35 miles Karl Richter was forced to eject. Unfortunately, Richter landed badly on the sharp, limestone karst and was severely injured. When an HH-3E arrived a PJ, SSgt Charles D Smith, was lowered 150 feet down on the hoist and found that Richter had been critically injured with multiple broken bones indicating that he had probably snagged his parachute on a rock or a tree and then fallen some distance. Karl Richter died in the helicopter on the way back to safety. Despite his youth and the fact that he had only been in the USAF for three years at the time of his death,

Karl Richter was regarded as one of the most experienced, dedicated and proficient F-105 pilots in Southeast Asia. He had shot down a MiG-17 on 21 September 1966 during a raid on SAM sites northwest of Haiphong and flew his 100th mission just three weeks later. After persistent requests he was allowed to return to Thailand to start another tour and it is thought that Richter may actually have passed the 200 mission mark before being killed.

KA-3B 142658   Detachment G, VAH-4, USN, USS *Oriskany*
Ens Bruce Merle Patterson (KIA)
AE2 Charles David Hardie (KIA)
1 crew, name unknown (survived)

A KA-3B suffered a double engine failure while on a tanker mission over the Gulf of Tonkin about 150 miles northeast of Da Nang. Unable to rectify the problem, all three crew abandoned the aircraft but only the pilot was found and rescued. This aircraft had only just been converted in June to KA-3B tanker standard at the Naval Air Rework Facility at Alameda, California.

29 July 1967

F-105D 58-1163   357 TFS, 355 TFW, USAF, Takhli
1Lt J Benton West (survived)

Another F-105 was lost on an armed reconnaissance mission the day after Richter's death. 1Lt West was about 25 miles north of Haiphong checking a road for activity when his aircraft was hit by ground fire. He tried to make for the sea and almost made it but was forced to eject about six miles east of Hon Gay where he was rescued by an HH-3E. The inaccessibility of much of the countryside of North Vietnam, even sometimes very close to major towns and cities, was often a major factor in the successful recovery of a downed airman. 1Lt West was sent to hospital in Japan but returned to active duty in 1968. He later flew with Eastern Airlines after retiring from the USAF.

The USS Forrestal *Fire*

A-4E   *149996, 150064, 150068, 150084, 150115, 150118, 150129, 152018, 152024, 152036, 152040*
F-4B   *153046, 153054, 153060, 153061, 153066, 153069, 153912*
RA-5C *148932, 149284, 149305 RVAH-11*

One of the greatest tragedies of the war in Southeast Asia occurred as the result of a simple electrical malfunction. The Atlantic Fleet carrier USS Forrestal had left Norfolk, Virginia on 6 June after a major refit and was assigned to TF 77 on 8 July. After working up in the South China Sea, the Forrestal took up her position at Yankee Station on 25 July for her combat debut off Vietnam. Four days later, after flying just 150 combat sorties, she was limping away from Vietnam towards Subic Bay in the Philippines for temporary repairs before returning to Norfolk, Virginia on 14 September for a major refurbishment.

On the morning of 29 July as a launch was under way, a stray voltage ignited a Zuni rocket pod suspended under F-4B 153061. One of the rockets fired and zoomed across the deck to hit a Skyhawk's fuel tank, causing a chain reaction of explosions and fire on the flight deck. The Skyhawk pilot, Lt(jg) D Dollarhide, was incredibly fortunate to escape and be rescued by his plane captain. The aircraft on the deck were soon well ablaze, the fire fed by over 40,000 gallons of aviation fuel together with bombs and other ordnance. Bombs detonated blowing holes in the armoured deck through which fell burning fuel and ordnance that set fire to six lower decks. After the inferno was eventually brought under control the next day a total of 134 men were dead, 62 more injured and 21 aircraft destroyed with another 34 damaged. Many of the dead were pilots who were trapped in their ready rooms below the hangar deck. Sixteen of the 20 men who jumped or were blown into the sea were rescued. This represented

the worst loss of life in the history of carrier aviation outside of the Second World War and was one of the most tragic incidents of the entire war.

The Forrestal never returned to the war in Southeast Asia. It eventually returned to Fleet service after a seven month, $72 million dollar refit that included rebuilding much of the aft end of the ship. The ship became a training carrier in February 1992 but was decommissioned on 10 September 1993 and is currently stored at Newport, Rhode Island, pending plans for preservation. Eighteen months after the Forrestal fire a similar accident happened to the Enterprise as it worked off Hawaii in preparation for a return to Southeast Asia. The ship caught fire on 14 January 1969 when a Zuni rocket on a Phantom ignited causing a series of explosions on the flight deck that killed 28 men and destroyed 15 aircraft.

30 July 1967

F-4C   64-0693   559 TFS, 12 TFW, USAF, Cam Ranh Bay
Capt Thomas Ray Allen (KIA)
1Lt Ronald Lyle Packard (KIA)

A Phantom on a night-time road reconnaissance mission was lost near Ba Binh, just eight miles north of the DMZ. Capt Allen had spotted a truck on a road and rolled in to attack the target. Allen's wingman saw a huge explosion on the ground close to the road and realised when he could not raise him on the radio that it was his leader's aircraft crashing. Whether the aircraft was shot down by ground fire or flew into the ground by accident could not be ascertained. The crew's remains were discovered during an excavation of the crash site in 1994 and formally identified three years later. Phantom 64-0693 was the first USAF aircraft to shoot down a MiG-17 when flown by Capt K E Holcombe and Capt A C Clark of the 45th TFS on 10 July 1965.

31 July 1967

F-8C   146984   VF-111, USN, USS *Oriskany*
Lt(jg) Charles Peter Zuhoski (POW)

The *Oriskany* had had an extremely tough re-introduction to combat in Southeast Asia with the loss of 12 aircraft and seven airmen since the ship started combat operations on 14 July. An SA-2 claimed the last victim of the month. Lt Zuhoski was flying as escort to an Iron Hand operation to the east of Hanoi. The aircraft found what they were looking for and started manoeuvring to avoid a volley of missiles. Lt Zuhoski was climbing through 11,000 feet when his aircraft was hit in the rear fuselage by a SAM. The engine seized and with the rear of the aircraft a mass of flames the pilot ejected and landed near the village of Ngu Nghi, 10 miles east of Hanoi. Like many pilots now coming into Southeast Asia, Charles Zuhoski was on his first operational tour

of duty after completion of flying and combat training. He joined VF-111 in March 1967, got married on 3 June, departed Alameda on the *Oriskany* on 16 June and became a POW on his 14th mission on 31 July. He was released by the North Vietnamese on 14 March 1973.

1 August 1967

A-4C   147670   VA-15, USN, USS *Intrepid*
Lt D W Thornhill (survived)

One of the first missions of August was a bombing raid on a large ammunition and explosives storage site close to Hon Gay. One of the aircraft assigned to flak suppression was a Skyhawk flown by Lt Thornhill. As the A-4 began to pull out of a 45-degree dive on its target, it was hit by anti-aircraft fire. Although Lt Thornhill could not see any damage from the cockpit he instinctively turned out to sea and shortly afterwards a fire warning light came on and his wingman reported that the aircraft was indeed on fire and pieces were falling off the rear fuselage. Lt Thornhill ejected amongst the numerous islands that line the coast around Hon Gay and was rescued by a Navy SAR helicopter

RF-101C 56-0207   20 TRS, 432 TRW, USAF, Udorn
Capt Charles C Winston (KIA)

A few hours after Lt Thornhill was shot down a USAF RF-101 was flying at 18,000 feet over Vinh Yen, 20 miles northwest of Hanoi, on its way to photograph a military storage area at Gia Du. The aircraft was hit by an SA-2 missile that blew off the Voodoo's starboard wing. The pilot may have been wounded or killed by the explosion, as he was not seen to eject from the blazing wreck as it crashed.

F-100D 56-3437   3 TFW, USAF, Bien Hoa
Capt Richard Eugene Woodson (KIA)

Later in the day an F-100 was lost along with its pilot while on a close air support mission over 100 miles southwest of Saigon. Capt Woodson's flight had been called in to strafe a force of around 150 VC who were dug in on a tree line near Ap Ta Diep, south of the Mekong Delta. Capt Woodson crashed close to the target, presumably a victim of small arms fire from the troops he was attacking.

2 August 1967

RF-4C 65-0848   11 TRS, 432 TRW, USAF, Udorn
Col Wallace Gourley Hynds (KIA)
Capt Carey Allen Cunningham (KIA)

Two RF-4C crews were tasked with a daylight photographic reconnaissance mission along Route 15 near Vinh. The lead aircraft was hit by small arms fire as it started its photo run at low level about five miles west of the city. Col Hynds immediately put

The devastating fire on board the USS *Forrestal* on 29 July 1967 resulted in the deaths of 134 men and the destruction of 21 aircraft. The ship resumed Fleet duty following a seven-month refit but she never returned to Vietnam. USN

the aircraft into a hard right turn but the Phantom crashed a few moments later killing both the crew. In 1989 the Vietnamese handed over a box of remains claiming them to be those of Col Hynds. However, in 1999 these remains were re-examined and found to be those of Capt Cunningham. Personal items from both the crew have been seen in a Vietnamese war museum.

F-100D 56-3041   531 TFS, 3 TFW, USAF, Bien Hoa
                   1Lt J V Fiorelli (survived)
After dark a flight of F-100s took off from Bien Hoa to attack a VC unit that was besieging a US Navy fuel dump. However, the flight had only reached about 10 miles east of the airfield when one of the aircraft was hit by ground fire. 1Lt Fiorelli attempted to turn back to Bien Hoa but had to eject and was rescued by one of the base's HH-43 Huskies.

A-4C 149632   VA-55, USN, USS *Constellation*
                1 pilot, name unknown (survived)
Shortly after launching on a combat mission, a Skyhawk suffered an engine flameout while climbing through 4,000 feet. Unable to restart the engine the pilot was forced to eject and was quickly rescued.

The C-7 Caribou
The Canadian-built C-7 Caribou was first sent to Southeast Asia with the US Army's 1st Aviation Company when it deployed to Thailand on 23 July 1962. The Company moved to Vung Tau in South Vietnam in December 1962 where a second company joined it in July 1963. By 1966 the Army was operating six companies with a total of 96 Caribous in Vietnam. However, early in that year the Army and the Air Force agreed to the transfer of all C-7s to USAF control in a rationalisation of roles and missions. The aircraft had a remarkable STOL performance and was particularly suited to operating into short, primitive airstrips where the C-123 or C-130 could not land. Replacement of Army personnel in the Caribou squadrons by Air Force air and ground crew began in July 1966 but the aircraft were not officially handed over until 1 January 1967. Meanwhile the 483rd TCW was activated at Cam Ranh Bay on 15 October 1966 to take over the C-7s from the Army. Six squadrons were activated to replace the six Army companies, two at Cam Ranh Bay, two at Vung Tau and two at Phu Cat. Even before the hand over six USAF personnel assigned to the 6252nd Operations Squadron were killed flying Caribous while still under Army control. The Caribou squadrons were usually dedicated to supporting Army units in specific military regions of South Vietnam. The 537th TAS was even more specifically assigned and worked primarily for the 1st Cavalry Division flying logistics, troop transport, courier, aeromedical evacuation and radio relay missions. The Caribou's finest hours would come during emergency resupply operations to remote Special Forces camps and fire bases such as Dak Pek, Dak Seang and Duc Lap. The aircraft was also used by Air America in Laos where its short-field performance again proved very useful.

3 August 1967

F-105D 58-1154   13 TFS, 388 TFW, USAF, Korat
                   Capt Wallace Grant Newcomb (POW)
The railway yard at Kep was once more the target for an F-105 raid. Pistol flight was still 15 miles to the northeast of the target and about to let down from 11,000 feet to start the bombing run when Capt Newcomb's aircraft was hit in the fuselage by an 85mm anti-aircraft shell. Within a couple of minutes Capt Newcomb had to give up a losing battle and eject from his crippled aircraft. He was quickly captured and spent the rest of the war as a POW until being released on 14 March 1973. After retirement from the regular Air Force he joined the New York ANG.

F-105D 62-4240   333 TFS, 355 TFW, USAF, Takhli
                   Capt John William Bischoff (KIA)

F-105D 61-0139   333 TFS, 355 TFW, USAF, Takhli
                   1 pilot, name unknown (survived)
The USAF lost two more F-105s in a mid-air collision on the 3rd when one of them struck the other as it disconnected from a KC-135 tanker over Laos en route to a mission. One of the pilots

was killed in the collision but the remainder of the strike force proceeded to its target in North Vietnam.

F-4C 64-0719   557 TFS, 12 TFW, USAF, Cam Ranh Bay
                 Maj John Albert DeBock (KIA)
                 1 crew, name unknown (survived)
In another accident, a Phantom crashed into runway lighting poles when it aborted its take off due to an engine failure. One of the crew ejected safely but the other was killed.

C-7B 62-4161   459 TAS, 483 TAW, USAF, Phu Cat
                 Capt Alan Eugene Hendrickson (KIA)
                 Capt John Dudley Wiley (KIA)
                 TSgt Zane Aubry Carter (KIA)
Three airmen died in a tragic friendly fire incident on 3 August. A C-7 Caribou was approaching the Duc Pho Special Forces camp, about 20 miles south of Quang Ngai, when it was hit by a shell from a US Army 155mm howitzer. The aircraft had flown into the line of fire and the shell blew off its entire rear fuselage and tail section. There is a well-publicised photograph of the aircraft taken during its fatal dive into the ground on the outskirts of the camp. Following this accident the Army and Air Force tightened up their coordination procedures for air operations near artillery fire zones.

4 August 1967

A-4E 150052   VA-163, USN, USS *Oriskany*
                Lt(jg) Ralph Campion Bisz (KIA)
As a formation of A-4s approached a POL storage site at Luc Nong, about eight miles northwest of Haiphong, four SA-2 missiles were seen to be fired from a SAM site near the target. Lt Bisz put his aircraft into a climb but the Skyhawk was hit by a SAM at about 10,500 feet and became a mass of flames and falling debris. No one in the flight saw any sign of a parachute and it was assumed by his wingman that Lt Bisz had died in his aircraft. For some reason Bisz was put on the official list as captured but the Navy now appears to accept that Lt Bisz died on 4 August. Ralph Bisz was serving on his second tour in Southeast Asia with VA-163 when he was killed.

The Cessna O-2
The Cessna O-2 was a militarised version of the Cessna 337 Skymaster six-seat light aircraft. The aircraft was first ordered into production for the USAF in December 1966 and was adapted to carry marker rockets and other ordnance for the role of forward air control. The first O-2As arrived in South Vietnam on 9 June with the intention that the type would eventually replace the older and smaller O-1 Bird Dog. Most were assigned to the 20th TASS and the 23rd TASS as these squadrons encountered the heaviest opposition. The 19th, 21st and 22nd TASS also received O-2s but still retained a large number of O-1s. Indeed, by January 1968 there were still 181 USAF O-1s based in Southeast Asia compared to 137 O-2s. Although the O-2 performed well in Southeast Asia it never entirely replaced the older aircraft. The O-2 could not operate from some of the smaller airstrips that the O-1 could fly into and visibility from the O-2 was not as good as that from the Bird Dog. The O-2 certainly had a better performance than the O-1 including the added safety that comes from two engines, especially as the engines were situated on the aircraft's centreline so that the failure of one engine did not produce a marked assymetrical flight condition. Many pilots never really warmed to the O-2 and it was regarded by most as a stop gap aircraft until the introduction of the specialist OV-10 Bronco in the following year.

6 August 1967

F-4C 64-0752   390 TFS, 366 TFW, USAF, Da Nang
                 Capt Albert Linwood Page (KIA)
                 1Lt Donald Richard Kemmerer (KIA)
Two Phantoms were sent to attack a suspected storage site near Thach Ban, 10 miles north of the DMZ. Opposition appeared fairly light so the aircraft set up a strafing pattern but as Capt Page's aircraft came round for its fourth run it was hit by automatic weapons fire. The aircraft was apparently hit in one of the

engines and was seen to be on fire. The crew radioed that they were ejecting and the aircraft was seen to crash into the sea about five miles offshore. No parachutes were seen nor SAR beepers heard and a search of the area revealed no sign of the crew who probably perished in their aircraft. Phantom 64-0752 was the first USAF aircraft to shoot down a MiG-21 when it was flown by Maj P J Gilmore and 1Lt W T Smith of the 480th TFS on 26 April 1966.

F-100D 55-3639   90 TFS, 3 TFW, USAF, Bien Hoa
                   Capt C C Clark (survived)
The 3rd TFW lost its third F-100 in less than a week when an aircraft was shot down during a close air support mission 10 miles southeast of Saigon. A flight of aircraft were attacking VC troops and Capt Clark was making his third bombing run on the target when his aircraft was hit by shrapnel from the explosion of one of his own bombs. He struggled to point the F-100 away from the target area but had to eject within a few seconds. He was rescued by an Army helicopter that was in the vicinity.

F-4C 63-7639   390 TFS, 366 TFW, USAF, Da Nang
                 Maj D R Conway (survived)
                 1Lt F W Dahl (survived)

O-1F 57-2825   20 TASS, 504 TASG, USAF, Da Nang

O-1E 56-2536,   20 TASS, 504 TASG, USAF, Da Nang
      56-2672

O-2A 67-21317, 20 TASS, 504 TASG, USAF, Da Nang
      67-21322
     A flight of Phantoms from Da Nang was despatched on a night road reconnaissance mission near the Mu Gia Pass when it encountered several trucks. Maj Conway made one pass over the target and then came round for a second run but his aircraft was hit by AAA. The Phantom remained airworthy and the crew nursed their crippled aircraft all the way back to Da Nang where Maj Conway made a crash landing. Unfortunately the aircraft veered off the runway and hit a line of parked FAC aircraft belonging to the 20th TASS. Three O-1s and two of the new O-2s were destroyed by impact damage and fire fed by fuel from the Phantom. Although the crew of the Phantom escaped unharmed the aircraft was so badly damaged by the flak and the subsequent crash landing that it had to be scrapped.

7 August 1967

F-4C 64-0656   559 TFS, 12 TFW, USAF, Cam Ranh Bay
                 Capt Glenn Hubert Wilson (POW)
                 1Lt Carl Dennis Chambers (POW)
During an armed reconnaissance mission just north of the DMZ a flight of F-4s spotted a barge on an inland waterway near Van Xuan, 10 miles south of Dong Hoi. Capt Wilson put his Phantom into a 45-degree dive from 9,000 feet to bomb the target but his aircraft was hit by AAA and caught fire. The crew ejected safely but were captured by NVA troops before they could be rescued. They were both imprisoned for the rest of the war and released on 14 March 1973. 1Lt Chambers was on his 101st mission of his tour when he was shot down.

RF-4C 65-0839   11 TRS, 432 TRW, USAF, Udorn
                  Capt N J Otto (survived)
                  1Lt R E Meeks (survived)
An RF-4C was returning from a reconnaissance mission in the Steel Tiger region of southern Laos when it was hit by ground-fire near the Laotian border with North Vietnam, a few miles northwest of the DMZ. The aircraft was hit in the wing as it was flying at 10,000 feet and the crew managed to cross into Laos before having to eject. Both men were rescued by an HH-3E having suffered only minor injuries.

8 August 1967

A-4C 147719   VA-146, USN, USS *Constellation*
                1 pilot, name unknown (survived)
A Skyhawk suffered an engine failure during a catapult launch from the USS *Constellation* and crashed into the sea after the pilot ejected.

C-1A   146016   USN, USS *Hornet*
            5 other crew, names unknown (survived)
A C-1A Trader was taking off from the *Hornet* on a logistics flight when one of its engines failed. Unable to maintain sufficient airspeed the aircraft settled into the sea and sank. All the occupants escaped from the aircraft and were rescued. The USS *Hornet* made three war cruises as an ASW carrier in Southeast Asia and served as a SAR base for the Sea Kings of HS-2, seven of which were lost during the war. The carrier was decommissioned on 26 June 1970 and was sold for scrap on 14 April 1993 but was saved and is now preserved as a floating museum at the former naval base at Alameda.

9 August 1967

A-1E   52-132678   602 ACS, 56 ACW, USAF, Udorn
            Capt Allen Sheldon Cherry (KIA)
A flight of Skyraiders found a truck park in a remote corner of North Vietnam close to the border with Laos, about 100 miles northwest of Vinh. As Capt Cherry started his strafing run on the target from 13,000 feet his aircraft was seen to continue past the truck park until it hit the ground and exploded. It was surmised that the pilot may have been hit by ground fire as he apparently made no attempt to eject.

RF-4C   64-1059   16 TRS, 460 TRW, USAF, Tan Son Nhut
            Capt Lauren Robert Lengyel (POW)
            1Lt Glenn Leo Myers (POW)
A lone RF-4C sent to photograph a railway bridge in North Vietnam failed to return with no indication as to the fate of the aircraft or the crew. 1Lt Myers was posted as missing in action until 9 March 1970 when he was at last allowed to write a letter home. Both crew had in fact escaped from the aircraft and were captured and imprisoned. Both men were released on 14 March 1973.

RF-101C   56-0225   Detachment 1, 45 TRS, 460 TRW, USAF,
            Tan Son Nhut
            1 pilot, name unknown (survived)
Another reconnaissance aircraft was lost on the 9th when a Voodoo had a mid-air collision with a US Army UH-1 Huey in South Vietnam, possibly 66-01099 of the 175th AHC which was lost with all four crew on this date.

10 August 1967

O-1G   51-12409   19 TASS, 504 TASG, USAF, Bien Hoa
            detached to Rach Gia
An O-1 FAC aircraft was destroyed by a hand grenade explosion during a VC attack on the airstrip at Rach Gia in the southern tip of South Vietnam.

11 August 1967

A-4E   151088   VMA-211, MAG-12, USMC, Chu Lai
            1Lt Kenneth Allen Berube (KIA)
A flight of Marine Corps A-4s was providing close air support to friendly troops near Hiep Duc, 20 miles west of Tam Ky, when one of the aircraft was hit by ground fire as it rolled in on the target. 1Lt Berube may have been wounded as he was not seen to eject from his aircraft before it crashed.

F-4C   63-7593   390 TFS, 366 TFW, USAF, Da Nang
            Maj R G Dilger (survived)
            1Lt G L Rawlings (survived)
The 390th TFS lost its third aircraft during the month of August during an attack on a truck convoy near Thanh Lang Xa, in the hills 55 miles northwest of Dong Hoi. The aircraft was damaged by 57mm anti-aircraft fire but limped back to towards Da Nang. However, the crew were forced to eject and came down in the sea just south of Marble Mountain off the coast near Da Nang and were immediately picked up by a rescue helicopter.

F-4C   63-7634   389 TFS, 366 TFW, USAF, Da Nang
            Maj Kenneth Richard Hughes (KIA)
            1Lt H B Cox (survived)
Another 366th TFW Phantom crashed as it was landing at Da Nang when returning from a close air support mission over South Vietnam. One of the crew was killed in the crash.

12 August 1967

F-8C   146993   VF-111, USN, USS *Intrepid*
            Lt Cdr Foster Schuler Teague (survived)
A road bridge at Ke Sat was the target of a Navy strike on the 12th. As the formation was returning from the target it encountered a SAM battery about 15 miles southeast of Hanoi and the aircraft took evasive action. One of the escorting Crusaders made a high-G turn to avoid a SAM but the pilot felt the aircraft hit by what he considered was anti-aircraft fire. The aircraft flew normally for a few minutes but then the hydraulics and flying control systems started to fail. Control was lost just off the coast, about 15 miles south of Haiphong, and the pilot ejected and was rescued from right under the noses of the North Vietnamese coastal defences by a Navy helicopter. 'Tooter' Teague later converted to the F-4 and commanded VF-51 in 1971 and later captained the USS *Kitty Hawk*.

F-105D   62-4278   469 TFS, 388 TFW, USAF, Korat
            Capt Thomas Elmer Norris (POW)
On the morning of 11 August the huge mile-long Paul Doumer railway and road bridge on the northeastern outskirts of Hanoi was finally released for a major strike. This bridge was of prime strategic importance to the North Vietnamese as it was the only railway crossing point over the Red River into Hanoi for the railways converging from Haiphong in the east, and the lines from China from the northeast and the northwest. The Doumer Bridge was on the original JCS target list of April 1964 but for political reasons it was not attacked until August 1967. The Doumer Bridge was just one of several targets in and around Hanoi that were released for attack by Washington at this time. The first raid was hurriedly despatched that very afternoon and one span of the railway bridge and two spans of the road bridge were dropped into the water. The Seventh Air Force decided on a follow up raid the next day, led by Col Bill Norris, the CO of the 333rd TFS, who had planned the 11 August raid. This target was psychologically as well as materially one of the most important targets in North Vietnam and the loss of the bridge, even for a short time, would pose a major problem for the North Vietnamese and boost the morale of the US airmen.

As usual the raid was accompanied by an Iron Hand flight to keep the SAM sites occupied. As the Iron Hand aircraft approached Gia Lam Airport, between the city and the bridge, one of the bombers was hit in the rear fuselage by AAA. Capt Norris left the target area in an attempt to get back to base but he had to eject near Phuc Yen, 17 miles northwest of Hanoi, and was captured. Despite the loss of the F-105 and its pilot the raid was a success, causing further damage to the bridge that kept it out of commission until October. Capt Norris was released from captivity on 14 March 1973. Allegedly, Capt Norris's USAF and Geneva Convention identity cards recently turned up in the hands of a Ukrainian militaria collector. It is not known if this report has been confirmed or if the cards have been returned to the USA.

RF-4C   65-0882   11 TRS, 432 TRW, USAF, Udorn
            Capt Edwin Lee Atterberry (POW - died)
            Capt Thomas Vance Parrot (POW)
Minutes after the last of the bombers had struck the bridge at Hanoi, an RF-4C prepared to make a run over the target to obtain BDA photographs. While flying at 18,000 feet about seven miles northeast of Hanoi the pilot received a SAM warning and started to jink the aircraft in the hope of evading the incoming SA-2. Unfortunately, the manoeuvre failed to break the missile's radar lock on the Phantom and it struck the aircraft, blowing its tail off. The crew ejected and were quickly captured. On 10 May 1969 Capt Atterberry and Capt John Dramesi made a dramatic escape attempt by squeezing through the roof of their cell. They were on the loose for 12 hours but were eventually recaptured and returned to the Zoo POW camp. Both men were severely beaten and tortured for days after the attempt and Edwin Atterberry apparently died of his mistreatment at the hands of the North Vietnamese guards. Almost the entire POW population suffered from beatings after this escape attempt and as a result senior POWs banned future attempts unless outside help was available, which in effect meant that there would be no more attempts to escape from North Vietnam. On 13 March 1974 the remains of Edwin Atterberry, who had been pomoted to the rank of Maj during his imprisonment, were returned to the USA for burial. Capt Parrot was released on 14 March 1973.

O-1C   140100   H&MS-16, MAG-16, USMC, Marble Mountain
            2 crew, names unknown (survived)
The Headquarters and Maintenance Squadron of the helicopter-equipped MAG-16 lost a Bird Dog when it stalled and crashed as it was taking off on a visual reconnaissance mission. Both crew escaped with injuries.

13 August 1967

RA-5C   151634   RVAH-12, USN, USS *Constellation*
            Lt Cdr Leo Gregory Hyatt (POW)
            Lt(jg) Wayne Keith Goodermote (POW)
The *Constellation* lost one its RA-5C reconnaissance aircraft and crew on the 13th. The aircraft was on a mission to photograph railway yards at Na Phuc near Lang Son, in the extreme northeast of North Vietnam and less than 10 miles from the Chinese border. As Lt Cdr Hyatt put the huge aircraft into a descending turn at over 720 knots it was hit in the wings and tail by anti-aircraft fire. Within seconds a fire developed and the tail started to disintegrate. The crew ejected as control of the aircraft was lost and they were quickly captured. Both men were on their 33rd mission when they were shot down and were released together on 14 March 1973 and both eventually retired from the Navy with the rank of Captain.

A-4E   152054   VMA-223, MAG-12, USMC, Chu Lai
            Capt Wesley Robert Phenegar (KIA)
Capt Phenegar was attached to MAG-12's Headquarters and Maintenance Squadron and he was killed flying a VMA-223 Skyhawk that suffered engine failure while it was returning from a combat mission. The aircraft crashed in Quang Tin province.

14 August 1967

A-4E   150122   VMA-211, MAG-12, USMC, Chu Lai
            Capt C H Wood (survived)
During a close air support mission in Military Region I in South Vietnam, a Marine Corps Skyhawk was hit by small arms fire as it pulled up from its second pass over a target. Capt Wood ejected safely and was rescued by helicopter.

17 August 1967

F-105D   62-4378   44 TFS, 388 TFW, USAF, Korat
            Maj Albert C Vollmer (survived)
An F-105 was shot down during an armed reconnaissance mission near the DMZ, an area that was becoming distinctly unhealthy for US airmen. Maj Vollmer was pulling up from an attack on a storage area near Ba Binh, eight miles north of the DMZ, when his aircraft was hit by flak. He turned out to sea with the aircraft on fire and ejected about five miles offshore where he was rescued 15 minutes later by an HH-3 from the 37th ARRS that was supported by Vollmer's wingman and two Skyraiders.

This was the second time that Albert Vollmer had been shot down over Southeast Asia, having had to eject from an F-105 near Ban Ken in northern Laos on 13 January 1965. This time he was seriously injured during the ejection and spent 11 months flat on his back in a hospital bed in a full body cast. He eventually resumed flying but his injuries precluding him from flying in aircraft fitted with ejector seats so he retired from the USAF and flew corporate jets for a living.

RA-5C   149302   RVAH-12, USN, USS *Constellation*
            Cdr Laurent Norbert Dion (KIA)
            Lt(jg) Charles David Hom (KIA)
On the 17th the *Constellation* lost another of its RA-5C crews when their aircraft crashed in the sea off the coast of North Vietnam during a photographic reconnaissance mission. The loss was thought to have been accidental, although the exact cause could not be determined due to the lack of evidence.

18 August 1967

F-100D 56-3114 309 TFS, 31 TFW, USAF, Tuy Hoa
1 pilot, name unknown (survived)

A Super Sabre crashed in South Vietnam due to an accidental engine failure. The pilot ejected safely and was rescued.

19 August 1967

B-57B 52-1550 13 TBS, 405 FW attached to 35 TFW, USAF, Phan Rang
Maj Richard Michael Secanti (KIA)
Maj Martin Weigner Andersen (KIA)

A Canberra was shot down with the loss of both crew during a close air support mission 25 miles north of Saigon. The aircraft was orbiting near its target, a VC storage area five miles west of Lai Khe, when it was hit by ground fire and crashed immediately before either of the crew could escape. Like many of the early B-57Bs and Cs, 52-1550 was originally used by the 3510th CCTW at Randolph AFB, Texas, to convert pilots and navigators to the Canberra before posting to operational units.

A-1H 137575 VA-25, USN, USS *Coral Sea*
Lt Cdr Frederick Horatio Gates (KWF)

The *Coral Sea* returned to TF 77 control on 10 August for her third war cruise but was not due to resume her position on the line for another 10 days until her squadrons were fully worked up. During the training period a Skyraider was lost in the South China Sea along with its pilot when the aircraft suffered an engine problem.

The A-37 Dragonfly

The Cessna A-37 Dragonfly was a modified version of the T-37 primary trainer that had been in service with the USAF since 1957. The Air Force had been interested in a counter-insurgency version of the T-37 since 1963 but it was the higher than anticipated attrition rate of the A-1E in Southeast Asia that finally decided the issue. The airframe of the basic T-37 was strengthened to withstand the higher stresses and loads encountered in combat and the T-37's J69 engines were replaced by J85s that had more than twice the thrust. The wing was rebuilt to take eight hardpoints for carrying up to 4,855lbs of ordnance and a GAU-2B/A Minigun was mounted in the nose. The aircraft was fitted with wingtip fuel tanks, although even with these its range was only some 390 miles. The first 25 A-37As were assigned to the 604th ACS at England AFB, Louisiana, which moved to Bien Hoa in August 1967. The Squadron was to undertake a four-month combat evaluation programme named Combat Dragon. Flying at Bien Hoa commenced on 15 August and within three weeks the daily sortie rate had increased from 12 to 60 per day. In October a detachment of aircraft was sent to Pleiku to participate in Tiger Hound operations in Laos. The evaluation was completed in mid-December with more than 4,300 sorties flown for the loss of only two aircraft. As a result of the evaluation a new version, the A-37B, was put into production. Modifications to the aircraft included the installation of a flight-refuelling probe to allow increased endurance. After the Combat Dragon trial was completed the 604th continued to operate the A-37 at Bien Hoa and had flown a total of 10,000 sorties by May 1968. A large number of A-37Bs were later supplied to the VNAF, which eventually operated 10 squadrons of the type. The USAF only equipped three squadrons with the A-37 in Southeast Asia.

21 August 1967

F-4B 152247 VF-142, USN, USS *Constellation*
Cdr Robin H McGlohn (survived)
Lt(jg) J M McIlrath (survived)

Monday the 21st of August proved to be a very expensive day for both the US Navy and the Air Force with the loss of eight aircraft and 10 men in combat. The four naval aircraft lost during the day all came from the *Constellation*, where morale must have been badly shaken. The first to fall was a Phantom from VF-142, which was part of the flak suppression element on an early morning raid on a road bridge at Chap Khe near Uong Bi,

12 miles northeast of Haiphong. Cdr McGlohn, CO of VF-142, was pulling up from a run on a target when an anti-aircraft shell holed the aircraft's starboard wing. Within a few seconds the hydraulic flight controls began to fail and the crew ejected when all control was lost. Despite coming down in one of the 'hottest' parts of North Vietnam, they were both rescued by a Navy SAR helicopter and returned to their carrier. This particular Phantom had shot down a MiG-21 on 10 August when being flown by Lt G H Freeborn and Lt(jg) R J Elliot.

F-105D 60-0437 354 TFS, 355 TFW, USAF, Takhli
1Lt Lynn Kesler Powell (KIA)

F-105D 59-1720 354 TFS, 355 TFW, USAF, Takhli
Capt Merwin Lamphrey Morrill (KIA)

Later in the morning the Takhli Wing flew a strike against the Yen Vinh railway marshalling yards near Hanoi. Two of the F-105s from Bear flight were lost during the raid. The first, flown by 1Lt Powell, was seen to be hit by AAA as it dived on the target. The pilot may have been wounded as he was not seen to eject before the aircraft crashed in the outskirts of Hanoi. As Bear flight was leaving the target area another of its aircraft was hit by AAA and crashed about seven miles southeast of Hanoi. Again none of the other aircrew saw a parachute or heard a beeper but Capt Morrill was carried as missing in action as no one was sure that he had not actually ejected. When the US prisoners were released in 1973 Powell and Morrill were not amongst their number but it was not until 10 years later, on 3 June 1983, that the mortal remains of both men were handed over to the US by the Vietnamese. 59-1720 may have belonged to the 333rd TFS at the time of its loss.

A-6A 152638 VA-196, USN, USS *Constellation*
Cdr Leo Twyman Profilet (POW)
Lt Cdr William Morgan Hardman (POW)

A-6A 152627 VA-196, USN, USS *Constellation*
Lt(jg) Dain Vanderlin Scott (KIA)
Lt(jg) Forrest George Trembley (KIA)

A-6A 152625 VA-196, USN, USS *Constellation*
Lt Cdr Jimmy Lee Buckley (KIA)
Lt Robert James Flynn (POW)

At exactly the same time as the USAF strike was going in at Yen Vinh, a naval strike consisting of four A-6 Intruders of Milestone flight from VA-196 was being unleashed on the nearby Duc Noi railway yard, five miles northeast of Hanoi. The Intruders were led by Cdr Profilet, the CO of VA-196, and it was his aircraft that was hit first. The flight had received several SAM warnings and there was intense anti-aircraft fire in the vicinity of the target. The cloud base was between 3,000 and 5,000 feet and storm clouds were building up. As Cdr Profilet's aircraft rolled into a 30-degree dive from 7,500 feet, an SA-2 exploded close by, which badly damaged the aircraft's starboard wing. A few moments later the wing came off and the aircraft cartwheeled towards the ground. The crew ejected and landed close to Hanoi and were quickly captured and taken to the Hanoi Hilton. A total of 51 SAMs were fired at the *Constellation's* aircraft during a series of strikes on this day. Cdr Profilet and Lt Cdr Hardman were on their 59th mission together when they were shot down. Leo Profilet was a veteran of the Korean War where he had flown 98 combat missions in the Skyraider. Both men were released from captivity on 14 March 1973.

Of the three remaining aircraft of Milestone flight, two of them, flown by Lt Cdr Buckley and Lt Scott, became separated from the deputy leader in the other aircraft but were tracked on his radar screen and those of an orbiting E-2 Hawkeye and on the *Constellation* itself. The two Intruders flew northeast away from the target but instead of turning out to sea they continued heading northeast until they crossed into China, almost 110 miles from Hanoi. It was possible that low cloud and thunderstorms forced them to head further north than had been planned and they apparently missed their pre-planned turning points. Whatever the cause, when the aircraft crossed into Chinese airspace they were attacked and shot down by Chinese MiG-19s and the event was loudly proclaimed on Peking Radio.

Of the four occupants of the Intruders only Lt Flynn survived the incident to be captured. Flynn was well-known throughout his Air Wing for carrying his cornet with him on combat missions with which to sound the US Cavalry charge into a keyed microphone just before roll-in. He spent no less than 2,030 consecutive days in solitary confinement in a Chinese prison but was flown to Hong Kong and repatriated on 15 March 1973. On 16 December 1975 the Chinese Government handed over the ashes of Lt Cdr Buckley.

A-37A 67-14508 604 ACS, 3 TFW, USAF, Bien Hoa
Maj G Shannon (survived)

The A-37 had been in Vietnam for just one week before the first aircraft was lost. Maj Shannon had completed a close air support mission and was approaching Bien Hoa when his aircraft was hit in the tail by small arms fire. He ejected three miles east of the airfield and was badly injured during the ejection sequence. This Dragonfly was originally T-37A 55-4310 and had served for many years with Air Training Command before conversion.

A-26A 64-17662 606 ACS, 56 ACW, USAF, Nakhon Phanom
Maj John Creighton Gille Kerr (KIA)
Capt Burke Henderson Morgan (KIA)

The last aircraft lost on the 21st was an A-26A from Nakhon Phanom, which disappeared during a road reconnaissance mission in northern Laos. Radio and radar contact was lost with the aircraft and a search revealed no trace of wreckage or crew.

22 August 1967

F-100D 56-3264 510 TFS, 3 TFW, USAF, Bien Hoa
Capt H D Canterbury (survived)

An F-100 was shot down as it was attacking a strong force of VC dug into bunkers about 10 miles northwest of Rach Gia in the southern tip of South Vietnam. Capt Canterbury's aircraft was hit by small arms fire so he flew a few miles out to sea and ejected. He was rescued by an Army helicopter.

F-4D 66-7517 435 TFS, 8 TFW, USAF, Ubon
1Lt Francis Barnes Midnight (KIA)
1Lt A M Silva (survived)

A flight of Phantoms from Ubon was tasked for a night strike against a ferry complex at Mi Le, 10 miles south of Dong Hoi. As 1Lt Midnight's aircraft rolled in to the attack from 10,500 feet it was hit by ground fire. The WSO ejected safely and was eventually rescued by a USAF helicopter but the pilot was killed. This was the first aircraft lost by the 435th TFS since it converted from the F-104C to the F-4D. The conversion not only entailed a change of aircraft but a move of base from Udorn to Ubon and the addition of navigators to the previously single-seat squadron.

23 August 1967

F-105D 59-1752 357 TFS, 355 TFW, USAF, Takhli
Maj Elmo Clinnard Baker (POW)

The 23rd was another bad day for the United States in the skies over Southeast Asia with a total of seven aircraft lost during the day. The first aircraft to be lost was an F-105 on an 18-aircraft Rolling Thunder strike on the Bac Giang rail and road bridge near Phu Lang Thuong, northeast of Hanoi. Maj Baker was assigned to flak suppression for the mission and his aircraft was hit in the fuselage by flak as it dived on to a target. He turned the burning aircraft southeast towards the sea but was forced to eject ten miles northwest of Hon Gay when the hydraulics failed. Maj Baker broke his leg on ejection and landed in a paddy field where he was beaten by villagers. He was taken to Hanoi by a Mil helicopter and was again beaten by a mob before being thrown into Hoa Lo prison for the customary torture session which all newcomers had to face at this period. Maj Baker, who was on his 61st mission, was eventually released on 14 March 1973. Thunderchief 59-1752 was painted as 'Yankee Sky Dog' while with the 357th TFS.

An F-105D of the 354th TFS from Takhli flies over the wooded hills of Laos en route to its target with a load of 500lb and 750lb bombs. USAF

F-4B   149498   VF-142, USN, USS *Constellation*
                          Lt Cdr Thomas Walter Sitek (KIA)
                          Ens Patrick Lawrence Ness (KIA)

Another aircraft lost on a flak suppression mission was a Phantom from the *Constellation* during a Navy strike on railway sidings at Lac Dao, to the east of Hanoi. Over the target the aircraft encountered intense flak and SAMs in profusion. Lt Cdr Sitek's aircraft was seen to successfully evade two missiles but was hit by a third as the F-4 levelled out momentarily at 8,000 feet. The aircraft quickly became a mass of flames from wingtip to wingtip and the fire spread to the fuselage as the fuel cells exploded. Neither of the crew escaped, probably having been wounded by the explosion of the SA-2. On 10 April 1986 the remains of Patrick Ness were returned to the USA from Vietnam and laid to rest at Fort Snelling National Cemetery in the Minneapolis/St Paul area.

F-4D   66-0238   555 TFS, 8 TFW, USAF, Ubon
                          Maj Charles Robert Tyler (POW)
                          Capt Ronald Nichalis Sittner (KIA)

F-4D   66-0247   555 TFS, 8 TFW, USAF, Ubon
                          Capt Larry Edward Carrigan (POW)
                          1Lt Charles Lane (KIA)

F-4D   65-0726   555 TFS, 8 TFW, USAF, Ubon
                          Maj Robert Ralston Sawhill (POW)
                          1Lt Gerald Lee Gerndt (POW)

F-4D   66-0260   555 TFS, 8 TFW, USAF, Ubon
                          Maj C B Demarque (survived)
                          1Lt J M Piet (survived)

Later in the day the Triple Nickel Squadron from Ubon took part in a strike against the Yen Vien railway yard that turned to disaster with the loss of four Phantoms and three crews. The strike consisted of nine flights of F-105s and four flights of F-4s, one of which was designated as the MiGCAP flight. As Ford flight approached the target at 15,000 feet it was intercepted by several MiG-21s. A dogfight ensued resulting in two Phantoms being shot down by the MiG's missiles just north of Thud Ridge, about 50 miles northwest of Hanoi. Maj Tyler ejected and was knocked unconscious and taken prisoner but his WSO, Capt Sittner, was not captured although another POW claimed to have seen Sittner in one of the Hanoi prisons. The pilot of the other MiG-victim, Capt Carrigan, also survived and was captured three days later. Once on the ground he saw another airman, who he took to be his WSO, Charles Lane, moving in the distance. US intelligence reports appeared to indicate that Lane was being held in a POW camp in 1968 but when Tyler and Carrigan were released on 14 March 1973, Charles Lane was unaccounted for and had not been seen by any other US POW.

During a 1991 JTF-FA investigation of this incident eye witnesses reported seeing three or four parachutes from the two Phantoms but only two airmen were captured. However, local villagers reported finding the body of an airman hanging from a tree by his parachute. The body was buried nearby and the investigation team disinterred the remains and sent them to Hawaii for identification. The remains were determined to be those of Capt Sittner. The witnesses also stated that a Chinese military unit arrived and removed the wreckage of one of the aircraft. Soon after the two Phantoms had been shot down 1Lt David Waldrop, an F-105 pilot from the 44th TFS, shot down two MiG-17s.

Following close on the heels of Ford flight was Falcon flight. Maj Sawhill avoided the MiGs but ran into an intense barrage of AAA as he dived on the target. His aircraft was hit and the crew ejected close to Gia Lam Airport on the outskirts of Hanoi. Both men were quickly captured and spent the rest of the war as prisoners until released on 14 March 1973.

Another of the 555th's Phantoms was hit by the intense AAA over the target but managed to escape from the area and head towards home. Maj Demarque crossed North Vietnam and Laos into Thailand but he and his WSO were forced to eject near Wanon Niwat, about 60 miles northwest of Nakhon Phanom, when they ran out of fuel before reaching a tanker. They were both picked up by a rescue helicopter, having suffered only minor injuries. The loss of four aircraft on a single raid was a severe blow to the 555th TFS and the threat of the MiG-21 was becoming very apparent. The VPAF had revised its tactics by approaching the strike force at low level and zooming up to attack with a single pass before heading for base or China. The tally might have been worse as an F-4C crew launched two Sparrow missiles at what they thought was a MiG but was then identified as another Phantom. The crew broke radar lock and the missiles went ballistic and fell into the jungle.

O-1E   56-2589   20 TASS, 504 TASG, USAF, Da Nang
                          Capt Derex S Williams (KIA)
                          1 crew, name unknown (survived)

To round off a bad day the USAF lost a forward air controller during a visual reconnaissance mission near Khe Sanh as night fell. The aircraft was flying at about 50 feet when its engine was hit by small arms fire. Capt Williams attempted a crash landing but he was killed and his observer, who was probably a Marine, was injured but recovered.

24 August 1967

F-105D 62-4268   357 TFS, 355 TFW, USAF, Takhli
                          Capt Jay Criddle Hess (POW)

The USAF fared better the following day losing only one aircraft during a raid on a railway marshalling yard at Lang Dang, 25 miles northeast of Kep. Capt Hess started his dive on the target but his aircraft was hit in the fuselage by 37mm flak as it passed through about 5,500 feet. He ejected a few miles northeast of the target and was soon captured. Jay Hess was shot down on his 33rd mission and was released from prison on 14 March 1973.

25 August 1967

A-4C   148440   VA-15, USN, USS *Intrepid*
                          Lt(jg) R W Gerard (survived)

A flight of A-4s from the *Intrepid* found a number of barges on a waterway eight miles north of Vinh. As Lt Gerard was pulling up from his second attack with his unguided rockets, his aircraft was hit by AAA in the nose and starboard wing. He headed out to sea and flew towards the carrier but after 20 minutes the hydraulic system began to fail and a fire broke out in the wing. Lt Gerard ejected close to the ship and was picked up by helicopter.

RA-3B 144835   VAP-61, USN, Cubi Point
                          Cdr Edward James Jacobs (KIA)
                          Lt(jg) James John Zavocky (KIA)
                          ADJ2 Claire Ronald Alan Bois (KIA)

A Skywarrior based at Cubi Point, but probably operating from Da Nang on temporary duty, went missing on a night road reconnaissance over North Vietnam. The aircraft was equipped with infra-red sensors to assist in finding targets in the dark. Nothing was heard from the aircraft and a search failed to reveal any sign of wreckage on land or in the sea. This Skywarrior had been damaged by anti-aircraft fire during a mission on the night of 15 August and lost 3,000lb of fuel from a punctured wing fuel tank but was able to land safely.

F-4C   64-0692   558 TFS, 12 TFW, USAF, Cam Ranh Bay
                          Capt William Otis Fuller (KIA)
                          1Lt Thomas Michael Killcullen (KIA)

Another aircraft lost over North Vietnam during the night of 25 August was an F-4C from Cam Ranh Bay. Capt Fuller was flying a road reconnaissance mission along Route 1A near Xom Quan, 10 miles north of the DMZ, when his aircraft was hit by AAA. The aircraft was seen to crash and explode near Xom Quan but there was no indication that either of the crew had escaped. This aircraft had shot down a MiG-21 during Operation Bolo on 2 January when flown by 1Lt L J Glynn and 1Lt L E Cary of the 433rd TFS.

Misty FACs and Commando Sabre

The need for an FAC aircraft that could survive in the skies of North Vietnam as well as the 'hot' areas of South Vietnam became apparent as the war progressed. The O-1 and O-2 had been used over the DMZ and into North Vietnam itself but by early 1967 enemy air defences had been greatly improved and the slow propeller-driven aircraft proved too vulnerable. As the F-4 was in heavy demand for strike and CAP roles it was decided to evaluate the two-seat F-100F as a fast FAC aircraft. The project was code named Commando Sabre and the specially selected crews used the radio call sign Misty. The unit was initially designated as Detachment 1 of the 612th TFS and was attached to the 37th TFW at Phu Cat on 28 June 1967. Although the crews were assigned to the 612th, most of the aircraft seemed to have belonged to the 416th TFS. Each crew, both pilots, would alternate flying and observing and controlling the strike fighters. All Misty FAC crews were volunteers with at least 100 combat missions in South Vietnam and 1,000 flying hours. The F-100F was well suited for the role but was in short supply and aircraft had to be borrowed from the other F-100 squadrons. The aircraft carried a belly-mounted panoramic stike camera and the observer also used a hand-held camera to obtain target photographs. The Commando Sabre unit later expanded its role to include RESCAP, artillery spotting, photographic reconnaissance, weather reconnaissance and participating in hunter-killer teams with flights of F-100s. Maj 'Bud' Day was the first commander of the Commando Sabre unit but within two months of the program starting up he was lost in combat.

26 August 1967

F-100F 56-3954   612 TFS, 37 TFW, USAF, Phu Cat
Maj George Everett Day (POW)
Capt Corwin N Kippenhan (survived)

On 26 August Misty 3 was flying an FAC mission just north of the DMZ. Maj 'Bud' Day was leading a flight of F-105s in a search for a suspected SAM site just north of Thon Cam Son. This was an area where several aircraft had been shot down by SAMs in recent weeks but the North Vietnamese were very adept at moving SAM batteries between sites and building dummy sites that were surrounded by anti-aircraft guns. As the F-100F came in over the target at 4,500 feet it was hit in the engine by AAA and burst into flames. The aircraft turned towards the sea but the crew had to eject about two miles short of the coast. Capt Kippenhan, who was on his first mission as an FAC, was rescued by an HH-3E but 'Bud' Day was captured before he could be picked up. During the ejection sequence Day's left arm was broken in three places, his left knee was dislocated and he was blinded in one eye by a blood clot. He was captured by North Vietnamese militia but after a short while he managed to escape from his captors. Despite his injuries he walked throughout the night and covered about 20 miles before resting as daylight broke. He was awakened by explosions all around him, either artillery or bombs, which further injured him. When he felt better a couple of days later he set off walking again but after several days he was starving and hallucinating. He eventually walked into a VC patrol near Quang Tri having unknowingly crossed into South Vietnam. He tried to escape but was shot twice, recaptured and eventually taken to Hanoi. He had been free for almost two weeks and was the only American to escape across the DMZ into the South from North Vietnam. Once in Hanoi, Maj Day suffered many severe torture sessions, some of them at the hands of Cuban interrogators, which left 'Bud' Day close to death on several occasions. George Day was eventually released from Hanoi on 14 March 1973.

Maj Day was on his 139th mission (67th over the North) when he was shot down. He had joined the US Marine Corps in 1942 after dropping out of high school and served over two years in the Pacific theatre. He joined the Army Reserve after demobilisation but then joined the USAF in 1951 and served tours flying the F-84 in Korea and the United Kingdom. He flew 72 missions in the F-100 in Vietnam before being selected to command the Misty FAC detachment. Colonel George Everett Day was awarded the Medal of Honor for his courageous escape attempt and for his outstanding example of resistance in several North Vietnamese prison camps. Said to be the most decorated officer after General MacArthur, Bud Day wrote a book titled *Return with Honor* and, following his retirement from the USAF in 1977, he became a practising attorney in Florida.

A-26A 64-17642   606 ACS, 56 ACW, USAF, Nakhon Phanom
Lt Col Bruce Allan Jensen (KIA)
Capt Francis Edward Smiley (KIA)

Tragedy struck the 606th ACS on the night of the 26th when the squadron commander was shot down and killed during an armed reconnaissance mission in Laos. Lt Col Jensen was flying about 85 miles northwest of Nakhon Phanom when his aircraft disappeared, almost certainly the victim of anti-aircraft fire.

A-6A 152639   VMA(AW)-533, MAG-12, USMC, Chu Lai
Maj Vladimir Henry Bacik (KIA)
Capt Paschal Glenn Boggs (KIA)

VMA(AW)-533 was the second Marine Corps A-6 squadron to deploy to Southeast Asia and had arrived at Chu Lai on 1 April. Like VMA(AW)-242, the Squadron flew mainly in support of Marine ground forces in the northern provinces of South Vietnam, but it also flew Rolling Thunder strikes against targets in the North. The Squadron lost its first aircraft during a night strike on storage buildings a few miles to the east of Hon Gay. Maj Bacik was making his run over the target at about 1,500 feet and 450 knots when the aircraft was hit by AAA and crashed. It appears that the crew did not have a chance to escape from the Intruder before it crashed.

28 August 1967

A-4E 150038   VMA-211, MAG-12, USMC, Chu Lai
Maj Charles Franklin Wallace (KIA)

The Marines lost another aircraft two days later when a Skyhawk was shot down two miles north of the DMZ. Maj Wallace was attacking an anti-aircraft gun site and was pulling up from his bombing run when the aircraft hit by AAA. The aircraft crashed just off the coast but the pilot was not seen to eject.

29 August 1967

A-4E 151025   VA-153, USN, USS *Coral Sea*
Lt Michael John Allard (KIA)

A flight of A-4s was assigned to attack a cave storage site at Nhan Thap near Vinh. Lt Allard rolled in to drop his M-117 bombs but appeared to misjudge the manoeuvre and rolled the aircraft too steeply which led to a high speed stall and spin. The aircraft spun into the ground before Lt Allard could regain control or eject.

30 August 1967

A-1H 135390   VA-25, USN, USS *Coral Sea*
Lt(jg) L E Gardiner (survived)

A section of Skyraiders from the *Coral Sea* found a number of small boats just offshore, about 30 miles north of Vinh. Lt Gardiner made one attack and came round for his second pass when his aircraft was hit by ground fire. He abandoned the aircraft a few miles out to sea and was picked up by a Navy helicopter before the North Vietnamese boats could reach him.

31 August 1967

A-4E 149975   VA-163, USN, USS *Oriskany*
Lt Cdr Hugh Allen Stafford (POW)

A-4E 152028   VA-163, USN, USS *Oriskany*
Lt(jg) David Jay Carey (POW)

A-4E 151991   VA-164, USN, USS *Oriskany*
Lt Cdr Richard Clark Perry (KIA)

On the last day of the month the *Oriskany* despatched 10 Skyhawks from VA-163 and VA-164 against a railway bridge at Vat Cach Thuong near Haiphong. A concerted campaign had started the previous day to isolate Haiphong through which about 85 per cent of the North's imports arrived. As the ships bringing in the supplies could not be attacked or the harbour mined, the only alternative was to try to cut all routes out of the city. About 13 miles southwest of Haiphong on the approach to the target the formation encountered a volley of SAMs. One of the missiles exploded directly in the path of Lt Cdr Stafford and his wingman, Lt Carey. Lt Cdr Stafford was flying at about 16,000 feet and the force of the explosion blew him out of the cockpit of his aircraft still strapped to his ejection seat. Fortunately, his seat separated and his parachute deployed automatically and, although badly injured, he was lucky to survive at all. Lt Carey, who was on his first mission over North Vietnam, was also in trouble. His engine wound down and the rear end of his aircraft was on fire. He ejected from the aircraft and, like his leader, was quickly captured. Lt Cdr Stafford and Lt Carey were both released on 14 March 1973.

A few minutes after the first two aircraft went down, the aircraft of Lt Cdr Perry, the leader of the VA-164 element, was hit by another SA-2. Streaming fuel, Lt Cdr Perry turned out to sea escorted by two other VA-164 aircraft. About two miles off the coast the aircraft became uncontrollable and Perry ejected. A SAR helicopter was already on the scene and a helicopter crewman saw Lt Cdr Perry hanging limp in his parachute. When he entered the water he failed to surface and when the pararescueman reached him he was found to be dead, probably from a chest wound. As the parachute lines were twisted around the pilot's body and the North Vietnamese were firing mortars at the helicopter from the shore, Lt Cdr Perry's body had to be left in the water. The body was recovered by the Vietnamese but it was not until February 1987 that Lt Cdr Perry's remains were handed over to the US government.

2 September 1967

F-105D 62-4338   333 TFS, 355 TFW, USAF, Takhli
Maj William George Bennett (KIA)

A flight of four F-105s from Takhli was flying a strike on a sector of roads in the hills 20 miles west of Dong Hoi when one of the aircraft was shot down. Maj Bennett was pulling up from his bombing run when his aircraft was hit by ground fire. It was thought that the pilot had probably been wounded as he was not seen to eject from the stricken aircraft before it impacted into the side of a steep karst ridge. 62-4338 was the personal mount of Col Jack Broughton, the vice-commander of the 355th TFW and was named 'Alice's Joy'. At this time Col Broughton was facing a courts martial for protecting two of his pilots who had fired on a Soviet ship during a raid on Cam Pha on 2 June.

3 September 1967

F-105D 61-0078   469 TFS, 388 TFW, USAF, Korat
Capt Herbert William Moore (KIA)

A flight of four F-105s was sent on a strike against a road bridge at Xom Cul in the hills, 55 miles northwest of Dong Hoi. As Capt Moore dived his aircraft at the target it was hit by anti-aircraft fire and he ejected close to the bridge. A SAR helicopter crew later spotted his empty parachute on the ground and his emergency beeper was heard. Voice contact could not be made with Capt Moore but the beeper was heard again several hours later. Although the search resumed the next day, Capt Moore was never heard of again and is presumed to have perished in the hills either as a result of the ejection or at the hands of the North Vietnamese. Thunderchief 61-0078 was painted as 'Sitting Pretty' during its service with the 469th.

4 September 1967

F-4D 65-0723   555 TFS, 8 TFW, USAF, Ubon
Maj Carl Dean Miller (KIA)
1Lt Thomas Patterson Hanson (KIA)

During a night-time armed reconnaissance mission in the southern provinces of North Vietnam a flight of Phantoms spotted trucks on a road near Mai Xa Ha, 15 miles southeast of Dong Hoi. During the attack one of the aircraft hit the ground and exploded either as a result of ground fire or misjudgement over the unlit terrain. It was thought that both crew died in the crash. During the period they were posted as missing in action Maj Miller was promoted to Colonel and 1Lt Hanson to Major.

C-123K 54-0621   19 ACS, 315 ACW, USAF, Phan Rang
Lt Col Merle Deane Turner (KIA)
Capt Edward Louis Goucher (KIA)
A1C James Russell Mayo (KIA)
8 passengers (KIA)

A Provider, captained by the CO of the 19th ACS, disappeared in South Vietnam during a flight from Bien Hoa to Nha Trang with the loss of all on board. The wreckage of the aircraft was found two days later near Bao Loc, its first scheduled stop. The cause of the accident was attributed to pilot error. Four of the passengers, Capt W B Mahone, Capt V K Kelley, TSgt J M Boatwright and MSgt H C Cook, were a Ranch Hand crew on their way to Nha Trang to collect one of their aircraft that had been under repair for battle damage.

5 September 1967

A-1G 52-132579   1 ACS, 14 ACW, USAF, Pleiku
Maj J O Gassman (survived)

A flight of Skyraiders from Pleiku crossed into southern Laos on a daytime armed reconnaissance mission. The flight discovered troops and a truck park near Ban Phiaha in the southern tip of Laos and commenced an attack. Maj Gassman made a strafing run but his aircraft was hit in the port wing by AAA and caught fire. He managed to fly a few miles away from the truck park before ejecting and was picked up safely by a VNAF helicopter

F-4C   63-7547   557 TFS, 12 TFW, USAF, Cam Ranh Bay
Capt Donald William Downing (KIA)
1Lt Paul Darwin Raymond (KIA)

A Phantom from Cam Ranh Bay was lost during a night armed reconnaissance mission just north of the DMZ. Two aircraft were attacking a truck park that had been discovered five miles north of Thon Cam Son when they flew into a barrage of 37mm flak. The wingman saw a huge fireball fall to the ground a few miles to the north west. It appears that neither of the crew escaped from the aircraft. During the period they were maintained as missing in action Capt Downing was promoted to the rank of Lieutenant Colonel and 1Lt Raymond to the rank of Captain.

RF-4C   66-0387   16 TRS, 460 TRW, USAF, Tan Son Nhut
2 crew, names unknown (survived)

A reconnaissance Phantom crashed in South Vietnam due to accidental engine failure. This was the first of eight US reconnaissance aircraft lost during September.

6 September 1967

O-1F   57-2978   21 TASS, 504 TASG, USAF, Nha Trang
Lt Col Norris Ray Smith (KIA)
1 crew, name unknown (survived)

A Bird Dog FAC aircraft crashed near Pleiku as the result of pilot error. The pilot was killed in the accident.

7 September 1967

O-1E   56-4177   19 TASS, 504 TASG, USAF, Bien Hoa
Capt Albert Francis Sayer (KIA)
Capt J J Cappel (survived)

A Bird Dog on a visual reconnaissance sortie was hit by automatic weapons fire from a group of VC troops. The aircraft crashed just two miles south of the town of Bien Hoa killing the pilot and slightly injuring the observer.

F-105F   63-8260   13 TFS, 388 TFW, USAF, Korat
2 crew, names unknown (survived)

A two-seat Thunderchief crashed in Thailand when it suffered an engine failure. Fortunately, both the crew ejected safely.

8 September 1967

F-4B   152238   VMFA-323, MAG-13, USMC, Chu Lai
Maj J B Caskey (survived)
Capt R L Drage (survived)

A Marine Corps Phantom from Chu Lai was shot down during a bombing mission against buildings near Thon Cam Son within the DMZ buffer zone. Maj Caskey was making his second pass over the target when his aircraft was hit by ground fire. He flew out to sea and along the coast in the hope of reaching Da Nang, however, he and his navigator were forced to eject about six miles off the coast near Hué. Maj Caskey was picked up by a Marine Corps coastal vessel and Capt Drage by a USAF helicopter.

F-8C   146929   VF-111, USN, USS *Oriskany*
1 pilot, name unknown (survived)

While on an armed reconnaissance mission a Crusader from the *Oriskany* suffered an electrical failure that resulted in a loss of power. The pilot ejected and was rescued.

9 September 1967

F-4D   66-7516   435 TFS, 8 TFW, USAF, Ubon
Lt J Silliman (survived)
Maj Ivan Dale Appleby (survived)

During a flight over Thailand a Phantom from the Wolfpack suffered an engine flame out forcing the crew to eject. The wreckage was recovered and the cause of the engine failure was traced to a faulty fuel line. Maj Appleby died on 7 October when he was shot down near Hanoi.

F-4C   64-0835   480 TFS, 366 TFW, USAF, Da Nang
2 crew, names unknown (survived)

Another Phantom was lost in an accident in South Vietnam the same day. An aircraft was taking off from Da Nang on an armed reconnaissance mission when one of its tyres blew out. The aircraft slewed off the runway and was so badly damaged that it had to be scrapped.

10 September 1967

B-57B   52-1510   8 TBS, 405 FW attached to 35 TFW, USAF,
Phan Rang
Maj Norris M Overly (POW)
Capt Gaylord Dean Petersen (KIA)

The elderly B-57s were still being used over North Vietnam at night, especially in the less well-defended southern provinces although even here the defences were becoming more and more efficient. Maj Overly was on a night armed reconnaissance mission when he spotted an oil tanker on a road about eight miles northwest of Dong Hoi. He put the aircraft into a dive but it was hit in the starboard engine by AAA. Both crew ejected but only Maj Overly survived to reach captivity. While in the Plantation prison in Hanoi, Maj Overly nursed fellow POWs 'Bud' Day and John McCain back from the brink of death. On 16 February 1968 Norris Overly was one of three POWS who were released into the hands of peace activists in order to obtain useful propaganda for the North Vietnamese cause. This early release caused a great deal of consternation amongst the remaining POWs but Overly and the other two men were able to give useful information on other prisoners and the location, layout and occupants of the camps they had been in.

A-4E   150047   VA-163, USN, USS *Oriskany*
1 pilot, name unknown (survived)

The Skyhawk could be fitted out with an in-flight refuelling pod for tanker sorties. An aircraft configured as a tanker was being catapulted from the *Oriskany* when its engine lost power. The pilot ejected safely and the aircraft crashed in the sea just in front of the ship.

11 September 1967

RF-4B   153104   VMCJ-1, MAG-11, USMC, Da Nang
Maj Richard William Hawthorne (KIA)
Capt Richard Raymond Kane (KIA)

Although VMCJ-1 had been operating the RF-4B from Da Nang since September 1966 it was not until a year later that the unit lost the first aircraft of this type in Southeast Asia. The RF-4B was used for photographic reconnaissance missions over the northern provinces of South Vietnam in support of Marine air and ground operations but, in common with Marine strike aircraft, it also flew a small number of sorties over Laos and North Vietnam. The aircraft that was lost on the 11th set off on an early morning sortie to photograph suspected enemy-occupied huts about 50 miles west of Da Nang on the South Vietnamese border with Laos. A bright flash was seen as the aircraft hit high ground en route to the target near Ben Giang, about 35 miles southwest of Da Nang, and both crew were posted missing. It was not possible to determine the cause of the aircraft's loss but it was either due to ground fire or flying into terrain when using the aircraft's radar to fly at low level.

F-8E   150910   VF-162, USN, USS *Oriskany*
Lt James Shaw (survived)

During an armed reconnaissance mission a Crusader pilot found that he had two bombs that would not release. As it was safer to land on a long runway with hung ordnance than attempt a carrier landing, Lt Shaw was ordered to make for Da Nang. Unfortunately, due to a navigation error the aircraft ran out of fuel before it reached Da Nang and the pilot had to eject. This Crusader was a MiG-killer, having been flown by Lt Gene Chancy on 21 June 1966 when he shot down a MiG-17.

12 September 1967

RF-4C   65-0857   12 TRS, 460 TRW, USAF, Tan Son Nhut
Capt J E Birmingham (survived)
1Lt R A Kopp (survived)

An RF-4C from Tan Son Nhut was flying a photographic reconnaissance mission along Route 1A, the main coastal road that stretched from the DMZ to Haiphong. As the aircraft was pulling up from a photo run it was hit by AAA near the village of Bo Trach, eight miles up the coast from Dong Hoi. Capt Birmingham immediately crossed the coast and flew south in the hope of reaching Da Nang. However, the crew were forced to eject about nine miles off the coast near Quang Tri and were picked up by a USAF helicopter.

14 September 1967

O-2A   67-21314   20 TASS, 504 TASG, USAF, Da Nang
Capt Gardner Brewer (KIA)

Although two O-2s had been lost during an airfield attack on 6 August, the first O-2 to be lost in the air was shot down on 14 September. Capt Brewer was returning to Da Nang from an FAC mission when he was shot down by ground fire about seven miles northeast of Quang Ngai. The aircraft crashed in flames and Capt Brewer was killed instantly.

15 September 1967

F-100D   55-2904   510 TFS, 3 TFW, USAF, Bien Hoa
Maj A E Munsch (survived)

Maj Munsch was flying a close air support mission in support of the 559th Infantry Regiment about 15 miles west of the town of My Tho in the Mekong Delta region when he was shot down. As he came down to low level to make his first napalm drop on the target his aircraft was hit by automatic weapons fire and badly damaged. He managed to fly towards My Tho and ejected close to the town where he was rescued by an Army helicopter.

16 September 1967

RF-101C   56-0180   20 TRS, 432 TRW, USAF, Udorn
Maj Bobby Ray Bagley (POW)

The 16th of September was a bad day for the USAF reconnaissance fraternity with the loss of three aircraft and three airmen. The object of attention in the North was the northwest railway line. Maj Bagley had obtained the required photographs and was on his way back to Udorn at 24,000 feet when he was jumped by a MiG-21 that shot him down. Bagley ejected and landed in the hills near Son La, 60 miles southwest of Yen Bai. He was badly beaten by the villagers who found him and then tortured by the NVA troops who took him into custody before being imprisoned and suffering further torture. After his release from captivity on 14 March 1973, Maj Bagley resumed his Air Force career at Shaw AFB and retired as a Colonel. He had spent 13 months in a staff job in South Vietnam before requesting an extension of his posting to Southeast Asia so that he could return to flying. Following the loss of this aircraft, RF-101s were rarely sent to Route Package 6 targets.

RF-101C   56-0181   20 TRS, 432 TRW, USAF, Udorn
Capt R E Patterson (survived)

The loss of the photographs of the northwestern railway prompted the 20th TRS to despatch another Voodoo on a repeat mission. Unfortunately, Capt Patterson fared little better although he eventually made it back to Udorn but without his aircraft or the photographs. Like Maj Bagley, he had also reached the target, made a successful photo run and was heading back home when he ran into trouble. His aircraft was damaged by AAA but it kept flying until he was forced to eject near Ban Ban in northern Laos, about 150 miles short of Udorn. He was rescued with only minor injuries by a USAF helicopter. Capt Patterson had been shot down a few months earlier on 21 June and was fortunate to survive both incidents.

RF-4C   64-1037   16 TRS, 460 TRW, USAF, Tan Son Nhut
Maj William Lee Nellans (KIA)
1Lt Peter Arthur Grubb (KIA)

The third reconnaissance aircraft to be lost on the 16th failed to return from a night mission over the southern provinces of North Vietnam. It was thought that the Phantom had been shot down by ground fire about five miles north of the DMZ but there was no trace of either of the crew.

17 September 1967

RF-4C 65-0894   11 TRS, 432 TRW, USAF, Udorn
Maj John Edward Stavast (POW)
Lt Gerald Santo Venanzi (POW)

Another reconnaissance Phantom was lost the very next day. Maj Stavast was flying at 24,000 feet near one of his targets at Hoang Lien, 10 miles northeast of Phuc Yen, when the aircraft was damaged by the explosion of an SA-2 missile. The aircraft flew for several minutes and reached a position about 17 miles south-west of Hanoi before the situation became hopeless and the crew had to eject. Both men were soon captured and imprisoned. Maj Stavast was flying his 91st mission and Lt Venanzi, who had been based at Udorn since June 1962, was flying his 62nd when they were shot down. They were both released on 14 March 1973.

18 September 1967

A-4C 149590   VA-34, USN, USS *Intrepid*
Lt Cdr S H Hawkins (survived)

Remarkably, the US Navy had not lost any aircraft in combat since the beginning of the month. However, on the 18th this run of good fortune was brought to a halt when a Skyhawk was shot down near Haiphong. Lt Cdr Hawkins was leading five other Skyhawks of the *Intrepid's* flak suppression flight to cover a raid on the main railway yard at Haiphong. As the flight approached the target at 5,000 feet and 320 knots, they received a SAM warning and took evasive action. As Lt Cdr Hawkins levelled out at 3,000 feet his aircraft was bracketed by two SA-2s, one of which exploded less than 100 feet from his Skyhawk causing extensive damage. With no radio, oxygen or aileron control he headed out to sea but ejected about 10 miles from the coast when he realised his aircraft was on fire. He was picked up safely by a Navy SAR helicopter.

19 September 1967

F-4D 66-7533   435 TFS, 8 TFW, USAF, Ubon
Maj L Boothby (survived)
1 other crew, name unknown (survived)

A Phantom of Spitfire flight was shot down following a raid on railway sidings at Thang Quang on the 19th. Maj Boothby was returning from the target when his aircraft was hit in the star-

board wing by 57mm anti-aircraft fire, 10 miles north of Phuc Yen. The aircraft was badly damaged but remained airborne until it reached a position 35 miles south of Udorn where it became uncontrollable and both the crew ejected.

F-100D 56-3330   90 TFS, 3 TFW, USAF, Bien Hoa
Capt Clyde Walter Carter (KIA)

An F-100D exploded over Bien Hoa as it prepared to approach for landing, killing the pilot. The cause of the explosion was not thought to have been due to enemy action.

21 September 1967

RF-8G 144623   Detachment 43, VFP-63, USN,
USS *Coral Sea*
Lt Cdr Milton James Vescelius (KIA)

As part of a major strike on bridges around Haiphong, the *Coral Sea* sent an RF-8 to photograph damage at the Kien An road bridge. As Lt Cdr Vescelius was making his run over the target at 3,000 feet and 600 knots, just as the last of the strike aircraft left the area, his aircraft was hit by AAA and the starboard wing burst into flames. The aircraft commenced a shallow starboard turn and the pilot ejected just to the north of Haiphong harbour. The aircraft exploded shortly afterwards. Lt Cdr Vescelius was seen alive on the ground by other pilots but he may have been killed by North Vietnamese troops. His remains were eventually returned to US authorities on 14 August 1985.

O-1E 56-2516   20 TASS, 504 TASG, USAF, Da Nang
Capt James H Bennett (KIA)
1 crew, name unknown (survived)

An O-1 was hit in the engine by small arms fire soon after taking off from Khe Sanh. With the aircraft on fire Capt Bennett attempted to crash-land the aircraft but he was killed and his observer, probably a US Marine, was injured.

23 September 1967

F-105D 59-1749   469 TFS, 388 TFW, USAF, Korat
Maj D S Aunapu (survived)

When not flying Rolling Thunder strikes or armed reconnaissance missions in the North, the F-105s occasionally flew Combat Skyspot radar bombing missions over North Vietnam or Laos. This usually involved a flight of four F-105Ds led by an

F-105F or an EB-66 that signalled the other aircraft when to release their bombs. This technique was often employed during periods of bad weather when the aircraft had to operate above cloud. Maj Aunapu was flying a Skyspot mission when his aircraft was hit and damaged by AAA (probably radar-directed 85mm) near Ban Katoi, 30 miles northwest of the DMZ. The aircraft almost reached Korat before Maj Aunapu was forced to eject. 59-1749 was painted as 'Marilee' and 'Mr Toad' with appropriate nose art while at Korat.

25 September 1967

EA-1F 133770   VAW-13, USN, Cubi Point
4 crew, names unknown (survived)

A VAW-13 Skyraider ditched in the sea during a logistics flight from Cubi Point after the engine began to run rough and lost power. All four crewmembers were rescued safely.

26 September 1967

F-4B 148422   VMFA-542, MAG-13, USMC, Chu Lai
Maj P M Cole (survived)
1Lt Harold John Moe (KIA)

VMFA-542 lost its third F-4 of the year during an attack on an anti-aircraft gun site on the coast two miles north of the DMZ. The aircraft was hit in the engine compartment by ground fire as it pulled up from its first attack. Maj Cole turned out to sea but he and his navigator were forced to eject about seven miles out to sea. Although a US Navy ship rescued Maj Cole, 1Lt Moe was killed during the incident.

F-105F 63-8267   357 TFS, 355 TFW, USAF, Takhli
2 crew, names unknown (survived)

A second F-105F was lost in an accident during the month when an aircraft struck the top of a tree during an approach to Takhli in bad weather at night. The crew escaped but the aircraft had to be scrapped.

F-4D 66-7534   435 TFS, 8 TFW, USAF, Ubon
Capt D J Ankeny (survived)
Lt J D Mynar (survived)

Another Air Force aircraft was lost in Thailand when a Phantom crashed due to pilot error. Again, both crew survived.

27 September 1967

A-4E 152056   VMA-311, MAG-12, USMC, Chu Lai
Maj Gerald L Ellis (survived)

Another Marine Corps aircraft was lost during an attack on an anti-aircraft gun site. On this occasion it was an A-4 that was bombing a gun pit close to the village of Thon Cam Son within the DMZ buffer zone. The Skyhawk was hit by AAA and caught fire as it dived on the target. Maj Ellis flew five miles out to sea before ejecting and being picked up by a USAF helicopter.

US-2C 133371   VC-5, USN, Cubi Point
4 crew, names unknown (survived)

VC-5 lost one of its Trackers while on a logistics flight to the USS *Hornet* in the Gulf of Tonkin. The aircraft suffered a loss of oil pressure in the starboard engine and the propeller had to be feathered but the aircraft could not maintain altitude and had to be ditched. All four crew were picked up safely.

29 September 1967

F-4B 151429   VMFA-115, MAG-13, USMC, Chu Lai
Lt Col Kenny C Palmer (survived)
Capt Charles S Cahaskie (survived)

Lt Col Palmer, the CO of VMFA-115, was leading a close air support mission just one mile north of the DMZ and close to the coast. The aircraft was hit by ground fire as it was pulling up from a target and Lt Col Palmer immediately pointed the stricken aircraft towards the sea. The crew ejected over the sea just south of the DMZ and Palmer was picked up by a USAF HH-3 and taken to Da Nang. Capt Cahaskie injured his back probably during the ejection, and had to be lifted on board a Navy frigate. VMFA-115 had arrived at Chu Lai on 14 May and

VFP-63 provided detachments for most of the aircraft carriers operating in the Gulf of Tonkin. This RF-8G belongs to Detachment G and is seen on board the USS *Oriskany* in August 1967. VFP-63 lost a total of 30 Crusaders between January 1964 and the end of the conflict. USN

stayed there until August 1970. Lt Col Palmer took command of the Squadron on 28 July and handed over his command to Lt Col R E Carey a week after this incident. Although the Squadron was on its third deployment and had been conducting operations in South Vietnam for almost two years, this was its first aircraft lost due to enemy action. This particular Phantom was another of the ex-Navy F-4Bs that had been loaned to the USAF for use by the 4453rd CCTW in 1963.

TA-4F 153499 H&MS-12, MAG-12, USMC, Chu Lai
Maj Cullen George Starnes (KIA)
1 crew, name unknown (survived)

The Headquarters and Maintenance Squadron of MAG-12 had a small number of two-seat TA-4F Skyhawks for continuation training, liaison flights and other purposes. As one of its TA-4Fs was approaching to land at Chu Lai it touched down heavily short of the runway demolishing the landing gear. The aircraft caught fire and one of the crew was killed in the crash.

30 September 1967

F-4B 151020 VMFA-115, MAG-13, USMC, Chu Lai
2 crew, names unknown (survived)

After losing an aircraft in combat on the 29th VMFA-115 was unfortunate enough to lose another aircraft the following day. A Phantom caught fire just after taking off on a strike mission and the crew ejected safely. The crash was attributed to a techical malfunction.

2 October 1967

AC-47D 43-48591 4 ACS, 14 ACW, USAF, Nha Trang
detached to Phu Cat
Lt Col Van Harold Newville (KIA)
Capt Arthur Raymond Coughlin (KIA)
Maj William Whitby Duck (KIA)
MSgt Charles Joseph Rogiers (KIA)
TSgt James Charles Krouse (KIA)
A2C William Ward Scoville (KIA)
A2C Walter Clarence Wright (KIA)

An AC-47 Spooky was shot down during a daylight mission over Hué City on 2 October. The location where the aircraft was hit was given in a US official document as being over the DMZ yet it crashed near Hué, 40 miles to the south. This aircraft had previously been used as a hack by the 48th TFW at RAF Lakenheath, Suffolk.

RF-4C 66-0403 11 TRS, 432 TRW, USAF, Udorn
Maj L Browne (survived)
Maj D M Miller (survived)

A reconnaissance Phantom was lost in Thailand when its engines flamed out following a fuel system malfunction.

2/3 October 1967

F-8E 150912 VMF(AW)-235, MAG-11, USMC, Da Nang
1Lt Patrick Lewis Ott (KIA)

During the night of 2 October a Marine Corps F-8 flew into high ground about 10 miles northwest of Da Nang as it was returning from a TPQ-10 radar bombing sortie and preparing to land. It is not known if enemy action played a part in the aircraft's loss but it was thought unlikely.

3 October 1967

F-4D 66-7564 435 TFS, 8 TFW, USAF, Ubon
Maj Joseph D Moore (survived)
1Lt S B Gulbrandson (survived)

A raid on the Cao Bang road bridge resulted in the loss of one of the raiders. About 50 miles southwest of Hanoi the formation was attacked by several MiG-21s and Maj Moore's aircraft was damaged by an air-to-air missile. The aircraft was on fire and its port engine had to be shut down but Maj Moore flew it to the border with Laos where he and his WSO ejected. They were both rescued by a USAF helicopter. Maj Moore redressed the balance a few weeks later when he shared a MiG-17 kill with an F-105F on 19 December.

F-105D 59-1727 469 TFS, 388 TFW, USAF, Korat
Maj Robert Warren Barnett (POW)

A formation of F-105s flew a raid on the Dap Cau road bridge, 25 miles northwest of Haiphong. As the aircraft approached the target at 16,000 feet they heard a SAM warning and a missile exploded close to Maj Barnett's aircraft causing major damage including hydraulic failure and an engine fire. Maj Barnett ejected close to Uong Bi, 15 miles northeast of Haiphong, and was captured by Vietnamese using tracker dogs on the morning of the 5th. Maj Barnett was on his 43rd mission when he was shot down and although he was flying an aircraft from the 469th TFS, he appears to have been a member of the 44th TFS. He was released from captivity on 14 March 1973.

A-4B 142114 VSF-3, USN, USS Intrepid
Lt(jg) A D Perkins (survived)

VSF-3 lost its second aircraft during the Intrepid's tour during a raid on a road and railway bridge at Haiphong. Lt Perkins was part of the flak suppression force that accompanied the bombers. As he started his dive to fire his Zuni rockets the aircraft was hit by AAA. He jettisoned his ordnance and headed towards the coast but the aircraft was hit again and further damaged and Lt Perkins was struck in the left leg by shrapnel. Smoke filled the cockpit and the most of the instruments failed. Lt Perkins jettisoned the cockpit canopy to clear the smoke but the aircraft was either hit by flak again or the engine may have exploded. The pilot ejected at 8,000 feet over Haiphong Harbour and was rescued from within yards of a ship by a Navy UH-2 flown by Lt Tim Melecosky from HC-1. Lt Melecosky was shot down by ground fire the next day while operating from the USS Coontz on another SAR mission. Although the helicopter, UH-2B 150153 was lost when it ditched off Haiphong, all the crew were rescued by a Seaking from HS-2.

F-105D 59-1824 354 TFS, 355 TFW, USAF, Takhli
Lt Col Ronald Runyon King (KIA)

A Thunderchief crashed in the Gulf of Tonkin when it ran out of fuel returning from a mission. The pilot was killed in the accident.

4 October 1967

A-4C 149619 VA-15, USN, USS Intrepid
Lt Cdr Peter VanRuyter Schoeffel (POW)

Lt Cdr Schoeffel was flying a flak suppression mission during a raid on a ferry one mile northeast of Haiphong when he was shot down and captured. He had just fired his rockets at a gun site and was pulling up when the aircraft was hit by AAA and instantly became uncontrollable. With the aircraft rolling and on fire and the cockpit full of smoke, the pilot ejected. He was soon captured and taken to the Hanoi Hilton. He was released on 14 March 1973. Peter Schoeffel was flying his 125th combat mission over Southeast Asia when he was shot down.

U-10B 63-13110 5 ACS, 14 ACW, USAF, Nha Trang
Capt David Hartzler Zook (KIA)

Capt Zook was flying a U-10B on a leaflet dropping mission near Lai Khe, 20 miles north of Saigon, when his aircraft was involved in a mid-air collision with another aircraft. The Courier crashed about five miles west of the village of Ben Cat but Capt Zook's body was not recoverd. David Zook was from an Amish family but had joined the Air Force and was an assistant professor of history at the USAF Academy in 1962. Capt Zook was promoted to the rank of Colonel during the period he was listed as missing.

4/5 October 1967

F-105F 63-8346 13 TFS, 388 TFW, USAF, Korat
Maj Morris Larosco McDaniel (KIA)
Capt William Allen Lillund (KIA)

During a night raid on the Lang Con railway bridge an F-105F was thought to have been shot down by ground fire 40 miles northwest of Hanoi. The last contact with the aircraft was when it took on fuel from a KC-135 tanker prior to crossing into North Vietnam and the last known position was about 10 miles north-

west of the town of Phu Tho. Maj McDaniel had almost reached his magic figure of 100 sorties and was only days from being posted back to the USA. This was probably a modified Project Northscope aircraft of the 'Ryan's Raiders' unit.

5 October 1967

F-8C 146938 VF-111, USN, USS Oriskany
Ens David Paul Matheny (POW)

During a raid on a pontoon bridge at Nho Quan, 20 miles southwest of Nam Dinh, one of the Crusader escorts was lost. Ens Matheny was in a turn at 10,000 feet and 400 knots when he felt an explosion and saw the rear end of his aircraft become a mass of flames. As his engine failed he attempted to glide to the sea but was forced to eject over land and was captured. It was never determined whether the aircraft had been shot down or had suffered a catastrophic engine failure. Ens Matheny was captured but spent only four months as a prisoner as he was released by the North Vietnamese as a propaganda measure on 16 February 1968 along with Capt J D Black and Maj N Overly.

F-105D 58-1169 13 TFS, 388 TFW, USAF, Korat
Capt Konrad Wigand Trautman (POW)

A Thunderchief was shot down near Kep as a formation was en route to bomb the railway line at Quang Hien. Capt Trautman was about to start his bombing run when his aircraft was hit by AAA. With the aircraft on fire he ejected about 15 miles northwest of Kep and was captured within a few minutes of hitting the ground. Capt Trautman had joined the USAF in 1948 and had flown 20 combat missions in the F-84 during the Korean War. He was flying his 62nd mission over Vietnam when he was shot down. He was released on 14 March 1973 having been the senior POW in the Zoo Annex prison camp. F-105D 58-1169 was painted as 'Dragon' during its time at Korat.

F-105D 62-4329 354 TFS, 355 TFW, USAF, Takhli
1 pilot, name unknown (survived)

Another F-105 was lost on the 5th when it crash-landed at Takhli due to an accidental engine failure.

6 October 1967

A-1E 52-132663 1 ACS, 14 ACW, USAF, Pleiku
Maj Frank Alton Armstrong (KIA)

Two Skyraiders from Pleiku were on a Steel Tiger strike against troops near Ban Pakha, close to the meeting point of the borders of South Vietnam, Laos and Cambodia. As the leader, Maj Armstrong, rolled in to drop his bombs his aircraft was hit by 12.7mm anti-aircraft fire. The aircraft rolled inverted and crashed a few miles from the target. Maj Armstrong may have been wounded as he was not seen to eject from the aircraft before it crashed.

F-105F 63-8272 44 TFS, 388 TFW, USAF, Korat
2 crew, names unknown (survived)

An F-105F (probably a Wild Weasel aircraft) ran off the runway at Korat when its drag chute failed on landing. The aircraft was damaged beyond repair.

F-4C 63-7612 433 TFS, 8 TFW, USAF, Ubon
1Lt J L Fuller (survived)
1Lt J E Nicholson (survived)

A Phantom crashed on take off from Ubon. Both the crew survived the accident.

7 October 1967

A-4E 152086 VA-164, USN, USS Oriskany
Lt David Lawton Hodges (KIA)

An Iron Hand flight of A-4s was searching for a Fan Song radar site that was known to be active south of Hanoi in association with an SA-2 battery. When the flight was at 11,000 feet about 15 miles south of the city, one of the pilots spotted two SAMs heading towards the aircraft. He called to Lt Hodges who was slow to respond and probably did not have the missiles in sight. The first missile passed safely behind the flight in a ballistic trajectory but the second SA-2 guided towards Lt Hodges's aircraft and exploded. The Skyhawk burst into flames, rolled to the right and

dived into a karst ridge near Hoang Xa. No ejection was seen and it was assumed that Lt Hodges might have been incapacitated by the blast from the SAM. In 1995 and 1996 joint US-Vietnamese excavation teams recovered the remains of Lt Hodges from the crash site.

F-4D   65-0727   555 TFS, 8 TFW, USAF, Ubon
          Maj Ivan Dale Appleby (KIA)
          Capt William Renwick Austin (POW)

Maj Appleby and Capt Austin were assigned to escort a reconnaissance mission over North Vietnam. About six miles north of Hanoi the flight was targeted by a SAM battery. Maj Appleby's aircraft was hit by an SA-2 that caused the aircraft to catch fire, inflicted damage to the hydraulics and caused the port engine to fail. The aircraft headed back in the direction of Thailand but Maj Appleby was unable to control the Phantom when the hydraulics failed completely and it crashed about 35 miles southwest of Hanoi. Only one parachute was seen as Capt Austin ejected into captivity. Maj Appleby apparently did not survive and was presumptively declared dead in 1976. Capt Austin was on his 81st mission when he was shot down. He was eventually released from North Vietnam on 14 March 1973. It was not until January 1995 that remains from the Phantom crash site were excavated and returned to the USA and positively identified in October as being those of Maj (since promoted to Colonel) Appleby. Ivan Appleby was buried at Arlington National Cemetery in December 1995.

F-105F   63-8330   13 TFS, 388 TFW, USAF, Korat
          Capt Joseph D Howard (survived)
          Capt George L Shamblee (survived)

F-105D   60-0444   34 TFS, 388 TFW, USAF, Korat
          Maj Wayne Eugene Fullam (KIA)

Just over two hours after Maj Appleby's Phantom was lost the Korat Wing hit the railway marshalling yard at Kep. As usual, the bombers were preceded by an Iron Hand flight of F-105F Wild Weasels and associated F-105D bombers. The Iron Hand flight had battled its way to the target and was heading east away from Kep when it was intercepted by MiG-21s. Capt Howard's aircraft was hit in the rear fuselage by an air-to-air missile but the F-105 escaped out to sea and headed south in an attempt to reach the safety of Da Nang. The aircraft crossed much of the Gulf of Tonkin but the crew were eventually forced to eject over the sea about 75 miles north of Da Nang. One man was rescued from the sea by a Marine Corps helicopter from the amphibious assault ship USS *Tripoli* and the other by a USAF helicopter.

About 20 minutes after the Iron Hand flight had left the target, one of the F-105D bombers was shot down. Maj Fullam rolled in on the target from 12,000 feet but the aircraft was struck in the starboard wing by 85mm flak. He radioed that he was ejecting and a parachute was seen and a strong SAR beeper signal was picked up, however, voice contact could not be made. Maj Fullam landed about 30 miles east of Kep and a Navy rescue helicopter attempted a rescue but could not get close due to intense ground fire. The helicopter crew saw Maj Fullam's parachute being pulled down from a tree and noted that the beeper signals ceased at the same time. A subsequent intelligence report claimed that Fullam had been captured by a Chinese anti-aircraft unit operating in North Vietnam and that he was handed over to the North Vietnamese and driven away in a jeep. This report could not be verified even after Operation Homecoming but on 24 September 1987 remains were handed over by the Vietnamese that were later identified as being those of Maj Fullam. The cause of his death remains a mystery.

8 October 1967

E-1B   148132   Detachment 34, VAW-111, USN, USS *Oriskany*
          Lt(jg) Andrew Gilbert Zissu (KIA)
          Lt(jg) Norman Lee Roggow (KIA)
          Lt(jg) Donald Findling Wolfe (KIA)
          ATC Roland Robert Pineau (KIA)
          Seaman Raul Antonio Guerra (KIA)

On the morning of the 8th an E-1B Tracer (call sign Sea Bat 700) was launched from the *Oriskany* on a combat mission over the Gulf of Tonkin. The Tracer was often used to monitor strikes over North Vietnam and provide MiG warnings and other intelligence. Instead of landing back on board the *Oriskany*, Lt Zissu landed at Chu Lai and refuelled for another mission. On board the aircraft in addition to the normal crew was Seaman R A Guerra who was listed as a Journalist Petty Officer, Third Class. He was probably accompanying the mission in order to write a story for one of the official newspapers or newsletters that abounded in Southeast Asia during the war. The crew took off from Chu Lai in poor weather conditions and, as planned, flew towards Da Nang where the aircraft would then make straight for the *Oriskany*. Da Nang radar monitored the aircraft as it approached from Chu Lai but radar contact was lost as the aircraft approached the airfield. Radar contact was briefly re-established showing the aircraft about 10 miles northwest of Da Nang close to mountainous terrain. Sea Bat 700 was instructed to turn right immediately, which the crew acknowledged, but radio and radar contact was lost with the aircraft moments later. An extensive SAR mission was launched despite low cloud, poor visibility and driving rain. Eventually wreckage was spotted by a SAR helicopter crew on a cliff face on Monkey Mountain but the terrain was so difficult that it was not possible to reach the wreck site to recover the crew's remains. There was no doubt that all the occupants had died instantly in the tragedy.

C-130B   61-2649   773 TAS, 463 TAW, USAF, Clark
          Lt Col Christopher Braybrooke (KIA)
          Maj Robert William Anderson (KIA)
          Capt Scott McClelland Burkett (KIA)
          A1C Terry Michael Rehm (KIA)
          A2C Ronald Paul Ruyf (KIA)
          19 crew/passengers, names unknown (KIA)

A C-130 Hercules took off from Phu Bai airfield near Hué for the short flight to Da Nang. The weather was poor with low cloud and ground fog and 10 minutes after taking off the aircraft flew into a mountain about 15 miles to the southeast of Phu Bai. The aircraft struck the mountain about 150 feet below its 1,850 feet summit and all 24 on board were killed in the accident. The wreckage was discovered two days later.

F-4C   63-7499   557 TFS, 12 TFW, USAF, Cam Ranh Bay
          1Lt David E Wieland (KIA)
          Lt Col E G Weaver (survived)

A Phantom suffered a fuel system malfunction that resulted in both engines flaming out simultaneously. Both the crew ejected but one of them was killed in the accident.

F-4C   63-7645   433 TFS, 8 TFW, USAF, Ubon
          2 crew, names unknown (survived)

Another Phantom was lost on the 8th during a CAP mission when two aircraft were involved in a mid-air collision, one of which had to be abandoned. The crew was probably Capt D R Calvert and Lt J V Macnab.

9 October 1967

A-4E   152085   VA-164, USN, USS *Oriskany*
          Lt(jg) L J Cunningham (survived)

A flight of Skyhawks attacked a pontoon bridge at Nao Quan in North Vietnam. A few minutes after the aircraft crossed the coast on their way back to the carrier, Lt Cunningham heard his engine suddenly flame out. The pilot attempted to relight the engine several times without success and at 3,000 feet he decided to eject. He was later picked up by a Navy helicopter. It was assessed that the aircraft may have been hit by ground fire as it was pulling up from its attack on the target as the bridge was well defended by AAA, automatic weapons and small arms fire.

F-105D   60-0434   34 TFS, 388 TFW, USAF, Korat
          Maj James Arlen Clements (POW)

Another Thunderchief fell victim to a MiG during a Rolling Thunder strike on North Vietnam. A formation of aircraft was flying at 15,000 feet en route to bomb the railway at Quang Hein when it was jumped by several MiG-21s. One of the F-105s was hit in the tailpipe by an Atoll missile about 25 miles northwest of Thai Nguyen. Maj Clements flew northeast for about 15 miles

before he was forced to eject. He was captured and imprisoned until the Operation Homecoming release of 14 March 1973. Sadly, James Clements died of cancer on 27 March 1997. His aircraft, 60-0434, was called 'Damn you Charlie Brown'.

12 October 1967

O-1G   51-12098   19 TASS, 504 TASG, USAF, Bien Hoa
          Maj W Siebert (survived)

During a visual reconnaissance mission near Khu Tru Mat, 10 miles north of Bien Hoa, a Bird Dog was hit in the engine by small arms fire. Maj Siebert was badly injured during the ensuing crash landing but was recovered by an Army helicopter.

F-4C   64-0710   557 TFS, 12 TFW, USAF, Cam Ranh Bay
          Capt Thomas Gardner Derrickson (KIA)
          1Lt John Kay Hardy (KIA)

A flight of Phantoms was conducting an armed reconnaissance just north of the DMZ at night when it ran into trouble. As the two aircraft were following Route 101 near Xuan Hoa, 15 miles north of the DMZ, they spotted a target and the leader commenced an attack. Shortly afterwards the wingman saw a flash on the ground followed by a fire. It was assumed that the aircraft had either been shot down, as their was intense ground fire at the time, or had flown into the ground during the attack.

C-130A   57-0467   21 TAS, 374 TAW, USAF, Naha
          Capt Reed (survived)
          4 crew, names unknown (survived)

Conditions at the airstrip at Dak To (like many other airstrips in South Vietnam) were often chaotic with US Army and ARVN soldiers operating on or close to the airfield, construction work taking place adjacent to the runway and aircraft parked in confined spaces. Twice in September, C-130s had collided with Army trucks at Dak To and on 12 October a Hercules hit a bulldozer that had moved onto the runway just as the aircraft was taking off. The bulldozer driver was killed and although the Hercules eventually landed safely at Cam Ranh Bay, it had to be scrapped as it was deemed to be unrepairable with the resources available.

13 October 1967

F-4B   150477   VMFA-323, MAG-13, USMC, Chu Lai
          Lt Col Edison Wainwright Miller (POW)
          1Lt James Howie Warner (POW)

The CO of VMFA-323 was shot down when he was diverted to attack two tracked vehicles that had been seen just north of the DMZ. As Lt Col Miller was pulling up from his attack, the aircraft was hit by 37mm AAA. Edison Miller headed south but both crew had to eject just inland from Cap Mui Lay, while still over the DMZ buffer zone. Aircrew who came down within the buffer zone normally stood a good chance of being rescued but luck was not on their side on the 13th and both Miller and Warner were soon captured and imprisoned. Edison Miller and Cdr W E Wilber alienated themselves from the rest of the POWs by making propaganda tapes and cooperating with the North Vietnamese in other ways while in prison. Lt Col Miller was eventually released on 12 February and Warner on 14 March 1973.

14 October 1967

RA-3B   144844   VAP-61, USN, Cubi Point
          Lt Cdr Robert Reddington Vaughan (KIA)
          Lt(jg) M M Moser (survived)

The RA-3Bs of VAP-61 from Cubi Point made frequent deployments to Da Nang to fly reconnaissance missions over North Vietnam and Laos. On the 14th an aircraft was detailed to fly a daylight photographic reconnaissance along the North Vietnamese coast. When the aircraft reached a point about 15 miles south of Thanh Hoa it encountered ground fire and sustained damage to the fuselage. Lt Cdr Vaughan flew out to sea to find a SAR destroyer but the aircraft crashed about 10 miles from the coast. Lt Moser ejected safely and was rescued by a Navy helicopter but Lt Cdr Vaughan did not survive.

The most welcome sight that a downed airman could hope for was a hovering helicopter and a PJ on his way down to assist in the rescue. The HH-53 arrived in Southeast Asia in September 1967 and 10 of these huge helicopters were lost on SAR missions during the war. USAF

15 October 1967

F-4C   63-7538   480 TFS, 366 TFW, USAF, Da Nang
Col R W Maloy (survived)
Capt W S Paul (survived)

A flight of Phantoms from Da Nang was sent on an armed reconnaissance mission that resulted in an attack on a military storage area on the coast about eight miles southeast of Dong Hoi. As Col Maloy dived on the target his aircraft was hit by AAA, which caused the starboard engine to fail. The aircraft sped out to sea but it soon became obvious that it was not going to reach Da Nang and the crew ejected about five miles off the coast. They were both rescued by a USAF helicopter.

C-130E   64-0548   50 TAS, 314 TAW, USAF, Ching Chuan Kang
Capt Erie Lawrence Bjorke (KIA)
1Lt James Randall Hottenroth (KIA)
TSgt Edward Mosley (KIA)
A2C John Herbert Snyder (KIA)
Sgt Charles Lynn Baney, US Army (KIA)
1 crew, name unknown (survived)

During a resupply mission to the Marine Corps base at Khe Sanh, a Hercules crashed short of the runway during a GCA and caught fire, killing all but one of the crew. The aircraft was attempting to deliver a load of sandbags by flying low and slow over the runway and pushing them out of the back. The sandbags were needed as part of a major reconstruction programme at the base and had to airdropped as the runway was being rebuilt. The weather was poor at the time with a low cloud base and the accident was thought to have been due to pilot error rather than enemy action. Sgt Baney was a US Army loadmaster. The only survivor was the aircraft commander who escaped through one of the cockpit windows.

15/16 October 1967

RF-4C   65-0855   12 TRS, 460 TRW, USAF, Tan Son Nhut
Capt Richard Duane Appelhans (KIA)
Capt George William Clarke (POW – died)

As night fell a reconnaissance Phantom from Tan Son Nhut flew north to perform a mission over the South Vietnamese border with Laos to the west of Khe Sanh. Not only was the area a major component of the Ho Chi Minh Trail but it was also becoming apparent that North Vietnamese forces were using the region to threaten the Marine Corps bases in Military Region I. Radio and radar contact was lost with the RF-4C when the aircraft was flying over Saravane province in Laos, about 12 miles west of Khe Sanh. A SAR mission was instigated but the results were negative. However, the three American prisoners who were released early in 1968 reported that they had seen George Clarke alive in a POW camp, although this was later refuted. Neither Clarke nor Appelhans emerged when the North Vietnamese released their prisoners in 1973 and they were both later presumed dead.

16 October 1967

O-1E   56-2503   20 TASS, 504 TASG, USAF, Da Nang
Maj M H Alexander (survived)

An O-1 from Da Nang was flying a visual reconnaissance sortie and was hit by small arms fire as it was approaching to land at an airstrip near An Hoa, 17 miles south of Da Nang. The aircraft crash-landed short of the airstrip but the pilot was only slightly injured.

F-105D   60-0461   469 TFS, 388 TFW, USAF, Korat
1 pilot, name unknown (survived)

A Thunderchief suffered an undercarriage malfunction as it retracted its wheels following take off. The problem could not be resolved and as it was deemed to be unsafe to attempt a landing the pilot ejected near the airfield.

17 October 1967

F-105D   60-0425   34 TFS, 388 TFW, USAF, Korat
Maj Dwight Everett Sullivan (POW)

F-105D   62-4326   34 TFS, 388 TFW, USAF, Korat
Maj Donald Eugen Odell (POW)

F-105D   61-0205   34 TFS, 388 TFW, USAF, Korat
Capt Anthony Charles Andrews (POW)

On the 17th the Korat Wing flew a major Rolling Thunder strike against the Dap Cau railway yards near Bac Ninh, 15 miles northeast of Hanoi. The raid turned out to be a costly affair for the USAF with three aircraft lost and three pilots taken prisoner. All three aircraft came from Hotrod flight of the 34th TFS. The flight approached the target at 19,000 feet but ran into an intense barrage of radar directed 85mm anti-aircraft fire. Maj Sullivan's and Maj Odell's aircraft were both hit at 19,000 feet as they rolled in to attack the target. About a minute later Maj Andrews dived down to drop his bombs and was pulling up through 6,000 feet when his aircraft was hit by smaller calibre flak. All three pilots ejected from their aircraft and landed close to the railway yard. After more than five years of imprisonment the three airmen were released together on 14 March 1973. Anthony Andrews later retired from the Air Force and flew for a major airline. Donald Odell had spent 10 years flying F-86, F-102 and F-106 interceptors before converting to the F-105 in July 1967. He was on his 17th mission when he was shot down. After his release Odell gave a graphic account of the torture and death of at least two American prisoners at the hands of Cuban interrogators who were even more brutal than the North Vietnamese guards. F-105D 61-0205 was painted as 'Mr Blackbird' while with the 34th.

A-4E   152038   VA-155, USN, USS Coral Sea
Lt(jg) Frederick John Fortner (KIA)

A section of Skyhawks was assigned to attack a military storage site near Dao Cai Bau island, 20 miles northeast of Hon Gay. The attack was made using 2.75 inch rockets but as Lt Fortner pulled up from his dive on the target his aircraft was seen to be trailing smoke and streaming fuel. The pilot turned for the open sea but then radioed that his controls were locked. The aircraft crashed and Lt Fortner was not seen to eject. The cause of the loss was attributed to a malfunction of one of the 2.75 inch rockets that resulted in a fuel or hydraulics fire. On 3 November 1988 the Vietnamese returned the mortal remains of Lt Fortner.

O-1E   probably 56-2601 21 TASS, 504 TASG, USAF, Nha Trang
2 crew, names unknown (survived)

A Bird Dog FAC aircraft was destroyed in an accident in South Vietnam.

18 October 1967

RF-101C   56-0212   20 TRS, 432 TRW, USAF, Udorn
Maj Nicholas A Pishvanov (survived)

A Voodoo was shot down during a reconnaissance mission over the Ho Chi Minh Trail in southern Laos. The aircraft was flying straight and level at 480 knots at 500 feet when it was hit by ground fire. Maj Pishvanov ejected a few seconds later and was lucky to be picked up by a USAF rescue helicopter. This Voodoo, like many that saw service in Vietnam, had previously served with the 66th TRW based at Laon in France.

A-4E   152048   VA-164, USN, USS Oriskany
Lt Cdr John Frederick Barr (KIA)

A raid on the Haiphong shipyards was supported by an Iron Hand flight provided by VA-164. The flight engaged a SAM site close to Haiphong but the SAM battery was protected by numerous anti-aircraft gun positions. As Lt Cdr Barr dived on the target his aircraft was hit by AAA and exploded. No parachute was seen and it was assumed he was killed in the aircraft. The remains of John Barr were returned in April 1988 and September 1989.

19 October 1967

F-4B   151457   VMFA-542, MAG-13, USMC, Chu Lai
Maj Glenn Gates Jacks (KIA)
1Lt Fred Ernest MacGeary (KIA)

A Marine Corps Phantom suffered an engine failure as it was taking off from Chu Lai on a strike mission. The aircraft crashed and both the crew were killed.

21 October 1967

F-100D   56-2965   612 TFS, 37 TFW, USAF, Phu Cat
Capt Clarence Joseph Hemmel (KIA)

A Super Sabre was lost during a close air support mission near Thanh Binh on the coast, about 30 miles southeast of Da Nang. Capt Hemmel's aircraft was probably hit by ground fire as it flew out over the coast and crashed into the sea. There was no sign of an ejection and it was thought that the pilot might have been wounded.

KA-3B   142655   Detachment G, VAH-4, USN, USS Oriskany
4 crew, names unknown (survived)

The Skywarrior was fitted with JATO bottles in the rear fuselage that were sometimes used to give extra thrust for heavy weight take offs. As a KA-3B tanker was taking off from the Oriskany on a logistics flight the JATO bottles ignited accidentally. Control of the aircraft was lost and the crew ejected safely.

22 October 1967

A-4E   150116   VA-163, USN, USS *Oriskany*
Lt(jg) James Edward Dooley (KIA)

The *Oriskany's* Air Wing mounted a major strike on Haiphong's railway yard on the 22nd. Lt Dooley made his first run to drop his bombs and started to pull up. Another pilot noticed that Dooley's aircraft started to stream fuel and made a gentle descending turn until it crashed into the water at the mouth of the Cua Cam River. Lt Dooley did not eject and may have been incapacitated by ground fire during the attack.

23 October 1967

F-4B   150469   VMFA-122, MAG-11, USMC, Da Nang
Capt W F Tremper (survived)
Maj J L Eddy (survived)

VMFA-122 arrived at Da Nang on 1 September from El Toro MCAS, California and lost their first aircraft on 23 October. An F-4B took off from Da Nang on a ferry flight to the naval air station at Cubi Point in the Philippines. The aircraft crashed during the flight but both crew escaped and were recovered.

F-105D 62-4335   333 TFS, 355 TFW, USAF, Takhli
Maj Rodney W McLean (KIA)

F-105D 61-0181   333 TFS, 355 TFW, USAF, Takhli
1 pilot, name unknown (survived)

An F-105 pilot was killed on the 23rd when two Thuds collided and crashed southwest of Udorn. The other pilot suffered a broken leg and arm during the ejection and was the first airman to be rescued in Southeast Asia by one of the newly-arrived HH-53B Super Jolly Green Giants. The first of these new helicopters had arrived at Udorn for the 37th ARRS in mid-September but the HH-53B was an interim model until the improved HH-53C became available. The new helicopter made its first combat pick-up in enemy-held territory on 25 November when an Air America pilot was rescued. Four HH-53s had arrived by January 1968 and they started to share alert duty with the HH-3s at Nakhon Phanom. The first HH-53Cs began to arrive at Udorn in the third week in February.

24 October 1967

F-105D 62-4262   354 TFS, 355 TFW, USAF, Takhli
Capt M D Scott (survived)

The Takhli Wing had not lost a single aircraft in combat during October until a raid on Kep airfield on the 24th. Capt Scott's aircraft was hit by an 85mm shell as he rolled in to the attack at 13,000 feet over the airfield. Despite a faltering engine, Capt Scott flew east for several minutes until he was eventually obliged to eject. He came down about 45 miles east of Kep and 22 miles inland from Hon Gay and was most fortunate to be rescued by a Navy helicopter.

A-4E   149963   VA-163, USN, USS *Oriskany*
Lt(jg) Ralph Eugene Foulks (survived)

The *Oriskany* flew another raid on the Haiphong railway yard on the 24th with the loss of another aircraft. Lt Foulks had hit the target and was just south of the city heading for the coast at 6,500 feet when, despite jinking to avoid anti-aircraft fire, his aircraft was hit by AAA. The engine failed but the aircraft remained controllable. Lt Foulks attempted to relight the engine without success and ejected about three miles from the coast. He was picked up by a Navy helicopter after having spent less than 10 minutes in the water. Tragically, Ralph Foulks was killed during an armed reconnaissance mission on 5 January 1968.

F-4B   150421   VF-151, USN, USS *Coral Sea*
Cdr Charles Rogers Gillespie (POW)
Lt(jg) Richard Champ Clark (KIA)

F-4B   150995   VF-151, USN, USS *Coral Sea*
Lt(jg) Robert Franchot Frishman (POW)
Lt(jg) Earl Gardner Lewis (POW)

Seven hours after Kep airfield was bombed, the Navy and Air Force made a coordinated attack on Phuc Yen, the first time this major air base had been attacked. The raid was accompanied by several flights of Phantoms that flew CAPs over various points in North Vietnam. Cdr Gillespie, the CO of VF-151, led one of the Phantom sections. As the raid was flying down Thud Ridge, still some 13 miles north of the target, it was engaged by a SAM battery. Cdr Gillespie saw one of the SA-2s and dived to 14,000 feet to avoid it but moments later the aircraft was hit by another missile that the crew had not spotted. The aircraft burst into flames and the hydraulics failed leading to loss of control. The cockpit filled with smoke, the intercom went dead and Cdr Gillespie had to use hand signals to order abandonment. He ejected safely but was not able to tell if his NFO escaped from the aircraft although other members of the section reported seeing two parachutes. It seems that Lt Clark did not appear in any of the POW camps.

The other members of Cdr Gillespie's flight remained overhead near Thud Ridge to provide cover for any possible rescue attempt. About 15 minutes later another Phantom was hit by a SAM. Lt Frishman was flying straight and level at 10,000 feet when it was damaged by a missile that exploded behind the Phantom. One of the engines failed and caught fire but before the crew could take any action another SA-2 exploded just in front of the aircraft. The Phantom immediately rolled out of control and both crew ejected. Lt Frishman thought his NFO, Lt Lewis, had been killed but the pair met up after more than four hours on the ground. However, both men were found and captured by the Vietnamese.

Lt Frishman's arm was badly injured when the SAM exploded but a North Vietnamese doctor operated on the arm removing the elbow joint and shortening the arm by eight inches. On 5 August 1969, after 18 months of constant pain and solitary confinement, Robert Frishman was released along with Seaman D B Hegdahl, who had fallen overboard from the cruiser USS *Canberra* on 6 April 1967, and 1Lt W L Rumble who was shot down on 28 April 1968. The North Vietnamese early release ploy backfired when Frishman and Hegdahl told the world of the torture and atrocious conditions of the POW camps. On 5 September 1969 Lt Frishman was awarded the DFC, the Naval Commendation Medal, the Purple Heart, and several Air Medals. Cdr Gillespie and Lt Lewis were both released on 14 March 1973. Frishman's aircraft was one of those that had been loaned to the USAF in 1963 to train the Air Force's first Phantom crews.

25 October 1967

F-105D 58-1168   354 TFS, 355 TFW, USAF, Takhli
Maj Richard Eugene Smith (POW)

Soon after dawn on the morning of the 25th a total of 21 F-105s from the Takhli Wing carrying 3,000lb bombs struck the Paul Doumer Bridge over the Red River on the outskirts of Hanoi. Maj Smith of Wildcat flight pulled up from dropping his bombs on the target and felt his aircraft being hit by medium calibre anti-aircraft fire. The aircraft started to burn as Maj Smith raced across Hanoi in a vain attempt to reach safety. He was forced to eject about 25 miles west of Hanoi and injured his left leg as he left the aircraft. Richard Smith was shot twice through the thigh during his capture. He was imprisoned until his release on 14 March 1973 after which he returned to flying duties following a period of recuperation. Following retirement he served as National President of the Air Force Association. His son also joined the USAF and flew several missions in the F-16 during Operation Desert Storm. Maj Richard Smith is sometimes reported as being a member of the 333rd TFS when he was shot down. It is possible he was flying an aircraft from another squadron on 25 October. 58-1168 had been flown by another 354th TFS pilot when it shot down a MiG-17 on 19 April 1967 and carried nose art with the name 'Betty's Boy'. The Paul Doumer Bridge was badly damaged with two spans dropped into the water but it was repaired by December and had to be attacked again.

F-105D 59-1735   333 TFS, 355 TFW, USAF, Takhli
Capt Ramon Anton Horinek (POW)

Later in the morning the Taklhi bombers also struck Phuc Yen airfield. Capt Horinek was in the flak suppression flight that had the task of subduing the anti-aircraft gunners who protected the airfield. As he started to dive on the target his aircraft was hit by 57mm AAA. The F-105 caught fire and Capt Horinek ejected practically over Phuc Yen airfield itself. He broke his ankle when he landed and was quickly captured and spent the next five years in various POW camps. He was on his third tour when he was shot down having previously flown tours as an A-1 and FAC pilot. In February 1966 Horinek landed his O-1 Bird Dog at a Special Forces Camp to control air strikes from the ground as the situation was too fluid to follow from the air. He controlled strikes from the Camp for more than 24 hours and was awarded the AFC for his heroism. He converted to the F-105 and returned to Southeast Asia for his third tour. He was released on 14 March 1973 and resumed flying duties until retiring in February 1983.

A-4E   150086   VA-163, USN, USS *Oriskany*
Lt Jeffrey Martin Krommenhoek (KIA)

In the afternoon of the 25th the Navy joined in the attack on Phuc Yen airfield. As a formation of Skyhawks and their escorts approached the target area they were met by a barrage of anti-aircraft fire and SAMs. Lt Krommenhoek's aircraft was last seen by his Squadron just prior to rolling in on the target. After the raid was over he failed to respond to radio calls but a search of the area was impossible due to the intensity of the defences. No further information appears to have been received on the demise of Lt Krommenhoek who was declared killed in action 10 years later.

F-105D 59-1737   469 TFS, 388 TFW, USAF, Korat
Maj Aquillan Friend Britt (KIA)

C-123K 54-0667   315 ACW, USAF, Phan Rang
Capt Jack M Dole (survived)
3 other crew, names unknown (survived)

A Provider from Phan Rang landed at Tan Son Nhut as its penultimate port of call during a long day shuttling around South Vietnam's airfields. As the aircraft was about to take off for its return flight to Phan Rang, the pilot saw a huge thunderstorm directly in its path and decided to abort the flight. He was ordered to taxi along the runway to return to the parking area and had covered about 2,000 feet when the tower warned him to clear the runway immediately. However, before the Provider could turn off the runway it was hit by a Thunderchief as it landed in poor visibility. The F-105's starboard wing sliced through the left side of the C-123's fuselage and the jet's fuselage tore off both the Provider's engines from its port wing. The Thunderchief pilot died in the collision and the burning aircraft tumbled down the runway for another 5,000 feet. All the C-123 crew escaped with burns, although one of them died from his injuries a few days later. Apparently, Maj Britt had been ordered to Tan Son Nhut to take part in a special ceremony to celebrate his 100th mission. F-105D 59-1737 was painted as 'Cherry Boy' during its time with the 469th.

26 October 1967

A-4E   150059   VA-155, USN, USS *Coral Sea*
Cdr Verlyne Wayne Daniels (POW)

The Navy suffered at the hands of the North Vietnamese SAM batteries on the 26th. The first aircraft was lost during another raid on Phuc Yen. Cdr Daniels was leading the second division of Skyhawks towards the target area at about 9,000 feet when a barrage of SAMs was fired at the aircraft. Cdr Daniels started evasive manoeuvres but his aircraft received a direct hit from an SA-2 that hit the rear fuselage. The aircraft was engulfed in flames and went out of control when the hydraulics failed. Cdr Daniels ejected about 15 miles northwest of Thai Nguyen and was soon captured. Verlyne Daniels was a Korean War veteran having flown Skyraiders with VA-155 in 1953 and returned to his old squadron in 1967 as executive officer. He was released on 14 March 1973 and retired from the Navy as a Captain.

A-4E   149959   VA-163, USN, USS *Oriskany*
Lt Cdr John Sidney McCain (POW)

A little later in the morning the *Oriskany* launched a strike on a thermal power plant at Hanoi. Again the target was well

protected by SAM batteries and two aircraft were shot down. Lt Cdr McCain was in the leading division of the raid but as he started his dive on the target his aircraft was hit by an SA-2 which blew most of the starboard wing off. Unable to control the remnants of his aircraft, McCain ejected over Hanoi itself and landed in a small lake in the city. During the high-speed ejection he broke both arms and his right leg and was barely able to save himself from drowning. Lt Cdr McCain was captured and spent the next five years as a prisoner until released on 14 March 1973. After the end of the war, John McCain visited Vietnam to see the lake where he had landed and saw a small monument that celebrated his capture.

John McCain was a member of a well-known Navy family, his father and his grandfather having both been naval admirals and aviators. His grandfather commanded the USS *Ranger* in the later 1930s and became Chief of the Bureau of Aeronautics in 1942 before commanding the Second Carrier Task Force in the Pacific in the final year of the Second World War. His father had flown from the USS *Hancock* to destroy Japanese shipping in Saigon harbour in January 1945. His father later became Commander-in-Chief Pacific Command in July 1968 and as such commanded the Army, Navy and Air Force units that fought the war in Southeast Asia. John McCain had been sat in his A-4 ready to launch from the *Forrestal* on 29 July when the disastrous fire started on that unlucky ship. Incredibly, he had also been on board the *Oriskany* on 26 October 1966 when that ship caught fire. After his release from Vietnam, John Sidney McCain resumed his naval career until he retired to enter politics. He was elected to the House of Representatives in 1982 and 1984 and won the Arizona Senate seat vacated by Barry Goldwater in 1986. During his time in the Senate John McCain was prominent in highlighting the POW/MIA issue. In March 2000 John McCain was narrowly beaten for the nomination as the Republican candidate for President by Senator George Bush.

F-8E 150310 VF-162, USN, USS *Oriskany*
Lt(jg) Charles Donald Rice (POW)

About an hour after Lt Cdr McCain had been shot down, another raid of 25 aircraft attacked the thermal power plant at Hanoi. A flight of four F-8s was assigned to flak suppression but one of the aircraft had to return to the carrier with a malfunction. As the three remaining aircraft approached the target the flight received SAM warnings and the Crusaders took immediate evasive action. Two SAMs were fired and Lt Rice's aircraft was hit by a missile at 15,000 feet as the F-8 was inverted during a split-S manoeuvre. The aircraft's port wing was blown off and the pilot ejected to land three miles northwest of Hanoi. He was quickly captured and imprisoned in the Hanoi Hilton. He was released on 14 March 1973.

27 October 1967

F-105D 62-4231 469 TFS, 388 TFW, USAF, Korat
Col John Peter Flynn (POW)

F-4D 66-7513 435 TFS, 8 TFW, USAF, Ubon
Capt Jon David Black (POW)
1Lt L Conner (KIA)

F-105D 61-0122 357 TFS, 355 TFW, USAF, Takhli
Maj Robert Lewis Stirm (POW)

On the morning of the 27th the USAF flew a major raid against the Canal des Rapides Bridge about five miles northeast of Hanoi. Col John Flynn, the 388th TFW's vice-commander, led the raid. As Col Flynn rolled his Thunderchief at 15,000 feet to dive on the target it was rocked by an explosion from an SA-2 missile. The aircraft became a mass of flames and Col Flynn ejected near the target. He was quickly captured and became the highest-ranking American officer to be held as a POW. With his fellow leaders, Cdr Jim Stockdale and Lt Col 'Robbie' Risner, he organized the POWs and, when conditions relaxed later in the war, formed the Fourth Allied POW Wing.

Within seconds of Col Flynn's Thunderchief being shot down, one of the CAP flight Phantoms was hit by AAA as it orbited over Thud Ridge, about 20 miles northwest of Phuc Yen. The aircraft's port engine caught fire and the pilot ejected a few minutes

later. The fate of the WSO, 1Lt Conner, was unknown at the time, but it appears that he was unable to eject and died in the crash. Capt Black was captured and taken to the Plantation prison in the centre of Hanoi.

About half an hour after the loss of the first two aircraft Maj Stirm was leading Zebra flight over the target when his aircraft was hit by an SA-2 as he was climbing through 12,000 feet to commence his attack. Maj Stirm ejected and was captured as soon as he hit the ground.

Col Flynn had joined the USAAF in 1942 and had flown P-51 Mustangs with the 31st FG in the Italian theatre. He became one of the first US pilots to fly jet fighters when he converted to the P-80 in 1946. He flew P-80s with the 49th FW in the ground attack role during the Korean War and was stationed in the UK and Germany during the 1950s and 1960s. In August 1967, with almost 4,000 hours flying time to his credit, he was assigned to Korat as the vice-commander of the 388th TFW. Following his release from captivity on 14 March 1973 he became the commandant of the Air Command and Staff College and then Inspector General of the USAF. He retired from the Air Force in the rank of Lieutenant General in October 1978 and died on 5 March 1997 after a long illness.

Capt Jon Black was only held in captivity for four months. On 16 February 1968 he and two other POWs were released into the custody of two US peace activists and flown back to the USA. This early release caused huge consternation amongst the other POWs and much criticism was directed at Capt Black in particular. However, he did greatly assist US intelligence agencies by providing detailed maps and sketches from memory of the Hanoi Hilton and the Plantation prisons as well as names of many other US prisoners.

Maj Stirm had converted to the F-105 after many years flying interceptors including the F-86D, F-89, F-94, F-102 and F-106. In at least one record he is reported to have been a member of the 333rd TFS when he was shot down. He was released on 14 March 1973 and flew corporate jets from San Francisco after retirement from the Air Force.

F-105D 61-0126 469 TFS, 388 TFW, USAF, Korat
Capt Russell Edward Temperley (POW)

Later in the day the F-105s were back over Hanoi, this time bombing a storage area about 10 miles southwest of the city. As the formation approached the target area and rolled in, one of the aircraft was damaged by AAA. With the rear end of his aircraft on fire, Capt Temperley turned southwest but only flew for about 10 miles before he was forced to eject. He landed in a tree and was immediately captured and taken to the New Guy Village in the Heartbreak Hotel area of the Hanoi Hilton. The irony of Capt Temperley's situation was that he had taken off from Korat as the airborne spare that accompanied most strikes up to a certain point and then turned back if the rest of the formation was serviceable. On this occasion one of the F-105s had to abort due to mechanical problems and Capt Temperley took his place. He was finally released from prison on 14 March 1973. 61-0126 was painted as 'Miss Texas' and 'Ol' Red Jr' at various times during its career in Southeast Asia.

F-105D 61-0195 354 TFS, 355 TFW, USAF, Takhli
1 pilot, name unknown (survived)

A Thunderchief suffered an engine failure as it was taking off from Takhli. The aircraft caught fire and the pilot was forced to eject.

28 October 1967

F-105D 61-0169 357 TFS, 355 TFW, USAF, Takhli
Lt Col Thomas Henry Kirk (POW)

The attack on Hanoi's bridges continued with another raid on the Paul Doumer Bridge on the 28th. Lt Col Kirk, the CO of the 357th, delivered his bombs and started to pull up from his dive. As the aircraft passed through 6,000 feet it was hit by AAA, either 37mm or 57mm. He immediately turned south but the rear end of the aircraft was on fire and Lt Col Kirk had to eject as he passed over Van La, 10 miles south of Hanoi. He was captured and joined the five other F-105 pilots who had been captured

during the last four days of fighting over North Vietnam. Lt Col Kirk was released on 14 March 1973. Thomas Kirk had flown 49 missions as a T-6 Mosquito FAC pilot in the Korean War before converting to F-86 Sabres at Kimpo. 61-0169 was painted as 'Every man a tiger', 'Hazel' and 'Moose mobile' at various times while at Takhli.

F-105D 62-4356 34 TFS, 388 TFW, USAF, Korat
1 pilot, name unknown (survived)

Another F-105 was lost at Korat through an engine malfunction. The pilot ejected safely.

29 October 1967

F-4B 151423 VMFA-323, MAG-13, USMC, Chu Lai
Maj Daniel I Carroll (survived)
Capt James J Hare (survived)

A strike on a target in the DMZ buffer zone claimed a Marine Corps Phantom on the 29th. Maj Carroll had commenced his second pass on the target near Con Thien when his aircraft was hit in the wing by automatic weapons or small arms fire. The aircraft remained controllable long enough for Maj Carroll to head out to sea near Da Nang where he and his navigator ejected and were picked up by a USAF SAR helicopter.

O-1E 56-2640 21 TASS, 504 TASG, USAF, Nha Trang
Capt G L Nenninger (survived)

A Bird Dog was flying a visual reconnaissance mission under a 600 feet-cloud base 70 miles northeast of Saigon and 15 miles northwest of the town of Bao Loc. As it was forced to fly so low it was easy prey to ground fire and sure enough it was hit in the engine by small arms fire. Capt Nenninger skilfully crash-landed the aircraft and emerged completely unscathed. He was rescued by a USAF helicopter.

30 October 1967

F-4B 150629 VF-142, USN, USS *Constellation*
Lt Cdr Eugene P Lund (survived)
Lt(jg) James R Borst (survived)

During a raid on the Thanh Hoa Bridge several MiGCAP flights were placed to protect the strike force. The northern Phantom CAP flight was vectored onto a flight of four MiG-17s near Haiphong. Lt Cdr Lund shot down one of the MiGs with an AIM-7E Sparrow missile and then positioned his Phantom behind the MiG's wingman and fired another Sparrow. The missile accelerated away from the aircraft but suddenly exploded about 100 feet in front of the Phantom. The crew saw debris from the missile pass down the starboard side of the aircraft and shortly afterwards noted a loss of power from the starboard engine but continued to fight the MiGs for a while. However, the engine would only produce 73 per cent power and it was later discovered that the undercarriage would not lower. Although the Phantom was able to reach the *Constellation*, without a serviceable undercarriage it was unable to complete an arrested landing. Lt Cdr Lund flew alongside the carrier at 5,000 feet and both he and his NFO ejected and were picked up by one of the carrier's helicopters. The Navy flew 97 sorties and dropped 215 tons of bombs on the Thanh Hoa Bridge from April to September 1967 with little to show for its effort. Gene Lund commanded VF-31 in 1972 while Lt Borst later got his pilot's wings but was killed in an A-7 in the USA during an air combat training mission.

A-6A 152601 VMA(AW)-242, MAG-11, USMC, Da Nang
Capt Hugh Michael Fanning (KIA)
Capt Stephen Jay Kott (KIA)

As night fell another bridge in North Vietnam was attacked. Two Marine Corps Intruders from Da Nang were despatched to bomb the Canal des Rapides Bridge near Hanoi. It was thought that immediately after Capt Fanning's aircraft had dropped its bombs it crashed near Gia Lam airport, close to the target. Nothing further was discovered about the loss although an unconfirmed report claimed that Capt Kott had been killed but Capt Fanning had been captured. However, neither men were released during Operation Homecoming but in August 1984 the Vietnamese handed over remains that were claimed to be those

of Hugh Fanning. The remains were buried with full military honours in Oklahoma City but 11 months later Mrs Fanning discovered that the remains were incomplete and, significantly, did not include skull or teeth, which the Marine Corps told Mrs Fanning had been the means of identification. The remains were exhumed and examined by an independent forensic expert who concluded that it was not possible to identify the remains and the identification was rescinded.

2 November 1967

A-4E   151985   VA-164, USN, USS *Oriskany*
                  Lt(jg) Frederic Woodrow Knapp (KIA)

Two Skyhawks from VA-164, led by Lt Knapp, were despatched on an armed reconnaissance mission north of Vinh. The pilots spotted a truck on a road about five miles west of Cho Giat, 30 miles north of Vinh. Lt Knapp commenced a 30-degree dive from 9,000 feet to fire his Zuni rockets. His wingman saw the aircraft continue its dive until it crashed into the ground. There was no apparent attempt to eject and it was thought probable that Lt Knapp had been hit by AAA and incapacitated. A Vietnamese source later claimed that villagers had recovered the remains of the pilot and had buried them nearby. On 14 October 1982 the Vietnamese handed over a Geneva Convention card belonging to Lt Knapp proving that his body had been found at some point but, as yet, no remains have been located.

A-6A   152629   VA-196, USN, USS *Constellation*
                  Lt Cdr Richard David Morrow (KIA)
                  Lt James Joseph Wright (KIA)

An Intruder from the *Constellation* failed to return from a DST seeding mission on the night of the 2nd. The Mk36 DST was a 500lb bomb fitted with a very sensitive magnetic fuse that was armed some 30 minutes after the weapon was dropped. The DSTs were often dropped along the Ho Chi Minh Trail and would explode whenever a truck came close enough to trigger the magnetic fuse. The target was a ferry at Kim Quan but as the A-6 started its bomb run contact with the aircraft was lost near Van La, 10 miles south of Hanoi. There was intense AAA and SAM activity in the target area at the time and three other pilots saw a fireball near Van La, which they presumed was the Intruder being shot down. A search for wreckage or crew proved negative.

3 November 1967

O-2A   67-21328   20 TASS, 504 TASG, USAF, Da Nang
                  Maj John Culbertson Egger (KIA)

The O-2A was gradually replacing many of the O-1s for FAC missions in the higher threat areas such as the region around the DMZ. Maj Egger was controlling an air strike on an anti-aircraft gun position near Vinh Linh, five miles north of the DMZ, when he was shot down and killed. The aircraft was seen to pull up over the gun site but then was hit in the tail by ground fire and burst into flames. The aircraft crashed before the pilot could escape. Remains recovered during an investigation in 1994 were identified as being those of Maj Egger.

KA-3B   147653   Detachment 64, VAH-8, USN,
                  USS *Constellation*
                  Lt Cdr Peter Herman Krusi (KIA)
                  Lt(jg) Hans Hubert Grauert (KIA)
                  Lt Richard W Sanifer (KIA)

A KA-3B Skywarrior was lost with all hands in the Gulf of Tonkin about 55 miles northeast of Dong Hoi as it was launched from the *Constellation* on a tanker mission. As the aircraft was being catapulted down the deck the catapult bridle separated prematurely and the Skywarrior failed to achieve flying speed. The aircraft settled into the water and sank taking with it the pilot and co-pilot. The body of Lt Sanifer was recovered from the sea.

A-37A   67-14503   604 ACS, 3 TFW, USAF, Bien Hoa
                  Maj Phillip Ward Broom (KIA)

The second A-37 Dragonfly lost in Southeast Asia crashed due to pilot error during a close air support mission in Bien Hoa province, South Vietnam. This aircraft was the first example of 39 A-37As to be produced and was originally the USAF's 14th T-37A serial 55-4303 first delivered in 1956. Maj Broom had commenced his tour in Vietnam on 20 August.

4 November 1967

F-4C   64-0795   390 TFS, 366 TFW, USAF, Da Nang
                  Maj R R Lester (survived)
                  1Lt G L Rawlings (survived)

A flight of Phantoms was providing close air support to friendly troops just south of the DMZ when one of the aircraft was lost. The target was enemy troops who were occupying trenches near the coast about 15 miles north of Hué. Maj Lester was pulling up from his third pass over the target when his aircraft was hit in the starboard wing by small arms fire. The crew ejected almost immediately and had to be rescued under fire by an Army helicopter.

5 November 1967

F-105D   61-0173   333 TFS, 355 TFW, USAF, Takhli
                  Capt Billy R Sparks (survived)

F-105F   62-4430   357 TFS, 355 TFW, USAF, Takhli
                  Maj Richard Allen Dutton (POW)
                  Capt Earl Glenn Cobeil (POW – died)

Phuc Yen airfield was once again the target for a major strike by the F-105 force. As usual the bombers were preceded by an Iron Hand flight but it was one of the bombers in the last flight that was shot down first on this raid. Capt Sparks, as Marlin lead, was leaving the target towards the north when three SAMs were fired at his flight about 10 miles west of Thai Nguyen. He took the flight down to low level but his F-105D was hit by at least three 57mm shells. The aircraft started to burn as Capt Sparks jettisoned his cockpit canopy and turned west. When the fire became too bad he ejected at around 24,000 feet about 16 miles to the south of Yen Bai and close to the Red River. His flight set up a RESCAP orbit over his position until a SAR task force arrived. As an HH-3 from the 37th ARRS, piloted by Capt Harry Walker, hovered over tall trees four MiG-17s made a single pass and fired at a Skyraider but the pick-up continued successfully.

Just after Capt Sparks's aircraft was hit, an F-105F Wild Weasel of the Iron Hand flight was also in trouble. The flight was tackling a SAM site to the west of the target when Maj Dutton's aircraft was hit by 37mm anti-aircraft fire that set the rear fuselage alight. Dutton tried to reach high ground but the crew were forced to eject near the Red River about five miles south of Piu Tho. Dutton and Cobeil were captured and flown to Hanoi in a VPAF Mil helicopter. When they arrived at the Hanoi Hilton they were both tortured for several days. Maj Dutton survived the ordeal but Earl Cobeil was beaten senseless by Vietnamese and Cuban interrogators and eventually died in captivity on 5 November 1970 after great suffering. His remains were eventually returned on 4 March 1974 and buried at Arlington. Richard Dutton was on his second tour in Southeast Asia when he was shot down. He had flown 100 missions with the 469th TFS before returning to Thailand to complete about 30 more before being taken prisoner. He was released on 14 March 1973. Like Capt Temperley on 27 October, Dutton and Cobeil had taken off as the airborne spare on 5 November 1967 but continued with the mission when one of the other Wild Weasels was forced to abort. They are recorded as belonging to the 333rd TFS in some records.

6 November 1967

F-105D   62-4286   469 TFS, 388 TFW, USAF, Korat
                  Maj Robert Warren Hagerman (KIA)

The first SAM kill of November took place during a raid on a storage area at Gia Thuo near Hanoi. Maj Hagerman was flying at 19,000 feet over Gia Lam Airport when an SA-2 exploded close to his aircraft, damaging his port wing. The aircraft crashed a few minutes later about 20 miles east of Bac Ninh and there was no indication that the pilot had survived. Thunderchief 62-4286 carried the name 'The Mad Bomber' while with the 469th.

7 November 1967

F-105D   60-0430   469 TFS, 388 TFW, USAF, Korat
                  Maj William Calvin Diehl (POW – died)

The Lang Gia railway yard, 30 miles northeast of Kep, was attacked on the 7th. One of the F-105s was hit by AAA as it was pulling up from its bomb run. With the aircraft's port wing on fire, Maj Diehl headed southeast but had to eject after flying less than 10 miles. It is suspected that he was captured but died at sometime during his imprisonment. Maj Diehl had started his tour at Korat on 23 September.

A-4C   148566   VA-34, USN, USS *Intrepid*
                  Lt(jg) M A Krebs (survived)

As a section of Skyhawks was en route to an armed reconnaissance one of the aircraft was seen to be streaming fuel about 20 miles west of Mu Ron Ma. Lt Krebs turned out to sea as the aircraft's port wing started to burn and he jettisoned his ordnance and headed towards the nearest SAR destroyer. The fire went out for a while but started again so Lt Krebs ejected close to the destroyer and was picked up.

F-4C   63-7600   390 TFS, 366 TFW, USAF, Da Nang
                  Capt Kenneth Fisher (POW)
                  Lt Leon Francis Ellis (POW)

The 390th lost another aircraft during the first week of November during a strike on a 37mm anti-aircraft gun position near Tho Ngoa, 20 miles northwest of Dong Hoi. Capt Fisher put his Phantom into a dive and released his bombs but the aircraft was hit by 57mm AAA immediately afterwards. The aircraft caught fire and broke up and the crew ejected and were captured. Although this was the first time that this crew had flown together, Capt Fisher had flown 57 missions in Southeast Asia and Lt Ellis had flown 53. They were both released on 14 March 1973. Leon Ellis later requalified as a pilot and became an instructor and later a squadron commander of a T-38 training squadron.

8 November 1967

F-100F   56-3764   416 TFS, 37 TFW, USAF, Phu Cat
                  Capt C B Neel (survived)
                  1Lt Guy Dennis Gruters (survived)

The second Misty FAC aircraft to be lost went down during a strike on POL tanks on the coast close to Dong Hoi. Capt Neel was flying over the target at around 6,500 feet when his Super Sabre was hit in the fuselage centre section by AAA and caught fire. He turned out to sea and the crew ejected a short distance from the coast from where they were rescued by a USAF SAR helicopter. Guy Gruters was shot down and captured during a Misty FAC mission on 20 December.

F-4D   66-0250   555 TFS, 8 TFW, USAF, Ubon
                  Maj William S Gordon (survived)
                  1Lt Richard Charles Brenneman (POW)

A flight of Phantoms from the 555th TFS tangled with several MiG-21s during a CAP mission on the 8th. The engagement started at 17,000 feet about 25 miles northeast of Yen Bai and, for Maj Gordon and 1Lt Brenneman, finished about 40 miles to the southwest when the Phantom's tail broke off after having been hit by an air-to-air missile. The crew ejected and parachuted down to earth in hilly terrain near the town of Lao Phou Van, about 25 miles from the border with Laos. A rescue attempt was made but only the pilot, Maj Gordon, could be found and rescued. Richard Brenneman was eventually captured and spent the next five years as a POW until released on 14 March 1973. Maj Gordon had shot down a MiG-17 with 1Lt J H Monsees on 26 October.

F-105D   61-0094   354 TFS, 355 TFW, USAF, Takhli
                  Capt Lawrence Gerald Evert (KIA)

A Rolling Thunder strike took place on the Dai Loy railway bypass just to the west of Phuc Yen on the 8th. During the attack one of the F-105s was hit by AAA and crashed near the target. There was no evidence to suggest that Capt Evert survived as he was not seen to eject from the aircraft before it hit the ground.

9 November 1967

F-4C 64-0751 480 TFS, 366 TFW, USAF, Da Nang
Lt Col John William Armstrong (KIA)
1Lt Lance Peter Sijan (POW – died)

As part of the night interdiction effort against the Ho Chi Minh Trail, the CO of the 480th TFS took off to bomb a ford at Ban Loboy in southern Laos, about 25 miles northwest of the DMZ. As Lt Col Armstrong was making his second pass over the target, his aircraft was engulfed in a ball of flame as it was either hit by 37mm AAA or damaged by the premature detonation of its own bombs. Armstrong probably reckoned that he had a better chance of making it to the Thai border to the west rather than attempt to fly eastwards towards Da Nang. In the event the aircraft crashed a few minutes later near Ban Thapachon about 50 miles short of the Thai border. Lt Col Armstrong was probably killed in the crash but 1Lt Sijan ejected and started an epic struggle for survival that lasted until his death three months later. Sijan was badly injured when he landed in the Laotian jungle and narrowly missed being rescued by helicopter but managed to evade capture for six weeks despite being unable to walk and while suffering from shock and starvation. Crawling through jungle and rugged terrain his only thought was to reach friendly forces but he was eventually captured around Christmas by North Vietnamese forces and taken to a holding camp in the jungle. Despite his poor physical condition 1Lt Sijan overpowered one of his guards and crawled into the jungle only to be captured again a few hours later. He was transferred to another camp near Vinh and was interrogated and tortured for several days despite his already pitiful condition. He was taken to the Hanoi Hilton along with two other airmen, Maj R R Craner and Capt G D Gruters, who had been shot down on 20 December and who cared for Sijan as best they could. Gruters had been in Sijan's squadron at the Air Force Academy. Sijan told his two cellmates the story of his evasion and capture as they tried to revive him but he succumbed to pneumonia on 22 January 1968. 1Lt Sijan's remains were returned to the USA on 13 March 1974. Two years later, in March 1976, Lance Sijan was posthumously awarded the Medal of Honor for his invincible courage and extraordinary devotion to duty and the Code of Conduct for POWs. He was the first graduate of the Air Force Academy to receive the Medal of Honor.

10 November 1967

F-4C 64-0669 389 TFS, 366 TFW, USAF, Da Nang
Maj James Sheppard Morgan (KIA)
1Lt Charles Jerome Honeycutt (KIA)

F-4C 64-0834 389 TFS, 366 TFW, USAF, Da Nang
Lt Col Kelly Francis Cook (KIA)
1Lt James Alan Crew (KIA)

Two Phantoms took off from Da Nang for an MSQ-77 drop above cloud on a target near Dong Hoi. The MSQ-77 radar bombing technique was similar to the Marines' use of the TPQ-10 ground-based radar. The aircraft climbed to about 26,000 feet and were tracked on radar but the weather proved unsuitable for their primary target so they were diverted to a secondary target. Radio and radar contact was lost when the aircraft were about 10 miles southeast of Dong Hoi just at the time when the aircraft were to commence their bombing run on the target. Although a North Vietnamese general was quoted in a journal article stating that two F-4s were shot down on this day by a women's militia unit and two airmen were captured, none of the four airmen appear to have survived. The USAF records the loss as probably being due to a mid-air collision although there is little evidence for this theory. In March 1991 the US authorities received remains that were later identified as being those of 1Lt Honeycutt.

11 November 1967

A-1E 52-132569 602 ACS, 56 ACW, USAF, Udorn
Maj William C Griffith (survived)

Two days after the loss of Lt Col Armstrong and 1Lt Sijan, the Sandys from Udorn were still searching for signs of wreckage or survivors. Maj Griffith was orbiting near Ban Loboy close to where the Phantom had gone down as his leader, Lt Col Ralph Hoggatt, descended to check out a radio contact. Suddenly Griffith's Skyraider was hit by 37mm AAA and burst into flames. Maj Griffith managed to fly a few miles to the south before ejecting from his crippled aircraft. Lt Col Hoggatt attacked enemy gun positions close to Grifiths and he diverted the SAR helicopters to his location. As Maj Griffith was caught in a tree, a PJ, A1C Roy Taylor, was lowered from an HH-3E to cut him free. Lt Col Hoggatt resumed his search for Armstrong and Sijan despite damage to his own aircraft but had to return to Udorn without locating either of the missing men. Ralph Hoggatt, a veteran of 204 combat missions, was awarded the AFC for his actions on this day.

14 November 1967

U-10A 63-13101 5 ACS, 14 ACW, USAF, Nha Trang
2 crew, names unknown (survived)

One of the 5th ACS's U-10 Couriers hit a truck and was destroyed when taking off from Cu Chi on a psychological warfare mission.

15 November 1967

O-1G 51-16876 22 TASS, 504 TASG, USAF, Binh Thuy
Capt E F Saunders (survived)
1 crew, name unknown (survived)

An O-1 Bird Dog had its engine put out of action by ground fire while on an FAC mission over an island in the mouth of the Mekong Delta, 15 miles east of Soc Trang. Capt Saunders crash-landed his aircraft near the village of Tie Can and he and his observer were rescued by an Army helicopter.

C-130E 62-1865, 63-7827 776 TAS, 314 TAW, USAF, Ching Chuan Kang

One of the bloodiest battles of the war was fought in the Central Highlands near Dak To between 3 and 22 November. After three weeks of heavy fighting the US 4th Infantry Division and the 173rd Airborne Brigade forced the NVA to retire, leaving many casualties on both sides. Having noted the pattern of early morning arrivals of C-130s at Dak To, the North Vietnamese waited until three Hercules were sitting on the parking ramp before firing 10 rockets into the area. Two Hercules were hit and soon engulfed in flames. A third aircraft was backed out of the way of the inferno by Capt J H Glenn and his crew during a lull in the attack and a fourth aircraft, which had landed moments before the first rounds exploded, took off again rapidly. The attack also destroyed 17,000 gallons of fuel and over 1,300 tons of ordnance when the ammunition dump was hit by artillery. The airfield was closed for two days and when it re-opened only one C-130 was permitted on the ground at a time.

16 November 1967

F-4B 152987 VF-151, USN, USS *Coral Sea*
Lt Cdr Paul Henry Schulz (POW)
Lt(jg) Timothy Bernard Sullivan (POW)

The *Coral Sea* launched a Rolling Thunder strike on the Hai Duong railway bridge but lost a Phantom on the way to the target. Lt Cdr Shulz was leading the flak suppression flight at 12,000 feet when suddenly four SAMs shot up through an overcast below the formation. Although Lt Cdr Schulz had started evasive manoeuvres, it was too late and his aircraft was hit by an SA-2. The aircraft was riddled with shrapnel all along its port side causing a fire and engine failure. Seconds later the entire tail unit disintegrated and the crew ejected, landing near Vinh Ninh, 15 miles southeast of their target. Both men were captured and imprisoned until their release on 14 March 1973.

17 November 1967

F-105D 62-4258 354 TFS, 355 TFW, USAF, Takhli
Maj Charles Edward Cappelli (KIA)

The next four days proved extremely costly for the USAF and Navy over North Vietnam with a total of 17 aircraft lost in combat. Nine of these aircraft were lost during strikes on airfields or SAM sites. An early morning strike on Bac Mai airfield on the southern outskirts of Hanoi resulted in the first loss of the 17th. Maj Cappelli was climbing through 14,000 feet over the target when his aircraft was badly damaged by a nearby SAM detonation. He tried to nurse his crippled aircraft back to Thailand but it crashed near Hoa Binh, nearly 40 miles to the southwest of Hanoi. A wingman observed Maj Cappelli ejecting from the aircraft and reported that the parachute descent looked normal. However, there is no evidence that Charles Cappelli was ever captured alive as he was not seen in any of the prison camps by other POWs. On 15 December 1988 remains were returned to the US that were identified on 5 May 1989 as being those of Maj Cappelli.

A-4C 149546 VA-34, USN, USS *Intrepid*
Lt Wilson Denver Key (POW)

A formation of A-4s were on an Iron Hand strike in the Hanoi area and were egressing from their target, a barge construction yard, when one of the aircraft went down. Lt Key was the wingman to Lt Cdr Teter and the pair encountered SAMs on the way to the Hanoi area. They evaded the first volley of missiles and attacked an active SAM site, which they destroyed. As they were heading back towards the coast the section was tracked by another missile site and SAMs were launched. Lt Key put his aircraft into a hard right turn at 1,200 feet but an SA-2 struck his aircraft and he was forced to eject at about 700 feet after the engine failed. 'Denny' Key landed safely about 10 miles southeast of Hanoi and was captured after a few minutes on the ground. Lt Key was shot down on his 90th mission and was eventually released from captivity on 14 March 1973.

F-4B 151488 VF-161, USN, USS *Coral Sea*
Cdr William Darrell McGrath (KIA)
Lt Roger Gene Emrich (KIA)

About an hour after Lt Key had been shot down another wave of aircraft headed towards the Hanoi area. One of the flak suppression aircraft was flown by Cdr McGrath of VF-161. The aircraft came under fire from a SAM battery when they were still 18 miles southeast of Hanoi. Cdr McGrath took evasive action but his aircraft was seen to be in a spin and passing through 3,500 feet. The other aircrew did not observe any battle damage on the aircraft and had not seen any SAMs or AAA in the aircraft's vicinity. It was thought possible that the pilot had lost control of the aircraft during a high-G SAM evasion manoeuvre resulting in a spin at too low an altitude to recover. There was also the possibility that the aircraft had, in fact been hit by AAA or a SAM, even though none had been seen. F-4B 151488 was flown by Cdr L Page and Lt J C Smith of VF-21 when they shot down a MiG-17 on 17 June 1965.

RF-4C 65-0899 11 TRS, 432 TRW, USAF, Udorn
Maj R F Ross (survived)
Capt F L Hobbs (survived)

An RF-4C was returning from a photographic reconnaissance mission to Bac Giang, northeast of Hanoi, when it was hit by a SAM. Maj Ross had just completed his photo run over the target at 24,000 feet and was jinking in an attempt to throw off the AAA and SAMs. Unfortunately, a missile exploded just underneath the aircraft, badly damaging its tail surfaces. Maj Ross immediately headed towards the coast and he and his navigator ejected safely over the Gulf of Tonkin, about 60 miles south of Haiphong. They were rescued by a Navy helicopter.

EB-66C 54-0473 41 TEWS, 355 TFW, USAF, Takhli
Maj Max Nichols (KIA)
Lt Ted Johnson (KIA)
Maj Karl D Hezel (KIA)
Maj William McDonald (KIA)
Capt Rey L Duffin (KIA)
Capt Robert Peffley (survived)
Capt James Stamm (survived)

Shortly after taking off from Takhli the No 2 engine of an EB-66C failed. Maj Nichols attempted to land and at first it appeared that he would be successful but then the aircraft sank rapidly on the approach and touched down with its wheels up on rough ground about 1,200 feet short of the runway. The aircraft slid along the ground but caught fire and exploded. Only two of the EWOs from the crew of seven escaped the inferno.

F-4C Phantom 63-7680 was a double MiG-killer with the 8th TFW having shot down a MiG-21 during Operation Bolo on 2 January 1967 when flown by Col Robin Olds and 1Lt C Clifton and a MIG-17 on 13 May when flown by another crew. On 20 November 1967 this Phantom was shot down during a raid near the DMZ while flying with the 480th TFS. USAF

18 November 1967

F-105F 63-8295	34 TFS, 388 TFW, USAF, Korat	Maj Oscar Moise Dardeau (KIA)
		Capt Edward William Lehnhoff (KIA)
F-105D 60-0497	469 TFS, 388 TFW, USAF, Korat	Lt Col William N Reed (survived)
F-105D 62-4283	469 TFS, 388 TFW, USAF, Korat	Maj Leslie John Hauer (KIA)
F-105D 62-4221	34 TFS, 388 TFW, USAF, Korat	Col Edward Burke Burdett (POW - died)

A raid on the MiG base at Phuc Yen turned out to be a disaster for the Korat Wing with the loss of four out of the 16 participating F-105s. This raid was flown in poor weather under the direction of the recently-commissioned TSQ-81 bombing navigation radar site at LS85 on Phou Pha Thi mountain in northern Laos. As usual the strike force was preceded by an Iron Hand flight of F-105F Wild Weasels and F-105D bombers. However, the flight was jumped by MiG-21s, one of which fastened onto Maj Dardeau's tail. The MiG fired a missile that hit the Wild Weasel causing it to disintegrate over the village of Van Du near the Song Lo River, some 40 miles northwest of Phuc Yen. It was not known at the time if the crew had ejected but it appears that they did not and their remains were handed over by the Vietnamese on 25 November 1987. As an illustration of the way the return of remains was used as a political tool, the Vietnamese first notified the US that it had located the remains of Dardeau and Lehnhoff in June 1977 and had promised to repatriate them. However, the promise was not fulfilled for another 10 years. Thunderchief 63-8295 was named 'Mugley Other' at the time it was lost.

The remainder of the Iron Hand flight was still under attack by MiGs and one of the bombers, flown by Lt Col Reed, was also hit by an air-to-air missile. Although badly damaged, the aircraft remained flyable and Lt Col Reed headed southwest and crossed into Laos before he was forced to eject about 12 miles northwest of the Pathet Lao stronghold of Sam Neua. Luckily, he was picked up by a USAF SAR helicopter before the Pathet Lao could find him.

The next aircraft to fall during this mission was flown by Maj Hauer, leader of Vegas flight, who was shot down as he approached the target from the north. He was preparing to roll in on his target from 16,500 feet when his aircraft was hit squarely by a SAM and was blown to pieces. Without the protection of the Wild Weasel flight the SAMs had a much better chance of success. Maj Hauer was seen to eject and a beeper signal was heard as he descended in his parachute about 10 miles northwest of Phuc Yen. His flight lost sight of the parachute as it descended into low cloud and nothing more was ever heard of Maj Leslie Hauer. His remains were eventually located and returned by the Vietnamese on 11 September 1990. Thunderchief 62-4283 was named 'Miss M Nookie' during its time at Korat.

The fourth and final aircraft lost during this costly raid was flown by Col Burdett, the wing commander of the 388th TFW. Having received numerous SAM warnings he was taking evasive action at 18,000 feet over Phuc Yen when his aircraft was damaged by a SAM that exploded close by. Col Burdett turned his burning aircraft southwest and ran for home but it crashed about 15 miles west of Hanoi. The pilot ejected and was thought to have been captured but died soon after either from injuries received during the SAM explosion or from the ejection or from torture. The loss of the wing commander and the vice-commander was a crushing blow to the 388th TFW. Edward Burdett's remains were repatriated on 6 March 1974. Col Burdett's aircraft was painted as 'The Fighting Irishman' and 'Wild Child' during its time in Southeast Asia.

19 November 1967

F-105F 63-8349	333 TFS, 355 TFW, USAF, Takhli	Maj Gerald C Gustafson (survived)
		Capt Russell F Brownlee (survived)

If the 18th was a bad day for the US airmen, the 19th was going to be even worse. The day started badly with yet another Wild Weasel lost during an attack on a SAM site. An Iron Hand flight was attacking a SAM battery near Cat Ngoi, 7 miles west of Hanoi, when Maj Gustafson's aircraft was hit by a missile as it was turning near the target at 9,000 feet. Fortunately the aircraft did not catch fire and Maj Gustafson was able to exit the area and head towards home. Escorted by another F-105F flown by Maj Bruce Stocks, he crossed into Laos and he and his 'Bear' ejected near the village of Sopka, 20 miles west of Sam Neua. Maj Stocks, despite being injured and his aircraft damaged by a near miss by a SAM, flew cover over Gustafson and Brownlee until rescue aircraft arrived and then refuelled from a tanker before landing his badly damaged Thud at Takhli. An Air America helicopter rescued the two airmen. Maj Gustafson continued to complete 101 missions in Southeast Asia but not before he and Capt Brownlee had to eject from another F-105 on 6 January 1968. Maj Stocks was awarded the AFC and the Korren Kolligian Jnr Trophy for 1967 for his actions in protecting his two colleagues.

F-4B 150997	VF-151, USN, USS *Coral Sea*	Lt Cdr Claude Douglas Clower (POW)
		Lt(jg) Walter O Estes (KIA)
F-4B 152304	VF-151, USN, USS *Coral Sea*	Lt(jg) James Erlan Teague (KIA)
		Lt(jg) Theodore Gerhard Stier (POW)

Switchbox flight from VF-151 was providing TARCAP coverage in the vicinity of Haiphong during strikes by aircraft from the *Intrepid* on airfields and bridges near the city. The two Phantoms were stalking a flight of MiGs when they were themselves engaged by other MiGs just south of Haiphong. The MiGs were from Gia Lam but were operating undetected from a forward airfield at Kien An. Lt Cdr Clower's aircraft was hit by an air-to-

air missile and its starboard wing was blown off. Lt Cdr Clower ejected and was captured but Lt Estes may have been injured as he was not seen to escape. Moments later Lt Teague's aircraft was also hit and damaged. The NFO, Lt Stier, thought that the aircraft was hit by cannon fire from a MiG but it is also possible that the aircraft was damaged by debris from Lt Cdr Clower's aircraft, which had just exploded close by. Lt Stier, a veteran of 155 missions, ejected but his pilot was not seen to escape from the aircraft. Lt Cdr Clower and Lt Stier were both released from captivity in 14 March 1973 and the remains of Lt Estes and Lt Teague were repatriated on 30 September 1977. Lt Cdr Clower's aircraft was one of the 27 Navy F-4Bs that had been loaned to the USAF for use by the 4453rd CCTW in 1963.

F-100D 56-3040	510 TFS, 3 TFW, USAF, Bien Hoa	Capt Duncan Padgett Smyly (KIA)

It had been almost two months since the 3rd TFW had lost a Super Sabre in combat. The run of good fortune came to end on the 19th when Capt Smyly was shot down and killed during a close air support mission near Loc Ninh, 60 miles north of Saigon. He had been scrambled to assist friendly troops who were engaged by a strong enemy force and was making his second pass dropping napalm when his aircraft caught fire and crashed, probably as the result of small arms fire.

RF-4C 65-0880	11 TRS, 432 TRW, USAF, Udorn	Lt Col Vernon Peyton Ligon (POW)
		Capt David Edward Ford (POW)

The SA-2 claimed a second victim on the 19th when a reconnaissance Phantom was shot down about seven miles southwest of Phuc Yen. Lt Col Ligon, the CO of the 11th TRS, had received SAM warnings and was jinking his aircraft at 15,000 feet but to no avail. The SAM exploded near the aircraft and damaged its tail surfaces forcing the crew to eject a few monments later. Both men were captured and taken to the Hoa Lo POW camp. Unfortunately, for Vern Ligon capture and imprisonment was not a new experience. He had joined the Army Air Corps in March 1942 and had flown P-47 Thunderbolts with the 362nd FG until he was shot down over Brussels on his 35th mission in November 1943. He escaped from a German Stalag but was quickly recaptured and held until his release in May 1945. He continued a long and varied Air Force career that included command of a SAC B-47 squadron. He was shot down on his 26th mission in his second war but the experiences of imprisonment in Germany could not prepare him for the new horrors he had to face in the North Vietnamese prison camps. Lt Col Ligon and Capt Ford were both released on 14 March 1973.

F-105D 58-1170	34 TFS, 388 TFW, USAF, Korat	Maj Raymond Walton Vissotzky (POW)
F-105D 61-0208	469 TFS, 388 TFW, USAF, Korat	Capt Harrison Hoyt Klinck (KIA)

Later in the day the Korat Wing flew a raid against a barge construction yard at Thuy Phoung on the Red River just north of

Hanoi. Barges and other shallow-draught vessels were critical elements in North Vietnam's attempts to resupply its troops in South Vietnam. The barge yard was close to several of the SAM sites that ringed Hanoi and as the strike force approached the target it was met by a volley of missiles. Maj Vissotzky was jinking at 16,000 feet but failed to shake one of the missiles, which exploded close to his aircraft. The aircraft crashed 15 miles west of Hanoi and Maj Vissotzky ejected and was captured. Raymond Vissotzky was released from captivity on 14 March 1973.

Another formation of F-105s was a few minutes behind the first wave. The SAMs were still very active and Capt Klinck's aircraft was hit by a missile at 11,000 feet just south of the target. The aircraft headed north and crashed near Vinh Yen, almost 20 miles away from where it was hit. Capt Klinck may have been wounded as he was not seen to eject from the aircraft. 61-0208 was painted as 'Mr Bulldog' while with the 469th. Four US aircraft had been shot down by SAMs during the day in which 94 SA-2 missile launches had been counted.

F-4C   64-0696   559 TFS, 12 TFW, USAF, Cam Ranh Bay
                   1Lt Charles Carter Nelson (KIA)
                   1Lt S Marenka (survived)

The final combat loss of the day occurred during a night close air support mission. Enemy troops had been spotted eight miles east of Dak To and a flight of Phantoms was scrambled from Cam Ranh Bay. 1Lt Nelson made an attack and was seen to pull up from the target with his aircraft on fire. The WSO ejected and was rescued by an Army helicopter but 1Lt Nelson did not escape and was killed.

F-8C   147004   VF-111, USN, USS Oriskany
                   Lt Edwin Ward Van Orden (KIA)

If the combat losses sustained on the 19th were not bad enough, the Oriskany lost a pilot when his Crusader fell into the water during a faulty catapult launch. This brought the day's tally to nine aircraft and 11 men lost and was one of the worst days of the war for the US air services.

20 November 1967

RF-4C   66-0394   11 TRS, 432 TRW, USAF, Udorn
                    Lt Col J C Scholtz (survived)
                    Capt J Ciminero (survived)

An RF-4C was tasked with photographing targets in and around Hanoi and was pulling up through 12,000 feet just to the west of the city when it was hit by 85mm AAA. Lt Col Scholtz and Capt Ciminero kept the aircraft flying for 80 miles until they were forced to eject just short of the Laotian border and came down near the village of Muong Min. A USAF helicopter dashed in and picked up the crew before they could be captured.

F-4C   63-7680   480 TFS, 366 TFW, USAF, Da Nang
                   Capt John Murray Martin (KIA)
                   Lt James Linsday Badley (survived)

A flight of F-4s from Da Nang was sent to look for a suspected SAM site about five miles north of the DMZ. The flight found the site and began an attack. As Capt Martin was pulling up from his third pass, his aircraft was hit twice in the fuselage by AAA. He turned towards the coast and the WSO ejected safely just as they crossed the beach. However, for some reason, Capt Martin was not able to escape and died when the aircraft hit the sea. John Martin was listed as missing even though it was clear he had not ejected. It was not until September 1990 that Martin's daughter learned of the details of her father's death. Lt Badley returned to operations but was killed on 27 March 1968. F-4C 63-7680 was flown by Col Robin Olds and 1Lt C Clifton on 2 January 1967 when they shot down one of seven MiG-21s during Operation Bolo. This aircraft also shot down a MiG-17 on 13 May 1967 when flown by Lt Col F A Haeffner and 1Lt M R Bever of the 433rd TFS.

F-105D   61-0124   469 TFS, 388 TFW, USAF, Korat
                     Capt William Wallace Butler (POW)

Later in the day the Korat bombers flew a mission to the Lang Lau railway and road bridge. About 20 miles southeast of Yen Bai, while still en route to the target, one of the flights of Thun-

derchiefs was intercepted by MiG-21s that got past the F-4 escorts. Capt Butler's aircraft was in a tight turn at 17,000 feet when it was hit by an air-to-air missile. The aircraft entered an uncontrollable spin and the pilot ejected and was captured. The rest of the F-105 flight jettisoned their bombs and aborted the mission. William Butler was released on 14 March 1973 and later became a veterinary surgeon. When serving with the 34th TFS 61-0124 was painted as 'Eight Ball'.

S-2E   150602   VS-21, USN, USS Kearsarge
                  2 crew, names unknown (KWF)

An S-2E Tracker disappeared over the South China Sea while on a local training flight during one of the Kearsarge's two-week stand-down periods.

23/24 November 1967

RF-4C   65-0844   11 TRS, 432 TRW, USAF, Udorn
                    Maj Brendan Patrick Foley (KIA)
                    Lt Ronald Michael Mayercik (KIA)

An RF-4C disappeared during a weather reconnaissance flight at night over North Vietnam. One report states that the aircraft was shot down near the Plain of Jars in Central Laos, however, no wreckage was ever found. Maj Foley was 48 years of age when he died, well above the average age for a fast jet pilot.

25 November 1967

A-6A   152612   VMA(AW)-242, MAG-11, USMC, Da Nang
                  Lt Col Lewis Herbert Abrams (KIA)
                  1Lt Robert Eugene Holdeman (KIA)

The CO of VMA(AW)-242 and his navigator flew an attack on Kien An airfield near Haiphong on the night of the 25th. Radio and radar contact was lost with the aircraft and a Peking radio broadcast claimed that an aircraft had been shot down in the vicinity of Haiphong. Nothing more was known of the fate of the crew until a joint US and Vietnamese team of investigators excavated a crash site in Haiphong province in 1993 and 1995. Some remains were found at the site and other bone fragments were handed over by villagers. On 26 June 1997 the mortal remains of the two Marine airmen arrived at Travis AFB for final burial at home. Lt Col Abrams was buried at Arlington National Cemetery on 9 July.

C-130E-I   64-0563   Detachment 1, 314 TAW, USAF, Nha Trang

The Vietnam war was a unique testing ground for a myriad of clandestine operations and systems. One of the most important of these programmes was known initially as Combat Spear. Four C-130E-I Combat Talon aircraft (known more popularly as Blackbirds due to their paint scheme and their role) arrived at Nha Trang in December 1966. The unit was designated Detachment 1 of the 314th TAW, code named Stray Goose and was deployed from Ching Chuan Kang AB, Taiwan. The aircraft were highly modified with APQ-115 terrain-following radar, electronic countermeasures systems and the Fulton Recovery System. Their role was to support the operations of the Special Forces and the MACVSOG, one of the most secret organisations in the theatre. The Detachment was redesignated as the 15th ACS in March 1968.

A mortar attack on Nha Trang air base destroyed one of the valuable Combat Talon Hercules and damaged three other aircraft. Thirty rounds were fired during the attack wounding 31 men but causing no fatalities.

O-1G   51-4799   19 TASS, 504 TASG, USAF, Bien Hoa

Another enemy attack took place on an airstrip at Nam Can on the banks of the Song Cua Lon River in the Cau Mau Peninsula, on the very southern tip of South Vietnam. The only aircraft lost was a Bird Dog FAC aircraft.

A-4E   150037   VA-155, USN, USS Coral Sea
                  Cdr William H Searfus (KIA)

As a Skyhawk was taxiing along the deck of the Coral Sea, it was blown over the ramp and into the sea by the jetblast from another aircraft. Sadly, the pilot, who had taken command of VA-155 in June, was unable to escape and drowned when the aircraft sank.

26 November 1967

F-4C   64-0697   390 TFS, 366 TFW, USAF, Da Nang
                   Col Herbert Owen Brennan (KIA)
                   1Lt Douglas Craig Condit (KIA)

A Phantom was lost during a strike on a bridge on Route 137B a few miles north of the Ban Karai Pass and about 20 miles west of Dong Hoi. Col Brennan, the assistant director of operations of the 366th, was making his second attack on the target when his aircraft crashed. Although it was assumed at first that the aircraft had been shot down the F-4 squadrons had also suffered a number of mysterious losses at the moment of bomb release in recent months and suspicion fell on the fuses. Col Brennan's aircraft crashed close to the target and it was assumed that both men had been killed, although a beeper signal was heard after the crash. In 1992 and 1993 investigations on this crash site found wreckage and personal equipment but no remains were discovered.

A-4B   142742   VSF-3, USN, USS Intrepid
                  1 pilot, name unknown (survived)

One of VSF-3's A-4B Skyhawks suffered an engine flameout during a training flight on the 26th. The pilot could not restart the engine and so ejected and was rescued. This was the last aircraft lost by the Intrepid before it sailed for its homeport of Norfolk, Virginia on 9 December.

28 November 1967

O-1G   51-12861   19 TASS, 504 TASG, USAF, Bien Hoa
                    detached to Rach Gia

A Bird Dog was destroyed in a VC mortar attack on the airstrip at Rach Gia on the 28th. This was the second O-1 lost on the ground at Rach Gia, the first aircraft having been destroyed on 10 August 1967.

29 November 1967

F-4C   64-0701   558 TFS, 12 TFW, USAF, Cam Ranh Bay
                   Maj Louis Farr Jones (KIA)
                   1Lt L J Lemoine (survived)

Losses in the Steel Tiger campaign in southern Laos were relatively few during 1967. However, casualties in the region suddenly increased from the end of November to the end of the year. On the 29th a flight of F-4s was attacking a road junction on the Trail near Ban Kala, 30 miles west of Khe Sanh. Maj Jones was pulling up from his second pass over the target when his Phantom was hit by AAA. The rear end of the aircraft caught fire and the aircraft crashed near the town of Sepone. It appears that only the WSO was able to escape from the aircraft and he was rescued soon afterwards by a helicopter.

30 November 1967

C-7B   62-4175   458 TAS, 483 TAW, USAF, Cam Ranh Bay
                   Maj Thomas Dewey Moore (KIA)
                   Maj William Jerome Clark (KIA)
                   SSgt Arturo Delgado-Marin (KIA)
                   SSgt Stanley Joseph Yurewicz (KIA)
                   22 passengers (KIA)

A C-7 Caribou crashed during a routine air transport flight in South Vietnam. As the aircraft approached Qui Nhon the pilot was advised that the weather at the airfield had fallen below safety minima. He replied that he would proceed to Nha Trang where the weather was better but the aircraft hit a mountain at 1,850 feet about five miles south of Qui Nhon. The weather at the time consisted of low cloud and rain that reduced visibility to about two miles. The four crew and 22 passengers, including two US civilians, were killed in the accident.

3 December 1967

F-4B   149440   VMFA-122, MAG-11, USMC, Da Nang
                   2 crew, names unknown (survived)

As a Marine Corps Phantom was taking off from Da Nang on a strike mission one of its tyres blew out causing the aircraft to swerve off the runway. The aircraft was destroyed but the crew survived unscathed.

5 December 1967

F-8C   146907   VF-111, USN, USS *Oriskany*
Lt H J Meadows (survived)

Lt Meadows was flying as escort to a reconnaissance aircraft (probably a Vigilante) that was photographing a section of Route 1A, the main coastal road that ran down virtually the entire length of North Vietnam. As the aircraft finished the photo run and headed out to sea Lt Meadows suddenly lost one of his flight control systems. A fire started in the rear of the aircraft and hydraulic fluid was seen to be streaming from the aircraft. As Lt Meadows flew over the southern SAR destroyer, about 25 miles off the coast to the northeast of Vinh, he lost his remaining flight control and hydraulic systems and the engine failed. He ejected and was rescued by a Navy helicopter. The probable cause of the loss was attributed to automatic weapons fire.

F-105D   59-1758   333 TFS, 355 TFW, USAF, Takhli
Maj Donald Myrick Russell (KIA)

The USAF had suffered very few casualties in the Barrel Roll campaign in northen Laos during the year and, in fact, had not lost an F-105 in this area since January. Maj Russell was leading a flight of four F-105s on an attack on a storage area 15 miles southeast of Sam Neua when his aircraft was hit by AAA. The rear fuselage of the F-105 caught fire and the aircraft entered a spin and crashed close to the target. Maj Russell, who was flying his 59th combat mission, was not observed to escape from the aircraft. Donald Russell's remains and identity tags were recovered during a JTF-FA invesatigation in Laos in May 1994 and positively identified two years later. The remains were flown to Kirtland AFB, New Mexico for burial in Albuquerque.

O-1F   52-2862   19 TASS, 504 TASG, USAF, Bien Hoa
2 crew, names unknown (survived)

A Bird Dog was damaged beyond repair when it veered off the runway as the pilot attempted to avoid a collision with another aircraft.

6 December 1967

EB-66C   54-0462   41 TEWS, 355 TFW, USAF, Takhli
Lt Col Jack M Youngs (KIA)
Capt Larry A Moore (KIA)
1Lt Paul S Krzynowek (KIA)
3 crew, names unknown (survived)

An EB-66C electronic warfare aircraft crashed while landing at Takhli due to a control system failure. Unfortunately, three of the six-man crew were killed in the accident.

7 December 1967

F-4C   64-0768   391 TFS, 12 TFW, USAF, Cam Ranh Bay
Maj R B Ray (survived)
1Lt F M Cerrato (survived)

Hammer 2 was an F-4C flown by Maj Ray and 1Lt Cerrato on a strike in the Steel Tiger zone of southern Laos. The aircraft was attacking a truck that had been spotted near Ban Talan Nua and was pulling up from the first pass when the Phantom was hit by ground fire. Ray and Cerrato ejected almost instantly and evaded enemy troops until they were picked up safely by a USAF helicopter.

8 December 1967

C-123K   54-0582   310 ACS, 315 ACW, USAF, Phan Rang
5 crew, names unknown (survived)

A Provider crashed in South Vietnam and was destroyed. The accident was attributed to pilot error.

10 December 1967

F-4C   64-0807   389 TFS, 366 TFW, USAF, Da Nang
Maj G L Nordin (survived)
1Lt R R Reddick (survived)

A Phantom was approaching Da Nang after a ferry flight, probably from Clark AFB in the Philippines. As the aircraft was descending through 3,000 feet near Giang Hoa, 15 miles southwest of the airfield, it was hit by ground fire. The crew ejected and were picked up by an Army helicopter that was in the vicinity.

12 December 1967

O-2A   67-21369   22 TASS, 504 TASG, USAF, Binh Thuy
2 crew, names unknown (survived)

The fifth Cessna O-2A to be destroyed in Vietnam was lost during a landing accident without injury to either of the crew.

13 December 1967

F-4C   64-0774   558 TFS, 12 TFW, USAF, Cam Ranh Bay
Capt W T Sakahara (survived)
1Lt Robert Elwood Bennett (KIA)

Two Phantoms were despatched from Cam Ranh Bay on a landing zone preparation mission on the northern bank of the Mekong River six miles north of Phu Vinh. One of the aircraft was just finishing its third pass when it was shot down, probably by a .50 calibre weapon. The aircraft crashed on the south bank of the river after both crew had ejected. Capt Sakahara and 1Lt Bennett both landed in the river but unfortunately Robert Bennett was dragged under the water by his parachute before rescuers could reach him. His body was never found.

C-7A   61-2387   535 TAS, 483 TAW, USAF, Vung Tau
Capt Kenneth L Chrisman (survived)
2Lt R Callahan (survived)

The first USAF C-7 Caribou lost to enemy action was shot down by VC ground fire while on a resupply flight. A single bullet severed a fuel manifold causing the engines to stop through fuel starvation. The pilot crash-landed the Caribou in a rice paddy near Binh Thuy and all the crew escaped.

14 December 1967

F-105D   59-1750   469 TFS, 388 TFW, USAF, Korat
Capt James Eldon Sehorn (POW)

The Paul Doumer Bridge was once more the target for an F-105 strike. Capt Sehorn's aircraft was lost when it was hit by AAA as it pulled up off the target. He ejected and was captured to spend over five years as a POW. Capt Sehorn was only on his seventh mission when he was shot down. After repatriation on 14 March 1973 James Sehorn continued his military career and eventually retired with the rank of Brigadier General in the Air Force Reserve. F-105D 59-1750 was painted as 'The Flying Anvil IV' while at Korat. This raid and another on the same target on 18 December put five consecutive spans of the bridge out of action for many months causing significant disruption to the flow of supplies into Hanoi although a pontoon-type railway bridge was constructed a few miles away by April 1968.

16 December 1967

F-4D   66-7631   555 TFS, 8 TFW, USAF, Ubon
Maj James Frederick Low (POW)
1Lt Howard John Hill (POW)

A Triple Nickel Phantom was lost in a dogfight during an early morning combat air patrol over Kep. Maj Low and 1Lt Hill were shot down by an air-to-air missile fired by a MiG-21 as they tried to egress and both men were captured when they ejected about five miles west of Kep. James Low was a Korean War ace with nine aircraft to his credit and had apparently had a reputation for nonconformity. Later he criticised his flight leader for staying in the fight until they were low on fuel. He was one of three men who the North Vietnamese selected for early release to a group of American peace activists on 18 July 1968. This early release caused a great deal of controversy and concern amongst those prisoners left behind. 1Lt Hill stayed the full course and was finally released on 14 March 1973.

F-4B   151492   VF-21, USN, USS *Ranger*
Lt Cdr Duke E Hernandez (survived)
Lt(jg) S L Vanhorn (survived)

The USS *Ranger* returned to TF 77 for its third war cruise on 3 December. The ship's first combat loss occurred during a raid on a road ferry at Kien An, just south of Haiphong. Lt Cdr Hernandez and Lt Vanhorn were flying as part of the flak suppression flight. As the flight was leaving the target area, Lt Hernandez's aircraft was hit by AAA causing the flight control system to fail. Controlling the aircraft by rudder alone, Lt Cdr Hernandez steered the aircraft out over the sea and he and his NFO ejected. They were both picked up by a Navy SAR helicopter. Lt Cdr Hernandez ejected from another Phantom over the Gulf of Tonkin on 28 April 1968

O-1G   51-12097   21 TASS, 504 TASG, USAF, Nha Trang
Maj Ommie Truman Cox (KIA)
1 crew, name unknown (survived)

An O-1 Bird Dog on an FAC mission was shot down near Phu Tuc, some 50 miles west of Tuy Hoa. The pilot may have been hit as the aircraft crashed out of control. The observer was probably from another service or he may have been South Vietnamese.

17 December 1967

F-4D   66-7774   497 TFS, 8 TFW, USAF, Ubon
Maj Kenneth Raymond Fleenor (POW)
1Lt Terry Lee Boyer (POW)

The North Vietnamese MiGs scored two more victories on the 17th during major coordinated attacks by large groups of MiG-17s and MiG-21s. A MiGCAP Phantom on a raid on the Lang Lau railway bridge fell to the cannon of a MiG-17 during a dogfight near Yen Bai. The crew ejected and came down near the town of Piu Tho on the Red River. The crew were both captured and taken to the Hanoi Hilton to start their five-year sentence, which ended in repatriation on 14 March 1973. Maj Fleenor was on his 87th mission when he was shot down, while 1Lt Boyer was on his 40th. Kenneth Fleenor was one of the first USAF pilots to convert to the Phantom and commanded the 12th FTW after his release and attained the rank of Brigadier General before retiring from the Air Force on 1 August 1980.

F-105D   60-0422   469 TFS, 388 TFW, USAF, Korat
1Lt Jeffrey Thomas Ellis (POW)

On the way to bomb the Lang Lau railway bridge, a formation of F-105s, flying at 16,000 feet, was jumped by several MiG-21s. On this occasion it appears that the MiG-21s were targeted at the bombers while the MiG-17s took on the CAP flight. An Atoll missile struck 1Lt Ellis's aircraft, which immediately snapped into a spin. He ejected safely moments before the aircraft exploded and landed about 10 miles west of Thai Nguyen. Jeffrey Ellis had only been in Southeast Asia since October but he had flown 44 missions during that time. He was soon captured and spent the next five years in four different prison camps before his release on 14 March 1973. He resumed his Air Force career after repatriation and eventually became the commander of the 47th Flying Training Wing and the Inspector General of Air Training Command before retirement as a Brigadier General. F-105D 60-0422 was painted as 'The Red Baron' during its time at Korat.

F-4C   64-0782   559 TFS, 12 TFW, USAF, Cam Ranh Bay
Col C Brett (survived)
1Lt Myron F Smith (KIA)

A Phantom was shot down near Vinh Linh, five miles north of the DMZ, during an armed reconnaissance mission. The aircraft was making its second pass over an automatic weapons site when it was hit by 57mm AAA. The aircraft crashed close to the target but only the pilot, Col Brett, survived the ejection and was rescued by an HH-3E of the 37th ARRS.

F-4D   66-7757   497 TFS, 8 TFW, USAF, Ubon
Maj Laird Guttersen (survived)
1Lt S P Sox (survived)

As night fell a third Phantom was shot down over North Vietnam. The aircraft was taking part in a strike on a ferry at Huu Hung, four miles south of Dong Hoi. It was hit by ground fire during the attack but Maj Guttersen coaxed the damaged aircraft out over the sea. He and his WSO ejected about eight miles off the coast and were rescued by a Navy helicopter. Maj Guttersen's good fortune ran out on 23 February 1968 when he was shot down over North Vietnam and captured.

F-100F	56-4005	612 TFS, 37 TFW, USAF, Phu Cat
		Maj Robert Roger Craner (POW)
		Capt Guy Dennis Gruters (POW)

The third Misty FAC Super Sabre and its crew was lost on this day. The aircraft was shot down by 57mm flak over the Annamites about 25 miles west of Dong Hoi. Craner and Gruters were both captured and imprisoned although Veith claims in *Code Name Bright Light* that a half-hearted attempt was made by their captors to exchange the crew for a sum of gold. These two airmen looked after 1Lt Lance Sijan during the final few days of his life in the Hanoi Hilton. It was largely due to their testimony that Sijan's story became known resulting in his posthumous award of the Medal of Honor. Maj Craner and Capt Gruters were released on 14 March 1973. Guy Gruters had been shot down and rescued during an earlier Misty FAC mission on 8 November.

The A-7 Corsair

The LTV A-7 Corsair II was designed to the Navy's requirements to replace the A-4 Skyhawk in the light attack role. Based in general on the design of the F-8 Crusader, the A-7 could carry up to 15,000lb of bombs, had advanced avionics and was powered by the newly developed TF30 turbofan. The aircraft first flew on 27 September 1965 and was first delivered to the Navy in September 1966. VA-147 was the first operationally ready A-7A squadron and deployed on board the USS Ranger to introduce the new aircraft to Vietnam. The carrier took up its position on the line on 3 December and the A-7 made its combat debut the following day. Despite problems with its engine, the aircraft soon proved a success and did eventually replace most of the A-4 squadrons of TF 77 in the light attack and Iron Hand roles. Later variants include the A-7B, A-7C and the A-7E while the USAF was so impressed with the Corsair that it later ordered the A-7D version.

22 December 1967

| A-4E | 152071 | VA-155, USN, USS *Coral Sea* |
| | | Lt Cdr Wilmer Paul Cook (KIA) |

During an armed reconnaissance mission a section of Skyhawks found and bombed a pontoon bridge 13 miles south of Vinh. After Lt Cdr Cook dropped his bombs his wingman saw that his leader's aircraft was on fire, probably as a result of damage from its own bombs. The wingman lost sight of Lt Cdr Cook's aircraft but later found its wreckage just two miles from the coast. A SAR helicopter arrived and saw Wilmer Cook's body, still strapped into his parachute, lying about 300 feet from the wreckage. The helicopter was unable to land due to intense ground fire but the helicopter crew got close enough to see that Lt Cdr Cook had died from wounds. The Vietnamese returned a set of remains on 21 June 1988 and these were positively identified as being those of Wilmer Cook on 28 September 1989.

| A-7A | 153239 | VA-147, USN, USS *Ranger* |
| | | Lt Cdr James Martin Hickerson (POW) |

The Navy lost its first A-7 Corsair in Southeast Asia on 22 December less than three weeks after the aircraft's combat debut. The aircraft was configured for an Iron Hand mission and was taking part in an attack on a Firecan AAA fire control radar situated eight miles southwest of Haiphong. Lt Cdr Hickerson approached the target at 15,000 feet and prepared to launch his Shrike missile. A Fan Song radar signal was picked up on the aircraft's radar warning receiver and three SA-2s were seen heading towards the formation. One of the missiles exploded about 200 feet under Lt Cdr Hickerson's Corsair, which was seen to roll

and dive towards the ground as the engine and hydraulic system failed. Hickerson ejected and was soon captured. After five years as a POW he was released on 14 March 1973.

F-4B	148388	VMFA-122, MAG-11, USMC, Da Nang
		Capt Gary Henry Fors (KIA)
		1Lt Guy K Lashlee (survived)

A Marine Corps F-4 was lost during a Steel Tiger strike just inside southern Laos, about 40 miles southwest of Hué. The target was a road (Route 922) that wound its way through the jungle and which, if cut, could prove an obstacle to trucks taking supplies to the south. Capt Fors and 1Lt Lashlee were on their second pass over the target when their Phantom was hit in the wing by 23mm anti-aircraft fire. The aircraft started to burn and the crew ejected almost immediately. One reports claims that as 1Lt Lashlee was descending in his parachute he saw that Capt Fors had landed near the crash site but was already surrounded by enemy troops. Lashlee drifted away and was rescued about 30 minutes later by a Marine Corps UH-1E from Khe Sanh. Despite tantalising but unsubstantiated reports that Gary Fors had been captured and was seen in captivity, he has never returned from the jungles of Laos.

| F-100D | 56-2922 | 531 TFS, 3 TFW, USAF, Bien Hoa |
| | | Capt Robert Lynne Long (KIA) |

The vast Michelin rubber plantations west of Lai Khe, some 30 miles northwest of Saigon, were well known to be the focal point for VC activity. However, the plantations were no sanctuary as the VC were constantly harried by fixed-wing aircraft and helicopters of the USAF and Army. On the 22nd Capt Long was attacking enemy troops who were engaged in a firefight with friendly forces about 10 miles west of Lai Khe. On the second strafing pass the Super Sabre was hit by automatic weapons fire and crashed before the pilot could eject.

25 December 1967

TF-9J	147381	H&MS-13, MAG-13, USMC, Chu Lai
		Maj G W Fritschi (survived)
		Capt A D Smiley (survived)

Air operations over Southeast Asia did not stop even for Christmas Day. The only TF-9J Cougar to be lost during the war in Southeast Asia was shot down during a visual reconnaissance mission in the A Shau Valley, 20 miles southwest of Hué. H&MS-11 and H&MS-13 had a small number of ageing, two-seat TF-9 Cougars in South Vietnam to fly visual reconnaissance or Tactical Air Coordination (Airborne) missions, a similar role to the USAF's fast FACs. The Cougars were also used for artillery observation during coastal bombardments of North Vietnam by the Navy's USS *New Jersey* battleship and other vessels. Using the colourful radio call sign of Furbritches, Maj Fritschi and Capt Smiley were diving through 1,700 feet to mark a target when their aircraft was hit in the aft fuselage by ground fire. Maj Fritschi headed east towards the coast in an attempt to reach the sea or Da Nang if the aircraft held together long enough. Unfortunately, the old Cougar did not quite make it and the crew had to eject about 12 miles southwest of Hué. They were both picked up safely by a USAF helicopter. This Cougar had previously had its windscreen shattered by small arms fire during a mission over the A Shau Valley on 27 October and was hit and damaged again during a mission on 17 December. The TF-9Js were retired and replaced by the TA-4F soon after this incident.

| O-2A | 67-21337 | 20 TASS, 504 TASG, USAF, Da Nang |
| | | Maj Billy E Lankford (KIA) |

An O-2 was shot down during an FAC mission near the village of Ngoc Tri, seven miles south of the Marine Corps airfield at Chu Lai. Maj Lankford was killed in the crash.

T-28D	49-1558	606 ACS, 56 ACW, USAF, Nakhon Phanom
		Capt Terry Treloar Koonce (KIA)
		1 crew, name unknown (KIA)

One of the Zorros of the 606th ACS was lost during an armed reconnaissance over Route 23 near the Ban Karai Pass in southern Laos. Capt Koonce had spotted a target (possibly a vehicle) and dived down to attack it. His T-28 was damaged by shrapnel from his own bomb or by target debris and the aircraft crashed without either Capt Koonce or his observer escaping. The observer was probably a Lao Air Force or Army man who were sometimes used for their local knowledge.

O-2A	67-21390	20 TASS, 504 TASG, USAF, Da Nang
		Maj Jerry A Sellers (KIA)
		Capt Richard W Budka (KIA)

The second O-2 to be lost on Christmas Day went down within the DMZ buffer zone. The aircraft was flying a visual recon-

In 1968 the A-7 Corsair began to replace the A-4 Skyhawk as the Navy's main light attack aircraft. Despite suffering serious engine problems, the A-7 was a fine combat aircraft and was often tasked with Iron Hand missions. This A-7A of VA-147 is about to be catapulted off the USS *Ranger* in January 1968 with an RA-5C Vigilante of RVAH-6 taxying up to the other catapult. USN

naissance mission and was struck by automatic weapons fire. It crashed three miles south of the village of Thon Cam Son killing both the crew. Maj Sellers was awarded a posthumous AFC for deliberately provoking enemy ground fire in an attempt to locate enemy positions for the strike aircraft. It is noteworthy that from the four O-2s that had been shot down during the year, not one crewmember had managed to escape, whereas 15 of the 36 occupants of O-1s had survived being shot down during the year.

RF-4B 153114   VMCJ-1, MAG-11, USMC, Da Nang
                 Maj D C Escalera (survived)
                 1Lt Thomas Anthony Grud (KIA)

A Marine Corps Phantom crashed at Da Nang as it was attempting to land after a reconnaissance mission. The aircraft touched down and attempted to catch the MOREST arrester cable but the cable broke and struck the aircraft's tail forcing the horizontal stabilizer to the full nose-up position. The aircraft pitched up sharply and the pilot attempted to climb away by using afterburner but the aircraft was flying too slowly and stalled at low altitude. Maj Escalera ejected and survived but 1Lt Grud's parachute did not fully open before he hit the ground and he was killed. VMCJ-1 was operating eight RF-4Bs at this stage of the war in addition to eight EF-10Bs and four EA-6As.

26 December 1967

A-4E 151029   VMA-211, MAG-12, USMC, Chu Lai
                1 pilot, name unknown (survived)

One of VMA-211's Skyhawks was lost during a test flight when the aircraft's hydraulic system failed. The pilot ejected and was picked up and the aircraft crashed into the sea.

27 December 1967

F-4B 153005   VF-114, USN, USS *Kitty Hawk*
                Lt Cdr Leonard Murray Lee (KIA)
                Lt(jg) Roger Burns Innes (KIA)

A section of two Phantoms from the *Kitty Hawk* was attacking a target on Cape Falaise, 25 miles north of Vinh, when one of the aircraft disappeared. The cloud base was only 1,000 feet but the section decided to perform a loft bombing manoeuvre which required the aircraft to run in at low level, pull up sharply and release the bomb as the aircraft approached the vertical. The low ceiling precluded the aircraft climbing very high without penetrating cloud but Lt Cdr Lee's wingman put his bombs on the target. Lee went in and pulled up into the clouds and was not seen again by his wingman. His radar trace disappeared off the screen of an E-2 Hawkeye that was monitoring the raid. No sign of any wreckage or survivors could be found and no SAR beepers were heard. It was assumed that the aircraft had crashed during the recovery from the loft manoeuvre.

F-4C 63-7489   390 TFS, 366 TFW, USAF, Da Nang
                Maj H W Miller (survived)
                1Lt Sammy Arthur Martin (KIA)

The USAF also lost a Phantom on the 27th when an aircraft was shot down during an armed reconnaissance mission. Maj Miller and 1Lt Martin were flying over Tho Ngoa, 20 miles northwest of Dong Hoi, when their aircraft was hit by automatic weapons fire. The aircraft started to burn as Maj Miller headed out over the coast. Both crew ejected at a point about 20 miles off the coast. A Navy SAR helicopter rescued Maj Miller but as 1Lt Martin was being hoisted out of the water he slipped through the rescue sling and dropped back into the sea. A large wave swept him away and the helicopter crew could not locate him again. The helicopter that made the rescue was one of the newly arrived twin-engined UH-2Cs from HC-1's Detachment 63 from the USS *Kitty Hawk*.

28/29 December 1967

C-130E-I 64-0547   Detachment 1, 314 TAW, USAF, Nha Trang
                    Capt Edwin Nelms Osborne (KIA)
                    Capt Gerald Gordon Van Buren (KIA)
                    Maj Charles Peter Claxton (KIA)

Maj Donald Ellis Fisher (KIA)
Capt Frank Claveloux Parker (KIA)
Capt Gordon James Wenaas (KIA)
TSgt Jack McCrary (KIA)
SSgt Wayne Alvin Eckley (KIA)
SSgt Gean Preston Clapper (KIA)
A1C Edward Joseph Darcy (KIA)
A1C James Randall Williams (KIA)

Shortly after midnight on the 28th a Combat Talon C-130E-I, flown by crew S-01, took off from Nha Trang and headed at low-level towards Hanoi on a special operations mission. The aircraft was to make a leaflet drop west of the city followed by a diversionary resupply drop in the Song Da Valley in North Vietnam. Diversionary drops were sometimes made by the Combat Talon aircraft to fool the enemy into thinking that a clandestine team was working in a particular area. The aircraft made a radio transmission about four hours later indicating that the mission was progressing normally. After that message there was no further radio contact and the aircraft was posted as missing on the morning of the 29th. It was presumed that the aircraft had either been shot down by ground fire over North Vietnam or had flown into the ground as it was returning at low-level in the dark. A two-week search along the aircraft's planned route failed to reveal any sightings of wreckage. Investigations at a crash site in mountains in the Lau Chau province of North Vietnam in 1992 and 1993 failed to provide conclusive evidence or human remains. The aircraft had crashed about 32 miles northeast of Dien Bien Phu and the site had already been scavenged by villagers. However a subsequent investigation did discover some scant remains but these are still awaiting positive identification. The wreckage was found just below the summit of a high karst cliff indicating that the aircraft had probably flown into high ground as it was returning from its mission.

F-4D 66-7521   435 TFS, 8 TFW, USAF, Ubon
                Capt R W Coburn (survived)
                Capt H Altman (survived)

A Phantom was lost the same night but on a different mission. Capt Coburn and Capt Altman were on a strike in southern Laos and were attacking a convoy of at least nine trucks on Route 911 near Ban Soppeng when they were hit by 37mm AAA. The crew ejected almost immediately as their aircraft caught fire but they were later rescued.

29 December 1967

F-4B 150449   VF-161, USN, USS *Coral Sea*
                Lt J F Dowd (survived)
                Lt(jg) G K Flint (survived)

Two Phantoms were flying a weather reconnaissance mission over the many small islands that hug the coastline near Cam Pha when one of the aircraft was lost. Lt Dowd felt the aircraft struck by ground fire, which was followed by dense smoke filling the cockpit. The pilot jettisoned the cockpit canopy in an effort to clear the smoke but it became worse and the cockpit began to get hot. The two crew ejected about 10 miles south of Cam Pha and were subsequently rescued by a Navy helicopter.

A-26A 64-17641   609 ACS, 56 ACW, USAF, Nakon Phanom
                  Capt Carlos Rafael Cruz (KIA)
                  Capt William Joseph Potter (KIA)
                  A1C Paul Leonard Foster (KIA)

Capt Cruz and his crew took off from Nakhon Phanom on a night interdiction mission over the Ho Chi Minh Trail in southern Laos. The crew found a convoy of at least 10 trucks near Ban Phoukachgi, 35 miles northwest of Khe Sanh. The aircraft made three successful passes over the convoy dropping bombs and napalm but as it rolled in on its fourth pass the Invader was hit by 37mm anti-aircraft fire. The aircraft crashed in flames and none of the crew were able to escape. On a Department of Defense list dated December 1996, all three crewmen of this aircraft are listed as having their remains returned to the USA at some time in the past. By a curious coincidence, a SSgt Raphael Cruz was killed in an Invader that was shot down over South Vietnam on 2 September 1963.

30 December 1967

F-100F 56-3878   612 TFS, 37 TFW, USAF, Phu Cat
                  Maj D A Sibson (survived)
                  Capt D Snyder (survived)

A strike on a suspected SAM site in the hills southwest of Dong Hoi was due to be controlled by one of the 612th's Misty FAC aircraft. Maj Sibson was approaching the target area and climbing to start his search for the site, when his aircraft was hit by a 57mm anti-aircraft shell. He turned east and crossed the coast where both the crew ejected about 10 miles out to sea. They were both rescued by a USAF helicopter. This was the fourth Misty FAC lost since 'Bud' Day was shot down in the first aircraft in August.

F-4C 63-7658   480 TFS, 366 TFW, USAF, Da Nang
                Maj Smith J Swords (KIA)
                1Lt Murray Lamar Wortham (KIA)

A Phantom was lost during a Steel Tiger mission at night over southern Laos. Maj Swords was searching the Ho Chi Minh Trail for traffic when he spotted a truck convoy near Ban Loupoum, 35 miles west of the DMZ. The aircraft crashed as it attacked the convoy, probably as a result of being hit by ground fire or the premature detonation of its own bombs. Apparently neither of the crew survived the crash.

31 December 1967

F-4C 63-7621   390 TFS, 366 TFW, USAF, Da Nang
                Maj Jake I Sorensen (survived)
                1Lt John C Aarni (survived)

Three aircraft were lost on the final day of 1967. Da Nang lost another Phantom, this time during an escort mission for a Ranch Hand defoliation flight of C-123s. The original mission near the DMZ was scrubbed due to fog so the C-123s and their escorts flew to Dak To in the Central Highlands to defoliate an infiltration route into South Vietnam from Cambodia. After the C-123s had finished their runs the escort flight was then diverted to provide close air support for an Army company that was under attack west of Dak To. Maj Sorensen was pulling up from his second pass when his aircraft was hit by automatic weapons fire. The engines began to fail and one of the aircraft's Sparrow missiles launched itself while another fired but did not leave the aircraft, causing it to accelerate. In addition, shells from the podded SUU-23 cannon started to cook off and explode. The crew ejected and were quickly picked up by an Army helicopter.

A-1E 52-135007   1 ACS, 56 ACW, USAF, Nakhon Phanom
                  1Lt Glenn Arthur Belcher (KIA)

The 1st ACS had started to move from Pleiku to Nakhon Phanom late in October to be closer to the Ho Chi Minh Trail in southern Laos and to take part in dropping gravel munitions as a component of the Igloo White programme. It lost its 10th Skyraider of the year during a Steel Tiger strike on New Year's Eve. 1Lt Belcher was making his third pass against vehicles on a road near Ban Phahoy, some 40 miles southeast of Nakhon Phanom. The pilot may have been hit by ground fire as the aircraft rolled uncontrollably and dived into the ground close to the target without any apparent escape attempt by 1Lt Belcher. In 1994 and 1995 joint US-Lao investigations unearthed aircraft wreckage and human remains and personal effects. The remains were subsequently identified as being those of Glenn Belcher.

A-6A 152917   VA-75, USN, USS *Kitty Hawk*
                Lt Cdr John Darlington Pearce (KIA)
                Lt Gordon Samuel Perisho (KIA)

An A-6A Intruder was launched from the *Kitty Hawk* for a singleton daylight strike on a storage cave about three miles east of Vinh. The aircraft was tracked to the target by an E-2 Hawkeye but several indications of SAM activity were received and transmitted to the crew. No radio message was received from the Intruder, which was apparently experiencing radio problems and the aircraft disappeared at the same time as the SAM warnings. A visual and signals search of the area proved negative. It was assumed that the aircraft had become the 62nd and final SAM victim of 1967.

Chapter Five

1968

The Tet Offensive, Khe Sanh and the End of Rolling Thunder

1 January 1968

RA-3B 144847   VAP-61, USN, NAS Cubi Point
Lt Cdr James Richard Dennison (KIA)
Lt(jg) Terence Higgins Hanley (KIA)
CPO Henry Howard Herrin (KIA)

The first aircraft lost in combat in 1968 failed to return from a night reconnaissance mission over North Vietnam. One of VAP-61's Skywarriors set out on a reconnaissance mission and was damaged by ground fire a few miles inland from its landfall causing the pilot to fly out to sea and head south. The aircraft crashed into the sea about 30 miles off Dong Hoi and despite an extensive search no trace of the three crewmen was ever found. VAP-61 and VAP-62 maintained detachments of aircraft at Da Nang and Don Muang to fly reconnaissance missions over North Vietnam and Laos. Using infra-red, video and normal photographic cameras, the aircraft worked over the Ho Chi Minh Trail searching for trucks and other targets. The aircraft even used special camouflage detection film that could distinguish between live and dead foliage thereby revealing camouflaged trucks and enemy positions. Like most of VAP-61's aircraft, 144847 wore a special camouflage paint scheme rather than the normal gull gray worn by fleet aircraft. This aircraft was the last Skywarrior lost in combat during the war.

A-4E 151133   VA-164, USN, USS *Oriskany*
Lt George Frank Schindelar (survived)

During an armed reconnaissance sortie a Skyhawk pilot was suddenly faced with a total electrical failure which, amongst other things, locked the aileron controls solid. Unable to control the aircraft the pilot was forced to eject over the sea but was picked up safely 30 miles northeast of Da Nang. Lt Schindelar completed two tours in Southeast Asia flying 204 combat missions before retiring from the Navy to fly DC-9s for Delta Airlines.

2 January 1968

F-8C 146989   VF-111, USN, USS *Oriskany*
Lt(jg) Craig M Taylor (survived)

A Crusader from VF-111 was assigned to escort an RF-8 reconnaissance aircraft on a mission over North Vietnam. As the aircraft approached Thanh Hoa the escorting aircraft suddenly lost power and suffered total electrical failure. With the engine providing only partial thrust, Lt Taylor dived the aircraft towards the coastline, which he crossed at 1,200 feet. With little engine power, the aircraft eventually stalled and Lt Taylor ejected over the sea about seven miles from the shore. He saw a number of Vietnamese junks heading towards him but a section of Skyhawks appeared and kept the junks at bay until Lt Taylor could be rescued by a Navy SAR helicopter. It was thought that anti-aircraft fire had hit the aircraft and had caused damage to the engine and may also have caused the undercarriage to drop creating excessive drag. Craig Taylor was on his first combat mission of his tour of duty. Unfortunately, he was killed in a flying accident at Miramar, California, after returning from Southeast Asia.

T-28D 49-1572   606 ACS, 56 ACW, USAF, Nakhon Phanom
Maj John Patee (survived)

During a night armed reconnaissance mission over Laos a T-28 suffered engine failure that resulted in the loss of the aircraft. The pilot escaped unharmed and was rescued by a USAF SAR helicopter early the next morning. The 606th ACS lost two of its eight T-28s during January.

F-105D 61-0149   355 TFW, USAF, Takhli
1 pilot, name unknown (survived)

Following a strike mission a Thunderchief, critically low on fuel, attempted to join up on a KC-135 tanker. Unfortunately, the F-105 ran out of fuel and flamed out before it could reach the tanker and the pilot was forced to eject.

3 January 1968

A-4C 148486   VA-112, USN, USS *Kitty Hawk*
Lt Cdr Edward Dale Estes (POW)

The first aircraft lost to a SAM in 1968 went down during an Iron Hand mission on the 3rd. The target was a SAM site near the Kien An road bridge just south of Haiphong. Lt Cdr Estes was leading the Iron Hand flight and as he approached Haiphong from the north at 11,000 feet he saw three SA-2s tracking towards the flight. The Skyhawks dived towards the missiles in an attempt to break their radar lock but one of the SAMs hit the leader's aircraft. The A-4 began to disintegrate and Lt Cdr Estes ejected about eight miles southwest of Kien An airfield as his cockpit filled with smoke. Edward Estes was captured and became the first US POW of 1968. After nearly five years in captivity he was released on 14 March 1973. He had flown over 90 missions over Southeast Asia during two combat cruises.

F-105D 58-1157   469 TFS, 388 TFW, USAF, Korat
Col James Ellis Bean (POW)

The MiGs also scored their first victory of 1968 on the 3rd. A force of F-105s on its way to bomb the Kinh No railway yard was intercepted by several MiG-21s at 10,000 feet, 25 miles west of Thai Nguyen. One of the MiGs evaded the F-4 escorts and Col Bean's aircraft was hit by an air-to-air missile, forcing him to eject. Col Bean, the Wing's deputy for operations, was the third senior officer to be lost by the 388th TFW in just over three months. James Bean had joined the USAAF in 1942 and had flown 41 combat missions in P-47 Thunderbolts over Europe. He had been flying the F-105 since 1960 and had helped to devise the flight-training programme for the aircraft. James Bean had served in Southeast Asia on several temporary detachments from the 8th TFW during the early phase of the war. He was released from imprisonment in North Vietnam on 14 March 1973. 58-1157 was painted as 'Shirley Ann' and 'Bubbles' during its time at Korat.

F-4B 151447   VMFA-122, MAG-11, USMC, Da Nang
An enemy attack on Da Nang resulted in the destruction of a Marine Corps Phantom. Twenty other aircraft were damaged to some degree but personnel casualties were limited to just two men who were wounded. A total of 49 mortar and rocket rounds were counted landing on the airfield during this attack.

4 January 1968

F-8E 150865   VF-162, USN, USS *Oriskany*
Lt(jg) Richard Willis Minnich (KIA)

The TARCAP aircraft assigned to protect the strike force over the target were particularly vulnerable to SAMs as they usually flew at high altitude and had to stay in the target area for the entire duration of the strike. One of two TARCAP Crusaders was lost as it was retiring from a strike on a road bridge at Hai Duong. The aircraft was flying at about 15,000 feet when it was hit by a SAM. The F-8 burst into flames, rolled and pitched down and then spun until it hit the ground about 10 miles north of Haiphong. It was assumed that Lt Minnich had been killed in the incident as

there was no indication of an ejection. His remains were eventually returned to the USA on 4 December 1985.

F-100D 55-3765   308 TFS, 31 TFW, USAF, Tuy Hoa
Capt J E Pollak (survived)

The F-100 was still the most numerous USAF aircraft in South Vietnam in January 1968 with a total of 193 aircraft in 13 squadrons soon to be supplemented by five more squadrons. The first combat loss in South Vietnam of 1968 took place near Ban Ti Srenh, 20 miles southeast of Ban Me Thuot City in the Central Highlands. Capt Pollak was pulling up from his second pass against a gun site when his aircraft was struck by ground fire. The aircraft caught fire and Capt Pollak ejected a couple of miles from the target area. A USAF helicopter rescued him a short while later.

5 January 1968

F-105F 63-8356   357 TFS, 355 TFW, USAF, Takhli
Maj James Cuthbert Hartney (KIA)
Capt Samuel Fantle (KIA)

An Iron Hand flight lost a Wild Weasel F-105F during a raid on a railway bridge at Dong Luc, near Kep. Maj Hartney and Capt Fantle were leading the flight of four aircraft and had fired a Shrike missile when they were attacked by MiGs. Cannon fire from a MiG-17 hit the F-105F causing a fire in the port wing. Both crew ejected as the aircraft rolled out of control. One of the wingmen saw two parachutes but no voice contact could be made. The North Vietnamese said that Capt Fantle had hit a rock as he landed and had been killed. No mention was made at the time of Maj Hartney. Capt Fantle's remains were released to the USA on 30 September 1977 but it was not until 20 November 1989 that Maj Hartney's remains were identified after being handed over by the Vietnamese. F-105F 63-8356 carried the name 'Miss Molly'.

RF-4C 65-0865   11 TRS, 432 TRW, USAF, Udorn
Lt Col W T Rodenbach (survived)
Lt E T Pizzo (survived)

A Phantom was tasked with a photographic reconnaissance mission in the Phuc Yen area. As the aircraft was flying straight and level at 7,000 feet, about 10 miles west of Phuc Yen airfield, it flew into a hail of anti-aircraft fire and was damaged. Lt Col Rodenbach coaxed the aircraft back across North Vietnam and Laos into Thailand but he and his navigator were forced to eject about 45 miles northeast of Udorn.

A-4E 152074   VA-144, USN, USS *Kitty Hawk*
Cdr Robert James Schweitzer (POW)

After the loss of Lt Cdr Estes on the 3rd, another Iron Hand mission on the 5th resulted in the loss of another Skyhawk. Cdr Schweitzer was leading his formation against a SAM site just to the west of Haiphong and Schweitzer's aircraft was hit by 37mm flak just as the last of the aircraft had dropped its bombs. The aircraft suffered complete electrical and hydraulic failure making it impossible for the pilot to maintain control. Cdr Schweitzer ejected close to Haiphong and was captured. For a time while in prison Robert Schweitzer allied himself with Cdr W E Wilber and Lt Col E W Miller and made propaganda tapes for the enemy. However, he later recanted and rejoined the ranks of the majority of the prisoners and returned from the camps with honour. After five years as a prisoner, Cdr Schweitzer was released on 14 March 1973. Robert Schweitzer was killed in an automobile accident on 24 January 1974. He was promoted to Captain posthumously and buried at sea from the USS *Ranger*.

The highly modified OP-2E Neptunes of VO-67 were tasked with dropping electronic sensors along the Ho Chi Minh Trail in southern Laos as part of the Igloo White surveillance system. VO-67 only spent eight months in Southeast Asia before returning to the USA after the loss of three aircraft. USN

F-105D 61-0068   469 TFS, 388 TFW, USAF, Korat
                  Capt William Eugene Jones (KIA)
The Korat Wing flew a strike on Kep airfield on the 5th. Capt Jones of Crossbow flight was pulling up through 9,000 feet after having released his bombs when an 85mm anti-aircraft shell hit his aircraft. Capt Jones turned towards the coast but after a couple of minutes he was seen to eject about 15 miles southeast of Kep. His parachute was seen to land and his emergency beeper was activated but there was no voice contact. Nothing more was heard of Capt Jones until his remains were returned from Vietnam in 1985. F-105D 61-0068 was painted as 'Barbara E' while at Korat.

A-4E   150131   VA-163, USN, USS *Oriskany*
                  Lt(jg) Ralph Eugene Foulks (KIA)
As darkness fell a section of Skyhawks flew an armed reconnaissance mission over coastal roads in North Vietnam. Trucks were seen on a road about 25 miles southwest of Nam Dinh and the aircraft commenced an attack. Lt Foulks followed his leader in the attack but after the leader dropped his bombs he could not contact his wingman nor was there any sign of burning wreckage. There was flak in the area at the time and it was assumed that Lt Foulks had either been shot down or had flown into the ground in the dark. Ralph Foulks had been shot down and rescued on 24 October 1967 during a raid on Haiphong. The remains of Lt Foulks were repatriated by the Vietnamese on 15 December 1988.

6 January 1968

F-105F 62-4441   333 TFS, 355 TFW, USAF, Takhli
                  Maj Gerald C Gustafson (survived)
                  Capt Russell F Brownlee (survived)
A two-seat Thunderchief crashed near Takhli when it suffered engine failure during a strike mission. This Wild Weasel crew had been shot down and rescued on 19 November 1967 during a mission over North Vietnam. This particular aircraft was one of a small number of F-105Fs that had been selected to be modified to carry the huge AGM-78 Standard ARM missile. However, it crashed before the modification could be carried out.

7 January 1968

F-100D 55-3619   612 TFS, 37 TFW, USAF, Phu Cat
                  Maj D P Wright (survived)
The USAF lost a second F-100 in South Vietnam within the space of four days. Maj Wright was taking part in a close air support mission near Ha Tan, 15 miles southwest of Da Nang, when he was shot down. His aircraft was hit in the fuselage by ground fire as he rolled in on his second pass on a group of VC. Maj Wright

headed east, crossed the beach and ejected over the sea, about 10 miles off Da Nang.

7/8 January 1968

RF-4C 65-0913   16 TRS, 460 TRW, USAF, Tan Son Nhut
                  Capt Hallie William Smith (KIA)
                  1Lt Charles Lawrence Bifolchi (KIA)
A Phantom on a night photographic mission to the area around Dak To in Kontum province went missing near the Laotian border. No trace of the aircraft or its crew was ever found but it was assumed to have been shot down somewhere north of Dak To.

9 January 1968

F-8E   150917   VMF(AW)-235, MAG-11, USMC, Da Nang
                 Capt D W Lorenzo (survived)
The Marines lost a Crusader during a Steel Tiger mission in southern Laos. Capt Lorenzo was bombing a choke point in a road near Ban Laipo when his aircraft was hit by automatic weapons fire. With his aircraft on fire Capt Lorenzo headed south but had to eject while still over Laos. He was rescued by a USAF helicopter.

F-4D   66-8729   497 TFS, 8 TFW, USAF, Ubon
                  Lt Col Norman Morgan Green (KIA)
                  1Lt Wayne Charles Irsch (KIA)
A Wolfpack Phantom was lost during a night interdiction mission over the Ho Chi Minh Trail in southern Laos. Lt Col Green and 1Lt Irsch were attacking a truck they had seen on a road when their aircraft was hit by ground fire. The aircraft crashed in a valley near Ban Kapay, about 20 miles west of the DMZ. There was no evidence at the time to suggest that either of the crew had been able to escape from the aircraft.

10 January 1968

F-4D   66-8704   13 TFS, 432 TRW, USAF, Udorn
                  Capt Keith Norman Hall (POW)
                  1Lt Earl Pearson Hopper (KIA)
On the 10th the USAF flew a raid on the Hoa Loc airfield, 15 miles west of Hanoi. As the TARCAP flight approached Hai Duong en route to the target, it came under attack from a SAM battery. Capt Hall's aircraft was at 20,000 feet when it was rocked by a nearby explosion from an SA-2 missile. The aircraft's hydraulic system was badly damaged and Capt Hall ejected, followed a few minutes later by 1Lt Hopper, who came down in a rugged mountainous area. Landing about 20 miles apart, both men activated their emergency SAR beepers. Capt Hall was captured after about 40 minutes on the ground but Earl Hopper's radio signal was tracked for three days. A Laotian ground search team was

inserted into the region and located Hopper's radio but found no trace of him. It was conjectured that Hopper had left his radio on and hid it as he was about to be captured.

Capt Hall and 1Lt Hopper were on their first mission together when they were shot down although Keith Hall had flown 58 missions with other WSOs during his tour in Southeast Asia. He was released on 14 March 1973. Classified information was received in the early 1980s that implied that Earl Hopper was still alive and imprisoned by the Pathet Lao. However, attempts to obtain further information from Laos have come to nought. This was the first Phantom lost by the 13th TFS since the Squadron had converted from the Thunderchief in October 1967 and moved from Korat to Udorn to become part of the 432nd TRW.

F-4B   151506   VF-154, USN, USS *Ranger*
                 2 crew, names unknown (survived)

F-4B   151499   VF-154, USN, USS *Ranger*
                 2 crew, names unknown (survived)
Two Navy Phantoms flew a radar-directed bombing mission over low cloud in Laos. As the aircraft set course for the return trip to the *Ranger* the leader inadvertently homed onto the TACAN of the northern SAR destroyer instead of that of the carrier. When the Phantoms broke out from the cloud they were over 100 miles from the *Ranger* and the aircraft had to be abandoned when they ran out of fuel.

F-4B   153063   VF-114, USN, USS *Kitty Hawk*
                 2 crew, names unknown (survived)
The Navy lost another Phantom in an accident on the 10th. During a CAP mission an aircraft from VF-114 suffered a complete loss of hydraulic pressure, which affected the flight control system. The crew ejected when they lost control. The occupants of the three Navy F-4s lost on the 10th were Lt(jg) T Beckwith, Lt R A Fleming, Lt(jg) T L Hart, Lt Cdr L N Mitchell, Lt(jg) J A Thorn and Lt(jg) D A Yost but it is not known who was in which aircraft.

VO-67 *and Igloo White*

The problem of North Vietnamese infiltration down the Ho Chi Minh Trail was proving extremely difficult to counter by conventional means. The lack of timely intelligence was one of the major problems. Special Forces and indigenous Hmong and Meo guerillas collected intelligence but often sustained heavy casualties. However, late in 1967 the USAF started to implement a plan to place hidden sensors along the Trail to send information back to orbiting aircraft, which in turn relayed the information back to the Infiltration Surveillance Center at Nakhon Phanom, code named Eagle White. As part of Project Igloo White, large numbers of acoustic and seismic sensors were dropped in Laos to intersect the Trail and to detect movement. The extensive barrier of sensors led to the project being nicknamed McNamara's Fence. The sensors were dropped by a variety of aircraft including A-1s, O-2s and helicopters but the task became the primary mission of VO-67, a special US Navy squadron, which arrived at Nakhon Phanom in November 1967. The signals from the sensors were picked up by high-flying aircraft which then relayed the information back to the Infiltration Surveillance Center from where orders were issued to strike aircraft to hit potential targets. The relay aircraft were operated by the 553rd RW and consisted initially of EC-121 Bat Cat aircraft later supplemented by QU-22s.

Twelve SP-2E Neptunes were modified to OP-2E standard for VO-67 by removing the Magnetic Anomaly Detector tail cone and installing an AN/ALE-29 chaff dispenser, a rearward looking camera and an AN/APQ-131 radar. The sensors had to be dropped at low level by the large aircraft and the attrition rate was expected to be high, despite the fact that the Neptunes were

be escorted by flights of F-4s. In fact the attrition rate was so high that the Squadron was withdrawn in June 1968, after only eight months of operations. After the Neptunes were withdrawn, Phantoms flew most of the sensor delivery missions.

1 January 1968

P-2E	131436	VO-67, USN, Nakhon Phanom
		Cdr Delbert Austin Olson (KIA)
		Lt(jg) Phillip Paul Stevens (KIA)
		Lt(jg) Denis Leon Anderson (KIA)
		Lt(jg) Arthur Charles Buck (KIA)
		PO2 Donald Nellis Thoresen (KIA)
		PO2 Kenneth Harry Widon (KIA)
		PO2 Michael Land Roberts (KIA)
		PO2 Richard Michael Mancini (KIA)
		PO3 Gale Robert Siow (KIA)

The first of three Neptunes lost by VO-67 during its brief career in Southeast Asia went missing during a daylight sensor delivery mission over Laos in poor weather. Radio and radar contact with the aircraft was lost during the mission and when it became overdue an extensive visual and electronic search of the operational area was commenced. Initially nothing was found, but 12 days later a Skyraider pilot found what he thought was a crash site near Ban Napoung, 45 miles northwest of the DMZ. An O-2 from the 23rd TASS obtained photographs of the site confirming that it was indeed the remains of Cdr Olson's aircraft. The Neptune had crashed into the north face of a sheer cliff just 150 feet below a 4,580 feet ridge. It was highly unlikely that anyone could have survived the impact and due to the extremely difficult terrain and the proximity of enemy troops in the area it was decided not to insert a search party to look for the bodies. On 23 February the entire crew were redesignated from missing in action to presumed killed in action. Cdr Olson was the Squadron's executive officer.

A-4E	151152	VA-164, USN, USS *Oriskany*
		Lt Cdr D R Weichman (survived)

During a Steel Tiger mission a section of Skyhawks attacked a small bridge 10 miles north of Ban Dong Pang in southern Laos. As Lt Cdr Weichman was pulling up from his third pass over the target he felt a thump as the aircraft was hit by small arms fire and the engine temperature rose as it started to vibrate. By reducing power he was able to fly the aircraft back across Laos and South Vietnam and out over the sea. However, when still about 25 miles from the *Oriskany* the engine caught fire and the flight control cables were burnt through causing a complete loss of control. Lt Cdr Weichman ejected and was picked up by a Navy helicopter.

14 January 1968

F-105D	60-0489	469 TFS, 388 TFW, USAF, Korat
		Maj Stanley Henry Horne (KIA)

The Korat Wing flew a strike on Yen Bai airfield with the loss of one of the F-105 bombers. As the strike force was leaving the target it was intercepted by several flights of MiGs and Maj Horne's aircraft was hit by an Atoll missile fired by a MiG-21. The aircraft crashed near the Red River east of Yen Bai and there was no indication that Maj Horne had survived. On 8 April 1990 the Vietnamese handed over human remains from an aircraft crash site. On 14 November 1990 it was announced that these remains had been positively identified as being those of Maj Stanley Horne.

O-1G	51-12750	21 TASS, 504 TASG, USAF, Nha Trang
		1Lt W H Trisko (survived)

A Bird Dog FAC was controlling a close air support operation about 10 miles east of Phan Rang airfield when it was hit by ground fire. With a faltering engine and the aircraft on fire, 1Lt Trisko flew the aircraft away from known enemy positions but he suffered major injuries during the subsequent crash-landing. He was rescued by a USAF helicopter.

EB-66C	55-0388	41 TEWS, 355 TFW, USAF, Takhli
		Maj Pollard Hugh Mercer
		(survived – died later)

Maj Irby David Terrell (POW)
Maj Thomas Wrenne Sumpter (POW)
Capt Hubert C Walker (POW)
1Lt Ronald Merl Lebert (POW)
Lt Thompson (survived)
Lt Pete Pedroli (survived)

The MiGs struck again later in the day and this time scored an even more significant victory. The VPAF had been trying to shoot down one of the USAF's EB-66 electronic warfare aircraft ever since the MiGs had been brought into service. SAMs had shot down several of these important aircraft but it was not until 14 January that the MiGs claimed their first and only EB-66. The aircraft, operating as Preview 01, was on station at 29,000 feet about 40 miles west of Thanh Hoa and was listening for enemy radar and jamming in support of a strike when it was intercepted by a MiG-21. The EB-66 was hit by an air-to-air missile that destroyed the aircraft's starboard engine. Maj Mercer headed southwest towards Laos but the crew had to abandon the aircraft over mountainous terrain while still over North Vietnam. The crew were spread out over inhospitable terrain when they landed. 1Lt Lebert landed in a tree and was suspended in his parachute straps for 17 hours unable to release himself and climb to the ground. He was eventually captured by local militia.

A large SAR effort was mounted as soon as the EB-66 went down. Voice contact was made with four of the survivors but due to poor weather and approaching darkness it was decided to delay a rescue attempt until first light on the 15th. Continuing bad weather delayed the rescue attempt and it was not until the afternoon of the 15th that Jolly Green 20, an HH-3E 64-14233 from the 37th ARRS, could make its way to the survivors. As the helicopter descended through a solid overcast it suffered a loss of power (probably due to ground fire) and hit the side of a hill before the pilot could enter autorotation. The aircraft came down about 40 miles east of Sam Neua, just inside North Vietnam in a mountainous area. Although the helicopter was destroyed the crew was unhurt and two more HH-3s were scrambled from Lima Site 36 to recover the helicopter crew. However, low cloud frustrated this attempt and one of the helicopters was damaged by small arms fire as it was leaving the area. It was not until the afternoon of the 17th that Jolly Green 71 flew in and rescued the crew of the helicopter. During the rescue Jolly Green 71 was also hit by ground fire, which put one of its engines out of action. On the same day Maj Mercer, Lt Pedroli and Lt Thompson were also rescued by an HH-3. Unfortunately Sonnie Mercer was badly injured and died of his injuries in hospital at Clark AFB on the 20th. An attempt to insert a Bright Light team to search for the other crew had to be aborted when a suitable landing site could not be found. On 22 January the North Vietnamese used a SAR beeper to lure another helicopter into a flak trap. The helicopter escaped with minor damage. Terrell, Sumpter, Walker and Lebert were all released from captivity on 14 March 1973.

F-100D	56-3429	510 TFS, 3 TFW, USAF, Bien Hoa
		1Lt Paul Douglas Strahm (KIA)

During a close air support mission near Bien Hoa a Super Sabre suffered an accidental engine failure and crashed killing the pilot.

15 January 1968

U-10D	66-14334	unit ..?, USAF, base ..?
		A mortar attack on the airfield at Luang

Prabang in Laos destroyed a U-10D Courier. The aircraft may have been used by the Ravens or Air America.

16 January 1968

F-4C	64-0927	480 TFS, 366 TFW, USAF, Da Nang
		Maj C E Lewis (survived)
		1Lt J L Kelley (survived)

F-4D	66-8706	480 TFS, 366 TFW, USAF, Da Nang
		Capt Scott B Stovin (survived)
		1Lt Thomas Nelson Moe (POW)

As two Phantoms were approaching the Mu Gia Pass at 24,000 feet on a Rolling Thunder strike they were suddenly blown apart

as one of their 750lb bombs detonated, presumably as it was being armed ready for dropping. The four crewmen ejected safely and came down about 20 miles northeast of the Pass. Three of the men were eventually rescued but 1Lt Moe was captured and spent the next five years as a POW until released on 14 March 1973. He was on his 85th mission when he was brought down. 64-0927 was the penultimate aircraft of 583 F-4Cs built for the USAF.

EF-10B	125831	VMCJ-1, MAG-11, USMC, Da Nang
		Capt William David Moreland (KIA)
		1Lt Paul Stuart Gee (KIA)

One of VMCJ-1's venerable EF-10B Skynights was lost during a daylight mission on the 16th. The aircraft was returning from a jamming mission over North Vietnam when it crashed into the sea about 15 miles north of Da Nang with the loss of both crew. There was no indication that enemy action had caused the loss of the aircraft.

C-1A	146054	USN, USS *Kitty Hawk*
		Lt Cdr William Joseph Thompson (KIA)
		Lt Orville Dale Cooley (KIA)
		AO3 William Henry Reeder (KIA)
		7 passengers and crew, names unknown
		(survived)

During a catapult launch one of the *Kitty Hawk's* C-1A Trader transport aircraft veered off the port side of the ship and crashed into the sea. Seven passengers and crew were pulled out of the water but three of the crew were lost in the accident.

17 January 1968

O-2A	67-21327	20 TASS, 504 TASG, USAF, Da Nang
		Capt Samuel Festis Beach (KIA)
		Sgt Donald Lee Chaney, US Army (KIA)

Throughout December 1967 and early January 1968 increased enemy activity around the Marine outpost at Khe Sanh had become serious enough for plans for the aerial reinforcement of the base to be put into action. A number of O-2 aircraft from the 20th TASS were detached to Khe Sanh, which was used as a forward operating location for Covey FAC missions over Laos. Moments after Capt Beach took off from Khe Sanh's steel mat runway, his aircraft was hit by small arms fire and crashed. Neither the pilot nor his observer, a Special Forces sergeant, survived the crash.

A-1H	serial ..?	602 ACS, 56 ACW, USAF, Udorn
		Lt Col Robert Frederick Wilke (KIA)

Although two of the four men who were brought down by their own bomb near the Mu Gia Pass on the 16th, the other two were still at large. On the 17th another SAR attempt was made and, as usual, the helicopters were preceded by Skyraiders reconnoitring the area and softening up any defences. As Lt Col Wilke flew over 1Lt Moe's position his aircraft was hit by automatic weapons fire and crashed just a few hundred yards from the F-4 survivor. There was no time for Lt Col Wilke to escape from his stricken aircraft. This was the first single-seat Skyraider lost by the USAF apart from a small number that had been lost while on loan from the VNAF. The Air Commandos started to receive the single-seat A-1H in late 1967. Stocks of the A-1E were running low whereas there were still plenty of single-seaters available in storage and the requirement to carry a Vietnamese observer in US combat aircraft had long since been dropped.

18 January 1968

F-4D	66-8720	435 TFS, 8 TFW, USAF, Ubon
		Maj Kenneth Adrian Simonet (POW)
		1Lt Wayne Ogden Smith (POW)

F-4D	66-7581	435 TFS, 8 TFW, USAF, Ubon
		Capt Robert Bruce Hinckley (POW)
		1Lt Robert Campbell Jones (POW)

The 8th TFW flew a strike on the Bac Giang thermal power plant 20 miles northeast of Hanoi on the 18th. Once again the MiGs were waiting for the strike force and pounced on Otter flight as

the Phantoms approached the target at 7,000 feet. Maj Simonet shot down one of the MiG-17s but then his own aircraft was hit and was seen to be on fire as the crew ejected close to the target. Three minutes later Capt Hinckley's aircraft was also shot down by a MiG-17. Hinckley and his WSO ejected about 15 miles southeast of Kep and they joined the other crew in the Hoa Lac prison. Ken Simonet was unusual in that he had served in three of America's fighting Services. He joined the Marine Corps straight from high school in 1942 and saw service in the Southwest Pacific. He re-enlisted with the Army after the War and served with the 11th Airborne Division in Japan. He graduated from West Point Academy in 1952 and received a commission in the USAF. He was on his second tour in Southeast Asia when he was shot down. All four were released on 14 March 1973.

A-6A   152636   VMA(AW)-533, MAG-12, USMC, Chu Lai
                  Maj Hobart McKinley Wallace (KIA)
                  Capt Patrick Peter Murray (KIA)
A Marine Corps Intruder failed to return from a night attack on a target near Vinh Yen, 20 miles northwest of Hanoi. It was thought that the aircraft reached its target and had pulled up through very low cloud to commence its bombing run. There was no trace of the aircraft or its crew and it was assumed to have been either shot down or crashed as it dived on the target through cloud.

F-4B   153055   VF-114, USN, USS *Kitty Hawk*
                  Lt(jg) Warren William Boles (KIA)
                  Lt(jg) Ronald Roehrich (KIA)
Two Phantoms were launched from the *Kitty Hawk* to fly a BARCAP mission for the carrier. This entailed protecting the carrier and its escorting vessels from enemy aircraft and ships. The vast majority of these patrols were uneventful as the North Vietnamese Navy rarely challenged US Navy vessels on the open sea and the ships operated out of range of the MiGs. Lt Boles was directed to investigate an unidentified surface target off the North Vietnamese coast, about 45 miles southeast of Thanh Hoa. The Phantom descended through a low overcast and the crew reported that the target was merely a cargo vessel. Moments later the Phantom disappeared from the *Kitty Hawk's* radar screen and radio contact was lost. SAR helicopters found a fuel slick and some debris from the aircraft but no sign of either of the crew. It was presumed that the aircraft had inadvertently hit the water as the crew was trying to identify the cargo ship.

20 January 1968

F-4C   64-0797   389 TFS, 366 TFW, USAF, Da Nang
                   Capt Tilden S Holley (KIA)
                   1Lt James Alan Ketterer (KIA)
A flight of two Phantoms flying an armed reconnaissance along Route 1A spotted several trucks near the mouth of the Sou Giang River, 15 miles northwest of Dong Hoi. As Capt Holley was making his second pass his aircraft was hit by 37mm anti-aircraft fire. The Phantom crashed immediately and neither of the crew were seen to escape, although a faint beeper signal was heard briefly. Allegedly, there is a report in the Defense Intelligence Agency's files that claims that Capt Holley did manage to eject from the aircraft but was killed in a shootout with North Vietnamese troops. F-4C 64-0797 was a MiG-killer, having been used by Maj R W Moore and 1Lt J F Sears of the 389th TFS to shoot down a MiG-21 on 26 April 1967.

The Seige of Khe Sanh
Coinciding with the Tet Offensive, the siege of Khe Sanh had all the hallmarks of disaster for the American forces. Vulnerable and remote from other major US bases, the taking of Khe Sanh would be a major victory for the North Vietnamese and a massive blow for American morale. However, the use of air power and the determination of the Marine Corps defenders turned a potentially disastrous defeat into a military and propaganda victory. The North Vietnamese build-up in the area started in December 1967 and by 20 January about 20,000 North Vietnamese troops stood ready to attack the base. However, any hopes that the North Vietnamese may have had in replicating

their famous victory over the French at Dien Bien Phu, which effectively marked the end of the Indo-China War in May 1954, were soon dashed. The major difference between the sieges at Dien Bien Phu and Khe Sanh was the availability of aerial firepower. In what became known as Operation Niagara, the US forces were able to muster the full strength of over 5,000 fixed-wing aircraft and helicopters against the enemy in the defence of Khe Sanh. A major factor in the ability to defend Khe Sanh on the ground was the resupply operations flown by C-123s and C-130s. Altogether these aircraft made 452 landings and 658 parachute drops to the encircled Marines bringing in 12,400 tons of ammunition and other supplies. Throughout the 77-day siege, US tactical aircraft together with B-52s maintained an unrelenting cascade of bombs, napalm and rockets on enemy positions while transport aircraft and helicopters kept the garrison supplied with ammunition, food and reinforcements. The B-52s alone flew 2,548 sorties dropping over 60,000 tons of bombs in defence of Khe Sanh, sometimes within 1,000 feet of the perimeter wire. It was the availability of air power at a sufficiently high level that made the difference between defeat and victory for the US forces at Khe Sanh.

21 January 1968

A-4E   151140   VMA-311, MAG-12, USMC, Chu Lai
                  Capt Bobby G Downing (survived)
The expected attack on Khe Sanh finally erupted on the 21st. The Marine Corps squadrons at Da Nang and Chu Lai began an almost constant bombardment of the enemy forces dug into the hills surrounding the base. The first fixed-wing aircraft lost during the siege was a Skyhawk that was shot down as it was strafing enemy troops six miles north of the base. Capt Downing tried to reach Khe Sanh but he was forced to eject about one mile short of the camp. A Marine Corps UH-1E helicopter rescued Capt Downing as his wingman made runs against advancing enemy troops.

22 January 1968

F-4B   151414   VMFA-323, MAG-13, USMC, Chu Lai
                  Lt Col Harry T Hagaman (survived)
                  Capt Dennis F Brandon (survived)
The next aircraft to fall victim to the North Vietnamese defences around Khe Sanh was a Phantom from Chu Lai. Lt Col Hagaman, VMFA-323's CO, was leading a flight of Phantoms against anti-aircraft gun positions around the base. As his Phantom was pulling up from a low-level pass it was hit by .50 calibre gunfire and burst into flames. Hagaman and Brandon ejected as the burning aircraft tumbled out of control just 100 feet above the ground. They both landed in tall elephant grass close to the base and were rescued by a Marine Corps helicopter as enemy troops searched for them. Lt Col Hagaman was the third CO of VMFA-323 to have ejected from a Phantom during the war.

23 January 1968

A-4E   150053   VMA-311, MAG-12, USMC, Chu Lai
                  Maj William E Loftus (survived)
The third Marine Corps aircraft lost in as many days was shot down on the 23rd. Maj Loftus was commencing a strafing run at 1,500 feet on an enemy troop concentration near Khe Sanh when his Skyhawk was hit in the fuselage by small arms fire. Realising that he could not reach his airfield or even the coast, he managed to reach Khe Sanh and ejected directly over the base. Loftus landed on the perimeter of the base and his parachute became entangled in the concertina wire that was used extensively to protect US bases in South Vietnam. He was freed by Marines from the base before the North Vietnamese, who were beginning to encircle the camp, could reach him.

A-6A   152932   VA-165, USN, USS *Ranger*
                  Lt Cdr Gerald Lee Ramsden (KIA)
                  Cdr L S Kollmorgen (survived)
When flying at low level and high speed the difference between safety and disaster can be measured in split seconds. Even in peacetime low-level flying can be dangerous but in a combat

situation the danger can be multiplied many times. The danger of low-level flying was illustrated by an Intruder crew whose aircraft hit the sea during a low-level ingress to a target in North Vietnam. One of the crew escaped but the other was killed. On this day the USS *Pueblo* was seized by the North Korean Navy and the USS *Enterprise* was diverted from heading towards Vietnam for its third war cruise and was sent to Korea to prepare for air strikes. The situation was later settled peacefully, but the *Pueblo* crisis came at a very bad time for the Americans as they were about to face one of the greatest challenges of the Vietnam War.

25 January 1968

A-4E   150057   VA-153, USN, USS *Coral Sea*
                  Cdr T E Woolcock (survived)
The SAMs had had little success during January but on the 25th they claimed their fourth victim of 1968. The CO of VA-153 was leading a strike on coastal defences and was approaching the target from inland at 12,000 feet when his Skyhawk was hit by a missile about 15 miles south of Vinh. The formation had received a warning of a SAM threat and Cdr Woolcock had started jinking his aircraft to break the missile's radar lock but to no avail. He managed to cross the coast and ejected two miles offshore. He was rescued by a Navy helicopter and returned to the *Coral Sea*.

26 January 1968

A-6A   152901   VA-165, USN, USS *Ranger*
                  Lt Cdr Norman Edward Eidsmoe (KIA)
                  Lt Michael Edward Dunn (KIA)
The Intruder's navigation and attack system was by now much more reliable than it had been in the early days of the aircraft's service and it was common for single aircraft to be sent on low-level strike missions at night. Lt Cdr Eidsmoe and Lt Dunn were flying just such a mission to bomb Vinh airfield, which is situated three miles north of the city. Two Skyhawks and two Corsairs were also airborne to provide support if needed. The Intruder was tracked in on radar until it descended to low-level shortly before it reached the target. The aircraft failed to reappear on radar and did not respond to radio calls. A search the following day found no sign of the aircraft but it was later discovered that the A-6 had crashed a few miles north of the target. The cause of the crash was undetermined.

27 January 1968

F-4C   63-7668   390 TFS, 366 TFW, USAF, Da Nang
                   Maj R W Phillips (survived)
                   1Lt B R Core (survived)
A flight of Phantoms was attacking a target on the coast of North Vietnam, three miles south of Dong Hoi, when one of the aircraft was struck by 37mm AAA. Maj Phillips headed out to sea and tried to nurse his crippled aircraft to a safe landing at Da Nang. Unfortunately, the crew were forced to eject and the aircraft crashed into the sea just off Monkey Mountain, north of Da Nang. A waiting USAF helicopter picked them up almost as soon as they parachuted into the water. Phantom 63-7668 was flown by Col Robin Olds and 1Lt W D Lafever of the 8th TFW on 4 May 1967 when they shot down a MiG-21.

28 January 1968

T-28D   49-1586   606 ACS, 56 ACW, USAF, Nakhon Phanom
                    Capt Charles W Brown (survived)
During a night armed reconnaissance sortie over the Ho Chi Minh Trail in southern Laos, a T-28 Zorro suddenly lost oil pressure, which eventually caused total engine failure. Capt Brown was just about to take over from an O-2 FAC who was directing strikes against trucks on the Trail when trouble struck. The O-2 followed the burning T-28 as it tried to make for a safe area but Capt Brown had to bail out after a few minutes, still over enemy-held territory. He landed safely and hid from enemy troops who were searching for him in the dark. In the morning the SAR force realised that Capt Brown had come down next to an NVA

battalion base camp but was picked up by a USAF SAR helicopter after suppressive fire and a smoke screen was laid down.

29 January 1968

A-4E   149976   VMA-211, MAG-12, USMC, Chu Lai
             Capt James Dale Mills (KIA)

January had been a costly month for Marine Corps aviation in Southeast Asia. The seventh Marine Corps aircraft lost in January was shot down during a close air support mission near Hoi An, just south of Da Nang. Capt Mills was strafing enemy troop positions when his Skyhawk was hit, probably by small arms fire. Capt Mills did not escape before the aircraft crashed and he may have been wounded by the ground fire.

A-4E   151055   VA-144, USN, USS *Kitty Hawk*
             1 pilot, name unknown (survived)

During a strike mission a Skyhawk suffered a mechanical failure that led to engine failure. The pilot had to eject but was rescued by a Navy helicopter.

F-105D 60-0478   355 TFW, USAF, Takhli
             1 pilot, name unknown (survived)

As a Thunderchief was taking off from Takhli on a night strike mission its engine failed and the aircraft settled back onto the ground. The pilot survived but the aircraft was destroyed.

The Tet Offensive

Tet is the holiday that celebrates the Vietnamese lunar New Year and during the war the event was usually marked by a cease-fire to allow the South Vietnamese to enjoy their celebrations and observe their religion. However, intelligence information collected in the early weeks of 1968 indicated that the Viet Cong, with assistance from NVA units in South Vietnam, was going to mount a large scale offensive. The attack was not expected until February so when the Tet Offensive opened on 30/31 January it was unexpected not only in its severity but also in its timing. It was estimated that around 80,000 communist troops were involved in the offensive and that as many as 10,000 of these were killed or captured. However, while the offensive might have been a military defeat for the VC and North Vietnam, it was certainly a huge political and psychological victory for the communist forces. Until Tet the American public had been told that the communist threat was being blunted in South Vietnam and that the North was about to buckle under the pressure of the Rolling Thunder campaign. The Tet Offensive made it clear that the communist threat in South Vietnam was still very real and that the 486,000 Americans based in that country were unable to destroy the VC. Coupled with increasingly heavy aircraft losses over North Vietnam, 1968 was probably the lowest point of the war in Southeast Asia with the exception of the final defeat in 1975.

The Tet Offensive opened on the night of 30/31 January with simultaneous attacks on a number of South Vietnamese cities and towns as well as 23 US and Vietnamese air bases. However, some VC units in the northern and central provinces of South Vietnam moved prematurely and attacked seven bases, including Da Nang and Pleiku, in the early hours of the 30th. These attacks further warned the Americans and South Vietnamese of the imminent major offensive. Within hours of the main offensive starting the American Embassy in Saigon was occupied by enemy troops and the old Vietnamese imperial capital at Hué was captured. The success of the airfield attacks encouraged the Viet Cong and North Vietnamese Army as the incidence of such attacks increased massively after Tet.

29/30 January 1968

F-4C   64-0826   366 TFW, USAF, Da Nang
F-4B   151407, 152273 VMFA-122, MAG-11, USMC, Da Nang
A-6A   152588   VMA(AW)-242, MAG-11, USMC, Da Nang

The North Vietnamese units assigned to attack the bases at Da Nang and Pleiku are thought to have mis-timed their assault, which was launched 24 hours before the main offensive. No aircraft were lost at Pleiku but three Phantoms and an Intruder were destroyed at Da Nang and another 25 aircraft were damaged. Around 40 mortars or 122mm rockets were fired at the base during the attack and one man was killed.

30/31 January 1968

A-37A   67-14517   604 ACS, 3 TFW, USAF, Bien Hoa
F-100D 55-3568   3 TFW, USAF, Bien Hoa

The VC attacks in battalion strength on Bien Hoa and Tan Son Nhut were among the most spectacular air base raids of the war. Although only two aircraft were destroyed and 17 damaged at Bien Hoa and none were lost at Tan Son Nhut, the raids had a major affect on morale. Being so close to Saigon the aftermath of the attacks was well documented by the news media and the deaths of four American servicemen underlined the tragedy. A total of 45 rounds were fired at Bien Hoa during the raid and the airfield perimeter was breached in many places by sappers and infantry.

F-4B   151508, 152287, 152289 VMFA-314, MAG-13,
             USMC, Chu Lai

The Marine Corps airfield at Chu Lai also came under attack resulting in the loss of three Phantoms. The MAG-13 area received 48 rounds of 122mm rockets and at least two Marine airmen, Capt Arthur De la Houssaye and 1Lt Richard Allen Kerr, were killed. Chu Lai's bomb dump was also hit and exploded with such force that it created a small lake and damaged buildings all over the base including VMA(AW)-533's hangar. Despite the damage, aircraft were operating from the base within hours of the attack. The US forces had now lost nine aircraft on the ground in the first two nights of the Tet Offensive. With the loss of 13 aircraft (seven of them on the ground), January 1968 was overall the worst month of the war for the Marines as far as fixed-wing aircraft losses are concerned.

1 February 1968

O-1E   51-4741, 56-422320 TASS, 504 TASG, USAF, Da Nang
O-1F   57-2864, 57-287019 TASS, 504 TASG, USAF, Bien Hoa

O-2A   67-21339, 67-21347, 67-21357, 67-21359
             20 TASS, 504 TASG, USAF, Da Nang

During the Tet Offensive the Citadel at Hué was captured by enemy troops and many hundreds of Vietnamese civilians were executed for collaborating with the Americans. The small airfield near the city was attacked by rocket and mortar fire and eight FAC aircraft were destroyed on the ground during the day. The O-2s had only been detached to Hué a few days before the attack took place.

2 February 1968

F-4C   63-7580   366 TFW, USAF, Da Nang

The VC mounted another rocket and mortar attack on Da Nang air base on the 2nd. Only one aircraft was destroyed on this occasion.

F-8E   150667   VF-191, USN, USS *Ticonderoga*
             Lt Peter Frederick Cherney (KIA)

The *Ticonderoga* arrived back on the line on 13 January, the first aircraft carrier to start a fourth cruise of the war. The first aircraft lost during this cruise was a Crusader that crashed in the Gulf of Tonkin as it was escorting a photographic reconnaissance aircraft, probably an RF-8G from the VFP-63 detachment on board the carrier. The aircraft's engine failed after a sudden loss of oil pressure and the pilot was lost in the subsequent crash. The loss was not thought to have been due to enemy action.

3 February 1968

F-102A 56-1166   509 FIS, 405 FW, USAF, Udorn
             1Lt Wallace Luttrell Wiggins (KIA)

The F-102 squadrons on rotation to Udorn provided CAPs for air strikes but do not appear to have had much success against the few MiGs they encountered. One of the rare F-102 vs MiG engagements resulted in victory for the MiG. 1Lt Wiggins and his leader were flying at 36,000 feet along the North Vietnamese border with Laos on an abortive escort mission when Wiggins was attacked by a MiG-21 about 35 miles east of Sam Neua. 1Lt Wiggins reported that he had a problem and when his leader checked his aircraft over he was amazed to see what appeared to be the remains of an air-to-air missile embedded in the Delta Dagger's tail. As the pair headed towards Laos they were attacked by two more MiG-21s. The leader, Maj A L Lomax, turned and fired three AIM-4D Falcon missiles, which missed but scared the MiGs away. When Maj Lomax looked for his wingman all he saw was a fireball and pieces of aircraft falling to earth. There was no sign of a parachute.

VMFA-122 lost two Phantoms on the ground at Da Nang during the opening night of the 1968 Tet offensive. A total of 20 US fixed-wing aircraft were lost at several airfields during the first week of the Tet offensive. USMC

4 February 1968

RF-4C 66-0443 14 TRS, 432 TRW, USAF, Udorn
1Lt William Tod Potter (KIA)
1Lt Robert John Edgar (KIA)

A reconnaissance Phantom was lost during a mission over southern Laos. The aircraft was cleared into its operational area by a forward air controller and the Phantom let down through cloud to start its photo run. 1Lt Potter reported that he had the target in sight but moments later the FAC pilot saw an explosion on the ground and assumed that the Phantom had crashed. The aircraft's wreckage was seen on Phakap mountain near Ban Phonsangphai, some 50 miles due east of Nakhon Phanom. There was no sign of the crew and a report by friendly Laotian troops stated that the crew had died in the aircraft. This was the first aircraft lost by the 14th TRS since its arrival from Bergstrom AFB, Texas on 28 October 1967.

F-105D 60-5384 34 TFS, 388 TFW, USAF, Korat
Capt Carl William Lasiter (POW)

The MiGs scored another victory when they shot down one of the F-105 bombers during a raid on barracks at Thai Nguyen. The strike force was still some 30 miles to the west of the target when it was intercepted by several MiG-21s. The MiGCAP flight Phantoms gave chase but lost the MiGs, which then closed on the rear of the F-105 flight. Capt Lasiter ejected from his aircraft at 18,000 feet after it was hit by an Atoll missile. He was captured and spent the next five years as a POW until his release on 14 March 1973. He was on his 52nd mission when he was shot down.

O-1E 56-4201 22 TASS, 504 TASG, USAF, Binh Thuy

A VC mortar attack on the airfield at Binh Thuy on the banks of the Mekong resulted in the destruction of a Bird Dog FAC aircraft.

5/6 February 1968

P-3B 153440 VP-26, USN, U-Tapao
(on TDY from Sangley Point)
Lt Cdr Robert F Meglio (KIA)
Lt(jg) Thomas Paul Jones (KIA)
Lt(jg) Lynn Michael Travis (KIA)
Lt(jg) Roy Arthur Huss (KIA)
AXC Donald Frederick Burnett (KIA)
AOC Donald Louis Gallagher (KIA)
AMH2 Homer Eugene McKay (KIA)
ADR1 James Clifford Newman (KIA)
AE1 Melvin Carl Thompson (KIA)
ADJ2 Billy W McGhee (KIA)
AX3 Armando Chapa (KIA)
AX3 William Farrell Farris (KIA)

Since November 1964 US Navy P-3 Orion squadrons had been based in Southeast Asia on rotation from bases in the Pacific and the USA. The aircraft were used primarily for coastal reconnaissance as part of the Market Time campaign to reduce the amount of infiltration and resupply of enemy forces by sea. An Orion took off from U-Tapao on the morning of the 5th for a 24-hour Market Time sortie over the Gulf of Thailand and along the coast of South Vietnam. The aircraft was flown by Crew Eight of VP-26, which was normally based at NAS Brunswick, Maine, but had been deployed to Sangley Point in the Philippines on 24 November 1967 for operations in Southeast Asia. Soon after midnight on the 5th the aircraft reported the first of a small number of surface contacts. Its last radio report was timed at 0300 hours. When the aircraft became overdue on the morning of the 6th an extensive search was started. Wreckage was located in the Gulf of Thailand at a position about 65 miles southwest of Rach Gia. It was soon apparent that all 12 men on board had been lost. Salvage operations commenced on 11 February and ceased on 21 March but no evidence was found to indicate whether enemy action or mechanical failure had caused the crash. The wreckage was located in 100 feet of water and two bodies, those of Lt Cdr Meglio and ADJ2 McGhee, were recovered. It was conjectured that there might have been a problem with the aircraft's autopilot causing it to fly into the sea. Another P-3 accident in

the South China Sea on 5 April was also thought to have been caused by problems with the aircraft's autopilot.

6 February 1968

O-1E 53-7994 19 TASS, 504 TASG, USAF, Bien Hoa
detached to Tay Ninh

A VC mortar attack on the airfield at Tay Ninh near the Cambodian border destroyed a single Bird Dog with a direct hit.

8 February 1968

F-4D 66-7769 555 TFS, 8 TFW, USAF, Ubon
Capt T K Dorsett (survived)
Capt J A Corder (survived)

The recent success that the MiGs had been having was a cause of great concern to the planners as well as the airmen who had to run their gauntlet. In an effort to subdue the VPAF, Phuc Yen airfield, one of the main MiG bases, was attacked on the 8th. Anti-aircraft fire hit one of the bombers as it swept across the airfield at 500 feet to deliver its bombs. Capt Dorsett pulled up with his port engine winding down and on fire. He flew back towards Thailand but he and his WSO were forced to eject over Laos, about 30 miles west of Sam Neua. Both men were picked up by an HH-3E having suffered only minor injuries.

A-1H '52-135043' 1 ACS, 56 ACW, USAF, Nakhon Phanom
Maj Robert Granthan Lapham (KIA)

The pressure on Khe Sanh continued despite almost continuous air strikes by B-52 and tactical aircraft. A new and worrying development was the employment of tanks by the North Vietnamese. Three tanks had been seen near the recently captured Special Forces camp at Lang Vei, about five miles southwest of Khe Sanh and practically on the border with Laos. Maj Lapham, along with three other Skyraider pilots, fought through intense anti-aircraft fire to attack the tanks with napalm. On its second pass, Maj Lapham's aircraft was hit by ground fire and crashed before the pilot could escape. Robert Lapham was posthumously award the Silver Star for his courage in the face of huge odds. The serial 52-135043 may be incorrect as it belongs to an A-1G.

10 February 1968

KC-130F 149813 VMGR-152, MAG-15, USMC, Da Nang
CWO Henry Wildfang (survived)
Maj Robert E White (survived)
MSgt John D'Adamo (KIA)
LCpl David Ralf Devik (KIA)
LCpl Jerry Wayne Ferren (KIA)
1 crew (survived)
5 US Marine passengers (KIA)

One of the main reasons that Khe Sanh was resisting the siege so successfully was its resupply by air. This became particularly important when 1,500 tons (representing 98 per cent of the base's ammunition supply) was hit and detonated by enemy rockets and artillery on the first day of the siege. Much of the resupply was performed by USAF C-123s and C-130s and the Marine Corps' own KC-130s. Normally a detachment of four aircraft from VMGR-152 was based at Da Nang for transport and air-to-air refuelling duties. Prior to 10 February seven C-130s had been hit and damaged on resupply missions into Khe Sanh. The first transport aircraft lost during the siege was a KC-130 that was hit in the cockpit and fuselage several times by .50 calibre gunfire as it approached the airfield on the 10th. The aircraft was carrying a load of flamethrowers and several large rubber bladders full of jet fuel for the Marine's turbine-engined helicopters. The No 3 engine caught fire and a fuel bladder was ruptured and trailed burning fuel. Despite extensive smoke and flames the aircraft touched down normally but then burst into flames as the fuel bladders exploded. The pilot and co-pilot escaped through the cockpit windows after they turned the aircraft off the runway and firefighters rescued another occupant before fire consumed the aircraft. Eight of the 11 men on board the aircraft were killed and LCpl Ferren died of his injuries on 1 March. One of the passengers who was killed was Col C E Peterson from the 1st MAW headquarters. Two days after this incident

the Seventh Air Force prohibited landings by C-130s at Khe Sanh although the prohibition was lifted briefly towards the end of the month. Henry Wildfang was awarded his fifth DFC for his skill in landing the aircraft at Khe Sanh.

11 February 1968

F-4C 63-7663 unit ..?, USAF, base ..?
O-1E 56-2491 19 TASS, 504 TASG, USAF, Bien Hoa
O-2A 67-21362 19 TASS, 504 TASG, USAF, Bien Hoa

Bien Hoa was hit by the Viet Cong again on 11 February, although only 16 rockets were fired and only three aircraft were destroyed during this raid. However, shrapnel and fire damaged another 26 aircraft. The Bird Dog was the fourth aircraft lost by the 19th TASS in base attacks during February.

O-2A 67-21401 22 TASS, 504 TASG, USAF, Binh Thuy

The Viet Cong had even less success when they attacked Binh Thuy where they only destroyed a single O-2 after firing nine mortar rounds.

12 February 1968

A-1H 54-135324 602 ACS, 56 ACW, USAF, Udorn
Capt P F Kimminau (survived)

It was not just at Khe Sanh that enemy tanks had been seen and engaged. During an armed reconnaissance mission 10 miles west of the Pathet Lao stronghold of Sam Neua, a flight of Skyraiders came upon a number of North Vietnamese tanks. Whether the tanks were on their way south to take part in the siege of Khe Sanh or the Tet offensive or were being used to support the Pathet Lao is not known. Wherever the destination, the Skyraiders attacked the tanks but Capt Kimminau's aircraft was hit by ground fire. He managed to fly about 10 miles to the west before he had to eject from the aircraft. He was rescued by an Air America helicopter.

O-1G 51-11993 19 TASS, 504 TASG, USAF, Bien Hoa
1 pilot, name unknown (survived)

A Bird Dog crashed into a fuel truck at Dak To airstrip in South Vietnam during a reconnaissance sortie. The accident was attributed to an error of judgement by the pilot.

14 February 1968

A-1H 134499 VA-25, USN, USS Coral Sea
Lt(jg) Joseph Patrick Dunn (KIA)

Lt Dunn must have thought himself lucky to be chosen to collect one of his Squadron's aircraft from Cubi Point NAS in the Philippines where it had been undergoing repairs. He took off from Cubi Point for the ferry flight back to the Coral Sea, which was having a 10-day stand down from operations. Lt Dunn was accompanied by another aircraft on the flight back to the carrier. During the flight the pair drifted north of their intended track and came close to the east coast of the Chinese island of Hainan. The aircraft were intercepted by Chinese MiGs, one of which fired on Lt Dunn's aircraft. The Skyraider came down about seven miles from the coast, offshore from the village of Kao-lung. The other US pilot saw Lt Dunn eject and watched the parachute deploy. He reported the incident but was under the impression that he was off the coast of North Vietnam so the SAR forces were directed to the wrong location. When the pilot eventually arrived at a South Vietnamese airfield he realised his mistake and the search was redirected towards Hainan. Eight hours after Lt Dunn was shot down a SAR beeper transmission was heard near Hainan, however, there has been no further evidence of the fate of Joseph Dunn since that day. Lt(jg) Dunn was promoted successively to the rank of Commander during the time he was posted as missing until his death was presumed for administrative purposes. This was the last Navy Skyraider lost during the war in Southeast Asia as the single seat model made its last flight with VA-25 on 10 April and the EA-1F flew its last operational mission on 18 September 1968. VA-25 flew the last operational Navy Skyraider sortie of the war on 20 February, after which the Squadron returned to the USA on the Coral Sea and re-equipped with the A-4F Skyhawk.

F-105D 60-0418   34 TFS, 388 TFW, USAF, Korat
                 Capt Robert Malcolm Elliot (KIA)

The Paul Doumer Bridge came in for another pounding on St Valentine's Day. Capt Elliot was part of an Iron Hand flight that was keeping the SAM batteries busy while the strike force hit the bridge. As the flight was retiring at the conclusion of the raid, Capt Elliot's aircraft was hit by a SAM at 8,000 feet and burst into flames. Capt Elliot radioed that he had been hit and was ejecting but none of his flight saw a parachute. The aircraft crashed near the Red River, about 15 miles south of Hanoi. A number of reports indicate that Robert Elliot did eject and was captured but he did not return in 1973. In 1988 the Vietnamese handed over remains that they claimed to be those of Capt Elliot along with his military ID card. However, it was not until December 1999 that the remains were positively identified as those of Robert Elliot. Apparently he had been buried by local villagers at the time of his death and subsequently disinterred and handed over to the government for repatriation. 60-0418 wore the name 'Sugar Bugger' with a cartoon character during its time at Korat.

F-8E 150909   VF-194, USN, USS *Ticonderoga*
              Lt(jg) Robert Charles McMahan (KIA)

Lt McMahan was escorting a photographic reconnaissance aircraft on a mission to Vinh airfield when he was shot down by one of the SAM batteries that protected the air base. The Crusader was flying at 5,000 feet when it was struck by the missile and although an emergency beeper was heard briefly there was no sign of a parachute. It appears that Lt McMahan did not survive the incident as his remains were handed over in September 1990 and formally identified on 29 November 1990.

F-100D 56-3304   90 TFS, 3 TFW, USAF, Bien Hoa
                 Capt J K Lewis (survived)

A flight of F-100s stood on strip alert every night at Bien Hoa, Phu Cat, Phan Rang and Tuy Hoa in case air support was needed in a hurry during the night. As the Viet Cong often preferred to attack at night, the F-100s were frequently called upon. Capt Lewis was scrambled to attack a VC gun position that had been discovered near the village of Cau Ke on the banks of the Mekong, 17 miles southeast of Can Tho. As he made his third strafing pass over the target, his aircraft was hit by small arms fire. Capt Lewis flew up the Mekong and ejected close to Binh Thuy airfield from where a USAF HH-43 from Detachment 10 of the 38th ARRS came out to rescue him.

14/15 February 1968

AC-47D 43-49859   14 ACS, 14 ACW, USAF, Nha Trang
                  detached to Phan Rang
                  Lt Col Karl Merritt Waldron (KIA)
                  Capt Edward Beeding Quill (KIA)
                  Capt Thomas Joseph Margle (KIA)
                  SSgt Warren Mitchell Dixon (KIA)
                  SSgt Robert Kiyoshi Kawamura (KIA)
                  SSgt Roger Gail Lee (KIA)
                  Sgt James Harvey Bennett (KIA)
                  Sgt Brent Tosh (KIA)

On the night of the 14th a Spooky gunship from Phan Rang was shot down just five miles south of the air base during a close air support mission. All eight crewmembers were killed when the aircraft crashed in flames. This was the only confirmed loss suffered by the short-lived 14th ACS. The Squadron was activated on 25 October 1967 but did not become operational until 15 January 1968 and was redesignated as the 3rd ACS on 1 May 1968.

15 February 1968

F-4D 66-7586   389 TFS, 366 TFW, USAF, Da Nang
               Capt Joseph V Carpenter (POW)
               Capt Lawrence Daniel Writer (POW)

A Da Nang Phantom was lost during a raid on trucks near Dong Hoi. Capt Carpenter was making his second strafing run when his aircraft was hit by 37mm anti-aircraft fire. Both crew ejected and were quickly captured. It took three weeks for the two men to reach their first prison camp in Hanoi. Capt Carpenter was only in prison for five months and became one of the three airmen released by the North Vietnamese as a propaganda stunt on 18 July. Capt Writer had arrived in Vietnam on the eve of the Tet Offensive and had only flown seven missions when he was shot down. He was released on 14 March 1973.

17 February 1968

F-100F 56-3959   614 TFS, 35 TFW, USAF, Phan Rang
                 Lt Col B M Fields (survived)
                 Capt William David Canup (survived)

The Mekong Delta area was always regarded as a Viet Cong stronghold and fighting was particularly heavy in the region during the Tet Offensive. All the F-100 units were very busy providing close air support during the Offensive. Lt Col Fields and Capt Canup were flying a mission in a two-seat F-100F to bomb enemy troops five miles southwest of Can Tho in the Delta. On their second pass their aircraft was hit by small arms fire forcing the pair to eject. Lt Col Fields was rescued by a VNAF aircraft and Capt Canup by a US Army aircraft or helicopter. Capt Canup was killed in an F-100 a few weeks later on 6 April.

OP-2E 131486   VO-67, USN, Nakhon Phanom
               Cdr Glenn Miller Hayden (KIA)
               Lt Curtis Frank Thurman (KIA)
               Lt(jg) James Stephen Kravitz (KIA)
               Ens James Charles Wonn (KIA)
               ATN1 Paul Nicholas Donato (KIA)
               AO2 Clayborn Willis Ashby (KIA)
               ADJ2 Chester Leroy Coons (KIA)
               AN Frank Arthur Dawson (KIA)
               AN James Edward Martin (KIA)

VO-67 lost its second aircraft and crew on 17 February. Cdr Glenn Hayden and his crew took off from Nakhon Phanom on a sensor delivery mission over southern Laos. The aircraft started its first delivery run to drop sensors near Ban Namm, 30 miles west of the DMZ. As it completed the first run, Cdr Hayden radioed to his fighter escort that the aircraft had been hit by small arms fire but that he would continue with the second run as there appeared to be no serious damage. As the Neptune was dropping its next load of sensors the pilot of the escorting fighter saw the

Neptune's starboard engine burst into flames. Cdr Hayden aborted the run and turned towards Nakhon Phanom. The fighter climbed through a low overcast to wait for the Neptune but it never appeared so the fighter descended back through the clouds to search for the aircraft. An area of burning wreckage was seen on the side of a ridge about two miles northwest of the village of Muang Phine. There was no sign of any survivors so it was presumed that all on board had perished in the crash. In 1993 a team of investigators recovered the remains of the crew and brought them home to the USA.

17/18 February 1968

F-100F 56-3923   3 TFW, USAF, Bien Hoa

Bien Hoa was once more the target for a Viet Cong attack on the 17th. Seven rockets or mortar rounds were fired destroying one Super Sabre and damaging three more. This Super Sabre first arrived in Vietnam when it deployed to Tan Son Nhut for five months with the 481st TFS in 1965.

C-130B 58-0743   772 TAS, 463 TAW, USAF, Mactan
RF-4C 63-7749   460 TRW, USAF, Tan Son Nhut
RF-101C 56-0182 Detachment 1, 45 TRS, 460 TRW,
                 USAF, Tan Son Nhut

The Viet Cong were more successful with their rockets at Tan Son Nhut where not only did they destroy a Hercules, the largest aircraft destroyed on the ground so far during the Tet Offensive, but they also hit two of the valuable reconnaissance aircraft. The VC used both 122mm rocket projectiles and 75mm recoilless rifles and about 100 rounds fell on the base within 20 minutes. 63-7749 was the 10th production RF-4C variant to be built. One of the rounds that hit the Hercules entered the fuselage through the overhead escape hatch and was described as a perfect hole-in-one!

18 February 1968

F-105F 63-8293   44 TFS, 388 TFW, USAF, Korat
                 Maj M S Muskat (survived)
                 Capt K Stouder (survived)

A two-seat Thunderchief was lost during a Barrel Roll mission in northern Laos. Maj Muskat and Capt Stouder were strafing a storage and bivouac area 10 miles west of Sam Neua when their aircraft was in the fuselage hit by AAA. The aircraft made it back into Thailand but the crew had to eject a few miles west of Udorn.

RF-4C 64-1043, 66-0391 460 TRW, USAF, Tan Son Nhut

Following their success on the previous day, the Viet Cong struck again at Tan Son Nhut resulting in the destruction of two more RF-4Cs. Four separate attacks were made on the airfield during the day with about 65 rockets or mortar rounds being fired.

A pair of RF-4Cs sit in their revetment at Tan Son Nhut as a fire burns on the far side of the base. Mortar, rocket and sapper attacks on airfields by VC units resulted in the loss of 113 American fixed-wing aircraft during the war. USAF

The 481st TFS was one of several F-100 squadrons that deployed to Southeast Asia on temporary duty before wings were permanently assigned. This F-100F sitting in the dark at Tan Son Nhut in October 1965 remained in South Vietnam after the 481st TFS returned to the USA in November 1965 and was destroyed during a VC attack on Bien Hoa on 17 February 1968. USAF

C-47B 43-48471   probably 6250 ABS, 377 CSG, USAF,
                  Tan Son Nhut
                  3 crew, names unknown (survived)
A C-47 Skytrain crashed as it was taking off on a transport flight. The accident was attributed to pilot error. This aircraft had previously been operated by the 12th TFW from Cam Ranh Bay.

19 February 1968

F-4C 64-0803 390 TFS, 366 TFW, USAF, Da Nang
               Capt P A Brandt (survived)
               1Lt P J Seiler (survived)
A Phantom was hit by ground fire seconds after taking off from Da Nang for a strike in the Khe Sanh area. The crew must have thought that the aircraft was undamaged as they apparently continued the mission. However, the aircraft crashed in the A Shau Valley, 10 miles southeast of Khe Sanh after the crew ejected. They were fortunate to be picked up from this well-known 'hot spot' by a USAF SAR helicopter.

RF-4C 65-0842   460 TRW, USAF, Tan Son Nhut
Tan Son Nhut lost a fourth reconnaissance Phantom in the space of three days during another day of Viet Cong rocket attacks on the airfield. Four attacks were made in the early hours and only 21 rockets were fired in total.

23 February 1968

F-4D 66-8725 497 TFS, 8 TFW, USAF, Ubon
               Maj Laird Guttersen (POW)
               1Lt Myron Lee Donald (POW)
As a flight of Phantoms was returning from a CAP mission over North Vietnam it was jumped by several MiG-21s about 35 miles north of Hon Gay. Maj Guttersen's aircraft was badly damaged by an air-to-air missile and he tried to make for the coast. Unfortunately, the crew had to eject about 10 miles short of the coast when the aircraft became uncontrollable. Both men were captured, tortured and kept in solitary confinement like most other POWs. Maj Guttersen was in his third war having flown B-25s in the Second World War and F-51s and F-86s in the Korean conflict. Ironically, he had served as an instructor at the Air University at Maxwell AFB where he had specialised in POW matters and had helped to write the manual on how to teach the Code of Conduct to be adopted by American POWs. His experience came in useful in the long years of brutal captivity in North Vietnam. He had flown C-130s in Southeast

Asia during 1965 and 1966 and had been shot down once before on his second tour when he had to be rescued from the Gulf of Tonkin on 15 December 1967. Maj Guttersen and 1Lt Donald were released on 14 March 1973. This Phantom would be the last USAF fixed-wing aircraft lost to a MiG until 18 December 1971.

A-6A 152631   VMA(AW)-533, MAG-12, USMC, Chu Lai
               1Lt R V Smith (survived)
               1 crew, name unknown (survived)

F-8E 150857   VMF(AW)-235, MAG-11, USMC, Da Nang
               Capt George Lawrence Hubler (KIA)
A Marine Corps Intruder on a strike mission collided with a Crusader on a non-combat flight a few miles out to sea near Da Nang. The two crew from the Intruder ejected and were rescued but the Crusader pilot was killed.

24 February 1968

A-6A 152644   VMA(AW)-533, MAG-12, USMC, Chu Lai
               Maj Jerry Wendell Marvel (POW)
               Capt Lawrence Victor Friese (POW)
A Marine Corps Intruder was shot down during a night strike on Hoa Lac airfield, 17 miles west of Hanoi. It was thought that the aircraft had probably been brought down by a SAM although this could not be confirmed. Capt Friese, who was on his 138th mission when he was shot down, evaded the North Vietnamese for four days before he was finally caught. Both men were released from captivity on 14 March 1973. Jerry Marvel later became commander of New River MCAS and retired from the Marines as a Colonel but died of a heart attack in 1995. Soon after returning from Vietnam, Capt Friese transferred from the Marines to the Navy and finally retired as a Commander in 1985.

F-8E 150335   VF-191, USN, USS Ticonderoga
               Lt Wendell Brown (survived)
A Crusader was lost during a night BARCAP mission when it ran out of fuel. The night was very dark and stormy and Lt Brown had difficulty engaging the basket of an A-3 tanker. Eventually his flight-refuelling probe hit the basket and damaged it so the Ticonderoga scrambled an A-4 with a buddy refuelling pack as a replacement. Just as Lt Brown plugged into the tanker's basket the A-4 pilot inadvertently disconnected him and the F-8 flamed out. Lt Brown ejected and was eventually picked up by a Navy helicopter after spending two and a half days in his life raft in the Gulf of Tonkin.

25 February 1968

F-100D 56-3261   355 TFS, 354 TFW attached to 37 TFW,
                  USAF, Phu Cat
                  Capt Bernard E Flanagan (survived)
A flight of F-100s from Phu Cat was sent on a Steel Tiger mission in southern Laos. The target was a group of North Vietnamese troops who had been seen near the village of Ban Kandon, 25 miles east of Saravan. As Capt Flanagan rolled in for his second pass his aircraft was hit by 37mm AAA. He flew towards Saravan and ejected safely. He was rescued within the hour by a USAF HH-3E.

O-1E 56-2512   20 TASS, 504 TASG, USAF, Da Nang
                Maj L J Severson (survived)
A Bird Dog was damaged by ground fire during an FAC mission 10 miles southwest of Da Nang. Maj Severson crash-landed the aircraft and was picked up by an Army helicopter before the VC could reach him.

A-4E 150104   VMA-211, MAG-12, USMC, Chu Lai
               Maj V P Hart (survived)
A flight of Skyhawks was sent to attack an enemy village near Hoi An, 10 miles southeast of Da Nang, which was defended by bunkers and fortified positions. Maj Hart's aircraft was hit by small arms fire on its fourth pass over the village. He ejected close by and was rescued by helicopter before the Viet Cong could find him.

26 February 1968

F-100D 55-3762   90 TFS, 3 TFW, USAF, Bien Hoa
                  Capt C D Sissell (survived)
Another F-100 was shot down in the Mekong Delta region. Capt Sissell was making his third strafing pass against a number of troops near Ap Nhut, 13 miles northeast of Can Tho, when his aircraft was hit by ground fire. He flew towards Can Tho and ejected a few miles west of the town. Capt Sissell survived to be shot down again on 6 March.

27 February 1968

OP-2E 131484   VO-67, USN, Nakhon Phanom
                Cdr Paul Lloyd Milius (KIA)
                Lt Bernie Walsh (survived)
                Ens H G Wells (survived)
                PO2 John Francis Hartzheim (KIA)
                5 crew, names unknown (survived)
The third and last Neptune lost by VO-67 was shot down on the 27th. The aircraft was on a mission to drop sensors in the area along Route 912, about 15 miles southwest of the Ban Karai Pass. As the aircraft was making its sensor drop it was hit in the radar bay by a 37mm anti-aircraft shell, which mortally wounded PO2 Hartzheim. The aircraft caught fire and the fuselage began to fill with dense smoke. Cdr Milius immediately took over the controls and ordered the crew to abandon the aircraft. John Hartzheim collapsed and died as he was carried to the rear of the aircraft. As Cdr Milius struggled to keep the Neptune airborne the remaining crew bailed out leaving Hartzheim's body in the aircraft. The Neptune crashed a few miles south of the Ban Laboy Ford. Although seven of the crew were rescued by SAR helicopters over the next five hours, the fate of Cdr Milius was unclear at the time. A SAR beeper was heard in the general locality of the crash and was thought at first to have been that of Cdr Milius. A Bright Light team was immediately prepared for insertion but approval from the US ambassador in Laos could not be obtained for a whole day.

Eventually the team went in but was met by strong opposition and had to be extracted. The contact was later thought to have possibly been one of the RF-4C crew listed below who were shot down only about 10 miles away. In 1994 US investigators discovered witnesses who claimed that Cdr Milius had escaped from the aircraft just moments before it crashed but that he was killed when his parachute failed to deploy before he hit the ground. Investigations by joint US/Lao teams in 1994, 1995 and 1996 recovered human remains and other items from the wreckage. Some of the remains were identified in March 1999 as those of PO2 Hartzheim. In November 1996 an *Arleigh Burke*-class guided-missile destroyer was named the USS *Milius* in honour of the Neptune's commander. Paul Milius had spent much of his 18-year naval career flying AEW and ASW aircraft but had also been Catapult Officer aboard the USS *Kearsarge*. Following the loss of this aircraft the minimum altitude for the sensor-dropping missions was raised to 5,000 feet. Although no more aircraft were lost, VO-67 was deactivated on 1 July and the task of dropping sensors was passed on to the F-4s of the 25th TFS.

RF-4C 66-0431 14 TRS, 432 TRW, USAF, Udorn
    Maj Gilbert Swain Palmer (KIA)
    Capt Thomas Thawson Wright (KIA)
A Phantom failed to return to Udorn from a solo reconnaissance mission over North Vietnam. It was thought that the aircraft had probably been shot down over southern Laos, not far from where the OP-2E came down. According to Veith in *Code Name Bright Light*, at least one of the Phantom crew is thought to have survived long enough to use his survival radio and fire a flare at the request of the SAR force. However, due to delays in authorising the rescue mission and a problem with a rescue hoist, no one was ever recovered. An intelligence report suggested that a black USAF officer had been seen in a temporary POW camp in this area and this report has been tentatively correlated to Capt Wright.

28 February 1968

C-130E 64-0522 776 TAS, 314 TAW, USAF, Ching Chuan Kang
    Maj Leland R Filmore (survived)
    1Lt Caroters (survived)
    1Lt Paul Burns (survived)
    TSgt Marcus Looper (survived)
    Sgt Gary Henke (survived)
    5 passengers (survived)
A Hercules was hit in the port wing by intense small arms fire just as it took off from an airstrip at Song Be, 25 miles northeast of An Loc. Maj Filmore and his co-pilot turned to the left, away from the direction of the enemy fire, and flew over a village south of the airfield where they came under another withering hail of fire. The port wing caught fire but the crew managed to crash-land the burning aircraft back on the runway at Song Be and all the passengers and crew escaped unharmed before the aircraft was completely gutted by fire. Maj Filmore was awarded a Silver Star for his part in the drama. This was the only transport aircraft to be shot down during the Tet Offensive, although another 83 transports were damaged by ground fire during this period. At this date there was a total of 96 USAF C-130 transports temporarily based in South Vietnam. The majority, 51, were based at Cam Ranh Bay, 27 were at Tan Son Nhut, 10 at Tuy Hoa, and eight at Nha Trang.

F-105D 62-4385 354 TFS, 355 TFW, USAF, Takhli
    Capt Gene I Basel (survived)
A flight of F-105s was sent to attack a POL storage site on the Ho Chi Minh Trail near Ban San in southern Laos. Capt Basel was making his second run on the target when his aircraft was

The 311th ACS lost three C-123 Providers in the first week of March 1968 during the siege of Khe Sanh. The C-123s and C-130s, together with Marine Corps helicopters, kept the base supplied throughout the long siege thereby averting a major communist victory. USMC

hit by ground fire. The engine started to wind down and caught fire. Capt Basel, who was on his 79th mission, ejected a few miles from where he was hit and was rescued by a USAF helicopter. Gene Basel later wrote an excellent account of his tour at Takhli titled *Pak Six*.

A-6A 152938 VA-35, USN, USS *Enterprise*
    Lt Cdr Henry Albert Coons (KIA)
    Lt Thomas Stegman (KIA)
An Intruder failed to return from a night strike on a coastal defence site at Do Son in North Vietnam. The pilot's last radio message stated that he was 14 minutes from the target and was about to start his run in. After the aircraft went missing an extensive land and sea search was made. Wreckage was spotted about 20 miles off the coast east of Thanh Hoa. A helmet, a liferaft and the flak-damaged tail fin were found floating a few miles from the aircraft's last known position but there was no sign of either of the crew.

29 February 1968

F-4D 66-7528 435 TFS, 8 TFW, USAF, Ubon
    Lt Col C D Smith (survived)
    1Lt Francis Murtaugh Driscoll (KIA)
A formation of F-4s was sent to attack a truck park during a Steel Tiger mission in southern Laos. The park was near the village of Ban Topen, about 30 miles west of the DMZ. Lt Col Smith's aircraft was hit by 14.5mm anti-aircraft fire during the attack. Lt Col Smith was able to fly the aircraft back to Ubon, however, the aircraft crashed while attempting to make an emergency landing. 1Lt Driscoll was killed and Lt Col Smith was badly injured when his parachute failed to deploy properly following ejection.

F-105F 63-8312 44 TFS, 388 TFW, USAF, Korat
    Maj Crosley James Fitton (KIA)
    Capt Cleveland Scott Harris (KIA)
The second Wild Weasel lost during 1968 was shot down during a strike on a major military vehicle depot in Hanoi. The Iron Hand flight of four F-105s approached Hanoi from the southwest at 12,000 feet but when it was over Van La, about 10 miles from the city, it came under attack from SAMs. Maj Fitton's aircraft was seen to be hit and its starboard wing caught fire and disintegrated. Both pilot and WSO were seen to eject by other members of the flight and emergency beepers were also heard. Although both men are thought to have survived their ejection, neither appeared in the POW camps and they were declared as missing in action at the end of the war. Maj Fitton's remains were handed over on 21 December 1975. Capt Harris's remains were not returned to the USA until April 1985. The cause of their deaths is still not known. Thunderchief 63-8312 was painted as 'Midnight Sun' at the time of its loss.

1 March 1968

C-123K 54-0694 311 ACS, 315 ACW, USAF, Phan Rang
    detached to Da Nang
    4 crew, names unknown (survived)
    6 passengers (survived)
A Provider was hit by fragments from the explosion of a mortar shell just as it was lifting off from Khe Sanh following a resupply flight. One engine was put out of action and the pilot quickly forced the aircraft back on the ground. The aircraft veered off the runway and caught fire. All the occupants escaped, six of them with injuries, and enemy mortar fire then hit the aircraft again causing it to burn out.

A-6A 152944 VA-35, USN, USS *Enterprise*
    Lt Cdr Thomas Edwin Scheurich (KIA)
    Lt(jg) Richard Clive Lannom (KIA)
As darkness fell three Intruders were launched from the *Enterprise* to make independent attacks on various targets in North Vietnam. Lt Cdr Scheurich and Lt Lannom were assigned to attack army barracks at Cam Pha. The three aircraft rendezvoused just off the North Vietnamese coast and each crew checked their aircraft's systems and weapons before heading off towards their respective targets. A search was instigated when Lt Cdr Scheurich's aircraft failed to return but no trace was found of the aircraft or its crew. It was assumed that the Intruder had been shot down or had flown into the sea among the islands south of Cam Pha.

2 March 1968

RF-4B 153115 VMCJ-1, MAG-11, USMC, Da Nang
    Maj R J Morley (survived)
    Capt D C Richards (survived)
VMCJ-1 lost one of its RF-4Bs during a reconnaissance mission in South Vietnam. The aircraft was shot down by ground fire near the village of Muang Bac, 50 miles southwest of Da Nang. Both the crew were rescued by an Army helicopter.

C-130A 56-0549 21 TAS, 374 TAW, USAF, Naha
    5 crew, names unknown (survived)
    5 passengers (KIA)
A Hercules was destroyed in a night landing accident in light rain at Hué/Phu Bai. Although none of the five crew were killed, six of the troops the aircraft was carrying were killed in the accident.

3 March 1968

A-37A 67-14521 604 ACS, 3 TFW, USAF, Bien Hoa
    1Lt John Thomas Welshan (KIA)
An A-37 was lost during a close air support mission near Bac Lieu on the southern tip of South Vietnam. 1Lt Welshan was

making his third pass over his target when his aircraft crashed either as a result of ground fire or by inadvertently flying into the ground. John Welshan was posted missing until administratively declared dead on 15 July 1975.

C-130E 62-1814   50 TAS, 314 TAW, USAF, Ching Chuan Kang
6 crew, names unknown (survived)

Another Hercules was destroyed in a landing accident, this time at Cam Ranh Bay. Again all the occupants escaped largely unscathed from the accident, which was thought to have been caused by an electrical fire on board the aircraft.

5 March 1968

O-1F 57-2813   21 TASS, 504 TASG, USAF, Nha Trang
Capt W T Abbey (survived)

An O-1 was shot down by ground fire in South Vietnam as it was en route to its assigned area for a visual reconnaissance mission. Capt Abbey was rescued having sustained only minor injuries.

EB-66E 54-0524   41 TEWS, 355 TFW, USAF, Takhli
3 crew, names unknown (survived)

An EB-66E electronic warfare aircraft crashed in Thailand following an engine failure during a radar jamming mission. This was the first EB-66E variant of the Destroyer to be lost during the war. The EB-66E was a modified version of the EB-66B and was fitted with more powerful ECM jamming equipment than its predecessors.

6 March 1968

F-100D 56-3269   510 TFS, 3 TFW, USAF, Bien Hoa
1Lt W V Tomlinson (survived)

Although the Tet Offensive was officially over, many of the air-fields in South Vietnam were still under the threat of Viet Cong attack. 1Lt Tomlinson was almost home when his Super Sabre was shot at as he approached Bien Hoa. He managed to eject and the aircraft crashed about a mile to the east of the airfield's perimeter fence. The pilot was rescued before the Viet Cong could reach him.

C-123K 54-0590   311 ACS, 315 ACW, USAF, Phan Rang
detached to Da Nang
Lt Col Frederick Jordan Hampton (KIA)
1Lt Ellis Eugene Helgeson (KIA)
Sgt Jeffrey Francis Conlin (KIA)
SSgt William Frank Anselmo (KIA)
SSgt Noel Luis Rios (KIA)
45 passengers (KIA)

A Provider was hit by ground fire as it approached Khe Sanh. The aircraft was delivering troops and spare parts from Hué/Phu Bai to Khe Sanh. The aircraft was forced to go around from its first approach to the airfield as a VNAF light aircraft was obstructing the runway. The Provider circled at low altitude to make another approach but it was hit by ground fire in the port jet engine. The pilot radioed that he was turning back to Da Nang but the air-craft spiralled into the ground minutes later. All 49 on board, including the five crew, 44 US Marines and a civilian photogra-pher, were killed in the crash. The aircraft crashed about a mile southeast of the runway. Sgts Anselmo and Rios were from the 15th Aerial Port Squadron.

F-105D 62-4336   333 TFS, 355 TFW, USAF, Takhli
Capt F E Peck (survived)

Although the war in South Vietnam was causing great concern at this time, the Steel Tiger campaign in southern Laos was also claiming more aircraft. A flight of F-105s was assigned to attack a road near Ban Vangthon, 20 miles west of the DMZ. The target was part of the Ho Chi Minh Trail and its destruction could cause significant delays to supplies moving south. Capt Peck's aircraft was hit by ground fire damaging the engine. He ejected and was badly injured but was picked up by a USAF helicopter.

F-100D 55-3587   90 TFS, 3 TFW, USAF, Bien Hoa
Capt C D Sissell (survived)

The 3rd TFW lost another F-100 on the 6th. Capt Sissell was attacking enemy troops six miles east of Quan Long in the south-ern tip of South Vietnam. The aircraft was hit in the tail by ground fire as it was pulling up off the target. The aircraft became uncontrollable so Capt Sissell ejected immediately. He was fortunate to be rescued before the troops he was bombing found him. This was the second time that Capt Sissell had ejected from his F-100 in the space of just over a week.

A-6A 152922   VA-75, USN, USS *Kitty Hawk*
Lt Richard Crawford Nelson (KIA)
Lt Gilbert Louis Mitchell (KIA)

An Intruder was lost during a night low-level strike on a railway yard at Haiphong. It was last plotted on radar as it crossed the coast seven miles southeast of Haiphong. Hanoi Radio reported the next day that an aircraft had been shot down near Haiphong during the night and a film was made by the North Vietnamese showing attempts to salvage the wreckage of the Intruder. A report in Nhan Dan, a North Vietnamese newspaper, also reported the incident and implied that the crew had been killed. The remains of Lt Nelson were returned on 1 July 1984 and were buried at Arlington National Cemetery.

7 March 1968

C-123K 54-0594   311 ACS, 315 ACW, USAF, Phan Rang
detached to Da Nang

Shortly after Lt Col Hampton's aircraft was shot down at Khe Sanh on the 6th, another Provider had its tail damaged by mor-tar fire as it was taxying on the airfield. The aircraft was repairable but further mortar fire on the 7th completed its destruction. Following the loss of three 311th ACS Providers at Khe Sanh within the last seven days, the 315th ACW started to rotate aircraft from other squadrons into Da Nang to share the burden of resupplying Khe Sanh.

O-1G 51-12013   19 TASS, 504 TASG, USAF, Bien Hoa
2 crew, names unknown (survived)

A Bird Dog crashed on landing at an airstrip at Bearcat as a result of pilot error following an observation flight.

11 March 1968

EC-47P 44-77016   361 TEWS, 460 TRW, USAF, Nha Trang
Lt Col Robert E Dobyns (survived)
2Lt Stanley R Marks (survived)
Maj John J Polites (survived)
SSgt David J Lott (survived)
SSgt Louis R Stennes (survived)
SSgt Kenneth J Corbin (survived)

The second EC-47 radio intelligence aircraft lost in combat was shot down during a mission over southern Laos on the 11th. The aircraft took off from Nha Trang and was orbiting at 9,500 feet near Ban Tok, about 45 miles west of Kham Duc, when it was hit by 37mm ground fire. The port engine was damaged and caught fire briefly, the undercarriage fell down and the hydraulics failed. The aircraft was over mountainous, forested terrain deep in enemy-held territory but it remained airborne. About 15 min-utes after being hit, the struggling EC-47 was joined by an O-2 FAC, which escorted the aircraft towards Pleiku. The aircraft was losing altitude as the remaining engine lost power and the pilot made a forced landing at the Ben Het Special Forces Camp, close to where the borders of Laos, South Vietnam and Cambodia meet. All the crew escaped and were eventually recovered, leav-ing the aircraft to be cannibalised. Lt Col Dobyns was awarded the Silver Star and the other crewmembers were each awarded the DFC for this mission. This EC-47 had been delivered to the Royal Air Force in 1945 and was used by 51 Squadron until handed back to the USAF in September 1948.

F-4D 66-7719   480 TFS, 366 TFW, USAF, Da Nang
Maj Ernest Arthur Olds (KIA)
1Lt Albert Eduardo Rodriguez (KIA)

A flight of Phantoms from Da Nang was flying an armed recon-naissance mission when the leader spotted vehicles on Route 1A, the main coast road, 15 miles south of Mu Ron Ma. One of the

aircraft was shot down by automatic weapons fire as the flight attacked the vehicles. One or both of the crew may have been hit, as there was no apparent attempt to eject before the aircraft crashed close to the road. The remains of the crew were returned to the USA in 1989.

A-37A 67-14506   604 ACS, 3 TFW, USAF, Bien Hoa
Maj Ronald Dale Bond (KIA)

The 604th ACS lost its fifth Dragonfly during a close air support mission near Lang Phuoc Hai, 12 miles northeast of Vung Tau. Maj Bond was strafing a target when his aircraft was hit by ground fire and crashed. He may have been wounded as he did not eject from the aircraft.

A-1E 52-135165   1 ACS, 56 ACW, USAF, Nakhon Phanom
1 pilot, name unknown (survived)

A Skyraider crashed due to engine failure during an armed reconnaissance mission. Enemy action was not suspected as the cause of the crash. By 1968 the USAF had used up most of the surplus Navy A-1E stock and other sub-models were now being converted and delivered to Southeast Asia. Skyraider 135165 was originally built as an AD-5W airborne early warning aircraft and was fitted with a huge underbelly radome. Redesignated as an EA-1E in 1962 this aircraft, and many like it, was subsequently converted to basic A-1E configuration for the USAF.

F-105D 60-0501   357 TFS, 355 TFW, USAF, Takhli
1 pilot, name unknown (survived)

During a strike mission a Thunderchief pilot noticed his air-craft's engine suddenly losing oil pressure. Eventually the engine failed and the pilot had to eject near Takhli. A technical malfunction was suspected rather than enemy action. This aircraft had shot down a MiG-17 during the great air battle of 13 May 1967.

12 March 1968

A-6A 152943   VA-35, USN, USS *Enterprise*
Cdr Glenn Edward Kollman (KIA)
Lt John Gary Griffith (KIA)

The *Enterprise* launched four Intruders on a strike mission in poor weather. As one of the aircraft left the catapult it was seen to pitch up and spin into the sea. Both the crew were lost includ-ing Cdr Kollman, the CO of VA-35. It was suspected that the air-craft had stalled and spun into the sea after the premature retraction of the flaps.

F-8E 150306   VF-53, USN, USS *Bon Homme Richard*
Lt Jerry Weber (survived)

Two Crusaders on a BARCAP mission were diverted to Da Nang due to deteriorating weather over the Gulf of Tonkin. Unfortu-nately, the weather at Da Nang was no better and Lt Weber had to rely on his leader as his own radar and TACAN were inoperative. As the two aircraft let down through cloud and rain Lt Weber suddenly saw trees in front of him and he hit several before ejecting as his Crusader rolled into the ground. The aircraft had just grazed the top of a ridge and crashed into the jungle near the Marine Corps facility on Monkey Mountain, close to Da Nang. However, Lt Weber had no idea where he was and spent a couple of anxious hours on the ground before he was located and rescued by a helicopter. Lt Weber had to eject again three months later when he ran out of fuel over the Gulf on 24 June.

O-1G 51-12030   19 TASS, 504 TASG, USAF, Bien Hoa

The Tet Offensive may have fizzled out but the Viet Cong were still attacking airfields, albeit at a reduced tempo. A mortar attack on Song Be badly damaged an O-1G FAC aircraft. The destruction of the aircraft was completed when it was accidentally dropped by a helicopter as it was being airlifted out of Song Be.

13 March 1968

A-1E 52-132587   602 ACS, 56 ACW, USAF, Udorn
Maj Donald Elliot Westbrook (KIA)

The USAF had a number of forward radar sites in Laos that were vital to monitor and control the air war over Laos and North

Vietnam. One of the most northerly and exposed sites was Lima Site 85, situated near the top of a 5,860 feet mountain called Phou Pha Thi, some 17 miles west of Sam Neua. The area around Sam Neua was the stronghold of the Pathet Lao so the Lima Sites in this region were guarded by Hmong tribesmen and were resupplied by Air America helicopters and fixed-wing aircraft. The Air Force men who operated the TSQ-81 radar and TACAN beacon at LS85 wore civilian clothes and were, on paper at least, employees of Lockheed. The site was protected on three sides by high, almost vertical, cliffs but intelligence information suggested that the North Vietnamese, who were fully aware of the site's vital function, were going to attempt to destroy the site. The radar site started operations under the code name Commando Club on 1 November 1967. However, the site's career was to be short-lived. The expected attack took place on 11 March and although several men were eventually evacuated by helicopter, 11 were lost to enemy action. Air support arrived too late to stop the radar site being overrun, but a search went on for several days in the hope of finding survivors, and strikes were conducted to destroy the sensitive radar equipment. On the morning of the 13th Maj Westbrook was flying one of four Skyraiders assigned to destroy the radar on LS85 and search for any survivors. By now the mountain was occupied by North Vietnamese infantry and Maj Westbrook's aircraft was shot down by ground fire as he flew just below the summit. Maj Westbrook was not seen to eject before the aircraft crashed although a rescue beeper was heard for a few seconds. The area was considered too 'hot' and the terrain too difficult to attempt a SAR mission.

A-1E   52-133888   1 ACS, 56 ACW, USAF, Nakhon Phanom
Lt Col Joseph Henry Byrne (KIA)
Lt Col Guy Fletcher Collins (KIA)

Since the loss of VO-67's Neptunes the sensor-seeding mission was reassigned to other aircraft types including Phantoms and Skyraiders. However, the Skyraider was also vulnerable as it had to fly low and slow to deliver the sensors. An A-1E was shot down near Muang Xepon, about 25 miles west of the DMZ. Flying at 200 feet and 220 knots, the crew had no chance to escape when the aircraft was hit by automatic weapons fire and crashed.

A-4E   152088   VA-144, USN, USS *Kitty Hawk*
Lt R E Curtis (survived)

A section of Skyhawks was sent to attack a location on Route 9 in southern Laos, about 20 miles west of Khe Sanh. The area was suspected to be used for the storage of trucks as they made their way up and down the Ho Chi Minh Trail. Lt Curtis was making his third strafing run when his aircraft was hit by automatic weapons fire. The engine began to vibrate as it lost power and the pilot ejected a few miles south of the target. He was rescued by an HH-3 after about 30 minutes on the ground.

14 March 1968

F-4D   66-7508   390 TFS, 366 TFW, USAF, Da Nang
Maj Gary L Tresemer (survived)
1Lt James Edward Hamm (KIA)

A flight of two Phantoms from Da Nang was scrambled to fly a diversionary strike for a helicopter evacuation that was planned to take place about 15 miles southwest of Hué. Marine Corps troops in the area were heavily engaged by soldiers from the NVA's 304th Division and were in need of assistance. Maj Tresemer made three runs over the target dropping napalm but on the fourth run the aircraft was hit by ground fire. Both the crew ejected but came down some distance from each other. Maj Tresemer was injured on landing but he was able to contact 1Lt Hamm using their survival radios and awaited their rescue. The first SAR helicopter sent to attempt a rescue was shot at and badly damaged. Maj Tresemer was rescued at the next attempt. James Hamm directed air strikes on the approaching enemy forces as he was waiting for rescue. Unfortunately, the North Vietnamese must have reached James Hamm first, as he was never found. Investigations in 1992 indicate that 1Lt Hamm was shot by a militia woman as he tried to defend himself with his pistol when he was discovered.

15 March 1968

F-4C   63-7701   391 TFS, 12 TFW, USAF, Cam Ranh Bay
Capt R C Fairlamb (survived)
1Lt P E Hubler (survived)

A truck park was discovered in southern Laos, about 80 miles west of Da Nang. A flight of Phantoms was despatched from Cam Ranh Bay to attack the target. As Capt Fairlamb was making his third pass his aircraft was hit by ground fire and burst into flames. The engines started to wind down and the crew were forced to eject a few miles from their target. They were both rescued by a USAF HH-3.

16 March 1968

F-8E   149225   VMFA(AW)-235, MAG-11, USMC, Da Nang
Capt G L Post (survived)

VMFA(AW)-235 lost a Crusader over the DMZ during an attack on enemy troops in contact with Marines. Capt Post was making his second bombing run on the troops when his aircraft ran into .50 calibre gunfire. He turned out to sea losing fuel rapidly and ejected a few miles off the coast. He was later rescued by a Navy helicopter.

O-2A   67-21408   23 TASS, 504 TASG, USAF, Nakhon Phanom
1Lt Albert A Engelhardt (KIA)

As dusk fell a Nail FAC from Nakhon Phanom went down 10 miles northwest of Khe Sanh. The cause of the loss was unknown.

AC-47D   43-49330   14 ACW, USAF, Binh Thuy

A Viet Cong attack on the airfield at Binh Thuy resulted in the destruction of an AC-47 Spooky gunship. This aircraft had originally been delivered to the USAAF in November 1944.

16/17 March 1968

A-6A   152940   VA-35, USN, USS *Enterprise*
Lt Cdr Edwin Arthur Shuman (POW)
Lt Cdr Dale Walter Doss (POW)

The A-6 Intruder crews must have thought they were the only people bombing North Vietnam at this time. Certainly, no other Navy aircraft type had been lost over the North since mid-February as bad weather kept most aircraft, other than the A-6s, grounded. VA-35 was particularly hard hit as it lost four aircraft and three crews within a little over two weeks. On the night of the 16th a division of four Intruders was launched from the *Enterprise* on a low-level strike. The target for Lt Cdr Shuman's aircraft was a railway yard at Khe Nu. However, when the aircraft was a few miles north of Hanoi, flying at 400 knots and at 200 feet, it was hit by a large calibre anti-aircraft shell. The aircraft's windscreen was shattered and the crew ejected when they became disoriented. Both men were quickly captured and became POWs, their capture being reported by Hanoi Radio the next day. Shuman and Doss were released on 14 March 1973. Edwin Shuman had flown 17 missions before being shot down and was a graduate of the US Naval Test Pilot School. Both men retired from the Navy with the rank of Captain. In 1991 Ned Shuman returned to Hanoi as part of a medical team that performed reconstructive surgery on children who had been born with facial deformities.

17 March 1968

F-4D   66-8780   390 TFS, 366 TFW, USAF, Da Nang
Maj P D Lambrides (survived)
1Lt J L Tavenner (survived)

A flight of Phantoms from Da Nang on an armed reconnaissance mission lost one of their number during an attack on boats just off the North Vietnamese coast a few miles north of the DMZ. Automatic weapons fire hit the aircraft's wings and Maj Lambrides headed further out to sea before he and his WSO ejected.

F-105D   61-0162   469 TFS, 388 TFW, USAF, Korat
Capt Thomas Truett Hensley (KIA)

The Pathet Lao headquarters at Sam Neua was the target of a raid by the F-105s from Korat on the 17th. One aircraft was lost during the raid. As Capt Hensley was pulling up through 5,000 feet after releasing his bombs, his aircraft was hit by AAA and caught fire. Capt Hensley was not observed to escape from his aircraft before it crashed near Sam Neua. Capt Hensley's aircraft carried road runner artwork but no name.

S-2E   149274   VS-23, USN, USS *Yorktown*
Cdr Donald Richard Hubbs (KIA)
Lt(jg) Lee David Benson (KIA)
AX2 Randall John Nightingale (KIA)
ADR Thomas David Barber (KIA)

An S-2 Tracker was launched from the *Yorktown* for a night surveillance patrol off the coast of North Vietnam near Vinh. About one hour after take off the pilot reported that they were having problems with their radar. No other radio messages were received and the aircraft disappeared from the *Yorktown*'s radar screen. The last known position was about 30 miles from the coast and 25 miles southeast of a small island known as Hon Me. North Vietnamese fishing boats were seen in the area the following day. On the 20th part of the Tracker's starboard wing was found but it was not possible to determine the cause of the aircraft's loss.

This was the last aircraft lost by the *Yorktown* during its three war cruises off Southeast Asia. In total the ship had lost two SH-3As and two fixed-wing aircraft during 192 days spent on the line. The four men lost in the Tracker were the only fatalities suffered in these losses. After this last cruise ended on 16 June the ship left Southeast Asia forever and was finally decommissioned on 27 June 1970. It is currently preserved as a memorial at Patriot's Point, Charleston, North Carolina.

18 March 1968

F-100F   56-3784   355 TFS, 354 TFW attached to 37 TFW,
USAF, Phu Cat
Capt Howard Keith Williams (KIA)
Capt B R Williams (survived)

A Misty FAC Super Sabre was lost during a strike on a storage area near Ban Katoi, a few miles north of the Ban Karai Pass, close to the North Vietnamese border with Laos. The aircraft was struck by AAA while at 5,000 feet and, although both crew ejected, only the rear seater was rescued by a USAF helicopter. It appears that the Commando Sabre unit was using aircraft from any of the Phu Cat squadrons.

O-1G   51-12108   21 TASS, 504 TASG, USAF, Nha Trang
Maj R P Greer (survived)

A Bird Dog was shot down while controlling an air strike close to the town of Ninh Hoa, 15 miles north of the aircraft's base at Nha Trang. Maj Greer's aircraft was hit by small arms fire at 1,000 feet but he crash-landed without injury about one mile from the town and was safely recovered.

A-1H   52-139678   602 ACS, 56 ACW, USAF, Udorn
Capt Edward W Leonard (survived)

One of the USAF's newly acquired single-seat Skyraiders was lost during an armed reconnaissance sortie over northern Laos. The aircraft was strafing an enemy strong point near Ban Hat Den, 30 miles southwest of Dien Bien Phu, when its engine was damaged by automatic weapons fire. Capt Leonard coaxed the aircraft back towards base but had to make a forced landing about 25 miles northeast of Udorn.

19 March 1968

O-1E   51-4899   21 TASS, 504 TASG, USAF, Nha Trang
Maj Charles Edward Blair (KIA)
A1C Victor Romero (KIA)

The 21st TASS lost another aircraft on the 19th but with more serious consequences. Maj Blair and his observer, A1C Romero, were flying a visual reconnaissance sortie over a mountainous region about 65 miles west of Nha Trang. The aircraft failed to return to base and its wreckage was later found on the slopes of Yook Nam Rmay, a 4,731 feet mountain near Duc Xuyen. The cause of the loss remains unknown. Maj Blair was successively promoted to the rank of Colonel, and Airmen Romero to Senior Master Sergeant during the time they were listed as missing.

20 March 1968

F-100D 55-3606   416 TFS, 37 TFW, USAF, Phu Cat
Maj Frederick N Thompson (POW)

Maj Thompson was taking part in an attack on a truck convoy in hilly terrain about 35 miles south of Vinh. He was using the Misty call sign but, unusually, was flying a single-seat F-100D rather than the two-seat F-100F normally flown by the Misty FACs. Maj Thompson was making his third pass over the target dropping napalm when his aircraft was hit by ground fire. He ejected close to the road and was captured. However, his stay at the Plantation POW camp was comparatively brief as he was one of the three prisoners who were released into the custody of American pacifists on 18 July 1968.

O-1G 51-16871   19 TASS, 504 TASG, USAF, Bien Hoa
Maj Louis C Zucker (KIA)
Capt Bruce A Couillard (KIA)

The FACs were having a bad month with a total of eight O-1s and O-2s lost during March. Two airmen were killed during a visual reconnaissance flight when their aircraft was shot down near the village of Xom Rach Bap, 20 miles northwest of Bien Hoa.

O-2A 67-21338   20 TASS, 504 TASG, USAF, Da Nang
Maj Allen Eugene Fellows (KIA)

Another FAC aircraft lost on this day was an O-2 that disappeared in southern Laos somewhere in the vicinity of Ban Gnang, near the Xé Banghrang River. No trace of the aircraft or its pilot was ever found. This aircraft used the radio call sign Covey which became specific to 20th TASS aircraft operating over Laos or North Vietnam from about this time.

21 March 1968

F-4D 66-8767   390 TFS, 366 TFW, USAF, Da Nang
1Lt Peter Dean Hesford (KIA)
1Lt Aubrey Eugene Stowers (KIA)

A flight of two Phantoms on a night strike mission over southern Laos spotted three trucks making their way along Route 918 near Ban Kapay. The Phantoms rolled in to the attack but the second aircraft of the flight was hit by 37mm AAA and crashed into the side of a mountain. No ejections were seen and nothing was heard by the FAC who stayed in the area for over two hours, so it was presumed that the crew died in the aircraft. Peter Hesford's brother spent some time in Laos trying to find out more about the incident and at one stage was told by a high-ranking Pathet Lao that Peter was alive. However, neither of the crew has yet been recovered.

A-4E 151077   VMA-311, MAG-12, USMC, Chu Lai
Maj John A Herber (survived)

A Skyhawk was lost during a night-time TPQ-10 beacon bombing mission near Hoi An, south of Da Nang. The pilot ejected safely and was later recovered uninjured.

22 March 1968

F-4C 64-0830   559 TFS, 12 TFW, USAF, Cam Ranh Bay
Lt Col Theodore Wilson Guy (POW)
Maj Donavan Loren Lyon (KIA)

A flight of Phantoms was sent on a Steel Tiger strike to destroy a gun site on the road between Khe Sanh and Tchepone, about 15 miles west of Khe Sanh and just across the border into Laos. On the third pass, as the aircraft was strafing the target, it was damaged by an explosion and disintegrated. Although attributed by the Air Force to AAA, Ted Guy thinks that one of his 750lb bombs exploded prematurely. Lt Col Guy was ejected as the cockpit broke up and he landed in the jungle. He was unaware of his WSO ejecting from the aircraft. Ted Guy was lucky to be captured alive as he killed two North Vietnamese soldiers on the ground. He was tied to a tree and was about to be executed when a North Vietnamese officer arrived to take him into custody. After several torture sessions he was eventually transferred to the Plantation POW camp in Hanoi where he became senior officer of all prisoners captured in Laos, Cambodia and South Vietnam. Ted Guy was severely tortured throughout his POW years, even during 1972 when treatment for most prisoners had improved significantly. He became convinced that the North Vietnamese systematically grouped their prisoners in different camps according to where they had been captured. The Hanoi Hilton was reserved for those shot down over North Vietnam and the Plantation held those captured in Laos and South Vietnam. Ted Guy was a Korean War veteran and had 5,600 hours flying time and 287 combat mission to his credit. He was the operations officer of the 559th TFS at the time he was shot down.

Following his release on 16 March 1973, Ted Guy brought charges against eight POWs who he considered had behaved treacherously while in the camps. He was later persuaded not to pursue the charges further. He retired as a Colonel in 1975 with a medical disability attributed to his harsh treatment in the POW camps. He then became very active in various POW/MIA organisations. Until 1991 he believed that no prisoners had been left behind after Operation Homecoming but he then changed his opinion, especially regarding the many men who came down in Laos and never returned. For some years he ran a POW/MIA awareness group on the Internet called *Operation Just Cause*. Ted Guy died of cancer on 23 April 1999.

23 March 1968

F-100D 56-3152   614 TFS, 35 TFW, USAF, Phan Rang
Capt Eugene Phillip McKinney (KIA)

A flight of F-100s was making an attack on Viet Cong buildings near An Nhon, eight miles southeast of the airfield at Phu Cat, when one of the aircraft was lost. Capt McKinney was pulling up from his fourth attack when his aircraft was hit by ground fire and crashed. An Army helicopter quickly arrived at the scene and confirmed that Capt McKinney had died in the aircraft.

O-1F 57-2796   21 TASS, 504 TASG, USAF, Nha Trang
2 crew, names unknown (survived)

Two Bird Dog FAC aircraft were destroyed in separate accidents on the 23rd. One of the aircraft crashed following engine failure but both crewmen survived a crash landing.

O-1F 57-2814   19 TASS, 504 TASG, USAF, Bien Hoa
Capt Larry Jack Clanton (KIA)

Another pilot was not so fortunate and was killed when his aircraft collided with another Bird Dog during a visual reconnaissance mission.

24 March 1968

UC-123K 54-0589   606 ACS, 56 ACW, USAF, Nakhon Phanom
5 crew, names unknown (survived)

A UC-123 flareship was operating over the Ho Chi Minh Trail in southern Laos when its port engine was damaged by AAA near Ban Namchalo. The pilot aborted the mission and carefully made his way back to Nakhon Phanom where he made an emergency landing. The aircraft was so badly damaged that it had to be scrapped.

The B-57 Canberra was the first jet attack aircraft to be based in South Vietnam. Unfortunately, the type was the subject of two major ground incidents in November 1964 and May 1965 involving the loss of 15 aircraft. 52-1592 was damaged on 25 March 1968 during a mission in southern Laos and crashed with the loss of both crewmembers while trying to make an emergency landing at Da Nang. USAF

The General Dynamics F-111A's introduction to combat was disastrous with the loss of three Combat Lancer detachment aircraft in less than a month. The aircraft was sent into combat before it had been fully tested and the poor results in Southeast Asia only stirred up more controversy over the F-111's future. USAF

A-4E   152068   VMA-211, MAG-12, USMC, Chu Lai
                  Capt Charles Wilbur Porterfield (KIA)

As a Skyhawk was taking off from Chu Lai on a strike mission it developed a problem and the pilot aborted the take off. Unfortunately, the aircraft veered off the runway and was destroyed killing the pilot.

25 March 1968

B-57B   52-1592   8 TBS, 35 TFW, USAF, Phan Rang
                    Capt Richard Whan Hopper (KIA)
                    Maj Donald Lyle McHugo (KIA)

A Canberra on an armed reconnaissance mission was damaged by small arms fire as it was making its second bombing run on a ford at Ban Te Bang in southern Laos, about 20 miles southwest of the A Shau Valley. The aircraft's port engine was damaged but Capt Hopper managed to fly the crippled aircraft back to Da Nang. Unfortunately the aircraft became uncontrollable during the single-engined landing at Da Nang and crashed with the loss of both crew. This B-57 had originally flown with the 38th TBG at Laon AB in France.

26 March 1968

F-105D   60-0462   469 TFS, 388 TFW, USAF, Korat
                     Capt Ralph J Hornaday (KIA)

As a Thunderchief was taking off from Korat its right mainwheel tyre burst. The pilot aborted the take off and engaged the barrier cable at the end of the runway but the cable snapped and the aircraft crashed killing the pilot. Thunderchief 60-0462 was named 'Huntress' when it served with the 34th TFS earlier in the war.

27 March 1968

F-4D   66-8801   480 TFS, 366 TFW, USAF, Da Nang
                   Capt Richard Lee Whitteker (KIA)
                   1Lt James Linsday Badley (KIA)

The danger of multiple passes over the same target was illustrated once more when a Phantom was shot down during a strike near Ban Katoi. On his third run Capt Whitteker was using his external cannon pod to strafe trucks on a road leading to the Ban Karai Pass when his aircraft was hit by automatic weapons or small arms fire. The Phantom crashed immediately and neither of the crew were seen to eject from the aircraft. Lt Badley had survived being shot down on 20 November 1967 near the DMZ with Capt Martin who was killed in the incident.

The F-111 and Combat Lancer

The General Dynamics F-111 strike aircraft had first flown in December 1964 and had gathered a dubious reputation during its testing and evaluation programme. A complex design in terms of both aerodynamics and avionics, the swing-wing F-111 did have its share of problems but was ultimately to prove to be a superb aircraft for low-level strike, especially in weather conditions that precluded normal operations. The most advanced combat aircraft in the world at the time of its deployment, the F-111A's performance was impressive. The aircraft had a top speed of 1,650 mph and a range of 1,500 miles with its maximum bomb load of up to 30,000lbs. Its advanced terrain-following and blind-bombing radars gave it a unique capability as a low-level, all-weather bomber. The first production aircraft made its initial flight on 12 February 1967 and was delivered to Nellis AFB, Nevada in July of that year. In an attempt to answer some of the criticisms of the aircraft's performance, it was decided to form a small detachment for an operational deployment to Southeast Asia. The 4480th TFW was formed at Nellis AFB on 15 July 1967 and Detachment 1 of the 4481st TFS was prepared for the deploy-ment to Takhli under the command of Col Ivan Dethman. The unit of six F-111As was redesignated as Detachment 1 of the 428th TFS when the Wing was upgraded to the 474th TFW. Despite misgivings by the air and ground crews that the aircraft was not yet ready for combat, the Detachment took off from Nellis on 15 March 1968 and deployed to Thailand under the code name Combat Lancer. Col Dethman and Capt Rick Matteis flew the first combat mission on 25 March, the first mission of a short and unhappy deployment.

28 March 1968

RF-8G   144616   Detachment 14, VFP-63, USN,
                   USS *Ticonderoga*
                   Lt Cdr Michael Walter Wallace (KIA)

An RF-8G Crusader was accompanying a formation of five Skyhawks on a Steel Tiger strike in southern Laos. The Crusader followed the Skyhawks as they rolled in on their target near Ban Tampank, 17 miles southeast of Khe Sanh. However, moments later the FAC pilot who was controlling the strike saw the Crusader hit the ground in a tight spin. It was suspected that Lt Cdr Wallace had lost control of the aircraft as he tried to roll in with the Skyhawks which normally performed this manoeuvre at a much lower airspeed than was normal for a Crusader. However, there was also the possibility that the aircraft had been hit by ground fire. By 1988 Laotian-US relations were beginning to thaw a little. The US assisted a private humanitarian organisation to build medical clinics in Laos. In return Laos agreed to investigate a limited number of aircraft crash sites to recover human remains. One of the first sites visited was that of Lt Cdr Wallace's Crusader. A joint US and Laotian team discovered the remains of Michael Wallace and returned them to the USA for burial in December 1988.

O-1F   57-2809   21 TASS, 504 TASG, USAF, Nha Trang
                   Capt T Davies (survived)
                   Capt K L Peterson (survived)

An O-1 was shot down by small arms fire during an FAC mission near Thon Ta Lu Ha, 12 miles north of Phang Rang airfield. Both crewmen survived the crash and were eventually recovered.

F-111A   66-0022   Detachment 1, 428 TFS, 474 TFW
                     attached to 355 TFW, USAF, Takhli
                     Maj Henry Elmer MacCann (KIA)
                     Capt Dennis Lee Graham (KIA)

The first F-111 to be lost in Southeast Asia went missing on a low-level night strike on a truck park at Chanh Hao just north of the DMZ. The aircraft (using the radio call sign Omaha 77) was last seen on radar in a figure-of-eight holding pattern about 10 miles west of Dong Hoi and close to the target but heading away from it. It was never established if the aircraft had a malfunction and was orbiting while the crew worked on the problem or if it was shot down or had flown into the ground as it tried to return to Takhli. Whatever the cause, the loss was a heavy blow so early on in the Combat Lancer deployment. The aircraft was thought to have come down near the North Vietnam/Laos border but the wreckage has never been found.

29 March 1968

O-2A   67-21302   23 TASS, 504 TASG, USAF, Nakhon Phanom
                    Lt Col H C Johnson (survived)
                    Maj J T Doran (survived)

During an FAC mission over the North Vietnamese coast near Xuan Hoa, 15 miles southeast of Dong Hoi, an O-2 had its rear engine put out of action by ground fire. Lt Col Johnson flew back towards base on his remaining engine but he and his observer were forced to bail out of the aircraft in Laos 45 miles short of Nakhon Phanom. This was the first confirmed occasion that anyone had survived being shot down in an O-2 since the first aircraft was shot down on 14 September 1967 and must have been a great relief to the O-2 community. The event was repeated a few days later.

30 March 1968

F-111A   66-0017   Detachment 1, 428 TFS, 474 TFW
                     attached to 355 TFW, USAF, Takhli
                     Maj Alexander A Marquandt (survived)
                     Capt Joseph W Hodges (survived)

An F-111 crew (call sign Hotrod 76) encountered control problems during a night mission while the aircraft was still in Thai airspace. The aircraft began to pitch and roll and when control was lost the crew ejected safely using the aircraft's unique escape module that separates the entire cockpit section from the aircraft and descends by parachute. Unfortunately, soon after landing near the wreck of their aircraft the M61A-1 Vulcan cannon's shells started to 'cook off' and the detonations were interpreted by the crew as enemy ground fire as they were unsure if they were in Laos or Thailand. Sandy Marquandt and Joe Hodges started escape and evasion procedures and were eventually rescued by an HH-3E flown by Maj W Oldermann who informed the crew that they were, in fact, in friendly territory within Thailand. The cause of the accident was traced to a capsule of solidified sealant that was fouling the pitch/roll mixer assembly, which in turn caused the stabiliser actuator to jam. On 8 May an F-111 crashed near Nellis AFB, Nevada and the same cause was suspected. 66-0017 was the last US aircraft lost on a Rolling Thunder raid before President Johnson announced the immediate cessation of bombing north of the 20th Parallel. On 3 April the bomb line was moved even further south to the 19th Parallel. This effectively confined future Rolling Thunder strikes to the southernmost provinces of North Vietnam. President Johnson's dramatic speech also announced his intention to retire at the end of his term.

Only two P-3 Orions were lost on Market Time operations during the war and both were lost by VP-26 within two months of each other in 1968 resulting in the deaths of 24 men. USN

31 March 1968

C-123K 54-0653   315 ACW, USAF, Phan Rang
                 4 crew, names unknown (survived)

A Provider suffered a mechanical failure as it was taking off on a trooping flight and crash-landed. None of the occupants were killed.

1 April 1968

O-2A 67-21406   23 TASS, 504 TASG, USAF, Nakhon Phanom
                Maj Gerald T Dwyer (survived)
                TSgt B C Cote (survived)

The 23rd TASS lost another O-2 within four days of losing an aircraft on the 29th March. Again the crew escaped with their lives thereby proving that it was possible to escape from the O-2 in the right circumstances. Maj Dwyer's aircraft was damaged by ground fire during a daylight FAC mission over southern Laos. As with Lt Colonel Johnson's aircraft on the 29th, it was the aft engine that was put out of action. Maj Dwyer flew the aircraft on its one remaining engine but he and his observer had to abandon the aircraft about 25 miles southeast of Nakhon Phanom. The hot and humid climate of Southeast Asia severely reduced the single-engine performance of some aircraft types to the point where the aircraft could not remain airborne for long on just one engine. Maj Dwyer was shot down a second time over Laos on 21 May 1968.

F-100D 55-3717   510 TFS, 3 TFW, USAF, Bien Hoa
                 Capt James Martin Brinkman (KIA)

A Super Sabre was lost in tragic circumstances during a close air support mission 40 miles northwest of Saigon. Capt Brinkman was attacking enemy vehicles seven miles north of Dau Tieng and was delivering his second load of napalm when the aircraft was hit by the blast from the explosion of its own ordnance. The Super Sabre crashed immediately giving Capt Brinkman no chance to eject.

P-3B 153445   VP-26, USN, U-Tapao (TDY from
              Sangley Point)
              Lt(jg) Frank E Hand (KIA)
              Lt(jg) Stuart M McLellan (KIA)
              Lt(jg) Brian J Mathison (KIA)
              Lt(jg) Michael J Purcell (KIA)

AME2 Donald W Burnside (KIA)
AT1 Kenneth L Crist (KIA)
AO2 William S Cutting (KIA)
AXC Donald E Kulacz (KIA)
AX3 Delmar L Lawrence (KIA)
AE1 Donald F Wood (KIA)
ADJ2 Edward O Wynder (KIA)
AX1 Alvin G Yoximer (KIA)

Just two months after losing a P-3 with all hands off the coast of South Vietnam, the VP-26 detachment at U-Tapao lost another aircraft, this time due to enemy action. Crew One reported that they were being shot at near the island of Hon Doc, 10 miles out to sea from Ha Tien, which sits astride South Vietnam's coastal border with Cambodia. The Orion was hit in the starboard wing by automatic weapons fire. One of the aircraft's engines caught fire and the pilot headed out to sea in an attempt to return to U-Tapao. However, after a few minutes the fire became more intense and the aircraft crashed near the small island of Hon Vang, one of a small group of islands just off the southern tip of the large island of Dao Phu Quoc. All 12 crew were killed in the crash. It was a tragic coincidence that VP-26 should suffer two of the three fatal incidents involving US Navy patrol aircraft during the war and in such a short space of time.

2 April 1968

F-100D 55-2875   510 TFS, 3 TFW, USAF, Bien Hoa
                 1Lt K S Peterson (survived)

The 510th TFS lost another aircraft the following day but with happier consequences for the pilot. A Viet Cong base consisting of buildings and bunkers had been discovered on the southern outskirts of Saigon itself. A flight of Super Sabres was despatched to attack the target but as 1Lt Peterson was pulling up from his second pass his aircraft was hit by ground fire. The pilot ejected safely and was quickly recovered by ground troops.

3 April 1968

B-57B 52-1586   8 TBS, 35 TFW, USAF, Phan Rang
                Maj Richard Zock (survived)
                A1C T L Tillotson (survived)

A Canberra was damaged by 37mm ground fire as it pulled up from its second pass over a ford at Ban Te Bang in southern Laos,

about 20 miles southwest of the A Shau Valley. Although the left wing was damaged the pilot managed to fly the Canberra back to Phan Rang to make an emergency landing. Unfortunately the aircraft was damaged beyond repair during the landing. Like 52-1592 that crashed on 25 March, 52-1586 was an ex-38th TBG aircraft.

RF-4C 65-0909   11 TRS, 432 TRW, USAF, Udorn
                Capt Ronald Reuel Rexroad (KIA)
                Capt John Charles Hardy (KIA)

Although bombing operations were now restricted to a small section of North Vietnam, reconnaissance missions still continued much as before in order to keep information on potential targets up to date. A reconnaissance Phantom disappeared over North Vietnam during a mission to photograph sections of major roads for possible future attack. No further information was received regarding the fate of the aircraft or its crew.

5 April 1968

F-4B 150463   VF-96, USN, USS *Enterprise*
              Ens S D Graber (survived)
              Lt C J Schwartze (survived)

A Navy Phantom suffered an in-flight electrical failure during a combat mission. The aircraft's power controls failed and the crew had to eject when the pilot lost control.

F-4C 63-7684   391 TFS, 12 TFW, USAF, Cam Ranh Bay
               Capt G L Butler (survived)
               Maj J G Kondracki (survived)

The USAF also lost a Phantom accidentally on the 5th. During an interdiction mission, an F-4 crew had difficulty refuelling from a tanker. Unable to take on more fuel the crew were forced to eject when the engines flamed out.

6 April 1968

F-100D 55-2911   615 TFS, 35 TFW, USAF, Phan Rang
                 Capt William David Canup (KIA)

The third Super Sabre to be lost in April was shot down while attacking enemy troops 10 miles northwest of An Khe and about 35 miles west of Phu Cat. Capt Canup was making his second run on his target when his aircraft was hit by automatic weapons fire and crashed before he could eject. A few weeks earlier Capt

Canup had survived an ejection from an F-100F on 17 February. The serial number of this F-100D is also quoted for an aircraft that was shot down on 26 January 1967.

7 April 1968

F-100F 56-3839   416 TFS, 37 TFW, USAF, Phu Cat
Maj T F Tapman (survived)
Capt E D Jones (survived)

A Misty FAC was lost during a strike mission on a truck park on Route 191 near Xom Duong Quan, just north of the Mu Gia Pass. Maj Tapman and Capt Jones were diving on the target to mark it for the strike fighters when their aircraft was hit by 37mm AAA. The aircraft caught fire but Maj Tapman flew west for about 20 miles before he and Capt Jones ejected. They were both safely recovered by a USAF SAR helicopter.

11 April 1968

TA-4F 153511   H&MS-11, MAG-11, USMC, Da Nang
Col L T Frey (survived)
Maj D F Newon (survived)

By April 1968 the TA-4F had replaced the TF-9J in the Tactical Air Coordination (Airborne) and visual reconnaissance roles. A three-aircraft detachment was operated by H&MS-11 as fast FACs in areas that were considered to be too dangerous for the slow flying O-1 FAC aircraft. Known as Playboys after their radio call sign, the TA-4Fs became much sought after assets in the area around the DMZ. Col Frey and Maj Newon were attacking an enemy village just seven miles south of Da Nang when they were shot down by small arms fire on their second pass. The crew ejected but were rescued by a Marine Corps helicopter.

A-4F 154995   VA-93, USN, USS *Bon Homme Richard*
Cdr Frederick H Whittemore (KWF)

The new A-4F variant of the Skyhawk was distinguishable from earlier versions primarily by its large dorsal 'hump', which contained additional avionics. Other improvements include an uprated engine, nosewheel steering, wing spoilers and a new zero-zero ejector seat that permitted escape at ground level with no forward speed. An A-4F took off from Cubi Point NAS in the Philippines for a ferry flight to the *Bon Homme Richard*. When the aircraft did not arrive at the expected time an extensive search was instigated over a large area of the South China Sea. However, there was no trace of the aircraft or its pilot. Cdr Whittemore had previously served as the executive officer with VA-212 and had survived being shot down over North Vietnam on 20 July 1967.

13 April 1968

RF-4C 66-0383   12 TRS, 460 TRW, USAF, Tan Son Nhut
Maj Walter Morris Stischer (POW)
Capt D L Verhees (survived)

An RF-4C was despatched on a reconnaissance mission to photograph a section of Route 165 on the Ho Chi Minh Trail in the southern tip of the Laotian panhandle. Maj Stischer was making his second photo run over the road when the Phantom was damaged by ground fire. The aircraft burst into flames and the crew ejected a few miles from the road, near the village of Ban Thakkapang. Capt Verhees was fortunate enough to be rescued by a USAF helicopter but Maj Stischer was captured by North Vietnamese troops. He was sent on a long and difficult journey to the prison camps in Hanoi and was eventually released from captivity on 28 March 1973.

C-130B 61-0967   774 TAS, 463 TAW, USAF, Mactan
7 crew, names unknown (survived)

As a Hercules was landing at Khe Sanh it suffered an engine failure and suddenly veered off the runway. The aircraft hit six recently dropped pallets, still containing cargo, and then continued into a truck and a forklift vehicle before coming to a halt and bursting into flames. The aircraft was damaged beyond repair but all the crew were rescued, although a civilian who was on board later died of his injuries. In an effort to determine the cause of the engine failure, nos 3 and 4 propellers were placed in

a cargo sling and a Marine Corps helicopter lifted off for Da Nang. Unfortunately the load was unbalanced and started to swing wildly, endangering the helicopter, so it had to be cut loose. As the load fell in enemy-held territory it could not be recovered so the cause of the accident remained undetermined.

14 April 1968

F-4B 150644   VF-154, USN, USS *Ranger*
Cdr Don Pringle (survived)
Lt(jg) G E Rose (survived)

A Phantom was lost when taking off on a ferry flight from Cubi Pont to the USS *Ranger* when the aircraft caught fire. Both the crew ejected safely but the aircraft crashed into an ammunition storage area near the airfield.

15 April 1968

F-105F 63-8337   357 TFS, 355 TFW, USAF, Takhli
Col David W Winn (survived)

A flight of F-105s was sent on a strike against trucks near Van Xuan, 10 miles south of Dong Hoi. Col Winn's aircraft was hit in the tail by 37mm flak at 5,000 feet causing a fire in the rear fuselage. He flew out to sea and headed south for Da Nang, the nearest airfield capable of taking a Thunderchief. However, the fire increased in intensity and Col Winn had to eject over the sea about 25 miles northeast of the airfield. He was rescued by an HH-3E. Col Winn had been appointed the assistant deputy commander of the 355th TFW in March and was shot down again and captured on 9 August. F-105F 63-8337 was painted as 'Bed Check Charlie' when serving at Korat earlier in the war.

F-105D 61-0206   34 TFS, 388 TFW, USAF, Korat
Maj James Hardin Metz (POW- died)

About two hours after Col Winn was shot down another flight of Thunderchiefs arrived in the Dong Hoi area, this time to attack a target near Van Loc, some 10 miles northwest of the town. During the attack Maj Metz reported that his aircraft had been hit by AAA. He was advised to head for the sea and eject as his aircraft was on fire. Maj Metz turned the aircraft towards the coast but had to eject before he could cross the beach. His wingman saw his parachute land in a clump of trees near a road. A SAR helicopter arrived about 45 minutes later but by then there was no sign of Jim Metz or his parachute. A Hanoi Radio report claiming that a US pilot had been captured that day was presumed to refer to Maj Metz as no other American pilot was lost over North Vietnam on the 15th. An intelligence report was received confirming that Maj Metz had been seen in captivity shortly after he was shot down. However, Jim Metz did not survive his captivity. He did not return with the rest of the prisoners released in 1973 and nothing further was known until his remains were handed over by the Vietnamese on 18 March 1977.

F-4B 153002   VF-114, USN, USS *Kitty Hawk*
2 crew, names unknown (survived)

F-4B 153043   VF-114, USN, USS *Kitty Hawk*
2 crew, names unknown (survived)

Two Phantoms from the *Kitty Hawk* collided in mid-air during a strike mission. All four crewmembers were rescued. The occupants of these two aircraft were Lt(jg) G K Baer, Lt Cdr J F Farnsworth, Lt(jg) R L McCready and Lt(jg) J Sarnecky but it is not known who was in which aircraft.

O-1G 51-7480   19 TASS, 504 TASG, USAF, Bien Hoa
1 pilot, name unknown (survived)

As a Bird Dog was taking off its undercarriage collapsed causing one wing to strike the ground and igniting one of the aircraft's marker rockets. The aircraft came to rest but the wing caught fire and the aircraft was burnt out.

16 April 1968

C-130A 56-0480   35 TAS, 374 TAW, USAF, Naha
5 crew, names unknown (survived)

As a Hercules was attempting to land at an airstrip at Bunard its approach was obscured by a cloud of dust blown up by the rotor

downwash from an Army helicopter. The Hercules landed heavily and was damaged beyond repair.

17 April 1968

A-37A 67-14518   604 ACS, 3 TFW, USAF, Bien Hoa
Capt John Wayne Held (KIA)

An A-37 Dragonfly was lost with its pilot during a close air support mission near Song Be, 70 miles north of Saigon. The aircraft had been scrambled from Bien Hoa and was hit by automatic weapons fire as Capt Held made his third pass attacking a Viet Cong gun pit. He ejected from the aircraft as it burst into flames and was seen to parachute to the ground. Although a US Army helicopter arrived within 20 minutes and medevaced a man to the ground all he could find was an empty parachute. A USAF HH-43F from the 38th ARRS also joined the search but Capt Held was never found. It was presumed that he had been captured and killed by the VC.

19 April 1968

A-4E 150063   VMA-211, MAG-12, USMC, Chu Lai
Capt K E Cook (survived)

A Skyhawk from VMA-211 fell victim to small arms fire as it made its seventh pass over a target near Hué. Capt Cook headed out to sea and ejected about three miles off the coast near Hué, from where he was rescued by helicopter.

20 April 1968

F-100D 55-3643   306 TFS, 31 TFW, USAF, Tuy Hoa
1 pilot, name unknown (survived)

As a Super Sabre climbed through 3,000 feet after taking off from Tuy Hoa, a flame was seen to shoot out from the tailpipe. The engine flamed out and the pilot ejected as he was too low to attempt a restart or return to the airfield.

21 April 1968

O-2A 67-21420   20 TASS, 504 TASG, USAF, Da Nang
Capt W D Parr (survived)

An O-2 was hit by ground fire in the tail boom during a visual reconnaissance flight at 4,000 feet in the Khe Sanh area. Capt Parr made a crash landing at Khe Sanh. The aircraft was damaged beyond repair and Capt Parr was injured and medevaced back to Da Nang.

F-4D 66-8778   389 TFS, 366 TFW, USAF, Da Nang
Maj Robert Paul Riggins (KIA)
1Lt William Chomyk (KIA)

Two Phantoms were scrambled from Da Nang to attack enemy troops in trenches about seven miles southwest of Hué. The leader, Maj Riggins, made the first attack but as the aircraft pulled off the target it was hit by automatic weapons fire. The pilot may have been hit as neither he nor his WSO ejected before the aircraft crashed west of Hué.

F-4D 66-7600   480 TFS, 366 TFW, USAF, Da Nang
Maj C R Webster (survived)
1Lt N C Vasser (survived)

As dusk fell another Da Nang Phantom was shot down, this one over North Vietnam. Maj Webster was bombing a target near Mai Xa Ha, 15 miles southeast of Dong Hoi when the aircraft was damaged by ground fire. Maj Webster flew the aircraft well out to sea and he and his WSO ejected about 35 miles off the coast near the DMZ. They were both rescued by a Navy SAR helicopter.

22 April 1968

F-111A 66-0024   Detachment 1, 428 TFS, 474 TFW
attached to 355 TFW, USAF, Takhli
Lt Col Edwin David Palmgren (KIA)
Lt Cdr David Leo Cooley, US Navy (KIA)

The third aircraft to be lost from the Combat Lancer detachment disappeared during a night low-level strike on a ferry at Phoung Chay in southern Laos, 30 miles west of the A Shau Valley. The ferry was an important crossing point over the Xé Lanong River

for traffic on the Ho Chi Minh Trail and was well defended. When the aircraft, using the call sign Tailbone 7, failed to return a search was commenced but after four days it was called off as no wreckage had been spotted and there was no evidence that the crew were still alive. Although the North Vietnamese claimed to have shot the aircraft down, it was thought more likely that the aircraft had flown into the ground near the target during the low-level approach. This incident resulted in the suspension of combat operations for the F-111 detachment although the crews continued to fly local training flights until 22 November when the Combat Lancer detachment returned to the USA having flown a total of just 55 combat sorties. It would be another four years before the F-111 returned to Southeast Asia to finally prove itself in combat. Four of the returning Combat Lancer aircraft were later converted to EF-111A Raven status and two of them saw action over Iraq in Operation Desert Storm. 66-0024 was one of two replacement aircraft that arrived at Takhli on 1 April following the loss of the first two aircraft.

Much earlier in his career Lt Col Palmgren had been a member of the Thunderbirds aerobatic team and had survived a dead stick landing in an F-84F near Maxwell AFB, Alabama. Lt Cdr Cooley was a US Navy officer on exchange duties with the USAF. The Navy had ordered the F-111B carrier-based variant of the F-111 and had a number of air and ground crew attached to the USAF to gain experience before their own aircraft were delivered. In the event the Navy cancelled the F-111B and relied on updated versions of the Intruder for its low-level strike capability.

23 April 1968

C-7A   61-2399   483 TAW, USAF, Vung Tau
A Viet Cong mortar attack at Vung Tau destroyed a Caribou transport on the ground.

F-100D   55-2923   615 TFS, 35 TFW, USAF, Phan Rang
Maj Amos Oliver Fox (KIA)
An F-100 crashed into a ridge of high ground near Phan Rang when it was forced to make a missed approach as it was returning from a close air support mission.

O-1G   53-7997   20 TASS, 504 TASG, USAF, Da Nang
2 crew, names unknown (survived)
A Bird Dog crashed after a mid-air collision with a similar aircraft of the VNAF. It is not known if the aircrew were on the same mission.

24 April 1968

F-4D   66-7541   480 TFS, 366 TFW, USAF, Da Nang
Lt Col Bobby Gene Vinson (KIA)
1Lt Woodrow Wilson Parker (KIA)
A pair of F-4s made a night attack on a storage area near Van Loc, some 10 miles northwest of Dong Hoi. As Lt Col Vinson approached the target area he radioed that he was descending to try to spot the target and drop flares. Moments later the wingman saw a fireball on the ground, which he presumed to be Vinson's aircraft exploding. It was not determined whether the aircraft had been shot down or had simply flown into the ground. There was no evidence at the time to suggest that the crew had survived. In 1992 and 1993 joint US-Vietnamese teams investigated the crash site and recovered human remains and personal effects confirming the identity as the crew of 66-7541.

25 April 1968

A-1J   52-142048   602 ACS, 56 ACW, USAF, Nakhon Phanom
Lt Col H D Schultz (survived)
A Skyraider was lost during a night mission over the Ho Chi Minh Trail in southern Laos, about 30 miles west of the A Shau Valley. Lt Col Schultz was pulling up from an attack on trucks he had found on a road when his aircraft was hit in the central fuselage by 37mm flak. With the aircraft on fire he ejected almost immediately and evaded until he was rescued.

F-4D   66-8736   497 TFS, 8 TFW, USAF, Ubon
Maj Albert Cook Mitchell (KIA)
1Lt Gregory John Crossman (KIA)

A Phantom was also lost on a night strike on the 25th. A flight of aircraft was attacking a convoy of at least 15 trucks near Ha Loi, 20 miles northwest of Dong Hoi when Maj Mitchell's aircraft was shot down. There was no indication that either of the crew had survived the crash.

F-105D   60-0436   34 TFS, 388 TFW, USAF, Korat
Maj Billy R Givens (KIA)
A Thunderchief crashed on landing when returning from a strike mission. The pilot was killed in the accident. At the time of the accident the aircraft was painted with the name 'Rebecca' and was one of a number of Thunderchiefs that had seen service with the 36th TFW at Bitburg AB, West Germany before arriving in Southeast Asia.

26 April 1968

C-130B   60-0298   29 TAS, 463 TAW, USAF, Clark
Maj Lilburn R Stow (KIA)
Capt James J McKinstry (KIA)
Maj John Lewis McDaniel (KIA)
TSgt Russell Rickland Fyan (KIA)
SSgt Beryl Stanley Blaylock (KIA)
Sgt Daniel Jerome O'Connor (KIA)
Sgt Larry Richard Todd (KIA)
A1C Kenneth Lee Johnson (KIA)
In early 1968 reports started coming in to indicate that new roads were being constructed in the A Shau Valley, one of the main North Vietnamese infiltration routes into the South. Operation Delaware started on 19 April to contest an enemy build-up in the A Shau Valley and on the 25th the US Cavalry landed at the abandoned airstrip at A Loui. On the next day C-130s from Cam Ranh Bay, Bien Hoa and Tan Son Nhut dropped supplies to the troops on the airfield. The airdrops were made under a low overcast without the benefit of air strikes, which had been cancelled due to the low cloud. Seven C-130s were hit by ground fire during the first 20 airdrops but on the 21st mission an aircraft from Tan Son Nhut was shot down. As the Hercules broke out through the cloud it was hit by .50 calibre and 37mm ground fire. The crew tried to jettison the load, which had caught fire in the cargo bay. The aircraft turned towards the airstrip to attempt a landing but it then hit some trees and crashed and exploded. All on board, including six crew and two USAF photographers, were killed. No more airdrops were attempted at A Loui on the 26th although they were resumed with more success the next day.

A-1E   52-132582   1 ACS, 56 ACW, USAF, Nakhon Phanom
Lt Col J A Saffell (survived)
A Skyraider on a dusk patrol over the Ho Chi Minh Trail was hit by 37mm ground fire. Lt Col Saffell was flying at 4,500 feet near Ban Thapachon in southern Laos when the aircraft took hits in the port wing. The pilot ejected safely and was eventually rescued by helicopter.

27 April 1968

A-4E   151070   VA-144, USN, USS *Kitty Hawk*
Lt Cdr Robert Saavedra (KIA)
A section of Skyhawks on a night-time armed reconnaissance mission over North Vietnam spotted a number of trucks on a road 30 miles south of Vinh. Lt Cdr Saavedra told his wingman that he was rolling in on the target and about 30 seconds later the wingman saw a large fireball on the ground near the road. Although sporadic anti-aircraft fire had been seen in the area it could not be determined whether Lt Cdr Saavedra had been shot down or had flown into the ground during his attack.

28 April 1968

RF-4C   66-0398   16 TRS, 460 TRW, USAF, Tan Son Nhut
Lt Col William Richard Cook (KIA)
Maj Joseph Chester Bors (KIA)
An RF-4C from Tan Son Nhut was lost during a reconnaissance mission over Quang Tin province in the north of South Vietnam. The aircraft is thought to have come down about 10 miles west of the Marine Corps base at Chu Lai. The crew are presumed to have been killed when the aircraft crashed.

F-4D   66-8757   389 TFS, 366 TFW, USAF, Da Nang
Lt Col John Stewart Finlay (POW)
1Lt Wesley L Rumble (POW)
Almost at the same moment as the RF-4C was lost near Chu Lai, another Phantom was shot down in North Vietnam. Lt Col Finlay was bombing a ferry near Phoung Thieu, seven miles north of the DMZ, when an 85mm anti-aircraft shell hit his aircraft. Unable to maintain control of the aircraft he and his WSO ejected and landed near the village of Mai Xa Ha. Both men were captured but 1Lt Rumble was badly injured and was put in a body cast by North Vietnamese doctors. The reason for his better than average treatment became obvious when he was released to US peace activists in Hanoi on 5 August 1969 along with Lt(jg) R F Frishman and Seaman D B Hegdahl. Wesley Rumble had memorised the names of many of the POWs he had met or was told about during his time in prison and this information was invaluable to the US intelligence services. Lt Col Finlay, who was on his 68th mission when he was shot down, was released on 14 March 1973. He had enlisted in the Navy in October 1944 and had served as a radio operator on PBMs and PB4Ys. He was commissioned in the USAF in 1949 and flew F-84Fs and F-100s before converting to the F-4. Following retirement from the Air Force in 1975 he worked for Lockheed at the Kennedy Space Centre.

F-4B   153014   VF-21, USN, USS *Ranger*
Lt Cdr Duke E Hernandez (survived)
Lt(jg) David J Lortscher (survived)
When dusk fell a section of Navy Phantoms bombed storage caves at Ben Thuy, just to the south of Vinh. As the leader's aircraft was pulling up from its attack it was hit by anti-aircraft fire. The port wing caught fire and the port engine had to be shut down. Lt Cdr Hernandez headed out to sea but within a few minutes the starboard engine also caught fire. The hydraulic system failed and the aircraft went out of control so the crew ejected close to a SAR destroyer about 15 miles offshore. They were quickly rescued by a Navy helicopter. After his return to the USA at the end of his combat tour David Lortscher ejected from another F-4 near San Diego on 14 September 1970. He repeated the performance on 22 September 1971, again near San Diego, when the canopy of his F-4 separated. David Lortscher made aviation history on 15 October 1973 when he ejected from a Phantom for the fourth time, this time during an exchange posting with the Royal Navy. This was not the only ejection for Duke Hernandez either as he had ejected from a Phantom during a raid on Haiphong on 16 December 1967.

O-2A   67-21367   20 TASS, 504 TASG, USAF, Da Nang
Capt James F Lang (KIA)
The area west of Hué was becoming extremely unhealthy for US aircraft. An O-2 was shot down by ground fire close to where the Hercules had crashed two days earlier. The O-2 was flying a visual reconnaissance mission at night, possibly in connection with the loss of the Hercules. Capt Lang was killed when the O-2 crashed, although it appears that a USAF helicopter reached the wreck site and recovered his body.

30 April 1968

O-1G   51-12438   19 TASS, 504 TASG, USAF, Bien Hoa
Capt I S Payne (survived)
SSgt J Applebey (survived)
Capt Payne was on his way to control a strike in his Bird Dog when he came under small arms fire about 5 miles west of Cao Lanh on the banks of the Mekong. The engine stopped but Capt Payne brought the aircraft down to an almost perfect forced landing. Both crew were later rescued by an HH-43.

A-26A   67-17648   609 ACS, 56 ACW, USAF, Nakhon Phanom
Capt Robert Edward Pietsch (KIA)
Capt Louis Fulda Guillermin (KIA)
An A-26 Invader was lost during a night interdiction mission over the Ho Chi Minh Trail in southern Laos. Capt Pietsch was making his second pass to drop napalm on two trucks he had found near Ban Boung, 35 miles west of the DMZ. The aircraft was hit by 37mm AAA and crashed immediately. It was presumed that the crew did not have a chance to escape.

F-4B   153003   VF-114, USN, USS *Kitty Hawk*
                  2 crew, names unknown (survived)
A Phantom had to make a barricade landing on board the *Kitty Hawk* when returning from a strike mission. The aircraft engaged the barrier but then went off the port side of the ship into the water. Both crew ejected and were rescued by the plane guard helicopter.

1 May 1968

F-4B   149424   VMFA-314, MAG-13, USMC, Chu Lai
                  Capt D C Evans (survived)
                  1Lt I F Hunsaker (survived)
May got off to a bad start as far as the 1st MAW was concerned. A Chu Lai Phantom was lost on the morning of the 1st during an attack on an enemy position 12 miles west of Da Nang. Capt Evans was making his second napalm run when his aircraft was hit by ground fire and burst into flames. The crew ejected and were quickly rescued by a USAF helicopter.

A-6A   151578   VMA(AW)-242, MAG-11, USMC, Da Nang
                  Capt G H Christensend (survived)
                  1 crew, name unknown (survived)
A Marine Corps Intruder crashed during a strike mission as a result of an accidental structural failure. The two crew ejected safely and were rescued.

2 May 1968

A-6A   154164   VMA(AW)-533, MAG-12, USMC, Chu Lai
                  1Lt Robert D Avery (KIA)
                  1Lt Thomas D Clem (KIA)
The Marines lost another Intruder during a dawn strike on vehicles five miles northwest of Dong Hoi on the 2nd. Radar contact was lost with the aircraft, which was presumed to have crashed near the target killing the crew. The cause of the loss was probably ground fire. In 1991 a US investigation team found North Vietnamese documents that recorded the shooting down of an Intruder on this date with the loss of both crew.

3 May 1968

F-8E   149173   VMF(AW)-235, MAG-11, USMC, Da Nang
                  Capt Stephen William Clark (KIA)
The Marines lost their fourth aircraft in three days during a close air support mission just south of the DMZ. Capt Clark had been scrambled to attack enemy troops who were engaging US Marines about eight miles northeast of Dong Ha. As the Crusader started its strafing run it was seen to take a hit in the cockpit from a .50 calibre weapon. The aircraft crashed and Capt Clark, who may have been wounded, did not eject. VMF(AW)-235 left for Iwakuni seven days after this incident thereby bringing an end to Marine Corps Crusader fighter operations in Southeast Asia. The three Marine F-8 fighter squadrons that had served at Da Nang had flown almost 21,000 sorties, the majority of them in the air-to-ground role. From December 1965 when the first Marine Corps Crusader fighters arrived at Da Nang, MAG-11's three F-8 squadrons had lost a total of 17 F-8Es while four more had been lost in 1965 during a cruise on the USS *Oriskany*.

4 May 1968

O-1G   51-11976   19 TASS, 504 TASG, USAF, Bien Hoa
                  Maj C R Gregory (survived)
                  1Lt R F Cook (survived)
An O-1 was shot down by ground fire during an FAC mission 20 miles north of Vung Tau. Maj Gregory was flying near the village of Xa Binh Gia when his engine was put out of action by enemy fire. He crash-landed the Bird Dog and he and his observer were rescued by a USAF helicopter.

The port side of an AC-47D Spooky gunship shows the aircraft's three 7.62mm mini-guns which were capable of firing 6,000 rounds per minute. USAF

4/5 May 1968

AC-47D   43-76207   4 ACS, 14 ACW, USAF, Nha Trang
                  detached to Phu Cat
                  Capt Donald Lewis Merry (KIA)
                  Maj Richard William Wackerfuss (KIA)

AC-47D   43-16159   4 ACS, 14 ACW, USAF, Nha Trang
                  detached to Phu Cat
                  Lt Col Leslie Earl Harris (KIA)
                  Maj Teddy James Tomchesson (KIA)
                  Sgt Nacey Kent (survived)

                  Also KIA in the aircraft were:
                  Lt Barry Lynn Brown (KIA)
                  Capt Edward Chester Krawczyk (KIA)
                  SSgt James Edgar Bowman (KIA)
                  Sgt Douglas Joseph Cradeur (KIA)
                  Sgt Roy Leo Lede (KIA)
On the night of 4/5 May the VC and NVA started a widespread offensive, called Mini Tet by the Americans, which involved attacks on 109 towns and cities in South Vietnam resulting in major casualties on both sides. Two Spooky gunships were scrambled to attack rocket and mortar launching sites that were bombarding Pleiku air base. The two gunships were shot down by automatic weapons fire within minutes of each other. Sgt Nacey Kent, the flight engineer in one of the AC-47s, was awarded the AFC for his efforts in re-entering the aircraft wreckage and rescuing a number of the crew from his aircraft despite having sustained a broken leg in the crash landing.

5 May 1968

A-1H   52-137612   6 ACS, 14 ACW, USAF, Pleiku
                  Capt Lyn Douglas Oberdier (KIA)
The 6th ACS had arrived in Southeast Asia in February 1968. Unlike the other Skyraider squadrons in Southeast Asia at this time, the 6th was equipped entirely with single-seat aircraft, although at least one A-1G was later used. In fact many of the Squadron pilots had ferried the ex-Navy aircraft from Davis-Monthan to the Navy's rework facility at Quonset Point, Rhode Island, where the aircraft were refurbished for service with the USAF. The Squadron's A-1Hs and A-1Js were shipped to Cam Ranh Bay on board an aircraft carrier and then flown to Pleiku. The Squadron's first casualty was Capt Oberdier, who was killed as he was returning from a close air support mission. His aircraft crashed near Muang Buk, 50 miles north of Pleiku, presumably as a result of ground fire. He did not eject from his Skyraider and may have been wounded or incapacitated.

RA-5C   149278   RVAH-1, USN, USS *Enterprise*
                  Lt Giles Roderick Norrington (POW)
                  Lt Richard George Tangeman (POW)
For all its strength and size, an aircraft like the RA-5C Vigilante could just as easily be destroyed by light anti-aircraft fire as a smaller aircraft like the A-1 or the A-4. One of the *Enterprise's* Vigilantes was conducting a photographic reconnaissance along Route 1A near Ha Tinh when it was shot down. As the aircraft was approaching the village of Xom Hoai, 15 miles to the west of Ha Tinh, at around 6,500 feet it was seen to burst into a huge fireball about twice the size of the aircraft. The aircraft then snapped rolled to the right as the starboard wing separated from the fuselage. Miraculously, both the crew ejected but were injured and soon captured. It was presumed that an anti-aircraft shell had hit a critical part of the aircraft's structure causing the catastrophic break-up. Lts Norrington and Tangeman had flown together as a crew since they converted to the Vigilante in 1965. They had flown 22 missions over North Vietnam before being shot down and were both repatriated on 14 March 1973.

A-4E   151105   VMA-121, MAG-12, USMC, Chu Lai
                  1Lt T M Aiton (survived)
A section of Skyhawks was scrambled from Chu Lai to bomb a force of NVA troops who were entrenched in a tree line near Ba Long, seven miles southwest of Quang Tri. 1Lt Aiton was pulling up from his third pass when his aircraft was hit by .50 calibre gunfire. He ejected close to his target but was soon rescued by a Marine Corps helicopter.

6 May 1968

A-4C   145096   VMA-223, MAG-12, USMC, Chu Lai
                  Capt Manuel A Guzman (survived)
A-4E   151198   VMA-311, MAG-12, USMC, Chu Lai
                  1 pilot, name unknown (survived)
Capt Guzman was leading a two-plane section of Skyhawks towards the A Shau Valley on a strike mission when his aircraft collided at 10,000 feet with a Skyhawk from VMA-311 that was just leaving the target area. Guzman lost control of his aircraft immediately and had to eject but the other pilot made it to the coast before ejecting. Both men were subsequently rescued by helicopter.

F-4D   66-8687   433 TFS, 8 TFW, USAF, Ubon
                  2 crew, names unknown (survived)
A Phantom crashed in Thailand due to pilot error during an armed reconnaissance mission.

7 May 1968

A-1J 52-142059 6 ACS, 14 ACW, USAF, Pleiku
Capt H G Hayes (survived)

Having suffered its first casualty on the 5th, it was not long before the 6th ACS lost another aircraft. Capt Hayes was making his fourth strafing pass against an enemy gun position near Chu Lai when his aircraft was damaged in the starboard wing, probably by ground fire. Another possibility is that the Spad's cannon exploded damaging the wing, as a number of burst cannon incidents plagued the 6th ACS at this time. Capt Hayes flew away from the target area before ejecting and was rescued by an Army helicopter.

F-4B 151485 VF-92, USN, USS *Enterprise*
Lt Cdr E S Christensen (survived)
Lt(jg) W A Kramer (survived)

A section of Phantoms became engaged in a running fight with several MiGs north of Vinh during a combat air patrol. During a confused fight the normally reliable radar and jamming support failed leaving the Phantom crews blind. Lt Cdr Christensen was forced to disengage as he was running low on fuel and headed for the sea without his wingman. As he returned to straight and level flight at 8,000 feet over the coast, his aircraft was hit by an Atoll air-to-air missile fired by a MiG-21. The Phantom burst into flames and started a nose-down spiral towards the sea. Both crew ejected about five miles off the coast and were eventually rescued.

A-4F 154214 VA-113, USN, USS *Enterprise*
Lt Cdr Paul Warren Paine (KIA)

Lt Cdr Paine was part of the RESCAP force that assisted in the rescue of Lt Cdr Christensen and Lt Kramer. The Skyhawks returned to the *Enterprise* but Lt Cdr Paine was waved off his first approach as the deck was not yet clear for him to land. As he flew downwind in the pattern for his next approach, his aircraft was seen to suddenly pitch nose down and crash into the sea. Lt Cdr Paine ejected at 100 feet but this was outside his ejection seat's envelope and he was killed. It was standard practice for aircrew to check each other's aircraft for signs of damage prior to landing but no damage was seen on Lt Cdr Paine's aircraft. For some reason the Skyhawk suddenly lost elevator control at an altitude that was too low to recover.

C-7B 62-4176 537 TAS, 483 TAW, USAF, Phu Cat
5 crew, names unknown (survived)

A Caribou suddenly lost engine power after take off and crashed while it was attempting to return to land. All the crew survived the incident.

8 May 1968

A-4E 152005 VA-56, USN, USS *Enterprise*
Lt D A Lawrence (survived)

During an armed reconnaissance mission, a section of Skyhawks attacked a group of trucks 12 miles south of Ha Tinh. Lt Lawrence fired his 2.75in rockets and pulled up but as his aircraft was climbing through 3,500 feet it was hit by ground fire. The engine started vibrating and the aircraft caught fire. Within seconds the engine stopped and Lt Lawrence was forced to eject. He was rescued by a Navy SH-3 which penetrated 20 miles inland to pick up the downed pilot.

9 May 1968

A-4E 152092 VMA-121, MAG-12, USMC, Chu Lai
Maj L D Tyrell (survived)

VMA-121 lost another Skyhawk during a close air support mission on the 9th. Maj Tyrell tried to reach Da Nang after sustaining battle damage but he was forced to eject over the sea near Monkey Mountain and had to be rescued.

O-2A 67-21399 20 TASS, 504 TASG, USAF, Da Nang
Maj Robert E Staley (KIA)
Capt George J Bedrossian (KIA)

An O-2 lost power just after take and crash-landed. Unfortunately, the aircraft burst into flames killing the two crew. The

names of the crew are assumed as these were the only two airmen lost on this date in Southeast Asia.

O-2A 68-6858 20 TASS, 504 TASG, USAF, Da Nang
2 crew, names unknown (survived)

The 20th TASS lost another aircraft on the same day when an O-2 ran out of fuel during a photographic reconnaissance mission. Both crew survived the subsequent crash-landing.

10 May 1968

O-1E 56-2469 20 TASS, 504 TASG, USAF, Da Nang
Maj B R Telshaw (survived)

Maj Telshaw was flying his Bird Dog just south of Hué when his engine was damaged by ground fire. He flew away from the area but was forced to crash-land a few miles to the west of the city.

F-105D 60-0415 357 TFS, 355 TFW, USAF, Takhli
Maj David B Coon (survived)

As the bombing restrictions in North Vietnam reduced the number of strike missions flown by the F-105 wings, more sorties could be allocated for support of the war in Laos and South Vietnam. A formation of Thunderchiefs was assigned to a close air support mission in South Vietnam, 15 miles west of Ben Het at the point where the borders of South Vietnam, Laos and Cambodia converge. Maj Coon was pulling up from his bombing run when his aircraft was struck by ground fire. He ejected close by and was picked up by an Army helicopter. This was the only occasion during the entire war that an F-105 was lost on a combat mission over South Vietnam. Prior to conversion to the F-105, Maj Coon had flown almost 4,000 hours in the KC-135 and had flown 60 combat missions in Southeast Asia.

O-2A 67-21370 22 TASS, 504 TASG, USAF, Binh Thuy
2 crew, names unknown (survived)

Having lost an O-2 on the 9th through running out of fuel, a second aircraft was lost the next day for the same reason. Again, both crew survived the ensuing crash-landing.

The Seige of Kham Duc

Kham Duc Special Forces camp (designated A-105) was situated in the Annamite Mountains 55 miles west of Chu Lai. It was extremely remote and by the spring of 1968 was the last remaining border camp in Military Region 1 still in American hands. The camp was on a narrow plain surrounded by dense forest and high mountains. Its only contact with the main operating bases was by air. The camp had been occupied by US Special Forces since September 1963 and had an airstrip that could take C-123s and C-130s. Five miles to the south was a small forward operating base at Ngoc Tavak defended by just over 100 men. In the early hours of 10 May the Ngok Tavak outpost was attacked by an NVA infantry battalion using mortars and rockets. Fierce fighting continued as night turned into day and two Marine Corps CH-46s were lost attempting to extract the survivors. Simultaneous with the attack on Ngoc Tavak, the North Vietnamese started a mortar attack on Kham Duc. Reinforcements were brought in by helicopter throughout the 11th despite enemy fire and low-lying fog. The enemy assault intensified in the early hours of the 12th and the perimeter defences were soon overrun. A massive enemy assault on the main compound started around noon but this was thwarted by accurate and devastating air strikes. However, it became obvious that the situation was hopeless and the decision was taken to evacuate the camp by helicopter and transport aircraft. USAF C-130s and C-123s ran the gauntlet of anti-aircraft and small arms fire in the air, and mortar and rocket fire on the ground as they helped to extract the survivors. The last of the defenders were evacuated from the camp at 4:33pm on the 12th. That night US aircraft bombed and strafed the camp's new occupants. Despite the loss of the camp, the evacuation of Kham Duc stands out as one the most heroic episodes in the history of the war in Vietnam.

12 May 1968

A-1H 52-135272 6 ACS, 14 ACW, USAF, Pleiku
Lt Col J N Swain (survived)

Early on the morning of the 12th the Skyraiders from Pleiku were already over the camp at Kham Duc trying to keep the enemy's heads down as US Army helicopters arrived to evacuate the camp. As the first Chinook landed it was hit by enemy fire and burst into flames. Moments later one of the Skyraiders was shot down as it was bombing enemy troops two miles north of the camp. The aircraft was hit in the port wing by .50 calibre gunfire and Lt Col Swain ejected and was lucky to be picked up by an Army helicopter.

O-2A 67-21333 20 TASS, 504 TASG, USAF, Da Nang
Capt Griffin Eli Scarborough (KIA)
1Lt Omar David Jones (KIA)

Later in the morning an O-2 was shot down as it was controlling an air strike near Ngoc Tavak, five miles south of Kham Duc. As the aircraft was diving to fire its rockets to mark the target, it was hit by ground fire, burst into flames and crashed. Neither of the crew was able to escape from the aircraft.

O-2A 67-21336 20 TASS, 504 TASG, USAF, Da Nang
Capt Phillip R Smotherman (survived)

About one hour after the first O-2 went down, another FAC aircraft was lost. Capt Smotherman had been working with the 23rd (Americal) Infantry Division in the area around Kham Duc for some time and was therefore well acquainted with the area and the desperate situation. He was controlling a flight of Marine Corps A-4s that was making rocket attacks on enemy positions near the camp when his aircraft was hit by ground fire. The starboard wing tip and aileron were damaged but with difficulty he guided the aircraft down to a forced landing on Kham Duc's airstrip, despite having to dodge a C-123 as it climbed away from the camp. The O-2 was badly damaged and was quickly destroyed on the ground by enemy mortar fire. Capt Smotherman was ordered to stay at the camp as the Air Liaison Officer and he continued to radio targeting information for air strikes for five hours while he was on the ground. Towards the end he was directing aircraft to drop ordnance within 25 yards of the defenders. He was later evacuated from Kham Duc by the last C-130 to leave the camp.

C-130B 60-0297 773 TAS, 463 TAW, USAF, Clark
Maj Bernard Ludwig Bucher (KIA)
1Lt Stephan Craig Moreland (KIA)
Maj John Lee McElroy (KIA)
SSgt Frank Monroe Hepler (KIA)
A1C George Wendell Long (KIA)
Capt Warren Robert Orr,
5th Special Forces Group, US Army (KIA)
Also killed were an unknown number of
South Vietnamese civilians

Maj Bucher's C-130 was one of the last aircraft to fly out of Kham Duc. The aircraft took off with an unknown number of passengers, many of them Vietnamese irregular troops and their dependants but also at least one US Army Special Forces officer. The aircraft took several hits as it took off and a few minutes later an FAC pilot who was airborne in the vicinity reported that the Hercules had exploded in mid-air and crashed into a ravine about one mile from the camp. Although it was not possible to reach the wreckage, the aircraft was completely burnt out and there was no chance of any survivors. It has been estimated that possibly as many as 150 Vietnamese were crammed on board the aircraft and died in the crash. Whatever the precise number of casualties, this incident was undoubtedly the worst air disaster of the war until the loss of a C-5A near Saigon on 4 April 1975. Maj Bucher's aircraft was temporarily based at Tan Son Nhut.

C-130A 56-0548 21 TAS, 374 TAW, USAF, Naha
Lt Col John R Delmore (survived)
TSgt John K McCall (survived)
3 crew, names unknown (survived)

Lt Col Delmore's aircraft was hit repeatedly by small arms fire as it was landing at Kham Duc. The linkage to the power levers on all four engines was damaged and the engines could not be throttled back for the landing so Lt Col Delmore had to feather all four props so he could set the aircraft down on Kham Duc's runway. With the brakes shot out the aircraft veered off to one

side of the runway, struck the wreckage of the Chinook that had been shot down earlier and came to rest with its nose stuck in the earth. Twenty minutes later a Marine Corps CH-46 evacuated all five crew out of Kham Duc. A little while later C-130 flights into Kham Duc ceased as most of the camp's defenders had by then been evacuated but a breakdown in communications resulted in a C-130 returning to Kham Duc to offload three men from a combat control team after the last of the defenders had left. When the mistake was realised the three men were rescued under heavy enemy fire by a C-123 Provider flown by Lt Col Joe M Jackson and Maj Jesse W Campbell of the 311th ACS. North Vietnamese troops were occupying the airfield when the Provider landed and fired at it continuously until it took off with the three men safely on board. Lt Col Jackson received the Medal of Honor for this feat of skill and courage under fire. A total of eight aircraft were lost at Kham Duc on the 12th including a Marine Corps CH-46, an Army UH-1C and an Army CH-47 in addition to the USAF aircraft. Lt Col Delmore and his crew were temporarily deployed to Cam Ranh Bay.

13 May 1968

A-6A   152951   VA-35, USN, USS *Enterprise*
            Lt Bruce B Bremner (survived)
            Lt Jack T Fardy (survived)

The *Enterprise* was not having a good month. The carrier lost its fifth aircraft of the month during a low-level night strike on Vinh airfield. Lt Bremner's Intruder crossed the target at 1,400 feet and successfully dropped 18 Mk36 DSTs magnetic-fused bombs. The aircraft was hit by a 57mm shell in the port wing, which caught fire. Lt Bremner turned out to sea and climbed to 35,000 feet in an attempt to put out the fire by starving it of oxygen. However, the fire would not go out so the crew decided to attempt an approach to the *Enterprise*. As the aircraft descended the fire increased in intensity resulting in an explosion that forced the crew to eject close to the *Enterprise*. They were both rescued by the carrier's plane guard helicopter and went on to fly another 90 missions before going home.

14 May 1968

A-4F   154198   VA-93, USN, USS *Bon Homme Richard*
            Lt(jg) Barry Edwin Karger (KIA)

Lt Karger was on a weather reconnaissance flight along the coast of North Vietnam when he saw and attacked a bridge on the main coastal road, 13 miles south of the Mu Ron Ma peninsula. His wingman saw him roll in on the bridge in a vertical dive. The Skyhawk started to pull out but then rolled through 180 degrees and dived into the ground. It could not be determined if the aircraft had been hit by ground fire or if Lt Karger had lost control during the dive. Barry Karger's remains were discovered at the wreck site during a joint US-Vietnamese investigation and positively identified in January 1994.

F-105D   61-0132   34 TFS, 388 TFW, USAF, Korat
            Maj Seymour R Bass (KIA)

An F-105 pilot was killed in a mid-air collision with his leader over Thailand during an attack mission. The other pilot involved managed to return to base and land safely. 61-0132 was painted as 'Hanoi Special' and had shot down a MiG-17 on 23 August 1967 when being flown by 1Lt Dave Waldrop of the 34th TFS.

15 May 1968

C-130E   63-7875   779 TAS, 464 TAW, USAF, Pope
            7 crew, names unknown (survived)

A TAC Hercules crash-landed at Song Be in South Vietnam due to engine failure and was destroyed.

16 May 1968

F-4D   66-7630   435 TFS, 8 TFW, USAF, Ubon
            Maj David J Rickel (KIA)
            1Lt Gerald Joseph Crosson (KIA)

Maj Rickel and 1Lt Crosson were flying a Night Owl mission in the Xuan Son area, 15 miles northwest of Dong Hoi, when they were shot down. Maj Rickel spotted a target and dived to attack it but the aircraft was hit by AAA. The Phantom crashed near the village of Ha Loi with no indication that either of the crew had managed to escape. A search the next day failed to reveal any sign of wreckage or the two men.

17 May 1968

F-100D   56-2949   416 TFS, 37 TFW, USAF, Phu Cat
            Capt J T Mattox (survived)

The US bases in South Vietnam were still under constant threat of Viet Cong attack and air strikes close to the airfields were becoming common. Capt Mattox was bombing enemy troops just five miles to the west of Phu Cat when he was shot down. He was making his third pass when his Super Sabre ran into ground fire. He ejected and was rescued by a USAF HH-43 from Phu Cat's detachment of the 38th ARRS.

O-1F   57-2980   21 TASS, 504 TASG, USAF, Nha Trang
            Maj Wilbur A Skaar (KIA)

Maj Skaar was controlling an air strike on an enemy automatic weapons position 15 miles west of Kontum when he was killed. His Bird Dog was hit by ground fire and crashed before he could bail out to safety.

A-4E   149970   VMA-311, MAG-12, USMC, Chu Lai
            Maj R W Wardlaw (survived)

Although the siege of Khe Sanh was over, it still remained a very active area. A formation of A-4s was attacking enemy troops seven miles north of the Marine Corps base when Maj Wardlaw was shot down. He was making his second pass when his aircraft was hit by small arms fire. He ejected safely and was lucky to be rescued from this extremely 'hot' area.

18 May 1968

RA-5C   149283   RVAH-11, USN, USS *Kitty Hawk*
            Cdr Charlie Negus James (POW)
            Lt Cdr Vincent Duncan Monroe (POW - died)

A Vigilante was on its way to photograph potential targets in the Vinh Son region when it ran into trouble. The aircraft was hit by AAA and burst into flames when it was about 25 miles northwest of Vinh. The aircraft began to disintegrate at which point the crew ejected. Two SAR beepers were heard and the SAR forces were called in. The air defences in the area proved to be too intense for an attempted rescue and the search had to be called off. Radio Hanoi later reported the capture of two American pilots in the Vinh Son area and both men were listed as POWs. However, it appears that Lt Cdr Monroe did not survive as he was not seen in any of the POW camps and did not return during Operation Homecoming.

    This was the last aircraft lost by the *Kitty Hawk* before finishing its third war cruise on 1 June and returning to the USA. The carrier had lost eight aircraft in combat and another seven in accidents during its 125 days on the line. Twelve of the *Kitty Hawk's* aircrew had been killed and another three were taken prisoner. Cdr James was released on 14 March 1973 while the remains of Lt Cdr Monroe were returned to the USA as a result of a visit to Hanoi by Congressman Montgomery on 23 August 1978. Vincent Monroe was later buried at Arlington National Cemetery. Charlie James had enlisted in the US Navy in 1947 and was commissioned as a naval aviator in 1951. He flew 64 combat missions over Korea in the Skyraider with VA-55 and later became a flying instructor before converting to the A-3 and then the A-5. He was the executive officer for RVAH-11 at the time of his shooting down.

RF-4C   66-0442   14 TRS, 432 TRW, USAF, Udorn
            Capt Terry Jun Uyeyama (POW)
            Capt Tommy Emerson Gist (KIA)

The USAF also lost a reconnaissance aircraft on the 18th. Capt Uyeyama and Capt Gist went missing during a mission near Dong Hoi in North Vietnam. Capt Uyeyama was captured and spent the rest of the war as a prisoner but Capt Gist was killed. Terry Uyeyama had flown 101 combat missions before being shot down. He was released on 14 March 1973.

F-100D   55-3548   531 TFS, 3 TFW, USAF, Bien Hoa
            Capt Roland Robert Obenland (KIA)

An F-100 flight was scrambled to attack enemy troops who were being engaged six miles southeast of Bien Hoa air base. Capt Obenland was making a low-level run to drop napalm when his aircraft was hit by automatic weapons fire. The aircraft crashed before the pilot could eject. This aircraft originally served with the 481st TFS at Cannon AFB, New Mexico.

O-1E   56-2520   22 TASS, 504 TASG, USAF, Binh Thuy
            1 pilot, name unknown (survived)

An O-1 Bird Dog FAC aircraft crashed in South Vietnam due to engine failure.

18/19 May 1968

F-4D   66-8695   497 TFS, 8 TFW, USAF, Ubon
            Capt Joseph Edwin Davies (KIA)
            1Lt Glenn Dewayne McCubbon (KIA)

A flight of two Phantoms from the Wolfpack was tasked with a night armed reconnaissance mission over the Trail in southern Laos. The wingman dropped his ordnance and set off back towards Ubon after seeing three explosions on the ground that he assumed were bombs dropped by his leader. However, Capt Davies's aircraft failed to rejoin at the appointed time and a search was instigated. A voice contact was made and the transmission was pinpointed to an area about 25 miles west of the DMZ. Another voice contact was then made that appeared to come from a totally different location but neither were thought to have come from the Phantom crew. Post-war investigations confirmed that the aircraft had been shot down with the loss of both men.

21 May 1968

A-4F   154988   VA-93, USN, USS *Bon Homme Richard*
            Lt(jg) J A Douglass (survived)

During a strike on a road bridge at Trang Song, 15 miles north of Vinh, one of the attacking Skyhawks was hit by automatic weapons fire. The aircraft began to trail flames from the rear fuselage and the controls started to stiffen. Lt Douglass headed out to sea and gained altitude but about 10 miles from the coast the hydraulic system failed completely and the pilot lost control. Lt Douglass ejected safely and was rescued by a Navy helicopter.

O-2A   67-21382   23 TASS, 504 TASG, USAF, Nakhon Phanom
            Maj Gerald T Dwyer (survived)

Having survived being shot down in an O-2 on 1 April, Maj Dwyer had another lucky escape on the 21st. Maj Dwyer was controlling an air strike on Route 968 of the Ho Chi Minh Trail near Kay Bong, 25 miles southeast of Ban Talan, when he was shot down again. The aircraft was hit in the starboard wing by a 37mm shell and Maj Dwyer had to bail out. During the descent he heard shots being fired at him by enemy troops on the ground. Upon landing he was pursued by five North Vietnamese soldiers. The North Vietnamese closed in as a rescue helicopter approached but Maj Dwyer shot three of them with his .38 calibre revolver and was successfully rescued once more.

22 May 1968

RF-8G   146886   Detachment 31, VFP-63, USN,
            USS *Bon Homme Richard*
            Lt(jg) Edwin Frank Miller (POW)

An RF-8 Crusader was assigned to photograph the Lang Met road bridge near Vinh. Lt Miller started jinking at 5,000 feet and 520 knots in an attempt to avoid flak while on his photo run. Although the flak was reported to be light, Lt Miller's aircraft was hit by 37mm anti-aircraft fire. The engine started to run down and the hydraulics failed resulting in a complete loss of control. Lt Miller ejected and was quickly captured. He was flying his 85th mission when he was shot down and he was released on 14 March 1973.

A-4F   154974   VA-212, USN, USS *Bon Homme Richard*
            Lt Cdr R S Thomas (survived)

The Cessna A-37 Dragonfly light attack aircraft was a modified version of the T-37 trainer and, despite its short range and poor performance compared to larger jets, acquitted itself well from 1967 to the end of the war. 2Lt D H Whitehill was killed in A-37A 67-14527 of the 604th ACS when it crashed during an escort mission on 23 May 1968. USAF

Lt Cdr Thomas and his flight was on an Iron Hand mission when Lt Miller's Crusader was shot down. He was directed to take his flight to Vinh and provide RESCAP for any rescue that might be attempted. As he flew just to the east of the city at 3,200 feet, his Skyhawk was hit in the wing root by flak. Lt Cdr Thomas headed out to sea with his aircraft on fire, all his cockpit warning lights flashing and his fuel dropping rapidly indicating a massive fuel leak. Eventually the fire burned through the wing spar and the wing separated from the fuselage at which point Lt Cdr Thomas ejected. He was picked up by a Navy SAR helicopter.

F-4D   66-0246   433 TFS, 8 TFW, USAF, Ubon
       Capt John Hunter Crews (KIA)
       1Lt Dean Paul St Pierre (KIA)

Another Night Owl Phantom was lost on the night of the 22nd. Capt Crews had spotted a convoy of six trucks on a road 20 miles west of Dong Hoi and rolled in to the attack. The aircraft crashed near the road, possibly as a result of being hit by 85mm AAA. There was no sign of any ejection and it was presumed that both men had been killed in the crash.

C-130A   56-0477   41 TAS, 374 TAW, USAF, Naha
       Lt Col William Henderson Mason (KIA)
       Capt Thomas Barry Mitchell (KIA)
       Maj Jerry Lee Chambers (KIA)
       Capt William Thomas McPhail (KIA)
       SSgt Calvin Charles Glover (KIA)
       Sgt Gary Pate (KIA)
       A1C John Quincy Adam (KIA)
       A1C Thomas Edward Knebel (KIA)
       A1C Melvin Douglas Rash (KIA)

The 41st TAS maintained a detachment of C-130s at Ubon for flare-dropping duties over the Ho Chi Minh Trail. Known as Blind Bat, this detachment provided flare support and forward air control at night for the fast jets, A-26s and A-1s that operated over the Trail. The mission started at Da Nang in early 1965 under the 6315th Operations Group. The detachment moved to Ubon in March 1966. On the night of the 22nd one of the Blind Bat aircraft failed to return from a flare mission over southern Laos. It was determined that the aircraft was lost somewhere near Muang Nong, about 20 miles southwest of the A Shau Valley, where another aircraft had reported a large fire on the ground. In 1989 and 1991 identity documents belonging to Sgt Pate were reported to have been discovered.

22/23 May 1968

F-4B   151500   VMFA-115, MAG-13, USMC, Chu Lai
       Capt J W Proctor (survived)
       Capt R Cox (survived)

A Marine Corps Phantom was lost during a night-time TPQ-10 radar-directed bombing mission about 15 miles south of Saravan in southern Laos. Capt Proctor was making his third run over the target when his aircraft was damaged by ground fire. He and his navigator ejected and were later rescued by an Army helicopter. Phantom 151500 was flown by Lt W M McGuigan and Lt(jg) R M Fowler of VF-161 on 13 July 1966 when they shot down a MiG-17.

23 May 1968

F-4B   151507   VMFA-542, MAG-11, USMC, Da Nang
       Capt J E Crowell (survived)
       Capt W S Poole (survived)

Another Marine Corps Phantom was lost the following day during a close air support mission just south of Da Nang. Capt Crowell's aircraft was struck by small arms fire as he overflew his target. Both crew ejected three miles north of Hoi An and were soon rescued.

A-37A   67-14527   604 ACS, 3 TFW, USAF, Bien Hoa
       2Lt David H Whitehill (KIA)

As an A-37 was flying an escort mission for a Ranch Hand spray flight it came under attack from an enemy gun position near Rang Rang, 30 miles northeast of Bien Hoa. 2Lt Whitehill made two passes over the gun but on his third strafing run his aircraft crashed, possibly as a result of ground fire. The pilot was unable to eject before the aircraft impacted close to the target.

UC-123B   54-0588   12 ACS, 315 ACW, USAF, Bien Hoa
       Lt Col Emmet Rucker (KIA)
       Maj James L Shanks (KIA)
       Sgt Herbert E Schmidt (KIA)

In an incident unrelated to the loss of the A-37A listed above, a Ranch Hand Provider was shot down during a spray run on a Viet Cong base camp area near Xom Rach Goc at the extreme southern tip of South Vietnam. The six Ranch Hand aircraft came under heavy automatic weapons fire as they were spraying in formation and at the end of the run smoke was seen trailing from the port engine of the number two aircraft. The Provider's wing caught fire and the aircraft rolled and crashed into the sea about a mile off the coast with the loss of all three on board. During April the 12th ACS had received the first of the upgraded UC-123Ks, which had two additional J-85-17 jet engines and other improvements. The extra performance was useful in enabling the spray aircraft to climb more rapidly and thereby spend less time at low altitude and to be able to survive the loss of one its piston engines.

A-1E   52-135202   1 ACS, 56 ACW, USAF, Nakhon Phanom
       1 pilot, name unknown (survived)

A Skyraider suffered an accidental engine failure as it was escorting a helicopter on a mission in South Vietnam. The pilot ejected and was rescued.

24 May 1968

O-2A   67-21335   20 TASS, 504 TASG, USAF, Da Nang
       Maj R T Loftus (survived)
       1 crew, name unknown (survived)

An O-2 FAC was shot down as it was controlling an air strike near Ha Tan, 15 miles southwest of Da Nang. The rear engine was put out of action by .50 calibre gunfire but Maj Loftus eased the aircraft down from 1,000 feet and force-landed without injury. The crew were airlifted out by an Army helicopter and the O-2 was destroyed.

A-4C   148549   VMA-223, MAG-12, USMC, Chu Lai
       Capt Steven J Driscoll (survived)

Capt Driscoll's Skyhawk was hit by .50 calibre ground fire as he was attacking Viet Cong gun positions near Tien Phuoc, 20 miles west of Chu Lai. He flew several miles south of the target before ejecting and being picked up by a USAF helicopter.

A-1H   52-137620   6 ACS, 14 ACW, USAF, Pleiku
       Lt Col Wallace A Ford (KIA)

A flight of Skyraiders from Pleiku was directed north to attack enemy troops 15 miles west of Tam Ky. Lt Col Ford was making his third strafing run at 500 feet when he was shot down by .50 calibre ground fire. The aircraft crashed before the pilot could escape. Wallace Ford was the first CO of the recently arrived 6th ACS. A base facility at Pleiku was named in his honour after his death.

25 May 1968

F-4D   66-7569   435 TFS, 8 TFW, USAF, Ubon
       Capt D J Ankeny (survived)
       1Lt A A Turner (survived)

The Wolfpack lost a fifth Phantom during May when an aircraft was shot down during a strike on an anti-aircraft gun position near Xom Duong Quan, just north of the Mu Gia Pass in North Vietnam. The aircraft was hit by AAA as it pulled up through 6,500 feet from its first pass. The port engine was damaged and had to be closed down as the aircraft flew towards Thailand. However, the crew had to eject near Ban Sappeng in southern Laos. Although both men were injured they were successfully rescued from the jungle by a USAF SAR helicopter.

28 May 1968

F-105D   61-0194   34 TFS, 388 TFW, USAF, Korat
       Maj Roger Dean Ingvalson (POW)

A flight of F-105s attacked troops and trucks five miles northwest of Dong Hoi during a Rolling Thunder mission. Maj Ingvalson, the 34th's operations officer, was shot down by ground fire as he was strafing the target from 1,800 feet. The aircraft caught fire and the pilot ejected a mile from the target and was quickly captured. Maj Ingvalson was lost on his 87th mission and was released on 14 March 1973. After retirement from the Air Force he founded a prison ministry, which he ran for 15 years before retiring. F-105D 61-0194 was painted as 'The Avenger' during its time with the 34th TFS.

A-4F   154982   VA-212, USN, USS *Bon Homme Richard*
       1 pilot, name unknown (survived)

A Skyhawk was lost during a strike mission due to accidental engine failure.

O-1G   51-4949   19 TASS, 504 TASG, USAF, Bien Hoa
       2 crew, names unknown (survived)

A Bird Dog was destroyed when its engine failed on take off on a reconnaissance mission.

29 May 1968

C-7B   62-4189   458 TAS, 483 TAW, USAF, Cam Ranh Bay
26 passengers and crew, names unknown
(survived)

A Caribou on a trooping flight was hit by small arms fire on the approach to Dak To and undershot the runway and swiped off the landing gear. A wing was then torn off and the aircraft was damaged beyond repair but all the passengers and crew survived.

30 May 1968

A-4F   154174   VA-212, USN, USS *Bon Homme Richard*
Lt J E Killian (survived)

VA-212 lost another aircraft during an attack on an oil storage site 12 miles northwest of Vinh. Lt Killian had just started his fifth dive on the target firing 2.75in rockets when his Skyhawk's engine began to vibrate and lose power. He headed for the coast, losing altitude all the time, but managed to fly about 30 miles out to sea before having to eject when he could no longer maintain flying speed. He was rescued by a Navy helicopter and it was determined that the engine failure was probably due to the ingestion of debris from the LAU-60 rocket pod carried by the Skyhawk.

O-2A   67-21405   20 TASS, 504 TASG, USAF, Da Nang
Capt Lewis Philip Smith (KIA)

A Covey FAC was lost during a forward air control mission in the Steel Tiger area of southern Laos. Capt Smith is thought to have come down near Ban Daktring, about 25 miles southwest of Kham Duc, probably as the result of anti-aircraft fire. Another aircraft in the area heard an emergency beeper signal but a search failed to find any trace of Capt Smith.

F-105D   60-0511   469 TFS, 388 TFW, USAF, Korat
Col N P Phillips (survived)

A flight of F-105s on a Steel Tiger strike in southern Laos spotted two trucks on a road near Ban Kate, 20 miles west of the DMZ. Col Phillips was strafing the trucks from an altitude of just 100 feet when his aircraft was hit by automatic weapons fire. He zoomed up to gain as much altitude as possible before ejecting. He was rescued after dark by a USAF SAR helicopter from Detachment 1 of the 40th ARRS. During the rescue the PJ, Sgt Thomas A Newman, was lowered to the ground. He sent the helicopter out of the area as he spent some time searching in the dark, risking detection by the enemy by calling out the pilot's name. When Sgt Newman eventually found Col Phillips he called for the helicopter to return for the pick up. Thomas Newman was awarded the AFC for his actions during this rescue. 60-0511 carried the name 'Sweet Sal' during its time at Korat.

31 May 1968

F-105D   60-0409   469 TFS, 388 TFW, USAF, Korat
Maj Eugene Paul Beresik (KIA)

Tiger Island is a small island about a mile across situated about 15 miles off the coast just north of the 17th Parallel. The island was occupied by the North Vietnamese who had several gun sites that threatened any aircraft that came close to the island. It was subjected to many air attacks throughout the war. On one such attack Maj Beresik was shot down and killed. He was making a low-level strafing run over one of the gun sites when his F-105 was hit by ground fire and crashed in the sea less than a mile from the island. The aircraft was too low for the pilot to have time to eject successfully. Thunderchief 60-0409 was known as 'Thunder Valley' and 'Bunny Baby' at various times while at Korat.

A-7A   153255   VA-82, USN, USS *America*
Lt K W Fields (survived)

Two Corsairs were assigned to attack a storage area near Ban Kate in southern Laos at dusk on the 31st. The leader, Lt Fields, made his first pass and noticed at least three anti-aircraft guns firing at him. During his second pass, Lt Fields felt a thump and the aircraft started rolling uncontrollably. A large section of the wing had been shot off and Lt Fields ejected close to his target.

He landed safely but was injured while evading North Vietnamese troops intent on capturing him. He was eventually rescued by a USAF SAR helicopter.

A-1H   52-135282   602 ACS, 56 ACW, USAF, Nakhon Phanom
Capt Edward W Leonard (POW)

When Lt Fields was shot down near Ban Kate, a USAF Skyraider, which was already in the area, was directed to search for the downed airman. Night was drawing in rapidly but Capt Leonard came down to 500 feet in an effort to protect the Corsair pilot until the rescue forces arrived. Unfortunately the Skyraider was hit by automatic weapons fire about 10 miles to the southwest of Lt Fields's position. Capt Leonard ejected but was captured by North Vietnamese soldiers. He was eventually sent to Hanoi and was released on 28 March 1973. Capt Leonard had flown over 250 missions in Southeast Asia and had been shot down during a mission over northern Laos on 18 March but managed to fly most of the way back to base before having to eject on that occasion.

A-7A   153258   VA-82, USN, USS *America*
1 pilot, name unknown (survived)

The *America* lost a second Corsair on this day when an aircraft suffered an engine flame out during in-flight refuelling. The pilot ejected and was quickly rescued.

1 June 1968

F-4C   64-0779   391 TFS, 12 TFW, USAF, Cam Ranh Bay
Maj Glenn Thomas Ciarfeo (KIA)
Capt M P Rhodes (survived)

A flight of Phantoms was scrambled to attack a force of enemy troops near Van Ninh on the coast, 40 miles north of Cam Ranh Bay. Maj Ciarfeo was making his seventh pass over the troops when his luck finally ran out. The Phantom was hit by ground fire and crashed two miles away from the enemy position. Only the WSO, Capt Rhodes, was able to eject, and he suffered severe injuries in doing so but was rescued.

A-1E   52-139584   602 ACS, 56 ACW, USAF, Nakhon Phanom
Maj W G Palank (survived)

The effort continued to find Lt Fields and Capt Leonard, who had been shot down near Ban Kate on the 31st. Another Skyraider was lost during the search but this time the pilot was rescued. Maj Palank was orbiting at 4,000 feet about six miles southwest of Khe Sanh when his engine was hit by a 37mm shell. With the engine producing reduced power he started back towards Thailand but was forced to eject near Ban Alao, 15 miles southwest of Ban Kate. He was rescued by a USAF SAR helicopter.

2 June 1968

F-4B   150453   VF-92, USN, USS *Enterprise*
Lt Cdr P A Carroll (survived)
Lt Cdr E P Sierra (survived)

During a combat air patrol a Phantom suffered a suspected double failure of the power control hydraulics system. With the aircraft out of control, both the crew ejected and were later picked up.

4 June 1968

F-4J   155554   VF-33, USN, USS *America*
Lt Eric Parker Brice (KIA)
Lt(jg) William A Simmons (survived)

When the USS *America* arrived off Vietnam on 12 May it was carrying the first squadron of the new F-4J variant of the Phantom to reach the theatre. The F-4J was a development of the Navy's F-4B and had a more powerful engine, strengthened undercarriage and modifications to the tailplane and wing to permit better handling on take off and approach. A flight of F-4Js was attacking a road intersection near Don Cay, 15 miles south of Vinh, when one of the aircraft was damaged by 37mm AAA. Lt Brice's aircraft was hit as he was pulling up through 4,500 feet, having just dropped his Mk82 bombs on the target. The utility hydraulics failed and the controls were damaged with the throttles stuck in full military power. Lt Brice managed to fly the aircraft using rudder only for control. The aircraft crossed

the coast safely but about 25 miles out to sea the Phantom caught fire. Lt Brice ordered his NFO to eject but the pilot's canopy then failed to jettison and Eric Brice was last seen desperately trying to push the canopy free so that his ejection seat could fire. Sadly, this was one of many instances when Phantom front-seaters failed to escape from their aircraft.

6 June 1968

A-1E   52-132667   1 ACS, 56 ACW, USAF, Nakhon Phanom
Capt E E Kirkpatrick (survived)
Maj David James Gunster (KIA)

A-1E   52-133925   1 ACS, 56 ACW, USAF, Nakhon Phanom
Maj Rodolph Lee Nunn (KIA)

Two Skyraiders were flying a seeding mission as part of the Igloo White sensor programme. The two aircraft were flying in close formation at 4,500 feet just south of the DMZ and nine miles north of Khe Sanh when they collided in mid-air. Both aircraft crashed and only Capt Kirkpatrick managed to eject. He was recovered, badly injured, by a USAF SAR helicopter.

7 June 1968

F-4B   150994   VF-92, USN, USS *Enterprise*
Lt(jg) W R McClendon (survived)
Lt(jg) R J Edens (survived)

VF-92 lost another aircraft in an accident five days after the first when the pilot's control column locked immediately after a catapult launch. With no way of controlling the aircraft, the crew were forced to eject. Either foreign object damage or a broken linkage may have been the cause of the accident.

8 June 1968

F-105D   61-0055   34 TFS, 388 TFW, USAF, Korat
Maj Carl B Light (survived)

A flight of F-105s was sent to bomb a truck park that had been discovered near Ba Binh, five miles north of the DMZ. As Maj Light was pulling up through 6,000 feet from his first run, his aircraft was hit by 37mm AAA and badly damaged. He ejected near the village of Xom Quan, about five miles deeper into North Vietnam. A SAR effort soon swung into action and Maj Light was eventually rescued by a USAF SAR helicopter the following day although a Phantom was lost during the attempt. This was the first rescue mission in which a Misty FAC was used for RESCAP duties and to direct air strikes. 61-0055 was painted as 'Dorothy II' while serving with the Korat Wing.

9 June 1968

A-4E   151080   VMA-121, MAG-12, USMC, Chu Lai
1Lt Walter Roy Schmidt (KIA)

A section of Skyhawks from Chu Lai was assigned to attack a weapons cache that had been discovered in a NVA base area about 20 miles southwest of Hué. 1Lt Schmidt (call sign Hellborne 215) was making his fifth pass and was using his cannon to strafe the target when his engine was hit by .50 calibre ground fire. He ejected over densely wooded hills and broke his leg either during the ejection or when he landed. He spoke to his wingman and a SAR helicopter on his survival radio and told them that North Vietnamese troops were approaching. In fact 1Lt Schmidt had ejected over a large NVA encampment area and was surrounded by enemy soldiers. Jolly Green 22 attempted a pick up but was forced to withdraw due to intense ground fire and shortage of fuel after three attempts. After a suppressive strike Jolly Green 23, HH-3E 67-14710 flown by Lt Jack C Rittichier and his crew, approached 1Lt Schmidt but as the helicopter drew close to the survivor it was hit by ground fire and burst into flames. The helicopter crash-landed in a small clearing but exploded on impact and no one was seen to escape from the wreckage. A further attempt to rescue 1Lt Schmidt was considered but the mission was then aborted as it was felt that he was being used as bait to trap the SAR helicopters. In addition to Lt Rittichier the HH-3 crew from the 37th ARRS at Da Nang consisted of Capt Richard C Yeend, SSgt Elmer Larry Holden and Sgt James Douglas Locker.

More Super Sabres were shot down in South Vietnam than any other strike aircraft. The nearest aircraft of this pair is 55-2914 that was shot down by small arms fire as it was taking off from Phan Rang on 18 June 1968 while serving with the 615th TFS. USAF

Lt Rittichier was flying with the USAF on exchange from the US Coast Guard and was the only fatality out of 10 Coast Guard helicopter pilots who were attached to the USAF in Southeast Asia from 1968. Jack Rittichier was no stranger to the USAF having served as a B-47 pilot with SAC until transferring to the Coast Guard in 1963. He was awarded a posthumous Silver Star for his attempt to complete the rescue. A rescue attempt the next day found no sign of 1Lt Schmidt. He was not known to have been in any of the POW camps and the most likely conclusion is that he was killed by enemy troops while resisting capture. JTF-FA investigations were mounted in 1998 using information provided by a flight simulation of the mission conducted at Hurlburt Field AFB, Florida in an attempt to find the location of the A-4 and HH-3 wreckage.

F-4D   66-8746   497 TFS, 8 TFW, USAF, Ubon
                   Maj William B Bergman (survived)
                   1Lt David A Willett (survived)
A flight of Phantoms from Ubon participated in the rescue attempt to recover Maj Light, who had been shot down north of the DMZ on the 8th. Unfortunately, one of the F-4s, Hudson 82, was hit by AAA as it orbited about four miles north of the DMZ. Maj Bergman headed out to sea and he and his WSO ejected 10 miles off the coast. They were both picked up by a USAF helicopter.

O-1E   56-4176   20 TASS, 504 TASG, USAF, Da Nang
                   Maj Robert Ball (KIA)
Maj Ball was controlling an air strike near the village of Kinh Mon in the DMZ buffer zone when he was shot down. The target was a network of enemy bunkers and Maj Ball was making his second run over the target when his Bird Dog was hit at 2,250 feet by 12.7mm anti-aircraft fire.

10 June 1968

A-7A   153265   VA-86, USN, USS *America*
                   Lt Cdr Randolph W Ford (POW- Died)
The Corsair had more advanced avionics than the Skyhawk and was better suited to night operations, although it was not in the same class as the Intruder. On the night of the 10th a section of Corsairs flew a road reconnaissance mission along the main coastal road, 30 miles southeast of Vinh. Lt Cdr Ford dropped a flare for his wingman to see if there was any traffic on the road. Moments later the wingman saw a huge fireball on the ground and then heard Lt Cdr Ford's voice on his survival radio. The pilot was descending in his parachute but had a broken right arm and other injuries. There was no indication as to the cause of the loss. Information was later received that Lt Cdr Ford had died of his wounds a few days after capture.

13 June 1968

O-2A   67-21415   20 TASS, 504 TASG, USAF, Da Nang
                    Maj David George Brenner (KIA)

An O-2 FAC was on its way to a mission when the aircraft collided with a UH-1D helicopter (66-01016) of the Army's 174th Aviation Company near Quang Ngai. The Huey had just taken off from LZ Dottie and was manoeuvring to avoid machine gun fire when it collided with the O-2 at about 1,000 feet. Maj Brenner was killed when his aircraft crashed into a canal as were the four crew and three infantrymen on board the helicopter. One of the dead was Lt Col F A Barker, CO of the 4th Battalion, 3rd Infantry Regiment.

14 June 1968

O-1E   56-2635   22 TASS, 504 TASG, USAF, Binh Thuy
                   Capt Harold Raymond Vogel (KIA)
A low flying Bird Dog collided with a radio tower in Sa Dec province, South Vietnam, killing the pilot.

U-3B   60-6058   unit ..?, USAF, base ..?
                   A Cessna U-3 liaison aircraft was the only casualty of a Viet Cong attack on Tan Son Nhut on the 14th. The U-3 was a military version of the Cessna 310 five-seat light twin-engined aircraft and a small number were used for communications or administrative flying between the US bases in South Vietnam and Thailand. The aircraft was also used on a courier service to deliver photographs and intelligence information to airfields and airstrips throughout Southeast Asia. This was the only aircraft of its type lost during the war.

15 June 1968

A-4E   149665   VA-56, USN, USS *Enterprise*
                   Lt J M Wright (survived)
Lt Wright was on his way to bomb a POL target at Trang Mao when he felt two small hits (probably from small arms fire) on his Skyhawk near Xom Dong, 15 miles west of Vinh. On leaving the target the aircraft's oil pressure began to fluctuate and eventually fell to zero. Lt Wright was within 20 miles of the *Enterprise* when his engine finally seized solid. He ejected at about 4,000 feet and was rescued within minutes.

16 June 1968

O-1F   57-2932   21 TASS, 504 TASG, USAF, Nha Trang
                   Maj Wayne A Ferguson (KIA)
An O-1 was shot down during an FAC mission near Phuoc Long, 25 miles southwest of Qui Nhon. Maj Ferguson was diving his aircraft at a target when the aircraft was hit by ground fire and crashed before he could bail out.

F-4J   155548   VF-102, USN, USS *America*
                   Cdr Walter Eugene Wilber (POW)
                   Lt(jg) Bernard Francis Rupinski (KIA)
During a CAP mission northwest of Vinh, a pair of Phantoms from the USS *America* were vectored towards an unidentified

aircraft. Due to the existing rules of engagement, the Phantoms had to turn back at the 19th Parallel. However, the MiG-21s also turned back and attacked the Phantoms from behind. One of the MiGs launched a missile that guided to the tailpipe of Cdr Wilber's aircraft. The aircraft exploded and the crew ejected, although only Cdr Wilber appears to have survived the ejection and was captured. Cdr Wilber had suffered major injuries during his ejection and alienated himself, along with a small number of colleagues, from the rest of the POWs to the extent that Cdr Stockdale accused Wilber of mutiny. Cdr Wilber, who was VF-102's executive officer and was on his 20th mission when he was shot down, was released with the first batch of POWs on 12 February 1973. This Phantom was the last US Navy aircraft that would be lost to a MiG until 27 April 1972, although an F-4B was lost during a dogfight on 17 August when it was shot down by one of its own kind.

18 June 1968

F-100D   55-2914   615 TFS, 35 TFW, USAF, Phan Rang
                     Maj G J Butler (survived)
The vulnerability of the US air bases in South Vietnam was illustrated once more on the 18th. A Super Sabre was hit by small arms fire just moments after taking off from Phan Rang. With his aircraft burning fiercely, Maj Butler ejected 10 miles southwest of the air base and was soon recovered.

19/20 June 1968

F-4J   155546   VF-33, USN, USS *America*
                   Lt Cdr John W Holtzclaw (survived)
                   Lt Cdr John A Burns (survived)
As night fell a pair of Phantoms started an armed reconnaissance mission with an A-6C Intruder looking for trucks on the roads north of Vinh. The aircraft received a SAM warning and Lt Cdr Holtzclaw jinked to evade two missiles but his aircraft was hit by a third SA-2 at an altitude of 2,600 feet. The Phantom's starboard wing was blown off and both crew ejected near the village of Van Tap, 20 miles northwest of Vinh. This was the first aircraft lost to a SAM in almost four months. The two airmen landed in rice paddies between two villages and made their way slowly to a densely forested hillside to hide and hopefully await rescue. A Seasprite flown by Lt Clyde E Lassen with Lt(jg) C L Cook, AE2 B B Dallas and ADJ3 D West of Detachment 104 of HC-7 was based on the destroyer USS *Preble*. Lassen made a daring flight into North Vietnam in total darkness over unfamiliar terrain. the helicopter was shot at by ground fire including two SAMs but eventually Lassen located the burning wreckage of the Phantom. Lt Lassen landed in a rice paddy about 600 feet from the downed airmen but had to lift off again when enemy troops opened fire at the helicopter as it sat on the ground. A flight of Navy aircraft arrived and started to drop flares so Lt Lassen attempted to pick up the survivors from among tall trees in the forest. As the rescue sling was being lowered the flares went out and the helicopter hit a tree in the pitch dark. Despite damage to the helicopter Lt Lassen made several passes over the downed airmen so that his door gunner could fire at enemy troops approaching the survivors' position. Eventually Holtzclaw and Burns made it down the hill to the flat rice paddies and Lt Lassen made another landing but the airmen were too far away and the helicopter again came under fire so Lassen took off, circled and landed, for the third time, closer to the survivors. Another SAM was fired as the helicopter was about to touch down and enemy troops could be heard crashing through the jungle trying to reach the survivors before they could get to the helicopter. For three minutes the helicopter sat in the rice paddy while Holtzclaw and Burns struggled their way through the mud and vegetation to reach the Seasprite. Under fire from three sides, Lassen

took off as soon as the men were aboard after a total of 56 minutes over North Vietnam and 45 minutes under fire. The helicopter was fired on by AAA as it crossed the coast and the side door was torn off during evasive manoeuvres. Short of fuel and his helicopter badly damaged, Lt Lassen headed for the nearest ship and landed on the destroyer USS *Jouett* with only five minutes of fuel remaining. For his outstanding efforts to complete the rescue, one of the few successful night rescues of the war, Lt Lassen was awarded the Medal of Honor at the White House on 16 January 1969.

21 June 1968

A-7A 153269   VA-86, USN, USS *America*
     1 pilot, name unknown (survived)
A Corsair from the USS *America* had a flying control hydraulics failure and crashed during a test flight.

22 June 1968

A-7A 153257   VA-82, USN, USS *America*
     1 pilot, name unknown (survived)
A Corsair had a catastrophic engine failure just moments after being catapulted off the deck of the USS *America* on a strike mission. The engine exploded and the pilot was forced to eject.

23 June 1968

F-105D 59-1765   333 TFS, 355 TFW, USAF, Takhli
     Maj J W Alder (survived)
As the worthwhile targets in the Iron Triangle around Hanoi were denied to them, the F-105 squadrons were reduced to shooting up trucks on the roads in southern North Vietnam and Laos. While not as dangerous as facing the defences in the north, this still took its toll. Maj Alder was making his third strafing pass on three trucks on a road near Van Loc, 10 miles northwest of Dong Hoi, when his aircraft was hit by 37mm flak. He turned east to cross the coast and tried to reach Da Nang but had to eject 30 miles off the coast northeast of the DMZ. He was rescued by a USAF SAR helicopter.

A-4F 154216   VA-113, USN, USS *Enterprise*
     Lt E E Christensen (survived)
A Skyhawk was lost during a bombing raid on Vinh on the 23rd. Lt Christensen left the target and crossed the coast to rendezvoused with the other aircraft that had taken part in the raid. As the formation joined up about 60 miles out to sea, Lt Christensen realised he had no throttle control. His engine then flamed out and, despite two attempts to relight, he had to eject. He was soon picked up by a Navy helicopter.

F-4D 66-8724   497 TFS, 8 TFW, USAF, Ubon
     Lt Col Donald Francis Casey (KIA)
     1Lt James Ervin Booth (KIA)
Lt Col Casey and 1Lt Booth were flying a night mission to attack a target in the mountains near Xom Sung, north of the Mu Gia Pass in North Vietnam. Just as their aircraft rolled in to drop its bombs, the wingman saw a flash and a large fire on the side of a mountain. Attempts to contact Lt Col Casey met with no success and it became obvious that the Phantom had crashed. Whether the aircraft had been shot down or had flown into high ground in the dark remains uncertain.

A-1H 52-134568   6 ACS, 14 ACW, USAF, Pleiku
     Capt Richard Lee Russell (KIA)
A Skyraider returned to Pleiku from a strike mission still carrying some of its ordnance. The aircraft landed badly and a bomb exploded destroying the aircraft and killing the pilot.

24 June 1968

F-100D 56-3339   90 TFS, 3 TFW, USAF, Bien Hoa
     Lt Col W G Savage (survived)
A Super Sabre was hit by ground fire as it was orbiting at 2,000 feet one mile south of Quan Long City in the extreme southern tip of South Vietnam during a close air support mission. The aircraft caught fire and Lt Col Savage ejected immediately.

A-6A 152949   VA-35, USN, USS *Enterprise*
     Lt Nicholas M Carpenter (KIA)
     Lt(jg) Joseph Scott Mobley (POW)
A single Intruder set out on a night low-level interdiction sortie from the *Enterprise*. The target was a waterway about five miles southwest of Vinh. The Intruder approached the waterway at 250 feet and 420 knots when it encountered anti-aircraft fire. A shell burst in the cockpit, injuring the pilot and causing the aircraft to roll. The NFO ejected and but Lt Carpenter is thought to have died in the aircraft. Lt Mobley broke his leg when he was shot down and was then tied to a post, beaten and put on public display where he was pelted with sticks and stones thrown by villagers. He had to set his leg himself although a North Vietnamese medic later put a splint on it. Joseph Mobley was released from North Vietnam on 14 March 1973 and eventually attained the rank of Rear Admiral.

F-8E 149158   VF-53, USN, USS *Bon Homme Richard*
     Lt Jerry Weber (survived)
At the end of a night BARCAP mission a Crusader tried to refuel from an A-4 tanker but was unable to do so because of a mechanical malfunction. The engine flamed out due to fuel exhaustion before the aircraft could reach the carrier or divert to Da Nang airfield and the pilot had to eject. Jerry Weber's luck, which had saved him from death on 12 March when he crashed in bad weather, held again as he was rescued from the sea.

25 June 1968

F-100D 55-3535   416 TFS, 37 TFW, USAF, Phu Cat
     1Lt Robert Miller Scott (KIA)
An F-100 was shot down during a close air support mission near Thach Khe, 10 miles southwest of Qui Nhon. 1Lt Scott was making his third bombing run over enemy troops when his aircraft was hit by ground fire and crashed. The pilot may have been wounded as he did not eject from his aircraft before it hit the ground. Super Sabre 55-3535 belonged to the 429th TFS when the Squadron deployed to Bien Hoa for five months in 1965.

C-130E 62-1861   50 TAS, 314 TAW, USAF, Ching Chuan Kang
     1Lt Fletcher A Hatch (survived)
     Lt Lee Blaser (survived)
     Lt Jon Alexander (survived)
     Sgt Joseph Basilico (survived)
     A1C Jerry Willard (survived)
A Hercules from Tuy Hoa had just taken off from Katum on an airlift flight when it was hit in the port wing by .50 calibre machine gun fire. The No1 engine burst into flames and fire spread along the port wing. As the runway at Katum was judged to be too short for an emergency landing, 1Lt Hatch decided to make for the airfield at Tay Ninh, about 20 miles to the southwest. As the aircraft approached the airfield the fire burnt through the aileron on the port wing and the wing spar began to bend downwards outboard of the No1 engine. With only the nose and left main gear extended the aircraft touched down and veered off the runway and exploded as it came to a stop. Despite the explosion and fire the crew managed to escape through the cockpit overhead hatch before the aircraft was destroyed by fire.

A-4C 147804   VMA-223, MAG-12, USMC, Chu Lai
     Capt Charles B Coltrin (survived)
Despite the successful American defensive action, Gen Westmoreland had decided to withdraw the Marines from Khe Sanh after the seige was lifted. Operation Charlie, the process of evacuation and demilitarization, concluded on 6 July but the area was a constant hive of activity. Capt Coltrin's aircraft was hit by ground fire as he was attacking a .50 calibre gun position five miles southwest of Khe Sanh. The aircraft went out of control and he ejected over enemy-held territory but he was fortunate enough to be picked up safely by helicopter. Capt Coltrin had had another lucky escape on 6 June when his Skyhawk suffered a brake failure as he was taxying to the flight line at Chu Lai. The aircraft veered off the taxyway, hit several obstructions, ran into soft sand and tipped upside down. Coltrin was uninjured and extricated from the aircraft, which was later repaired.

RF-4C 63-7755   11 TRS, 432 TRW, USAF, Udorn
     Capt M S Jones (survived)
     Maj F J McKenna (survived)
An RF-4C on a reconnaissance mission over southern Laos was shot down by ground fire near the village of Ban Nakok, 20 miles east of Nakhon Phanom. Both crewmen were able to eject and were later picked up by a USAF SAR helicopter.

A-7A 153271   VA-86, USN, USS *America*
     1 pilot, name unknown (survived)
A Corsair suffered a generator failure during a strike mission. Smoke entered the cockpit, the oxygen system failed and the aircraft then caught fire. The pilot ejected safely and was soon picked up.

C-123K 54-0595   310 ACS, 315 ACW, USAF, Phan Rang
     4 crew, names unknown (survived)
A Provider was landing at an airfield in South Vietnam when it veered off the runway and hit a parked helicopter.

26 June 1968

O-2A 68-6879   20 TASS, 504 TASG, USAF, Da Nang
     Maj Robert F Woods (KIA)
     1Lt Johnnie C Cornelius (KIA)
An O-2 and its crew was lost during an FAC mission about two miles north of the DMZ, close to the border with Laos. Maj Woods commenced a 45-degree dive to mark a target but the aircraft continued its dive until it hit the ground. Neither of the crew were able to escape and may have been wounded by ground fire.

F-105D 58-1150   34 TFS, 388 TFW, USAF, Korat
     1 pilot, name unknown (survived)
The starboard main undercarriage leg sheared off a Thunderchief as it was landing after returning from a strike mission. This aircraft was the fifth F-105D to be built and was painted with the names 'The Boss' and 'Cobra' during its service with the 34th TFS.

28 June 1968

A-1H 52-135291   6 ACS, 14 ACW, USAF, Pleiku
     Maj Paul Frederick Johns (KIA)
A Skyraider was shot down close to the South Vietnam/Laos border, 15 miles southeast of the A Shau Valley. Maj Johns was attacking a truck he had spotted on Route 922 and was making a run to drop napalm when his aircraft was hit by .50 calibre gunfire. The aircraft came down on the South Vietnamese side of the border, 30 miles to the west of Hué, and Maj Johns was killed in the crash.

30 June 1968

F-100D 56-3372   352 TFS, 35 TFW, USAF, Phan Rang
     Capt F F Davis (survived)
The fourth F-100 to be lost in combat during June was shot down on a close air support mission near Tan An, 18 miles southwest of Tan Son Nhut. Capt Davis was pulling up from an attack on enemy bunkers when his aircraft was hit by ground fire. The port wing caught fire and Capt Davis ejected two miles to the north and was picked up by an Army helicopter.

1 July 1968

F-105D 61-0118   333 TFS, 355 TFW, USAF, Takhli
     Lt Col Jack Modica (survived)
While on an afternoon strike mission just north of the DMZ, a flight of F-105s came upon a rare target. An SA-2 missile was seen being transported to a SAM site on a carrier vehicle. The flight attacked the vehicle immediately but in the process, Lt Col Modica's aircraft (Scotch 03) was damaged by automatic weapons fire. He attempted to head to a safe area but was forced to eject a few miles north of the DMZ. He was located in the jungle by a Misty FAC F-100F and a SAR mission was launched. The first attempts to pick up the downed pilot had to be aborted due to heavy ground fire so he had to spend the night in hiding. The

next morning a SAR task force arrived but on the first attempt the helicopter was hit by ground fire and had to withdraw. A few hours later another attempt was made by a helicopter from the 37th ARRS flown by Lt L Eagan, one of a small number of US Coast Guard pilots who served with the USAF. During the rescue A1C Joel E Talley, the PJ, was lowered to the ground and spent 15 minutes searching for the downed pilot in the dense undergrowth. Lt Col Modica had a broken pelvis and could not be moved far so Talley called in the helicopter, which immediately came under fire. A1C Talley strapped the injured pilot and himself to the jungle penetrator and were hoisted clear of the trees, however the helicopter had to leave the area with the pair still dangling from the rescue cable until it reached a safe area where they could be safely hoisted on board. Joel Talley was on his very first rescue mission and became the fifth PJ to be awarded the AFC for bravery in Southeast Asia.

2 July 1968

F-100D 56-3122 306 TFS, 31 TFW, USAF, Tuy Hoa
1Lt Lance Lagrange (KIA)

F-100s were often used for landing zone preparation in advance of a helicopter assault. On such a mission near Thuan An, 40 miles north of Phu Cat, an F-100 was dropping napalm on its first pass when it was hit by ground fire and crashed near the target. The pilot did not eject and was killed.

A-1H 52-137601 6 ACS, 14 ACW, USAF, Pleiku
Maj Henry Albert Tipping (KIA)

Maj Tipping was flying RESCAP for the SAR attempt to find Lt Col Modica, who had ejected near the DMZ on the 1st. The Skyraider was orbiting at 5,000 feet near Thon Cam Son within the DMZ buffer zone when it was damaged by 37mm AAA. The aircraft crashed in flames a few miles away and Maj Tipping was unable to escape and was killed.

3 July 1968

F-100D 56-2936 90 TFS, 3 TFW, USAF, Bien Hoa
1 pilot, name unknown (survived)

At the end of a combat sortie an F-100 landed back at Bien Hoa with its wheels up and was damaged beyond repair. Whether this was caused by a technical malfunction or by pilot error is not known.

4 July 1968

F-4C 63-7496 391 TFS, 12 TFW, USAF, Cam Ranh Bay
1Lt J B Jaeger (survived)
Maj D A Hamilton (survived)

A flight of Phantoms were scrambled to attack enemy troops who were being engaged by US ground troops 10 miles north of Cam Ranh Bay. 1Lt Jaeger made eight passes over the troops but had still not expended all his ordnance. He came in for a strafing pass but the Phantom was hit by ground fire in the port engine. The crew ejected almost immediately and were lucky to be picked up by an Army helicopter that was in the vicinity.

F-4B 151467 VMFA-115, MAG-13, USMC, Chu Lai
Maj Jay N Bibler (survived)
Capt Daniel J Coonon (survived)

The area around Khe Sanh was still a dangerous place for US forces. During a close air support mission five miles south of Khe Sanh a VMFA-115 Phantom was hit by .50 calibre ground fire during its strafing run and suffered damage to the starboard engine. The aircraft caught fire and the crew ejected just as they crossed the coast about five miles north of Hué. The crew was rescued by an Army helicopter but three months later, on 8 October, Capt Coonon was shot down again and this time he did not survive.

F-100D 55-2900 352 TFS, 35 TFW, USAF, Phan Rang
Maj J S Ellard (survived)

As a Super Sabre was climbing away from Phan Rang on a night mission it was hit by small arms fire. However, it seems that Maj Ellard was unaware of this fact as he continued with his mission. Later he noticed a rapid loss of fuel and tried to make an emer-

gency landing at Binh Thuy in the Mekong Delta. The aircraft crashed during the landing and Maj Ellard was badly injured.

A-4F 155002 VA-192, USN, USS *Ticonderoga*
1 pilot, name unknown (survived)

F-8E 149165 VF-194, USN, USS *Ticonderoga*
Lt(jg) J F Strahm (survived)

When returning from a combat mission an A-4 and an F-8 practised air-to-air combat over the Gulf of Tonkin. During the manoeuvring, the two aircraft collided and both pilots had to eject from their damaged aircraft.

5 July 1968

F-100F 58-1226 614 TFS, 35 TFW, USAF, Phan Rang
Col P B Hardy (survived)
Capt D W Jenny (survived)

The destruction of a SAM on its transporter on the 1st confirmed that the SAM sites just north of the DMZ were active. A Misty FAC led a strike mission against a SAM battery near Thach Ban, 10 miles north of the DMZ. Col Hardy was flying over the target at 4,000 feet when his aircraft was hit in the tail by 37mm flak. He coaxed the crippled aircraft back across the DMZ before he and Capt Jenny had to abandon the F-100. Col Hardy was rescued by a USAF helicopter while Capt Jenny was picked up by a Marine Corps helicopter.

F-4D 66-7756 433 TFS, 8 TFW, USAF, Ubon
Lt Col Carl Boyette Crumpler (POW)
1Lt Michael Thomas Burns (POW)

A formation of Phantoms was sent to bomb a gun site near Ha Loi, 20 miles northwest of Dong Hoi. Lt Col Crumpler's aircraft was hit by 37mm AAA as it dived on the target. He turned east to make for the relative safety of the sea but he and his WSO had to eject near Van Loc, six miles short of the coast. They were both captured and became the first USAF POWs in over a month. It took 35 days for the two men to reach Hanoi in a truck. Both men were released from captivity on 14 March 1973. Carl Crumpler had enlisted in the US Navy during the Second World War and was commissioned into the USAF in 1950. He spent most of his career flying in Air Defense Command and was involved in training Imperial Iranian Air Force pilots prior to the delivery of their Phantoms.

O-1G serial ..? unit ..?, USAF, base ..?
Maj Herman Smits (KIA)
Maj B F Hill (survived)

Very little is recorded about the loss of this Bird Dog FAC and the death of Maj Smits. It is known that the incident occurred in Phu Yen province in South Vietnam and Maj Hill was rescued.

F-4C 63-7713 557 TFS, 12 TFW, USAF, Cam Ranh Bay
Maj Edward R Silver (KIA)
1Lt Bruce E Lawrence (KIA)

A night attack on the Mi Le ferry, 20 miles southeast of Dong Hoi, resulted in the loss of an F-4 crew. Maj Silver's Phantom burst into flames and exploded as it approached its target. The wingman did not see an ejection nor could he make contact on his survival radio. It was presumed that the aircraft had been shot down by ground fire and that both men had been killed. Later a returning POW remembered seeing a North Vietnamese propaganda film that showed a dead airmen with the name 'Silver' on his flight suit.

8 July 1968

F-4B 148432 VMFA-122, MAG-11, USMC, Da Nang
Lt Col E R Howard (survived)
Capt R D Hess (survived)

A flight of Phantoms from Da Nang was scrambled to attack enemy troops just three miles southwest of the air base. Lt Col Howard made no less than seven passes over the troops but on his eighth pass, which was a strafing run at 400 feet and 450 knots, the aircraft ran into a barrage of machine gun fire and was damaged. The Phantom remained airborne just long enough to cross the coastline and the crew ejected safely.

F-4D 66-7671 433 TFS, 8 TFW, USAF, Ubon
1Lt Charles W Mosley (survived)
1Lt Don M Hallenbeck (survived)

A pair of Phantoms (call signs Roman 01 and Roman 02) on an armed reconnaissance mission at dusk over North Vietnam attacked several trucks near the Mi Le ferry, close to where Maj Silver's aircraft had been lost the previous night. 1Lt Mosley rolled in on a 20-degree dive to fire his rockets but the aircraft was hit by ground fire as he pulled up. The aircraft climbed but lost its hydraulics forcing Mosley and Hallenbeck to eject about 12 miles east of the Mu Gia Pass. The crew were picked up by a USAF SAR helicopter after a two day SAR operation coordinated by a Misty FAC.

9 July 1968

A-1E 52-139575 602 ACS, 56 ACW, USAF, Nakhon Phanom
Lt Col William A Buice (survived)

A flight of Skyraiders was engaged in landing zone preparation near the village of Sopka, 25 miles west of Sam Neua in northern Laos, when one of the aircraft was shot down. Lt Col Buice was climbing away from a run over the target when his Skyraider was hit by small arms fire as the aircraft passed through 1,500 feet. He flew a few miles to the southeast before abandoning the aircraft and was later rescued by a USAF SAR helicopter.

F-100D 56-3124 309 TFS, 31 TFW, USAF, Tuy Hoa
Maj M K Ryan (survived)

A Super Sabre was shot down as it was bombing an enemy gun position two miles west of Khe Sanh. Maj Ryan ejected from the burning aircraft and was eventually rescued by a Marine Corps helicopter.

10 July 1968

A-1H 52-135251 602 ACS, 56 ACW, USAF, Nakhon Phanom
Maj H R Jennings (survived)

Another Skyraider was lost during a Barrel Roll mission in northern Laos. Maj Jennings was strafing military buildings near Ban Pa Kha when he was shot down by small arms fire. Ejecting close by he was fortunate to be rescued by an Air America helicopter before the Pathet Lao or North Vietnamese could reach him.

13 July 1968

F-4B 150650 VMFA-115, MAG-13, USMC, Chu Lai
Capt John Clark Hurst (KIA)
1Lt Leonard Adrian Bird (KIA)

A Marine Corps Phantom was lost 10 miles south of Khe Sanh during a close air support mission. The aircraft was making its second pass over the target at 500 feet and 450 knots when it was hit by ground fire, burst into flames and crashed, killing both crew.

F-105D 60-0453 34 TFS, 388 TFW, USAF, Korat
1Lt G R Confer (survived)

A POL transshipment point had been discovered in the hills near Xom Duong Quan just north of the Mu Gia Pass. Barrels of petrol were stored for use by the many trucks that were still plying the roads and trails of North Vietnam and Laos despite the USAF's best efforts. A flight of F-105s was sent to destroy the POL storage site but one of the aircraft was hit in the rear fuselage by AAA as it rolled in to the attack from 6,000 feet. 1Lt Confer flew the aircraft back across Laos but realised he could not reach Korat and decided to make an emergency landing at Udorn instead. During the landing the aircraft was damaged beyond repair but the pilot walked away with only minor injuries.

13/14 July 1968

F-105D 62-4367 333 TFS, 355 TFW, USAF, Takhli
Maj Robert Keith Hanna (survived)

A flight of F-105s made a night strike on truck traffic near Van Loc, 10 miles northwest of Dong Hoi. Maj Hanna was about to commence a strafing run from 8,000 feet when his Thud was rocked by hits from a 37mm anti-aircraft gun. His aircraft began

to burn and he ejected about 10 miles to the west, near the village of Ha Loi, breaking his ankle on landing. He evaded capture until he could be rescued by a USAF HH-3 from Nakhon Phanom on the 15th. Maj Hanna was on his 82nd combat mission when he was shot down.

The Air National Guard

The seizure of the USS Pueblo *by North Korean naval vessels on 23 January resulted in the immediate activation of 11 Air National Guard groups. The* Pueblo *crisis was resolved without resort to force but in the meantime the Tet Offensive had erupted in South Vietnam. It was decided to send four squadrons of F-100s to bolster the Super Sabre wings in South Vietnam. The first to deploy was the Colorado Air National Guard's 120th TFS from Denver, which arrived at Phan Rang on 3 May. Next to deploy were the 136th TFS from Niagara Falls, New York; the 174th TFS from Sioux City, Iowa; and the 188th TFS from Albuquerque, New Mexico. The 120th was attached to the 35th TFW at Phan Rang while the 174th was attached to the 37th TFW at Phu Cat and the 136th and 188th to the 31st TFW at Tuy Hoa. In addition ANG personnel predominantly manned the 355th TFS, a regular USAF squadron, soon after it deployed to the 37th TFW at Phu Cat in February. The four Guard squadrons stayed in Southeast Asia for one year before returning to the USA, leaving behind an enviable record and reputation. The average flying time of the ANG F-100 pilots was over 1,000 hours in the aircraft compared to about 150 for regular squadron pilots. The 120th had no less than 21 airline pilots, all of whom had previously flown the F-100 or other types in their regular Air Force service. This higher level of experience resulted in a greater degree of proficiency in flying and weapons delivery. The Guard squadrons brought their own highly experienced maintenance crews as the F-100C was different in many respects from the F-100D used by the regular Air Force squadrons in South Vietnam.*

14 July 1968

F-100D 55-3722 612 TFS, 37 TFW, USAF, Phu Cat
Capt J T Piner (survived)

A Super Sabre was lost during a close air support mission in the hills 25 miles southwest of Hué. Capt Piner was making his second napalm run over the target at 1,500 feet when he ran into intense 37mm anti-aircraft fire. He ejected within seconds but was soon picked up by a Marine Corps helicopter.

F-100C 54-2004 174 TFS, 37 TFW, USAF, Phu Cat
1Lt Warren K Brown (KIA)

About one and a half hours later the 37th TFW lost another aircraft on the same target, sadly the pilot was killed in this incident. 1Lt W K Brown was also on his second napalm run when he, like Capt Piner before him, ran into a barrage of anti-aircraft fire. The aircraft was only flying at 200 feet when it was hit and although 1Lt Brown ejected, he was too low for his parachute to deploy fully before he hit the ground and he was killed. He was the first of six Air National Guard airmen to lose their lives during the deployment of the F-100 squadrons to Vietnam.

15 July 1968

F-105F 63-8353 44 TFS, 388 TFW, USAF, Korat
Maj Gobel Dale James (POW)
Capt Larry Eugene Martin (KIA)

A raid on a suspected SAM site resulted in the loss of the first Wild Weasel for nearly five months. The site was close to Phu Qui, seven miles northwest of Dong Hoi. Maj James and Capt Martin were pulling up from their first attack when the aircraft was hit by 37mm AAA. Maj James turned towards the coast but he and

Capt Martin had to eject just seconds before they crossed the beach and landed about one mile north of Dong Hoi. Maj James ejected successfully but was captured. He was unsure if Capt Martin's seat had left the aircraft before it crashed. Maj James was on his 34th mission and was eventually released on 14 March 1973. On 8 November 1989 it was announced that the remains of Capt Martin had been returned by the Vietnamese. Thunderchief 63-8353 was painted as 'Billie Fern' and 'Thunderchief' while at Korat.

16 July 1968

A-7A 153234 VA-97, USN, USS *Constellation*
1 pilot, name unknown (survived)

The USS *Constellation* arrived back on the line on 28 June to start its fourth war cruise. The first aircraft lost during this cruise was a Corsair that ran out of fuel while it was waiting its turn for recovery on board the ship following an armed reconnaissance mission.

F-102A 56-0963 509 FIS, 405 FW, USAF, base ..?
1 pilot, name unknown (survived)

One of the F-102 air defence fighters on temporary deployment from Clark AB was lost on the 16th when it suffered an engine failure during an escort mission. This Delta Dagger had been used by the 40th FIS at Yokota AB, Japan before being transferred to the 509th FIS.

17 July 1968

O-2A 67-21384 23 TASS, 504 TASG, USAF, Nakhon Phanom
Lt Col S C Ferguson (survived)
Capt R P Lappin (survived)

A Nail FAC of the 23rd TASS was flying near Ban Dong Hene in southern Laos on an Igloo White mission when its front engine was shot out by small arms fire. Lt Col Ferguson crash-landed the aircraft on small airstrip and he and his observer were later rescued by a USAF SAR helicopter.

EF-10B 125793 VMCJ-1, MAG-11, USMC, Da Nang
1Lt Ariel Lindley Cross (KIA)
1Lt Lionel Parra (KIA)

One of VMCJ-1's ancient EF-10Bs was lost during a radar-jamming mission close to the DMZ. The cause of the loss and the fate

of the crew were not determined. This was the fifth and final EF-10B lost during the four years that VMCJ-1 operated the type from Da Nang. The Skynight pioneered electronic-countermeasures during the war despite its age and poor performance in comparison with more modern jets. Using the radio call sign Cottonpicker, VMCJ-1's aircraft flew over 9,000 sorties and provided stand-off electronic jamming in support of thousands of strikes both day and night. The EF-10s were withdrawn from Da Nang in October 1969 and transferred to the 3rd MAW at El Toro until retired on 31 May 1970.

18 July 1968

O-1G 51-12555 21 TASS, 504 TASG, USAF, Nha Trang
Capt A R Ziaseker (survived)

One of Nha Trang's Bird Dogs was lost during a FAC mission seven miles southwest of the airfield on the 18th. Capt Ziaseker was flying at low-level en route to a target when his aircraft was hit in the engine by automatic weapons fire. He crash-landed without injury and was swiftly picked up by a USAF helicopter.

19 July 1968

EB-66B 53-0491 41 TEWS, 355 TFW, USAF, Takhli
2 crew, names unknown (survived)

An EB-66B landed short of the runway at Takhli during a ground-controlled approach and was damaged beyond repair. The fact that there were only two pilots on board indicates that the aircraft was most likely on a training sortie.

21 July 1968

F-100D 56-2905 355 TFS, 37 TFW, USAF, Phu Cat
Lt Col Sherman E Flanagan (KIA)

A Super Sabre and its pilot was lost during a mission to destroy an anti-aircraft gun position on the South Vietnam/Laos border, in the hill country 25 miles southwest of Hué. Lt Col Flanagan was making his first strafing pass from 3,000 feet when his aircraft was hit by ground fire and dived into the ground near the target. The pilot may have been wounded by the anti-aircraft fire as he did not eject. Lt Col Flanagan was a member of the District of Columbia ANG who had volunteered for service with the 355th.

The OV-10A Bronco was designed specifically for counter-insurgency and forward air control in limited war scenarios. The aircraft were delivered in protective cocoons as deck cargo and offloaded at Cam Ranh Bay for flight testing before delivery to operational units. The USAF's 67-14625 survived the war to serve with the 601st TCW at Sembach AB, Germany. USAF

A-1E   52-132668   1 ACS, 56 ACW, USAF, Nakhon Phanom
                    Maj B M Mobley (survived)
A Skyraider was returning from an escort mission (probably for a helicopter or an FAC) and was shot down 10 miles northwest of the DMZ and 10 miles southeast of the Ban Karai Pass. Maj Mobley ejected when his engine was hit by ground fire and he was rescued by helicopter.

RF-8G   145642   Detachment 11, VFP-63, USN, USS *Intrepid*
                    Lt F W Pfluger (survived)
The USS *Intrepid* returned to TF 77 control on 6 July and was working up for its return to the line on the 24th. Three days before it was due to commence combat operations it lost one of its RF-8Gs during a test flight. The aircraft suffered engine failure, thought to have been due to a fuel pump problem. The pilot ejected safely and was rescued.

22 July 1968

F-100D   56-3066   531 TFS, 3 TFW, USAF, Bien Hoa
                    1Lt Lynn Arthur Hoffman (KIA)
A Super Sabre was struck by lightning and damaged during a combat mission over South Vietnam. The pilot lost control of the aircraft during an emergency landing at Bien Hoa and the aircraft crashed. Unfortunately 1Lt Hoffman was killed in the accident.

23 July 1968

RF-4C   65-0895   460 TRW, USAF, Tan Son Nhut
                    Maj Gen Robert Franklin Worley (KIA)
                    Maj Robert F Brodman (survived)
It was not uncommon in Southeast Asia for senior officers to fly operational missions. Squadron and wing commanders regularly flew combat missions and often led strikes into North Vietnam. Occasionally a higher-ranking officer would fly operationally, both for personal reasons and to experience what he was sending his men to do on a daily basis. Maj Gen Worley was the vice-commander of the Seventh Air Force. On the 23rd he and Maj Brodman took off from Tan Son Nhut in their RF-4C, call sign Strobe 1, for a photographic reconnaissance mission in the Military Region I area. As the aircraft was flying near the coast, about 10 miles northwest of Hué, it was hit in the forward fuselage by ground fire. As was usual in the Phantom the rear seat navigator ejected first, but Maj Gen Worley in the front seat was unable to eject and was killed. This incident prompted an investigation into the Phantom's ejection system, focussing on the canopy separation. It was discovered that under certain conditions the front canopy would fail to separate following the firing of the rear seat. Several previous incidents where Phantom front-seaters had failed to survive an ejection were probably due to this phenomenon. A modification programme was quickly introduced to add extra gas-operated pistons to the canopy rails, which seemed to solve the problem. Similar problems had also been encountered with US Navy and Marine Corps Phantoms

and a number of pilots had been lost when their canopies failed to separate. Another result of this incident was an order from Gen Momyer banning very senior officers from flying combat missions in Southeast Asia.

Gen Worley had joined the Air Corps in October 1940 and flew 120 combat missions in P-40s and P-47s in the Mediterannean and Far East during the Second World War. He was shot down on his very first combat mission while flying close air support for American troops in North Africa and had to evade through enemy lines to return to his unit. Post-war he commanded the USAF's first jet training school at Williams AFB and later served in a number of senior appointments including Director of Operations for the USAF in Europe.

A-4F   154189   VA-23, USN, USS *Ticonderoga*
                    Lt Cdr Lawrence Dean Gosen (KIA)
Lt Cdr Gosen was launched from the *Ticonderoga's* port catapult on a combat RESCAP mission. It appears that the catapult launched the aircraft with about 16 knots excess airspeed and the aircraft crashed into the sea about 200 yards in front of the ship and exploded. This was the last aircraft lost by the *Ticonderoga* before it finished its fourth war cruise on 9 August. It had lost two aircraft (both Crusaders) in combat and five aircraft and one helicopter in accidents during 120 days on the line.

F-4D   66-8716   13 TFS, 432 TRW, USAF, Udorn
                    2 crew, names unknown (survived)
A Phantom crew experienced a complete hydraulic failure over Thailand during a combat mission. Unable to control the aircraft the crew ejected and were recovered safely.

24 July 1968

F-4J   155551   VF-33, USN, USS *America*
                    Cdr O G Elliott (survived)
                    Lt(jg) Andris Dambekaln (survived)
A strike on a road ferry 12 miles west of Vinh was accompanied by a flight of Phantoms to provide flak suppression. Cdr Elliott dropped his bombs on an anti-aircraft gun position and pulled up but as he was passing through 4,500 feet his aircraft was hit by AAA. The hydraulic system began to fail as he headed towards the sea and he had to use the rudder to keep the aircraft straight and level. About five miles off the coast the port engine overheat light came on and the crew ejected. They were both rescued by a Navy helicopter from a SAR destroyer. In a repeat of the incident that killed Maj Gen Worley the previous day, 'Tex' Elliott's canopy failed to release after his back-seater's ejection seat fired. Fortunately, Cdr Elliott managed to push the canopy free and his seat then fired. 'Tex' Elliott, VF-33's executive officer, survived and wrote a report about the problem and it was discovered that a venturi effect occurred between 400 and 500 knots that kept the front canopy from releasing. Phantoms were later fitted with gas-operated pistons that pushed up the leading edge of the front canopy after the rear canopy had left the aircraft.

F-4D   66-7703   497 TFS, 8 TFW, USAF, Ubon
                    Capt T O Gill (survived)
                    1Lt R G Pierce (survived)

F-4D   66-7682   497 TFS, 8 TFW, USAF, Ubon
                    Capt Harley Benjamin Hackett (KIA)
                    1Lt John Robert Bush (KIA)
The Night Owls of the 497th TFS had a bad night on the 24th. A flight of two Phantoms took off from Ubon on an armed reconnaissance of the southern provinces of North Vietnam, but neither returned. The aircraft attacked road traffic on a road south of Mu Ron Ma but Capt Gill's aircraft was hit by ground fire and badly damaged. Capt Hackett vectored his leader's aircraft out over the water in an attempt to reach Da Nang. As Capt Gill headed south, the crew of a Navy aircraft saw a flash on the surface of the sea about 15 miles from the coast. This was later presumed to be Capt Hackett's aircraft, which apparently crashed into the sea without either he or his WSO being able to escape. Meanwhile Capt Gill and 1Lt Pierce were trying to reach Da Nang. However, as the aircraft approached the airfield from the north the crew were forced to eject and landed safely in Da Nang Bay. Capt Gill was rescued by a USAF helicopter and 1Lt Pierce was picked up by a US Navy vessel.

A-7A   153253   VA-82, USN, USS *America*
                    Lt Cdr David Scott Greiling (POW - died)
A few minutes after Capt Gill and 1Lt Pierce ejected from their Phantom near Da Nang, another drama was unfolding in the North. Two Corsairs from the USS *America* were flying an armed reconnaissance mission in the region around the Mu Ron Ma peninsula. Lt Cdr Greiling and his wingman saw moving lights that they suspected was truck traffic on a road near the village of Dong Rung. Lt Cdr Greiling reported rolling in on the target and this was followed a few moments later by a fireball on the ground, which his wingman at first took to be a truck full of fuel exploding. After completing his own attack the wingman tried to contact his leader but without success and then realised that the fireball he had seen was probably Lt Cdr Greiling's aircraft hitting the ground. Other aircraft arrived on the scene and dropped flares in an attempt to find the downed pilot. The crash site was 500 feet below a ridge on a heavily wooded hillside. It was presumed that the pilot had most probably died in the crash of the aircraft. However, on 17 July 1969 David Greiling was reclassified as a POW as a result of intelligence from an unusual source. Ships from Eastern Europe often visited Haiphong to bring in military and other supplies and a Polish seaman was shown the identity cards of 30 Americans by a Vietnamese in a bar in Haiphong. Greiling's card was said to be among these cards and indeed 28 of the 30 men were released during Operation Homecoming in 1973 but David Greiling and one other was not.

The OV-10 Bronco
The O-1 and O-2 had performed sterling work as FAC aircraft but neither was designed specifically for the role and both had limited performance, especially in terms of speed, range and weapons-carrying capability. From the outset the North American OV-10 Bronco was designed as a counter-insurgency aircraft with the secondary role of forward air control. Originating as a Marine Corps requirement, the OV-10 was eventually used by the Marines, the Air Force and the Navy in the reconnaissance and FAC roles. The aircraft's performance was significantly better than the types it replaced and even more important from the crew's point of view, its huge canopy and high seating position gave it excellent visibility and the inclusion of ejection seats greatly increased crew confidence and survivability. The OV-10's major deficiency was the loud and distinctive noise produced by its turboprop engines and high-speed propellers, which tended to give its position away to the enemy. The Marines were the first to introduce the Bronco to Southeast Asia with the arrival of the first six aircraft at Marble Mountain on 6 July. VMO-2 flew the

Another victim of a Viet Cong attack was this Marine Corps A-6A Intruder which was destroyed at Da Nang either during the Tet raid or during an attack in July 1968. USMC

first combat mission with the OV-10A within four hours of the first aircraft arriving on the 6th. By the end of the year a total of 26 Broncos had arrived in South Vietnam and VMO-2 and VMO-6 racked up around 3,000 sorties during 1968. The USAF received its first OV-10 on 23 February 1968 and the first Air Force aircraft arrived in South Vietnam on 31 July. Within a few months the five USAF tactical air support squadrons started to receive OV-10s to supplement their O-1s and O-2s. The third operator of the Bronco in Southeast Asia was the US Navy, which equipped a single squadron in support of riverine operations in the Mekong Delta.

25 July 1968

OV-10A 155412   VMO-2, MAG-16, USMC, Marble Mountain
Capt Alfred Leonard Tripp (KIA)
1Lt Michael Franc Hendrickson (KIA)
The first OV-10 Bronco to be lost in combat in Southeast Asia was shot down as it was marking enemy positions for a strike near the village of Binh Son, 25 miles south of Da Nang. The aircraft was hit by small arms fire as it dived on the target and it crashed before either of the crew could escape.

F-4J   155540   VF-102, USN, USS *America*
Lt Charles Carroll Parish (KIA)
Lt Robert StClair Fant (POW)
Another of the *America's* new F-4Js was lost during a raid on North Vietnam. The target on this occasion was the railway marshalling yard at Vinh. As the Phantom was pulling up having released its bombs the NFO saw a bright orange flash and the aircraft snap rolled onto its back. The pilot attempted to regain control but the Phantom started a series of barrel rolls, which eventually ceased. As the aircraft descended through 1,000 feet the NFO initiated a command ejection. However, although Lt Fant was ejected successfully, it appears that Lt Parish's seat never left the aircraft. Lt Fant was captured immediately after landing and spent the rest of the war as a POW until being released on 14 March 1973. The cause of the aircraft's loss was either AAA or the premature detonation of one of its own bombs.

F-100C 54-1912   136 TFS, 31 TFW, USAF, Tuy Hoa
Capt Joseph A L Huillier (KIA)
The third Air National Guard F-100 pilot to be killed in Southeast Asia was lost on the night of the 25th during a close air support mission. Capt Huillier was bombing an enemy storage area near the village of Thon Ba, 20 miles west of Tam Ky, and was making his second pass when his aircraft was hit by ground fire. The aircraft crashed in the target area and although an Army

helicopter arrived a few minutes later, it quickly became obvious that the pilot had died in the incident.

A-6A   154166   VMA(AW)-533, MAG-12, USMC, Chu Lai
Maj Curtis G Lawson (survived)
1Lt Paul Gordon Brown (POW)
An Intruder (call sign Hellborn 20) was despatched on an armed reconnaissance sortie just north of the DMZ when it was hit by intense 37mm flak at 3,000 feet. Both crew ejected and came down about 10 miles northwest of Thon Cam Son. The pilot, Maj Lawson, came down in the Dai River and swam to the river bank where he stayed in the water and hid. Several hours later he contacted a Misty FAC that was looking for him. The area was too well defended to attempt a rescue until it could be softened up by air strikes. As it was getting dark Maj Lawson was told to stay put until the next morning. A Misty FAC put in a series of strikes after first light on the 26th. Following a number of abortive attempts, Jolly Green 31 of the 37th ARRS (flown by Maj C E Wicker and Maj R E Booth) approached the survivor over the river and came under heavy ground fire. The escorting A-1s and the helicopter's door gunners put down a fierce suppressive fire as the helicopter swept along the river at 70 knots until it reached Capt Lawson. The fight engineer, SSgt J Enriquez and the PJ, Sgt S M Northern, continued firing with their M-60s as they deployed the jungle penetrator into the water. Capt Lawson swam towards the helicopter as it landed in the water and was dragged on board before a rapid departure under the protective fire of the four A-1s. The two crewmen had fired a total of 2,400 rounds from their M-60s before both guns seized due to overheating. 1Lt Brown was not so fortunate as his pilot as he landed in a populated area and was captured. He was sent to Hanoi and was released on 14 March 1973.

C-7B   63-9761   457 TAS, 483 TAW, USAF, Cam Ranh Bay
Capt Kenneth James Hoffman (KIA)
A1C Gary Raymond McKendrick (KIA)
2 crew, names unknown (survived)
A Caribou crashed near Pleiku when the pilot lost control as it was flying close to the stall, probably during an air drop. The aircraft struck a tree and fell to the ground killing two of the four crew.

26 July 1968

A-4F   154182   VA-93, USN, USS *Bon Homme Richard*
Lt Cdr Frank Eugene Fullerton (KIA)
Capt Fullerton was leading another Skyhawk pilot on an armed night reconnaissance mission in the Vinh area. He spotted truck lights on a road near Bai Duc Thon, 16 miles south of Ha Tinh,

Although not pictured in Southeast Asia this HC-130P shows the Fulton recovery system, which could be used to snag a helium balloon on the end of a cable as part of a rescue system. This aircraft is still in service with the 71st Rescue Squadron at Moody AFB, Georgia. USAF

and commenced an attack. The wingman saw Lt Cdr Fullerton's bombs detonate followed by a very large explosion that threw burning debris high into the air. At first the wingman assumed the second, larger explosion to be the result of the bombs hitting a truck but when Lt Cdr Fullerton failed to call in or rendezvous at the appropriate position it became apparent that all was not well. It was later presumed that the Skyhawk had either flown into the ground or had been blown up by its own bombs.

27 July 1968

A-4E   151143   VMA-121, MAG-12, USMC, Chu Lai
Maj Donald Bruce Campbell (KIA)
A Marine Corps Skyhawk and its pilot was lost during a landing zone preparation near Ha Tan, 20 miles southwest of Da Nang. Maj Campbell was dropping napalm on his first run over the target when his aircraft struck the ground. It could not be determined if the aircraft had been hit by ground fire or had inadvertently flown into the ground or had been hit by its own ordnance.

A-6A   152595   VMA(AW)-242, MAG-11, USMC, Da Nang
An enemy attack on Da Nang air base destroyed one of VMA(AW)-242's Intruders and damaged four other aircraft. Only six rounds were fired during the attack and five airmen were wounded.

F-100F 56-3750   37 TFW, USAF, Phu Cat
2 crew, names unknown (survived)
A two-seat Super Sabre crashed due to engine failure while on a training flight. The crew ejected safely and were soon rescued by a US Navy Swift Boat PCF-53 operating from Cat Lo. This F-100 may have been a Misty FAC aircraft.

28 July 1968

F-100D 55-3608   510 TFS, 3 TFW, USAF, Bien Hoa
Maj Elwin Rex Shain (KIA)
During a close air support mission an F-100 pilot spotted enemy soldiers on a raft on a small river 10 miles northeast of Song Be City. As the aircraft started its strafing run it was hit in the starboard wing by ground fire. The aircraft burst into flames and crashed close to the river. Maj Shain did not have time to eject and was killed.

29 July 1968

HC-130P 66-0214, 39 ARRS, 3 ARRG, USAF, Tuy Hoa
66-0218

The most serious air base attack during July took place at Tuy Hoa on the 29th. Viet Cong sappers infiltrated the base and lay in long grass between the runways for several hours before placing their satchel charges. Two HC-130s were destroyed and another seven aircraft were damaged including five more C-130s, a C-47 and an F-100. Nine of the attackers were killed but the loss of two valuable aircraft was a major blow for the 3rd ARRG. This was one of the very few occasions that the VC actually penetrated the defences of an American base and was able to place charges undetected.

30 July 1968

O-2A 68-6891 20 TASS, 504 TASG, USAF, Da Nang
detached to Chu Lai
Capt Thomas John Beyer (KIA)

An O-2 from the 20th TASS's detachment at Chu Lai was lost along with its pilot during a FAC mission in South Vietnam. Capt Beyer radioed that his mission was progressing normally and that he was heading for Kham Duc. When he did not return to Chu Lai at the expected time the SAR forces were alerted. The search continued for five days and focussed on his last known position about 10 miles east of Kham Duc. However, there was no sign of Capt Beyer or his aircraft.

1 August 1968

A-4C 148599 VA-66, USN, USS *Intrepid*
Lt(jg) Edward James Broms (KIA)

Lt Broms was last man in a flight of four Skyhawks on a morning strike on a target at Dong Dun, 30 miles south of Vinh. After bombing the target the section leader heard Lt Broms radio that he was under heavy anti-aircraft fire as he began his bomb run. No further calls were made and despite an immediate search of the area, there was no sign of the Skyhawk or its pilot. Radio Hanoi later reported the shooting down of an American aircraft south of Vinh on this day but no mention was made of the fate of the pilot who had most likely been killed in his aircraft.

F-4D 66-8822 389 TFS, 366 TFW, USAF, Da Nang
Maj William James Thompson (KIA)
1Lt Joseph Shaw Ross (KIA)

At dusk a flight of Phantoms was flying an armed reconnaissance mission north of the DMZ when the leading aircraft was lost. Maj Thompson and 1Lt Ross observed trucks close to the Ban Karai Pass and 15 miles southwest of Dong Hoi. Maj Thompson dropped several flares over the trail and told his wingman to stand off while he made the first attack. The wingman then saw a huge explosion near the target and tried to contact Maj Thompson's aircraft without success. A search at first

light failed to reveal any sign of wreckage or the crew, although parachutes from the flares were sighted near the burnt out wreck of a truck close to Ban Katoi village.

2 August 1968

F-100C 54-1775 136 TFS, 31 TFW, USAF, Tuy Hoa
1Lt Michael J Laskowski (survived)

The 136th TFS lost its second aircraft in Vietnam during an attack on enemy bunkers that were thought to hold supplies and weapons 10 miles southeast of the A Shau Valley and close to the Laotian border. Maj Laskowski was making his second strafing run at 1,000 feet when his aircraft was hit by automatic weapons fire. Maj Laskowski headed away from the target and ejected 15 miles west of Hué. He was spotted by an FAC and an Army UH-1, but the helicopter was not equipped with a hoist and could not rescue 1Lt Laskowski through the tall trees. However, about 30 minutes later he was rescued by a USAF helicopter captained by Maj Vernon Dander from the 37th ARRS.

F-4B 149449 VMFA-323, MAG-13, USMC, Chu Lai
Maj D I Carroll (survived)
1Lt R C Brown (survived)

A Phantom was hit by small arms fire as it was making its sixth pass over an enemy target near An Hoa, 17 miles southwest of Da Nang. The aircraft was dropping napalm from 400 feet and was hit in the starboard wing. Maj Carroll flew the burning aircraft back towards Chu Lai and attempted to land but could not get the landing gear to extend. The crew ejected about a mile off the coast and were both rescued by an Army helicopter that was in the vicinity.

6 August 1968

RF-101C 56-0215 Detachment 1, 45 TRS, 460 TRW, USAF,
Tan Son Nhut
Maj G D Harlow (survived)

Maj Harlow took off from Tan Son Nhut and flew the length of South Vietnam to photograph enemy targets north of the DMZ. His Voodoo was damaged by AAA as he made his second run over a potential target near Thach Ban, about 10 miles north of the DMZ. With the rear fuselage in flames Maj Harlow headed out to sea and ejected off the coast near Hué. He was later picked up by a Navy ship. This was the last RF-101C to be lost during the war in Southeast Asia although the type was not finally withdrawn until the deactivation of the 45th TRS on 1 November 1970. The RF-101C, which was rapidly being replaced by the RF-4C version of the Phantom, had performed sterling work since its first deployment to Southeast Asia in October 1961. A total of 38 RF-101Cs was lost during the war, 28 of them over North Vietnam. Despite the aircraft's tricky handling characteristics, only five Voodoos were lost in accidents during 10 years of operations in Southeast Asia.

8 August 1968

F-4B 148420 VMFA-122, MAG-11, USMC, Da Nang
Capt C R Cusack (survived)
Capt S M Creal (survived)

Another Marine Corps Phantom was lost while attacking an enemy position five miles north of An Hoa, close to where Maj Carroll's aircraft had been hit on the 2nd. Capt Cusack was dropping napalm on his third bombing run over the target when his Phantom was hit by .50 calibre gunfire that put the starboard engine out of action. With his aircraft on fire Capt Cusack attempted to return to base but he and his navigator were forced to eject from the aircraft seven miles offshore from Da Nang. A Navy ship rescued Capt Cusask, while Capt Creal was recovered by a USAF helicopter.

F-100C 53-1713 136 TFS, 31 TFW, USAF, Tuy Hoa
1 pilot, name unknown (survived)

The unlucky 136th TFS lost another aircraft on the 8th. The aircraft crashed when its engine failed but the pilot ejected safely. This aircraft was the fifth F-100C to be built for the USAF and had spent the early part of its career at Edwards AFB as a test aircraft.

9 August 1968

F-105D 62-4292 357 TFS, 355 TFW, USAF, Takhli
Col David W Winn (POW)

The North Vietnamese defences north of the DMZ claimed yet another aircraft on the 9th. A flight of Thunderchiefs was bombing an anti-aircraft gun position but Col Winn's aircraft was hit by 37mm AAA as it pulled up through 5,000 feet after his attack. The rear of the aircraft started to burn as Col Winn headed for the coast. However, about two miles short of the sea he was forced to eject and landed close to the village of Xom Quan where he was captured. David Winn was the deputy wing commander of the Takhli Wing and was flying with the 333rd TFS in a 357th aircraft when he was shot down. He became one of the most senior officers in the POW camps. Col Winn joined the Air Force in 1943 and flew B-26 Marauders and P-38 Lightnings with the Twelfth Air Force during the Second World War. He flew Hawker Hunters and English Electric Lightnings while on an exchange tour with the Royal Air Force at Leconfield in the 1960s. He had been shot down on 15 April 1968, close to where he came down on 9 August, but his luck did not hold the second time. He was released on 14 March 1973 and resumed a successful USAF career. He served in a number of senior positions in NORAD, eventually commanding the Combat Operations Center at Cheyenne Mountain with the rank of Brigadier General before retiring from the Air Force on 1 July 1978.

A-1H 52-135326 6 SOS, 633 SOW, USAF, Pleiku
Maj Wayne Benjamin Wolfkeil (KIA)

On 1 August all the Air Commando units in the USAF were redesignated as Special Operations units and the first aircraft lost from one of the newly-designated squadrons was a Skyraider from Pleiku. Two Skyraiders were despatched on a Steel Tiger strike into southern Laos but Maj Wolfkeil's aircraft was hit by ground fire during an attack on enemy troops on the Ho Chi Minh Trail. The aircraft crashed eight miles northeast of Ban Pakha, in the extreme southern tip of the Laotian panhandle and there was no sign that the pilot had ejected. Maj Wolfkeil was promoted to the rank of Colonel during the time he was missing and was declared dead for administrative purposes in 1979.

11 August 1968

A-1E 52-139594 1 SOS, 56 SOW, USAF, Nakhon Phanom
Lt Col Charles Teague (KIA)

On returning from a combat mission a Skyraider crashed during a ground controlled approach to Nakhon Phanom killing the pilot

The RF-101C Voodoo tactical reconnaissance aircraft was finally withdrawn from service in Southeast Asia in 1970 having been one of the first USAF aircraft to be deployed to the theatre. USAF

The Cessna O-2A began to supplement the O-1 Bird Dog as a FAC aircraft in mid-1967. Despite the O-2's higher performance and increased armament, many pilots preferred the O-1 as it was more manoeuvrable, had better visibility and could operate from shorter airstrips. USAF

15 August 1968

RF-4C 66-0447   14 TRS, 432 TRW, USAF, Udorn
Capt Terrin Dinsmore Hicks (KIA)
Capt Joseph Francis Shanahan (POW)

A Phantom from Udorn was despatched on a solo reconnaissance mission in Route Package I. The aircraft was hit by ground fire as it was flying over the mouth of the Sou Giang River, 15 miles northwest of Dong Hoi. Both the crew managed to eject and spoke to each other as they descended by parachute. They landed about one mile from each other, on opposite sides of a hill. Capt Shanahan landed in a village and was captured almost immediately and heard gunshots from the other side of the hill. Shanahan was later given Capt Hicks's boots to wear as his own had been stolen. It would appear that Capt Hicks was killed by North Vietnamese militia during his attempt to evade capture. His identity cards were handed over by the Vietnamese in November 1985. The following month the Vietnamese handed over seven sets of remains, one of which was claimed to be those of Capt Hicks, but this could not be confirmed. Maj Shanahan had flown 192 missions during two tours in Southeast Asia and was released from captivity on 14 March 1973.

16 August 1968

F-100F 56-3865   612 TFS, 37 TFW, USAF, Phu Cat
Maj Michael Owen McElhanon (KIA)
Maj John Francis Overlock (KIA)

A Misty FAC was lost along with its crew on a mission north of the DMZ. The aircraft had taken on fuel from a tanker once during the mission and Maj McElhanon later reported that he was heading out over the Gulf of Tonkin to rendezvous with the tanker again. When a flight of fighters crossed the DMZ and called for the Misty to designate their target it was realised that the aircraft was missing. A search proved fruitless and it was presumed that the aircraft was either lost over the sea or was shot down near Dong Hoi. In one document at least, these men are recorded as being members of the 309th TFS and it is possible that they were on detachment to the 612th.

F-4D 66-8754   389 TFS, 366 TFW, USAF, Da Nang
Maj L N Cain (survived)
1Lt M Metcalfe (survived)

Enemy troops near the village of Thon Binh An, 20 miles northwest of Da Nang, were the object of a raid by a flight of Phantoms on the 16th. Maj Cain had just commenced his strafing run on the troops when his aircraft was hit by small arms fire in the rear fuselage and started to burn. Maj Cain headed due north to where a waiting USAF SAR helicopter was orbiting. The crew ejected and were soon picked up safely.

17 August 1968

F-100F 56-3834   355 TFS, 37 TFW, USAF, Phu Cat
Capt Charles A Shaheen (survived)
Capt Richard G Rutan (survived)

A second Misty FAC was lost the day after Maj McElhanon and Maj Overlock went down. Capt Shaheen and Capt Rutan were controlling a strike on a truck park that had been discovered in the hills, 40 miles northwest of Dong Hoi. As their aircraft was pulling up from its third strafing run it was struck by a 37mm anti-aircraft shell, which damaged the engine. The aircraft caught fire as it climbed out towards the sea and the crew ejected about 12 miles off the coast of North Vietnam. They were both rescued by a USAF SAR helicopter after spending more than three hours in a life raft. This flight was to have been Chuck Shaheen's last mission of his tour with the Commando Sabre unit. Dick Rutan flew a total of 325 combat missions in Southeast Asia, 105 of them in the Misty FAC role. He retired from the Air Force in 1978 and joined his brother's aircraft design and manufacturing company test flying the successful series of Vari-Eze and LongEz series of sports aircraft until forming his own company, Voyager Aircraft Inc, in 1981. In December 1986 he and his co-pilot, Jeana Yeager, made aviation history when they made the first non-stop, unrefuelled flight around the world in a time of just over nine days in the Voyager aircraft.

F-4B 151404   VF-142, USN, USS Constellation
Lt(jg) Markham Ligon Gartley (POW)
Lt William John Mayhew (POW)

A flight of Phantoms on a CAP mission engaged a number of MiG-21s approximately 20 miles northwest of Vinh. Lt Gartley started a split-S manoeuvre at 10,000 feet just as his flight leader fired a Sidewinder missile. The Sidewinder missed its intended victim and instead guided itself towards the heat

signature of Gartley's Phantom. The missile hit the Phantom's tail and the aircraft's port engine caught fire. The hydraulics soon failed and with the aircraft out of control, the crew ejected but were both captured. Lt Gartley was one of three men to be released into the hands of US peace activists on 25 September 1972 while Lt Mayhew served the full term and was released on 14 March 1973.

F-4D 66-7565   555 TFS, 432 TRW, USAF, Udorn
1Lt William Elmo Powell (KIA)
1Lt Arthur Thomas Hoffson (POW)

A Triple Nickel Phantom was lost on the 17th during a strike on a target in the hills 20 miles northwest of Dong Hoi. 1Lt Powell had just started his bombing run when his aircraft was hit by ground fire. The WSO ejected first but it is not certain if the pilot had actually left the aircraft before it crashed. 1Lt Hoffson was captured on his 97th mission, with just three more to go before he could have returned home. He was repatriated on 14 March 1973. A set of human remains were handed over by the Vietnamese in 1985 and two years later these were identified as being those of William Powell.

F-105D 61-0219   469 TFS, 388 TFW, USAF, Korat
Capt Noble Ray Koontz (KIA)

A Thunderchief landed at Korat after a ferry flight but its drag chute failed to deploy properly. The aircraft engaged the runway barrier at high speed but the aircraft's tailhook sheared off and the aircraft crashed into the overshot area and the pilot was killed. This particular aircraft was variously known as 'The Traveller', 'Linda Lou' and 'Foreign Aid' during its time in Southeast Asia.

18 August 1968

F-4D 66-8811   480 TFS, 366 TFW, USAF, Da Nang
Capt A R Thomas (survived)
1Lt G M Green (survived)

Another Da Nang Phantom was lost during a close air support mission over the DMZ. Capt Thomas started his bombing run against an enemy troop position but the F-4 was hit in the fuselage by .50 calibre gunfire. The crew subsequently ejected near Cam Lo, on the southern edge of the DMZ buffer zone, and was rescued by a US Army helicopter.

19 August 1968

F-8H   147924   VF-24, USN, USS *Hancock*
     Lt(jg) L R Plotz (survived)

The *Hancock* was due to start operations on the 23rd having recently arrived in the South China Sea for its fourth war cruise. The F-8H was a remanufactured F-8D with a strengthened wing and undercarriage and other minor modifications. As the Air Wing was training for operations it lost one of the newly-modified Crusaders when it ran out of fuel before it could return to the carrier. This was an inauspicious start for the Crusader's swansong in Southeast Asia.

20 August 1968

A-4C   148470   VA-36, USN, USS *Intrepid*
     1 pilot, name unknown (survived)

During an attack mission two Skyhawks collided in mid-air. One of the aircraft managed to return to the carrier but the other had to be abandoned as it was too badly damaged.

A-6B   151560   VA-196, USN, USS *Constellation*
     Lt W A Neal (survived)
     Lt(jg) D C Brandenstein (survived)

The A-6B variant of the Intruder was a modification of the basic A-6A for the specialised Iron Hand defence suppression mission. The aircraft could carry the huge AGM-78 Standard ARM and also had an array of associated radars and other avionics. Only 19 A-6Bs were converted from standard A-6As but they were extensively used by a number of Intruder squadron in Southeast Asia. The first A-6B to be lost was being launched from the *Constellation* when it was found that its leading edge slats would not fully retract so the aircraft lost lift and hit the water. Both crew ejected as the aircraft ditched in the Gulf of Tonkin

23 August 1968

F-100C   54-1922   136 TFS, 31 TFW, USAF, Tuy Hoa
     1Lt J J Thurn (survived)

Yet another 136th TFS aircraft was lost during a close air support mission over South Vietnam. A flight of F-100s had been called in to attack enemy troops near Duc Lap, close to the border with Cambodia and 30 miles southwest of Ban Me Thuot. 1Lt Thurn was making his second pass dropping napalm when his Super Sabre was shot down by automatic weapons fire. He ejected safely and was rescued by an Army helicopter.

O-2A   67-21348   20 TASS, 504 TASG, USAF, Da Nang
     detached to Chu Lai
     Capt Lon Davis Richards (KIA)

An O-2 detachment at Chu Lai provided aircraft to control strikes on the surrounding area, which was becoming more and more hostile. Capt Richards was controlling a strike on a series of enemy bunkers and trenches about six miles southwest of the base when his aircraft was shot down from 2,000 feet by machine gun fire. The pilot may have been hit, as he did not abandon the aircraft.

RF-4C   66-0466   14 TRS, 432 TRW, USAF, Udorn
     1Lt Francis Leslie Setterquist (KIA)
     1Lt Charles Lee Bergevin (KIA)

An RF-4C disappeared during a night low-level reconnaissance sortie over North Vietnam. 1Lt Setterquist and 1Lt Bergevin were assigned to photograph potential targets in an area 50 miles to the northwest of Dong Hoi. When the aircraft failed to return at the time its fuel would have been exhausted, an electronic and radio search was made without results. A North Vietnamese news report later stated that a Phantom had been shot down during the night of the 23rd.

24 August 1968

F-4D   66-8694   497 TFS, 8 TFW, USAF, Ubon
     Maj Charles Harold W Read (KIA)
     1Lt Melvin Earl Ladewig (KIA)

Two Phantoms on an armed reconnaissance mission commenced an attack on a storage area 17 miles northwest of Dong

Hoi. Following the attack the leader saw a large fireball on the ground and he soon realised that it was the wreckage of Maj Read's aircraft. The cause of the loss remains undetermined but was probably ground fire or target fixation. Neither of the crewmembers are thought to have ejected from the aircraft.

A-7A   154359   VA-27, USN, USS *Constellation*
     Lt J R Lee (survived)

During an armed reconnaissance mission a flight of Corsairs attacked an anti-aircraft gun site on the outskirts of the city of Vinh using their Walleye bombs. Lt Lee rolled in on the target and prepared to fire his missile but his aircraft was hit by flak before he could fire. The aircraft burst into flames as Lt Lee headed towards the coast. As the aircraft crossed the coast at 4,000 feet the hydraulics suddenly failed and the aircraft went out of control. Lt Lee ejected safely and parachuted into the sea close to the shore but was protected by other A-7s from VA-27. He was later rescued by a SH-3 SAR helicopter from HC-7.

F-8H   148694   VF-211, USN, USS *Hancock*
     Lt(jg) B S Foster (survived)

During a BARCAP mission a Crusader suffered a hydraulic failure that led to a total loss of control. The pilot ejected and was picked up safely.

F-4B   150434   VF-143, USN, USS *Constellation*
     Lt William Arthur Heep (KIA)
     Lt(jg) T L McPherson (survived)

As a Phantom was being launched from the *Constellation* for an armed reconnaissance sortie over North Vietnam the catapult bridle connection failed and the aircraft fell into the sea. Unfortunately, only one of the crew was able to escape before the aircraft sank.

25 August 1968

F-105F   63-8323   357 TFS, 355 TFW, USAF, Takhli
     2 crew, names unknown (survived)

A two-seat Thunderchief suffered an oil system failure that resulted in the engine seizing up. Both crew ejected safely near Takhli.

26 August 1968

C-7B   62-4177   457 TAS, 483 TAW, USAF, Cam Ranh Bay
     Capt Robert George Bull (KIA)
     1Lt Ralph William Manners (KIA)
     A1C David Frederick Sleeper (KIA)

A Caribou was hit by ground fire in the starboard wing as it was flying close to the Cambodian border on an airlift flight, about 10 miles southwest of An Loc. The aircraft crashed and exploded killing the three crewmen.

F-4D   66-7531   480 TFS, 366 TFW, USAF, Da Nang
     Maj Donald William Pick (KIA)
     1Lt Samuel F Wilburn (survived)

The growing threat to operations from even the largest American bases was once more graphically illustrated as a Phantom was climbing out of Da Nang on a strike mission. The aircraft was hit by ground fire damaging the starboard engine and the aircraft burst into flames. Maj Pick flew the aircraft about five miles out to sea where his WSO ejected. Sadly, Maj Pick was killed in the incident. 1Lt Wilburn was shot down again and rescued on 19 October 1968.

28 August 1968

A-6B   151561   VA-85, USN, USS *America*
     Lt(jg) Robert Ray Duncan (KIA)
     Lt(jg) Alan Frederick Ashall (KIA)

A flight of Intruders encountered an active SAM battery on a night-time Iron Hand mission in the Vinh Son area, 20 miles northwest of Vinh. As the aircraft were searching the area from 15,000 feet, Lt Duncan reported seeing three SAM launches. Two A-7 pilots saw a detonation at about 14,000 feet followed later by a second explosion on or near the ground. Although the precise sequence of events could not be confirmed, it would appear that

Lts Duncan and Ashall had fallen victim to an SA-2. The missiles had been fired from the same general area where the *America* had lost a Phantom to a SAM on 18 June. This was last of only two A-6B Intruders to be lost during the war.

A-1E   52-135139   56 SOW, USAF, Nakhon Phanom
     A Skyraider was damaged when it landed at a forward strip in Laos. The aircraft was moved to a revetment so that repairs could take place but the aircraft fell from trestles and was so badly damaged that the repairs were abandoned and the aircraft scrapped.

29 August 1968

AC-47D   43-49499   14 SOW, USAF, Phan Rang
     A Spooky gunship was destroyed during a VC rocket attack on Phan Rang air base. This aircraft had originally been delivered to the USAAF as a C-47B in November 1944.

30 August 1968

A-4F   154981   VA-93, USN, USS *Bon Homme Richard*
     Lt Cdr H A Eikel (survived)

Another aircraft was lost in the Vinh Son region when a section of Skyhawks was scouting over the area on an armed reconnaissance mission. The section found an anti-aircraft gun position and were jinking to avoid its deadly fire prior to commencing a bombing run. Lt Cdr Eikel's aircraft was hit as it was in a turn at 5,000 feet causing a partial loss of control. All the aircraft's systems failed in quick succession leading to a total loss of control forcing Lt Cdr Eikel to eject 25 miles northwest of Vinh. Despite being some 30 miles inland, the pilot was rescued from capture by a Navy SH-3 helicopter. Lt Cdr Eikel later converted to the A-7 and was shot down by a SAM while flying with VA-94 from the USS *Coral Sea* on 24 May 1972.

31 August 1968

RF-4C   65-0858   12 TRS, 460 TRW, USAF, Tan Son Nhut
     Capt T G Dorsett (survived)
     Capt D G Kenny (survived)

The third RF-4C to be lost during August was shot down during a photographic reconnaissance mission near the abandoned Special Forces Camp at Kham Duc in the Annamites. The aircraft was making a photo run at 2,000 feet and 480 knots when it was hit by .50 calibre gunfire that damaged one of the engines. Capt Dorsett flew due north to a position about 25 miles southwest of Da Nang before he and his navigator were forced to abandon the aircraft. They were both picked up by a US Army helicopter, having suffered only minor injuries.

F-4D   66-8688   432 TRW, USAF, Udorn
     Capt J R Wilson (survived)
     1Lt William Louis Kinkade (KIA)

Another Phantom was lost after night fell during a strike on trucks on a mountain road 25 miles west of Dong Hoi. Capt Wilson commenced a dive from 6,000 feet but the aircraft burst into flames after being hit by ground fire. Capt Wilson ejected but 1Lt Kinkade may have been wounded or killed by the flak burst and did not escape. The pilot was badly injured but was rescued the next day by a USAF SAR helicopter in a dramatic rescue mission. The on-scene commander for the rescue attempt at first light was Lt Col William A Jones, the CO of the 602nd SOS. Lt Col Jones led four Skyraiders on an intensive search for 1Lt Kinkade who was in intermittent radio contact with the SAR force. His aircraft was hit several times but Lt Col Jones persisted in trolling up and down valleys to find the downed survivor. Just as he found 1Lt Kinkade and guided the HH-53 toward him, Jones's Skyraider was hit and the cockpit engulfed in flames as the ejection seat's rocket motor ignited just behind his head. He jettisoned the canopy to prepare to bail out but decided to stay with the aircraft when the flames died down. Despite severe burns he flew all the way back to Nakhon Phanom and landed safely in poor weather in a barely controllable aircraft. As Lt Col Jones lay on the operating table he insisted on reporting the exact location of 1Lt Kinkade thus enabling a successful

rescue later that day. Lt Col William A Jones was subsequently awarded the Medal of Honor for his actions on his 98th mission. Sadly, William Jones was killed in the crash of a private aircraft in the USA on 15 November 1969 after taking up an appointment at Andrews AFB. The Skyraider flown by Lt Col Jones on his epic mission was destroyed on 28 September 1972, it was the last USAF Skyraider to be lost during the conflict. Phantom 66-8688 was credited with a MiG-21 on 6 February 1968 when it was being flown by Capt R H Boles and 1Lt R B Battista of the 433rd TFS.

F-8H   147897   VF-24, USN, USS *Hancock*
                  Lt Cdr John Eugene Bartocci (KIA)

As a Crusader was returning from a night combat air patrol it developed a high sink rate and hit the *Hancock's* ramp. The aircraft broke in two and exploded killing the pilot.

F-4C   64-0837   559 TFS, 12 TFW, USAF, Cam Ranh Bay
                   Lt Col P A Kauttu (survived)
                   1Lt G A D'Angelo (survived)

During a training flight over South Vietnam a Phantom suffered a control system failure and the aircraft had to be abandoned just off Cam Ranh Bay.

1 September 1968

F-105D   60-0512   34 TFS, 388 TFW, USAF, Korat
                     Capt D K Thaete (survived)

An F-105 was lost during a Barrel Roll mission in central Laos. The aircraft was at 15,000 feet en route to bomb a North Vietnamese storage area when it was hit by AAA. The engine was damaged and the aircraft was seen to be on fire. Capt Thaete headed southwest back towards Thailand but had to eject after flying about 20 miles. He was rescued from the Laotian jungle by a USAF helicopter. His F-105 carried the name 'The Mercenary' under the starboard wing root.

O-2A   67-21315   20 TASS, 504 TASG, USAF, Da Nang
                    Maj Jack Clare Plumb (KIA)

An O-2 suffered an engine failure during an FAC mission in Quang Ngai province and crashed killing the pilot.

2 September 1968

A-4E   150100   VMA-311, MAG-12, USMC, Chu Lai
                  Maj Donald S Carr (survived)

A flight of Skyhawks from Chu Lai was tasked with an armed reconnaissance mission in the hill country near the A Shau Valley. Maj Carr's aircraft was damaged by ground fire as it pulled up after bombing a target near the village of Nong Tru'ong Nam Dong, 30 miles to the west of Da Nang. He headed east with the rear end of the Skyhawk on fire and ejected near Phu Loc, 25 miles northwest of Da Nang, where he was soon picked up by a helicopter.

A-7A   153225   VA-86, USN, USS *America*
                  1 pilot, name unknown (survived)

During an attack mission a Corsair pilot inadvertently hit the water and was forced to eject from his damaged aircraft. He was fortunate that the initial impact did not destroy the aircraft and that he could escape to be rescued by a helicopter.

3 September 1968

F-4C   64-0681   558 TFS, 12 TFW, USAF, Cam Ranh Bay
                   Maj T E Assalone (survived)
                   1Lt C P Parlatore (survived)

Air strikes close to US air bases were by now quite common and this was especially so at those deemed most vulnerable like Tan Son Nhut and Da Nang, which were surrounded by numerous villages that were suspected of harbouring Viet Cong forces. A flight of Phantoms from Cam Ranh Bay was called in to bomb VC positions just two miles west of Tan Son Nhut air base on the 3rd. Maj Assalone was making a run over his target at 600 feet when his aircraft was hit by small arms fire. The crew ejected immediately and were fortunate to be rescued from the area before the VC could exact their revenge.

6 September 1968

C-130E   62-1785   345 TAS, 314 TAW, USAF, Ching Chuan Kang
                     Capt David Horace Risher (KIA)
                     Capt Leonard Selaniko (KIA)
                     Maj Eugene Winfield Hartman (KIA)
                     TSgt Ralph James Lund (KIA)
                     Sgt Jesus Ochoa (KIA)

A Hercules on an airlift flight from Tuy Hoa was damaged by ground fire about a mile south of Tan Phat airfield near the city of Bao Loc, 85 miles southwest of Cam Ranh Bay. The pilot tried to land the aircraft but it crashed before he could set it down. However, one source claims that the aircraft was not lost to enemy action but crashed into a hill in bad weather.

A-6A   154127   VA-85, USN, USS *America*
                  Cdr Kenneth Leon Coskey (POW)
                  Lt Cdr R G McKee (survived)

The CO of VA-85 set off on a night low-level attack on targets near the city of Vinh. Carrying 10 Mk36 bombs and four CBUs, the aircraft first bombed a road ferry at Linh Cam, 10 miles southeast of Vinh, before proceeding to the Ben Thuy road ferry, two miles to the southeast of the city. After it dropped CBUs on the target the aircraft started a climbing turn but was hit by a 37mm shell in the fuselage. The aircraft started to pitch and roll violently and, unable to regain control of the stricken Intruder, the crew ejected. The aircraft crashed on a small island in the Song Ca River just to the east of Vinh and the two men came down close to the wreck but were separated. By the time the SAR helicopter arrived the rescue forces had made voice contact with Cdr Coskey who told them that he had injured his leg but would try to make his way to the wreck of the Intruder. However, when the helicopter approached the wreck it was fired at by North Vietnamese militia and had to depart after picking up Lt Cdr McKee. Cdr Coskey was captured on the island and was held as a POW until his release on 14 March 1973. He had only taken command of VA-85 on 28 June 1968 and was the Squadron's fourth CO to be lost since 1965.

A-4F   154187   VA-93, USN, USS *Bon Homme Richard*
                  1 pilot, name unknown (survived)

A Skyhawk configured as a tanker aircraft suffered an accidental explosion, probably due to an engine or fuel system fault. The pilot managed to escape before the aircraft plunged into the sea.

7 September 1968

F-4B   152994   VMFA-115, MAG-13, USMC, Chu Lai
                  Capt J R Denton (survived)
                  1Lt J C Church (survived)

A Marine Corps Phantom was lost during a close air support mission seven miles south of Hué on the 7th. Capt Denton was making his second run over the target dropping napalm on enemy positions when small arms fire damaged his port engine and set the aircraft alight. He headed east but he and his navigator had to eject near the Marine Corps base at Phu Bai. They were quickly rescued by one of the helicopters from the base.

F-105F   63-8289   44 TFS, 388 TFW, USAF, Korat
                     2 crew, names unknown (survived)

The two crewmembers of an F-105F were forced to eject over Thailand when the aircraft suffered a catastrophic engine failure.

8 September 1968

F-4J   155744   VMFA-334, MAG-11, USMC, Da Nang
                  Capt M H Branum (survived)
                  1Lt H W Hibbs (survived)

It was not just the Navy that received the new F-4J version of the Phantom. The Marines started to replace the F-4B in June 1967 when VMFA-334 received the Corps' first J-models at MCAS El Toro. The Squadron arrived at Da Nang on 30 August 1968 and a week later it lost its first aircraft during a close air support mission two miles south of Hoi An and about 15 miles southeast of Da Nang. The target was an enemy weapons cache situated on the banks of the Song Thu Bon River. Capt Branum was making

his fourth pass over the target to drop napalm when his aircraft was struck by ground fire. He immediately set course for Da Nang and almost made it but he and his navigator had to eject from the aircraft on the final approach about a mile short of the airfield. Both men were hauled out of Da Nang Bay by a helicopter from the base.

10 September 1968

F-100F   56-3772   355 TFS, 37 TFW, USAF, Phu Cat
                     Capt D A McGrath (survived)
                     Capt R D Uffley (survived)

A two-seat Super Sabre was taking part in a close air support mission in South Vietnam. Capt McGrath was making his second strafing pass against North Vietnamese troops near the village of Bon Dro, 20 miles southwest of the city of Ban Me Thuot. The aircraft was hit by ground fire that damaged the engine and set the aircraft alight. The crew ejected close to the enemy troops and were fortunate to be picked up by a USAF helicopter.

F-4B   148409   VMFA-314, MAG-13, USMC, Chu Lai
                  Lt Col F E Petersen (survived)
                  Capt K D Edlen (survived)

Marine ground operations within the DMZ buffer zone continued throughout the summer of 1968 and much of the Marine close air support effort was in direct support of the 'grunts' involved in these operations. A flight of Phantoms was attacking enemy troops in trenches and bunkers about 12 miles northeast of Khe Sanh when one of the aircraft was lost. Lt Col Petersen was pulling up from his third pass over the target when his F-4 was hit by .50 calibre gunfire. The port engine had to be shut down and the rear of the aircraft started to burn. The crew ejected shortly after the aircraft was hit and they were fortunate to be rescued by an Army helicopter that happened to be nearby.

F-8H   148680   VF-51, USN, USS *Bon Homme Richard*
                  Lt J N Quisenberry (survived)

A Crusader assigned to a TARCAP mission was abandoned following an engine explosion. The cause was thought to have been a mechanical failure rather than enemy action.

Phantom FACs

While the Commando Sabre programme had proved the value of fast FAC aircraft that could operate in high threat areas, the F-100F Misty FAC was not an ideal vehicle for the role, especially as replacement aircraft were scarce. In early 1968 Seventh Air Force flew a small number of test flights with Misty pilots in the back seats of F-4Ds. The Phantom also had its disadvantages including a poor view downward from the rear seat and high fuel consumption rate. It was not as manoeuvrable as the F-100 and it had a persistent engine smoke trail that made it easier to sight. However, its power and load-carrying capacity, its advanced avionics and its better availability outweighed the disadvantages. The 366th TFW at Da Nang was selected to pioneer the Phantom FAC programme and the aircraft used the call sign Stormy. The 366th started training its first Stormy FAC crews on 12 August using Misty crews as instructors. The Wing flew its first FAC mission in Route Package I on 2 September and lost its first aircraft in this new role just nine days later. In November 1968 the 8th TFW at Ubon also started FAC training for selected crews and implemented their Wolf FAC programme in the Steel Tiger area in December. Wolf FACs were also used to lead bombing raids in poor weather by using their LORAN equipment to identify targets and compute bomb release points. Next to adopt the fast FAC was the 388th TFW at Korat. On 19 March 1969 the Wing flew its first Tiger FAC mission and concentrated much of its effort on the Barrel Roll region of northern Laos and flew strike control missions in support of General Vang Pao's indigenous forces. All the fast FACs flew visual reconnaissance missions as well as pre-planned strike control missions and were often used to control strikes during SAR operations. In April 1969 the 432nd TRW started a unique fast FAC programme that consisted of an RF-4C and an F-4D fast FAC working as a team. The Falcon FAC F-4D carried out visual reconnaissance and called in the RF-4C (call sign Atlanta) to take photographs if necessary. Similarly the

RF-4C could call the Falcon FAC in to control a strike if it spotted a target. The Falcon/Atlanta team was very successful in finding and striking targets in the Barrel Roll and Steel Tigers areas. The 432nd TRW also developed the Laredo F-4E FAC hunter-killer mission, which consisted of a single F-4E leading and directing formations of up to 20 Phantoms.

The final Phantom FAC development was the Night Owl missions flown by the Wolfpack's night flying 497th TFS. Although the other fast FAC units experimented with night operations it was the 497th that specialised in this role. From October 1969 Night Owl F-4D FACs flew night missions over the Ho Chi Minh Trail concentrating on the strategic Mu Gia and Ban Karai passes. The aircraft were equipped with laser target designators and the accompanying Phantoms carried 1,000lb and 2,000lb laser-guided bombs. Night Owl FAC missions ceased in January 1970 when it was assessed that the dangers involved did not warrant the risk of operating low level at night in bad weather. In 1972 the 8th TFW developed the Pave Wolf fast FAC programme using Paveway laser illuminators, which immediately improved the FAC's success rate. Overall, the various fast FAC programmes developed in Southeast Asia were very successful in that they greatly improved the success rate of armed reconnaissance and air strikes. The one feature that characterised all the programmes was the high loss rate, approximately four times that of 'ordinary' strike aircraft. Unfortunately, the USAF have done little to maintain or develop the fast FAC role since Vietnam although the OA-10A now specialises in the FAC role.

11 September 1968

F-4D 66-8752 389 TFS, 366 TFW, USAF, Da Nang
Maj L E Bustle (survived)
1Lt Richard Haven Vandyke (KIA)

The first Stormy FAC to be lost went down barely a week after the start of the programme. A flight of F-4s, led by Maj Bustle, was attacking trucks that had been spotted on a road near Van Loc, 10 miles northwest of Dong Hoi. Maj Bustle was just pulling up from his attack when his aircraft was hit twice by 37mm flak. The fuselage quickly became a mass of flames but the pilot managed to cross the coast before he ejected. A USAF SAR helicopter picked up Maj Bustle but for some reason the WSO, 1Lt Vandyke, did not survive the incident.

12 September 1968

F-100D 56-3245 510 TFS, 3 TFW, USAF, Bien Hoa
Capt Ronald R Fogleman (survived)

It is a curious fact that several airmen who later attained very high rank in the USAF did so only after surviving being shot down in Southeast Asia.

A flight of Super Sabres took off from Bien Hoa for a close air support mission near Vam Song Ong Doc on the western coast of the extreme southern tip of South Vietnam. Having dropped his bombs, Capt Fogleman was firing his cannon on his fourth run over the enemy positions. As he cleared the target his F-100 was hit in the fuselage by automatic weapons fire. He ejected moments later and came down in mangrove swamps. A US Army AH-1G Cobra helicopter was flying nearby and landed so that Capt Fogleman could ride out by standing on one of the helicopter's skids and holding onto a open gun panel. In December Capt Fogleman volunteered for Commando Sabre fast FAC duties with the 37th TFW and finished his tour in Vietnam in September 1969 with 315 combat missions to his credit. Ronald Fogleman later flew the F-4 and F-15 and rose through the ranks of the Air Force commanding the 836th AD, the Seventh Air Force and Air Mobility Command until he was appointed the USAF's Chief of Staff on 26 October 1994. He retired early from the USAF on 1 September 1997 following a disagreement with the Secretary of Defense over accountability for the Khobar Towers terrorist bombing in Dhahran in June 1996.

F-105D 59-1762 357 TFS, 355 TFW, USAF, Takhli
Maj Samuel Chapman Maxwell (KIA)

During a mission over North Vietnam a flight of F-105s came upon a line of small boats sailing up the Song Ron River, 15 miles south of Mu Ron Ma. Maj Maxwell started a strafing run on the boats but his aircraft was hit by ground fire and crashed. The Vietnamese returned Maj Maxwell's remains to the USA in 1989.

C-123K 54-0714 19 SOS, 315 SOW, USAF, Phan Rang
3 crew, names unknown (survived)

As a Provider was landing at an airfield in South Vietnam one of the propellers went into reverse due to a malfunction. The aircraft veered off the runway and was damaged beyond repair.

F-105D 62-4359 469 TFS, 388 TFW, USAF, Korat
1 pilot, name unknown (survived)

A Thunderchief returning from a combat mission was diverted to Takhli because of bad weather at Korat. Unfortunately, the aircraft ran out of fuel and crashed after the engine flamed out. This particular aircraft was painted as 'Twelve o'clock High' while at Korat.

14 September 1968

F-105D 60-0522 357 TFS, 355 TFW, USAF, Takhli
Capt D M Tribble (survived)

Capt Tribble's flight was bombing three trucks that had been found on a road eight miles west of Dong Hoi. His aircraft was hit by AAA and the rear end of the aircraft caught fire. He set off back towards Thailand and crossed into Laos but was forced to eject near Ban Pongdong from where he was rescued by a SAR helicopter from Nakhon Phanom. 60-0522 was one of five Thunderchiefs each credited with a MiG-17 during a major air battle on 13 May 1967.

A-7A 154344 VA-27, USN, USS *Constellation*
Cdr George T Pappas (survived)

The second Corsair lost by VA-27 almost resulted in the loss of the Squadron's CO. Cdr Pappas was leading a flight of aircraft on a raid on the ferry across the Ngan Pho River at Linh Cam, 10 miles southeast of Vinh. As Cdr Pappas was pulling up from his first dive on the target, his aircraft was hit in the starboard wing by AAA. The flying control system was damaged and the starboard aileron was deflected fully up, which required full left aileron to fly level. The aircraft was also losing fuel and a fire threatened to burn the port wing off. Cdr Pappas flew his badly damaged aircraft back to Da Nang but as he started on the final approach the fire increased in intensity. The aircraft engaged the runway arrester gear but the cable broke and the aircraft veered off the runway. As this point Cdr Pappas ejected and landed close to the burning remains of his Corsair. George Pappas returned to the *Constellation* and continued to lead his squadron until February 1969, despite a knee injury.

16 September 1968

F-4B 149443 VF-143, USN, USS *Constellation*
Lt Cdr W R Lambertson (survived)
Lt(jg) T L McPherson (survived)

A Phantom was lost from the *Constellation* in a most unusual accident. The aircraft had just been catapulted off the deck when part of the aircraft's instrument panel became dislodged. The resulting confusion caused the pilot to stall the aircraft but both crewmen ejected safely and were rescued.

F-102A 56-0970 509 FIS, 405 FW, USAF, Udorn
1 pilot, name unknown (survived)

Upon returning from a training flight, an F-102 landed at Udorn but collided with an RF-4C on the runway and was so badly damaged that the Delta Dagger had to be scrapped. F-102A 56-0970 had served with both the 2nd FIS and the 5th FIS at Suffolk County AFB, New York before transferring to the 509th FIS in 1960.

17 September 1968

RF-4C 65-0915 11 TRS, 432 TRW, USAF, Udorn
Capt L L Paul (survived)
Capt Edgar Felton Davies (KIA)

An RF-4C was despatched to photograph a section of Route 914, part of the Ho Chi Minh Trail, near Ban Vangthon in southern Laos. During its photo run the aircraft was hit by ground fire and the crew had to eject close to the road. A USAF HH-53 arrived on the scene but its crew could only locate Capt Paul, who was rescued. There was no sign of Capt Davies who is presumed to have died in the incident, possibly at the hands of North Vietnamese troops after landing.

F-8H 148648 VF-24, USN, USS *Hancock*
Lt(jg) Paul Eugene Swigart (survived)

A section of Crusaders on a BARCAP mission engaged a number of MiG-21s near Vinh. After a long, indecisive engagement, Lt Cdr Red Isaacks and Lt Swigart had to break away from the fight when their fuel began to run low. The pair climbed towards the coast to rendezvous with a tanker for the return flight to the *Hancock*. However, minutes later the engine of Lt Swigart's Crusader flamed out due to fuel starvation and the pilot ejected, coming down in the sea five miles from the island of Hon Nieu off the coast near Vinh. A SAR helicopter later picked him up safely. Lt Swigart was killed in a ramp strike accident on 4 February 1969.

O-1E 56-2556 20 TASS, 504 TASG, USAF, Da Nang
Capt J R Compton (survived)

An O-1 pilot was controlling a landing zone preparation air strike a couple of miles to the west of the city of Hué when he was shot down. The aircraft's engine was damaged when it was hit by .50 calibre machine gun fire, so Capt Compton made a radio call for assistance, flew a few miles to the north and crash-landed his aircraft to await rescue. A US Army helicopter responded to his radio call and picked him up.

A-7A 153214 VA-97, USN, USS *Constellation*
Lt Cdr Brian Dunstan Woods (POW)

Lt Cdr Woods was flying the last aircraft in a formation of five Corsairs that bombed a road eight miles south of Vinh. An Intruder crew saw a Corsair hit by AAA at about 10,000 feet near Vinh. The Corsair burst into flames and dived into the ground. Although no parachute was seen an emergency beeper was heard briefly. Lt Cdr Woods had ejected but was captured within minutes of landing and sent to Hanoi. He was released from prison on 12 February 1973 and resumed his naval career. He was included in the first batch of released prisoners at the request of the US government so that he could fly straight back to the USA to visit his mother who was terminally ill in hospital. Thus, Brian Woods became the first POW to return to the USA as a result of Operation Homecoming.

19 September 1968

F-105D 60-0428 469 TFS, 388 TFW, USAF, Korat
Maj Elwyn Rex Capling (KIA)

The increasingly 'hot' region just north of the DMZ claimed yet another pilot on the 19th. A flight of F-105s was sent to bomb a storage area six miles northwest of Thon Cam Son. As Maj Capling was making his second run at the target his Thud was hit by 37mm anti-aircraft fire. He turned towards the coast but Maj Capling had to eject and the aircraft crashed near Vinh Linh, three miles short of the sea. The other pilots in the flight saw him land and spoke to him on his survival radio. Capling told them that his leg was broken. This was the last message received from Elwyn Capling and it appears that he was killed by his captors as he did not appear in any of the known POW camps. His remains were returned to the USA on 18 March 1977. Thunderchief 60-0428 was the first F-105D to reach 3,000 flying hours and had flown more than 500 combat missions before it was lost. It was painted as 'Pollyana' and 'Cajun Queen' during its time at Korat.

F-4B 152232 VMFA-542, MAG-11, USMC, Da Nang
Capt John Allen Lavoo (KIA)
Capt Robert Alan Holt (KIA)

A storage dump near the village of Mai Xa Ha, 13 miles north of the DMZ, was the object of a strike by Marine Corps Phantoms on the 19th. Capt Lavoo was making his second dive on the target when his aircraft was hit by small arms fire. The aircraft continued its dive until it slammed into the ground close to its target. Neither of the crew were seen to escape from the aircraft. In

September 1994, after several attempts at excavation, human remains were discovered and returned to the USA. The remains were later identified as being those of Capt Lavoo and Capt Holt and were buried at Arlington National Cemetery on 19 July 1999.

A-37A   67-14513   604 SOS, 3 TFW, USAF, Bien Hoa
1 pilot, name unknown (survived)

As a Dragonfly was taking off on an escort mission, one of its tyres burst and shredded and the aircraft ran off the side of the runway. The pilot escaped unharmed but the aircraft had to be scrapped.

F-4D   66-8692   435 TFS, 8 TFW, USAF, Ubon
Maj Roger O Clemens (KIA)
1Lt Peter Nash (survived)

A Phantom crash-landed during a night landing at Ubon and veered off the runway. 1Lt Nash ejected and survived but the pilot was killed in the accident.

21 September 1968

F-4B   150459   VMFA-115, MAG-13, USMC, Chu Lai
Capt Robert F Conley (KIA)
1Lt Steven R Major (KIA)

The Marines lost another Phantom while attacking enemy troops during a close air support mission near Phu Bai south of Hué. Both crew were killed when the aircraft was hit by ground fire during its first pass on a target. The pilot was the son of Brig Gen Robert F Conley, a well-known Marine aviator who had shot down a MiG-15 at night during the Korean War and who had commanded VMF(AW)-312 at Da Nang in 1965 and MAG-11 in 1966.

B-57B   52-1498   8 TBS, 35 TFW, USAF, Phan Rang
Lt Col D D Klein (survived)
1Lt R P Erickson (survived)

A Canberra on a night strike on a truck park near Ban Loumpoum in southern Laos was making its fifth dive on the target when it was hit by 37mm flak. The aircraft's port engine was put out of action but Lt Col Klein managed to fly almost 100 miles towards a Navy SAR destroyer off Hué. The crew ejected and were quickly picked up by the vessel. Built in August 1954, 52-1498 was the sixth B-57B and had been used as a development aircraft by the manufacturers and at Edwards AFB, California.

22 September 1968

A-1H   52-139739   602 SOS, 56 SOW, USAF, Nakhon Phanom
Maj Charles Frederic Kuhlmann (KIA)

The second USAF aircraft lost during a Barrel Roll mission in September was a Skyraider from Nakhon Phanom. Maj Kuhlmann was on RESCAP escort duties and was orbiting over a remote part of central Laos, about 15 miles northeast of Ban Ban, in case a SAR mission was required. The Skyraider was hit by small arms fire and although Maj Kuhlmann managed to leave the area his aircraft crashed and he was killed. He may well have been wounded by the ground fire and was unable to eject before his aircraft crashed. Some time prior to December 1996 his remains were returned for burial in the USA.

23 September 1968

A-4F   155015   VA-55, USN, USS Hancock
Lt Cdr Dale H Osborne (POW)

On an armed reconnaissance mission a section of Skyhawks made an attack on a barge using Zuni unguided rockets. The barge had been found on a waterway 10 miles north of Vinh but the area was well defended by AAA. The section leader made his first run and fired his Zunis but as he was pulling up Lt Cdr Osborne reported flak and was then hit himself. A 37mm shell entered the cockpit and severely injured Lt Cdr Osborne to the extent that he was unable to control the aircraft. He was knocked unconscious but he came round and, with difficulty, managed to eject and was soon captured. Shrapnel from the anti-aircraft round had shredded Osborne's left leg and he was so badly wounded that twice on the long journey to Hanoi his captors

thought he had died and were about to bury him when he regained consciousness just in time. Once in a POW camp he received medical treatment from the North Vietnamese that saved his life and he was nursed back to health by his cellmate, Lt Cdr Brian Woods who had been shot down on the 17th. Dale Osborne was still in poor health in 1973 and was released in the first batch of POW repatriations on 12 February 1973. He had served with the USAF in the early 1950s but joined the Navy in 1956. He had flown a variety of aircraft including the P-2 Neptune and T-28 trainer and had also flown the S-2 Tracker from the USS Kearsarge during its deployment to Southeast Asia in 1966.

A-4E   152091   VA-106, USN, USS Intrepid
Lt Cdr David Francis Callaghan (KWF)

During a test flight over the Gulf of Tonkin a Skyhawk suffered a generator failure. Lt Cdr Callaghan radioed that he was returning to the ship and set up a long straight approach to the carrier. All went well until the last few seconds before touchdown when the aircraft started to bank to the left. The nose dropped and the aircraft crashed into the LSO's platform before plunging into the sea.

24 September 1968

O-1G   51-4570   19 TASS, 504 TASG, USAF, Bien Hoa
Capt George Michael Cunningham (KIA)
Maj Norman Northrop Cunningham,
US Army (KIA)

A Bird Dog was shot down during an FAC mission near Phu Giao, 15 miles north of Bien Hoa. Both pilot and observer were killed in the crash. It is not known if the crew were related to each other.

F-100D   55-3602   308 TFS, 31 TFW, USAF, Tuy Hoa
1Lt Norman MacLeod Paulsen (KIA)

A Super Sabre crashed in Phu Yen province, South Vietnam, possibly due to pilot error.

26 September 1968

A-4E   150094   VMA-121, MAG-12, USMC, Chu Lai
Capt Dale Alan Luster (KIA)

A Marine Corps A-4 was lost during a close air support mission near Phuoc An, nine miles west of Tam Ky on the 26th. Capt Luster was dropping napalm on enemy troop positions when his aircraft was hit by automatic weapons fire. The Skyhawk crashed near the target and Capt Luster may have been hit, as he did not eject from the aircraft.

27 September 1968

F-100C   53-1765   174 TFS, 37 TFW, USAF, Phu Cat
1Lt J W Vinapuu (survived)

The 174th TFS lost its second aircraft since its deployment to Vietnam during a close air support mission. 1Lt Vinapuu took off from Phu Cat and was climbing through 3,000 feet about 15 miles northeast of the airfield when the aircraft was hit by .50 calibre ground fire. When the engine failed he ejected just off the coast near Vinh Loi and was rescued by an Army helicopter.

28 September 1968

A-4F   155011   VA-55, USN, USS Hancock
Lt D J Wright (survived)

A Rolling Thunder strike on the Tam Da railway bypass 11 miles north of Vinh resulted in the loss of one of the raiders. Lt Wright was pulling up from his attack on the target when his aircraft was hit by 37mm flak as it climbed through 4,000 feet. The aircraft began to stream fuel and a large hole was observed near the port wing root. The engine flamed out just as the aircraft crossed the coast and Lt Wright ejected a few miles offshore. He was rescued by a Navy SH-3 under the protection of a flight of A-7s and returned safely to his carrier.

29 September 1968

A-1H   52-135305   6 SOS, 633 SOW, USAF, Pleiku
Capt Wayne Ellsworth Newberry (KIA)

The 6th SOS lost a pilot on the 29th when an aircraft was shot down over southern Laos. North Vietnamese troops had been reported 20 miles west of Kham Duc and a flight of Skyraiders was scrambled from Pleiku. Capt Newberry was making his second strafing run under low cloud when his aircraft was hit by return fire from enemy troops. The aircraft crashed immediately and the pilot was not seen to eject. Capt Newberry was the seventh pilot lost by the 6th since its arrival earlier in the year.

30 September 1968

F-105F   63-8317   333 TFS, 355 TFW, USAF, Takhli
Capt Clifford Wayne Fieszel (KIA)
Maj Howard Horton Smith (KIA)

A Wild Weasel was lost during a strike on a SAM site near Phu Qui, five miles west of Dong Hoi. The aircraft was hit by 37mm AAA as it rolled in on the target. Capt Fieszel's wingman had been hit earlier and was heading out to sea and so did not see what happened to his leader. The F-105F went down in the vicinity of the target and an emergency beeper was heard for 24 hours after the aircraft crashed. The next day Radio Hanoi reported that two aircraft had been shot down, although in fact only one had actually been lost on the raid, and that one of the pilots had been captured. Nothing more was heard about Capt Fieszel or Maj Smith and they were presumed dead after the end of the war. 63-8317 had been painted as 'Half Fast' when serving with the 13th TFS and was later nicknamed 'Root Pack Rat'. The aircraft was credited with a MiG-17 kill on 19 December 1967.

A-6A   154149   VA-196, USN, USS Constellation
Lt(jg) Larry Jack Van Renselaar (KIA)
Lt Domenick Anthony Spinelli (KIA)

Three Intruders were despatched from the Constellation on a night armed reconnaissance mission north of Vinh using their radar to look for road traffic along Route 1A, the main coastal road. When the aircraft were about 17 miles northwest of Vinh, a SAM warning was received and Lt Van Renselaar subsequently reported two SAMs being launched in his direction. The other Intruder crews saw two explosions at about 5,000 feet followed about 20 seconds later by another explosion on the ground. An E-2 Hawkeye orbiting over the Gulf of Tonkin observed that the Intruder's IFF disappeared from the radar screen at about the same time. Wreckage was sighted on the ground not far from the coast during a search the next day. It was presumed that a SAM had hit the Intruder or the aircraft may have crashed when trying to avoid a missile. The crew were believed to have been killed in the incident, however, information obtained by the crew's families in the late 1980s suggested that the crew may have been captured. Any doubt as to Lt Van Renselaar's fate was dispelled in 1989 when his remains were returned to the USA from Vietnam. In a cruel twist of fate, 'Spike' Spinelli's wife Raye had lost her first husband during the Second World War when he was shot down over enemy territory.

1 October 1968

TA-4F   153523   H&MS-11, MAG-11, USMC, Da Nang
Capt J A Spaith (survived)
1Lt U S Grant (survived)

The 1st of October was not a good day for Marine Corps Skyhawks in Southeast Asia. The two-seat TA-4Fs of H&MS-11 were used for artillery observation as well as FAC and training duties. Capt Spaith and 1Lt Grant were on an artillery spotting mission when their aircraft was damaged by ground fire three miles southwest of Thon Cam Son, in the DMZ buffer zone. The aircraft sustained hits to the central fuselage and, although it did not catch fire, the Skyhawk had to be abandoned about eight miles off the coast. Both men were later rescued by a US Navy ship.

A-4E   151159   VMA-121, MAG-12, USMC, Chu Lai
1 pilot, name unknown (survived)

A VMA-121 Skyhawk aborted its take off on a combat mission and ran off the end of the runway. The aircraft caught fire and burnt out but the pilot escaped.

The USAF strike aircraft that fought the air war over North Vietnam relied on the KC-135 Stratotanker detachments to provide in-flight refuelling, without which much of North Vietnam would have been outside the range of aircraft based in Thailand. During the war KC-135s transferred about 1.4 billion gallons of fuel. *USAF*

A-4C   147767   VMA-223, MAG-12, USMC, Chu Lai
                            1Lt David I Habermacher (survived)

The second Skyhawk lost at Chu Lai this day belonged to VMA-223. As the aircraft was taking off on a ground-controlled bombing mission the starboard mainwheel tyre blew and separated from the wheel. The aircraft swerved and struck an arrester gear engine and a revetment. The Skyhawk then settled back onto the runway and 1Lt Habermacher ejected safely moments before the aircraft crashed and exploded.

Young Tigers: KC-135 Tankers

Although receiving little publicity, it is true to say that without the KC-135 tanker force the USAF's air war in Southeast Asia simply could not have taken place. The KC-135 was still in the process of replacing the ageing KB-50s and KB-97s in the tanker role when the war began. Eventually 729 KC-135 tankers were delivered to the USAF, the majority of them flying under SAC control.

Clark AB in the Philippines was the first temporary base for KC-135 tankers used in the early months of the war but more permanent bases were needed. In January 1965 the 4252nd SW was established at Kadena on the island of Okinawa in preparation for the start of Arc Light B-52 raids later in the year. Forward operating locations were also established at Don Muang and Takhli to provide support for tactical aircraft operations under the generic code name of Young Tiger. By the middle of 1965 there were 45 KC-135s based in the Southeast Asian theatre, the majority of them at Kadena. Refuelling areas for B-52s from Guam were situated near the northern tip of the Philippines while those for tactical aircraft were sited over Thailand, Laos and the Gulf of Tonkin. Occasionally, in cases of dire emergency, tankers would even cross the border to refuel aircraft over North Vietnam itself, although the risks of SAMs and MiGs made this a risky business.

To satisfy the ever-increasing requirement for more tanker support, more KC-135s started operations from Takhli in August 1966. By the end of the year there was a total of 75 KC-135s based in Southeast Asia. However, the basing of tankers at Takhli was not enough and a new airfield at Ching Chuan Kang on the Chinese Nationalist island of Taiwan was constructed to take KC-135s as well as a C-130 wing. Due to various delays in construction the first tankers did not move in to CCK, as it was invariably known, until February 1968.

In 1972 the number of KC-135s deployed to Southeast Asia began to swell as the tempo of the air war increased. By the end of June there were 60 KC-135s at Kadena with 46 at U-Tapao, 28 at Clark, 20 at Takhli, 13 at Don Muang and seven at Korat. Of the nominal total of 172 KC-135s available, 114 were earmarked for Young Tiger tactical missions and 58 for Arc Light and other strategic missions. September 1972 was the peak month of the war for tanker activity with a total of 2,661 Young Tiger and 1,241 Arc

Light sorties being flown. These 3,902 sorties involved the transfer of 159.6 million pounds of fuel in 12,509 refuellings.

In addition to supporting combat missions over Southeast Asia, tankers also made possible the rapid deployment of aircraft to the theatre from the USA, especially in 1972 when a large number of deployments were made. Bullet Shot deployments involved the move of B-52s to Andersen and KC-135s to U-Tapao and Kadena while a series of Constant Guard deployments brought in a number of A-7D, F-111 and F-4E units while redeploying other units that were displaced by the newer aircraft.

From June 1964 to August 1973 USAF tankers flew a total of 194,687 sorties in support of missions in Southeast Asia. During these sorties the aircraft made 813,878 refuellings and transferred a grand total of 8,963,700,000lbs of fuel, which equates to about 1.4 billion gallons.

In addition to the three KC-135s lost in Southeast Asia in 1968 and 1969, one other aircraft should be mentioned, as it was lost in connection with the war. On 24 September 1968 KC-135A 55-3133 of the 509 BW, attached to the 4258 SW, was returning SAC personnel from the war zone to the USA when it suffered an engine failure over the Pacific. The aircraft diverted to Wake Island but crashed during a missed approach killing 11 of the 52 on board. The accident was due to the failure to retract the spoilers (which had been deployed during the descent) during the overshoot.

2 October 1968

A-4E   151126   VA-164, USN, USS *Hancock*
                            Cdr Donald Edward Erwin (KIA)

A section of A-4s on a road reconnaissance mission ran into 85mm AAA near the village of Ngoc Long Ha, 20 miles northwest of Vinh. Cdr Erwin was jinking his aircraft in an attempt to avoid being tracked by the gunners but to no avail as his aircraft was hit in the wing. He turned his burning aircraft towards the sea, streaming a trail of leaking fuel. Cdr Erwin was unable to jettison his bombs and the fire was growing in intensity, so as soon as he crossed the coast he ejected. However, a split second after his seat fired, the aircraft exploded. The explosion probably stunned or killed Cdr Erwin as he did not surface after parachuting into the sea. One of the many small fishing boats seen in the area at the time probably retrieved the Commander's body as his remains were handed over to the US and identified in March 1990.

O-1F   57-2827   21 TASS, 504 TASG, USAF, Nha Trang
                            Maj A F Mason (survived)
                            Capt R Meadows (survived)

A Bird Dog was shot down by ground fire during an FAC mission about 10 miles northwest of Da Lat and 55 miles from its base at Nha Trang. The two crew survived their ordeal and were rescued by a US Army helicopter.

F-100D   55-3661   352 TFS, 35 TFW, USAF, Phan Rang
                            Maj D R Barron (survived)

On the night of the 2nd a flight of F-100s was scrambled from Phan Rang to bomb enemy troops and bunkers near That Son in the extreme southwestern corner of South Vietnam. Maj Barron's aircraft was damaged by small arms fire but it must have appeared not to have been serious as, instead of landing at Bien Hoa or Tan Son Nhut, he flew over 250 miles across South Vietnam, by-passed Phan Rang and attempted to land at Cam Ranh Bay. However, he had to eject over the sea close to the airfield and was rescued by a Navy boat.

KC-135A 55-3138   93 BW attached to 4258 SW, USAF, U-Tapao
                           Maj Dean L Beach (KIA)
                           1Lt Richard M Welch (KIA)
                           1Lt Robert C Profilet (KIA)
                           TSgt Earl B Estep (KIA)

The Number 4 engine of a KC-135 failed during its take off roll from U-Tapao on a tanker sortie over Thailand and Laos. The aircraft had already passed the point where it was committed to take off giving the pilot no option but to continue. However, the asymmetric thrust and the aircraft's heavy weight caused both nosewheel tyres to fail. The aircraft became airborne but hit the reinforced concrete and steel runway light stanchions 1,800 feet past the end of the runway and crashed, killing all on board.

3 October 1968

RF-8G   144620   Detachment 19, VFP-63, USN, USS *Hancock*
                          Lt James Lee Merrick (KIA)

During a photographic reconnaissance mission a Crusader suffered a control failure and pitched down into a 60-degree dive until it hit the water off the South Vietnamese coast. The pilot was killed in the accident.

C-7B   63-9753   537 TAS, 483 TAW, USAF, Phu Cat
                          Capt Wayne Philip Bundy (KIA)
                          1Lt Ralph Schiavone (KIA)
                          SSgt Donald Gene Cleaver (KIA)
                          SSgt James Kenneth Connor (KIA)
                          9 US Army passengers (KIA)

A C-7 collided with an Army CH-47A Chinook helicopter 66-19041 of the 228th Combat Support Aviation Battalion, 1st Cavalry Division, near Camp Evans. The Caribou took off from Camp Evans and made a climbing right hand turn before reaching the end of the runway. The CH-47, flown by CW2 T E Johnson and WO1 R L Conroy, was approaching Camp Evans from LZ Nancy on a regular shuttle flight with troops and mail and the two aircraft collided at 1,100 feet. One of the Chinook's rotor blades sliced through the Caribou's cockpit and another blade hit

the port engine. The Caribou spiralled into the ground and the Chinook's rear rotors separated and struck the helicopter's fuselage causing it to fall to the ground and explode. All four crew and nine passengers were killed in the Caribou and the five crew and six passengers were killed in the Chinook. This was the worst of a number of airspace control incidents during the war. Unfortunately several of these incidents involved the Caribous which the Army had turned over to USAF control in 1967.

5 October 1968

F-4D   66-8751   480 TFS, 366 TFW, USAF, Da Nang
Capt S L Lustfield (survived)
1Lt R E Walkup (survived)

A flight of Phantoms was scrambled to attack enemy mortar positions near Giang Hoa, 15 miles to the southwest of Da Nang. Capt Lustfield put his aircraft into a 10-degree dive to deliver his ordnance when he took several .50 calibre hits in the rear fuselage. The aircraft was soon engulfed in flames and the crew ejected a couple of miles from the target area. They were rescued by a USAF helicopter before the VC could reach them.

B-57B   52-1570   8 TBS, 35 TFW, USAF, Phan Rang
Maj Miller (survived)
Maj R Dyer (survived)

One of Phan Rang's Canberras crashed during a combat mission due to an accidental engine failure. This B-57 was yet another of its type that had served with the 38th TBG at Laon AB in France but it had also been flown by the Nevada ANG before transfer to Southeast Asia.

6 October 1968

A-7A   153273   VA-27, USN, USS Constellation
Lt(jg) G M Biery (survived)

The Corsair would become a very useful Iron Hand aircraft in due course of time and indeed was still being used in that role during Operation Desert Storm in Iraq in 1991. The Corsair was soon put to work as an Iron Hand aircraft in Vietnam equipped, like its predecessor the Skyhawk, with the Shrike anti-radar missile. However, on one of the aircraft's early SAM raids, the North Vietnamese came out on top. A strike force including an Iron Hand flight of Corsairs made a night raid on a SAM site that was known to be active near Phuc Bien, 15 miles north of Vinh. Lt Biery made his run against the site to launch his Shrike just as a missile lifted off. Unfortunately, the Shrike failed to fire and Lt Biery almost stalled as he made a high-G pull out at 10,000 feet. He saw the SAM detonate about 200 feet behind his aircraft, which immediately went out of control. The pilot ejected soon after crossing the beach and was quickly rescued by a Navy helicopter from the destroyer USS Richmond K Turner.

7 October 1968

C-7B   63-9745   535 TAS, 483 TAW, USAF, Vung Tau
3 crew, names unknown (survived)

A Caribou crashed in South Vietnam due to pilot error.

8 October 1968

O-2B   67-21457   9 SOS, 14 SOW, USAF, Nha Trang
1Lt Charles Henry Richardson (KIA)
A1C John Bradford Stevens (KIA)

The 9th SOS had been activated in January 1967 from a nucleus provided by the 5th SOS to perform psychological warfare operations in the two northernmost Corps regions of South Vietnam while the 5th SOS retained responsibility for the two southernmost Corps. In addition to its original C-47s and U-10s, the 9th SOS had received a number of Cessna O-2Bs. The mission included dropping millions of Chieu Hoi leaflets, which urged the Viet Cong to defect to the South Vietnamese government. The 9th SOS's aircraft could also be fitted with loudspeakers for broadcasting propaganda messages to the VC and their supporters. The first aircraft lost by the 9th was an O-2 that was shot down by small arms fire 15 miles northwest of Nha Trang during a leaflet dropping mission. This was one of only two O-2Bs to be lost during the entire war.

F-4B   152329   VMFA-115, MAG-13, USMC, Chu Lai
Capt Joseph W Jones (KIA)
Capt Daniel J Coonon (KIA)

A section of Phantoms from Chu Lai was attacking enemy positions 15 miles southwest of Da Nang when an aircraft failed to pull out of its dive, probably hit by ground fire. The navigator, Capt Coonon, had survived being shot down near Khe Sanh on Independence Day with a different pilot but this time there was no rescue possible for him.

13 October 1968

A-6A   154141   VA-52, USN, USS Coral Sea
Cdr Quinlen Roberts Orell (KIA)
Lt James D Hunt (KIA)

The USS Coral Sea took up its position on the line on 10 October for its fourth tour of duty in the war. Just three days later the ship lost its first aircraft in combat. An Intruder was launched on a night armed reconnaissance mission looking for traffic on the roads south of Vinh. Cdr Orell and Lt Hunt completed their mission and were egressing through a known AAA belt when they received a signal in their aircraft that told them a nearby Fan Song SAM radar had just 'lit them up'. The crew reported this to an orbiting EKA-3B, which promptly jammed the enemy radar. However, just as the Intruder was crossing the coast near the mouth of the Song Kanh Can River, 20 miles southeast of Vinh, it suddenly disappeared from the radar screen of a ship that had been tracking it. Despite an extensive search, no trace of the aircraft or its crew was ever found and the cause of its loss could not be determined.

A-1G   52-132542   602 SOS, 56 SOW, USAF, Nakhon Phanom
Capt Michael John Masterson (KIA)

Capt 'Bat' Masterson was flying a night mission near Ban Kangthat in central Laos when his aircraft's gyro toppled and his attitude indicator failed. He became disorientated in the darkness and radioed that he was ejecting. Although an extensive search of the area was made over the next few days, there was no sign of Capt Masterson who is presumed to have died in the jungles of Laos. Capt Masterston was of Canadian origin.

16 October 1968

O-1E   51-5001   19 TASS, 504 TASG, USAF, Bien Hoa
Maj Freddie Dale Dickens (KIA)

Maj Dickens was landing at the airfield at Tay Ninh after an FAC mission when his Bird Dog was shot down by ground fire just outside the base.

O-1E   56-2651   19 TASS, 504 TASG, USAF, Bien Hoa
1Lt George Barker Hamilton (KIA)

Another Bird Dog and its pilot were lost from Bien Hoa on the 16th when an aircraft crashed after its engine stalled accidentally.

17 October 1968

F-100D   55-2929   615 TFS, 35 TFW, USAF, Phan Rang
1Lt Mark Constant Chenis (KIA)

A Super Sabre pilot died when he aborted his take off from Phan Rang and overran the runway and crashed.

18 October 1968

RF-4B   151976   VMCJ-1, MAG-11, USMC, Da Nang
Maj J W Quist (survived)
1Lt D T Schanzenbach (survived)

VMCJ-1 lost one of its RF-4Bs during a photographic reconnaissance mission north of the DMZ. Maj Quist was making his photo run at 2,100 feet and at 600 knots when the aircraft was hit by ground fire. The port engine had to be shut down and the aircraft was turned out to sea. The crew had to eject five miles off the coast and about 30 miles north of Hué but they were soon pulled out of the water by a USAF SAR helicopter. This was the fourth and final RF-4B lost by the Marines during the Vietnam War although the type was still being used extensively up to the time VMCJ-1 left Da Nang in July 1970.

19 October 1968

F-4D   66-7740   480 TFS, 366 TFW, USAF, Da Nang
Lt Col Donald R D'Amico (survived)
1Lt Samuel F Wilburn (survived)

A Phantom (call sign Dover 01) was shot down by AAA during an armed reconnaissance mission just south of Dong Hoi. Lt Col D'Amico was strafing a gun emplacement when his aircraft was hit and one of the engines damaged. With the aircraft on fire, he flew out to sea and he and his WSO ejected about 15 miles off the coast northeast of the DMZ. Both men were eventually recovered by a USAF rescue helicopter although HH-3E 66-13282 from the 37th ARRS was hit by enemy fire from Tiger Island as it made a water landing and had to be abandoned. The helicopter crew was also rescued by other HH-3s. 1Lt Wilburn was doubly fortunate to be rescued in that he had been shot down a few weeks earlier while taking off from Da Nang on 26 August 1968.

O-2A   68-6870   19 TASS, 504 TASG, USAF, Bien Hoa
Capt Ralph Robert Wensinger (KIA)
Capt Anthony Joseph Pearson (KIA)

An O-2 crew was controlling an air strike on a VC base camp near the Perfume River, 10 miles south of Saigon, when their aircraft was shot down. Both men were killed when the aircraft crashed before they could escape.

20 October 1968

C-47D   45-0934   460 TRW, USAF, Tan Son Nhut
Lt Col Howard Elmer Van Vliet (KWF)
Lt Col Robert Brooks Richardson (KWF)
Lt Col Council Lee Royal (KWF)
Maj Gerald Eugene Burgener (KWF)
Maj Basil Lincoln Ciriello (KWF)
Maj Gerald Dean Ziehe (KWF)
Capt Gayland Omer Scott (KWF)
MSgt William Parker Bowman (KWF)
TSgt Donald William Bruck (KWF)
TSgt Billy Ray Morris (KWF)
TSgt John Derral Thomas (KWF)
SSgt Eugene William Hendricks (KWF)
11 passengers (KWF)

Most wings and bases in South Vietnam and Thailand had a C-47 for communications flying at some time in the war. They were used to fly personnel between bases and sometimes to rest and recuperation centres, Bangkok and Hong Kong being particular favourites. In the early morning the 460th TRW's C-47 took off from Tan Son Nhut for a flight to Hong Kong with a refuelling stop at Da Nang. As the aircraft was flying over mountainous terrain near Ban Me Thuot the pilot made a Mayday call saying that the Number 2 engine had failed and the propeller could not be feathered. He requested vectors to the airfield at Ban Me Thuot but the aircraft crashed in poor weather and pre-dawn darkness. The wreckage was found about 20 miles south of Ban Me Thuot at an elevation of 2,300 feet and all 23 passengers and crew, including two US civilians, had been killed. Curiously, 12 of the occupants are listed as crew members on this flight.

21 October 1968

RB-57E   55-4264   Detachment 1, 460 TRW, USAF, Tan Son Nhut
Maj J W Johnston (survived)
Maj Philip N Walker (survived)

In over five years of operations the Patricia Lynn detachment had only lost a single aircraft until 21 October 1968. One of the unit's aircraft was making a sensor run over a VC position three miles southeast of the town of Truc Giang in the Mekong Delta when it was hit. Flying straight and level at 2,000 feet, the aircraft ran into small arms fire that damaged the starboard engine causing it to catch fire. Moments later the two crew ejected and were later recovered with only minor injuries. The Patricia Lynn missions continued until the unit was inactivated in August 1971 and the four surviving RB-57s returned to the USA.

A-4E   151160   VA-106, USN, USS Intrepid
Lt Kenneth Keith Knabb (KIA)

A section of Skyhawks found a truck on a road in the hills about 20 miles south of Ha Tinh during a strike mission. Lt Knabb started a strafing run on the truck from about 6,500 feet but his aircraft was then seen to explode as it hit the ground. A partially deployed parachute was seen lying close to the wreck but there was no sign of Lt Knabb. By the time a rescue helicopter arrived the parachute had been spread out on the ground in a perfect circle indicating either that Lt Knabb was trying to attract his rescuers' attention or that the North Vietnamese were using the parachute as a lure to trap the helicopter. The cause of the aircraft's loss was never determined and Lt Knabb was presumed to have been killed in the incident. This Skyhawk was the last aircraft to be lost before the end of the *Intrepid's* third and final tour of duty in Southeast Asia. The ship returned to Norfolk, Virginia, on 8 February 1969 and and decommissioned on 15 March 1974. The carrier has been moored in New York Harbour since 1982 as a floating museum.

A-1E   52-132646   1 SOS, 56 SOW, USAF, Nakhon Phanom
Maj W L Bagwell (survived)
A North Vietnamese storage area had been discovered near the village of Ban Nakok, 20 miles east of Nakhon Phanom. A flight of Skyraiders was despatched to destroy the site but it was well protected. Maj Bagwell was making his second dive-bombing run on the target when his aircraft was hit in the port wing by enemy fire. The aircraft caught fire and the pilot was obliged to eject a couple of miles from the target. Maj Bagwell was safely rescued the following day by a USAF HH-53 flown by Lt Col Royal Brown and his crew from Nakhon Phanom. Maj Bagwell was also shot down over the Plain of Jars on 28 June 1969 and once more survived the incident.

A-4E   151122   VMA-223, MAG-12, USMC, Chu Lai
Capt David A Wellman (survived)
As a Skyhawk was landing back at Chu Lai from a night attack mission the aircraft was displaced to the right of the runway centreline and its wing struck the arresting gear revetment. As the aircraft continued along the runway its starboard wing separated and Capt Wellman was lucky to escape with just an injured shoulder. The aircraft was damaged beyond repair.

22 October 1968

OV-10A   155422   VMO-2, MAG-16, USMC, Marble Mountain
Capt Eugene William Kimmel (KIA)
Capt Rodney Rene Chastant (KIA)
VMO-2 lost its second Bronco during a tactical air control mission near the village of Giang Hoa, 12 miles southwest of Da Nang. The aircraft was hit by ground fire as it marked targets for strike aircraft under a low cloud base. Both the crew were killed when the aircraft crashed. A Marine Corps UH-1E landed and recovered the body of one of the crew before being forced to leave the area as the VC closed in. The UH-1 then called in an air strike on the area. Capt Chastant, a Marine infantry officer, had started his tour in Vietnam in July 1967.

KC-135A   61-0301   99 BW attached to 4252 SW, USAF,
Ching Chuan Kang
Capt Kent V Allison, 454 BW (KWF)
Capt Mark F White, 454 BW (KWF)
1Lt James J Hayes, 454 BW (KWF)
SMSgt Howard B Benge, 454 BW (KWF)
SSgt Robert T Goyette, 99 BW (KWF)
Sgt Robert Dudek, 99 BW (KWF)
During a night approach at the end of a logistics support flight a KC-135 tanker from the Ching Chuan Kang detachment descended below the minimum safe approach altitude and struck a mountain about 1,000 feet below its 7,300 feet summit and some 47 miles from Ching Chuan Kang. The flight crew were on temporary deployment from the 901st ARS of the 454th BW, Columbus AFB, while two maintenance men and the aircraft belonged to Westover's 99th BW.

23 October 1968

F-100D   55-2921   612 TFS, 37 TFW, USAF, Phu Cat
1Lt R E Bryan (survived)

A flight of F-100s from Phu Cat flew north to fly a close air support mission in Military Region I a few miles southwest of Hué. 1Lt Bryan was strafing enemy positions when he ran into a hail of .50 calibre gunfire. He headed towards the sea and ejected about five miles off the coast where he was rescued by a Navy ship. 1Lt Bryan was shot down again during a Misty FAC sortie on 12 January 1969.

O-2A   67-21394   20 TASS, 504 TASG, USAF, Da Nang
Maj Marion E Reed (KIA)
The 20th TASS lost two O-2 pilots in two separate incidents on the 23rd. Maj Reed was marking a target in the DMZ buffer zone within two miles of the coast when he was lost. His aircraft was hit by ground fire as he rolled in on his target and he was unable to escape from the O-2 before it crashed.

O-2A   68-6883   20 TASS, 504 TASG, USAF, Da Nang
Capt Richard L Edwards (KIA)
About one hour after Maj Reed was killed, Capt Edwards was marking an enemy position for an air strike about 15 miles south of Da Nang. His aircraft was hit by ground fire at 1,500 feet and crashed in flames before he could escape.

24 October 1968

F-4D   66-0264   390 TFS, 366 TFW, USAF, Da Nang
Maj George Edward Tyler (KIA)
1Lt Darrell L Richardson (survived)
A Phantom was lost in North Vietnam during a night strike on a truck park near Phu Qui, five miles west of Dong Hoi. As Maj Tyler turned over the target at 3,000 feet, his aircraft was hit by 57mm AAA and burst into flames. Both crew ejected close to the target and 1Lt Richardson spent the night suspended in his parachute from a tree. He was rescued at first light by a USAF HH-3 of the 40th ARRS from Nakhon Phanom. Maj Tyler could not be found and did not appear as a POW so is presumed to have been killed in the incident or during capture.

27 October 1968

A-1H   52-139735   6 SOS, 633 SOW, USAF, Pleiku
Lt Col V J Cole (survived)
A flight of Skyraiders from Pleiku was despatched on a Steel Tiger mission to bomb a storage area 15 miles northeast of Muang Fangdeng in the extreme southern tip of Laos. Lt Col Cole was making his first run dropping napalm when his aircraft was hit by 37mm AAA. The pilot ejected close to the target but managed to evade enemy forces until a USAF helicopter rescued him.

F-105D   62-4264   34 TFS, 388 TFW, USAF, Korat
1Lt Robert Clifton Edmunds (KIA)
A flight of F-105s was sent out on a night-time armed reconnaissance mission over the hills northwest of Dong Hoi. The flight found a target near Quang Khe, about 25 miles northwest of Dong Hoi, but one of the aircraft was hit in the fuselage by AAA during the attack. The aircraft crashed in flames shortly afterwards and the pilot may have been wounded, as he was not observed to eject. 62-4264 was named 'Rompin Rudy' and carried a stylised painting of a reindeer.

27/28 October 1968

RF-4C   65-0846   11 TRS, 432 TRW, USAF, Udorn
Capt William Harry Stroven (KIA)
Capt Kenneth Arnold Stonebraker (KIA)
A reconnaissance Phantom set off from Udorn on a night-time Sea Dragon mission along the coast of North Vietnam. The aircraft failed to return from the mission and was presumed lost just to the west of Dong Hoi. No sign of the aircraft or its crew has ever been found as far as is known.

28 October 1968

TA-4F   154304   H&MS-13, MAG-13, USMC, Chu Lai
Capt Charles R Connor (KIA)
Lt William Ernest Ricker, USN (KIA)

A two-seat Skyhawk from MAG-13, using the call sign Love Bug 50, was returning from a target spotting mission south of Hué when it disappeared. The crew had reported that they had completed their mission and were over the sea and flying down the coastline to return to Chu Lai. The reason for its loss could not be determined. Lt Ricker was a US Navy officer flying with the Marines on an exchange posting.

30 October 1968

RF-4C   66-0457   11 or 14 TRS, 432 TRW, USAF, Udorn
Maj R E Boucher (survived)
Capt R D Smith (survived)
A reconnaissance Phantom crashed in Thailand due to accidental engine failure.

31 October 1968

A-7A   153175   VA-27, USN, USS *Constellation*
1 pilot, name unknown (survived)
A Corsair crashed due to accidental engine failure during a combat mission. The pilot ejected safely.

The End of Rolling Thunder
On 31 October President Johnson, under growing pressure from public opinion at home and with no signs that the North Vietnamese were about to back down, announced that the bombing of North Vietnam would cease the following day. The Rolling Thunder bombing campaign against North Vietnam had started on 2 March 1965 but during its 44-month history its overall effectiveness was severely restricted by political limitations and the resourcefulness of the North Vietnamese. So began a three-and-a-half year bombing halt against North Vietnam that would last until April 1972. In the meantime reconnaissance missions could still be flown and these were often escorted by F-4s or F-105s. The defences in North Vietnam at the time of the bombing halt were formidable and consisted of 8,000 anti-aircraft guns, 400 radars, 150 MiGs and 40 SA-2 sites. During the halt the North Vietnamese took the opportunity to reinforce their air defences in all areas in case the Americans should resume their bombing.

1 November 1968

F-4J   155742   VMFA-334, MAG-11, USMC, Da Nang
Capt G S Libey (survived)
1Lt W H Frizell (survived)
The last missions of Rolling Thunder were flown on the afternoon of 1 November and the last aircraft lost in the campaign was a Marine Corps Phantom. VMFA-334 lost the second of its new F-4Js during an attack on NVA positions near Vinh Linh, two miles north of the DMZ. Capt Libey had started his second bombing run when his Phantom was struck by groundfire that damaged the port wing. Capt Libey flew the aircraft out over the sea where he and his navigator ejected about six miles from the coast. A Navy helicopter picked up the pilot while the navigator was rescued by the Australian destroyer HMAS *Perth*.

5 November 1968

A-4E   152046   VMA-211, MAG-12, USMC, Chu Lai
1 pilot, name unknown (survived)
On the day that Richard Nixon was elected as the 37th President of the USA a Marine Corps Skyhawk suffered engine failure during a strike mission and had to be abandoned just off the coast of South Vietnam.

9 November 1968

F-100D   56-3446   615 TFS, 35 TFW, USAF, Phan Rang
Capt Roger Edward Wichman (KIA)
A flight of F-100s was returning to Phan Rang from a close air support mission when one of the aircraft was hit by ground fire near the village of Thon Vu Bon, 10 miles southwest of the airfield. Capt Wichman tried to reach Phan Rang but the aircraft caught fire and although he appears to have ejected north of the airfield, he was killed during the incident.

The F-105 Thunderchief was the USAF's main strike aircraft during the Rolling Thunder campaign during which nearly 350 F-105s were lost. All these Takhli Wing aircraft eventually survived the war and served with Air National Guard squadrons. USAF

F-4B   152209   VMFA-115, MAG-13, USMC, Chu Lai
                  2 crew, names unknown (survived)

During the monsoon season in Southeast Asia one of the extra hazards that aircrew had to contend with was that of wet runways. Heavy rain often did not drain away from the runway surfaces fast enough and when mixed with rubber residue from thousands of take offs and landings, the result was a very slick surface. On the 9th a Marine Corps Phantom ran off a wet runway as it was taking off from Chu Lai. The aircraft was damaged and caught fire as it hit obstructions and was completely burnt out.

11 November 1968

O-1F   57-2952   21 TASS, 504 TASG, USAF, Nha Trang
                   Maj J R Albright (survived)

A Bird Dog was hit by small arms fire during an FAC mission about 15 miles southwest of Nha Trang. The aircraft did not appear to be too badly damaged at first but later in the mission the engine stopped. Maj Albright was injured in the ensuing crash landing but was recovered by a US Army helicopter.

A-4E   149660   VMA-311, MAG-12, USMC, Chu Lai
                  Capt Phillip D Barger (KIA)

The Marines lost a Skyhawk on the 11th during a close air support mission near Phu Loc, 25 miles northwest of Da Nang. Capt Barger was preparing to make a second pass to drop napalm when his aircraft was hit by small arms fire. The aircraft crashed close to the target before Capt Barger could eject.

OV-10A 67-14631   19 TASS, 504 TASG, USAF, Bien Hoa
                   2 crew, names unknown (survived)

The 19th TASS began to receive the OV-10 in August and lost its first aircraft (and the first USAF OV-10 to be lost in Southeast Asia) when it suffered an engine failure during a training flight. Both crew ejected safely, becoming the first men to survive the crash of a Bronco in Southeast Asia.

12 November 1968

F-100D 56-3438   306 TFS, 31 TFW, USAF, Tuy Hoa
                   1 pilot, name unknown (survived)

A Super Sabre crashed due to engine failure during an attack mission in South Vietnam. The engine failure was caused by a mechanical fault rather than by enemy action.

13 November 1968

F-4C   64-0800   559 TFS, 12 TFW, USAF, Cam Ranh Bay
                   Maj Joseph W Buchanan (KIA)
                   1Lt Jose C Santos (KIA)

A Phantom was lost during a close air support mission near Katum close to the border with Cambodia. Maj Buchanan was making a napalm run on an enemy position from 200 feet when his aircraft was hit by automatic weapons fire. The aircraft crashed before either of the crew could escape. Friendly troops later arrived on the scene and confirmed that the crew had been killed.

14 November 1968

O-1E   56-4207   19 TASS, 504 TASG, USAF, Bien Hoa
                   Capt William Hillric Fabian (KIA)
                   Capt C B Gannaway (survived)

A Bird Dog was hit by ground fire as it was orbiting at 1,500 feet during an FAC mission near Phuoc Vinh, 35 miles north of Saigon. The aircraft crashed close to enemy troops and although the pilot was killed, the observer survived the crash and was later rescued by an Army helicopter. Capt Fabian's remains were recovered post-war and were buried at Arlington National Cemetery.

15 November 1968

F-8H   147923   VF-211, USN, USS Hancock
                  Lt P R Scott (survived)

As a Crusader was returning from a combat air patrol it struck the ramp of the Hancock as it was about to touch down. The pilot was fortunate to survive.

16 November 1968

F-100D 56-2935   615 TFS, 35 TFW, USAF, Phan Rang
                   Maj C R Hollis (survived)

A night-time close air support mission near the town of Vi Thanh in the southwestern tip of South Vietnam was badly affected by poor weather. Maj Hollis was dropping napalm on his second pass when his Super Sabre was struck by automatic weapons fire. The aircraft burst into flames and the pilot ejected safely to be picked up later by an Army helicopter.

O-1F   57-2820   21 TASS, 504 TASG, USAF, Nha Trang
                   detached to Pleiku
                   Maj Carl Frederick Karst (KIA)
                   Capt Nguyen X Quy, VNAF (KIA)

An O-1 failed to return to Pleiku from a visual reconnaissance mission about 20 miles to the southeast. When the aircraft became overdue a search was commenced but was called off three days later when nothing was found. A few months later a Vietnamese villager reported that he had heard from an NVA propaganda team that Maj Karst and his Vietnamese observer had been shot down by small arms fire. According to the North Vietnamese, Capt Quy had been killed and Maj Karst had been captured and then executed in a village in northern Phu Bon province. The veracity of this story could not be checked but in December 1983 a Vietnamese refugee in Malaysia handed over two bone fragments and an identity tag bearing Maj Karst's name. Again, it is known whether these artefacts were genuine or fake. However, in 1989 the Vietnamese turned over some human remains that were eventually identified as being those of Maj Karst. The Major's remains were buried at Arlington National Cemetery in October 1993.

F-100D 55-3653   615 TFS, 35 TFW, USAF, Phan Rang
                   Maj Robert Charles Wiechert (KIA)

A Super Sabre crashed off the coast during a mission in South Vietnam. It was concluded that the pilot had probably suffered from spatial disorientation during a manoeuvre and lost control of the aircraft.

17 November 1968

F-4B   149456   VMFA-115, MAG-13, USMC, Chu Lai
                  Capt Paul D Derby (KIA)
                  1Lt Thomas A Reich (KIA)

A Marine Corps Phantom was shot down during a close air support mission against enemy troops three miles southwest of Ha Thanh and 25 miles southwest of Chu Lai. The aircraft was making its first run at 500 feet to drop napalm canisters when it was hit by ground fire in the cockpit area, possibly incapacitating the pilot. The aircraft crashed in the target area and both crew died in the crash.

F-105D serial ..?   34 TFS, 388 TFW, USAF, Korat
                      1 pilot, name unknown (survived)

During a strike mission a Thunderchief started to lose oil pressure, which eventually led to the engine seizing up. The pilot ejected safely and was rescued.

F-100D 56-3452   309 TFS, 31 TFW, USAF, Tuy Hoa
                   Capt Welch (survived)

O-2A   67-21378   23 TASS, 504 TASG, USAF, Nakhon Phanom
                   Capt Grenoble (survived)

An F-100 and an O-2 collided in mid-air over South Vietnam. It is possible that the O-2 was controlling the strike for the F-100 flight. Fortunately, both pilots survived their ordeal and were rescued by Jolly Green 15, an HH-3 captained by Lt Col Royal Brown.

OV-10A Bronco 67-14625 is seen in action over the Mekong Delta in August 1969. The aircraft is firing smoke rockets to mark a target for the strike aircraft under its control.
USAF

18 November 1968

B-52D 55-0103   367 BS, 306 BW attached to 4252 SW,
                   USAF, Kadena
                   Capt Charles D Miller (KIA)
                   5 crew, names unknown (survived)

The increasing need for Arc Light B-52 sorties following the Tet Offensive and the USS *Pueblo* incident outstripped the resources of U-Tapao and Andersen and the USAF decided to deploy a single squadron of 15 aircraft to Kadena and 11 more aircraft to Andersen. This brought the total number of B-52s available for Arc Light operations to 105, the peak figure until the 1972 Bullet Shot reinforcement. The first squadron was provided by the 91st BW from Glasgow AFB, Montana, but later the 306th BW from McCoy AFB, Florida, arrived on rotation from Guam and was parented by the tanker-equipped 4252nd SW. The mission times for aircraft based at Kadena was half that of those based at Andersen, although the weather was more of a factor than on Guam. The Kadena squadron flew Arc Light missions until September 1970 when the B-52s at Andersen and Kadena were stood down and returned to the USA leaving U-Tapao to continue B-52 operations.

The first of two B-52s lost at Kadena crashed on take off when the aircraft failed to accelerate sufficiently. The pilot aborted the take off but the aircraft went off the end of the runway and ran into soft earth. The fuel tank in the fuselage burst and fuel sprayed onto the ECM operator who was burned to death. The rest of the crew escaped with minor injuries before the bomb load exploded. This crash resulted in riots and demonstrations by Okinawan students and trade union members who were opposed to the presence of the B-52s on the island.

19 November 1968

F-4D   66-8807   390 TFS, 366 TFW, USAF, Da Nang
                   Maj Yale Rezin Davis (KIA)
                   1Lt John Norman Reilly (KIA)

A Phantom was hit by automatic weapons fire as it was about to land back at Da Nang following an escort mission. The aircraft crashed immediately and neither of the crew were able to escape before it hit the ground.

20 November 1968

F-100F 56-3775   416 TFS, 37 TFW, USAF, Phu Cat
                   Capt Frank T Kimball (survived)
                   Capt Lawrence K Irving (survived)

The Commando Sabre detachment was losing aircraft at a rate of about four times that of the standard F-100 squadrons in South Vietnam. The sixth aircraft lost in 1968 was the first Misty to be shot down in Laos. The aircraft was hit by ground fire near the village of Ban Pro in southern Laos as the crew were checking out enemy positions on the Trail. Capt Kimball headed east but the crew had to abandon the aircraft when the engine failed. They were both rescued by an HH-3E flown by Lt Col John J Devlin, commander of the 37th ARRS.

21 November 1968

A-4C   148608   VA-216, USN, USS *Coral Sea*
                   Cdr Marvin Joel Naschek (KIA)

A Skyhawk was catapulted off the *Coral Sea* on a strike mission but instead of climbing away it was seen to lose altitude until it crashed into the sea. Sadly, the pilot did not survive the accident.

RF-4C 66-0432   14 TRS, 432 TRW, USAF, Udorn
                   Capt P N Shiraishi (survived)
                   Capt E U Larue (survived)

Both engines of an RF-4C flamed out due to fuel starvation as it was returning to Udorn from a photographic reconnaissance mission. The crew ejected close to the airfield.

22 November 1968

O-2A   68-6859   23 TASS, 504 TASG, USAF, Nakhon Phanom
                   Maj Richard C Swift (KIA)
                   Capt Ivan J Campbell (KIA)

An O-2 FAC struck a tree and crashed near Nakon Phanom, killing both the crew.

23 November 1968

RF-4C 66-0445   14 TRS, 432 TRW, USAF, Udorn
                   Capt Bradley Gene Cuthbert (KIA)
                   Capt Mark John Ruhling (POW)

The 14th TRS lost its second aircraft within three days on the 23rd, but this time it also lost a crew. Capt Cuthbert and Capt Ruhling were photographing a SAM site and sections of a road near Van Loc, 10 miles northwest of Dong Hoi, when their aircraft was hit by ground fire. The port wing started to burn and the crew ejected close to Dong Hoi itself. Capt Ruhling was captured soon after he landed but Capt Cuthbert did not survive to reach a POW camp and was probably killed by his captors. Mark Ruhling was on his 84th mission when he was shot down and was released from captivity on 14 March 1973. Bradley Cuthbert was shot down on his 28th birthday. His remains were returned in 1990 and positively identified on 20 December 1991. This was the first US aircraft lost over North Vietnam since the end of the Rolling Thunder campaign.

25 November 1968

RA-5C 149293   RVAH-5, USN, USS *Constellation*
                   Cdr Ernest Albert Stamm (POW – died)
                   Lt(jg) Richard Cobb Thum (KIA)

The second US reconnaissance aircraft lost over North Vietnam during November was a Vigilante which was flying a photographic reconnaissance mission near the 19th Parallel. The aircraft was tracked by an anti-aircraft battery near Van Tap, 20 miles northwest of Vinh, causing Cdr Stamm to jink the aircraft in an attempt to throw the gunners off their aim. As the Vigilante was flying at 5,500 feet and 550 knots, the escorting pilots saw the aircraft suddenly explode and break into four major pieces. One of the escorts saw flak burst near the aircraft a few seconds prior to the explosion but others also heard a Fan Song SAM radar. Two parachutes were seen although neither crew survived even though it was thought that Cdr Stamm was captured but probably died before he reached a POW camp.

F-4D   66-7523   555 TFS, 432 TRW, USAF, Udorn
                   Maj Joseph Castleman Morrison (KIA)
                   1Lt San Dewayne Francisco (KIA)

An escort for another photographic reconnaissance mission was shot down on the 25th. An F-4 from Udorn was shot down by AAA near the Ban Karai Pass. Both the crew ejected safely but they landed close to an NVA encampment in the jungle. Voice contact was made with Maj Morrison and 1Lt Francisco and it is known that Morrison evaded successfully throughout the night. The rescue forces spoke to Maj Morrison in the morning but were unable to attempt a pick up due to bad weather. By the time the weather had improved contact had been lost with both men and they were never heard from again. It would appear that they were captured and killed by enemy forces. The crew's identity papers and other personal effects were later displayed in the museum of the 280th Air Defence Regiment and an official North Vietnamese photograph clearly shows the dead body of Maj Morrison.

Commando Hunt

The ending of the Rolling Thunder campaign against North Vietnam released a large number of aircraft for use in the interdiction campaign over the Ho Chi Minh Trail. The first Commando Hunt interdiction campaign started on 15 November 1968 and eventually seven such campaigns were flown over southern Laos, corresponding to wet or dry seasons as dictated by the monsoon climate of Southeast Asia. The campaigns were intended to reduce the flow of arms and men from North Vietnam to the South and to destroy as much equipment and ordnance as possible. However, the problems of finding and destroying targets on the Trail remained as difficult as ever and the resourceful North Vietnamese always found ways to keep the troops in South Vietnam supplied with enough arms and reinforcements. The US employed its full range of available air power in the Commando Hunt operations and also introduced a number of new weapons and techniques. The B-52s, tactical fighters and the AC-119 and AC-130 gunships played a major part in the campaigns and the AC-130 Spectre was claimed to be the most effective aircraft in killing trucks. Unfortunately, most of the evidence since the war indicates that the number of trucks killed and the amount of supplies destroyed was greatly exaggerated. The series of campaigns came to an end on 10 April 1972 when Operation Linebacker started and just weeks after North Vietnam had proved its success in resupplying troops in the field by launching the Spring Invasion.

26 November 1968

O-2A   67-21419   20 TASS, 504 TASG, USAF, Da Nang
                   Capt Gregg Hartness (KIA)
                   1Lt A S Shepherd (survived)

In the very early hours of the 26th an O-2 took off from Da Nang for a visual reconnaissance of the Ho Chi Minh Trail in Laos, southwest of the DMZ. Just over one hour into the flight the aircraft was hit in the tail by 37mm anti-aircraft fire as it was flying near the village of Ban Katao at 8,000 feet. As the aircraft started to spin down out of control, Capt Hartness ordered 1Lt

Shepherd to bail out, which he did successfully. 1Lt Shepherd was picked up by a USAF helicopter about three hours later but there was no sign of Capt Hartness and he may not have escaped from the aircraft before it crashed.

27 November 1968

A-4E   150111   MAG-12, USMC, Chu Lai
A Skyhawk was destroyed at Chu Lai when its jumped it chocks and smashed into a building near fuelpits.

28 November 1968

C-130B   61-2644   772 TAS, 463 TAW, USAF, Clark
5 crew, names unknown (survived)
At the conclusion of a ferry flight, the nose gear of a Hercules failed on landing at Tonle Cham in South Vietnam causing irreparable damage to the aircraft.

F-4D   66-7646   390 TFS, 366 TFW, USAF, Da Nang
Maj Thomas Laird Brattain (KIA)
1 crew, name unknown (KIA)
A wet runway caused another accident when a Phantom veered off the runway and exploded, killing the crew.

29 November 1968

F-100D   56-3237   352 TFS, 35 TFW, USAF, Phan Rang
1Lt W L Cook (survived)
A Super Sabre was lost during a close air support mission near Phu Hiep, 45 miles west of Phan Rang. A flight of F-100s was attacking enemy troops in a mountainous region that overlooked Phu Hiep and Dalat. 1Lt Cook's aircraft was hit by small arms fire during the attack causing him to eject. He was rescued by a USAF helicopter before the enemy troops could find him.

2 December 1968

O-1G   156685   VMO-6, MAG-36, USMC, Quang Tri
1Lt James Robert Reese (KIA)
1Lt Richard Eli Latimer (KIA)
VMO-6 had deployed to South Vietnam in August 1965 equipped with the UH-1E for observation and gunship support of MAG-36's helicopter squadrons. However, in July 1968 the Squadron received a small number of O-1 aircraft for reconnaissance and forward air control duties. The O-1 flight soon took over FAC and observation duties from the UH-1Es allowing the helicopters to concentrate on the gunship role to which they were more suited. VMO-6 lost its first O-1 while it was on a visual reconnaissance mission about 15 miles southwest of Quang Tri. The crew spotted enemy troops and the pilot dived on them to mark their position but the aircraft was hit by .30 calibre gunfire and crashed. 1Lt Reese and his infantry observer, Lt Latimer, were killed. Although this was the sixth Bird Dog the Marines had lost in Vietnam, it was the first one to be lost in combat. The O-1G was an FAC conversion of the basic O-1A Bird Dog and only eight were completed for the Marines.

B-52D   55-0115   367 BS, 306 BW attached to 4252 SW,
USAF, Kadena
The 306th BW lost another B-52 at Kadena when an aircraft burnt out in a ground fire accident prior to an Arc Light mission.

3 December 1968

OV-10A   155411   VMO-2, MAG-16, USMC, Marble Mountain
1Lt Robert Lyon Norton (KIA)
1Lt Robert Arthur Carney (KIA)
VMO-2 lost its third Bronco during a visual reconnaissance mission for an artillery unit six miles southwest of Da Nang. The crew had finished their mission and were about to return to base but radioed that they were going to take a look at an area known as 'Happy Valley'. The aircraft's wreckage was later found in the jungle having dived in vertically, killing both the crew. It was presumed that the aircraft had been shot down by ground fire in the valley, which was shrouded by low cloud forcing the aircraft to fly very low.

F-4D   66-7499   497 TFS, 8 TFW, USAF, Ubon
Maj C L Gallanger (survived)
1Lt D K Chastain (survived)
A Phantom was lost in southern Laos during a Night Owl mission over the Ho Chi Minh Trail. Maj Gallanger's aircraft was hit by AAA as it patrolled over a road near Ban Senphan, south of the Mu Gia Pass. Both crew ejected safely and were later rescued by a USAF HH-53 flown by Capt Harwood from Nakhon Phanom.

6 December 1968

F-105D   61-0053   357 TFS, 355 TFW, USAF, Takhli
Capt R M Walker (survived)
Another USAF aircraft was lost during a Steel Tiger mission in southern Laos. Dallas flight was a flight of four F-105s that was bombing a POL storage site near Ban Soppeng, when one of its aircraft was hit by 57mm anti-aircraft fire as it dived on the target. Capt Walker flew a few miles away from the target before ejecting. He was picked up by an HH-3 flown by Lt Col Royal Brown and his crew from Nakhon Phanom.

8 December 1968

A-1J   52-142033   602 SOS, 56 SOW, USAF, Nakhon Phanom
Maj T H O'Connor (survived)
Two Skyraiders were lost in northern Laos during a Barrel Roll mission against enemy troops near Sopka, 20 miles west of Sam Neua. Maj O'Connor was strafing on his third pass against the troops when his aircraft was hit by small arms fire. The fuselage started to burn and the pilot ejected after flying a few miles away from the enemy forces. He was eventually rescued by a USAF SAR helicopter but not before another Skyraider and its pilot had been lost trying to rescue him.

A-1J   52-142035   602 SOS, 56 SOW, USAF, Nakhon Phanom
Capt Joseph Samuel Pirrucello (KIA)
Two hours after Maj O'Connor was shot down, Capt Pirrucello was flying RESCAP for the rescue helicopters. There was sporadic ground fire from many enemy positions around Sopka and the Skyraiders were bombing and strafing in order to suppress the fire long enough for the Jolly Greens to make the rescue. Capt Pirrucello was making a strafing run when his aircraft was hit by small arms fire. He may have been wounded by the ground fire, as he was not seen to eject.

F-105D   61-0150   354 TFS, 355 TFW, USAF, Takhli
1Lt Robert Alan Rex (KIA)
About 20 minutes after Capt Pirrucello was shot down, another USAF aircraft was shot down on an unrelated Barrel Roll mission. A flight of four F-105s was sent to bomb a truck storage site in the mountains near Ban Na Kham, 12 miles west of Sam Neua. The FAC controlling the strike saw 1Lt Rex's aircraft start its dive on the target and continue, without dropping its bombs, until it hit the ground. No ejection was seen and it was presumed that the pilot had died in the incident. In 1994 a joint US and Laotian investigation team excavated the site of an aircraft crash near Sopka and recovered human remains and personal items. The remains were taken to the US Army's Central Identification Laboratory in Hawaii and positively identified as being those of Robert Rex in July 1996. Mitochondrial DNA testing was used to confirm identification in addition to normal forensic methods.

9 December 1968

RF-4C   64-1048   11 TRS, 432 TRW, USAF, Udorn
Maj R I McCann (survived)
Capt J B Koebberling (survived)
The 11th TRS had a particularly bad month, losing three aircraft and two men during December. The first aircraft to be brought down was on a photographic reconnaissance mission over the Sou Giang River near Trung Tan, 25 miles northwest of Dong Hoi, when it was hit. Maj McCann was making his second photo run in the area at 7,000 feet and 540 knots when his Phantom was hit by 37mm AAA. Maj McCann turned east towards the coast and he and Capt Koebberling ejected one mile offshore. They were subsequently rescued by a USAF SAR helicopter.

10 December 1968

A-1H   52-134508   602 SOS, 56 SOW, USAF, Nakhon Phanom
Capt J J Jenkinson (survived)
The area around Sopka in northern Laos was still the centre of attention for the Skyraiders from NKP. A flight of aircraft was attacking enemy troops and mortar postions about five miles to the southeast of the village, when one of the aircraft was hit by 12.7mm anti-aircraft fire as it dived on the target for the third time. Capt Jenkinson coaxed his burning aircraft a few miles to the south, away from the enemy forces, before ejecting from the Skyraider. He was later rescued by a USAF SAR helicopter.

12 December 1968

RF-4C   65-0820   11 TRS, 432 TRW, USAF, Udorn
Capt Harlan J Drewry (survived)
Capt Russell Dale Galbraith (KIA)
The second RF-4C lost during December was on a night photographic reconnaissance mission over the Steel Tiger area of southern Laos. Capt Drewry was flying along a road near Ban Muangsen when his aircraft was hit by ground fire. Drewry lost control of the aircraft and ejected and thought that Capt Galbraith had also managed to eject, although he never saw him again. Capt Drewry was rescued by an HH-3 from Nakhon Phanom the following morning and a Road Watch team searched for Galbraith but found nothing. Russell Galbraith never returned from Southeast Asia and was declared dead for administrative purposes in August 1978.

13 December 1968

B-57E   55-4284   8 TBS, 35 TFW, USAF, Phan Rang
Maj Thomas Wayne Dugan (KIA)
Maj Francis Jay McGouldrick (KIA)

C-123K   54-0600   606 SOS, 56 SOW, USAF, Nakhon Phanom
Lt T M Turner (survived)
1Lt Joseph Peter Fanning (KIA)
1Lt John Scott Albright (KIA)
1Lt Douglas Vincent Dailey (KIA)
1Lt Morgan Jefferson Donahue (KIA)
SSgt Samuel Franklin Walker (KIA)
TSgt Frederick Lee Clarke (KIA)
The tactical fighter-bombers that worked over the Ho Chi Minh Trail at night often relied on the light of flares provided by Candlestick C-123s from the 606th SOS. These aircraft would patrol the trail all night often working in conjunction with the B-57s from Phan Rang as well as A-1s, A-26s, F-4s and T-28s from Thailand. The Candlestick C-123 was both an FAC and a flareship combined. Using Starlight Scopes the C-123s did much to find and mark targets in the northern sector of the Steel Tiger area, while the Blind Bat C-130s concentrated on the southern sector. However, the mission had its dangers, not just from the enemy but from the operational hazards of flying at night with few precision navigational aids over mountainous terrain. At 3:30 in the morning of the 13th A Candlestick aircraft spotted a target near Ban Nampakhon, 20 miles southwest of the Ban Karai Pass in southern Laos. A pair of B-57s was called in to hit the target but during the bomb run one of the Canberras struck the C-123. The Canberra crashed immediately, killing both the crew, and the Provider started a slow spin towards the ground. The Provider's pilot, Lt Turner, was temporarily knocked unconscious, and when he came to he saw that the other flight deck crew had already gone. Lt Turner bailed out and landed in a tree where he stayed until he was rescued at dawn by an HH-3 flown by Capt Harwood and his crew from Nakhon Phanom. As Lt Turner floated down he saw at least one other parachute below him, but no more men were rescued from the aircraft. Information received since the war lends credence to claims that the navigator, 1Lt Donahue, may have survived the crash and been captured. As late as 1987 1Lt Donahue's family received seemingly credible information that indicated he was still being held captive in Laos. However, there have been no new developments since then and, officially at least, he remains listed as killed in action.

AC-47D 43-49274 3 SOS, 14 SOW, USAF, Nha Trang det to
Bien Hoa
Maj F D Reeder (survived)
1Lt P N Rose (survived)
Several other crew, unknown (survived)

OV-10A 67-14627 19 TASS, 504 TASG, USAF, Bien Hoa
Capt Charles Farrell Griffin (KIA)
Capt Bruce Briant Greene (KIA)

By a strange coincidence, another mid-air collision resulted in the loss of two more USAF aircraft at the opposite end of Indo-China on the night of the 13th. A Viet Cong night attack on an outpost six miles southeast of Truc Giang in the Mekong Delta resulted in the scramble of a number of aircraft from Bien Hoa. An AC-47 was directed to the target and started to drop flares to assist the defenders as it orbited at 3,500 feet. The crew of the Dakota felt a bump and the aircraft became difficult to control. The aircraft had been hit by an OV-10 FAC that was co-ordinating the aircraft in the vicinity of the target. Both aircraft headed back towards Bien Hoa but the OV-10 crashed northwest of Saigon killing both the crew. The AC-47 gunship eventually landed at Bien Hoa but its undercarriage collapsed and the aircraft was so badly damaged that it was scrapped. This was the only aircraft lost by the 3rd SOS during it 17-month existence in Vietnam.

TA-4F 153501 H&MS-11, MAG-11, USMC, Da Nang
2 crew, names unknown (survived)
One of MAG-11's two-seat Skyhawks crashed during an attack mission after the aircraft suffered an electrical failure.

14 December 1968

O-2A 67-21308 19 TASS, 504 TASG, USAF, Bien Hoa
1 pilot, name unknown (survived)
An O-2 FAC crashed in South Vietnam following a control failure. The pilot was injured but survived.

16 December 1968

F-100D 55-2920 612 TFS, 37 TFW, USAF, Phu Cat
Capt J A Nugent (survived)
A Super Sabre was damaged by ground fire during a night close air support mission in the hill country, 35 miles northwest of Nha Trang. With his engine showing signs of damage, Capt Nugent was directed to fly west towards the town of Lac Thien where he ejected and was picked up by an Army helicopter.

17 December 1968

C-123K 54-0708 309 SOS, 315 SOW, USAF, Phan Rang
Capt Kenneth Roy Crist (KIA)
1Lt Roger Henry Strout (KIA)
SSgt Jesse John Bradshaw (KIA)
1 crew, name unknown (survived)
During a ferry flight a Provider crashed due to a fuel transfer problem that eventually led to engine failure. Three of the four crewmen were killed in the accident. The names of the crew are assumed from the Vietnam Wall database as being the only USAF personnel killed while flying in Military Region I on this day.

18 December 1968

A-6A serial ..? VA-196, USN, USS Constellation
Lt(jg) John Richards Babcock (KIA)
Lt Gary Jon Meyer (KIA)
An Intruder was lost during a daylight Steel Tiger strike on a road just within Laos, about 15 miles southeast of the A Shau Valley. Four aircraft were working on the target under the control of a USAF FAC aircraft. Lt Babcock's aircraft was rolling in on the target at 10,000 feet when it suddenly became enveloped in flames and dived into the ground. No ejection or parachutes were seen and it was assumed that the crew had died in the aircraft. The loss of the aircraft was put down to either anti-aircraft fire or the premature detonation of its own bombs.

F-100C 54-1931 136 TFS, 31 TFW, USAF, Tuy Hoa
1Lt H W Roberts (survived)
The New York ANG squadron lost an aircraft during an air interdiction mission on the 18th. A flight of aircraft took off from Tuy Hoa but one of the F-100s was hit by small arms fire five miles west of the airfield as it climbed away. For some reason, instead of returning to Tuy Hoa, 1Lt Roberts flew his damaged F-100 all the way to Da Nang where he ejected off the coast. He was rescued by a USAF helicopter. This was the fifth and final aircraft lost by the 136th TFS before it returned home to Niagara Falls on 25 May 1969.

A-1H 52-137546 22 SOS, 56 SOW, USAF, Nakhon Phanom
Maj Gregory Inman Barras (KIA)
The 22nd SOS started operations at Nakhon Phanom in late October and replaced the T-28s of the 606th SOS in the night interdiction role. A night armed reconnaisance mission over the Ho Chi Minh Trail ended in disaster on the night of the 18th. Maj Barras was attacking trucks on Route 12 near the village of Ban Sang, 10 miles west of the Mu Gia Pass, when his aircraft was seen to crash and explode. He may have flown into the ground or he may have been wounded by ground fire as there was no indication that he had escaped from his aircraft before it crashed. Apparently the pilot's body was buried near the wreck by a Laotian villager and Maj Barras's remains were recovered and identified in 1998.

19/20 December 1968

A-6A 154152 VA-196, USN, USS Constellation
Lt Michael Lora Bouchard (KIA)
Lt Robert W Colyar (survived)
Another Intruder was lost in December during a night strike on a truck park on the Trail near Ban Tanook, 20 miles southwest of the A Shau Valley. An FAC cleared Lt Bouchard's aircraft in for its bombing run at 5,500 feet and 510 knots under the light of flares. Suddenly the aircraft's starboard wing was blown off by flak and the crew ejected. It is not known if Lt Bouchard ejected safely although other aircraft in the area picked up two emergency beepers for a short time. Once on the ground Lt Colyar searched for his pilot for about half an hour but the area was crawling with enemy troops so he left the area and was fortunate to be picked up by a USAF helicopter the following day. Three Bright Light search teams also failed to find any trace of Lt Bouchard despite searching for several days.

20 December 1968

F-100D 55-3647 306 TFS, 31 TFW, USAF, Tuy Hoa
Maj Forrest B Fenn (survived)
The Tuy Hoa Wing lost a Super Sabre from one of its regular squadrons during a strike at dusk in southern Laos. Maj Fenn was making his second pass over the target near Ban Kate, close to the DMZ, when his aircraft was hit in the forward fuselage by AAA. He ejected close to his target and evaded successfully until he was picked up by an HH-3E of the 40th ARRS the next day. Maj Fenn was the 1,500th man to be saved by the SAR forces in Southeast Asia since the beginning of the war. Lt L Eagan, who was a US Coast Guard pilot attached to the Squadron, captained the helicopter on this mission. Maj Fenn had already had a narrow escape on 24 August 1968 when he force landed a badly damaged F-100D at Binh Thuy after receiving battle damage over Laos.

21 December 1968

F-105D 61-0089 354 TFS, 355 TFW, USAF, Takhli
Capt Richard Kenneth Allee (KIA)
A flight of four F-105s was sent on a Steel Tiger mission against enemy troop positions near Ban Senphan, just south of the Mu Gia Pass. As Capt Allee made his first dive on the target his Thud was hit by ground fire, burst into flames and dived into the jungle near the target. Capt Allee did not eject and may have been wounded by the enemy fire. In 1996 a crash site that had been located two years earlier was excavated and humans remains discovered that were identified in May 1998 as those of Capt Allee.

22 December 1968

RF-4C 65-0906 11 TRS, 432 TRW, USAF, Udorn
Capt Terry Lynn Greenhalgh (KIA)
1Lt R E Hoffman (survived)
The 11th TRS lost its third RF-4C of December (and its eighth of the year) during a Steel Tiger mission. The aircraft was hit in the port wing by anti-aircraft fire during a photographic reconnaissance mission over southern Laos. Capt Greenhalgh managed to fly the badly damaged aircraft all the way back to Udorn but was killed during the subsequent crash landing. His navigator, 1Lt Hoffman, survived with only minor injuries.

24 December 1968

F-4B 149427 VMFA-314, MAG-13, USMC, Chu Lai
Capt Robert Duane Kent (KIA)
1Lt Richard Girard Morin (KIA)
A Marine Corps F-4 was lost in the early hours of the 24th during a night mission over the Trail in southern Laos. Capt Kent was bombing several trucks on a road near Ban Palin, 30 miles southwest of Khe Sanh, when his aircraft was hit by AAA and crashed. Neither of the crew were seen to eject.

F-105D 62-4234 354 TFS, 355 TFW, USAF, Takhli
Maj Charles Richard Brownlee (KIA)
The loss of a Thunderchief and its pilot during a Steel Tiger strike in southern Laos resulted in a sequence of events that also led to the death of a PJ. Maj Brownlee's flight was attacking trucks on a road near Ban Topen near the Ban Karai Pass. His aircraft was hit by ground fire but he managed to fly a few miles to the west before ejecting near Ban Paphilang. Maj Brownlee spoke to his wingman on his emergency radio and reported that he was injured. As it was getting dark Brownlee was told to take cover for the night and expect a rescue attempt at first light. At dawn on Christmas Day an HH-3 flown by Maj Reinhart from Detachment 1 of the 40th ARRS arrived on the scene and A1C Charles Douglas King, the PJ, was lowered about 100 feet to the ground. He found Maj Brownlee hanging in his parachute suspended from branches but A1C King freed him and fastened the pilot's body to the jungle penetrator. Suddenly enemy troops closed in and started firing at King and the hovering helicopter. King told the helicopter pilot that he was hit and to move away. The helicopter began to pull up but the cable snagged a tree and both A1C King and Maj Brownlee fell to the ground. The helicopter was hit in the cockpit and a fuel tank and had to leave the area. A two-day search failed to find any trace of the missing men. According to a Laotian refugee who arrived in the USA in February 1986, A1C King had been captured and taken away in a truck but his eventual fate remains unknown although his identity papers were later seen on display in Hanoi's Central Army Museum. A1C King was posthumously awarded the AFC. Maj Brownlee's aircraft was painted as 'Sweet Thirza May' during its time at Takhli.

26 December 1968

F-100D 56-2968 416 TFS, 37 TFW, USAF, Phu Cat
Capt N H Duncan (survived)
An F-100 was lost during a Steel Tiger strike on a truck park in southern Laos. Capt Duncan was returning from the raid when his aircraft was hit by small arms fire near the village of Ding in southern Laos, 40 miles west of Kham Duc. Although the engine was damaged, Capt Duncan continued into South Vietnam and almost made it home but was forced to eject just three miles short of Phu Cat's runway.

29 December 1968

F-100C 54-1973 120 TFS, 35 TFW, USAF, Phan Rang
Capt J E O'Neill (survived)
The last aircraft to be lost during 1968 was another F-100 that was shot down during a close air support mission over South Vietnam. Capt O'Neill was making his third pass on a target near Vi Thanh in the extreme southwest of the country when his aircraft was damaged by ground fire. Capt O'Neill attempted to fly back to Phan Rang but was forced to eject when the aircraft became uncontrollable. An Army helicopter quickly picked him up.

1969

Interdiction on the Ho Chi Minh Trail

3 January 1969

A-4C 147764 VA-216, USN, USS *Coral Sea*
Lt(jg) R M Aaron (survived)

The only Navy aircraft lost in combat during the whole of January was a Skyhawk that was shot down while on a Steel Tiger mission in southern Laos. A pair of Skyhawks was attacking a 37mm gun position near Ban Thakkapang, about 20 miles northeast of Muang Fangdeng. As Lt Aaron was pulling up from his bomb run he felt the engine vibrate so he pushed the throttles wide open to climb to 21,000 feet to give himself plenty of altitude. He crossed the coast near Chu Lai but the engine settings began to fluctuate so he tried to restart the engine twice without success. He ejected about 10 miles off the coast and was rescued by a Marine Corps helicopter.

4 January 1969

F-100C 54-2051 188 TFS, 31 TFW, USAF, Tuy Hoa
Maj Bobby Gene Neeld (KIA)

F-100C 54-2030 188 TFS, 31 TFW, USAF, Tuy Hoa
Capt Mitchell Sim Lane (KIA)

Following a successful attack mission a flight of two New Mexico ANG F-100s was diverted from landing back at Tuy Hoa because of bad weather. The pair headed towards Cam Ranh Bay and requested a VFR radar approach to the airfield. Nothing more was heard from either pilot and a search was instigated but without result. It was suspected that the aircraft had collided and crashed a few miles to the northwest of the air base.

6 January 1969

F-4D 66-8763 435 TFS, 8 TFW, USAF, Ubon
Capt R B Meyers (survived)
Capt S Faulkner (survived)

A Wolfpack Phantom had to be abandoned over Thailand when it ran out of fuel as it was returning to base.

The F-102 Delta Dagger

The F-102 Delta Dagger first began to re-equip PACAF fighter interceptor squadrons in March 1959. By June 1960 five squadrons had received the F-102; the 4th FIS at Misawa AB, Japan, the 16th FIS at Naha AB, Okinawa, the 40th FIS at Yokota AB, Japan, the 68th FIS at Itazuke AB, Japan, and the 509th FIS at Clark AB, Philippines. It was the last named squadron that bore much of the burden of combat duty in Southeast Asia. The F-102 first arrived in the war zone for air defence duties as early as August 1961 when four aircraft from the 509th FIS deployed to Bangkok's Don Muang Airport in Thailand under the code name Bell Tone. The 509th FIS also sent four aircraft to Tan Son Nhut on 22 March 1962 following reports of possible North Vietnamese aircraft activity south of the DMZ. The early F-102 rotations to Southeast Asia consisted of routine GCI missions but no threat ever transpired. The F-102 detachments returned to Clark in May 1963. On 5 August 1964, following the escalation of the war after the Gulf of Tonkin Incident, six F-102s of the 16th FIS

were sent to Tan Son Nhut and operated as a detachment of Clark's 405th FW. A further six aircraft from the 509th FIS arrived at Da Nang the same day. F-102 detachments remained in Southeast Asia but by July 1965 the 509th FIS was the last F-102 squadron left in PACAF as all the other squadrons had re-equipped with the F-4C. Despite an inventory of 42 Delta Daggers the 509th FIS had difficulty maintaining the detachments at Bien Hoa, Da Nang, Tan Son Nhut, Udorn and Don Muang, so two F-102 squadrons were transferred from the USA as reinforcements. The 82nd FIS arrived at Naha on 18 February 1966 while the 64th FIS deployed to Clark on 11 June 1966. The 64th joined the 509th FIS in providing detachments to the bases in Southeast Asia.

Although air defence was the F-102's primary task the aircraft was also used for combat air patrol, Arc Light escort, and even close air support and air interdiction. The F-102s were known to have used their infra-red seekers to search for traffic on the Ho Chi Minh Trail and fire Falcon air-to-air missiles at blips on the radar. The aircraft also used 2.75 inch unguided rockets against ground targets, but without much success. On 15 December 1969 the 64th FIS was inactivated at Clark leaving the 509th to soldier on until 24 July 1970. The last F-102 squadron in PACAF was the 82nd FIS, which inactivated at Naha on 31 May 1971, thereby bringing to an end the F-102's 12-year service in PACAF.

7 January 1969

F-4C 63-7588 557 TFS, 12 TFW, USAF, Cam Ranh Bay
Capt W F Needham (survived)
1Lt S D Adams (survived)

A Phantom was shot down as it was attacking Viet Cong positions only two miles north of Tan Son Nhut airport. Capt Needham was making his third pass when his aircraft was hit in the tail and set alight by ground fire. The crew ejected seconds later but being so close to Tan Son Nhut they were quickly picked up by one of the base HH-43s.

F-102A 56-1186 509 FIS, 405 FW, USAF, Don Muang or Udorn
Capt Thomas B Orr (KIA)

During an escort mission an F-102 pilot reported a loss of engine oil pressure. The aircraft subsequently crashed in Thailand and the pilot was killed. This particular aircraft had previously protected the US capital when it served with the 95th FIS at Andrews

AFB, Maryland and was the last of 14 F-102s lost in Southeast Asia during eight years of detachments to a variety of bases.

10 January 1969

A-1H 52-137496 6 SOS, 633 SOW, USAF, Pleiku
Maj J B Wheeler (survived)

The 6th SOS lost two Skyraiders within about an hour of each other on the 10th. Maj Wheeler was attacking enemy positions in the A Shau Valley when his aircraft was hit by .50 calibre ground fire. Maj Wheeler headed away from the Valley but was forced to eject over the hills 25 miles southwest of Da Nang. He was later recovered and returned to Pleiku.

A-1H 52-137559 6 SOS, 633 SOW, USAF, Pleiku
Maj Arthur Roy Sprott (KIA)

When Maj Wheeler went down Maj Sprott and others hurried to his aid to provide cover for a rescue attempt. On the way to his downed colleague, Maj Sprott's aircraft was shot down by ground fire about 12 miles southwest of Da Nang. Although Maj Wheeler was lucky and was eventually rescued, Maj Sprott ejected but was killed and became yet another Spad pilot to die in an attempt to save a downed airman. His body and partially deployed parachute were later found by a pararescueman but as Maj Sprott's body was being lifted into a Jolly Green Giant it fell from the hoist and could not be recovered as it was getting dark.

11 January 1969

O-1G 51-16951 22 TASS, 504 TASG, USAF, Binh Thuy
Capt Francis Joseph Birchak (KIA)
2Lt V T Nguyen, VNAF (KIA)

A Bird Dog was shot down during a visual reconnaissance mission at Cao Lanh near the Mekong River and 65 miles southwest of Saigon. Capt Birchak and his Vietnamese observer were both killed when the aircraft crashed in flames.

F-105D 61-0072 354 TFS, 355 TFW, USAF, Takhli
Maj W M Thompson (survived)

A flight of Thunderchiefs bombed a truck park that had been found on the Trail near Ban Nammi in southern Laos. Maj Thompson's aircraft was hit by 37mm anti-aircraft fire causing serious damage that forced him to eject a few miles to the west. He was later rescued by an HH-3E flown by Lt Col Royal Brown and his crew.

The F-102 Delta Dagger saw just over a decade of service in Southeast Asia as detachments from Clark AB and bases in Japan rotated into five bases in South Vietnam and Thailand. Only 14 F-102s were lost during the war, four of them in airbase attacks. USAF

The F-4E variant of the Phantom was the first model to be fitted with an integral gun and was first deployed to Southeast Asia in November 1968. This aircraft, which later served with the 21st Composite Wing at Elmendorf AFB, Alaska, is from Korat's 469th TFS. USAF

12 January 1969

F-100F 56-3995   612 TFS, 37 TFW, USAF, Phu Cat
Capt R F Cassaro (survived)
1Lt R E Bryan (survived)

The first Misty FAC to be shot down in 1969 was lost during a mission near Ban Tok in southern Laos. Capt Cassaro was pulling up through 2,000 feet from his second pass over a target when the Super Sabre was hit by ground fire. Capt Cassaro crossed back into South Vietnam but he and 1Lt Bryan were forced to eject about 30 miles west of Da Nang and were later rescued. 1Lt Bryan had been shot down before while on a close air support mission near Hué on 23 October 1968.

F-4B 151441   VMFA-323, MAG-13, USMC, Chu Lai
1Lt W C Ryan (survived)
1Lt Gary L Bain (survived)

During a strike mission the crew of a Phantom noticed flames coming from the portside rear fuselage and was forced to eject. The loss was attributed to mechanical failure rather than enemy action. This was the last of 11 Phantoms lost by VMFA-323 during its long residence at Chu Lai. Apart from two brief rotations to Iwakuni the Squadron had been in South Vietnam since December 1965 and had flown around 17,000 close air support, escort and strike sorties. The Squadron left Vietnam in March and transferred to the 3rd MAW at El Toro MCAS in California.

13 January 1969

B-57B 52-1561   8 TBS, 35 TFW, USAF, Phan Rang
Lt Col Norman Dale Eaton (KIA)
Capt Paul Everett Getchel (KIA)

A Canberra failed to return from a Steel Tiger night interdiction mission over southern Laos. The aircraft was seen to go down in flames about 10 miles south of the A Shau Valley and although no ejection or parachutes were seen, a faint emergency beeper was heard briefly by an FAC pilot in the area. However, a search the next day revealed no sign of the two crew, who are presumed to have perished in the incident.

The F-4E Gunfighter

One of the main problems with the otherwise superb F-4 Phantom was the lack of an internal cannon to supplement its air-to-air missiles and its air-to-ground ordnance. The Phantom was designed at a time when reliance on the missile was thought to have made a gun unnecessary. However, operational use in Vietnam had proved that there were still occasions when a gun was vital. Although the aircraft could carry an external gun pod this resulted in a loss of performance due to the extra weight and drag. A major redesign of the aircraft culminated in the production of the F-4E version. This model had a M61A1 Vulcan rotary cannon in an extended nose as well as other improvements over previous models. The F-4E was first delivered to the 33rd TFW at Eglin AFB in early 1968. The 40th TFS from Eglin supplied the first aircraft and crews which deployed to Korat on 17 November to re-equip the 469th TFS, replacing its F-105s. The 469th flew its first combat mission with the new aircraft on 26 November. The Korat-based 34th TFS re-equipped with the F-4E during May

1969 and the 366th TFW at Da Nang received two F-4E squadrons during the spring.

14 January 1969

F-4E 67-0294   469 TFS, 388 TFW, USAF, Korat
Maj Emil E Boado (KIA)
1Lt Joseph G Wilson (KIA)

The first F-4E variant of the Phantom to be lost in Southeast Asia was destroyed in an accident in Thailand. Unfortunately, neither of the crew escaped from the aircraft.

16 January 1969

A-4F 155059   VA-155, USN, USS *Ranger*
Cdr John Herbert Weaver (KIA)

The *Ranger* had rejoined TF 77 on 12 November 1968 for its fourth war cruise, commencing operations on the line 17 days later. Its first casualty was a Skyhawk that apparently made a normal catapult launch only to descend into the sea and explode. Sadly, the pilot was killed in the accident, the cause of which was never positively identified.

17 January 1969

F-4D 66-8773   390 TFS, 366 TFW, USAF, Da Nang
Capt Victor Arlon Smith (KIA)
1Lt J R Fegan (survived)

A Stormy FAC was lost when a flight of Phantoms was despatched on an armed reconnaissance mission over southern Laos. The flight spotted an anti-aircraft gun position in a valley near Ban Vangthon and rolled in to bomb it. The aircraft were met by a light barrage of 37mm ground fire and Capt Smith's aircraft was hit, setting the wing on fire. The WSO ejected first, as was normal for the Phantom, but it is not known if Capt Smith ejected from the aircraft before it crashed. In a large-scale rescue effort 1Lt Fegan was eventually rescued by a USAF HH-53 but Capt Smith, who had served in the US Marine Corps before joining the USAF, was never found. The rescue of 1Lt Fegan was probably the most intensive rescue effort of the war so far involving 284 aircraft sorties over several days.

A-1H 52-134632   602 SOS, 56 SOW, USAF, Nakhon Phanom
Lt Col Lurrie J Morris (survived)

About 90 minutes after Capt Smith's Phantom was shot down a flight of Skyraiders was orbiting near the crash site providing RESCAP coverage for the SAR helicopters. One of the Skyraiders was hit by AAA at 5,500 feet and limped away a few miles to the south before Lt Col Morris ejected safely. He was picked up by a 40th ARRS rescue helicopter the following day although not before another helicopter had been shot down. Jolly Green 67 was an HH-53B (66-14430 of the 40th ARRS from Nakhon Phanom) that was taking part in the SAR mission for the Stormy FAC crew and Lt Col Morris. The helicopter was recovering Lt Col Morris when it was hit by intense ground fire, lost it's hydraulic system and made a crash landing nine miles southeast of Tchephone, Laos. Pararescueman Sgt Thomas Pope was hit in the leg and was saved from falling out of the helicopter by his fellow PJ, Don Johnson. Minutes later Jolly Green 70 landed in the face of heavy

ground fire and picked up everyone from Jolly Green 67 as well as Lt Col Morris. A little while later strike aircraft were ordered to destroy Jolly Green 67 to prevent the NVA from capturing it intact. Lt Col Morris was the CO of the 602nd SOS

A-6A 152586   VMA(AW)-242, MAG-11, USMC, Da Nang
Capt Edwin James Fickler (KIA)
1Lt Robert John Kuhlman (KIA)

A Marine Corps Intruder failed to return from a low-level strike mission at night in the A Shau Valley border region. The aircraft was almost certainly shot down by ground fire or flew into the ground during a low-level attack. There was no indication that either of the crew had ejected from the aircraft.

C-7A 60-5434   536 TAS, 483 TAW, USAF, Vung Tau
5 crew, names unknown (survived)

A Caribou transport veered off the runway as it was landing and was damaged beyond repair.

18 January 1969

A-1H 52-134588   602 SOS, 56 SOW, USAF, Nakhon Phanom
Capt Robert Franklin Coady (KIA)

As the SAR effort to rescue Lt Col Morris and the Phantom crew continued, the 602nd lost another aircraft and its pilot. On the morning of the 18th four Skyraiders arrived on the scene a few miles south of Ban Kate. The flight attacked enemy troops in the area in the face of intense 37mm anti-aircraft fire. Capt Coady was seen in a shallow dive over the target when his aircraft was hit by AAA and crashed into a wooded hillside. He was not seen to eject from the aircraft. Robert Coady was declared dead in 1978. In July 1992 the crash site of this aircraft was investigated by a Joint US/Laotian team that found a number of personal items in the wreckage but no remains.

O-2A 67-21350   20 TASS, 504 TASG, USAF, Da Nang
Maj G H Blair (survived)
2Lt W E Townsley (survived)

As the search for the downed airmen was going on between Ban Kate and Ban Vangthon, an O-2 was going about its business about 15 miles to the south. The aircraft was flying near the village of Ban Palin in order to assess damage done to trucks on the Trail during the previous night. As the aircraft was flying at 7,500 feet it was hit by AAA and the tail was damaged. Unable to control the aircraft, the pilot and observer bailed out and landed near the wreckage. They were both rescued by a USAF HH-53 helicopter from the 40th ARRS although 2Lt Townsley was badly injured. The A-1 escorts dropped CBU-19 tear gas cannisters during the rescue to keep NVA troops away from the downed crew.

20 January 1969

F-100D 55-3704   615 TFS, 35 TFW, USAF, Phan Rang
1Lt J D James (survived)

Five USAF F-100s were lost in separate incidents over three days from 20 January. 1Lt James was dropping napalm on a target five miles south of Vinh Long in the Mekong Delta when he was shot down by ground fire. The Super Sabre's wing caught fire and he ejected near his target but was later rescued by an HH-43.

21 January 1969

F-100D 56-3113   352 TFS, 35 TFW, USAF, Phan Rang
Capt F E Davis (survived)

A Super Sabre was damaged by ground fire during a close air support mission in South Vietnam. Capt Davis ejected just off the coast 10 miles south of Phan Thiet and was rescued by a Navy vessel. This pilot may have been the 'F F Davis' was who shot down with the 352nd TFS on 30 June 1968.

F-100D 55-3513 612 TFS, 37 TFW, USAF, Phu Cat
1Lt J R Nichols (survived)

A flight of F-100s was sent to attack a truck storage area just to the west of the Ban Karai Pass on the border between Laos and North Vietnam. One of the aircraft was hit by AAA and badly damaged. 1Lt Nichols headed southeast and eventually crossed the coast. However, he was forced to eject from his crippled aircraft just off the coast near the Marine Corps airfield at Chu Lai.

F-100D 56-3158 615 TFS, 35 TFW, USAF, Phan Rang
Capt Milo George Maahs (KIA)

A Super Sabre pilot was killed during a close air support mission 10 miles southeast of Katum near the Cambodian border. His aircraft was damaged by ground fire during a napalm run. Capt Maahs then flew south and reached Bien Hoa but he was killed when his aircraft crashed on the approach to the airfield.

22 January 1969

F-4B 152260 VMFA-115, MAG-13, USMC, Chu Lai
1Lt W E Collins (survived)
1Lt Daniel Joseph Minahan (KIA)

The first Marine Corps Phantom lost to enemy action in 1969 was shot down during a close air support mission 17 miles south of Hué. The aircraft was dropping napalm on enemy troops when it was hit in the cockpit by ground fire. Although the pilot tried to make for the coast the aircraft only managed to fly a couple of miles before the crew were forced to eject. Both crew were recovered by helicopter, but the navigator, 1Lt Minahan, was found to be dead and the pilot badly injured.

F-100F 56-3886 355 TFS, 37 TFW, USAF, Phu Cat
Maj J M Grathwol (survived)
Capt Colin Arnie Clarke (survived)

Another Misty FAC was lost during a Steel Tiger mission. Maj Grathwol and Capt Clarke were flying a visual reconnaissance mission over southern Laos when their aircraft was damaged by automatic weapons fire. The aircraft headed back towards base but the crew were forced to eject over the hills 40 miles west of Chu Lai and 12 miles east of the deserted camp at Kham Duc. They were both rescued by a USAF SAR helicopter. Capt Clarke had been shot down very early in the war on 18 August 1964 in a single-seat F-100 and later distinguished himself while flying an A-7D Corsair during a RESCAP mission on 16 November 1972.

24 January 1969

F-4C 64-0767 558 TFS, 12 TFW, USAF, Cam Ranh Bay
Maj R D Russ (survived)
1Lt R J Rybak (survived)

A Phantom was lost during a close air support mission in the A Shau Valley region. Maj Russ was making his second bomb run from 3,000 feet when his aircraft was hit by .50 calibre ground fire. The port engine was damaged and caught fire and the crew ejected close to the border between South Vietnam and Laos, 25 miles southwest of Hué. Maj Russ and 1Lt Rybak were later rescued by a USAF SAR helicopter.

A-4E 151097 VMA-223, MAG-12, USMC, Chu Lai
Capt Michael P Green (survived)

While flying a close air support mission for the 1st Marine Division, Capt Green's Skyhawk was hit by small arms fire on its fourth pass near Thuong Duc, 20 miles southeast of Da Nang. He flew due east and ejected three miles out to sea where he was picked up by a US Navy vessel and returned safely to Chu Lai. This was the last of 14 Skyhawks lost by VMA-223 before its final departure from South Vietnam on 28 January 1970. The Squadron had flown a total of 32,068 sorties in 38,375 flying hours and dropped 34,260 tons of ordnance during its time in Southeast Asia.

Super Sabre 56-3158 of the 614th TFS is seen here flying over Phan Rang, home of the 35th TFW. On 21 January 1969 this aircraft was damaged by ground fire during a strike near Katum and Capt M G Maahs of the 615th TFS was killed when he attempted to make an emergency landing at Bien Hoa. USAF

F-4D 65-0725 433 TFS, 8 TFW, USAF, Ubon
Lt Col R W Clement (survived)
Capt J A Nash (survived)

The Wolfpack suffered its first combat loss of 1969 during a Steel Tiger mission in southern Laos. A flight of Phantoms scouted along a road about 10 miles east of Ban Talan on the lookout for trucks or other targets. The flight attacked a target but Lt Col Clement's aircraft was hit in the fuselage by 37mm AAA. The aircraft burst into flames and the crew ejected safely a few miles to the west. The crew was eventually recovered by an HH-53B piloted by Lt Eagan of the US Coast Guard.

F-100F 56-3731 614 TFS, 35 TFW, USAF, Phan Rang
1Lt J D Muller (survived)
Capt G G Potter (survived)

One of Phan Rang's two-seat Super Sabres was taking part in a close air support mission near Truc Giang in the Mekong Delta, 40 miles southwest of Saigon. 1Lt Muller was diving at a target when his aircraft was hit by ground fire. The crew ejected a few miles to the south and 1Lt Muller was rescued by an Army helicopter while Capt Potter was picked up by a USAF HH-43.

25 January 1969

F-4C 64-0739 557 TFS, 12 TFW, USAF, Cam Ranh Bay
Maj P E Gushwa (survived)
1Lt W J Arland (survived)

A formation of Phantoms attacked a .50 calibre gun site near A Sap, 25 miles southwest of Hué. One of the aircraft was damaged by return fire during the attack and burst into flames. Maj Gushwa headed towards Hué but he and his WSO had to eject about 15 miles from the city. The crew was rescued by friendly ground troops. This particular aircraft had shot down a MiG-17 on 15 May 1967 when flown by Maj W L Kirk and 1Lt S A Wayne of the 433rd TFS.

F-4E 67-0286 469 TFS, 388 TFW, USAF, Korat
Maj Russell Keith Utley (KIA)
1Lt Daniel Everett Singleton (KIA)

The first F-4E version of the Phantom lost in combat in Southeast Asia was shot down on a night interdiction mission over the Ho Chi Minh Trail. Maj Utley and 1Lt Singleton made an attack on an intersection point near Ban Kate. During the attack the aircraft was seen to crash, probably as a result of anti-aircraft fire. No parachutes were seen or emergency beepers heard and it was presumed that both men had been killed in the crash.

25/26 January 1969

F-100C 54-1956 120 TFS, 35 TFW, USAF, Phan Rang
F-100D 56-3301 35 TFW, USAF, Phan Rang

Two Super Sabres, including one from the Colorado Air National Guard squadron, were destroyed on the ground during an attack by the NVA's H-13 Sapper Company on the night of the 25/26th at Phan Rang. A total of 74 rounds of 82mm mortars and 107mm rockets were fired at the base and 11 other aircraft were damaged and 15 men wounded. Fourteen of the enemy soldiers were killed and one was captured during the raid. The damage might have been even worse had a sapper attack, using satchel charges and grenades, not been discovered and turned back by the base's security police.

27 January 1969

C-130E 63-7780 776 TAS, 314 TAW, USAF, Ching Chuan Kang
A Hercules was caught on the ground and destroyed during a Viet Cong mortar attack at night on the airfield at Tonle Cham, near the Cambodian border with South Vietnam.

F-4C 63-7441 559 TFS, 12 TFW, USAF, Cam Ranh Bay
Maj Robert J Cameron (KIA)
Capt Thomas G Burge (KIA)

As a Phantom was taking off from Cam Ranh Bay on a close air support mission it struck the runway barrier equipment, veered off the runway and started to travel across rough ground. One of the bombs it was carrying exploded and the aircraft was blown to pieces, killing both crew instantly.

28 January 1969

F-4D 66-8690 435 TFS, 8 TFW, USAF, Ubon
Capt G M Smith (survived)
1Lt H R Dobbs (survived)

This was the first Wolf fast FAC to be lost since the 8th TFW started the mission in December. Capt Smith was controlling a strike on a 37mm anti-aircraft gun position when his aircraft was shot down. The gun site was near the village of Ban Xam Tai, just south of the Mu Gia Pass. Capt Smith's Phantom was hit by AAA at 4,000 feet and caught fire. The crew ejected a few miles to the southeast and were rescued by an HH-53. This particular Phantom was flown by Lt Col A E Lang and 1Lt R P Moss of the 435th TFS when they shot down a MiG-21 on 12 February 1968.

29 January 1969

F-4D 66-7474 497 TFS, 8 TFW, USAF, Ubon
　　　　　　　Maj William Edward Campbell (KIA)
　　　　　　　Capt Robert Edwin Holton (KIA)

At dusk on the 29th a flight of Phantoms attacked a truck convoy near Ban Xam Tai, in almost exactly the same location where Capt Smith's Phantom had been hit on the previous day. The defences were still very active and a 37mm shell hit Maj Campbell's aircraft at 4,500 feet. It is possible that the crew were incapacitated by the ground fire as neither were observed to eject from the aircraft before it crashed. In 1989 Capt Campbell's gold finger ring was acquired from a Laotian villager. The ring was eventually given to Bill Campbell's family in 1991. Apparently his Smith and Wesson service revolver is displayed in a museum in Hanoi.

RF-4C 67-0447 16 TRS, 460 TRW, USAF, Tan Son Nhut
　　　　　　　Maj Harper Brown Keeler (KIA)
　　　　　　　Maj Ludwig George Baumann (KIA)

While en route on a photographic reconnaissance mission an RF-4C crashed into a hill five miles south of Nha Trang. It was not determined whether the aircraft had been shot down or had crashed as the result of an accident.

30 January 1969

OV-10A 67-14642 19 TASS, 504 TASG, USAF, Bien Hoa
　　　　　　　Capt Remi Hendricus Greeff (KWF)

During a training flight over Gia Dinh province, South Vietnam, the engine of an OV-10 failed and the aircraft crashed, killing the pilot.

31 January 1969

F-100C 54-2041 188 TFS, 31 TFW, USAF, Tuy Hoa
　　　　　　　Capt J N Williams (survived)

The New Mexico ANG squadron lost an aircraft during a close air support mission against a VC base camp near Song Be City. The aircraft was hit by small arms fire as it dived on the target. Capt Williams headed back to Tuy Hoa and almost made it but he was forced to abandon his aircraft near the village of My Thanh, 15 miles southwest of the airfield. He was rescued by one of the base's HH-43 Pedros.

1 February 1969

O-2A 67-21432 23 TASS, 504 TASG, USAF, Nakhon Phanom
　　　　　　　detached to Ubon
　　　　　　　Maj Donald Alfred Luna (KIA)

An O-2 FAC aircraft on a visual reconnaissance mission over southern Laos disappeared somewhere near the town of Muang Phine. It was presumed that the aircraft had been shot down by North Vietnamese troops.

4 February 1969

F-8H 147919 VF-24, USN, USS Hancock
　　　　　　　Lt(jg) Paul Eugene Swigart (KIA)

A Crusader commenced its approach to land back on board the USS Hancock after returning from a CAP mission. As the aircraft was about to touch down its port main undercarriage struck the carrier's ramp and the aircraft veered to the left until it fell off the deck. Unfortunately, Lt Swigart did not escape from the aircraft. Paul Swigart had ejected from a Crusader on 17 September 1968 when he ran out of fuel after a fight with MiGs.

5 February 1969

EC-47Q 45-1133 362 TEWS, 460 TRW, USAF, Pleiku
　　　　　　　Maj Homer Morgan Lynn (KIA)
　　　　　　　Capt Walter Francis Burke (KIA)
　　　　　　　Maj Harry Tilman Niggle (KIA)
　　　　　　　Maj Robert Eugene Olson (KIA)
　　　　　　　MSgt Wilton Neil Hatton (KIA)
　　　　　　　SSgt James Vernon Dorsey (KIA)
　　　　　　　SSgt Rodney Herschel Gott (KIA)
　　　　　　　SSgt Hugh Leslie Sherburn (KIA)
　　　　　　　TSgt Louis John Clever (KIA)
　　　　　　　Sgt Clarence Leon McNeill (KIA)

An EC-47 was shot down by ground fire near Ban Phan, 25 miles southeast of Saravan in southern Laos. The aircraft was on a radio direction finding mission in an attempt to locate enemy forces on the Ho Chi Minh Trail. A search was initiated after the aircraft failed to make a scheduled stop at Phu Bai. Despite six days of searching no crash site was found and nothing was heard from any of the 10 crew. However, in October 1969 the wreckage of an aircraft was discovered near Ban Phan and a team visited the site to confirm its identity as that of the missing EC-47. The starboard wing was found about 500 yards away from the rest of the wreckage and showed sign of fire damage originating from the engine. Human remains were recovered from the crash site and were eventually returned to the USA for burial in a communal grave at Jefferson Barracks National Cemetery in St Louis as positive identification could not be made for all the crew. Most of the enlisted crewmembers who operated the classified listening and encryption equipment were members of the 6994th Security Squadron.

F-105D 62-4364 355 TFW, USAF, Takhli
　　　　　　　This Thunderchief was damaged beyond repair in a ground accident at Takhli.

7 February 1969

F-4J 155762 VMFA-334, MAG-13, USMC, Chu Lai
　　　　　　　Capt Richard Augustine Deleidi (KIA)
　　　　　　　1Lt J W Maxwell (survived)

One of Chu Lai's Phantoms was damaged during a close air support mission only three miles to the west of Da Nang. Capt Deleidi was pulling up from his second attack on enemy troops when his aircraft was hit by .50 calibre ground fire. The aircraft caught fire as it headed out over the sea. 1Lt Maxwell ejected just off the coast and was badly injured in the process but was rescued by a Marine Corps helicopter. However, Capt Deleidi was killed when the aircraft crashed in the sea.

8 February 1969

F-100D 55-3562 416 TFS, 37 TFW, USAF, Phu Cat
　　　　　　　Capt Thomas Edward Clark (KIA)

With the war in the North halted the North Vietnamese increased their defences on the Ho Chi Minh Trail and the USAF responded by flying more defence suppression sorties in southern Laos. A flight of Super Sabres was sent to destroy an anti-aircraft gun position near Ban Kapay, 25 miles west of the DMZ. Capt Clark's aircraft was hit by 23mm ground fire as he prepared to attack the target and he crashed before he was able to eject.

A-4E 151103 VA-164, USN, USS Hancock
　　　　　　　Lt Cdr Roger Allen Meyers (KIA)

The Hancock suffered its second non-combat loss within the space of five days. A Skyhawk was launched on a night strike from one of the ship's catapults but was seen to pitch down and crash into the sea and explode. The pilot was killed. This was a particularly tragic accident in that the Hancock was due to finish its spell of line duty the very next day. The ship returned to North Island on 3 March having lost three A-4s and an F-8 in combat and six F-8s and a single A-4 in accidents during its fifth war cruise.

11 February 1969

F-105D 62-4256 34 TFS, 388 TFW, USAF, Korat
　　　　　　　temporarily operating from Takhli
　　　　　　　1Lt Robert John Zukowski (KIA)

North Vietnamese trucks travelling along the Trail required large amounts of fuel and oil that had to be stored in concealed dumps at regular intervals. Whenever these POL storage sites were found they became prime targets. A flight of two F-105s was despatched to attack a POL store near Ban Topen, 15 miles southwest of the Ban Karai Pass. 1Lt Zukowski put his aircraft into a 45-degree dive over the target but as he passed through 5,000 feet the Thunderchief rolled inverted and continued its dive straight into the ground. 1Lt Zukowski was not seen to eject and was posted as missing in action. His status was changed to killed in action on 15 January 1979. Robert Zukowski had arrived at Korat on 12 June 1968 and had flown 122 missions in Southeast Asia before being killed. During three joint field investigations by US and Laotian personnel in 1993 and 1996, human remains and personal items including identity tags, a watch and a St Christopher medallion, were found at the crash site and formally identified on 30 October 1996 as being those of Robert Zukowski. The watch was one of four that 1Lt Zukowski had purchased and had had engraved for his father, his brothers and himself. The watch, along with one of the identity tags, was placed in his coffin when he was buried at Justice, Illinois.

F-4D 66-8690 of the 435th TFS was shot down near the Mu Gia Pass during a Wolf FAC sortie on 28 January 1969. The aircraft had shot down a MiG-21 over North Vietnam on 12 February 1968. USAF

By the late 1960s the only Skywarriors left in service were tankers, reconnaissance and electronic warfare aircraft. This KA-3B of VAQ-130 was photographed in August 1969 while operating from the USS *Franklin D Roosevelt*. USN

12 February 1969

F-105D 60-0417   333 TFS, 355 TFW, USAF, Takhli
Maj Vincent Colasuonno (KIA)

Another F-105 and its pilot was lost on a Steel Tiger mission the following day. Maj Colasuonno's aircraft was damaged by automatic weapons fire during a strike on a storage area near Ban Kok Nak, 35 miles west of the DMZ. He flew back across Laos into Thailand but he was killed when the hydraulics failed and his aircraft crashed about 50 miles northwest of Ubon.

14 February 1969

F-4D 65-0651   497 TFS, 8 TFW, USAF, Ubon
Lt Col Stanley Scott Clark (KIA)
1Lt Gordon K Breault (survived)

A Wolfpack Phantom was lost during a raid by two aircraft on a ford on the Trail near Ban Bouang Nam, 20 miles northeast of Saravan in southern Laos. Lt Col Clark had started his second bombing run on the target when his aircraft was hit by 37mm AAA. Lt Col Clark climbed the aircraft to about 12,000 feet before ordering his WSO to eject. The aircraft crashed in a river and 1Lt Breault did not see his pilot eject. Gordon Breault spoke to the crew of the other Phantom as he parachuted down. He was later rescued by an HH-53 from Nakhon Phanom, but not before a Skyraider had been shot down during the rescue attempt. Enemy ground fire from the area around the downed airman was intense and the Skyraiders had to drop CBU-19 tear gas munitions to disable the enemy gun crews before the helicopter could make the rescue. The fate of Lt Col Clark was not determined.

A-4C 148547   VA-216, USN, USS *Coral Sea*
Lt Cdr J F Meehan (survived)

A-4C 149529   VA-216, USN, USS *Coral Sea*
Lt(jg) Larry James Stevens (KIA)

A pair of Skyhawks was assigned to accompany an Intruder on a night interdiction mission over the Ho Chi Minh Trail in southern Laos. The Intruder was using the airborne moving target indicator function of its AN/APQ-148 multi-mode radar to search for moving traffic on the roads and trails and the two Skyhawks were in close formation just behind. As the three aircraft headed west near Ban Kate at 14,000 feet, Lt Cdr Meehan saw anti-aircraft fire moments before his aircraft was rocked by two massive explosions. He saw the aircraft of his wingman, Lt Stevens, crash into the ground and explode with no indication that the pilot had been able to escape. Lt Cdr Meehan's own Skyhawk was badly damaged, probably by the explosion of Lt Stevens's aircraft, and suffered an elevator control restriction that resulted in a nose high attitude and pitch oscillations. Lt Cdr Meehan flew his damaged aircraft for 35 minutes until he reached the coast and ejected about 20 miles off Hué and was picked up by a USAF SAR helicopter. The aircraft was close to the stall throughout the flight due to the damaged elevator controls.

A-7A 153181   VA-105, USN, USS *Kitty Hawk*
Lt(jg) William Clinton Niedecken (KIA)

The third Navy aircraft lost on the night of the 14th was a Corsair that was shot down as it was attacking a truck park near Muang Nong, 20 miles west of the A Shau Valley. Lt Niedecken had already made three bombing runs and was on a 45-degree strafing run when his aircraft dived into the ground. Lt Niedecken had reported anti-aircraft fire during his dive on the target and it was thought that either his aircraft had been hit or he had left his recovery too late after being distracted by the anti-aircraft fire.

15 February 1969

A-1J 52-142080 602 SOS, 56 SOW, USAF, Nakhon Phanom
Lt Col Richard Ambrose Walsh (KIA)

At first light on the 15th two Skyraiders arrived near the last known location of Clark and Breault's Phantom and began searching for the crew in the hope of a rescue attempt. Lt Col Walsh became the on-scene commander and was soon joined by two more Spads and two HH-3s. Walsh made several low passes in an attempt to spot 1Lt Breault, who he had contacted by radio. As the helicopters were about to move in, Lt Col Walsh reported that he was receiving 37mm anti-aircraft fire. The Skyraider was hit and crashed into the jungle from about 1,000 feet. Lt Col Walsh's wife was apparently told that friendly forces reached the crash site about three months later but found no sign of the pilot's remains. In 1985 an unconfirmed report spoke of Richard Walsh being seen alive in Laos with a number of other US POWs. However, it seems more likely that Richard Walsh died when his aircraft was shot down 25 miles northeast of Saravan.

17 February 1969

F-4J 155760   VF-21, USN, USS *Ranger*
Lt Cdr D J Weaver (survived)
Lt(jg) J H Akin (survived)

A Phantom was lost during a CAP mission when it caught fire and then suffered a complete hydraulic failure. Both crew survived the accident and were quickly rescued from the Gulf of Tonkin.

KA-3B 138943   Detachment 43, VAH-10, USN, USS *Coral Sea*
Lt Cdr Rodney Max Chapman (KIA)
PO1 Stanley Milton Jerome (KIA)
PO1 Eddie Ray Schimmels (KIA)

A more serious accident occurred to another Navy aircraft on the 17th. A KA-3B Skywarrior from the *Coral Sea* was lost with all hands during a night tanker mission. The aircraft was patrolling over the Gulf of Tonkin, about 80 miles off Dong Hoi in case it was needed to refuel aircraft on their way back to their carriers. On his return to the *Coral Sea*, Lt Cdr Chapman overflew the carrier and started a wide circuit to make a GCA approach. The aircraft started to descend and Lt Cdr Chapman was told to turn towards the ship. However, he did not respond to the message and the aircraft continued straight ahead until it was lost from the carrier's radar screen. A search was initiated throughout the night and into the next day but with no success. The probable cause of the accident was recorded as controlled flight into the sea probably due to pilot fatigue. The tankers often flew very long and tiring missions in their unceasing efforts to support the combat forces.

18 February 1969

F-105D 60-0505   34 TFS, 388 TFW, USAF, Korat
temporarily operating from Takhli
Capt John Martin Brucher (KIA)

A flight of two F-105s on an FAC-controlled strike in southern Laos attacked a truck POL storage site near Ban Son, just to the west of the Ban Karai Pass. Capt Brucher's aircraft had its tail blown off by AAA as it dropped its bombs on the target. The pilot ejected and was seen by his wingman to parachute into a tree. He made contact on his emergency radio and reported that he was

suspended from a branch and unable to free himself. He also stated that he had a dislocated shoulder. The first rescue attempt had to be abandoned because of intense enemy ground fire and when the rescue helicopter arrived on the scene the following day, Brucher's parachute was found to be empty. Whatever happened to John Brucher, he did not return home. During its time at Korat F-105D 60-0505 was painted variously as '25 Ton Canary', 'The Tar Heel' and 'Fighting Irishman'.

20 February 1969

F-4J 155763   VF-21, USN, USS *Ranger*
Lt(jg) David Phillip Neislar (KIA)
1 crew, name unknown (survived)

As a Phantom was being catapulted from the *Ranger*, the catapult bridle separated from the aircraft prematurely and the aircraft's nose dropped to the deck. The Phantom became airborne but then crashed into the sea just in front of the carrier. Only one of the crew managed to escape from the aircraft before it crashed.

22 February 1969

F-4D 66-8717   555 TFS, 432 TRW, USAF, Udorn
Capt Wayne Edward Pearson (KIA)
1Lt M E Heenan (survived)

The first aircraft lost on a Barrel Roll mission in 1969 was a Phantom that was shot down during a strike on enemy positions in the Plain of Jars. Capt Pearson was attacking his target under the control of a Raven FAC and his aircraft was shot down in flames near Ban Thuang. Capt Pearson may have been wounded and ordered the WSO to eject moments before the aircraft hit the ground. 1Lt Heenan blacked out during the high speed ejection and came to suspended under a tree, bleeding heavily from his initial contact with the tree trunk. He spoke to the Raven pilot on the survival radio and sprained his ankle as he released himself from his parachute. After about 45 minutes a group of North Vietnamese soldiers started approaching towards Heenan's position. The Raven FAC guided Heenan away from the enemy troops and directed him to a clearing where an HH-53 from Udorn rescued him just in the nick of time. At some time prior to April 1994 Capt Pearson's remains were returned to the USA and identified.

F-4C 63-7586   558 TFS, 12 TFW, USAF, Cam Ranh Bay
Maj R C Roth (survived)
1Lt C H Gray (survived)

Another Phantom was lost on the 22nd during a close air support mission in South Vietnam. A flight of F-4s was attacking a target five miles south of Da Lat when one of the aircraft was hit by 12.7mm anti-aircraft fire. Maj Roth was making his fourth pass over the target at 2,500 feet when his Phantom burst into flames. He flew a few miles to the south before he and his WSO ejected. They were both picked up safely by an Army helicopter.

B-57B 52-1532   8 TBS, 35 TFW, USAF, Phan Rang
Lt Col Donald Elmer Paxton (KIA)
Maj Charles Macko (KIA)

Although the Canberras from Phan Rang were operating over the Trail primarily at night by this date, the aircraft did make

occasional daylight raids as well. Lt Col Paxton and Maj Macko were bombing trucks on a road seven miles southeast of Ban Kate when their aircraft was shot down by ground fire. Neither of the crew were thought to have ejected from the aircraft before it crashed on a slope close to the road.

O-1E   56-4227   504 TASG, USAF, Dau Tieng

A Bird Dog was destroyed by a VC satchel charge during a night attack on the base at Dau Tieng near the Michelin rubber plantations 35 miles northwest of Saigon.

F-100D 55-2918   3 TFW, USAF, Bien Hoa
U-10B 63-13107   14 SOW, USAF, Bien Hoa

A more serious VC attack on Bien Hoa resulted in the loss of a Super Sabre and one of the Air Commando's U-10B Couriers. Thirty-nine rockets were fired during the attack and eight other aircraft were damaged. Fortunately, there were no fatalities and only four men were wounded.

28 February 1969

O-2A   67-21412   23 TASS, 504 TASG, USAF, Nakhon Phanom
                    1Lt Stephen G Long (POW)
                    SMSgt D W Morrell (survived)

A Nail FAC from Nakhon Phanom was flying an Igloo White mission near Ban Senphan, south of the Mu Gia Pass, when it was shot down. The aircraft was flying at 6,000 feet when its port wing was damaged by AAA. The pilot and observer both survived the incident although the pilot, 1Lt Long, suffered a broken left femur and was captured. He spent months in the Laotian jungle until he was transferred to Hanoi. He became one of the very few men to survive captivity in Laos and to be transferred to North Vietnam and repatriated during Operation Homecoming. While he was in Laos he was told that he had been sentenced to 'live forever in a cave'. Stephen Long was released from Hanoi on 28 March 1973 and returned to flying, serving in F-4E, F-105G and F-16A squadrons before retiring from the Air Force and flying for an airline. SMSgt Morrell was a photographer and managed to evade capture until he was rescued by an HH-3E captained by Maj Silver.

1 March 1969

F-4D   66-8814   433 TFS, 8 TFW, USAF, Ubon
                    Maj Wendell Richard Keller (KIA)
                    1Lt Virgil Kersh Meroney (KIA)

A Phantom was lost on a night mission over the Trail in southern Laos. Maj Keller and 1Lt Meroney were attacking a storage area and truck park near Ban Topen, 15 miles southwest of the Ban Karai Pass, when their aircraft was shot down. The aircraft was rolling in on its ninth pass over the target when it was hit by AAA. Neither of the crew was thought to have ejected from the aircraft.

A-1J   52-142023   602 SOS, 56 SOW, USAF, Nakhon Phanom
                    1Lt Clyde William Campbell (KIA)

Four F-105Ds from Korat's 34th TFS return from a mission on 16 December 1968. The second aircraft from the left, 60-0505, was shot down on a POL strike in southern Laos on 18 February 1969. The pilot, Capt J M Brucher, ejected safely but, like many others, never returned from Laos alive. USAF

A flight of Skyraiders was sent on an armed reconnaissance mission in the vicinity of Lima Site 36 near Na Khang, about 25 miles north of Ban Ban in central Laos. LS 36 was the northernmost outpost in Laos with the exception of the radar site at LS85. The North Vietnamese had been gradually building up the pressure on these remote sites as they served as excellent bases for guerrilla attacks by General Vang Pau's indigenous Laotian troops. 1Lt Campbell was attacking enemy positions about 10 miles to the west of LS36 when he was shot down. He was not seen to escape from his aircraft before it crashed.

A-1H   52-139641   602 SOS, 56 SOW, USAF, Nakhon Phanom
                    1 pilot, name unknown (survived)

Another of the 602nd SOS's Skyraiders crashed in Thailand when it suffered engine failure during a training flight.

C-7B   63-9762   459 TAS, 483 TAW, USAF, Phu Cat
                    3 crew, names unknown (survived)

A C-7 Caribou was damaged beyond repair when it landed short of the runway due to pilot error.

2 March 1969

F-105D 61-0109   333 TFS, 355 TFW, USAF, Takhli
                    Maj Christos Constantine Bogiages (KIA)

Another strike aircraft was lost over the Plain of Jars as more missions were flown over the region as a result of increased pressure from the Pathet Lao and North Vietnamese and the greater aircraft availability resulting from the end of the Rolling Thunder campaign. A flight of F-105s was attacking a storage area near Ban Thuang when one of the aircraft was hit during its fourth strafing run. Maj Bogiages was not seen to eject from his Thud before it crashed. This aircraft was painted as 'Big Kahuna' at some stage during its career with the Takhli Wing.

F-4J   155770   VMFA-334, MAG-13, USMC, Chu Lai
                    Lt Col S E D'Angelo (survived)
                    1Lt P E Daly (survived)

A Phantom with the radio call sign of Love Bug 46 was shot down during a close air support mission at dusk, 20 miles south of Da Nang. A flight of aircraft had been scrambled to attack enemy troops in the open and Lt Col D'Angelo was making his third run dropping napalm from 1,000 feet when his aircraft was hit by ground fire. The aircraft caught fire and both the crew ejected safely and were picked up by helicopter shortly afterwards. 1Lt Daly was shot down again a few weeks later with another pilot on 12 May.

5 March 1969

F-4D   66-7637   390 TFS, 366 TFW, USAF, Da Nang
                    Capt E A Davis (survived)
                    1Lt C J Wiles (survived)

One of the local Phantoms was lost during an attack on enemy troops seven miles south of Da Nang. Capt Davis was pulling up from his third pass when his aircraft was hit by automatic weapons or small arms fire. Capt Davis headed towards the open sea and he and his WSO ejected about four miles off the coast near Da Nang, from where they were rescued by helicopter.

F-100D 56-3174   355 TFS, 37 TFW, USAF, Phu Cat
                    Lt Col G J Kertesz (survived)

A flight of F-100s was overflying a target at 11,000 feet near Dak To when one of the aircraft took a hit from AAA. Lt Col Kertesz headed southeast and ejected about 15 miles northwest of Kontum. He was later recovered by friendly ground troops.

6 March 1969

O-2A   67-21386   23 TASS, 504 TASG, USAF, Nakhon Phanom
                    Maj T A Scanlan (survived)

A Nail FAC was shot down by AAA 12 miles east of Muang Phine in southern Laos as it was controlling an air strike on a target. Maj Scanlan bailed out safely but was injured on landing. He was later rescued by a USAF HH-3.

F-100D 56-3270   90 TFS, 3 TFW, USAF, Bien Hoa
                    1Lt M D Martin (survived)

The 3rd TFW had not lost a Super Sabre in the air since September 1968 but this run of good fortune came to an end on 6 March. A flight of aircraft was attacking suspected enemy positions near Ap Dao Du, 35 miles southwest of Binh Thuy, when one of the aircraft was shot down. 1Lt Martin was making his fifth pass and was flying low to deliver napalm when his F-100 was hit by small arms fire. He ejected close to the target and was picked up by a US Army helicopter before the Viet Cong could reach him.

8 March 1969

C-130E 64-0545   50 TAS, 314 TAW, USAF, Ching Chuan Kang
                    Col Ralph A Cone (KWF)
                    Lt Col Paul E Garrett (KWF)
                    Maj Warren L Long (KWF)
                    Maj Raymond L Tacke (KWF)
                    Major William J Griffin (Died)
                    MSgt William B Terry (KWF)
                    TSgt John W Israel (KWF)
                    SSgt Barry W Murtaugh (KWF)
                    SSgt Gordon L Wheeler (KWF)
                    Sgt Alan C Martin (KWF)
                    Sgt Eugene Pizzino (Died)
                    SSgt Robert L Wilson (Died)

A Hercules crashed short of the runway at Ching Chuan Kang on the island of Taiwan at the conclusion of a flight from Vietnam. The weather at Ching Chuan Kang was below minimums at the time forcing the crew to make several attempts to land. Nine of the occupants were killed in the accident while Maj Griffin died on the 14th, SSgt Wilson on the 15th and Sgt Pizzino on the 16th of March.

9 March 1969

O-2A   67-21425   23 TASS, 504 TASG, USAF, Nakhon Phanom
      Capt Robert F Rex (KIA)
      SSgt Tim Leroy Walters, US Army (KIA)

Another Nail FAC was lost in Laos. The observer in this aircraft was a Staff Sergeant from the MACVSOG, the organisation that specialised in clandestine operations behind enemy lines in Southeast Asia. The aircraft was shot down near Ban Nathon, about 10 miles west of the DMZ. The wreckage was later inspected by a ground team but they were unable to recover the bodies due to the proximity of enemy forces, although they did recover important maps, cameras and the weapons. The remains of SSgt Walters were discovered during JTF-FA investigations in early 1999 and positively identified in December.

A-7B   154473   VA-25, USN, USS *Ticonderoga*
      1 pilot, name unknown (survived)

The USS *Ticonderoga* returned to TF 77 control on 18 February and started air operations on 4 March. The first aircraft lost by the carrier was also the first A-7B lost during the war. The A-7B was similar to the A-7A but with a slightly more powerful version of the TF30 turbofan engine. As one of the new aircraft was established on the approach to the *Ticonderoga* following a combat mission, its engine suddenly lost thrust and the pilot had to eject. The cause of the engine failure was thought to have been due to a technical failure.

10 March 1969

F-100D   56-3380   612 TFS, 37 TFW, USAF, Phu Cat
      Capt Arthur William Cofer (KIA)

Phu Cat lost its sixth F-100 of the year during a close air support mission over the hills 25 miles west of Nha Trang. Capt Cofer was killed when his aircraft was hit by ground fire as he was pulling up from his third pass against enemy buildings and bunkers. The pilot may have been wounded as he was not observed to eject from his aircraft.

F-4D   65-0722   435 TFS, 8 TFW, USAF, Ubon
      Lt Col Carter Purvis Luna (KIA)
      Capt Aldis P Rutyna (survived)

Two Phantoms were despatched from Ubon to attack a truck park and an associated POL storage site near Ban Loumpoum, 25 miles southwest of the Ban Karai Pass. Lt Col Luna's aircraft was hit by ground fire as it was making its fifth run over the target. He headed west but the crew was forced to eject less than 10 miles from the target. Both men landed safely and were in voice contact with the SAR forces. However, they were surrounded by enemy troops and Lt Col Luna was thought to have been killed or captured. Capt Rutyna used his emergency radio to call down air strikes on NVA troops who were within yards of his position. He was rescued by a SAR helicopter about three hours after ejecting.

A-26A   64-17673   609 SOS, 56 SOW, USAF, Nakhon Phanom
      Capt Neal E Monette (KIA)
      Maj John V Callanan (KIA)

An Invader crashed in the circuit at Nakhon Phanom when it ran out of fuel causing engine failure as it was returning from an interdiction mission. The crew were circling at low level trying to establish whether the gear was down or not as they had an unlocked gear light in the cockpit. The port engine failed first and the aircraft rolled into the ground. The A-26 crews were frequently faced with warnings that the undercarriage was not safely down and locked. In almost all cases these warnings were found to be spurious.

O-1E   56-2497   22 TASS, 504 TASG, USAF, Binh Thuy
      2 crew, names unknown (survived)

A Bird Dog FAC crashed in South Vietnam as a result of pilot error.

13 March 1969

F-4B   153018   VF-114, USN, USS *Kitty Hawk*
      Lt(jg) E L Brazil (survived)
      Lt(jg) K J Oden (survived)

During a CAP mission a Phantom pilot discovered that his left throttle was stuck at 100 per cent. Eventually the port engine flamed out and the aircraft became uncontrollable forcing the crew to eject.

14 March 1969

F-100C   53-1740   174 TFS, 37 TFW, USAF, Phu Cat
      1Lt C J Grewell (survived)

An F-100 was lost near Dak To on the 14th. A flight of aircraft was bombing a road intersection point about 15 miles southwest of the town when 1Lt Grewell's aircraft was hit by automatic weapons fire on his second pass. He ejected close to the target and was rescued by an Army helicopter soon afterwards. F-100C 53-1740 had previously been flown by the Thunderbirds aerobatic team. This was the last aircraft lost by the 174th TFS before it returned home to Sioux City, Iowa on 14 May. This Guard squadron had flown 6,359 missions and had logged 11,399 combat hours during its stay in Southeast Asia. During its deployment it had dropped 12.9 million pounds of bombs, 3 million pounds of napalm, 512,000lbs of cluster munitions, and had fired 1.8 million rounds of 20mm ammunition. Three aircraft had been lost in combat during the deployment but only one pilot had been killed.

15 March 1969

B-57B   52-1567   8 TBS, 35 TFW, USAF, Phan Rang
      Lt Col E Tiddy (survived)
      Maj Michael A De Sousa (survived)

A Canberra was hit by ground fire and damaged during an attack on a North Vietnamese rocket launching position near the A Shau Valley. Lt Col Tiddy flew all the way back to Phan Rang but had to crash-land the aircraft close to the airfield when both engines flamed out. Both men were recovered by the base HH-43. B-57B 52-1567 had seen service with the 38th TBG at Laon AB in France, the Nevada ANG, the Kentucky ANG and the 405th FW before transfer to the 35th TFW.

A-1H   52-134562   602 SOS, 56 SOW, USAF, Nakhon Phanom
      1 pilot, name unknown (survived)

A Spad pilot had a lucky escape on the 15th when he aborted take off and his aircraft slid off the runway, exploded and burned.

17 March 1969

F-105D   61-0104   34 TFS, 388 TFW, USAF, Korat
      1Lt David Thomas Dinan (KIA)

An F-105 was lost during a Barrel Roll mission on the eastern edge of the Plain of Jars. A flight of Thuds was attacking a mobile anti-aircraft gun when 1Lt Dinan's aircraft was hit by return fire while on his second strafing run. He flew away from the target but had to eject a short while later. He was killed when his parachute was torn as he descended into trees and fell a considerable height and rolled down a hillside.

A-6A   154160   VMA(AW)-533, MAG-12, USMC, Chu Lai
      1Lt Steven Ray Armistead (KIA)
      Capt Charles Elbert Finney (KIA)

VMA(AW)-533 lost an aircraft and crew on a low-level night mission near Muang Nong in southern Laos. The aircraft had just bombed enemy positions when it was hit by AAA and crashed. A search over the next few days failed to find any sign of aircraft wreckage or the crew. This was the last aircraft lost by VMA(AW)-533 before the Squadron left Chu Lai for Iwakuni in October as part of the general withdrawal announced by President Nixon. During 30 months of operations in Southeast Asia the Squadron had flown a total of 11,058 sorties for the loss of seven aircraft. In 1999 a joint US/Lao investigation team excavated

a crash site after a villager handed in 1Lt Armistead's identification tag. Personal items and scant human remains were discovered but so far only those of Capt Finney have been positively identified.

18 March 1969

F-100D   55-3635   308 TFS, 31 TFW, USAF, Tuy Hoa
      1Lt T J Ebdon (survived)

The 308th TFS suffered one of its rare losses on the 18th during an attack on a VC encampment near Ap Nam, 15 miles northwest of Quan Long, in the extreme southern tip of South Vietnam. 1Lt Ebdon was diving on the target when his aircraft was hit by small arms fire at about 900 feet. He ejected a few moments later and was rescued by a US Army helicopter.

A-1E   52-139579   22 SOS, 56 SOW, USAF, Nakhon Phanom
      1Lt M A Riopelle (survived)

The 22nd SOS lost an aircraft during a Barrel Roll armed reconnaissance mission on the southeastern edge of the Plain of Jars. The aircraft was bombing military structures near Ban Pho Xiangkhoang and was just pulling up from its third pass when automatic weapons fire damaged its starboard wing. The aircraft began to burn and 1Lt Riopelle ejected near his target. He successfully evaded capture until he was rescued by an HH-53 from the 40th ARRS piloted by Capt Rieddle.

20 March 1969

A-4E   151045   VMA-211, MAG-12, USMC, Chu Lai
      Maj A D Miller (survived)

Due to the bombing restrictions it had been several months since an aircraft had been lost in the area just to the north of the DMZ. Bombing raids still took place in the area and a Marine Corps Skyhawk was shot down there on the 20th. Maj Miller was pulling up from his third attack on an enemy position about five miles north of the village of Thon Cam Son when ground fire hit his aircraft's tail. With the aircraft on fire he decided to eject immediately and was lucky to be rescued by a USAF SAR helicopter before he could be captured by the North Vietnamese.

21 March 1969

A-4E   150041, 151043, 151060, 151124, 151127, 151149
      MAG-12, USMC, Chu Lai

The Viet Cong achieved a major success at Chu Lai on the night of the 21st when they destroyed six Skyhawks on the airfield, four of them from VMA-311. The bases at Cam Ranh Bay, Da Nang, Phan Rang and Pleiku were also attacked on the same night but no aircraft were lost at these locations.

22 March 1969

A-26A   64-17667   609 SOS, 56 SOW, USAF, Nakhon Phanom
      Capt James Wesley Widdis (KIA)
      Capt Robert Charles Davis (KIA)

An Invader was lost during a night interdiction mission over the Ho Chi Minh Trail as it was attacking trucks on Route 911. The aircraft was hit by 37mm AAA and brought down near Ban Pakhiat, about 25 miles west of the Ban Karai Pass. An FAC pilot saw a fireball on the ground near the road but did not see any parachutes and it was presumed that the crew had died in their aircraft. Investigations by US and Laotian teams in 1994 and 1995 recovered remains that were identified in October 1996 as being those of the Invader crew.

24 March 1969

O-1E   serial ..?   20 TASS, 504 TASG, USAF, Da Nang
      Capt K G Herron (survived)

The A Shau Valley maintained its infamous reputation of being a particularly 'hot' area and claimed yet another aircraft on the 24th. Capt Herron was flying an FAC mission over the Valley at low level when his aircraft was hit by small arms fire. He was too low to bail out so he crash-landed the Bird Dog and was injured. He was later extricated by friendly ground troops and evacuated out of the area.

25 March 1969

F-100D 56-2960 615 TFS, 35 TFW, USAF, Phan Rang
Maj W R Chaffer (survived)

A pair of F-100s was scrambled for a night-time close air support mission 20 miles northeast of Bien Hoa. Enemy troops in contact had been reported near the village of Ap Thanh Dang and air support was called for. As Maj Chaffer was making his second napalm drop his aircraft was hit by ground fire and he ejected seconds later. He was rescued from the clutches of the Viet Cong by a US Army helicopter.

A-1E 52-135201 22 SOS, 56 SOW, USAF, Nakhon Phanom
Capt K E Gilmore (survived)

Later the same night a Skyraider pilot on an armed reconnaissance sortie over the Trail in southern Laos spotted a number of trucks on a road 15 miles east of Ban Napoung. Capt Gilmore made his first bombing run but as he came around for his second pass his aircraft was hit by AAA and went out of control. He ejected close to the road and was rescued the next day by a USAF HH-53 helicopter captained by Maj Smith.

F-4B 150447 VF-151, USN, USS *Coral Sea*
2 crew, names unknown (survived)

The last aircraft lost by the *Coral Sea* before completing its fourth war cruise was a Phantom that crashed following engine failure while on a combat air patrol. Both crew ejected and were rescued. The ship left the line five days later and returned to Alameda having spent a total of 110 days on the line with just four combat and four operational losses.

26 March 1969

A-1H 52-134515 1 SOS, 56 SOW, USAF, Nakhon Phanom
1Lt Michael J Faas (survived)

The next day another Skyraider was lost on yet another Steel Tiger strike mission. 1Lt Faas attacked a group of trucks that were protected by a Russian-made ZPU mobile anti-aircraft gun near Ban That, 30 miles northeast of Nakhon Phanom. The aircraft was hit by ground fire and the pilot ejected close to the target. He was fortunate to evade capture and be rescued by the same HH-53 that rescued Capt Gilmore. 1Lt Faas was shot down again on 18 March 1972 during a second tour with the 1st SOS.

27 March 1969

B-57B 52-1508 8 TBS, 35 TFW, USAF, Phan Rang
Lt Col Richard W Burkholder (survived)
Lt Col H V Wright (survived)

A Canberra was damaged by AAA during a dawn strike on a river ford near the town of Tavouac in southern Laos, 20 miles southwest of the A Shau Valley. As the aircraft was pulling up from its second pass, it was struck by 37mm flak causing a fire in the fuselage. Lt Col Burkholder nursed the crippled aircraft for as long as he could but he and his navigator were forced to eject near Phu Cat. This aircraft was the last B-57B lost in Southeast Asia. A total of 54 B-57Bs, two B-57Es and a B-57C had been lost in Southeast Asia since the first aircraft arrived at Bien Hoa in August 1964. By June 1969 there were only six B-57s left at Phan Rang and these were operating almost exclusively at night by then. The 8th TBS started to run down in September and left Phan Rang at the end of October 1969 after five years in Southeast Asia. However, this was not the end of the Canberra's contribution to the war in Southeast Asia.

F-100C 54-1897 120 TFS, 35 TFW, USAF, Phan Rang
Maj Clyde Seiler (KIA)

Although the 120th TFS had lost an aircraft on 29 December, it had not lost a pilot since its deployment from Colorado in April 1968. However, on 27 March the Squadron's run of good fortune came to an end when Maj Seiler was killed when he was shot down during a close air support mission near Song Be City. The Squadron flew its last combat mission on 8 April before returning to Buckley ANG Base at Denver. The 120th had flown 6,127 sorties in the year spent at Phan Rang. It had dropped 14.3 million pounds of bombs, 5.6 million pounds of napalm, 227,070 pounds of cluster munitions, and had fired 423,000 rockets and

1.8 million rounds of 20mm ammunition. The Squadron had lost only two aircraft and one pilot on operations and had another aircraft destroyed during a VC attack on Phan Rang.

28 March 1969

F-4D 66-8764 389 TFS, 366 TFW, USAF, Da Nang
Maj Robert Arthur Belcher (KIA)
1Lt Michael Andrew Miller (KIA)

A mortar site and associated bunkers near Bo Ho Su in the DMZ buffer zone were the target for a strike by a pair of Phantoms from Da Nang. One of the aircraft was hit by automatic weapons or small arms fire and crashed before either of the crew could escape.

F-4D 66-8685 555 TFS, 432 TRW, USAF, Udorn
Capt Robert Dean Davenport (KIA)
Capt William Paul Justice (KIA)

Another Phantom was lost on the 28th after nightfall during a Barrel Roll mission over the Plain of Jars in northern Laos. Capt Davenport and Capt Justice were making their second bombing run on a supply and storage area about six miles south of Ban Naxa when their aircraft was hit by 37mm AAA. The aircraft was seen to crash close by, apparently killing both the crew.

Fast Jet Defoliation

The use of UC-123 Providers in Ranch Hand defoliation operations was becoming increasingly dangerous, especially in high-threat areas such as the Ho Chi Minh Trail in southern Laos. In an effort to increase survivability the use of fast jets as spray aircraft was proposed and experiments were conducted in the field. It was thought that the use of fast jets would not require escort or suppression aircraft to accompany the spray aircraft as was necessary with the Providers. The 390th TFS was chosen to perform trials and at least three of the Squadron's F-4Ds were fitted with modified underwing tanks fitted with spray nozzles. The first spray test mission took place over Da Nang on 17 January 1969 and the first of only seven combat spray missions was flown on 25 January. The missions involved three spray aircraft flying in a V-formation at 500 knots and 100-200 feet above the jungle. The area to be sprayed was marked by an FAC and a 10-mile swath some 300 feet wide could be sprayed in 70 seconds. Several tank failures occurred and when an aircraft was shot down on 29 March the programme was terminated. Attempts to revive the fast jet spray project later in the year eventually came to nought. All Ranch Hand defoliation operations in Southeast Asia came to an end on 9 May 1970 after which the C-123-equipped 12th SOS devoted its efforts to psychological warfare and flare dropping missions in support of the Cambodian incursion.

29 March 1969

F-4D 66-8809 390 TFS, 366 TFW, USAF, Da Nang
Capt W J Popendorf (survived)
1Lt Frederick William Hess (KIA)

Capt Popendorf and 1Lt Hess were assigned a mission to defoliate a segment of Route 915 that lay near Ban Topen, 15 miles southwest of the Ban Karai Pass. As the formation of three aircraft came round for its second run at 100 feet and 500 knots, Popendorf's Phantom was hit by small arms fire. Capt Popendorf pulled up but the aircraft started rolling uncontrollably and he and 1Lt Hess ejected moments before the aircraft crashed into a hillside. Capt Popendorf was injured but was rescued three hours later by a USAF SAR helicopter. However, despite a 10-hour search, Frederick Hess could not be located and was posted as missing in action. In May 1979 his status was changed to presumptively killed in action.

F-105D 62-4270 34 TFS, 388 TFW, USAF, Korat
1Lt R A Stafford (survived)

The only Thud lost on a Steel Tiger mission in March was shot down during a strike on a road intersection 25 miles southeast of Saravan. 1Lt Stafford was on his fourth pass when his aircraft was hit by AAA at 9,000 feet. He ejected a few miles away from his target and was later rescued by a USAF helicopter. This Thunderchief carried the names 'The Liquidator' and the legend

'Noli Non Legitime Carbor Undum Est' which was intended to be translated as 'Don't let the bastards grind you down'!

31 March 1969

RA-5C 150842 RVAH-6, USN, USS *Enterprise*
Cdr Danforth Ellithorpe White (KIA)
Lt Ramey Leo Carpenter (KIA)

A Vigilante and its fighter escort were flying a reconnaissance mission about 30 miles northeast of Nakhon Phanom when the Vigilante suddenly exploded. The aircraft was in an 80-degree starboard turn at 5,000 feet and 420 knots when it suddenly burst into a huge fireball and disintegrated. The major section of the wreckage was seen to enter a flat spin and crash without any indication of an ejection. No flak was seen before the incident but the escort was fired at afterwards. The cause was put down either to ground fire, a fuel tank explosion, or structural failure due to the aircraft being overstressed in a tight turn. The site of the crash was excavated in 1997 and remains of the crew recovered and identified.

The *Enterprise* had set sail from Alameda, California on 6 January for its fourth war cruise off Southeast Asia. It was due to spend several weeks working up its Air Wing in the Pacific before proceeding to the South China Sea. On 14 January, while the *Enterprise* was about 75 miles from Hawaii, the ship suffered a major fire when a Zuni rocket on F-4J 155804 accidentally exploded due to it being heated by the exhaust of an engine starter cart. Twenty-seven men were killed and another 344 injured and eight F-4Js, six A-7Bs and a single EKA-3B tanker were destroyed in the blaze. After a six-week refit at Pearl Harbor costing over $56 million the ship left Hawaii on 26 February and continued on its way to Vietnam, arriving on Yankee Station on 31 March.

1 April 1969

F-100F 56-3863 355 TFS, 37 TFW, USAF, Phu Cat
Maj R G Standerfer (survived)
1Lt C L Veach (survived)

The third Misty FAC to be shot down in 1969 was lost during a mission in poor weather 10 miles northeast of Ban Talan in southern Laos. Maj Standerfer and 1Lt Veach were making their second dive on a target to mark it for a formation of F-4s when their aircraft was hit by ground fire. Maj Standerfer headed southeast but after a few miles he and 1Lt Veach had to eject and landed close to the border with South Vietnam. They were subsequently rescued by a USAF SAR helicopter. Maj Standerfer had landed in a tree and fallen to the ground and was further injured when he was dragged through the trees on the jungle penetrator as he was being rescued. His injuries caused him severe discomfort on the long Misty FAC missions and he returned to a normal F-100 strike squadron to finish his tour.

2 April 1969

F-4D 66-8771 390 TFS, 366 TFW, USAF, Da Nang
Lt Col C G Foster (survived)
1Lt J P McMahon (survived)

A flight of Phantoms bombed a road intersection point on the Trail in southern Laos, about 20 miles west of Kham Duc. Lt Col Foster was making his third dive bombing run on the target when a 37mm anti-aircraft gun found its mark. The Phantom's starboard wing was badly damaged and caught fire. The crew ejected safely a short time later and came down about 30 miles southwest of Da Nang from where they were picked up by a USAF SAR helicopter.

3 April 1969

A-6A 155587 VA-65, USN, USS *Kitty Hawk*
Lt Cdr E G Redden (survived)
Lt J F Ricci (survived)

An Intruder was assigned to fly a strike near the Mu Gia Pass in southern Laos under the control of a Nail FAC aircraft from Nakhon Phanom. A fuel storage area near the town of Ban Sang was marked as a target but the Intruder developed a systems fault that meant that the crew had to attack the target visually. As L

Cdr Redden put the Intruder into a climbing turn to position for the attack, it was hit in the nose by an anti-aircraft shell. The starboard engine failed and the canopy was covered in oil or hydraulic fluid. Unable to jettison its bombs the aircraft could not maintain altitude on one engine and the crew had to eject. They were both rescued from the jungle by USAF SAR helicopters from the 40th ARRS.

F-105D 62-4269   34 TFS, 388 TFW, USAF, Korat
          Maj Peter Bugbee Christianson (KIA)

A Thud pilot was lost during a Barrel Roll mission over the Plain of Jars in northern Laos. Maj Christianson was bombing a storage area about five miles south of Ban Naxa when his aircraft was damaged by automatic weapons fire. Although he managed to fly his burning aircraft away from the immediate target area he was killed when his aircraft crashed. During its career in Southeast Asia 62-4269 carried the nicknames 'Big Mike', 'Okie Judy', 'The Impossible Dream', 'On Target' and 'Phylus I'.

4 April 1969

A-4E 151993   VMA-211, MAG-12, USMC, Chu Lai
          1Lt Ronald Dean Layton (KIA)

A flight of Skyhawks was bombing a target near Phuoc Binh, 20 miles southwest of Da Nang, when one of the aircraft was shot down. 1Lt Layton was on his third attack against the target when his aircraft was hit by .30 calibre ground fire. The Skyhawk crashed a few miles from the target and 1Lt Layton was killed.

5 April 1969

F-4D 66-0233   497 TFS, 8 TFW, USAF, Ubon
          Capt R Brandt (survived)
          1Lt C R Koster (survived)

A Night Owl Phantom was lost during the night of the 5th when it was bombing a storage area near Nam Theun, 35 miles northeast of Nakhon Phanom. Capt Brandt was pulling up from his first pass over the target when his aircraft was hit by ground fire. The crew ejected close to the target but were later rescued by a USAF helicopter.

8 April 1969

OV-10A 155420   VMO-2, MAG-16, USMC, Marble Mountain
          1Lt Joseph L Stone (survived)
          1Lt M R Cathey (survived)

The first OV-10 lost in action in 1969 belonged to the Marines. It was on a visual reconnaissance mission about 20 miles south of Da Nang when the crew attacked a river crossing point. As it was making its third strafing pass the aircraft's port engine was stuck by small arms fire. The aircraft soon became uncontrollable and the other engine failed forcing the crew to eject. They landed close together in the middle of at least two companies of NVA soldiers but fortunately a Marine Corps UH-1E pilot saw the ejection and landed close by. Stone and Cathey did not have time to get in the helicopter but stood on the skids and clung on as it took off and returned them safely to Da Nang.

EB-66B 53-0498   42 TEWS, 355 TFW, USAF, Takhli
          Lt Col Edwin P Anderson (KIA)
          Lt Col James Ellsworth Ricketts (KIA)
          Capt Joseph M Orlowski (KIA)

An EB-66 was taking off from Takhli when one of its engines was seen to emit smoke. The tower warned the pilot and suggested that he abort the take off. Unfortunately, the aircraft was already beyond the point where it could safely stop on the runway available so the pilot continued the take off. The aircraft lifted off and started to climb away on the one remaining engine but then lost altitude and crashed, killing the crew.

9 April 1969

TA-4F 154299   H&MS-11, MAG-11, USMC, Da Nang
          Maj Robert S Miecznikowski (survived)
          Capt James C Buffington (survived)

The Marines lost one of their Playboy fast FACs during a Steel Tiger mission on the 9th. The crew were attacking a storage area

and encampment 15 miles south of the A Shau Valley and were making their second pass when their aircraft was hit by 37mm AAA. Maj Miecznikowski flew away from the target area but he and Capt Buffington were soon obliged to eject from their crippled aircraft. They were rescued six hours later by two USAF HH-53 helicopters. This particular Skyhawk had been hit by 14.5mm anti-aircraft fire and badly damaged during an armed reconnaissance mission on 6 August 1968 when the rear seat pilot was injured.

A-1E 52-133990   22 SOS, 56 SOW, USAF, Nakhon Phanom
          Maj R H Shumock (survived)

A Skyraider was lost over the Plain of Jars during a Barrel Roll mission. Maj Shumock was flying an armed reconnaissance mission at night over Pathet Lao-held territory and attacked a storage area near the village of Ban Pho, on the eastern edge of the Plain. The target must have been only lightly defended because Maj Shumock's aircraft was not hit until its ninth pass when small arms or automatic weapons fire damaged the aircraft. He headed south and flew back into Thailand but was forced to eject about 55 miles northwest of Nakhon Phanom.

12 April 1969

F-4D 66-8766   390 TFS, 366 TFW, USAF, Da Nang
          Maj Ernest Leo Desoto (KIA)
          1Lt Frederick Mervyn Hall (KIA)

A flight of three F-4s was despatched on a mission to destroy a cluster of six .50 calibre gun sites that were in action about 10 miles southwest of Katum. Maj Desoto's aircraft was climbing over the target area when it was hit by automatic weapons fire. The aircraft crashed a few miles from the target and both airmen were killed.

A-7A 153222   VA-147, USN, USS Ranger
          1 pilot, name unknown (survived)

A Corsair had to be abandoned during a combat mission when it suffered an engine flameout. The cause was thought to have been due to a failure of the engine accessory gear train. This was the fourth and last aircraft lost by the Ranger before it completed its fourth tour of duty on 16 April. All the aircraft had been lost in accidents, which indicates the reduced risk of operations since the end of the Rolling Thunder campaign.

RF-4C 67-0446   16 TRS, 460 TRW, USAF, Tan Son Nhut
          Capt Arnold William Lamp (KIA)
          Capt C E Mattern (survived)

A reconnaissance Phantom pilot experienced problems with his aircraft attitude indicator and became so disorientated that he lost control of the aircraft. One of the crew was killed in the accident, which occurred in Lam Dong province in central South Vietnam.

16 April 1969

O-2A 67-21437   19 TASS, 504 TASG, USAF, Bien Hoa
          Capt William O Burkett (KIA)
          Capt Leon J Pierce (KIA)

A Viet Cong bunker complex had been discovered near Long Thanh, about 15 miles east of Saigon and an air strike was arranged to destroy the target. An O-2 FAC from Bien Hoa was assigned to control the strike but as the aircraft dived on the target to mark it for the fighters, the FAC was hit by small arms fire that damaged the starboard wing. The aircraft crashed near the bunkers before either of its occupants could escape.

F-4D 66-8796   25 TFS, 8 TFW, USAF, Ubon
          Maj D W Winkels (survived)
          Capt R P Andersen (survived)

A Phantom was lost during a Steel Tiger strike on a storage area close to the Mu Gia Pass. Maj Winkels was on his second pass over the target when his Phantom was damaged by ground fire. He headed west immediately and crossed into Thailand but he and his WSO had to eject about 10 miles northwest of Nakhon Phanom and were rescued by an HH-3E. The 25th TFS transferred to the Wolfpack at Ubon from the 33rd TFW at Eglin AFB on 29 May 1968, replacing the 555th TFS which moved to the 432nd TRW. The 25th TFS had been in Southeast Asia for almost

a year before it lost its first aircraft. This was also the first F-4D lost to have been modified with an ARN-92 LORAN-D receiver to enable night and bad weather precision bombing. A total of 72 aircraft were thus modified under the Pave Phantom programme, most of them serving with the 8th TFW. The LORAN-equipped aircraft were often used as pathfinders for other strike aircraft so that they could drop their bombs through cloud cover. The accuracy of these attacks was debatable according to many of the crews who flew these missions.

F-100D 56-3403   309 TFS, 31 TFW, USAF, Tuy Hoa
          1Lt Robert Vincent Willett (KIA)

A flight of F-100s from Tuy Hoa was making a night strike on a group of trucks near Tavouac in southern Laos. 1Lt Willett was seen to put his Super Sabre into a dive from 5,000 feet but his aircraft was then hit by 37mm anti-aircraft fire and crashed near the truck convoy. Robert Willett, who had been married only six weeks before he left for Vietnam, was not seen to eject and was presumed killed.

OV-10A 67-14691   19 TASS, 504 TASG, USAF, Bien Hoa
          2 crew, names unknown (survived)

An OV-10 and an A-1G collided in mid-air and the Bronco had to be abandoned. The Skyraider managed to land safely.

17 April 1969

F-4C 64-0843   558 TFS, 12 TFW, USAF, Cam Ranh Bay
          Capt J L Beavers (survived)
          1Lt G K Muellner (survived)

A bunker complex 15 miles southwest of Katum was the target for a flight of Phantoms on the 17th. As Capt Beavers pulled up from his fourth pass over the target his aircraft was damaged by small arms fire. He managed to maintain control and flew the aircraft towards Saigon in the hope of making an emergency landing at Tan Son Nhut. Unfortunately, the crew were forced to eject just four miles away from the airfield but they were both recovered safely by a US Army helicopter. Capt Beavers was shot down again on 9 August 1972 while serving with the 49th TFW.

RF-4C 66-0405   14 TRS, 432 TRW, USAF, Udorn
          Capt R Bartholomew (survived)
          Capt B F Doyle (survived)

The USAF fast jet reconnaissance units had been very fortunate so far in 1969 having lost just one aircraft and crew in January and another aircraft in an accident on 12 April. However, another aircraft was lost on 17 April but the crew were recovered. Capt Bartholomew and Capt Doyle were assigned to a dawn mission to photograph bridges and other likely targets along Route 912 in southern Laos, west of the Ban Karai Pass. The aircraft was damaged by automatic weapons fire as it flew near the town of Ban Topen at 3,500 feet. Capt Bartholomew flew the Phantom back across Laos and into Thailand but he and his navigator were forced to eject 10 miles east of Ubon when they were just minutes away from a safe landing.

O-1F 57-2833   504 TASG, USAF, Da Lat
          A Bird Dog was destroyed during a Viet

Cong rocket and mortar attack on the airstrip at Da Lat, 40 miles northwest of Phan Rang.

22 April 1969

F-100D 55-3632   416 TFS, 37 TFW, USAF, Phu Cat
          1Lt R C Detwiler (survived)

Sunvalley 6 was the call sign of one of a flight of F-100s sent to bomb a truck park 25 miles east of Saravan in southern Laos. 1Lt Detwiler was making his second 45-degree dive on the target when his aircraft was hit by AAA. He ejected a few miles from the target and was later rescued by a USAF SAR helicopter.

F-4D 65-0649   480 TFS, 37 TFW, USAF, Phu Cat
          Lt Col Walter Shelby Van Cleave (KIA)
          1Lt Vincent Calvin Scott (KIA)

Half an hour after Sunvalley 6 was shot down, an F-4D with the call sign Cobra 2, went down a few miles to the north. The target was another truck park about 15 miles east of Ban Talan.

Lt Col Van Cleave and 1Lt Scott were were shot down by automatic weapons fire as they dived to bomb the target. The aircraft crashed a couple of miles away and no one was seen to escape from the Phantom. In April and May the 37th TFW at Phu Cat replaced its four F-100 squadrons with two F-4D squadrons, both of them transferring from the 366th TFW at Da Nang. The 480th TFS had only been at Phu Cat for a week before losing its first aircraft from its new base.

F-100D 56-3305   355 TFS, 37 TFW, USAF, Phu Cat
                  1 pilot, name unknown (survived)
During a close air support mission an F-100 pilot delivered his attack at such a low altitude that his aircraft hit a tree. This was a not infrequent occurrence but in this instance the damage was such that the pilot was forced to eject, thereby bringing Phu Cat's score to three aircraft lost on this day.

23 April 1969

F-100D 56-3335   531 TFS, 3 TFW, USAF, Bien Hoa
                  1Lt R M Hargett (survived)
Another F-100 was lost during a close air support mission in South Vietnam. A huge complex of Viet Cong bunkers had been discovered 12 miles west of Binh Thuy. 1Lt Hargett was making his second pass over the target when his aircraft was shot down by small arms fire. He ejected safely and was picked up by a USAF helicopter, probably an HH-43 Huskie. This pilot also escaped from an F-100 when it was was shot down on 10 July 1969.

The EC-121R Bat Cat

An integral part of the Igloo White sensor system for detecting enemy activity on the Ho Chi Minh Trail was the EC-121R Bat Cat aircraft. Lockheed Air Services converted thirty surplus US Navy EC-121K and EC-121P aircraft to EC-121R configuration in 1966-1967. The 553rd RW was formed at Otis AFB, Massachusetts in February 1967 to operate the aircraft. The Wing deployed to Korat in October 1967 and was tasked with the collection of electronic intelligence information. Normally the aircraft orbited over South Vietnam, Laos or even North Vietnam for about eight hours while its seven-man combat information crew tuned into radio transmissions from air-dropped sensors. A variety of these sensors were used with names like Acoubuoy, Spikebuoy, Adsid and Acousid and they relayed acoustic and seismic information from the nearby movement of trucks and people on the Ho Chi Minh Trail. The information received from these sensors could be relayed to the Task Force Alpha centre at Nakhon Phanom or it could be analysed on board the EC-121Rs by its mission crew of radio and electronic specialists. The information thus received was used for the targeting of air strikes on sections of the Trail which were known to be active. By mid-1970 the number of EC-121Rs at Korat had been reduced from the original 27 to nine aircraft and the Wing was inactivated on 15 December 1970.

25 April 1969

EC-121R 67-21493 554 RS, 553 RW, USAF, Korat
                  Lt Col Emerson E Heller (KIA)
                  Maj Paul R Lunsford (KIA)
                  Lt Col William C McCormick (KIA)
                  Maj Thomas M Brandom (KIA)
                  Capt George R Kidd (KIA)
                  1Lt John A Marsh (KIA)
                  TSgt James H Belflower (KIA)
                  TSgt Albert N Booker (KIA)
                  TSgt Warren C Delaney (KIA)
                  TSgt Kenneth W Fowler (KIA)
                  SSgt Jerald C Davis (KIA)
                  SSgt Paul Faulk (KIA)
                  SSgt James D Moore (KIA)
                  Sgt Mitchel Messing (KIA)
                  Sgt Mark M Steeley (KIA)
                  Sgt William D Stepp (KIA)
                  A1C Michael J Cotterill (KIA)
                  A1C Ronald C Deforrest (KIA)

An EC-121R Bat Cat aircraft crashed two minutes after taking off from Korat on an operational mission on the afternoon of the 25th killing all 18 crew on board. The aircraft took off in a thunderstorm and the pilot requested vectors to the right in order to clear the storm. The aircraft climbed to about 500 feet against a 20-knot headwind before flying into turbulence and a severe wind shear that changed the headwind into a 60-knot tailwind. The pilot lost control and could not recover before the aircraft hit the ground in a rice paddy and exploded as it hit trees and broke up. The base HH-43 Pedro was scrambled when the tower could not get a response from the EC-121 and the wreckage was located about four miles southwest of Korat airbase. Lt Col Heller was a very experienced pilot with 5,583 flying hours to his credit, including 1,109 in the C-121, while the co-pilot, Maj Lunsford, had 4,388 hours in the C-121 and 6,607 hours in total. This aircraft had started life as a WV-2 with the US Navy and had flown from Barbers Point NAS in Hawaii for several years before being converted to EC-121R configuration for the USAF.

26 April 1969

A-1J   52-142029 602 SOS, 56 SOW, USAF, Nakhon Phanom
                  Maj James Boyd East (KIA)
The third aircraft to be lost over the Plain of Jars during April was a Skyraider from Nakhon Phanom that was lost on a night strike. Maj East was attacking enemy troops and mortar positions on the northeastern edge of the Plain when his aircraft was hit by 12.7mm anti-aircraft fire while on its third pass. The aircraft continued its dive on the target and flew into the ground killing Maj East. In 1994 a Laotian witness to the incident reported the location of the crash site and a joint US/Laotian team excavated the site later the same year. Bone fragments found were identified by mitochondrial DNA testing as being those of Maj East in July 1997. James East was finally laid to rest at Fort Sam Houston National Cemetery near San Antonio on 22 August 1997.

F-8J   150341   VF-51, USN, USS *Bon Homme Richard*
                  1 pilot, name unknown (survived)
A Crusader hit the *Bon Homme Richard's* ramp as it was landing from a CAP mission. The pilot was lucky to survive. This was the first F-8J model to be lost in the war and was simply a remanufactured F-8E with a strengthened wing and undercarriage and a few other minor modifications.

28 April 1969

F-4B   148427   VMFA-314, MAG-13, USMC, Chu Lai
                  Capt J S Garzik (survived)
                  Capt F L Massey (survived)
A flight of F-4Bs was attacking a target in the hills about 30 miles west of the city of Hué when one of the aircraft was damaged by ground fire. Capt Garzik was pulling up through 2,000 feet on his first pass when his aircraft was damaged and caught fire. He immediately turned east but he and his navigator had to eject when about 10 miles from Hué. They were both rescued by an Army helicopter having received only minor injuries.

A-7A   153164   VA-37, USN, USS *Kitty Hawk*
                  1 pilot, name unknown (survived)
During an attack mission a Corsair suffered an engine breakup which caused an explosion and fire. The pilot ejected safely and the cause was put down to a mechanical failure.

F-8J   150320   VF-53, USN, USS *Bon Homme Richard*
                  Lt(jg) M E Mansell (survived)
The *Bon Homme Richard* lost another Crusader when an aircraft developed an engine problem while on a CAP mission. The engine began to lose thrust as fuel and smoke were seen to be streaming from the aircraft's tailpipe. As an explosion appeared imminent, the pilot ejected and was rescued from the sea.

29 April 1969

C-130B 61-2637   29 TAS, 463 TAW, USAF, Clark
                  Maj R E Fromm (survived)
                  1Lt D L Hickson (survived)
                  Several other crew, unknown (survived)

A Hercules on a resupply flight from Tan Son Nhut was hit by ground fire as it was landing at the airfield at Loc Ninh, 70 miles north of Saigon. The aircraft was hit in the starboard wheel well and caught fire but the pilot carried out a crash landing and all the occupants escaped before the aircraft burnt out

30 April 1969

F-100D 56-3075   416 TFS, 37 TFW, USAF, Phu Cat
                  Maj R E Gibson (survived)
In addition to Skyraiders and Phantoms, Super Sabres were also used to drop acoustic and magnetic sensors near infiltration routes and trails. Maj Gibson was dropping sensors from 500 feet on a trail 15 miles north of Bien Hoa when he ran into ground fire. He headed southwest but was forced to eject near the town of Cu Chi, some 15 miles northwest of Saigon, where he was picked up by an Army helicopter.

RF-4C 66-0390   16 TRS, 460 TRW, USAF, Tan Son Nhut
                  Maj Glenn Allyn Gordon (KIA)
                  Maj Francis Ernest Stewart (KIA)
An RF-4C had been shot down on 17 April when trying to obtain photographs of Route 912 near Ban Topen, west of the Ban Karai Pass. On the last day of the month another RF-4C was despatched to try to obtain photographs of the same route. Maj Gordon and Maj Stewart were flying at about 5,000 feet when their Phantom was hit by ground fire and badly damaged. The aircraft caught fire but Maj Gordon managed to fly his crippled aircraft all the way to Da Nang. Unfortunately, the aircraft was destroyed and the crew killed during an attempted emergency landing at the base. The decision to attempt a landing in a badly damaged aircraft in the hope of returning the precious film was always a difficult one, as the mission would only have to be repeated until the required photographs had been obtained. Sadly, in this case, luck was against the crew.

2 May 1969

A-7A   153180   VA-105, USN, USS *Kitty Hawk*
                  Lt Cdr W J O'Connor (survived)
VA-105 lost a Corsair during a dusk strike on a suspected storage site near Route 920 just south of the A Shau Valley. Lt Cdr O'Connor was pulling up from a strafing run when his aircraft was hit by ground fire. The engine and electrical system failed and the pilot ejected a few miles from the target. He was later recovered by a USAF SAR helicopter.

O-2A   67-21305 23 TASS, 504 TASG, USAF, Nakhon Phanom
                  1Lt Phillip Louis Mascari (KIA)
A short time after the Corsair was shot down, a Nail FAC disappeared during a dusk mission near Tavouac in southern Laos, 20 miles southwest of the A Shau Valley. 1Lt Mascari was an F-4 pilot serving a tour as an FAC and was on his 33rd mission when he was lost. His parents visited Laos after the war in an attempt to discover their son's fate and were told by a Laotian villager that he had been buried near his aircraft.

F-105F 62-4445   354 TFS, 355 TFW, USAF, Takhli
                  2 crew, names unknown (survived)
Loss of oil pressure due to a mechanical failure caused an F-105F's engine to fail during a strike mission. The crew ejected safely near Takhli and were later rescued.

4 May 1969

F-100C 53-1741   188 TFS, 31 TFW, USAF, Tuy Hoa
                  Capt Michael T Adams (KIA)
The New Mexico ANG squadron lost a pilot on the 4th when an F-100 was shot down on a strike in the Steel Tiger area. Capt Adams was bombing a storage area near Ban Nathom Mai, 40 miles west of the DMZ, when his aircraft was hit by automatic weapons fire. Capt Adams ejected but was killed and his body was retrieved by an HH-53. Capt Adams was the last casualty suffered by the 188th TFS before its redeployment back to Kirtland AFB, New Mexico on 18 May having lost four aircraft and three pilots during its tour in Vietnam. This particular aircraft had earlier been damaged in a crash-landing incident at Da Nang.

The AC-130 Spectre Gunship II was one of them most successful weapons in the interdiction campaign against infiltration and resupply along the Ho Chi Minh Trail. Six AC-130s were shot down over southern Laos with the loss of a total of 52 aircrew. USAF

F-8J   150877   VF-53, USN, USS *Bon Homme Richard*
1 pilot, name unknown (survived)
A Crusader had to be abandoned during a combat air patrol when its afterburner blew out as the result of a fuel supply problem.

6 May 1969

O-1G   156682   VMO-6, MAG-39, USMC, Quang Tri
1Lt Norman Karl Billipp (KIA)
1Lt John Robert Hagan (KIA)
A Marine Corps Bird Dog and crew disappeared while on a visual reconnaissance flight. The aircraft had last been seen flying along Route 9 near the Laotian border. Although it was presumed to have been shot down neither the wreckage nor the crew were ever found. This was the second O-1G FAC conversion of the Bird Dog lost by the Marines in Vietnam. Norman Billip was declared dead in July 1976 and John Hagan in March 1978.

A-4E   152043   VA-94, USN, USS *Bon Homme Richard*
1 pilot, name unknown (survived)
A Skyhawk landed on board the *Bon Homme Richard* after a combat mission but then skidded off the deck into the sea. The pilot escaped safely.

8 May 1969

F-4C   64-0805   559 TFS, 12 TFW, USAF, Cam Ranh Bay
Maj William James Brashear (KIA)
1Lt Henry Gerald Mundt (KIA)
A flight of four Phantoms was bombing a section of road on the Ho Chi Minh Trail near the village of Ding, some 40 miles to the west of the abandoned Special Forces camp at Kham Duc. Bombing under a low cloud base, one of the aircraft was seen to be hit by AAA and burst into flames. The aircraft then dived into the ground and although parachutes were reported and a SAR aircraft spoke to one of the crew on the survival radio, neither of the men returned home alive.

F-8J   149226   VF-51, USN, USS *Bon Homme Richard*
Lt Cdr R G Snow (survived)
The *Bon Homme Richard* was having an unlucky time with the loss of five aircraft in accidents within the space of two weeks. The fifth aircraft to be lost was a Crusader that hit the ramp on landing. Fortunately, the pilot in this incident, as in the preceding four, escaped with his life.

9 May 1969

F-100D   55-3522   90 TFS, 3 TFW, USAF, Bien Hoa
1Lt J V Williford (survived)
A flight of F-100s was scrambled in response to a call for an air strike on enemy troops who were engaging friendly forces 30 miles northeast of Bien Hoa. 1Lt Williford made three successful passes but on his fourth run, as he was about to drop napalm, his aircraft was hit by 12.7mm anti-aircraft fire. Williford managed to get about 10 miles south of the target area before he had to abandon the aircraft. An Army helicopter later rescued him.

O-2A   67-21329   20 TASS, 504 TASG, USAF, Da Nang
1 pilot, name unknown (survived)
An O-2 crashed near Da Nang and was destroyed following an engine failure.

10 May 1969

B-52D   56-0593   509 BW attached to 4133 BW(P),
USAF, Andersen
Capt James L Sipes (KIA)
1Lt Larry Ivan Broadhead (KIA)
Capt Russell L Platt (KIA)
1Lt Maurice E Lundy (KIA)
1Lt Thomas R McCormick (KIA)
MSgt Harold B Deel (KIA)
A B-52 crashed into the Pacific Ocean shortly after take off from Andersen AFB on Guam, killing all on board.

11 May 1969

F-4B   152988   VMFA-115, MAG-13, USMC, Chu Lai
1Lt Gary L Bain (survived)
1Lt William Cornelius Ryan (KIA)
A section of Phantoms from VMFA-115 was tasked with a strike on a storage area near Ban Kate in the Steel Tiger area of southern Laos. As one of the aircraft pulled up from the target it was hit by ground fire and crashed shortly afterwards. Only one of the crew managed to eject from the stricken aircraft and he was rescued by a USAF SAR helicopter but had suffered a broken arm and leg. This was second time lucky for 1Lt Bain as he had already survived the crash of a Phantom on 12 January 1969. William Ryan may have been the same W C Ryan who survived the crash of a VMFA-323 Phantom on 12 January 1969.

12 May 1969

F-4J   155788   VMFA-334, MAG-13, USMC, Chu Lai
1Lt D H Matzko (survived)
1Lt P E Daly (survived)
Another Marine Corps Phantom was lost the following day when a VMFA-334 aircraft was shot down during a close air support mission in the DMZ buffer zone. 1Lt Matzko was delivering napalm on a target near the village of Bo Ho Su when ground fire damaged the aircraft's starboard wing. The aircraft sped out to sea and the crew had to eject about 10 miles off the coast near Da Nang. This was the second time within a little over two months that 1Lt Daly had been shot down as he had survived an incident on 2 March. This was the last aircraft lost by VMFA-334 before it redeployed to Iwakuni on 30 August. The Squadron was one of the first Marine Corps units to be redeployed from Vietnam as part of the gradual withdrawal from Southeast Asia.

A-7B   154441   VA-25, USN, USS *Ticonderoga*
1 pilot, name unknown (survived)
A Corsair pilot ran out of fuel and out of luck when his engine flamed out just as he was about to hook up to a tanker during a combat mission. Unable to regain contact with the tanker's hose the pilot had no option but to eject.

14 May 1969

F-105F   62-4435   354 TFS, 355 TFW, USAF, Takhli
Maj A M Yahanda (survived)
A two-seat F-105F was being flown by a single pilot as a normal strike aircraft on a mission over southern Laos. Maj Yahanda was attacking a truck on a road near Ban Naden, about 20 miles west of the Mu Gia Pass. On its second pass, the aircraft was damaged by ground fire. Maj Yahanda flew back across Laos into Thailand but was forced to eject just five miles from Udorn. This aircraft was painted as 'Roman Knight' while at Takhli.

16 May 1969

U-10B   66-14372   14 SOW, USAF, Bien Hoa
A U-10 was being recovered by a heavy lift helicopter, probably from a forced landing near an airfield, the aircraft was damaged beyond repair when it fell from the sling.

F-4B   153037   VMFA-314, MAG-13, USMC, Chu Lai
2 crew, names unknown (survived)
As a Phantom was taking off from Cubi Point NAS in the Philippines for a ferry flight to Chu Lai the pilot over-rotated the aircraft and the Phantom lifted off at too low an airspeed and stalled. Both the crew ejected safely.

17 May 1969

F-4D   serial ..?   unit ..?, USAF, base ..?
1Lt Virgil Grant Stewart (KIA)
1 crew, name unknown (survived)
A Phantom was hit by ground fire over the Mu Gia Pass during an armed reconnaissance mission. The crew ejected but only one man was picked up successfully. 1Lt Stewart radioed that he was on the ground with a broken arm and leg. One of the two SAR helicopters had to abort the mission as it was unable to refuel, however, rescue forces spotted 1Lt Stewart as they came under fire from a nearby anti-aircraft gun. A helicopter from the 40th ARRS lowered a PJ to the ground but he discovered that 1Lt Stewart was dead. As NVA troops were closing in it was not possible to recover Virgil Stewart's body.

18 May 1969

C-123K   54-0639   310 SOS, 315 SOW, USAF, Phan Rang
1Lt Neil William Hayden (KIA)
1Lt Douglas McArthur Evans (KIA)
MSgt Duane Leland Hartenhoff (KIA)
TSgt Kermit Bruce Roberts (KIA)
SSgt Carl Joseph Wanner (KIA)
Sgt Milton Jackson Bush (KIA)
A Provider on an airlift sortie had its port engine damaged by 12.7mm ground fire near Tanh Linh, 50 miles east of Bien Hoa. The crew struggled to keep the burning aircraft airborne and headed for Bien Hoa to try to make an emergency landing. Tragically, the aircraft crashed just six miles northeast of the airfield killing all on board.

KC-130F   149814   VMGR-152, MAG-15, USMC, Da Nang
Maj Jimmie Dwayne Sells (KIA)
Maj John Clarence Williamson (KIA)
MGSgt Carroll Franklin Hersey (KIA)
MSgt Edmond Chester Polenski (KIA)
Sgt Robert Allen Bonebright (KIA)
Cpl James Allen Cox (KIA)

F-4B   151001   VMFA-542, MAG-11, USMC, Da Nang
1Lt Charles William Pigott (KIA)
Capt John Laurence Nalls (KIA)

F-4B 151450 VMFA-314, MAG-13, USMC, Chu Lai
Maj J D Moody (survived)
1Lt Griffiths (survived)

One of the worst air accidents suffered by the Marines during the war in Southeast Asia took place on 18 May near Phu Bai, just south of the DMZ. Two Phantoms from VMFA-314 were plugged into a KC-130F tanker taking on fuel when a Phantom from VMFA-542 on an opposite track slammed into the tanker's starboard wing near the Number 3 engine. The crew from one of the VMFA-314 fighters managed to eject over the sea after jettisoning their bombs and the other aircraft (flown by Maj A Gillespie and 1Lt V Maddox) returned safely to Chu Lai. Tragically, the VMFA-542 aircraft and the Hercules crashed with the loss of all on board. 1Lt Pigott had recently arrived in theatre and was on an orientation flight with an experienced navigator.

21 May 1969

F-8J 150926 VF-194, USN, USS *Oriskany*
Lt Obar (survived)

The USS *Oriskany* returned to the line on 16 May to commence its fourth tour of the war. Six days after it started operations over Laos, the ship lost a Crusader when it suffered a fuel system malfunction during a CAP mission. On 9 July 1968 this particular Crusader was flown by Lt Cdr John Nichols of VF-191 when he shot down a MiG-17 while escorting an RF-8G reconnaissance aircraft.

23 May 1969

A-4E 150119 VMA-311, MAG-12, USMC, Chu Lai
1Lt Peter W Otis (survived)

A flight of Skyhawks from Chu Lai was assigned to a close air support mission about 16 miles northwest of Da Nang. 1Lt Otis was preparing to attack the target with napalm but his aircraft was hit by ground fire and he ejected almost immediately after making a brief Mayday call. He was soon recovered and returned to Chu Lai.

The AC-130 Spectre Gunship

The limitations of the AC-47 as a gunship became apparent soon after the type's introduction to combat. However, the gunship concept was so promising that work on a successor system started and a number of types were considered. Eventually the C-130 Hercules was selected for a variety of reasons including its better performance, longer endurance, ability to carry more and heavier weapons and better avionics. Known as the Gunship II programme, the first AC-130A test aircraft arrived at Nha Trang on 21 September 1967 for a 10-week operational trial over Laos and South Vietnam. The aircraft returned to Nha Trang in February 1968 after a brief refurbishment in the USA and continued operational trials until December. A host of technical and supply problems constantly delayed the delivery of further AC-130s but eventually enough aircraft arrived in Southeast Asia to form a squadron. The 16th SOS was activated at Ubon under the 8th TFW on 30 October 1968 using the original test crews and aircraft as a nucleus. The AC-130A programme was code-named Pave Pronto but the aircraft was more commonly known as Spectre after the Squadron's radio call sign. Four more AC-130s had arrived at Ubon by the end of 1968 allowing the prototype, 54-1626, to return to the USA for refurbishment.

From December 1968 many Spectre missions were flown with F-4 escorts provided by the Night Owls of the 497th TFS. Each gunship sortie would be accompanied by up to three F-4s, which cycled to and from tankers to provide a continuous presence to increase the firepower available and to help protect the AC-130 from ground attack. Late in 1969 modified AC-130s under the code name Surprise Package began to arrive at Ubon. These aircraft had improved armament including 20mm Gatling guns and 40mm Bofors cannon and a Paveway 1 laser designator.

24 May 1969

F-100D 55-3555 355 TFS, 31 TFW, USAF, Tuy Hoa
Capt Charles Jerome Manske (KIA)

Capt Manske's Super Sabre was damaged by ground fire during a close air support mission over South Vietnam. He was bombing enemy troops in contact with friendly forces when his aircraft was hit by small arms fire. He crossed the coast and headed for his base but the aircraft crashed in the sea about 25 miles northeast of Tuy Hoa and he was killed.

AC-130A 54-1629 16 SOS, 8 TFW, USAF, Ubon
Lt Col William H Schwehm (survived)
Maj Gerald H Piehl (survived)
SSgt Cecil Taylor (KIA)
SSgt Jack Wayne Troglen (KIA)
9 crew, names unknown (survived)

The first AC-130 gunship to be lost during the war was on a night armed reconnaissance mission over southern Laos checking Routes 914 and 920 for truck traffic. The aircraft was about to attack a truck convoy on a road near the village of Ban Tanbok, about 20 miles southwest of the A Shau Valley, when it was hit. It took two rounds of 37mm AAA in the tail and fuselage as it orbited at 6,500 feet. The hydraulic system failed and the aircraft started climbing uncontrollably until the pilot and co-pilot wrestled the control columns to full forward and brought all the crewmembers to the flight deck to make the aircraft nose-heavy. It was then discovered that the elevator trim, rudder control and autopilot were no longer functioning but the pilots regained partial control by the use of aileron trim and differential engine power. Unfortunately SSgt Troglen, the illuminator operator, had been mortally wounded and died before the aircraft landed. Lt Col Schwehm nursed the damaged aircraft back to Ubon and ordered most of the crew to bail out near the airfield before attempting a landing. As the aircraft touched down the starboard undercarriage collapsed and the AC-130 veered off the runway shearing off the starboard wing when it hit the barrier cable housing causing the aircraft to catch fire. SSgt Taylor, the flight engineer, was unable to escape and died in the incident.

RF-8G 146844 Detachment 34, VFP-63, USN, USS *Oriskany*
Lt(jg) S L Ritchey (survived)

The *Oriskany* lost its second Crusader within five days when an aircraft had an engine flameout during a photographic reconnaissance mission. The cause was presumed to be accidental rather than battle damage.

25 May 1969

F-100D 56-3119 352 TFS, 35 TFW, USAF, Phan Rang
1Lt D G Stanford (survived)

The last of four F-100s shot down during May was lost during a close air support mission in South Vietnam. The target was VC troops in the open near the Saigon River, about 10 miles southwest of Lai Khe. 1Lt Stanford had completed his attack and was leaving the target area at low level when his aircraft was damaged by small arms fire. The aircraft must have been too badly damaged to permit a safe landing so 1Lt Stanford flew southeast and crossed the coast to eject over the sea about 30 miles east of the city of Vung Tau. He was rescued by a US Navy ship that had been notified to look out for the pilot.

O-2A 67-21361 19 TASS, 504 TASG, USAF, Bien Hoa
3 crew, names unknown (survived)

An O-2 crashed in South Vietnam following an engine failure.

27 May 1969

C-130A 56-0472 21 TAS, 374 TAW, USAF, Naha
Maj A M Moore (survived)
1Lt C A Peterson (survived)
Several other crew, unknown (survived)

The USAF transport fleet was going through a bad patch with three aircraft lost in combat within four weeks. The third of these was a Hercules that was damaged by ground fire as it was about to land at Katum with a load of construction equipment. As it approached the runway fuel started streaming from the starboard wing and when the propellers went into reverse pitch after touchdown the fuel was sucked up into the engines and ignited. The resulting fire ignited more fuel in the starboard wing tanks,

which then exploded, and the aircraft came to a halt just off the runway. All the crew evacuated safely but the aircraft was damaged beyond repair by the fire.

29 May 1969

OV-10A 155403 VMO-6, MAG-39, USMC, Quang Tri
Capt John R Morgan (survived)
1Lt Robert J Moriarty (survived)

In November 1968 VMO-6 received the first of its new OV-10A Broncos to supplement the O-1s it had received only four months earlier. The OV-10 was a significant improvement over the O-1 in terms of speed and firepower and was used in the higher threat areas. The Squadron's first OV-10 to be lost was shot down during a visual reconnaissance mission on 29 May. A Bronco crew spotted a raft on a river near Lang Chei, seven miles south of Khe Sanh. Rafts were frequently used by the VC and NVA to transport supplies to their forces in the field. The aircraft dived to attack the raft but as it was pulling up from its attack it was hit by AAA. The port engine caught fire and the crew ejected a few miles from the river. They were later rescued by a Marine Corps CH-46 helicopter and quickly returned to Quang Tri.

1 June 1969

O-2A 67-21319 20 TASS, 504 TASG, USAF, Da Nang
1Lt Kennard E Svanoe (KIA)
Capt Jackie L Dickens (KIA)

June would turn out to be a bad month for the O-2 operators with four aircraft lost and seven airmen killed. The first aircraft was shot down by small arms fire during an FAC mission 20 miles northwest of Da Nang. The crew were controlling an air strike on enemy buildings and both men died in the crash of their aircraft, a fact verified by an Army helicopter crew who later reached the site.

2 June 1969

O-2A 67-21316 20 TASS, 504 TASG, USAF, Da Nang
1Lt James Robson Gilmore (KIA)

The second O-2 FAC lost in June was shot down by .30 calibre ground fire during a visual reconnaissance mission near Tam Ky. The aircraft crashed in flames and the pilot was unable to bail out before it hit the ground.

3 June 1969

F-100D 55-3790 614 TFS, 35 TFW, USAF, Phan Rang
1Lt Donald Francis Ginart (KIA)

A Super Sabre was lost during a close air support mission 10 miles southwest of Quan Long in the extreme southern tip of South Vietnam. 1Lt Ginart was making his second strafing pass against VC structures when his F-100 was hit by automatic weapons fire. He may have been wounded as he was unable to eject before the aircraft crashed close to the target. An Army helicopter later visited the crash site and recovered his body.

5 June 1969

RF-4C 66-0388 11 TRS, 432 TRW, USAF, Udorn
Col R F Findlay (survived)
Capt D M Moy (survived)

An RF-4C was sent off on a mission to photograph sections of Route 101 in North Vietnam close to Dong Hoi. As the aircraft flew just to the west of the town at 4,500 feet it was hit by a 57mm shell. Col Findlay turned out to sea and he and his navigator ejected just two miles offshore. They were rescued by a USAF SAR helicopter in full sight of the residents of Dong Hoi. This was the first US aircraft to be lost over North Vietnam for six months, the three previous aircraft in November and December 1968 also being involved in reconnaissance missions.

O-1F 57-2981 504 TASG, USAF, Phan Thiet

A Bird Dog FAC aircraft was destroyed by a 107mm rocket during a Viet Cong night attack on the airstrip at Phan Thiet. This aircraft was the last of the 310 TL-19D instrument training variant of the Bird Dog to be built. It was later redesignated as an O-1D and then converted to an O-1F model.

6 June 1969

OV-10A 67-14665 19 TASS, 504 TASG, USAF, Bien Hoa
1 pilot, name unknown (survived)

As a Bronco was accelerating for take off at Bien Hoa, one of its tyres burst and the aircraft slewed off the runway and was damaged beyond repair.

O-1G 51-12824 20 TASS, 504 TASG, USAF, Da Nang
O-2A 67-21325 20 TASS, 504 TASG, USAF, Da Nang
Two of the 20th TASS's FAC aircraft were destroyed by 122mm rockets during a Viet Cong strike on the airfield at Da Nang on the night of the 6th. A total of 20 rockets were fired during the attack and a further 12 aircraft were damaged and four men killed.

7 June 1969

EC-47P 43-49547 362 TEWS, 460 TRW, USAF, Pleiku
8 crew, names unknown (survived)

One of the 362nd's venerable EC-47 RDF aircraft was destroyed following an engine failure during an operational mission.

8 June 1969

A-7B 154383 VA-215, USN, USS *Enterprise*
1 pilot, name unknown (survived)

During a combat mission a Corsair pilot was warned of fire coming from his tailpipe. With his engine winding down he ejected safely and was picked up by a Navy helicopter. The incident was attributed to a mechanical failure rather than enemy action.

A-1H 52-135356 22 SOS, 56 SOW, USAF, Nakhon Phanom
1Lt Lloyd M Scott (KIA)

A Skyraider pilot was killed when the aircraft's engine failed during an armed reconnaissance sortie and the aircraft crashed in Thailand. The cause was thought to be a mechanical failure rather than combat damage. The date of 1Lt Scott's death is given as 9 June on the Vietnam Wall in Washington, DC.

The QU-22B was one of several highly modified types designed for the collection of data from the sensors dropped as part of the Igloo White programme. The aircraft could be flown by remote control although most flights in Southeast Asia were flown by a pilot. USAF

The QU-22

One of the integral parts of the Igloo White surveillance system was the little QU-22, a unique aircraft in Southeast Asia in that it could be flown either with or without a pilot. The QU-22 was a highly modified version of the Beech A36 Bonanza light aircraft under the Pave Eagle II programme. Although the aircraft could be operated by remote control as a pilotless drone, it was usually flown with a pilot on board in Southeast Asia. The aircraft was fitted with wingtip fuel tanks and a Continental IO-520-B engine with a special reduction gearbox to turn the propeller at a very low rpm to reduce the aircraft's noise signature. The aircraft was also fitted with avionics equipment that received the information transmitted by the acoustic and seismic sensors that littered the Ho Chi Minh Trail. The information was retransmitted either to an orbiting EC-121R or direct to the Eagle White facility at Nakhon Phanom for analysis. A total of six YQU-22As and 27 QU-22Bs were produced and the first aircraft arrived at Nakhon Phanom in March 1969. Many of the survivors were later converted back to a more standard configuration and sold to private owners in the USA.

11 June 1969

F-4D 66-7493 390 TFS, 366 TFW, USAF, Da Nang
Maj W R Deans (survived)
Maj C A Thomas (survived)

A pair of Phantoms was despatched to fly escort for an attack mission on an automatic weapons site near Hiep Duc, 17 miles west of Tam Ky. Maj Deans was on his second low-level pass over the target when his aircraft was struck by small arms fire. The aircraft was hit in the aft fuselage and the crew ejected a few miles from the target. Both men were later rescued by a USAF SAR helicopter.

YQU-22A 68-10531 553 RW, USAF, Nakhon Phanom
1 pilot, name unknown (survived)

The first QU-22 to be destroyed in Southeast Asia crashed following engine failure during an operational sortie. This aircraft was the prototype YQU-22A and the first of 33 QU-22 aircraft.

12 June 1969

A-1H 52-134614 602 SOS, 56 SOW, USAF, Nakhon Phanom
1Lt Neal Clinton Ward (KIA)

Two Skyraider pilots on an armed reconnaissance mission over the Barrel Roll area of northern Laos came across a truck convoy near the town of Ban Ban. The aircraft set up an attack pattern but 1Lt Ward was shot down as he dived on the target for the fifth time. Hit by automatic weapons fire, the aircraft crashed close to the convoy and the pilot was not seen to escape before the aircraft hit the ground and exploded.

14 June 1969

F-105D 60-5381 354 TFS, 355 TFW, USAF, Takhli
Maj Harold Kahler (KIA)

Another pilot was lost on a Barrel Roll mission on the 14th. Two Thuds were searching for trucks on a road in northern Laos but failed to find any. However, they did find a bridge and a ford near Ban Na Muang and requested permission to attack this new target. The lead aircraft rolled in to drop its bombs followed by Maj Kahler. The leader saw a flash of light in his rear-view mirror and tried to contact Kahler without success. Assuming that Maj Kahler had been shot down by AAA, the leader quickly searched the area before he was forced to return for lack of fuel. A search team later located the wreckage of Maj Kahler's F-105 but found no sign of the pilot. On the same day, the Pathet Lao claimed to have shot down an American aircraft and that the pilot had been 'suitably punished'! Whatever the punishment was, Harold Kahler, a Second World War veteran, was never seen again. Thunderchief 60-5381 was painted as 'Miss Marie' when it served with the Korat Wing.

F-4D 66-7574 497 TFS, 8 TFW, USAF, Ubon
Capt James William Grace (KIA)
1Lt Wayne J Karas (survived)

A Wolf fast FAC was lost in southern Laos during a BDA mission. As the aircraft approached a bridge it was hit by ground fire from a ZPU anti-aircraft gun site. Some time later Capt Grace and 1Lt Karas ejected near Ban Kapay. A USAF CH-3C Special Forces helicopter from the 20th SOS reached the area and rescued 1Lt Karas but as Capt Grace was being hauled up on the jungle penetrator, the helicopter hit a tree and he fell, most probably to his death. His body could not be found despite a ground search later in the year and in June 1976 he was officially declared dead. In 1997 the cockpit canopy of 66-7574 was found in the jungle and recovered by a JTF-FA team as a potential memorial for the 8th TFW.

The Cessna O-2B was used exclusively by the 9th SOS in Southeast Asia. Along with C-47s and U-10s, the O-2B was employed in psychological warfare roles and two aircraft were shot down with the loss of four crewmen. USAF

An F-100 was damaged by ground fire during a close air support mission in South Vietnam. Capt Casper flew his burning aircraft out over the coast near Phan Rang and ejected about five miles out to sea. He was later rescued by a USAF helicopter. During the rescue attempt an HH-43F (59-1590 of Detachment 1 from the 38th ARRS at Phan Rang) crashed, probably due to ground fire. None of the crew suffered any major injuries.

28 June 1969

A-1E   52-133927   1 SOS, 56 SOW, USAF, Nakhon Phanom
                  Lt Col W D Neal (survived)
                  Maj W L Bagwell (survived)
A Skyraider on a Barrel Roll armed reconnaissance mission strafed enemy forces at an abandoned Lima Site at Muong Soui on the western edge of the Plain of Jars. During the attack the aircraft was hit in the starboard wing by automatic weapons fire and the wing started to burn. The aircraft crashed seconds later but both the crew escaped and were recovered. Maj Bagwell had been shot down in southern Laos on 21 October 1968.

2 July 1969

A-1H   52-137543   1 SOS, 56 SOW, USAF, Nakhon Phanom
                  Capt John Leroy Flinn (KIA)
Another Skyraider was lost near Muong Soui while on an armed reconnaissance sortie. Capt Flinn spotted a truck on a road and dived to strafe it. His aircraft was hit by ground fire and crashed close to the road. Capt Flinn apparently did not have time to eject from his aircraft before it crashed.

3 July 1969

F-4B   153015   VF-213, USN, USS *Kitty Hawk*
                  2 crew, names unknown (survived)
The *Kitty Hawk* lost a Phantom that went out of control during a reconnaissance escort mission. The probable cause was a control malfunction of some kind, possibly a foreign object jamming the controls. Both the crew ejected safely and were rescued.

F-8J   150656   VF-162, USN, USS *Ticonderoga*
                  Lt T R Weinal (survived)
A control malfunction was also the probable cause of the loss of a Crusader during a CAP mission on the same day. Again, the pilot ejected and was soon rescued.

4 July 1969

A-1H   52-137512   602 SOS, 56 SOW, USAF, Nakhon Phanom
                  Col Patrick Martin Fallon (KIA)
Col Fallon was the vice-commander of the 56th SOW. Like many wing staff, he insisted on flying operational missions to remain current and to inspire the aircrew and ground crew under his command. He and his wingman were flying an armed reconnaissance mission over the southern half of the Plain of Jars when they were directed to a group of enemy troops that had been sighted near the village of Muang Pot, on the southwestern edge of the Plain. Col Fallon was pulling up from his second pass over the troops when his aircraft was hit by 12.7mm anti-aircraft fire. He ejected near the enemy troops and came down between two high ridges. Both ridges were occupied by enemy troops and Fallon's wingman attacked them until his aircraft was damaged forcing him to return to base. Col Fallon was in voice contact with the rescue forces but he was surrounded by enemy troops and was wounded. His final message was to request the Spads to bomb the enemy all around him as, in his own words 'They have zapped me. I've had it.' It was presumed that he was killed by the enemy soldiers in a final stand of defiance. A few months later a report was received to the effect that a US airmen had been killed by grenades while defending himself with a pistol. Patrick Fallon had flown

---

16 June 1969

F-105D   60-0530   354 TFS, 355 TFW, USAF, Takhli
                  1Lt J L Devoss (survived)
A flight of F-105s was sent to attack a cluster of three 14.5mm gun sites that had been pinpointed near the town of Ban Ban in northern Laos. 1Lt Devoss was making his first strafing run on the target when his aircraft was hit at 3,000 feet by return fire from the guns. He left the area and flew back towards Thailand but was forced to eject from his aircraft near Ban Thasi, 35 miles north of the Thai border. He was later rescued by a USAF HH-53 helicopter having suffered a broken leg and arm during the ejection. F-105D 60-0530 was painted as 'Tandem Turtle' when it flew with the 34th TFS.

F-4D   66-7510   389 TFS, 366 TFW, USAF, Da Nang
                  Maj G G Fulghom (survived)
                  1Lt Harmon Polster (survived)
An anti-aircraft gun was also the target for a US air strike in South Vietnam. A flight of Phantoms from Da Nang was sent to destroy a .50 calibre gun site near Duc Pho, 15 miles south of Quang Ngai. Again, one of the attacking aircraft was hit and damaged by return fire. Maj Fulghom headed northeast, crossed the coast and he and his WSO ejected about 10 miles off the coast near Chu Lai. They were quickly pulled out of the water by an Army helicopter. Sadly, Harmon Polster was killed when he was shot down again a few weeks later on 15 July with another pilot.

19 June 1969

O-2A   68-6869   19 TASS, 504 TASG, USAF, Bien Hoa
                  Capt James Dean Hoag (KIA)
                  1Lt George Richard Dover, USMC (KIA)
Capt Hoag and his Marine Corps observer, 1Lt Dover, were killed while on an FAC mission near Lang Phuoc Hai, 15 miles northeast of Vung Tau. They were controlling an air strike on Viet Cong rocket and mortar launching sites when their O-2's tail was blown off by ground fire. Both men died when the aircraft crashed before they could bail out.

22 June 1969

O-2B   67-21455   9 SOS, 14 SOW, USAF, Nha Trang
                  Maj Erich Carl Engelhard (KIA)
                  1Lt Michael Anthony Seagroves (KIA)
The fourth O-2 lost during June was an O-2B psychological warfare aircraft or 'leaflet bomber' from the 9th SOS. The aircraft was directed towards a group of enemy troops 20 miles north of Nha Trang, probably to use its loudspeakers to broadcast messages designed to incite defection, rather than to drop leaflets. The aircraft was shot down near Ninh Hoa and, once again, both the crew died in the crash.

A-4E   152029   VA-144, USN, USS *Bon Homme Richard*
                  Lt(jg) Leland Charles Cooke Sage (KIA)

Lt Sage led his wingman on a Steel Tiger strike at night under the control of an FAC. He rolled in on the target near Ban Soppeng, 15 miles west of the Mu Gia Pass, but for some reason did not drop any bombs. Lt Sage rolled in from 11,000 feet for his second attempt and stated that he would pull up and egress to the left of the target. Two FACs in the area saw his aircraft dive towards the target and continue in a straight line until it exploded on the ground near the target. Although there was light flak in the area and he may have been hit, there was a strong possibility that Lt Sage, in his anxiety to deliver his bombs on target, became preoccupied with his bomb switch settings and flew into the ground.

23 June 1969

C-130B   61-0965   773 TAS, 463 TAW, USAF, Clark
                  Capt Gary Edward Brunner (KIA)
                  Maj William Howard Condit (KIA)
                  1Lt Terry Michael Reed (KIA)
                  Lt Col Jean Arthur Kearby (KIA)
                  SSgt Billy Wallace McDonald (KIA)
                  SSgt George Charles Peters (KIA)
The only transport aircraft to be lost during June was a Hercules from Tan Son Nhut that was shot down at Katum during a resupply mission to the Special Forces camp. The aircraft was flying at 3,000 feet and was hit in the port wing by a quad .50 calibre radar-directed anti-aircraft gun causing a fire and engine failure. The Hercules stalled and spun into the ground killing the crew who were on their first shuttle together as a crew. The aircraft was carrying three pallets of 105mm howitzer ammunition at the time of the incident. The remains of four of the crew were recovered and identified soon after the incident but it was not until October 1994 that a joint US/Vietnamese investigation team excavated the wreck site and found remains that were identified four years later as those of Maj Condit and 1Lt Reed.

25 June 1969

F-4B   151416   VMFA-542, MAG-11, USMC, Da Nang
                  1Lt A Vadyak (survived)
                  1Lt S S Talbot (survived)
A flight of Phantoms was flying a close air support mission near Dong Ha just south of the DMZ when one of the aircraft was shot down. 1Lt Vadyak was pulling up through 5,000 feet after a 20-degree dive on his target when ground fire struck the aircraft's fuselage. Seconds later the crew were forced to eject but they were later recovered.

26 June 1969

F-100D   55-3516   614 TFS, 35 TFW, USAF, Phan Rang
                  Capt J H Casper (survived)

over 100 combat mission during his time in Southeast Asia and had flown 125 missions as an FAC pilot in the Korean War.

5 July 1969

F-100D 55-3589   531 TFS, 3 TFW, USAF, Bien Hoa
                    1Lt S L Shook (survived)

An F-100 was lost during a close air support mission near the town of My Tho in the Mekong Delta, about 30 miles southwest of Saigon. 1Lt Shook was making his fourth run on the target, which consisted of Viet Cong buildings and bunkers, and was preparing to drop napalm canisters. As he came down to 100 feet to make his delivery the aircraft was hit by small arms fire. The pilot pulled up into a climb and ejected moments later, landing safely less than a mile from his target. An Army helicopter that was in the vicinity rescued him before the VC could reach him.

6 July 1969

F-8H 148636   VF-111, USN, USS *Ticonderoga*
                    Lt G P Hahn (survived)

The *Ticonderoga* lost another Crusader while on a CAP mission during July when an aircraft suffered a loss of oil pressure leading to total engine failure.

8 July 1969

A-26A 64-17646   609 SOS, 56 SOW, USAF, Nakhon Phanom
                    Maj James Elmo Sizemore (KIA)
                    Maj Howard Vincent Andre (KIA)

As well as flying night interdiction missions over the Ho Chi Minh Trail in southern Laos, the Invaders of the 609th SOS also flew Barrel Roll missions in northern and central Laos. Maj Sizemore and Maj Andre were on a night mission and were directed to strafe enemy troops near Ban Keo Koong on the southern edge of the Plain of Jars. The aircraft was seen to make its strafing run but then flew into a hill, either as a result of ground fire or pilot error. Both the crew were killed in the crash. This was the last A-26 to be lost in Southeast Asia. The 609th SOS flew its last mission over the Trail on the night of 9 November and then flew its weary Invaders to Clark AB in the Philippines for eventual return to the USA and retirement at the boneyard at Davis-Monthan AFB, Arizona. Of the 30 aircraft used in Southeast Asia, 12 had been lost on operational flights. The aircraft had built itself an enviable reputation and was claimed by many to be the most effective night interdiction weapon over the Ho Chi Minh Trail with the exception of the AC-130 gunship.

9 July 1969

O-1G 51-5103   21 TASS, 504 TASG, USAF, Nha Trang
                    Capt H Hiu (survived)

A Bird Dog FAC was flying just north of the Song Da Rang River when it was hit by small arms fire. The engine was damaged so the pilot made a crash-landing about six miles northwest of Tuy Hoa suffering major injuries in the process. He was picked up by an Army helicopter and evacuated to a medical facility, possibly to one of the ships that served as floating hospitals just off the South Vietnamese coast.

10 July 1969

F-100D 56-3049   531 TFS, 3 TFW, USAF, Bien Hoa
                    1Lt R M Hargett (survived)

1Lt Hargett had been shot down in his F-100 near Binh Thuy on 23 April so he must have thought himself doubly unlucky but also doubly blessed when he survived another shoot down on 10 July. He was making his second strafing attack on a group of enemy troops in sampans near Cao Lanh when his aircraft was struck by ground fire. The Super Sabre's engine began to wind down and 1Lt Hargett ejected safely near Sa Dec a few miles to the south and was later recovered.

12 July 1969

F-100D 55-2849   309 TFS, 31 TFW, USAF, Tuy Hoa
                    Capt F T Brady (survived)

A Super Sabre was shot down during a close air support mission 30 miles northwest of Phan Rang. Capt Brady was strafing Viet Cong buildings near Ap Lac Vien when his aircraft ran into a hail of small arms fire. He ejected immediately and was fortunate to be picked up by a USAF helicopter before he fell into the hands of the VC.

F-4D 66-7697   433 TFS, 8 TFW, USAF, Ubon
                    Maj Paul Wedlake Bannon (KIA)
                    1Lt Peter Xavier Pike (KIA)

The third Wolf FAC to be lost went missing during a visual reconnaissance mission over the northern sector of the Ho Chi Minh Trail in the Laotian panhandle. The target area was shrouded by low cloud and Maj Bannon radioed that he was trying to find a break in the cloud to move to another part of the Trail. The transmission suddenly stopped in mid-sentence at the same time as the aircraft's radar return disappeared. The aircraft was lost in a remote mountainous area south of Ban Nathon and it was thought unlikely that either of the crew had survived the incident. Whether the aircraft had been shot down or flew into a mountain could not be determined. Maj Bannon was the Wolf FAC operations officer while 1Lt Pike was on his first Wolf mission.

14 July 1969

O-1E 51-12505   19 TASS, 504 TASG, USAF, Bien Hoa
                    detached to Quan Loi
                    Maj F J Floyd (survived)

An Loc was under increasing pressure from enemy forces and operations in and out of the airfield were never free from a degree of risk. On the 14th a Bird Dog aircraft was hit by automatic weapons fire as it took off on a visual reconnaissance mission. The engine stopped but Maj Floyd made a successful crash-landing and was recovered by an Army patrol and brought back to the base.

15 July 1969

F-105D 60-0518   44 TFS, 388 TFW, USAF, Korat
                    Maj R E Kennedy (survived)

A flight of F-105s was sent to bomb a storage area near Ban San, just west of the Ban Karai Pass. Maj Kennedy's aircraft was hit by ground fire and badly damaged. The aircraft caught fire but Maj Kennedy was able to return across Laos and into Thailand but was forced to eject about 10 miles southwest of the town of Maha Sarakham while heading for Korat. This aircraft was credited with a MiG-17 when flown by Maj R S Dickey on 4 December 1966. It was painted as 'Thud Protector of SEA' and 'Billie Babe' while at Korat.

F-4D 66-7603   389 TFS, 37 TFW, USAF, Phu Cat
                    Capt Michael Stephen Walker (KIA)
                    1Lt Harmon Polster (KIA)

As night fell a flight of Phantoms set out to bomb a 37mm anti-aircraft gun site near Ban Dakvo in southern Laos, 25 miles west of Kham Duc. As one of the aircraft was pulling up from its first attack it was seen to be hit by AAA and crash into the jungle. There was no evidence that either of the crew had been able to escape from the aircraft. 1Lt Polster had survived being shot down with another pilot almost exactly a month earlier.

16 July 1969

F-100D 56-3420   416 TFS, 31 TFW, USAF, Tuy Hoa
                    Capt James Vernon Dawson (KIA)

A Super Sabre was lost in an accident just off the coast of South Vietnam during an attack mission in which the pilot was killed.

17 July 1969

F-105D 62-4394   333 TFS, 355 TFW, USAF, Takhli
                    Maj Fred W Shattuck (Died)

A Thunderchief pilot died in a tragic accident at Takhli when one of the tyres burst as the aircraft was taking off. The undercarriage collapsed and the aircraft exploded and burnt out. A firefighter and a medic, who had arrived on board one of the 38th ARRS's

HH-43s soon after the crash, removed the pilot from the cockpit but he died in hospital in Okinawa two days later. F-105D 62-4394 was named 'Big Bunny' and was credited with a MiG-17, which it shot down when being flown by Maj D M Russell on 18 October 1967.

The Black Ponies

VAL-4, the Black Ponies, was formed at North Island NAS, California in January 1969 to fly the OV-10A in the light attack role in Southeast Asia. A total of 18 OV-10As were transferred from the Marine Corps to the Navy for use by VAL-4. The Squadron deployed to South Vietnam in late March and took up residence at Binh Thuy from where it flew its first combat missions on 19 April. Squadron Headquarters and Detachment A with five aircraft were based at Binh Thuy in the Mekong Delta while Detachment B and its five aircraft was based 80 miles away at Vung Tau on the coast southeast of Saigon. The Squadron's mission was to provide close air support to naval riverine forces in III and IV Corps, especially in the Mekong Delta and the waterways around Saigon. It was the only OV-10 squadron based in Southeast Asia with an attack role as opposed to forward air control and artillery observation in which the Air Force and Marine Corps squadrons specialised. The Navy aircraft were equipped with Zuni rockets, 2.75-inch rocket pods and the 20mm gun pod. The operations consisted of air patrols, overhead air cover and escort, close air support, scramble alert, reconnaissance and artillery spotting. The Vung Tau detachment was closed down on 1 July 1970 and moved to Binh Thuy to join the rest of the Squadron.

19 July 1969

OV-10A 155490   VAL-4, USN, Binh Thuy
                    Lt Aubrey Grady Martin (KIA)
                    Lt(jg) Roy Dean Sikkink (KIA)

The first aircraft and crew lost by VAL-4 was shot down during a Game Warden surveillance mission near Ap Bac, 45 miles west of Saigon. The crew were en route to their patrol sector at 2,500 feet when they came under intense automatic weapons fire. The aircraft entered a shallow dive and crashed onto the summit of a hill. Neither of the crew ejected and may have been wounded by the ground fire. These were not the first combat casualties suffered by the Squadron. On 23 May Lt Peter Fransson Russell was killed by a single shot as his aircraft (155472) was strafing an enemy target in Kien Giang province. The aircraft was landed safely by the rear-seat pilot, Lt(jg) Johnson. Both crewmembers in the Navy OV-10s were pilots although the rear seat only had a limited set of flight controls.

A-7B 154423   VA-87, USN, USS *Ticonderoga*
                    1 pilot, name unknown (survived)

The Corsair's engine continued to give trouble. During an attack mission, one of VA-87's aircraft suffered compressor stalls resulting in a loss of power. The pilot ejected safely.

A-1H 52-137520 probably 6 SOS, 633 SOW, USAF, Pleiku
                    1 pilot, name unknown (survived)

A Skyraider had to be abandoned when its engine failed during a SAR escort mission over South Vietnam.

B-52D 55-0676   70 BW attached to 4133 BW(P),
                    USAF, Andersen
                    6 crew, names unknown (survived)

As a B-52 was taking off in heavy rain from U-Tapao on an Arc Light mission the pilot's and co-pilot's airspeed indicators gave different readings. The pilot eventually aborted the take off but the nose gear collapsed and the aircraft caught fire as it came to a halt at the end of the runway. An HH-43B (59-1562 from Detachment 12 of the 38th ARRS) arrived on the scene with a fire suppressant kit and although most of the B-52 crew were seen to have escaped from the aircraft it was thought that the tail gunner was still on board (he had in fact escaped unseen). The helicopter hovered near the burning Stratofortress in an attempt to locate the tail gunner but the aircraft's bombs and fuel tanks started to explode and the HH-43 was blown some distance away. Maj Warren K Davis and TSgt Harry Cohen were killed when the

helicopter crashed while Sgt Thomas Miles survived with major injuries. Four KC-135s parked near the inferno were started and taxied to a safe distance by their crew chiefs thereby averting an even greater tragedy. The B-52 was on detachment to Andersen from the 70th BW from Clinton-Sherman AFB, Oklahoma and had probably recovered at U-Tapao following an Arc Light raid. Guam-based aircraft often landed at U-Tapao and flew several missions from there before returning to Andersen thereby reducing crew fatigue on the long-range missions from Guam. The HH-43 had only been transferred from Udorn to U-Tapao five days before it was lost.

20 July 1969

A-4F   154993   VA-23, USN, USS *Oriskany*
                         Lt Stanley Kutz Smiley (KIA)

A pair of Skyhawks completed an air strike in southern Laos under the control of an FAC and were looking for targets of opportunity on their way back to the coast. Lt Smiley, leading the pair, radioed that he had spotted what he thought was a truck on a road near Ban Houn, about 20 miles southwest of the A Shau Valley. He reported that he was turning round to check out the potential target but when his wingman pulled up to take a position behind Lt Smiley's aircraft, he was horrified to see it fly into the ground in a shallow dive. There was no anti-aircraft fire in the area at the time or during the subsequent search and there was no indication as to why the aircraft had flown into the ground. It was presumed that Lt Smiley had died when his aircraft crashed but in 1988 a former Royal Lao Army officer, Somdee Phommachanh, claimed that he had been held with two Americans, David Nelson and Stanley Smiley. He also said that Nelson had died and Smiley was taken away by the Vietnamese. As with so many stories about missing Americans in Southeast Asia, the details of this case have not yet been confirmed independently.

21 July 1969

A-4F   154199   VA-192, USN, USS *Oriskany*
                         1 pilot, name unknown (survived)

A-4F   155003   VA-192, USN, USS *Oriskany*
                         1 pilot, name unknown (survived)

On the day that Neil Armstrong became the first man to walk on the moon the war in Southeast Asia continued unabated and the *Oriskany* lost two Skyhawks when they collided in mid-air during a combat mission. Both the pilots managed to eject and were rescued.

22 July 1969

A-4C   148310   VA-112, USN, USS *Ticonderoga*
                         1 pilot, name unknown (survived)

A Skyhawk ditched in the sea when the catapult bridle failed during a launch from the *Ticonderoga*. The pilot ejected before the aircraft hit the water.

OV-10A 155421   VMO-2, MAG-16, USMC, Marble Mountain
                       1Lt Roland Charles Hamilton (KIA)
                       1 crew, name unknown (survived)

A Bronco lost engine power and crashed into the side of a mountain in the Steel Tiger area of southern Laos. The pilot survived the accident and was rescued by a Marine Corps task force consisting of OV-10s, CH-46s and AH-1s. Unfortunately, the observer died in the crash.

23 July 1969

A-1G   52-133883 6 SOS, 633 SOW, USAF, Pleiku
                   Maj Franklin William Picking (KIA)
                   Maj Thomas Hubert McCarty (KIA)

A Skyraider was bombing a Viet Cong target about 25 miles northwest of Phu Cat when it was shot down. Both crew died when their aircraft was hit by ground fire at 2,500 feet on its third pass over the target. The starboard wing burst into flames and the aircraft crashed before either of the crew could escape. Although recorded as an A-1G this aircraft was originally built as an A-1E and may have been converted in service.

O-2A   68-10851 20 TASS, 504 TASG, USAF, Da Nang
                   detached to Phu Bai
                   1Lt K W Haman (survived)

During a visual reconnaissance mission near the city of Hué an O-2 was shot down by a .30 calibre weapon as the pilot was observing troops in combat from 1,500 feet. 1Lt Haman survived the incident and was rescued by a USAF helicopter having suffered only minor injuries.

24 July 1969

F-100D 56-3252   510 TFS, 3 TFW, USAF, Bien Hoa
                    1Lt S H Morehouse (survived)

A Super Sabre was lost during a strike on a VC staging area in South Vietnam. The aircraft was hit as it was pulling up from its third pass and the pilot ejected a few miles north of the target. He was later rescued by a USAF helicopter.

25 July 1969

F-4J   155809   VMFA-232, MAG-13, USMC, Chu Lai
                       Capt J C Stokes (survived)
                       1Lt R P Devere (survived)

VMFA-232 returned to Vietnam in March 1969 having served a previous tour with the Crusader in 1966/1967. The Squadron lost its first F-4 on 25 July when Marine ground forces called in an air strike on an enemy position eight miles southwest of Tam Ky and just 15 miles west of Chu Lai. One of the Phantoms that responded to the call was pulling up from its first run at the target when it was hit by small arms fire. Both crew ejected and were later rescued, Capt Stokes was picked up by an Army helicopter and 1Lt Devere by one from the Marine Corps.

26 July 1969

OV-10A 67-14633 19 TASS, 504 TASG, USAF, Bien Hoa
                   Capt B W Hawkins (survived)
                   1Lt W G Stegemann (survived)

An OV-10 FAC was shot down near Ben Cat, 15 miles northwest of Bien Hoa. The aircraft was flying over its intended target at 4,000 feet when its port wing was hit by .50 calibre anti-aircraft fire. The crew ejected safely and were picked up by a US Army helicopter.

A-4C   147833   VA-112, USN, USS *Ticonderoga*
                       Lt Richard David Brenning (KIA)

The *Ticonderoga's* run of accidental aircraft losses in July came to a tragic finale on the 26th when a Skyhawk crashed into the sea after a catapult launch about 70 miles northeast of Dong Hoi, this time the pilot did not survive. The ship had lost five aircraft during the month and completed its last tour of duty off Vietnam on 1 August. During its 97 days on the line it had lost a total of seven aircraft, including two A-4s, three A-7s and two F-8s, all of them from accidental causes. The *Ticonderoga* was decommissioned on 16 November 1973 and was scrapped the following year.

C-7B   62-4186   537 TAS, 483 TAW, USAF, Phu Cat
                   1Lt James Fielding Wohrer (KIA)
                   4 crew, names unknown (survived)

One of the crew of a Caribou transport aircraft died when it crashed in Phuoc Tuy province, South Vietnam following an engine failure.

27 July 1969

B-52D 56-0630   70 BW attached to 4133 BW(P),
                   USAF, Andersen
                   Lt Col Robert Howard Barr (KIA)
                   Capt Edward William Wyatt (KIA)
                   Capt John Anthony Albasio (KIA)
                   Capt Donald Joseph Maccio (KIA)
                   Capt Edward Anthony Miskowski (KIA)
                   1Lt Gary Paul Leach (KIA)
                   TSgt Clinton Eugene Tibbetts (KIA)
                   TSgt Richard Piskula (KIA)

A B-52 crashed on take off from Andersen after suffering a structural failure in the starboard wing. TSgt Piskula was a maintenance man who is listed as being killed on this date and may have been on board the aircraft as an extra crewmember on this occasion.

29 July 1969

A-4F   154184   VA-23, USN, USS *Oriskany*
                         1 pilot, name unknown (survived)

A Skyhawk was refuelling from a tanker when some fuel sprayed from the hose and was ingested into the Skyhawk's air intakes

B-52s from Andersen often continued on to U-Tapao following an Arc Light sortie so that the crews could fly some shorter range missions before making the 3,000 mile-journey back to Guam. On 19 July 1969 a B-52 caught fire on take off at U-Tapao and exploded resulting in the destruction of an HH-43 rescue helicopter. USAF

and into the engine. A fire started in the engine bay followed by an explosion and engine failure. The pilot ejected and was safely rescued.

1 August 1969

A-4E   150074   VMA-211, MAG-12, USMC, Chu Lai
Capt P H Courtney (survived)

A Marine Corps Skyhawk was damaged during an attack on an enemy position not far from the DMZ. Capt Courtney was rolling in on his target when he felt his aircraft hit by flak. He immediately headed out to sea and ejected two miles off the coast near the DMZ. He was rescued by a SAR helicopter.

F-4E   67-0323   421 TFS, 366 TFW, USAF, Da Nang
Capt Tommy Leon Callies (KIA)
1Lt Douglas Glenn Burd (KIA)

The 421st TFS had been reactivated at Eglin AFB, Florida with F-4Es in April 1969 and spent two months at Misawa, Japan before arriving at Da Nang on 26 June. The Squadron lost its first aircraft and crew on 1 August during a dusk strike on enemy troops in the open about 20 miles southwest of Quang Ngai. The aircraft came in low to drop napalm but was hit by ground fire and crashed soon afterwards killing both the crew.

A-7A   153185   VA-37, USN, USS *Kitty Hawk*
Lt Cdr George Francis Talken (KIA)

The last aircraft lost by the *Kitty Hawk* before it left the line on 16 August and returned to the USA was a Corsair that had an engine problem as it was returning from a combat mission. The aircraft crashed as the pilot was flying a radar-directed approach to the carrier. Battle damage was not thought to be the cause but could not be ruled out either. The *Kitty Hawk* had spent a total of 111 days on the line during its fourth tour off Vietnam. During this time the ship had lost three aircraft in combat and four due to accidental causes.

2 August 1969

F-8J   149214   VF-53, USN, USS *Bon Homme Richard*
Lt G Wells (survived)

The pilot had to eject from a Crusader when the engine exploded during a BARCAP mission over the Gulf of Tonkin. He was rescued by a Navy helicopter.

O-2A   67-21332   20 TASS, 504 TASG, USAF, Da Nang
1Lt Hal Kent Henderson (KIA)

An O-2 FAC collided in mid-air in Quang Nam province with an Army CH-47C Chinook 67-18513 from C Company of the 159th ASHB, 101st Airborne Division. The five crew of the Chinook (consisting of pilot WO T L Dives, CWO R A Vaquera, Sgt D A Irelan, Sgt T K Ryan and SP4 J S Stacey) were also killed in the accident.

3 August 1969

F-4D   66-7599   390 TFS, 366 TFW, USAF, Da Nang
Capt A C Stripe (survived)
1Lt A G Hendrick (survived)

A Phantom was damaged during a strike on enemy bunkers in southern Laos about 20 miles west of Khe Sanh. The aircraft was hit in the starboard wing by 37mm anti-aircraft fire as it made its second pass over the target. Capt Stripe headed towards Thailand rather than attempt to make it back towards Da Nang but he and his WSO were forced to eject near Ubon.

F-4E   67-0291   4 TFS, 366 TFW, USAF, Da Nang
Capt James David White (KIA)
Capt James Edward Morton (KIA)

The 4th TFS had been transferred to Da Nang from the 33rd TFW at Eglin AFB, Florida on 12 April and had been operating in Southeast Asia for four months before it suffered its first casualties. Capt White and Capt Morton were assigned to attack enemy lines of communications in hilly terrain 30 miles southwest of Da Nang. As the aircraft came in low to drop napalm, it was hit by 12.7mm anti-aircraft fire and crashed before either of the crew could escape.

4 August 1969

F-4E   67-0325   421 TFS, 366 TFW, USAF, Da Nang
Col George Stanton Dorman (KIA)
1Lt Roy Donald Bratton (KIA)

Another Da Nang F-4E was lost attacking Viet Cong lines of communications the following day. Col Dorman and 1Lt Bratton were attacking a target near Ba Gia, 10 miles northwest of Quang Ngai when they were shot down. The aircraft had just pulled up from its fourth pass when it was hit in the fuselage by .50 calibre gun fire. The aircraft crashed about a mile from the target and, once again, neither of the crew was able to eject before the impact.

6 August 1969

F-100D   56-3090   308 TFS, 31 TFW, USAF, Tuy Hoa
1Lt R P Busico (survived)

The first of four Super Sabres lost during August was shot down during a strike on enemy positions near Ap Long Lam, 25 miles northeast of the city of Phan Thiet in South Vietnam. As the aircraft made its initial dive on the target it was hit by small arms fire forcing the pilot to eject a few miles away when the aircraft caught fire. He was picked up by an Army helicopter.

8 August 1969

F-100D   55-3581   614 TFS, 35 TFW, USAF, Phan Rang
1Lt E L Daniel (survived)

Another Super Sabre was lost during an attack on a Viet Cong weapons cache that was thought to include rockets and mortars. 1Lt Daniel had just finished making his fourth run over the target when his aircraft was hit by ground fire about 15 miles southeast of Song Be City. He flew all the way back to Phan Rang but was forced to eject about five miles from the airfield and was picked up by an HH-43 helicopter of Detachment 1 of the 38th ARRS from the airfield.

RA-3B   144826   VAP-61, USN, Cubi Point on TDY to Da Nang
4 crew, names unknown (survived)

One of the Skywarriors from the Navy reconnaissance detachment at Da Nang was lost on the 8th while on a logistics flight. The fuel flow became erratic and while the crew were trying to sort out the problem, both engines flamed out. Unable to restart the engines, the four crew abandoned the aircraft and were later rescued.

9 August 1969

F-100F   56-3734   416 TFS, 31 TFW, USAF, Tuy Hoa
Capt Laurent Lee Gourlet (KIA)
1Lt Jefferson Scott Dotson (KIA)

A Misty FAC was lost about 15 miles southwest of the A Shau Valley during a visual reconnaissance mission over the Trail to scout for suitable targets. Other aircrew heard Capt Gourlet and 1Lt Dotson radio that the aircraft had been hit and that they were about to eject. One of the witnesses reported seeing at least one parachute but neither man has yet been recovered.

OV-10A   155455   VMO-6, MAG-39, USMC, Quang Tri
2 crew, names unknown (survived)

During a training mission a Marine Corps Bronco developed a problem with its starboard engine. The engine subsequently burst into flames and the crew had to eject from the aircraft.

F-4E   67-0261   34 TFS, 388 TFW, USAF, Korat
Capt P M Lang (survived)
Capt C W Magsig (survived)

The Korat Wing flew its first Tiger FAC mission in March 1969 and lost its first aircraft in this role on 9 August during a Barrel Roll strike on a truck park in Laos. The aircraft was damaged by ground fire on its third pass over the target and the crew attempted to reach their base in Thailand. The aircraft became uncontrollable and had to be abandoned near Muong Soumi and the huge Nam Ngum Reservoir, 45 miles north of Vientianne. The crew were rescued the next day by a USAF SAR helicopter from the 40th ARRS.

10 August 1969

A-4E   151131   VA-144, USN, USS *Bon Homme Richard*
Lt William Emil Mickelsen (KIA)

A Skyhawk pilot was killed during a night mission when returning to the *Bon Homme Richard* as the ship was steaming about 70 miles northeast of Dong Hoi. The aircraft undershot slightly on the approach and it struck the carrier's ramp and disintegrated. A number of men on the deck were injured by flying debris from the aircraft and the central drop tank ruptured and caught fire as the aircraft fell into the sea, killing the pilot.

12 August 1969

F-8J   150330   VF-53, USN, USS *Bon Homme Richard*
Lt D Manlove (survived)

A Crusader was lost due to an engine problem during a BARCAP mission over the Gulf of Tonkin. The engine lost thrust and the pilot had to eject.

13 August 1969

A-4E   152003   VA-144, USN, USS *Bon Homme Richard*
1 pilot, name unknown (survived)

The *Bon Homme Richard's* run of bad luck continued with another aircraft accident on the 13th, its fifth of the month. A Skyhawk stalled immediately after a catapult launch and the pilot ejected safely.

14 August 1969

O-1G   51-5097   22 TASS, 504 TASG, USAF, Binh Thuy
Capt Kenneth J Hamrick (KIA)

A Bird Dog FAC aircraft was shot down by automatic weapons fire near Ap Bac, about 40 miles southwest of Saigon. The pilot was found dead in the wreckage of his aircraft when an Army helicopter arrived at the scene a short while later.

U-10D   63-13102   5 SOS, 14 SOW, USAF, Nha Trang
detached to Bien Hoa
1Lt Roger David Brown (KIA)

One of the 5th SOS's psywar U-10s was being ferried from one airfield to another on the night of the 14th when it was hit by ground fire. 1Lt Brown attempted an emergency landing about 10 miles east of Bien Hoa but was killed when the aircraft crashed.

15 August 1969

A-4F   154206   VA-195, USN, USS *Oriskany*
1 pilot, name unknown (survived)

A Skyhawk burst a tyre during a catapult launch for a training flight and during the subsequent landing the main landing gear collapsed. The aircraft was so badly damaged that it was scrapped.

F-100D   56-3283   531 TFS, 3 TFW, USAF, Bien Hoa
Capt Humberto Robles Hernandez (KIA)

As an F-100 took off from Bien Hoa for a close air support mission it was seen to adopt an abnormally nose-high attitude. The aircraft then stalled and crashed killing the pilot.

18 August 1969

RF-4C   65-0921   16 TRS, 460 TRW, USAF, Tan Son Nhut
Maj Wolf (survived)
Capt R Richardson (survived)

An RF-4C crashed soon after taking off from Tan Son Nhut on a photographic reconnaissance flight. Both the crew ejected safely and were recovered.

19 August 1969

F-4B   149416   VMFA-542, MAG-11, USMC, Da Nang
Lt Col Robert Norman Smith (KIA)
Capt John Norlee Flanigan (KIA)

The Marines lost two Phantom crews from different squadrons on the 19th. Lt Col Smith and Capt Flanigan were escorting a photographic reconnaissance aircraft over North Vietnam, probably a Marine Corps RF-4B, on a mission to Bat Lake near

On 1 January 1967 the US Army handed over its entire inventory of C-7 Caribous to the USAF and six squadrons were formed on that date in South Vietnam. The Caribou made a name for itself in the often difficult and dangerous resupply of remote Special Forces camps such as Dak Seang and Ben Het. USAF

Thach Ban, 12 miles north of the DMZ. The two aircraft made their first run over the target then separated and were supposed to rendezvous again for the second pass. However, Lt Col Smith's aircraft did not return and was presumed to have been shot down by AAA. Both crew were presumed to have died in their aircraft. On 26 June 1997 the USAF announced that the remains of Capt Flanigan had been identified. The remains had been handed over by the Vietnamese in 1989 but at that time there was no corroborating evidence of their identity. However, investigations into the crash site during two expeditions in 1993 and 1995 uncovered personal items and the remains were then re-examined and identified using mitochondrial DNA testing.

F-4B   151012   VMFA-115, MAG-13, USMC, Chu Lai
1Lt James Richard Bohlig (KIA)
Capt Richard Thomas Morrisey (KIA)
The second Marine Corps Phantom lost on the 19th went missing as it was returning from a night-time TPQ-10 radar bombing mission over North Vietnam. The aircraft is thought to have come down in the sea about 20 miles northeast of Chu Lai. It was not thought that the loss was due to enemy action.

21 August 1969

YQU-22A 68-10532 553 RW, USAF, Nakhon Phanom
1 pilot, name unknown (KIA)
The pilot of one of NKP's QU-22As was killed when his aircraft crashed in Thailand following engine failure.

22 August 1969

O-1E   56-2663   unit ..?, USAF, base ..?
A Bird Dog was being retrieved by an Army CH-47 Chinook heavy lift helicopter when it dropped from the sling and was destroyed.

23 August 1969

F-100D 55-2895   612 TFS, 35 TFW, USAF, Phan Rang
Capt D M Wanless (survived)
A pair of F-100s was dropping napalm in an effort to burn Viet Cong food crops about 55 miles southwest of Phan Rang when one of the aircraft was lost. Capt Wanless was making his second pass when his aircraft was badly damaged by the blast from one of his napalm canisters. He ejected a few miles to the north of the target and was rescued by an Army helicopter.

25 August 1969

F-105D 59-1818   357 TFS, 355 TFW, USAF, Takhli
Maj Steven Roy Sanders (KIA)
The Thunderchief squadrons were spending much of their time on Barrel Roll missions in northern and central Laos at this stage of the war. Maj Sanders was killed during an attack on enemy troops in the jungle near Ban Then Phoun, 30 miles to the east of the Plain of Jars. He had expended his ordnance on his first five passes and then began a strafing run. The aircraft was hit by ground fire and crashed, apparently before Maj Sanders could eject.

27 August 1969

F-4D   65-0634   480 TFS, 37 TFW, USAF, Phu Cat
Capt C J Wingert (survived)
Maj J J Baick (survived)
A Phantom from Phu Cat was lost during an attack on an automatic weapons site near the town of Duc Pho, 25 miles south of Quang Ngai. Capt Wingert was diving on the target for the second time when his port engine was put out of action by ground fire. The aircraft was on fire as he turned east and headed out to sea where he and his WSO ejected about five miles from the coast. They were both injured during the ejection but were rescued by an Army helicopter.

29 August 1969

F-4B   153041   VMFA-542, MAG-11, USMC, Da Nang
Capt Jerry Allen Zimmer (KIA)
1Lt Albert Stephen Graf (KIA)
The Marines lost their third Phantom during the month of August on a close air support mission near Ap Hai, 20 miles south of Da Nang. Capt Zimmer was pulling up from his first pass over a target when his aircraft was hit in the tail by .50 calibre gun fire. The Phantom burst into flames and crashed near the target before either of the crew could eject.

OV-10A 155456   VMO-6, MAG-39, USMC, Quang Tri
Capt Jack Ervin Schober (KIA)
1Lt Richard Didacus Krupa (KIA)
August had been a bad month for the Marines with three Phantoms missing and six crew killed and then an OV-10 and its crew were lost on the 29th. The Bronco crashed soon after what appeared to be a normal take off from Quang Tri on a visual

reconnaissance flight. The starboard engine lost power and the aircraft rolled to the right and crashed into a newly constructed hanger. The observer ejected as the aircraft crashed through the hanger roof but he was killed when he hit a roof beam. This was the last of three OV-10s to be lost by VMO-6 before it departed for Futema MCAS on Okinawa in November 1969. The Squadron had also lost two O-1s and a number of UH-1Es during its four-year tour of duty in South Vietnam.

1 September 1969

AC-47D 43-49021   4 SOS, 14 SOW, USAF, Nha Trang
detached to Bien Hoa
Capt Robert Paul Acher (KIA)
Capt James Sutherland Pitches (KIA)
1Lt Ray Colon Williams (KIA)
MSgt Harry Herr Wecker (KIA)
TSgt Willie Warnie Alley (KIA)
TSgt Lester Melvin Cavallin (KIA)
TSgt Albert Carl McBride (KIA)
SSgt Fred Winston Smith (KIA)
A Spooky gunship on a night patrol was directed to assist friendly troops who were under attack from enemy forces about 20 miles east of Bien Hoa. The aircraft arrived at the scene and started firing but it was hit in the starboard wing by ground fire and the aircraft crashed in Long Khanh province. This was the last USAF Spooky lost during the war. The 3rd SOS was inactivated on this day and its aircraft passed on to the VNAF and the 4th SOS followed suit by the end of the year. A total of 19 AC-47s had been lost during four years of service with the USAF. While the aircraft had its limitations and was too vulnerable for employment in daylight or over the Ho Chi Minh Trail, the AC-47 had certainly proved the value of the gunship concept and the pioneering work done by the Spooky crews was greatly developed by the AC-119 and AC-130 units.

3 September 1969

F-4D   66-8791   25 TFS, 8 TFW, USAF, Ubon
Col D N Stanfield (survived)
1Lt C E Dorn (survived)
A Phantom was flying over northern Laos on a LORAN validation flight when it was damaged by ground fire about 10 miles southwest of Sam Neua. The 25th TFS flew many unarmed cross-country sorties code named Operation Diogenes in order to recalibrate the LORAN ground stations distributed throughout Southeast Asia. Col Stanfield flew the aircraft back into Thailand and he and his WSO ejected safely five miles south of the airfield at Udorn. They were picked up a few minutes later by one of the HH-43s from Detachment 5 of the 38th ARRS that was based on the airfield.

6 September 1969

EC-121R 67-21495 554 RS, 553 RW, USAF, Korat
Lt Col John L Jones (survived)
1Lt Donald D Thompson (survived)
Maj Joyful J Jenkins (KIA)
Maj John B Tersoly (survived)
Capt Terry A Thomas (survived)
MSgt Eddie J Vickers (survived)
MSgt Perry J Wiley (survived)
TSgt Thomas M Tasaki (survived)
SSgt Billie J Black (survived)
SSgt Gunther H Rehling (KIA)
SSgt William C Werner (survived)
Sgt Julius C Houlditch (KIA)

Sgt Arnold Noel Jaco (KIA)
Sgt Jerry R Orth (survived)
Sgt David C Smith (survived)
Sgt Gary L Sobotta (survived)

One of the 554th RS's EC-121R Bat Cat aircraft crashed as it was attempting an instrument approach and landing in a heavy rainstorm at Korat in the early morning of the 6th. The aircraft took off during the afternoon of the 5th for a 13-hour mission, much of which was flown in poor weather which deteriorated further as the aircraft approached Korat. The pilot aborted the first attempt to land due to poor visibility in driving rain and was given radar vectors for another approach. The second approach appeared normal until about one mile from touchdown when the aircraft suddenly lost altitude and crashed into the approach lights, about 3,000 feet from the runway. The fuselage broke into three sections, which then caught fire. Within minutes a HH-43 from Detachment 4 of the 38th ARRS arrived with a fire suppression kit but the rescue was hampered by poor visibility caused by smoke and torrential rain while flooded streams and concertina wire impeded ground movement. Eventually 12 of the 16 crew were rescued from the wreck, four of them by the HH-43. Unfortunately, the navigator and three other crewmen died and four local Thais on the ground were also killed when the aircraft hit them. Like 67-21493, which crashed on 25 April, this aircraft had previously flown from Barbers Point NAS, Hawaii, with a Navy AEW squadron until it was converted into an EC-121R for the USAF in 1967.

9 September 1969

F-4D   66-7686   555 TFS, 432 TRW, USAF, Udorn
2 crew, names unknown (survived)

A 555th TFS Phantom crashed on landing after a combat mission as the result of pilot error.

11 September 1969

C-7B   62-4187   537 TAS, 483 TAW, USAF, Phu Cat
1Lt Robert Paul Wiesneth (KIA)
1Lt Neil Norman Greinke (KIA)
1Lt Charles Brent Ross (KIA)
SSgt Frederick Wilhelm (KIA)

A Caribou, using the radio call sign Soul 47, was en route to a Special Forces camp near Plei Djereng, 20 miles west of Pleiku, when it was shot down by small arms fire. All four crewmen were killed in the incident.

F-4D   66-7530   390 TFS, 366 TFW, USAF, Da Nang
Capt Roger Danny Helwig (KIA)
Capt Roger Horace Stearns (KIA)

A Stormy FAC was controlling an air strike 12 miles east of Ban Kate in southern Laos when it was lost. As the aircraft pulled up from its target it was seen to be hit in the wing by ground fire. Fuel streamed from the wing and the aircraft rolled inverted and crashed into a stream bed close to the target. No ejection was seen before the impact and the men were presumed killed in action. In May 1990 a joint US/Lao investigation of the crash site recovered the remains of Roger Stearns along with his identity card and an aircraft data plate. As yet no remains of Roger Helwig have been found.

F-8J   150861   VF-194, USN, USS Oriskany
Lt C Riddle (survived)

As a Crusader returned from a BARCAP mission it struck the ramp of the Oriskany and the pilot lifted off to go around for another approach. However, the aircraft's fuel state was already critical and during the circuit to land the aircraft ran out of fuel and the pilot was forced to eject.

12 September 1969

O-2A   68-10987   19 TASS, 504 TASG, USAF, Bien Hoa
Maj Mannifred Yates (KIA)
Capt Thomas Wiley Norman (KIA)

An O-2 was shot down by small arms fire during a visual reconnaissance patrol in the Saigon area. The aircraft's tail was dam-

aged and Maj Yates attempted an emergency landing about five miles south of Saigon but the aircraft crashed and both crew were killed.

F-100D   55-3512   612 TFS, 35 TFW, USAF, Phan Rang
Maj A W Steinhauss (survived)

A flight of F-100s was despatched to bomb a bunker complex that had been discovered just three miles northeast of Bien Hoa. These bunkers were probably being used by the VC to store supplies for their frequent night attacks on the airbase. Maj Steinhauss was pulling up from his attack on the target when his aircraft was hit by ground fire. He ejected almost immediately from his burning aircraft but was soon rescued without a scratch by a US Army helicopter.

14 September 1969

O-2A   68-10854   21 TASS, 504 TASG, USAF, Nha Trang
detached to Kontum
Capt T S Rankin (survived)

An O-2 from the 21st TASS's detachment at Kontum was shot down by ground fire during a visual reconnaissance mission 20 miles to the northeast of Dak To. The rear engine was hit and put out of action and the aircraft crashed but Capt Rankin stepped out of the wreck with just minor injuries. A US Army helicopter quickly rescued him.

18 September 1969

F-4B   152213   VMFA-122, MAG-13, USMC, Chu Lai
2 crew, names unknown (survived)

A Marine Corps Phantom was destroyed when it skidded off the runway during an arrested landing at Chu Lai. VMFA-122 had only arrived at the airfield on 5 September from Iwakuni for its second tour in Vietnam.

F-100D   either 55-2903 or 56-2903
308 TFS, 31 TFW, USAF, Tuy Hoa
1 pilot, name unknown (survived)

A Super Sabre crashed during a close air support mission following accidental engine failure. The pilot ejected safely and was rescued.

19 September 1969

F-4B   151405   VMFA-314, MAG-13, USMC, Chu Lai
Capt Walter Vann Lemmond (KIA)
1Lt Robert Edward Lavender (KIA)

A Marine Corps Phantom was shot down by ground fire as it was returning from a night-time TPQ-10 radar bombing mission. Both the crew were killed when the aircraft crashed about 10 miles west of Chu Lai.

21 September 1969

A-6A   155611   VMA(AW)-225, MAG-11, USMC, Da Nang
Maj P M Busch (survived)
1Lt R W Hargrave (survived)

A North Vietnamese command post had been located in the DMZ buffer zone about seven miles north of the village of Cam Lo. Maj Busch and 1Lt Hargrave took part in a daylight raid on the target under a low cloudbase. The aircraft was hit by AAA over the target and the starboard wing caught fire. Both men ejected and sustained serious injuries. However, Maj Busch was rescued by an Army helicopter and 1Lt Hargrave by a Marine Corps helicopter.

24 September 1969

F-100D   55-3737   614 TFS, 35 TFW, USAF, Phan Rang
1 pilot, name unknown (survived)

A Super Sabre crashed near Phan Rang through pilot error while on an attack mission. The pilot was picked up by an HH-43 Huskie from Phan Rang's Detachment 1 of the 38th ARRS. This particular F-100 had been flown by the Thunderbirds aerobatic team in the mid-1960s before the aircraft was transferred to Southeast Asia.

27 September 1969

F-8J   149172   VF-53, USN, USS Bon Homme Richard
Lt Cdr J Taylor (survived)

A Crusader from the Bon Homme Richard was lost when it suffered a control failure. The pilot ejected safely and was quickly rescued. This was the last aircraft lost by the Bon Homme Richard before it completed its fifth tour and left the line for its homeport of Alameda on 8 October. During 97 days on the line the ship had only had one combat loss but had lost a further 11 aircraft in accidents. The ship was fortunate in the sense that only two airmen were killed during the cruise.

29 September 1969

A-6A   155696   VMA(AW)-242, MAG-11, USMC, Da Nang
Maj Luther Albert Lono (KIA)
1Lt Patrick Robert Curran (KIA)

An Intruder from Da Nang disappeared during a night-time armed reconnaissance sortie over southern Laos. The mission was being flown under the control of a USAF FAC. The mission appeared to be going smoothly until the FAC lost contact with the Intruder. The last known position was variously reported as either being 25 miles west of Khe Sanh or to the southeast of the A Shau Valley. A search failed to find any sign of the aircraft or its crew although an emergency transmission was heard briefly during the night. Maj Lono was the executive officer of VMA(AW)-242. These were the last casualties suffered by the Squadron before it returned to the USA in September 1970, taking up residence at El Toro MCAS in California. VMA(AW)-242 spent 47 months of continuous service in Southeast Asia, a Marine Corps record surpassed only by VMCJ-1. During its time at Da Nang VMA(AW)-242 flew 16,782 combat sorties and lost seven Intruders due to enemy action (two of them in airbase attacks) and two more aircraft in accidents.

30 September 1969

EC-47Q   43-48959   362 TEWS, 460 TRW, USAF, Pleiku
8 crew, names unknown (survived)

One of the EC-47 radio direction-finding aircraft crash-landed on the last day of September as the result of an engine failure. This aircraft had previously been a VC-47D VIP transport and had served with the 322nd AD.

1 October 1969

F-4D   66-7546   555 TFS, 432 TRW, USAF, Udorn
Capt R A Gieleghem (survived)
1Lt G R Zesinger (survived)

The 432nd TRW started its own fast FAC programme in April 1969 and lost its first aircraft in this role on 1 October. A truck park and storage site was discovered to the east of Ban Ban, about 35 miles east of the Plain of Jars in northern Laos. A flight of Phantoms was sent to attack the target and Capt Gieleghem and 1Lt Zesinger were acting as the FAC for the mission using the call sign Laredo. As they pulled up from their first pass over the target their aircraft was hit by 37mm AAA. One of the engines failed and the aircraft caught fire. The aircraft remained airborne long enough to get close to the Thai border before the crew ejected. They were rescued by USAF SAR helicopters. This Phantom had been flown by Capt W S Gordon and 1Lt J H Monsees when they shot down a MiG-17 on 26 October 1967.

A-7A   153252   VA-97, USN, USS Constellation
Lt P E Mullowney (survived)

A section of Corsairs from the Constellation attacked a truck park near Ban Napoung, 25 miles south of the Mu Gia Pass, during a night-time Steel Tiger armed reconnaissance mission. Lt Mullowney completed two passes over the target and joined up with his wingman on their way back to the carrier. He then felt a slight jolt and the aircraft's electrical system suddenly failed. The engine wound down rapidly and although hydraulic power was regained when the pilot extended the emergency turbine, the electrics stayed off line. Attempts to relight the engine failed and Lt Mullowney ejected at 5,000 feet. He was rescued by a USAF HH-53 helicopter from the 40th ARRS.

The AC-119 Gunship III was intended as a stop gap aircraft until the AC-130 was available in quantity. Unfortunately the AC-119G Shadow was grossly underpowered and two aircraft were lost through engine failures killing a total of 12 airmen. USAF

2 October 1969

F-4D   66-8697   13 TFS, 432 TRW, USAF, Udorn
1Lt R D Ballentine (survived)
1Lt M E Stone (survived)

A flight of Phantoms was sent to bomb the truck park near Ban Ban in northern Laos that had been the object of a raid the previous day. In a repeat of the earlier incident, one of the Phantoms was hit by 37mm AAA over the target and its starboard engine was damaged. The aircraft caught fire but in this instance the pilot was able to fly the aircraft all the way back to Udorn where he made a crash-landing. Although the aircraft was damaged beyond repair, both the crew walked away with just minor injuries.

F-4C   63-7708   559 TFS, 12 TFW, USAF, Cam Ranh Bay
Capt John Arnold Quinn (KIA)
Capt P E Rider (survived)

A Phantom was shot down during a close air support mission in Ninh Thuan province in South Vietnam. The aircraft was hit by small arms fire as it pulled up from its dive to attack enemy troops and crashed, killing the pilot. Capt Rider ejected and was later recovered.

C-2A   152796   VRC-50, USN, Cubi Point NAS
Lt Herbert Hugh Dilger (KWF)
Lt Richard Allen Livingstone (KWF)
PO3 Paul Kierstead Moser (KWF)
PO3 Michael James Tye (KWF)
PO3 Rayford Jerome Hill (KWF)
21 passengers (KWF)

The aircraft carriers in the South China Sea and the Gulf of Tonkin were kept supplied with stores and ordnance while at sea by replenishment ships of TF 77. However, aircraft such as the C-1 Trader and the newer C-2 Greyhound were used for flying personnel and mail between ship and shore. Disaster struck on 2 October when a C-2 went missing during a flight from Cubi Point in the Philippines to the USS *Constellation*, which was operating in the Gulf. VRC-50 was a US Naval Reserve squadron that was based at Atsugi NAS in Japan with a detachment at Cubi Point and operated a mixed fleet including C-1As, C-2As, CT-39Es and KC-130Fs on transport duties throughout the Western Pacific and Far East area. The 21 passengers were from a variety of units and some were going to be transferred from the *Constellation* to other ships in the Gulf. The aircraft had made contact with the USS *Constellation* and reported that all was normal. The carrier's radar tracked the aircraft until it disappeared from the screen about 10 miles from the ship. Helicopters took off immediately to search the area and a small amount of debris was spotted near an oil slick. The indications were that the aircraft had dived steeply into the sea and disintegrated. The

cause of the accident was never established despite a salvage operation that lasted over a month although the most likely cause was thought to be an engine problem. All Navy C-2s were grounded for some time after this crash until modifications to the engine gearbox and mounting structure were made. A location of 70 miles northeast of Dong Hoi is given in one document for the location of the C-2's loss.

A-1J   52-142030   602 SOS, 56 SOW, USAF, Nakhon Phanom
1Lt Donald R Moore (KIA)

A Skyraider ground looped as it was taking off on a combat mission and caught fire. The aircraft's bombs exploded before the pilot could get clear and he was killed.

4 October 1969

F-100D   55-2935   510 TFS, 3 TFW, USAF, Bien Hoa
1 pilot, name unknown (survived)

An F-100 developed a fuel system problem during a close air support mission and had to be abandoned after the engine failed.

6 October 1969

C-130B   58-0718   774 TAS, 463 TAW, USAF, Clark
Maj Robert Hayes (KIA)
Capt Bruce Cardy (KIA)
1Lt Wendell Curry (KIA)
SSgt Isaac Corbett (KIA)
SSgt Norman Sweat (KIA)

A Hercules exploded in mid-air near the Marine Corps base at Chu Lai during a night cargo flight to Da Nang. The crew were on their first shuttle to Vietnam. There was speculation that the aircraft had strayed into an artillery firing range by mistake and had been hit by a shell. However, there was also the strong possibility of the aircraft having been a victim of sabotage.

O-2A   68-10995   21 TASS, 504 TASG, USAF, Nha Trang
2 crew, names unknown (survived)

As an O-2 was taking off for a reconnaissance sortie its front engine failed and the aircraft was damaged beyond repair during the subsequent crash-landing.

7 October 1969

F-105D   62-4243   333 TFS, 355 TFW, USAF, Takhli
1 pilot, name unknown (survived)

A Thud was lost as it was attempting to land back at Takhli when the aircraft suffered engine failure. A series of photographs published on the Internet show this aircraft parked near VMCJ-1's flight line when it was visiting Da Nang in August 1965. The Marines quickly 'zapped' the Thunderchief, adorning it with 'Marines' titles and the RM tail codes of VMCJ-1.

8 October 1969

F-4C   63-7498   558 TFS, 12 TFW, USAF, Cam Ranh Bay
Capt N A Jacobs (survived)
Capt D L Stevenson (survived)

A flight of Phantoms from the 12th TFW attacked enemy troops near Ban Vangthon in southern Laos. As Capt Jacobs put his aircraft into a 45-degree dive to deliver his bombs it was hit by groundfire and badly damaged. He headed east towards the border and was directed out over the coast where he and his WSO ejected near the island of Hon Giai, 15 miles southeast of Da Nang. The crew were rescued by a waiting USAF HH-53 from the 40th ARRS.

O-2A   67-21343   23 TASS, 504 TASG, USAF, Nakhon Phanom
2 crew, names unknown (survived)

OV-10A   67-14635   23 TASS, 504 TASG, USAF, Nakhon Phanom
2 crew, names unknown (survived)

An O-2 and an OV-10 from the same FAC squadron collided in mid-air as they orbited over a downed airman during a SAR mission. All four crew escaped from the two aircraft and were subsequently rescued by HH-3s and HH-53s.

EC-47P   43-49100   361 TEWS, 460 TRW, USAF, Phu Cat
1Lt Ronald Harold Knight (KIA)
1Lt Max Emmanuel Rosen (KIA)
Capt Bradley Rogers Ransom (KIA)
TSgt Sylvester William Redman (KIA)
SSgt Elmore L Hall (KIA)
SSgt Michael L Stiglich (KIA)

Prong 33 took off from Phu Cat on the afternoon of the 8th on a planned seven-hour RDF mission. However, just 20 minutes after take off the pilot radioed that he was returning to base because of a problem with the doppler navigation equipment. The aircraft landed safely and although the doppler was fixed, the aircraft's weather radar was found to be unusable. Despite bad weather in the flight area, the pilot was told to take off again but to return before dark if the weather worsened. When the aircraft reached its intended area of operations it was found that the weather was too bad to operate safely so 1Lt Knight flew towards the coast to return to Phu Cat. The pilot was guided through bad weather towards Phu Cat by the GCA controller but during the approach 1Lt Knight reported an inverter fire followed by the loss of his gyros and attitude indicators. The GCA controller gave instructions to direct the aircraft to the airfield but radio and radar contact was lost during the approach. Search operations were hampered by bad weather and it was not until 12 October that the wreckage was located by a SAR helicopter about 15 miles southeast of Phu Cat.

10 October 1969

C-123K   54-0642   19 SOS, 315 SOW, USAF, Phan Rang
Capt William F Unckrich (KIA)
1Lt Charles Franklin Burrell (KIA)
TSgt Harry Clifton Shepard (KIA)
SSgt Lavoyn Augustus Jones (KIA)
A1C Leland Craig Johnson (KIA)

As a Provider was taking off from an airfield in Kien Giang province of South Vietnam it suddenly banked sharply to the left and crashed. All five crew were killed in the accident.

F-100D   55-3642   308 TFS, 31 TFW, USAF, Tuy Hoa
1 pilot, name unknown (survived)

As a Super Sabre was landing at Tuy Hoa its drag parachute separated prematurely and the aircraft ran into a tow truck causing so much damage that the aircraft (and most probably the tow truck as well) had to be scrapped.

The AC-119 Shadow and Stinger

Development of the AC-130 Gunship II was delayed by numerous problems resulting in an interim solution being put forward. The USAF still had a number of ageing C-119 transport aircraft in service, mostly with Air National Guard and Air Force Reserve units. It was decided that this aircraft could be modified to a basic gunship configuration in short order and could fill the requirement until the AC-130 was available in some numbers. Under project Combat Hornet a total of 52 AC-119s were withdrawn from service for modification to Gunship III standard by Fairchild-Hiller. The basic model was the AC-119G, 26 of which were produced. This was followed by a further 26 examples of the more sophisticated jet engine-augmented AC-119K. The 71st SOS was activated at Lockbourne AFB, Ohio and was manned largely by Air Force Reserve crews. The Squadron deployed to South Vietnam in December 1968 and established its headquarters at Nha Trang with detachments at Tan Son Nhut and Phan Rang. On 1 June 1969, with most of the reservists replaced by regular personnel, the 71st was redesignated as the 17th SOS. It was soon discovered that the AC-119G was grossly underpowered for the task it was being called upon to perform and could not even maintain altitude on a single engine. Its poor performance and lack of sophisticated avionics and weapons meant that the AC-119G was largely confined to operations within South Vietnam where it performed sterling work in the protection of remote outposts and Special Forces units as well as supporting troops in contact with enemy forces, mostly at night. The AC-119K was fitted with two J-85 jet engines, 20mm Vulcan cannons, and improved radar and night vision devices including a FLIR system. The first AC-119K was delivered to the 18th SOS at Nha Trang on 3 November 1969. The AC-119K squadron concentrated its efforts on night armed reconnaissance over the Ho Chi Minh Trail in Laos. By the end of 1970 AC-119 detachments were operating from Phan Rang, Tan Son Nhut, Da Nang and Nakhon Phanom.

The AC-119G was known as Shadow after its radio call sign while the AC-119K was known as Stinger. The aircraft of the 17th SOS were handed over to the VNAF's 819th Squadron in September 1971 and the 18th SOS's aircraft formed the 821st Squadron in December 1972.

11 October 1969

AC-119G 52-5907 Detachment 1, 17 SOS, 14 SOW, USAF, Phan Rang detached to Tan Son Nhut
Lt Col Bernard Richard Knapic (KIA)
Maj Moses Lopes Alves (KIA)
Maj Jerome James Rice (KIA)
Capt John Hooper V Hathaway (KIA)
SSgt Ellsworth Smith Bradford (KIA)
SSgt Abraham Lincoln Moore (KIA)
4 crew, names unknown (survived)

An AC-119, radio call sign Shadow 76, crashed as it was taking off from Tan Son Nhut when an engine failed and caught fire. With all its armament and ammunition together with a full fuel load the single-engined performance of the AC-119G was insufficient to enable it to stay airborne. Six of the 10 crew were killed in the accident.

14 October 1969

F-100D 56-3069 615 TFS, 35 TFW, USAF, Phan Rang
Capt George Robert Andrews (KIA)

During a close air support mission a flight of F-100s attacked an enemy sampan near Thuy Dong, about 30 miles west of Saigon. Capt Andrews came in low to drop his ordnance but his aircraft was hit by ground fire and crashed. He may have been wounded by the enemy fire as he did not eject.

17 October 1969

A-4E 150107 VMA-311, MAG-12, USMC, Chu Lai
1 pilot, name unknown (survived)

A Skyhawk was destroyed by fire following an aborted take off from Chu Lai as it was setting off on a close air support mission. The pilot ejected safely.

19 October 1969

OV-10A 68-3786 19 TASS, 504 TASG, USAF, Bien Hoa
Lt Col Frank H Briggs (KIA)
Capt James C Woods (KIA)

A Bronco was conducting a training flight from Bien Hoa when it was shot down by small arms fire. Lt Col Briggs and Capt Woods were practising GCA and ADF approaches to the airfield when the starboard engine was hit and caught fire. The aircraft crashed near Long Thanh, 12 miles southeast of Bien Hoa and neither of the crew escaped.

21 October 1969

O-2A 68-10975 21 TASS, 504 TASG, USAF, Cam Ranh Bay
1Lt Glenn R Cook (KIA)
Maj John Lee Espenshield (KIA)

An FAC aircraft was controlling an air strike on Viet Cong positions in the hills 25 miles west of Nha Trang when it disappeared. The precise cause of the loss could not be ascertained, as the wreckage was not located by US forces. In December 1988 the Vietnamese returned the remains of Maj Espenshield to the USA.

24 October 1969

F-100F 56-3887 309 TFS, 31 TFW, USAF, Tuy Hoa
1Lt A D Muller (survived)
Capt J K Clapper (survived)

A Misty FAC was flying over the complex road and trail network in southern Laos on the search for possible targets when it ran into ground fire. As the aircraft approached the village of Ban Bouang Nam, 20 miles southeast of Ban Talan, it was hit by enemy fire at 1,500 feet and the two crew ejected immediately. The pair evaded capture and were found by an HH-3E (66-13281) from the 37th ARRS. 1Lt Muller had a broken leg so the PJ, TSgt Donald G Smith, was lowered to the ground to prepare him for the stretcher hoist. As they were being lifted into the helicopter enemy troops began firing and the hoist was damaged. Smith and Muller had to be cut free and they both fell back into the jungle as Jolly Green 28 escaped to make an emergency landing in a clearing about a mile away. The helicopter crew was quickly rescued by another HH-3E (66-13290) but Jolly Green 28 had to be destroyed by strike aircraft to prevent it from falling into enemy hands. For the next few hours TSgt Smith protected 1Lt Muller, directed air strikes on enemy positions and defended against enemy attack until another helicopter arrived to complete the rescue. TSgt Smith later received the AFC for his actions. Capt Clapper was rescued by yet another SAR helicopter despite intense enemy ground fire.

25 October 1969

F-4D 65-0751 435 TFS, 8 TFW, USAF, Ubon
Capt Gray Dawson Warren (KIA)
1Lt Neil Stanley Bynum (KIA)

A Wolf FAC Phantom and its crew were lost during an air strike near Ban Son close to the Ban Karai Pass in southern Laos. Capt Warren was controlling the strike, the target being construction equipment including a bulldozer that had been found on a road 15 miles west of the DMZ. On the third pass the bulldozer was hit by rockets and destroyed but the Phantom hit the ground about 100 yards from its target and exploded. SAR forces encountered 37mm anti-aircraft fire during a two-hour search and it is possible that the aircraft was shot down or failed to pull out of the dive in time.

26 October 1969

F-8J 150284 VF-191, USN, USS *Oriskany*
Lt T L Letter (survived)

The *Oriskany* was due to finish its fourth war cruise off Southeast Asia on 31 October but six days before operational flying ceased it lost a Crusader. The aircraft landed back on the carrier after a BARCAP mission but its nose gear failed and the aircraft was damaged beyond repair. The ship completed its 116 days on the line with a total of nine aircraft lost, only one of them due to enemy action.

27 October 1969

A-1H 52-137539 602 SOS, 56 SOW, USAF, Nakhon Phanom
1Lt James Wayne Herrick (KIA)

A flight of Skyraiders was on a Barrel Roll armed reconnaissance mission flying along Route 7 in northern Laos. 1Lt Herrick spotted a truck and dived down to attack it. His aircraft flew into the side of a mountain near Ban Paka Noy, close to the border with North Vietnam and some 40 miles east of the Plain of Jars. It was not determined whether he had been shot down or had flown into the ground as a result of target fixation or some other problem. James Herrick was killed the day before his 25th birthday.

1 November 1969

F-100F 56-3796 416 TFS, 31 TFW, USAF, Tuy Hoa
Lt Col Lawrence William Whitford (KIA)
1Lt Patrick Henry Carroll (KIA)

Another Misty FAC was lost during a visual reconnaissance flight over the Ho Chi Minh Trail in southern Laos. Lt Col Whitford was running low on fuel and called for a tanker but the Super Sabre failed to meet the tanker and was posted missing. The aircraft's last known position was about 35 miles west of Dak To, just within Laos. The fate of the crew remains a mystery.

A-1E 52-132455 602 SOS, 56 SOW, USAF, Nakhon Phanom
Maj Richard Walter Lytle (KIA)
1 crew, name unknown (survived)

A Skyraider developed an engine fault during a RESCAP mission over Laos and crashed killing one of the crew.

3 November 1969

F-4C 63-7528 557 TFS, 12 TFW, USAF, Cam Ranh Bay
Capt Stanley L Adams (KIA)
1Lt William D Smith (KIA)

A flight of Phantoms on a Steel Tiger interdiction mission found enemy troops in the open near Ban Soppeng, 10 miles south of the Mu Gia Pass. The aircraft started their attack but it was not until Capt Adams's 10th pass that his aircraft was shot down by ground fire. The aircraft was dropping napalm at the time, which would have required a low-level delivery.

4 November 1969

OV-10A 67-14676 20 TASS, 504 TASG, USAF, Da Nang
Capt Charles L Karr (KIA)
Maj Harry Jay Coates (KIA)

A Bronco was marking the position of a VC unit about 10 miles northeast of Quang Ngai when it failed to pull out of a dive and crashed close to the target. An Army helicopter arrived to search for survivors but the crew were found to be dead at the scene.

F-105D 59-1734 357 TFS, 355 TFW, USAF, Takhli
Capt Larry James Hanley (KIA)

A flight of F-105s attacked anti-aircraft gun positions near Ban Soppeng, possibly as a result of the loss of the Phantom on the previous day. Capt Hanley was pulling up from his second pass when his aircraft was hit by ground fire. He headed east to try to reach the coast but crashed a few miles short of the North Vietnamese border. Capt Hanley was presumed to have died.

5 November 1969

F-4D 66-7748 497 TFS, 8 TFW, USAF, Ubon
Capt Douglas Paul Lefever (KIA)
Capt Joseph Ygnacio Echanis (KIA)

Capt Lefever and Capt Echanis were leading a dawn strike on a Night Owl FAC mission on roads in the Mu Gia and Ban Karai Passes and were directing a pair of Navy aircraft to a target. Contact was lost with Capt Lefever's aircraft near Ban Senphan, a few miles south of the Mu Gia Pass, and a fireball was seen on the ground. Presuming that the Phantom had been shot down an electronic search was initiated but there was no indication that either of the crew had survived and the wreckage was never located. This Phantom had shot down a MiG-21 on 3 January 1968 when being flown by Maj B J Bogoslofski and Capt R L Huskey of the 433rd TFS.

F-4C   63-7604   559 TFS, 12 TFW, USAF, Cam Ranh Bay
                 1Lt Frederick J Carter (KIA)
                 Capt Wade A Greer (KIA)
A Phantom was being guided to a radar controlled landing at Cam Ranh Bay after an interdiction mission when it suddenly disappeared from the screen. The cause of the aircraft's loss was never ascertained and the crew were never recovered.

O-1G   156680   unit ..?, USAF, base ..?
                A Bird Dog was destroyed during a Viet Cong attack on an American base in South Vietnam. Although listed as a USAF aircraft this Bird Dog was one of a batch of eight aircraft serialled by the Navy's Bureau of Aeronautics in 1967.

7 November 1969

O-2A   68-10852   probably 20 TASS, 504 TASG,
                  USAF, Da Nang
An O-2 was being airlifted to Da Nang for repairs under an Army CH-47 Chinook when it fell from the sling and was destroyed. This was the third such incident of this kind since May although this must be balanced by the many hundreds of aircraft and helicopters that were successfully retrieved by heavy lift helicopters during the war.

11 November 1969

A-1E   52-135211   22 SOS, 56 SOW, USAF, Nakhon Phanom
                   Capt G H Porter (survived)
A Skyraider was hit by AAA near Ban Ban, 35 miles east of the Plain of Jars, during a Barrel Roll strike. Capt Porter ejected successfully and was later rescued by a USAF HH-53 from the 40th ARRS.

F-4D   65-0643   497 TFS, 8 TFW, USAF, Ubon
                 Maj C W Killen (survived)
                 1Lt J G Hoyler (survived)
The night of the 11th turned out to be a bad night for the Thailand-based Phantom squadrons with the loss of three aircraft and two crews. The first aircraft to be lost was bombing a target in the Mu Gia Pass. The aircraft was hit by AAA and the crew ejected. Miraculously, the pair were rescued from this very heavily defended area by a USAF HH-53 from the 40th ARRS.

F-4D   66-8718   13 TFS, 432 TRW, USAF, Udorn
                 Capt Robert Leon Tucci (KIA)
                 Maj James Eugene Dennany (KIA)
A few hours after the first Phantom had been shot down, another aircraft was lost as it was attacking trucks on the Trail near Ban Soppeng. The aircraft was seen to be hit by ground fire and crashed and exploded. No parachutes were observed or beeper signals heard indicating that the crew had probably been killed in their aircraft. Robert Tucci was on his second tour of duty in Southeast Asia having flown 181 missions from Da Nang on his first tour.

F-4E   67-0219   34 TFS, 388 TFW, USAF, Korat
                 Capt Jon Keith Bodahl (KIA)
                 Capt Harry Winfield Smith (KIA)
A SAR helicopter was sent to search for possible survivors just in case Capt Tucci or Maj Dennany had been able to escape from their aircraft. The helicopter was damaged by ground fire and a flight of F-4Es from Korat arrived to provide cover for the rescue forces. Unfortunately, one of the Phantoms was also shot down by 37mm anti-aircraft fire near Ban Senphan and the crew was killed.

12 November 1969

A-1H   52-139821   6 SOS, 633 SOW, USAF, Pleiku
                    Maj Gerald Robert Helmich (KIA)
In the early hours of the 12th the search for possible survivors of the shoot downs near the Mu Gia Pass was still continuing. Having already lost three Phantoms during the night, the rescue forces then lost one of their Skyraiders and its pilot. Capt Helmich was orbiting about a mile south of Ban Senphan when he was shot down by ground fire. It was not known whether he managed

to eject or not but he did not survive and became the fifth airman to be lost that night. This was the last of 15 Skyraiders lost by the 6th SOS before it was closed down and its aircraft and pilots dispersed among the other Skyraider squadrons based in Southeast Asia. The Squadron officially inactivated three days after Maj Helmich's death. Skyraider 139821 was the last of 713 A-1Hs to be built.

13 November 1969

F-4J   155802   VMFA-232, MAG-13, USMC, Chu Lai
                Maj G Lindgren (survived)
                Maj T Leach (survived)
During a training mission in South Vietnam a Phantom stalled as the pilot rolled in on a practice target. The crew ejected safely before the aircraft crashed. The squadron quoted for this Phantom may be incorrect as VMFA-232 left Chu Lai for Iwakuni on 7 September and did not return to Vietnam until April 1972.

15 November 1969

A-6A   155701   VMA(AW)-225, MAG-11, USMC, Da Nang
                1Lt D R Jessen (survived)
                1Lt R D Tutor (survived)
An Intruder was damaged by ground fire as it was on its way to bomb a target in the northernmost province of South Vietnam on the night of the 15th. The aircraft's starboard engine had to be shut down and the crew headed back towards Da Nang but had to eject over Da Nang Bay, approximately eight miles north of the airfield.

A-7A   153156   VA-27, USN, USS Constellation
                1 pilot, name unknown (survived)
An A-7 from the Constellation crashed during a strike mission when the engine suffered a bearing failure. The pilot escaped and was recovered safely.

A-7A   152679   VA-86, USN, USS Coral Sea
                1 pilot, name unknown (survived)
The Coral Sea also lost an A-7 on the 15th when an aircraft on an escort mission developed an oil leak that eventually led to engine failure. The pilot ejected and was soon picked up.

16 November 1969

O-1F   57-2867   21 TASS, 504 TASG, USAF, Cam Ranh Bay
                 Maj G R Lattin (survived)
                 2Lt W C Phillips, US Army (survived)
A Bird Dog FAC was controlling an air strike near Bu Krak on the South Vietnamese border with Cambodia about 100 miles north of Saigon. The target was an NVA anti-aircraft gun position and Maj Lattin was pulling up from marking the target for the second time when the aircraft was hit by ground fire, which damaged the engine. Maj Lattin crash-landed a few miles from the target and he and his Army observer were safely recovered.

F-4C   64-0842   557 TFS, 12 TFW, USAF, Cam Ranh Bay
                 Maj L L Davis (survived)
                 1Lt A A Ernst (survived)
Yet another Phantom was lost at the southern end of the Mu Gia Pass. Maj Davis and 1Lt Ernst were on a daylight strike mission on a choke point on a road a few miles north of Ban Senphan. The aircraft was hit by ground fire as it dived on the target and the crew ejected close by. Once again the rescue forces swung into action and a 40th ARRS HH-53C plucked the two airmen from the clutches of the North Vietnamese.

RF-4C   66-0468   14 TRS, 432 TRW, USAF, Udorn
                  Capt C P Sloan (survived)
                  1Lt A L Guise (survived)
Bullwhip 1 was sent on a photographic reconnaissance mission into northern Laos and was damaged by 37mm flak about 10 miles south of the Pathet Lao's headquarters at Sam Neua. The aircraft was flying at 250 feet and 540 knots when it was hit. Capt Sloan nursed his crippled Phantom back across Laos and into Thailand. He reached Udorn but he and his navigator were forced to eject about seven miles southeast of the airfield. This

crew had the misfortune to be shot down again on 21 December 1969.

RF-4C   65-0916   16 TRS, 460 TRW, USAF, Tan Son Nhut
                  Maj E P Morphew (survived)
                  Capt R C Cotton (survived)
Coincidentally, another RF-4C was lost about 40 minutes later on a totally different mission. This aircraft was from Tan Son Nhut and was flying a photographic reconnaissance mission over southern Laos when it was hit. The aircraft's port wing was damaged by 37mm flak about 30 miles southeast of Ban Talan. Maj Morphew headed east and managed to reach the coast where he and his navigator ejected about seven miles from Da Nang. The pair were picked up from the sea by a USAF helicopter.

OV-10A   67-14644   19 TASS, 504 TASG, USAF, Bien Hoa
                    detached to Tay Ninh
                    Maj Philippe B Fales (KIA)
The last of the five USAF aircraft lost on the 16th was a Bronco on a visual reconnaissance mission near Katum. Maj Fales was flying without an observer when his aircraft was shot down by ground fire about eight miles southeast of the city. The pilot was found to be dead when an Army helicopter arrived at the scene shortly after the crash.

17 November 1969

F-4D   66-7567   390 TFS, 366 TFW, USAF, Da Nang
                 Capt J J Rabeni (survived)
                 Maj D A Bowie (survived)
A Phantom crashed one mile short of the runway as it was approaching Da Nang following an interdiction mission in southern Laos.

20 November 1969

O-2A   67-21301   20 TASS, 504 TASG, USAF, Da Nang
                  Lt Col Walter A Renelt (KIA)
                  Capt John R Baldridge (KIA)
A forward air controller was checking the roads and trails along the South Vietnamese border with Laos about 20 miles west of Kham Duc when the aircraft was shot down. Neither of the crew escaped from the aircraft before it crashed.

O-1E   56-2657   19 TASS, 504 TASG, USAF, Bien Hoa
                 1 pilot, name unknown (survived)
A Bird Dog was taking off on a visual reconnaissance flight when it was caught in the wake turbulence of another aircraft. The pilot lost control and the aircraft crashed.

22 November 1969

F-4J   155889   VF-143, USN, USS Constellation
                Lt(jg) Herbert C Wheeler (recovered)
                Lt(jg) Henry James Bedinger (POW)
A section of F-4s from the Constellation was assigned to bomb a trail near Ban Nampakhon, 20 miles southwest of the Ban Karai Pass. The cloud base was around 8,000 feet, which necessitated a flatter than usual roll in on the target. Lt Wheeler rolled in at 360 knots and lit his afterburner but the aircraft failed to respond when he tried to level the wings. The aircraft continued rolling and pitched steeper nose down. With not enough altitude to effect a safe recovery, the crew ejected. Lt Wheeler was eventually rescued by a USAF HH-53 helicopter but Lt Bedinger was surrounded by enemy troops and captured. He became one of a handful of prisoners who survived being captured in Laos. During his captivity he was put in a cell with Ernie Brace, a civilian pilot with Bird and Son, who had been taken prisoner on 21 May 1965 when his Pilatus Porter was captured at an airstrip in Laos. Brace became the longest held civilian POW and the longest held survivor to return from Laos. His amazing story can be found in A Code to Keep written by Brace himself in 1988. Lt Bedinger was transferred to a prison in North Vietnam and was released on 28 March 1973. The exact cause of the aircraft's loss was never determined but was thought to have been either a control failure, a stall, or anti-aircraft fire.

The lengths to which the SAR forces would go to rescue a downed airman are illustrated by the rescue of 1Lt W J Bergeron in December 1969. A total of 366 sorties were flown during the rescue, which was finally made by an HH-53C of the 40th ARRS. USAF

F-4E   67-0314   4 TFS, 366 TFW, USAF, Da Nang
Capt C E Williams (survived)
Capt J T Harrison (survived)

A flight of Phantoms was sent from Da Nang to attack Viet Cong positions seven miles northeast of Quang Ngai. As Capt Williams was pulling up from the target his aircraft was struck by ground fire. He flew north to attempt an emergency landing but he and his WSO were forced to eject over the sea about five miles from Da Nang.

A-6A   155613   VA-196, USN, USS Ranger
Cdr L W Richards (survived)
Lt(jg) Richard Carl Deuter (KIA)

A section of Intruders from the Ranger was assigned to hit a target under the control of an FAC near Tavouac, about 15 miles south of the A Shau Valley in southern Laos. The aircraft rolled in on the target but as it started to pull out of its dive the wing failed and the aircraft disintegrated. Miraculously, the pilot escaped and was rescued within 30 minutes but his NFO was not found and probably was not able to eject. The cause of the wing failure could not be positively identified but was either caused by flak or a fatigue failure in the wing itself.

RF-4C   66-0441   14 TRS, 432 TRW, USAF, Udorn
Capt L P Wright (survived)
1Lt F O Paige (survived)

The third RF-4C to be lost during November was shot down during a photographic reconnaissance mission in southern Laos on the 22nd. Capt Wright was making a photo run at 300 feet and 540 knots over a damaged truck on a road three miles south of Ban Topen, west of the Ban Karai Pass. The aircraft was hit by ground fire and the port engine was damaged. Nevertheless, Capt Wright flew across Laos and into Thailand where he and his navigator ejected safely a few miles from Nakhon Phanom.

A-6A   155607   VA-196, USN, USS Ranger
Lt Cdr Richard F Collins (KIA)
Lt Michael Edward Quinn (KIA)

VA-196 lost another Intruder on the same day when an aircraft failed to return from a night armed reconnaissance mission over the Ho Chi Minh Trail. The crew were using the aircraft's airborne moving target indicator radar to locate trucks on the Trail and were being followed by another Intruder, which had been delayed by technical problems, and was about 25 miles behind. The crew of the second aircraft saw a huge fireball estimated to be near the village of Ban Tampanko, about 25 miles southwest of Khe Sanh. Attempts to raise Lt Cdr Collins on the radio met with no response and it was presumed that the Intruder had crashed. A subsequent search revealed no trace of the aircraft or its crew.

24 November 1969

F-105D   61-0060   357 TFS, 355 TFW, USAF, Takhli
Capt James Blair White (KIA)

A flight of two F-105s was sent on a Barrel Roll mission to attack troop positions about five miles southwest of Ban Ban in northern Laos. Capt White was shot down on his second pass and was not seen to eject from his aircraft before it dived into the ground. Jim White was the brother of astronaut Lt Col Edward White who had flown in Gemini 4 in June 1965 and was one of three astronauts killed in the Apollo 204 capsule fire at Cape Canaveral on 27 January 1967. Jim had applied for the astronaut programme and was hoping to start training when he returned to the USA.

C-130A   56-0533   41 TAS, 374 TAW, USAF, Naha
Capt Earl Carlyle Brown (KIA)
1Lt Peter Richard Matthes (KIA)

Maj Michael Dimitri Balamonti (KIA)
Capt Richard Owen Ganley (KIA)
SSgt Charles Richard Fellenz (KIA)
SSgt Larry Irwin Grewell (KIA)
SSgt Donald Lee Wright (KIA)
Sgt Rexford John DeWispelaere (KIA)

On the night of the 24th a Blind Bat C-130 forward air control aircraft from Ubon was orbiting at 9,000 feet in the Ban Bak area to the east of Saravan in southern Laos. The aircraft was above a 4,000 feet cloud base when it was hit by several rounds of 37mm flak and burst into flames. The aircraft crashed about 15 miles east of Ban Talan and all on board were killed. The remains of the crew were returned from Laos in November 1993 and positively identified in October 1995. The Blind Bat mission ceased in mid-1970 after five years of operations over the Ho Chi Minh Trail with the loss of two aircraft plus another two lost at Da Nang during a sapper attack in July 1965.

25 November 1969

F-4D   66-7562   13 TFS, 432 TRW, USAF, Udorn
Capt G J Skaret (survived)
1Lt D M Tye (survived)

A Laredo fast FAC aircraft went down during a Barrel Roll mission in northern Laos. A flight of Phantoms was sent on a strike on Route 7 with the Laredo aircraft, flown by Capt Skaret, directing the raid. As Capt Skaret pulled up from attacking a target on the road 10 miles southeast of Ban Ban, his aircraft was hit in the fuselage by 37mm AAA. He turned south and he and his WSO ejected near Ban Xon, 30 miles north of the Nam Ngum Reservoir. The crew were later rescued by an Air America helicopter that was in the vicinity.

28 November 1969

F-8J   150349   VF-211, USN, USS Hancock
Lt G W Warrell (survived)

The USS Hancock arrived back on the line on 1 September for its fifth tour off Vietnam. After nearly three months of trouble-free operations the ship lost a Crusader on the 28th. The aircraft struck the ramp and crashed when returning from a CAP mission but the pilot escaped.

F-105D   61-0196   333 TFS, 355 TFW, USAF, Takhli
1 pilot, name unknown (survived)

F-105D   60-0435   333 TFS, 355 TFW, USAF, Takhli
1 pilot, name unknown (survived)

As a group of aircraft were taking on fuel from a KC-135, the wake turbulence from a Phantom caused two Thunderchiefs to collide and cause enough damage for both pilots to eject from their aircraft. 60-0435 was painted with the name 'Satisfaction' when it flew with the 34th TFS and 61-0196 was painted as 'Mary Sabre' in early 1968.

1 December 1969

F-4C   63-7438   559 TFS, 12 TFW, USAF, Cam Ranh Bay
Capt Frederick W Seibert (KIA)
Capt Patrick J Hayes (KIA)

A Phantom was shot down by ground fire during a dusk strike on enemy positions near Bu Krak on the South Vietnamese border with Cambodia, about 100 miles north of Saigon. The aircraft burst into flames as it dived on the target and crashed before either of the crew could escape.

A-1G   52-132546   602 SOS, 56 SOW, USAF, Nakhon Phanom
1 pilot, name unknown (survived)

A Skyraider crashed when its engine failed as it was taking off on a strike mission from Nakhon Phanom.

3 December 1969

F-4D   66-7763   433 TFS, 8 TFW, USAF, Ubon
Maj Brad L Sharp (survived)
1Lt J C Mangels (survived)

A Wolf FAC crew was directing a strike 15 miles southwest of Ban Senphan in southern Laos when their aircraft was shot down. The two men escaped and were eventually recovered by a USAF SAR helicopter. Brad Sharp was the commander of the Wolf FAC unit at the time of his shoot down. He later took command of the 25th TFS and survived the crash of a Phantom in a take off accident at Ubon on 10 July 1972.

4 December 1969

A-37A   67-14523   604 SOS, 3 TFW, USAF, Bien Hoa
1 pilot, name unknown (survived)

During a close air support mission a Dragonfly came so low as it was dropping napalm that it hit the top of a tree. This was not an uncommon occurrence but on this occasion the damage was so great that the pilot was forced to eject. This was the first Dragonfly to be lost in Vietnam since September 1968.

5 December 1969

F-4C   63-7444   558 TFS, 12 TFW, USAF, Cam Ranh Bay
Capt Benjamin Franklin Danielson (KIA)
1Lt Woodrow J Bergeron (survived)

Two Phantoms were sent on a raid on a choke point on the Trail near the village of Ban Phanop in southern Laos. The second aircraft (call sign Boxer 22) was pulling up from its first high angle dive bomb delivery when it was hit by a 37mm shell at 6,000 feet. Capt Danielson turned to the east but the crew ejected a few miles from the target when they lost control. Both men landed less than 200 yards apart on either side of a river in a valley. Voice contact was made with them and the rescue forces were called in on what became one of the largest rescue efforts of the war. However, the crew had landed in one of the best defended areas of the Trail and the North Vietnamese had geography and time on their side.

On the 5th no less than seven SAR helicopters from Nakhon Phanom and Udorn made attempts to rescue the survivors but each time they came close they were hit by ground fire and had to withdraw, some suffering considerable damage. On that first day a total of 88 sorties were flown including 47 by A-1s, 12 by F-105s, seven by F-4s, two by F-100s, 10 by various helicopters, seven by FACs and three by HC-130P King airborne mission control aircraft. From first light on the 6th until midday, Sandys and other aircraft hosed down the area around the downed airmen in the hope of suppressing ground fire. During the morning 1Lt Bergeron radioed that he heard shouts and gunshots across the river and then heard a scream after which he could no longer contact Capt Danielson. It was assumed that the North Vietnamese had discovered his hiding place and killed him in a shootout. A huge smoke screen was put down to protect the helicopters as they made their run in towards the remaining survivor. The first helicopter to make the attempt was hit and lost part of its flight control system while the second got stuck in the branches of a tree as it backed towards 1Lt Bergeron. The pilot only managed to free the HH-53 by backing further towards the tree and breaking off a branch with its badly damaged tail boom. More fighter attacks took place and another smoke screen put down for further attempts after midday but three more helicopters were damaged by enemy fire during the afternoon. Another attempt just before dusk also failed and 1Lt Bergeron had to spend a second night on the ground as North Vietnamese soldiers with dogs searched for him in the long grass and bamboo. A total of 154 sorties had been flown on the second day including 74 by Sandys, 50 by fighters, 14 by FACs, five by HC-130Ps and 11 by HH-53s. At dawn on the 7th F-4 FACs directed flights of F-105s to strike anti-aircraft gun positions in the valley while Sandys attacked enemy troops who were close to the survivor. The first helicopter was driven away by ground fire and more air strikes were called in. A smoke corridor was built up again and Jolly Green 77, an HH-53C flown by Lt Col Shipman of the 40th ARRS, started its run in with flights of Sandys on either side blasting away at muzzle flashes from the enemy's guns. 1Lt Bergeron saw the helicopter draw near and made a dash for the river waving a white escape and evasion map. The PJ lowered the rescue hoist and Bergeron grabbed hold as the helicopter started reeling him in. Woodrow Bergeron was at last rescued from almost certain death. The entire operation had lasted 51 hours during which a total of 366 sorties had been flown resulting in severe damage to 12 helicopters and five A-1s as well as the tragic death of a PJ, A1C David M Davison, who was killed on the 5th. This SAR operation gives an indication of the extent to which the US forces are willing to go to rescue those in peril. Although the Bat 21 rescue in April 1972 received more publicity, the rescue of Woodrow Bergeron remains as one of the most outstanding episodes of the war in Southeast Asia.

F-4E   67-0300   469 TFS, 388 TFW, USAF, Korat
                   Capt John Calvin Clark (KIA)
                   1Lt Patrick Kendal Harrold (KIA)
As night fell another Phantom was lost in Laos, this one during a Barrel Roll mission in the north of the country. Capt Clark

located a truck on a road about 15 miles east of Ban Ban and commenced an attack. As it dived steeply on the truck the aircraft was hit by 37mm AAA and crashed in flames near the road. There was no indication that either of the crew had been able to eject before the aircraft crashed. However, it was not until investigations in 1994 and 1995 that the remains of the crew were recovered from Laos and were then buried at Arlington on 21 November 1997.

OV-10A 67-14628   19 TASS, 504 TASG, USAF, Bien Hoa
                    2 crew, names unknown (survived)
A Bronco crash-landed at Dian airfield in South Vietnam and was damaged beyond repair. The cause of the accident was attributed to pilot error.

6 December 1969

A-4E   150080   VMA-311, MAG-12, USMC, Chu Lai
                   1 pilot, name unknown (survived)
A Skyhawk burst a tyre as it was taking off from Chu Lai on a combat mission. The pilot abandoned the take off but the aircraft veered off the runway and was damaged beyond repair.

8 December 1969

F-105F 63-8352   357 TFS, 355 TFW, USAF, Takhli
                   Maj Carl Richard Dice (KIA)
                   1Lt B N Cox (survived)
A two-seat F-105F was damaged by 37mm AAA during a Barrel Roll mission three miles south of Ban Ban on the 8th. The aircraft was hit in the port wing as it was bombing a storage area. Although the aircraft caught fire, the flames subsequently went out and Maj Dice headed back towards base. He decided to attempt an emergency landing at Udorn but he was killed when the aircraft crashed on landing. The WSO, 1Lt Cox, survived with only minor injuries. 63-8352 was a historic aircraft in that it was the aircraft flown by Maj Merlyn Dethlefsen on a mission on 10 March 1967 for which he subsequently received the Medal of Honor. The aircraft was painted as 'Ramp Tramp' and 'Mr Flak Bait' during its time at Takhli.

10 December 1969

F-100D 56-3332   355 TFS, 31 TFW, USAF, Tuy Hoa
                   Maj R F Boyle (survived)
A Super Sabre was lost during a Steel Tiger strike near Kay Bong, 30 miles southeast of Saravan. Maj Boyle put his aircraft into a 45-degree dive at 500 knots but it was hit by 37mm AAA forcing him to eject immediately. He was later rescued by a USAF SAR helicopter.

11 December 1969

F-100F 58-1215   3 TFW, USAF, Bien Hoa
A Viet Cong attack on Bien Hoa on the night of the 11th resulted in fairly light damage except for the loss of a two-seat Super Sabre. Eleven 122mm rockets were fired and three men were wounded by shrapnel.

13 December 1969

C-130A 56-0499   41 TAS, 374 TAW, USAF, Naha
                   5 crew, names unknown (survived)
A Hercules crashed on take off from Bu Dop near the Cambodian border as it attempted a three-engined take off. This small airstrip often suffered from enemy mortar attacks and three-engined departures were not uncommon as they were preferable to staying on the ground overnight until spares could be flown in. Three successful three-engined take offs had been made by C-130s from Bu Dop in recent months but the fourth attempt failed.

16 December 1969

RF-8G   145611   Detachment 19, VFP-63, USN,
                  USS Hancock
                  Lt Victor Patrick Buckley (KIA)
An RF-8G crashed into the Gulf of Tonkin about 60 miles east of Dong Hoi and its pilot was killed when it was returning to the Hancock from a photographic reconnaissance mission. The cause of the aircraft's loss was presumed to have been accidental.

17 December 1969

A-37A   67-14526   604 SOS, 3 TFW, USAF, Bien Hoa
                    Lt Col William Robert Spillers (KIA)
An A-37 Dragonfly was lost during a close air support mission near Phuoc Binh, 35 miles north of Saigon. The aircraft was dropping napalm on VC bunkers and buildings when its crashed close to the target, probably as a result of ground fire.

A-7B   154542   VA-56, USN, USS Ranger
                   1 pilot, name unknown (survived)
The Corsair was still prone to engine problems. An aircraft developed an engine malfunction on the approach to the Ranger when returning from a strike mission and the pilot was eventually forced to eject as the engine failed.

A-1H   52-135273   22 SOS, 56 SOW, USAF, Nakhon Phanom
                     1 pilot, name unknown (survived)
A Skyraider crashed accidentally during a close air support mission.

C-123K 55-4562   310 SOS, 315 SOW, USAF, Phan Rang
                   1 crew, name unknown (KIA)
                   4 crew, names unknown (survived)
A Provider undershot the runway at Gia Nghia, 90 miles northeast of Saigon, and crashed killing one of the five crewmen on board. The aircraft broke up and was destroyed by fire.

19 December 1969

F-4E   67-0253   4 TFS, 366 TFW, USAF, Da Nang
                   Capt T R Webb (survived)
                   Capt L M Bonner (survived)
A Stormy FAC Phantom was directing a strike on a target 15 miles northeast of Ban Talan in southern Laos when it was damaged by flak. The aircraft was hit in the fuselage by 23mm AAA

The 602nd SOS lost at least 80 Skyraiders during the war. However, both the Skyraiders seen here at Nakhon Phanom in December 1969 just before the squadron deactivated, survived the war. Lt Col D Feld

but Capt Webb managed to exit from the target area and fly back across Laos and into Thailand. The crew almost made it to Ubon but ejected about two miles from the airfield.

KC-135A 56-3629 93 BW attached to 4220 ARS, 4252 SW, USAF, Ching Chuan Kang
Maj Gene T Wright, 7 BW (KIA)
Capt Jon M Olsson, 7 BW (KIA)
Capt Douglas W Murphey, 7 BW (KIA)
SMSgt Howard G Benford, 7 BW (KIA)

Three KC-135s took off from Ching Chuan Kang in succession to form a refuelling cell for an Arc Light support mission over the South China Sea. Soon after take off the last aircraft in the cell encountered very severe turbulence from which it was unable to recover and it crashed out of control into the sea. Very little wreckage and none of the crew were ever found. The aircraft was from the 93rd BW, Castle AFB, California but the crew were from the 7th BW at Carswell AFB, Texas and were temporarily attached to the 4220th ARS during their tour on Taiwan. This was the last of four KC-135s lost in connection with the war in Southeast Asia. By the end of the war in 1973 the tanker force had flown a total of 194,687 sorties in a total of 911,364 flying hours. During these sorties the KC-135s conducted 813,878 in-flight refuellings off-loading more than eight billion pounds of fuel. The tanker effort received little publicity during or after the war but, quite simply, without the tanker force there would have been no air war over North Vietnam. Not only did the KC-135s and their Navy equivalents enable the US forces to carry out the air offensive, but the tankers also saved many aircraft and their crews by emergency refuellings, often breaking safety regulations in an endeavour to save their fellow airmen.

20 December 1969

F-4D 66-7543 390 TFS, 366 TFW, USAF, Da Nang
Capt D S Catchings (survived)
1Lt W R Daley (survived)

In a repeat of the previous day's event, another Stormy FAC Phantom was lost during an FAC mission in southern Laos. The aircraft was flying near Ban Namm, 30 miles west of the DMZ, when it was also hit by 23mm ground fire. Capt Catchings managed to fly the aircraft to within a few miles of Ubon before he and his WSO were forced to eject.

OV-10A 155503 VAL-4, USN, Binh Thuy detached to Vung Tau
Lt(jg) Joel Alexis Sandberg (KIA)
Capt Carl Edwin Long, USMC (KIA)

Lt Sandberg and his Marine Corps observer, Capt Long, were patrolling the Saigon Long Tau shipping channel, a task that VAL-4 did every day. The pilot radioed that he was descending to investigate a suspicious-looking sampan but nothing further was heard from him. The aircraft was found to have crashed near the mouth of the Song Thi Va River in the Rung Sat Special Zone, about eight miles north of Vung Tau. The cause was probably small arms or automatic weapons fire and neither of the crew survived. The largely intact aircraft was embedded deeply in thick mud and an Army CH-47 Chinook was called in to recover the wreck. As the helicopter attempted to haul the OV-10 out of the mud the strop broke under the strain and the helicopter shot upwards out of control and almost crashed. It was then decided to destroy the aircraft where it lay in the mud after the bodies of the crew were removed. Bronco 155503 was the final aircraft of an order of 114 OV-10As for the Marine Corps and was one of 18 aircraft loaned to the Navy.

21 December 1969

RF-4C 66-0396 14 TRS, 432 TRW, USAF, Udorn
Capt C P Sloan (survived)
1Lt A L Guise (survived)

The crew of an RF-4C was shot down for the second time in just over a month. Capt Sloan and 1Lt Guise had ejected from their aircraft near Udorn following battle damage during a Barrel Roll mission on 16 November. On 21 December the pair were flying another Barrel Roll mission (still using the call sign Bullwhip 1) when their Phantom was hit by 37mm AAA 20 miles

southeast of Ban Ban. This time the damage was too serious to be able to return to Thailand and the crew ejected moments after the aircraft was hit. However, their good luck held and they were rescued by a 40th ARRS HH-53 having suffered only minor injuries during the ejection and landing.

A-1H 52-139811 602 SOS, 56 SOW, USAF, Nakhon Phanom
1 pilot, name unknown (survived)

A Skyraider was taking off on an escort mission when it lost oil pressure causing the engine to fail. The pilot escaped from the subsequent crash-landing.

24 December 1969

O-2A 68-10999 19 TASS, 504 TASG, USAF, Bien Hoa
Sgt Lauren Dean Fritz (KWF)
A1C Patrick Robert Martin (KWF)

On Christmas Eve two airmen stole an O-2 and took off on an unauthorised flight over Phuoc Tuy province. The aircraft crashed after about 12 minutes and both men were killed. Neither of the men were actually aircrew.

26 December 1969

C-7B 63-9723 459 TAS, 483 TAW, USAF, Phu Cat
1Lt David Bicknel Bowling (KIA)
1Lt R J Patterson (survived)
TSgt E J Welch (KIA)

A Caribou was hit by small arms fire as it approached Tien Phuoc, west of Tam Ky during a cargo flight from Phu Cat. The pilot, 1Lt Bowling, was wounded in the chest and the aircraft crashed inverted into a rice paddy near the village of Phuoc An. Although the co-pilot survived, the flight mechanic, TSgt Welch, was crushed to death by the cargo when it broke loose on impact.

OV-10A 67-14657 19 TASS, 504 TASG, USAF, Bien Hoa
Maj David Lloyd Knott (KIA)

A Bronco had just taken off from the airfield at An Loc for an FAC mission when it was shot down by small arms fire killing the pilot, the only occupant.

A-6A 152891 VA-35, USN, USS Coral Sea
Lt(jg) Dustin Cowles Trowbridge (KIA)
Lt(jg) Walter Henry Kosky (KIA)

An Intruder configured for a tanker sortie crashed in the Gulf of Tonkin killing both its crew. The cause of the accident could not be confirmed.

A-7B 154517 VA-56, USN, USS Ranger
1 pilot, name unknown (survived)

As an A-7 Corsair was being launched from the catapult of the USS Ranger, the aircraft's engine lost thrust and the aircraft settled towards the sea. The pilot ejected safely and was quickly rescued.

27 December 1969

TA-4F 154621 H&MS-11, MAG-11, USMC, Da Nang
Maj Richard E Lewis (survived)
1Lt Paul E Phillips (survived)

H&MS-11 lost one of its Playboy TA-4F fast FACs during a Steel Tiger mission in southern Laos. Maj Lewis was manoeuvring to avoid anti-aircraft fire at 1,000 feet near the town of Ban Kate when his aircraft was hit by 23mm ground fire. The engine wound down and the crew ejected but were recovered the next day by a rescue helicopter after strike forces suppressed intense ground fire around the downed airmen. This was the second TA-4F lost in about 1,700 reconnaissance and FAC sorties over Laos during 1969.

F-4C 63-7524 558 TFS, 12 TFW, USAF, Cam Ranh Bay
2 crew, names unknown (survived)

When a Phantom was returning from an interdiction mission the crew experienced problems with the aircraft's navigation system and radios. Unable to obtain an accurate steer for base the aircraft ran out of fuel before it could land. Both the crew ejected safely and were rescued.

O-1G 50-1719 unit ..?, USAF, Tuy Hoa

A Bird Dog was destroyed as the indirect result of a VC attack on Tuy Hoa in the night. It was being towed rapidly away from the flight line under fire when it struck a tree and was so badly damaged that it had to be scrapped.

28 December 1969

F-4B 149429 VMFA-122, MAG-13, USMC, Chu Lai
1Lt E M Franger (survived)
Lt D K McClennan (survived)

A flight of Phantoms was amongst the aircraft that provided escort and firepower for the rescue forces that were looking for Maj Lewis and 1Lt Phillips who had been shot down the previous day. About seven miles southeast of Muang Phine the Phantoms found and attacked a 37mm anti-aircraft gun position. As 1Lt Franger rolled in for his second pass his aircraft was hit by a 37mm shell that exploded in the engine bay. The crew ejected and were rescued the following day by a USAF SAR helicopter.

F-100D 55-3511 308 TFS, 31 TFW, USAF, Tuy Hoa
Lt Col C W Meyers (survived)

A Super Sabre had just taken off from Tuy Hoa and was heading inland on a close air support mission when it was hit by ground fire and crashed about 20 miles west of the airfield. The pilot ejected and was rescued by an Army helicopter. This particular Super Sabre had been used for flight test duties by the Sacramento Air Material Area in the early 1960s and had been painted in a vivid red and white high-visibility colour scheme.

C-117D 17284 H&MS-13, MAG-13, USMC, Chu Lai
Lt Col Douglas Lee Snead (KWF)
Capt Donald Joseph Berger (KWF)
Sgt William Lloyd Bunch (KWF)
Cpl Ronald Francis Liscum (KWF)

MAG-13's Skytrain logistics transport crashed in Quang Tin province on a training flight killing the crew. This aircraft had entered service with the US Navy at San Diego as an R4D-6 in September 1944 but was later modified to C-117D standard and had served with H&MS-13 since at least the end of 1966.

29 December 1969

A-1H 52-137552 602 SOS, 56 SOW, USAF, Nakhon Phanom
1Lt N E Frisbie (survived)

A Skyraider was lost during a night armed reconnaissance mission in southern Laos. 1Lt Frisbie found several trucks on a road near Ban Dong Pang, 45 miles southeast of Nakhon Phanom. As he dived on the target his aircraft was hit by 37mm anti-aircraft fire. He maintained control and headed back towards Nakhon Phanom but was forced to eject about eight miles south of the airfield and had to be picked up by an HH-3E.

30 December 1969

F-4D 66-7590 555 TFS, 432 TRW, USAF, Udorn
Capt Fielding Wesley Featherston (KIA)
1Lt Douglas David Ferguson (KIA)

Five Phantoms, led by a Laredo FAC flown by Capt Featherston and 1Lt Ferguson, were sent to destroy a fuel dump 25 miles north of Ban Ban in northern Laos. The dump was estimated to hold around 1,200 drums of petrol, which was used by trucks supplying North Vietnamese forces in Laos. Capt Featherston's aircraft was hit during a strafing run and exploded in a fireball with no sign of ejection. However, the next day the crash site was photographed and two empty parachutes were seen hanging from nearby trees. There was no trace of the crew and the parachutes may have been used to lure rescue helicopters into a trap.

31 December 1969

OV-10A 68-3812 23 TASS, 504 TASG, USAF, Nakhon Phanom
Capt R R Russell (survived)

A Bronco on a visual reconnaissance mission over southern Laos was shot down by 37mm flak 10 miles west of Ban Thapachon. Capt Russell ejected as the aircraft spun into the ground. He was recovered by an HH-3E having suffered only minor injuries.

Chapter Seven

1970

The Year of Withdrawal

2 January 1970

F-4D 66-8784 25 TFS, 8 TFW, USAF, Ubon
Capt John Thomas West (KIA)
1Lt Ronnie George Lindstrom (KIA)

Two Phantoms from Ubon were sent on a LORAN validation flight over southern Laos. As the aircraft approached the town of Ban Tampanko at 4,500 feet one of the Phantoms was seen to be hit by ground fire and crashed without any sign of an ejection or parachutes. This was the second aircraft lost on a LORAN calibration flight.

A-6A 152937 VA-196, USN, USS *Ranger*
Lt Bruce Carlton Fryar (KIA)
Lt Nicholas George Brooks (KIA)

Two Intruders were despatched on a raid on a storage dump near the Mu Gia Pass in southern Laos under the control of a USAF FAC. As Lt Fryar made his second 40-degree dive on the target the aircraft was seen to explode at about 5,400 feet and the starboard wing separated from the fuselage. Two good parachutes were seen by both the FAC and the other Intruder crew, indicating that both men had ejected. A SAR mission was launched immediately and orbiting aircraft picked up emergency beeper signals. One of the crew was seen lying on the ground still attached to his parachute. A pararescueman was lowered to the ground and tried to attach a hoist to the airman, who was identified as Lt Fryar and was apparently dead, but heavy ground fire forced the helicopter away and the pararescueman only just escaped with his life. Encroaching darkness put an end to further rescue attempts that day and when the rescue forces arrived at the scene the following morning they found that the pilot and his parachute were gone. Although an emergency beeper was heard intermittently later that day there was no further sign of either of the Intruder crew and the search was called off several days later. The Brooks family later received information from an unspecified and uncorroborated source that Lt Brooks had been captured and had escaped three times before being killed by his captors. His remains were returned to the USA by Laotian freedom fighters in 1982 and were buried at sea on 25 March of that year. The most probable cause of the Intruder's demise was a hit from 23mm flak that was present at the time. However, it was also thought possible that the explosion might have been caused by a premature detonation of the aircraft's ordnance. It was still carrying six Mk82 bombs when it blew up.

3 January 1970

C-123K 54-0688 19 TAS, 315 TAW, USAF, Phan Rang
5 crew, names unknown (survived)

A Provider was damaged beyond repair when it suffered a nose gear malfunction. On 1 January the 315th SOS was redesignated as the 315th TAW, reflecting its primary role of in-theatre tactical airlift.

5 January 1970

F-4B 152283 VMFA-542, MAG-11, USMC, Da Nang
Maj Larry Warren Robinson (KIA)
1Lt Robert Wayne Burnes (KIA)

A flight of Phantoms from VMFA-542 was escorting a Playboy TA-4F fast FAC when they attacked 37mm anti-aircraft gun positions near Ban Kapay, 30 miles west of the DMZ. Maj Robinson was making his second attack on the target when his aircraft was hit by 37mm flak and crashed close to the gun positions.

Neither of the crew had time to eject from the Phantom and may have been wounded as a round was seen to strike the cockpit. Larry Robinson was actually a Playboy FAC pilot but on this occasion was flying a Phantom as part of a hunter-killer team with a Playboy TA-4F. Phantom 152283 had previously served with VF-96 on board the USS *Enterprise* before it was passed to the Marine Corps.

7 January 1970

A-7A 153231 VA-86, USN, USS *Coral Sea*
Lt Cdr Michael George Hoff (KIA)

A section of A-7s from the *Coral Sea* was sent on an armed reconnaissance mission over the Trail in southern Laos. The aircraft found trucks on a road near Ban Namm, some 30 miles west of the DMZ and commenced an attack. As Lt Cdr Hoff was pulling up from his fourth strafing pass on the trucks his aircraft was hit by AAA and he reported that he had a fire warning light and was going to eject. He pulled up to 2,000 feet but then the aircraft rolled inverted and dived into the ground. No parachute was seen and it was presumed that the aircraft crashed before Lt Cdr Hoff was able to escape.

F-4E 67-0357 421 TFS, 366 TFW, USAF, Da Nang
Capt Robert Ochab (KWF)
1Lt Campbell (survived)

A pair of Phantoms was practising air combat manoeuvring against each other on a training flight near Da Nang. One of the aircraft crashed when it started a manoeuvre at too low an altitude to pull out safely. One of the crew was killed in the accident.

9 January 1970

A-1G 52-132612 602 SOS, 56 SOW, USAF, Nakhon Phanom
Capt J L Hudson (survived)

A Skyraider was damaged during a mission over a particularly remote and mountainous area of northern Laos about 70 miles west of Sam Neua. Capt Hudson was attacking enemy troops, almost certainly Pathet Lao, and was making his fifth pass when his aircraft was damaged by small arms fire. He headed south but was forced to eject near Muang Poi on the southwestern edge of the Plain of Jars. He was rescued by a USAF HH-53C helicopter from the 40th ARRS, which had to send a PJ down to extricate Capt Hudson from the trees.

A-4E 152082 VMA-211, MAG-12, USMC, Chu Lai
1Lt Dennis Lee Peek (KIA)

A flight of A-4s from Chu Lai was sent to attack enemy troops that were engaging friendly forces 20 miles south of Da Nang. 1Lt Peek was making his second attack on the troops when his aircraft was hit by ground fire and crashed before he could escape.

F-100D 55-3569 308 TFS, 31 TFW, USAF, Tuy Hoa
1 pilot, name unknown (survived)

During a training flight over South Vietnam a Super Sabre suffered a compressor stall that resulted in engine failure. Unable to restart the engine, the pilot ejected and was soon picked up. This aircraft first saw service in Vietnam with the 481st TFS in 1965.

10 January 1970

O-2A 68-6863 20 TASS, 504 TASG, USAF, Da Nang
1Lt John A Lehecka (KIA)
SFC James Henry Zumbrun, US Army (KIA)

The highly secret and highly dangerous MACVSOG Shining Brass patrols along the Ho Chi Minh Trail were renamed Prairie Fire in 1969. An O-2 on a Prairie Fire support mission was lost 20 miles west of Dak To, near the point where the borders of South Vietnam, Laos and Cambodia meet. 1Lt Lehecka and his SOG observer were controlling an air strike when their aircraft was hit by small arms fire and crashed, killing both the crew.

O-1G 51-7441 504 TASG, USAF, base ..?
2 crew, names unknown (survived)

Another FAC aircraft was lost on the 10th when a Bird Dog crashed on take off injuring the crew and destroying the aircraft.

11 January 1970

A-1H 52-134570 602 SOS, 56 SOW, USAF, Nakhon Phanom
1Lt Richard David Chorlins (KIA)

A Skyraider was taking part in a night strike on truck traffic in the Mu Gia Pass when it was shot down. 1Lt Chorlins was turning at 7,500 feet in preparation for his second pass when his aircraft was hit by 37mm AAA. The Spad caught fire and crashed before the pilot had a chance to escape.

F-4J 155750 VF-154, USN, USS *Ranger*
Lt Terence Patrick Ryan (KIA)
1 crew, name unknown (survived)

A Phantom crashed into the sea shortly after being launched from the *Ranger* on a BARCAP mission. One of the crew was killed in the accident.

13 January 1970

F-100D 55-3777 35 TFW, USAF, Phan Rang
1 pilot, name unknown (survived)

An F-100 had to be abandoned when it lost engine oil pressure causing complete engine failure during a close air support mission.

14 January 1970

F-100D 56-3097 531 TFS, 3 TFW, USAF, Bien Hoa
1Lt W H Baker (survived)

The threat to operations at even the larger airbases in South Vietnam was once more illustrated on the 14th when a Super Sabre was hit by small arms fire as it climbed through 2,000 feet after taking off from Bien Hoa. The pilot continued heading east until he had to eject about 15 miles from the airfield. He was picked up by an Army helicopter.

15 January 1970

F-4D 66-8820 390 TFS, 366 TFW, USAF, Da Nang
Maj Tommy Ray Warren (KIA)
1Lt R D Leblanc (survived)

A Stormy FAC Phantom was shot down during an armed reconnaissance mission in southern Laos. Maj Warren was flying at 3,200 feet near Ban Kate when the aircraft was hit in the forward fuselage by ground fire. The pilot may have been wounded as he did not appear to eject after his WSO left the aircraft. 1Lt Leblanc was later rescued by a USAF SAR helicopter.

18 January 1970

F-100F 56-3975 416 TFS, 31 TFW, USAF, Tuy Hoa
1Lt J L Merrill (survived)
Capt H D Scott (survived)

The Commando Sabre unit lost two aircraft on consecutive days on Steel Tiger missions in southern Laos thereby maintaining its unenviable record of the highest loss rate of any F-100 unit in Southeast Asia. The first Misty FAC aircraft was shot down as it circled its target at 1,000 feet near the village of Ban Tok, 45 miles southeast of Saravan. The aircraft was hit by 23m AAA and 1Lt Merrill headed for Thailand. However, he and Capt Scott had to eject from their burning aircraft about 25 miles northwest of Saravan and were later rescued by a USAF SAR helicopter.

O-2A   68-10864   21 TASS, 504 TASG, USAF, Cam Ranh Bay
                  1Lt Steven A Mueller (KIA)
A 'slow' FAC was also lost on the 18th. 1Lt Mueller was flying over a target at 1,500 feet about 35 miles west of Pleiku, close to the border with Laos, when his aircraft was hit by small arms fire. He headed east but the aircraft crashed near Plei Djereng and 1Lt Mueller was killed.

19 January 1970

F-100F   56-3847   416 TFS, 31 TFW, USAF, Tuy Hoa
                   Capt D F Brown (survived)
                   Capt E L Farnsworth (survived)
The second Misty FAC to be lost in January was damaged by 23mm flak about 10 miles northeast of Ban Talan. Capt Brown coaxed the damaged aircraft back into South Vietnam and took it out over the sea where he and Capt Farnsworth ejected about 12 miles off the coast near Tam Ky. After a short while in the water they were both picked up by a USAF helicopter. This was the first of two ejections made by Capt Farnsworth as he was shot down and rescued during another mission near Ban Talan exactly two months later.

22 January 1970

A-1H   52-139799   22 SOS, 56 SOW, USAF, Nakhon Phanom
                   Capt E F Anderson (survived)
A flight of Skyraiders was assigned to attack a truck park to the west of Ban Senphan in southern Laos. Capt Anderson had just completed his eighth pass over the target, having used up most of the Skyraider's prodigious ordnance load, when his aircraft was damaged by automatic weapons fire. Capt Anderson turned his burning aircraft west and headed back to base but he was forced to eject 20 miles northeast of Nakhon Phanom and was rescued by a USAF SAR helicopter that had already been alerted.

26 January 1970

F-100D   55-3574   615 TFS, 35 TFW, USAF, Phan Rang
                   1 pilot, name unknown (survived)
A Super Sabre pilot lost control of his aircraft as he was making a low-level pass to drop napalm on a target in South Vietnam. The aircraft hit several trees and the pilot ejected before the aircraft crashed. He was rescued by helicopter shortly afterwards.

27 January 1970

F-105D   59-1772   333 TFS, 355 TFW, USAF, Takhli
                   Maj D W Livingston (survived)
The first Thud to be lost in 1970 was shot down while on a Barrel Roll mission in northern Laos. A flight of F-105s was attacking a bivouac and storage area about 12 miles south of Sam Neua when Maj Livingston's aircraft was hit by ground fire at 5,000 feet as he was rolling in on his third pass. He turned south but did not get very far as he was forced to eject near the village of Ban Nampang from where he was rescued by a USAF HH-53C from the 40th ARRS. This particular F-105D was credited with shooting down a MiG-17 on 26 March 1967 while being flown by Col Robert R Scott and another MiG on 28 April 1967 while being flown by a pilot from the 357th TFS.

More F-100s were lost in South Vietnam, than any other strike aircraft, a total of 189 between August 1964 and May 1971. F-100D 56-3097 was shot down on 14 January 1970 as it was climbing out from Bien Hoa, home of the 3rd TFW. The pilot, 1Lt W H Baker, ejected safely. USAF

OV-10A   67-14680   23 TASS, 504 TASG, USAF, Nakhon Phanom
                    detached to Ubon
                    Capt N E James (survived)
A Bronco pilot (Nail 35) spotted several trucks on a road near Ban Nathon, 12 miles west of the DMZ. The OV-10 was flying at 11,000 feet as the pilot kept his eye on the trucks but the aircraft was hit by 37mm flak and badly damaged. Capt James headed towards Thailand and ejected safely about 15 miles northwest of Nakhon Phanom and was picked up by an HH-53C from the 40th ARRS.

A-1E   52-132674   22 SOS, 56 SOW, USAF, Nakhon Phanom
                   1 pilot, name unknown (survived)
A Skyraider's engine failed as it was returning from an armed reconnaissance mission. The aircraft crash-landed, caught fire and burnt out but the pilot escaped serious injury.

28 January 1970

F-105G   63-8329   44 TFS, 355 TFW, USAF, Takhli
                   Capt Richard Joseph Mallon (KIA)
                   Capt Robert Joseph Panek (KIA)
The F-105G was an updated version of the F-105F Wild Weasel and had arrived in Thailand as early as April 1968 but had not seen much action due to the bombing halt imposed at that time. The F-105G carried an internal ALQ-101 ECM pod and more modern radar homing and warning receiving equipment in addition to improved versions of the AGM-78 Standard ARM missile.
An F-105G (call sign Seabird 02) was part of the escort for an RF-4C on a photographic reconnaissance mission over North Vietnam. The object of the mission was a SAM site in the hills about 25 miles west of Mu Ron Ma. The aircraft were fired at from the ground so, under the rules of engagement, they retaliated in kind. As the F-105G was pulling up from its second pass over the target it was hit by AAA and burst into flames. The aircraft turned southwest but it crashed near the village of Xom Duong Quan, north of the Mu Gia Pass. Both the crew were seen to eject and land safely. A rescue mission rapidly swung into action and four HH-53s from the 40th ARRS were despatched together with a Crown HC-130P and a flight of Sandies to attempt a pick up. An SA-2 was fired at one of the A-1s as it was searching for the downed airmen and several MiG warnings were received but it was not realised just how close the MiGs were. As the HC-130 was refuelling one of the helicopters in a safe area to the west, two other helicopters, Jolly Green 71 and Jolly Green 72, were orbiting about 20 miles northwest of where the Thud went down. Suddenly two MiG-21s made a run through the SAR formation and an air-to-air missile hit Jolly Green 71 (66-14434), which exploded and crashed. All on board the helicopter were killed including the pilot, Maj Holly Gene Bell, and the rest of the crew consisting of Capt Leonard Charles Leeser, SMSgt William David Pruett, TSgt William Carl Sutton, Sgt

William Charles Shinn and Sgt Gregory Lee Anderson. The rest of the SAR task force escaped to the west although the MiGs were taking no chances and headed for home without making a second pass. Meanwhile Mallon and Panek were surrounded by enemy troops and at least one account claims that they were captured and executed by North Vietnamese militia.
The remains of the F-105G crew and Maj Bell (misidentified by the North Vietnamese as MSgt Sutton as his identity cards were found near the body) were amongst a group of remains handed over by the Vietnamese in December 1988. The MiG pilot credited with the destruction of the HH-53 was Lt Vu Ngoc Dinh of the 921st Regiment. During its career in Southeast Asia 63-8329 was painted as 'Rosemary's Baby', 'Protestor's Protector' and 'My Diane'. The Wild Weasel crew are listed in some documents as belonging to the 354th rather than the 44th TFS. These were the first USAF aircraft lost in North Vietnam since August 1969.

29 January 1970

O-1F   57-2868   21 TASS, 504 TASG, USAF, Cam Ranh Bay
                 detached to Ban Me Thuot
                 1Lt J L Denalt (survived)
                 1Lt W G Uhls (survived)
A crew from the 21st TASS were flying a visual reconnaissance mission from their forward operating base at Ban Me Thuot. The Bird Dog was about five miles northwest of the airfield when it was hit by small arms fire. With a dead engine and the aircraft on fire, 1Lt Denalt skilfully crash-landed his aircraft resulting in only minor injuries to him and his observer. An Army helicopter rescued them both shortly afterwards.

5 February 1970

A-7B   154391   VA-93, USN, USS *Ranger*
                Lt Richard C Stephenson (KIA)
Radar contact was lost with a Corsair shortly after it was launched on a strike mission. The aircraft was tracked until it was about two miles from the ship but it then disappeared from the screen and presumably crashed into the Gulf of Tonkin.

6 February 1970

A-6A   155618   VA-196, USN, USS *Ranger*
                Lt Cdr E P Reese (survived)
                Lt(jg) E R Frazer (survived)
VA-196 lost an Intruder during a Steel Tiger mission at dusk on the 6th. Lt Cdr Reese was attacking two trucks that had been found on a road near Ban Kapay, 30 miles west of the DMZ. The Intruder rolled in from 12,500 feet but as it passed through 7,000 feet the aircraft was hit by AAA and started to spiral to the right. The violent gyrations caused the port wing to disintegrate and the two crew ejected. The crew were rescued by a 40th ARRS HH-53 helicopter at first light the next day.

In 1970 the sprawling US air base at Cam Ranh Bay housed the USAF's 12th TFW and 483rd TAW as well as detachments of C-130s and Navy P-3 Orions. Its proximity to local villages (My Ca at lower left) illustrate the problems faced by air base security forces, although Cam Ranh Bay itself fared much better than some other bases in this respect. USN

F-4B   152322   VMFA-314, MAG-13, USMC, Chu Lai
                  Capt J E Sharkey (survived)
                  1Lt C E Stewart (survived)
A Marine Corps Phantom crashed due to engine failure during a strike mission in South Vietnam. Both the crew ejected safely and were rescued.

8 February 1970

F-4B   149467   VMFA-314, MAG-13, USMC, Chu Lai
                  Maj J B Leonard (survived)
                  1Lt J C Coon (survived)
A Marine Corps Phantom was thought to have been a victim of its own ordnance during a close air support mission in South Vietnam. Maj Leonard was dropping napalm on enemy troops near Duc Pho, 40 miles southeast of Chu Lai, when its port wing suddenly caught fire. Although there was .50 calibre ground fire reported at the time, there seems a strong possibility that the aircraft had been hit by the blast from the napalm. Maj Leonard flew the burning aircraft out to sea and he and 1Lt Coon ejected off the coast about 25 miles southeast of Da Nang and were picked up by helicopter.

OV-10A 67-14646   19 TASS, 504 TASG, USAF, Bien Hoa
                    Capt Langston (survived)
                    Capt Coker, US Army (survived)
During a visual reconnaissance flight north of Siagon a Bronco crew spotted what appeared to be an enemy base camp near Bau Tram, 15 miles southeast of Katum. The aircraft was hit by .50 calibre ground fire as it rolled in from 3,000 feet to mark the target. The crew ejected safely before the aircraft crashed close to the target and they were subsequently recovered by an Army patrol.

9 February 1970

A-4F   155005   VA-212, USN, USS Hancock
                  Lt John Arthur Griner (KIA)
A Skyhawk from the Hancock was diverted to Da Nang following a strike mission. The aircraft blew a tyre on landing and the aircraft crashed, killing the pilot.

10 February 1970

F-100D 55-3585   612 TFS, 35 TFW, USAF, Phan Rang
                   1Lt Phillips (survived)
An F-100 was damaged during a mission near Katum. 1Lt Phillips was attacking enemy bunkers when his aircraft was hit by small arms fire on his fourth pass. He flew across South Vietnam, crossed the coast and ejected about 10 miles from Phan Ly Cham. He was rescued from the sea by a USAF helicopter. This may have been the same Lt J V Phillips of the 612th TFS who was shot down on 16 September 1970.

A-4F   155023   VA-164, USN, USS Hancock
                  1 pilot, name unknown (survived)
A Skyhawk configured for a tanker mission developed a fuel system malfunction that led to an explosion as it was refuelling another aircraft. The tanker pilot ejected and was rescued and the other aircraft landed safely.

11 February 1970

A-1E   52-135195   22 SOS, 56 SOW, USAF, Nakhon Phanom
                     Lt Col William Lewis Kieffer (KIA)
A Skyraider was lost along with its pilot during a Barrel Roll mission on the 11th. Lt Col Kieffer was bombing Pathet Lao troop positions near Ban Len in the Plain of Jars when his aircraft was shot down by small arms fire while in a 40-degree dive. The pilot may have been wounded by ground fire as he was not observed to eject from the aircraft before it hit the ground.

12 February 1970

F-4B   151454   VMFA-122, MAG-13, USMC, Chu Lai
                  Lt Robert S Bradshaw (KIA)
                  1Lt Michael Hugh Breeding (KIA)
A VMFA-122 Phantom failed to return from a combat mission near Quang Tri but the loss was listed as 'probably not enemy action'.

15 February 1970

O-2A   67-21358   20 TASS, 504 TASG, USAF, Da Nang
                    Capt Gerald Edward Hull (KWF)
                    1Lt James Stephen Baird (KWF)
The crew of an O-2 was killed during a training flight over Thua Thien province, South Vietnam, when the aircraft flew into the side of a ridge, presumably through an error of judgement.

17 February 1970

F-100D 56-3147   614 TFS, 35 TFW, USAF, Phan Rang
                   1 pilot, name unknown (survived)
During a close air support mission an F-100 lost oil pressure resulting in engine failure. The pilot ejected and was subsequently rescued.

18 February 1970

F-4D   66-7526   435 TFS, 8 TFW, USAF, Ubon
                   Maj Thomas Eldon Gillen (KIA)
                   Capt Robert S Dotson (survived)
A Phantom was on a munitions delivery flight along Route 7 near Ban Paka, 40 miles east of the Plain of Jars and close to the border with North Vietnam. The aircraft was probably dropping small mines on the road rather than actually bombing a target. The aircraft was hit in the nose by ground fire as it was flying at 700 feet and 500 knots. The WSO, Capt Dotson, ejected but Maj Gillen may have been wounded, as he was not seen to escape from the aircraft before it crashed. Capt Dotson was rescued at dusk the same day by a HH-53 piloted by Lt Col Shipman of the 40th ARRS. Robert Dotson was shot down again on 21 April 1971 during a Wolf FAC mission in southern Laos.

F-4C   63-7671   557 TFS, 12 TFW, USAF, Cam Ranh Bay
                   Capt Thomas Carl Daffron (KIA)
                   1Lt Charles Frank Morley (KIA)
Another Phantom was lost over Laos during a night strike on enemy troops on the Trail about 10 miles southwest of the Ban Karai Pass. Capt Daffron was rolling in from 10,000 feet when the aircraft was hit by 37mm flak and burst into flames. There was no indication that either of the crew had managed to escape from the aircraft before it crashed. Nothing more was heard or seen of the crew despite a four-day aerial search of the area. This was the 179th and final F-4C Phantom to be lost in Southeast Asia. The 559th TFS flew the last USAF F-4C combat mission on 22 March. Three excavations in 1993 and 1995 recovered personal equipment and human remains that were positively identified by anthropological analysis in 1999 as being those of the Phantom crew.

19 February 1970

F-4B   150427   VMFA-314, MAG-13, USMC, Chu Lai
                  1Lt D W Vanhorne (survived)
                  1Lt W K Meyer (survived)
VMFA-314 lost a Phantom during a night close air support mission south of Da Nang. The aircraft was pulling out of dive over a target when it was hit by ground fire and the port wing burst into flames. The crew ejected moments later and were rescued up by a Marine Corps helicopter.

AC-119K 53-3156   18 SOS, 14 SOW, USAF, Phan Rang
                    detached to Da Nang
                    10 crew, names unknown (survived)
An AC-119K Stinger returning from a night-time armed reconnaissance mission over the Trail landed short at Da Nang and was damaged beyond repair. About two miles from touchdown the engines on the port wing suddenly lost power due to fuel starvation and the pilot was unable to maintain control. The crew escaped with minor injuries.

21 February 1970

F-105G 63-8281   354 TFS, 355 TFW, USAF, Takhli
                   Maj G B Hurst (survived)
                   Capt C S Bevan (survived)
The USAF lost its second F-105G during a Barrel Roll mission over the Plain of Jars. Maj Hurst and Capt Bevan were taking part in a strike on Pathet Lao troops near the northern edge of the Plain when their aircraft was hit by small arms fire during their third pass. The aircraft caught fire but this subsequently went out as Maj Hurst set course for Thailand. The aircraft stayed airworthy long enough to reach Udorn but the crew had to eject a few miles from the airfield and completed their mission by rescue helicopter. This aircraft had been painted as 'Little Annie Fanny' when serving with the 388th TFW.

25 February 1970

F-4B   152286   VF-161, USN, USS *Coral Sea*
Lt A Gilchrist (survived)
Lt(jg) T Young (survived)

A Phantom from the *Coral Sea* was lost due to a rare failure of a tanker aircraft not being in the correct position to give fuel when it was needed. The Phantom eventually ran out of fuel, the engines failed and the crew ejected and were rescued from the sea.

26 February 1970

A-4E   151135   VMA-311, MAG-13, USMC, Chu Lai
1Lt J E Barksdale (survived)

During a dusk flight over the border country about 30 miles southwest of Hué, a section of Skyhawks came upon a number of trucks stopped on a mountain road. The aircraft attacked immediately but on its third pass 1Lt Barksdale's aircraft was hit by ground fire. The port side of the fuselage was holed and a small fire started. The pilot headed southeast but by the time he reached Chu Lai it was dark so instead of risking an emergency landing he ejected a few miles off the coast and was picked up by a Marine Corps helicopter. VMA-311 had been reassigned to the Phantom-equipped MAG-13 on 12 February as MAG-12 prepared to leave Vietnam.

28 February 1970

A-7A   153143   VA-27, USN, USS *Constellation*
Lt R E Karp (survived)

A Corsair was shot down during a Steel Tiger strike in southern Laos. Lt Karp was taking part in a raid on a truck park near Ban Kate and was pulling up from his first pass when his aircraft was struck by 23mm ground fire. He lost control of the aircraft and ejected immediately. He was later rescued by an HH-53C from the 40th ARRS.

A-6A   155605   VA-196, USN, USS *Ranger*
Lt R R Wittenberg (survived)
Lt H W Paul (survived)

An Intruder was seen to be on fire as it accelerated down the deck of the *Ranger* during a catapult launch for a training flight. The crew ejected moments later and were picked up from the sea by the carrier's plane guard helicopter.

3 March 1970

A-7A   153136   VA-86, USN, USS *Coral Sea*
Lt John Jackson Parker (KIA)

The *Coral Sea* was sailing about 100 miles northeast of Dong Hoi when Lt Parker was catapulted off the deck for a strike mission in southern Laos. Moments after take off the aircraft crashed into the sea and although a helicopter was on the scene immediately there was no sign of the pilot.

4 March 1970

A-1E   52-133914   602 SOS, 56 SOW, USAF, Nakhon Phanom
Capt D E Friestad (survived)

Capt Friestad was flying a Steel Tiger armed reconnaissance sortie at night over southern Laos when he was shot down. He found and attacked several trucks on a road near Ban Boung, 35 miles west of the DMZ. As he pulled up from his first pass his aircraft was hit by a 37mm shell and he ejected almost immediately. He evaded capture and was rescued the next day by a USAF HH-53C helicopter from the 40th ARRS. Capt Friestad was shot down again a few weeks later during a RESCAP on 22 April.

F-100D   56-3121   308 TFS, 31 TFW, USAF, Tuy Hoa
Capt Robert Page Rosenbach (KIA)

Two Super Sabres took off from Tuy Hoa on a night-time Combat Skyspot radar-controlled bombing mission near the DMZ. Capt Rosenbach lost his UHF transmitter after take off but could receive his leader and responded by clicking his microphone button. The mission proceeded as planned and the pair headed back towards their base. As they approached Tuy Hoa they started a wide circling approach to land. Capt Rosenbach was cleared to land first while his leader followed close behind. Capt Rosenbach's aircraft was seen on radar as it overshot the runway and headed out to sea. About 10 miles northeast of the airfield Capt Rosenbach switched his IFF transponder to the emergency setting indicating that he had a problem. Moments later the aircraft disappeared from the radar screen and an extensive sea and air search was put into action. The search was terminated three days later with no sign of Capt Rosenbach or his aircraft.

8 March 1970

A-4F   154994   VA-212, USN, USS *Hancock*
1 pilot, name unknown (survived)

A Skyhawk suffered engine failure as it was being launched from the *Hancock* and ditched in front of the carrier. The pilot ejected and was rescued.

F-100D   56-3377   308 TFS, 31 TFW, USAF, Tuy Hoa
1 pilot, name unknown (survived)

A Super Sabre crashed on landing at Tuy Hoa due to pilot error when it returned from an interdiction mission.

9 March 1970

F-100D   55-2890   352 TFS, 35 TFW, USAF, Phan Rang
Capt R F Clay survived)

A Super Sabre was lost during a landing zone preparation mission near Duc Phong, 20 miles west of Song Be City. Capt Clay was pulling up from his second pass when his aircraft was hit by ground fire causing the engine to fail. He ejected immediately and was soon picked up by an Army helicopter.

F-100D   56-3384   615 TFS, 35 TFW, USAF, Phan Rang
Capt Richard John Cowell (Died)

Another Super Sabre was lost later the same day during a Steel Tiger strike on the border between South Vietnam and Laos, about 21 miles west of Kham Duc. Capt Cowell was making his second dive bombing attack on an intersection point when his aircraft was hit by AAA and burst into flames. He ejected and was recovered by a USAF helicopter but he died of his injuries the following day.

F-4E   67-0282   4 TFS, 366 TFW, USAF, Da Nang
Capt Lothar Gustav Thomas Terla (KIA)
1Lt Larry William Cotten (KIA)

On the night of the 9th a flight of Phantoms was sent to attack trucks that had been located on the Ho Chi Minh Trail near Chanum in southern Laos, 35 miles southwest of Kham Duc. Capt Terla's aircraft was hit by 37mm flak and crashed in the target area. Apparently neither of the crew escaped from their aircraft before it crashed.

F-4J   155775   VF-21, USN, USS *Ranger*
Lt Leonard John Schoeppner (KIA)
Lt(jg) Rex Lewis Parcels (KIA)

Lt Schoeppner and Lt(jg) Parcels were launched from the *Ranger* for a photographic reconnaissance escort mission over Laos. Due to bad weather over the target area the mission was cancelled so the Phantom was diverted to its secondary mission of providing a combat air patrol for the carrier. Contact with Lt Schoeppner's aircraft was lost about three hours into the flight when the aircraft should have joined up with another Phantom over the Gulf of Tonkin. A large number of ships and aircraft commenced a search for the Phantom but no trace of the aircraft or its crew were ever found. Another pilot reported seeing a Phantom in a dive over the sea and it was thought possible that if this was Lt Schoeppner's aircraft then it may have crashed due to pilot disorientation in cloud or through manoeuvring at too low an altitude to recover safely.

10 March 1970

A-1E   52-132445   602 SOS, 56 SOW, USAF, Nakhon Phanom
Capt D R Combs (survived)
Capt G E Luck (survived)

The Plain of Jars was one of the few parts of northern Laos where tracked vehicles could be used effectively and the North Viet-namese were supplied with T-34, T-54 and PT-76 tanks, some of which were used in Laos. Tanks had been reported near Ban Len in the centre of the Plain and a flight of Skyraiders was sent out to attack them. Capt Combs and Capt Luck found a tank and made five passes before their Skyraider was shot down by small arms fire. They ejected close to their target and were fortunate to be rescued by an Air America helicopter.

11 March 1970

O-2A   68-6884   20 TASS, 504 TASG, USAF, Da Nang
1Lt Paul F Klug (KIA)
Maj James W Clement (KIA)

An O-2 failed to return to Da Nang from an FAC mission over a choke point on the Ho Chi Minh Trail. The crew had completed their task and were returning to base but never arrived. Their fate still remains a mystery.

14 March 1970

A-4F   155010   VA-55, USN, USS *Hancock*
Lt(jg) P A Schranz (survived)

A pair of Skyhawks on a night strike on the Trail spotted two trucks near Ban Kate in southern Laos. Lt Schranz followed his leader and rolled in from 12,000 feet. As he was passing 10,000 feet he felt a thump as the aircraft was hit by 37mm flak so he jettisoned his ordnance and pulled out of the dive. The electrics suddenly failed and the engine flamed out. Unable to relight the engine, Lt Schranz ejected a few miles from the target and was later rescued by a USAF helicopter.

A-1H   52-134471   602 SOS, 56 SOW, USAF, Nakhon Phanom
Maj Donald B Fincher (KIA)

A Skyraider crashed in Thailand due to engine failure during an armed reconnaissance mission and the pilot was killed.

15 March 1970

A-4F   155044   VA-212, USN, USS *Hancock*
Lt Cdr R W Hunter (survived)

The *Hancock* lost a second Skyhawk within 24 hours when an aircraft was damaged during another Steel Tiger strike. Lt Cdr Hunter was on a daylight strike on a section of road near Ban Topen, west of the Ban Karai Pass, when his aircraft was hit by 37mm AAA as it was pulling up from its first bombing run. The aircraft's control cables must have been hit as the control column went slack and the aircraft started rolling and could barely be controlled using rudder and elevator trim. Lt Cdr Hunter skilfully guided his rolling aircraft across Laos and North Vietnam and out over the sea until he ejected close to the carrier about 90 miles northeast of Dong Hoi. One of the ship's helicopters picked him up out of the water.

OV-10A   67-14682   23 TASS, 504 TASG, USAF, Nakhon
Phanom detached to Ubon
Capt D J Erickson (survived)

A Bronco was flying a visual reconnaissance sortie at dusk in southern Laos just to the west of the DMZ when it was shot down. Capt Erickson was flying near the village of Ban Vat at 9,000 feet when his aircraft was hit by 37mm AAA forcing him to eject. He was later rescued by a USAF helicopter.

16 March 1970

F-105D   62-4230   354 TFS, 355 TFW, USAF, Takhli
Maj W J Wycoff (survived)

A formation of Thuds was despatched to attack a storage area five miles southeast of Ban Ban in northern Laos. Following release of his bombs Maj Wycoff was pulling up through 5,000 feet when a 37mm shell hit his aircraft. Turning south he kept his crippled aircraft flying as long as possible but was forced to eject 10 miles south of Udorn and was picked up by an HH-53.

EC-121M   145927   VQ-1, USN, Atsugi
Lt Cdr Harvey C K Aiua (KWF)
Lt Cdr Harry C Martin (KWF)
Lt Robin A Pearce (KWF)

Lt George L Morningstar (KWF)
Lt(jg) James M Masters (KWF)
Lt(jg) Charles E Pressler (KWF)
Lt(jg) Jean P Souzon (KWF)
CPO William J Risse (KWF)
PO1 Larry O Marchbank (KWF)
PO1 Arthur D Simmons (KWF)
PO1 Donald W Wilson (KWF)
PO2 Floyd E Andrus (KWF)
PO2 Gregory J Asbeck (KWF)
PO2 William P Bletsch (KWF)
PO2 Guy T Denton (KWF)
PO2 Joseph S Saukaitis (KWF)
PO2 John S Schaefer (KWF)
PO2 Stuart J Scruggs (KWF)
PO2 Barry M Searby (KWF)
PO3 John M Birch (KWF)
PO3 Thurle E Case (KWF)
PO3 Ben A Hughes (KWF)
PO3 Ralph S Purhum (KWF)
8 crew, names unknown (survived)

F-4D   66-7503   366 TFW, USAF, Da Nang

An EC-121M of VQ-1 was being ferried to Da Nang from Taiwan when it crashed as it was landing. One of the aircraft's engines had been shut down during the flight due to a generator over-heating. The first 1,000 feet of Da Nang's runway was closed for repair work necessitating a different approach from normal. At a late stage of the approach another aircraft taxied onto the run-way forcing the EC-121 to attempt an overshoot but the aircraft banked until it wings were vertical and it crashed into a concrete revetment and a hangar before disintegrating. The wreckage hit a USAF Phantom, which was also destroyed. Sadly, only eight of the 31 people on board the EC-121 could be saved. One of the crew survived the crash but then succumbed to a heart attack. VQ-1 was based at Atsugi NAS in Japan but detached EC-121s to Da Nang to fly patrols over the Gulf of Tonkin. The EC-121s monitored operations over North Vietnam and were credited with assisting in the destruction of numerous MiGs as well as enemy patrol boats. From 1969 the Constellations were supple-mented by the EP-3 Aries I aircraft, a highly modified variant of the Orion. The squadron also operated Skywarriors from Da Nang, Cubi Point, Don Muang and from aircraft carriers in the Tonkin Gulf.

19 March 1970

A-1H   52-135275   602 SOS, 56 SOW, USAF, Nakhon Phanom
Maj J Evenson (survived)

A truck park near Ban Len in the Plain of Jars was the target for a flight of Skyraiders on the 19th. Maj Evenson's aircraft was damaged by ground fire as he was returning from the raid but he crossed back into Thailand and ejected 25 miles west of Nakhon Phanom.

F-100F   56-3945   306 TFS, 31 TFW, USAF, Tuy Hoa
Capt E L Farnsworth (survived)
1Lt J D Davies (survived)

A Misty FAC aircraft was controlling a strike on a road intersec-tion point 10 miles northeast of Ban Talan in southern Laos when it was shot down. The aircraft burst into flames when it was hit by 37mm anti-aircraft fire and the crew ejected a few miles to the east of their target. They were later rescued by a USAF heli-copter. Capt Farnsworth had been shot down in the same area exactly two months earlier when he was flying a back-seat mis-sion with Capt Brown.

F-4D   66-8696   435 TFS, 8 TFW, USAF, Ubon
Capt William A Rash (survived)
1Lt Dennis Gerald Pugh (KIA)

Another FAC aircraft was lost on the 19th when a Phantom (using the radio call sign Wolf 6) was shot down when controlling a strike near Ban Senphan at the southern end of the Mu Gia Pass. The aircraft was hit by 37mm AAA and burst into flames. Both the crew ejected safely and both were in voice contact with other air-craft once on the ground. A rescue attempt was delayed until the morning of the 20th due to enemy activity and approaching darkness. When the rescue task force returned in the morning Dennis Pugh reported that he was surrounded by enemy troops and several attempts to rescue him had to be abandoned after intense ground fire had shot down a Skyraider. In Pugh's final transmission he told the orbiting aircraft to bomb his position as the enemy were closing in. He kept his finger on the transmit key and the horrified listeners heard North Vietnamese voices and between 15 to 20 gunshots followed by silence. The aircraft then bombed the position. On the 21st another Skyraider was shot down but Capt Rash was then rescued by a 40th ARRS HH-53C from his hiding place in a cave, despite being badly injured. Den-nis Pugh could not be found and was presumed to have been killed during or after capture. Lt Pugh's identity documents were later displayed in the Hanoi Central Military Museum.

20 March 1970

A-1E   52-135154   602 SOS, 56 SOW, USAF, Nakhon Phanom
1Lt D P Townsend (survived)

On the first day of the search for Capt Rash and 1Lt Pugh near Ban Senphan one of the escorting Spads was shot down. 1Lt Townsend was attacking enemy troops from low-level to protect the downed aircrew and the rescue helicopter when his aircraft was hit by 37mm AAA. He flew about 10 miles away from the scene before having to eject and was picked up by one of the 40th ARRS HH-53s he had been escorting.

21 March 1970

OV-10A   68-3794   23 TASS, 504 TASG, USAF, Nakhon Phanom
Capt J A Richmond (survived)

The Nail FACs from Nakhon Phanom flew FAC missions for the Barrel Roll campaign as well as for the Steel Tiger strikes. On the 21st Capt Richmond was flying near Ban Muangphan on the eastern edge of the Plain of Jars when his Bronco was hit twice by 37mm flak. The port wing caught fire and the pilot ejected and was rescued by an Air America helicopter.

A-1J   52-142065   602 SOS, 56 SOW, USAF, Nakhon Phanom
Maj Edward Monroe Hudgens (KIA)

The search for Wolf 6 near Ban Senphan continued on the 21st after the loss of a Skyraider the previous day. Maj Hudgens was attacking enemy air defences when he was shot down. He was making his ninth pass over the same target at 1,000 feet when his aircraft was shattered by 37mm flak. Capt Hudgens was not seen to eject from his aircraft and was presumed to have died in the crash. Shortly afterwards the rescue mission was called off after Capt Rash was picked up.

30 March 1970

OV-10A   155393   VAL-4, USN, Binh Thuy
Lt Cdr John P Westerman (survived)
Lt(jg) Peter W Ford (survived)

A Black Pony OV-10 took part in an attack on two .50 calibre gun sites near Hue Duc, 20 miles north of Rach Gia. The aircraft was strafing the target on its third pass when it was hit by return fire and its port engine caught fire. The crew ejected close to the gun positions but were rescued by an Army helicopter. Lt Ford was shot down again on 29 September 1970.

F-4D   66-8707   13 TFS, 432 TRW, USAF, Udorn
Lt Col W E Brown (survived)
Lt Col L L Melton (survived)

A formation of Phantoms was despatched to attack a SAM site in North Vietnam, presumably after a reconnaissance aircraft had been fired at, but one of the aircraft was damaged en route. Lt Col Brown's Phantom was hit by AAA as it crossed the North Viet-namese border 15 miles northwest of the Mu Gia Pass. He turned around and flew back to Thailand on one engine but he and his WSO had to eject five miles northwest of Nakhon Phanom.

31 March 1970

O-1F   57-2883   504 TASG, USAF, Gia Nghia
A Bird Dog FAC aircraft was the sole victim of a Viet Cong night attack on the airstrip at Gia Nghia. The air-craft was hit and destroyed by a 60mm rocket projectile.

The Siege of Dak Seang

The region to the west of Dak To in the Central Highlands was particularly vulnerable to enemy attack, as it was close to the point where the borders of South Vietnam, Cambodia and Laos met. Enemy artillery in Laos and Cambodia could reach some of the Special Forces camps such as Ben Het and Dak Seang, which often had to be resupplied by air when enemy activity cut the roads leading to the camps. The small camp at Dak Seang, 35 miles northwest of Kontum, was situated in a valley which was wide enough for airdrops in any direction. The camp was often resupplied by US transport aircraft operating from the airfield at Pleiku, 60 miles to the south. On 1 April a strong NVA force besieged the camp and an airdrop of ammunition and supplies was made by three C-7s during the afternoon. The NVA had posi-tioned anti-aircraft guns along the likely air corridors that trans-port aircraft might use during their airdrops. Light ground fire was encountered on these first missions and one aircraft received two hits that did little damage. Enemy pressure on the camp con-tinued throughout the night and on the following morning two more Caribous set off from Pleiku to make another drop. Ground fire proved to be heavier on the second day and one of the aircraft was hit and crashed. Despite the obvious danger a further 11 air-drops were made by C-7 crews later on the 2nd with three aircraft being damaged by ground fire. The airdrops continued despite intense ground fire that eventually claimed three C-7s and dam-aged many more. However, by 13 April the situation at Dak Seang had improved enough for the air resupply mission to be largely taken over by US Army helicopters although C-7s made a small number of night airdrops towards the end of April. On 7 May C-123s resumed daylight airdrops at Dak Seang and on 11 May

Caribous of the 483rd TAW take off from a South Vietnamese airfield that is under attack from Viet Cong. The Air Force lost twenty of the rugged Caribous during the war, three of them during the siege of the Special Forces camp at Dak Seang in April 1970. USAF

The E-2 Hawkeye AEW aircraft flew its first missions over the Gulf of Tonkin in November 1965 but it did not replace the elderly E-1B Tracer completely until after the end of the war. Two E-2s were lost in accidents during the war resulting in the deaths of 10 men. USN

C-7s resumed landing at the camp's airstrip. Between 1 April and 1 May the C-7s of the 483rd TAW had flown 127 sorties to Dak Seang dropping 240 tons of supplies, 90 per cent of which was recovered by the defenders from within the perimeter of the 200 feet-square camp itself. The successful resupply of Dak Seang illustrated the resourcefulness and bravery of the airlift crews and planners but also highlighted the vulnerability of slow-flying transport aircraft to ground fire in this type of situation.

2 April 1970

C-7A   61-2406   537 TAS, 483 TAW, USAF, Phu Cat
       1Lt Steve Warren Train (KIA)
       1Lt Charles E Suprenant (KIA)
       MSgt Dale Elling Christensen (KIA)

Two Caribous arrived overhead at Dak Seang in the early morning of the 2nd to drop ammunition to the besieged defenders of the camp. The aircraft approached the camp from the east under the guidance of an FAC who was also directing strikes by fighter aircraft on enemy positions. The first aircraft dropped successfully but reported ground fire as it made a steep right-hand turn after delivering its load. The second aircraft, flown by 1Lt Train, made a left-hand turn to try to avoid the ground fire but was hit by automatic weapons fire at an altitude of 400 feet. The Caribou flew off to the south, possibly trying to make for Dak To, but it burst into flames and crashed about five miles from Dak Seang, killing the crew.

3 April 1970

A-7A   154358   VA-97, USN, USS *Constellation*
       Lt H P Hoffman (survived)

A section of Corsairs from VA-97 was tasked to bomb a section of road on Route 920 near Ban Tambok, 20 miles southwest of the A Shau Valley, under the control of an FAC. Lt Hoffman's aircraft was hit by shrapnel from a 37mm shell as he made his bombing run but he continued his dive and dropped his bombs before pulling out and heading away from the target. The wingman confirmed damage to the Corsair's rear fuselage on the starboard side and after about 20 minutes the engine seized and the aircraft became uncontrollable. Lt Hoffman ejected close to the South Vietnamese border with Laos, about 50 miles west of Da Nang from where he was rescued by a US Army helicopter.

4 April 1970

O-2A   68-11058   20 TASS, 504 TASG, USAF, Da Nang
       1Lt John Everett Duffy (KIA)

An O-2 was flying under low cloud on a visual reconnaissance mission in the Quang Ngai region when it failed to return to its base at Da Nang. The aircraft is thought to have been shot down near the village of Ba To, about 20 miles south of Quang Ngai, and 1Lt Duffy was probably killed in the crash. His remains were returned to the USA in May 1993 and identity confirmed in March 1996.

C-7B   62-4180   537 TAS, 483 TAW, USAF, Phu Cat
       Capt James Anthony Gray (KIA)
       Maj Frederick W Dauten (KIA)
       MSgt Russell Leo Klein (KIA)

After the Caribou was shot down at Dak Seang on the 2nd the airlift was briefly suspended by the Air Force but was resumed at the insistence of MACV and a fleet of 18 C-7s was assembled at Pleiku. Eleven more drops were made later in the day on the 2nd and although three aircraft were hit, none were lost. A total of 31 more sorties were made on the 3rd and the 4th but another aircraft was lost and 13 others damaged. A five-aircraft drop was being made in the afternoon when the fourth aircraft in the formation was hit by heavy ground fire shortly after releasing its load. The aircraft crashed two miles from the camp killing the crew.

F-4B   150416   VMFA-314, MAG-13, USMC, Chu Lai
       1Lt R K Cecka (survived)
       1Lt G K Bruce (survived)

A flight of Phantoms from Chu Lai was sent to provide close air support to ground forces just below the DMZ. 1Lt Cecka was pulling up from his third pass over the target when his aircraft was hit by ground fire and burst into flames. He headed east and the crew ejected about four miles off the coast from where they were picked up by a Navy ship.

5 April 1970

F-4B   152325   VF-151, USN, USS *Coral Sea*
       Lt Thomas Terrill (survived)
       Lt Curtis Henry Cropper (KIA)

When returning from a BARCAP mission a Phantom crashed following an accidental fire and explosion that led to a loss of control. Both the crew ejected over the Gulf of Tonkin about 90 miles northeast of Dong Hoi. The aircraft was diving at high speed and the force of the ejection stunned both men. Lt Cropper, the NFO, appeared to be unconscious when he hit the water and he was not able to inflate his life jacket or release his parachute. The parachute quickly sank beneath the waves taking Lt Cropper with it. Lt Terrill was eventually rescued from the sea.

6 April 1970

C-7B   63-9746   457 TAS, 483 TAW, USAF, Cam Ranh Bay
       Capt Julius Patrick Jaeger (KIA)
       1Lt Theron Carl Fehrenbach (KIA)
       TSgt Gordon Manson Gaylord (KIA)

The resupply of Dak Seang continued on the 5th when seven Caribous successfully made airdrops, although very few of the loads could be recovered. On the 6th the last of three Caribous to be lost during the siege of Dak Seang was shot down by ground fire as it was pulling up from its dropping run. The aircraft burst into flames and crashed close to the camp killing the crew. Six Caribou sorties were flown on the 6th but, again, most of the loads could not recovered. The next night three successful drops were made by Caribous in conjunction with an AC-119 gunship that provided spotlight illumination during the final moments of the run in. This technique was used successfully for 68 drops over the next five nights, which enabled the defenders to hold on until the situation improved enough for daylight drops and then landings to be made at the camp.

F-100D   56-3278   308 TFS, 31 TFW, USAF, Tuy Hoa
       Capt Michael Lee Klingner (KIA)

A POL dump consisting of oil or petrol drums was discovered on the Trail 25 miles west of Kham Duc, just within Laos. A flight of F-100s was sent to destroy the dump but as Capt Klingner made his first strafing run his aircraft was hit by small arms fire and crashed before he could escape.

F-4D   66-7695   555 TFS, 432 TRW, USAF, Udorn
       Maj R S Vanbrunt (survived)
       1Lt O H Loyd (survived)

The 432nd TRW lost another Laredo FAC on 6 April during a visual reconnaissance mission over northern Laos. Two trucks were seen stopped on Route 7 about 10 miles southeast of Ban Ban, probably broken down. The aircraft attacked the trucks but they were well protected by automatic weapons positions and one of the Phantoms was hit as it was pulling up through 6,000 feet while on its second pass. The aircraft burst into flames and the crew ejected close to the road but were rescued the next day by a USAF HH-53 SAR helicopter from the 40th ARRS flown by Lt Col Hegewood.

A-1H   52-139621   602 SOS, 56 SOW, USAF, Nakhon Phanom
       1Lt J R Matthews (survived)

As it began to get dark the rescue forces were still looking for Maj Vanbrunt and 1Lt Loyd near Ban Ban. As usual the Skyraiders were busy suppressing ground fire and 1Lt Matthews was orbiting about a mile away from the downed airmen when his Skyraider was hit by 23mm anti-aircraft fire. He ejected and landed safely and was rescued by an HH-53C from the 40th ARRS that reportedly also rescued a Raven FAC during the evening.

7 April 1970

A-7A   153233   VA-97, USN, USS *Constellation*
       Lt M P Hamilton (survived)

VA-97 lost another aircraft during a Steel Tiger mission four days after Lt Hoffman's aircraft was shot down. Lt Hamilton was bombing a truck park near Ban Dakpok, 30 miles north of Muang Fangdeng, when he was shot down. He was pulling up from his second pass over the target when his Corsair was hit by 23mm AAA. He continued to climb to about 7,500 feet and ejected as the aircraft started to nose over into its terminal dive. He was rescued by an Air America helicopter which was in the vicinity at the time.

8 April 1970

E-2A   151711   VAW-116, USN, USS *Coral Sea*
       Lt(jg) Charles Brooks Pfaffmann (KWF)
       Lt Larry Coleman Knight (KWF)
       SN Brian Lee Bushnell (KWF)
       SN Andrew Anthony Horchar (KWF)
       AMEC Jack Lee Wright (KWF)

The *Coral Sea* was operating in the Gulf of Tonkin about 70 miles northeast of Dong Hoi on the 8th. Immediately after launching from the carrier on a ferry flight, Lt Pfaffmann reported a fire in the cockpit of his E-2 and that he was going to return to the ship. Unfortunately, the aircraft crashed about three miles ahead of the carrier and although a helicopter and a destroyer were at the scene within minutes, all five crew were lost.

A-7A   153153   VA-97, USN, USS *Constellation*
       1 pilot, name unknown (survived)

Another VA-97 Corsair had to be abandoned during a combat mission when a loss of oil pressure caused its engine to fail. The pilot was recovered safely. This was the last aircraft lost by the *Constellation* on its fifth cruise of the war before leaving for the USA on 17 April. During 128 days on the line the carrier had lost five aircraft to enemy action and two more in accidents.

OV-10A 67-14656 19 TASS, 504 TASG, USAF, Bien Hoa
                 1 pilot, name unknown (survived)
A Bronco crashed on take off on an FAC mission when it one of its engines failed.

10 April 1970

RF-4C 65-0863 11 TRS, 432 TRW, USAF, Udorn
              Maj J L Leaphart (survived)
              Capt J C Bernholtz (survived)
An RF-4C was damaged by AAA during a photo run at 4,500 feet over a segment of road in northern Laos while on a Barrel Roll mission. Despite major damage to the starboard wing, Maj Leaphart flew the aircraft back to Udorn but he and his navigator were forced to eject as it went out of control during the approach to land. Both the crew suffered injuries during the ejection and landing.

11 April 1970

A-4E 152099 VMA-311, MAG-13, USMC, Chu Lai
             1Lt Jan H Nelson (KIA)
A pair of Skyhawks from Chu Lai bombed an enemy base camp that had been discovered in the hills about 12 miles southwest of Da Nang. 1Lt Nelson rolled in and dived on the target but his aircraft was then seen to dive into the ground and explode. It was possible that the aircraft had been damaged by ground fire or had crashed due to disorientation or target fixation by the pilot.

15 April 1970

F-105D 61-0220 355 TFW, USAF, Takhli
               1 pilot, name unknown (survived)
A Thud had to be abandoned due to engine failure and fire during a combat mission. The aircraft had been painted as 'I dream of Jeanie' when it flew from Korat in 1968.

F-105G 62-4415 354 TFS, 355 TFW, USAF, Takhli
               2 crew, names unknown (survived)
Another Thud was lost on the 15th when a two-seat G-model made a wheels up landing at Takhli due to pilot error. The bombs exploded destroying the aircraft and the crew were lucky to survive. This aircraft was painted as 'SAM Seducer', 'Night Bird' and with flower-power decoration as 'Dawn Daddie's Rickie Tickie Go-go Chine'.

16 April 1970

RF-4C 66-0409 12 TRS, 460 TRW, USAF, Tan Son Nhut
              Maj Richard Lee Ayers (KIA)
              Capt Robert Ernest Rausch (KIA)
An RF-4C from Tan Son Nhut went missing during a photographic reconnaissance sortie over southern Laos and the DMZ area. After refuelling from a KC-135 tanker the Phantom headed north for another target. The aircraft's last known position was just west of Tavouac near the heavily defended A Shau Valley. There were several known 37mm AAA sites in this area and it was presumed that the aircraft had been shot down by ground fire. However, Hanoi Radio claimed to have shot down an RF-4C on this date in the Vinh Linh Special Zone, just north of the DMZ, although the North Vietnamese would never have admitted shooting down an aircraft in Laos.

17 April 1970

F-4D 66-7598 389 TFS, 12 TFW, USAF, Phu Cat
             Maj Loel F Rexroad (KIA)
             1Lt Robert W Smith (KIA)
A flight of Phantoms was called in to attack enemy troops that were being engaged by friendly forces 15 miles northwest of Phu Cat. Maj Rexroad put his aircraft into a 10-degree dive to attack the troops but the Phantom was hit by small arms fire and crashed before either of the crew could escape. This was the first aircraft lost by the 12th TFW since its move from Cam Ranh Bay to Phu Cat at the end of March.

20 April 1970

F-105D 60-0451 333 TFS, 355 TFW, USAF, Takhli
               Capt Douglas Frank Mahan (KIA)
Two Pathet Lao howitzers in operation near Bouam Long just northeast of the Plain of Jars were the object of a raid by a flight of F-105s on the 20th. Capt Mahan's aircraft was hit by automatic weapons fire as it dived on the guns. The F-105 crashed close to its target and the pilot was not seen to eject. F-105D 60-0451 was painted as 'Little Lancer' and 'Billie Babe II' during its time at Takhli.

21 April 1970

OV-10A 155423 VMO-2, MAG-11, USMC, Da Nang
               Maj Eugene Lacy Wheeler (KIA)
               Capt Charles E Hatch (survived)
In addition to its role as an FAC and close air support aircraft, the Bronco carried cameras that gave it a photographic reconnaissance capability. Maj Wheeler and Capt Hatch were taking photographs of a road near the border between South Vietnam and Laos about 12 miles west of Kham Duc when they were shot down. Flying at about 1,000 feet the aircraft was hit in the rear fuselage by either 37mm or 57mm AAA and caught fire. The crew ejected and Capt Hatch was recovered the next morning by helicopter but although Maj Wheeler was in voice contact with the rescue forces he was not recovered. It was assumed he had been killed by an enemy patrol that he reported was closing in on his position. Maj Wheeler had only started his tour of duty with VMO-2 the day before he was shot down.

A-1H 52-135336 22 SOS, 56 SOW, USAF, Nakhon Phanom
                Capt J M Dyer (survived)

A-1J 52-142070 602 SOS, 56 SOW, USAF, Nakhon Phanom
                Maj C E Whinery (survived)
About four hours after Maj Wheeler's OV-10 was shot down west of Kham Duc two USAF Skyraiders flying RESCAP during the search for the aircrew were also shot down. Capt Dyer was making his second pass over an enemy position just west of where the Bronco went down when the aircraft was hit by 23mm AAA. Capt Dyer ejected from his burning aircraft and landed safely to await rescue. Half an hour later another of the escorting Skyraiders was lost at almost exactly the same location. Maj Whinery was making his fourth pass from just 300 feet on a target close to where Capt Dyer had landed when his Spad was hit by 14.5mm ground fire. Maj Whinery ejected and landed safely close to Capt Dyer. They were both rescued by one of the SAR helicopters of the 40th ARRS, making the Squadron's 99th and 100th combat rescues.

22 April 1970

AC-130A 54-1625 16 SOS, 8 TFW, USAF, Ubon
                 Maj William Leslie Brooks (KIA)
                 1Lt John Cline Towle (KIA)
                 Lt Col Charlie Brown Davis (KIA)
                 Lt Col Charles Stoddard Rowley (KIA)
                 Maj Donald Garth Fisher (KIA)
                 MSgt Robert Newell Ireland (KIA)
                 SSgt Thomas Yuji Adachi (KIA)
                 SSgt Eugene Fields (survived)
                 SSgt Stephen Warren Harris (KIA)
                 SSgt Ronnie Lee Hensley (KIA)
                 A1C Donald Michael Lint (KIA)
In the early hours of the 22nd an AC-130 Spectre gunship (call sign Adlib 1) took off from Ubon on a Commando Hunt mission over the Ho Chi Minh Trail in southern Laos. The gunship was later joined by two fighters to form a truck hunter-killer team and the aircraft started work over Route 96A about 25 miles east of the town of Saravan. As the attack proceeded the AC-130 was hit by 37mm AAA and the port wing caught fire near the wing root. Some of the crew attempted to fight the blaze but the fire was too intense. Sgt Fields groped his way forward through darkness and smoke but found the gunner's position vacant and a hatch open. Fields strapped on a parachute and abandoned the

aircraft. Killer 2, one of the accompanying fighters, made voice contact with one of the crew who identified himself as Adlib 12, which was Maj Fisher's call sign. Sgt Fields had suffered burns on his face and hands and his parachute snagged on a tree. He eventually climbed down and hid until morning when he was rescued by a SAR task force. As has happened in several incidents, various rumours and claims relating to the missing crewmembers have persisted since the war. Returned POWs claimed to have seen Maj Fisher and Lt Col Rowley in prison camps but none of this information was ever substantiated. However, in November 1993 the remains of the missing crew were recovered from the wreck site near Ban Tang Lou and identified at the US Army's Central Identification Laboratory in Hawaii. The remains were buried in a group burial plot at Arlington National Cemetery on 8 November 1995. Even then some families did not accept proof of death as not all crew members were thought to be represented by the 1,400 small fragments of bone and teeth that were returned from Laos and that barely filled a single coffin. The name of SSgt Harris was omitted from the gravestone at Arlington at the request of his family. Like most of the AC-130s that served in Southeast Asia this aircraft was painted with distinctive nose art and carried the name 'War Lord'.

A-4C 148484 VA-172, USN, USS Shangri-La
             Lt(jg) John Bryan Golz (KIA)
The Hancock-class aircraft carrier the USS Shangri-La arrived from Mayport and started its first, and only, tour of duty on the line on 12 April. The Shangri-La had been redesignated as an anti-submarine carrier in 1969 but, like the Intrepid, she served in Southeast Asia as an attack carrier. The first aircraft lost by the ship and, incidentally, her only combat loss from the total of nine aircraft lost during the cruise, was a Skyhawk from VA-172. Lt Golz was taking part in a night strike on trucks on the Trail 10 miles northeast of Ban Talan and made his attack just as dawn was breaking. The aircraft was seen by the FAC to start its dive on the target but it then flew into the ground and exploded. No flak was seen prior to the crash and there was no indication that Lt Golz had ejected. The cause of the crash was undetermined but was most probably due to either ground fire or target fixation resulting in a loss of orientation.

F-4D 66-8702 13 TFS, 432 TRW, USAF, Udorn
             Maj T A Rush (survived)
             Capt B E Foster (survived)
A Falcon FAC Phantom was damaged by 37mm AAA during a Barrel Roll mission in northern Laos. Maj Rush was bombing an interdiction point on a road seven miles southwest of Ban Ban when his aircraft was hit in the starboard wing as it pulled up through 8,000 feet after the first pass. Maj Rush climbed and headed south and made it back to Udorn but he and his WSO ejected about 10 miles south of the airfield.

EC-47P 43-48402 362 TEWS, 460 TRW, USAF, Pleiku
                 1Lt George M Wall (KIA)
                 1Lt R M Nasipak (survived)
                 SSgt Michael R Conner (KIA)
                 6 crew, names unknown (survived)
Further south in Laos one of the RDF EC-47s was shot down during a mission to the south of the A Shau Valley. The aircraft was flying at 5,500 feet as the crew attempted to locate and fix enemy radio broadcasts when it was hit by automatic weapons fire or 37mm AAA. With the aircraft losing oil and power 1Lt Wall flew east in the hope of reaching an airfield but he was forced to crash-land the aircraft about 20 miles southwest of Hué. 1Lt Wall and SSgt Conner were killed in the crash-landing but the others were rescued by USAF SAR helicopters. This C-47 had been operated by the 5001st Operations Squadron from Fairbanks AFB, Alaska in the late 1950s.

A-1J 52-142015 602 SOS, 56 SOW, USAF, Nakhon Phanom
                Capt D E Friestad (survived)
The search for the Marine Corps Bronco crew that was shot down on the 21st claimed a third Skyraider on the 22nd. Capt Friestad was orbiting the crash sites of the two Skyraiders that had been shot down the previous day and was jinking to avoid ground fire

when his aircraft was hit twice by 37mm flak. The starboard wing caught fire and the pilot ejected close to where his colleagues had landed. He was later rescued by a USAF helicopter. This was the second time that Capt Friestad had been shot down and rescued, the first occasion being on 4 March 1970.

O-2A   68-11005   19 TASS, 504 TASG, USAF, Bien Hoa
1 pilot, name unknown (survived)

An O-2 crashed on landing due to pilot error following a visual reconnaissance patrol.

23 April 1970

F-4D   66-7639   433 TFS, 8 TFW, USAF, Ubon
Capt Albin Earl Lucki (KIA)
1Lt Robert Arthur Gomez (KIA)

A Wolf FAC crew was shot down and killed while on a Steel Tiger mission. They found a truck on a road near Ban Topen west of the Ban Karai Pass and had just rolled in on it when their aircraft was hit by AAA. The aircraft was seen to crash without any sign of an ejection or parachute and it was presumed that the crew died in the incident.

F-4D   66-8775   390 TFS, 366 TFW, USAF, Da Nang
Capt M W Nelson (survived)
1Lt J D Holmquist (survived)

A couple of hours later on the morning of the 23rd another Phantom was lost in southern Laos. The aircraft was a Stormy FAC from the 366th TFW. Capt Nelson and 1Lt Holmquist were flying an armed reconnaissance mission near Tavouac when their aircraft was hit in the fuselage by 23mm AAA at 4,800 feet. The crew ejected almost immediately and were subsequently rescued by a USAF helicopter.

25 April 1970

A-1H   52-139668   602 SOS, 56 SOW, USAF, Nakhon Phanom
detached to Da Nang
Maj D E Detar (survived)

Although the siege at Dak Seang was winding down by the 25th, the NVA was still very active. A flight of Skyraiders from the 602nd SOS's Operating Location Alpha detachment at Da Nang responded to a request for air support as enemy troops were once again attacking the camp. Maj Detar was making his fourth pass over the enemy troops at 500 feet when his aircraft received at least two hits from small arms or automatic weapons fire. The aircraft was hit in the rear fuselage and burst into flames forcing the pilot to eject close to the enemy forces. However, Maj Detar was recovered by friendly troops, having suffered only minor injuries during the ejection.

F-4E   67-0214   34 TFS, 388 TFW, USAF, Korat
Capt Charles K Hackett (KIA)
1Lt S R Hancock (survived)

A Phantom was lost during a Barrel Roll mission when it was seeding a road with either mines or sensors. Capt Hackett was pulling up from his run over the road about seven miles southwest of Ban Ban when his Phantom was shot down by AAA. The WSO, 1Lt Hancock, ejected and survived to be rescued by a USAF helicopter, but Capt Hackett died in the incident.

27 April 1970

AC-119G   53-8155   Detachment 1, 17 SOS, 14 SOW, USAF,
Phan Rang detached to Tan Son Nhut
1Lt Thomas Lambert Lubbers (KIA)
1Lt Charles Milford Knowles (KIA)
Maj Meredith Glenn Anderson (KIA)
Maj Robert Bokern (survived)
MSgt Joseph Cobden Jeszeck (KIA)
SSgt Allen Chandler (survived)
SSgt Robert Frederick Fage (KIA)
Sgt Michael J Vangelisti (KIA)

An AC-119G, radio call sign Shadow 78, had an engine failure at about 100 feet just as it was taking off from Tan Son Nhut on a mission over the Trail. The crew struggled to keep the aircraft airborne but it crashed about two miles beyond the end of the

runway. Six of the eight men on board were killed in the crash. This was the second Shadow lost to an engine failure on take off and following this latest accident the USAF limited the AC-119G's gross take off weight in order to achieve a safe rate of climb on a single engine.

28 April 1970

A-4C   147803   VA-12, USN, USS Shangri-La
1 pilot, name unknown (survived)

As a Skyhawk was returning to the Shangri-La it made an unsuccessful attempt to refuel from a tanker. The Skyhawk subsequently ran out of fuel and had to be abandoned.

29 April 1970

OV-10A   68-3824   19 TASS, 504 TASG, USAF, Bien Hoa
detached to Cu Chi
Capt Wendell Lee Brown (KIA)
1Lt Jose Hector Ortiz (KIA)

The 19th TASS maintained a small detachment of aircraft at an airstrip at Cu Chi about 15 miles northwest of Saigon. One of the detachment's Broncos was taking off for an FAC mission when it was hit in the tail by small arms fire. The aircraft crashed about four miles southwest of Cu Chi and neither of the crew survived.

F-8H   148650   VF-162, USN, USS Shangri-La
Lt J Jackson (survived)

The Shangri-La lost two aircraft in accidents in two days in succession. The second aircraft was a Crusader that was launched with insufficient airspeed following a cold catapult shot. The pilot ejected before the aircraft hit the sea just ahead of the carrier.

1 May 1970

A-7A   152680   VA-82, USN, USS Coral Sea
1 pilot, name unknown (survived)

The Coral Sea lost a Corsair from engine failure as it was en route to its target in Laos. This was the twelfth Corsair lost through engine failure since January 1969.

Cambodia

American frustration at the continued infiltration of South Vietnam following the end of the Rolling Thunder offensive led eventually to the secret bombing of enemy sanctuaries in Cambodia by B-52s. The first strike took place on 18 March 1969 and by 26 May 1970 the B-52s had flown a total of 4,308 sorties over Cambodia, mostly at night under ground radar control. In March 1970 Prince Sihanouk was deposed by a military junta led by General Lon Nol who formed the Khmer Republic. The new government was more sympathetic to the cause of South Vietnam and soon found itself at odds with Hanoi. The North Vietnamese responded by openly occupying much of eastern Cambodia and attempting to cut off Phnom Penh. Lon Nol asked for US assistance which gave President Nixon a legitimate excuse to attack the NVA and VC sanctuaries in Cambodia that had been a thorn in America's side ever since the war began.

Tactical air strikes commenced on 24 April and five days later 42,000 American and 48,000 ARVN troops began a limited incursion into Cambodia. Initially at least, the air strikes were limited to 18 miles across the border in support of the ground troops. Most of the allied troops had been withdrawn back into South Vietnam by 29 June having captured thousands of tons of weapons and supplies and killed or captured many NVA and VC soldiers. However, although the enemy forces close to the South Vietnamese border had been hit hard, those deeper in Cambodia still threatened the new government. On 30 June US air strikes commenced against NVA forces west of the Mekong River who were threatening provincial towns close to Phnom Penh. American air strikes in Cambodia continued for the next three years but by the end of 1970 the North Vietnamese still occupied about half of the country. Phnom Penh itself was largely cut off and supplies to the capital had to be taken up the Mekong River under heavy air and naval escort. A number of small-scale ground incursions by

ARVN troops in 1971 and 1972 met with varying success. Air strikes continued after the cease-fire in South Vietnam in January 1973 and in May of that year air power thwarted an attempt by Khmer Rouge rebels to cut off and capture Phnom Penh. However, the US Congress was by now tired of the war in Southeast Asia and forced President Nixon to cut off funds for the bombing of Cambodia with the result that the last combat missions were flown on 15 August 1973.

2 May 1970

F-4D   66-8721   13 TFS, 432 TRW, USAF, Udorn
Capt B R Bodenheim (survived)
1Lt G R Jackman (survived)

Another Falcon fast FAC was lost on 2 May. Capt Bodenheim was shot down by anti-aircraft fire just to the north of the DMZ. The aircraft was rolling in on a target when it was hit and the crew ejected safely moments later. They were subsequently rescued by a USAF SAR helicopter. This was the first USAF aircraft to be shot down in North Vietnam since 30 March.

F-4D   65-0628   480 TFS, 12 TFW, USAF, Phu Cat
Maj T Herring (survived)
Maj F C Peters (survived)

The first US fixed-wing aircraft to be lost during the incursion into Cambodia was a Phantom that was shot down as it was bombing a North Vietnamese staging area about 12 miles west of Loc Ninh and four miles within Cambodia. Maj Herring and Maj Peters ejected as their aircraft burst into flames on the third pass over the target and they were later recovered by US ground troops.

O-2A   68-11064   19 TASS, 504 TASG, USAF, Bien Hoa
Capt Jerry Newton Phillips (KIA)
Capt Rodney Harold Stone (KIA)

An O-2 FAC collided in mid-air with a US Army AH-1G Cobra helicopter (68-15121) over Cambodia and crashed killing both crew in each aircraft. The Cobra was from the 11th Armored Cavalry Regiment from Quan Loi and was being flown by CW2 William Wesley Davis and WO1 Steven Joseph Greenlee. The O-2 was in a climbing right turn and the AH-1G was in a descending orbit at the time of the collision. The helicopter's rotor blades sliced off a large section of the O-2's port wing and also damaged the cockpit area. The Cobra's rotor hub separated from the mast and both aircraft fell into dense jungle.

3 May 1970

F-4D   66-7613   497 TFS, 8 TFW, USAF, Ubon
Lt Col Lawrence Yerges Conaway (KIA)
1Lt Carl Russell Churchill (KIA)

A Phantom was lost during a Barrel Roll seeding mission. The aircraft was flying at 1,000 feet and 450 knots about 15 miles southeast of Ban Ban when it ran into 37mm ground fire. The aircraft burst into flames and crashed into a river before the crew could escape.

5 May 1970

RF-4C   65-0914   12 TRS, 460 TRW, USAF, Tan Son Nhut
Maj R E Moffitt (survived)
Lt Col D A Kellum (survived)

An RF-4C was assigned to photograph enemy lines of communications in the hill country about 25 miles to the southwest of Hué. As Maj Moffitt rolled in to start his photo run at 500 feet his aircraft was hit by 37mm AAA and became uncontrollable within minutes. The crew ejected a few miles to the east and were rescued by a USAF helicopter.

7 May 1970

F-4E   67-0293   469 TFS, 388 TFW, USAF, Korat
Capt T G Sweeting (survived)
1Lt D L Yates (survived)

The second Tiger FAC to be lost was shot down on a mission over northern Laos on 7 May. Capt Sweeting was tasked as controller for a strike on a Pathet Lao recoilless rifle position about eight

miles northwest of Ban Ban. As the strike commenced Capt Sweeting came in low to strafe the target but his Phantom was hit by 12.7mm ground fire. He flew a few miles to the eastern perimeter of the Plain of Jars where he and his WSO were forced to eject. An Air America helicopter picked them both up and returned them to Thailand.

OV-10A 68-3827   23 TASS, 504 TASG, USAF, Nakhon
                   Phanom detached to Ubon
                   Capt M L Taylor (survived)
Another aircraft was lost during an FAC mission in Laos. An OV-10 was hit twice by ground fire as it flew at 7,000 feet near Ban Tanbok, about 20 miles southwest of the A Shau Valley. One of the engines caught fire and Capt Taylor ejected to be rescued later by a USAF helicopter.

8 May 1970

F-100F 56-3827   416 TFS, 31 TFW, USAF, Tuy Hoa
                   Maj G M Marks (survived)
                   1Lt J P Richards (survived)
A Misty FAC aircraft was assigned to control an air strike in the tri-border region where the borders of South Vietnam, Laos and Cambodia converge. As the F-100 pulled up from marking a truck on a road near Ban Pakha, the aircraft was hit by 23mm AAA. The aircraft burst into flames and seconds later the crew ejected. They evaded the North Vietnamese until they could be rescued by a USAF helicopter. This was the last of at least 20 Misty FACs of the Commando Sabre unit to be lost since the inception of the programme in June 1967. The last Misty mission was flown on 14 May bringing to an end a programme that pioneered the use of fast jet aircraft for the FAC role and which led to the use of the Phantom as a fast FAC in Southeast Asia.

F-100D 55-3782   355 TFS, 31 TFW, USAF, Tuy Hoa
                   1 pilot, name unknown (survived)
A Super Sabre crashed on landing due to pilot error when it returned from a close air support mission.

9 May 1970

O-1E 56-2519   22 TASS, 504 TASG, USAF, Binh Thuy
                 1Lt R M Blackman (survived)
The third fixed-wing aircraft lost in Cambodia was a Bird Dog that was providing forward air control in support of ground troops near Vott Prek Cham, 25 miles southeast of Phnom Penh and on the banks of the Mekong River. The Bird Dog was flying at about 4,000 feet when it was hit by automatic weapons or small arms fire. 1Lt Blackman crash-landed the aircraft a few miles to the south and was rescued by a US Army helicopter.

A-7B 154555   VA-93, USN, USS Ranger
                1 pilot, name unknown (survived)
A Corsair was lost over the side of the Ranger when its arrester hook failed as it took one of the wires on landing. The pilot ejected and was recovered. The Ranger left the line three days later having spent 103 days on line duty on the cruise. It had lost four Intruders to enemy action and seven other aircraft to other causes during its tour.

The SR-71 in Southeast Asia

The first SR-71 Mach-3 high-altitude reconnaissance aircraft was delivered to the USAF on 6 January 1966 following four years of operations by the highly secret, CIA-sponsored Lockheed A-12. The aircraft's unsurpassed performance and intelligence-gathering capability made it a prime candidate for deployment to Southeast Asia. Such was the sensitivity and secrecy of the SR-71 programme that the aircraft were based in special facilities at Kadena AB on the island of Okinawa. The first aircraft arrived at the 9th SRW's Operating Location-8 on 8 March 1968, followed by two more aircraft in the next few days. This and subsequent deployments to and from the USA were code named Glowing Heat while the SR-71 programme as a whole was named Senior Crown and the operational missions in Southeast Asia were called Giant Scale. The aircraft was soon nicknamed the Habu, after a type of deadly black snake found on Okinawa. The

SR-71 flew its first operational mission from Kadena on 21 March 1968 and averaged about one sortie a week for the first two years and two sorties a week in 1970, culminating in a sortie every day by 1972. Operating at altitudes of up to 80,000 feet and speeds of around 2,000 mph, the SR-71 could easily outrun SA-2s and MiGs and employed its impressive array of cameras, radar and ELINT equipment to obtain coverage of North Vietnam. Even though the SR-71 arrived in the theatre towards the end of Rolling Thunder, the intelligence provided was of immense importance. Each flight took off from Kadena and refuelled from special KC-135Q tankers before entering the Gulf of Tonkin for a high-speed pass over North Vietnam. The SR-71 would then refuel again from a tanker over Thailand or Laos prior to making a second run over the target area before heading back to Kadena, refuelling once more en route. Several occasions arose when SR-71s had to make emergency landings at U-Tapao and the aircraft suffered badly from engine flameouts, especially in the early days. The Kadena detachment was increased from three to four aircraft in the spring of 1970 but soon afterwards the detachment lost its first aircraft.

10 May 1970

SR-71A 64-17969   Det OL-8, 9 SRW, USAF, Kadena
                    Maj William E Lawson (survived)
                    Maj Gilbert Martinez (survived)
An SR-71 had completed its first pass over North Vietnam and had filled up with its special JP7 fuel from a KC-135Q tanker over Thailand in readiness for its second run over enemy territory. The SR-71 disconnected from the tanker and lit its afterburners to climb back to altitude. However, all around the aircraft there were now huge banks of cloud reaching up to 50,000 feet and containing thunderstorms. In an effort to climb above the storms, Maj Lawson began to climb more steeply but with a full fuel load the SR-71 was sluggish until it reached supersonic speed. Before the aircraft could pick up speed it entered clouds and air turbulence caused both engines to flame out. The aircraft pitched up and stalled and without enough airspeed to attempt an engine restart, the crew was forced to eject and the aircraft crashed near Korat.

11 May 1970

O-2A 67-21341   20 TASS, 504 TASG, USAF, Da Nang
                  Lt Col Jerry William Pyle (KIA)
An O-2 on an FAC sortie was shot down by .50 calibre ground fire near Hoi An, about 12 miles southeast of Da Nang. The pilot may have been wounded as he did not bail out of the aircraft before it hit the ground.

12 May 1970

F-4D 66-7643   390 TFS, 366 TFW, USAF, Da Nang
                 Capt P W Harbison (survived)
                 1Lt J E Shelton (survived)
An NVA unit was reported to be occupying bunkers and huts about 15 miles west of Plei Djering. A flight of Phantoms was called in to hit the target but one of the aircraft was hit by small arms fire as it swept in at 700 feet. The rear fuselage burst into flames and the crew ejected seconds later. They landed safely and were soon rescued by an Army helicopter.

13 May 1970

F-4D 65-0607   480 TFS, 12 TFW, USAF, Phu Cat
                 Capt Alan Robert Trent (KIA)
                 1Lt Eric James Huberth (KIA)
A Phantom was lost during a strike on a bridge just five miles inside Cambodia and about 40 miles to the west of Kontum. As the aircraft made its second dive on the target it was struck by machine gun fire and crashed before either of the crew could escape. The aircraft exploded with almost a full bomb load on board and the wreckage was spread over a large area. A ground team was inserted into the area the next day but found no sign that the crew had ejected. This aircraft had previously served with the 36th TFW at Bitburg in West Germany.

15 May 1970

F-4B 150424   VMFA-115, MAG-13, USMC, Chu Lai
                1Lt R C Rissel (survived)
                1Lt J F Fitzmaurice (survived)
Viet Cong bunkers had been spotted near an anti-aircraft gun position near the Song Cu De River about seven miles northwest of Da Nang and a flight of Phantoms was sent to attack the target. As 1Lt Rissel was making his third pass his aircraft was hit in the rear fuselage by .50 calibre ground fire and burst into flames. He flew the short distance to Da Nang but the crew had to abandon the aircraft before they could put it down on the runway. They were both safely recovered by one of the base rescue helicopters.

F-8J 150326   VF-53, USN, USS Bon Homme Richard
                Lt(jg) Lloyd George Howie (KIA)
A Crusader pilot was waved off from his first approach to the Bon Homme Richard after returning from a BARCAP sortie. The aircraft overshot and climbed away to start another approach but the ship lost radar contact with it and it was presumed that the aircraft crashed into the sea while the pilot was concentrating on his approach.

16 May 1970

EKA-3B 142657   VAQ-135, USN, NAS Cubi Point
                 Cdr Richard Robert Skeen (KWF)
                 Lt Cdr Eugene Floyd McNally (KWF)
                 ADCS Edwin Ray Conner (KWF)
An EKA-3B Skywarrior was being ferried from Cubi Point NAS in the Philippines to the USS Coral Sea in the Gulf of Tonkin when it had to be diverted to Da Nang due to a shortage of fuel, possibly as a result of bad weather. During the diversion to Da Nang radar contact with the aircraft was lost and it was subsequently found to have crashed off the coast of South Vietnam. One of the crew's bodies was found during an extensive search but there was no sign of the other two men.

17 May 1970

F-4B 152239   VF-161, USN, USS Coral Sea
                Lt Norman Philip Westwood (KIA)
                Lt J Kane (survived)
The Coral Sea lost another aircraft the next day when a Phantom's starboard engine caught fire immediately after the aircraft was launched on a night strike mission. The aircraft was only airborne for about five seconds before it hit the water. During that time the command ejection sequence was initiated and the NFO ejected but the pilot's seat had not left the aircraft before it crashed. The plane guard helicopter rescued Lt Kane but an extensive search by aircraft, helicopters and the destroyer USS George K Mackenzie failed to find any sign of Lt Westwood.

19 May 1970

RF-4C 65-0827   11 TRS, 432 TRW, USAF, Udorn
                  Maj C A Crawford (survived)
                  Capt F P Norton (survived)
The centre of attention in northern Laos was still the Ban Ban Valley to the east of the Plain of Jars and another aircraft was lost in the valley on the 19th. An RF-4C was sent to obtain photographs of a segment of road about five miles southeast of the town of Ban Ban. As the aircraft flew over the road at almost 5,000 feet it was hit by ground fire and Maj Crawford immediately turned for home. However, after about 10 miles the crew had to eject but they came down in mountainous terrain and were later rescued by an Air America helicopter.

EC-47N 43-15133   362 TEWS, 460 TRW, USAF, Pleiku
One of the venerable EC-47 RDF aircraft was destroyed and two other aircraft damaged during a rocket attack on the airfield at Pleiku. Only four rockets were fired, one of which made a direct hit on the EC-47, and no injuries were reported. This C-47 had served as a communications aircraft with the 7101st ABS at Wiesbaden in West Germany before conversion to EC-47N standard.

20 May 1970

F-4J   155738   VF-92, USN, USS *America*
Lt(jg) J Hapgood (survived)
Lt(jg) R Williamson (survived)

The USS *America* arrived back under TF 77 control on 12 May from Norfolk, Virginia for its second tour of duty off Southeast Asia. It was not due to take its place on the line until the 26th but it lost a Phantom during its training period in the week prior to operations. The crew had to eject from the aircraft due to a control failure and were quickly rescued.

22 May 1970

O-2A   68-11002   20 TASS, 504 TASG, USAF, Da Nang
Capt Richard W Meacham (KIA)
1 crew, name unknown (KIA)

An O-2 Covey FAC was shot down in the vicinity of the abandoned Marine Corps camp at Khe Sanh on the 22nd and both occupants were killed. Capt Meacham's observer was probably a VNAF officer.

23 May 1970

F-4B   152319   VMFA-115, MAG-13, USMC, Chu Lai
1Lt J D Brewer (survived)
1Lt J Nelson (survived)

A Phantom caught fire soon after taking off from Chu Lai on a combat mission. The crew ejected safely before the aircraft crashed.

25 May 1970

F-4D   66-0245   433 TFS, 8 TFW, USAF, Ubon
1Lt G M Rubus (survived)
1Lt J T Sornberger (survived)

A cluster of four 23mm anti-aircraft gun positions had been located near Ban Dakbong Noy in southern Laos, 30 miles west of Kham Duc. A flight of Phantoms from the Wolfpack was sent to attack the guns but one of the aircraft was damaged by return fire. 1Lt Rubus headed east and crossed the coast over 70 miles away before he and his WSO ejected from the aircraft. They were then picked up by a USAF helicopter.

26 May 1970

F-100D   56-3136   309 TFS, 31 TFW, USAF, Tuy Hoa
Capt W D Croom (survived)

A flight of F-100s took off from Tuy Hoa for an interdiction sortie over the Trail but one of the aircraft was hit by small arms fire just 15 miles west of the airfield. Capt Croom turned back towards Tuy Hoa but he was forced to eject some 10 miles northwest of the base and had to be picked up by the base HH-43.

A-4E   149993   VA-152, USN, USS *Shangri-La*
1 pilot, name unknown (survived)

A Navy pilot abandoned his Skyhawk during a tanker mission when the engine suddenly lost power. It was suspected that the aircraft had ingested fuel into the engine air intakes as the aircraft was taking on fuel from another tanker.

27 May 1970

F-4D   66-0275   480 TFS, 12 TFW, USAF, Phu Cat
Capt George R Keller (KIA)
1Lt Glen Hung Nin Lee (KIA)

A strike on buildings in Cambodia near the village of Phum Chas Yang, about 45 miles west of Ban Me Thuot, resulted in the loss of a Phantom crew. Capt Keller and 1Lt Lee were making their sixth pass over the target when their aircraft was hit by small arms fire as it pulled up. The starboard wing burst into flames and separated from the fuselage causing the aircraft to roll into the ground. 1Lt Lee's remains were not recovered from Cambodia until 23 August 1994.

F-4B   149403   VMFA-314, MAG-13, USMC, Chu Lai
Capt R E Dahart (survived)
1Lt R C Blakely (survived)

A flight of Marine Corps Phantoms was bombing a truck park near Ban Tampanko in southern Laos when one of the aircraft was damaged by ground fire. Capt Dahart was pulling up from his second attack when his starboard engine was hit and caught fire. He headed east in an attempt to reach Da Nang or the coast but he and his navigator were forced to eject from the aircraft near Quang Tri City and were subsequently rescued by a US Army helicopter. 1Lt Blakely was shot down again two weeks later.

29 May 1970

F-100D   55-3803   614 TFS, 35 TFW, USAF, Phan Rang
Capt W H Rutherford (survived)

Another aircraft was lost on a raid in Cambodia. A flight of Super Sabres was sent to attack an enemy position near Phum Chiphu, 35 miles west of Saigon and just within Cambodia. Capt Rutherford came down to 500 feet as he strafed the target on his fourth pass. His aircraft was damaged by small arms fire and he ejected a few miles away and was later rescued by an Army helicopter.

A-7A   153146   VA-82, USN, USS *Coral Sea*
1 pilot, name unknown (survived)

The last aircraft lost by the *Coral Sea* before it completed its fifth tour of duty with TF 77 was a Corsair of VA-82. The pilot reported smoke in the cockpit followed by an internal explosion and a loss of oil pressure. The pilot ejected safely and was rescued. The ship had spent 125 days on the line and had lost a single Corsair due to enemy action and another 10 aircraft in accidents. Twelve men had died in the accidents as well as the Corsair pilot lost in combat.

O-2A   68-11033   20 TASS, 504 TASG, USAF, Da Nang
1 pilot, name unknown (survived)

For the second time in May, an O-2 FAC collided in mid-air with another aircraft and crashed. However, in this instance the pilot survived.

30 May 1970

F-100D   56-3242   531 TFS, 3 TFW, USAF, Bien Hoa
Maj A E Ruth (survived)

A Super Sabre was lost on the 30th during a strike on VC positions in South Vietnam itself. Maj Ruth was on his third pass over the target near Phuoc Long, about 20 miles northeast of Quan Long City in the southernmost tip of the country. His F-100 was hit by .30 calibre ground fire and crashed a few miles from the target after Maj Ruth ejected. An Army helicopter later picked him up.

4 June 1970

O-1E   56-2620   22 TASS, 504 TASG, USAF, Binh Thuy
detached to Chau Doc
Maj J E Zahm (survived)
Lt Col W C English (survived)

A Bird Dog was hit by small arms fire as it took off from a strip at Chau Doc close to the border with Cambodia, about 90 miles west of Saigon. The aircraft's engine was damaged and Maj Zahm crash-landed near the airstrip. Both men vacated the wrecked aircraft without a scratch and were picked up by a VNAF helicopter.

RF-4C   66-0385   12 TRS, 460 TRW, USAF, Tan Son Nhut
Maj Bobby Gene Huggins (KIA)
Maj Alvin Eugene Mather (KIA)

An RF-4C went missing during a night-time photographic reconnaissance sortie in South Vietnam. An Army forward fire support base reported seeing a low-flying aircraft crash and explode close to the border with Cambodia, about 20 miles north of Song Be City. A search team located the crash site the next day and found remains including a hand that was identified as that of Maj Mather. The family of Maj Huggins had to wait another 27 years until confirmation of his death. A JTF-FA investigation team excavated the wreck site in 1995 and remains were found that were later identified by DNA testing as being those of Maj Huggins. His remains were buried at Arlington National Cemetery in October 1997.

6 June 1970

AC-119K   52-5935   18 SOS, 14 SOW, USAF, Phan Rang
detached to Da Nang
TSgt Clyde Douglas Alloway (KIA)
9 crew, names unknown (survived)

As an AC-119K Stinger took off from Da Nang for a night gunship mission it suffered a runaway propeller on the Number 1 engine. The pilot tried to return to the airfield to attempt an emergency landing but he could not control the aircraft. The crew abandoned the aircraft over the sea just to the east of Da Nang and all but one man was rescued. The aircraft continued flying out to sea and caused a brief panic when it seemed to be heading for Chinese airspace around Hainan Island. However, the aircraft crashed into the South China Sea well before it reached Hainan.

7 June 1970

F-4B   151478   VMFA-122, MAG-13, USMC, Chu Lai
1Lt Kurt Michael Wilbrecht (KIA)
1Lt W T Pepper (survived)

A pair of Marine Corps Phantoms were attacking an enemy position near An Hoa, 15 miles southwest of Da Nang, when one of the aircraft was shot down. The aircraft flew into a barrage of .50 calibre gunfire at 500 feet as it made a shallow dive on the target. The ground fire hit the cockpit area and 1Lt Wilbrecht may have been hit as he flew west, deeper into enemy held territory, rather than making for the coast to the east. The aircraft crashed about 15 miles from where it was hit and although the navigator ejected and was rescued by helicopter, 1Lt Wilbrecht died in the crash.

A-4E   150062   VMA-311, MAG-13, USMC, Chu Lai
Capt Frederick Palka (survived)

The Marines lost another aircraft later the same day during a close air support mission near Ben Het, 30 miles northwest of Kontum. Capt Palka commenced his second dive on the target when his aircraft was hit by ground fire and burst into flames. He ejected close to the target as the aircraft rolled out of control and landed in the middle of a firefight but was rescued 40 minutes later by an Army helicopter and taken to Pleiku.

OV-10A   155495   VAL-4, USN, Binh Thuy
Lt Cdr Jere Alan Barton (KIA)
Lt Cdr James D Hanks (survived)

As well as their prime role of hunting down Viet Cong riverine traffic, the Broncos of VAL-4 were also used for close air support of friendly troops if necessary. An aircraft flown by Lt Cdr Barton and Lt Cdr Hanks was directed to attack enemy troops who had been engaged on a large island in the Mekong River, five miles northeast of Vinh Long. On the eighth pass their Bronco was hit by .30 calibre machine gun fire and the port engine and wing burst into flames. Lt Cdr Barton was wounded by the ground fire but apparently managed to command eject both himself and Lt Cdr Hanks at low level. Lt Cdr Hanks was located and rescued by an Army helicopter but Lt Cdr Barton was killed in the incident.

A-4F   154215   VA-144, USN, USS *Bon Homme Richard*
1 pilot, name unknown (survived)

A Skyhawk from VA-144 had to be abandoned when its engine exploded and the aircraft caught fire during a combat mission. The cause was thought to have been mechanical failure and the pilot was rescued. This was the second and last aircraft lost by the *Bon Homme Richard* during its fifth tour with TF 77. The ship left its position on 20 October having spent 101 days on the line with the loss of a Crusader and a Skyhawk. The carrier was decommissioned on 2 July 1971 but was not stricken for disposal until 20 September 1989 and was scrapped at San Pedro in 1992.

9 June 1970

O-1F   57-2890   21 TASS, 504 TASG, USAF, Cam Ranh Bay
detached to Pleiku
1Lt John Leslie Ryder (KIA)
Capt Barry Wayne Hilbrick, US Army (KIA)

An O-1 went missing during a visual reconnaissance flight in the Central Highlands. The aircraft took off from Pleiku and headed for Ben Het, the crew's first destination, before proceeding to Dak Seang Camp. However, at some stage in the flight the crew failed to report in by radio and calls from various ground stations were not answered. The weather was very poor at the time and a search could not be mounted until the next day. The search continued until the 19th but to no avail. Capt Hilbrick was an Operations Officer with the Army's 5th Special Forces Group.

F-4E   67-0295   469 TFS, 388 TFW, USAF, Korat
                   Capt R L Clingaman (survived)
                   Capt C W Ripple (survived)

A Phantom from Korat was shot down on a night mission over the Ho Chi Minh Trail near Tavouac in southern Laos. Capt Clingaman was flying escort for a gunship that was searching the Trail for signs of movement when the Phantom was hit by 37mm AAA. The aircraft was badly damaged and the crew ejected almost immediately but were later rescued by a USAF helicopter.

C-7B   63-9724   459 TAS, 483 TAW, USAF, Phu Cat

A C-7 Caribou was being airlifted by a CH-54 Skycrane helicopter when it fell from the sling and was destroyed. Sometime in May the aircraft had run off the end of the runway as it was landing at a strip at Tra Bong, 25 miles northwest of Quang Ngai city. None of the crew was injured in the crash and it was decided to airlift the Caribou out for repair. The propellers and outboard wing sections were removed before the airlift was attempted. The Caribou was one of the largest aircraft that could be lifted by heavy lift helicopters but unfortunately on this occasion the sling snapped and the aircraft fell to the ground breaking in two. By the time 63-9724 was finally destroyed the 459th TAS had been inactivated, leaving five Caribou squadrons in Southeast Asia.

11 June 1970

F-4B   153022   VMFA-314, MAG-13, USMC, Chu Lai
                   Capt B A Rindt (survived)
                   1Lt R C Blakely (survived)

A Phantom was damaged by ground fire during a close air support mission in the northern provinces of South Vietnam. Capt Rindt flew the aircraft out to sea and he and his navigator ejected about three miles off the coast near Chu Lai. This was the second time within two weeks that 1Lt Blakeley had been forced to abandon a Phantom having ejected near Quang Tri on 27 May. On the second occasion he was pulled from the water by a Navy ship while his pilot was rescued by helicopter.

12 June 1970

F-4D   66-8770   25 TFS, 8 TFW, USAF, Ubon
                   Capt Richard D Massari (KIA)
                   1Lt E Payne (survived)

A LORAN-modified Phantom returned from an escort mission and joined the landing pattern at Ubon. During the circuit to land one its engines failed and the Phantom crashed. Only one of the crew managed to eject before the aircraft hit the ground.

17 June 1970

OV-10A   68-3815   23 TASS, 504 TASG, USAF, Nakhon
                     Phanom detached to Ubon
                     Capt K E Loar (survived)

A Bronco was flying a visual reconnaissance mission southeast of the A Shau Valley when the pilot spotted what looked like a road repair vehicle near the village of Tala. As he flew over the vehicle at 6,500 feet the Bronco was hit by AAA and badly damaged. Capt Loar headed southwest and eventually ejected near Muang Khongxedon from where he was rescued by an Air America helicopter that was based nearby.

18 June 1970

F-4E   67-0297   421 TFS, 366 TFW, USAF, Da Nang
                   Maj Harry Lawrence McLamb (KIA)
                   Maj Carl Wilson Drake (KIA)

A Phantom crew was lost during a raid in Cambodia on the 18th. The aircraft was strafing a truck on a road near Sre Chas, close to the Mekong River, when it was hit by small arms fire. The Phantom crashed near the road before either of the crew had a chance to eject.

19 June 1970

F-4B   150653   VMFA-122, MAG-13, USMC, Chu Lai
                   1Lt F Hall (survived)
                   1Lt G Mitchell (survived)

A Marine Corps Phantom crashed on landing back at Chu Lai. The cause of the accident was attributed to the aircraft landing with an asymmetric ordnance load for which the pilot was unable to compensate.

20 June 1970

OV-10A   68-3802   23 TASS, 504 TASG, USAF, Nakhon Phanom
                     1 pilot, name unknown (survived)

A Bronco pilot had to abandon his aircraft after it was hit in mid-air by an RF-4C on a reconnaissance mission. The Phantom landed safely and the Bronco pilot was recovered by an HH-53 from the 40th ARRS.

22 June 1970

A-4C   148495   VA-172, USN, USS Shangri-La
                  Lt John Stiles Earle (KIA)

On the evening of the 22nd a Skyhawk was launched from the catapult of the Shangri-La but did not climb away as normal. The pilot radioed that the aircraft would not accelerate or climb and the aircraft ditched about two miles in front of the ship. A search started immediately and continued throughout the night and the following day but there was no sign of Lt Earle.

24 June 1970

A-37B   69-6346   604 SOS, 3 TFW, USAF, Bien Hoa
                    1Lt Russell Earl Voris (KIA)

A pair of A-37s was sent to attack bridges about 10 miles east of the town of Kratie in Cambodia. 1Lt Voris was pulling up from his second pass when his aircraft was hit by ground fire and crashed nearby. Although 1Lt Voris survived the crash and was rescued from the wreck by the crew of an Army helicopter, he died later in the day of his injuries. This was the first of the more capable A-37B variants of the Dragonfly to be lost during the war.

25 June 1970

A-7B   154525   VA-155, USN, USS Oriskany
                  1 pilot, name unknown (survived)

The Oriskany arrived back on the line on 14 June for its fifth cruise of the war. The ship lost its first aircraft when a Corsair lost power during a night-time catapult shot. The pilot ejected just before the aircraft crashed into the sea ahead of the carrier.

28 June 1970

A-7A   153176   VA-153, USN, USS Oriskany
                  Cdr Donald Deane Aldern (KIA)

The Oriskany's first and, as it happened only, combat loss of its fifth cruise occurred during a night Steel Tiger mission. The pilot was Cdr Aldern, the commander of Air Wing 19, who was leading his wingman on an FAC-controlled strike 10 miles south of Muang Fangdeng in the southern tip of Laos. His Corsair was seen by the FAC and his wingman to start its bomb run, drop its bombs and then fly into the ground near the target and explode. Although no flak was seen at the time it was possible that ground fire or target fixation or disorientation were possible causes. An attempt to examine the crash site had to be abandoned when the ground party encountered heavy enemy resistance.

30 June 1970

F-4E   67-0279   34 TFS, 388 TFW, USAF, Korat
                   Capt Mitchell Olen Sadler (KIA)
                   1Lt Gordon Clark Hill (KIA)

A Tiger FAC Phantom disappeared over Laos while on a weather reconnaissance mission. Although satellites and ground-based meteorological observations provided much valuable weather information, these methods were sometimes insufficient for the detail required for planning missions over enemy-held territory and aircraft had to be used. The crew of this Phantom was posted missing and never returned.

OV-10A   68-3807   23 TASS, 504 TASG, USAF, Nakhon Phanom
                     Capt William Stephen Sanders (KIA)
                     TSgt Albert H Mostello, US Army (survived)

A Bronco Nail FAC was shot down in southern Laos during an FAC mission in support of a MACVSOG reconnaissance team. The aircraft was hit in the cockpit area by automatic weapons fire near Ban Kapay, just west of the DMZ. The Special Forces observer ejected but the pilot of the OV-10 was probably wounded by the ground fire and did not eject. When the Bronco went down a SAR task force was quickly despatched to the area but the first attempt failed when an HH-3 had to withdraw due to heavy ground fire. Jolly Green 54, an HH-53C 68-8283 from the 40th ARRS, then arrived and made an attempt amidst suppression from several A-1s but the helicopter was hit by ground fire and crashed inverted, killing all on board. The helicopter's crew consisted of Capt Leroy Clyde Schaneberg, Maj John Winfred Goeglein, MSgt Paul Laverne Jenkins, SSgt Marvin Earl Bell and SSgt Michael Frank Dean. TSgt Mostello was rescued by another HH-3 SAR helicopter after tear gas was dropped to keep enemy troops away from the survivor. In December 1993 the helicopter's crash site was excavated and the crew's remains were identified as a group on 7 March 1995 and buried at Arlington. The helicopter had been shot down by Company 1, 35th Battalion, Group 559 of the NVA.

F-100D   56-3287   308 TFS, 31 TFW, USAF, Tuy Hoa
                     1 pilot, name unknown (survived)

The last aircraft lost in June was a Super Sabre that crashed due to pilot error on a close air support mission in South Vietnam.

3 July 1970

OV-10A   68-3788   20 TASS, 504 TASG, USAF, Da Nang
                     detached to Pleiku
                     Capt William Allen Justice (KIA)

An OV-10 was shot down during an FAC mission in Cambodia on the 3rd. Capt Justice was flying near Sre Mat close to the Tonle Srepok River when his aircraft was hit by ground fire and burst into flames. The pilot did not have a chance to eject before the aircraft crashed.

4 July 1970

EKA-3B   142400   VAQ-132, USN, USS America
                    3 crew, names unknown (survived)

An EKA-3B overshot from a landing approach to the USS America following a tanker mission. Unfortunately, as the aircraft started to climb away its drag parachute accidentally deployed and the pilot lost control. All three crew ejected from the aircraft before it plunged into the sea.

8 July 1970

F-100D   55-2943   615 TFS, 35 TFW, USAF, Phan Rang
                     1Lt D P Egelston (survived)

A Super Sabre was shot down during an attack on an enemy position 10 miles northeast of Phan Thiet. The aircraft was on its third pass over the target when it was hit by ground fire. 1Lt Egelston headed back to base but was forced to eject over the sea about 35 miles south of Phan Rang and was picked up by a USAF helicopter.

9 July 1970

F-100D   55-3572   31 TFW, USAF, Tuy Hoa
                     1Lt G K Newsome (survived)

Another Super Sabre was lost during a close air support mission in South Vietnam on the 9th. 1Lt Newsome was pulling up from his first attack on an enemy position near Loi Tan, 35 miles

The A-37B was a modified version of the A-37A that had improved avionics and an in-flight refuelling capability. A total of 22 A-37s were lost by the USAF in Southeast Asia, five of them in Cambodia in 1970/71. USAF

northeast of Bien Hoa, when his aircraft was hit by small arms fire and burst into flames. He ejected a couple of miles away from his target and was recovered by a USAF helicopter.

11 July 1970

TA-4F 154646 H&MS-11, MAG-11, USMC, Da Nang
Capt R T Rasmussen (survived)
1Lt W W Mills (survived)

A Playboy TA-4F was marking a target in the A Shau Valley when it was hit by .50 calibre gunfire as it pulled up from its first pass. The crew ejected about a mile from the target and were rescued six hours later by a USAF SAR helicopter despite intense enemy anti-aircraft fire that put 15 holes into the helicopter. This Skyhawk had been hit by ground fire five times in the two months prior to being shot down.

17 July 1970

C-47A 43-15583 probably 14 SOW, USAF, base ..?
Maj Lloyd Arthur McGrew (KWF)
3 crew, names unknown (survived)

A C-47 transport crashed during a training flight when it suffered an engine failure. It is not known for sure which unit owned the aircraft as it is erroneously recorded as belonging to '14 TRW' in one official document. The eventual fate of the aircraft is in doubt as at least one source claims that 43-15583 later flew with Air Laos as XW-PFY.

24 July 1970

OV-10A 67-14672 20 TASS, 504 TASG, USAF, Da Nang
detached to Duc Co
1Lt James Michael Butler (KIA)

The 20th TASS maintained a detachment of aircraft at an airstrip at Duc Co, six miles from the Cambodian border and 25 miles southwest of Pleiku. At dusk 1Lt Butler had just taken off from Duc Co when his Bronco was hit by ground fire and crashed about 10 miles east of the strip. The pilot was killed in the crash.

F-4D 66-7761 555 TFS, 432 TRW, USAF, Udorn
Capt James William Reed (KIA)
1Lt Donald Bruce Bloodworth (KIA)

A flight of three Phantoms was flying as escort to a C-123 (possibly a Black Spot night FAC aircraft) on a night-time Barrel Roll mission when they attacked a truck on a road on the eastern edge of the Plain of Jars. As Capt Reed, a Falcon fast FAC pilot, made his second strafing pass on the truck his aircraft was seen to be hit by ground fire. The C-123 crew saw the Phantom crash and explode close to the truck but did not see any ejection or parachutes and it was presumed that both crew died in the crash. In 1993 a joint US-Lao investigation team excavated a crash site and discovered human remains that were later identified as being those of 1Lt Bloodworth.

25 July 1970

F-4D 65-0693 433 TFS, 8 TFW, USAF, Ubon
Lt Col Richard W Pennington (Died)
Capt R L Rigel (survived)

During a night escort mission over the Trail a Phantom bombed a 37mm anti-aircraft gun site near the village of Ban Pha Bong-tai, 12 miles west of the DMZ. As Lt Col Pennington came in for his second pass on the target his aircraft was hit by return fire from the gun and both crew ejected. Both men were rescued by a 37th ARRS helicopter but Lt Col Pennington died of his wounds the following day.

F-4J 155789 VF-92, USN, USS America
Lt Paul Anthony Gregory (KIA)
1 crew, name unknown (survived)

The third and final aircraft lost by the USS America before it completed its second war cruise was a Phantom that crashed into the Gulf of Tonkin following control problems during a CAP mission. Sadly, one of the crew died in the accident. The ship had spent exactly 100 days on the line before it departed on 8 November and this was its only air fatality of the tour.

28 July 1970

A-1H 52-139776 602 SOS, 56 SOW, USAF, Nakhon Phanom
detached to Da Nang
Maj Otis Cleveland Morgan (KIA)

Two Skyraiders were shot down on the 28th. The first aircraft was on an escort mission when it was hit by ground fire near Cang Dong, 20 miles south of Da Nang. Maj Morgan did not eject from his aircraft and was killed in the crash.

A-1H 52-135263 1 SOS, 56 SOW, USAF, Nakhon Phanom
Maj Petter B Lee (survived)

The other Skyraider lost on the 28th was flying a night-time Steel Tiger strike over the Trail in southern Laos. Maj Lee had found a convoy of five trucks a few miles southwest of the Ban Karai Pass and commenced to attack his target. On his final pass the aircraft was hit by 37mm flak and the Skyraider's rear fuselage caught fire. He ejected at 4,000 feet and landed on the side of a hill just above a river. Maj Lee climbed up the hill as far as he could and dug in under the foliage for the rest of the night. FAC aircraft orbited near Maj Lee throughout the night and spoke to him via his emergency radio every 30 minutes. A first light rescue attempt had to be postponed due to low cloud and while waiting for rescue Maj Lee radioed the positions of enemy troops and guns to the FAC overhead who then brought in air strikes. By late afternoon the weather had cleared enough for a 37th ARRS HH-53 flown by Maj G C Hitt to make an attempt. The helicopter swept in along a valley protected by smoke screens laid down by the Sandys as more A-1s, F-4s and F-105s continued to pound enemy positions to keep them away from the survivor. Maj Lee was quickly hoisted to safety after more than 18 hours on the ground.

29/30 July 1970

RF-4C 66-0436 14 TRS, 432 TRW, USAF, Udorn
Capt Gary Anthony Chavez (KIA)
Capt Donald Alan Brown (KIA)

An RF-4C failed to return from a photographic reconnaissance mission over southern Laos during the night of the 29/30th. The aircraft's last known position was just to the east of a ridge which marks the edge of the Plateau des Bolovens, about 25 miles north of Muang Fangdeng. Despite an extensive search, no trace of the aircraft or its crew was found.

6 August 1970

A-4C 149553 VA-12, USN, USS Shangri-La
1 pilot, name unknown (survived)

As a Skyhawk was being launched on a combat mission from the Shangri-La the catapult linkage broke and the aircraft was launched at too low an airspeed. The pilot ejected before the aircraft crashed into the sea.

10 August 1970

C-123K 55-4527 315 TAW, USAF, Phan Rang
Maj Grant Reed Waugh (KWF)
Capt Dwaine Elbyrne Mattox (KWF)
TSgt Bernard Francis Morrill (KWF)
1 crew, name unknown (survived)

A Provider on a ferry fight crashed in Khanh Hoa province in South Vietnam when one of its engines failed. Only one of the four crewmen on board survived the accident.

12 August 1970

F-8H 148660 VF-162, USN, USS Shangri-La
Cdr M Wright (survived)

A Crusader was abandoned during a combat air patrol following problems with the aircraft's fuel system. The pilot was rescued from the Gulf of Tonkin.

13 August 1970

OV-10A 67-14660 20 TASS, 504 TASG, USAF, Da Nang
Capt John Parker Powell (KIA)

No US aircraft had been lost within the DMZ buffer zone since September 1969 until a Bronco went down as it was controlling a strike near Kinh Mon on 13 August. The target was a .50 calibre gun site and the Bronco crashed when it collided in mid-air with one of the strike aircraft. The fighter landed safely but Capt Powell was killed when his aircraft crashed.

14 August 1970

A-1H 52-135242 56 SOW, USAF, Da Nang
1 pilot, name unknown (survived)

A Skyraider from the 56th SOW's Operating Location Alpha suffered engine failed as it was taking off from Da Nang on a close air support mission. The aircraft crashed but the pilot survived with only minor injuries.

17 August 1970

F-4E 67-0312 366 TFW, USAF, Da Nang
Capt David Leroy Ramsey (KIA)
Maj Phillip Rogerson Wellons (KIA)

F-4E 67-0257 366 TFW, USAF, Da Nang
Capt James Watson Wood (KIA)
Capt Stephen Bernard Melnick (KIA)

During a night strike on an enemy position 10 miles southwest of Da Nang two Phantoms collided in mid-air and crashed, killing the four airmen involved.

21 August 1970

F-100D 56-3435   612 TFS, 35 TFW, USAF, Phan Rang
         1Lt Charles Edward McLeish (KIA)

1Lt McLeish had recently arrived at Phan Rang and was flying an orientation flight in company with another aircraft in order to familiarise himself with the Wing's operational area. As the aircraft approached Ben Het 1Lt McLeish's aircraft was shot down by ground fire and he was killed.

30 August 1970

OV-10A 68-3798   20 TASS, 504 TASG, USAF, Da Nang
         Capt Michael John McGerty (KIA)
         MSgt Charles Howard Gray, US Army (KIA)

A Covey FAC was lost while on an FAC mission about 60 miles southwest of Da Nang. The aircraft was shot down by ground fire close to the border between South Vietnam and Laos and both the pilot and the Special Forces observer were killed.

1 September 1970

A-4E 150028   VMA-311, MAG-13, USMC, Chu Lai
         1Lt John David Lawson (KIA)

VMA-311 lost a pilot during a close air support mission to assist troops of the ARVN's 1st Division near Ba Long, 15 miles southwest of Quang Tri. Two aircraft were dropping napalm at low level when one of them was hit, burst into flames and crashed into a hill near the target without dropping its ordnance. The Skyhawk crashed before 1Lt Lawson had a chance to eject.

2 September 1970

F-4B 150466   VMFA-115, MAG-13, USMC, Chu Lai

In a tragic ground accident VMFA-115 lost an aircraft and three ground crew. A Phantom had just been taxied to the fuel pits when for some reason its fuel tanks were jettisoned. The area soon became an inferno and the aircraft exploded killing three ground crew and injuring several more. Apparently the fire spread rapidly when the fire extinguisher available failed to work properly. This was the last aircraft lost during Marine Corps operations from Chu Lai. In accordance with the general withdrawal of American units from South Vietnam the last unit, VMFA-122, left Chu Lai on 8 September and the base was handed over to the US Army's Americal Division.

5 September 1970

O-2A 68-10992   21 TASS, 504 TASG, USAF, Cam Ranh Bay
         1Lt Robert Douglas Hauer (KIA)

An O-2 went down about 20 miles northwest of Nha Trang during an FAC mission. It was presumed that the aircraft had been shot down by ground fire and the pilot killed but the wreck was never found to confirm this assumption.

8 September 1970

TA-4F 154302   H&MS-11, MAG-11, USMC, Da Nang
         1 pilot, name unknown (survived)

A TA-4F developed a problem with its fuel system during a test flight from Da Nang. The pilot was forced to eject when the engine stopped through fuel starvation. TA-4F 154302 had received slight damage when it was hit by a 12.7mm round during a visual reconnaissance mission on 1 August.

11 September 1970

A-4E 151165   VMA-311, MAG-11, USMC, Da Nang
         1Lt Bernard Herbert Plassmeyer (KIA)

On the night of the 10/11th a flight of two Skyhawks was called to attack enemy troops who were occupying a ridgeline in the hills near the A Shau Valley, 25 miles southwest of Hué and were fighting elements of the 101st Airborne Division. 1Lt Plassmeyer made one successful pass but as he came around for the second time his aircraft was hit by ground fire, burst into flames and crashed. It was thought that the pilot did not have time to eject before the aircraft crashed. 1Lt Plassmeyer had completed about

100 sorties since arriving in Vietnam in February 1970. This aircraft was the last of 28 Skyhawks lost by VMA-311 during its many deployments to South Vietnam, 23 of these had been lost to enemy action, six of them during Viet Cong attacks on Chu Lai. The Squadron had flown a total of 54,625 combat sorties during the war and had lost eight pilots killed due to enemy action or accidents. Although the Squadron would return to South Vietnam in May 1972 it did not lose any further aircraft or personnel.

16 September 1970

F-100D 55-3806   612 TFS, 35 TFW, USAF, Phan Rang
         1Lt J V Phillips (survived)

The Cambodian incursion continued and a Super Sabre was lost in that country on the 16th. 1Lt Phillips was bombing boats and a storage area five miles southeast of the town of Kratie when he was shot down as he pulled up from his seventh pass. He ejected safely and was picked up by a USAF helicopter.

17 September 1970

OV-10A 68-3800   20 TASS, 504 TASG, USAF, Da Nang
         1Lt Jerry Eugene Bevan (KWF)
         1 crew, name unknown (survived)

A Bronco had an accidental engine failure during a ferry flight and the aircraft crashed in South Vietnam. One of the crew was killed in the accident.

22 September 1970

A-4C 149525   VA-172, USN, USS *Shangri-La*
         1 pilot, name unknown (survived)

The *Shangri-La* suffered its third faulty catapult shot of its tour on the 22nd. A Skyhawk was being launched on a strike mission when the catapult failed and the aircraft crashed into the sea just ahead of the carrier. The pilot managed to eject safely and was rescued.

23 September 1970

F-105D 61-0153   355 TFW, USAF, Takhli
         Capt J W Newhouse (survived)

A flight of F-105s was despatched to bomb a ford in southern Laos 10 miles southeast of the A Shau Valley. Capt Newhouse's aircraft was hit by 37mm flak during the attack and he headed northwest into South Vietnam to try to reach Da Nang or the sea. He was forced to eject about 10 miles west of Hué and finished the rest of his journey by USAF helicopter. This aircraft was the last F-105 Thunderchief lost from Takhli RTAB. On 7 October the 355th TFW ceased combat operations and prepared for deactivation on 10 December. Most of the aircraft and pilots were sent to McConnell AFB but a few went to the 12th TFS at Kadena. The only Thunderchiefs left in theatre after the 355th left was a handful of Wild Weasels at Korat.

28 September 1970

O-2A 67-21409   504 TASG, USAF, base ..?
         1 pilot, name unknown (survived)

Two O-2s collided in mid-air during an FAC mission over South Vietnam. One of the aircraft managed to land safely but the other was too badly damaged and had to be abandoned.

29 September 1970

OV-10A 155479   VAL-4, USN, Binh Thuy
         Lt(jg) Ed A Bastarache (survived)
         Lt(jg) Peter W Ford (survived)

The Black Ponies lost an aircraft during a close air support mission 30 miles west of Saigon on the 29th. The aircraft was on its sixth pass over enemy troop positions near the village of Xom Thong Xoai when it was hit by small arms fire. The fuselage caught fire and the occupants ejected near the enemy troops but were safely recovered. Being shot down in an OV-10 was not a new experience for Lt Ford as he had been forced to eject from an aircraft near Rach Gia on 30 March 1970.

1 October 1970

O-2A 68-10839   19 TASS, 504 TASG, USAF, Bien Hoa
         1Lt Garrett Edward Eddy (KIA)
         1Lt Michael Stephen Vrablick (KIA)

The radio call sign Rustic was used by O-2 and OV-10 FACs during missions over Cambodia from June 1970 to August 1973. The observers were usually French-speakers as they had to communicate with Cambodian government troops who often spoke French but no English. The 19th TASS flew most of the Rustic missions from Bien Hoa and Tan Sonh Nhut until the mission was transferred to Ubon in November 1971. An O-2 Rustic crew was shot down and killed during an FAC mission in Cambodia. 1Lt Eddy's aircraft was hit by automatic weapons fire about 25 miles northwest of Kampong Cham and crashed in flames.

2 October 1970

C-130E 64-0536   776 TAS, 314 TAW, USAF, Ching Chuan Kang
         Maj Irwin Mayer (KWF)
         Maj Ronald Stelter (KWF)
         1Lt Richard Thomas (KWF)
         SSgt Bernard Ehle (KWF)
         A1C Frank Wilson (KWF)
         A1C Walter Bosnick (KWF)
         37 passengers (KWF)

A Hercules crashed into Cha Tien Shan Mountains after taking off from Taipei, Taiwan on a flight to Ching Chuan Kang. All the occupants, many of whom were C-130 crewmembers, were killed in the accident.

6 October 1970

F-8J 150289   VF-191, USN, USS *Oriskany*
         Lt John Bernard Martin (KIA)

A Crusader pilot was killed when his aircraft hit the ramp and disintegrated on an approach to the *Oriskany* following a BARCAP mission over the Gulf of Tonkin.

7 October 1970

O-2A 68-10969   21 TASS, 504 TASG, USAF, Cam Ranh Bay
         detached to Ban Me Thuot
         1Lt W W Galvani (survived)
         Lt Dau, VNAF (survived)

Another FAC was shot down during a mission in Cambodia on the 7th. 1Lt Galvani and his Vietnamese observer were supporting special forces on a mission near O Rang, just across the Cambodian border near Bu Krak. The O-2 was hit by ground fire as it was orbiting at 2,000 feet near the friendly forces. 1Lt Galvani crash-landed the aircraft and he and Lt Dau were rescued by a VNAF helicopter.

A-1H 52-139789   1 or 602 SOS, 56 SOW, USAF, Nakhon
         Phanom
         Maj John Vinson Williams (KIA)

A Skyraider crashed during a strike mission over Quang Tri province, South Vietnam when the aircraft's engine failed, probably due to a mechanical problem rather than enemy action. The pilot was killed.

8 October 1970

RF-4C 68-0610   14 TRS, 432 TRW, USAF, Udorn
         Capt William August Ott (KIA)
         Capt Donald Emerson Shay (KIA)

An RF-4C failed to return from a photographic reconnaissance mission at dusk over southern Laos on the 8th. The aircraft was thought to have been shot down as it was photographing roads on the Trail to the southwest of the DMZ. This aircraft was fitted with an AN/ARN-92 LORAN system that provided precision navigation and was linked to the aircraft's AN/APQ-102A sideways-looking radar.

11 October 1970

OV-10A 67-14696   23 TASS, 504 TASG, USAF, Nakhon Phanom
         Capt Robert W Brunson (KIA)

Another FAC was lost in Cambodia but, unlike other aircraft up to this point, this particular aircraft was shot down near the northern border with Thailand. Capt Brunson was shot down and killed near Samrong.

20 October 1970

F-8H   148643   VF-162, USN, USS *Shangri-La*
                  Lt H Kesler (survived)

A Crusader's engine failed shortly after the aircraft was launched from the *Shangri-La* on a CAP mission. The pilot ejected and was soon rescued. This was the ninth and final aircraft lost by the ship before it left the line on 5 November. All but one of the aircraft were lost to operational causes and only a single Skyhawk was shot down. Two pilots had been killed during the tour, which saw the ship spend a total of 120 days on the line. The *Shangri-La* returned to Mayport on 17 December and was decommissioned on 30 June 1971 but was not scrapped until 1988.

24 October 1970

EB-66C 55-0384   42 TEWS, 388 TFW, USAF, Korat
                  6 crew, names unknown (survived)

An EB-66C crashed accidentally during a combat mission but all six crewmembers escaped and were recovered safely.

25 October 1970

F-100D 56-3383   614 TFS, 35 TFW, USAF, Phan Rang
                  1 pilot, name unknown (survived)

An F-100 returning from a strike mission crashed short of Phan Rang's runway and was destroyed. The pilot survived the accident.

5 November 1970

O-2A   68-10965 20 TASS, 504 TASG, USAF, Da Nang
                  Lt Col Robert Keith Milbrath (KIA)
                  1Lt Peter Joseph Landry (KIA)

An O-2 FAC was shot down on the South Vietnamese coast 10 miles east of Hué during a visual reconnaissance patrol. Lt Col Milbrath and 1Lt Landry were killed when their aircraft was hit by small arms fire and crashed before either could escape from the aircraft.

13 November 1970

RF-4C   66-0420   14 TRS, 432 TRW, USAF, Udorn
                  Maj David Irvin Wright (KIA)
                  1Lt William Warner Bancroft (KIA)

Maj Wright and 1Lt Bancroft took off on a mission to obtain photographic coverage of four SAM sites in the southern provinces of North Vietnam. As the aircraft was making a photo run over one of the sites at 500 feet and 520 knots one of the escorting pilots saw it take hits from 23mm AAA. The Phantom exploded and crashed before either of the crew could escape. The aircraft crashed near Ha Tinh, about 35 miles south of Vinh. This was the first US aircraft to be lost over North Vietnam since an F-105G was shot down on 28 January 1970.

14 November 1970

RF-8G   145624   Detachment 34, VFP-63, USN, USS *Oriskany*
                  Lt Joseph Russell Klugg (KIA)

Shortly before it was due to finish it fifth war cruise, the *Oriskany* lost a Crusader pilot in a tragic accident. The aircraft was being launched on a photographic reconnaissance mission when the Crusader's starboard main undercarriage failed as it accelerated down the catapult. On leaving the deck the aircraft rolled to the right and crashed into the sea Lt Klugg ejected as the aircraft rolled off the ship but there was not enough time for the seat to separate and he was drowned. The ship finished it line duty on 22 November having lost four aircraft, only one of them due to enemy action, during 90 days on the line.

15 November 1970

F-105G 63-8311   6010 WWS, 388 TFW, USAF, Korat
                  2 crew, names unknown (survived)

A two-seat Thunderchief crashed in Thailand during an escort mission when its engine failed. Both the crew ejected safely and were recovered. This aircraft was nicknamed 'SAM Fighter' when it flew with the 354th TFS at Takhli as a F-105F earlier in the war.

The Son Tay Raid

One of the most daring special operations of the entire war took place on the night of the 20/21st of November. After six months of detailed planning and rehearsal, a task force took off from Udorn to attempt the rescue of American POWs from a prison camp at Son Tay, just 20 miles west of Hanoi. The plan called for an HH-3E to crash-land inside the prison compound carrying 13 troops of the assault force who would blast a hole in the prison perimeter wall for the main force assault troops who were carried by five HH-53Cs. The helicopters were supported by an HC-130P tanker, two Combat Talon C-130Es and five A-1E Skyraiders. A huge supporting force totalling 116 Air Force and Navy aircraft flew diversionary and supporting missions during the raid. Five Wild Weasels arrived in the Son Tay area before the task force to keep the nearby SAM sites busy as the helicopters approached. Ten F-4s flew a MiGCAP orbit over northeastern Laos while Navy F-4s and F-8s flew CAPs just off the North Vietnamese coastline. Intruders and Corsairs made numerous feints east of Hanoi to confuse the North Vietnamese defences into thinking that a major raid was building up in that area. The raid was brilliantly executed despite two of the helicopters making their initial landing at the wrong building. Unfortunately, when the assault troops stormed the prison camp they found it deserted except for a few guards, the American prisoners having been moved to another camp some time earlier. The HH-3E, 65-12785 call sign Banana 1 of the 40th ARRS, was destroyed by the assault troops before they left in the HH-53s.

Even if the Son Tay raid had failed to recover any American prisoners, it certainly shocked the North Vietnamese. By focussing world attention on the plight of the POWs and showing the North Vietnamese to what lengths the American armed forces were willing to go, the raid helped in the general improvement of conditions for the POWs. The outlying camps were closed and the prisoners concentrated in the two main camps in Hanoi where the men could live in groups rather than in solitary confinement. News of the raid also greatly enhanced the POW's morale.

20/21 November 1970

F-105G 62-4436   6010 WWS, 388 TFW, USAF, Korat
                  Maj Donald W Kilgus (survived)
                  Capt Clarence T Lowry (survived)

The Wild Weasels were successful in protecting the Son Tay task force as only 18 SAMs were fired from the eight nearby sites during the raid. However, two of the missiles found their mark and one Weasel limped back to base but the other had its fuel tank holed and the crew were later forced to eject near Pa Doung, about 10 miles south of the Plain of Jars in northern Laos. Two of the returning HH-53s heard the Wild Weasel crew's plight and diverted to attempt a rescue after taking on fuel from an HC-130P tanker. An Air America C-123 also heard the radio calls and arrived at the scene to drop flares for the helicopters. However, the helicopters could not locate the downed airmen and started to take ground fire so the HC-130P aircraft commander ordered the HH-53s to orbit with him away from the area until dawn. At first light four Skyraiders arrived and soon found the Weasel crew and put down suppressive fire as the two helicopters swept in to pick up Maj Kilgus and Capt Lowry thereby ensuring that the rescue force did not return to Udorn entirely empty-handed. Don Kilgus had flown three previous tours in Southeast Asia in O-1s and F-100s and was thought to have shot down a MiG-17 on 4 April 1965 although this remains an unconfirmed kill.

22 November 1970

O-1E   56-4189   22 TASS, 504 TASG, USAF, Binh Thuy
                  2 crew, names unknown (survived)

A Bird Dog crashed on an FAC mission in South Vietnam following an accidental control failure. This was the last aircraft lost by the 22nd TASS before it was inactivated and absorbed into the 19th TASS on 15 January 1971.

23 November 1970

OV-10A 67-14688 19 TASS, 504 TASG, USAF, Bien Hoa
                  Maj D L Brooks (survived)
                  SSgt G B Bellefeuille (survived)

Another Rustic FAC was shot down in Cambodia as it was controlling an air strike on enemy troops in a marshy area just west of Kampong Cham, an important provincial capital. The aircraft caught fire at 3,000 feet when it was hit by ground fire and both the crew ejected and were later rescued by helicopter.

27 November 1970

C-123K 55-4574   315 TAW, USAF, Phan Rang
                  1Lt Marvin S Arthington (KIA)
                  Maj Robert Lee Baker (KIA)
                  1Lt Frederick M Rader (KIA)
                  TSgt William Brandon O'Kieff (KIA)
                  Sgt Allen James Bodin (KIA)
                  A1C Frederick Richard Neff (KIA)
                  73 ARVN troops (KIA)

A Provider on a flight from Tan Son Nhut to Nha Trang crashed into a mountain in Khanh Hoa province while in thick cloud about 15 miles southwest of its destination. The aircraft crashed at an elevation of 4,600 feet, some 500 feet below the top of a ridge. All six crew and 73 ARVN troops on board died in the accident and the aircraft's burnt out wreckage was found nine days later.

29 November 1970

C-123K 54-0649   310 TAS, 315 TAW, USAF, Phan Rang
                  Capt Cecil Gerald Moyer (KIA)
                  Capt Norbert Albert Podhajsky (KIA)
                  1Lt James Francis Saxby (KIA)
                  SSgt Grayson Henry Newberry (KIA)
                  SSgt Harry Allen Watson (KIA)
                  About 39 US and ARVN troops (KIA)
                  2 personnel (survived)

In a repeat of the incident just two days previous, a Provider disappeared on a trooping flight. The aircraft crashed about 15 miles southwest of Cam Ranh Bay while on a troop deployment flight from Phan Rang. The aircraft took off from Phan Rang in low cloud, high winds and poor visibility and was last seen flying through a valley with high ridges on both sides. The aircraft crashed into high ground at 2,700 feet while in thick cloud. The wreckage was found five days later with only two men still alive. Eleven USAF personnel are recorded as being killed in the accident along with about 20 ARVN troops.

1 December 1970

F-4E   67-0329   366 TFW, USAF, Da Nang
                  Capt J R Robinson (survived)
                  1Lt D A Boulet (survived)

A Stormy FAC Phantom was lost during a night armed reconnaissance sortie over southern Laos. Capt Robinson was flying at 5,000 feet when his aircraft was hit by AAA near Tavouac. The aircraft burst into flames and the crew ejected and were later recovered.

3 December 1970

A-7E   157483   VA-25, USN, USS *Ranger*
                  1 pilot, name unknown (survived)

The A-7E Corsair was an unpdated model of the basic A-7 with greatly improved avionics, a 20mm M61-A1 cannon and an Allison TF41 engine based on the Rolls Royce Spey. The first A-7E squadrons arrived in Southeast Asia on board the USS *America* in May 1970. A new A-7E for VA-25 set off on a ferry flight from Cubi Point in the Philippines to the *Ranger*, which had started its sixth tour of the war on 21 November. However, the aircraft ran out of fuel before it could reach the ship and the aircraft had to be abandoned.

12 December 1970

F-100D 56-3132 352 TFS, 35 TFW, USAF, Phan Rang
1 pilot, name unknown (survived)

A Super Sabre was lost near Kampong Cham, 40 miles north of Phnom Penh, during a strike on a target in Cambodia. The pilot ejected and was later rescued.

B-57G 53-3931 13 TBS, 8 TFW, USAF, Ubon
Lt Col Paul R Pitt (survived)
Lt Col Ed Buschette (survived)

O-2A 67-21428 23 TASS, 504 TASG, USAF, Nakhon Phanom
1Lt Thomas Allen Duckett (KIA)
Maj Owen George Skinner (KIA)

Following operational trials in Southeast Asia in 1968 with modified B-57Bs in the night intruder role, 16 aircraft were modified to B-57G standard for the night interdiction role. Under the project name Tropic Moon III the aircraft were fitted with forward-looking radar, infra-red sensors, a low-light television and a laser rangefinder in a modified nose section. The aircraft could find and identify a target on the darkest of nights, mark it with the laser and drop up to four 500lb laser-guided bombs with a high degree of accuracy. Thus one of the oldest jet aircraft still in the USAF inventory became one of the most technologically advanced weapons in the war in Southeast Asia. The 13th TBS was reactivated at MacDill AFB, Florida on 8 February 1970 and deployed to Ubon to join the 8th TFW in September.

During the B-57G's 20-month tour of duty at Ubon only one aircraft was lost. The squadron commander, Lt Col Paul Pitt, and the squadron sensor officer, Lt Col Ed Buschette, were flying a night mission over the Ho Chi Minh Trail in southern Laos when their aircraft was hit and they had to eject near Ban Vangthon, 25 miles west of the DMZ. After spending an uncomfortable night in the jungle they were picked up by helicopter the next morning. The loss of the aircraft was initially put down to AAA but when an O-2A Nail FAC from Nakhon Phanom also failed to return from its mission in the same area, it was assumed that the two aircraft had probably collided in the darkness.

The following day the largely intact wreckage of the O-2A was spotted on the ground along with what was thought to be an empty parachute hanging from a tree. Radio contact was made with an unidentified individual and SAR beepers were heard for two days but as they were constantly moving a fix on their location could not be made. Like many other airmen brought down in Laos, Duckett and Skinner disappeared and were never seen again.

The 13th TBS left Ubon for Clark AFB in April 1972 having built up an impressive record of night operations on the Trail. Although fraught with technical difficulties and expensive to operate, the B-57G programme proved the effectiveness of its various sensors and laser technology. The advanced weapons and targeting systems of today's US military aircraft owe much to the pioneers of the Tropic Moon programme.

An A-7E Corsair of VA-27 is launched from the USS *Enterprise*. This type was a great improvement on earlier versions and was often used in the Iron Hand role. USN

15 December 1970

C-2A 155120 VRC-50, USN, Atsugi NAS, Japan
Lt Meril Olen McCoy (KWF)
Lt(jg) Anthony J Piersanti (KWF)
PO3 Clyde Chilton Owen (KWF)
AMS3 John Frank Szlapa (KWF)
5 passengers (KWF)

Fourteen months after VRC-50 lost one of its C-2 Greyhounds in the Gulf of Tonkin, the Squadron lost another aircraft in equally tragic circumstances. The aircraft had landed on board the USS *Ranger* to deliver passengers and cargo and was setting off on the next leg of its journey. The C-2A was catapulted off the *Ranger* but moments later it was seen to pitch up and stall before crashing into the sea. None of the five passengers and four crew survived the disaster, which occurred about 80 miles north-northeast of Da Nang. During an extensive search two bodies were recovered from the sea.

17 December 1970

F-4B 150649 VMFA-115, MAG-11, USMC, Da Nang
Col Albert C Pommerenk (survived)
Maj Noel E Douglas (survived)

VMFA-115 had returned to Vietnam on 24 August 1970 and was assigned as the only Phantom squadron at Da Nang. Indeed, after the last of the Chu Lai Phantoms left in September, VMFA-115 was the only Marine Corps Phantom unit in Southeast Asia and by December it was one of only three Marine Corps fixed-wing squadrons left in the war (the others being VMA-311 and VMO-2). On 17 December Col Pommerenk led a section of Phantoms to the Mu Gia Pass to hunt for trucks. When Col Pommerenk's aircraft was pulling up from its target it was hit in the port engine by AAA. The engine ran down and the crew heard a muffled explosion but the aircraft flew for a further 70 miles before the controls froze and the crew were forced to eject near Ban Bamran in southern Laos. They were both picked up by an Army helicopter. Albert Pommerenk eventually became a Brigadier General and commanded MAG-11 in 1971.

18 December 1970

OV-10A 68-3821 20 TASS, 504 TASG, USAF, Da Nang
Maj James Pattee Allenberg (KIA)

A Bronco suffered an accidental engine failure during an FAC mission and crashed off the coast near Da Nang killing the pilot.

19 December 1970

F-4D 66-7624 555 TFS, 432 TRW, USAF, Udorn
Capt D H Rotz (survived)
1Lt W K Louis (survived)

A Phantom crew were acting as a Laredo FAC for a strike in northern Laos. As the aircraft was flying about 10 miles south of the Plain of Jars it was hit in the cockpit by ground fire. Although injured, both crew ejected safely from their burning aircraft and were later rescued.

21 December 1970

RF-4C 68-0601 14 TRS, 432 TRW, USAF, Udorn
1Lt M M Nullis (survived)
Maj A F Rush (survived)

The 432nd TRW lost another aircraft on an FAC mission just two days later. An RF-4C Atlanta aircraft was sent on a mission to photograph roads on the Trail in southern Laos with an accompanying Falcon F-4D FAC. The RF-4C was turning at 4,500 feet over a road as it prepared to make a photo run when it was hit by anti-aircraft fire. The crew ejected a few miles from where the aircraft was hit and landed near Ban Kapay, 25 miles west of the DMZ. They were later rescued by a USAF SAR helicopter. The loss of this aircraft prompted major strikes on air defences in the Ban Karai and Mu Gia passes.

24 December 1970

A-1E 52-139598 1 SOS, 56 SOW, USAF, Nakhon Phanom
Maj Albro Lynn Lundy (KIA)

Maj Lundy and another A-1 pilot volunteered to escort two Air America helicopters on a medevac mission in northern Laos. The mission was to evacuate badly wounded troops from the heavily defended Ban Ban Valley and it was considered so dangerous that volunteers were called for rather than assigned. On the return journey from Ban Ban Maj Lundy reported that his engine was backfiring (possibly as a result of small arms fire) and that he had to eject. Other pilots saw an ejection but one of the pilots noticed that the parachute was empty with straps and harness dangling as it descended to the ground about five miles east of the town of Ban Ban. It was thought that Maj Lundy had slipped from his harness, which may not have been properly fastened. He was declared 'Dead – body not recovered' two days later. Maj Lundy was due to return to the USA after Christmas and then serve as an air attaché in Europe. In 1991 a photograph emerged from Laos purporting to show May Lundy in captivity, however, as with so many reports and artefacts that have emerged since the war, this has not been substantiated or confirmed even thought the photograph was said to have been accompanied by fingerprints.

28 December 1970

OV-10A 67-14661 20 TASS, 504 TASG, USAF, Da Nang
Capt James Leonard Smith (KIA)
SSgt Roger Lynn Teeter, US Army (KIA)

A Covey FAC Bronco was lost during a Steel Tiger reconnaissance patrol over southern Laos in support of a MACVSOG reconnaissance team. Capt Smith's aircraft was thought to have been shot down by AAA near Ban Bamran just west of the DMZ and he and his observer, a Special Forces sergeant, were killed in the crash.

A-7E 157509 VA-25, USN, USS *Ranger*
Lt Cdr Robert W Castle (survived)

The first of the new A-7Es to be lost in combat was an aircraft on a night-time Steel Tiger mission in southern Laos. Lt Cdr Castle was pulling up from a bombing run when he noticed that his oil quantity gauge was reading low. He jettisoned the remainder of his bombs and headed towards Nakhon Phanom, his emergency diversion airfield. During the flight the oil pressure began to drop and the engine started to vibrate and the wingman reported flames coming from the Corsair's tailpipe. Lt Cdr Castle secured the engine at 13,000 feet and glided for eight minutes down to 5,000 feet when he ejected and landed safely about 16 miles southeast of Nakhon Phanom. A SAR team was put together consisting of an HH-43 of Detachment 9 of the 38th ARRS, flown by Capt Bobby Lay, and four A-1 Sandies, while an OV-10 Nail FAC that had been controlling the air strike also assisted. The HH-43 was confined primarily to base rescue at this stage of the war but it was the only available helicopter on this occasion. Lt Cdr Castle was picked up by the HH-43 after spending just 19 minutes on the ground. The cause of the loss could not be positively attributed to enemy action and may well have been caused by a mechanical failure.

Chapter Eight

1971

A Much Reduced Presence

2 January 1971

F-4E   67-0359   469 TFS, 388 TFW, USAF, Korat
                   Capt H D Wier (survived)
                   1Lt R K Brown (survived)

The first aircraft lost in the New Year was a Tiger FAC Phantom that was shot down while controlling a strike on the northern edge of the Plain of Jars. The aircraft was damaged by AAA as it dived on a group of trucks. Capt Wier headed southeast but he and his navigator had to eject just west of the Ban Ban Valley and were rescued by a USAF helicopter.

3 January 1971

F-4E   66-0380   34 TFS, 388 TFW, USAF, Korat
                   Maj James Henry Ayres (KIA)
                   Capt Charles Wayne Stratton (KIA)

A pair of Phantoms was sent on a night-time strike mission on enemy positions in southern Laos. As the leading aircraft made its first pass it was hit by AAA and crashed near the village of Ban Namalou, five miles southeast of Ban Muangsen. There was no indication that either of the crew had been able to escape.

5 January 1971

F-4J   155577   VF-21, USN, USS *Ranger*
                  Lt L Rinne (survived)
                  Lt(jg) Carleton Pierce Miller (KIA)

A Phantom was returning to the *Ranger* at about 4:00 am after a night BARCAP mission and was set up for a GCA landing. About a mile from the carrier the crew took over the approach and flew it visually. The aircraft touched down too far down the deck and missed the arrester wires. As the aircraft left the deck the crew ejected and witnesses saw two parachutes land in the sea. Lt Rinne, the pilot, was picked out of the water by one of the *Ranger*'s SH-3G Seaking helicopters. However, there was no sign of Lt Miller, who was presumed to have drowned.

8 January 1971

A-6C   155647   VA-145, USN, USS *Ranger*
                  Cdr Keith Royal Wilson Curry (KIA)
                  Lt Cdr Gerald L Smith (survived)

The *Ranger* lost another aircraft and its pilot in an accident on the 8th. An Intruder crashed into the sea 400 yards in front of the carrier seconds after launch and only one of the crew was found and rescued. The A-6C TRIM (Trails, Roads, Interdiction, Multisensor) was a specialised version of the Intruder designed for the interdiction role over the Ho Chi Minh Trail. The aircraft was fitted with a variety of sensors including LLTV and FLIR which were supposed to significantly enhance the aircraft's ability to spot and target traffic on the Trail at night and in bad weather. Only 12 aircraft were produced, modified from basic A-6As, and they were used by VA-35 and VA-165 in addition to VA-145. On their last deployment in 1972 the A-6Cs were fitted with a laser target designator to mark targets for Paveway laser-guided bombs.

13 January 1971

C-7B   62-12584   483 TAW, USAF, Cam Ranh Bay
                    4 crew, names unknown (survived)

A Caribou crashed in South Vietnam due to pilot error during a cargo flight. This was the last of 20 Caribou to be destroyed in Southeast Asia while under USAF control. At least 38 C-7s from the

483rd TAW were handed over to the VNAF in 1972 prior to the American withdrawal from South Vietnam. Six VNAF Caribous were flown to Thailand when South Vietnam fell in 1975 but about 30 other aircraft were captured by the NVA as the C-7s had not been flown for some time before the final defeat and were in storage.

17 January 1971

F-4E   66-0288   421 TFS, 366 TFW, USAF, Da Nang
                   Maj Robert Henry Mirrer (KIA)
                   Maj J D Siderius (survived)

A flight of Phantoms was sent to bomb an NVA storage area near Ban Kaloung in southern Laos on the 17th. Maj Mirrer's aircraft was struck by AAA as it dived on the target from 7,000 feet. He turned his burning aircraft to the east and eventually crossed the coast. The crew ejected over the sea about 15 miles east of Da Nang but although Maj Siderius was found and rescued by a USAF helicopter, Maj Mirrer could not be located. In one document the crew are listed as being members of the 4th rather than the 421st TFS.

20 January 1971

F-4E   67-0267   366 TFW, USAF, Da Nang
                   Capt D A Warner (survived)
                   Maj H E Kiefer (survived)

A Phantom was hit by small arms fire seconds after it took off from Da Nang and was climbing through 1,000 feet. One of the aircraft's engines caught fire so Capt Warner turned the Phantom out over the sea and he and Maj Kiefer ejected a few miles off the coast. They were both picked up safely by a USAF helicopter.

26 January 1971

A-4F   154980   VA-164, USN, USS *Hancock*
                  1 pilot, name unknown (survived)

The *Hancock* arrived back on the line on 20 November 1970 for its sixth tour of duty of the war. Its first aircraft loss was a Skyhawk that crashed soon after being launched on a strike mission. The pilot ejected and was rescued.

27 January 1971

F-100D   56-3197   352 TFS, 35 TFW, USAF, Phan Rang
                     Capt John Mautz Neill (KIA)

A flight of F-100s was sent to bomb a mortar position in Cambodia. As Capt Neill pulled up through 1,000 feet from his second pass over the target his aircraft by ground fire and burst into flames. The aircraft crashed close to the target and the pilot was killed.

28 January 1971

OV-10A   67-14638   23 TASS, 504 TASG, USAF, Nakhon
                      Phanom detached to Ubon
                      Maj Harold Benton Lineberger (KIA)

Maj Lineberger was controlling an air strike on Route 13 about 20 miles northeast of the town of Kratie in Cambodia when he was shot down. Route 13 was the main road running from Saigon through Cambodia and into Laos and was being used by the North Vietnamese to bring men and supplies into South Vietnam. Maj Lineberger had destroyed several motorised sampans in the area in the two days before he was shot down and had seen

an abandoned truck on Route 13. He was returning to destroy the truck when his aircraft was hit by ground fire and crashed. A search was conducted for several days but there was no sign of the pilot who probably died when his aircraft crashed.

31 January 1971

O-2A   68-10841   21 TASS, 504 TASG, USAF, Cam Ranh Bay
                    1Lt J Hoenninger (survived)
                    1Lt F R Platt (survived)

An air strike was called to deal with North Vietnamese troops who were attacking friendly forces about 35 miles south of Pleiku during the night of the 31st. 1Lt Hoenninger and 1Lt Platt were controlling the air strike from their O-2 when it was hit by ground fire. The pilot crash-landed the aircraft in the dark and the crew were later rescued by an Army helicopter.

1 February 1971

A-37B   69-6356   8 SOS, 35 TFW, USAF, Bien Hoa
                    1Lt James Craig Harris (KIA)

A Dragonfly was shot down during a strike on NVA positions just inside Cambodia, about 40 miles southwest of Pleiku. The pilot apparently did not eject before the aircraft crashed close to the target.

3 February 1971

F-4D   66-8777   25 TFS, 8 TFW, USAF, Ubon
                   Lt Col Robert Lauren Standerwick (KIA)
                   Maj Norbert Anthony Gotner (POW)

A Phantom was dropping sensors over the Ho Ch Minh Trail when it was shot down by AAA near Ban Kantaloung about 10 miles southwest of the Ban Karai Pass. Both the crew ejected and were in voice contact with each other and with other aircraft. A rescue attempt could not be made straight away due to approaching darkness and bad weather. Later Lt Col Standerwick was heard to say that he had been shot and was being surrounded by enemy troops. Both men were listed as missing in action but Maj Gotner had been captured and was sent to the camps in North Vietnam. Like other men captured in Laos and sent to North Vietnam he was kept apart from prisoners captured in North and South Vietnam for much of the time. He was the first airman to arrive in Hanoi as a prisoner since Lt Bedinger in November 1969. Lt Col Standerwick, who had been a SAC pilot flying EC-135 Looking Glass airborne command post aircraft, did not return from Southeast Asia and was declared dead by the USAF on 20 June 1980. At some stage during its time at Ubon 66-8777 was named 'Miss Magic'.

F-4D   66-0263   13 TFS or 555 TFS, 432 TRW, USAF, Udorn
                   Capt Thomas A Mravak (KIA)
                   1Lt Lennart G Langhorne (KIA)

Another Phantom was lost on the 3rd when it crashed as it was landing at Udorn following a strike mission in Laos. Both the crew were killed in the crash.

5 February 1971

F-8J   149197   VF-211, USN, USS *Hancock*
                  Lt J Bodanske (survived)

A Crusader was destroyed in a ramp strike accident as it returned to the *Hancock* from a combat air patrol on the 5th. The pilot survived the accident.

8 February 1971

QU-22B 69-7705 56 SOW, USAF, Nakhon Phanom
Maj Lennox Lee Ratcliff (KIA)

A QU-22B pilot was killed when his aircraft's engine failed during a surveillance flight over Laos as part of the Igloo White programme.

10 February 1971

UC-123K 56-4373 310 TAS, 315 TAW, USAF, Phan Rang
detached to Tan Son Nhut
1Lt Charles Milton Deas (KIA)
1Lt Richard William O'Keefe (KIA)
Lt Col Daniel H Harrison Tate (KIA)
MSgt Donald Louis Dunn (KIA)
TSgt Clyde Wendell Hanson (KIA)

The Ranch Hand defoliation programme was drawing to a close and the last herbicide mission had been flown in South Vietnam on 7 January. The 12th ACS had been inactivated on 31 July 1970 and the Ranch Hand crews had been posted to A Flight of the 310th TAS. On 28 January the six Providers and the crews of A Flight were absorbed into the rest of the Squadron to take up conventional transport duties. However two aircraft were retained for insecticide spraying in an attempt to combat the mosquitoes that thrived in the swampy regions of South Vietnam. On 10 February one of the two insecticide sprayers crashed at Phan Rang killing all five crew on board. The flight was 1Lt Deas's last mission before returning to the USA and he had asked several squadron members to take photographs of his aircraft as he made low passes over the airfield. No evidence of damage from enemy action was found and the crash was determined to have been caused by pilot error. Insecticide spraying continued for another year until the last Ranch Hand aircraft left Vietnam in February 1972.

11 February 1971

F-4D 66-7473 12 TFW, USAF, Phu Cat
Capt M W Ford (survived)
1Lt Robert Arthur Eisenbeisz (KIA)

A Phantom was shot down in South Vietnam as it was providing close air support to friendly ground forces near Ba Long, 12 miles southwest of Quang Tri. Capt Ford was pulling up from his third attack on enemy troops when his aircraft was hit by automatic weapons fire. Capt Ford ejected and was later recovered by the ground troops he had been supporting but 1Lt Eisenbeisz apparently did not eject and was killed.

F-100D 55-2901 35 TFW, USAF, Phan Rang
Capt Michael Donald McGovern (KIA)

A Super Sabre was destroyed in a landing accident at Pleiku following a strike mission. The crash was attributed to pilot error.

16 February 1971

F-4D 66-8787 25 TFS, 8 TFW, USAF, Ubon
Lt Col W R Cox (survived)
Maj W C Allen (survived)

Two Wolfpack Phantoms were shot down on separate Steel Tiger missions in southern Laos on the 16th. Lt Col Cox and Maj Allen were bombing a road on the Trail near Ban Son, just west of the Ban Karai Pass, when their aircraft was hit by AAA. One of the engines caught fire and had to be shut down. As they headed west towards Thailand the aircraft became uncontrollable and the crew ejected about 40 miles east of Nakhon Phanom and were rescued by a USAF helicopter. Phantom 66-8787 was painted as 'Dragon Wagon', the 25th TFS being named the Assam Dragons.

F-4D 66-8750 497 TFS, 8 TFW, USAF, Ubon
Maj Ralph Nathan Pattillo (KIA)
Capt Charles Lee Hoskins (KIA)

The second Ubon Phantom to be lost on the 16th was on a night mission to attack a couple of 37mm gun positions that had been spotted on the Trail. The aircraft was shot down in flames by ground fire near Ban Thakkapang, 20 miles north of Muang Fangdeng. An air search was initiated but nothing was found and the area was too heavily defended to insert a ground team.

19 February 1971

O-2A 68-11001 20 TASS, 504 TASG, USAF, Da Nang
1Lt James Larry Hull (KIA)
Sgt William Matthew Fernandez, US Army (KIA)

A Covey FAC crew was killed on the 19th during a search for an Army helicopter that was lost in southern Laos. UH-1H 68-15255 of the 101st Airborne Division had been attempting to recover a Special Forces reconnaissance team in the A Shau Valley on the 18th when it was shot down and crashed killing all on board. The O-2 crashed in the jungle near Ban Pelou, some 55 miles west of Da Nang and neither of the occupants survived. The next day another UH-1 airlifted in a Special Forces team that recovered the body of Sgt Fernandez but 1Lt 'Woodstock' Hull's body was trapped in the wreckage and could not be recovered.

20 February 1971

O-1F 57-2872 21 TASS, 504 TASG, USAF, Cam Ranh Bay
1Lt P Peacock (survived)

1Lt Peacock was ferrying a Bird Dog from one airfield to another when he was shot down near Plei Djereng, 20 miles west of Pleiku. He survived a crash-landing and was subsequently rescued by a USAF SAR helicopter.

21 February 1971

C-130B 61-2642 463 TAW, USAF, Clark

In the early hours of the 21st a C-130 was destroyed and three more aircraft damaged during a Viet Cong rocket attack on Da Nang. Six rounds were fired at the base and only one man was wounded. Hercules 61-2642 had just had its load of munitions unloaded as two of its engines required maintenance when it was hit by a 122mm rocket. The port wing was blown off outboard of the engines and the aircraft was gutted by fire. Four other aircraft were damaged in the attack but there were no serious casualties. The loss of a single Hercules had little effect on the huge airlift effort in support of the Lam Son 719 offensive in the northern provinces that was going on at this time.

24 February 1971

A-6A 156994 VA-145, USN, USS *Ranger*
Lt Cdr W Galbraith (survived)
Lt D D Waters (survived)

An Intruder crashed moments after being launched on a strike mission. The crew ejected and were soon picked up.

25 February 1971

F-4D 66-8691 366 TFW, USAF, Da Nang
Maj Richard Keith Somers (KIA)
Capt J S Talley (survived)

Again, two Phantoms were shot down during two unrelated Steel Tiger missions in southern Laos. Maj Somers was bombing enemy troops in contact with friendly forces near Ban Tampanko, 17 miles southwest of Khe Sanh. The aircraft was hit in the cockpit at 1,000 feet on its fourth pass. Maj Somers may have been wounded or his ejection seat damaged, as he did not follow Capt Talley out of the aircraft. The WSO was subsequently rescued by a USAF helicopter.

F-4D 65-0637 12 TFW, USAF, Phu Cat
Capt Hedditch (survived)
1Lt T McLaughlin (survived)

A total of 20 C-7 Caribous were lost by the USAF in Southeast Asia. The aircraft's rough field capability was legendary but the 38 C-7s that were passed onto the VNAF appear to have been used only infrequently before the final collapse. USAF

The second Phantom lost on this day was taking part in a night mission in the same area. Capt Hedditch was making his third pass on a target near Ban Tampanko when his aircraft was struck by ground fire. In this instance both the crew ejected successfully and were rescued by a USAF helicopter.

26 February 1971

F-4D   66-8774   8 TFW, USAF, Ubon
            Capt Rodney D Collins (KIA)
            1 crew, name unknown (survived)

February had been a bad month for the USAF's accident record in Southeast Asia. A total of 10 men were killed in five accidents during the month, two more than had been killed due to enemy action. The last USAF aircraft lost in an accident was a Phantom that crashed in Thailand while on an escort mission. One of the crew survived but the other was killed.

27 February 1971

A-7E   157458   VA-195, USN, USS Kitty Hawk
            1 pilot, name unknown (survived)

A Corsair had to be abandoned during a strike mission when the engine flamed out and the pilot was unable to get a relight. Amazingly, this was the only aircraft lost by the Kitty Hawk during her fifth tour of duty in Southeast Asia. The ship took up her position on the line on 8 December 1970 and departed for the USA on 23 June after spending a total of 138 days on operations.

F-4J   155884   VF-21, USN, USS Ranger
            Lt(jg) Larry Gene Lewis (KWF)
            Lt(jg) James Carroll (survived)

A Phantom suffered an engine failure as it was being catapulted off the Ranger on a training flight at night. One of the afterburners was seen to go out as the aircraft was hurtling down the deck and as the Phantom started to descend towards the water the pilot initiated a command ejection. Both seats were seen to fire but the Ranger's helicopter could only find Lt Carroll despite a search that continued throughout the night and all next day. This was the last of eight aircraft lost by the Ranger during 123 days spent on the line on her sixth tour in Southeast Asia. Three Corsairs had been lost to enemy action with one pilot missing but another three airmen were killed in accidents during the tour.

6 March 1971

A-1H   52-139734   1 SOS, 56 SOW, USAF, Nakhon Phanom
            1Lt C L Tipton (survived)

1Lt Tipton was taking part in a SAR mission about 15 miles west of Khe Sanh when he was shot down. The Skyraiders were attacking enemy forces in the vicinity and it was during his ninth pass that 1Lt Tipton was eventually shot down by small arms fire as he flew just above the treetops. The Skyraider's starboard wing caught fire and the pilot ejected and was soon picked up by a USAF SAR helicopter.

10 March 1971

EB-66C   55-0389   42 TEWS, 388 TFW, USAF, Korat
            4 crew, names unknown (survived)

An EB-66 crashed on take off from Korat due to a control failure. This aircraft was the last of 36 EB-66C models to be built and had first flown in 1956.

11 March 1971

F-100D   56-3181   35 TFW, USAF, Phan Rang
            1 pilot, name unknown (survived)

The engine of a Super Sabre caught fire during a combat mission and the pilot was forced to abandon the aircraft. The cause of the engine problem was thought to have been a mechanical failure rather than combat damage.

12 March 1971

F-100D   56-3415   614 TFS, 35 TFW, USAF, Phan Rang
            1Lt Clive Garth Jeffs (KIA)

A flight of Super Sabres was despatched from Phan Rang to attack an enemy position in Khang Hoa province of South Vietnam. One of the aircraft was shot down in flames about 40 miles northwest of Nha Trang and its pilot was posted missing. Other aircraft nearby heard a good beeper signal after 1Lt Jeffs ejected but could not make voice contact with him. A 10-day search failed to find any trace of the pilot. The crash site of an F-100 was discovered in 1974 and investigated by the JTF-FA in 1990 but so far there is no new information on the fate of 1Lt Jeffs. 56-3415 also saw service with the 31st TFW at Tuy Hoa during its time in Vietnam.

13 March 1971

A-7E   157589   VA-113, USN, USS Ranger
            Lt Barton Sheldon Creed (KIA)

The reduced role of TF 77 at this period of the war is indicated by the fact that it had been nearly three months since a US Navy aircraft had been lost in action in Southeast Asia. On 13 March the Ranger lost a Corsair and its pilot during a Steel Tiger strike. Lt Creed was strafing a truck on a road near Ban Sung, 30 miles southwest of the A Shau Valley, when his aircraft was hit by 23mm AAA. The Corsair's starboard wing separated at the wingfold joint and Lt Creed ejected at about 2,000 feet. He was severely injured with a broken leg and a broken arm but was in voice contact with his wingman and rescue forces. An FAC located Lt Creed and attempted to lure enemy troops away by firing marker rockets at a false location. Three attempts were made to rescue the pilot over the next two days but heavy ground fire prevented the rescue and wounded some of the helicopter crew. Two of the helicopters were badly damaged by small arms fire and had to force-land on their way back to base. At night a pararescueman was lowered on a jungle penetrator and spent some time looking for Lt Creed but did not find him. Lt Creed is presumed to have either died of his injuries in the jungle or been killed by his captors.

16 March 1971

O-2A   68-6860   20 TASS, 504 TASG, USAF, Da Nang
            1Lt Stephen Russell Scrivener (KIA)
            Capt Douglas Milton Seeley (KIA)

An O-2 on an FAC mission over the Trail in southern Laos was hit by by 37mm anti-aircraft fire near the village of Ban Bamran, just west of the DMZ. Both the crew were killed when the aircraft crashed.

F-8J   150294   VF-211, USN, USS Hancock
            Lt R Amber (survived)

The Crusader was always regarded as a 'hot ship' and appears to have been much more prone to ramp strikes than any other Navy aircraft of its generation. During the war 13 Crusaders were lost in ramp strike accidents compared to just two for all other aircraft types (both A-4s). VF-211 lost an aircraft on 16 March when it hit the ramp of the USS Hancock after returning from a BARCAP mission. The Hancock left the line on 3 May after 100 days of operations during which it lost just two Crusaders and a Skyhawk with no fatalities.

19 March 1971

C-123K   54-0650   19 TAS, 315 TAW, USAF, Phan Rang
            4 crew, names unknown (survived)

A Provider caught fire after the nose gear oleo strut collapsed on landing at an airstrip at Thein Ngon in South Vietnam. The crew escaped without injury. This was the last of 54 C-123 Providers to be lost by the USAF in Southeast Asia, 20 of them due to enemy action. In June 1972 the last Air Force Providers in Southeast Asia were handed over to the VNAF, which operated three squadrons until their replacement by C-130s in 1973. The rugged and reliable C-123, along with the smaller C-7, performed much of the resupply of Special Forces camps and other units at remote locations throughout South Vietnam. Its rough field capability enabled it to operate from the uneven runway surfaces often found at the up-country strips. Despite its age, the aircraft was one of the mainstays of the ground war in Southeast Asia.

22 March 1971

F-4D   '67-0655'   13 TFS, 432 TRW, USAF, Udorn
            Maj R D Priest (survived)
            Maj R L Cubberly (survived)

A flight of Phantoms was flying an escort mission for a reconnaissance aircraft over the southern provinces of North Vietnam when one of the aircraft was lost. The formation was about 10 miles southwest of Dong Hoi when a SAM was launched at the aircraft. Maj Priest's aircraft, a Falcon fast FAC Phantom, was hit by the missile and burst into flames. The crew ejected immediately and evaded capture until they could be rescued by a USAF SAR helicopter. This was the first US aircraft to be lost to an SA-2 since October 1968. The serial quoted for this aircraft is incorrect, as 67-0655 is the serial of a Minuteman ICBM.

F-100D   56-3180   614 TFS, 35 TFW, USAF, Phan Rang
            Capt Peter Gibney Moriarty (KIA)

Sightings of tanks in southern Laos were becoming a more regular occurrence as the NVA became bolder. However, when caught in the open tanks became priority targets and every effort was made to destroy them wherever they were found. A flight of F-100s was sent on a raid to attack a group of four tanks that had been seen just inside Laos, about 10 miles to the west of Khe Sanh. Capt Moriarty was making his first pass when his aircraft was hit by 12.5mm ground fire and burst into flames. The aircraft crashed before the pilot could eject.

24 March 1971

OV-10A   67-14693   20 TASS, 504 TASG, USAF, Da Nang
            1Lt Jack M Butcher (POW)

During a Covey FAC mission an OV-10 was shot down by AAA about five miles east of Ban Talan in southern Laos. As Lt Butcher was searching for enemy activity at a ford on the Trail a 37mm anti-aircraft shell hit the nose of his Bronco causing him shrapnel injuries. 1Lt Butcher ejected immediately, blacked out from pain and came to on the ground but was quickly captured by North Vietnamese troops. He was taken to a large base camp in the jungle and five days later he escaped from his guards but was recaptured a few hours later. Following interrogation and a threatened execution Butcher and his armed guards set off on the long walk to Hanoi on 4 May. Five days later he slipped away from his guards again and escaped into the jungle. This time he was free for 10 days during which time the JPRC in Saigon, using information gained from enemy radio transmissions, mounted several search missions and even inserted a Bright Light team into the area where Butcher was thought to be. Unfortunately, Jack Butcher was recaptured on May 19 when he stumbled into a Laotian village near Tchepone. He eventually arrived in Hanoi in June and was imprisoned with the other men who had been captured in Laos. Jack Butcher had arrived at Da Nang in February and was only on his eleventh mission when he was shot down but he became one of the fortunate few to survive being captured in Laos. He was released from captivity on 28 March 1973.

26 March 1971

A-37B   69-6351   8 SOS, 35 TFW, USAF, Bien Hoa
            1Lt Dean Wilbur Krueger (KIA)

A Dragonfly was lost in Cambodia during an air strike on enemy troops who were entrenched in a series of bunkers about 17 miles northwest of Kampong Cham. The aircraft was dropping napalm from 100 feet when it was hit by ground fire and crashed, killing the pilot.

4 April 1971

F-100D   56-3120   352 TFS, 35 TFW, USAF, Phan Rang
            1Lt Joseph Stanley Smith (KIA)

Another aircraft was lost in Cambodia when a flight of Super Sabres attacked a storage area about 30 miles north of Kampong Cham. 1Lt Smith was strafing the target on his fifth pass when ground fire hit the aircraft's port wing. The aircraft crashed before the pilot could eject. This was the twentieth US fixed-wing aircraft lost in Cambodia since the incursion started in May 1970.

6 April 1971

A-1J 52-142077 1 SOS, 56 SOW, USAF, Nakhon Phanom
Capt J W Stewart (survived)

A Skyraider was lost during an escort mission in the Barrel Roll area of northern Laos. Capt Stewart was flying near Ban Nam, 30 miles northwest of the Nam Ngum Reservoir, when his aircraft was hit by ground fire forcing him to eject. An Air America helicopter later rescued him. Since December 1970 when the 602nd SOS deactivated, the 1st SOS was the last remaining USAF A-1 Skyraider squadron left in Southeast Asia. Most of the aircraft left behind by departing squadrons were passed on to the VNAF.

11 April 1971

F-100D 56-2937 614 TFS, 35 TFW, USAF, Phan Rang
Capt William Carl Buerk (KIA)

A flight of F-100s was flying a close air support mission a few miles to the southwest of Dak To when one of the aircraft was shot down. Capt Buerk was making his first pass on a target when he was shot down and killed before he could escape from his aircraft.

13 April 1971

F-100D 55-3749 614 TFS, 35 TFW, USAF, Phan Rang
1 pilot, name unknown (survived)

Another 614th TFS aircraft from Phan Rang was lost during a raid in Cambodia. The aircraft was hit by 37mm AAA as it was pulling up from an attack and crashed just inside Cambodia, about 25 miles west of Katum, after the pilot ejected.

15 April 1971

F-100D 56-2955 352 TFS, 35 TFW, USAF, Phan Rang
Capt J C Hauck (survived)

The 35th TFW was going through a rough patch during April 1971. The Wing lost its fourth aircraft of the month during a strike on suspected enemy positions four miles southwest of Ben Het, near Dak To. Capt Hauck's aircraft was pulling up from its second pass when it was hit by small arms fire at 1,000 feet. Capt Hauck headed southeast and ejected close to Kontum and was recovered by an Army unit.

17 April 1971

A-7E 157511 VA-113, USN, USS Ranger
Lt R E Forman (survived)

As dusk began to darken the skies of southern Laos a section of Corsairs from the Ranger found a number of trucks on a road near the village of Ding, 35 miles north of Muang Fangdeng. Lt Forman's aircraft was hit in the lower fuselage by 23mm AAA during his bombing run. He ejected safely a few miles from the road and was rescued the next day by a helicopter.

21 April 1971

F-4D 66-7717 497 TFS, 8 TFW, USAF, Ubon
Capt Robert S Dotson (survived)
Capt B D Smith (survived)

A Wolf FAC Phantom was shot down as it was directing a mission in southern Laos. Both the crew ejected safely and were subsequently recovered. Capt Dotson had survived being shot down on 18 February 1970 during a Barrel Roll mission in northern Laos.

OV-10A 67-14645 504 TASG, USAF, base ..?
Maj William Esley Wood (KWF)
Maj Herbert Miller (KWF)

The crew of an OV-10 Bronco died in an accident in South Vietnam during a non-operational flight on the 21st.

24 April 1971

F-4D 66-7616 unit ..?, USAF, base ..?
Capt Jeffrey Charles Lemon (KIA)
1Lt Walter Harrison Sigafoos (KIA)

A Phantom was lost during a night-time Steel Tiger mission on the 24th. Capt Lemon and 1Lt Sigafoos were posted missing when their aircraft went down in a hilly region about 30 miles east of Saravan. The aircraft was attacking a truck and was either shot down or flew into the ground by accident. Other aircrew in the area saw a huge explosion but no trace of the aircraft or its crew was found during the subsequent search of the area.

26 April 1971

O-2A 67-21388 23 TASS, 504 TASG, USAF, Nakhon Phanom
1Lt G L Mellor (survived)
1Lt G J Fleming (survived)

In a worrying development in the air war over southern Laos, an O-2 Nail FAC was shot down by a SAM about 30 miles east of Nakhon Phanom. The aircraft was flying at 80 knots at 7,000 feet and was damaged by a huge explosion on its starboard side forcing the crew to bail out. They both landed safely and were later rescued. The existence of the SAM site had only been confirmed a few weeks earlier.

28 April 1971

OV-10A 155450 H&MS-11, MAG-11, USMC, Da Nang
1Lt David Warren Windsor (KIA)
CWO2 Gerald Calvin Seybold (KIA)

When VMO-2 departed from Da Nang on 31 March it passed on some of its OV-10s to H&MS-11. This squadron then became the last remaining Marine Corps fixed-wing unit in Southeast Asia until it too left on 1 June. The unit flew a few FAC missions before it departed and on one of these missions it lost an aircraft and its crew. The aircraft was marking a small harbour for attack about eight miles northwest of Da Nang when it was shot down by small arms fire. CWO2 Seybold was in the Marine Corps intelligence branch. This was the only Marine Corps fixed-wing aircraft lost in Southeast Asia in 1971 and the last to be lost until the return of several Marine Corps squadrons in April 1972. On 8 May 1971 a VMCJ-1 EA-6A flew what was thought to be the last Marine Corps fixed-wing combat sortie in Southeast Asia before the few remaining units left the theatre. Few could have guessed that in less than a year two Marine Aviation Groups would return to fight in South Vietnam once again.

F-100D 55-3550 615 TFS, 35 TFW, USAF, Phan Rang
1Lt Benjamin Gaines Lang (KIA)

A flight of F-100s was scrambled from Phan Rang to bomb a VC position in South Vietnam on the night of the 28th. As the aircraft were returning to the airfield, one of the Super Sabres was hit by ground fire near Ap Vinh Hoa on the coast about 20 miles southwest of Phan Rang. 1Lt Lang was killed when the aircraft crashed. This aircraft was the last of 242 F-100 Super Sabres to be lost during the wars in Southeast Asia. The F-100 had been the workhorse of the air war in South Vietnam since the escalation of the conflict in 1965 and had also flown missions over North Vietnam, Laos and Cambodia. The peak years for losses were 1968 and 1969 with a total of 116 aircraft lost. According to USAF figures the F-100 flew 360,283 combat sorties during the war.

6 May 1971

F-4E 67-0335 4 TFS, 366 TFW, USAF, Da Nang
Maj Arthur S Blissett (survived)
Capt J E Seaton (survived)

A flight of Phantoms was sent on a raid on a large number of sampans that had been spotted on a tributary of the Tonle Kong River 10 miles southwest of Muang Fandeng in the southern tip of Laos. During the attack one of the aircraft was shot down but the crew was later rescued. This was the only fixed-wing aircraft lost to enemy action during the month. Maj Blissett was shot down and survived again on 17 December.

20 May 1971

O-2A 67-21389 20 TASS, 504 TASG, USAF, Da Nang
2 crew, names unknown (survived)

An O-2 crashed short of the runway after a reconnaissance flight on the 20th and was damaged beyond repair.

4 June 1971

OV-10A 67-14692 20 TASS, 504 TASG, USAF, Da Nang
2 crew, names unknown (survived)

A Covey FAC was shot down while on a mission in southern Laos. The aircraft was damaged by ground fire about 15 miles northeast of Muang Fangdeng and crashed near the village of Ban Thakkapang, a few miles to the north.

11 June 1971

E-2B 151719 VAW-115, USN, USS Midway
5 crew, names unknown (KWF)

After an absence of six years during which it underwent a major reconstruction at San Francisco Navy Yard, the USS Midway returned to the South China Sea and took up her position on the line on 18 May. Within a month tragedy had struck the ship when one of her E-2B Hawkeye AEW aircraft disappeared during a ferry flight. The names of the crew are not recorded on the Vietnam Wall in Washington, DC as the Midway was taking a break from operations in the war zone and therefore the men were technically not eligible for inclusion.

18 June 1971

A-1H 52-135314 1 SOS, 56 SOW, USAF, Nakhon Phanom
Capt Roger Earl Witte (KIA)

A Skyraider and its pilot was lost on a Barrel Roll mission on the morning of the 18th. Capt Witte was attacking enemy troops near Ban Na on the southern rim of the Plain of Jars and had put his aircraft into a 20-degree dive when it was hit by small arms fire and crashed before he could escape.

EKA-3B 147649 Detachment 3, VAQ-130, USN, Da Nang
Lt John Robert Painter (KIA)
Lt(jg) Raymond Vincent DeBlasio (KIA)
ADJ2 Barry Alan Bidwell (KIA)

A Skywarrior and its three crew were lost on a tanker mission on the 18th due to a control failure. VAQ-130 normally operated detachments of aircraft on board aircraft carriers in the tanker and electronic warfare roles but the Squadron also based aircraft at Da Nang on occasions. The aircraft crashed into the Gulf of Tonkin about 200 miles north of Da Nang and despite an extensive search none of the crew was ever found.

20 June 1971

OV-10A 67-14668 20 TASS, 504 TASG, USAF, Da Nang
Maj B R Ross (survived)
1Lt A L Moxon (survived)

Another Covey FAC OV-10 was lost in southern Laos. Maj Ross and 1Lt Moxon were 15 miles southeast of Muang Fangdeng when their aircraft was damaged by ground fire. They ejected near the conjunction of the borders of South Vietnam, Laos and Cambodia and were later rescued.

21 June 1971

F-8J 150868 VF-194, USN, USS Oriskany
Cdr Charles David Metzler (KIA)

The Oriskany arrived back from Alameda, California on 16 June for its sixth war cruise off Southeast Asia. Just five days after she started operational flying the ship lost a Crusader pilot who ejected while he was in the landing pattern about 40 miles northeast of the DMZ. The aircraft was returning from a strike mission and the pilot drowned before he could be rescued. The reason for the ejection was never determined.

27 June 1971

A-37B 68-10778 8 SOS, 35 TFW, USAF, Bien Hoa
Capt Richard Warren Jones (KIA)

An A-37 Dragonfly was lost along with its pilot during a night strike on a target in Cambodia. Capt Jones died when his aircraft dived into the ground near his target, probably as a result of ground fire. The aircraft crashed near Phum Khsach Sa, 30 miles southeast of Phnom Penh.

The 1st SOS lost at least 74 Skyraiders during its long career in Southeast Asia. A-1H 52-139730 was damaged beyond repair on 26 July 1971 during a landing accident at Nakhon Phanom. Lt Col D Feld

29 June 1971

F-4D   66-8686   435 TFS, 8 TFW, USAF, Ubon
                   Capt W R Ricks (survived)
                   1Lt B D Buffkin (survived)
A Wolf FAC Phantom was badly damaged by 37mm flak during a daylight raid on a target on the western edge of the DMZ buffer zone. Capt Ricks headed east in the hope of reaching Da Nang but he and his WSO ejected upon final approach to the airfield.

5/6 July 1971

OV-10A 67-14634 23 TASS, 504 TASG, USAF, Nakhon Phanom
                   1Lt Daniel Wayne Thomas (KIA)
                   Capt Donald Gene Carr, US Army (KIA)
A Nail FAC Bronco disappeared while on a flight over the southernmost region of Laos. The aircraft is thought to have come down about 20 miles east of Muang Fandeng. Capt 'Butch' Carr was an Army Special Forces officer from Mobile Launch Team 3 of Task Force 1 Advisory Group, which specialised in cross-border infiltration and intelligence operations. Capt Carr was being taken on an orientation flight at the time of the incident. The crew had encountered poor weather and they did not return at the appointed time. A five-day search failed to produce any evidence of the fate of the aircraft or its crew and, despite a report that an OV-10 pilot had been seen in captivity in early July, neither of the crew ever returned from Southeast Asia.

10 July 1971

RF-4C   66-0392   12 TRS, 460 TRW, USAF, Tan Son Nhut
                   Capt R C Wheeler (survived)
                   1Lt J F Stuermver (survived)
An RF-4C took off from Tan Son Nhut for a photographic reconnaissance mission in Cambodia. The aircraft was hit by automatic weapons fire at 200 feet and the starboard wing burst into flames as it flew near the town of Stoeng Treng on the Mekong River, 60 miles north of Kratie. The fire went out and Capt Wheeler coaxed his aircraft back towards South Vietnam. However, the crew had to eject about 45 miles west of Saigon and was rescued by a USAF helicopter.

18 July 1971

A-1H   52-135314 1 SOS, 56 SOW, USAF, Nakhon Phanom
                   1 pilot, name unknown (survived)
A Skyraider was shot down by small arms fire during a Barrel Roll escort mission in northern Laos. The aircraft crashed near Ban Sun Visay, 15 miles east of Luang Prabang but the pilot was later rescued. The serial number of this aircraft conflicts with that of a Skyraider that was lost in northern Laos exactly one month before this incident.

22 July 1971

RF-4C   65-0847   12 TRS, 460 TRW, USAF, Tan Son Nhut
                   Lt Col W Musgrove (survived)
                   1Lt J F Stuermver (survived)
The 12th TRS lost another Phantom during a mission over Cambodia. Lt Col Musgrove was making his second photo run near Phum Prey Rumdeng, 55 miles south of Phnom Penh, when his aircraft was damaged by ground fire. The crew ejected a few miles from their target and were picked up by an Army helicopter. For the second time within a fortnight 1Lt Stuermver found himself completing a mission in a rescue helicopter instead of his Phantom as he had been shot down on 10 July during an earlier combat mission over Cambodia.

26 July 1971

A-1H   52-139730 1 SOS, 56 SOW, USAF, Nakhon Phanom
                   1 pilot, name unknown (survived)
A Skyraider had to be scrapped after sustaining damage in a landing accident at Nakhon Phanom.

28 July 1971

A-1H   52-139702 1 SOS, 56 SOW, USAF, Nakhon Phanom
                   Maj D H Putton (survived)
An enemy troop concentration came under attack from a pair of Skyraiders 10 miles west of Khe Sanh, on the border with Laos. Maj Putton was making his second pass when his aircraft was shot down by small arms fire. He ejected moments before it crashed and he was later rescued by an Army helicopter.

2 August 1971

A-1J   52-142053 1 SOS, 56 SOW, USAF, Nakhon Phanom
                   1Lt Glen Johnson Taliferro (KIA)
A Skyraider was on its way to a target in northern Laos when it was damaged by ground fire about 20 miles north of the huge Nam Ngum Reservoir. The aircraft crashed some minutes later and 1Lt Taliferro was killed.

QU-22B 70-1538   554 RS, 56 SOW, USAF, Nakhon Phanom
                   1 pilot, name unknown (survived)
A QU-22B crashed following engine failure during a reconnaissance mission.

5 August 1971

O-1   51-12768   unit ..?, USAF, base ..?
                   1 pilot, name unknown (survived)
A Bird Dog crashed following an engine malfunction during an FAC flight. This aircraft may have been a Raven FAC.

12 August 1971

OV-10A 67-14662 19 TASS, 504 TASG, USAF, Bien Hoa
                   detached to Phan Rang
                   1Lt John Michael Rydlewicz (KIA)
A Bronco was shot down by ground fire during an FAC mission 15 miles northwest of the South Vietnamese town of Xa Phan Thiet. The pilot was unable to escape before the aircraft crashed.

KA-6D   152598   VA-115, USN, USS Midway
                   Lt Cdr B S Wade (survived)
                   Lt J S McMahon (survived)
The KA-6D was a conversion of the A-6A airframe optimised for the tanker role. The KA-6D was fitted with a refuelling hose and drum unit and could transfer around 12,000lb of fuel per sortie. The aircraft's complex attack avionics suite was removed as it was not intended to take part in combat strikes. The first KA-6D to be lost had to be abandoned when a fire started in the refuelling unit. The crew were subsequently rescued. This was the second and final aircraft lost by the Midway before completing her tour and leaving the line on 10 October. Her abbreviated 74-day tour of duty had been marred from the very start by the loss of one of her E-2Bs but the ship would return the following year.

16 August 1971

O-2A   68-11030   20 TASS, 504 TASG, USAF, Da Nang
                   1Lt John William Kennedy (KIA)
An O-2 set off from Chu Lai for an FAC mission to the south of Da Nang in support of the 23rd Infantry Division. The aircraft was shot down by ground fire near Ton Bon, 20 miles southwest of Quang Tri and the pilot was posted missing. The area was searched for a week but there was no sign of 1Lt Kennedy or his aircraft. Unlike many FAC pilots, 1Lt Kennedy was relatively inexperienced having only received his wings in October 1970. His remains were recovered from Vietnam during field investigations in 1992 and 1993 and positively identified on 25 June 1996.

2 September 1971

F-4D   66-8731   13 TFS, 432 TRW, USAF, Udorn
                   Maj J R Compton (survived)
                   Capt R E Fitzgerald (survived)
A Phantom (using a Falcon FAC call sign) was lost during a Barrel Roll strike near Ban Len on the northern edge of the Plain of Jars. The aircraft was attacking a troop concentration and had just rolled in on its second attack when it was hit by small arms fire and burst into flames. The crew ejected and were rescued by an Air America helicopter although both had received serious injuries.

8 September 1971

A-7A   153223   VA-153, USN, USS Oriskany
                   1 pilot, name unknown (survived)
VA-153 lost one of its Corsairs when the aircraft's engine failed as it was being catapulted from the deck of the Oriskany. The pilot had no option but to eject and was quickly rescued by the ever-present plane guard helicopter.

9 September 1971

O-2A   68-11038   19 TASS, 504 TASG, USAF, Bien Hoa
                   1 pilot, name unknown (survived)
As an O-2 was about to land it flew into the wake turbulence of another aircraft and crashed out of control near the runway. The pilot was injured but survived.

10 September 1971

F-4D   66-8712   13 TFS, 432 TRW, USAF, Udorn
                   Capt Andrew Ivan (KIA)
                   Capt Leroy Jason Cornwell (KIA)
A Phantom acting as a Laredo FAC for a Barrel Roll mission was shot down over northern Laos. The aircraft was hit by ground fire near Ban Ban and Capt Cornwell spoke briefly to a wingman on the survival radio but no sign of the crew was found during an extensive aerial search of the area. The wreckage of the aircraft was discovered close to a 37mm anti-aircraft gun site. The remains of the crew were eventually returned from Laos during a joint US/Lao investigation in August 1994 and identified in March 1996.

12 September 1971

A-1H   52-134589   '530 TFS', USAF, Pleiku
                   1 pilot, name unknown (survived)

A Skyraider was lost on this date but nothing more is known about the incident. The unit is recorded as the '530th TFS' but the only USAF unit still operating Skyraiders in Southeast Asia by this date was the 1st SOS. The unit in question was probably the VNAF's 530th FS, which was activated at Pleiku on 1 December 1970.

16 September 1971

A-1H   52-134622   1 SOS, 56 SOW, USAF, Nakhon Phanom
                   Capt Frederick C Boli (survived)

A pair of Skyraiders was making a dusk strike near Ban Len in the Plain of Jars when one of the aircraft was damaged by small arms fire. As Capt Boli was making his sixth pass on a Pathet Lao troop concentration, he heard bullets strike the aircraft's fuselage and the engine began to lose oil pressure. He headed south and attempted to land the Skyraider at a short airstrip at Ban Nam Tia code-named LS 20A. On touching down the tyres blew and the aircraft left the runway at which point Capt Boli retracted the undercarriage to stop the aircraft before it ran into a cliff. The aircraft was damaged but repairable but it was then totally wrecked when it was dragged off the runway destroying the undercarriage and then dropped by a CH-54 Skycrane which was attempting to fly it out of the airstrip in a high wind. At this stage of the war the 1st SOS was operating a mixture of Skyraider models made up of seven A-1Es, two A-1Gs, 13 A-Hs and six A-1Js.

22 September 1971

A-7B   154430   VA-215, USN, USS *Oriskany*
               1 pilot, name unknown (survived)

The *Oriskany* lost a Corsair through engine failure when the pilot had to eject from his aircraft during a strike mission.

26 September 1971

OV-10A   67-14664   19 TASS, 504 TASG, USAF, Bien Hoa
                    Lt Lansford E Trapp (survived)
                    1 other crew, name unknown (survived)

A Rustic FAC was controlling an air strike about 10 miles northwest of Kampong Cham in Cambodia when the aircraft was hit by ground fire. The target was a cluster of four 12.7mm anti-aircraft guns and the Bronco was hit at 3,500 feet and burst into flames. Both the crew ejected safely and were rescued by a USAF helicopter. The observer was thought to have been a Cambodian army officer. Lt Trapp eventually flew more than 700 hours as an FAC in Southeast Asia and later flew the A-7D, F-4E and the F-16A. He later commanded the 355th and 366th Wings and the Twelfth Air Force before becoming vice commander of PACAF in September 1999 as a Lieutenant General.

30 September 1971

A-1E   52-135187   1 SOS, 56 SOW, USAF, Nakhon Phanom
                   1Lt George Wayne Kamenicky (KIA)
                   Capt H Ramsay Vincent (KIA)

Yet another Skyraider was lost on a mission over the Plain of Jars on the 30th. The aircraft was bombing a troop concentration on the southeastern edge of the Plain when it was hit by small arms fire as it started a 20-degree dive on the target. The aircraft crashed before either of the crew could eject. Capt Vincent was on his first combat sortie since arriving at Nakhon Phanom.

F-4E   68-0316   421 TFS, 366 TFW, USAF, Da Nang
                 Capt Michael Leo Donovan (KIA)
                 1Lt Ronald Leslie Bond (KIA)

A Stormy FAC Phantom was sent out on an armed reconnaissance sortie over southern Laos. The aircraft had refuelled twice from KC-135 tankers to extend its patrol time but then failed to return to Da Nang as scheduled. An extensive search was made in the region to the southwest of the A Shau Valley where it was thought that the aircraft had been brought down, but there was no sign of aircraft or crew. 1Lt Bond was apparently a member of the 390th TFS and was training for fast FAC duties when he was lost.

1 October 1971

RF-4C   serial ..?   14 TRS, 432 TRW, USAF, Udorn
                     Capt James Vernon Newendorp (KIA)
                     Capt J J Sigler (survived)

An RF-4C on a photographic reconnaissance mission was shot down about 5 miles northeast of An Loc in South Vietnam. The pilot was killed but the navigator ejected safely and was recovered by an Army patrol.

12 October 1971

A-7E   156866   VA-97, USN, USS *Enterprise*
               1 pilot, name unknown (survived)

The *Enterprise* arrived back on the line on 16 July for her fifth war cruise. After nearly three months of trouble-free operations, the ship lost a Corsair during a catapult launch on 12 October. The cause was thought to be a mechanical failure of the aircraft's main undercarriage. The pilot ejected before the aircraft crashed and was subsequently rescued.

17 October 1971

RA-5C   156634   RVAH-5, USN, USS *Enterprise*
                 Cdr Lauren Ray Everett (KWF)
                 Lt Cdr Paul Amos Stokes (KWF)

Five days after losing a Corsair the *Enterprise* suffered a tragedy when one of her huge Vigilante reconnaissance aircraft flew into the sea during a training flight killing both the crew. This was the first RA-5C lost in Southeast Asia since March 1969. The *Enterprise* did not lose any more aircraft before it departed on 24 January 1972 having spent a total of 88 days on the line.

18 October 1971

O-1   serial ..?   483 TAW, USAF, Cam Ranh Bay
                   Capt J Partridge (survived)
                   Capt D Busch (survived)

A Bird Dog was shot down by small arms fire near Phan Rang city.

29 October 1971

OV-10A   155394   VAL-4, USN, Binh Thuy
                  Lt R L Segars (survived)
                  Lt E A Smith (survived)

A Black Pony OV-10 was making an attack on a Viet Cong target near one of the mouths of the Mekong about 15 miles southeast of Phu Vinh when it was hit by ground fire. The pilot had just fired rockets from about 1,200 feet on his third pass over the target when the aircraft was damaged. He flew south to the coast where he and his observer ejected and were later rescued by an Army helicopter.

30 October 1971

O-2A   67-21439   20 TASS, 504 TASG, USAF, Da Nang
                  1Lt Robert Edward Ryan (KIA)

An O-2 FAC aircraft crashed near Savannakhet in southern Laos after being hit in the engine by ground fire. The pilot was killed in the incident.

1 November 1971

A-7A   153189   VA-153, USN, USS *Oriskany*
               Cdr Thomas Paul Frank (KIA)

As a Corsair was being catapulted from the deck of the *Oriskany* the aircraft's nose gear collapsed. The aircraft failed to achieve flying speed and ditched just ahead of the carrier. Sadly the pilot was unable to escape and died in his aircraft. This was the last of four aircraft (including three Corsairs) lost by the *Oriskany* during her 75 days on the line. She departed for Alameda on 19 November at the completion of her sixth tour.

23 November 1971

F-4E   69-7562   4 TFS, 366 TFW, USAF, Da Nang
                 Capt Robert Wayne Altus (KIA)
                 1Lt William Phelps (KIA)

A flight of Phantoms set off from Da Nang on a night mission over southern Laos. When the flight was about 20 miles northwest of the town of Chanum one of the pilots witnessed a huge fireball on the ground. After attempting to contact Capt Altus without success it was deduced that the fireball was his Phantom exploding as it hit the ground. Whether the aircraft had been shot down or simply flew into the rugged terrain could not be determined.

25/26 November 1971

F-4D   66-7752   497 TFW, 8 TFW, USAF, Ubon
                 Capt James Eugene Steadman (KIA)
                 1Lt Robert Donald Beutel (KIA)

Capt Steadman and 1Lt Beutel were flying a Night Owl FAC mission in southern Laos controlling other strike aircraft when they were lost. The aircraft failed to return from its sortie and was presumed to have been shot down near the Ban Karai Pass. The men were posted as missing in action for seven years until the Air Force changed their classification to killed in action. 1Lt Beutel was flying his last mission before flying to Australia on a spell of Rest and Recuperation leave.

29 November 1971

A-37B   69-6352   8 SOS, 315 TAW, USAF, Bien Hoa
                  Capt Alan W Moore (survived)

Small-scale ground operations continued in Cambodia, often against Khmer Rouge rebels as well as NVA soldiers. A call for close air support from US ground forces was answered by a flight of A-37s from Bien Hoa. As Capt Moore was pulling up from an attack on enemy troops his aircraft was hit in the port engine by ground fire. Capt Moore ejected 25 miles northwest of Kampong Cham but was soon recovered by a USAF helicopter.

10 December 1971

F-105G   63-8326   17 WWS, 388 TFW, USAF, Korat
                   Lt Col Scott Winston McIntire (KIA)
                   Maj Robert E Belli (survived)

The 17th WWS was activated on 1 December from the 6010th WWS, which was itself created from a detachment of the 12th TFS at Korat on 1 November 1970. It was known that the North Vietnamese had been constructing SAM sites in southern Laos to protect key points on the Ho Chi Minh Trail since March 1971. These missiles posed a threat not only to the tactical aircraft that roamed over the Trail day and night but also to the flights of B-52s, which over the years had dropped thousands of tons of bombs on the Trail from high altitude. On 10 December a pair of F-105Gs took off from Korat in support of a B-52 strike near the Mu Gia Pass. The Thuds found an active SAM site near the Pass and attacked it with AGM-45 Shrike anti-radar missiles. After firing two missiles Lt Col McIntire's aircraft (Ashcan 02) was itself hit by a SAM at 18,000 feet. Maj Belli was momentarily knocked unconscious but came to and initiated a command ejection sequence. In a major rescue mission, Maj Belli was located and rescued by a helicopter but Lt Col Scottie McIntire was seen by a helicopter crew the following day to be hanging limp in his parachute in a tall tree. He was presumed to be dead as he appeared lifeless and had been hanging in this position for over 20 hours in appalling weather and would have died from hypothermia within six hours. The helicopter crew was unable to retrieve Scott McIntire's body due to heavy ground fire.

12 December 1971

C-2A   152793   VRC-50, USN, Cubi Point
               4 crew, names unknown (KWF)

A C-2 Greyhound disappeared during a logistics flight over the South China Sea with the loss of its crew of four. This accident happened almost a year to the day of the crash of another C-2 from VRC-50 that was lost in the Gulf of Tonkin. The names of the crew are not recorded on the Vietnam Wall in Washington, DC as the aircraft was not flying an operational mission in the war zone at the time and therefore the men are technically not eligible for inclusion.

16 December 1971

F-4D   66-8744   433 TFS, 8 TFW, USAF, Ubon
                   Maj K S Morris (survived)
                   1Lt W J King (survived)

A Phantom was shot down in Cambodia as it was attacking enemy troops 25 miles west of the capital, Phnom Penh. Maj Morris's aircraft was hit by 12.7mm AAA as it made a 45-degree dive on the target. With a damaged engine Maj Morris flew the aircraft to Phnom Penh and he and his WSO ejected close to the capital and were quickly rescued by a helicopter.

17 December 1971

F-4E   69-7559   4 TFS, 366 TFW, USAF, Da Nang
                   Lt Col Arthur S Blissett (survived)
                   1Lt Michael H Murray (survived)

The newly-discovered SAM site just north of the Mu Gia Pass in Laos scored another hit during the night of the 17th. Lt Col Blissett and 1Lt Murray (Gunfighter 82) were escorting an RF-4C when a missile hit their Phantom. The crew ejected a few miles away from where they were hit and were recovered early the next morning by two HH-53s from the 40th ARRS escorted by four A-1s and assisted by a Nail FAC that controlled air strikes to keep enemy troops away from the survivors. Lt Col Blissett spent nine hours suspended in his parachute from the branches of a tree 70 feet above the ground before being rescued. Jolly Green 30, an HH-53 of the 40th ARRS flown by Maj Clyde E Bennett, actually made the pick up. This was the second time that Lt Col Blissett had been shot down in southern Laos in a Phantom, the first occasion being on 6 May 1971 when he was still a Major.

18 December 1971

F-4D   66-0241   555 TFS, 432 TRW, USAF, Udorn
                   Maj Kenneth R Johnson (POW)
                   1Lt Samuel R Vaughan (POW)

There had been little opportunity for air-to-air combat since the end of Rolling Thunder and the North Vietnamese MiGs had not shot down a USAF fixed-wing aircraft since 23 February 1968. Falcon 66 was one of a pair of Phantoms that was flying top cover for a helicopter that was extracting a Special Forces team from behind enemy lines in northeastern Laos. As the mission proceeded the Phantoms were attacked by MiG-21s and during the engagement Maj Johnson's aircraft was shot down by an air-to-air missile near Ban Poung Ban. The crew ejected and attempted to evade capture but were surrounded and taken prisoner by North Vietnamese troops. The pair was lucky in that they were eventually sent to the camps in North Vietnam and survived captivity. Maj Johnson was released on 14 March 1973 and 1Lt Vaughan was released in the last batch on 28 March 1973. Maj Johnson had flown 220 missions in the F-100D with the 510th TFS in 1967. He later assisted in the delivery of F-5s to the VNAF and flew a number of combat missions with them. He converted to the F-4 and was shot down on his 55th Phantom mission. 1Lt Vaughan had arrived at Udorn on 10 October and was on his 49th mission when he was shot down.

F-4D   65-0799   13 TFS, 432 TRW, USAF, Udorn
                   Maj W T Stanley (survived)
                   Capt L O'Brien (survived)

F-4D   64-0954   13 TFS, 432 TRW, USAF, Udorn
                   1Lt Kenneth R Wells (POW)
                   Maj Leland L Hildebrand (POW)

As soon as Falcon 66 was shot down the rescue task force swung into action in the hope of recovering the Phantom crew before they could be captured. A formation of Phantoms from a sister squadron at Udorn took part in the attempted rescue but two of the aircraft became casualties themselves. Nearly three hours after Falcon 66 went down Maj Stanley was heading southeast away from the area to refuel when he was attacked by a MiG and was shot down. Both crew ejected and were eventually picked up by a USAF SAR helicopter. Half an hour later another Phantom flying CAP coverage over the rescue force was also lost, the aircraft running out of fuel as it tried to reach a tanker following an engagement with a MiG. 1Lt Wells and Maj Hildebrand ejected but were captured before they could be rescued and joined Maj Johnson and 1Lt Vaughan in captivity. Wells and Hildebrand were also sent to North Vietnam and were both released on 28 March 1973. Leland Hildebrand was on his 20th mission when he was shot down while Ken Wells was only on his 9th mission having arrived at Udorn on 9 November. Capt O'Brien survived the crash of his Phantom at Udorn on 1 February 1972.

19 December 1971

F-4D   66-0237   555 TFS, 432 TRW, USAF, Udorn
                   Capt Leo Tarlton Thomas (KIA)
                   1Lt Daniel Roberts Poynor (KIA)

The Udorn Wing lost another Phantom on the 19th and this time the crew were killed in the incident. Capt Thomas and 1Lt Poynor, a Falcon FAC crew, were taking part in a strike on a group of three 23mm anti-aircraft gun positions on the eastern edge of the Plain of Jars when they were killed. The aircraft was hit by a 37mm shell and crashed before either of the crew could escape. The crew's remains were discovered during a Joint US/Lao investigation and were positively identified on 27 June 1995 and returned for burial at Arlington National Cemetery. This particular Phantom was one of a small number of aircraft fitted with a device known as Combat Tree that could locate and plot enemy IFF transmissions thereby providing beyond visual range identification of MiGs. The equipment was fitted with an explosive charge which was detonated when the ejection seats were fired to prevent it from falling into enemy hands.

24 December 1971

OV-10A 67-14667   20 TASS, 504 TASG, USAF, Da Nang
                   detached to Pleiku
                   Capt Timothy Michael Tucker (KIA)
                   1Lt William Robert Finn (KIA)

A Covey FAC from Pleiku was lost about 15 miles southwest of Muang Fangdeng in the extreme southern tip of Laos. The exact cause of the aircraft's loss and the fate of the crew could not be determined.

Proud Deep

Operation Proud Deep was a five-day limited air campaign which commenced on 26 December against specified North Vietnamese targets including fuel and supply depots, airfields, SAM sites and truck parks below the 20th parallel. Ostensibly the offensive was mounted in response to the build up of North Vietnamese SAM sites and MiG activity in the southern provinces of the North. The campaign was to consist of no more than about 1,000 bombing sorties but it got off to a bad start due to bad weather caused by the northeast monsoon.

26 December 1971

F-4D   66-8818   433 TFS, 8 TFW, USAF, Ubon
                   Capt Lawrence Gene Stolz (KIA)
                   1Lt Dale Francis Koons (KIA)

Four Phantoms from Ubon flew a Proud Deep strike against a storage complex at Thanh Hoa in North Vietnam on Boxing Day. About 10 miles south of Thanh Hoa the flight came under fire from a SAM site and one of the aircraft was hit by an SA-2. The aircraft entered cloud and was not seen again. It is not known if the crew were able to eject before the aircraft crashed but a few days later the North Vietnamese published a photograph, which was reprinted in a Dutch newspaper, showing identification papers and other personal items of Capt Stolz and 1Lt Koons. The original photograph had a note stating that the crew were killed when their aircraft crashed near the Ham Rong or Dragon's Jaw Bridge. On 3 January 1990 it was announced by the US Government that remains previously handed over by the Vietnamese had been identified as those of the Phantom crew.

OV-10A 67-14648   23 TASS, 504 TASG, USAF, Nakhon Phanom
                   Capt Lynn E Guenther (POW)

A Nail FAC was controlling an air strike just to the south of the Ban Karai Pass when the Bronco was shot down by ground fire. Capt Guenther injured his left eye and shoulder during ejection, he was captured and sent to North Vietnam where his injuries were treated. He was released on 12 February 1973. Capt Guenther had previously flown KC-135 tankers with the 909th ARS in the USA before volunteering as an FAC in Southeast Asia

30 December 1971

F-4B   150418   VF-111, USN, USS *Coral Sea*
                   Lt Cdr David Wesley Hoffman (POW)
                   Lt(jg) Norris Alphonzo Charles (POW)

A flight of Phantoms from the *Coral Sea* was sent on a Proud Deep strike on the city of Vinh. Lt Cdr Hoffman was orbiting at 20,000 feet some five miles east of the city when an SA-2 shot through the overcast beneath the aircraft and exploded near the Phantom damaging its tail. The aircraft became difficult to control but Lt Cdr Hoffman managed to cross the coast before he and Lt Charles had to eject. The pair were captured before they could be rescued and became POWs. These were the first naval airmen to be taken prisoner in North Vietnam since September 1968 although Lt Bedinger, who was captured in Laos, had been taken prisoner in November 1969. Lt Norris Charles, one of the few black naval aviators to be captured during the war, was one of three prisoners who were released early to US peace activists in Hanoi on 25 September 1972 along with Lt(jg) M L Gartley and Maj E Elias. David Hoffman, who had ejected from a Phantom on 25 February 1967, served the full term and was released in Operation Homecoming on 28 March 1973. He was on his 205th combat mission when he was shot down, having previously served two tours with VF-96 on board the *Enterprise*. He was actually serving as Air Wing 15's LSO on board the *Coral Sea* but still flew the occasional operational sortie.

A-6A   155677   VA-165, USN, USS *Constellation*
                   Lt Cdr Frederick Lee Holmes (KIA)
                   Lt C W Burton (survived)

Shortly after the Phantom was shot down the Navy lost another aircraft during a Proud Deep strike on Yen Dung near Vinh. A formation of Intruders, Corsairs and Phantoms from the *Constellation* crossed the coast eight miles north of Vinh at 12,000 feet en route to the target. Because cloud covered the target area it was planned for an Intruder to lead the other aircraft to the target as a pathfinder and locate the target by radar. The Intruder would drop its bombs in straight and level flight above the clouds as would the accompanying Corsairs and Phantoms. Unfortunately this tactic put the aircraft at great risk from SAMs and radar-directed AAA. Lt Cdr Holmes was approaching the target when a SAM shot up through the cloud layer 6,000 feet below the aircraft and exploded just in front of it. The aircraft became engulfed in flames and the starboard wing separated. The NFO, Lt Burton, and possibly the pilot were ejected unintentionally by the break up of the aircraft. Lt Burton survived, albeit badly injured, and was rescued by a Navy helicopter from the sea near Hon Nieu island off the coast near Vinh. Enemy boats were kept at bay by the Corsairs and Phantoms, which made several strafing runs near the survivor. However, although one of the SAR crew reported seeing another man in the water there was no sign of Lt Cdr Holmes who probably did not survive the ejection. Due to the presence of a large number of small boats in the area the SAR helicopter could not stay long to investigate.

31 December 1971

F-4D   '66-0753' 497 TFS, 8 TFW, USAF, Ubon
                   Maj William Young Duggan (KIA)
                   Capt Frederick John Sutter (KIA)

A Night Owl aircraft set off from Ubon on a night FAC mission over the Trail. The aircraft failed to return from the mission and was thought to have been shot down near Ban Senphan, just south of the Mu Gia Pass. Capt Sutter's father, Herman, had been a POW during the Second World War when his aircraft was shot down, but Frederick Sutter was not so fortunate and did not survive his ordeal. The serial number quoted for this aircraft is incorrect, as 66-0753 is the serial of a UH-1D Huey helicopter. As a captain, William Duggan had been shot down in a Skyraider while flying with the 1st ACS on 10 February 1965.

Chapter Nine

1972

The Spring Invasion and the Linebacker Campaigns

18 January 1972

A-7E   156880   VA-94, USN, USS *Coral Sea*
                  1 pilot, name unknown (survived)
A Corsair was lost when its starboard main landing gear collapsed as it was being catapulted from the USS *Coral Sea*. The pilot ejected and was quickly rescued.

20 January 1972

RF-4C 68-0573   14 TRS, 432 TRW, USAF, Udorn
                  Maj R K Mock (survived)
                  1Lt J L Stiles (survived)
A reconnaissance Phantom was shot down 15 miles south of the Ban Ban Valley in northern Laos during a Barrel Roll mission. The crew ejected and were rescued by an Air America helicopter.

F-4E   67-0247   421 TFS, 366 TFW, USAF, Da Nang
                  Capt C J Davis (survived)
                  Capt R K Venables (survived)
The second Phantom lost on the 20th was a Stormy FAC aircraft that was taking part in a bombing mission on a section of road on the Ho Chi Minh Trail about 20 miles west of Khe Sanh. The aircraft was hit in the fuselage by 23mm AAA and burst into flames. The crew ejected a few miles from the road and were eventually rescued by a US Army helicopter.

22 January 1972

A-7E   156849   VA-146, USN, USS *Constellation*
                 1 pilot, name unknown (survived)
The *Constellation* lost a Corsair when the aircraft's engine failed due to a mechanical problem during a strike mission. The pilot ejected and was rescued.

1 February 1972

F-4D   serial ..?   13 TFS, 432 TRW, USAF, Udorn
                    Capt Paul G Bast (KIA)
                    Capt L O'Brien (survived)
A Phantom crashed upon take-off from Udorn killing one of the crew. Capt O'Brien had earlier survived being shot down by a MiG during a RESCAP in northern Laos on 18 December 1971.

2 February 1972

F-105G serial ..?   17 WWS, 388 TFW, USAF, Korat
                    Maj Charles H Stone (KIA)
                    1 crew, name unknown (survived)
After the loss of the Phantom on the 1st, another aircraft crashed when taking off from a Thai base, this time it was an F-105G Wild Weasel from Korat that had an engine problem. Once again, only one of the crew survived the accident.

4 February 1972

A-7E   156870   VA-22, USN, USS *Coral Sea*
                 Lt Daniel Dean Cooper (KIA)
A Corsair pilot was killed when his aircraft was seen to fly into the sea off the coast of South Vietnam, probably as a result of disorientation or misjudgement.

9 February 1972

OV-10A 155461   VAL-4, USN, Binh Thuy
                 Lt Robert Edward Lutz (KIA)
                 1Lt Eugene Brindle (survived)

During a Sea Dragon mission a Black Pony OV-10 accidentally flew into the water and was destroyed. Only one of the crew survived the crash. This was the last aircraft lost by VAL-4 during its three year tour of duty in South Vietnam. The Squadron had lost seven Broncos and seven aircrew during this time, all but the last of these aircraft were shot down by ground fire. The Squadron flew its last combat mission on 31 March before it was deactivated on 10 April. It had flown more than 21,000 sorties over the southern provinces of South Vietnam and Cambodia and had dropped about 11,000 tons of ordnance.

10 February 1972

F-4E   66-0371   34 TFS, 388 TFW, USAF, Korat
                  Capt John S Murphy (survived)
                  1Lt Thomas W Dobson (survived)
A Tiger FAC was shot down during a Steel Tiger strike at dusk on the 10th. The aircraft was hit by ground fire as it attacked a target 15 miles northeast of Muang Fangdeng. Both the crew ejected safely and were rescued by HH-53s, one of them using the newly-introduced Limited Night Recovery System that enabled a rare night-time recovery. Capt Murphy was shot down again on 8 June but on that occasion was captured.

13 February 1972

F-4D   66-8741   435 TFS, 8 TFW, USAF, Ubon
                  1Lt J F McCarthy (survived)
                  Capt G Profitt (survived)
A Phantom suffered a hydraulic failure during a strike mission and had to be abandoned. The cause was not thought to be attributable to enemy action.

16 February 1972

F-4D   66-7601   25 TFS, 8 TFW, USAF, Ubon
                  Capt William R Schwertfeger (POW)
                  1Lt Ralph W Galati (POW)
In readiness for their planned invasion of South Vietnam the North Vietnamese moved a number of SAM batteries into the DMZ. On 17 February one US pilot counted 81 SA-2s fired from within the DMZ zone. On the 16th a flight of Phantoms was taking part in a strike on a target just north of the DMZ when one of the aircraft was badly damaged by the nearby explosion of an SA-2 missile. Capt Schwertfeger flew to the coast before he and his WSO ejected. However, they were both captured and became POWs. Both men were released from prison on 28 March 1973 and resumed their Air Force careers. In some documents this crew is listed as being members of the 433rd TFS rather than the 25th and may have been involved in the Wolf fast FAC program. Capt Schwertfeger had flown no less than 350 missions in Southeast Asia having served his first tour as a navigator. 1Lt Galati was on his 69th mission when he was captured. F-4D 66-7601 was a triple MiG-killer having shot down two MiG-17s on 6 November 1967 when flown by Capt D D Simmonds and 1Lt G H McKinney of the 435th TFS and another MiG-17 on 19 December 1967 when flown by Maj J D Moore with 1Lt McKinney again.

17 February 1972

O-2A   serial ..?   21 TASS, 504 TASG, USAF, Cam Ranh Bay
                    detached to Tan Son Nhut
                    1Lt Richard Neil Christy (KIA)
                    SSgt W E Silva (survived)

An O-2 FAC was shot down during a mission over Cambodia and the pilot killed when the cockpit was shattered by ground fire. The observer, SSgt Silva, survived the subsequent crash and was recovered.

F-105G 63-8333   17 WWS, 388 TFW, USAF, Korat
                  Capt James D Cutter (POW)
                  Capt Kenneth James Fraser (POW)
Another aircraft was downed by a SAM just north of the DMZ. A Wild Weasel was hit near the coastal village of Xom Quan Cat about 13 miles north of the DMZ. Although Capt Cutter and Capt Fraser ejected four miles off the coast they were captured by the North Vietnamese. Capt Cutter had previously served in Southeast Asia as a KC-135 tanker pilot before converting to the Thud. Capt Fraser was on his 90th mission when he was shot down and suffered a broken arm and temporary amnesia as a result of the ejection. Both men were released on 28 March 1973. This aircraft was the 800th F-105 Thunderchief of all models to be built for the USAF.

F-4D   serial ..?   432 TRW, USAF, Udorn
                    Maj Robert Harry Irwin (KIA)
                    Capt Edwin Alexander Hawley (POW)
About one hour after the Wild Weasel went down a Phantom Falcon FAC that was flying RESCAP for an attempted rescue was also lost. The aircraft was shot down by ground fire near Xom Quan just inland from the coast. Capt Hawley, the back seater, ejected first as per normal but it appears that Maj Irwin was not able to eject and was killed. Capt Hawley was released on 12 February 1973, still not recovered from the injuries he sustained during the ejection from his Phantom. On 20 November 1989 the US Government announced that remains previously handed over by the Vietnamese had been identified as those of Maj Irwin.

18 February 1972

F-4J   157266   VF-92, USN, USS *Constellation*
                 Lt Bruce Phillip Rowe (KIA)
                 Lt(jg) D E Spence (survived)
A flight of Phantoms from the *Constellation* was sent to attack a group of anti-aircraft gun sites in southern Laos. One of the aircraft was damaged by AAA as it pulled up from its attack. The port engine was damaged and Lt Rowe headed back towards the coast. The aircraft almost made it back to the carrier but about 75 miles northeast of the DMZ the aircraft's hydraulic system suddenly failed and the flaps dropped causing the aircraft to stall on the approach. Both the crew ejected but sadly only the NFO, Lt Spence, was found and rescued by a Navy ship.

24 February 1972

OV-10A 67-14620   23 TASS, 504 TASG, USAF, Nakhon Phanom
                  1 pilot, name unknown (survived)
A Bronco suffered an engine failure and crashed as it was taking off on an FAC flight.

2 March 1972

OV-10A 67-14658   20 TASS, 504 TASG, USAF, Da Nang
                  Capt M H Long (survived)
A Covey FAC was shot down by AAA as Capt Long was controlling an air strike about 15 miles north of Saravan in southern Laos. Capt Long ejected and was subsequently rescued.

3 March 1972

F-4B 150417 VF-51, USN, USS *Coral Sea*
Lt K T Moore (survived)
Lt G H Westfall (survived)

A Phantom had to be abandoned by its crew following an accidental control failure during a BARCAP mission.

6 March 1972

F-4E 69-7552 4 TFS, 366 TFW, USAF, Da Nang
1Lt Carter Avery Howell (KIA)
1Lt Stephen Arthur Rusch (KIA)

A flight of Phantoms from Da Nang was sent on a strike on the Ho Chi Minh Trail in southern Laos. One of the aircraft was hit by AAA as it dived on its target about 20 miles northeast of Saravan. The aircraft was seen to dive into the ground but no ejection or parachutes were seen and it was presumed that neither of the crew were able to escape.

A-7E 158655 VA-195, USN, USS *Kitty Hawk*
Cdr Donald L Hall (KWF)

During a night sortie off the northern coast of the Philippines the CO of VA-195 was killed when his Corsair accidentally crashed into the sea astern of the *Kitty Hawk*. The cause of the accident was undetermined.

8 March 1972

A-4F 154205 VA-55, USN, USS *Hancock*
Cdr George J Fenzl (survived)

The CO of VA-55 was leading a section of Skyhawks on a Steel Tiger strike on the 8th when his aircraft was badly damaged by flak. He was making his sixth 45-degree dive bombing run when the aircraft was hit by AAA rupturing a fuel cell. Cdr Fenzl headed east towards Da Nang but he was forced to eject just 12 miles to the northwest of the city and was picked up by a USAF helicopter.

14 March 1972

OV-10A serial ..? 23 TASS, 504 TASG, USAF, Nakhon Phanom
1Lt Arthur Hans Hardy (KIA)

A Bronco was lost while on an FAC mission in southern Laos. 1Lt Hardy was killed when his aircraft was shot down by anti-aircraft fire approximately 20 miles northeast of Saravan. The following day the 504th TASG was inactivated and control of the 23rd TASS was transferred to the 56th SOW as part of the general reduction and consolidation of the United States forces in Southeast Asia.

17 March 1972

A-37B 69-6355 8 SOS, 377 ABW, USAF, Bien Hoa
1Lt John Michael Minor (KIA)

A Dragonfly pilot was killed when his aircraft crashed as it was landing back at Bien Hoa after a close air support mission.

18 March 1972

OV-10A 68-3823 23 TASS, 56 SOW, USAF, Nakhon Phanom
1Lt David G Breskman (survived)
Capt Steven L Boretsky (survived)

The third Bronco to be lost in March was shot down as it was controlling a strike on a river ford about 10 miles east of Pakse in southern Laos, in an area known to American pilots as the 'Catcher's Mitt'. The aircraft, Nail 31, was hit in the fuselage by anti-aircraft fire and set ablaze at 8,000 feet. Both of the crew managed to eject safely and although the first rescue attempt had to be aborted due to a technical malfunction of one of the helicopters, the men were eventually recovered at first light the following day by a USAF HH-53C. One of the Bronco crew killed an NVA soldier who was attempting to capture him and brought the soldier's AK-47 back with him. This was the first time that a USAF aircraft had been lost so close to Pakse which is situated on the banks of the Mekong close to the border with Thailand.

A-1J 52-142063 1 SOS, 56 SOW, USAF, Nakhon Phanom
Capt Michael J Faas (survived)

A Skyraider was flying an escort for the SAR mission for Nail 31. The OV-10 had come down in what was apparently a heavily defended area near Route 23, one of the busiest parts of the Ho Chi Minh Trail. Capt Faas was flying near the village of Ban Gnang in southern Laos, about 40 miles west of the A Shau Valley, when his aircraft was hit in the starboard wing by anti-aircraft fire. The pilot ejected and was quickly rescued by an Air America UH-34D helicopter flown by Ben Van Etten who happened to be on a routine flight from Udorn to Pakse at the time. The North Vietnamese gunners also damaged three other Skyraiders during the rescue. Mike Faas was on his second tour with the 1st SOS and had been shot down on 26 March 1969 during his first tour.

19 March 1972

A-7E 157529 VA-192, USN, USS *Kitty Hawk*
Lt Frederick Knee (survived)

A Corsair was lost when it suffered an engine failure following a catapult launch at night from the *Kitty Hawk*. Lt Knee was climbing away to rendezvous with another A-7 when the engine vibrated and failed. The pilot turned towards the carrier and ejected safely and was rescued by one of the *Kitty Hawk's* helicopters.

23 March 1972

F-4D 66-8792 25 TFS, 8 TFW, USAF, Ubon
Maj James Edward Whitt (KIA)
Capt James Terry Jackson (KIA)

A truck park five miles south of Tavouac in southern Laos was the object of a strike in the early hours of the 23rd. Maj Whitt's aircraft was hit by ground fire as it was leaving the target and was seen to crash inverted and explode. No ejection or parachutes were seen and it was apparent that the crew had not been able to escape before the aircraft crashed.

A-7E 157520 VA-192, USN, USS *Kitty Hawk*
Lt Dennis Stanley Pike (KIA)

The fourth Corsair lost by the *Kitty Hawk* during March crashed due to an engine malfunction. A flight of A-7s was sent on a close air support mission just south of the DMZ. Cdr Robert Taylor, the CO of VA-192 later recalled the mission: 'We were on a mission just south of the DMZ,' remembers Taylor. 'Government forces were being overrun by the Viet Cong, and a T-28 with an American pilot and Vietnamese observer also went down. We were on target about forty minutes and finally had to leave. I watched Pike disappear on the way out, and that scene, those 10 or 15 seconds, are embedded in my mind, lived over and over. I was about a mile-and-a-half behind him, saw the smoke come out of his tailpipe and called him up asking if there were any problems. He replied, 'Yeah, I've got some oil pressure problems.' We were only about twenty miles inside of Laos, and I told him to take a heading toward Da Nang. He rolled out and made the turn from southwest all the way around to the east at five thousand feet. I told him, 'If you pass three thousand feet and don't have anything left, then [get] out.' He replied, 'Roger that,' followed by an 'Uh oh, there goes the engine. Well, see you guys later.'

Cdr Taylor saw Lt Pike eject but the parachute did not deploy and Lt Pike, veteran of about 175 combat missions, was killed. Following the loss of Lt Pike's aircraft and another Corsair on the 19th the aircraft was briefly grounded for investigations into the engine. The problem was thought to involve failure of the Allison TF41 engine spacers. However, although evidence was scanty, it was also suggested that the two aircraft may have been lost through foreign object damage causing the engines to break up.

A-1H 52-137622 '514 TFS', USAF, Bien Hoa
1 pilot, name unknown (survived)

A Skyraider crashed in Thailand following engine failure and the pilot survived the accident. The unit is quoted as the '514th TFS', which may refer to the VNAF's 514th FS that was equipped with A-1s at Bien Hoa at this time.

28 March 1972

AC-130A 55-0044 16 SOS, 8 TFW, USAF, Ubon
Maj Irving Burns Ramsower (KIA)
Capt Curtis Daniel Miller (KIA)
Maj Henry Paul Brauner (KIA)
1Lt Charles Joseph Wanzel (KIA)
Maj Howard David Stephenson (KIA)
Capt Richard Castillo (KIA)
Capt Richard Conroy Halpin (KIA)
Capt Barclay Bingham Young (KIA)
SSgt James Kenneth Caniford (KIA)
SSgt Merlyn Leroy Paulson (KIA)
SSgt Edwin Jack Pearce (KIA)
SSgt Edward DeWilton Smith (KIA)
A1C Robert Eugene Simmons (KIA)
A1C William Anthony Todd (KIA)

On the night of the 28th an AC-130 Spectre gunship set off from Ubon on a truck hunting mission over the Ho Chi Minh Trail in southern Laos. As the aircraft approached the town of Muang Phine, about 35 miles west of Khe Sanh, it was seen to be hit by an SA-2 missile fired from one of the newly-established SAM sites in Laos. The aircraft burst into flames, crashed and exploded. No parachutes were seen but an emergency beeper signal was picked up briefly. A SAR task force found no sign of any survivors although the search of the area was limited due to intense ground fire. The Pathet Lao subsequently issued a news release claiming that they had shot down the aircraft. This AC-130 was painted with nose art and the name 'Prometheus' and had previously suffered battle damage in December 1971 when both propellers on the starboard engines were shot off.

Following a joint US/Laotian excavation of the crash site in February 1986, the remains of at least nine of the crew were returned on 1 March. However, as the identification in at least two cases rested on the identity of a single tooth or piece of bone, and because the USAF had earlier excavated another crash site and claimed it to be the AC-130, some of the families of the deceased do not accept the identification.

The Spring Invasion

Encouraged by the gradual withdrawal of US forces from Southeast Asia and the poor performance of South Vietnamese forces, the North Vietnamese General Vo Nguyen Giap planned an ambitious invasion of the South in an effort to bring the war to a victorious close. Known as the Nguyen Hue Offensive to the North Vietnamese, and the Spring or Easter Invasion to the Americans, the offensive was launched on 30 March and took the South by surprise. The North Vietnamese made three main thrusts into South Vietnam. The largest and most successful of the North Vietnamese offensives took place in Military Region 1 where enemy troops swarmed across the DMZ and from Laos capturing Quang Tri and Hué and threatening Da Nang. The second major invasion took place in the Central Highlands to the north and west of Pleiku where major battles were fought at Kontum and Dak To. Lastly, Communist forces attempted to threaten Saigon itself by making a major thrust through Binh Long province to the north of the city. However, after capturing Tay Ninh and the US airfield at Quan Loi the North Vietnamese were repulsed during the bitter siege of An Loc. Unwilling to send ground troops back to Vietnam, President Nixon's response was to use air power to blunt the offensive. Reinforcements began to flood back into Southeast Asia within hours of the start of the offensive. The first squadron to arrive was the 36th TFS that flew its F-4Ds from Osan AB, Korea to Da Nang to join the 366th TFW the day after the start of the Invasion. The Marines despatched three F-4 squadrons to Da Nang in April and two A-4 squadrons to Bien Hoa in May. The US Navy ordered four of its carriers to join the two already on duty at Yankee Station. On 31 March the USAF had a total of 365 aircraft based in Southeast Asia. By the end of May this figure had increased to 501 and, when all six carriers had arrived, the US Navy added another 400 combat aircraft available for operations.

The series of USAF deployments from the USA commenced in early April under the code name Constant Guard. For the record

the Constant Guard I deployment commenced on 7 April and consisted of the 561st TFS (F-105G) to Korat, 334th TFS and 336th TFS (F-4E) to Ubon, and eight EB-66s from the 39th TEWS to Korat to supplement the squadrons there. Constant Guard II started on 1 May and saw the deployment of the 58th TFS and 308th TFS (F-4E) to Udorn. Constant Guard III was the largest of the deployments and involved the move of all four squadrons of the 49th TFW (F-4D) from Holloman AFB, New Mexico to Takhli, starting 7 May. Constant Guard IV started on 13 May and involved the 36th TAS and 61st TAS (C-130E) deploying to the 347th TAW at Ching Chuang Kang AB, Taiwan. Constant Guard V saw the return of the F-111A to Southeast Asia with the 429th TFS and 430th TFS moving to Takhli on 27 September. Finally, Constant Guard VI involved the deployment of three squadrons of the 354th TFW with their new A-7Ds to Korat. In conjunction with the move of tactical aircraft in Constant Guard deployments, SAC began a series of deployments of B-52s to Southeast Asia under the code name Bullet Shot that resulted in a total of 153 bombers deploying to Andersen and another eight to U-Tapao.

30 March 1972

AC-130E 69-6571   16 SOS, 8 TFW, USAF, Ubon
                            Capt Waylon O Fulk (survived)
                            Capt E N Bolling (survived)
                            13 crew, names unknown (survived)

Another Spectre gunship was lost on the night of the 30th, this time without casualties. The aircraft was one of the newer AC-130E Pave Spectre gunships that were supplementing the ageing AC-130As. The first AC-130E arrived at Ubon on 25 October 1971. The aircraft had more powerful engines and were more heavily armed with a larger ammunition load and more protective armour than the old A-models. From February 1972 under the Pave Aegis programme AC-130s were refitted with a huge 105mm howitzer that replaced the two rear 40mm guns.

Spectre 22 spotted a convoy of trucks on the Trail 35 miles north of Muang Fangdeng in southern Laos. The aircraft destroyed three of the trucks and was about to fire again to make sure of the kill when it was hit by ground fire. The aircraft was flying at 195 knots and 7,500 feet when 57mm anti-aircraft shells hit its starboard wing and fuselage. The AC-130 caught fire when fuel leaking from the starboard pylon tank ignited. Capt Fulk headed northwest towards Thailand in the hope of reaching Ubon but the crew were forced to abandon the aircraft which crashed about 15 miles southeast of Saravan. The abandonment set in motion one of the largest SAR missions ever mounted by

the US forces. An HC-130 soon arrived on the scene and took over as on-scene commander of what proved to be a massive and complex rescue mission. Numerous aircraft including Nail FACs and other Spectres conducted a radio and visual search throughout the night to locate the survivors in preparation for a pick-up attempt at first light. It was discovered that two of the survivors had bailed out soon after the aircraft had been hit and were some 40 miles to the east of the main group of survivors. At first light in a well-coordinated operation four HH-53s from the 40th ARRS picked up 13 men from the main group, one of whom had a broken leg. A few minutes later two Air America UH-34D helicopters protected by A-1s rescued the two other survivors from a well-defended area near the Trail to the east. The huge operation on the night of the 30th/31st had involved seven HH-53s, eight A-1s, three HC-130s, 11 flights of strike aircraft (seven of which made attacks), four EB-66s, six F-105s, 14 Nail FACs, three Raven FACs, three Air America helicopters, four AC-130s and an F-4 Fast FAC. Unfortunately, the successful rescue of the entire crew of Spectre 22 was overshadowed by the attempted rescue of Bat 21 that followed in the next few days but these two operations epitomise the high points and low points that rescue crews faced in Southeast Asia.

2 April 1972

O-2A   68-10842   20 TASS, 366 TFW, USAF, Da Nang
                                  1Lt Richard L Abbot (survived)

An O-2 had one of its engines damaged by ground fire as it was orbiting south of the DMZ preparing to control an air strike. 1Lt Abbot flew out over the sea but had to bail out when the aircraft started to spin. Although he broke his arm as he left the aircraft, 1Lt Abbot was soon picked up by the USS *Hamner*.

EB-66C   54-0466   42 TEWS, 388 TFW, USAF, Korat
                                Maj Wayne Louis Bolte (KIA)
                                Lt Col Iceal E Hambleton (survived)
                                Lt Col Anthony Robert Giannangeli (KIA)
                                Lt Col Charles Allen Levis (KIA)
                                Maj Henry Muir Serex (KIA)
                                1Lt Robin Frederick Gatwood (KIA)

The saga of Bat 21 started on the afternoon of the 2nd when two EB-66s (radio call signs Bat 21 and Bat 22) were flying as jamming escorts for a cell of three B-52s on a strike against NVA invasion forces near Camp Carroll, just south of the DMZ. SA-2 batteries had recently been moved into South Vietnam and the extra jamming power of the EB-66s was required to protect the B-52s. As the B-52s drew close to their target at least 10 missiles

were fired in two salvos, but all missed. When the EB-66s turned northwest to clear the target area a SAM site to the north of the DMZ launched three more missiles, one of which hit Bat 21 at 24,000 feet. Lt Col Hambleton ejected from the aircraft and parachuted down near the Cam Lo River, about two miles northeast of the village of Cam Lo. No other parachutes were seen or SAR beepers heard. Hambleton used his survival radio to speak to an O-2 pilot who had seen the incident. The FAC pilot remembered that a planned evacuation of Quang Tri had just been cancelled so he called the Sandy flight involved and within minutes the Skyraiders swept over Hambleton's position and blasted enemy troops who were closing in on him. The first rescue attempt involved four US Army helicopters that were scrambled from Phu Bai. Two UH-1H troop transport helicopters from F Troop, 8th Cavalry Regiment, 196th Infantry Brigade were escorted towards Hambleton's location by a couple of AH-1G Cobras. As the helicopters approached Dong Ha the leading UH-1 and AH-1 were both hit by heavy ground fire. The Cobra limped away and made a forced landing on the coast from where the crew was rescued by an HH-53. The UH-1H (67-17801 callsign Blueghost 39) caught fire and crashed a few miles northwest of Dong Ha. The door gunner, SP4 J M Astorga, survived and was captured by the North Vietnamese but the rest of the crew, consisting of 1Lt B K Kulland, WO1 J W Frink and SP5 R P Paschall, were killed. The remains of these three men were recovered in 1993 and positively identified on 2 April 1994. Astorga was eventually taken to Hanoi and was released on 5 March 1973.

Meanwhile the Joint SAR Center in Saigon not fully realising that Hambleton had come down in the path of a major enemy advance, promptly imposed a no-fire zone of 17-miles radius around the downed airman. This was later the source of great controversy as it severely limited the freedom of action of US and ARVN ground troops to use artillery and air strikes to counter the enemy offensive. Under a low ceiling of cloud on the 3rd two OV-10s pinpointed Hambleton's precise position by using LORAN navigational fixes. Once his location had been accurately plotted Seventh Air Force put in up to 90 strike sorties a day for the next 10 days, many of them bombing through low cloud, in an attempt to keep the enemy away from Hambleton's position.

On the 6th another attempt to rescue Lt Col Hambleton and 1Lt Clark, who had been shot down on the 3rd, was made by a SAR task force under the direction of Sandy lead, Capt Fred Boli. The attempt ended in disaster when an HH-53C (68-10365 call sign Jolly Green 67) of the 37th ARRS from Da Nang was shot down by ground fire as it approached Hambleton's position from the southwest. The helicopter crashed about half a mile south of 1Lt Clark's hiding place and three miles to the east of Cam Lo village. The crew consisted of Capt Peter Hayden Chapman, 1Lt John Henry Call, TSgt Roy Drewitt Prater, TSgt Allen Jones Avery, Sgt William Roy Pearson and a photographer from the 601st Photo Flight, Sgt James Harold Alley. After the war the crash site of the HH-53 was visited by US and Vietnamese investigation teams on three separate occasions in 1989, 1992 and 1994. Some human remains were eventually recovered in 1994 and returned to the USA. Three of the crew were identified individually using mitochondrial DNA testing and the remains were finally laid to rest in a group burial at Arlington National Cemetery on 19 November 1997. The burial ceremony included a flyover by two MH-53J Pave Low III helicopters, the successors of the Vietnam-era Jolly Green Giants.

After this tragedy the area was declared to be too 'hot' for conventional SAR operations so the JPRC organised a Special Forces team led by Lt Col A Anderson, USMC and Navy SEAL Lt Tom Norris to attempt a rescue by infiltrating enemy territory in darkness. On the night of 9 April Norris and his team of five

The EB-66 electronic warfare aircraft provided jamming support and collected electronic intelligence for much of the war, often in the highly dangerous skies of North Vietnam. However, the EB-66 is probably best remembered for being the aircraft involved in the Bat 21 saga of April 1972. A total of 14 EB-66s were lost in the war, four of them shot down by SAMs. USAF

Vietnamese SEALs moved along the Mieu Giang River and rescued Mark Clark at daybreak and returned to a forward operating base. The base was then shelled by North Vietnamese artillery and two more rescue attempts had to be postponed. On the night of the 12th Norris and his team disguised themselves as Vietnamese fishermen and, despite heavy enemy fire, successfully rescued Lt Col Hambleton bringing an end to his 10-day ordeal. Lt Norris was badly wounded in another action in October 1972 and was himself rescued from certain death by another Navy Seal, PO Michael Thornton. Both men were later awarded the Medal of Honor for their bravery in these two actions. Tom Norris became a special agent with the FBI after retiring from the Navy.

The successful recovery of Lt Col Hambleton was tempered by the loss of the helicopter crews and the knowledge that, despite an all out effort involving hundreds of sorties, the airborne SAR forces could not complete the rescue. This highlights both the achievements and the limitations of the SAR mission in Southeast Asia. The air defence environment near the DMZ proved too prohibitive for the SAR forces and would probably have resulted in the loss of further aircraft and men had the efforts continued. However, without the SAR effort and the constant air strikes, Lt Col Hambleton would probably have been captured early on in the incident. It was only through the efforts of the SAR forces that he was able to make his own way to a position where Lt Norris and his SEAL team could complete the rescue. The Bat 21 rescue has received a large amount of publicity including a 1988 feature film starring Gene Hackman and Danny Glover in a highly dramatized and factually inaccurate account of the incident. More valuable is *The Rescue of Bat 21* written by Darrell Whitcomb, an OV-10 FAC pilot who was involved in the incident.

3 April 1972

OV-10A 68-3789 23 TASS, 56 SOW, USAF, Nakhon Phanom
1Lt William Joseph Henderson (POW)
1Lt Mark N Clark (survived)

Nail 38 was one of the many aircraft involved in the search for Lt Col Hambleton. 1Lt Henderson and 1Lt Clark took over the watch from another Pave Nail FAC on the morning of the 3rd. The aircraft was orbiting near Dong Ha at 5,000 feet with a couple of A-1s when it was hit by a SAM fired from within the DMZ. Both crew ejected immediately and landed safely but were separated from each other. An immediate attempt at a rescue failed when a UH-1 and two escorting AH-1s received heavy ground fire as they approached the downed airmen. 1Lt Henderson was captured by NVA troops as night fell after hiding in a bamboo thicket for eight hours. 1Lt Clark landed on the banks of the Cam Lo River and hid for seven days before being rescued by the SEAL team led by Lt Norris. Lt Henderson was released on 27 March 1973 after spending just under a year as a POW.

4 April 1972

QU-22B 69-7700 554 RS, 56 SOW, USAF, Nakhon Phanom
1 pilot, name unknown (survived)

A QU-22B on a surveillance mission crashed in Thailand following engine failure.

Operation Freedom Train

As reinforcements arrived in Southeast Asia in response to the North Vietnamese invasion, President Nixon gave the military authority to start a new bombing campaign. Operation Freedom Train was a limited air campaign that commenced on 5 April against North Vietnamese supply lines below the 20th parallel. Unlike during Rolling Thunder the planners of the new campaign were given much more freedom to prosecute the war and were not micro-managed from the White House. The campaign expanded quickly and by the middle of April Washington was allowing air strikes above the 20th parallel and close to Hanoi and Haiphong. It was during Freedom Train that SAC's B-52s flew their first missions north of the DMZ on 9 April when 15 aircraft bombed railway and POL targets at Vinh and the big bombers flew their first mission into Route Package VI on 16 April. Freedom Train operations were terminated on 7 May. In this and in other respects, Freedom Train, limited though it was in scope, was the forerunner of the more extensive Linebacker campaigns that followed.

6 April 1972

A-7E 158006 VA-195, USN, USS *Kitty Hawk*
Cdr Mace C Gilfry (survived)

Another CO of a Corsair squadron was shot down following Cdr Frenzl's escape on 8 March. A section of Corsairs was flying near Dong Hoi on a road reconnaissance mission when a volley of six SAMs was fired at the aircraft. One of the missiles damaged the tail of Cdr Gilfry's aircraft, which caught fire. He managed to steer his stricken aircraft out over the sea and ejected about 15 miles north of Dong Hoi when the aircraft's hydraulic system failed. He was rescued by a Navy HH-3A SAR helicopter.

A-7E 157590 VA-22, USN, USS *Coral Sea*
Cdr Thomas Earl Dunlop (KIA)

About 50 minutes later yet another Corsair was shot down, only this time the pilot did not escape and the pilot was the *Coral Sea's* CAG or commander of Air Wing 15. The aircraft (call sign Beefeater 300) was on a road reconnaissance mission about seven miles south of Dong Hoi when it was also hit by a SAM. The section of two A-7s had approached from the sea under broken cloud and poor visibility and ran into intense ground fire. Soon after starting their reconnaissance the wingman saw Cdr Dunlop's aircraft take a direct hit from a SAM. The Corsair exploded and hit the ground and no parachute was seen to indicate that the pilot had been able to eject. Cdr Dunlop was the sixth and last CAG to be lost during the war. Five of them were shot down while the sixth was killed in the *Oriskany* fire.

7 April 1972

OV-10A 68-3820 20 TASS, 366 TFW, USAF, Da Nang
1Lt Bruce Charles Walker (KIA)
1Lt Larry Fletcher Potts, USMC (KIA)

As the NVA swept south through Military Region I the vital fire support bases were overrun denying the defenders artillery support. To compensate the Navy brought in more ships to provide naval gunfire support and Marine Corps observers were attached to USAF FAC units to act as artillery observers. The ships included the mighty battleship the USS *New Jersey* with its 16-inch guns that had a range of 23 miles. An Air Force Bronco with a Marine Corps observer on board was tasked with spotting for artillery just south of the DMZ. While it was on station the aircraft was hit by a SAM and crashed three miles northwest of Dong Ha. The missile was one of a total of 83 SAMs spotted in the DMZ area on this day. The location of the crash was about four miles northeast of where Lt Col Hambleton and 1Lt Clark were still hiding but the the loss of this aircraft is not directly connected with the attempt to rescue the pair. Both the OV-10 crew ejected from their aircraft and 1Lt Walker evaded capture for 11 days. During this time he used his survival radio to direct air strikes on camouflaged enemy positions. A survival kit was dropped to him and he was told to make his way northeast to the coast for an attempted rescue. On the morning of the 18th his last radio message to rescue aircraft was to warn them not to attempt a pick up as enemy soldiers were chasing him and closing in. When he was last seen, 1Lt Walker was lying in a ditch surrounded by about 20 North Vietnamese soldiers who were clearly heard on the Lieutenant's survival radio. It has also been reported that 1Lt Potts was captured and died of wounds in Quang Binh prison. Larry Potts was shot down on his 25th birthday.

9 April 1972

F-4D 66-7764 25 TFS, 8 TFW, USAF, Ubon
Capt W M Banks (survived)
Capt M J Jacobs (survived)

A Wolf FAC Phantom was shot down during a Steel Tiger mission over southern Laos. Capt Banks was preparing to control a strike near Ban Kate, about 27 miles west of Khe Sanh, when his aircraft was hit by ground fire. The crew ejected almost immediately and were later rescued.

A-6A 155652 VMA(AW)-224, USMC, USS *Coral Sea*
Major Clyde D Smith (survived)
1Lt Scott Douglas Ketchie (KIA)

Along with the Navy squadrons on board the *Coral Sea* when she deployed for her sixth combat cruise to Southeast Asia was a Marine Corps A-6 Intruder squadron, VMA(AW)-224. This was the only occasion during the entire war that a Marine Corps A-6 squadron operated from an aircraft carrier and VMA(AW)-224 flew interdiction missions over the Ho Chi Minh Trail at night and attack missions against North Vietnam by day.

Major Smith was flying a road interdiction mission at dusk over the Trail in southern Laos when he spotted a small group of trucks near Ban Bamran just across the border from the DMZ. As he was about to leave the target area following his third pass over the trucks Maj Smith felt a thump and the aircraft started to shake having been hit by AAA. The crew could see the reflection of a fire from the rear of the aircraft and within a few seconds the controls froze and the aircraft pitched up into an inverted spin. Maj Smith ejected and thought his NFO had also left the aircraft although no trace was ever found of 1Lt Ketchie. The aircraft was at 12,000 feet when Maj Smith ejected and, although the light was fading, he was clearly visible in his parachute as he came floating down towards the jungle and landed close to the aircraft's wreckage. The North Vietnamese threw a cordon around the downed pilot and set a trap to shoot down the SAR helicopter, which they knew would soon arrive.

The SAR effort to rescue the crew of Bengal 505 became one of the most intensive and best known of the war. A USAF HH-53C was already in the area when the Intruder was shot down but was not allowed to attempt a rescue because there were no escorts available at the time. Later a Pave Nail OV-10A from the 23rd TASS entered the area and monitored the pilot's location and enemy movement using its night vision equipment. Maj Smith remained hidden during the night and for the following three days and nights as rescue attempts were made and foiled by a combination of bad weather and enemy activity. Unfortunately, he was in a bad position for an attempted rescue and the SAR commander had to be careful not to give Smith's position away. Despite a coded attempt to get Maj Smith to move out of the area he remained in his position and the North Vietnamese were showing signs of impatience. On the fourth day (13 April) the SAR forces decided that they could wait no longer and started a brilliantly coordinated and excecuted rescue under the on-scene commander, Maj James C Harding of the 1st SOS. Skyhawks from VA-55 attacked SAM sites nearby using Shrike missiles as other Navy aircraft, under control of an OV-10 FAC, swept in low to bomb and strafe North Vietnamese troops surrounding Maj Smith. An HH-53C, 69-5793 from the 40th ARRS flown by Capt Bennie D Orrell and Lt James R Casey, swooped down under the low cloud and spotted Maj Smith. He hooked himself to the jungle penetrator and was hoisted up by the PJ as NVA soldiers fired on the helicopter and the survivor. Clyde Smith had been on the ground in one of the most heavily defended areas of Laos for four days and his rescue was an outstanding example of the work of the SAR forces in Southeast Asia. Capt Orrell was awarded the AFC for this mission. Maj Smith flew a further 32 missions from the *Coral Sea* including the mining of Haiphong Harbour on 9 May. He later commanded two Marine Corps squadrons at MCAS Cherry Point before retiring in 1979.

12 April 1972

EA-6A 156979 VMCJ-1, MAG-15, USMC, Da Nang
Capt David Leverett Leet (KIA)
1Lt John Michael Christiansen (KIA)

In response to the North Vietnamese invasion of the South, VMCJ-1 sent a detachment of EA-6As from Iwakuni to Cubi Point NAS in the Philippines on 3 April. From Cubi Point the aircraft flew to Da Nang each day to provide electronic warfare support to US aircraft operating over the northern provinces of South Vietnam before returning to the Philippines each evening. The EA-6A, which made its debut with VMCJ-1 in Southeast Asia as long ago as October 1966, was a highly modified ECM variant of the A-6 Intruder that carried a large radome on the top of its tail

fin and could carry four underwing electronic pods. Its main role was stand off jamming and electronic location of enemy radars. Only 28 EA-6As were built, most of them were delivered to Marine Corps VMCJ squadrons to replace the EF-10 Skynights.

The first of two EA-6As to be lost in Southeast Asia went missing during a jamming mission in support of a Navy air strike. The exact cause was unknown but it was thought possible that the aircraft may have been shot down by flak or a SAM as it left its orbit and headed for Da Nang at the end of the mission.

EC-47P 45-1102   362 TEWS, 366 TFW, USAF, Da Nang

It had been more than a year since the US forces had lost a fixed-wing aircraft in an attack on an airfield in South Vietnam. However, on the night of 12 April enemy forces mounted an attack on Da Nang during which an EC-47 was destroyed and another five aircraft damaged. One man was killed and 10 injured by the 24 rockets that were fired during the attack. 45-1102 had been a VC-47D VIP transport prior to conversion to EC-47 standard.

14 April 1972

F-4J 157252   VF-114, USN, USS *Kitty Hawk*
Lt Joseph Gales Greenleaf (KIA)
Lt Clemie McKinney (KIA)

A North Vietnamese POL dump just below the DMZ and 17 miles west of Quang Tri was the target of a raid on the 14th. As one of a flight of three Phantoms dived on the target it was hit by 37mm flak and continued its dive until it crashed close to the target near the village of Cam Lo. The FAC pilot controlling the attack saw that the aircraft had taken a hit in the cockpit and that neither of the crew had been able to escape. On 14 April 1985 the Vietnamese returned human remains said to belong to Lt McKinney. The Navy confirmed the identity in February 1988 although the McKinney family has disputed the claim.

15 April 1972

F-4E 66-0324   421 TFS, 366 TFW, USAF, Da Nang
1Lt Larry Allen Trimble (KIA)
Maj Gale A Despiegler (POW)

A convoy of about 40 trucks was seen near Dong Hoi in North Vietnam on the 15th during an armed reconnaissance mission by a flight of Phantoms. One of the aircraft was hit by a SAM at 8,000 feet and crashed about four miles west of Dong Hoi. Maj Despiegler ejected and was soon captured. It was not known if 1Lt Trimble had ejected but he apparently did not survive the incident. Gale Despiegler, who had already flown 100 missions over Southeast Asia as a B-52 navigator before converting to the F-4, was released from captivity on 28 March 1973. The remains of Larry Trimble were handed over on 21 July 1989 and positively identified in the following October.

16 April 1972

F-105G 63-8342   17 WWS, 388 TFW, USAF, Korat
Capt Alan Paul Mateja (KIA)
Capt Orvin Clarence Jones (KIA)

One of the responses to the North Vietnamese invasion of the South was Operation Freedom Porch Bravo, a limited attack on targets in the Hanoi/Haipong area of the North. This was the first time US aircraft had bombed the heartland of North Vietnam since March 1968. The offensive began on the 16th with co-ordinated Air Force and Navy raids on SAM sites and POL storage in the Haiphong area. The raid was spearheaded by a 17-aircraft B-52 strike that was protected by a number of Iron Hand aircraft, stand-off jammers and chaff bombers. Over 250 SAMs were fired during these initial raids but only one USAF aircraft was lost. One of the F-105G Wild Weasels was hit by a SAM as it attacked a SAM support depot on the outskirts of Haiphong. The aircraft crashed near the harbour and neither of the crew were able to escape.

A-7E 156860   VA-94, USN, USS *Coral Sea*
Cdr David L Moss (survived)

One of the first strikes of the new campaign almost resulted in the loss of yet another Navy A-7 squadron commander. Cdr Moss

was leading an Alpha Strike on a target in Haiphong and was approaching the city from the sea when a volley of SAMs was launched at the aircraft. All the aircraft started to take evasive action and Cdr Moss saw one missile streak overhead and another go underneath his aircraft, which was then rocked by an explosion. Due to the amount of large calibre AAA in the sky at the time, Cdr Moss was not sure if his aircraft had been hit by a missile or by flak. Whatever the cause the result was a loss of hydraulic pressure and a number of warning lights in the cockpit. Cdr Moss made for the open sea and managed to get close to a destroyer that had come to within 20 miles of the North Vietnamese coast on SAR duty. Although injured on ejection, he was picked up safely by the destroyer.

F-4D 65-0771   390 TFS, 366 TFW, USAF, Da Nang
1Lt V Parkhurst (survived)
1Lt M De Long (survived)

During a flak suppression mission a Phantom suffered an accidental utility hydraulic failure that led to loss of control. Both the crew ejected safely before the aircraft crashed.

18 April 1972

C-130E 63-7775   Detachment 1, 374 TAW, USAF, Tan Son Nhut
Capt Donald B Jensen (survived)
Maj L R Pratt (survived)
3 crew, names unknown (survived)

For several days the 374th TAW's detachment at Tan Son Nhut had been trying to drop ammunition and supplies to the defenders of An Loc, which came under heavy attack from 12 April following the loss of Loc Ninh seven days earlier. Several attempts were made but most of the loads fell into enemy hands and antiaircraft fire was becoming more ferocious so a change of tactics to low level CDS drops was required. The CDS drops started with a high-speed, low-level approach (250 knots and below 200 feet) until the aircraft climbed rapidly to about 600 feet and slowed to 130 knots for the actual drop. On the 18th a Hercules flown by Capt Jensen approached An Loc at 200 feet to drop its load. It was hit by automatic weapons fire and damaged as it climbed to commence the final run in. The starboard wing caught fire and the load had to be jettisoned but Capt Jensen headed south in the hope of reaching Tan Son Nhut. However, Donald Jensen had to crash-land the aircraft in a swamp near Lai Khe and all the crew were recovered by Army helicopters. CDS drops were suspended after this incident but later attempted again during the resupply of An Loc.

19/20 April 1972

F-4D 65-0602   421 TFS, 366 TFW, USAF, Da Nang
Capt Thomas Hugh Amos (KIA)
Capt Mason Irwin Burnham (KIA)

A Phantom was lost during a night mission with an AC-130 gunship in the Steel Tiger area of southern Laos. A target had been found and marked and Capt Amos and Capt Burnham were lining up for an attack when several of the AC-130 crew saw a huge fireball on the ground. The Phantom did not respond to radio calls and the crew was posted missing. The aircraft had crashed near the South Vietnamese border with Laos about 15 miles to the west of Kham Duc. Aerial searches lasted for three days without result. In May 1993 a joint US-Vietnamese team found two villagers who had discovered a crash site and had collected artefacts including ID tags for Amos and Burnham. Between 1994 and 1998 excavations recovered human remains that were positively identified in November 1999 as those of the missing airmen. As an indication of the danger of these excavations, the last dig in June 1998 had to be halted and the site closed to further work due to the large amount of unexploded ordnance found in the area. The mortal remains of Capt Amos and Capt Burnham were buried at Arlington National Cemetery on 25 May 2000.

20 April 1972

RF-4C 68-0598   14 TRS, 432 TRW, USAF, Udorn
Maj Edward Knight Elias (POW)
1Lt Ernest S Clark (survived)

An RF-4C was despatched on a reconnaissance mission to obtain photographs of a truck park near Dong Hoi. Near the target the aircraft dived to avoid a SAM but was hit by a second missile at 6,000 feet five miles west of the town. The aircraft's tail and rear fuselage burst into flames and the crew ejected a few seconds later when it became obvious that the aircraft was no longer flyable. 1Lt Clark's parachute was ripped as he fell through the jungle canopy and he sustained several broken ribs when he hit the ground. 'Woody' Clark was eventually rescued by an HH-53C after spending two days and two nights hiding from NVA troops who hacked their way through the jungle trying to find him. Maj Elias was less fortunate and was captured after evading for three days. Edward Elias was taken to Hanoi where he and several other prisoners were visited by the actress and peace activist Jane Fonda. On 25 September 1972 Edward Elias, together with Lt(jg) M L Gartley and Lt(jg) N A Charles, was released to The Coalition, a US peace organisation that was visiting Hanoi.

21 April 1972

F-4D 66-7494   334 TFS, 4 TFW attached to 8 TFW, USAF, Ubon
Capt D P Brown (survived)
Capt L W Peters (survived)

The 334th TFS and 336th TFS had deployed from the 4th TFW, Seymour-Johnson AFB, North Carolina to Ubon on attachment to the Wolfpack on 11 and 12 April. The first aircraft lost by the newly-arrived squadrons was shot down by a SAM during a Freedom Train mission near Thanh Hoa. The aircraft was egressing from its target at 20,500 feet when it was damaged by the explosion of a missile. Capt Brown turned out to sea and he and his WSO ejected about 25 miles southeast of Thanh Hoa. They were both picked up by a Navy HH-3A SAR helicopter.

22 April 1972

QU-22B 67-1548   554 RS, 56 SOW, USAF, Nakhon Phanom
1 pilot, name unknown (survived)

A QU-22B surveillance aircraft crashed in Thailand due to a control failure. 67-1548 was the last of 27 QU-22Bs that had been built for the Air Force.

23 April 1972

F-4E 69-7564   390 TFS, 366 TFW, USAF, Da Nang
Maj C Hall (survived)
Capt L R Boughner (survived)

The SAMs scored another kill when a formation of Phantoms bombed a storage site at Trung Ngia, two miles west of Dong Hoi on the 23rd. Maj Hall and Capt Boughner ejected close to the coast and were soon rescued by a Navy HH-3A.

25/26 April 1972

C-130E 64-0508   Detachment 1, 374 TAW, USAF, Tan Son Nhut
Maj Harry Arlo Amesbury (KIA)
1Lt Kurt Frederick Weisman (KIA)
1Lt Richard Lee Russell (KIA)
TSgt Donald Russell Hoskins (KIA)
SSgt Calvin Coolidge Cooke (KIA)
SSgt Richard Edward Dunn (KIA)

The airdrops to the beleaguered forces at An Loc continued at night as it had become too dangerous to attempt the low-level drops in daylight. Night-time CDS drops had been reinstated after poor results using the GRADS system of radar-directed airdrops. On the night of the 25th a C-130 attempting to drop at An Loc was shot down. The aircraft approached the drop zone at 500 feet and 170 knots when it was hit by ground fire and crashed shortly afterwards about five miles south of An Loc. All on board were killed. Two other Hercules had already been hit by ground fire during the night's operation and when Maj Amesbury's aircraft was lost the airdrop was brought to a halt for the night. In February 1975 South Vietnamese forces located and returned the remains of 1Lt Weisman but the bodies of the other crewmembers remain missing. The aircraft was from the 345th TAS from Ching Chuan Kang AB on Taiwan. This same crew had airdropped supplies to ARVN forces on the 24th at Kompong Trach

in Cambodia and their aircraft had been hit by ground fire no less than 86 times on that mission.

27 April 1972

F-4B   153025   VF-51, USN, USS *Coral Sea*
     Lt Albert R Molinare (POW)
     Lt Cdr James Burton Souder (POW)

The first US aircraft lost in air-to-air combat during the renewed bombing of North Vietnam was a Navy Phantom from the *Coral Sea*. This was the first US Navy aircraft shot down by a MiG since 16 June 1968. Lt Molinare and Lt Cdr Souder were on a two-aircraft MiGCAP mission when they were vectored towards several MiG-21s near Bai Thuong. The Phantoms could not see the MiGs but followed Red Crown's directions until one of the aircraft was suddenly hit at 8,000 feet by an Atoll air-to-air missile that guided towards the heat of the starboard engine. The MiG pilot was Hoang Quoc Dung of the 921st Fighter Regiment. The Phantom caught fire causing engine failure and hydraulic seizure. The crew ejected about 30 miles northwest of Thanh Hoa and were captured. After less than a year as POWs the men were released on 28 March 1973. Lt Cdr Souder had served two previous tours in Southeast Asia with VF-143 and had flown a total of 325 missions during the war. He assumed the role of medical officer while a POW despite having no formal medical training.

F-4B   151472   VMFA-115, MAG-15, USMC, Da Nang
     Maj Thomas Knowles Duffy (KIA)
     Capt Darryl F Dziedic (survived)

Within days of the start of the North Vietnamese invasion, the US Marine Corps began to deploy a number of its fighter, attack and helicopter squadrons back to South Vietnam. Among the first units to return to Da Nang were two squadrons of F-4s, VMFA-115 and VMFA-232, which arrived on 6 April under the control of MAG-15. In taking up residence at Da Nang VMFA-115 returned to where it had first entered the war in Southeast Asia in October 1965. The only loss suffered by the Squadron on its last tour of Vietnam duty occurred on 27 April when a Phantom flown by the Squadron's executive officer collided with an O-1 Bird Dog of the VNAF during a combat mission. The navigator ejected but Maj Duffy was killed in the crash. The Squadron had lost 20 aircrew and 23 aircraft during 33,553 combat sorties up until the ceasefire on 27 January 1973. Thirteen of these aircraft had been lost as a result of enemy action. VMFA-115 left Nam Phong, where it had moved on 16 June 1972, and deployed to Naha on 31 August 1973.

28 April 1972

F-4   serial ..?   366 TFW, USAF, Da Nang
     Capt M C Francisco (survived)
     Capt A S Arthur (survived)

Another aircraft was lost on an Freedom Train mission on the 28th. Capt Francisco and Capt Arthur ejected from their aircraft over the sea after it was damaged by ground fire during an armed reconnaissance mission in North Vietnam. Both men were subsequently rescued by a USAF SAR helicopter.

1 May 1972

O-2A   serial ..?   20 TASS, 366 TFW, USAF, Da Nang
     1Lt W L Jankowski (survived)

On 1 May the city of Quang Tri fell to the North Vietnamese invaders. Four HH-53s made a daring emergency evacuation of 132 American and South Vietnamese troops under intense close quarter fire. Throughout the day FAC aircraft brought in air strike after air strike on the enemy forces surrounding the city. The only fixed-wing aircraft lost during the evacuation was an O-2 FAC that was shot down near Quang Tri on 1 May. 1Lt Jankowski bailed out safely from his aircraft and was later recovered. This was the first confirmed US fixed-wing aircraft lost to the new SA-7 Strela man-portable missile. The 57 inch-long missile guided to the heat produced by the aircraft's engines and was a particular threat to slow-moving aircraft and helicopters, especially at altitudes below about 6,000 feet. While the missile's 1.15-kg warhead was large enough to cause fatal damage to an

aircraft's structure, a hit by an SA-7 did not always result in total destruction. Between 1972 and 1975 the North Vietnamese fired 589 SA-7s resulting in 204 hits, although not every hit resulted in a shoot down.

A-7E   156888   VA-94, USN, USS *Coral Sea*
     Lt M G Surdyk (survived)

The ever-increasing threat from SA-2s resulted in a lot of emphasis being put on Iron Hand strikes by both the Navy and the Air Force. An A-7 was lost on an Iron Hand mission on the 1st during an attack on a SAM site near Van Loc, 12 miles northwest of Dong Hoi. Lt Surdyk was manoeuvring to avoid a missile at 14,000 feet when an SA-2 exploded about 250 feet below his aircraft. The aircraft's electrical system failed instantly and a few minutes later Lt Surdyk lost control just after he crossed the coast. He was quickly rescued by a Navy HH-3A SAR helicopter.

A-1H   52-134551   1 SOS, 56 SOW, USAF, Nakhon Phanom
     1Lt William Joseph Seitz (survived)

As dusk drew on another USAF aircraft fell victim to the SA-7. A SAR task force was looking for 1Lt Jankowski when one of the Skyraider escorts (Sandy 08) was hit by a missile as the aircraft orbited at 3,500 feet about 10 miles south of Quang Tri. The aircraft's engine caught fire but 1Lt Seitz managed to reach the coast, escorted by an OV-10, and ejected about four miles off the beach where he was eventually picked up by an Army helicopter. This Skyraider was painted with the nickname 'Jello Liver' with with the 1st SOS and had suffered extensive battle damage from a 57mm shell during a SAR mission in March.

A-37B   69-6348   8 SOS, 377 ABW, USAF, Bien Hoa
     Maj F A Marano (survived)

Another aircraft was shot down on the 1st, this one at the furthest point in South Vietnam from Quang Tri. A Dragonfly was taking part in a close air support mission at dusk near Kien Long on the southernmost tip of South Vietnam when it was damaged by ground fire. Maj Marano made it back to land at Bien Hoa but the aircraft was so badly damaged that it had to be scrapped.

2 May 1972

A-1E   52-135141   1 SOS, 56 SOW, USAF, Nakhon Phanom
     Maj James C Harding (survived)

A-1G   52-133865   1 SOS, 56 SOW, USAF, Nakhon Phanom
     Capt D R Screws (survived)

Two more Skyraiders were downed within seconds of each other as they searched for Sandy 08 just south of Quang Tri. Maj Harding and Capt Screws were flying at 5,500 feet and 6,500 feet respectively when their aircraft were hit by SA-7s. Both missiles hit close to the aircraft's engine, the source of heat to which they guided. The pilots ejected from the aircraft and were both picked up by Army helicopters although Capt Screws was badly injured. Maj Harding had played a major role in the successful rescue of Maj Clyde Smith (Bengal 505 Alpha) on 13 April and for which he was awarded the AFC.

AC-119K   53-7826   18 SOS, 56 SOW, USAF, Nakhon Phanom
     Capt Terrance Francis Courtney (KIA)
     Lt Jim Barkalow (survived)
     Capt David Roddy Slagle (KIA)
     Lt Col Tashioglou (survived)
     Lt Larry Barbee (survived)
     SSgt Bare (survived)
     SSgt Kenneth R Brown (KIA)
     SSgt Dale Iman (survived)
     SSgt Ski Sledzinski (survived)
     A1C Craig Corbett (survived)

The first, and indeed only, AC-119 lost to enemy action by the USAF during the war was shot down during a daylight mission on 2 May. Six AC-119s were deployed to Bien Hoa on 15 April to assist in the defence of An Loc. It was rare for the slow and vulnerable AC-119s to fly during daylight hours but a C-130 had dropped ammunition to the defenders of An Loc and the load had fallen into enemy-held territory and had to be destroyed before the NVA found it. The AC-119, call sign Stinger 41, orbited over An Loc, which was still under intense siege, and waited to

take its turn on the target. The AC-119 and an accompanying FAC were fired on by a 37mm anti-aircraft gun, which immediately became their new target. As the aircraft circled at 4,700 feet it was hit in the starboard wing by 37mm flak and limped away with the wing on fire. The piston engine on the starboard wing failed, the jet engine was blown off and the undercarriage leg swung down causing extra drag that the pilot was unable to counter. Seven of the crew bailed out as Capt Courtney fought to maintain control of the aircraft, but he and two other men were killed when the aircraft crashed about five miles from An Loc. The FAC was monitoring the bail out and the survivors were rescued over the next four hours by two HH-53s and a US Army UH-1 with the assistance of much suppressive fire from AC-130s, strike fighters and helicopter gunships. Stinger daylight missions were terminated following this incident.

KA-6D   152597   VA-115, USN, USS *Midway*
     Lt R K A Bendel (survived)
     Lt J G Houser (survived)

The USS *Midway* returned on 30 April to take up its position on the line for the third time. Just two days after commencing operations the ship lost its first aircraft. A KA-6D Intruder had to be abandoned while on a tanker mission due to an accidental fire in the cockpit. Both crewmen were subsequently rescued.

3 May 1972

A-6A   155709   VMA(AW)-224, USMC, USS *Coral Sea*
     1Lt Joseph William McDonald (KIA)
     Capt David Beryl Williams (KIA)

The second Marine Corps Intruder lost from the *Coral Sea* failed to return from a daylight mission northwest of Dong Hoi. The target was a bridge and 1Lt McDonald and Capt Williams had completed their bombing run and had their leader in sight as they sped towards the coast. After the leader crossed the coast he searched for his wingman but could not see him nor could he be raised on radio. The cause of the loss of the aircraft is still unknown although the remains of Capt Williams were returned from Vietnam and identified on 26 October 1989.

F-4E   69-7221   25 TFS, 8 TFW, USAF, Ubon
     Capt Timothy Robert Ayres (POW)
     1Lt Theodore S Sienicki (POW)

A Wolf FAC Phantom was lost during a raid just north of the DMZ. The aircraft was controlling a strike on a SAM site four miles north of Thon Cam Son when it was shot down by ground fire. The aircraft broke up immediately forcing the crew to eject. Both men were captured and sent to Hanoi from where they were released on 28 March 1973 during Operation Homecoming. This crew normally flew the F-4D but was allocated an E-model at short notice, which probably reduced their competence on this mission. Also the strike force was late in taking off giving the North Vietnamese more time to prepare. Capt Ayres had flown over 460 missions in Southeast Asia (most of them as an O-2 FAC pilot based at Quang Ngai) while Ted Sienicki had flown 55 missions up to the point he was shot down. Timothy Ayres retired from the Air Force and went to fly for a major airline.

C-130E   62-1797   Detachment 1, 374 TAW, USAF, Tan Son Nhut
     Capt Donald Lee Unger (KIA)
     Capt Alexander McIver (KIA)
     1Lt Thomas Carl Widerquist (KIA)
     SSgt Lester Bracey (KIA)
     SSgt Joseph Clifford Hopper (KIA)
     SSgt Freddie Leon Slater (KIA)

The resupply of An Loc claimed yet another Hercules on the night of 3 May, the third since 18 April. Capt Unger had made his low level CDS drop and was pulling up from 500 feet to return to Tan Son Nhut when his aircraft was hit by automatic weapons fire. The Hercules crashed a few miles from An Loc and all the crew were killed. The aircraft was from the CCK's 50th TAS. After this incident no more low level drops were made at An Loc. The USAF resumed high altitude GRADS drops at An Loc on 4 May having solved some of the earlier problems with the system and achieved a 90 per cent success rate using this radar-directed drop procedure.

5 May 1972

F-4E   69-7230   334 TFS, 4 TFW attached to 8 TFW, USAF, Ubon
Capt R W Comstock (survived)
Capt P G Kulzer (survived)

Capt Comstock and Capt Kulzer were on a Wolf FAC mission when they were shot down by AAA near Ba Long, 10 miles southwest of Quang Tri. The crew ejected and were later rescued.

6 May 1972

A-7E   156879   VA-22, USN, USS *Coral Sea*
Lt Marvin Benjamin Christopher Wiles (KIA)

A pair of A-7s on an armed reconnaissance mission south of Vinh spotted a SAM launch a few miles to the south of their position. The leading aircraft was flown by Cdr Roger Sheets, the air wing commander of CVW-5. The aircraft turned south and Cdr Sheets made a bombing run on the SAM site. At the same time an Iron Hand aircraft from another flight fired a Shrike missile at the SAM radar which, combined with the A-7's bombs, destroyed much of the site. As Cdr Sheets came round to start his next pass he saw an aircraft on fire diving towards the ground. Lt Wiles's aircraft had been hit by a missile from another SAM site but the pilot ejected and came down 15 miles northwest of Dong Hoi. Cdr Sheets saw Marvin Wiles land right in the middle of a small village but the ground fire was so intense that the Commander had to leave the area and return to the carrier. It was presumed that as Lt Wiles had landed in a village that he had been captured and would have been among the prisoners returned at the end of the war. However, Marvin Wiles apparently never made it to a POW camp and information subsequently received suggests that he was killed in the village while trying to resist capture. He was originally buried in the village but his body was later exhumed by Vietnamese officials and has not yet been traced.

OV-10A   67-14686   probably 20 TASS, 366 TFW, USAF, Da Nang
An enemy night attack on Da Nang airfield destroyed a Bronco and damaged another two aircraft. Sixteen rockets were fired in the attack which left three men wounded.

7 May 1972

F-4J   155576   VMFA-212, MAG-15, USMC, Da Nang
Capt John Wadsworth Consolvo (KIA)
CWO3 J J Castonguay (survived)

VMFA-212 was the third Marine Corps Phantom squadron to deploy to Southeast Asia in 1972, arriving from its base at Kaneohe Bay in Hawaii on 14 April to join MAG-15. A flight of Phantoms from VMFA-212 attacked a rarely seen target just north of the DMZ. On a road about eight miles northwest of the village of Thon Cam Son a small convoy of trucks carrying SA-2 missiles had been spotted. They were probably being taken to one of the several new SAM sites that had been built near the DMZ in recent months. Capt Consolvo was pulling up from his second pass when his aircraft was hit by AAA and caught fire. He flew south for as long as the aircraft remained controllable so as to reach a safer area to eject. About 10 miles to the east of Khe Sanh Capt Consolvo ordered his navigator to eject but it is not known if John Consolvo had been able to follow him. Only CWO3 Castonguay was found and rescued by a USAF SAR helicopter. Capt Consolvo had served two tours at Da Nang and had flown more than 150 missions.

RA-5C   151618   RVAH-7, USN, USS *Kitty Hawk*
Cdr Clarence Ronald Polfer (POW)
Lt(jg) Joseph Eugene Kernan (POW)

A Vigilante was sent to take BDA photographs of a truck park near Thanh Hoa that had just been attacked. As the aircraft was on its photo run at 4,500 feet and 600 knots it was hit by AAA near the Dragon's Jaw Bridge. The rear of the aircraft caught fire and Cdr Polfer and Lt Kernan ejected and were captured. Both men were released from North Vietnam on 28 March 1973. Clarence Polfer had flown over 200 missions during three tours in Southeast Asia, the first two as a Phantom pilot with VF-154 operating from the *Coral Sea* and the *Ranger*. He was serving as the executive officer with RVAH-7 when he was shot down. After retiring

from the Navy Joseph Kernan became involved in State politics and became the Mayor of South Bend, Indiana and the Lieutenant Governor of Indiana.

Linebacker I

The shock of the Spring Invasion and the failure of South Vietnamese forces to hold back the invaders without American assistance resulted in the resumption of US bombing raids on North Vietnam. The limited Freedom Train operation that commenced on 5 April had little obvious effect so President Nixon decided on a large-scale campaign against the North, code named Linebacker, which started on 10 May. The campaign was later known as Linebacker I and ended on 23 October.

The aims of the campaign were to restrict supplies entering North Vietnam from abroad; to destroy military targets and stockpiles of supplies within North Vietnam; and to restrict the flow of supplies throughout North Vietnam and along the Ho Chi Minh Trail into South Vietnam. The major difference between Linebacker I and Rolling Thunder was the decision to mine North Vietnam's major ports. Operation Pocket Money was initiated on 9 May when A-6s and A-7s from the USS Coral Sea dropped mines in the waterways leading to Haiphong Harbour. In addition, the harbours at Cam Pha, Hon Gay, Vinh and Thanh Hoa were also mined. All the mines were set to become live at 6.00pm Hanoi time on the 11th thereby giving foreign ships the opportunity to leave the mined harbours safely until that time.

The day after the mining operation commenced the bombing of North Vietnam resumed with a vengeance. The Navy made the first strikes when about 90 aircraft from the Coral Sea, Constellation and Kitty Hawk attacked POL, railway and bridge targets in and around Haiphong. Between 6 April and the end of June the USAF's 8th TFW had destroyed 106 bridges in North Vietnam, including the Paul Doumer and Thanh Hoa bridges, using the new laser-guided bombs for the first time in the North. North Vietnamese opposition to the new campaign was vigorous. In addition to a huge increase in the number of anti-aircraft guns that now faced the US aircrew, the VPAF's MiGs also put up strong resistance. However, the US fighter crews now had the upper hand. The new air combat training programme that had been instituted by the US Navy resulted in improved tactics and a greater level of exposure to realistic air combat training for the fighter crews. The introduction of the APX-80 Combat Tree equipment allowed USAF F-4's to interrogate the MiG's IFF and verify that a distant radar target was an enemy aircraft which resulted in a major advantage for US pilots. On 10 May USAF and Navy Phantoms shot down a total of 11 MiGs for the loss of just two USAF F-4s to the enemy aircraft.

10 May 1972

F-4D   65-0784   555 TFS, 432 TRW, USAF, Udorn
Maj Robert Alfred Lodge (KIA)
Capt Roger C Locher (survived)

On the first day of the Linebacker offensive the loss of a Phantom over North Vietnam triggered one of the most remarkable stories of escape and evasion to come from the wars in Southeast Asia. A strike force of 32 Phantoms was launched on the first raid of the offensive against the vital Paul Doumer Bridge and the Yen Vien railway marshalling yard near Hanoi. This was the first raid on the Doumer Bridge since February 1968 and was followed up by another raid on the 11th that effectively put the bridge out of action for the rest of the war. Maj Lodge and Capt Locher, using the call sign Oyster 1, were leading the MiGCAP flight for the strike and were flying an aircraft fitted with the Combat Tree IFF detection system. Lodge and Locher were regarded as one of the USAF's best fighter teams and Bob Lodge was a driving force behind the success of the 432nd TRW's success in MiG-hunting. As they were orbiting at 18,000 feet about 25 miles west of Thai Nguyen they were engaged head-on by a flight of four MiG-21s. The two formations passed each other and the Phantoms turned quickly to get behind the MiGs. Three of the MiG-21s were shot down, one by Lt John Markle and his WSO Capt Steve Eaves, one by Capt Steve Ritchie and his WSO Capt Chuck DeBellevue and one by Maj Lodge and Capt Locher. Moments later a flight of four

MiG-19s zoomed up and closed on Maj Lodge's aircraft. Lt Markle warned Bob Lodge that there were MiGs on his tail but Lodge was chasing another MiG-21 and made no attempt to manoeuvre. Moments later, just as he fired another Sparrow missile, Lodge's Phantom was hit in the tail by cannon fire from one of the MiG-19s. The hydraulic system failed and Lodge ordered Locher to eject as the aircraft was on fire and in a flat spin but it appears unlikely that Maj Lodge himself managed to eject before the aircraft crashed. None of the other Phantom crews reported seeing any parachutes from the burning Phantom as it spun into the ground. The Wing at Udorn presumed that both the crew had died in the incident until on 1 June, three weeks later, a Phantom crew reported that they had heard a beeper and had made voice contact with Capt Locher who had been in hiding for three weeks.

A SAR task force was quickly diverted to the area but the Sandys and the helicopters received intense anti-aircraft fire and, as the helicopters were attempting to pinpoint Locher's precise position, a MiG-21 made two high speed passes. As the helicopters were also running short of fuel, it was decided to abandon the attempt for the day. Gen John Vogt, Commander of the Seventh Air Force, cancelled all planned missions over North Vietnam for the next day and directed that all forces be diverted to the rescue of Capt Locher. The rescue attempt on the 2nd began with a diversionary attack on nearby Yen Bai airfield and attacks on known AAA positions in the area. The rescue force consisted of a total of 119 aircraft including SAR helicopters, A-1 Sandys, F-4s, F-105G Wild Weasels, EB-66 jammers and KC-135 tankers. Heavy ground fire met the Sandys and the helicopters as they swept in at low level and more Phantoms were called in to attack the guns. Every gun in every village seemed to open up on the helicopters as they came in literally at tree top height. The brand new electronic location finders carried by the HH-53s were instrumental in finding Locher's position precisely. As the lead helicopter (69-5786 flown by Capt Dale E Stovall of the 40th ARRS) approached the survivor the crew lowered a jungle penetrator and Roger Locher jumped on and was hauled aboard under a hail of bullets and shrapnel.

The rescue force had, right up to the last moment, half-expected a trap set by the North Vietnamese as they could not believe that a downed airman could survive for so long in enemy territory. Roger Locher had landed safely on a steep, heavily wooded hillside, not far from the burning wreck of his aircraft and within sight of the MiG base at Yen Bai. He had walked about 12 miles from where he had been shot down and had stayed alive by eating wild fruit, nuts, berries and the shoots of weeds. He was lucky in that he could obtain food from various plants and fresh water from the many streams that flow through that part of Vietnam. Having been on the ground for 23 days Roger Locher holds the unenviable record for the longest duration between shoot down and rescue and also for the deepest penetration rescue of the war. Locher was flying his 407th combat mission when he was shot down and had been credited with three MiG kills along with Maj Lodge on 21 February and 8 and 10 May flying 65-0784 on each occasion. Roger Locher later retrained as a pilot and in 1985-87 commanded the 4453rd Test and Evaluation Squadron, which was resposible for testing the F-117A stealth fighter.

At first it was hoped that Locher's pilot, Maj Lodge, had also managed to escape. However, this was not to be and Lodge's remains were returned to the USA on 30 September 1977. Bob Lodge had shot down three MiGs and was regarded as an outstanding pilot and combat leader. He was the 432nd TFW's weapons officer and knew more about the APX-80 Combat Tree system than any other pilot in Southeast Asia. Lodge and Locker's Phantom was the first American loss to the VPAF's MiG-19s. Fifty-four Shenyang J-6s, the Chinese-built version of the MiG-19, had been delivered to Yen Bai where the 925th Fighter Regiment was formed in February 1969. During the bombing halt the new unit had little opportunity for action until the start of Linebacker I but it had used the time well in training and building up to full strength. The MiG-19 that shot down Lodge and Locker was thought to have been flown by either Lt Pham Hung Son or Lt Le Thanh Dao and two of the eight aircraft that took off from Yen Bai on this day were lost.

An F-4E Phantom of the 469th TFS drops its load of 500lb bombs, some of them fitted with fuse extenders to ensure that the bombs detonate at ground level instead of burying themselves in earth before exploding. USAF

F-4E   67-0386   58 TFS, 432 TRW, USAF, Udorn
Capt Jeffrey Lyndol Harris (KIA)
Capt Dennis Edward Wilkinson (KIA)

It was probably the same MiGs that were involved in the shooting down of Roger Locher's Phantom that also destroyed another F-4 a few minutes later. Capt Harris and Capt Wilkinson were flying in one of the strike escort flights on the Paul Doumer Bridge raid when they were attacked by MiG-19s about 15 miles northeast of Yen Bai as the strike force was egressing. A MiG-19 got behind Harlow flight and fired its cannon at a Phantom, blowing its port wing off. Neither of the crew was seen to escape from the fireball as it fell to earth. The MiG was then chased away by the leader of Harlow flight before it could do any more damage. Several sets of human remains were handed over on 26 August 1978 and one of these sets was identified the following month as being those of Capt Wilkinson. The crash site of this Phantom was excavated in 1993, 1995 and 1996 by joint US/Vietnamese teams and on the final dig, human remains, along with personal effects including a blood chit, were discovered. The remains were positively identified in May 1997 as belonging to Capt Harris.

F-4J   155797   VF-92, USN, USS *Constellation*
Cdr Harry Lee Blackburn (POW - died)
Lt Stephen Anthony Rudloff (POW)

Later in the morning the Navy flew a second strike consisting of about 90 aircraft from the *Coral Sea, Constellation,* and *Kitty Hawk.* The target was Hai Duong, 30 miles east of Hanoi on the railway line to Haiphong where there was a railway yard, a POL storage site and a bridge. Cdr Blackburn and Lt Rudloff were flying as part of the CAP over the target. Just after the last of the strike aircraft left the target Cdr Blackburn's F-4 was hit in the tail by 85mm AAA. The engines failed, followed by the electrical power system and a fierce fire started to burn away the rear fuselage. Both crew managed to eject and to land only about 100 yards apart. Lt Rudloff was temporarily blinded during the incident and was taken to the Hanoi Hilton but he had no further direct contact with his pilot. Stephen Rudloff, who was on his third tour of the war and his 295th combat mission, was released on 28 March 1973 and later became an F-14 Tomcat instructor pilot. Cdr Blackburn, the Squadron's executive officer, is presumed to have been killed either during or soon after capture. A report that Cdr Blackburn committed suicide by swallowing a cyanide pill circulated after the prisoners returned from Hanoi, but this seems fanciful and cannot be substantiated. His remains were returned to the USA on 10 April 1986.

F-4J   155800   VF-96, USN, USS *Constellation*
Lt Randy H Cunningham (survived)
Lt(jg) Willie P Driscoll (survived)

Seconds after Cdr Blackburn's aircraft was shot down another of the *Constellation's* Phantoms ran into trouble. Lt Cunningham and Lt Driscoll were in the flak suppression flight on the Hai Duong raid and had just released their cluster bombs when they were attacked by two MiG-17s. The MiGs overshot and Lt Cunningham fired a Sidewinder that destroyed one of the enemy aircraft. By this time there were several groups of MiG-17s, MiG-19s and MiG-21s in the air near Haiphong and it was obvious that the VPAF had launched an all-out effort against the raid. Lt Cunningham and his wingman dived into a group of eight MiGs that were attacking three other Phantoms of VF-96. With his second Sidewinder Cunningham shot down another MiG-17 that was on the tail of Cdr Dwight Timm's Phantom. As four MiG-21s dived on Cunningham he evaded and headed for the coast. On the way out he spotted another MiG-17 and decided to attack it. What followed was one of the most famous dogfights of the entire war with the aircraft and crews equally matched in performance and skill. After a series of vertical rolling scissors manoeuvres Cunningham fired a Sidewinder that hit the MiG which then dived into the

ground. This third kill of the mission made Randy Cunningham and Willie Driscoll the first 'aces' of the Vietnam War as they had previously shot down two MiGs on 19 January and 8 May. What is more the fifth MiG was thought to have been flown by a pilot known to the Americans as 'Colonel Tomb' who had built up an enviable reputation in the skies over North Vietnam.

Cunningham and Driscoll had little time to celebrate their new 'ace' status. They headed out towards the coast passing several more MiGs but as they approached Nam Dinh climbing through 16,000 feet their aircraft was damaged by an explosion from an SA-2 missile. Shrapnel peppered the rear underside of the fuselage and the starboard wing tip was blown off. At first the aircraft appeared to be flying normally but soon afterwards the hydraulics started to fail. The aircraft pitched nose up and Cunningham flew along for several minutes causing the aircraft to alternately climb and dive as he rolled it using rudder and throttle. In this manner they reached the coast but the aircraft was on fire and started to spin. Unable to pull out of the spin Cunningham and Driscoll ejected about five miles out to sea. The pair were soon rescued by SH-3 Sea King helicopters from HC-7 and were taken to the USS *Okinawa.* The incident is described in detail in Cunningham's book *Fox Two.*

The Unknown/Known Warrior

In the early 1980s the US government decided to bury the remains of an unidentified serviceman to represent the Vietnam War in the Tomb of the Unknowns in Washington, DC. On 13 April 1984 the Department of Defense selected a set of unidentified remains that were being kept at the Central Identification Laboratory in Hawaii. The remains finally chosen had been found by an ARVN reconnaissance team near An Loc in October 1972. The remains only consisted of six bones comprising just three per cent of the skeleton. Associated with the remains when they were originally found were pieces of a parachute and a flying suit, a pistol holster and a one-man inflatable life raft and, amazingly, an identity card bearing the name of 1Lt Michael Blassie. This identity card was stolen before the remains reached the mortuary in Saigon and only a tentative identification was attached to the remains. In 1980 this tentative identification was downgraded to an 'unidentifiable' status. Thus it was apparent from the very start that the Unknown Warrior had been known to be an airman and was even tentatively identified as 1Lt Michael Blassie. Nevertheless, in 1984 the by now unidentified remains were buried with full honours at the Arlington National Cemetery beside the Tomb of the Unknown Warriors from World War One, World War Two and the Korean War.

Several aircraft went down near An Loc during the war including two C-130s and an AC-119, in which a total of 15 men were killed; five O-2s; and two A-37 Dragonflys, and several helicopters. The items found with the remains point very strongly to the remains being associated with the A-37s or O-2s as helicopter crews were not equipped with parachutes and the C-130 and AC-119 did not carry one-man life rafts.

With the development of mitochondrial DNA testing as a means of forensic identification, the possibility of an identification of the Vietnam Unknown became a reality. It was strongly suspected by some researchers that the remains recovered near An Loc in 1972 were those of 1Lt Michael Blassie and this speculation encouraged President Clinton to order the opening of the Tomb on 14 May 1998 to allow an examination. A very thorough forensic examination did eventually prove that the scant remains belonged to 1Lt Michael Blassie and he was laid to rest with full military honours at Jefferson Barracks National Cemetery near St Louis, Missouri, on 10 July 1998.

11 May 1972

A-37B   69-6345   8 SOS, 377 ABW, USAF, Bien Hoa
1Lt Michael Joseph Blassie (KIA)

The USAF lost three aircraft in the defence of An Loc on 11 May when the NVA made an all-out attempt to capture the city. Maj James Connally and his wingman, 1Lt Blassie, were dropping napalm about two miles northwest of the defended perimeter when Blassie's Dragonfly was hit by 23mm ground fire. The leader and an FAC pilot saw 1Lt Blassie's aircraft stream fuel from the wings as it slowly rolled inverted, crashed and exploded in the jungle but they did not see any sign of an ejection or a parachute. The aircraft crashed close to enemy positions and it was not until 31 October that friendly forces could reach the area to investigate the crash site. A graduate of the Air Force Academy, Michael Blassie had arrived at Bien Hoa in January 1972 and was on his 132nd combat mission when he was shot down.

O-2A   68-11000   21 TASS, 377 ABW, USAF, Tan Son Nhut
Capt Barry Kenneth Allmond (KIA)

Two of the three USAF aircraft lost at An Loc on this day were O-2 FACs that were controlling the hundreds of aircraft which were contributing to the defence of the camp. Capt Allmond, using the call-sign Chico 1, was controlling a strike when his aircraft was hit by AAA and crashed before he could bail out. Some sources claim that the two O-2s lost on the 11th were shot down by SA-7 SAMs which were seen in some numbers around An Loc from the 11th onwards. Capt Allmond had earlier controlled the strike on which 1Lt Blassie was shot down.

O-2A   68-11004   21 TASS, 377 ABW, USAF, Tan Son Nhut
1Lt John Herbert Haselton (KIA)

The second FAC lost at An Loc was shot down about four hours after the first and was flown by 1Lt Haselton as Sundog 3. Again, the aircraft was hit by flak and crashed before the pilot could escape. Also shot down near An Loc on this day was an Army AH-1 Cobra and a VNAF Skyraider.

F-105G   62-4424   17 WWS, 388 TFW, USAF, Korat
Maj William Hansen Talley (POW)
Maj James Phillip Padgett (POW)

An Iron Hand flight lost a Wild Weasel, Icebag 01, during a strike mission in North Vietnam on the 11th. The flight was tackling a

SAM site about 20 miles southwest of Hanoi and the attention of the Weasel crew was directed at the site as a barrage of six missile were fired in their direction from other sites. Although the SAMs missed their mark they had distracted the Weasels who failed to notice a flight of MiG-21s that attacked from their six o'clock position. This combination of an SA-2 barrage to distract the US aircraft from a MiG threat was an oft-used ploy, especially in the fierce air battles of 1972. Maj Talley and Maj Padgett ejected from their aircraft a few minutes after it was hit by an Atoll missile at 13,000 feet. The crew came down in hilly terrain about 25 miles southwest of Hanoi and a SAR mission could not be launched until the following day due to the distance involved and hours of daylight left in which to organise and mount a mission. Unfortunately, Maj Talley was captured before the SAR forces arrived the next morning but Maj Padgett remained at large for another 24 hours before also being captured. Both men were released on 28 March 1973. Maj Talley was on his third tour in Southeast Asia and had flown a total of 182 combat missions whereas Maj Padgett was on his first tour and was only on his 13th mission when he was shot down. F-105G 62-4424 was painted as 'Tyler Rose' during its time at Korat.

F-4D   66-0230   555 TFS, 432 TRW, USAF, Udorn
                                 Lt Col Joseph W Kittinger (POW)
                                 1Lt William J Reich (POW)

About 10 minutes after the Wild Weasel went down the MiGs scored another victory. A flight of Phantoms was escorting a raid when they were engaged by several MiG-21s about five miles northwest of Thai Nguyen. Two aircraft were chasing a MiG when Lt Col Kittinger's Phantom was hit by an air-to-air missile that damaged the starboard wing and set the aircraft alight. The crew ejected a few miles from Thai Nguyen and were soon captured and taken to Hanoi. Kittinger's wingman, Capt S E Nichols, shot down the MiG they had been chasing. When Joe Kittinger was shot down he was already a living legend in the USAF. He had joined the Air Force in 1949 and eventually became a test pilot. He is best known for his part in Project Manhigh which was designed to test the pressure suit and other equipment that was going to be used in the US space programme. On 2 June 1957 he piloted an experimental balloon which ascended to 96,000 feet. On 16 August 1960 he made another record-breaking balloon ascent, this time to 102,800 feet at which point he climbed out of the balloon in his bulky pressure suit and literally jumped into space. His free fall lasted over four minutes during which he attained Mach 1 with a maximum speed of 614 mph. The parachute he was testing had been designed for astronauts in the event of an emergency in the earth's atmosphere. Joe Kittinger served three tours in Vietnam and had flown a staggering total of 485 missions before he was shot down just seven days before he was due to return home. The red-haired, 43-year old Kittinger had shot down a MiG-21 on 1 March and was known as the 'Red Baron' or 'Grandpa' in the POW camps. He had been one of the original Farm Gate B-26 pilots and finally retired from the Air Force in 1978. 1Lt William Reich had flown 125 missions before he was captured. Both men were released from Hanoi on 28 March 1973. Phantom 66-0230 had been flown by Capt F S Olmstead and Capt G R Volloy of the 13th TFS on 30 March 1972 when they shot down a MiG-21.

12 May 1972

F-4E   66-0299   390 TFS, 366 TFW, USAF, Da Nang
                                 Capt Samuel Young Adair (KIA)
                                 1Lt Dennis Clarke Cressey (KIA)

A Phantom from Da Nang was lost during a dusk Linebacker raid on North Vietnam. The aircraft was acting as an FAC when it was shot down and the crew killed. This aircraft had previously served with the 1st TFW at MacDill AFB in Florida.

F-4D   66-8799   435 TFS, 8 TFW, USAF, Ubon
                                 Capt Lonnie Pat Bogard (KIA)
                                 1Lt William Henry Ostermeyer (KIA)

One of the 8th TFW's Night Owl fast FACs was lost after dark during a mission over the Trail in southern Laos. All was going well until just after a scheduled refuelling session with a tanker.

Contact was lost with the F-4 near the Ban Karai Pass but the exact fate of the aircraft or crew was never determined.

14 May 1972

O-1   serial ..?   unit ..?, USAF, base ..?
                                   1 pilot, name unknown (survived)

An O-1 Bird Dog became the fifth confirmed American victim of the SA-7 when it was shot down during an FAC mission on the 14th. The aircraft was flying at 4,000 feet just to the west of An Loc when it was hit.

O-2A   serial ..?   21 TASS, 377 ABW, USAF, Tan Son Nhut
                                   1Lt H A McPhillips (survived)

Yet another FAC was brought down at An Loc when an O-2 was damaged by ground fire just west of the town. The pilot bailed out before the aircraft crashed and he was subsequently recovered by ground forces.

17 May 1972

A-7E   158015   VA-147, USN, USS *Constellation*
                                   Cdr T R Wilkinson (survived)

When the Linebacker I strikes commenced on the 10th armed reconnaissance flights over North Vietnam were also restarted. A flight of Corsairs on a road reconnaissance mission found and attacked an anti-aircraft gun position 20 miles northwest of Dong Hoi. As Cdr Wilkinson was on his fifth pass his aircraft was hit by 37mm AAA and caught fire. A fuel tank had been holed and the pilot turned towards the coast and ejected about five miles offshore just three minutes after the aircraft had been hit. The pilot was soon rescued by a Navy HH-3A. Cdr Wilkinson had taken command of VA-147 on 4 February and survived the war only to be lost during a routine sortie off the Philippines on 29 January 1973.

C-130E   63-7798   Detachment 1, 374 TAW, USAF, Tan Son Nhut
                                   Capt Richard Harold Hagman (KIA)
                                   1Lt Clarence Paul Lewis (KIA)
                                   Capt John Wilburn Adams (KIA)
                                   TSgt David Lee Wagner (KIA)
                                   1 crew, name unknown (survived)

It was not just at An Loc that a North Vietnamese siege was causing heavy casualties. Kontum had been cut off when the NVA captured Dak To on 24 April and cut the road from Pleiku. From then on the only method of resupply of fuel, food, ammunition and other supplies was by air. It once more fell to the C-130s based at Tan Son Nhut to provide the bulk of the airlift effort. A Hercules was climbing away from Kontum when one of its engines was hit by ground fire. It has been suggested that the ground fire was actually a lucky shot from a mortar or a rocket that had been fired at the airfield. Capt Hagman and all except one member of his crew died when the aircraft crashed seconds after being hit. The aircraft was from the 776th TAS.

F-105G   63-8347   Detachment 1, 561 TFS, 23 TFW
                                   attached to 388 TFW, USAF, Korat
                                   2 crew, names unknown (survived)

A Wild Weasel detachment of the 561st TFS arrived at Korat in April on a six-month deployment from McConnell AFB, Kansas to reinforce the 17th WWS. As an aircraft was landing back at Korat after an Iron Hand mission one of its tyres blew out on touch down. The aircraft veered off the runway and caught fire. Both the crew escaped but the aircraft was so badly damaged that it had to be scrapped. The aircraft was returning from an aborted mission and landed overweight causing the tyre to blow. This F-105G was painted as 'Dragon II' while at Korat in 1968 and transferred to Takhli to serve with the 44th TFS and was repainted as 'Mt Idan Flash' and 'Honky Tonk Woman'.

18 May 1972

F-4D   66-7612   421 TFS, 366 TFW, USAF, Da Nang
                                   1Lt Wesley Dallas Ratzel (KIA)
                                   1Lt Jonathan Bruce Bednarek (KIA)

Among the targets scheduled for the Linebacker I offensive were North Vietnam's airfields and especially the MiG bases. A raid on

Kep airfield resulted in the loss of one of the MiGCAP aircraft. 1[Lt] Ratzel and 1Lt Bednarek were flying at 6,000 feet three mile[s] north of the airfield when their Phantom was shot down, proba[-] bly by a MiG-19 from the 925th Fighter Regiment. There was n[o] evidence to suggest that either of the crew had escaped from the[ir] aircraft before it crashed. The remains of the crew were eventu[-] ally returned to the USA in December 1988. This Phantom wa[s] the last of only three American aircraft thought to have been sho[t] down by North Vietnamese MiG-19s although two Phantom[s] were claimed on 8 and 23 May but with no corroborating evi[-] dence. The MiG-19 had not proved a success in air combat an[d] suffered from a high attrition rate in combat and from acciden[ts] so it was phased out of operations during the summer of 197[2.]

19 May 1972

A-7B   154541   VA-56, USN, USS *Midway*
                                   Lt Aubrey Allen Nichols (POW)

An Iron Hand flight attacked an anti-aircraft gun position nea[r] the town of Ha Tinh, 25 miles south of Vinh. As Lt Nichols wa[s] pulling up through 6,000 feet his aircraft was hit in the tail b[y] AAA. Although Lt Nichols headed towards the coast the aircraf[t] became engulfed in flames, the engine began to lose power an[d] smoke and flames in the cockpit forced the pilot to eject. L[t] Nichols suffered facial burns but landed safely and was capture[d.] He was released on 28 March 1973.

OV-10A   67-14622   20 TASS, 366 TFW, USAF, Da Nang
                                   Capt David Phillip Mott (POW)
                                   CWO2 William Edwin Thomas, USMC (POW[)]

Naval gunfire control missions were still being flown to provid[e] artillery support to beleaguered ARVN troops near the coast. [A] Bronco was shot near Quang Tri with a Marine Corps observe[r] who specialised in artillery direction. During the mission the air[-] craft was hit by ground fire and the crew ejected but were quickl[y] captured by NVA troops. The crew was transported across th[e] DMZ and eventually taken to the Hanoi Hilton for imprisonme[nt] for the rest of the war. They were both released from captivity o[n] 27 March 1973. Capt Mott had flown more than 100 mission[s] during his tour in Southeast Asia.

20 May 1972

F-4D   65-0600   555 TFS, 432 TRW, USAF, Udorn
                                   1Lt John D Markle (survived)
                                   Capt James W Williams (POW)

Bowleg flight of four Phantoms was escorting a Linebacker rai[d] on the 20th and was orbiting about 35 miles west of Hanoi whe[n] it was jumped by several MiG-21s. Bowleg 02, 1Lt Markle's air[-] craft, was hit by an Atoll missile and he and Capt Williams ejecte[d] moments later. The two men landed safely and a SAR task forc[e] was ordered in to make a pick-up. Despite heavy ground fire [a] USAF HH-53 from the 40th ARRS rescued 1Lt Markle but Cap[t] Williams was captured and spent less than a year in a POW camp. Capt Williams was flying his 228th mission when he wa[s] shot down. He was repatriated on 28 March 1973 and retraine[d] as a pilot flying F-4s and F-15s in a number of assignments. 1L[t] Markle had shot down a MiG-21 flying 66-8734 during the epi[c] air battle on 10 May.

21 May 1972

F-4E   67-0358   4 TFS, 366 TFW, USAF, Da Nang
                                   Lt Col R E Ross (survived)
                                   1Lt W N Key (survived)

As dusk fell on the 21st a Phantom was flying about 10 miles we[st] of Quang Tri on a mining mission. The aircraft was damaged b[y] 23mm AAA and Lt Col Ross immediately headed east and crosse[d] the coast. The crew ejected over the sea about 25 miles north o[f] Da Nang and were subsequently picked up by a Navy ship. Lt Co[l] Ross survived the crash of another Phantom after it was dam[-] aged by a MiG on 8 July.

F-4B   153032   VF-151, USN, USS *Midway*
                                   Lt Cdr H Sampson (survived)
                                   Lt(jg) R G Draggett (survived)

A Phantom crashed into the sea as it was being launched from the *Midway*. Both the crew ejected safely and were picked up by the carrier's plane guard SH-3G Sea King.

22 May 1972

F-4D   serial ..?   35 TFS, 3 TFW attached to 366 TFW,
                      USAF, Da Nang
                      2 crew, names unknown (survived)

Another F-4 was lost near Quang Tri on the 22nd. The aircraft was pulling up from an attack when it was hit in the starboard wing by ground fire. The crew ejected safely and were soon rescued. It is possibile that this aircraft was shot down by an SA-7 missile although they usually posed little threat to the faster jets.

C-130E 62-1854   21 TAS, 374 TAW, USAF, Naha
                   A Hercules blew a tyre as it was making a
night landing at Kontum. The aircraft could not be repaired in the dark so it had to left on the airfield until the morning. However, the aircraft was hit in a rocket attack as dawn broke and was destroyed. This Hercules was painted as the 'Quan Loi Queen'.

23 May 1972

A-7B   154405   VA-93, USN, USS *Midway*
                  Cdr Charles Edward Barnett (KIA)

A naval alpha strike force bombed the thermal power plant at Nam Dinh to the southwest of Haiphong on the 23rd. As the Iron Hand flight was retiring from the target one of the Corsairs was shot down about 15 miles to the southeast of Nam Dinh. Cdr Barnett was in the trail position at 16,000 feet and had just received a SAM warning when he radioed that his aircraft had been hit by a SAM. No further transmissions were heard but the wingman saw what looked like aircraft wreckage on the ground about five miles from the coast. It was presumed that Cdr Barnett had died in his aircraft. On 3 November 1988 the Vietnamese returned remains that were later identified as being those of Cdr Barnett. Charles Barnett had previously been shot down by a SAM on 13 December 1966 when he was a flying a Skyhawk from the USS *Ticonderoga*.

F-4D   serial ..?   435 TFS, 8 TFW, USAF, Ubon
                      Capt William G Byrns (POW)
                      Capt William Raymond Bean (POW)

A Wolfpack Phantom was flying a Night Owl FAC sortie for a strike on a POL site about eight miles north of the DMZ when it was shot down by ground fire. Capt Byrns and Capt Bean ejected and Byrns were captured immediately. Capt Bean remained in hiding for 36 hours while fighters softened up the area but having learned the lessons of the Bat 21 rescue, the defences were considered too strong to attempt a rescue. The two men spent the rest of the war in a North Vietnamese prison until released on 28 March 1973. Capt Byrns was on his second tour when he was shot down having previously flown with the 469th TFS from Korat and had flown a total of 424 combat missions.

24 May 1972

F-8J   150311   VF-24, USN, USS *Hancock*
                  Lt Carrol Robert Beeler (POW)

A section of Crusaders from the *Hancock* was flying a CAP mission over North Vietnam on the 24th when one of the aircraft was lost. Lt Beeler had been vectored by Red Crown onto an unidentified aircraft which turned out to be another F-8. Lt Beeler lost visual contact with his wingman but arranged to rendezvous out to sea. On the way to the coast, Lt Beeler's aircraft was shot down by a SAM but he ejected and was captured. Carrol Beeler was released from captivity on 28 March 1973.

A-7E   156877   VA-94, USN, USS *Coral Sea*
                  Lt Cdr H A Eikel (survived)

Another Corsair was lost on an Iron Hand mission the day after Cdr Barnett was shot down. Lt Cdr Eikel launched two Shrike missiles at an SA-2 Fan Song radar that was emitting about eight miles northeast of Haiphong. Lt Cdr Eikel initiated a split-S manoeuvre as soon as he launched his missiles but as he was

diving vertically towards the ground he felt an explosion and saw two bright orange flashes from SAM bursts. He headed out to sea but a little while later he lost his hydraulics, flying controls and engine power and was forced to eject over the Gulf of Tonkin about 25 miles southeast of Haiphong. Lt Cdr Eikel was rescued by a Navy SH-3 helicopter. Lt Cdr Eikel had been shot down in a Skyhawk over North Vietnam during an earlier tour with VA-93 on 30 August 1968.

O-2A   68-11056   20 TASS, 366 TFW, USAF, Da Nang
                    1Lt Richard Scott Voigts (KIA)

1Lt Voigts was flying an FAC mission in support of a Ranger border camp about 10 miles northwest of Pleiku when his aircraft was seen to crash. It was presumed to have been a victim of ground fire and 1Lt Voigts apparently died in the crash.

25 May 1972

OV-10A 67-14678   20 TASS, 366 TFW, USAF, Da Nang
                    1Lt J W Twaddell (survived)
                    1Lt J W Shaw (survived)

An OV-10 was on an FAC mission to the northwest of Hué when it fell victim to an SA-7 SAM. The crew were controlling an air strike against enemy troops in contact with friendly forces and the Bronco was flying at 5,000 feet and 150 knots when it was hit by the missile. The crew ejected about seven miles north of Hué and were rescued by a VNAF helicopter.

A-4F   155045   VA-212, USN, USS *Hancock*
                  Cdr Henry Hooker Strong (KIA)

The CO of VA-212 was lost during a strike on the Ben Thuy road bridge three miles south of the city of Vinh. Cdr Strong's aircraft was last seen by his wingmen as he rolled in on the target. Several of the Skyhawks were hit and damaged by the intense flak that filled the air over the target. Some of the pilots thought they heard the Commander report 'feet wet' as he crossed the coast but there was no sign of an ejection or wreckage. The most likely cause of the loss is that the aircraft was shot down by flak.

26 May 1972

TA-4F   153508   H&MS-15, MAG-15, USMC, Da Nang
                  Capt W E Ramsbottom (survived)
                  CWO2 Bruce Edward Boltze (survived)

The Headquarters and Maintenance Squadron detachment that deployed to Da Nang on 16 April with MAG-15 had a small number of two-seat TA-4F Skyhawks for Fast FAC, visual reconnaissance and other duties. It was while on a reconnaissance mission that the crew of a TA-4F spotted an enemy tank about 15 miles northwest of Hué and decided to strafe it with 20mm cannon fire. As the aircraft pulled up through 4,500 feet from its first run it was suddenly hit in the aft fuselage by an SA-7 missile. Although the Skyhawk was badly damaged, Capt Ramsbottom flew back towards Da Nang but he and his observer were forced to eject over the sea about 10 miles southeast of the airfield. CWO2 Boltze was killed on 6 October while flying on a naval gunfire observation mission in a USAF OV-10.

F-4D   66-7621   366 TFW, USAF, Da Nang
                   Capt A N Arnold (survived)
                   Capt T F Kincaid (survived)

Another fast FAC was shot down as it was controlling a strike. The aircraft was hit by AAA just south of the old Marine Corps base at Khe Sanh and the crew ejected close to their target. Despite the fact that the area was very heavily defended, the crew were both picked up with only minor injuries by a USAF rescue helicopter.

27 May 1972

A-4F   155048   VA-55, USN, USS *Hancock*
                  Lt Thomas B Latendresse (POW)

A strike on a bridge near Ha Tinh was aborted due to bad weather at the target so the strike force went looking for targets of opportunity. Lt Latendresse flying Garfish 512 was part of the Iron Hand section tasked with flak suppression on the raid. As Lt Latendresse was pulling up from his attack on a flak site his aircraft was hit in the port wing by AAA. He ejected about 14 miles

south of Vinh and was captured having suffered severe injuries during the ejection. Lt Latendresse was released on 28 March 1973 and spent the next 11 months being treated for his injuries. He had served on two combat cruises with VAW-13 flying the EA-1F version of the Skyraider and had been released from the Navy in 1969 to fly for Northwest Airlines. However, in June 1970 he returned to active duty and converted to the A-4 and flew a tour in the Gulf of Tonkin with VA-55. He eventually retired from the Navy as a Captain.

A-4F   154197   VA-55, USN, USS *Hancock*
                  1 pilot, name unknown (survived)

VA-55 lost another Skyhawk from its flak suppression flight on the 27th when it crashed after its engine failed on launch from the carrier. The pilot ejected safely before the aircraft fell into the sea. It is not known if this aircraft was on the same mission in which Lt Latendresse was shot down.

29 May 1972

A-6A   155650   VMA(AW)-224, USMC, USS *Coral Sea*
                  Lt Cdr Philip Schuyler (survived)
                  Capt Lou J Ferracane (survived)

The *Coral Sea's* Marine Corps squadron lost an Intruder during a Linebacker strike on the Uong Bi railway yard 12 miles northeast of Haiphong. About five miles prior to reaching the target one of the aircraft was hit by light flak but seeing no apparent damage the crew continued their bombing run. As the aircraft pulled up for a 10-degree run to drop Snakeye bombs the aircraft was again hit by flak. Still pressing on the aircraft was hit for a third time as it released its bombs on the target. As the aircraft headed back out to sea the starboard wing was seen to be on fire and the crew ejected over the sea about 75 miles southeast of Haiphong as the fire burned through the wing spar. They were both picked up by a Navy HH-3A SAR helicopter.

1 June 1972

F-4E   serial ..?   308 TFS, 31 TFW attached to 432 TRW,
                      USAF, Udorn
                      Capt G W Hawks (survived)
                      Capt David B Dingee (survived)

The SAR effort for Capt Roger Locher who had been shot down near Yen Bai on 10 May swung into action on 1 June when he was able to contact a flight of aircraft on a Linebacker strike. Flights of aircraft were immediately diverted to the area to provide RESCAP coverage for a rescue attempt. Capt Hawks was just south of Yen Bai when his aircraft was damaged by the explosion from a SAM at 11,000 feet. He managed to fly his crippled aircraft back to Thailand but he and his WSO ejected a few miles from Udorn when it was decided that it was unsafe to attempt a landing. The WSO, Capt Dingee, became a POW on the 27th of the month when he was shot down with another pilot.

4 June 1972

F-4J   155819   VMFA-212, MAG-15, USMC, Da Nang
                  Capt Benjamin Lee Tebault (KIA)
                  1Lt Michael Jacob Konow (KIA)

VMFA-212 lost its second Phantom during its brief stay at Da Nang. A flight of Phantoms had been sent to provide close air support to ARVN troops about 10 miles north of Phu Cat when one of the aircraft was hit by AAA during its attack and crashed. It is likely that the crew had been wounded by the ground fire as no ejection was observed and it was presumed that the crew had died in the crash. VMFA-212 returned to Kaneohe Bay in Hawaii on 24 June after just over two months of service in Southeast Asia.

5 June 1972

O-2A   68-10981   21 TASS, 377 ABW, USAF, Tan Son Nhut
                    1Lt C P Dunn (survived)

An O-2 was damaged by ground fire during an FAC mission in South Vietnam. 1Lt Dunn crash-landed his aircraft about 10 miles northwest of Bao Loc but was badly injured. He was later rescued by a USAF rescue helicopter

6 June 1972

F-4D   66-0232   13 TFS, 432 TRW, USAF, Udorn
       Maj James Alan Fowler (KIA)
       Capt John Wayne Seuell (KIA)

Maj Fowler and Capt Seuell were assigned to lead a flight of four Phantoms on a CAP mission over North Vietnam in support of a Linebacker raid. The flight arrived near Yen Bai and took up station at 15,000 feet as planned. As the flight was about to withdraw and set course for base a SAM launch warning was received and the flight began evasive manoeuvres. A missile was seen to explode directly under the tail of the lead aircraft, which caught fire. No ejections were observed as the aircraft dived into the ground about five miles north of Yen Bai. About 30 minutes later two emergency beeper signals were heard briefly but voice contact was not made and there was no other indication that the crew had survived. Maj Fowler was the commander of B Flight of the 13thTFS and had previously flown F-100s and F-105s. Some of the crew's personal effects were scavenged by local villagers and the remains of the crew were buried near the crash site but the location of the graves has since been lost. This aircraft was fitted with the Combat Tree IFF detection equipment.

7 June 1972

RA-5C   156616   RVAH-1, USN, USS *Saratoga*
       Lt Cdr C H Smith (survived)
       Lt L G Kunz (survived)

The Atlantic Fleet carrier USS *Saratoga* arrived on the line on 18 May for its first and only tour of the war. With the arrival of the *Saratoga* the only available fleet carrier not to have served in Southeast Asia during the war was the USS *John F Kennedy*. The *Saratoga* lost its first aircraft on 7 June during a photographic reconnaissance sortie near Haiphong. A Vigilante was taking photographs of anchorages among the islands off Haiphong where foreign-registered merchant ships tied up before offloading supplies in the port. The aircraft began a pop-up manoeuvre at 3,000 feet to start a photo run when it received an indication of a nearby SAM launch. Lt Cdr Smith broke first to the left and then reversed his course at which point the SAM exploded as it hit the aircraft. The port engine lost power and had to be shut down and after Lt Cdr Smith headed out to sea and selected afterburner on the starboard engine, it also failed. The electrical power failed and the controls froze forcing the crew to eject about 15 miles southeast of Haiphong. A Sea King of HC-7 was directed towards the Vigilante and rescued the crew within minutes of their ejection.

8 June 1972

F-4E   67-0303   34 TFS, 388 TFW, USAF, Korat
       Capt John S Murphy (POW)
       1Lt L D Johnson (survived)

An F-4E was lost on a fast FAC mission near the DMZ. Capt Murphy was the leading FAC pilot with the 13th TFS and had flown 54 Tiger FAC missions from his total of 124 combat missions with this Squadron before he was shot down. The aircraft was damaged by ground fire and the crew ejected close to the shore near the northern edge of the DMZ buffer zone. Although 1Lt Johnson landed in the sea and was rescued by a Navy helicopter, Capt Murphy was not so fortunate and was captured on the beach and imprisoned. John Murphy started his flying career as a B-52 copilot before converting to the F-105 and flying 100 missions from Korat in 1968. He returned to Korat in October 1971 after a spell as a T-38 instructor pilot, and was shot down first on 10 February 1972 and then again near the end of his tour. Capt Murphy was released from captivity on 27 March 1973.

QU-22B   69-7697   554 RS, 56 SOW, USAF, Nakhon Phanom
       1 pilot, name unknown (survived)
A QU-22B was lost due to engine failure on a data collection flight.

OV-10A   68-3803   23 TASS, 56 SOW, USAF, Nakhon Phanom
       2 crew, names unknown (survived)
In an unusual accident a Bronco crashed due to double engine failure. Both crew ejected safely and were rescued.

11 June 1972

A-6A   154145   VMA(AW)-224, USMC, USS *Coral Sea*
       Capt Roger Eugene Wilson (KIA)
       Capt William Kerr Angus (POW)

Another of VMA(AW)-224's Intruders was lost during a Linebacker raid on an anti-aircraft gun position near Nam Dinh, 40 miles southeast of Hanoi. The aircraft dropped its bombs in a 45-degree dive but as it started to pull out of the dive its port wing was seen to separate inboard of the wing fold joint. The aircraft rolled rapidly to the left and the starboard wing also began to break up. With the aircraft streaming fuel and in an uncontrollable spiral dive the crew ejected, although only the navigator survived to be captured. This was one of several instances during the war when an Intruder had lost a wing. Although, as in this case, flak damage was often listed as the probable cause, structural failure due to the wing being overstressed also remained a distinct possibility. In the absence of wreckage to examine doubts still persisted as to the exact cause of the aircraft's demise. Capt Angus was repatriated from North Vietnam on 28 March 1973. This was the fourth and last Intruder lost by VMA(AW)-224 during its six-month cruise on the *Coral Sea*. The Squadron had flown 2,800 sorties in 4,500 flying hours during its tour and had taken part in the Operation Pocket Money mining of Haiphong harbour on 8 May.

13 June 1972

F-4E   67-0365   308 TFS, 31 TFW attached to 432 TRW, USAF, Udorn
       1Lt Gregg Omar Hanson (POW)
       1Lt Richard J Fulton (POW)

A flight of Phantoms from Udorn was assigned as a CAP for a Linebacker raid over North Vietnam. About 25 miles northeast of Yen Bai the CAP flight encountered and chased several MiG-19s and a dogfight ensued. Unfortunately the Phantom crews missed a warning radio call and a MiG-21 crept in behind and fired a missile which guided to the heat from the engines of 1Lt Hanson's aircraft. The aircraft remained flyable for a short while but the crew were then forced to eject. They both landed north of the town of Tuyen Quang and were soon captured. It was not until 24 August that the North Vietnamese announced that the two men had been captured. Both men were repatriated from North Vietnam on 28 March 1973.

A-7A   153206   VA-37, USN, USS *Saratoga*
       Lt Cdr Francis John Davis (KIA)
A section of Corsairs from the *Saratoga* was flying a night-time armed reconnaissance mission along the coast of North Vietnam on the lookout for enemy boats. A merchant ship was spotted between the islands of Hon Mat and Hon Nieu just off the coast near Vinh. Lt Cdr Davis descended to 5,000 feet to drop flares so that his wingman could attack. Lt Cdr Davis radioed that he had a SAM warning and soon afterwards his wingman saw a bright flash below him. Other aircrew in the vicinity saw what could have been a SAM launch followed by a larger explosion. A search revealed no sign of wreckage or the pilot and it was presumed that the aircraft had been hit by an SA-2 fired from Hon Nieu island.

16 June 1972

RF-8G   145613   Detachment 3, VFP-63, USN, USS *Midway*
       Lt P Ringwood (survived)
An RF-8G Crusader was damaged by AAA as it attempted to obtain photographs of the Thanh Hoa Bridge which been severely damaged on 27 April and 13 May by Phantoms from the 8th TFW using Paveway LGBs. The Crusader was in a turn at 4,500 feet and 450 knots when it was hit by 37mm flak. The aft section of the aircraft was set on fire and Lt Ringwood headed out to sea and ejected about 10 miles off the coast. He was quickly rescued by a Navy SH-3 SAR helicopter.

A-7A   153197   VA-105, USN, USS *Saratoga*
       Lt John Joseph Cabral (KIA)
The third aircraft to be lost by the *Saratoga* was a Corsair that crashed after being launched from the carrier on an armed

reconnaissance mission. Unfortunately, the pilot was killed in the accident.

17 June 1972

A-7E   157531   VA-192, USN, USS *Kitty Hawk*
       Cdr Darrel D Owens (survived)
On the 17th a strike group from the *Kitty Hawk* attacked important railway sidings at Thieu Giuong near Thanh Hoa. As the aircraft were leaving the target area and heading out to sea, the Corsairs of the RESCAP flight, which had been orbiting off the coast in case they were needed, swept in to drop their bombs before returning to the carrier. Cdr Owens, VA-192's executive officer, was leading the flight at 14,000 feet when he spotted two SAMs that had been launched in his direction. One of the missiles exploded about 150 feet off the port beam but the other exploded directly in front of the aircraft. Within seconds the hydraulic flight control system began to fail and the aircraft started to roll. Cdr Owens recrossed the coast and managed to guide his damaged aircraft back to the *Saratoga*. However, as he slowed down for a straight-in approach to the carrier, the nose dropped and the aircraft rolled uncontrollably to the right. The pilot ejected and was soon picked up by the ever-present plane guard helicopter. Cdr Owens became the squadron commander of VA-192 in May 1973.

A-1E   52-133857   1 SOS, 56 SOW, USAF, Nakhon Phanom
       Maj Esequiel Martinez Encinas (KIA)
A Skyraider was lost near Muang Khongxedon, 25 miles north of Pakse during a Steel Tiger mission in southern Laos. A flight of two aircraft was directed onto a target by a Covey FAC and made multiple passes. Maj Zeke Encinas was diving on his sixth pass when his aircraft was seen to start smoking and continue its dive until it crashed. There was no apparent attempt to escape and the pilot may have been wounded. A ground team later searched the wreck and found the pilot's remains as well as evidence of shrapnel damage to the aircraft's cockpit, probably from an exploding round of 23mm AAA.

A-7A   153230   VA-105, USN, USS *Saratoga*
       Lt Larry Ronald Kilpatrick (KIA)
After nightfall the *Saratoga* lost another of it's A-7s over North Vietnam. After completing a search for merchant ships off the coast, a section of two Corsairs flew inland to commence an armed reconnaissance patrol. About 10 miles south of Ha Tinh the two aircraft became separated and as he was trying to rejoin the leader, Lt Kilpatrick reported that he had sighted two trucks and was rolling in to attack them. The last message from Lt Kilpatrick was that he had completed his bombing run. No trace of the aircraft or its pilot was found in the subsequent search and it was presumed that the Corsair had either flown into high ground or had been shot down.

18 June 1972

F-4J   157273   VF-213, USN, USS *Kitty Hawk*
       Lt Cdr Roy Cash (survived)
       Lt R J Laib (survived)
A section of Phantoms was flying a BARCAP mission over Hon Nieu island near Vinh during a dawn attack on a merchant ship. Lt Cdr Cash was jinking at 1,000 feet in an attempt to throw the anti-aircraft gunners off their aim when his aircraft was hit by 23mm flak. The port wing caught fire and fuel streamed from the aircraft as Lt Cdr Cash headed out to sea towards his carrier. About 100 miles out to sea the pilot eventually lost control as the hydraulic system began to fail completely. The crew ejected safely and were quickly picked up by a Navy helicopter. Lt Cdr Cash and his NFO, Lt J E Kain, had shot down a Mig when serving with VF-33 on 10 July 1968

AC-130A   55-0043   16 SOS, 8 TFW, USAF, Ubon
       Capt Paul Faris Gilbert (KIA)
       Capt Robert Allan Wilson (KIA)
       Capt Gordon Bocher (survived)
       Maj Gerald Francis Ayres (KIA)
       Maj Robert Herman Harrison (KIA)

The jungle penetrator carried by SAR helicopters was designed to penetrate through dense foliage so that the rescue cable could reach survivors on the ground. The hinged seat could be swung out for the survivor to take the ride into the hovering helicopter. The PJ often rode the seat down to the ground to assist in the rescue. USAF

Capt Mark Giles Danielson (KIA)
2Lt Robert Reid (survived)
MSgt Jacob Edward Mercer (KIA)
TSgt Richard Milton Cole (KIA)
SSgt Donald Herman Klinke (KIA)
SSgt Larry Jerome Newman (KIA)
SSgt Richard E Nyhof (KIA)
Sgt Leon Andrew Hunt (KIA)
Sgt Stanley Lawrence Lehrke (KIA)
SSgt William B Patterson (survived)

An AC-130A Spectre gunship was operating over the border country about 25 miles southwest of Hué when it was shot down by an SA-7 missile. The first recorded SA-7 firing at an AC-130 took place on 5 May and the 16th SOS had been fortunate not to lose an aircraft to the SA-7 until this incident. Capt Paul Gilbert and his crew had taken off from Ubon for a patrol near the A Shau Valley. The missile hit the Number 3 engine and the wing was blown off moments later when a fuel tank exploded. At least three of the crew were able to escape from the aircraft by parachute and were rescued the next day by SAR helicopters. Since the war unconfirmed reports have circulated regarding the possibility that at least one of the 12 men listed as deceased actually survived the crash and was captured. However, as with so many uncorroborated reports, the possibility that anyone else had survived the crash appeared to be denied once and for all when the partial remains of 12 bodies were found at the crash site in 1993. Three members of the crew, Ayres, Danielson and Mercer, were identified individually by the Central Identification Laboratory in Hawaii, the remainder were identified as group remains in a USAF announcement of 21 October 1994. The remains, consisting of around 300 pieces of bone and several teeth, were buried as a group at Arlington National Cemetery on 17 November 1994. Even so, several of the families of the deceased still contest the identification of the remains.

A-37B   69-6349   8 SOS, 377 ABW, USAF, Bien Hoa
                    1 pilot, name unknown (survived)
A Dragonfly crashed accidentally in Thailand but the pilot escaped unharmed.

20 June 1972

F-8J   150923   VF-211, USN, USS *Hancock*
                  Cdr James W Davis (survived)
A Crusader, Nickel 102, was flying a mission over the border near the Mu Gia Pass when it was shot down by ground fire. Cdr Davis, the CO of VF-211, was strafing a storage area in a 45-degree dive when his aircraft was hit by 37mm flak on its second pass. A fire warning light came on in the cockpit and the hydraulic and flight control system began to fail. Cdr Davis ejected when the aircraft started to roll out of control and entered a flat spin. He was then protected by a constant stream of A-4s and F-8s that blasted any movement in the jungle near the downed pilot. Cdr Davis was rescued the following day by an HH-53 flown by Capt B D Orrell of the 40th ARRS. On 1 May 1967 this Crusader was flown by Lt Cdr M Wright when he shot down a MiG-17.

A-1J   52-142043   1 SOS, 56 SOW, USAF, Nakhon Phanom
                     Capt Larry G Highfill (survived)
About five hours after Cdr Davis was shot down one of the Sandys that was protecting him was also brought down. Capt Highfill, Sandy 07, had been suppressing ground fire about 25 miles west of Hué and was just climbing away to return to base to refuel when his aircraft was hit by 23mm AAA. One of the Skyraider's fuel cells was ruptured and caught fire forcing Capt Highfill to eject. He was also rescued at first light the next day by Capt Orrell's HH-53.

21 June 1972

F-4E   69-0282   334 TFS, 4 TFW attached to 8 TFW, USAF, Ubon
                  Capt George A Rose (POW)
                  1Lt Peter A Callaghan (POW)
A common feature of many raids during the Linebacker offensive was the extensive use of chaff to blind the North Vietnamese radars. Chaff consisted of strips of metallic foil cut to specific lengths to match particular band frequencies. When this foil was dropped in quantity it blotted out large areas on the enemy radar screens. Phantoms were often used to drop foil ahead of the strike force to deny the North Vietnamese knowledge of the exact location of the strike aircraft thereby making it more difficult for the MiGs to intercept and for the radar-controlled guns to find their targets. Capt Rose and 1Lt Callaghan were flying a chaff bomber in support of a raid on the 21st. Over the Red River near Piu Tho, about 40 miles northwest of Hanoi, the chaff flight was suddenly attacked by three MiG-21s and Capt Rose's aircraft was hit by an Atoll missile. The aircraft exploded scattering its load of chaff everywhere and the crew ejected but were soon captured. They were both released from Hanoi on 28 March 1973. George Rose had flown with the 12th TFW from Cam Ranh Bay in 1966/1967 and had served two tours in Germany before returning to the USA. He had arrived at Ubon with the 334th TFS in April 1972.

24 June 1972

F-4E   '66-0315'   421 TFS, 366 TFW, USAF, Da Nang
                     Capt David B Grant (POW)
                     Capt William David Beekman (POW)

F-4D   66-7636   25 TFS, 8 TFW, USAF, Ubon
                  1Lt James Lon McCarty (KIA)
                  1Lt Charles Allen Jackson (POW)
Two more Phantoms were lost to MiGs on the 24th. A large number of aircraft were sent to bomb the iron and steel plant at Thai Nguyen but as the aircraft neared the target they were jumped by several MiG-21s. The strike force lost its usual cohesion as it had to manoeuvre to avoid the chaff flight egressing the target area. It was at this point that the MiGs pounced on one of the escort flights about 40 miles west of Hanoi and a Phantom flown by Capt Grant and Capt Beekman was shot down from 20,000 feet by an air-to-air missile. The crew were soon captured and imprisoned. About 10 minutes later another Phantom, this time from the strike force, was shot down by a MiG near Thai Nguyen. The aircraft had just cleared the target when it was attacked by a pair of MiG-21s that dropped out of the overcast. The WSO, 1Lt Jackson, ejected safely and was captured but the pilot apparently did not escape and was killed in the incident. Despite severe ejection injuries, 1Lt Jackson escaped the night after he was captured but he was soon apprehended and imprisoned. McCarty and

Jackson are listed as being members of the 433rd TFS in some sources. 1Lt Jackson was repatriated on 12 February 1973 while Capt Grant (75 missions) and Capt Beekman (175 missions) were released on 28 March. The serial number for the 421st TFS aircraft is thought to be incorrect as 66-0315 was flying with the Thunderbirds aerobatic team at this time and later served at Nellis AFB.

25 June 1972

A-7E   157437   VA-22, USN, USS *Coral Sea*
Lt Geoffrey Raymond Shumway (KIA)

At dusk on the 25th two A-7s from the *Coral Sea* set off an armed reconnaissance mission in the area north of Vinh. Lt Shumway in the leading aircraft saw two trucks parked in hilly terrain near the village of Thung Lim, 30 miles north of Vinh. Lt Shumway was seen to roll in to a 20-degree dive attack but when his wingman next looked after setting up his own attack all he saw was a fireball on the ground near the target. It was suspected that Lt Shumway had flown into the ground in the poor light conditions of approaching night while he was concentrating on hitting the trucks. This was the last aircraft lost by the *Coral Sea* before the end of its sixth war cruise on 11 July 1972. The carrier returned for a seventh cruise on 20 March 1973 but did not lose any more aircraft. The *Coral Sea* was finally decommissioned on 30 April 1991 and was scrapped at Baltimore between 1993 and 1997.

O-2A   68-11015   20 TASS, 366 TFW, USAF, Da Nang
Capt C M Hovston (survived)

The situation around Hué was improving and the NVA showing signs of retreating to the north. Capt Hovston was flying a night FAC mission when his aircraft was shot down by automatic weapons fire 10 miles to the southwest of Hué. He bailed out safely and was later rescued by a US Army helicopter.

26 June 1972

O-2A   68-10982   21 TASS, 377 ABW, USAF, Tan Son Nhut
Capt David Lewis Yoakum (KIA)
Capt Thomas Joseph Jozefowski (KIA)

Another FAC was shot down the following day in South Vietnam, this time with the loss of both crew. The aircraft was hit by automatic weapons fire near Phu My, 12 miles north of Phu Cat, and crashed before either of the crew could escape.

27 June 1972

F-4E   67-0243   308 TFS, 31 TFW attached to 432 TRW, USAF, Udorn
Capt John P Cerak (POW)
Capt David B Dingee (POW)

The 27th of June turned out to be a bad day for the USAF with the loss of five aircraft in combat, three of them to MiGs, the worst day in terms of air-to-air casualties of the entire war as no MiGs were shot down in return. The first loss of the day occurred during a raid on Bac Mai airfield. One of the CAP flights for the mission was orbiting about 40 miles to the west of Hanoi when they received warning of a SAM launch. No SAMs were fired but the crews were distracted long enough for one of the aircraft to be hit by a missile from a MiG-21 forcing the crew to eject immediately. Both men were captured and spent the rest of the war in prison until released on 28 March 1973. This was a highly experienced crew having a combined total of nearly 600 combat missions under their belts. Capt Cerak had flown 254 missions when he was shot down. Capt Dingee had recently started on his second tour and had flown a total of 325 combat missions in Southeast Asia. He had been shot down with another pilot on the first day of June and had been rescued on that occasion. His son, Capt Steven Dingee, was credited with shooting down an Iraqi helicopter on 11 February 1991 while flying an F-15C during Operation Desert Storm.

F-4E   68-0314   308 TFS, 31 TFW attached to 432 TRW, USAF, Udorn
Lt Col Farrell Junior Sullivan (KIA)
Capt Richard Logan Francis (POW)

Simultaneously with the raid on Bac Mai another formation of aircraft from Udorn was attacking a major motor vehicle facility in Hanoi. During the raid one of the chaff bombers was hit by a SAM at 17,700 feet almost directly over Gia Lam Airport, just to the east of the city. Only the WSO, Capt Francis, survived the incident but he was captured. He was released on 28 March 1973 and is recorded as being a member of the 523rd TFS and had flown 57 combat missions at the time of his shoot down.

O-2A   68-11026   21 TASS, 377 ABW, USAF, Tan Son Nhut
Capt David Earle Baker (POW)

Operations in Cambodia were still continuing even though the concentration of activity was now once more in North Vietnam. The last US fixed-wing aircraft to be lost over Cambodia had been shot down in February 1972 but on 27 June an O-2 was lost during a visual reconnaissance mission. The aircraft was shot down by ground fire near Phum Prasol, 20 miles to the southwest of Tay Ninh. Remarkably, Capt Baker was the only US POW ever to be released from Cambodia when he was handed over to the US authorities on 12 February 1973 at Loc Ninh. David Baker had flown EC-121s in Southeast Asia earlier in the war and eventually rose to the rank of Brigadier General and was responsible for the Air Force's joint operations and interoperability programmes following service in Operation Desert Storm with the 4th TFW. Gen Baker retired from the USAF on 1 October 1997.

F-4E   69-7271   366 TFW, USAF, Takhli
Capt Lynn A Aikman (survived)
Capt Thomas J Hanton (POW)

F-4E   69-7296   366 TFW, USAF, Takhli
Maj R C Miller (survived)
1Lt Richard H McDow (POW)

The MiGs struck again on the 27th when they attacked a flight of four Phantoms that had been protecting the SAR forces as they were attempting to rescue Capt Cerak and Capt Dingee who had been shot down earlier in the day. Valent flight had completed their primary mission of dropping chaff for a strike on Hanoi when it was diverted to the SAR mission. The flight was searching an area about 80 miles to the west of Hanoi heading towards a flight of MiGs when two MiG-21s sneaked in unseen behind and fired their air-to-air missiles, hitting two of the Phantoms. The pilots from the two aircraft were subsequently rescued under heavy ground fire by HH-53s of the 40th ARRS but the luckless WSOs were both captured. Sgt Charles D McGrath, the PJ from one of the helicopters, was awarded the AFC for his actions in protecting a survivor during this rescue. Capt Hanton and 1Lt McDow were both released on 28 March 1973. The 366th TFW moved from Da Nang to Takhli towards the end of June and officially took up residence at the Thai base on the 27th. The move to Takhli was made as the security of Da Nang was becoming more difficult due to the increased threat from enemy forces since the Spring Invasion. The loss of two Phantoms on the first day of operations from Takhli was not an auspicious start to this new phase of the Wing's career.

29 June 1972

OV-10A   68-3804   20 TASS, 6498 ABW, USAF, Da Nang
Capt Steven Logan Bennett (KIA)
Capt Michael B Brown, USMC (survived)

In an inspiring display of courage and self-sacrifice, Capt Steve Bennett saved the life of his Marine Corps observer when their OV-10 Bronco was badly damaged by ground fire on the 29th. The pair was flying a naval gunfire support mission directing fire from the cruiser USS *Newport News* and the destroyer USS *R B Anderson* near Quang Tri. The mission was extended when the relief OV-10 was delayed and Bennett and Brown controlled a strike by a section of Navy Intruders just as darkness approached. As they were heading back to Da Nang Capt Bennett, flying as Covey 87, heard an emergency transmission from a platoon of South Vietnamese troops who were under heavy attack just west of Quang Tri. There was no air support or artillery immediately available with the exception of another OV-10, Nail 70 flown by Capt Darrel Whitcomb, who was directed to join Covey 87. The two aircraft started to make strafing attacks on the enemy troops.

Capt Bennett made four strafing runs against the North Vietnamese troops forcing them to pull back. On the fifth pass the aircraft was hit by an SA-7 missile at 6,500 feet. The missile hit the port engine, which burst into flames as the undercarriage hung down loosely. The aircraft headed towards the coast and was joined by Nail 70 as Capt Brown transmitted a May Day message. When over the sea Capt Brown discovered that his parachute had been shredded by shrapnel from the SA-7. Capt Bennett turned west in an attempt to reach Hué but the fire grew worse and it became apparent that he would not be able to reach land. The Bronco's ditching characteristics were known to be poor as the cockpit tended to break up as it hit the surface of the water. Nevertheless, in an attempt to save his observer, Capt Bennett decided to ditch his aircraft a few hundred yards off the South Vietnamese coast. Capt Whitcomb and another Nail FAC that had joined him directed the rescue forces to the incident. The undercarriage hit the water first and the Bronco cartwheeled breaking up the cockpit on impact. Capt Brown was able to escape through a hole in the side of the fuselage and was picked up by a Navy helicopter but Capt Bennett was trapped and drowned. His body was recovered from the wreckage the next day. Steven Bennett, who had been in combat for less than three months, was posthumously awarded the Medal of Honor, which was presented to his widow on 8 August 1974. As a tribute to Bennett's self-sacrifice a US Navy chartered commercial sealift ship was christened the *Capt Steven L Bennett* on 20 November 1997.

30 June 1972

OV-10A   67-14700   20 TASS, 6498 ABW, USAF, Da Nang
1Lt E E Steincamp (survived)
1 crew, name unknown (KIA)

Another Bronco was lost in the vicinity of Quang Tri the day after Steve Bennet's aircraft was brought down. 1Lt Steincamp was flying an FAC mission, probably with a Vietnamese observer, when their aircraft was hit by ground fire about eight miles southeast of Quang Tri. In this incident the observer was killed but the pilot survived and was recovered by ground troops.

1 July 1972

O-2A   68-11040   21 TASS, 377 ABW, USAF, Tan Son Nhut
1Lt R W Vincent (survived)
1Lt W C Brooks (survived)

Sundog 5 was an O-2 FAC that was shot down on a mission just on the Cambodian side of the border with South Vietnam about 30 miles northwest of Saigon. The aircraft was hit by 37mm flak and both the crew bailed out and parachuted safely into the jungle. An Army helicopter later rescued them.

F-4E   67-0277   34 TFS, 388 TFW, USAF, Korat
Maj Paul Kurtz Robinson (POW)
Capt Kevin Joseph Cheney (POW)

The Korat Wing flew a major strike on Kep airfield on the 1st of the month during which it lost one of its Phantoms from a CAP flight. The raid was met by the usual barrage of SAMs and all the CAP aircraft were jinking in an attempt to dodge the missiles. Maj Robinson was doing 520 knots at 19,000 feet when he was warned of a SAM launch. His aircraft was bracketed by two missiles that exploded and set his aircraft on fire. Both the crew ejected safely and came down about eight miles southeast of Kep but were soon captured after landing. Apparently, as they were floating down Maj Robinson was heard on his survival radio to jokingly tell Capt Cheney to meet him at base operations at Kep airfield when they landed! Both crew, who are listed as being members of the 469th TFS in some documents, were released on 28 March 1973. Maj Robinson had flown a tour in the F-100 in Vietnam during 1967/68 and had amassed an impressive total of 350 missions over South Vietnam (several as a Misty FAC) and 137 over the North by the time of his capture. After his release from Hanoi he resumed his Air Force career and flew A-10s from RAF Bentwaters and finally retired as the vice commander of the Tactical Fighter Weapons Centre at Nellis AFB. He later became a vice president of the Wells Fargo Bank. Capt Cheney had flown two consecutive tours at Korat and had flown 280 missions over

Laos, 20 over Cambodia, 40 over South Vietnam and 62 over North Vietnam, many of these missions as a Tiger FAC.

2 July 1972

O-1   serial ..?   unit ..?, USAF, base ..?
              1 pilot, name unknown (survived)

Little is known about this particular incident except that the aircraft was shot down by an SA-7 missile near Phum Luong, just inside Cambodia, about 50 miles west of Saigon. The fate of the pilot is unknown but a 1Lt John Michael Cole is listed as having been killed on this date but in Thua Thien province, just to the north of Da Nang.

3 July 1972

F-4E   69-0289   13 TFS, 432 TRW, USAF, Udorn
              Capt Stephen Howard Cuthbert (KIA)
              Capt Marion Anthony Marshall (POW)

A Phantom was lost during a Laredo fast FAC mission over North Vietnam on the 3rd. The target was a suspected underground fuel tank farm about 15 miles southwest of Ha Tinh. The aircraft's centre line fuel tank collapsed, probably as the result of small arms fire, during a dive on the target and the aircraft crashed nearby. The WSO, Capt Marshall, was command ejected by the pilot and was captured but Capt Cuthbert apparently did not survive the incident. Tony Marshall was released from captivity on 29 March 1973. He had flown a total of 266 combat missions during the war, 51 of them over North Vietnam and had extended his tour at Udorn for an extra six months. On 21 December 1990 the USAF announced that remains handed over by the Vietnamese in the previous September had been identified as those of Capt Cuthbert.

5 July 1972

A-37B   serial ..?   8 SOS, 377 ABW, USAF, Bien Hoa
              1 pilot, name unknown (survived)

Another victim of the diminutive SA-7 was an A-37 Dragonfly that was shot down 10 miles southwest of Hué on the 5th. The pilot was recovered safely.

F-4E   67-0339   34 TFS, 388 TFW, USAF, Korat
              Maj William J Elander (POW)
              1Lt Donald K Logan (POW)

F-4E   67-0296   34 TFS, 388 TFW, USAF, Korat
              Capt William A Spencer (POW)
              1Lt Brian J Seek (POW)

Bass flight was the Phantom escort element of a 16-aircraft strike force that was attacking a target near Hanoi when it was jumped by a number of MiG-21s just to the east of Kep. The escorting Phantoms were orbiting the strike aircraft at 18,000 feet as they were dropping LGBs on the target, a procedure that took longer than the usual visual dive bombing run. The MiGs were vectored through low cloud and popped up just long enough to launch their Atoll missiles before diving down back through the cloud. Two of the Phantoms were hit by the missiles within seconds of each other and all four crewmen involved survived but were captured. Maj Elander's aircraft came down about 20 miles northeast of Kep while Capt Spencer's aircraft crashed about eight miles east of the town. 1Lt Seek had a particularly harrowing escape. Unable to eject himself his life was saved by Capt Spencer who command ejected him as flames in the cockpit started to burn through his clothing. As 1Lt Seek fell from 18,000 feet his parachute failed to open automatically and he had to struggle to open his 'chute, which eventually deployed at 5,000 feet above the ground. All four Phantom crew were released eight months later on 29 March 1973. Maj Elander had flown a tour of 100 missions in the F-105 in 1965 and had been a pilot with the Thunderbirds demonstration team in 1969 before completing another 67 missions in the F-4 prior to being shot down. Don Logan had flown 133 combat missions in Southeast Asia and converted to the F-111A upon returning to the USA. He later worked for Rockwell International, Northrop and Boeing and is the author of a number of aviation books including

The 388th TFW at Korat RTAFB – 1972, which describes his own shoot down in detail. Although using 34th TFS aircraft all the crews involved were from the 469th TFS. MiG-21PFM serial number 5020 is currently displayed at the VPAF Museum in Hanoi and is claimed to be the aircraft that Nguyen Tien Sam of the 927th Fighter Regiment was flying when he shot down two F-4s on 5 July 1972. It is stated that Sam's engine flamed out as he flew through the explosion caused by his first missile but he restarted the engine and shot down the second Phantom. F-4E 67-0296 shot down a MiG-21 on 21 Jun 1972 when being flown by Lt Col V R Christiansen and Maj K M Harden.

F-4D   66-7680   433 TFS, 8 TFW, USAF, Ubon
              Capt Michael D Vanwagenen (survived)
              Maj E K Johnson (survived)

At the same time as the two Korat aircraft were being shot down a Ubon Phantom was also damaged just to the east of Kep. The aircraft was part of a strike force and was about to bomb a bridge in Route Package VI when one of the aircraft was hit by a SAM at 21,000 feet. The starboard wing was damaged and Capt Vanwagenen turned towards the sea. Luckily his aircraft remained airborne for some time and the crew eventually had to eject over the Gulf about 35 miles northeast of the DMZ. They were both rescued by a USAF SAR helicopter. This was the first Phantom fitted with the Pave Knife laser-guided bombing system to be lost during the war. Laser weapons were just being introduced in quantity at this stage of the war and the new technology was rapidly proving itself by hitting a number of pinpoint targets, including bridges, that had previously stood up to many conventional weapons. It was all the more important that the laser pod and associated avionics did not fall into enemy hands so Capt Vanwagenen saved not only himself and his WSO but also a valuable piece of equipment from capture.

6 July 1972

F-4D   65-0800   497 TFS, 8 TFW, USAF, Ubon
              Maj Harland M Davis (KIA)
              1Lt Frederick M Koss (KIA)

A Phantom crashed as it attempted to land in a heavy rainstorm at night at Ubon after a strike mission. One source suggests that it was hit by small arms fire on the approach to the airfield. Neither of the crew managed to escape before the aircraft crashed. Maj Davis was assigned to 435th TFS but the aircraft apparently belonged to the 497th. He had flown F-100s from Lakenheath with the 48th TFW in 1962 and had survived a tour with the 1st ACS in South Vietnam in 1965 flying 283 missions in the A-1E.

7 July 1972

A-6A   155690   VMA(AW)-533, MAG-15, USMC, Nam Phong
              1Lt Alan Joseph Kroboth (POW)
              Capt Leonard Robertson (KIA)

The enemy threat to US bases was particularly severe at Da Nang which was frequently under attack from enemy sappers even before the Spring Invasion. The ever-growing concern for security of MAG-15's aircraft and personnel drove the Marines to move the Group to an austere airfield in the middle of Thailand. The airfield at Nam Phong had been built by the Americans in 1967 as an emergency landing base and had rarely been used except as a Special Forces camp for the training of Laotian guerillas. It had a 10,000 feet paved runway and little else to commend it before the Marines moved in. The Marines formed Task Force Delta to open up the airfield and the first troops arrived on 24 May. VMFA-115 was the first squadron to arrive, transferring from Da Nang on 16 June. By the 20th VMFA-232 and VMA(AW)-533 had also arrived at Nam Phong. These were joined later by a detachment of KC-130s from VMGR-152 and four CH-46s of H&MS-36 for SAR duties. Although undeniably more secure than any of the bases in South Vietnam, Nam Phong's greatest drawback was its distance from MAG-15's targets, which necessitated in-flight refuelling and turnarounds at Da Nang before return missions to Nam Phong.

The first aircraft lost after the move to Nam Phong was an Intruder that was shot down during a raid on a storage area five

miles south of Khe Sanh. The aircraft was pulling up from its first pass over the target when it was hit in the starboard wing by AAA and set on fire. Only the pilot, 1Lt Kroboth, ejected and survived, although he was captured. His captors told him that his navigator had died in the crash. He was repatriated from North Vietnam on 27 March 1973.

8 July 1972

F-4E   69-7563   4 TFS, 366 TFW, USAF, Takhli
              Lt Col R E Ross (survived)
              Capt S M Imaye (survived)

Once again the escort element tackled the MiGs during a raid on Hanoi and lost one of their number while protecting the strike force. After the attack on a major vehicle repair facility in Hanoi the aircraft headed back to Thailand but about 45 miles southwest of Hanoi the MiGs made a concerted attack. Lt Col Ross's aircraft was damaged by an air-to-air missile that put the left engine out of action but he managed to make it back into Thailand before he and his WSO had to eject just north of Udorn. Capt Imaye was later credited with a MiG-21 when flying with Lt Col Gene Taft on 29 July. Lt Col Ross had been shot down on 21 May and was rescued from the Gulf of Tonkin.

B-52G   59-2600   72 SW(P), USAF, Andersen
              Lt Col James Lloyd Vaughan (KIA)
              6 crew, names unknown (survived)

A B-52G suffered a mechanical failure soon after taking off from Andersen en route to Vietnam and crashed into the sea, killing one of the crew. The 72nd SW(P) had been activated on 1 June 1972 with four provisional bomb squadrons to control the large number of B-52Gs deploying from the USA as part of the build-up for Operation Linebacker. By July Andersen was bursting at the seams with 12,000 deployed personnel on the base compared to 4,000 prior to the influx of reinforcements.

9 July 1972

A-4F   154972   VA-212, USN, USS *Hancock*
              Cdr Frank Clifford Green (KIA)

Cdr Green was leading a night-time armed reconnaissance mission over North Vietnam when he spotted the lights of a truck on a road near Dam Khanh, 50 miles south of Hanoi. The visibility in the dark was about 10 miles but was marred by a light haze. Soon after Cdr Green commenced his attack the wingman saw his aircraft fly into the ground and explode. There was no indication that he had escaped. The crash site was located by a SAR team but it had been camouflaged by the North Vietnamese and the area was well defended. It was presumed that Cdr Green had inadvertently flown into the ground through target fixation or poor visibility.

10 July 1972

F-4J   155803   VF-103, USN, USS *Saratoga*
              Lt Robert Irving Randall (POW)
              Lt Frederick J Masterson (POW)

A Phantom CAP flight over Kep was engaged by several MiGs from the airfield below. Lt Randall was dogfighting with a MiG-17 when his aircraft was hit, probably by cannon fire. The aft end of the Phantom caught fire and the crew ejected about seven miles west of Kep. The crew were soon captured and imprisoned and were repatriated on 29 March 1973. This Phantom was the last US aircraft shot down by a MiG-17 during the war. The MiG pilot was Hanh Vinh Tuong of the 923rd Fighter Regiment who is said to have been killed later during this engagement although no US aircraft claimed a MiG on this date. This was the only MiG-victim of 1972 that was confirmed to have been shot down by cannon fire rather than by an air-to-air missile.

F-4D   66-7707   25 TFS, 8 TFW, USAF, Ubon
              Lt Col Brad L Sharp (survived)
              1Lt Michael Pomphrey (survived)

As the CO of the 25th TFS was taking off from Ubon leading a raid of eight Phantoms, his starboard tyre blew out just at the 'abort/no go' decision point. Lt Col Sharp aborted the take off but

the wheel disintegrated and pieces of it punctured the drop tank, which caught fire. The aircraft engaged the barrier at the end of the runway and was quickly engulfed in flames. 1Lt Pomphrey rapidly left the aircraft and got clear of the flames but re-entered the inferno to assist his pilot who had injured his ankle on jumping to the ground. The aircraft burnt out igniting both ejection seats and two Mk84 LGBs. 1Lt Pomphrey and two maintenance men were awarded Airman's Medals for rescuing Lt Col Sharp. The airfield was closed for several hours and a Linebacker raid had to be cancelled. This was the second Pave Knife Phantom lost by the 25th in a matter of days. Lt Col Sharp had been shot down during a Wolf FAC mission in southern Laos on 3 December 1969.

11 July 1972

A-4F   155046   VA-55, USN, USS *Hancock*
   Lt Cdr Henry D Lesesne (POW)

An oil storage depot at Hai Duong, midway between Hanoi and Haiphong, was the target for a strike by the aircraft of the *Hancock* on the 11th. As the strike force hit the target the Iron Hand defence suppression flight attacked a SAM site near the Red River about 20 miles southwest of Hai Duong. Lt Cdr Lesesne had received a SAM launch warning and was diving in a split-S manoeuvre at 11,000 feet above a low cloud base when his aircraft was hit by an SA-2. The rear end of the Skyhawk was engulfed in flames and the aircraft soon started rolling uncontrollably. The pilot ejected and was quickly captured. After eight months imprisonment, Henry Lesesne was repatriated on 29 March 1973. He resumed his flying career after returning to the USA and converted to the A-7E Corsair.

12 July 1972

F-4E   69-0302   334 TFS, 4 TFW attached to 8 TFW, USAF, Ubon
   1Lt James Linton Huard (KIA)
   Capt Samuel O'Donnell (KIA)

A Wolf FAC failed to return from a solo mission over North Vietnam. The aircraft was thought to have been shot down near the mouth of the Sou Giang River, 15 miles northwest of Dong Hoi. During the subsequent three-day search for the aircraft two FAC pilots reported hearing a faint SAR beeper but nothing further

was heard or seen of the crew and intense AAA and SAM activity in the area precluded a more extensive search. Later information indicated that the aircraft crashed into a reservoir. Apparently one body was recovered from the site and buried by local villagers before being exhumed in 1976 and reburied in Hanoi. These remains were repatriated to the USA in 1988 along with 37 other sets of remains and eventually, by the use of mitochondrial DNA testing using samples of his mother's blood, the remains were proved to be those of 1Lt Huard. He was buried at Arlington National Cemetery in May 1997.

17 July 1972

F-4D   66-8772   497 TFS, 8 TFW, USAF, Ubon
   1Lt G K Tushek (survived)
   Capt Wayne Gordon Brown (KIA)

A-7C   156792   VA-86, USN, USS *America*
   Cdr William D Yonke (survived)

A-7C   156771   VA-86, USN, USS *America*
   Lt D K Anderson (survived)

In a remarkable incident a Night Owl FAC Phantom and two Navy Corsairs were lost on a night mission about 20 miles southwest of Hué. The Phantom was guiding the Corsairs to a target using its LORAN navigation system to pinpoint the target. The three aircraft were in close formation as the A-7s dropped their Mk82 bombs simultaneously on the Phantom's mark. One of the bombs exploded prematurely damaging all three aircraft. The Phantom became a mass of flame and both the crew ejected from the aircraft but Capt Brown was badly injured. At first light an OV-10 arrived on the scene and spoke to both survivors on their emergency radios. Capt Brown had injured his back and was unable to move. The FAC called in a strike to secure the area around the survivors and shortly afterwards a pair of Skyraiders arrived followed by two HH-53s. One of the helicopters descended below the low cloud but had to abort the rescue attempt when strong winds and turbulence over the mountains, in addition to ground fire, almost caused it to crash. However, before the next rescue attempt could be made gunshots were heard by 1Lt Tushek near where Capt Brown was thought to be hiding and the rescue commander could not regain radio contact with the Captain. The winds abated a little so the rescue

forces returned just before sunset and an HH-53 from the 37th ARRS eventually winched 1Lt Tushek to safety in most difficult conditions caused by weather, terrain and enemy action.

Both Corsairs had also been damaged in the incident and Cdr Yonke's aircraft caught fire. He turned towards the coast but lost control as the fire burned through the flying controls. The CO of VA-86 ejected just south of Hué and was soon recovered. His wingman, Lt Anderson, managed to make the coast but was losing fuel rapidly and flamed out about 15 miles northeast of Da Nang. He was rescued by a USAF SAR helicopter. Malfunctioning ordnance had been a minor but persistent cause of aircraft attrition throughout the war in Southeast Asia.

A-7B   154521   VA-155, USN, USS *Oriskany*
   Lt Leon Frederick Haas (KIA)

Later in the night and further to the north yet another Corsair was lost in action. Lt Haas was flying with another A-7 on an armed reconnaissance mission just off the coast of North Vietnam when he reported that he was taking evasive action after seeing what may have been a SAM launch. The aircraft apparently crashed into the sea near Hon Nieu island and the pilot was killed. It was presumed that Lt Haas had inadvertently flown into the water while trying to keep sight of the light he had seen earlier.

19 July 1972

F-4D   66-0253   7 TFS, 49 TFW, USAF, Takhli
   Capt H D Wier (survived)
   1Lt K G Edwards (survived)

The 49th TFW from Holloman AFB, New Mexico deployed with four squadrons consisting of 72 F-4Ds to Takhli in Operation Constant Guard III in early May. This was the largest overseas deployment that TAC had mounted up to that date. A total of 3,195 personnel and 1,600 tons of cargo was airlifted from Holloman to Takhli in just nine days. Takhli had been virtually abandoned since the 355th TFW deactivated in December 1970, so the base had to be reopened and virtually rebuilt. The 49th's first combat casualty took place during a close air support mission two miles east of Quang Tri on 19 July. Capt Wier was making his second 45-degree dive on enemy bunkers in a village when his aircraft was hit by 37mm flak. The aircraft's rear fuselage caught fire but the Phantom remained airborne long enough for the crew to eject about five miles out to sea. Capt Wier and 1Lt Edwards were later rescued by a US Navy vessel. This may have been the same Capt H D Wier who was shot down over northern Laos on 2 January 1971 while flying with 388 TFW.

20 July 1972

F-4D   66-0265   35 TFS, 3 TFW attached to 388 TFW,
   USAF, Korat
   Capt Joe Lee Burns (survived)
   1Lt M Nelson (survived)

On the 20th the Air Force flew a Linebacker strike on POL storage at Kep airfield. The strike force hit the target and retired to the south to fly out over the Gulf of Tonkin before climbing to altitude for the return flight to Thailand. As Capt Burns was a few miles north of Hon Gay and about to cross the coast at 5,000 feet, his aircraft was hit by AAA and burst into flames. The aircraft just made it to the sea before the crew were forced to eject. They came down in the water close to the North Vietnamese coast but were rescued by a Navy SH-3 helicopter. Capt Burns was on his second tour in Southeast Asia and had flown 222 combat missions. He later helped set up the T-38 Aggressor Squadron at Nellis AFB to teach air combat training with the benefit of experience from Southeast Asia. He later commanded the 44th TFS.

Operating from Kadena on the island of Okinawa, the SR-71A flew high-speed, high-altitude reconnaissance missions over North Vietnam from March 1968. Although largely invulnerable to enemy air defences, two of the aircraft were lost in accidents during the war. USAF

SR-71A 64-17978   Det-OL-KA, 9 SRW, USAF, Kadena
                   Capt Dennis K Bush (survived)
                   Capt James W Fagg (survived)
The second and final SR-71 lost during the war in Southeast Asia suffered a landing accident at Kadena on 20 July. The aircraft was returning from a reconnaissance flight over North Vietnam when the pilot was told that strong crosswinds were buffeting the airfield and making landings difficult. Capt Bush made a normal approach and deployed the aircraft's massive braking parachute in a rapid deploy-jettison technique designed to slow the aircraft down but not allow weathercocking to one side. After the parachute was jettisoned, Capt Bush decided that the aircraft was in danger of running off the runway so he accelerated and took off for another attempt. He touched down again but now, without the benfit of a drag parachute, he was unable to slow the aircraft down rapidly or keep it on the runway in the strong crosswind. The SR-71 left the runway and the undercarriage hit a concrete structure causing major damage to the airframe. Both the crew escaped unharmed but the aircraft was damaged beyond repair and it was later cannibalised for spare parts for the rest of the SR-71 fleet. Aircraft 64-17978 had a Playboy bunny painted on its tail fin and was known as the 'Rapid Rabbit'.

22 July 1972

RF-8G 146873   Detachment 3, VFP-63, USN, USS *Midway*
                Lt Cdr Gordon Curtis Paige (POW)
A Crusader was despatched from the *Midway* for a photographic reconnaissance mission along Route 116 south of Thanh Hoa. Lt Cdr Paige crossed the coast and started his descent to commence his photo run. As the aircraft was passing through 4,500 feet it was hit by ground fire. The starboard wing was hit first and started to stream fuel. Then as the aircraft started a turn to port the ejection seat was fired by a hit in the cockpit. Moments after Lt Cdr Paige ejected the wing separated and the fuselage broke in half. Lt Cdr Paige was captured near Phong Bai, about 35 miles south of Thanh Hoa, and was imprisoned in Hanoi. He was released on 29 March 1973.

23 July 1972

A-7B 154531   VA-56, USN, USS *Midway*
               Lt(jg) Gary Leslie Shank (KIA)
Just as dusk began to turn day into night on the 23rd a pair of Corsairs crossed the North Vietnamese coast south of Haiphong to commence an armed reconnaissance mission. The leader made a bombing run on a target in the Ho Doi military area about 15 miles south of Haiphong. The wingman, Lt Shank, was then sent to start his bomb run but just after bomb release and as the aircraft started to pull out of its dive there was a flash on the aircraft's nose as it was hit by flak. The pilot may have been incapacitated as he did not eject before the aircraft dived into the sea just off the coast.

A-37B 69-6359   8 SOS, 377 ABW, USAF, Bien Hoa
                 1Lt Stephen Howard Gravrock (KIA)
The siege of An Loc was offically declared to be over on 18 June but the area was still heavily infiltrated by NVA troops. During a dusk close air support mission at An Loc 1Lt Gravrock was about to drop a load of napalm when his aircraft was hit by ground fire and crashed before he could escape.

A-7B 154532   VA-56, USN, USS *Midway*
               Lt Cdr Clarence Orfield Tolbert (survived)
A section of Corsairs was flying a night-time armed reconnaissance mission during which a POL storage site was attacked at Da Thit, some 35 miles southwest of Thanh Hoa. Lt Cdr Tolbert's aircraft was hit in the port wing by AAA as he approached the target at 3,500 feet. He jettisoned his ordnance and headed for the coast. The engine may have ingested some debris as during the flight back to the carrier the aircraft's engine surged and the fuel flow became erratic. When the Corsair was about 40 miles from the coast flames were seen coming from the jetpipe and the engine flamed out. The pilot ejected and was rescued by a US Navy helicopter. Clarence Tolbert was shot down and killed during an armed reconnaissance mission on 5 November.

24 July 1972

F-4E 66-0369   421 TFS, 366 TFW, USAF, Takhli
                Capt S A Hodnett (survived)
                1Lt D Fallert (survived)
A Phantom was shot down by a MiG-21 during a Linebacker raid near Kep. The aircraft was part of the escort flight and was damaged by an air-to-air missile fired by the MiG. The Phantom headed for the coast and the crew eventually ejected over the sea about 25 miles southeast of Haiphong. Both the crew were rescued by a Navy HH-3A SAR helicopter.

29 July 1972

F-4E 66-0367   4 TFS, 366 TFW, USAF, Takhli
                Capt James D Kula (POW)
                Capt Melvin K Matsui (POW)

F-105G 62-4443   17 WWS, 388 TFW, USAF, Korat
                 Maj T J Coady (survived)
                 Maj H F Murphy (survived)
A raid on Kep ran into trouble when it was engaged by several MiGs. One of the Phantoms from the chaff-escort flight was hit by an Atoll missile fired by a MiG-21 at about 10,000 feet some 15 miles northeast of Kep. The crew ejected a few moments later when it was realised that their burning aircraft was no longer responding to the controls. Capt Kula and Capt Matsui were soon captured and spent the rest of the war in a POW camp until they were released on 29 March 1973. Two of the attacking MiGs were shot down during the engagement. Maj Kula was flying his 35th mission when he was shot down. He returned to flying after repatriation and later commanded the 68th TFS when it transitioned from the F-4 to the F-16A.

About 10 minutes later, as the strike force was retiring from the target and heading out to sea, one of the Iron Hand F-105Gs engaged a MiG. As the Thunderchief performed a split-S manoeuvre it fired a Sidewinder missile at the MiG but the missile exploded prematurely and damaged the F-105's starboard wing. Maj Coady managed to coax his badly damaged aircraft out over the Gulf of Tonkin and set course for Da Nang. The crew ejected about five miles offshore from Da Nang and were soon picked up by US Marine Corps helicopters.

30 July 1972

F-4D 66-7576   435 TFS, 8 TFW, USAF, Ubon
                Lt Col William J Breckner (POW)
                1Lt Larry D Price (POW)
Three USAF Phantoms were lost over North Vietnam on the 30th. One aircraft was shot down during a raid on a major bridge near Hanoi. As Lt Col Breckner approached the target his aircraft was hit by a SAM and the crew ejected about five miles east of Hanoi. Both men were captured immediately and imprisoned in Hanoi until their release on 29 March 1973. William Breckner had joined the USAF in 1955 and had flown the F-86H, F-100D, F-101B and the F-106 in addition to the F-4. He flew Skyhawks with the Navy on an exchange tour and was on the ill-fated cruise of the *Forrestal* when it caught fire in July 1967 and returned to combat on board the *Intrepid* in 1968. He eventually retired from the Air Force with the rank of Major General.

F-4D 66-7770   523 TFS, 405 FW attached to 432 TRW,
                USAF, Udorn
                Capt D A Crane (survived)
                1Lt D W Petkunas (survived)
The 523rd TFS deployed from Clark AB and was attached to the 432nd TRW at Udorn on 9 April for seven months. The first aircraft lost by the Squadron was abandoned over the Gulf of Tonkin about 60 miles northeast of Vinh when it ran out of fuel returning from an escort mission. The crew were rescued by a Navy HH-3A SAR helicopter.

F-4D 66-7597   523 TFS, 405 FW attached to 432 TRW,
                USAF, Udorn
                Capt G B Brooks (survived)
                Capt J M McAdams (survived)

The second Phantom from the 523rd to go down on the 30th was damaged by a MiG during a combat air patrol about three hours later. Capt Brooks flew out to sea before he and his WSO ejected 35 miles east of Thanh Hoa and were rescued by a Navy HH-3A SAR helicopter.

B-52D 56-0677   307 SW, USAF, U-Tapao
                 Capt Thomas W Reasor (KIA)
                 Capt Ronald A Ashe (KIA)
                 Maj James E Hudelson (KIA)
                 Capt David J Price (KIA)
                 Capt Joseph L Ruzicka (KIA)
                 1 crew, name unknown (survived)
A B-52 from U-Tapao was struck by lightning during a combat mission. Most of the aircraft's instruments were knocked out by the strike. The port wing caught fire and the aircraft crashed killing all on board except for one man who managed to escape.

F-4D 66-0274   8 TFW, USAF, Ubon
                2 crew, names unknown (survived)
The Wolfpack lost a Phantom on the 30th when it accidentally crashed on landing back at Ubon following a combat mission. This aircraft was credited with killing a MiG-17 on 26 October 1967 when being flown by Capt J D Logeman and 1Lt F E McCoy of the 555th TFS.

31 July 1972

A-7A 153193   VA-105, USN, USS *Saratoga*
               1 pilot, name unknown (survived)
The *Saratoga* lost another Corsair in an accident during a launch for a combat mission. The aircraft's engine failed and the Corsair crashed into the sea moments after the pilot ejected safely.

2 August 1972

F-4J 155817   VMFA-232, MAG-15, USMC, Nam Phong
               1Lt R O Lamers (survived)
               1Lt Sam Gary Cordova (survived)
VMFA-232 had arrived at Da Nang along with VMFA-115 on 6 April in response to the North Vietnamese invasion. The Marine Corps F-4 squadrons redeployed to Nam Phong in June when the threat to Da Nang from enemy ground troops increased to a dangerous level. VMFA-232 lost its first aircraft from its new base on 2 August. As a Phantom was approaching the runway at Nam Phong following a training flight the engines failed through fuel starvation and the aircraft crashed. Both crew ejected safely but 1Lt Cordova was killed on the 26th of the month when he was shot down by a MiG-21.

6 August 1972

A-7B 154508   VA-56, USN, USS *Midway*
               Lt(jg) Michael Gene Penn (POW)
Lt Penn was part of an Iron Hand flight that was tasked with supporting an alpha strike on a transhipment point at Loi Dong in North Vietnam. As the flight was retiring from the target and heading for the coast a SAM warning was received and the flight leader saw two missiles heading towards them from the port beam. Lt Penn started evasive action but a missile exploded close to his aircraft at about 8,000 feet and the aircraft burst into flames and nosed over into a steep dive. Lt Penn ejected just south of Uong Bi, about 10 miles northeast of Haiphong, and spoke to his leader on his survival radio. Unfortunately, the area was too well defended to attempt a rescue and Lt Penn was soon captured. He was repatriated on 29 March 1973. Michael Penn had been on his 75th mission when he was shot down.

A-7A 153147   VA-105, USN, USS *Saratoga*
               Lt J R Lloyd (survived)
Another Corsair was lost over North Vietnam on the 6th after nightfall. A section of aircraft was flying an armed reconnaissance mission near Vinh when the aircraft picked up a signal indicating that they were being tracked by a Fan Song SAM radar and that a missile had been launched. The aircraft started jinking but at 3,500 feet and 300 knots Lt Lloyd's Corsair was hit and

the port wing started to disintegrate. The aircraft caught fire, the hydraulics failed and the controls stiffened. Lt Lloyd ejected as the aircraft pitched nose down. He landed safely near My Ngoc, 20 miles northwest of Vinh and was later rescued by a Navy HH-3A SAR helicopter. It could not be determined whether the aircraft had been hit by a SAM or by 37mm AAA, which was also seen at the same time as the SAM launch.

9 August 1972

F-4D   65-0599   7 TFS, 49 TFW, USAF, Takhli
                   Capt J L Beavers (survived)
                   1Lt W A Haskell (survived)

A flight of Phantoms from Takhli was temporarily based at Da Nang to provide close air support for friendly ground troops about 12 miles southwest of Hué. Capt Beavers was on his fourth pass dropping Mk82 bombs on enemy troops when his aircraft was hit by automatic weapons or small arms fire. The Phantom's rear fuselage caught fire and Capt Beavers headed out to sea where he and his WSO ejected about 15 miles north of Da Nang. They were quickly picked up by a USAF SAR helicopter. Capt Beavers had been shot down while on a previous tour with the 12th TFW during a mission near Katum on 17 April 1969.

10 August 1972

F-4D   66-0281   497 TFS, 8 TFW, USAF, Ubon
                   Capt Patrick T Mathews (KIA)
                   1Lt Herbert D Stark (KIA)

A Phantom crashed near Ubon soon after taking off for a strike on Vinh airfield. Both the crew were killed when the aircraft crashed.

12 August 1972

C-130E 62-1853   Detachment 1, 374 TAW, USAF, Tan Son Nhut
                   Maj Jerry Duane Vance (KIA)
                   Capt Terry Kohler (KIA)
                   Maj James Wesley Fulk (KIA)
                   Capt Merrill Howard Masin (KIA)
                   Capt Charles Price Roberts (KIA)
                   Capt Timmie Joe Ward (KIA)
                   MSgt Ray Edwin Tannehill (KIA)
                   23 passengers (KIA)
                   1 crew, name unknown (survived)
                   13 passengers (survived)

A Hercules had one of its engines damaged by small arms fire soon after taking off from Soc Trang shortly before dawn on the 12th. The Hercules was hit as it reached about 500 feet and it crashed near the airfield killing 30 of the 44 men on board. The aircraft was from the 776th TAS. This was the last of 54 airlift C-130s lost by the USAF in Southeast Asia during the war. Five of these aircraft had been operating in the Blind Bat flare ship role and a further 11 aircraft were lost in the gunship, Special Forces and SAR roles. Between July 1965 and November 1972 USAF C-130s flew a total of 708,087 sorties within Southeast Asia, the peak month being May 1968 when 14,392 sorties were flown.

F-8J   150336   VF-24, USN, USS *Hancock*
                   Lt David Mathew Thompson (KIA)

VF-24 lost a pilot when a Crusader crashed into the sea as it approached for a night landing on board the *Hancock* following a combat air patrol. The cause of the accident was not determined.

13 August 1972

RF-4C   68-0604   14 TRS, 432 TRW, USAF, Udorn
                   Capt William Aaron Gauntt (POW)
                   1Lt Francis Wayne Townsend (KIA)

An RF-4C took off from Udorn on a daylight reconnaissance flight in the southernmost province of North Vietnam. The aircraft was shot down by 57mm AAA near Kinh Mon within the DMZ buffer zone. Capt Gauntt survived and was captured but 1Lt Townsend's fate is unknown although it was thought that he had

ejected from the aircraft. Capt Gauntt had flown 130 missions, including 57 over the North, before being shot down and was almost at the end of his tour of duty at Udorn. He was repatriated on 27 March 1973 and resumed flying the RF-4C.

16 August 1972

F-4J   157262   VF-114, USN, USS *Kitty Hawk*
                   Cdr John Russell Pitzen (KIA)
                   Lt Orland James Pender (KIA)

A flight of Phantoms from the *Kitty Hawk* was flying a CAP mission during a strike by a flight of Intruders on the night of the 16th on targets on North Vietnam's northeast railway line. After the Intruders had bombed their target and as the CAP flight was about to cross the coast the leading fighter was shot down, probably by a SAM, about 10 miles north of Haiphong. The Intruder crews saw at least five SAMs in the vicinity and one of the missiles was seen to explode in two large fireballs at 11,000 feet. The remains of the Phantom crew were discovered in 1994 and positively identified in March 1996.

17 August 1972

A-7A   153207   VA-37, USN, USS *Saratoga*
                   Lt Cdr Dale Virgil Raebel (POW)

An Iron Hand flight was supporting a strike in the Phu Ly area when it lost an aircraft. Soon after Lt Cdr Raebel fired a Shrike missile at a SAM radar, an SA-2 exploded about 300 feet in front of his aircraft causing major damage. He turned towards the coast with fuel streaming from his aircraft and flames coming from the fuselage. On the way to the coast Lt Cdr Raebel reported that he was losing oil pressure and his engine was winding down. He ejected 20 miles southwest of Haiphong when he could no longer control the Corsair and he was soon captured. Dale Raebel, who served as VA-37's administrative and maintenance officer, was released from captivity on 29 March 1973.

17/18 August 1972

O-2A   68-10980 20 TASS, 6498 ABW, USAF, Da Nang

The VC struck once more at the sprawling airbase at Da Nang destroying two aircraft and damaging 10 more with 122mm rockets. Da Nang suffered four such raids during the month of August alone. In addition to the O-2 the other aircraft lost was HH-53C 68-10361 of the 37th ARRS. This was one of five HH-53s that had participated in the ill-fated raid on the Son Tay POW camp in North Vietnam in November 1970.

19 August 1972

RF-4C   69-0355   14 TRS, 432 TRW, USAF, Udorn
                   Capt Roger Ernest Behnfeldt (KIA)
                   Maj Tamotsu Shingaki (POW)

An RF-4C on an early morning weather reconnaissance mission was shot down by a SAM as it was flying at 13,000 feet about eight miles northeast of Kep. Hawaiian-born Maj Shingaki ejected and was captured but the pilot, Capt Behnfeldt did not survive the incident. Maj Shingaki was released on 29 March 1973. Capt Behnfeldt's remains were returned by the Vietnamese on 24 September 1987 and formally identified in the following November.

A-6A   157018   VA-52, USN, USS *Kitty Hawk*
                   Lt Roderick Barnum Lester (KIA)
                   Lt Harry Seeber Mossman (KIA)

An Intruder disappeared during a night low-level strike on a transhipment point at Da Mon Toi near Cam Pha. The weather was poor with a 1,000 feet ceiling and several thunderstorms along the path of the aircraft. Another aircraft noted a flash of light under the low cloud near Hanoi which may have been associated with the loss of the Intruder. However, an oil slick was later seen just off the coast near the position of the aircraft's last radar fix. Lt Lester was on his 144th mission when he was lost.

QU-22B 70-1547   554 RS, 56 SOW, USAF, Nakhon Phanom
                   1 pilot, name unknown (survived)

A QU-22B intelligence gatherer crashed when the pilot lost control in turbulence.

22 August 1972

F-4E   68-0477   421 TFS, 366 TFW, USAF, Takhli
                   Maj Lee Morrow Tigner (KIA)
                   1Lt William James Crockett (KIA)

A flight of four Phantoms was providing close air support to friendly ground forces near Quang Tri when one of the aircraft was shot down. Maj Tigner was making his second run dropping napalm on troop positions when his aircraft was hit by 14.5mm ground fire. The starboard wing separated from the aircraft which rolled inverted and crashed into the Cua Viet River at Quang Tri City. The crash site was twice visited in 1974 by a USAF team and some human remains were discovered indicating that both men had died in the crash.

25 August 1972

F-4D   66-7482   13 TFS, 432 TRW, USAF, Udorn
                   Lt Col Carl G Bailey (survived)
                   Capt Jeffrey S Feinstein (survived)

During a morning MiGCAP mission a Phantom from Udorn was damaged by 37mm AAA about 30 miles north of Haiphong. Lt Col Bailey was at 3,000 feet at the time and immediately headed for the coast. He and Capt Feinstein ejected over the Gulf about 45 miles northeast of Vinh and were rescued by a USAF HH-53 from the 37th ARRS. Jerry Feinstein had already participated in four MiG kills and he became the USAF's third ace when his aircraft shot down a MiG-21 on 13 October. Phantom 66-7482 was fitted with the Combat Tree IFF detection system.

F-4B   153020   VF-161, USN, USS *Midway*
                   Lt Cdr Michael William Doyle (KIA)
                   Lt John Clyde Ensch (POW)

The Navy flew a major strike against a military storage area near Nam Dinh at dusk on the 25th. During the raid an SA-2 missile hit one of the CAP Phantoms as it was manoeuvring in an effort to avoid SAMs at 3,500 feet about 20 miles northeast of Nam Dinh. The missile exploded close to the aircraft's cockpit and Lt Ensch was badly injured by the blast but managed to eject. Another pilot reported seeing two parachutes but it is highly probable that Lt Cdr Doyle was severely injured during the incident. A SAR effort was terminated after two days due to heavy ground fire with no indication that there were any survivors. Lt Ensch was captured soon after he landed and had suffered a broken arm and other injuries. He was on his 285th mission when he was shot down (having served on three previous tours with VF-21 and VF-161) and was released from imprisonment on 29 March 1973. John Ensch was credited with two MiGs with his pilot, Lt Cdr R E McKeown, on 23 May 1972 while flying 153020. Lt Cdr Doyle's remains were returned to the USA on 14 August 1985.

QU-22B 70-1546   554 RS, 56 SOW, USAF, Nakhon Phanom
                   1 pilot, name unknown (survived)

Another QU-22B was lost in an accident in August when an aircraft suffered an engine failure when taking off from Nakhon Phanom. Once again, the pilot escaped with his life.

26 August 1972

F-4J   155811   VMFA-232, MAG-15, USMC, Nam Phong
                   1Lt Sam Gary Cordova (KIA)
                   1Lt D L Borders (survived)

In addition to their close air support and strike duties, the two Marine Corps Phantom squadrons based at Nam Phong also supplemented the USAF in flying combat air patrols over Laos. It was during a BARCAP mission over northern Laos that VMFA-232 lost an aircraft on the 26th. A flight of aircraft was orbiting over the North Vietnamese/Laotian border about 25 miles northeast of Sam Neua when it was vectored towards a MiG by Teaball, a newly-commissioned radar control facility that was not renowned for its reliability. As the Phantoms were approaching the MiGs, Teaball had a systems failure and before Red Crown could pass radar vectors to the Phantoms the MiGs had flashed past. 1Lt Cordova's aircraft was hit by an Atoll missile that struck the Phantom's tail and set it on fire. The crew ejected

from the stricken aircraft and 1Lt Cordova communicated with other aircraft in the vicinity on his survival radio as he was parachuting down to earth. Apparently he landed in a ravine and reported that he could hear enemy troops nearby. His last transmission spoke of imminent capture but it appears that he was killed either during or after capture as he did not appear in any of the known POW camps. His navigator, 1Lt Borders, was luckier as he was rescued by an HH-53. The mortal remains of Sam Cordova were eventually returned to the USA on 15 December 1988. This was the only Marine Corps Phantom lost to in air-to-air combat during the war. The North Vietnamese pilot credited with this kill was Lt Nguyen Duc Soat. 1Lt Cordova had ejected safely from a Phantom earlier in the month while on final approach to Nam Phong.

27 August 1972

F-4B   151013   VF-151, USN, USS *Midway*
Lt Theodore W Triebel (POW)
Lt(jg) David A Everett (POW)

A Phantom was shot down as it was escorting a photographic reconnaissance aircraft along Route 1A near Phu Ly in North Vietnam. The aircraft was flying at 5,000 feet and was already jinking as it had received a SAM warning. An SA-2 struck the rear fuselage and exploded, causing severe damage to all the Phantom's systems and resulting in a fuel fire. The crew ejected shortly afterwards and came down near Phu Nho Quan, about 40 miles south of Hanoi. Both of the crew were captured and both were released on 29 March 1973. Lt Triebel had flown two combat tours with VF-213 and had also served on an exchange posting at Ubon with the 8th TFW before flying his third and fourth tours with VF-151.

30 August 1972

A-37B   69-6358   8 SOS, 377 ABW, USAF, Bien Hoa
A Dragonfly was the only aircraft destroyed during a Viet Cong attack on the airfield at Bien Hoa, although another 10 aircraft were damaged and one man was wounded during the attack. This was the last USAF fixed-wing aircraft lost during an air base attack during the war. This was also the last of 10 A-37As and 12 A-37Bs lost during the war.

2 September 1972

F-4E   68-0335   421 TFS, 366 TFW, USAF, Takhli
Capt William Commodore Wood (KIA)
Maj Robert Roy Greenwood (KIA)

Two Phantoms were assigned to a Raven FAC who was working a target five miles east of the town of Ban Na Mai in the Plain of Jars. Capt R W Herold, Raven 23, marked the target for the Phantoms and Capt Wood made two passes over the target, dropping Mk82 bombs. On the third pass the other Phantom crew saw Capt Wood's aircraft burst into flames and crash near the village of Lat Sen. They also saw at least one parachute and then noticed that the Bird Dog FAC had also crashed. It was not known whether the FAC and the Phantom had collided or had both been shot down by the 12.7mm anti-aircraft gun site they were attacking at the time. Two ejection seats were seen on the ground but there was no trace of any of the aircrew and no SAR beepers were heard.

A-4E   152000   VMA-211, MAG-12, USMC, Bien Hoa
1Lt D R Eisenbrey (survived)

After the start of the Spring Invasion the communists made major advances in Military Region 3 north of Saigon capturing Loc Ninh and threatening An Loc, the regional capital. In response to the need for more close air support resources to defend An Loc and Saigon the Marines sent two squadrons of Skyhawks from MAG-12 to Bien Hoa. It was the first time during the war that Marine Corps jet squadrons had been based in the south of the country. Thirty-two Skyhawks from VMA-211 and VMA-311 began deploying from Iwakuni and Cubi Point to Bien Hoa on 17 May and combat operations began three days later. Few of the Marine Corps Skyhawk pilots had any combat experience so they flew indoctrination missions in the right-hand

seat of USAF A-37s and then flew missions with the Dragonflys leading until they became more proficient.

The Marine Corps A-4 squadrons at Bien Hoa were heavily involved in the defence of An Loc for much of the summer of 1972. The first Skyhawk lost from Bien Hoa was shot down during a close air support mission near An Loc on 2 September. The aircraft's port wing was badly damaged by ground fire over the target and 1Lt Eisenbrey attempted to return to Bien Hoa but had to eject about 12 miles north of the airfield when the aircraft became uncontrollable. He was picked up by an Army helicopter.

5 September 1972

RF-8G   146861   Detachment 1, VFP-63, USN, USS *Hancock*
Cdr R Harrison (survived)

F-8J   150299 (?)   VF-24, USN, USS *Hancock*
Lt J Schultz (survived)

The *Hancock* lost a photographic reconnaissance Crusader and its escort fighter when they collided as they were about to refuel from a tanker over the Gulf of Tonkin. Fortunately, both pilots managed to eject and were rescued.

6 September 1972

A-6A   155626   VA-75, USN, USS *Saratoga*
Lt Cdr Donald Frederick Lindland (KIA)
Lt Roger Gene Lerseth (POW)

An Intruder was shot down by two SAMs during a daylight raid on Kien An airfield near Haiphong. The aircraft was at 13,000 feet and was just about to roll in on the target when the first missile exploded in front of the aircraft. The Intruder was seen to emerge from the missile's fireball in a left-hand dive trailing fuel and flames. Another missile was seen to explode near the aircraft and the crew were then seen to eject and land near the airfield. Before being captured Lt Lerseth saw his pilot moving around on the ground. Lt Cdr Lindland, who was VA-75's operations officer, is thought to have evaded capture for 24 hours but Lerseth was later told during his interrogation that his pilot was dead. Roger Lerseth broke his left leg during the ejection and was repatriated on 12 February 1973. The remains of Donald Lindland were returned by the Vietnamese on 3 June 1983. Roger Lerseth, who was on his 96th mission when he was shot down, resumed flying in the A-6 and was on the maiden cruise of the USS *Nimitz*.

A-4F   155021   VA-212, USN, USS *Hancock*
Lt W F Pear (survived)

Later in the day a pair of Skyhawks on an armed reconnaissance mission found several trucks on a coastal road about 10 miles south of Thanh Hoa. As Lt Pear was about to pull up from his second pass at 5,000 feet his aircraft was hit in the tail by 23mm flak. He turned towards the sea with the aircraft on fire and the engine winding down slowly. About five miles out to sea the controls suddenly froze and the aircraft started to roll to the left so Lt Pear ejected. He was later rescued by a Navy helicopter. This was the last of 12 aircraft lost by the *Hancock* before completing its seventh tour on 25 September. The ship would return to Vietnam on 19 May 1973 for her eighth war cruise, a record for any TF 77 carrier, but no further aircraft were lost on her final tour. The USS *Hancock* was decommissioned on 30 January 1976 and was subsequently scrapped.

7 September 1972

A-7B   154393   VA-93, USN, USS *Midway*
Lt Cdr Donald Arthur Gerstel (KIA)

Two Corsairs were inbound over the Gulf of Tonkin towards Vinh on a night armed reconnaissance mission against enemy shipping when the leader's aircraft was struck by lightning. Lt Cdr Gerstel reported that the aircraft seemed OK but after that nothing more was heard from him. The aircraft is presumed to have crashed into the sea near Hon Nieu Island either as a direct result of the lightning strike, or pilot distraction or to enemy ground defences. An extensive search of the area failed to find any sign of wreckage or the pilot.

8 September 1972

F-4J   157302   VF-103, USN, USS *Saratoga*
Cdr R P Bordone (survived)
Lt J H Findley (survived)

One of the *Saratoga's* Phantoms was damaged by 23mm AAA as it flew along Route 1A about 25 miles north of Vinh during a road reconnaissance mission. The aircraft was hit in the fuselage and wing and the port engine began to run roughly. A small fire eventually went out but the aircraft's hydraulic and pneumatic systems failed as the Phantom reached the carrier's position 80 miles offshore and reduced speed. The pilot could not maintain control so both crew ejected successfully and were rescued by an SH-3G. Cdr Bordone had previously flown the A-6 Intruder and had survived being blown up by his own bombs during a Steel Tiger mission on 24 July 1965.

9 September 1972

F-4E   69-7565   307 TFS, 31 TFW attached to 432 TRW, USAF, Udorn
Capt William J Dalecky (survived)
Capt Terry M Murphy (survived)

A flight of four Phantoms was led by Capt John Madden and Capt Charles DeBellevue on a CAP mission to protect a Linebacker raid on Thai Nguyen. The flight had already shot down two MiG-19s and a MiG-21 and were returning when Capt Dalecky's aircraft was damaged by AAA about 10 miles north of Hanoi and started to lose fuel at a high rate. Capt Dalecky maintained control and followed the strike force back into Laos before he and his WSO were forced to eject from the aircraft. They were subsequently rescued by a USAF SAR helicopter.

10 September 1972

A-7C   156798   VA-82, USN, USS *America*
Lt(jg) Stephen Owen Musselman (KIA)

An Iron Hand flight of Corsairs from the USS *America* was attacking SAM sites during a Linebacker raid in the Hanoi area on the 10th. As the aircraft approached Hanoi from the south a large number of SAMs were fired and Lt Musselman and the other members of the flight started to take evasive action. A missile was seen to hit Lt Musselman's aircraft forcing him to eject about five miles south of the city. It is not known why Lt Musselman did not survive but the Vietnamese returned his remains to the USA on 8 July 1981.

F-4E   69-7251   335 TFS, 4 TFW attached to 8 TFW, USAF, Ubon
2 crew, names unknown (survived)

A Wolf FAC Phantom was flying a visual reconnaissance sortie just west of Dong Hoi when it was hit by 23mm ground fire as it flew over a bridge that had attracted attention. The crew later ejected and were both subsequently rescued.

11 September 1972

F-4E   69-0288   335 TFS, 4 TFW attached to 8 TFW, USAF, Ubon
Capt Brian M Ratzlaff (POW)
Capt Jerome Donald Heeren (POW)

During a Linebacker strike the flight of Phantoms that was tasked with dropping chaff ahead of the strike force was intercepted by MiG-21s about 15 miles northeast of Kep. The escort tried to warn the chaff flight about the MiGs but the chaff bombers turned the wrong way and one of the Phantoms was hit by an Atoll missile. Capt Ratzlaff and Capt Heeren ejected and were captured, although not until three days later in the case of Brian Ratzlaff. This was a highly experienced crew, Capt Ratzlaff having flown about 400 combat missions and Capt Heeren 312, both having flown previous tours in South Vietnam. Both men were released on 29 March 1973.

F-4J   155526   VMFA-333, USMC, USS *America*
Maj Lee T Lasseter (survived)
Capt John D Cummings (survived)

F-4J   154784   VMFA-333, USMC, USS *America*
Capt Andrew Scot Dudley (survived)
1Lt James W Brady (survived)

One of the two Phantom squadrons on board the USS *America* on its third and final combat cruise was VMFA-333 of the US Marine Corps. This was the only occasion when a Marine Corps Phantom squadron had deployed on board a carrier for duty in the war. On 11 September VMFA-333 provided a CAP flight of two F-4Js for a major strike on the Co Giang SAM assembly depot. During the mission the CAP flight engaged several MiGs and Maj 'Bear' Lasseter, the Squadron's executive officer, and Capt Cummings shot down a MiG-21 and damaged another near Phuc Yen airfield. The air battle had left the pair of F-4s short of fuel and they had to fly directly over Haiphong on their way to the Gulf and a waiting tanker. The air began to fill with SAMs and flak bursts and, despite evasive action, Maj Lasseter's Phantom was hit by an SA-2 at 15,000 feet damaging the wing and causing the aircraft to burst into flames. Eventually hydraulic failure led to loss of control and the crew ejected over the Gulf about 35 miles southeast of Haiphong, from where they were rescued by an SH-3 of HC-7 operating from the USS *England*.

Maj Lasseter's wingman was also hit as he flew over Haiphong on the way out to sea. Capt Dudley's aircraft was hit by flak in the wing and fuselage causing a massive fuel leak. The engines flamed out from lack of fuel when the aircraft was about 45 miles south of Haiphong and the crew joined their colleagues in the Gulf and were rescued by the SAR destroyer USS *Biddle*. All four men were returned to the carrier with barely a scratch to celebrate the only all-Marine Corps MiG-kill of the war. Maj Lasseter took command of VMFA-333 on Christmas Eve when Lt Col Cochran was shot down.

12 September 1972

F-4E   69-7266   336 TFS, 4 TFW attached to 8 TFW,
USAF, Ubon
Capt Rudolph V Zuberbuhler (POW)
Capt Frederick Charles McMurray (POW)

Another Phantom was lost during a chaff dropping mission in support of a Linebacker raid on storage caves at La Danh, 35 miles north of Hanoi. The chaff flight was engaged by MiG-21s which broke through the MiGCAP flight about 25 miles northeast of Haiphong before the target had been reached. Capt Zuberbuhler's aircraft was hit by an Atoll missile and the crew had to ejected before they reached the coast. Both men were eventually captured and both were released on 29 March 1973.

Capt Zuberbuhler was on his 368th mission of the war when he was shot down. The MiG that shot down this Phantom was later destroyed by a Sidewinder missile from an F-4E from the 388th TFW. Two more MiG-21s were shot down by USAF Phantoms during this engagement.

A-7A   153213   VA-37, USN, USS *Saratoga*
Lt G H Averett (survived)

After an uneventful night-time merchant shipping surveillance patrol off the coast of North Vietnam, a section of Corsairs crossed the coast to begin a road reconnaissance along Route 1A. A truck park was spotted about 30 miles north of Dong Hoi and one of the aircraft dropped flares as the other rolled in on the attack. As Lt Averett pulled up from his attack his aircraft was hit by flak and his wingman reported that it was on fire. The two aircraft flew out to sea and Lt Averett ejected about 12 miles east of Mu Ron Ma and was picked up by the destroyer USS *Wiltsie*.

13 September 1972

F-4J   153854   VF-74, USN, USS *America*
Lt Michael Paul Rice (KIA)
1 crew, name unknown (survived)

One of the crew of a Phantom died when the aircraft crashed during a landing accident at night on board the USS *America* as the aircraft returned from a BARCAP mission. The other occupant ejected and was picked up safely.

16 September 1972

F-4D   66-8785   523 TFS, 405 FW attached to 432 TRW,
USAF, Udorn
Capt W A Kangas (survived)
Capt Frederick R Cunliffe (survived)

North Vietnamese coastal artillery at Hon La, about 10 miles southwest of Dong Hoi, was shelling US Navy vessels offshore, so an air strike was mounted on the guns. During the attack a Laredo FAC Phantom was hit by AAA at 4,000 feet and badly damaged. Capt Kangas flew out to sea towards the destroyer USS *Preble* and he and his WSO ejected 35 miles northeast of Dong Hoi. Despite a very choppy sea the Phantom crew were spotted parachuting into the sea and two Marine Corps AH-1G Sea Cobras arrived to protect the downed airmen until the *Preble* launched its whaleboat. The crew spent less than 25 minutes in the water.

OV-10A   67-14640   20 TASS, 6498 ABW, USAF, Da Nang
Capt R L Poling (survived)
Capt J A Personnet (survived)

A Covey FAC was hit by AAA during a forward air control mission near Thach Tru, about 15 miles south of Quang Tri. The two crew ejected a few minutes later and were eventually rescued by an Army helicopter.

A-6A   15/028   VA-35, USN, USS *America*
Cdr Verne George Donnelly (KIA)
Lt Cdr Kenneth Richard Buell (KIA)

The CO of VA-35 was lost during an armed reconnaissance mission over North Vietnam's northeast railway line on the night of the 16th. The pilot of an Iron Hand aircraft over Haiphong reported seeing AAA bursts that appeared to be following an aircraft heading towards Hanoi culminating in a bright orange explosion after which all AAA activity ceased. It was presumed that this sighting was Cdr Donnelly's Intruder being shot down near the town of Hai Duong. Nothing more was heard of the crew until an announcement on 5 February 1991 that the remains of Cdr Donnelly had been identified from several sets of remains returned earlier by the Vietnamese. Cdr Donnelly had taken command of VA-35 on 24 May 1972 and he was the second CO lost by the Squadron in Southeast Asia.

17 September 1972

F-105G   63-8360   17 WWS, 388 TFW, USAF, Korat
Capt Thomas Oneal Zorn (KIA)
1Lt Michael Stephen Turose (KIA)

A Wild Weasel on an armed reconnaissance mission received indications that it was being tracked by a Fan Song radar about 20 miles north of Haiphong. The aircraft was badly damaged by the explosion of a SAM at 11,000 feet causing major damage to the rear fuselage. Capt Zorn headed towards the southeast and crossed the coast. However, the aircraft crashed in the sea about 25 miles southeast of Haiphong and both the crew were killed.

A-7C   156781   VA-82, USN, USS *America*
1 pilot, name unknown (survived)

As a Corsair from the USS *America* was landing at Da Nang after a close air support mission, one of its tyres blew and the aircraft veered off the runway damaging the aircraft beyond repair.

F-4D   65-0593   434 TFS, 35 TFW attached to 49 TFW,
USAF, Takhli
Capt E B Dyer (survived)
Capt D E Henneman (survived)

When the 49th TFW deployed to Takhli in May it brought all four of its regular squadrons with it. However, on 12 August the 7th TFS was replaced by the 434th TFS, which deployed on temporary duty from the 35th TFW at George AFB, California. The only aircraft lost by the 434th during its two-month stay at Takhli was a Phantom that suffered a systems failure resulting in a fire in the cockpit. The aircraft crashed as it was attempting to land at Ubon but the crew escaped.

OV-10A   68-3810   23 TASS, 56 SOW, USAF, Nakhon Phanom
2 crew, names unknown (survived)

Nail 60 crashed during a ferry flight when one of its engines failed just as it was crossing the Ho Chi Minh Trail in southern Laos. Both the crew ejected and landed safely. The rescue mission almost failed when two SAR helicopters from Da Nang both had to return to base with technical problems. However, two other helicopters had been scrambled from Nakhon Phanom and Jolly Green 65 completed the rescue although the Bronco observer was badly injured and had to be strapped to a Stokes litter on the ground by a PJ. The wreck of the OV-10 was completely destroyed by the accompanying flight of Sandies to prevent it from falling into enemy hands.

The A-1 Skyraider will forever be known as Sandy to many of the participants of the war in Southeast Asia. It played a major part in the successful rescue of many downed airmen, although the price was sometimes heavy. A total of at least 42 USAF A-1s were lost during rescue missions during the war. USAF

The F-111's return to combat in 1972 showed that it was a most capable low-level, all-weather strike aircraft which could reach targets in conditions that grounded other types. The HG code shows this aircraft to belong to the 347th TFW. Six aircraft were lost during the Linebacker offensives of 1972 with the loss of 10 airmen. USAF

19 September 1972

A-7E   158653   VA-192, USN, USS *Kitty Hawk*
Lt W A Robb (survived)

A formation of Corsairs from the *Kitty Hawk* attempted to bomb a bridge about 25 miles south of Vinh but were frustrated by bad weather. The flight headed north and flew along Route 1A looking for a target of opportunity and came across a bridge near Ninh Xa, about 10 miles south of Vinh. As Lt Robb pulled up from a 45-degree dive attack his aircraft was hit by flak and caught fire. He turned out to sea and managed to fly about 20 miles off the coast before being forced to eject when he lost control. As he was descending in his parachute he saw his Corsair dive into the sea below him and noted that the entire tail section had broken away.

F-4D   65-0647   49 TFW, USAF, Takhli
2 crew, names unknown (survived)

A Phantom crew on a strike mission were caught out when their aircraft ran short of fuel. Too far from a major airfield, they tried to land at the airstrip at Cu Chi to the northwest of Saigon but the aircraft crashed and was destroyed. Both the crew survived the incident.

20 September 1972

A-7B   154363   VA-155, USN, USS *Oriskany*
1 pilot, name unknown (survived)

A Corsair from the *Oriskany* had to be abandoned during a weather reconnaissance flight when the aircraft's engine failed. The cause was suspected to be a failure of the engine accessory drive.

21 September 1972

F-4D   66-8769   555 TFS, 432 TRW, USAF, Udorn
Maj Roger William Carroll (KIA)
Lt Dwight William Cook (KIA)

A Triple Nickel Phantom was lost during an armed reconnaissance mission in northern Laos. The flight attacked a cluster of anti-aircraft guns on the southern edge of the Plain of Jars and during the attack Maj Carroll's aircraft was hit by return fire and crashed near the target. A Raven FAC pilot, who was controlling the strike, observed the crash. He did not see any parachutes or any other indications that the crew had escaped although later reports claimed that one of the crew had been captured alive. In June 1994 the remains of the crew were returned to the USA and positively identified in October the following year. Maj Carroll had previously flown as a navigator in B-47 and B-52 bombers of SAC before taking pilot training and flying F-100s in South Vietnam.

22 September 1972

RF-4C   69-0351   14 TRS, 432 TRW, USAF, Udorn
Capt J G Watts (survived)
1Lt J H Pomeroy (survived)

A reconnaissance Phantom set off from Udorn to photograph the area around Bat Lake north of the DMZ on an Atlanta fast FAC mission. As Capt Watts was flying his photo run at 4,500 feet and 530 knots near Xuan Noa the aircraft was hit by 23mm flak, damaging an engine. The crew ejected safely less than three miles off the coast and were rescued by a USAF helicopter.

F-4E   67-0385   34 TFS, 388 TFW, USAF, Korat
Capt G A Lentz (survived)
1Lt N J Holoviak (survived)

On returning from a CAP mission the pilot of a Phantom lost control of the aircraft as it landed at Korat during a thunderstorm. The aircraft left the runway and the WSO ejected safely. The pilot remained in the Phantom and was uninjured even though the aircraft was damaged beyond repair during the crash.

24 September 1972

A-7B   154436   VA-155, USN, USS *Oriskany*
Lt Daniel Vernor Borah (KIA)

A flight of two A-7s was bombing enemy troops and trucks near Dong Ha just south of the DMZ when one of the aircraft was shot down. Lt Borah's wingman inadvertently dropped all his ordnance on his first pass so he then pulled up to 13,000 feet and watched as Lt Borah began to attack the target. He had just pulled up from his second pass when his aircraft was seen to burst into flames having been hit by 37mm flak. The aircraft climbed but then rolled inverted and Lt Borah was seen to eject. The pilot made radio contact with his wingman during the parachute descent and was seen to land in trees. Also an emergency beeper was heard to transmit briefly. A two-day SAR effort failed to reveal any further sign of Lt Borah. It seems probable that Daniel Borah was killed either during his parachute descent or on the ground during capture by North Vietnamese troops. Post-war investigation revealed that his aircraft was shot down by the 284th AAA Battalion of the NVA.

26 September 1972

OV-10A   67-14685   21 TASS, 377 ABW, USAF, Tan Son Nhut
1Lt Vincent Craig Anderson (KIA)

A Bronco on an FAC mission was strafing a target in the Mekong Delta with its 20mm cannon when it was hit by .50 calibre ground fire. The aircraft crashed 10 miles north of Phu Vinh killing the pilot, the only occupant.

A-4E   151099   VMA-211, MAG-12, USMC, Bien Hoa
Capt James P Walsh (POW)

Another of the Marine Corps Skyhawks from Bien Hoa was lost during a close air support mission in defence of An Loc. The target was enemy forces that had occupied Quan Loi airfield near the city and it was known to be well defended by many AAA sites. Two Skyhawks took off from Bien Hoa and rendezvoused with an FAC to start their attack. Capt Walsh's aircraft was hit by ground fire as he began to pull out of a 30-degree dive on the target. With the aircraft's tail on fire and the controls not responding, Capt Walsh ejected a few miles from An Loc and landed in a rubber plantation. A rescue helicopter was hit by ground fire and had to withdraw and Capt Walsh had landed in the middle of an enemy campsite and was already in captivity. He was the last US Marine to be taken prisoner during the war. Fortunately he was only imprisoned for five months before being released on 12 February 1973 having made an unsuccessful escape attempt en route to Hanoi.

27 September 1972

F-8J   150325   VF-194, USN, USS *Oriskany*
Lt Richard Bryan Lineberry (KWF)

A Crusader crashed killing the pilot when it caught fire as it was taking off from Da Nang. The aircraft was being ferried from Da Nang to the USS *Oriskany* in the Gulf of Tonkin at the time of the accident.

The Return of the F-111

After the return of the Combat Lancer F-111 detachment to the USA in November 1968 the F-111's career went through a series of ups and downs. A fatal accident in December 1969 resulted in the grounding of the entire F-111 fleet for seven months as a major structural test and inspection programme was undertaken. However, although accidents continued to happen, the aircraft and its avionics and weapon systems were continuously developed and improved and by 1972 most of the aircraft's problems were behind it, even if it still had its critics. In addition, the crews were now much more experienced and proficient. When Linebacker I commenced in May the 474th TFW at Nellis AFB, Nevada, was one of the units notified for deployment to Southeast Asia, thereby heralding the return of the F-111 to combat status. Commencing on 27 September the Wing deployed two squadrons of F-111s to Takhli as Constant Guard V and flew the first mission on the night of the 28th, 33 hours after leaving Nellis. The last of 48 F-111s arrived at Takhli on 5 October with seven more replacement aircraft arriving over the next seven months.

28 September 1972

A-1H   52-139738   1 SOS, 56 SOW, USAF, Nakhon Phanom
1Lt L L Smith (survived)

A flight of Skyraiders was assigned the task of providing cover for a medical evacuation of a friendly position in northern Laos. 1Lt Smith's aircraft was shot down by ground fire near Ban Nam Feng but he was later rescued by an Air America helicopter. This was the last of a grand total of 201 Skyraiders lost by the Air Force in Southeast Asia. The Skyraider took part in its last RESCAP mission on 7 November after which the 1st SOS was inactivated and its remaining aircraft turned over to the VNAF. The Sandy role, which the A-1 had performed so brilliantly for so long, was handed over to the newly-arrived A-7D Corsairs of the 354th TFW. Skyraider 52-139738 was a historic aircraft in that it was flown by Lt Col W A Jones on 1 September 1968 when he earned the Medal of Honor during a rescue mission. It was also the last aircraft to be lost by the 1st SOS during its nine years of service in Southeast Asia. During that time the Squadron had lost no less than 74 Skyraiders and 18 other aircraft.

F-111A   67-0078   429 TFS, 474 TFW on TDY, USAF, Takhli
Maj William Clare Coltman (KIA)
1Lt Robert Arthur Brett (KIA)

The first casualty from the newly-deployed F-111 squadrons failed to return from the very first mission over Laos on the night of the 28th. Six aircraft were rapidly turned round after arriving at Takhli on the evening of the 28th and were despatched on individual missions. Unfortunately, the hurried preparation led to equipment problems and only two of the six aircraft actually reached a target. Ranger 23 set off from Takhli to bomb a target to the southeast of Yen Bai and was either shot down, flew into the ground or was destroyed by the explosion from its own Mk84 bombs. The Mk84 requires a minimum drop height of 1,300 feet

to be sure of avoiding debris from the explosion. It was thought possible that the crew dropped from a lower altitude and were hit by shrapnel from their own bombs. The weather was poor that night and the aircraft's terrain-following radar, which was used to fly automatic at low level on night missions, could be deceived by dense rain showers and other phenomena. Whatever the cause, as with the Combat Lancer deployment, the tragic early loss of an aircraft and its crew was a major blow to the return to combat of the F-111 and resulted in a five-day standown to introduce revised tactics.

29 September 1972

F-105G 63-8302   17 WWS, 388 TFW, USAF, Korat
Lt Col James William O'Neil (POW)
Capt Michael Joseph Bosiljevac (KIA)

The second Wild Weasel to be shot down during September was lost during a raid on the 29th. The Iron Hand flight was locked onto by a Fan Song radar near Phuc Yen, about 12 miles northwest of Hanoi, and before Lt Col O'Neil in Crow 01 could fire a Shrike missile his aircraft was hit by a SAM at 8,000 feet. The aircraft caught fire and several minutes later the crew were forced to eject approximately 25 miles west of Hanoi. Lt Col O'Neil saw his EWO in his parachute as he descended and was later told by a prison guard that Capt Bosiljevac was alive and well. A SAR attempt was foiled when MiGs appeared and chased the Sandies out of the area. Only James O'Neil was released on 29 March 1973 during Operation Homecoming. The fate of Capt Michael Bosiljevac was unknown until remains claimed to be his were handed over by the Vietnamese on 24 September 1987. These remains were positively identified as such in January 1988 and Capt Bosiljevac was finally buried in Omaha, Nebraska on 10 February. It is still not known exactly how or when he died. 63-8302 was painted as 'Half a Yard', 'Jefferson Airplane' and 'The Smith Brother's Cough Drop Special' at various times in Southeast Asia.

5 October 1972

F-4D 66-8738   335 TFS, 4 TFW attached to 8 TFW,
USAF, Ubon
Capt Keith H Lewis (POW)
Capt John Hardesty Alpers (POW)

On the afternoon of the 5th the Wolfpack flew a Linebacker strike on a munitions depot at Tai Xouan near Yen Bai. The strike force was engaged by MiG-21s over the target and one of the Phantoms was shot down by an air-to-air missile and the crew ejected about 10 miles north of Yen Bai. Capt Lewis and Capt Alpers were captured and sent initially to the Hanoi Hilton. They were released six months later on 29 March 1973. Keith Lewis had served a tour with the 559th TFS at Cam Ranh Bay in 1966 and arrived at Ubon in July 1972. John Alpers had served as a B-52 navigator before converting to the F-4.

F-4E serial ..?   435 TFS, 8 TFW, USAF, Ubon
Capt James D Latham (POW)
1Lt Richard Lyman Bates (POW)

A Wolf FAC Phantom was shot down by ground fire near Xom Quan, 12 miles north of the DMZ as it flew at low level to check out a convoy of apparently burned out trucks as a potential target. The starboard wing was blown off and both men ejected safely but were shot at as they came down by parachute. Unharmed, they were captured immediately and kept in separate bunkers for several weeks until they were taken by truck to Hanoi for imprisonment. Before they were moved to Hanoi Jim Latham broke out of his bunker and evaded to the coast where he was recaptured as he attempted to push a small fishing boat into the sea. Both men were released on 29 March 1973. James Latham had flown a total of 378 combat missions in Southeast Asia, including a tour as a Nail FAC OV-10 pilot, while Richard Bates had flown 136 missions, 98 of them over North Vietnam. Latham later commanded the 20th and 432nd TFWs before retiring from the USAF as a Brigadier General on 1 August 1997. Richard Bates retrained as an F-4 pilot following his release from Hanoi.

6 October 1972

F-4E 69-7573   307 TFS, 31 TFW attached to 432 TRW,
USAF, Udorn
Capt J P White (survived)
Capt A G Egge (survived)

A Phantom from a CAP flight supporting a Linebacker strike on North Vietnam was damaged by a MiG but managed to make a safe exit. Losing fuel from a ruptured fuel cell the engines eventually flamed out and the crew ejected near the Thai/Laotian border about 60 miles northeast of Udorn and were picked up by an Air America helicopter.

F-4E 69-7548   25 TFS, 8 TFW, USAF, Ubon
Lt Col Robert Dale Anderson (KIA)
1Lt George Francis Latella (POW)

The Wolfpack flew a strike on a target near Son Tay on the 6th but lost an aircraft and its crew. As the strike force drew close to Hanoi at 16,500 feet Lt Col Anderson's aircraft was damaged by a SAM. The crew ejected a few minutes later about 25 miles south of Yen Bai. The other members of the flight saw two good parachutes and the crew landed within a few hundred yards of each other near the Red River. Voice contact was made with both men and Lt Col Anderson reported that he was uninjured and could not see any enemy troops. 1Lt Latella was captured almost immediately but Lt Col Anderson never appeared in any of the known POW camps and did not return home. George Latella was released on 29 March 1973.

OV-10A 67-14673   20 TASS, 6498 ABW, USAF, Da Nang
Lt Col Carl Otis McCormick (KIA)
CWO2 Bruce Edward Boltze, USMC (KIA)

A Covey FAC with a Marine Corps observer was directing naval gunfire on enemy positions near Da Nang when it was seen to explode and fall into the sea just off the coast about 12 miles north of Da Nang. No survivors were found from the incident. Bruce Boltze had survived being shot down near Da Nang in a TA-4F on 26 May but on the 6th his luck ran out.

10 October 1972

F-4E 67-0254   307 TFS, 31 TFW attached to 432 TRW,
USAF, Udorn
Capt Peter McArthur Cleary (KIA)
Capt Leonardo Capistrano Leonor (KIA)

Yet another fast FAC aircraft was lost in the southern provinces of North Vietnam. The Laredo aircraft from Udorn failed to return from a mission in Quang Binh province and was thought to have been shot down near the city of Ron. The crew are listed as being members of the 523rd TFS but they may have been flying a 307th aircraft at the time of the incident.

11 October 1972

A-6A 155700   VMA(AW)-533, MAG-15, USMC, Nam Phong
1Lt John Robert Peacock (KIA)
1Lt William Marshall Price (KIA)

A Marine Corps Intruder crew went missing while on a night-time road reconnaissance mission over North Vietnam. The aircraft is thought to have been brought down about 12 miles west of Dong Hoi and both the crew are assumed to have been killed in the incident. 1Lt Price was one of a number of Canadians who managed to join the US armed forces to fight in Southeast Asia.

12 October 1972

F-4E 69-0276   469 TFS, 388 TFW, USAF, Korat
Capt Myron A Young (POW)
1Lt Cecil H Brunson (POW)

During a Linebacker raid on the northeastern railway one of the escorting Phantoms was shot down by MiGs about 20 miles northeast of Kep. The aircraft was chasing two MiG-21s when it was hit at 18,000 feet by an Atoll missile fired by a third MiG flown by Lt Nguyen Duc Soat. The crew ejected a few moments later and were eventually captured, although it was 26 hours before the North Vietnamese tracked down Capt Young. He was beaten and almost killed before being taken to Hanoi for imprisonment.

Although the crew is listed as belonging to the 469th TFS, the aircraft may have belonged to the 34th TFS. They were both repatriated on 29 March 1973. 'Joe' Young was a veteran of 379 combat missions, 43 of them in Route Package 6. Phantom 69-0276 had shot down a MiG 21 just four days earlier while being flown by Maj G L Retterbush and Capt R H Jasperson of the 35th TFS and 1Lt Brunson had shared a credit for a MiG-19 kill on 6 October when flying 66-0313 with Maj G L Clouser.

15 October 1972

B-52D 55-0097   43 SW, USAF, Andersen
6 crew, names unknown (survived)

An Andersen-based B-52 sustained major damage at U-Tapao following an emergency landing. After languishing on the airfield for some months the aircraft was scrapped in February 1973 as it was deemed uneconomical to repair.

16/17 October 1972

F-111A 67-0066   429 TFS, 474 TFW on TDY, USAF, Takhli
Capt James Alan Hockridge (KIA)
1Lt Allen Upton Graham (KIA)

The 474th TFW lost its second aircraft on the night of the 16th when Capt Hockridge and 1Lt Graham, flying as Coach 33, failed to return from a low level strike on a railway bridge at Dia Loi near Phuc Yen. The aircraft crashed close to the target and, according to the North Vietnamese, both crew were killed in their escape module, which failed to deploy properly. Radio Hanoi also claimed the F-111 as the 4,000th US aircraft shot down over North Vietnam, which was something of an exaggeration. A later radio report stated that the crew's remains were buried near the Ca Lo River but on 30 September 1977 the remains of the crew were returned to the USA by the Vietnamese. The cause of the loss was never positively determined but in addition to the possibility of flak or SAMs there was still concern over the carriage of the Mk84 bombs, which had been found to detach fully armed without warning at low altitude. The large fragmentation pattern of the 2,000lb bomb at low level might well have caused the aircraft's demise. Soon after this incident the use of Mk84 bombs was restricted to medium or high altitude missions and most low level missions used the 500lb Mk82 'slick' or Snakeye bombs.

17 October 1972

F-4D 66-8708   435 TFS, 8 TFW, USAF, Ubon
2 crew, names unknown (survived)

A Phantom Night Owl FAC returning to Ubon crashed about 25 miles north of the airfield as it prepared to land. The crewmembers ejected safely and were soon picked up by helicopter.

23 October 1972

F-4D 65-0632   8 TFW, USAF, Ubon
2 crew, names unknown (survived)

Another Wolfpack Phantom was destroyed when it crashed while landing at Ubon after a combat mission. In the hope that North Vietnam would come to the negotiating table, President Nixon restricted Linebacker operations on 23 October. Bombing missions north of the 20th parallel were prohibited for the time being, although operations in the lower provinces of North Vietnam were still permitted. During the course of Linebacker I the USAF alone had flown 9,315 sorties over North Vietnam for the loss of 63 aircraft. The North Vietnamese had fired 2,750 SA-2 missiles during Linebacker I resulting in the loss of 46 aircraft, a kill rate of almost 60 missiles fired for each kill. In 1965 it only took an average of 18 SAMs to down an aircraft.

27 October 1972

F-4E 69-7273   25 TFS, 8 TFW, USAF, Ubon
Capt R B Jones (survived)
Capt E L Bleak (survived)

During a visual reconnaissance mission north of the DMZ a flight of Phantoms attacked two 57mm anti-aircraft gun sites near the village of Xom Quan, north of the DMZ. One of the

A total of 397 F-105 Thunderchiefs were lost in Southeast Asia representing 48 per cent of the total number of 833 constructed. However, F-105D 60-0464 survived the war having been modified to T-Stick standard. USAF

Phantoms, a Wolf FAC, was hit by AAA and Capt Jones flew out to sea where he and Capt Bleak ejected about 40 miles north of Hué. They were soon rescued by a USAF SAR helicopter.

A-7C   156775   VA-86, USN, USS *America*
                  Lt Cdr James Wayne Hall (KIA)
An Iron Hand flight was supporting a night strike close to Thanh Hoa when two SAMs were launched at the Corsairs. The aircraft were heading for the coast at 13,000 feet at the time and no warning was received from the RHAW equipment carried by the aircraft either before or after the launch, probably indicating that the missiles had been launched ballistically without initial radar guidance. Lt Cdr Hall called out the launch in his 12 o'clock position but then his aircraft was seen to sustain a direct hit and it crashed about two miles southwest of Thanh Hoa. It was thought unlikely that the pilot could have survived such catastrophic damage and there was no indication of an ejection or emergency transmissions. In 1989 the Vietnamese handed over 15 boxes of remains, one of which was believed to contain the remains of Lt Cdr Hall. Mitochondrial DNA testing, together with excavations at a crash site in 1993 and 1994 that recovered personal items, eventually confirmed the identity of the remains as being those of James Hall in March 2000.

29 October 1972

A-7C   156762   VA-86, USN, USS *America*
                  Lt Cdr James Edward Sullivan (KIA)
A section of Corsairs set off on an armed reconnaissance mission on the lookout for water-borne logistic craft just off the coast of North Vietnam. About 25 miles north of Vinh the aircraft made a low-level identification run over a ship when Lt Cdr Sullivan's aircraft was hit by automatic weapons fire. The aircraft burst into flames when its ordnance or a fuel tank was hit. The pilot ejected seconds before the port wing separated from the aircraft. Lt Cdr Sullivan was observed to be picked up by enemy boats but was last seen face down in one of the boats and may have been killed or drowned. Radio Hanoi reported the death of an American airman on this day, which apparently referred to Lt Cdr Sullivan. His remains were eventually handed over by the Vietnamese on 14 August 1985.

A-6A   155705   VA-115, USN, USS *Midway*
                  1 crew, name unknown (KIA)
                  1 crew, name unknown (survived)

F-4B   153031   USN, USS *Midway*
An Intruder made a hard landing on board the *Midway* causing the undercarriage to collapse. The aircraft ran into a Phantom, which was so badly damaged that it had to be scrapped. In addition to one of the Intruder's crew who was killed in the accident, four men were killed on the deck of the carrier when they were hit by debris from the crash.

2 November 1972

A-7E   157530   VA-192, USN, USS *Kitty Hawk*
                  Lt R G Deremer (survived)
The pilot of a Corsair felt his aircraft shudder as he pulled up after firing a Walleye missile at a railway bridge at Tap Phuc, 15 miles north of Vinh. He reduced power and lowered the nose which seemed to solve the problem but as he flew out to sea the Corsair's engine temperature rose and the engine suffered a series of compressor stalls. As the engine wound down the pilot ejected over the sea 50 miles north of the DMZ and was picked up by a Navy helicopter. The cause of the engine problem could not be determined. This was the final aircraft to be lost by the USS *Kitty Hawk* before the end of its sixth and last war cruise two days later. The ship is one of three carriers that served in South-

east Asia that are still in service today and the *Kitty Hawk* is not due to be decommissioned until 2008.

5 November 1972

A-7B   154540   VA-56, USN, USS *Midway*
                  Lt Cdr Clarence Orfield Tolbert (KIA)
A section of Corsairs on an armed reconnaissance mission were looking for a suspected SAM site near Route 1A, about 35 miles north of Vinh. As the Corsairs were flying at 3,500 feet and 400 knots, Lt Cdr Tolbert's aircraft was hit by 23mm AAA. The starboard wing caught fire briefly and the aircraft started to lose fuel. The aircraft turned towards the coast but it crashed near the beach killing the pilot. A puff of smoke had been observed in the cockpit area and it is possible that Lt Cdr Tolbert may have been incapacitated and was unable to eject. An article in the 15 November issue of Nhan Dan, a North Vietnamese newspaper, claimed that an aircraft had been shot down on the 5th and that the pilot had been killed when he ejected but his parachute failed to deploy. Lt Cdr Tolbert had been forced to eject from a Corsair on 23 July 1972 when his aircraft was hit by anti-aircraft fire. Clarence Tolbert's remains were returned by the Vietnamese on 3 November 1988.

7 November 1972

F-111A   67-0063   429 TFS, 474 TFW on TDY, USAF, Takhli
                     Maj Robert Mack Brown (KIA)
                     Maj Robert David Morrissey (KIA)
An F-111, call sign Whaler 57, went missing during a low-level night strike on a ferry and ford at Luat Son about 30 miles west of the Ban Karai Pass in southern Laos. The crew had dropped their bombs and were leaving the target area when they disappeared. The cause of their loss and the exact fate of the crew remains unknown despite an extensive search that lasted until 20 November. Apparently artefacts from this aircraft were later found to be on display in the Quang Binh Provincial Museum after the war. These items included an F-111A manual, Maj Brown's ID card and the aircraft's data plate. The aircraft was shot down by the 359th Company, Quang Binh forces. Maj Brown had a flown a tour in South Vietnam in 1966 in the F-100 and was awarded three DFCs on that tour. Parts of the F-111 were discovered in the possession of local villagers during a visit to the region in July 1992 by an American investigation team. It was also rumoured that parts of the aircraft had been recovered and sent to Russia for investigation.

9 November 1972

A-7C   156764   VA-86, USN, USS *America*
                  1 pilot, name unknown (survived)
As a Corsair returned to the USS *America* following a test flight it suffered a brake failure after landing. The aircraft rolled off the ship but the pilot ejected and was quickly rescued.

A-4E   151191   VMA-211, MAG-12, USMC, Bien Hoa
                  1 pilot, name unknown (survived)

A Skyhawk's engine failed as the aircraft was taking off from Bien Hoa on a close air support mission and the pilot ejected moments before it crashed. This was the third and last Skyhawk lost by the two MAG-12 squadrons based at Bien Hoa. All three aircraft had belonged to VMA-211 and all the pilots survived their ordeal, although one was captured. The other squadron, VMA-311, lost no aircraft during the eight-month deployment to South Vietnam. By the end of 1972 the two MAG-12 Skyhawk squadrons had flown a total of 12,574 combat sorties averaging about 50 sorties a day. The squadrons had dropped a total of 18,903 tons of bombs during this time. In over seven years of combat operations in Vietnam VMA-311 had flown a grand total of 54,625 combat sorties and dropped 105,000 tons of ordnance for the loss of 28 aircraft. MAG-12 began transferring back to Iwakuni on 29 January 1973.

10 November 1972

A-7B   154506   VA-93, USN, USS *Midway*
                  Lt M J Cobb (survived)
A flight of Corsairs came across two trucks on a road about 15 miles south of Thanh Hoa during an armed reconnaissance mission. As Lt Cobb was making his attack his aircraft was hit by 37mm flak and caught fire. He turned towards the coast and crossed the beach just as the aircraft's flight control system started to fail. Lt Cobb ejected about 10 miles off the coast when the aircraft became uncontrollable. He was subsequently rescued by a Navy HH-3A SAR helicopter.

A-7A   153161   VA-37, USN, USS *Saratoga*
                  Lt Cdr Frederick Williston Wright (KIA)
Later in the day another flight of Corsairs was sent on a road reconnaissance mission just north of the DMZ. The leader, Lt Cdr Wright, made an attack on a road intersection during which his wingman lost sight of him. The wingman later spotted aircraft wreckage on the ground near the road and about four miles north of the village of Thon Cam Son. Rescue aircraft encountered 23mm anti-aircraft fire and it was thought probable that Lt Cdr Wright was either shot down by ground fire or had stalled and crashed as he was pulling up off the target. There was no indication that the pilot had survived but his remains were not returned to the USA by the Vietnamese until September 1990 and positively identified on 12 December 1990. Frederick Wright was buried with full military honours at Arlington National Cemetery on 18 December. Lt Cdr Wright was on his second combat tour in Southeast Asia and had also flown combat patrol missions during the Cuban Missile Crisis of 1962.

A-7B   154399   VA-56, USN, USS *Midway*
                  Lt W P Lotsberg (survived)
After nightfall yet another Corsair was lost on the 10th. Lt Lotsberg was the Number 2 in a section of Corsairs on a road reconnaissance mission along Route 1A south of Vinh. The section discovered a truck about seven miles southeast of Ha Tinh but Lt Lotsberg's aircraft was hit by 23mm AAA just as he was about to roll in on the target. He headed towards the sea but his flying

controls froze almost immediately and he ejected at 15,000 feet just off the coast about 90 seconds after being hit. He was later rescued by a Navy helicopter.

16 November 1972

F-105G 63-8359 Detachment 1, 561 TFS, 832 AD attached to 388 TFW, USAF, Korat
Maj Norman Maier (survived)
Capt Kenneth Theate (survived)

The B-52 Arc Light raids that had been pounding South Vietnam, Laos and Cambodia for many years were extended into the southern provinces of North Vietnam in April 1972 in response to the North's invasion of the South. Each raid was supported by a large number of Iron Hand and ECM aircraft, chaff bombers and escort fighters. It was on a B-52 support raid on the night of the 16th on a target near Vinh that one of the support aircraft was lost. A Wild Weasel from an Iron Hand flight was hit by an SA-2 that suddenly emerged from cloud cover as the aircraft was escorting a cell of B-52s at 19,000 feet about 30 miles northwest of Vinh. The Thud crew ejected a few moments later and came down near the town of Dong Xuon where they both hid until morning. A SAR task force of some 75 aircraft coordinated by Maj Colin Arnie Clark of the 356th TFS in an A-7D Corsair attempted a rescue the next day. After several hours Maj Clark eventually found a way through the low cloud and enemy defences into a valley where the two downed airmen were then picked up by an HH-53. This was the first rescue mission supported by the A-7D Corsair in its new role as a Sandy replacement. It was during this first mission for the Corsairs that the increase in speed of the RESCAP aircraft became an obvious handicap. Unlike the Skyraider, the Corsair had to fly a race track pattern round the helicopter so as not to get too far ahead. This used up a lot of fuel and on this occasion required four visits to a tanker for refuelling. As a result of this mission revised RESCAP tactics were worked out for the better integration of the new aircraft. Maj Clark, a former Misty FAC pilot, spent a total of nine hours in the air on this mission, much of it in poor weather. His aircraft suffered a communications malfunction and was badly damaged by AAA and tracked by a SAM site. He received a well-earned AFC for his efforts and his aircraft is now preserved in the USAF Museum at Wright-Patterson AFB. He was well aware of the plight of the F-105 crew as he himself had been shot down twice during the war, the first time on 18 August 1964 and the second on 22 January 1969, both times while flying F-100s.

20 November 1972

F-4J 153849 VMFA-232, MAG-15, USMC, Nam Phong
Capt W D Anderson (survived)
Capt Donald Charles Breuer (KIA)

The last Phantom lost by VMFA-232 was shot down during a two-aircraft strike on a target in southern Laos on 20 November. The aircraft was hit by AAA near Ban Tampanko, about 20 miles west of the A Shau Valley. The pilot ejected and was rescued by a USAF SAR helicopter but the navigator was probably unable to

eject and did not survive. VMFA-232 had lost a total of five Phantoms and two crewmembers during its last two tours in Southeast Asia. The Squadron lost no further aircraft and left Nam Phong on 1 September 1973 for a two-month stay at Cubi Point before moving on to Iwakuni.

F-4J 157288 VF-103, USN, USS *Saratoga*
Lt Cdr V E Lesh (survived)
Lt(jg) D L Cordes (survived)

When the B-52 strikes had started against targets around Vinh in April it was realised that the huge bombers were vulnerable to interception by MiGs so a strong CAP force of US Air Force and Navy fighters accompanied each raid. On the night of the 20th VF-103 was providing the CAP flight for a B-52 strike on Vinh. One of the Phantoms was damaged by a SAM at 17,000 feet about 20 miles northeast of Vinh. The port wing caught fire and the port engine failed. Lt Cdr Lesh and Lt Cordes were fortunate in being able to keep the aircraft flying long enough to reach the sea and ejected safely off Thanh Hoa when the hydraulic system failed. They were picked up unharmed by a Navy SH-3G.

F-111A 67-0092 430 TFS, 474 TFW on TDY, USAF, Takhli
Capt Ronald Dean Stafford (KIA)
Capt Charles Joseph Caffarelli (KIA)

The fourth F-111 lost during the 1972 deployment failed to return from a night mission against a transhipment point at Co Giang in southern North Vietnam. Burger 54 is thought to have flown into the sea after successfully bombing the target as wreckage was later washed up on the coast just south of the DMZ. A number of incidents involving failures of the automatic terrain-following radar mode led other members of the 474th TFW to suspect that Stafford and Caffarelli's aircraft had entered a shallow descent when the radar failed to recognise the surface of the sea.

F-4D 66-7501 555 TFS, 432 TRW, USAF, Udorn
Capt Calvin B Tibbett (KWF)
1Lt William S Hargrove (KWF)

The crew of a Phantom were killed when it crashed following a control failure during a training sortie over Thailand. This particular aircraft was fitted with the Combat Tree modification that enabled the detection of enemy IFF transmissions at beyond visual range. This was a successful fighter crew who had shot down two MiG-21s on 9 and 16 September, the first one by 20mm cannon while flying an F-4D and the second by a Sidewinder missile while flying an F-4E. Phantom 66-7501 had also had a successful career having been flown by Lt Col C D Westphal and Capt J S Feinstein of the 13th TFS when they shot down a MiG-21 on 13 October.

21 November 1972

EC-47Q 43-49771 361 TEWS, 56 SOW, USAF, Nakhon Phanom
Capt Robert Alan Kohn (KIA)
MSgt John W Ryon (KIA)
8 crew, names unknown (survived)

Two of the 10-man crew of an EC-47 Dakota were killed when the aircraft, call sign Baron 56, crashed on landing after sus-

taining a control failure. This aircraft had been used as a VIP transport by the US Embassy in Copenhagen before being converted to an EC-47 RDF aircraft.

22 November 1972

B-52D 55-0110 96 BW attached to 307 SW, USAF, U-Tapao
Capt Norbert J Ostrozny (survived)
Capt Robert Estes (survived)
Capt P A Foley (survived)
SSgt Ron Sellers (survived)
2 crew, names unknown (survived)

Although 13 B-52s had been lost in accidents in Southeast Asia during eight years of Arc Light operations, the first Stratofortress lost as a direct result of enemy action was brought down on the night of 22 November 1972. The B-52 force had been bombing targets around Vinh for seven months and the number of SAM launches had increased noticeably during that time. Two aircraft had been damaged earlier in the month but had landed safely at U-Tapao. Capt Ostrozny and his crew from the 96th BW, Dyess AFB, Texas were on rotation at U-Tapao and were flying as Olive 2 (most B-52 cells used a colour as their call sign). The aircraft was at high altitude about 25 miles northwest of Vinh and had just dropped its bombs when it was rocked by a nearby SAM detonation that caused heavy damage. The aircraft was peppered by shrapnel and fire broke out in the rear fuselage and in both wings. The pilot headed back towards Thailand escorted by an F-105G Wild Weasel in the hope of making an emergency landing back at U-Tapao. SSgt Sellers in the gun turret at the back of the aircraft could hear but could not transmit on his radio. His compartment began to get hot as the fire in the fuselage took hold and he could see the wings gradually being burned away. About five miles from the Thai border the last of the engines stopped but Capt Ostrozny judged that he had enough altitude to glide the rest of the way despite a fiercely burning aircraft with no electrical power or flight instruments. Just as the aircraft crossed the Mekong River into Thailand the starboard wing tip broke away and the aircraft started an uncontrolled turn. All the crew abandoned the aircraft safely and the B-52 crashed about 15 miles southwest of Nakhon Phanom. An HH-53 was airborne as the crew ejected and picked them up within minutes of touching down.

23 November 1972

O-2A 68-11065 21 TASS, 377 ABW, USAF, Tan Son Nhut
1 pilot, name unknown (survived)

The area around An Loc was still highly dangerous and an FAC was shot down by an SA-7 missile at dusk on the 23rd. The pilot escaped and was soon picked up by a US Army helicopter.

A-7E 157592 VA-27, USN, USS *Enterprise*
1 pilot, name unknown (survived)

A Corsair returned from a flak suppression sortie over North Vietnam but made a hard touch down on the *Enterprise* and was waved off to go around for another attempt. As the aircraft was in the circuit its engine failed, most probably as a result of damage from the bad landing, and the pilot ejected and was rescued.

OV-10A 67-14632 23 TASS, 56 SOW, USAF, Nakhon Phanom
1 pilot, name unknown (survived)

A Bronco, call sign Nail 36, suffered an engine failure as it was taking off from Da Nang on an FAC mission. The aircraft crashed but the pilot survived. An HH-43 was already in the air when the OV-10 pilot radioed that he was in trouble and the helicopter had to avoid being hit by the OV-10 as it passed close by. Lt W Latham and Lt J Moulton saw the OV-10 pilot parachute into a rice paddy

The 14th TRS lost a total of 22 RF-4C Phantoms during its long tenure at Udorn RTAB. In all 83 RF-4Cs and 38 RF-101Cs were lost during the war illustrating the dangers of low-level tactical reconnaissance operations in a war zone. RF-4C 69-0350 was a LORAN-equipped aircraft that could be identified by a towel-rail antenna on the dorsal spine. USAF

The B-52D model of the Stratofortress flew most of the Arc Light sorties from 1966 to 1972 and also flew about 70 per cent of the B-52 sorties during Linebacker II when nine aircraft were shot down. USAF

and landed their HH-43 close by. The pilot was picked up one minute and 30 seconds after ejecting, probably the fastest rescue in the history of the war.

26 November 1972

F-8J   150887   VF-191, USN, USS *Oriskany*
                  Lt(jg) G E Weller (survived)

A Crusader caught fire as it was being launched from the *Oriskany* on a strike mission. The pilot ejected and the aircraft crashed into the sea just in front of the carrier.

28 November 1972

F-4D   serial ..?   432 TRW, USAF, Udorn
                      Capt Jack Rockwood Harvey (KIA)
                      Capt Bobby Marvin Jones (KIA)

A Phantom took off from Udorn to fly to Da Nang on a non-combat flight. On board was Capt B M Jones who was a flight surgeon and the purpose of the flight was to log flying hours to maintain his flight status. The aircraft suddenly disappeared from the radar screens about 18 miles west of Da Nang, as the Phantom started its approach to the airfield in heavy rain and low cloud. An emergency beeper was heard but bad weather and enemy activity hampered rescue efforts for three days and the crew was never found. Wreckage was later spotted on Bach Ma mountain in the Phu Loc district but it could not investigated at the time.

A-6A   155622   VA-75, USN, USS *Saratoga*
                  Cdr Charles M Earnest (KIA)
                  Lt Cdr G L Jackson (survived)

An Intruder from VA-75 crashed into the sea moments after being launched from the *Saratoga* on an armed reconnaissance mission over North Vietnam. Unfortunately, the Squadron's CO was killed although the NFO survived the accident. Cdr Earnest had been awarded the Silver Star for directing a successful inland rescue of Lt J R Lloyd of VA-105 near Vinh on the night of 6 August.

2 December 1972

A-7D   71-0310   353 TFS, 354 TFW, USAF, Korat
                   Capt Anthony Cameron Shine (KIA)

The success of the A-7 Corsair in US Navy service prompted the USAF to buy a version for its own use as a light attack aircraft. The A-7D differed from the earlier Navy models by using an Allison TF41 engine, a 20mm multi-barrel cannon and updated avionics. Many of these improvements were also incorporated into the Navy's A-7E variant of the Corsair. Eventually a total of 459 A-7Ds were built for the USAF but the type saw only brief action in Southeast Asia. The 354th TFW arrived at Korat from Myrtle Beach AFB, South Carolina on 10 October with 72 aircraft operated by its three squadrons. By the end of the year the Wing had flown around 4,000 sorties for the loss of just two aircraft. In addition to close air support the Wing was also given the Sandy role within a few weeks of its arrival in Southeast Asia. A rapid learning exercise then took place between the A-7 pilots and the A-1 pilots of the 1st SOS who were about to hand over their aircraft to the VNAF.

The first A-7D to be lost in Southeast Asia was performing the Sandy role of SAR helicopter escort. Capt Shine was escorting a helicopter into the Barrel Roll region of northern Laos when he went missing. He was flying near the Barthelmy Pass on the border between Laos and North Vietnam, about 95 miles northwest of Vinh, when he disappeared as he descended through low cloud to identify a target. A three-day search failed to discover any sign of Capt Shine or the wreckage of his Corsair. Two of Capt Shine's brothers had also served in Southeast Asia and one of them, 1Lt J C Shine, had been killed while serving with the Army on 15 October 1970. Capt Shine's daughter was determined to

find her father's remains and travelled to Vietnam in 1993 and searched the crash site herself. The discovery of Capt Shine's flying helmet led to a JTF-FA investigation that recovered his remains from a nearby grave. His remains were returned to the USA in June 1995 and formally identified on 2 August 1996. Capt Shine was buried with full military honours at Arlington National Cemetery later in 1996.

9 December 1972

RF-4C   68-0597   14 TRS, 432 TRW, USAF, Udorn
                    Maj Billie Joe Williams (KIA)
                    1Lt Hector Michael Acosta (POW)

The last USAF casualty before the start of the Linebacker II offensive was a reconnaissance Phantom from Udorn that was shot down on a road reconnaissance mission north of the city of Vinh. Maj Williams and 1Lt Acosta were escorted by a flight of four Phantoms as they photographed targets in preparation for the new offensive when their aircraft was hit by a SAM near Nghai Hung, about 35 miles north of Vinh. 1Lt Acosta ejected himself and his pilot and two parachutes were observed by the other Phantom crews. However, the missile damaged the aircraft's cockpit and Acosta thought that Maj Williams might already have been dead or at least severely injured. The next day an HH-53 from the 40th ARRS was fired on as it hovered over a body, thought to be that of Maj Williams, as it lay in a clearing near the wreckage. Two HH-53s were damaged by ground fire and several crewmen wounded during the futile rescue attempt. Hector 'Mex' Acosta was badly injured and was captured but spent less than three months as a POW before being released on 29 March 1973. He had flown 92 missions and his pilot had flown 100 missions before they were shot down. On 20 December 1990 it was announced that the remains of Maj Williams had been returned and identified.

13 December 1972

RF-8G   144608   Detachment 4, VFP-63, USN, USS *Oriskany*
                   Lt Thomas B Scott (survived)

A reconnaissance Crusader crashed as it was attempting to land back on board the *Oriskany* at the end of a training flight. The aircraft touched down short of the arrester wires which it then missed. Lt Scott ejected safely and was soon picked up but the aircraft fell in the sea. This aircraft was probably the most historic Crusader ever built as it was the aircraft that Maj John Glenn, USMC, flew at supersonic speed across the United States on Project Bullet on 16 July 1957. The aircraft took hundreds of photographs on the three hours and 23 minute-journey between Los Angeles and New York. The aircraft was later modified from its original F8U-1P configuration to RF-8G standard while John Glenn went on to become the first American astronaut to orbit the earth in February 1962 and the oldest man to fly in space in October 1998. This, one of the oldest Crusaders still in service, was the last of its type to be lost during the war. This Crusader was also the last aircraft lost by the *Oriskany* before it departed

Southeast Asia on 20 March 1973 at the conclusion of its seventh and final tour. The carrier was decommissioned on 15 May 1976 and was stricken on 25 July 1989 and is currently stored at Beaumont, Texas, awaiting its fate.

Linebacker II

Exasperated by the North Vietnamese reluctance to negotiate a peace treaty, President Nixon ordered an all-out bombing campaign of limited duration to commence on the night of 18th December. Although originally only planned to last for three days, the campaign eventually lasted 11 days and extended over the Christmas break. The campaign, named Linebacker II, saw the use of B-52s over Hanoi and Haiphong for the first time during the war in a truly strategic air campaign. In February 1972 B-52 reinforcements started arriving at both Andersen and U-Tapao under the code name Operation Bullet Shot and these deployments accelerated after the Easter Invasion. By the beginning of December a total of 206 B-52s were available for operations by the Eighth Air Force in Southeast Asia, more than half of SAC's entire inventory of the type. Andersen AFB on Guam had 99 B-52Gs and 53 B-52Ds while U-Tapao in Thailand had a further 54 B-52Ds. The Andersen aircraft had to fly a 6,000-mile round trip lasting 14 hours and some missions had to route further north to meet their tankers from Kadena resulting in a 8,200 mile, 18-hour round trip. The length of the missions had a major impact on the planning process particularly with regard to the time required to make modifications to tactics, targets and routings. This lack of flexibility was to cost the B-52 force dearly in the early days of the campaign. SAC's KC-135 tanker force in Southeast Asia, which totalled some 172 aircraft by mid-1972, made Linebacker II possible and throughout the campaign the tankers flew a total of 1,312 sorties involving 4,593 refuellings. Two different models of the B-52 were used, the B-52D that had been performing Arc Light missions for many years and the newer B-52G. Although a more recent model with a better performance the B-52G did not have such a sophisticated ECM fit as the D models. A modification programme was under way to improve the B-52G's ECM equipment but many of the aircraft deployed to Andersen and yet to be modified and SAC felt what turned out to be justifiable concern for the survivability of the B-52G in combat over North Vietnam. Also the B-52G was not fitted with external bomb racks nor had it had the Big Belly bomb bay conversions that the B-52D had and so could carry only 27 bombs whereas the B-52D could carry a staggering total of 108 x 500lb bombs. In practice while the U-Tapao aircraft did indeed carry 108 bombs, the Andersen-based aircraft normally only carried 66 as these aircraft had a much greater distance to travel on each mission.

The B-52s did not operate in total isolation. As well as tanker support, the whole range of USAF and US Navy tactical air power was employed, much of it in an effort to support the B-52 raids that were hoped would break North Vietnamese resistance and force them to the negotiating table. Tactical aircraft including

USAF and Navy F-4s and A-7s during the day and A-6s and F-111s during the night concentrated on enemy defences including airfields, AAA and SAM sites, assisted by F-105G Wild Weasels and Navy Iron Hand aircraft. Electronic warfare support was provided by EB-66s, EA-3s and EA-6As and the new EA-6B Prowlers for stand off jamming, while chaff was dropped by flights of F-4s to obscure enemy radar screens. Other F-4s flew MiGCAP missions during the raids while command and control was provided, as it had been for much of the war, by EC-121s orbiting over Laos and the Gulf of Tonkin and by Red Crown, a Navy ship sailing in the northern part of the Gulf. Added to this armada was the ever-present SAR task force of HC-130s, HH-53s, and the new Sandys, the A-7s. Each B-52 raid was supported by as many as 120 tactical aircraft, all requiring the most detailed and precise planning to ensure that the various components acted as a whole. However, no matter how many precautions or preparations could be taken beforehand, the viability of the B-52 force over Hanoi and Haiphong was still very much an unknown quantity. In the final analysis, SAC's reputation, indeed the reputation of US air power as a whole, depended largely on the men and machines that flew the Linebacker II missions.

18/19 December 1972

B-52G 58-0201   340 BS, 97 BW attached to 72 SW(P),
USAF, Andersen
Lt Col Donald Louis Rissi (KIA)
1Lt Robert James Thomas (KIA)
Maj Richard Edgar Johnson (POW)
Capt Robert Glenn Certain (POW)
Capt Richard Thomas Simpson (POW)
Sgt Walter Lee Ferguson (KIA)

The first night of Linebacker II saw a total of 129 B-52s attack North Vietnam in three waves with between four and five hours between each wave and 10 minutes between each three-aircraft flight or cell that made up each wave. This total was made up of 42 B-52Ds from U-Tapao and 54 B-52Gs and 33 B-52Ds from Andersen. The U-Tapao aircraft struck first, bombing the MiG-21 airfields at Hao Lac, Kep and Phuc Yen. The rest of the force struck the Yen Vien railway yard, the Kinh No storage complex, Hanoi radio station, and a railway repair depot in the city. Only two aircraft, both B-52Gs, failed to drop their bombs on target due to technical malfunctions.

The first B-52 to be lost during the Linebacker II offensive was from one of several cells of the first wave sent to bomb the Yen Vien railway yard two miles north of Hanoi. The aircraft, radio call sign Charcoal 1, was hit by two SA-2 missiles at 34,000 feet seconds before bomb release and crashed near Vinh Phu about five miles north of Hanoi. Three of the crew managed to escape from the blazing bomber but the other three were killed. The three POWs were released on 29 March 1973. The remains of Lt Col Rissi, the pilot, 1Lt Thomas, the co-pilot and Sgt Ferguson, the tail gunner, were returned by the Vietnamese on 23 August 1978. Ironically, this crew had been scheduled to rotate back home to the 97th BW at Blytheville AFB, Arkansas before the offensive started but their replacement crew had been delayed from leaving Loring AFB, Maine by a snowstorm and were not combat ready by the 18th. Pieces of wreckage from Charcoal 1 are currently on display at the Central Army Museum in Hanoi. During the first night of Linebacker II Sgt Samuel Turner, a tail gunner in Brown 3, made history when he became the first B-52 gunner to shoot down an enemy aircraft when his Stratofortress was attacked by a MiG-21. However, it was soon realised that it was the SA-2 that was going to be the major threat to the B-52s and a total of 164 missiles were counted on the first night, resulting in the loss of three of the bombers.

B-52G 58-0246   2 BW attached to 72 SW(P), USAF, Andersen
Maj Cliff Ashley (survived)
Capt Gary Vickers (survived)
Maj Archie Myers (survived)
1Lt Forrest Stegelin (survived)
Capt Jim Tramel (survived)
MSgt Ken Connor (survived)
Lt Col Hendsley Conner (survived)

About four hours later the second wave of B-52s hit the storage complex at Kinh No and other targets. As Peach cell was turning immediately after bomb release about two miles northwest of Hanoi, one of the aircraft was hit by a SAM causing major damage. Peach 2, flying at 38,500 feet, caught fire and the crew realised that they could not make Guam so decided to try to reach U-Tapao. The missile had exploded near the port wing and had ripped off the large underwing fuel tank and stopped the two port outer engines. Escorted by two F-4s the crew coaxed the aircraft across North Vietnam and Laos into Thailand but had to abandon the aircraft 20 miles east of Khon Khaen when the fire became worse and the wing began to disintegrate. All the crew were subsequently rescued by Marine Corps helicopters from Nam Phong. The crew was from the 2nd BW at Barksdale AFB, Louisiana. Lt Col Conner was the deputy airborne mission commander for the second wave and had to jump out of the aircraft through the hole in the floor left by the navigator's ejection seat as the B-52s were not fitted with an ejection seat for the seventh man they sometimes carried.

F-111A 67-0099   430 TFS, 474 TFW on TDY, USAF, Takhli
Lt Col Ronald Jack Ward (KIA)
Maj James Richard McElvain (KIA)

The only USAF tactical strike aircraft lost on the first night of the Linebacker II offensive was an F-111 (call sign Snug 40) that failed to return from a single-aircraft raid on the Hanoi International Radio communication transmitter. The F-111 squadrons were assigned a variety of targets during Linebacker II including railway yards, airfields, army barracks and SAM sites. A radio message was received by a C-130 Moonbeam ABCC aircraft reporting that the F-111 had bombed the target on schedule and had crossed the coast. After that nothing further was heard and the aircraft was posted missing when it became overdue back at Takhli. No trace of the aircraft or its crew was discovered. This loss was thought by some to have been another instance of the TFR failing to recognise the surface of the sea causing the aircraft to descend below the required altitude until it hit the sea. Lt Col Ward was the 430th's operations officer.

B-52D 56-0608   99 BW attached to 307 SW, USAF, U-Tapao
Capt Hal K Wilson (POW)
Maj Alexander Fernando (POW)
Capt Henry Charles Barrows (POW)
Capt Charles Arthur Brown (POW)
Capt Richard Waller Cooper (KIA)
TSgt Charlie Sherman Poole (KIA)

As dawn was breaking the last cell of the third wave of B-52s hit Hanoi's main radio station on the outskirts of the city. Just after dropping its bombs from 38,000 feet, Rose 1 was hit by a SAM during its post-target turn and caught fire. At least four of the crew abandoned the aircraft, which crashed near the village of Oai Than, five miles southwest of Hanoi. The crew was deployed from the 99th BW at Westover AFB, Massachusetts and the four surviving crewmembers were all released on 29 March 1973. Capt Wilson had flown 250 combat missions over Southeast Asia in his four tours of duty before being shot down. Hal Wilson converted to the FB-111A after returning from Hanoi. Henry Barrows was a German whose family had emigrated to the USA in 1958. He had previously flown 120 missions during a tour in the AC-130 from Ubon. Maj Fernando had joined the Air Force in 1952 and had been a navigator on B-29s and B-47s prior to converting to the B-52. In January 1996 part of the wreckage of Rose 1 was excavated from a pond by a JTF-FA team and remains thought to be those of TSgt Poole were discovered.

A-7C 156783   VA-82, USN, USS *America*
Lt Carl T Wieland (POW)

Before first light on the 19th an Iron Hand flight of two Corsairs from the USS *America* flew a strike on a SAM site 12 miles south of Haiphong. Soon after launching their Shrikes, the leader spotted two SAMs that had been launched at the aircraft. One of the missiles went over the flight and exploded harmlessly but the other missile hit the wingman's aircraft. Lt Wielend ejected immediately at 19,000 feet and was captured soon after landing. As he parachuted down he was almost hit by an A-6 Intruder that

was flying through cloud. He spent 100 days as a POW before being released on 29 March 1973. He became the first POW to return to operational flying status after returning to the USA.

19 December 1972

OV-10A serial ..?   20 TASS, 6498 ABW, USAF, Da Nang
Capt Francis Xavier Egan (KIA)
1 crew, name unknown (survived)

As the B-52s and tactical strike aircraft took the war to Hanoi and Haiphong, the pressure on the northern provinces of South Vietnam was maintained. A Bronco was hit by an SA-7 missile during an FAC mission near Quang Tri and brought down. The pilot was killed but the observer survived and was eventually rescued.

On the night of the 19th/20th a total of 93 B-52s (27 B-52Ds and 36 B-52Gs from Andersen along with 30 B-52Ds from U-Tapao) hit mostly the same targets as the night before although the Thai Nguyen thermal power plant was also added to the list. Tactics and routings were largely unchanged from the previous night. About 180 SAM launches were logged, about the same as on the first night. However, none of the B-52s were lost on the 19th/20th although a B-52D from the second wave had to make an emergency landing at the USMC airfield at Nam Phong in Thailand following battle damage.

20/21 December 1972

B-52G 57-6496   456 BW attached to 72 SW(P),
USAF, Andersen
Capt Terry Mercer Geloneck (POW)
1Lt William Youl Arcuri (POW)
Capt Craig Allan Paul (KIA)
Capt Warren Richard Spencer (KIA)
1Lt Michael Robert Martini (POW)
SSgt Roy Madden (POW)

B-52G 57-6481   42 BW attached to 72 SW(P),
USAF, Andersen
Capt John Ellinger (survived)
5 crew, names unknown (survived)

B-52D 56-0622   99 BW attached to 307 SW, USAF, U-Tapao
Maj John Franklin Stuart (KIA)
Maj Randolph Allen Perry (KIA)
Capt Irwin Stuart Lerner (KIA)
Capt Thomas J Klomann (POW)
1Lt Paul Louis Grainger (POW)
MSgt Arthur Vincent McLaughlin (KIA)

The good luck that the B-52 force had encountered on the previous night encouraged the SAC planners to continue with the same basic attack strategy for the third night running. By now it was known that the original three-day campaign had been extended indefinitely and in hindsight a change of tactics for the third night would have been sensible. The targets for 20th/21st were a composite of those that had been struck on the first two nights and included Kinh No, Thai Nguyen, Yen Vien and Hanoi itself. A total of 99 B-52s took part in the raid and the enemy responded by firing about 220 SAMs at the B-52s resulting in the loss of six aircraft. Thirty-three B-52Ds from U-Tapao together with 24 B-52Ds and 42 B-52Gs from Andersen took part in the third night of raids. During the raids MiG-21s were observed that MiG-21s were flying alongside several of the B-52s apparently reporting their altitude to the SAM and AAA command units. The MiGs also made several attempts to shoot down the huge bombers but only managed to damage one aircraft that was later brought down by a SAM.

Yen Vien was the target for the first wave and was approached by the formation through a narrow corridor to the northwest of Hanoi. As Quilt cell approached the target it started receiving SAM launch indications. About 30 seconds before bomb release time three or four SAMs were seen heading towards the B-52s but evasive manoeuvres could not be commenced until the bombs had been dropped. Quilt 3 started a hard turn as soon as its bombs had gone but just seconds later it was hit by one or two SAMs about 10 miles west of Hanoi. Capt Paul, the EWO, and SSgt Madden, the gunner, were badly injured, cabin pressurisa-

tion was lost and there was a fuel leak. Capt Geloneck ordered the crew to abandon the aircraft as it began to lose altitude but Capt Paul and Capt Spencer were killed. The crew was deployed from the 456th BW at Beale AFB in California. Capt Geloneck, 1Lt Arcuri and SSgt Madden were all released on 12 February due to their injuries but 1Lt Martini had to wait until 29 March 1973 for his release. SSgt Madden later had to have a leg amputated as a result of his injuries and the effects of gangrene. On 30 September 1977 the remains of the two missing crewmen were handed over by the Vietnamese.

Brass 2, like Quilt 3, was a B-52G with unmodified ECM equipment. The cell lost formation integrity on approach to the target with the result that the leader was some six miles ahead of Brass 2 over the target. Brass 2 was hit by two SAMs at 35,500 feet over Hanoi while in its post-target turn after bombing Yen Vien. The missiles damaged four of the engines but the crew managed to fly across North Vietnam and Laos into Thailand where they eventually had to abandon the aircraft 10 miles southwest of Nakhon Phanom. The crew of Brass 2 was deployed from the 42nd BW from Loring AFB, Maine.

The crew of Orange 3, captained by Maj J F Stuart, heard the emergency beepers from the crew of Quilt 3 as they started their bomb run on Yen Vien. Just seconds before bomb release the B-52D was attacked by a MiG resulting in damage and a small fire in the forward wheel well. Then a volley of three SAMs was fired at the aircraft, which received at least one direct hit at 35,500 feet about five miles north of Hanoi. The aircraft went into a flat spin with its starboard wing on fire and pieces falling off the aircraft. The cabin depressurised and the electrical power failed so the aircraft commander ordered the crew to abandon the aircraft, which then crashed in Yen Thuong village. Capt Klomann and 1Lt Granger managed to eject and were the only survivors of the six-man crew and Klomann was seriously injured and remained semi-conscious for two weeks but was nursed back to health by his fellow POWs. Between 15 and 20 SAMs were fired at Orange cell while in the target area.

Capt Klomann, who was flying as a substitute on Orange 3 on the 20th, was repatriated early on 12 February due to his wounds while 1Lt Granger was released on 29 March 1973. The crew had deployed with the 346th BS from the 99th BW at Westover AFB, Massachusetts although the aircraft actually belonged to the 7th BW.

A-6A 155594 VA-196, USN, USS *Enterprise*
Cdr Gordon R Nakagawa (POW)
Lt Kenneth Hill Higdon (POW)

The Navy's Intruder squadrons made a significant contribution to the Linebacker II offensive performing low-level strikes every night. One aircraft from the *Enterprise* was targeted against the Haiphong shipyards on the night of the 20th. As Cdr Nakagawa and Lt Higdon sped along under 500 feet at 420 knots their aircraft was hit by ground fire over Haiphong city. It was conjectured that the aircraft was hit by 37mm flak or even possibly by an SA-7 SAM, although most of these little missiles were allocated to the North Vietnamese forces in South Vietnam or Laos. Whatever hit the Intruder, it burst into flames and the engines and flight controls began to fail. The crew ejected about eight miles south of Haiphong and were soon captured. Lt Higdon was released on 12 February and Cdr Nakagawa on 29 March 1973. Gordon Nakagawa was the executive officer of VA-196 and had flown 185 missions at the time of his capture.

B-52D 56-0669 306 BW attached to 43 SW, USAF, Andersen
Capt Vincent Russo (survived)
Maj Frank Alton Gould (KIA)
Capt James Farmer (survived)
Lt Deverl Johnson (survived)
2 crew, names unknown (survived)

It was becoming apparent to SAC planners during the course of the raids that the B-52Gs with unmodified ECM equipment were faring particularly badly even when flying in their tight cell formation for mutual protection. In an attempt to reduce further losses two cells of B-52Gs from the second wave on 20th/21st were recalled while on their way to the target. Other unmodified B-52Gs had to continue, as their recall would have broken up

force integrity and reduced the bomb tonnage on particular targets to an unacceptably low level. The second wave hit the Thai Nguyen thermal power plant and the Bac Giang railway yard and suffered no losses.

One of the targets on the third wave was Gia Lam railway repair shops just east of Hanoi, which was attacked by three cells. Straw cell was engaged by at least 18 SAMs as it made its way towards Hanoi. Straw 2 was hit by a SAM and badly damaged shortly after it started its post-target turn. Two engines caught fire and the electrical power failed but the crew managed to fly southwest towards Thailand. However, the crew was unable to transfer fuel from one side of the aircraft to the other and it became difficult to control. Thirty minutes after it was hit and just after the aircraft crossed into Laos the aircraft became uncontrollable and the crew abandoned the B-52 about 10 miles northeast of the Ban Ban Valley. All the crew survived and were rescued by a USAF HH-53 from the 40th ARRS with the exception of the radar navigator, Maj Frank Gould, who was injured when the SAM struck the Stratofortress and was not thought to have escaped from the aircraft. However, conflicting information exists that suggests that Maj Gould did escape and may have been captured. Several live sightings of Maj Gould in Laos were claimed in the early 1990s together with other information from Laotian villagers giving fresh but ultimately false hope to his family. This was the first B-52D from Andersen to be shot down during the Linebacker raids. The crew were on detachment from the 306th BW at McCoy AFB, Florida

B-52G 58-0198 92 BW attached to 72 SW(P), USAF, Andersen
Lt Col James Yoshikazu Nagahiro (POW)
Capt Donovan Keith Walters (KIA)
Maj Edward Harvey Johnson (KIA)
Capt Lynn Richard Beens (POW)
Capt Robert Ray Lynn (KIA)
A1C Charles James Bebus (KIA)
Lt Col Keith Russell Heggen (POW – Died)

Most of the AC-130 gunships were painted with distinctive nose art during the war. This aircraft is AC-130A 56-0490 'Thor', which was shot down on a mission near Pakse on 21 December 1972 during the Linebacker II campaign. USAF

The B-52G version of the Stratofortress, despite being a later model than the B-52D, had a more basic ECM fit and was less able to defend itself from the SA-2 missile. Six of the 15 aircraft lost during Linebacker II were B-52Gs despite the fact they only flew 225 out of the 741 sorties flown. USAF

B-52G 58-0169 97 BW attached to 72 SW(P), USAF, Andersen
Capt Randall James Craddock (KIA)
Capt George Barry Lockhart (KIA)
Maj Bobby Alexander Kirby (KIA)
Capt Ronald Dwight Perry (KIA)
2Lt Charles Edward Darr (KIA)
SSgt James Leon Lollar (POW)

A few minutes behind the raid on Gia Lam, Olive 1 led a raid on Kinh No by four cells of aircraft from Guam just as dawn was beginning to break. Olive 1, another of the unmodified B-52Gs, was flown by Lt Col Nagahiro and also carried Lt Col Heggen, the deputy airborne mission commander, in addition to the normal crew. Olive 1 was hit by a SAM in the tail section at 35,000 feet two miles west of Hanoi moments after it had dropped its bombs and was turning on its course for the return flight. The aircraft crashed in flames and although all the crew are thought to have ejected only three of them successfully escaped from the bomber. Lt Col Nagahiro and Capt Beens were repatriated on 29 March 1973 but Lt Col Heggens died of his injuries soon after being captured. The remains of Lt Col Heggen were returned on 13 March 1974 but it was not until October 1988 that the remains of the other four missing crewmen were returned. Hawaiian-born James Nagahiro had started his flying career as a navigator in C-124 transports before pilot training and conversion to the B-47 and B-52. The crew were on deployment from the 92nd BW's base at Fairchild AFB in Washington.

Two cells behind Olive cell and also headed for Kinh No was Tan cell. Capt Craddock's Tan 3 was an unmodified B-52G that had lost its bombing and navigation radar and so had to rely on radar directions from the cell leader. By the time the cell reached the target Tan 3 was lagging well behind the other two aircraft and it was hit by two SAMs about eight miles northwest of Hanoi. Only the tail gunner, SSgt Lollar, ejected before the aircraft exploded and he was captured and was released on 29 March 1973. SSgt Lollar had previously served on ground tours in Southeast Asia with B-57 and AC-47 units before training as a

tail gunner on the B-52. The crew was from the 97th BW based at Blytheville AFB, Arkansas. The remains of Capt Perry were returned by the Vietnamese on 21 December 1975, three years to the day of his death, but it was not until 15 December 1988 that remains subsequently identified as belonging to the four remaining men missing from Tan 3 were returned.

Four unmodified B-52Gs and two B-52Ds had been lost on a single night with another B-52D (Brick 2) damaged and forced to make an emergency landing at U-Tapao. Five of the aircraft lost had been hit after bomb release during the post-target turn when the ECM was less effective and the crew unable to look for SAMs on one side of the aircraft. After this costly night the unmodified B-52Gs were not sent on raids over Hanoi again.

21/22 December 1972

A-6A   152946   VA-75, USN, USS *Saratoga*
        Lt Cdr Robert Stewart Graustein (KIA)
        Lt Cdr Barton Scott Wade (KIA)

Several Intruders from the *Saratoga* were despatched on low-level strikes throughout North Vietnam on the night of the 21st. Just after dusk Lt Cdr Graustein bombed Kien An airfield near Haiphong and reported by radio that he had dropped his bombs. The target was very heavily defended with a variety of AAA guns and moments after the radio call other aircraft in the vicinity saw an airborne explosion and a fire on the ground. When Lt Cdr Graustein and Lt Cdr Wade did not radio in or return to the carrier it was presumed that they had been shot down by flak over the target. This Intruder was the last fixed-wing aircraft lost by the *Saratoga* before the end of its only tour of duty in Southeast Asia, although two SH-3 helicopters were lost on the 23rd and the 31st of the month. The ship was eventually decommissioned on 30 September 1994 and is currently in storage at Newport, Rhode Island, awaiting its fate.

AC-130A   56-0490   16 SOS, 56 SOW, USAF, Ubon
        Capt Harry Roy Lagerwall (KIA)
        Capt Stanley Neal Kroboth (KIA)
        Maj Paul Oswald Meder (KIA)
        Maj Francis Anthony Walsh (KIA)
        Capt Joel Ray Birch (KIA)
        Capt Thomas Trammell Hart (KIA)
        Capt Robert Leonel Liles (KIA)
        2Lt George Duncan MacDonald (KIA)
        1Lt Delmar Ernest Dickens (KIA)
        A1C Charles Frederick Fenter (KIA)
        TSgt Robert Thomas Elliott (KIA)
        TSgt James Ray Fuller (KIA)
        TSgt John Quitman Winningham (KIA)
        Sgt Richard Williams (survived)
        Sgt Carl E. Stevens (survived)
        A1C Rollie Keith Reaid (KIA)

The war over the Ho Chi Minh Trail continued throughout the Linebacker II offensive but on the night of the 21st an AC-130 Spectre gunship was lost along with most of its crew. The aircraft, piloted by Capt Lagerwall, had found three trucks near Ban Laongam, 25 miles west of Saravan in southern Laos. It was firing at the target from an altitude of 7,800 feet when it was hit by 37mm AAA. The aircraft may have been hit in a fuel tank as it exploded and crashed in flames and 14 of the 16 men on board were killed. Two of the crew managed to bail out and were rescued by a 40th ARRS HH-53 some hours later, located by the night vision devices on board another AC-130 and the LNRS equipment on board the helicopter. Maj Walsh is listed as being a member of the 497th TFS and may have been along just for the ride. This aircraft was nicknamed 'Thor' and was painted with appropriate gunship nose art.

In February 1985 a joint excavation by US and Laotian investigators discovered numerous small bone fragments at the crash site and it was later announced that these had been positively identified as being the remains of the crew. The family of Capt Hart was dissatisfied with the investigation and sued the US Government. The US Army's Central Identification Laboratory came under scrutiny and its identification procedures were challenged. The family won the lawsuit and the identification of two

of the crew was rescinded, however, the 11th Circuit Court of Appeals later overturned the verdict.

B-52D   55-0061   96 BW attached to 307 SW, USAF, U-Tapao
        Capt Peter James Giroux (POW)
        Capt Thomas Waring Bennett (KIA)
        Lt Col Gerald William Alley (KIA)
        Capt Peter Paul Camerota (POW)
        1Lt Joseph Bernard Copack (KIA)
        MSgt Louis Edward LeBlanc (POW)

B-52D   55-0050   7 BW attached to 307 SW, USAF, U-Tapao
        Lt Col John Harry Yuill (POW)
        Capt David Ian Drummond (POW)
        Lt Col Louis Henry Bernasconi (POW)
        Lt Col William Walter Conlee (POW)
        1Lt William Thomas Mayall (POW)
        SSgt Gary Lee Morgan (POW)

The fourth day of the B-52 campaign against North Vietnam marked the second phase of the offensive and had been planned to involve mainly the B-52Ds from U-Tapao. This was fortuitous as it gave the planners time to revise their thinking about the employment of the more vulnerable B-52Gs. A total of just 30 U-Tapao aircraft flew the raid while another 30 aircraft from Andersen flew Arc Light sorties over South Vietnam. About 70 SAMs were thought to have been fired on this night, two of which found their mark.

The targets for Day 4 were the Bac Mai military storage area near Hanoi, the Van Dien storage depot and Quang Te airfield. Scarlet 1, a 96th BW aircraft from Dyess AFB, Texas, was being flown by a 22nd BW crew from March AFB, California under the leadership of Capt P Giroux and was assigned to the Bac Mai raid. When the crew were pre-flighting the B-52 they noticed that it had suffered a radar failure on a previous flight but that the fault could not be traced on the ground. However, as the aircraft approached the initial point to start its bomb run the radar failed again and Capt Giroux ordered Scarlet 2 to take the lead. As Scarlet 1 dropped back it became separated from its cell and before it could catch up the gunner warned the pilot that a MiG was on the aircraft's tail. Capt Giroux took evasive action as the tail gunner fired at the MiG and launched flares to decoy two air-to-air missiles that had been fired at the bomber. The MiG pulled away as the B-52s approached a SAM site and two SA-2s were fired at the cell. With the cell spread out and ECM protection reduced, both missiles guided towards Scarlet 1 and one of the missiles hit the aircraft in the centre fuselage. The port wing caught fire as did the two inboard engines on the starboard wing. After the bombs had gone the co-pilot, Capt Bennett, ordered the crew to abandon the aircraft and fired Capt Giroux's ejection seat manually as the pilot was semi-conscious at the time. MSgt LeBlanc later recollected that he saw six parachutes leave the aircraft. He and the pilot were captured immediately but Capt Camerota, the EWO, spent the next 12 days on the run in enemy territory including several days spent hiding in a cave. On 30 December Capt Camerota reached the top of a high hill in an attempt to contact someone on his survival radio. He eventually made contact with several aircraft but he could not be rescued due to intense enemy activity in the area. On 3 January, suffering from extreme exhaustion, he turned himself in to some Vietnamese villagers and was taken to the Hanoi Hilton. Capt Giroux was released on 12 February due to his severe injuries and Capt Camerota and MSgt LeBlanc were released on 29 March 1973. Lt Col Alley and 1Lt Copack's remains were returned by the Vietnamese on 15 December 1988 and their identity confirmed the following June. Capt Peter Giroux had flown 264 combat missions during the war including 104 missions flying EC-121Rs with the 553rd RS. A total of 43 of his 160 B-52 missions were over North Vietnam. At some stage in its career 55-0061 was painted as 'Big Country Bomber'.

A little way behind Scarlet cell on the Bac Mai raid, Blue 1 was hit by two SAMs just three minutes later about seven miles to the west of Hanoi soon after releasing its bombs. The crew had seen 10 SAMs between their initial point and the release point. The aircraft caught fire, the cabin depressurised and the electrical power failed. All the crew abandoned the aircraft safely and were

captured although four of the men were slightly wounded by shrapnel. 1Lt Mayall had to bail out manually through the navigator's hatch when his ejection seat failed to operate. With three Lieutenant Colonels on board the aircraft this crew was singled out for special interrogation by the North Vietnamese but the days of torture and inhumane treatment had long gone. This was the only complete B-52 crew to be captured alive during Linebacker II and they were all released on 29 March 1973. The crew was deployed from the 7th BW from Carswell AFB, Texas, but was using a 43rd SW aircraft from Andersen. The crew was flying their third mission in four days.

Lt Col Yuill had flown the F-86, F-102, B-58 and the C-130 before converting to the B-52. He had flown C-130s during a combat tour at Tan Son Nhut earlier in the war. His son, Michael Yuill, later joined the USAF and flew the B-52 and the B-1B. SSgt Gary Morgan had been a SAR helicopter crewman in Southeast Asia with the US Navy before joining the Air Force and becoming a B-52 tail gunner.

22/23 December 1972

F-111A   67-0068   429 TFS, 474 TFW on TDY, USAF, Takhli
        Capt Robert David Sponeybarger (POW)
        1Lt William Wallace Wilson (POW)

Although no B-52s were lost from the 30 aircraft from U-Tapao that struck POL and railway targets in Haiphong on the night of the 22nd, an F-111 (call sign Jackel 33) was shot down during a strike against port facilities on the Red River on the outskirts of Hanoi. The aircraft was hit by AAA moments after dropping its 12 x 500lb bombs but it headed west to escape the intense enemy defences. However, the starboard engine had to be shut down due to flak damage and the crew had to eject over rugged terrain about 55 miles west of Hanoi when the aircraft caught fire and the hydraulics failed. Capt Sponeybarger was captured three days after being shot down and 1Lt Wilson was almost rescued on the fourth day.

An HH-53C 68-10788 commanded by Capt R D Shapiro of the 40th ARRS from Nakhon Phanom made the rescue attempt but took heavy ground fire and had to withdraw. 1Lt Wilson was within inches of reaching the jungle penetrator that had been lowered from the helicopter when he lost his balance and fell down a slope. Jolly Green 73 had to leave the area when more enemy soldiers appeared and it then tried to refuel from an HC-130 but the helicopter's in-flight refuelling probe had been damaged by ground fire. Running short of fuel Maj Shapiro put the helicopter down on a mountain top northeast of Ban Ban and the crew was rescued by another helicopter. The HH-53 had to be abandoned in enemy-held territory and was then destroyed by a flight of A-7s.

1Lt Wilson evaded for two more days but was finally captured as he tried to reach a container of food and water that had been dropped to him by an A-7D. He activated a trip-wire that set off a small explosive charge that had been set by the North Vietnamese to trap the escapee. This was only F-111 crew to become POWs during the war and they were both released on 29 March 1973.

23 December 1972

F-4J   153885   VMFA-333, USMC, USS *America*
        Lt Col John K Cochran (survived)
        Maj H S Carr (survived)

The CO of VMFA-333 was assigned to escort a photographic reconnaissance aircraft on a mission over the North Vietnamese coast. The mission was to obtain intelligence on the location of the North Vietnamese Navy's torpedo boats, which could potentially pose a threat to TF 77 operations in the Gulf of Tonkin. The Phantom was hit in the tail by 85mm flak and badly damaged as the aircraft was flying over one of the many groups of islands off the coast near Hon Gay. A fuel cell was ruptured and the aircraft caught fire. Moments later the crew ejected and landed in the sea about 15 miles southeast of Hon Gay from where they were rescued by a Navy HH-3A SAR helicopter. Lt Col Cochran returned to the USA for hospitalisation for back injuries and command of the Squadron passed to Maj Lee Lasseter who had survived being shot down on 11 September.

EB-66B serial ..?   42 TEWS, 388 TFW, USAF, Korat
       Maj Henry James Repeta (KIA)
       Maj George Frederick Sasser (KIA)
       Capt William Robert Baldwin (KIA)

An EB-66 crashed at Korat as both engines failed when it was landing back from an electronic warfare mission over North Vietnam. All three crewmen were killed in the accident, although the pilot ejected but impacted the ground still in his seat. This was the 14th and final B-66 variant to be lost in Southeast Asia during the war. Four of the aircraft had been lost to SAMs, one to a MiG, one to an unknown cause and the remaining eight were lost in accidents.

Once again none of the B-52s flying raids over the North were lost on this night. Twelve B-52Ds from Andersen and 18 B-52Ds from U-Tapao attacked the railway yard at Lang Dang and SAM sites north of Haiphong.

24 December 1972

A-7D   71-0312   353 TFS, 354 TFW, USAF, Korat
              Capt Charles Francis Riess (POW)

During a Barrel Roll strike in northern Laos a USAF Corsair collided with the Raven FAC aircraft that was controlling the strike with the loss of both aircraft. The pilot of the Raven O-1G Bird Dog was Capt Paul Vernon Jackson. Capt Chuck Reiss was bombing a field gun about 10 miles southwest of the Ban Ban Valley when the FAC pulled up sharply into the path of the Corsair. The Corsair sliced through the Bird Dog's wing and the O-1 dived into the ground as the wing collapsed and Capt Jackson was killed. Chuck Hines, another Raven FAC pilot, flew low over the wreck to confirm that Capt Jackson had been killed. Capt Riess ejected from his badly damaged Corsair and was captured by North Vietnamese troops. He was sent to Hanoi and kept with nine other men who had also been captured in Laos and were kept separate from the POWs who had been captured in North Vietnam. He was released on 28 March 1973. Capt Riess had flown about 230 missions in F-4s and A-7s before being captured.

A-7E   157503   VA-113, USN, USS *Ranger*
              Lt Phillip Spratt Clark (KIA)

Three Navy Corsairs set off for a daylight mining mission on the Chateau Renaud Channel near Hon Gay. Low cloud and poor visibility meant that each aircraft had to make its own individual run to drop its mines rather than making the drop in formation in a single pass. As the last aircraft started its run the pilot saw a parachute descending through the clouds moments after Lt Clark reported that he had dropped his ordnance. Lt Clark came down in the sea about five miles south of Cam Pha and made three radio transmissions to the aircraft overhead. His emergency beeper was also heard several times but Lt Clark did not survive. Search and rescue efforts were frustrated by bad weather and approaching darkness. Whether he drowned or was killed during capture is not known. The mortal remains of Lt Clark were returned to the USA on 3 November 1988.

A force of 30 B-52Ds from U-Tapao flew missions over North Vietnam on Christmas Eve, striking railway yards at Thai Nguyen and Kep. Improved tactics including an overland approach over Laos and splitting the waves both in and out of the target area resulted in all the bombers emerging from North Vietnam virtually unscathed. The second of two MiG-21s to fall to a B-52 gunner (A1C Albert Moore of Ruby 3) was shot down during this raid.

26/27 December 1972

B-52D   56-0674   449 BW attached to 307 SW, USAF, U-Tapao
              Capt Robert John Morris (KIA)
              1Lt Robert Markham Hudson (POW)
              Capt Michael Harold LaBeau (POW)
              Capt Nutter Jerome Wimbrow (KIA)
              1Lt Duane Paul Vavroch (POW)
              TSgt James Raymond Cook (POW)

The last three nights of operations had seen no further B-52 losses since the disaster of Day 3 of the campaign. After a Christmas stand down the final phase of Linebacker II operations resumed on the night of the 26th. The tactics were changed again and involved 120 B-52s in 10 waves hitting nine separate targets around Hanoi, Haiphong and Thai Nguyen but within the space of just 15 minutes instead of spread out throughout the night as in previous large-scale raids. A total of 45 B-52Gs and 33 B-52Ds took part from Andersen as well as 42 B-52Ds from U-Tapao. It was planned that 72 of the huge bombers would be converging over Hanoi at almost exactly the same time. Precision planning and precision flying were the order of the day but the entire mission was almost scrubbed when tankers at Kadena had to take off 15 minutes late due to a C-141 transport having to make an emergency landing at the airfield. In the event this was one of the most successful raids of the entire war despite the loss of two aircraft.

The fourth wave consisted of 18 aircraft assigned to hit the railway yard at Giap Nhi on the southern outskirts of Hanoi. Ebony 2 in the fifth cell was hit by a SAM about 10 miles southeast of Hanoi and crashed about 25 miles southwest of the city. The pilot, Capt Morris, and the EWO, Capt Wimbrow, did not survive but the other four men were captured, although TSgt Cook was badly injured. 1Lt Hudson was shot in the left shoulder by a North Vietnamese militia man while Hudson was still descending in his parachute. TSgt Cook was released on 12 February due to his injuries and 1Lt Vavroch, Capt LaBeau and 1Lt Hudson were all released on 29 March 1973. The remains of Capt Morris and Capt Wimbrow were returned by the Vietnamese on 30 September 1977. The crew were flying a 96th BW aircraft at the time but they were actually deployed from the 449th BW at Kincheloe AFB, Michigan.

B-52D   56-0584   22 BW attached to 307 SW, USAF, U-Tapao
              Capt James Mack Turner (KIA)
              Lt Robert Hymel (survived)
              Lt Col Donald Arrington Joyner (KIA)
              Maj Lawrence Jay Marshall (KIA)
              Capt Roy Tom Tabler (KIA)
              TSgt Spencer Grippin (survived)

The railway yard at Kinh No was once more a target for the bombers and Ash cell was the last cell to bomb this target from the fifth wave. Ash 1 was hit by a SAM about 50 miles southwest of Hanoi as it was returning from making a successful strike. The aircraft was badly damaged with two engines knocked out and numerous fuel leaks. TSgt Grippin, the gunner, was injured by shrapnel from the SAM. At first the pilot headed out over the Gulf of Tonkin to make for Da Nang but he then decided that the aircraft could reach U-Tapao so he headed for Thailand with an escorting flight of F-4s. Soon after midnight the aircraft commenced a straight-in approach for an emergency landing at U-Tapao. Unfortunately, the pilot lost control of the aircraft during the final moments of the approach and the B-52 pitched up and then crashed about a mile from the runway. One of the first Americans to arrive at the crash site was Capt Brent Diefenbach who had just returned from a raid on the North. He entered the burning fuselage to find Lt Hymel, the co-pilot, trapped by his leg and still strapped to his live ejection seat. With great difficulty Diefenbach eventually freed Hymel and carried him out of the burning wreckage. Capt Diefenbach was later awared the Airman's Medal for his bravery. TSgt Grippin escaped when the tail section of the bomber broke away on impact.

Both Ebony 2 and Ash 1 were from two-aircraft cells as a B-52 from each cell had aborted before reaching North Vietnam. Two aircraft did not give the same degree of ECM protection that a three-aircraft cell could provide.

27 December 1972

F-4E   67-0292   13 TFS, 432 TRW, USAF, Udorn
              Maj Carl H Jeffcoat (POW)
              1Lt Jack R Trimble (POW)

The search for the F-111 crew that had been shot down on the night of the 22nd was still proceeding. A flight of Phantoms on a MiGCAP mission was involved in the search for the crew but when the flight was about 35 miles southwest of Hanoi it was attacked by MiG-21s. During the dogfight, one of the Phantoms became separated from the rest of the flight and was hit by an air-to-air missile forcing Maj Jeffcoat and 1Lt Trimble to eject. The crew landed safely but were soon captured and spent just over three months as POWs until they were repatriated on 29 March 1973. Phantom 67-0292 was flown by Lt Col T E Taft and Capt S M Imaye of the 4th TFS on 29 July 1972 when they shot down a MiG-21.

27/28 December 1972

A-6A   155666   VMA(AW)-533, MAG-15, USMC, Nam Phong
              Capt Ralph Jim Chipman (KIA)
              1Lt Ronald Wayne Forrester (KIA)

A Marine Corps A-6 Intruder disappeared during a night-time road reconnaissance mission over North Vietnam. The exact fate of the aircraft and its crew was never determined but it was thought to have been shot down on the coast near Xuan Noa, 15 miles southeast of Dong Hoi.

B-52D   56-0599   28 BW attached to 307 SW, USAF, U-Tapao
              Capt John Mize (survived)
              Capt Terrence Gruters (survived)
              Capt Dennis Anderson (survived)
              Capt William North (survived)
              Lt William Robinson (survived)
              TSgt Peter E Whalen (survived)

B-52Gs and B-52Ds take off from Andersen AFB on Guam to fly Linebacker II missions over North Vietnam, some of them lasting as long as 18 hours. USAF

245

Day 9 of Linebacker II involved a total of 60 B-52s consisting of 30 B-52Ds from U-Tapao and 21 B-52Gs and nine B-52Ds from Andersen. The force dropped its bombs in six waves in just 10 minutes thereby concentrating its effort and swamping the defences. The seven targets included the Lang Dang and Trung Quang railway yards, three SAM sites, and a supply depot. Another 30 B-52s from Andersen flew sorties over South Vietnam and the lower provinces of North Vietnam.

One cell was assigned to bomb a particularly 'hot' SAM site known as VN549 that was situated just to the southwest of Hanoi. Unfortunately, the SAM site lived up to its reputation and just after a successful bomb release Ash 2, which was actually bombing another nearby SAM site, was hit by one of VN549's missiles at 35,500 feet and badly damaged. The crew counted no less than 15 SAMs fired as a barrage towards the aircraft. Capt Mize was wounded by shrapnel in the left leg and right hand and the rest of the crewmembers were also wounded to some degree by shrapnel from the missile. Capt Mize regained control of the aircraft despite the loss of all the engines on the port side and the loss of power boost on the controls. By sheer determination and physical effort he flew the burning aircraft back towards Thailand. Most of the navigational and flight instruments had been damaged so the navigator had to use dead reckoning to guide the aircraft to safety. After just under an hour of exhausting struggle the aircraft crossed into Thailand but then the electrical system started to fail, the bomb bay doors dropped open and the undercarriage began to cycle up and down of its own accord. With total loss of control imminent Capt Mize ordered the crew to eject but Lt Robinson's seat failed to function and he had to abandon the aircraft manually. Capt Mize then held the aircraft steady for as long as he could until he was certain that Lt Robinson had jumped and then ejected himself. The crew came down about 15 miles southwest of Nakhon Phanom and was picked up by two SAR helicopters. Capt Mize and his crew were from the 28th BW at Ellsworth AFB, South Dakota but 56-0599 was a 7th BW aircraft. For his courage and skill in saving his crew, Capt Mize was awarded the AFC, the only member of SAC so honoured during the war. John Mize was on his fourth Linebacker II mission and his 295th mission of the war. The rest of the crew received DFCs for their actions.

B-52D	56-0605	7 BW attached to 43 SW, USAF, Andersen
		Capt Frank Douglas Lewis (POW)
		Capt Samuel Bolden Cusimano (POW)
		Maj James Carroll Condon (POW)
		Maj Allen Louis Johnson (KIA)
		1Lt Bennie Lamar Fryer (KIA)
		MSgt James Wayne Gough (POW)

Twelve aircraft were targeted on the railway yards at Trung Quang near Hanoi on the night of the 27th. Cobalt 1 was hit by a SAM at 25,000 feet near Bac Ninh, 15 miles northeast of Hanoi. The four cells had started their bombing run and encountered heavy flak and SAM activity. A total of about 45 SAMs were fired at the aircraft as they approached Hanoi. One minute before bomb release Cobalt 1 was locked onto by two SAMs and although Capt Lewis and his crew evaded those, they were not able to dodge a third missile that struck the B-52 as it was in a tight turn. All the crew were injured to some extent by the explo-

sion of the SAM and 1Lt Fryer was almost certainly killed at that point. The wings caught fire, the fuel tanks were ruptured and the electrical system failed. Forty seconds after being hit and unable to release his bombs, the captain gave the order to abandon the aircraft. Four of the crew ejected from the aircraft before it crashed near Hanoi. MSgt Gough was hit by pieces of burning debris from the engines and wings as he left the aircraft. Maj Johnson, the EWO, was thought to have ejected from the aircraft. A North Vietnamese interrogator told Capt Lewis that he knew that his navigator was a black man, indicating either that he had been captured or that his body had been found. The four survivors were all released on 29 March 1973. The crew was deployed from the 320th BW at Mather AFB, California and was flying an aircraft from Carswell's 7th BW. These two aircraft were the last B-52s to be lost during the Linebacker II raids.

1Lt Fryer's remains were returned by the North Vietnamese on 30 September 1977 and Maj Johnson's were returned on 4 December 1985 and formally identified the following June. Capt Cusimano had flown 144 missions in C-123K flareships from Nakhon Phanom before assignment to B-52s. Maj Condon had amassed over 6,000 hours in SAC B-47s and B-52s and had flown over 120 missions during the war.

F-4E	67-0234	4 TFS, 432 TRW, USAF, Udorn
		Capt John Wesley Anderson (POW)
		1Lt Brian H Ward (POW)

One of the Linebacker CAP flights that protected the B-52s was engaged by MiGs during a Linebacker strike. One of the Phantoms was shot down by an Atoll missile at low-level and Capt Anderson and 1Lt Ward ejected about 30 miles west of Hanoi. Not only was this the last USAF aircraft to be shot down by a MiG but it was also the only US aircraft lost in air-to-air combat at night during the war.

The crew ejected at high speed and at very low-level and Capt Anderson broke both his arms during the ejection and was released early on 12 February while 1Lt Ward, although also injured, was repatriated on 29 March 1973.

28 December 1972

RA-5C	156633	RVAH-13, USN, USS *Enterprise*
		Lt Cdr Alfred Howard Agnew (POW)
		Lt Michael Firestone Haifley (KIA)

An RA-5C had just completed its photo run over a POL storage site when its escort warned of a MiG in the Vigilante's eight o'clock position. The escort vectored the Vigilante towards the coast and turned to attack the MiG. However, before the MiG could be engaged it fired a missile which hit the Vigilante. The aircraft caught fire and crashed into the sea. The pilot ejected and was captured but his NFO was killed in the incident. Lt Cdr Agnew was released on 29 March 1973. Lt Cdr Agnew had served in AEW and ASW squadrons before converting to the reconnaissance role in the RA-5C. This was the 90th and last US aircraft shot down by a MiG during the war. This was also the last of 26 RA-5C Vigilantes to be lost in Southeast Asia.

Day 10 of the B-52 raids saw a total of 60 aircraft take part, 30 B-52Ds from U-Tapao together with 15 B-52Ds and 15 B-52Gs from Andersen. Four waves of aircraft attacked SAM sites around Hanoi, while two waves hit the Lang Dang railway yard on the

northeast railway again. On this night a total of 99 supporting aircraft, mostly F-4s, A-7s, F-105Gs and EB-66s, assisted the B-52 effort and fewer SAMs seemed to be fired than on previous nights. Andersen also sent 28 B-52s to other targets in Southeast Asia on the night of the 28th/29th.

29 December 1972

EA-6A	156982	VMCJ-2, USMC, NAS Cubi Point
		Capt Hal L Baker (survived)
		MSgt Frederick E Killebrew (survived)

An EA-6A crashed during a jamming mission when it suffered a hydraulic system malfunction causing the aircraft to catch fire near Cubi Point. Both the crew ejected and were rescued. MSgt Killebrew was over 50 at the time of the incident and was one of the oldest men to fly combat missions during the war. This aircraft was the last US Marine Corps fixed-wing aircraft to be lost during the wars in Southeast Asia.

The final day of the Linebacker II B-52 strikes was once again completed without loss to the attackers. On this day 30 B-52Ds from U-Tapao and 18 B-52Ds and 12 B-52Gs from Andersen hit SAM storage sites at Phuc Yen and Trai Ca as well as the Lang Dang railway yards yet again. Thirty more B-52Gs flew other missions against targets in North and South Vietnam. Only a handful of SAMs were launched at the raiders and only one MiG was seen during the raid. However, SAC was now running out of lucrative targets for the B-52s and so, with signs that the North Vietnamese were now willing to resume peace talks at Paris, the Linebacker II campaign came to an end. The B-52 force at Andersen and U-Tapao had completed a total of 729 out of a planned 741 sorties against targets around Hanoi, Haiphong and Thai Nguyen against some of the most formidable SAM and AAA air defences in the world. Around 15,287 tons of bombs were dropped on 34 targets by the B-52s and it was estimated by the USAF that some 1,600 military or industrial buildings had been destroyed or badly damaged. In addition the northeast railway had been interdicted in several places almost bringing train movements to a halt and some three million gallons of fuel had been destroyed. In addition to the B-52s, USAF and Navy tactical aircraft flew 1,041 day and 1,082 night sorties over North Vietnam during the campaign. Estimates of the number of SA-2s fired at the B-52s vary between 884 and 1,285. Only 24 missiles achieved hits giving the SA-2 a hit rate of 2.7 per cent if the lower figure is used. Fifteen B-52s were lost during Linebacker II, all of them to SAM hits, thereby reducing the SA-2's success rate to only 1.7 per cent of the number of missiles launched. Although the SA-2 might not have been as effective as some analysts feared and the B-52 loss rate amounted to only 2.06 per cent, the loss of 15 aircraft was still a heavy price to pay. The loss rate improved after Day 3 due to revised tactics, more flexible routings, compressed times-on-target, increased numbers of support aircraft and restrictions on the use of the B-52G. Of the 92 crewmembers flying in the 15 B-52s that were shot down, 59 survived, 33 of them as POWs. The effectiveness of Linebacker II must be judged against the fact that peace negotiations resumed in Paris on 8 January leading to the signing of a cease-fire agreement 19 days later and the release of the POWs in the weeks that followed.

31 December 1972

| OV-10A | 67-14643 | unit ..?, USAF, base ..? |
| | | 2 crew, names unknown (survived) |

During an armed reconnaissance mission an OV-10 was hit by ground fire near An Hoa, 15 miles southwest of Da Nang. Both the crew ejected safely and were later recovered. The serial number quoted for this aircraft may be incorrect as 67-14643 was noted in service with the 601st TCW at Sembach in the 1980s.

During the Linebacker II offensive the B-52s from Andersen and U-Tapao completed a total of 729 out of 741 planned sorties for the loss of 15 aircraft. The huge base at Andersen contributed 396 of these sorties and sustained eight of the losses. USAF

Chapter Ten

1973
Winding Up the War

3/4 January 1973

B-52D 55-0056   307 SW, USAF, U-Tapao
Lt Col Gerald Wickline (survived)
Capt Myles McTernan (survived)
4 crew, names unknown (survived)

Just five days after the end of Linebacker II another B-52 was lost when it was damaged by an SA-2 during a raid on Vinh. The aircraft was hit just as it released its bombs about 15 miles southwest of the city. The two port outer engines were knocked out and the hydraulic and electrical systems were damaged and the aircraft depressurised when the cockpit windows were shattered. Lt Col Wickline took the aircraft out to sea and tried to reach Da Nang. However, just 25 miles northeast of the airfield the aircraft became uncontrollable and the commander ordered the crew to abandon the aircraft. All the crew left safely with the exception of Capt McTernan, the navigator, whose ejection seat only moved a little way downwards out of the aircraft before it came to a sudden stop. Capt McTernan had great difficulty in unstrapping and climbing out of his seat so that he could bail out through an open hatch. He hit the aircraft structure on the way out and landed in the sea in a semi-conscious state and without a life raft in 8-10 feet-high waves. McTernan came down several miles from the rest of his crew who were quickly rescued by a USAF HH-53. By an amazing stroke of luck he was spotted after several hours by a rescue aircraft that overflew him as it was returning to Da Nang for fuel. Capt McTernan was then rescued by a Marine Corps helicopter.

4 January 1973

F-4D 65-0745   497 TFS, 8 TFW, USAF, Ubon
Capt J R Wallerstedt (survived)
Capt Steven Bryce Johnston (KIA)

A Phantom was shot down during an escort mission over southern Laos. The target was enemy artillery about five miles south of Muang Phine and the aircraft was hit by 23mm flak as it dived on the target. The aircraft crashed about 10 miles to the southwest and both the crew ejected. The crew landed close together and Capt Wallerstedt found Capt Johnston pinned to the ground by the branch of a tree. It seems that Capt Johnston had parachuted into the tree breaking off a large branch which then fell on him and killed him. Capt Wallerstedt was later rescued by a SAR helicopter but Capt Johnston's body had to be left behind due to approaching darkness and enemy forces that were closing in on the position.

6 January 1973

A-7B 154543   VA-56, USN, USS *Midway*
Lt John Carl Lindahl (KIA)

The *Midway* lost a Corsair as it was being launched for a strike mission about 40 miles off the DMZ. The launch appeared normal at first but then the aircraft dived into the sea and the pilot was killed in the accident. Although a helicopter dropped a diver near the aircraft within 45 seconds of the Corsair hitting the water, there was no sign of Lt Lindahl, who must have gone down in his aircraft.

7 January 1973

F-4D 66-8749   13 TFS, 432 TRW, USAF, Udorn
Capt T Wiles (survived)
Maj G B Nunez (survived)

A Phantom crashed near Udorn due to a mechanical failure during a strike mission. The two crew ejected and were rescued.

9 January 1973

A-6A 155693   VA-115, USN, USS *Midway*
Lt Michael Timothy McCormick (KIA)
Lt(jg) Robert Alan Clark (KIA)

Two Intruders were launched from the *Midway* on a low-level night strike on a SAM site 30 miles northwest of Vinh and close to the coast. The raid was being made in support of a B-52 strike near Vinh and the night was very dark with cloud cover at 1,500 feet. A barrage of missiles was fired at the raiders, including about a dozen at the B-52s and at least three at the Intruders. The low cloud made it difficult to spot the SAMs until they broke cloud and by then precious reaction time had been lost. After completing its mission, the other Intruder waited over the sea for Lt McCormick's aircraft but it never appeared. The surviving Intruder retraced the planned flight path at 15,000 feet and made numerous radio calls but without response. A SAR mission was mounted but there was no sign of the aircraft or its crew.

11 January 1973

A-7D 71-0316   355 TFS, 354 TFW, USAF, Korat
1 pilot, name unknown (survived)

A Corsair on an escort mission crashed about 20 miles northeast of Udorn when its engine failed from fuel starvation due to a fuel transfer problem. The pilot ejected safely and was soon picked up.

13 January 1973

B-52D 55-0116   307 SW, USAF, U-Tapao
6 crew, names unknown (survived)

A B-52 suffered battle damage during an Arc Light raid on North Vietnam and had to make an emergency landing at Da Nang. The aircraft was so badly damaged that it was deemed unrepairable and was scrapped at Da Nang late in March.

14 January 1973

F-4B 153068   VF-161, USN, USS *Midway*
Lt Victor T Kovaleski (survived)
Ens D H Plautz (survived)

A flight of Phantoms was escorting a Blue Tree photographic reconnaissance mission near Thanh Hoa when the formation ran into heavy flak about 10 miles southwest of the city. Lt Kovaleski's aircraft was hit by an 85mm anti-aircraft shell that caused a massive fuel leak, damaged the port engine and led to electrical failure. When the remaining engine failed just as the aircraft crossed the coast the crew ejected safely and were rescued by a Navy HH-3A SAR helicopter. Lt Kovaleski had achieved fame two days earlier when he shot down a MiG-17, the 197th and last MiG shot down during the war. Phantom 153068 had shot down a MiG-19 on 18 May 1972 when flown by Lt H A Bartholomay and Lt O R Brown. It was also the last aircraft lost by the USS *Midway* before the carrier left TF 77 control on 12 February having spent a record 208 days on the line during its third and final tour in Southeast Asia. The *Midway* was decommissioned on 11 April 1992 and has since been stored at Bremerton, Washington, awaiting possible preservation at San Diego.

21 January 1973

EKA-3B 142634   Detachment 4, VAQ-130, USN, USS *Ranger*
Lt Cdr Charles Leslie Parker (KIA)
Lt(jg) Keith Allen Christophersen (KIA)
PO2 Richard Daniel Wiehr (KIA)

An EKA-3B Skywarrior was lost as it was being launched at night on a tanker sortie from the USS *Ranger* about 100 miles east of Vinh. As the aircraft was travelling down the catapult there was an explosion and sparks were seen to come from the starboard engine. The aircraft pitched nose down and left the ship at a very slow speed and crashed into the sea. All three crew on board were lost in the accident. This was the last of 20 A-3s lost in Southeast Asia during the war, not including another RA-3B that crashed during a test flight from Cubi Point on 16 June 1967. Of the 20 aircraft lost only six were brought down by enemy action, three of these during night reconnaissance sorties. Six of the Skywarriors lost were RA-3Bs from VAP-61, four of them in combat. The remaining 14 aircraft were lost in accidents, six of them while being catapulted from a carrier.

24 January 1973

A-6A 157007   VA-35, USN, USS *America*
Lt C M Graf (survived)
Lt S H Hatfield (survived)

An Intruder was shot down by ground fire during a close air support mission six miles north of Quang Tri, the first US Navy aircraft to be lost in combat in South Vietnam since September 1972. The aircraft was hit either by 37mm AAA or a SAM and flew out to sea and almost made it back to the carrier but the two crew had to eject about 55 miles northeast of the DMZ and were later rescued by a Navy helicopter. This was the last aircraft lost by the *America* before it left TF 77 control on 24 March. The USS *America* continued to serve until it was decommissioned on 9 August 1996 and is currently in storage at Philadelphia awaiting final disposal.

27 January 1973

F-4J 155768   VF-143, USN, USS *Enterprise*
Cdr Harley Hubert Hall (KIA)
Lt Cdr Phillip Allen Kientzler (POW)

Another Navy aircraft was lost near Quang Tri on the very day that the Paris Peace Accords were signed between the USA and North Vietnam. A Phantom, flown by the CO of VF-143, was bombing a number of trucks on a road about eight miles north of the city and was hit by AAA as it pulled up from its third pass. The aircraft caught fire and the flying control system failed leading to a loss of control. Both crew ejected at 4,000 feet and were seen to land only about 100 feet apart near a village on an island in the Cua Viet River. Cdr Hall was seen to be moving about and to discard his parachute. Lt Cdr Kientzler was captured and was told that Cdr Hall had been killed by a North Vietnamese soldier. Phillip Kientzler, a veteran of over 500 combat missions in Southeast Asia, was the last Navy aviator to become a POW during the war. Two months later he was released on 27 March 1973. Cdr Hall had previously flown as leader of the Blue Angels aerobatic team. His remains were returned to the USA for burial in June 1995. This Phantom was the final aircraft lost by the USS *Enterprise* before it finished its sixth and last cruise of the war on 3 June 1973. The mighty *Enterprise* is scheduled to remain in service until 2013, when it will be the last of the Vietnam-era aircraft carriers still in service.

OV-10A 68-3806   23 TASS, 56 SOW, USAF, Nakhon Phanom
                   1Lt Mark Allan Peterson (KIA)
                   Capt George William Morris (KIA)
When the Navy Phantom went down near Quang Tri a Nail FAC Bronco was diverted to the area to search for any survivors. As the aircraft approached the site of the incident at 6,000 feet it was hit by an SA-7 missile and the crew were forced to eject as the aircraft spun down out of control. Observers saw two good parachutes and 1Lt Peterson made voice contact on his survival radio and stated that he was about to be captured. A rescue attempt failed due to intense enemy activity and the crew was posted missing in action. After his release Lt Cdr Kientzler reported that he saw about 30 Viet Cong firing at Peterson and Morris as they parachuted down. This was the last combat loss in South Vietnam before the cease fire took effect.

29 January 1973

A-7E 156837   VA-147, USN, USS *Constellation*
                Cdr T R Wilkinson (KWF)
On the day that the cease-fire came into effect, the Navy lost another aircraft in Southeast Asia. The CO of VA-147 disappeared in a Corsair after being launched on a training flight north of the Philippines. The cause of the loss of the aircraft and its pilot was never determined. Cdr Wilkinson was the last of about 50 naval squadron commanders involved in aircraft losses during the war, 27 of whom were killed. Five air wing commanders were also shot down during the war. Cdr Wilkinson had been shot down near Dong Hoi and rescued on 17 May 1972. The *Constellation* remained in Southeast Asia until it finally returned to North Island, California, on 11 October 1973. The carrier is one of three Vietnam veterans that still remain in service and is due to be decommissioned in 2003.

30 January 1973

F-4J 158361   VF-21, USN, USS *Ranger*
                Lt James Allyn Duensing (KIA)
                Lt(jg) Roy Elbert Haviland (KIA)

F-4J 158366   VF-21, USN, USS *Ranger*
                Lt(jg) J E Reid (survived)
                Lt E A Beaver (survived)
In the same month as it lost a Skywarrior with all hands, the *Ranger* suffered another tragedy in January when two of its Phantoms collided in mid-air during a BARCAP mission. Both aircraft crashed but only one crew managed to escape and were rescued. These Phantoms were the last aircraft lost by the *Ranger* before the end of its final war cruise in Southeast Asia. The carrier was decommissioned on 10 July 1993 and is currently in storage at Bremerton, Washington.

4/5 February 1973

EC-47Q 43-48636   361 TEWS, 56 SOW, USAF, Nakhon
                    Phanom detached to Ubon
                    Capt George Ross Spitz (KIA)
                    1Lt Robert Edward Bernhardt (KIA)
                    Capt Arthur Ray Bollinger (KIA)
                    2Lt Severo James Primm (KIA)
                    SSgt Todd Michael Melton (KIA)
                    Sgt Dale Brandenburg (KIA)
                    Sgt Peter Richard Cressman (KIA)
                    Sgt Joseph Andrew Matejov (KIA)
Although the Paris Peace Accords effectively ended US involvement over North Vietnam itself, operations continued over Laos, Cambodia and South Vietnam. On the night of 4/5 February an EC-47 RDF aircraft, using the call sign Baron 52, was on a mission to locate North Vietnamese tanks travelling along the Trail through Laos towards Kontum and Pleiku. The pilot radioed that the aircraft had been fired at by AAA and later failed to make a routine radio report. A search was initiated but the wreck was not found until the 7th. The aircraft had been shot down about 35 miles southeast of Saravan in southern Laos and the crew of eight was posted missing. Three PJs were lowered to the site on the 9th and saw at least four bodies but could only recover partial remains. In 1993 a JTF-FA team investigated the crash site of the EC-47 and recovered bone fragments and eight parachute rings indicating that none of the parachutes had been used. A group burial took place in December 1995 representing all the crew members of Baron 52 despite unsubstantiated reports that the four radio operators had escaped from the aircraft and been captured. The last EC-47 flight in Southeast Asia took place on 15 May 1974 bringing to an end eight years of intelligence gathering in Southeast Asia by this venerable old aircraft.

17 February 1973

A-7D 70-0949   354 TFS, 354 TFW, USAF, Korat
                 Maj J J Gallagher (survived)
Enemy forces were by this date dangerously close to the Thai border and a Corsair was shot down during a close air support mission just 15 miles east of Nakhon Phanom. Maj Gallagher's aircraft was hit by AAA at 15,000 feet and the engine was damaged. He headed back towards Thailand and ejected safely three miles south of Nakhon Phanom and was picked up by the base HH-43 Huskie.

When the 354th TFW deployed from Myrtle Beach AFB in October 1972 its A-7D Corsairs soon began to replace the A-1 in the Sandy rescue escort role. Only six A-7Ds were lost, four of them in 1973. USAF

20 February 1973

F-111A 67-0072   429 TFS, 474 TFW on TDY, USAF, Takhli
                   2 crew, names unknown (survived)
An F-111 crashed on take off from Takhli when the main landing gear pin sheared causing the undercarriage to collapse. The aircraft slid off the side of the runway with its full load of 24 Mk82 bombs and caught fire. The crew left the aircraft rapidly with only minor injuries and were rescued by the base police unit but the fire trucks could not get near the aircraft, which continued to burn all night as the bombs exploded one by one. Apparently, the fire and periodic explosions caused many of the personnel on the base to think that the airfield was under enemy attack.

7 April 1973

OV-10A 67-14659   23 TASS, 56 SOW, USAF, Nakhon Phanom
                    1Lt Joseph Gambino (KIA)
Operations were still continuing in Cambodia although no fixed-wing aircraft had been lost there since 2 July 1972. The Rustic FAC mission was transferred from the 19th TASS at Bien Hoa to the 23rd TASS in November 1971, with a detachment of aircraft operating from Ubon. On 7 April an OV-10 was shot down while on a Rustic FAC mission near Trapeang Veng, some 50 miles northwest of Kampong Cham. On the day of his 24th birthday, 1Lt Gambino was directing a strike on enemy mortar and gun positions when his aircraft was hit by .50 calibre gunfire from Khmer Rouge soldiers. The aircraft crashed in flames and the pilot was killed.

18 April 1973

F-4E 67-0281   421 TFS, 432 TRW, USAF, Udorn
                 Capt Samuel Larry James (KIA)
                 Capt Douglas Kent Martin (KIA)
A Phantom was lost during a strike on a target in Cambodia on the 18th. Capt James and Capt Martin were marking a target for a strike near Lomphat, 60 miles southwest of Pleiku, when their aircraft crashed. There was thick haze in the target area at the time and although none of the other aircrew on the raid saw the Phantom crash they did see a long swathe of destruction in the jungle near the target. An extensive air search of the area revealed no sign of the crew although unconfirmed intelligence reports suggested that one or both might have ejected. Following several years of post-war enquiries, a joint US/Cambodian investigation team found the wreck site in January 1998 and recovered the remains of the two crewmen. Phantom 67-0281 was flown by Lt Col L L Beckers and Capt J F Huwe of the 35th TFS when they shot down a MiG-19 on 23 May 1972.

4 May 1973

A-7D 71-0305   3 TFS, 388 TFW, USAF, Korat
                 1Lt T L Dickens (survived)
A flight of Corsairs was sent to attack enemy boats on the Mekong River about 20 miles northwest of Phnom Penh in Cambodia. 1Lt Dickens's aircraft was hit by ground fire as he pulled up through 8,000 feet from his initial pass to drop Mk82 bombs. He flew south and ejected close to Phnom Penh airport and was picked up by a USAF HH-53, the last combat rescue of the war.

25 May 1973

A-7D 70-0945   354 TFW, USAF, Korat
                 Capt Jeremiah Frederick Costello (KIA)
Another Corsair was lost during a close air support mission in Cambodia. Capt Costello had just climbed to 10,000 feet and levelled off for the return trip back to Korat when his aircraft was hit in the starboard wing by AAA. The aircraft caught fire and crashed near Siemreap, just north of the vast Tonle Sap Lake. Unfortunately, Capt Costello was killed in the incident and his body was recovered by an HH-53. This was the last of six USAF A-7D Corsairs that had been lost during the war.

26 May 1973

F-4D 65-0645 308 TFS, 31 TFW attached to 8 TFW,
USAF, Ubon
Maj Jerry Cox (survived)
Capt Wade A Hubbard (survived)

Yet another aircraft was lost in Cambodia when a Phantom was
shot down during an attack on a bridge near Kratie. Two Phantoms were flying an armed reconnaissance mission along Route
13, one of the major infiltration routes through southern Cambodia to South Vietnam. Maj Cox was escorting a Wolf FAC and
the pair were equipped with LGBs. Having already bombed a
bridge and refuelled from a tanker, the two Phantoms returned
to their search when Maj Cox's aircraft was hit by AAA at 6,000
feet and caught fire. Maj Cox set course for Ubon but when the
aircraft was 45 miles to the northwest of Kratie the crew were
forced to eject as the aircraft's systems failed and flames entered
the cockpit. Maj Cox's ejection seat failed to fire at first and he
had to manually jettison the canopy, which then allowed the seat
to fire. Maj Cox then landed in a tree and fell 40 feet to the ground
injuring his back. About four hours later an HH-53 from Udorn
arrived and rescued both men, although Maj Cox had to hospitalised with back injuries and severe burns.

5 June 1973

OV-10A serial ..? 23 TASS, 56 SOW, USAF, Nakhon Phanom
1Lt Richard Tenney Gray (KIA)

A Bronco Nail FAC crashed on take off from Nakhon Phanom for
a mission over Cambodia, killing the pilot. This was the last of 64
Broncos lost by the USAF during the war. The OV-10A had
proved to be a capable FAC aircraft during its first five years of
service. Its performance was significantly better than the O-1
and O-2 but it was still vulnerable to light weapons and SA-7s,
especially at the altitudes it was forced to fly at in order to perform its tasks. The aircraft had a long career with the USAF and
USMC in the FAC role until replaced by the OA-37 and OA-10.
The Bronco was one of only two aircraft types (the other being
the F-4 Phantom) to be used by the Air Force, Navy and the
Marines in Southeast Asia.

16 June 1973

F-111A 67-0111 430 TFS, 474 TFW on TDY, USAF, Takhli
Maj Robert P McConnell (survived)
Capt Richard Skeels (survived)

The last F-111 to be lost in Southeast Asia crashed following a
mid-air collision with another F-111 (67-0094 flown by Col
Kenneth M Alley and Maj Glen Perry) over Cambodia. One of the
aircraft suffered a radar malfunction and asked the other aircraft to pathfind for it when the collision took place. 67-0111
became uncontrollable and Maj McConnell and Capt Skeels were
forced to eject. 67-0094 lost six feet of its wing but Col Alley and
Maj Perry made an emergency landing at Udorn destroying one
of the runway arrester gear cables in the process. 67-0111 was
an attrition replacement and did not arrive at Takhli until 8 May
1973. This was the 11th and final F-111 loss of the war. Despite
its poor combat debut, the F-111 had proved itself to be an outstanding low level, all-weather strike aircraft and later served
with distinction during the US raid on Libya on 15 April 1986 and
in Operation Desert Storm in 1991.

F-4E 67-0374 336 TFS, 4 TFW attached to 8 TFW,
USAF, Ubon
Capt Samuel Blackmar Cornelius (KIA)
Capt John Jackie Smallwood (KIA)

The last US aircraft lost to enemy action during the war in
Southeast Asia was shot down during a strike mission in Cambodia. The aircraft was hit by ground fire as it attacked a target
near Lomphat, about 80 miles northeast of Kratie. The Phantom
crashed near the target and it was thought unlikely that the crew
could have escaped despite an unconfirmed report of three US
airmen being captured in Cambodia at about this time and being
taken to South Vietnam. Capt Cornelius and Capt Smallwood
were the last US airmen to die in combat during the war in
Southeast Asia.

29 June 1973

F-4D serial ..? 432 TRW, USAF, Udorn
2 crew, names unknown (survived)

A Phantom crashed on landing when it suffered an engine failure at the conclusion of a ferry flight. This was the last US aircraft to be lost in Southeast Asia before all US air combat
operations ceased on 15 August.

Conclusion: The Final Withdrawal

*The cease-fire in South and North Vietnam was signed on 27
January 1973 thereby heralding an end to US involvement in the
war in Southeast Asia. The last US air strikes in South Vietnam
were flown the following day. The long civil war in Laos theoretically came to end on 21 February when a cease-fire was signed
ending US air operations over that country. However, the bombing of North Vietnamese positions in Laos resumed briefly after
the NVA captured a town in the Plain of Jars. The last PACAF aircraft left South Vietnam on 28 March although the USAF still
maintained a formidable presence in Thailand and at sea. On
16 June the US lost its last fixed-wing aircraft on operations in
Southeast Asia, an F-4E and an F-111A. The last combat mission
of the war was flown by two A-7Ds of the 354th TFW on 15 August.
Official US figures for the war between October 1961 and March
1973 reveal that a total of 2,257 fixed-wing aircraft were lost
while flying a total of 5,226,701 sorties. This represents an average loss rate of just 0.04 per cent although particular types of aircraft in certain roles suffered much higher loss rates than the
average. Even so, compared to the aircraft loss rate for the Korean
War of 2 per cent and the Second World War of 9.7 per cent, the
air war in Southeast Asia was much less costly in terms of men
and machines. The development of the SAR role also did much to
reduce the level of personnel losses during the war while technological developments, particularly in the field of electronic warfare, also led to reduced losses.*

*The plight of the POWs at last came to an end early in 1973 as
Operation Homecoming was mounted to fly the men from Hanoi
to Clark AFB in the Philippines. The longest-serving POWs had
spent nine long years incarcerated in North Vietnam while those
shot down during Linebacker II had spent less than three months.
It is a well-known fact that fewer men were released than was
expected, but the fate of many of those who still remain missing*

**The F-111As of the 347th TFW were among some of the last
USAF aircraft to leave Southeast Asia. Eleven F-111s were
lost during the war.** USAF

*will probably remain a mystery forever, despite strenuous efforts
by US government agencies to account for all Americans missing
in Southeast Asia.*

*The last US troops left South Vietnam on 29 March 1973 leaving behind just a handful of men assigned to the office of the
defence attaché in Saigon. The US handed over hundreds of aircraft and thousands of tons of other military equipment to the
South Vietnamese and left them to continue to fight the war
against the North.*

*Gradually US forces withdrew from the rest of Southeast Asia
and the air bases began to shut down with the first major base at
Takhli being closed on 12 September 1974. However, the hijacking of the US merchant vessel SS Mayaguez by Cambodian troops
in international waters in May 1975 saw a minor action that
culminated in a disastrous attempt to land troops on the island
of Koh Tang. The ship and its crew were recovered on 15 May
but the US forces sustained a number of casualties and lost five
CH-53s of the 21st SOS.*

*The fighting in Vietnam abated for a while after the cease-fire
but continued on and off for another two years until North Vietnamese and Viet Cong troops finally stormed Saigon itself in
April 1975. Helicopters from the USMC and Air America evacuated the last Americans from the rooftop of the American embassy
in Saigon on 29 April in Operation Frequent Wind. During the
same month the US mounted Operation Eagle Pull to evacuate
foreign nationals from Phnom Penh as Cambodia eventually fell,
thereby starting that country's tragic period of rule by Pol Pot's
Khmer Rouge*

*Following the end of South Vietnam, American forces continued the withdrawal from Southeast Asia. The last B-52 left
U-Tapao on 8 June 1975 while Ubon was handed over to the
Royal Thai Air Force on 26 June. The A-7Ds of the 3rd TFS left
Korat on 15 December with the F-4s of the 432nd TRW leaving
Udorn five days later. The last operational US aircraft to leave
Southeast Asia were several KC-135s that departed U-Tapao on
22 December 1975, thereby bringing to an end a turbulent chapter in American history.*

United States Air Force Order of Battle

The following terms are used throughout this appendix:

Activated — Official formation date of units;
Assigned — Permanent placement within a higher organisation;
Attached — Temporary placement within a higher organisation;
Inactivated — Disbanded;
Redesignated — Change of name or number;
Reassigned — Transferred from one higher formation to another;
Deployed — Moved from USA or other theatres to Southeast Asia;
Moved — Transferred from one base to another without a change of assignment.

Higher Echelons

Seventh Air Force
Activated at Tan Son Nhut to replace 2 AD, 1 Apr 1966; moved to Nakhon Phanom RTAB, 29 Mar 1973; inactivated, 30 Jun 1975.

Eighth Air Force
Transferred to Anderson AFB, Guam from Westover AFB, Mass to replace 3 AD, 1 Apr 1970; moved to Barksdale AFB, La, 1 Jan 1975.

Thirteenth Air Force
Activated at Clark AB, Philippines, 16 May 1949; assigned to PACAF, 1 Jul 1957.

2nd ADVON
Activated at Tan Son Nhut under Thirteenth Air Force, 15 Nov 1961; inactivated and replaced by 2 AD, 8 Oct 1962.

2nd Air Division
Activated at Tan Son Nhut under Thirteenth Air Force to replace 2 ADVON, 8 Oct 1962; redesignated Seventh Air Force, 1 Apr 1966.

3rd Air Division
Activated at Andersen AFB, Guam under SAC, 18 Jun 1954; inactivated, 31 Mar 1970; reactivated at Andersen, 1 Jan 1975.

17th Air Division (Provisional)
Activated at U-Tapao RTAB under Eighth Air Force, 1 Jun 1972; inactivated, 1 Jan 1975.

57th Air Division (Provisional)
Activated at Andersen AFB, Guam under Eighth Air Force, 1 Jun 1972; inactivated, 15 Nov 1973.

315th Air Division
Activated at Tachikawa AB, Japan under PACAF, 25 Jan 1951; inactivated, 15 Apr 1969.

834th Air Division
Activated at Tan Son Nhut under Seventh Air Force, 25 Oct 1966; inactivated, 1 Dec 1971.

Pre-November 1965
Wings & Groups and other units

1st Air Commando Group, Detachment 2A
Redesignated from Detachment 2A, 4400 CCTS at Bien Hoa, c.17 Apr 1962; redesignated 1 ACS, 8 Jul 1963.
Aircraft: B-26B, RB-26L, SC-47D, T-28D, U-10A
Aircraft lost: 4 B-26B, 4 T-28D, 1 U-10A

14th Combat Support Group
Activated at Nha Trang, Apr 1966; inactivated 30 Sep 1971.

33rd Tactical Group
Activated at Tan Son Nhut, Apr 1963; redesignated 6250 CSG, Jun 1965. Squadrons attached or assigned: 8 TBS, 13 TBS, Detachment 1 41 TRS, Det 1, 460 TRW.

34th Tactical Group
Activated at Bien Hoa, 8 Jul 1963; redesignated 6251 TFW, 1 Aug 1965.
Squadrons attached or assigned: 1 ACS, 19 TASS, 602 ACS.

35th Tactical Group
Activated at Don Muang Airport, Bankok, 19 Jun 1963; inactivated, 8 Jul 1965.

315th Troop Carrier Group
Activated at Tan Son Nhut under 315 AD, 8 Dec 1962; redesignated 315 ACG, 8 Mar 1965; redesignated 315 ACW, 8 Mar 1966. Squadrons attached or assigned: 19 TCS, 309 TCS, 310 TCS, 311 TCS.

377th Combat Support Group
Activated at Tan Son Nhut, 8 Apr 1966; redesignated 377 ABW, 17 Jan 1972; inactivated, 28 Mar 1973. Squadrons attached or assigned: 8 SOS, 9 SOS, 21 TASS, 310 TAS, 360 TEWS.

504th Tactical Air Support Group
Activated at Bien Hoa, 8 Dec 1966; inactivated at Tan Son Nhut, 15 Mar 1972. Squadrons attached or assigned: 19 TASS, 20 TASS, 21 TASS, 22 TASS, 23 TASS.

505th Tactical Air Control Group
Activated at Tan Son Nhut from 6250 TASG, 8 Nov 1965 with numerous detachments; replaced by 504 TASG, 8 Dec 1966. Squadrons attached or assigned: 19 TASS, 20 TASS, 21 TASS, 22 TASS, 23 TASS.

630th Combat Support Group
Activated at Udorn RTAB, 8 Apr 1966; replaced by 432 TRW, 18 Sep 1966.

632nd Combat Support Group
Activated at Bin Thuy, Apr 1966; inactivated, 1969.

633rd Combat Support Group
Activated at Pleiku, May 1967; redesignated 633 SOW, 15 Jul 1968. Squadrons attached or assigned: 6 ACS.

634th Combat Support Group
Activated at Nakhon Phanom RTAB, 8 Apr 1966; replaced by 56 ACW, 8 Apr 1967. Squadrons attached or assigned: 606 ACS.

6010th Tactical Group
Activated at Don Muang Airport, Bankok, Jul 1962; redesignated 35 TG, Jul 1963.

6232nd Combat Support Group
Activated at Udorn RTAB under 6234 TFW, 18 Jul 1965; redesignated 630 CSG, 8 Apr 1966.

6234th Tactical Fighter Wing
Activated at Korat RTAB, 5 Apr 1965; inactivated and replaced by 388 TFW, 8 Apr 1966. Squadrons attached or assigned: 12 TFS, 67 TFS, 68 TFS, 357 TFS, 421 TFS, 469 TFS, 561 TFS, Wild Weasel I Det.

6235th Tactical Fighter Wing
Activated at Takhli RTAB, 8 Jul 1965; replaced by 355 TFW, 8 Nov 1965. Squadrons attached or assigned: 335 TFS, 562 TFS, 563 TFS.

6250th Combat Support Group
Activated at Tan Son Nhut, Jun 1965; replaced by 377 CSG, 8 Apr 1966. Squadrons attached or assigned: 4 ACS, 20 TRS, Detachment 1 460 TRW, 481 TFS.

6250th Tactical Air Support Group (Provisional)
Activated at Tan Son Nhut, 1 Aug 1965; redesignated 505 TACG, 8 Nov 1965. Squadrons attached or assigned: 19 TASS, 20 TASS, 21 TASS, 22 TASS.

6251st Tactical Fighter Wing
Redesignated from 34 TG at Bien Hoa, Jul 1965; replaced by 3 TFW, Nov 1965. Squadrons attached or assigned: 1 ACS, 307 TFS, 602 ACS.

6252nd Tactical Fighter Wing
Activated at Da Nang, 8 Jul 1965; replaced by 35 TFW, 8 Apr 1966. Squadrons attached or assigned: 8 TBS, 13 TBS, 390 TFS, 480 TFS.

6253rd Combat Support Group
Activated at Nha Trang, Jul 1965; replaced by 14 CSG, Apr 1966. Squadrons attached or assigned: 5 ACS, 602 ACS.

6254th Combat Support Group
Activated at Pleiku, Jul 1965; redesignated 633 CSG, May 1967.

6255th Combat Support Group
Activated at Binh Thuy, Jul 1965; redesignated 632 CSG, Apr 1966.

6256th Combat Support Group
Activated at Cam Ranh Bay, Jul 1965; replaced by 12 TFW, Oct 1965.

6258th Combat Support Group
Activated at Phan Rang, Oct 1965, replaced by 366 TFW, Mar 1966.

6441st Tactical Fighter Wing (Provisional)
Deployed to Takhli RTAB from Yokota AB, Japan, May 1965; replaced by 6235 TFW and returned to Yokota AB, 8 Jul 1965.

6492nd Combat Cargo Group (Troop Carrier)
Activated at Tan Son Nhut under 315 AD, Sep 1962; replaced by 315 TCG, Dec 1962.

Special Aerial Spray Flight (Ranch Hand)
Deployed to Tan Son Nhut, 7 Jan 1962 and attached to 464 TCW; reassigned to 315 TCG as Detachment 1, Jul 1964 and attached to 309 TCS; redesignated as 309 ACS, 8 Mar 1965; moved to Bien Hoa, December 1965; reassigned to 12 ACS, 315 ACW, Tan Son Nhut, 15 Oct 1966 but remained based at Bien Hoa; redesignated 12 SOS, 1 Aug 1968; moved to Phan Rang, Feb 1969; reassigned to 310 TAS, 315 TAW, Phan Rang, 31 Jul 1970; absorbed into 310 TAS, 28 Jan 1971.
Aircraft: UC-123B/K   Aircraft lost: 8

Wild Weasel I Detachment
Attached to 6234 TFW, Korat RTAB from Tactical Air Warfare Center, Eglin AFB, Fla, 26 Nov 1965-11 Jul 1966.
Aircraft: F-100F   Aircraft lost: 3

Tactical Wings

3rd Tactical Fighter Wing
Transferred to Bien Hoa from England AFB, La, 8 Nov 1965; reduced to paper status 31 Oct 1970; transferred to Kunsan AB, South Korea, 15 Mar 1971. Squadrons attached or assigned: 1 ACS, 8 AS, 10 FCS, 90 TFS/AS, 307 TFS, 308 TFS, 416 TFS, 429 TFS, 510 TFS, 531 TFS, 602 ACS, 604 ACS/SOS

8th Tactical Fighter Wing
Transferred to Ubon RTAB from 831 AD, George AFB, Calif, 8 Dec 1965; transferred to Kunsan AB, South Korea, 16 Sep 1974. Squadrons attached or assigned: 13 TBS, 16 SOS, 25 TFS, 58 TFS, 308 TFS, 334 TFS, 335 TFS, 336 TFS, 433 TFS, 435 TFS, 497 TFS, 555 TFS

12th Tactical Fighter Wing
Transferred to Cam Ranh Bay from MacDill AFB, Fla, 8 Nov 1965; moved to Phu Cat, 31 Mar 1970; inactivated, 17 Nov 1971. Squadrons attached or assigned: 43 TFS, 389 TFS, 391 TFS, 480 TFS, 555 TFS, 557 TFS, 558 TFS, 559 TFS.

14th Air Commando Wing
Activated at Nha Trang, 8 Mar 1966; redesignated 14 SOW, 1 Aug 1968; moved to Phan Rang, 15 Oct 1969; inactivated, 30 Sep 1971. Squadrons attached or assigned: 1 ACS, 3 ACS/SOS, 4 ACS/SOS, 5 ACS/SOS, 6 ACS, 9 ACS/SOS, 14 ACS, 15 ACS/SOS, 17 ACS, 18 SOS, 20 ACS/SOS, 71 SOS, 90 SOS, 602 ACS, 604 ACS/SOS.

31st Tactical Fighter Wing
Transferred to Tuy Hoa from Homestead AFB, Fla, 16 Dec 1966; returned to Homestead AFB, 15 Oct 1970. Squadrons attached or assigned: 136 TFS, 188 TFS, 306 TFS, 308 TFS, 309 TFS, 355 TFS, 416 TFS.

35th Tactical Fighter Wing
Activated at Da Nang, 8 Apr 1966 replacing 6252 TFW; moved to Phan Rang swapping designations with 366 TFW, 10 Oct 1966; inactivated, 31 Jul 1971. Squadrons attached or assigned: 8 TBS, 13 TBS, 120 TFS, 352 TFS, 390 TFS, 480 TFS, 612 TFS, 614 TFS, 615 TFS.

37th Tactical Fighter Wing
Activated at Phu Cat, 1 Mar 1967; inactivated, 31 Mar 1970. Squadrons attached or assigned: 174 TFS, 355 TFS, 389 TFS, 416 TFS, 480 TFS, 612 TFS.

49th Tactical Fighter Wing
Temporarily deployed to Takhli RTAB from Holloman AFB, N Mex, 4 May - 2 Oct 1972. Squadrons attached or assigned: 7 TFS, 8 TFS, 9 TFS, 417 TFS, 434 TFS.

56th Air Commando Wing
Activated at Nakhon Phanom RTAB, 8 Apr 1967; redesignated 56 SOW, 1 Aug 1968; transferred to MacDill AFB, Fla and redesignated 56th TFW, 30 Jun 1975. Squadrons attached or assigned: 1 ASC/SOS, 18 SOS, 21 TASS, 23 TASS, 361 TEWS, 554 RS, 602 ACS/SOS, 606 ACS/SOS, 609 ACS/SOS.

315th Air Commando Wing
Redesignated from 315 ACG at Tan Son Nhut, 8 Mar 1966; moved to Phan Rang, 15 Jun 1967; redesignated 315 SOW, 1 Aug 1968; redesignated 315 TAW, 1 Jan 1970; inactivated, 31 Mar 1972. Squadrons attached or assigned: 8 SOS, 9 SOS, 12 ACS/SOS, 19 ACS/SOS, 309 ACS/SOS/TAS, 310 ACS/SOS/TAS, 311 ACS/SOS/TAS, Detachments 1,5 and 6, 315 Air Division, Air Transport Flight RAAF.

347th Tactical Fighter Wing
Activated at Takhli RTAB, 30 Jul 1973; moved to Korat RTAB, 12 Jul 1974; inactivated, 30 Jun 1975. Squadrons attached or assigned: 428 TFS, 429 TFS.

354th Tactical Fighter Wing
Advanced Echelon deployed to Korat RTAB from Myrtle Beach AFB, SC, 10 Oct 1972; Rear Echelon remained at Myrtle Beach; Advanced Echelon returned to Myrtle Beach, 23 May 1974. Squadrons attached or assigned: 74 TFS, 353 TFS, 354 TFS, 355 TFS, 356 TFS, 358 TFS.

355th Tactical Fighter Wing
Transferred to Takhli RTAB from 835 AD, McConnell AFB, Kans, 8 Nov 1965; inactivated, 10 Dec 1970. Squadrons attached or assigned: 41 TRS/TEWS, 42 TRS/TEWS, 44 TFS, 333 TFS, 334 TFS, 335 TFS, 354 TFS, 357 TFS, 469 TFS, 562 TFS, 6460 TRS.

366th Tactical Fighter Wing
Transferred to Phan Rang from 832 AD, Holloman AFB, N Mex, 20 Mar 1966; moved to Da Nang swapping designations with 35 TFW, 10 Oct 1966; moved to Takhli RTAB, 27 Jun 1972; inactivated and designation transferred to 832 AD, Mountain Home AFB, Idaho, 31 Oct 1972. Squadrons attached or assigned: 4 TFS, 20 TASS, 35 TFS, 352 TFS, 362 TEWS, 389 TFS, 390 TFS, 391 TFS, 421 TFS, 480 TFS, 614 TFS, 615 TFS, Detachment 1 612 TFS.

377th Air Base Wing
Redesignated from 377 CSG at Tan Son Nhut, 17 Jan 1972; inactivated, 28 Mar 1973. Squadrons attached or assigned: 8 SOS, 9 SOS, 21 TASS, 310 TAS, 360 TEWS.

388th Tactical Fighter Wing
Activated at Korat RTAB, 8 Apr 1966; transferred to Hill AFB, Utah, 23 Dec 1975. Squadrons attached or assigned: 3 TFS, 7 ACCS, 13 TFS, 16 SOS, 17 WWS, 34 TFS, 35 TFS, 42 TEWS, 44 TFS, 421 TFS, 469 TFS, 553 RS, 6010 WWS, Detachment 1, 561 TFS.

405th Fighter Wing
Activated at Clark AB, Philippines, 9 Apr 1959; inactivated, 16 Sep 1974. The Wing maintained detachments of F-102s from the 64 FIS and 509 FIS and also controlled detachments from 16 FIS and 82 FIS from Naha AB, Okinawa. Detachments were based at Bien Hoa, Da Nang, Don Muang, Udorn and Tan Son Nhut from Mar 1962 until Jul 1970.

432nd Tactical Reconnaissance Wing
Activated at Udorn RTAB, 18 Sep 1966; redesignated 432 TFW, 15 Nov 1974; inactivated, 23 Dec 1975. Squadrons attached or assigned: 4 SOS, 4 TFS, 7 ACCS, 11 TRS, 13 TFS, 14 TRS, 18 TRS, 25 TFS, 41 TRS/TEWS, 58 TFS, 307 TFS, 308 TFS, 421 TFS, 523 TFS, 555 TFS, 6460 TRS, 6461 TRS.

460th Tactical Reconnaissance Wing
Activated at Tan Son Nhut, 18 Feb 1966; inactivated, 31 Aug 1971. Squadrons attached or assigned: 12 TRS, 16 TRS, 20 TRS, 41 TRS, 45 TRS, 360 TRS/TEWS, 361 TRS/TEWS, 362 TRS/TEWS, 6460 TRS.

460th Tactical Reconnaissance Wing, Detachment 1
Patricia Lynn detachment activated at Tan Son Nhut as Detachment 1, 33 TG, 7 May 1963; redesignated Detachment 1, 6250 CSG, Jun 1965; redesignated Detachment 1, 460 TRW, 18 Feb 1966; inactivated, 31 Aug 1971. Aircraft: RB-57E   Aircraft lost: 2

460th Tactical Reconnaissance Wing, Detachment 2
Activated at Tan Son Nhut, 8 Apr 1969; inactivated 1 Jun 1970.

474th Tactical Fighter Wing.
Temporarily deployed to Takhli RTAB from Nellis AFB, Nev, 27 Sep 1972; returned to Nellis, 30 Jul 1973 and squadrons passed on to 347 TFW. Squadrons attached or assigned: 428 TFS, 429 TFS, 430 TFS.

483rd Troop Carrier Wing
Activated at Cam Ranh Bay, 15 Oct 1966; redesignated 483 TAW, 1 Aug 1967; inactivated, 31 May 1972. Squadrons attached or assigned: 20 SOS, 90 SOS, 360 TEWS, 361 TEWS, 362 TEWS, 457 TCS/TAS, 458 TCS/TAS, 459 TCS/TAS, 535 TCS/TAS, 536 TCS/TAS, 537 TCS/TAS.

552nd Airborne Early Warning & Control Wing, Detachment 1
Detachment 1 transferred to Tan Son Nhut from McClellan AFB, Calif, 17 Apr 1965; moved to Ubon RTAB, Feb 1967; moved to Udorn RTAB, Jul 1967; moved to Korat RTAB, Oct 1967; returned to McClellan AFB, 2 Jun 1974. Squadrons attached or assigned: 963 AEW&CS, 964 AEW&CS, 965 AEW&CS, 966 AEW&CS. Aircraft: EC-121D/T.

553rd Reconnaissance Wing *Bat Cats*
Activated at Otis AFB, Mass, 9 Feb 1967; transferred to Korat RTAB, 31 Oct 1967; inactivated 15 Dec 1970. Squadrons attached or assigned: 553 RS, 554 RS.

633rd Special Operations Wing
Activated at Pleiku, 15 Jul 1968; inactivated 15 Mar 1970. Squadrons attached or assigned: 6 SOS.

C-130 Transports Wings
Based in the USA or the Pacific that sent squadrons and crews on detachment to Southeast Asia

Pacific Air Force Units

314th Troop Carrier Wing
Activated at Sewart AFB, Tenn, 1 Nov 1948; transferred to Ching Chuan Kang AB, Taiwan, 22 Jan 1966; redesignated 314 TAW, 1 Aug 1967; moved to Little Rock AFB, Ark, 31 May 1971. Detachments mainly at Tuy Hoa. Squadrons attached or assigned:

50th Troop Carrier Squadron
Assigned to 315 AD, Clark AB, Philippines, 26 Dec 1965; transferred to Ching Chuan Kang AB, 28 Jan 1966; reassigned to 314 TCW, 23 Feb 1966; redesignated 50 TAS, 1 Aug 1967; reassigned to 374 TAW, Ching Chuan Kang AB, 31 May 1971. Aircraft: C-130E   Code: DE   Aircraft lost: 4

345th Troop Carrier Squadron
Assigned to 314 TCW, 25 Mar 1966; redesignated 345 TAS, 1 Aug 1967; reassigned to 374 TAW, Ching Chuan Kang AB, 31 May 1971. Aircraft: C-130E   Code: DH   Aircraft lost: 3

346th Tactical Airlift Squadron
Assigned to 314 TAW from 516 TAW, Dyess AFB, Tex, 15 May 1969; inactivated, 31 May 1971. Aircraft: C-130E   Code: DY   Aircraft lost: 0

776th Troop Carrier Squadron
Assigned to 314 TCW, 25 Mar 1966; redesignated 776 TAS, 1 Aug 1967; reassigned to 374 TAW, Ching Chuan Kang AB, 31 May 1971. Aircraft: C-130E   Code: DL   Aircraft lost: 6

374th Troop Carrier Wing
Activated at Naha AB, Okinawa to replace 6315 OG, 8 Aug 1966; redesignated 374 TAW, 1 Aug 1967; moved to Ching Chuan Kang AB, Taiwan, 31 May 1971; moved to Clark AB, Philippines, 5 Nov 1973. Detachments mainly at Cam Ranh Bay. Squadrons attached or assigned:

21st Troop Carrier Squadron
Assigned to 6315 OG, Naha AB, 20 Oct 1964; reassigned to 374 TCW, 8 Aug 1966; redesignated 21 TAS, 1 Aug 1967; moved to Ching Chuan Kang AB, 31 May 1971; moved to Clark AB, 1 Nov 1973. Aircraft: C-130A/E   Code: YD   Aircraft lost: 4 C-130A, 1 C-130E

35th Troop Carrier Squadron
Assigned to 6315 OG, Naha AB, 8 Jan 1963; reassigned to 374 TCW, 8 Aug 1966; redesignated 35 TAS, 1 Aug 1967; inactivated, 31 Mar 1971. Aircraft: C-130A   Code: YJ   Aircraft lost: 2

36th Tactical Airlift Squadron
Attached to 374 TAW, 16 May - 7 Sep 1972 from 316 TAW, Langley AFB, VA. Aircraft: C-130E   Code: LM   Aircraft lost: 0

37th Tactical Airlift Squadron
Attached to 374 TAW, 6 Dec 1972 - 15 Mar 1973 from 316 TAW, Langley AFB, Va. Aircraft: C-130E   Code: LM   Aircraft lost: 0

38th Tactical Airlift Squadron
Attached to 374 TAW, 1 Sep - 29 Nov 1972 from 316 TAW, Langley AFB, Va. Aircraft: C-130E   Code: LM   Aircraft lost: 0

41st Troop Carrier Squadron
Assigned to 6315 OG, Naha AB, 21 Nov 1965; reassigned to 374 TCW, 8 Aug 1966; redesignated 41 TAS, 1 Apr 1967; inactivated, 28 Feb 1971. Aircraft: C-130A   Code: YP   Aircraft lost: 6

50th Tactical Airlift Squadron
Assigned to 374 TAW from 314 TAW, Little Rock AFB, Ark,
31 May 1971; became non-operational, 8 Feb 1973;
reassigned to 314 TAW, 15 Aug 1973.
Aircraft: C-130E   Code: DE   Aircraft lost: 0

61st Tactical Airlift Squadron
Attached to 374 TAW from 314 TAW, Little Rock AFB, Ark,
13 May - 8 Sep 1972. Aircraft: C-130E   Code: LK   Aircraft lost: 0

345th Tactical Airlift Squadron
Assigned to 374 TAW from 314 TAW, Little Rock AFB, Ark,
31 May 1971; transferred to Clark AB, 15 Nov 1973.
Aircraft: C-130E   Code: DH   Aircraft lost: 0

772nd Troop Carrier Squadron
Attached to 374 TAW from 463 TAW, Dyess AFB, Tex,
10 May - 6 Jun 1973.
Aircraft: C-130B   Code: QF   Aircraft lost: 0

773rd Troop Carrier Squadron
Attached to 374 TAW from 463 TAW, Dyess AFB, Tex,
28 Feb - 10 May 1973.
Aircraft: C-130B   Code: QG   Aircraft lost: 0

776th Tactical Airlift Squadron
Assigned to 374 TAW from 314 TAW, Ching Chuan Kang AB,
31 May 1971; moved to Clark AB, 15 Nov 1973; inactivated,
31 Oct 1975. Aircraft: C-130E   Code: DL   Aircraft lost: 0

815th Troop Carrier Squadron
Assigned to 315 AD, Tachikawa AB, 25 Jun 1960;
reassigned to 374 TAW, Naha AB, 1 Nov 1968; became
non-operational, 19 Oct 1969; inactivated, 15 Dec 1969.
Aircraft: C-130A   Code: YU   Aircraft lost: 0

817th Troop Carrier Squadron
Assigned to 6315 OG, Naha AB, 1963; reassigned to 374 TCW,
Naha AB, 8 Aug 1966; redesignated 817 TAS, 1 Aug 1967;
became non-operational, 10 Apr 1970; inactivated, 15 Jun 1970.
Aircraft: C-130A   Code: YU   Aircraft lost: 4

463rd Troop Carrier Wing
Activated at Memphis Municipal Airport, Tenn, 16 Jan 1953;
moved to Ardmore AFB, Okla, 1 Sep 1953; moved to Sewart
AFB, Tenn, 15 Jan 1959; moved to Langley AFB, Va, 1 Jul 1963;
transferred to Mactan AB, Philippines, 23 Nov 1965;
redesignated 463 TAW, 1 Aug 1967; moved to Clark AB,
Philippines, 15 Jul 1968; inactivated, 31 Dec 1971.
Detachments mainly at Tan Son Nhut.
Squadrons attached or assigned:

29th Troop Carrier Squadron
Attached to 463 TCW, Mactan AB from 313 TCW, Forbes AFB,
Kans, 30 Jan 1966 but based at Clark AB; assigned to 463 TCW,
25 Mar 1966; redesignated 29 TAS, 1 Aug 1967; became non-
operational, 1 Jul 1970; inactivated, 31 Oct 1970.
Aircraft: C-130B   Code: QB   Aircraft lost: 5

772nd Troop Carrier Squadron
Assigned to 463 TCW, Mactan AB, 7 Feb 1966;
redesignated 772 TAS, 1 Aug 1967; inactivated, 15 Jun 1971;
reactivated and attached to 374 TAW, Ching Chuan Kang AB,
Taiwan, 10 May 1973.
Aircraft: C-130B   Code: QF   Aircraft lost: 3

773rd Troop Carrier Squadron
Transferred to Clark AB with 463 TCW, 23 Nov 1965;
redesignated 773 TAS, 1 Aug 1967; inactivated, 31 Oct 1971;
reactivated under 463 TAW, 1 Jun 1972; attached to 374 TAW,
Ching Chuan Kang AB, Taiwan, 28 Feb 1973.
Aircraft: C-130B   Code: QG   Aircraft lost: 4

774th Troop Carrier Squadron
Transferred to Mactan AB with 463 TCW, 23 Nov 1965;
redesignated 774 TAS, 1 Aug 1967; reassigned to 405 FW,
Clark AB, 31 Dec 1971; inactivated, 15 Sep 1972.
Aircraft: C-130B   Code: QW   Aircraft lost: 4

6315th Operations Group
Activated at Naha AB, Okinawa, Jan 1963; redesignated 374
TCW, 8 Aug 1966. Squadrons attached or assigned: 21 TCS,
35 TCS, 815 TCS, 817 TCS. See 374th Troop Carrier Wing
for squadron details.

Tactical Air Command Units

64th Troop Carrier Wing
Activated at Sewart AFB, Tenn, 1 Jul 1966;
redesignated 64 TAW, 1 May 1967; moved to Little Rock AFB,
Ark, 9 Mar 1970; inactivated, 31 May 1971.
Squadrons attached or assigned: 61 TCS/TAS, 62 TCS/TAS.
Aircraft: C-130B/E   Codes: SR and ST   Aircraft lost: 1

313rd Troop Carrier Wing
Activated at Forbes AFB, Kans, 1 Oct 1964; redesignated 313
TAW, 1 May 1967; inactivated, 30 Sep 1973. Squadrons
attached or assigned: 29 TCS, 38 TAS, 47 TCS/TAS, 48 TCS/TAS
Aircraft: C-130B   Codes: FB and FH   Aircraft lost: 0

316th Troop Carrier Wing
Activated at Langley AFB, Va, 25 Nov 1965; redesignated 316
TAW, 1 May 1967; inactivated, 1 Oct 1975. Squadrons attached
or assigned: 29 TCS, 36 TCS/TAS, 37 TCS/TAS, 38 TCS/TAS.
Aircraft: C-130E   Codes: LM, LN and LO   Aircraft lost: 0

464th Troop Carrier Wing
Activated at Lawson AFB, Ga, 1 Feb 1953; moved to Pope AFB,
NC, 21 Sep 1954; redesignated 464 TAW, 1 May 1967;
inactivated, 31 Aug 1971. Squadrons attached or assigned:
775 TCS, 776 TCS, 777 TCS/TAS, 778 TCS/TAS, 779 TCS/TAS.
Aircraft: C-130E   Codes: PB, PG and PR   Aircraft lost: 1

516th Troop Carrier Wing
Activated at Dyess AFB, Tex, 1 Jan 1963;
redesignated 516 TAW, 1 May 1967; inactivated, 1 Jun 1972
Squadrons attached or assigned: 17 TCS, 18 TCS/TAS, 345 TCS,
346 TCS/TAS, 347 TCS/TAS, 348 TAS
Aircraft: C-130E   Codes: DB, DY and DZ   Aircraft lost: 0

Tactical Squadrons

1st Air Commando Squadron
Redesignated from Detachment 2A, 1 ACG at Bien Hoa under
34 TG, 8 Jul 1963; reassigned to 6251 TFW, Bien Hoa, 8 Jul
1965 but attached to 3 TFW, Bien Hoa, 21 Nov 1965-8 Mar 66;
moved to Pleiku, 5 Jan 1966; reassigned to 2 AD, 18 Feb 66;
reassigned to 14 ACW, Nha Trang, 8 Mar 1966 but remained at
Pleiku; reassigned to 56 ACW, Nakhon Phanom RTAB, 20 Dec
1967; redesignated 1 SOS, 1 Aug 1968; reassigned to 18 TFW,
Kadena AB, Okinawa, 15 Dec 1972 but a detachment operated
at Nakhon Phanom until 28 Jan 1973.
Aircraft: A-1E/G/H/J, B-26B, RB-26L, SC-47D, T-28D,
U-10A/B/D   Codes: EC and TC.
Aircraft lost: 53 A-1E, 5 A-1G, 12 A-1H, 4 A-1J, 5 B-26B,
1 RB-26L, 1 O-1F, 10 T-28D, 1 U-10A.

3rd Air Commando Squadron
Assigned to 14 ACW, Nha Trang, 1 May 1968;
redesignated 3 SOS, 1 Aug 1968; inactivated, 15 Sep 1969.
Aircraft: AC-47D   Code: EL   Aircraft lost: 1

3rd Tactical Fighter Squadron
Activated at Korat RTAB under 388 TFW, 15 Mar 1973;
reassigned to 3 TFW, Clark AB, Philippines, 15 Dec 1975.
Aircraft: A-7D   Code: JH   Aircraft lost: 1

4th Air Commando Squadron
Activated at Tan Son Nhut under 2 AD, 2 Aug 1965 and
attached to 6250 CSG on same day but did not actually arrive
at Tan Son Nhut until 14 Nov 1965; assigned to 14 ACW, Nha
Trang, 8 Mar 1966 but remained at Tan Son Nhut until 1 Jun
1966 when it moved to Nha Trang with detachments at Bien
Hoa, Da Nang, Nakhon Phanom RTAB, Phu Cat, Pleiku and
Ubon; redesignated 4 SOS, 1 Aug 1968; moved to Phan Rang,
1 Oct 1969; inactivated, 15 Dec 1969.
Aircraft: AC-47D, SC-47D, U-10A/B
Codes: EN and OS   Aircraft lost: 15 AC-47D

4th Tactical Fighter Squadron
Assigned to 366 TFW, Da Nang from 33 TFW, Eglin AFB, Fla,
12 Apr 1969; moved to Takhli RTAB, 27 Jun 1972; reassigned
to 432 TRW, Udorn RTAB, 31 Oct 1972; converted to F-4D by
Jan 1973; reassigned to 388 TFW, Hill AFB, Utah, 23 Dec 1975.
Aircraft: F-4D/E   Codes: LA and UD   Aircraft lost: 12 F-4E

5th Air Commando Squadron
Activated at Nha Trang probably under 6253 CSG, Aug 1965;
reassigned to 14 ACW, Nha Trang, 8 Mar 1966 with
detachments at Bien Hoa, Binh Thuy, Da Nang and Pleiku;
provided nucleus for 9 ACS, Mar 1967; redesignated 5 SOS,
1 Aug 1968; inactivated, 15 Oct 1969.
Aircraft: C-47B/D, SC-47D, U-10A/B/D   Code: EO
Aircraft lost: 1 C-47B, 1 U-10A, 5 U-10B, 1 U-10D

6th Air Commando Squadron
Assigned to 14 ACW, Nha Trang from 1 ACW, England AFB, La,
29 Feb 1968 but based at Pleiku; reassigned to 633 ACW,
Pleiku, 15 Jul 1968 with a detachment at Da Nang, 1 Apr 1968
- 1 Sep 1969; redesignated 6 SOS, 1 Aug 1968; inactivated,
15 Nov 1969. Aircraft: A-1E/G/H/J   Codes: ET and 6T
Aircraft lost: 13 A-1H, 1 A-1G, 1 A-1J

7th Airborne Command and Control Squadron
Activated at Da Nang under PACAF, 13 Feb 1968 but operated
from Udorn RTAB; reassigned to Seventh AF, 1 Mar 1968;
reassigned to 432 TRW, Udorn, 31 Oct 1968 but remained
attached to Seventh AF; moved to Korat RTAB, 15 Apr 1972
and reassigned to 388 TFW, Korat, 30 Apr 1972 but still
remained attached to Seventh AF until 22 May 1974;
reassigned to 374 TAW, Clark AB, Philippines, 22 May 1974
Aircraft: EC-130E   Code: JC   Aircraft lost: 0

7th Tactical Fighter Squadron
Deployed on TDY to Takhli RTAB with 49 TFW from Holloman
AFB, N Mex, 11 May-12 Aug 1972.
Aircraft: F-4D   Codes: HB and HO   Aircraft lost: 2

8th Tactical Bomber Squadron
Deployed to Bien Hoa as part of 405 FW ADVON 1 from 405 FW,
Clark AB, Philippines, 5 Aug-3 Nov 1964; attached to 33 TG,
Tan Son Nhut, 18-28 Jun 1965; moved to Da Nang under 2 AD,
28 Jun 1965; attached to 6252 TFW, Da Nang, 8 Jul-15 Aug 1965,
16 Oct-16 Dec 1965, 15 Feb-7 Apr 1966; attached to 35 TFW,
Da Nang, 8-18 Apr 1966, 15 Jun-15 Aug 1966; attached to
35 TFW, Phan Rang, 12 Oct-12 Dec 1966, 11 Feb-12 Apr 1967,
7 Jun-2 Aug 1967, 26 Sep-21 Nov 1967; alternated with 13 TBS
during these rotations from 405 FW at Clark AB; reassigned to
35 TFW, Phan Rang, 15 Jan 1968; re-equipped with A-37B
and redesignated 8 AS and reassigned to 3 TFW, Bien Hoa,
15 Nov 1969; redesignated 8 SOS and reassigned to 35 TFW,
Bien Hoa, 30 Sep 1970; reassigned to 315 TAW, Phan Rang
but remained at Bien Hoa, 31 Jul 1971; reassigned to 377 ABW,
Tan Son Nhut but remained at Bien Hoa, 15 Jan 1972;
reassigned to 405 FW, Clark AB, 1 Oct 1972.
Aircraft: B-57B/C/E (1964-1968), A-37B (1969-1972)
Codes: PQ (B-57) and CF (A-37B)
Aircraft lost: 55 B-57B/C/Es (includes aircraft flown by 13 TBS),
11 A-37B

8th Tactical Fighter Squadron
Deployed on TDY to Takhli RTAB with 49 TFW from Holloman
AFB, N Mex, 21 May-4 Oct 1972.
Aircraft: F-4D   Codes: HC and HO   Aircraft lost: 0

9th Air Commando Squadron
Activated under PACAF, 9 Jan 1967 and assigned to 14 ACW,
Nha Trang but based at Pleiku, 25 Jan 1967 with detachments
at Bien Hoa, Binh Thuy, Da Nang, Phu Cat, Tuy Hoa and Ubon
RTAB; moved to Nha Trang, Sep 1967; redesignated 9 SOS,
1 Aug 1968; moved to Tuy Hoa, 5 Sep 1969; moved to Phan
Rang, 15 Aug 1970; reassigned to 315 TAW, Phan Rang,
30 Sep 1971; attached to 377 ABW, Tan Son Nhut, 12 Jan 1972;
inactivated, 29 Feb 1972.
Aircraft: AC-47D, O-2B, U-10D   Code: ER
Aircraft lost: 2 O-2B

9th Tactical Fighter Squadron *Flying Knights*
Deployed on TDY to Takhli RTAB with 49 TFW from Holloman AFB, N Mex, 13 May-5 Oct 1972.
Aircraft: F-4D   Codes: HD and HO   Aircraft lost: 0

10th Fighter Commando Squadron
Redesignated from 4503 TFS(P) at Bien Hoa under 3 TFW, 8 Apr 1966; inactivated, 17 Apr 1967.
Aircraft: F-5C   Aircraft lost: 8

11th Tactical Reconnaissance Squadron
Assigned to 432 TRW, Udorn RTAB from 67 TRW, Mountain Home AFB, Idaho, 25 Oct 1966 taking over assets of 6461 TRS; reassigned to TAC and moved to Shaw AFB, SC, 10 Nov 1970 for inactivation on 24 Jan 1971.
Aircraft: RF-4C   Code: OO   Aircraft lost: 28

12th Air Commando Squadron
Activated from the Special Aerial Spray Flight at Tan Son Nhut and assigned to 315 ACW, 15 Oct 1966; moved to Bien Hoa, 1 Dec 1966; redesignated 12 SOS, 1 Aug 1968; inactivated, 31 Jul 1970. Aircraft: UC-123B/K
Aircraft lost: see Special Aerial Spray Flight (Ranch Hand)

12th Tactical Fighter Squadron *Dirty Dozen/Foxy Few*
Deployed on TDY to Da Nang under 2 AD from 18 TFW, Kadena AB, Okinawa, 1 Feb 1965; a portion of the Squadron deployed to Korat RTAB, 8 Feb 1965, the remainder moving from Da Nang to Korat, 20 Feb 1965; returned to 18 TFW, 15 Mar 1965; deployed on TDY to 6234 TFW, Korat from 18 TFW, 15 Jun-25 Aug 1965.
Aircraft: F-105D/F   Aircraft lost: 4 F-105D

12th Tactical Fighter Squadron, Detachment 1
Deployed to 388 TFW, Korat RTAB from 18 TFW, Kadena AB, Okinawa, 24 Sep 1970; redesignated 6010 WWS, 31 Oct 1970.
Aircraft: F-105F/G   Code: ZB   Aircraft lost: 0

12th Tactical Reconnaissance Squadron *Blackbirds*
Assigned to 460 TRW, Tan Son Nhut from 67 TRW, Mountain Home AFB, Idaho, 2 Sep 1966; inactivated, 31 Aug 1971 and reactivated same day under 67 TRW, Bergstrom AFB, Tex
Aircraft: RF-4C   Code: AC   Aircraft lost: 12

13th Tactical Bomber Squadron *Grim Reapers*
Deployed to Bien Hoa as part of 405 FW ADVON 1 from 405 FW, Clark AB, Philippines, 5 Aug 1964; moved temporarily to Tan Son Nhut, 16 May 1965; attached to 6252 TFW, Da Nang, 18 Jun 1965; attached to 35 TFW, Da Nang from 405 FW, 17 Apr-17 Jun 1966, 14 Aug-13 Oct 1966; attached to 35 TFW, Phan Rang, and alternated with 13 TBS on rotation with 405 FW at Clark AB and spent the following periods at Phan Rang 12 Dec 1966-11 Feb 1967, 11 Apr-8 Jun 1967, 1 Aug-26 Sep 1967, 21 Nov 1967 to inactivation at Phan Rang on 15 Jan 1968; reactivated and attached to 8 TFW, Ubon RTAB, 15 Sep 1970; reassigned to 8 TFW, 31 Oct 1970; became non-operational, 12 Apr 1972; reassigned to 405 FW, Clark AB, 24 Dec 1972; inactivated, 30 Sep 1973.
Aircraft: B-57B/C/E (1964-1968), B-57G (1970-1972)
Codes: PV, FK and FS   Aircraft lost: 55 B-57B/C/Es (includes aircraft flown by 8 TBS), 1 B-57G

13th Tactical Fighter Squadron *Panther Pack*
Activated under PACAF, 2 May 1966; assigned to 18 TFW, Kadena AB, Okinawa, 15 May 1966 but attached to 388 TFW, Korat RTAB same day; converted to F-4D, Oct 1967; attached to 432 TRW, Udorn RTAB, 15 Oct 1967; reassigned to 432 TRW, 15 Nov 1967; inactivated, 30 Jun 1975.
Aircraft: F-105D/F (1966-1967), F-4D/E (1967-1975)
Codes: OC and UD (F-4D)
Aircraft lost: 10 F-105D, 7 F-105F, 16 F-4D, 2 F-4E

14th Air Commando Squadron
Activated at Nha Trang under 14 ACW, 25 Oct 1967; not operational until 15 Jan 1968; redesignated 3 ACS, 1 May 1968.
Aircraft: AC-47D   Aircraft lost: 1

14th Tactical Reconnaissance Squadron
Assigned to 432 TRW, Udorn RTAB from 75 TRW, Bergstrom AFB, Tex, 28 Oct 1967; inactivated, 30 Jun 1975.
Aircraft: RF-4C   Codes: OZ and UD   Aircraft lost: 22

15th Air Commando Squadron
Activated at Nha Trang under 14 ACW from Detachment 1, 314 TAW, 15 Mar 1968; redesignated 15 SOS, 1 Aug 1968; inactivated, 31 Oct 1970. Aircraft: C-130E-I   Aircraft lost: 0

15th Tactical Reconnaissance Squadron *Cotton Pickers*
Pipe Stem detachment on TDY to Tan Son Nhut from 18 TFW, Kadena AB, Okinawa, 18 Oct-19 Nov 1961 and Able Mable detachment to Don Muang and Tan Son Nhut shared in rotation with 45 TRS, Nov 1961-Jan 1965; detachment to Udorn RTAB, 1 Apr 1965-2 Apr 1966.
Aircraft: RF-101C   Aircraft lost: 6

16th Fighter Interceptor Squadron *Tigers*
Assigned to 51 FIW, Naha AB, Okinawa, 9 Mar 1959; detachments on TDY to Bien Hoa, Da Nang, Don Muang and Tan Son Nhut; inactivated, 24 Dec 1964.
Aircraft: F-102A, TF-102A   Aircraft lost: 0

16th Special Operations Squadron
Activated at Ubon RTAB under 8 TFW, 30 Oct 1968; attached to 388 TFW, Korat RTAB, 19 Jul 1974; inactivated, 8 Dec 1975 and reactivated under 1 SOW, Hurlburt Field AFB, Fla four days later. Aircraft: AC-130A/E/H   Codes: EA, FT and WP
Aircraft lost: 5 AC-130A, 1 AC-130E

16th Tactical Reconnaissance Squadron
Deployed to Tan Son Nhut under 2 AD from 363 TRW, Shaw AFB, SC, 30 Oct 1965; assigned to 460 TRW, Tan Son Nhut, 18 Feb 1966; reassigned to 475 TFW, Misawa AB, Japan, 15 Mar 1970. Aircraft: RF-4C   Code: AE   Aircraft lost: 15

17th Special Operations Squadron
Activated at Nha Trang under 14 SOW, 1 Jun 1969 with detachments at Phan Rang, Phu Cat, Pleiku, Tan Son Nhut and Tuy Hoa; moved to Phan Rang, 15 Aug 1969; inactivated, 30 Sep 1971. Aircraft: AC-119G   Code: EF   Aircraft lost: 2

17th Wild Weasel Squadron
Activated from 6010 WWS and assigned to 388 TFW, Korat RTAB, 1 Dec 1971; inactivated, 15 Nov 1974.
Aircraft: F-105G   Codes: JB and ZB   Aircraft lost: 8

18th Special Operations Squadron
Activated at Lockbourne AFB, Ohio under 1 SOW, 25 Jan 1969; reassigned to 14 SOW, Phan Rang, 1 Oct 1969 with detachments at Da Nang, Phu Cat, Nakhon Phanom and Udorn RTAB; reassigned to 56 SOW, Nakhon Phanom RTAB, 25 Aug 1971; inactivated, 31 Dec 1972.
Aircraft: AC-119K   Code: EH   Aircraft lost: 3

19th Tactical Air Support Squadron
Activated at Bien Hoa under 34 TG, 17 Jun 1963 with detachments at various locations; inactivated, 8 Aug 1964; reactivated at Bien Hoa under 34 TG, 31 Oct 1964; assigned to 6250 TASG(P), Tan Son Nhut, 1 Aug 1965 but remained at Bien Hoa; reassigned to 505 TACG, Tan Son Nhut, 8 Nov 1965 but remained at Bien Hoa; reassigned to 504 TASG, Bien Hoa, 8 Dec 1966; inactivated 19 Jan 1972.
Aircraft: O-1E/F/G, O-2A, OV-10A
Aircraft lost: 16 O-1E, 20 O-1F, 17 O-1G, 12 O-2A, 16 OV-10A

19th Troop Carrier Squadron
Activated at Tan Son Nhut under 315 TCG, Oct 1964; redesignated 19 ACS, 8 Mar 1965; reassigned to 315 ACW, Tan Son Nhut, 8 Mar 1966; moved to Phan Rang, 15 Jun 1967; redesignated 19 SOS, 1 Aug 1968; redesignated 19 TAS, 1 Jan 1970; non-operational, 1 May 1971; inactivated, 10 Jun 1971.
Aircraft: C-123B/K   Code: WE   Aircraft lost: 7

20th Tactical Air Support Squadron
Activated at Da Nang under PACAF, 26 Apr 1965 with detachments at various locations; assigned to 2 AD, 8 May 1965; attached to 6250 TASG(P), Tan Son Nhut but based at Da Nang, 1 Aug 1965; reassigned to 505 TACG but remained at Da Nang, 8 Nov 1965; reassigned to 504 TASG, Bien Hoa but remained at Da Nang, 8 Dec 1966; reassigned to 366 TFW, Da Nang, 15 Mar 1972; reassigned to 6498 ABW, Da Nang, 27 Jun 1972; reassigned to 71 TASG, George AFB, Calif, 15 Jan 1973
Aircraft: O-1E/F/G, O-2A, OV-10A
Aircraft lost: 25 O-1E, 1 O-1F, 5 O-1G, 55 O-2A, 22 OV-10A

20th Tactical Reconnaissance Squadron *Green Pythons*
Assigned to 6250 CSG, Tan Son Nhut, 12 Nov 1965; reassigned to 460 TRW, Tan Son Nhut, 18 Feb 1966 with a detachment at Udorn; reassigned to 432 TRW, Udorn RTAB, 18 Sep 1966; inactivated, 1 Nov 1967. Aircraft: RF-101C   Aircraft lost: 19

21st Tactical Air Support Squadron
Activated at Pleiku under PACAF, 8 May 1965 with detachments at various locations; assigned to 6250 TASG(P), Tan Son Nhut but based at Pleiku, 1 Aug 1965; reassigned to 505 TACG, Tan Son Nhut but remained at Pleiku, 8 Nov 1965; reassigned to 14 ACW, Nha Trang, Sep 1966; reassigned to 504 TASG, Bien Hoa, 8 Dec 1966 but remained at Nha Trang; moved to Cam Ranh Bay, Oct 1969; reassigned to 377 ABW, Tan Son Nhut, 15 Mar 1972; inactivated, 23 Feb 1973.
Aircraft: O-1E/F/G, O-2A, OV-10A
Aircraft lost: 18 O-1E, 14 O-1F, 9 O-1G, 16 O-2A, 1 OV-10A

22nd Special Operations Squadron
Assigned to 56 SOW, Nakhon Phanom RTAB, 25 Oct 1968; became non-operational, 18 Jul 1970; inactivated, 30 Sep 1970
Aircraft: A-1E/G/H/J   Code: TS   Aircraft lost: 6 A-1E, 5 A-1H

22nd Tactical Air Support Squadron
Activated at Binh Thuy under PACAF with detachments at various locations, 26 Apr 1965; assigned to 2 AD, 8 May 1965; reassigned to 6250 TASG(P), Tan Son Nhut but based at Binh Thuy, 1 Aug 1965; reassigned to 505 TACG, Tan Son Nhut but remained at Binh Thuy, 8 Nov 1965; reassigned to 504 TASG, Bien Hoa, but remained at Binh Thuy, 8 Dec 1966; inactivated, 15 Jan 1971. Aircraft: O-1E/F/G, O-2A
Aircraft lost: 10 O-1E, 3 O-1G, 3 O-2A

23rd Tactical Air Support Squadron
Activated at Nakhon Phanom RTAB under 505 TACG, Tan Son Nhut, Apr 1966; reassigned to 504 TASG, Bien Hoa but remained at Nakhon Phanom, 8 Dec 1966 with a detachment at Udorn RTAB; reassigned to 56 SOW, Nakhon Phanom, 15 Mar 1972; inactivated, 30 Jun 1975.
Aircraft: O-1E/F, O-2A, OV-10A
Aircraft lost: 1 O-1E, 6 O-1F, 15 O-2A, 23 OV-10A

25th Tactical Fighter Squadron *Assam Dragons*
Assigned to 8 TFW, Ubon RTAB from 33 TFW, Eglin AFB, Fla, 28 May 1968; reassigned to 432 TRW, Udorn RTAB, 5 Jul 1974; inactivated, 18 Dec 1975 and reactivated next day under 18 TFW, Kadena AB, Okinawa.
Aircraft: F-4D/E   Codes: FA, WP and UD
Aircraft lost: 11 F-4D, 3 F-4E

34th Tactical Fighter Squadron *Fighting Rams*
Activated under 41 AD but attached to 388 TFW, Korat RTAB, 15 May 1966; reassigned to 347 TFW, Yokota AB, Japan, 15 Jan 1968 but remained attached to 388 TFW at Korat; operated from Takhli RTAB, 1-27 Feb 1969; converted to F-4E, May 1969; reassigned to 388 TFW, 15 Mar 1971; converted to F-4D, Jun-Jul 1974; inactivated, 23 Dec 1975 and reactivated the same day under 388 TFW, Hill AFB, Utah.
Aircraft: F-105D/F (1966-1969), F-4D/E (1969-1975)   Code: JJ
Aircraft lost: 34 F-105D, 2 F-105F, 11 F-4E

35th Tactical Fighter Squadron *Black Panthers*
Deployed on TDY to Korat RTAB from 41 AD, Yokota AB, Japan, 24 Sep-20 Nov 1964; deployed on TDY to Takhli RTAB under 2 AD from 6441 TFW, Yokota AB, 4 May-26 Jun 1965 and 19 Oct-15 Nov 1965; attached to 366 TFW, Da Nang from 3 TFW, Kunsan AB, South Korea, 3 Apr 1972; attached to 388 TFW, Korat from 3 TFW, 12 Jun 1972; returned to Kunsan AB, 12 Oct 1972
Aircraft: F-105D (1964-1965), F-4D (1972)   Code: UP (F-4D)
Aircraft lost: 2 F-4D

36th Tactical Fighter Squadron *Flying Fiends*
Deployed on TDY to Korat RTAB under 2 AD from 41 AD, Yokota AB, Japan, 9 Aug-5 Oct 1964; deployed on TDY to Takhli RTAB under 2 AD from 41 AD, 6 Mar-4 May 1965; deployed on TDY to Takhli from 6441 TFW, Yokota AB, 26 Aug-28 Oct 1965. Aircraft: F-105D/F   Aircraft lost: 9 F-105D

41st Tactical Reconnaissance Squadron
Assigned to Takhli RTAB under Thirteenth AF from 363 TRW, Shaw AFB, SC, 20 Oct 1965; attached to 355 TFW, Takhli, 8 Nov 1965; assigned to 460 TRW, Tan Son Nhut, 18 Feb 1966 but remained at Takhli until Jun 1966 still attached to 355 TFW; reassigned to 432 TRW, Udorn RTAB, 18 Sep 1966 but remained at Takhli; redesignated 41 TEWS, 15 Mar 1967; reassigned to 355 TFW, Takhli, 15 Aug 1967; inactivated, 31 Oct 1969. Aircraft: EB-66B/C/E Code: RC
Aircraft lost: 2 EB-66B, 6 EB-66C, 1 EB-66E

41st Tactical Reconnaissance Squadron Detachment 1
Attached to 33 TG, Tan Son Nhut, Apr 1965; attached to 6250 CSG, Tan Son Nhut, Jun 1965; inactivated, Apr 1966.
Aircraft: EB-66B/C   Aircraft lost: 1 EB-66B

42nd Tactical Electronic Warfare Squadron
Activated at Takhli RTAB under PACAF, 15 Dec 1967 and assigned to 355 TFW, Takhli, 1 Jan 1968; attached to 388 TFW, Korat RTAB, 23 Sep 1970; reassigned to 388 TFW, 15 Oct 1970; inactivated, 15 Mar 1974.
Aircraft: EB-66B/C/E Codes: RH and JW
Aircraft lost: 2 EB-66B, 3 EB-66C

43rd Tactical Fighter Squadron
Deployed on TDY to Cam Ranh Bay from 15 TFW, MacDill AFB, Fla via Clark AB, Philippines, 21 Oct 1965; attached to 12 TFW, Cam Ranh Bay, 8 Nov 1965-4 Jan 1966.
Aircraft: F-4C   Aircraft lost: 0

44th Tactical Fighter Squadron *Vampires*
Deployed on TDY to Korat RTAB under 2 AD from 18 TFW, Kadena AB, Okinawa, Aug 1964-25 Feb 1965, 21 Apr-23 Jun 1965 (attached to 6234 TFW from 5 Apr 1965) and 19-29 Oct 1965; reassigned to 388 TFW, Korat from 18 TFW, 25 Apr 1967 in Wild Weasel role; operated from Takhli RTAB, 1-27 Feb 1969; reassigned to 355 TFW, Takhli, 10 Oct 1969; reassigned to Thirteenth AF but remained at Takhli until inactivated, 10 Dec 1970. Aircraft: F-105D/F/G Codes: JE and RE
Aircraft lost: 7 F-105D, 5 F-105F, 1 F-105G

45th Tactical Fighter Squadron
Deployed to 2 AD at Ubon RTAB under 2 AD from 15 TFW, MacDill AFB, Fla, 4 Apr-10 Aug 1965.
Aircraft: F-4C   Aircraft lost: 2

45th Tactical Reconnaissance Squadron *Polka Dots*
Able Mable detachment on TDY to Don Muang Airport, Bankok from 39 AD, Misawa AB, Japan, Nov 1961-1 May 1962 and 14 Nov-14 Dec 1962; detachment on TDY to Tan Son Nhut from 39 AD, 14 Dec 1962-5 May 1963, 1 Nov 1963-3 May 1964 and 1 Feb-6 Nov 1965; detachment on TDY to Udorn RTAB from 39 AD, 1 Nov 1965-15 Aug 1966; deployed on TDY as Detachment 1, 45 TRS to 460 TRW, Tan Son Nhut, 8 Jul 1966; reassigned to 475 TFW, Misawa, 15 Jan 1968 but remained as Detachment 1, 45 TRS at Tan Son Nhut until withdrawn, 1 Nov 1970.
Aircraft: RF-101C Code: AH Aircraft lost: 13

47th Tactical Fighter Squadron
Deployed on TDY to Ubon RTAB from 15 TFW, MacDill AFB, Fla, 22 Jul-27 Nov 1965. Aircraft: F-4C Aircraft lost: 5

58th Tactical Fighter Squadron
Deployed on TDY to 432 TRW, Udorn RTAB from 33 TFW, Eglin AFB, Fla, 29 Apr-18 Oct 1972; deployed on TDY to 8 TFW, Udorn from 33 TFW, 8 Jun-14 Sep 1973.
Aircraft: F-4E Code: ED Aircraft lost: 1

64th Fighter Interceptor Squadron *Scorpions*
Assigned to 405 FW, Clark AB, Philippines, 10 Jun 1966; detachments on TDY to Bien Hoa, Da Nang, Don Muang and Tan Son Nhut; inactivated, 15 Dec 1969.
Aircraft: F-102A, TF-102A   Code: PE
Aircraft lost: 1 F-102A

67th Tactical Fighter Squadron *Fighting Cocks*
Deployed on TDY to Korat RTAB under 2 AD from 18 TFW, Kadena AB, Okinawa, Aug 1964-Jan 1965; deployed on TDY to 6234 TFW, Korat RTAB from 18 TFW, Kadena AB, Okinawa, 18 Feb-26 Apr 1965 and 16 Aug-23 Oct 1965; Wild Weasel F-4C detachment deployed to 388 TFW, Korat from 18 TFW, Kadena, 23 Sep 1972-18 Feb 1973 and 20 Apr-2 May 1975.
Aircraft: F-105D/F (1964-1965), F-4C (1972-1993)
Code: ZG (F-4C) Aircraft lost: 11 F-105D, 1 F-105F

68th Tactical Fighter Squadron
Deployed on TDY to 6234 TFW, Korat RTAB from 8 TFW, George AFB, Calif, 27 Aug-6 Dec 1965 but was based at Ubon RTAB from 24 Nov 1965. Aircraft: F-4C Aircraft lost: 1

71st Special Operations Squadron
Assigned to 14 SOW, Nha Trang, 20 Dec 1968 with detachments at Phan Rang and Tan Son Nhut; redesignated 17 SOS, 1 Jun 1969. Aircraft: AC-119G   Aircraft lost: 0

74th Tactical Fighter Squadron
Deployed on TDY to Korat RTAB from 23 TFW, England AFB, La, 2 Jul-28 Dec 1973 and attached to 354 TFW.
Aircraft: A-7D Code: EL Aircraft lost: 0

80th Tactical Fighter Squadron *Headhunters*
Deployed on TDY to Korat RTAB under 2 AD from 41 AD, Yokota AB, Japan, 30 Oct-29 Dec 1964; deployed on TDY to Takhli RTAB under 2 AD from 6441 TFW, Yokota, 27 Jun-26 Aug 1965. Aircraft: F-105D/F Aircraft lost: 1 F-105D

82nd Fighter Interceptor Squadron
Assigned to 51 FIW, Naha AB, Okinawa, 17 Feb 1966; detachments on TDY to Bien Hoa, Da Nang, Don Muang and Tan Son Nhut; inactivated, 31 May 1971.
Aircraft: F-102A, TF-102A Code: NV Aircraft lost: 0

90th Tactical Fighter Squadron *Pair o' Dice*
Assigned to 3 TFW, Bien Hoa from 401 TFW, England AFB, La, 8 Feb 1966; converted to A-37B and redesignated 90 AS, 12 Dec 1969; redesignated 90 SOS and reassigned to 14 SOW, Phan Rang but moved to Nha Trang, 31 Oct 1970; reassigned to 483 TAW, Cam Ranh Bay, 1 Sep 1971 but remained at Nha Trang; reassigned to 18 TFW, Kadena AB, Okinawa 15 Apr 1972.
Aircraft: F-100D/F (1966-1969), A-37B (1969-1972)
Codes: CB (F-100) and CG (A-37)
Aircraft lost: 12 F-100D, 2 F-100F

120th Tactical Fighter Squadron, Colorado Air National Guard
Assigned to 35 TFW, Phan Rang from 140 TFG, Denver, Colo, 30 Apr 1968-18 Apr 1969.
Aircraft: F-100C/F Code: VS Aircraft lost: 3 F-100C

136th Tactical Fighter Squadron,
New York Air National Guard *Rocky's Raiders*
Assigned to 31 TFW, Tuy Hoa from 107 TFG, Niagara Falls, NY, 14 Jun 1968-25 May 1969.
Aircraft: F-100C/F Code: SG Aircraft lost: 5 F-100C

174th Tactical Fighter Squadron, Iowa Air National Guard
Assigned to 37 TFW, Phu Cat from 185 TFG, Sioux City, Iowa, 14 May 1968-11 May 1969.
Aircraft: F-100C/F Code: HA Aircraft lost: 3 F-100C

188th Tactical Fighter Squadron,
New Mexico Air National Guard *Enchilada Air Force*
Assigned to 31 TFW, Tuy Hoa from 150 TFG, Kirtland AFB, N Mex, 7 Jun 1968-18 May 1969.
Aircraft: F-100C/F Code: SK Aircraft lost: 4 F-100C

306th Tactical Fighter Squadron
Deployed to Tuy Hoa from Homestead AFB, Fla with 31 TFW, 16 Dec 1966; returned to Homestead AFB with 31 TFW, 15 Oct 1970. Aircraft: F-100D/F Code: SD
Aircraft lost: 5 F-100D, 1 F-100F

307th Tactical Fighter Squadron
Deployed on TDY to 34 TG, Bien Hoa from 31 TFW, Homestead AFB, Fla, 24 Jun 1965; attached to 6251 TFW, Bien Hoa, Jul 1965; attached to 3 TFW, Bien Hoa, 21 Nov 1965; returned to 31 TFW, 6 Dec 1965; attached on TDY to 432 TRW, Udorn RTAB from 31 TFW, 29 Jul-28 Oct 1972.
Aircraft: F-100D/F (1965), F-4E (1972) Code: ZF (F-4)
Aircraft lost: 3 F-4E

308th Tactical Fighter Squadron *Emerald Knights*
Assigned to 3 TFW, Bien Hoa from 31 TFW, Homestead AFB, Fla, 2 Dec 1965; attached to 31 TFW, Tuy Hoa, 15 Nov 1966; assigned to 31 TFW, 25 Dec 1966; became non-operational, 10 Sep 1970; assigned to 4403 TFW, England AFB, La, 1 Oct 1970; converted to F-4E with 31 TFW at Homestead AFB; attached to 432 TRW, Udorn RTAB from 31 TFW, 28 Apr-29 Jul 1972; attached to 8 TFW, Ubon RTAB from 31 TFW, Homestead AFB, 11 Dec 1972-11 Jun 1973.
Aircraft: F-100D/F (1965-1970), F-4D/E (1972-1973)
Codes: SM (F-100) and ZF (F-4)
Aircraft lost: 17 F-100D, 1 F-4D, 4 F-4E

309th Troop Carrier Squadron
Assigned to 315 TCG, Tan Son Nhut, Jul 1963; redesignated 309 ACS, 8 Mar 1965; reassigned to 315 ACW, Tan Son Nhut, 8 Mar 1966; moved to Phan Rang, 15 Jun 1967; redesignated 309 SOS, 1 Aug 1968; redesignated 309 TAS, 1 Jan 1970; became non-operational, 1 Jul 1970; inactivated, 31 Jul 1970.
Aircraft: C-123B/K Code: WH Aircraft lost: 2

309th Tactical Fighter Squadron
Deployed to Tuy Hoa from Homestead AFB, Fla with 31 TFW, 16 Dec 1966; became non-operational, 10 Sep 1970; reassigned to 4403 TFW, England AFB, La, 9 Oct 1970.
Aircraft: F-100D/F Code: SS Aircraft lost: 8 F-100D, 1 F-100F

310th Troop Carrier Squadron
Assigned to 315 TCG, Tan Son Nhut, 8 Jul 1963; redesignated 310 ACS, 8 Mar 1965; moved to Nha Trang, 29 Jun 1965; reassigned to 315 ACW, Tan Son Nhut, 8 Mar 1966; moved to Phan Rang, 14 Jul 1967; redesignated 310 SOS, 1 Aug 1968; redesignated 310 TAS, 1 Jan 1970; reassigned to 377 ABW, Tan Son Nhut, 15 Jan 1972; inactivated, 15 Nov 1972.
Aircraft: C-123B/K, UC-123K Code: WM Aircraft lost: 11 C-123

311th Troop Carrier Squadron
Redesignated from 777 TCS and assigned to 315 TCG at Da Nang, 1 Jul 1963; redesignated 311 ACS, 8 Mar 1965; reassigned to 315 ACW, Tan Son Nhut, 8 Mar 1966; moved to Phan Rang, 15 Jun 1967 with detachments at Da Nang and Tan Son Nhut; redesignated 311 SOS, 1 Aug 1968; redesignated 311 TAS, 1 Jan 1970; became non-operational, 15 Sep 1971; inactivated, 5 Oct 1971.
Aircraft: C-123B/K Code: WV Aircraft lost: 7

333rd Tactical Fighter Squadron *Redleg Lancers*
Assigned to 355 TFW, Takhli RTAB from 4 TFW, Seymour-Johnson AFB, NC, 8 Dec 1965; reassigned to 23 TFW, McConnell AFB, Kans, 15 Oct 1970. Aircraft: F-105D/F
Code: RK Aircraft lost: 46 F-105D, 4 F-105F

334th Tactical Fighter Squadron *Eagles*
Deployed on TDY to 6235 TFW, Takhli RTAB (355 TFW from 8 Nov 1965) from 4 TFW, Seymour-Johnson AFB, NC, 2 Sep 1965-5 Feb 1966; converted to F-4E and deployed on TDY to 8 TFW, Ubon RTAB from 4 TFW, Seymour-Johnson AFB, 11 Apr-5 Aug 1972 and 30 Sep 1972-18 Mar 1973.
Aircraft: F-105D/F (1965-1966), F-4D/E (1972-1973)
Codes: SA and SJ (F-4) Aircraft lost: 6 F-105D, 1 F-4D, 3 F-4E

335th Tactical Fighter Squadron *Chiefs*
Deployed on TDY to 355 TFW, Takhli RTAB from 4 TFW, Seymour-Johnson AFB, NC, 6 Nov-6 Dec 1965; converted to F-4E and deployed on TDY to 8 TFW, Ubon RTAB from 4 TFW, Seymour-Johnson AFB, 6 Jul-22 Dec 1972.
Aircraft: F-105D/F (1965), F-4D/E (1972) Code: SJ (F-4)
Aircraft lost: 1 F-4D, 2 F-4E

336th Tactical Fighter Squadron
Deployed on TDY to 8 TFW, Ubon RTAB from 4 TFW, Seymour-Johnson AFB, NC, 12 Apr-30 Sep 1972 and 9 Mar-7 Sep 1973. Aircraft: F-4E   Codes: SC and SJ   Aircraft lost: 2

346th Troop Carrier Squadron
Deployed on TDY to Tan Son Nhut and Da Nang from 464 TCW, Pope AFB, NC, 2 Jan-Jun 1962. Aircraft: C-123B   Aircraft lost: 0

352nd Tactical Fighter Squadron
Assigned to 366 TFW, Phan Rang, 15 Aug 1966; reassigned to 35 TFW, Phan Rang, 10 Oct 1966; inactivated, 31 Jul 1971.
Aircraft: F-100D/F   Code: VM   Aircraft lost: 12 F-100D, 1 F-100F

353rd Tactical Fighter Squadron
Deployed to Korat RTAB with 354 TFW, Myrtle Beach AFB, SC, 10 Oct 1972-15 Mar 1973.
Aircraft: A-7D   Code: MB   Aircraft lost: 2

354th Tactical Fighter Squadron *Fighting Bulldogs*
Deployed on TDY to Korat RTAB under 2 AD from 355 TFW, McConnell AFB, Kans, 13 Mar 1965; attached to 6234 TFW, Korat, 5 Apr 1965; returned to 355 TFW, 18 Jun 1965; transferred to Takhli RTAB with 355 TFW, 28 Nov 1965; inactivated, 15 Oct 1970 and reactivated at Davis-Monthan AFB, Ariz same day; converted to A-7D and deployed to 354 TFW, Korat from 355 TFW, Davis-Monthan AFB, 14 Jan-4 Jul 1973.
Aircraft: F-105D/F/G (1965-1970), A-7D (1973)
Codes: RM (F-105) and MB (A-7D)
Aircraft lost: 50 F-105D, 9 F-105F, 2 F-105G, 1 A-7D

355th Tactical Fighter Squadron
Attached to 37 TFW, Phu Cat from 354 TFW, Myrtle Beach, SC, 3 Feb 1968; reassigned to 37 TFW, 5 Jul 1968; reassigned to 31 TFW, Tuy Hoa, 15 May 1969; inactivated, 30 Sep 1970 and reactivated under 354 TFW, Myrtle Beach AFB next day; converted to A-7D and deployed to Korat RTAB with 354 TFW, 10 Oct 1972-16 Mar 1973 and 15 Oct 1973-26 Apr 1974.
Aircraft: F-100D/F (1968-1970), A-7D (1972-1974)
Codes: HP and SP (F-100) and MB (A-7D)
Aircraft lost: 7 F-100D, 5 F-100F, 1 A-7D

356th Tactical Fighter Squadron
Deployed to Korat RTAB with 354 TFW, Myrtle Beach AFB, SC, 10 Oct 1972-4 May 1974.
Aircraft: A-7D   Code: MB   Aircraft lost: 0

357th Tactical Fighter Squadron *Lickin' Dragons*
Deployed on TDY to Korat RTAB under 2 AD from 355 TFW, McConnell AFB, Kans, Aug-12 Dec 1964; deployed on TDY to 6234 TFW, Korat RTAB from 355 TFW, 12 Jun-8 Nov 1965; deployed to Takhli RTAB with 355 TFW, 29 Jan 1966; inactivated, 10 Dec 1970. Aircraft: F-105D/F/G   Code: RU
Aircraft lost: 42 F-105D, 8 F-105F

358th Tactical Fighter Squadron
Deployed to 354 TFW, Korat RTAB from 355 TFW, Davis-Monthan AFB, Ariz, 28 Dec 1973-14 May 1974.
Aircraft: A-7D   Code: MB   Aircraft lost: 0

360th Tactical Reconnaissance Squadron
Activated at Tan Son Nhut under 460 TRW, 8 Apr 1966 with detachments at Phu Bai and Nakhon Phanom; redesignated 360 TEWS, 15 Mar 1967; reassigned to 483 TAW, Cam Ranh Bay, 31 Aug 1971; reassigned to 377 ABW, Tan Son Nhut, 1 Feb 1972; inactivated, 24 Nov 1972.
Aircraft: EC-47N/P/Q   Code: AJ   Aircraft lost: 0

360th Tactical Electronic Warfare Squadron, Detachment 1
Attached to 460 TRW, Tan Son Nhut, 1 Jun 1970; inactivated, 31 Aug 1971. Aircraft: EC-47N/P/Q   Code: AJ   Aircraft lost: 0

361st Tactical Reconnaissance Squadron
Activated at Tan Son Nhut under 460 TRW, 8 Apr 1966 but based at Nha Trang with detachments at Phu Cat, Pleiku and Vung Tau; redesignated 361 TEWS, 15 Mar 1967; moved to Phu Cat, 18 Sep 1969; reassigned to 483 TAW, Cam Ranh Bay, 31 Aug 1971; reassigned to 56 SOW, Nakhon Phanom RTAB with a detachment at Ubon RTAB, 1 Sep 1972; inactivated, 30 Jun 1974. Aircraft: EC-47N/P/Q   Code: AL
Aircraft lost: 3 EC-47P, 2 EC-47Q

361st Tactical Reconnaissance Squadron, Detachment 1
Activated at Tan Son Nhut under 460 TRW and based at Pleiku, 8 Sep 1966; inactivated, 1 Feb 1967
Aircraft: EC-47N/P/Q   Code: AL   Aircraft lost: 0

362nd Tactical Electronic Warfare Squadron
Activated at Tan Son Nhut under 460 TRW, 1 Feb 1967 but based at Pleiku with detachments at Da Nang and Nakhon Phanom RTAB; redesignated 362 TEWS, 15 Mar 1967; reassigned to 483 TAW, Cam Ranh Bay, 31 Aug 1971; reassigned to 366 TFW, Da Nang, 1 Feb 1972; inactivated, 27 Jun 1972. Aircraft: EC-47N/P/Q   Code: AN
Aircraft lost: 1 EC-47N, 4 EC-47P, 2 EC-47Q

389th Tactical Fighter Squadron
Deployed to Phan Rang with 366 TFW from Holloman AFB, N Mex, 14 Mar 1966; moved to Da Nang, 10 Oct 1966; converted to F-4D by Jan 1968; reassigned to 37 TFW, Phu Cat, 15 Jun 1969; reassigned to 12 TFW, Phu Cat, 31 Mar 1970; inactivated, 15 Oct 1971 and reactivated the same day at Mountain Home, Idaho under 347 TFW.
Aircraft: F-4C/D   Codes: AA-AZ and HB
Aircraft lost: 13 F-4C, 10 F-4D

390th Tactical Fighter Squadron
Assigned to 6252 TFW, Da Nang from 366 TFW, Holloman AFB, N Mex, 29 Oct 1965 but actually arrived at Da Nang c.17 Nov 1965; reassigned to 35 TFW, Da Nang, 8 Apr 1966; reassigned to 366 TFW, Da Nang, 10 Oct 1966; converted to F-4D by Jan 1968; became non-operational, 14 Jun 1972; inactivated, 30 Jun 1972 and reactivated the same day at Mountain Home, Idaho under 347 TFW.
Aircraft: F-4C/D/E   Codes: BA-BZ and LF
Aircraft lost: 25 F-4C, 20 F-4D, 2 F-4E

391st Tactical Fighter Squadron
Attached to 12 TFW, Cam Ranh Bay from 366 TFW, Holloman AFB, N Mex, 26 Jan 1966; reassigned to Seventh AF, 1 Apr 1966 but remained attached to 12 TFW; reassigned to 12 TFW, 23 Jun 1966; reassigned to 475 TFW, Misawa AB, Japan, 22 Jul 1968.
Aircraft: F-4C   Code: XT   Aircraft lost: 8

416th Tactical Fighter Squadron *Silver Knights*
Deployed on TDY to Da Nang from 3 TFW, England AFB, La, 14 Mar 1965; moved to Bien Hoa, Jun 1965; returned to 3 TFW, 21 Jul 1965; deployed to Bien Hoa with 3 TFW, 16 Nov 1965 but based at Tan Son Nhut; moved to Bien Hoa, 15 Jun 1966; reassigned to 37 TFW, Phu Cat, 15 Apr 1967; reassigned to 31 TFW, Tuy Hoa, 28 May 1969; became non-operational, 5 Sep 1970; reassigned to 4403 TFW, England AFB, La, 23 Sep 1970.
Aircraft: F-100D/F   Codes: HE and SE
Aircraft lost: 15 F-100D, 8 F-100F

417th Tactical Fighter Squadron
Deployed on TDY to Takhli RTAB with 49 TFW from Holloman AFB, N Mex, 4 May-2 Oct 1972.
Aircraft: F-4D   Codes: HE and HO   Aircraft lost: 0

421st Air Refuelling Squadron, Detachment 1
Deployed on TDY to Takhli RTAB from 41 AD, Yokota AB, Japan, Aug-Oct 1964. Aircraft: KB-50J   Aircraft lost: 1

421st Air Refuelling Squadron, Detachment 2
Deployed on TDY to Tan Son Nhut from 41 AD, Yokota AB, Japan, Jun-Oct 1964. Aircraft: KB-50J   Aircraft lost: 0

421st Tactical Fighter Squadron *Fighting Cavaliers*
Deployed on TDY to Korat RTAB under 2 AD from 835 AD, McConnell AFB, Kans, 15 Seo-23 Nov 1964; reassigned to 6234 TFW, Korat RTAB from 835 AD, 20 Nov 1965; reassigned to 388 TFW, Korat, 8 Apr 1966; reassigned to 15 TFW, MacDill AFB, Fla, 25 Apr 1967; converted to F-4E and reassigned to 366 TFW, Da Nang, 16 Apr 1969 but detached to 475 TFW, Misawa AB, Japan, 23 Apr 1969 and did not arrive at Da Nang until 26 Jun 1969; moved to Takhli RTAB, 27 Jun 1972; reassigned to 432 TRW, Udorn RTAB, 31 Oct 1972; moved to Clark AB, Philippines, 13 Dec 1975 for reassignment to 388 TFW, Hill AFB, Utah, 23 Dec 1975.
Aircraft: F-105D/F (1965-1967), F-4D/E (1969-1975)
Codes: LC and UD (F-4)
Aircraft lost: 27 F-105D, 2 F-4D, 13 F-4E

428th Tactical Fighter Squadron *Buccaneers*
Deployed TDY to Takhli RTAB from 474 TFW, Cannon AFB, N Mex, 18 May-3 Sep 1962; deployed on TDY to Da Nang and Takhli, Aug 1964-Mar 1965; converted to F-111A and deployed on TDY to Takhli with 474 TFW from Nellis AFB, Nev, 2 Jan 1973; reassigned to 347 TFW, Takhli, 30 Jul 1973; moved to Korat RTAB, 12 Jul 1974; inactivated, 15 Jun 1975.
Aircraft: F-100D/F (1962-1965), F-111A (1972-1975)
Codes: NA and HG (F-111A)   Aircraft lost: 3 F-100D

428th Tactical Fighter Squadron, Detachment 1
Activated at Nellis AFB, Nev under 474 TFW, 20 Jan 1968; deployed on TDY to Takhli RTAB, 18 Mar-22 Nov 1968.
Aircraft: F-111A   Aircraft lost: 3

429th Tactical Fighter Squadron *Black Falcons*
Deployed on TDY to 6251 TFW, Bien Hoa from 474 TFW, Cannon AFB, N Mex, 13 Jul 1965 on attachment to 27 TFW; attached to 3 TFW, 21 Nov 1965; returned to 474 TFW, 16 Dec 1965; converted to F-111A and deployed on TDY to Takhli RTAB with 474 TFW from Nellis AFB, Nev, 29 Sep 1972-26 Jan 1973 and 18 Mar-29 Jul 1973; reassigned to 347 TFW, Takhli, 30 Jul 1973; moved to Korat RTAB, 12 Jul 1974; reassigned to 474 TFW, Nellis AFB, 21 Jun 1975.
Aircraft: F-100D/F (1965), F-111A (1972-1975)
Codes: NA and HG (F-111A)   Aircraft lost: 5 F-100D, 5 F-111A

430th Tactical Fighter Squadron *Tigers*
Deployed on TDY to Takhli RTAB from 474 TFW, Cannon AFB, N Mex, 3 Sep-13 Dec 1962; converted to F-111A and deployed on TDY to Takhli with 474 TFW from Nellis AFB, Nev, 27 Sep 1972-23 Mar 1973.
Aircraft: F-100D/F (1962), F-111A (1972-1973)
Code: NA (F-111A)   Aircraft lost: 3 F-111A

433rd Tactical Fighter Squadron *Satan's Angels*
Deployed to Ubon RTAB from George AFB, Calif with 8 TFW, 8 Dec 1965; converted to F-4D, Oct 1967; inactivated, 23 Jul 1974.
Aircraft: F-4C/D   Codes: FG and WP
Aircraft lost: 22 F-4C, 14 F-4D

434th Tactical Fighter Squadron
Attached to 49 TFW on TDY at Takhli RTAB from 35 TFW, George AFB, Calif, 12 Aug-6 Oct 1972.
Aircraft: F-4D/E   Code: GA   Aircraft lost: 1 F-4D

435th Tactical Fighter Squadron *Eagle Squadron*
Deployed on TDY to 6252 TFW, Da Nang from 479 TFW, George AFB, Calif, 12 Oct-20 Dec 1965; detachment deployed on TDY to 8 TFW, Ubon RTAB from 479 TFW, 5 Jun 1966 but based at Udorn RTAB; reassigned to 8 TFW, 24 Jul 1966; converted to F-4D and moved to Ubon, 2 Aug 1967; inactivated, 8 Aug 1974.
Aircraft: F-104C (1965-1967), F-4D (1967-1974)
Codes: FO and WP (F-4D)
Aircraft lost: 9 F-104C, 25 F-4D, 1 F-4E

436th Tactical Fighter Squadron
Deployed on TDY to 6252 TFW, Da Nang from 479 TFW, George AFB, Calif, Jul-Oct 1965.
Aircraft: F-104C   Aircraft lost: 4

457th Troop Carrier Squadron
Activated from 134th Aviation Company, US Army, Can Tho under PACAF, 12 Oct 1966 and assigned to 483 TCW, Cam Ranh Bay, 1 Jan 1967 with a detachment at Don Muang Airport, Bankok; redesignated 457 TAS, 1 Aug 1967; became non-operational, 1 Apr 1972; inactivated, 30 Apr 1972.
Aircraft: C-7A/B   Code: KA   Aircraft lost: 3 C-7B

458th Troop Carrier Squadron
Activated from 135th Aviation Company, US Army, Dong Ba Thin under PACAF, 12 Oct 1966 and assigned to 483 TCW, Cam Ranh Bay, 1 Jan 1967 with a detachment at Nha Trang; redesignated 458 TAS, 1 Aug 1967; inactivated, 1 Mar 1972.
Aircraft: C-7A/B   Code: KC   Aircraft lost: 2 C-7B

459th Troop Carrier Squadron
Activated from 92nd Aviation Company, US Army, Qui Nhon under PACAF, 12 Oct 1966 and assigned to 483 TCW, Cam Ranh Bay, 1 Jan 1967 but based at Phu Cat with detachments at Da Nang and Pleiku; redesignated 459 TAS, 1 Aug 1967; became non-operational, 15 May 1970; inactivated, 1 Jun 1970
Aircraft: C-7A/B   Code: KE   Aircraft lost: 4 C-7B

469th Tactical Fighter Squadron *Fighting Bulls*
Deployed on TDY to Korat RTAB under 2 AD from 355 TFW, McConnell AFB, Kans, Jan-13 Mar 1965; attached to 6234 TFW, Korat RTAB from 355 TFW, 8 Nov 1965; assigned to 388 TFW, Korat, 8 Apr 1966; converted to F-4E, Nov 1968; inactivated, 31 Oct 1972.
Aircraft: F-105D/F (1965-1968), F-4E (1968-1972)
Code: JV   Aircraft lost: 56 F-105D, 7 F-4E

476th Tactical Fighter Squadron
Deployed on TDY to 6252 TFW, Da Nang from 479 TFW, George AFB, Calif, 20 Apr-Jul 1965.
Aircraft: F-104C   Aircraft lost: 1

480th Tactical Fighter Squadron
Assigned to 6252 TFW, Da Nang from 366 TFW, Holloman AFB, N Mex, 1 Feb 1966; attached to 35 TFW, Da Nang, 8 Apr 1966; assigned to 35 TFW, 23 Jun 1966; reassigned to 366 TFW, Da Nang, 10 Oct 1966; converted to F-4D by Mar 1968; reassigned to 37 TFW, Phu Cat, 15 Apr 1969; reassigned to 12 TFW, Phu Cat, 31 Mar 1970; inactivated 17 Nov 1971.
Aircraft: F-4C/D   Codes: CA-CZ and HK
Aircraft lost: 20 F-4C, 14 F-4D

481st Tactical Fighter Squadron *Crusaders*
Deployed on TDY to 6250 CSG, Tan Son Nhut from 27 TFW, Cannon AFB, N Mex, via Clark AB, Philippines, 29 Jun-30 Nov 1965. Aircraft: F-100D/F   Aircraft lost: 6 F-100D

497th Tactical Fighter Squadron *Night Owls*
Deployed to Ubon RTAB from George AFB, Calif with 8 TFW, 8 Dec 1965; converted to F-4D Nov 1967; inactivated, 16 Sep 1974.
Aircraft: F-4C/D   Codes: FP and WP
Aircraft lost: 14 F-4C, 26 F-4D

509th Fighter Interceptor Squadron
Assigned to 405 FW, Clark AB, Philippines, 9 Apr 1959; detachments on TDY to Bien Hoa, Da Nang, Don Muang and Tan Son Nhut from 21 Mar 1962 until inactivated, 24 Jul 1970.
Aircraft: F-102A, TF-102A   Code: PK
Aircraft lost: 12 F-102A, 1 TF-102A

510th Tactical Fighter Squadron *Buzzards*
Deployed on TDY to JTF 116 at Don Muang Airport, Bangkok from 405 FW, Clark AB, Philippines, 16 May-8 Jun 1962; detachment deployed to Takhli and Da Nang, Jun 1964; deployed to Bien Hoa from England AFB, La, with 3 TFW, 10 Nov 1965; inactivated, 15 Nov 1969.
Aircraft: F-100D/F   Code: CE   Aircraft lost: 16 F-100D

522nd Tactical Fighter Squadron *Fireballs*
Deployed on TDY to Takhli RTAB under 2 AD from 27 TFW, Cannon AFB, N Mex, 12 Dec 1962-15 Feb 1963, 16 Mar-6 May 1964 and 20 Sep-15 Nov 1964.
Aircraft: F-100D/F   Aircraft lost: 0

523rd Tactical Fighter Squadron
Deployed on TDY to 432 TRW, Udorn RTAB from 405 FW, Clark AB, Philippines, 9 Apr-24 Oct 1972.
Aircraft: F-4D   Code: PN   Aircraft lost: 3

524th Tactical Fighter Squadron *Hounds of Heaven*
Deployed on TDY to Takhli RTAB under 2 AD from 27 TFW, Cannon AFB, N Mex, 9-27 Jun 1963 and 21 Jan-19 Mar 1964.
Aircraft: F-100D/F   Aircraft lost: 0

531st Tactical Fighter Squadron
Deployed to Bien Hoa from England AFB, La with 3 TFW, 8 Nov 1965; inactivated, 31 Jul 1970.
Aircraft: F-100D/F   Code: HP   Aircraft lost: 18 F-100D

535th Troop Carrier Squadron
Activated from 57th Aviation Company, US Army, Vung Tau under PACAF, 12 Oct 1966 and assigned to 483 TCW, Cam Ranh Bay, 1 Jan 1967 but based at Vung Tau with detachments at Da Nang and Phu Cat; redesignated 535 TAS, 1 Aug 1967; moved to Cam Ranh Bay, Jul 1970; inactivated, 24 Jan 1972.
Aircraft: C-7A/B   Code: KH   Aircraft lost: 1 C-7A, 1 C-7B

536th Troop Carrier Squadron
Activated from 61st Aviation Company, US Army, Vung Tau under PACAF, 12 Oct 1966 and assigned to 483 TCW, Cam Ranh Bay, 1 Jan 1967 but based at Vung Tau with a detachment at Can Tho; redesignated 536 TAS, 1 Aug 1967; moved to Cam Ranh Bay, Jul 1970; inactivated, 15 Oct 1971.
Aircraft: C-7A/B   Code: KL   Aircraft lost: 1 C-7A

537th Troop Carrier Squadron
Activated from 17th Aviation Company, US Army, An Khe under PACAF, 12 Oct 1966 and assigned to 483 TCW, Cam Ranh Bay, 1 Jan 1967 but based at Phu Cat with a detachment at An Khe; redesignated 537 TAS, 1 Aug 1967; inactivated, 31 Aug 1971.
Aircraft: C-7A/B   Code: KN   Aircraft lost: 1 C-7A, 5 C-7B

553rd Reconnaissance Squadron
Activated at Otis AFB, Mass under 553 RW, 25 Feb 1967; moved to Korat RTAB, 31 Oct 1967 with QU-22s operating from Nakhon Phanom RTAB; reassigned to 388 TFW, Korat, 15 Dec 1970; inactivated, 31 Dec 1971.
Aircraft: EC-121R, QU-22B, YQU-22A   Aircraft lost: 0

554th Reconnaissance Squadron
Activated at Otis AFB, Mass under 553 RW, 25 Feb 1967; moved to Korat RTAB, 31 Oct 1967 with QU-22s operating from Nakhon Phanom RTAB; reassigned to 56 SOW, Nakhon Phanom, 15 Dec 1970; inactivated, 30 Sep 1972.
Aircraft: EC-121R, QU-22B, YQU-22A
Aircraft lost: 2 EC-121R, 6 QU-22B

555th Tactical Fighter Squadron *Triple Nickel*
Attached to 8 TFW, Ubon RTAB from 12 TFW, MacDill AFB, Fla via 51 FIW, Naha AB, Okinawa, 22 Feb 1966 but based at Udorn RTAB; reassigned to 8 TFW, 25 Mar 1966 but still based at Udorn; moved to Ubon, 20 Jul 1966; converted to F-4D, May 1967; assigned to 432 TRW, Udorn, 28 May 1968; inactivated, 5 Jul 1974 and reactivated same day under 58 TFTW, Luke AFB, Ariz
Aircraft: F-4C/D   Codes: FY and OY
Aircraft lost: 9 F-4C, 28 F-4D

556th Reconnaissance Squadron
Activated at Yokota AB, Japan, Jun 1967; detachments deployed to Don Muang Airport, Bankok from Jun 1967.
Aircraft: RB-57A/D, RC-130A   Code: GT   Aircraft lost: 0

557th Tactical Fighter Squadron
Deployed to Cam Ranh Bay with 12 TFW from MacDill AFB, Fla, 14 Nov 1965; became non-operational, 10 Mar 1970; inactivated, 31 Mar 1970.
Aircraft: F-4C   Code: XC   Aircraft lost: 19

558th Tactical Fighter Squadron
Deployed to Cam Ranh Bay with 12 TFW from MacDill AFB, Fla, 14 Nov 1965; detached to Kunsan AB, South Korea under 18 TFW control, 3 Feb-10 Mar 1968 and 26 Mar-22 Jul 1968; became non-operational, 10 Mar 1970; inactivated, 31 Mar 1970.
Aircraft: F-4C   Codes: XD and XT   Aircraft lost: 17

559th Tactical Fighter Squadron
Assigned to 12 TFW, Cam Ranh Bay from 836 AD, MacDill AFB, Fla, 27 Dec 1965; became non-operational, 23 Mar 1970; inactivated, 31 Mar 1970.
Aircraft: F-4C   Code: XN   Aircraft lost: 18

561st Tactical Fighter Squadron
Deployed on TDY to Takhli RTAB under 2 AD from 23 TFW, McConnell AFB, Kans, 6 Feb-10 Jul 1965 and attached to 6441 TFW from May 1965 and 6235 TFW from 8 Jul 1965.
Aircraft: F-105D/F   Aircraft lost: 0

561st Tactical Fighter Squadron, Detachment 1
Detachment deployed to 388 TFW, Korat RTAB from 23 TFW, McConnell AFB, Kans, 7 Apr 1972 (parent squadron reassigned to 832 AD, McConnell AFB, Kans, 1 Jul 1972); reassigned to 35 TFW, George AFB, Calif, 15 Jul 1973.
Aircraft: F-105G   Codes: MD and WW   Aircraft lost: 2

562nd Tactical Fighter Squadron
Deployed on TDY to 6235 TFW, Takhli RTAB from 23 TFW, McConnell AFB, Kans, 13 Aug 1965; attached to 355 TFW, Takhli, 8 Nov 1965; returned to 23 TFW, 6 Dec 1965.
Aircraft: F-105D/F   Aircraft lost: 6 F-105D

563rd Tactical Fighter Squadron *Ace of Spades*
Deployed on TDY to Takhli RTAB under 2 AD from 23 TFW, McConnell AFB, Kans, 8 Apr-15 Aug 1965 and attached to 6441 TFW from May 1965 and 6235 TFW from 8 Jul 1965.
Aircraft: F-105D/F   Aircraft lost: 11 F-105D

602nd Fighter Commando Squadron/Air Commando Sqn
Activated at Bien Hoa under 34 TG, 12 Oct 1964; attached to 6251 TFW, Bien Hoa, Jul 1965 with a detachment at Udorn RTAB; attached to 3 TFW, Bien Hoa, 21 Nov 1965; assigned to 6253 CSG, Nha Trang, Feb 1966 but remained attached to 3 TFW at Bien Hoa; reassigned to 14 ACW, Nha Trang, 8 Mar 1966 with a detachment at Nakhon Phanom RTAB; moved to Udorn, Apr 1966; reassigned to 56 ACW, Nakhon Phanom, 8 Apr 1967 but remained at Udorn until Mar 1968; redesignated 602 SOS, 1 Aug 1968; inactivated, 31 Dec 1970.
Aircraft: A-1E/G/H/J   Code: TT
Aircraft lost: 44 A-1E, 4 A-1G, 22 A-1H, 10 A-1J

603rd Air Commando Squadron, Detachment 1
Deployed to Nakhon Phanom RTAB from 1 ACW, England AFB, La and attached to 606 ACS, May 1966; inactivated, Apr 1967.
Aircraft: A-26A   Aircraft lost: 3

604th Air Commando Squadron
Assigned to 14 ACW, Nha Trang from 1 ACW, England AFB, La, Aug 1967 but detached to 3 TFW, Bien Hoa; redesignated 604 SOS, 1 Aug 1968; reassigned to 3 TFW, Bien Hoa, 1 Mar 1970; inactivated, 30 Sep 1970. Aircraft: A-37A/B   Code: CK
Aircraft lost: 10 A-37A, 1 A-37B

606th Air Commando Squadron
Activated at Nakhon Phanom RTAB under 634 CSG, 8 Mar 1966; assigned to 56 ACW, Nakhon Phanom, 8 Apr 1967; redesignated 606 SOS, 1 Aug 1968; inactivated, 15 Jun 1971
Aircraft: A-26A, C-123K, RT-28, T-28D, U-10D, UH-1F
Code: TO   Aircraft lost: 4 A-26A, 2 C-123K, 7 T-28D

609th Air Commando Squadron
Assigned to 56 ACW, Nakhon Phanom RTAB, 15 Sep 1967; redesignated 609 SOS, 1 Aug 1968; inactivated, 1 Dec 1969
Aircraft: A-26A   Code: TA   Aircraft lost: 5

612th Tactical Fighter Squadron
Deployed on TDY to Da Nang from 401 TFW, England AFB, La, Sep-Nov 1964; activated as Detachment 1, 612 TFS and attached to 366 TFW, Phan Rang, 15 May 1966; attached to 35 TFW, Phan Rang, 10 Oct 1966; attached to 37 TFW, Phu Cat, 8 Jun 1967; attached to 35 TFW, Phan Rang, 14 Apr 1969; redesignated 612 TFS, 35 TFW, 15 Mar 1971; reassigned to 401 TFW, Torrejon AB, Spain, 31 Jul 1971.
Aircraft: F-100D/F   Codes: HS and VS
Aircraft lost: 13 F-100D, 5 F-100F

613th Tactical Fighter Squadron
Deployed on TDY to Da Nang from 401 TFW, England AFB, La, Nov 1964-Jul 1965. Aircraft: F-100D/F   Aircraft lost: 6 F-100D

614th Tactical Fighter Squadron *Lucky Devils*
Deployed on TDY to Da Nang from 401 TFW, England AFB, La, Aug-Nov 1964; assigned to 366 TFW, Phan Rang, 18 Sep 1966; reassigned to 35 TFW, Phan Rang, 10 Oct 1966; reassigned to 401 TFW, Torrejon AB, Spain, 31 Jul 1971. Aircraft: F-100D/F
Code: VP   Aircraft lost: 16 F-100D, 3 F-100F

615th Tactical Fighter Squadron
Deployed on TDY to Da Nang from 401 TFW, England AFB, La via Clark AB, Philippines, Aug-Sep 1964 and Apr-Jun 1965; assigned to 366 TFW, Phan Rang, 16 Jul 1966; reassigned to 35 TFW, Phan Rang, 10 Oct 1966; inactivated, 31 Jul 1971
Aircraft: F-100D/F   Code: VZ   Aircraft lost: 20 F-100D, 1 F-100F

776th Troop Carrier Squadron
Deployed on TDY to Tan Son Nhut under 2 ADVON from 464 TCW, Pope AFB, NC, Jun 1962; redesignated 310 TCS, 1 Jul 1963.
Aircraft: C-123B   Aircraft lost: 0

777th Troop Carrier Squadron
Deployed on TDY to Da Nang and Don Muang Airport, Bankok under 2 ADVON from 464 TCW, Pope AFB, NC, 11 Jun 1962; redesignated 311 TCS, 1 Jul 1963.
Aircraft: C-123B   Aircraft lost: 2

4400th Combat Crew Training Squadron, Detachment 2A
Deployed to Bien Hoa, 5 Nov 1961; redesignated Detachment 2A, 1 ACG, c.17 Apr 1962; redesignated 1 ACS, 8 Jul 1963.
Aircraft: B-26B, RB-26, SC-47A, T-28D
Aircraft lost: 1 SC-47A

4503rd Tactical Fighter Squadron (Provisional)
Activated at Williams AFB, Ariz, 22 Jul 1965; deployed to Bien Hoa under PACAF, 26 Oct 1965; redesignated 10 FCS, 8 Apr 1966.
Aircraft: F-5C   Aircraft lost: 1

6010th Wild Weasel Squadron
Activated from Detachment 1, 12 TFS at Korat RTAB, 1 Nov 1970 and assigned to 388 TFW; redesignated 17 WWS, 1 Dec 1971.
Aircraft: F-105F/G   Code: ZB   Aircraft lost: 2 F-105G

6091st Reconnaissance Squadron, Detachment
Detachments deployed to Don Muang Airport, Bankok and Cam Ranh Bay from Yokota AB, Japan, from Jul 1964; redesignated 556 RS, June 1967.
Aircraft: RB-57A/D, RC-130A   Aircraft lost: 0

6460th Tactical Reconnaissance Squadron
Assigned to 460 TRW, Tan Son Nhut, 8 Jun 1966 but attached to 355 TFW, Takhli RTAB same day; reassigned to 432 TRW, Udorn RTAB, 18 Sep 1966; redesignated 6460 TEWS, 15 Mar 1967; reassigned to 355 TFW, 15 Aug 1967; inactivated, 1 Jan 1968.
Aircraft: EB-66B/C   Aircraft lost: 0

6461st Tactical Reconnaissance Squadron
Deployed to Udorn RTAB as Detachment 1, 9 TRS from 363 TRW, Shaw AFB, SC, 26 Jul 1966; redesignated 6461 TRS and assigned to 460 TRW, 29 Jul 1966 but still based at Udorn; reassigned to 432 TRW, Udorn 18 Sep 1966; merged with 11 TRS, 25 Oct 1966.
Aircraft: EB-66B/C, RF-4C   Aircraft lost: 0

Strategic Air Command Units

Strategic Air Command Wings

9th Strategic Reconnaissance Wing, Detachment
Detachment OL-8 activated at Kadena AB, Okinawa, 8 Mar 1968; redesignated Detachment OL-RK, 30 Oct 1970; redesignated Detachment OL-KA, 26 Oct 1971; redesignated Detachment 1, Aug 1974, inactivated, Jan 1990.
Aircraft: SR-71A   Aircraft lost: 2

43rd Strategic Wing
Activated at Andersen AFB, Guam under Eighth AF to replace 3960 SW, 1 Apr 1970; attached to 57 AD(P), 1 Jun 1972; reassigned to 8th AF, 15 Nov 1973; attached to 3 AD, 1 Jan 1975; inactivated, 30 Sep 1990.
Squadrons attached or assigned: 60 BS, 63 BS(P), 4182 BS
Aircraft: B-52D, KC-135A   Aircraft lost: 3 B-52D

72nd Strategic Wing (Provisional)
Activated at Andersen AFB, Guam under 57 AD(P) as holding wing for B-52G units on TDY, 1 Jun 1972; inactivated, 15 Nov 1973. Squadrons attached or assigned: 64 BS(P), 65 BS(P), 329 BS(P), 486 BS(P).
Aircraft: B-52G   Aircraft lost: 7

307th Strategic Wing
Activated at U-Tapao RTAB under Eighth AF to replace 4258 SW, 1 Apr 1970; attached to 17 AD(P), 1 Jun 1972; attached to 3 AD, 1 Jan 1975; inactivated, 30 Sep 1975.
Squadrons attached or assigned: 364 BS(P), 365 BS(P), 901 ARS(P), 4180 BS, 4181 BS.
Aircraft: B-52D, KC-135A   Aircraft lost: 11 B-52D

310th Strategic Wing (Provisional)
Activated at U-Tapao RTAB under 17 AD(P), 1 Jun 1972; inactivated, 1 Jul 1974.
Aircraft: KC-135A   Aircraft lost: 0

376th Strategic Wing
Activated at Kadena AB, Okinawa under Eighth AF to replace 4252 SW, 1 Apr 1970; attached to 3 AD, 1 Jan 1975; inactivated, 30 Oct 1991. Squadrons attached or assigned: 82 SRS, 909 ARS, 4102 ARS(P), 4180 BS, 4220 ARS.
Aircraft: B-52D, KC-135A, RC-135A   Aircraft lost: 0

3960th Strategic Wing
Activated at Andersen AFB, Guam under 3 AD and became holding wing for B-52D and B-52F units on TDY, 1 Apr 1955; inactivated and replaced by 43 SW, 31 Mar 1970.
Aircraft: B-52D/F   Aircraft lost: 2 B-52F

4080th Strategic Wing Detachment OL-20
Activated at Bien Hoa as a detachment of 4028 SRS, c.14 Feb 1964; redesignated as a detachment of 100 SRW, 25 Jun 1966 and detachment taken over by 349 SRS; moved to U-Tapao RTAB, 11 Jul 1970; redesignated 99 SRS, 1 Nov 1972; inactivated, 30 Jun 1976.
Aircraft: U-2A/C/F   Aircraft lost: 1 U-2C

4133rd Bombardment Wing (Provisional)
Activated at Andersen AFB, Guam, 1 Feb 1966; replaced by 43 SW and inactivated, 1 Jul 1970.
Aircraft: B-52D/F   Aircraft lost: 6 B-52D

4252nd Strategic Wing
Activated at Kadena AB, Okinawa, 12 Jan 1965; replaced by 376 SW and inactivated, 1 Apr 1970.
Aircraft: B-52D, KC-135A   Aircraft lost: 2 B-52D, 2 KC-135A

4258th Strategic Wing
Activated at U-Tapao RTAB as holding wing for B-52D units on TDY, 2 Jun 1966; replaced by 307 SW and inactivated, 1 Apr 1970
Aircraft: B-52D, KC-135A   Aircraft lost: 1 KC-135A

Strategic Air Command Squadrons

60th Bomb Squadron
Assigned to 43 SW, Andersen AFB, Guam, 1 Jul 1971 but non-operational until Feb 1972; inactivated, 30 Apr 1990.
Aircraft: B-52D

63rd Bomb Squadron (Provisional)
Attached to 43 SW, Andersen AFB, Guam, 15 Jun 1972; became non-operational, Nov 1973; inactivated, 30 Jun 1975.
Aircraft: B-52D

64th Bomb Squadron (Provisional)
Activated at Andersen AFB, Guam, under 72 SW(P), 15 Jun 1972; inactivated, 15 Nov 1973. Aircraft: B-52G

65th Bomb Squadron (Provisional)
Activated at Andersen AFB, Guam, under 72 SW(P), 15 Jun 1972; inactivated, 15 Nov 1973. Aircraft: B-52G

82nd Strategic Reconnaissance Squadron
Activated at Kadena AB, Okinawa under 3 AD, 25 Aug 1967; reassigned to 4252 SW, Kadena AB, 2 Jan 1968; reassigned to 376 SW, Kadena AB, 1 Apr 1970; inactivated, 30 Sep 1976
Aircraft: RC-135C/D/M

99th Strategic Reconnaissance Squadron, Detachment
Activated at U-Tapao RTAB under 100 SRW and attached to 307 SW, U-Tapao, 1 Jan to 30 Sep 1975. Aircraft: U-2C/R

329th Bomb Squadron (Provisional)
Activated at Andersen AFB, Guam, under 72 SW(P), 1 Jun 1972; inactivated, 15 Nov 1973. Aircraft: B-52G

350th Strategic Reconnaissance Squadron, Detachment
Activated from 4025 SRS under 100 SRW at Bien Hoa, 11 Feb 1966 with a detachment at Da Nang; moved to U-Tapao RTAB, 11 Jul 1970 with a detachment at Nakhon Phanom.
Aircraft: AQM-34, DC-130A

364th Bomb Squadron (Provisional)
Activated at U-Tapao RTAB under 307 SW, 1 Jul 1972; non-operational until 29 Jan 1973; inactivated, 30 Jun 1975.
Aircraft: B-52D

365th Bomb Squadron (Provisional)
Activated at U-Tapao RTAB under 307 SW, 1 Jul 1972; non-operational until 29 Jan 1973; inactivated, 1 Jul 1974.
Aircraft: B-52D

486th Bomb Squadron (Provisional)
Activated at Andersen AFB, Guam under 72 SW(P), 1 Jun 1972; inactivated, 15 Nov 1973. Aircraft: B-52G

901st Air Refuelling Squadron (Provisional)
Activated at U-Tapao RTAB under 310 SW(P), 1 Jun 1972; reassigned to Detachment 1, 43 SW, 1 Jul 1974; inactivated, 20 Mar 1976. Aircraft: KC-135A

902nd Air Refuelling Squadron (Provisional)
Activated at U-Tapao RTAB under 310 SW(P), 1 Jun 1972; inactivated, 1 Jul 1974. Aircraft: KC-135A

909th Air Refuelling Squadron
Assigned to 376 SW, Kadena AB, Okinawa from 22 BW, March AFB, Calif, 1 Jul 1971; reassigned to 18 Wg, Kadena, 1 Oct 1991. Aircraft: KC-135A/Q

4025th Strategic Reconnaissance Squadron
Deployed to Bien Hoa with a detachment at Da Nang under 4080 SRW, Aug 1964; redesignated 350 SRS, 11 Feb 1966.
Aircraft: AQM-34, DC-130A

4101st Air Refuelling Squadron (Provisional)
Activated at Takhli RTAB under 17 AD(P), 6 Jun 1972; inactivated, 15 Feb 1973. Aircraft: KC-135A

4102nd Air Refuelling Squadron (Provisional)
Activated at Clark AB, Philippines under 376 SW, 18 Dec 1971; moved to Ching Chuan Kang AB, Tawian, 7 Aug 1972; inactivated, 8 Nov 1972; reactivated at Clark AB under 376 SW, 18 Dec 1972; inactivated, 22 Jan 1973. Aircraft: KC-135A

4103rd Air Refuelling Squadron (Provisional)
Activated at Don Muang Airport, Bankok under 17 AD(P), 1 Jul 1972; inactivated, 10 Oct 1972. Aircraft: KC-135A

4104th Air Refuelling Squadron (Provisional)
Activated at Korat RTAB under 17 AD(P), 9 Jun 1972; moved to Takhli RTAB, 10 Oct 1972; inactivated, 8 Nov 1972.
Aircraft: KC-135A

4180th Bomb Squadron
Assigned to 376 SW, Kadena AB, Okinawa, 1 Apr 1970; reassigned to 307 SW, U-Tapao RTAB, 1 Oct 1970 but was non-operational until inactivated, 31 Dec 1971.

4181st Bomb Squadron
Activated at U-Tapao RTAB under 307 SW, 1 Apr 1970 but was non-operational until inactivated on 31 Mar 1972.

4220th Air Refuelling Squadron
Activated at Ching Chuan Kang AB, Taiwan under 4252 SW, 2 Feb 1968; reassigned to 376 SW, 1 Apr 1970; became non-operational, 15 Nov 1970; inactivated, 31 Jan 1971.
Aircraft: KC-135A

Rescue Units

All Air Rescue Squadrons were redesignated Aerospace Rescue and Recovery Squadrons on 8 Jan 1966.

Early Detachments

31st Air Rescue Squadron
Clark AB, Philippines, detachment to Da Nang, Jul 1964; detachment redesignated 37 ARS, Dec 1965 (HU-16B).

33rd Air Rescue Squadron
Naha AB, Okinawa, detachment to Korat RTAB, Jun 1964; detachments to Udorn and Da Nang (HU-16B); detachment to Nakhon Phanom, 20 Jun-Nov 1964 (HH-43B).

36th Air Rescue Squadron Detachment 4
Osan AB, South Korea detachment to Takhli RTAB, Aug-Nov 1964 (HH-43B).

36th Air Rescue Squadron
Tachikawa AB, Japan, detachment to Udorn RTAB, Jun 1965 (HC-54D, HC-130H).

79th Air Rescue Squadron
Andersen AFB, Guam detachment to Udorn RTAB, Jun 1965 (HC-54D, HC-130H).

Pacific Air Rescue Center

Provisional Detachment 1
Bien Hoa, 1 Sep 1964; moved to Takhli RTAB, Nov 1964; inactivated, Jan 1965 (HH-43B).

Provisional Detachment 2
Da Nang, 10 Aug 1964; moved to Nakhon Phanom RTAB, Nov 1964; inactivated, Jan 1965 (HH-43B).

Provisional Detachment 3
Ubon RTAB, Apr 1965 (HH-43B/F).

Provisional Detachment 4
Korat RTAB, 14 Aug 1964; inactivated, Jan 1965 (HH-43B).

Provisional Detachment 5
Udorn RTAB, May 1965 (HH-43B/F).

Detachment 3
Tan Son Nhut, 1 Apr 1962; redesignated 38 ARS, 1 Jul 1965 (HH-43B/F).

Detachment 4
Bien Hoa, 20 Oct 1964 (HH-43B/F).

Detachment 5
Da Nang, 20 Oct 1964 (HH-43B/F).

3rd Aerospace Rescue and Recovery Group

Activated at Tan Son Nhut, Jan 1966; assigned to 41 ARRW, Hickam AFB, Hawaii, 20 Aug 1972; inactivated, Jan 1976.

Detachment 1
Phan Rang, 1 Jul 1971; inactivated, 31 Jan 1972.

Detachment 2
Udorn RTAB, 1 Jul 1971; inactivated, 1972.

Detachment 3
Ubon RTAB, 1 Jul 1971; redesignated Detachment 3, 40 ARRS, 20 Aug 1972.

Detachment 4
Korat RTAB, 1 Jul 1971; redesignated 56 ARRS, 8 Jul 1972.

Detachment 5
Udorn RTAB, 1 Jul 1971; redesignated Detachment 5, 40 ARRS, 20 Aug 1972.

Detachment 6
Bien Hoa, 1 Jul 1971; inactivated, 1972.

Detachment 7
Da Nang, 1 Jul 1971; inactivated, 30 Nov 1972.

Detachment 8
Takhli RTAB, 10 May 1972; inactivated, 1972.

Detachment 9
Nakhon Phanom RTAB, 1 Jul 1971; inactivated, 1972.

Detachment 12
U-Tapao RTAB, 1 Jul 1971; redesignated Detachment 12, 40 ARRS, 20 Aug 1972.

Detachment 13
Phu Cat, 1 Jul 1971; inactivated, Nov 1971.

Detachment 14
Tan Son Nhut, 1 Jul 1971; redesignated Detachment 14, 40 ARRS, 15 Sep 1972.

Squadrons assigned:
37 ARRS, 38 ARRS, 39 ARRS, 40 ARRS, 56 ARRS.

37th Air Rescue Squadron

Activated at Da Nang, 8 Jan 1966; redesignated 37 ARRS, 8 Jan 1966; inactivated, 30 Nov 1972.
Aircraft: HC-130H/P, HH-3E, HH-43B/F, HH-53B/C, HU-16B
Aircraft lost: 5 HH-3E, 3 HH-53C, 1 HU-16B

Detachment 1
Udorn RTAB, 8 Jul 1966; redesignated 39 ARRS, 16 Jan 1967.

Detachment 2
Udorn RTAB, 16 Jan 1967; redesignated 40 ARRS, 18 Mar 1968.

38th Air Rescue Squadron

Activated at Tan Son Nhut, 1 Jul 1965; redesignated 38 ARRS, 8 Jan 1966; inactivated, 1 Jul 1971.
Aircraft: CH-3C, HC-54D, HH-3E, HH-43B/F, HU-16B
Aircraft lost: 1 CH-3C, 3 HH-3E, 11 HH-43B/F

Detachment 1
Nakhon Phanom RTAB, 1 Jul 1965; transferred to Udorn RTAB, Nov 1965; transferred to Phan Rang, 1966; inactivated 1 Jul 1971.

Detachment 1 (Provisional)
Cam Ranh Bay, Sep 1965.

Detachment 2
Takhli RTAB, 1 Jul 1965; inactivated, 15 Nov 1970.

Detachment 3
Ubon RTAB, 1 Jul 1965; transferred to 3 ARRG control, 1 Jul 1971.

Detachment 4
Korat RTAB, 1 Jul 1965; transferred to 3 ARRG control, 1 Jul 1971.

Detachment 5
Udorn RTAB, 1 Jul 1965; transferred to 3 ARRG control, 1 Jul 1971.

Detachment 6
Bien Hoa, 1 Jul 1965; transferred to 3 ARRG control, 1 Jul 1971.

Detachment 7
Da Nang, 1 Jul 1965; transferred to 3 ARRG control, 1 Jul 1971.

Detachment 8
Cam Ranh Bay, 18 Jan 1966; inactivated, 15 Sep 1970.

Detachment 9
Pleiku, 15 Sep 1965; moved to Nakhon Phanom RTAB, 16 Feb 1970; transferred to 3 ARRG control, 1 Jul 1971.

Detachment 10
Binh Thuy, 15 Sep 1965; inactivated, 20 Dec 1970.

Detachment 11
Tuy Hoa, 18 Jan 1966; inactivated, 15 Oct 1970.

Detachment 12
Nha Trang, 8 Apr 1966; moved to U-Tapao RTAB; transferred to 3 ARRG control, 1 Jul 1971.

Detachment 13
Phu Cat, 8 Jan 1966; transferred to 3 ARRG control, 1 Jul 1971; inactivated, Nov 1971.

Detachment 14
Da Nang, 8 Jan 1966; moved to Tan Son Nhut; transferred to 3 ARRG control, 1 Jul 1971.

39th Aerospace Rescue and Recovery Squadron

Activated at Udorn RTAB, 16 Jan 1967; from Detachment 1, 37 ARRS; moved to Tuy Hoa, 8 Jun 1967; moved to Cam Ranh Bay, 16 Sep 1970; moved to Korat RTAB, Mar 72; inactivated, 1 Apr 1972.
Aircraft: HC-130H/P   Aircraft lost: 2 HC-130P

40th Aerospace Rescue and Recovery Squadron

Activated at Udorn RTAB, 18 Mar 1968 from Detachment 2, 37 ARRS; moved to Nakhon Phanom RTAB, 21 Jul 1971; inactivated, 31 Jan 1976.
Aircraft: HC-130P, HH-3E, HH-43B/F, HH-53B/C
Aircraft lost: 1 HH-3E, 2 HH-53B, 5 HH-53C

Detachment 1
Nakhon Phanom RTAB, 18 Mar 1968; inactivated, 1 Jul 1971.

Detachment 3
Ubon RTAB, 20 Aug 1972; inactivated, 20 Aug 1974.

Detachment 5
Udorn RTAB, 20 Aug 1972; inactivated, 30 Sep 1975.

Detachment 7
Da Nang, 30 Nov 1972; inactivated, 10 Feb 1973.

Detachment 8
Takhli RTAB, 15 Oct 1972; inactivated, 31 Jan 1973.

Detachment 10
Takhli RTAB, 31 Jan 1971; inactivated, 30 Jul 1974.

Detachment 12
U-Tapao RTAB, 20 Aug 1972; inactivated, 31 Jan 1976.

Detachment 14
Tan Son Nhut, 15 Sep 1972; inactivated, 10 Feb 1973.

56th Aerospace Rescue and Recovery Squadron

Activated at Korat RTAB, 8 Jul 1972 from Detachment 4, 3 ARRG; inactivated, 15 Oct 1975.
Aircraft: HC-130H/P   Aircraft lost: 0

Notes on Codes

The first confirmed sighting of squadron code letters used on USAF aircraft in Southeast Asia was in January 1967 although code letters may have been used before the end of 1966. Some of the first squadron codes were worn by the F-4 squadrons of the 366th TFW at Da Nang and were unique in that each aircraft carried individual code letters in the series AA to AZ (389th TFS), BA to BZ (390th TFS) and CA to CZ (480th TFS). However, this system was soon discarded in favour of code letters for each squadron. Most tactical aircraft carried squadron codes by the end of 1967. The exceptions were helicopters; the H-3, H-43 H-53 and FAC aircraft; the O-1, O-2 and OV-10. Individual squadron codes were replaced towards the end of the war by code letters that merely identified the wing, often mnemonically, such as the letters UD for Udorn.

United States Navy Aviation Order of Battle

Aircraft Carriers

Information for each ship includes: the deployment dates when the carrier was assigned to and reassigned from the operational control of TF 77, the number of days spent on operations on the line, the air wing or group and its aircraft code letters, squadrons and detachments and their equipment, and number of aircraft lost.

USS Bon Homme Richard
24 Feb-16 Nov 1964 (39 days) CVW-19 (Code NM)
VF-191 (F-8E); VF-194 (F-8C); VA-192 (A-4C); VA-195 (A-4C); VA-196 (A-1H/J); VAH-4 Det E (A-3B); VFP-63 Det E (RF-8A); VAW-11 Det E (E-1B); HU-1 Det 1 Unit E (UH-2A). Aircraft lost: 1 F-8E

USS Ticonderoga
11 May-10 Dec 1964 (61 days) CVW-5 (Code NF)
VF-51 (F-8E); VF-53 (F-8E); VA-55 (A-4E); VA-56 (A-4E); VA-52 (A-1H/J); VAH-4 Det B (A-3B); VFP-63 Det B (RF-8A); VAW-11 Det B (E-1B); HU-1 Det 1 Unit B (UH-2A). Aircraft lost: 4 A-4E, 1 F-8E

USS Constellation
11 Jun 1964-24 Jan 1965 (68 days) CVW-14 (Code NK)
VF-142 (F-4B); VF-143 (F-4B); VA-144 (A-4C); VA-146 (A-4C); VA-145 (A-1H/J); VAH-10 (A-3B); VFP 63 Det F (RF-8A); VAW-11 Det F (E-1B); HU-1 Det 1 Unit F (UH-2A). Aircraft lost: 1 A-1H, 2 A-4C, 1 F-4B, 1 RF-8A

USS Kearsarge
11 Aug-8 Nov 1964 (58 days) CVSG-53 (Code NS)
VS-21 (S-2F); VS-29 (S-2F); HS-6 (SH-3A); VAW-11 Det R (EA-1E); VA-153 Det R (A-4B); HU-1 Det 1 Unit 5 (UH-2A). Aircraft lost: 0

USS Ranger
17 Aug 1964-25 Apr 1965 (103 days) CVW-9 (Code NG)
VF-92 (F-4B); VF-96 (F-4B); VA-93 (A-4C); VA-94 (A-4C); VA-95 (A-1H/J); VAW-2 Det M (A-3B); VFP-63 Det M (RF-8A); RVAH-5 (RA-5C); VAW-11 Det M (E-1B); HU-1 Det 1 Unit M (UH-2A). Aircraft lost: 2 A-1H, 2 F-4B, 1 RA-5C

USS Hancock
16 Nov 1964-11 May 1965 (82 days) CVW-21 (Code NP)
VF-24 (F-8C); VF-211 (F-8E); VA-212 (A-4E); VA-216 (A-4C); VA-215 (A-1H/J); VAH-4 Det L (A-3B); VFP-63 Det L (RF-8A); VAW-11 Det L (E-1B); HU-1 Det 1 Unit L (UH-2A). Aircraft lost: 5 A-1H, 1 A-3B, 3 A-4C, 1 A-4E, 1 F-8C, 1 F-8E

USS Coral Sea
23 Jan-23 Oct 1965 (167 days) CVW-15 (Code NL)
VF-151 (F-4B); VF-154 (F-8D); VA-153 (A-4C); VA-155 (A-4E); VA-165 (A-1H/J); VAH-2 (A-3B); VFP-63 Det D (RF-8A); VAW-11 Det D (E-1B); HU-1 Det 1 Unit D [became HC-1 Det 1 Unit D on 1 Jul 1965] (UH-2A/B). Aircraft lost: 2 A-1H, 1 A-3B, 6 A-4C, 5 A-4E, 6 F-8D, 3 RF-8A

USS Yorktown
9 Feb-28 Apr 1965 (57 days) CVSG-55 (Code NU)
VS-23 (S-2E); VS-25 (S-2E); HS-4 (SH-3A); VAW-11 Det T (EA-1E); VMA-223 Det T (A-4C). Aircraft lost: 1 EA-1F

USS Midway
22 Mar-14 Nov 1965 (144 days) CVW-2 (Code NE)
VF-21 (F-4B); VF-111 (F-8D); VA-22 (A-4C); VA-23 (A-4E); VA-25 (A-1H/J); VAH-8 (A-3B); VFP-63 Det A (RF-8A); VAW-11 Det A (E-1B); VAW-13 Det A (EA-1F); HU-1 Det 1 Unit A [became HC-1 Det 1 Unit A on 1 Jul 1965] (UH-2A). Aircraft lost: 1 A-1H, 6 A-4C, 4 A-4E, 1 EA-1F, 4 F-4B, 4 F-8D, 2 RF-8A

USS Oriskany
27 Apr-6 Dec 1965 (141 days) CVW-16 (Code AH)
VF-162 (F-8E); VMF(AW)-212 (F-8E); VA-163 (A-4E); VA-164 (A-4E); VA-152 (A-1H/J); VAH-4 Det G (A-3B); VFP-63 Det G (RF-8A); VAW-11 Det G (E-1B); HU-1 Det 1 Unit G [became HC-1 Det 1 Unit G on 1 Jul 1965 (UH-2A). Aircraft lost: 7 A-1H/J, 1 A-3B, 7 A-4E, 5 F-8E, 2 RF-8A

USS Bon Homme Richard
12 May 1965-4 Jan 1966 (136 days) CVW-19 (Code NM)
VF-191 (F-8E); VF-194 (F-8E); VA-192 (A-4C); VA-195 (A-4C); VA-196 (A-1H/J); VFP-63 Det E (RF-8A); VAW-11 Det E (E-1B); VAW-13 Det E (EA-1F); HU-1 Det 1 Unit E [became HC-1 Det Unit E on 1 Jul 1965] (UH-2A/B). Aircraft lost: 4 A-1H/J, 2 A-4C, 10 F-8E, 1 RF-8A

USS Independence
5 Jun-21 Nov 1965 (100 days) CVW-7 (Code AG)
VF-41 (F-4B); VF-84 (F-4B); VA-72 (A-4E); VA-86 (A-4E); VA-75 (A-6A); VAH-4 Det 62 (A-3B); RVAH-1 (RA-5C); VAW-12 Det 62 (E-1B); VAW-13 Det 1 (EA-1F); HU-2 Det 62 [became HC-2 Det 62 on 1 Jul 1965] (UH-2A). Aircraft lost: 3 A-4E, 4 A-6A, 2 C-1A, 1 E-1B, 5 F-4B, 2 RA-5C

USS Bennington
29 Jul-9 Sep 1965 (34 days) CVSG-59 (Code NT)
VS-33 (S-2E); VS-38 (S-2E); HS-8 (SH-3A); VAW-11 Det Q (E-1B); VA-113 Det Q (A-4B). Aircraft lost: 1 A-4B

USS Hornet
11 Oct 1965-8 Feb 1966 (50 days) CVSG-57 (Code NV)
VS-35 (S-2D/E); VS-37 (S-2E); HS-2 (SH-3A); VAW-11 Det N (E-1B); H&MS-15 Det N (A-4C). Aircraft lost: 1 S-2D, 1 SH-3A

USS Ticonderoga
25 Oct 1965-7 May 1966 (112 days) CVW-5 (Code NF)
VF-51 (F-8E); VF-53 (F-8E); VA-56 (A-4E); VA-144 (A-4C); VA-52 (A-1H/J); VAH-4 Det B (A-3B); VFP-63 Det B (RF-8A); VAW-11 Det B (E-1B); HC-1 Det 1 Unit B (UH-2A/B). Aircraft lost: 5 A-1H/J, 4 A-4C, 2 A-4E, 4 F-8E, 1 RF-8A

USS Kitty Hawk
15 Nov 1965-6 Jun 1966 (122 days) CVW-11 (Code NH)
VF-114 (F-4B); VF-213 (F-4G/B); VA-113 (A-4C); VA-115 (A-1H/J); VA-85 (A-6A); VAH-4 Det C (A-3B); RVAH-13 (RA-5C); VAW-11 Det C (E-2A); HC-1 Det 1 Unit C (UH-2A/B). Aircraft lost: 4 A-1H/J, 1 A-3B, 4 A-4C, 7 A-6A, 5 F-4B, 1 F-4G, 3 RA-5C.

USS Enterprise
21 Nov 1965-14 Jun 1966 (131 days) CVW-9 (Code NG)
VF-92 (F-4B); VF-96 (F-4B); VA-36 (A-4C); VA-76 (A-4C); VA-93 (A-4C); VA-94 (A-4C); VAH-4 Det M (A-3B); RVAH-7 (RA-5C); VAW-11 Det M (E-1B); HC-1 Det 1 Unit M (UH-2A/B). Aircraft lost: 1 A-3B, 12 A-4C, 6 F-4B, 1 RA-5C

USS Hancock
6 Dec 1965-21 Jul 1966 (143 days) CVW-21 (Code NP)
VF-24 (F-8C); VF-211 (F-8E); VA-212 (A-4E); VA-216 (A-4C); VA-215 (A-1H/J); VFP-63 Det L (RF-8A); VAW-11 Det L (E-1B); VAW-13 Det L (EA-1F); HC-1 Det 1 Unit L (UH-2A/B). Aircraft lost: 4 A-1H, 5 A-4C, 4 A-4E, 1 EA-1F, 1 F-8C, 6 F-8E, 3 RF-8A, 1 UH-2A

USS Ranger
3 Jan-18 Aug 1966 (137 days) CVW-14 (Code NK)
VF-142 (F-4B); VF-143 (F-4B); VA-55 A-4E); VA-146 (A-4C); VA-145 (A-1H/J); VAH-2 Det F (A-3B); RVAH-9 (RA-5C); VAW-11 Det F (E-2A); HC-1 Det F (UH-2A/B). Aircraft lost: 4 A-1H/J, 3 A-4C, 10 A-4E, 3 F-4B, 1 RA-5C

USS Yorktown
25 Feb-3 Jul 1966 (72 days) CVSG-55 (Code NU)
VS-23 (S-2E); VS-25 (S-2E); HS-4 (SH-3A); VAW-11 Det T (E-1B). Aircraft lost: 2 SH-3A

USS Intrepid
1 May-30 Oct 1966 (103 days) CVW-10 (Code AK)
VA-15 (A-4B); VA-95 (A-4B); VA-165 (A-1H); VA-176 (A-1H); HC-2 Det 11 (UH-2A/B). Aircraft lost: 3 A-1H, 1 A-4B, 1 UH-2A

USS Constellation
29 May-24 Nov 1966 (111 days) CVW-15 (Code NL)
VF-151 (F-4B); VF-161 (F-4B); VA-153 (A-4C); VA-155 (A-4E); VA-65 (A-6A); VAH-8 (A-3B); RVAH-6 (RA-5C); VAW-11 Det D (E-2A); HC-1 Det 1 Unit D (UH-2A/B). Aircraft lost: 3 A-4C, 5 A-4E, 2 A-6A, 3 F-4B, 2 RA-5C

USS Oriskany
11 Jun-8 Nov 1966 (87 days) CVW-16 (Code AH)
VF-111 (F-8E); VF-162 (F-8E); VA-163 (A-4E); VA-164 (A-4E); VA-152 (A-1H); VAH-4 Det G (A-3B); VFP-63 Det G (RF-8G); VAW-11 Det G (E-1B); HC-1 Det 1 Unit G (UH-2A/B). Aircraft lost: 6 A-1H, 8 A-4E, 9 F-8E, 1 RF-8G, 1 UH-2B

USS Kearsarge
11 Jul-11 Dec 1966 (70 days) CVSG-53 (Code NS)
VS-21 (S-2E); VS-29 (S-2E); HS-6 (SH-3A); VAW-11 Det R (E-1B). Aircraft lost: 1 S-2E, 2 SH-3A

USS Franklin D Roosevelt
25 Jul 1966-29 Jan 1967 (95 days) CVW-1 (Code AB)
VF-14 (F-4B); VF-32 (F-4B); VA-12 (A-4E); VA-72 (A-4E); VA-172 (A-4C); VAH-10 Det 42 (A-3B); VFP-62 Det 42 (RF-8G); VAW-12 Det 42 (E-1B); HC-2 Det 42 (UH-2A/B). Aircraft lost: 4 A-4C, 6 A-4E, 1 E-1B, 1 EA-1F, 2 F-4B, 1 RF-8G

USS Coral Sea
11 Aug 1966-16 Feb 1967 (109 days) CVW-2 (Code NE)
VF-21 (F-4B); VF-154 (F-4B); VA-22 (A-4C); VA-23 (A-4E); VA-25 (A-1H); VAH-2 Det A (A-3B); VFP-63 Det A (RF-8G); VAW-11 Det A (E-2A); VAW-13 Det A (EA-1F); HC-1 Det 1 Unit A (UH-2A/B). Aircraft lost: 2 A-1H, 1 A-3B, 6 A-4C, 3 A-4E, 6 F-4B, 1 RF-8G

USS Ticonderoga
27 Oct 1966-22 May 1967 (126 days) CVW-19 (Code NM)
VF-191 (F-8E); VF-194 (F-8E); VA-192 (A-4E); VA-195 (A-4C); VA-52 (A-1H); VAH-4 Det E (A-3B); VFP-63 Det E (RF-8G); VAW-11 Det E [became VAW-111 Det 14 on 20 Apr 1967] (E-1B); HC-1 Det 1 Unit E (UH-2A/B). Aircraft lost: 2 A-1H, 4 A-4C, 8 A-4E, 3 F-8E

The aircraft carriers of the US Navy, like the USS *Kitty Hawk* seen here, added the equivalent of three or four airfields for much of the war. Between August 1964 and August 1973 17 attack carriers made a cumulative total of 73 deployments to Southeast Asia. A total of 853 aircraft were lost by the attack carriers during the war. USN

USS *Kitty Hawk*
17 Nov 1966-12 Jun 1967   (118 days)   CVW-11 (Code NH)
VF-114 (F-4B); VF-213 (F-4B); VA-112 (A-4C); VA-144
(A-4C); VA-85 (A-6A); VAH-4 Det C (A-3B); RVAH-13
(RA-5C); VAW-11 Det C [became VAW-114 on 20 Apr 1967]
(E-2A); HC-1 Det 1 Unit C (UH-2A/B).
Aircraft lost: 1 A-3B, 3 A-4C, 3 A-6A, 8 F-4B, 2 RA-5C

USS *Enterprise*
3 Dec 1966-30 Jun 1967   (132 days)   CVW-9 (Code NG)
VF-92 (F-4B); VF-96 (F-4B); VA-56 (A-4C); VA-113 (A-4C);
VA-35 (A-6A); VAH-2 Det M (A-3B); RVAH-7 (RA-5C);
VAW-11 Det M [became VAW-112 on 20 Apr 1967] (E-2A);
VAW-13 Det M (EA-1F); HC-1 Det 1 Unit M (UH-2A/B).
Aircraft lost: 5 A-4C, 1 A-6A, 7 F-4B, 1 RA-5C

USS *Bennington*
21 Dec 1966-15 Apr 1967   (78 days)   CVSG-59 (Code NT)
VS-33 (S-2E); VS-38 (S-2E); HS-8 (SH-3A); VAW-11 Det Q
[became VAW-111 Det 20 on 20 Apr 1967] (E-1B).
Aircraft lost: 1 SH-3A

USS *Hancock*
20 Jan-14 Jul 1967   (102 days)   CVW-5 (Code NF)
VF-51 (F-8E); VF-53 (F-8E); VA-93 (A-4E); VA-94 (A-4C);
VA-115 (A-1H/J); VAH-4 Det B (A-3B); VFP-63 Det B (RF-
8G); VAW-11 Det B [became VAW-111 Det 19 on 20 Apr 1967]
(E-1B); HC-1 Det 19 (UH-2A/B).
Aircraft lost: 5 A-1H, 2 A-4C, 5 A-4E, 4 F-8E

USS *Bon Homme Richard*
10 Feb-17 Aug 1967   (112 days)   CVW-21 (Code NP)
VF-24 (F-8C); VF-211 (F-8E); VA-76 (A-4C); VA-212 (A-4E);
VA-215 (A-1H/J); VAH-4 Det L (A-3B); VFP-63 Det L (RF-8G);
VAW-11 Det L [became VAW-111 Det 31 on 20 Apr 1967]
(E-1B); VAW-13 Det 31 (EA-1F); HC-1 Det 1 Unit L (UH-2B).
Aircraft lost: 2 A-1H/J, 4 A-4C, 6 A-4E, 5 F-8C, 4 F-8E,
2 RF-8G, 1 UH-2B

USS *Hornet*
25 Apr-18 Oct 1967   (77 days)   CVSG-57 (Code NV)
VS-35 (S-2E); VS-37 (S-2E); HS-2 (SH-3A); VAW-11 Det N
[became VAW-111 Det 12 on 20 Apr 1967] (E-1B).
Aircraft lost: 1 C-1A, 6 SH-3A, 1 US-2C

USS *Constellation*
15 May-26 Nov 1967   (121 days)   CVW-14 (Code NK)
VF-142 (F-4B); VF-143 (F-4B); VA-55 (A-4C); VA-146 (A-4C);
VA-196 (A-6A); VAH-8 Det 64 (A-3B, KA-3B); RVAH-12 (RA-5C);
VAW-113 (E-2A); VAW-13 Det 64 (EA-1F); HC-1 Det 64 (UH-
2A/B). Aircraft lost: 4 A-4C, 4 A-6A, 5 F-4B, 1 KA-3B, 2 RA-5C

USS *Intrepid*
9 Jun-9 Dec 1967   (103 days)   CVW-10 (Code AK)
VF-111 Det 11 (F-8C); VSF-3 (A-4B); VA-15 (A-4C); VA-34
(A-4C); VA-145 (A-1H/J); VFP-63 Det 11 (RF-8G); VAW-121
Det 11 (E-1B); VAW-33 Det 11 (EA-1F); HC-2 Det 11
(UH-2A/B). Aircraft lost: 3 A-4B, 9 A-4C, 1 F-8C, 1 UH-2A

USS *Oriskany*
26 Jun 1967-23 Jan 1968   (122 days)   CVW-16 (Code AH)
VF-111 (F-8C); VF-162 (F-8E); VA-163 (A-4E); VA-164
(A-4E); VA-152 (A-1H/J); VAH-4 Det G (KA-3B); VFP-63 Det
G (RF-8G); VAW-111 Det 34 (E-1B); HC-1 Det G (UH-2A/B).
Aircraft lost: 1 A-1H, 23 A-4E, 1 E-1B, 6 F-8C, 6 F-8E, 2 KA-3B

USS *Forrestal*
8 Jul-22 Aug 1967   (5 days)   CVW-17 (Code AA)
VF-11 (F-4B); VF-74 (F-4B); VA-46 (A-4E); VA-106 (A-4E);
VA-65 (A-6A); RVAH-11 (RA-5C); VAH-10 Det 59 (KA-3B);
VAW-123 (E-2A); HC-2 Det 59 (UH-2A/B).
Aircraft lost: 11 A-4E, 7 F-4B, 3 RA-5C

USS *Coral Sea*
10 Aug 1967-29 Mar 1968   (132 days)   CVW-15 (Code NL)
VF-151 (F-4B); VF-161 (F-4B); VA-153 (A-4E); VA-155 (A-4E);
VA-25 (A-1H/J); VAH-2 Det 43 (KA-3B); VFP-63 Det 43
(RF-8G); VAW-116 (E-2A); VAW-13 Det 43 (EA-1F); HC-1
Det 43 (UH-2A). Aircraft lost: 3 A-1H, 6 A-4E, 8 F-4B, 1 RF-8G

USS *Kearsarge*
12 Oct 1967-28 Mar 1968   (75 days)   CVSG-53 (Code NS)
VS-21 (S-2E); VS-29 (S-2E); HS-6 (SH-3A); VAW-111 Det 33
(E-1B). Aircraft lost: 1 S-2E, 2 SH-3A

USS *Ranger*
20 Nov 1967-18 May 1968   (88 days)   CVW-2 (Code NE)
VF-21 (F-4B); VF-154 (F-4B); VA-22 (A-4C); VA-147 (A-7A);
VA-165 (A-6A); VAH-2 Det 61 (KA-3B); RVAH-6 (RA-5C);
VAW-13 Det 61 (EKA-3B); VAW-115 (E-2A); HC-1 Det 61
(UH-2B/C). Aircraft lost: 2 A-6A, 1 A-7A, 5 F-4B, 2 UH-2B/C

USS *Kitty Hawk*
6 Dec 1967-20 Jun 1968   (125 days)   CVW-11 (Code NH)
VF-114 (F-4B); VF-213 (F-4B); VA-112 (A-4C); VA-144
(A-4E); VA-75 (A-6A/B); VAH-4 Det 63 (KA-3B); RVAH-11
(RA-5C); VAW-13 Det 63 (EA-1F); VAW-114 (E-2A); HC-1
Det 63 (UH-2C). Aircraft lost: 1 A-4C, 4 A-4E, 2 A-6A, 1 C-1A,
6 F-4B, 1 RA-5C

USS *Ticonderoga*
13 Jan-9 Aug 1968   (120 days)   CVW-19 (Code NM)
VF-191 (F-8E); VF-194 (F-8E); VA-23 (A-4F); VA-192
(A-4F); VA-195 (A-4C); VAH-4 Det 14 (KA-3B); VFP-63 Det
14 (RF-8G); VAW-111 Det 14 (E-1B); VAQ-33 Det 14
(EA-1F); HC-1 Det 14 (UH-2B).
Aircraft lost: 2 A-4F, 4 F-8E, 1 RF-8G, 1 UH-2A

USS *Enterprise*
14 Jan-12 Jul 1968   (100 days)   CVW-9 (Code NG)
VF-92 (F-4B); VF-96 (F-4B); VA-56 (A-4E); VA-113 (A-4F);
VA-35 (A-6A); VAH-2 Det 65 (KA-3B); RVAH-1 (RA-5C);
VAW-13 Det 65 (EKA-3B); VAW-112 (E-2A); HC-1 Det 65
(UH-2C). Aircraft lost: 2 A-4E, 2 A-4F, 6 A-6A, 4 F-4B, 1 RA-5C

USS *Bon Homme Richard*
9 Feb-29 Sep 1968   (135 days)   CVW-5 (Code NF)
VF-51 (F-8H); VF-53 (F-8E); VA-93 (A-4F); VA-94 (A-4E);
VA-212 (A-4F); VFP-63 Det 31 (RF-8G); VAW-13 Det 31
(EKA-3B); VAW-111 Det 31 (E-1B); HC-1 Det 31 (UH-2C).
Aircraft lost: 9 A-4F, 2 F-8E, 1 F-8H, 1 RF-8G

USS *Yorktown*
13 Mar-16 Jun 1968   (63 days)   CVSG-55 (Code NU)
VS-23 (S-2E); VS-25 (S-2E); HS-4 (SH-3A); VAW-111 Det 10
(E-1B). Aircraft lost: 1 S-2E

USS *America*
12 May-20 Nov 1968   (112 days)   CVW-6 (Code AE)
VF-33 (F-4J); VF-102 (F-4J); VA-82 (A-7A); VA-86 (A-7A);
VA-85 (A-6A/B); VAH-10 Det 66 (KA-3B); RVAH-13 (RA-5C);
VAW-13 Det 66 [became VAQ-130 Det 66 on 1 Oct 1968]
(EKA-3B); VAW-122 (E-2A); HC-2 Det 66 (UH-2A/B).
Aircraft lost: 2 A-6A/B, 8 A-7A, 5 F-4J

USS *Constellation*
14 Jun 1968-23 Jan 1969   (129 days)   CVW-14 (Code NK)
VF-142 (F-4B); VF-143 (F-4B); VA-27 (A-7A); VA-97 (A-7A);
VA-196 (A-6A/B); VAH-2 Det 64 [became VAQ-132 Det 64 on
1 Nov 1968] (KA-3B); VAW-13 Det 64 [became VAQ-130
Det 64 on 1 Oct 1968] (EKA-3B); RVAH-5 (RA-5C); VAW-113
(E-2A); HC-1 Det 64 (UH-2C)
Aircraft lost: 4 A-6A/B, 6 A-7A, 3 F-4B, 1 RA-5C, 2 UH-2A/C

USS *Bennington*
25 Jun-20 Oct 1968   (64 days)   CVSG-59 (Code NT)
VS-33 (S-2E); VS-38 (S-2E); HS-8 (SH-3A); VAW-111 Det 20
(E-1B). Aircraft lost: 2 SH-3A

USS *Intrepid*
6 Jul 1968-16 Jan 1969   (106 days)   CVW-10 (Code AK)
VF-111 Det 11 (F-8C); VA-36 (A-4C); VA-66 (A-4C); VA-106
(A-4E); VFP-63 Det 11 (RF-8G); VAW-121 Det 11 (E-1B);
VAQ-33 Det 11 (EA-1F); HC-2 Det 11 (UH-2A/B).
Aircraft lost: 2 A-4C, 2 A-4E, 1 RF-8G

USS *Hancock*
6 Aug 1968-23 Feb 1969   (107 days)   CVW-21 (Code NP)
VF-24 (F-8H); VF-211 (F-8H); VA-55 (A-4F); VA-163 (A-4E);
VA-164 (A-4E); VFP-63 Det 19 (RF-8G); VAW-13 Det 19
[became VAQ-130 Det 19 on 1 Oct 1968] (EKA-3B); VAW-111
Det 19 (E-1B); HC-1 Det 19 (UH-2C).
Aircraft lost: 2 A-4E, 2 A-4F, 6 F-8H, 1 RF-8G

USS *Coral Sea*
23 Sep 1968-11 Apr 1969 (110 days) CVW-15 (Code NL)
VF-151 (F-4B); VF-161 (F-4B); VA-153 (A-4F); VA-216
(A-4C); VA-52 (A-6A); VAH-10 Det 43 (KA-3B); VFP-63 Det
43 (RF-8G); VAW-13 Det 43 [became VAQ-130 Det 43 on
1 Oct 1968] (EKA-3B); VAW-116 (E-2A); HC-1 Det 43 (UH-2C).
Aircraft lost: 4 A-4C, 1 A-6A, 1 F-4B, 1 KA-3B, 1 UH-2C

USS *Hornet*
3 Nov 1968-17 Apr 1969 (106 days) CVSG-57 (Code NV)
VS-35 (S-2E); VS-37 (S-2E); HS-2 (SH-3A); VAW-111 Det 12
(E-1B). Aircraft lost: 1 SH-3A

USS *Ranger*
12 Nov 1968-10 May 1969 (91 days) CVW-2 (Code NE)
VF-21 (F-4J); VF-154 (F-4J); VA-147 (A-7A); VA-155 (A-4F);
VA-165 (A-6A); RVAH-9 (RA-5C); VAH-10 Det 61 (KA-3B);
VAQ-130 Det 61 (EKA-3B); VAW-115 (E-2A); HC-1 Det 61
(UH-2C). Aircraft lost: 1 A-4F, 1 A-7A, 2 F-4J

USS *Kitty Hawk*
15 Jan-27 Aug 1969 (111 days) CVW-11 (Code NH)
VF-114 (F-4B); VF-213 (F-4B); VA-37 (A-7A); VA-105
(A-7A); VA-65 (A-6A/B); RVAH-11 (RA-5C); VAQ-131
(KA/EKA-3B); VAW-114 (E-2A); HC-1 Det 63 (UH-2C).
Aircraft lost: 1 A-6A, 4 A-7A, 2 F-4B

USS *Ticonderoga*
18 Feb-10 Sep 1969 (97 days) CVW-16 (Code AH)
VF-111 (F-8H); VF-162 (F-8J); VA-25 (A-7B); VA-87 (A-7B);
VA-112 (A-4C); VFP-63 Det 14 (RF-8G); VAQ-130 Det 14
(EKA-3B); VAW-111 Det 14 (E-1B); HC-1 Det 14 (UH-2C).
Aircraft lost: 2 A-4C, 3 A-7B, 1 F-8H, 1 F-8J

USS *Enterprise*
17 Mar-26 Jun 1969 (35 days) CVW-9 (Code NG)
VF-92 (F-4J); VF-96 (F-4J); VA-146 (A-7B); VA-215 (A-7B);
VA-145 (A-6A/B); RVAH-6 (RA-5C); VAQ-132 (KA/EKA-3B);
VAW-112 (E-2A); HC-1 Det 65 (UH-2C).
Aircraft lost: 1 A-7B, 1 RA-5C

USS *Bon Homme Richard*
6 Apr-19 Oct 1969 (97 days) CVW-5 (Code NF)
VF-51 (F-8J); VF-53 (F-8J); VA-22 (A-4F); VA-94 (A-4E);
VA-144 (A-4E); VFP-63 Det 31 (RF-8G); VAQ-130 Det 31
(KA/EKA-3B); VAW-111 Det 31 (E-1B); HC-1 Det 31 (UH-2C).
Aircraft lost: 4 A-4E, 7 F-8J, 1 UH-2C

USS *Kearsarge*
4 May-14 Aug 1969 (55 days) CVSG-53 (Code NS)
VS-21 (S-2E); VS-29 (S-2E); HS-6 (SH-3A); VAW-111 Det 33
(E-1B). Aircraft lost: 0

USS *Oriskany*
5 May-10 Nov 1969 (116 days) CVW-19 (Code NM)
VF-191 (F-8J); VF-194 (F-8J); VA-23 (A-4F); VA-192 (A-4F);
VA-195 (A-4E/F); VFP-63 Det 34 (RF-8G); VAQ-130 Det 34
(EKA-3B); VAW-111 Det 34 (E-1B); HC-1 Det 34 (UH-2C).
Aircraft lost: 5 A-4F, 3 F-8J, 1 RF-8G

USS *Hancock*
21 Aug 1969-6 Apr 1970 (115 days) CVW-21 (Code NP)
VF-24 (F-8H); VF-211 (F-8J); VA-55 (A-4F); VA-164 (A-4F);
VA-212 (A-4F); VAH-10 Det 19 (KA-3B); VFP-63 Det 19
(RF-8G); VAW-111 Det 19 (E-1B); HC-1 Det 19 (SH-3A).
Aircraft lost: 5 A-4F, 1 F-8J, 1 RF-8G, 1 SH-3G

USS *Constellation*
1 Sep 1969-29 Apr 1970 (128 days) CVW-14 (Code NK)
VF-142 (F-4J); VF-143 (F-4J); VA-27 (A-7A); VA-97 (A-7A);
VA-85 (A-6A/B); RVAH-7 (RA-5C); VAQ-133 (KA/EKA-3B);
VAW-113 (E-2A); HC-1 Det 5 (SH-3A).
Aircraft lost: 6 A-7A, 1 F-4J

USS *Coral Sea*
14 Oct 1969-18 Jun 1970 (125 days) CVW-15 (Code NL)
VF-151 (F-4B); VF-161 (F-4B); VA-82 (A-7A); VA-86 (A-7A);
VA-35 (A-6A); VFP-63 Det 43 (RF-8G); VAQ-135 (KA/EKA-3B);
VAW-116 (E-2A); HC-1 Det 9 (UH-2C).
Aircraft lost: 1 A-6A, 5 A-7A, 1 E-2A, 1 EKA-3B, 3 F-4B.

USS *Ranger*
4 Nov 1969-23 May 1970 (103 days) CVW-2 (Code NE)
VF-21 (F-4J); VF-154 (F-4J); VA-56 (A-7B); VA-93 (A-7B);
VA-196 (A-6A); RVAH-5 (RA-5C); VAQ-134 (KA/EKA-3B);
VAW-115 (E-2A); HC-1 Det 8 (SH-3A).
Aircraft lost: 5 A-6A, 4 A-7B, 2 F-4J

USS *Shangri-La*
30 Mar-24 Nov 1970 (120 days) CVW-8 (Code AJ)
VF-111 (F-8H); VF-162 (F-8H); VA-12 (A-4C); VA-152
(A-4E); VA-172 (A-4C); VFP-63 Det 38 (RF-8G); VAH-10
Det 38 [became VAQ-129 Det 38 on 1 Sep 1970] (KA-3B);
VAW-121 Det 38 (E-1B); HC-2 Det 38 (UH-2C).
Aircraft lost: 5 A-4C, 1 A-4E, 3 F-8H

USS *Bon Homme Richard*
21 Apr-3 Nov 1970 (101 days) CVW-5 (Code NF)
VF-51 (F-8J); VF-53 (F-8J); VA-22 (A-4F); VA-94 (A-4E);
VA-144 (A-4F); VFP-63 Det 31 (RF-8G); VAQ-130 Det 31
(EKA-3B); VAW-111 Det 14 (E-1B); HC-1 Det 3 (UH-2C).
Aircraft lost: 1 A-4F, 1 F-8J

USS *America*
12 May-23 Nov 1970 (100 days) CVW-9 (Code NG)
VF-92 (F-4J); VF-96 (F-4J); VA-146 (A-7E); VA-147 (A-7E);
VA-165 (A-6A/B/C); RVAH-12 (RA-5C); VAQ-132 (KA/EKA-3B);
VAW-124 (E-2A); HC-2 Det 66 (UH-2C).
Aircraft lost: 1 EKA-3B, 2 F-4J

USS *Oriskany*
1 Jun-29 Nov 1970 (90 days) CVW-19 (Code NM)
VF-191 (F-8J); VF-194 (F-8J); VA-153 (A-7A); VA-155
(A-7B); VFP-63 Det 34 (RF-8G); VAQ-130 Det 1 (EKA-3B);
VAW-111 Det 34 (E-1B); HC-1 Det 6 (UH-2C).
Aircraft lost: 1 A-7A, 1 A-7B, 1 F-8J, 1 RF-8G

USS *Hancock*
7 Nov 1970-19 May 1971 (100 days) CVW-21 (Code NP)
VF-24 (F-8J); VF-211 (F-8J); VA-55 (A-4F); VA-164 (A-4F);
VA-212 (A-4F); VFP-63 Det 1 (RF-8G); VAQ-129 Det 19
(EKA-3B); VAW-111 Det 3 (E-1B); HC-1 Det 7 (UH-2C).
Aircraft lost: 1 A-4F, 2 F-8J

USS *Ranger*
11 Nov 1970-9 Jun 1971 (123 days) CVW-2 (Code NE)
VF-21 (F-4J); VF-154 (F-4J); VA-25 (A-7E); VA-113 (A-7E);
VA-145 (A-6A/C); RVAH-1 (RA-5C); VAQ-134 (KA/EKA-3B);
VAW-111 Det 6 (E-1B); HC-1 Det 1 (SH-3G).
Aircraft lost: 2 A-6A/C, 4 A-7E, 1 C-2A, 2 F-4J

USS *Kitty Hawk*
27 Nov 1970-6 Jul 1971 (138 days) CVW-11 (Code NH)
VF-114 (F-4J); VF-213 (F-4J); VA-192 (A-7E); VA-195 (A-7E);
VA-52 (A-6A/B); RVAH-6 (RA-5C); VAQ-133 (KA/EKA-3B);
VAW-114 (E-2B); HC-1 Det 2 (UH-2C). Aircraft lost: 1 A-7E

USS *Midway*
7 May-24 Oct 1971 (74 days) CVW-5 (Code NF)
VF-151 (F-4B); VF-161 (F-4B); VA-56 (A-7B); VA-93 (A-7B);
VA-115 (A-6A, KA-6D); VFP-63 Det 3 (RF-8G); VAQ-130 Det
2 (EKA-3B); VAW-115 (E-2B); HC-1 Det 8 (SH-3G).
Aircraft lost: 1 E-2B, 1 KA-6D

USS *Oriskany*
4 Jun-8 Dec 1971 (75 days) CVW-19 (Code NM)
VF-191 (F-8J); VF-194 (F-8J); VA-153 (A-7A); VA-155
(A-7B); VA-215 (A-7B); VFP-63 Det 4 (RF-8G); VAQ-130
Det 3 (EKA-3B); VAW-111 Det 2 (E-1B); HC-1 Det 5 (UH-2C).
Aircraft lost: 2 A-7A, 1 A-7B, 1 F-8J

USS *Enterprise*
27 Jun 1971-2 Feb 1972 (88 days) CVW-14 (Code NK)
VF-142 (F-4J); VF-143 (F-4J); VA-27 (A-7E); VA-97 (A-7E);
VA-196 (A-6A/B, KA-6D); RVAH-5 (RA-5C); VAQ-130 Det 4
(EKA-3B); VAW-113 (E-2B); HC-1 Det 4 (SH-3G).
Aircraft lost: 1 A-7E, 1 RA-5C

USS *Constellation*
27 Oct 1971-24 Jun 1972 (169 days) CVW-9 (Code NG)
VF-92 (F-4J); VF-96 (F-4J); VA-146 (A-7E); VA-147 (A-7E);
VA-165 (A-6A, KA-6D); RVAH-11 (RA-5C); VAQ-130 Det 1
(EKA-3B); VAW-116 (E-2B); HC-1 Det 3 (SH-3G).
Aircraft lost: 1 A-6A, 2 A-7E, 3 F-4J, 1 SH-3G

USS *Coral Sea*
8 Dec 1971-11 Jul 1972 (148 days) CVW-15 (Code NL)
VF-51 (F-4B); VF-111 (F-4B); VA-22 (A-7E); VA-94 (A-7E);
VMA(AW)-224 (A-6A/B, KA-6D); VFP-63 Det 5 (RF-8G);
VAQ-135 Det 3 (EKA-3B); VAW-111 Det 4 (E-1B); HC-1 Det 6
(SH-3G). Aircraft lost: 4 A-6A, 8 A-7E, 3 F-4B, 1 SH-3G

USS *Hancock*
28 Jan-25 Sep 1972 (165 days) CVW-21 (Code NP)
VF-24 (F-8J); VF-211 (F-8J); VA-55 (A-4F); VA-164 (A-4F);
VA-212 (A-4F); VFP-63 Det 1 (RF-8G); VAQ-135 Det 5
(EKA-3B); VAW-111 Det 2 (E-1B); HC-1 Det 7 (SH-3G).
Aircraft lost: 7 A-4F, 4 F-8J, 1 RF-8G

USS *Kitty Hawk*
1 Mar-17 Nov 1972 (192 days) CVW-11 (Code NH)
VF-114 (F-4J); VF-213 (F-4J); VA-192 (A-7E); VA-195
(A-7E); VA-52 (A-6A/B, KA-6D); RVAH-7 (RA-5C); VAQ-135
Det 1 (EKA-3B); VAW-114 (E-2B); HC-1 Det 1 (SH-3G).
Aircraft lost: 1 A-6A, 8 A-7E, 3 F-4J, 1 RA-5C

USS *Midway*
21 Apr 1972-23 Feb 1973 (208 days) CVW-5 (Code NF)
VF-151 (F-4B); VF-161 (F-4B); VA-56 (A-7B); VA-93 (A-7B);
VA-115 (A-6A, KA-6D); VFP-63 Det 3 (RF-8G); VAQ-130 Det
2 (EKA-3B); VAW-115 (E-2B); HC-1 Det 2 (SH-3G).
Aircraft lost: 2 A-6A, 10 A-7B, 5 F-4B, 1 KA-6D, 2 RF-8G

USS *Saratoga*
8 May 1972-16 Jan 1973 (173 days) CVW-3 (Code AC)
VF-31 (F-4J); VF-103 (F-4J); VA-37 (A-7A); VA-105 (A-7A);
VA-75 (A-6A/B, KA-6D); RVAH-1 (RA-5C); VAW-123 (E-2B);
HS-7 (SH-3A/D).
Aircraft lost: 3 A-6A, 8 A-7A, 3 F-4J, 1 RA-5C, 2 SH-3A/D

USS *Oriskany*
21 Jun 1972-20 Mar 1973 (169 days) CVW-19 (Code NM)
VF-191 (F-8J); VF-194 (F-8J); VA-153 (A-7A); VA-155
(A-7B); VA-215 (A-7B); VFP-63 Det 4 (RF-8G); VAQ-130
Det 3 (EKA-3B); VAW-111 Det 6 (E-1B); HC-1 Det 5 (SH-3G).
Aircraft lost: 3 A-7B, 2 F-8J, 1 RF-8G

USS *America*
1 Jul 1972-4 Mar 1973 (158 days) CVW-8 (Code AJ)
VF-74 (F-4J); VMFA-333 (F-4J); VA-82 (A-7C); VA-86
(A-7C); VA-35 (A-6A/C, KA-6D); RVAH-6 (RA-5C); VAQ-132
(EA-6B); VAW-124 (E-2B); HC-2 Det 66 (SH-3G).
Aircraft lost: 2 A-6A, 8 A-7C, 4 F-4J

USS *Enterprise*
19 Sep 1972-3 Jun 1973 (183 days) CVW-14 (Code NK)
VF-142 (F-4J); VF-143 (F-4J); VA-27 (A-7E); VA-97 (A-7E);
VA-196 (A-6A/B, KA-6D); RVAH-13 (RA-5C); VAQ-131
(EA-6B); VAW-113 (E-2B); HS-2 Det 1 (SH-3G).
Aircraft lost: 1 A-6A, 1 A-7E, 1 F-4J, 1 RA-5C

USS *Ranger*
28 Nov 1972-14 Jun 1973 (120 days) CVW-2 (Code NE)
VF-21 (F-4J); VF-154 (F-4J); VA-25 (A-7E); VA-113 (A-7E);
VA-145 (A-6A/B, KA-6D); RVAH-5 (RA-5C); VAQ-130 Det 4
(EKA-3B); VAW-111 Det 1 (E-1B); HC-1 Det 4 (SH-3G).
Aircraft lost: 1 A-7E, 1 EKA-3B, 2 F-4J

USS *Constellation*
16 Jan-2 Oct 1973 (98 days) CVW-9 (Code NG)
VF-92 (F-4J); VF-96 (F-4J); VA-146 (A-7E); VA-147 (A-7E);
VA-165 (A-6A ,KA-6D); RVAH-12 (RA-5C); VAQ-134 (EA-6B);
VAW-116 (E-2B); HS-6 Det 1 (SH-3G). Aircraft lost: 1 A-7E

USS *Coral Sea*
20 Mar-30 Oct 1973 (84 days) CVW-15 (Code NL)
VF-51 (F-4B); VF-111 (F-4B); VA-22 (A-7E); VA-94 (A-7E);
VA-95 (A-6A, KA-6D); VFP-63 Det 5 (RF-8G); VAQ-135 Det 3
(EKA-3B); VAW-111 Det 4 (E-1B); HC-1 Det 6 (SH-3G).
Aircraft lost: 0

USS *Hancock*
19 May-24 Dec 1973   (29 days)   CVW-21 (Code NP)
VF-24 (F-8J); VF-211 (F-8J); VA-55 (A-4F); VA-164 (A-4F,
TA-4F); VA-212 (A-4F); VFP-63 Det 1 (RF-8G); VAQ-135
Det 5 (EKA-3B); VAW-111 Det 2 (E-1B); HC-1 Det 3 (SH-3G).
Aircraft lost: 0

Carrier-based Squadrons Summary

RVAH-1 *Tigers*
4 deployments on USS *Enterprise, Independence, Ranger*
and *Saratoga* between May 1965 and Feb 1973.
Aircraft: RA-5C   Code: AC, AG, NE, NG   Aircraft lost: 4

RVAH-5 *Savage Sons*
5 deployments on USS *Constellation, Enterprise* and *Ranger*
between Aug 1964 and Jun 1973.
Aircraft: RA-5C   Code: NE, NG, NK   Aircraft lost: 3

RVAH-6 *Fleurs*
5 deployments on USS *America, Constellation, Enterprise,
Kitty Hawk* and *Ranger* between May 1966 and Mar 1973.
Aircraft: RA-5C   Code: AJ, NE, NG, NH, NL   Aircraft lost: 3

RVAH-7 *Peacemakers of the Fleet*
4 deployments on USS *Constellation, Enterprise* and *Kitty
Hawk* between Oct 1965 and Nov 1972.
Aircraft: RA-5C   Code: NG, NH, NK   Aircraft lost: 3

RVAH-9 *Hoot Owls*
2 deployments on USS *Ranger* between Dec 1965 and May 1969.
Aircraft: RA-5C   Code: AC, NE   Aircraft lost: 1

RVAH-11 *Checkertails*
4 deployments on USS *Constellation, Forrestal* and *Kitty
Hawk* between Jun 1967 and Jul 1972.
Aircraft: RA-5C   Code: AA, NG, NH   Aircraft lost: 4

RVAH-12 *Speartips*
3 deployments on USS *America* and *Constellation* between
Apr 1967 and Oct 1973.
Aircraft: RA-5C   Code: NG, NK   Aircraft lost: 2

RVAH-13 *Bats*
4 deployments on USS *America, Enterprise* and *Kitty Hawk*
between Oct 1965 and Jun 1973.
Aircraft: RA-5C   Code: AE, NH, NK   Aircraft lost: 6

VA-12 *Flying Ubangis*
2 deployments on USS *Franklin D Roosevelt* and *Shangri-La*
between Jun 1966 and Dec 1970.
Aircraft: A-4C/E   Code: AB, AJ   Aircraft lost: 2 A-4C, 2 A-4E

VA-15 *Valions*
2 deployments on USS *Intrepid* between Apr 1966 and Dec 1967.
Aircraft: A-4B/C   Code: AK   Aircraft lost: 1 A-4B, 5 A-4C

VA-22 *Fighting Redcocks*
5 deployments with A-4 on USS *Bon Homme Richard, Coral
Sea, Midway* and *Ranger* between Mar 1965 and Nov 1970.
2 deployments with A-7 on USS *Coral Sea* between Nov 1971
and Nov 1973. Aircraft: A-4C/F, A-7E.
Code: NE, NF (A-4), NL (A-7)   Aircraft lost: 12 A-4C, 4 A-7E

VA-23 *Black Knights*
4 deployments on USS *Coral Sea, Midway, Oriskany* and
Ticonderoga between Mar 1965 and Nov 1969.
Aircraft: A-4E/F   Code: NE, NM   Aircraft lost: 7 A-4E, 3 A-4F

VA-25 *Fist of the Fleet*
3 deployments with A-1 on USS *Coral Sea* and *Midway*
between Mar 1965 and Apr 1968.
3 deployments with A-7 on USS *Ranger* and *Ticonderoga*
between Feb 1969 and Jun 1973.
Aircraft: A-1H/J, A-7B/E   Code: NE, NL (A-1), AH, NE (A-7)
Aircraft lost: 8 A-1H, 2 A-7B, 2 A-7E

VA-27 *Royal Maces*
4 deployments on USS *Constellation* and *Enterprise* between
May 1968 and Jun 1973.
Aircraft: A-7A/E   Code: NK   Aircraft lost: 6 A-7A, 1 A-7E

VA-34 *Blue Blasters*
1 deployment on USS *Intrepid* between May and Dec 1967.
Aircraft: A-4C   Code: AK   Aircraft lost: 4

VA-35 *Black Panthers*
4 deployments on USS *America, Coral Sea* and *Enterprise*
between Nov 1966 and Mar 1973. Aircraft: A-6A/C, KA-6D.
Code: AJ, NG, NL   Aircraft lost: 10 A-6A

VA-36 *Roadrunners*
2 deployments on USS *Enterprise* and *Intrepid* between
Oct 1965 and Feb 1969.
Aircraft: A-4C   Code: AK, NG   Aircraft lost: 5

VA-37 *Bulls*
2 deployments on USS *Kitty Hawk* and *Saratoga* between
Dec 1968 and Feb 1973.
Aircraft: A-7A   Code: AC, NH   Aircraft lost: 6

VA-46 *Clansmen*
1 deployment on USS *Forrestal* between Jun and Sep 1967.
Aircraft: A-4E   Code: AA   Aircraft lost: 0

VA-52 *Knightriders*
3 deployments with A-1 on USS *Ticonderoga* between Apr
1964 and May 1967. 3 deployments with A-6 on USS *Coral Sea*
and *Kitty Hawk* between Sep 1968 and Nov 1972.
Aircraft: A-1H/J, A-6A/B, KA-6D.
Code: NF, NM (A-1), NH, NL (A-6)
Aircraft lost: 5 A-1H, 2 A-1J, 2 A-6A

VA-55 *Warhorses*
8 deployments on USS *Constellation, Hancock, Ranger* and
Ticonderoga between Apr 1964 and Jan 1974.
Aircraft: A-4C/E/F   Code: NF, NK, NP
Aircraft lost: 1 A-4C, 12 A-4E, 7 A-4F

VA-56 *Champions*
4 deployments with A-4 on USS *Enterprise* and *Ticonderoga*
between Apr 1964 and Jul 1968. 3 deployments with A-7 on
USS *Midway* and *Ranger* between Oct 1969 and Mar 1973.
Aircraft: A-4C/E, A-7B   Code: NF, NG (A-4), NF (A-7)
Aircraft lost: 3 A-4C, 6 A-4E, 9 A-7B

VA-65 *Tigers*
3 deployments on USS *Constellation, Forrestal* and *Kitty
Hawk* between May 1966 and Sep 1969.
Aircraft: A-6A/B   Code: AA, NH, NL   Aircraft lost: 3 A-6A

VA-66 *Waldomen*
1 deployment on USS *Intrepid* between Jun 1968 and Feb 1969.
Aircraft: A-4C   Code: AK   Aircraft lost: 1

VA-72 *Blue Hawks*
2 deployments on USS *Independence* and *Franklin D
Roosevelt* between May 1965 and Feb 1967.
Aircraft: A-4E   Code: AB, AG   Aircraft lost: 6

VA-75 *Sunday Punchers*
3 deployments on USS *Independence, Kitty Hawk* and
Saratoga between May 1965 and Feb 1973.
Aircraft: A-6A/B, KA-6D   Code: AC, AG, NH
Aircraft lost: 9 A-6A

VA-76 *Spirits*
2 deployments on USS *Bon Homme Richard* and *Enterprise*
between Oct 1965 and Aug 1967.
Aircraft: A-4C   Code: NG, NP   Aircraft lost: 7

VA-82 *Marauders*
4 deployments on USS *America* and *Coral Sea* between Apr
1968 and Mar 1973. Aircraft: A-7A/C   Code: AE, AJ, NL.
Aircraft lost: 6 A-7A, 3 A-7C

VA-85 *Black Falcons*
4 deployments on USS *America, Constellation* and *Kitty
Hawk* between Oct 1965 and May 1970. Aircraft: A-6A/B.
Code: AE, NH, NK   Aircraft lost: 11 A-6A, 1 A-6B

VA-86 *Sidewinders*
1 deployment with A-4 on USS *Independence* between May
and Dec 1965. 3 deployments with A-7 on USS *America* and
Coral Sea between Apr 1968 and Mar 1973.
Aircraft: A-4E, A-7A/C   Code: AG (A-4), AE, AJ, NL (A-7).
Aircraft lost: 1 A-4E, 7 A-7A, 5 A-7C

VA-87 *Golden Warriors*
1 deployment on USS *Ticonderoga* between Feb and Sep 1969.
Aircraft: A-7B   Code: AH   Aircraft lost: 1

VA-93 *Blue Blazers*
4 deployments with A-4 on USS *Bon Homme Richard,
Enterprise, Hancock* and *Ranger* between Aug 1964 and Oct
1968. 3 deployments with A-7 on USS *Midway* and *Ranger*
between Oct 1969 and Mar 1973.
Aircraft: A-4C/E/F, A-7B   Code: NF, NG (A-4), NE, NF (A-7)
Aircraft lost: 1 A-4C, 5 A-4E, 6 A-4F, 5 A-7B

VA-94 *Mighty Shrikes*
6 deployments with A-4 on USS *Bon Homme Richard,
Enterprise, Hancock* and *Ranger* between Aug 1964 and Nov
1970. 2 deployments with A-7 on USS *Coral Sea* between Nov
1971 and Nov 1973. Aircraft: A-4C/E, A-7E   Code: NL
Aircraft lost: 6 A-4C, 1 A-4E, 4 A-7E

VA-95 *Skynights/Green Lizards*
1 deployment with A-1 on USS *Ranger* between Aug 1964 and
May 1965. 1 deployment with A-4 on USS *Intrepid* between
Apr and Nov 1966. 1 deployment with A-6 on USS *Coral Sea*
between Mar and Nov 1973.
Aircraft: A-1H/J, A-4B, A-6A/B, KA-6D.
Code: NG (A-1), AK (A-4), NL (A-6)   Aircraft lost: 2 A-1H

VA-97 *Warhawks*
4 deployments on USS *Constellation* and *Enterprise* between
May 1968 and Jun 1973.
Aircraft: A-7A/E   Code: NK   Aircraft lost: 6 A-7A, 1 A-7E

VA-105 *Gunslingers*
2 deployments on USS *Kitty Hawk* and *Saratoga* between
Dec 1968 and Feb 1973.
Aircraft: A-7A   Code: AC, NH   Aircraft lost: 6

VA-106 *Gladiators*
2 deployments on USS *Forrestal* and *Intrepid* between
Jun 1967 and Feb 1969.
Aircraft: A-4E   Code: AA, AK   Aircraft lost: 2

VA-112 *Bombing Broncos*
3 deployments on USS *Kitty Hawk* and *Ticonderoga* between
Nov 1966 and Sep 1969.
Aircraft: A-4C   Code: AH, NH   Aircraft lost: 5

VA-113 *Stingers*
4 deployments with A-4 on USS *Bennington, Enterprise* and
Kitty Hawk between Mar 1965 and Jul 1968. 2 deployments
with A-7 on USS *Ranger* between Oct 1970 and Jun 1973.
Aircraft: A-4B/C/F, A-7E   Code: NG, NH (A-4), NE (A-7).
Aircraft lost: 1 A-4B, 6 A-4C, 2 A-4F, 3 A-7E

VA-115 *Arabs*
2 deployments with A-1 on USS *Hancock* and *Kitty Hawk*
between Oct 1965 and Jul 1967. 2 deployments with A-6 on
USS *Midway* between Apr 1971 and Mar 1973.
Aircraft: A-1H/J, A-6A, KA-6D   Code: NH, NF (A-1), NF (A-6)
Aircraft lost: 6 A-1H, 3 A-1J, 2 A-6A, 2 KA-6D

VA-144 *Roadrunners*
6 deployments on USS *Bon Homme Richard, Constellation,
Kitty Hawk* and *Constellation* between May 1964 and Nov 1970.
Aircraft: A-4C/E/F   Code: NF, NH, NK
Aircraft lost: 6 A-4C, 7 A-4E, 1 A-4F

VA-145 *Swordsmen*
3 deployments with A-1 on USS *Constellation, Intrepid* and
Ranger between May 1964 and Dec 1967. 3 deployments with
A-6 on USS *Enterprise* and *Ranger* between Jan 1969 and
Jun 1973. Aircraft: A-1H/J, A-6A/B/C, KA-6D.
Code: NK, AK (A-1), NE, NG (A-6)
Aircraft lost: 4 A-1H, 1 A-1J, 1 A-6A, 1 A-6C

VA-146 *Blue Diamonds*
3 deployments with A-4 on USS *Constellation* and *Ranger*
between May 1964 and Dec 1967. 4 deployments with A-7 on
USS *America, Constellation* and *Enterprise* between Jan
1969 and Oct 1973. Aircraft: A-4C, A-7B/E.
Code: NK (A-4), NG (A-7)   Aircraft lost: 7 A-4C, 1 A-7E

VA-147 *Argonauts*
5 deployments on USS *America, Constellation* and *Ranger* between Nov 1967 and Oct 1973.
Aircraft: A-7A/E   Code: NE, NG   Aircraft lost: 2 A-7A, 2 A-7E

VA-152 *Wild Aces*
3 deployments with A-1 on USS *Oriskany* between Apr 1965 and Jan 1968. 1 deployment with A-4 on USS *Shangri-La* between Mar and Dec 1970.
Aircraft: A-1H/J, A-4E   Code: AH (A-1), AJ (A-4)
Aircraft lost: 13 A-1H, 1 A-1J, 1 A-4E

VA-153 *Blue Tail Flies*
5 deployments with A-4 on USS *Constellation, Coral Sea* and *Kearsarge* between Jun 1964 and Apr 1969. 3 deployments with A-7 on USS *Oriskany* between May 1970 and Mar 1973.
Aircraft: A-4B/C/E/F, A-7A   Code: NL (A-4), NM (A-7)
Aircraft lost: 9 A-4C, 2 A-4E, 3 A-7A

VA-155 *Silver Foxes*
4 deployments with A-4 on USS *Constellation, Coral Sea* and *Ranger* between Dec 1964 and May 1969. 3 deployments with A-7 on USS *Oriskany* between May 1970 and Mar 1973.
Aircraft: A-4E/F, A-7B   Code: NE, NL (A-4), NM (A-7)
Aircraft lost: 14 A-4E, 1 A-4F, 4 A-7B

VA-163 *Saints*
4 deployments on USS *Hancock* and *Oriskany* between Apr 1965 and Mar 1969.
Aircraft: A-4E   Code: AH, NP   Aircraft lost: 21

VA-164 *Ghost Riders*
8 deployments on USS *Hancock* and *Oriskany* between Apr 1965 and Jan 1974. Aircraft: A-4E/F, TA-4F
Code: AH, NP   Aircraft lost: 20 A-4E, 2 A-4F

VA-165 *Boomers*
2 deployments with A-1 on USS *Coral Sea* and *Intrepid* between Dec 1964 and Nov 1966. 5 deployments with A-6 on USS *America, Constellation* and *Ranger* between Nov 1967 and Oct 1973. Aircraft: A-1H/J, A-6A/B/C, KA-6D
Code: AK, NL (A-1), NE, NG (A-6)   Aircraft lost: 4 A-1H, 3 A-6A

VA-172 *Blue Bolts*
2 deployments on USS *Franklin D Roosevelt* and *Shangri-La* between Jun 1966 and Dec 1970.
Aircraft: A-4C   Code: AB, AJ   Aircraft lost: 7

VA-176 *Thunderbolts*
1 deployment on USS *Intrepid* between Apr and Nov 1966.
Aircraft: A-1H   Code: AK   Aircraft lost: 1

VA-192 *Golden Dragons*
5 deployments with A-4 on USS *Bon Homme Richard, Oriskany* and *Ticonderoga* between Jan 1964 and Nov 1969 2 deployments with A-7 on USS *Kitty Hawk* between Nov 1970 and Nov 1972.
Aircraft: A-4C/E/F, A-7E   Code: NM (A-4), NH (A-7)
Aircraft lost: 1 A-4C, 8 A-4E, 3 A-4F, 5 A-7E

VA-195 *Dambusters*
5 deployments with A-4 on USS *Bon Homme Richard, Oriskany* and *Ticonderoga* between Jan 1964 and Nov 1969 2 deployments with A-7 on USS *Kitty Hawk* between Nov 1970 and Nov 1972.
Aircraft: A-4C/E/F, A-7E   Code: NM (A-4), NH (A-7)
Aircraft lost: 5 A-4C, 1 A-4F, 3 A-7E

VA-196 *Main Battery*
2 deployments with A-1 on USS *Bon Homme Richard* between Jan 1964 and Jan 1966. 5 deployments with A-6 on USS *Constellation, Enterprise* and *Ranger* between Apr 1967 and Jun 1973.
Aircraft: A-1H/J, A-6A/B, KA-6D   Code: NM (A-1), NE, NK (A-6)
Aircraft lost: 3 A-1H, 1 A-1J, 13 A-6A, 1 A-6B

VA-212 *Rampant Raiders*
8 deployments on USS *Bon Homme Richard* and *Hancock* between Oct 1964 and Jan 1974.
Aircraft: A-4E/F   Code: NF, NP   Aircraft lost: 11 A-4E, 9 A-4F

VA-215 *Barn Owls*
3 deployments with A-1 on USS *Bon Homme Richard* and *Hancock* between Oct 1964 and Aug 1967.
3 deployments with A-7 on USS *Enterprise* and *Oriskany* between Jan 1969 and Mar 1973.
Aircraft: A-1H/J, A-7B   Code: NP (A-1), NG, NM (A-7)
Aircraft lost: 10 A-1H, 1 A-1J, 2 A-7B

VA-216 *Black Diamonds*
3 deployments on USS *Coral Sea* and *Hancock* between Oct 1964 and Apr 1969.
Aircraft: A-4C   Code: NL, NP   Aircraft lost: 12

VAH-2 *Royal Rampants*
9 deployments on USS *Constellation, Coral Sea, Enterprise* and *Ranger* between Aug 1964 and Oct 1968.
Aircraft: A-3B, KA-3B   Code: mainly ZA but also NK and NL
Aircraft lost: 2 A-3B

VAH-4 *Fourrunners*
16 deployments on USS *Bon Homme Richard, Enterprise, Hancock, Independence, Kitty Hawk, Oriskany* and *Ticonderoga* between Jan 1964 and Aug 1968.
Aircraft: A-3B, KA-3B   Code: mainly ZB but also AH
Aircraft lost: 4 A-3B, 3 KA-3B

VAH-8 *Fireballers*
3 deployments on USS *Constellation* and *Midway* between Mar 1965 and Dec 1967.
Aircraft: A-3B, KA-3B   Code: NE, NK, NL   Aircraft lost: 1 KA-3B

VAH-10 *Vikings*
8 deployments on USS *America, Constellation, Coral Sea, Forrestal, Franklin D Roosevelt, Hancock, Shangri-La* and *Ranger* between May 1964 and Aug 1970.
Aircraft: A-3B, KA-3B   Code: various   Aircraft lost: 1 KA-3B

VAQ-33 *Knight Hawks*
2 deployments on USS *Intrepid* and *Ticonderoga* between Dec 1967 and Feb 1969.
Aircraft: EA-1F   Code: NM, AK   Aircraft lost: 0

VAQ-129 *Vikings*
2 deployments on USS *Hancock* and *Shangri-La* between Sep 1970 and Jun 1971.
Aircraft: EKA-3B, KA-3B   Code: AJ, NP   Aircraft lost: 0

VAQ-130 *Zappers*
18 deployments on USS *America, Bon Homme Richard, Constellation, Coral Sea, Enterprise, Hancock, Midway, Oriskany, Ranger* and *Ticonderoga* between Oct 1968 and Jun 1973. Aircraft: EKA-3B, KA-3B   Code: various
Aircraft lost: 2 EKA-3B

VAQ-131 *Lancers*
1 deployment with KA-3 on USS *Kitty Hawk* between Dec 1968 and Sep 1969. 1 deployment with EA-6B on USS *Enterprise* between Sep 1972 and Jun 1973.
Aircraft: EA-6B, EKA-3B, KA-3B
Code: NH (KA-3), NK (EA-6B)   Aircraft lost: 0

VAQ-132 *Scorpions*
3 deployments with KA-3 on USS *America, Constellation* and *Enterprise* between Nov 1968 and Dec 1970. 1 deployment with EA-6B on USS *America* between Jun 1972 and Mar 1973 Detachment to Cam Ranh Bay between Jun 1972 and Feb 1973.
Aircraft: EA-6B, EKA-3B, KA-3B
Code: AJ, NP (KA-3), AJ (EA-6B)   Aircraft lost: 1 EKA-3B

VAQ-133 *Wizards*
2 deployments on USS *Constellation* and *Kitty Hawk* between Aug 1969 and Jul 1971.
Aircraft: EKA-3B, KA-3B   Code: NH, NK   Aircraft lost: 0

VAQ-134 *Garudas*
2 deployments with KA-3 on USS *Ranger* between Oct 1969 and Jul 1971. 1 deployment with EA-6B on USS *Constellation* between Jan and Oct 1973. Aircraft: EA-6B, EKA-3B, KA-3B
Code: NE (KA-3), NG (EA-6B)   Aircraft lost: 0

VAQ-135 *Black Ravens*
6 deployments on USS *Coral Sea, Hancock* and *Kitty Hawk* between Sep 1969 and Jan 1974. Aircraft: EKA-3B, KA-3B
Code: NH, NL, NP   Aircraft lost: 1 EKA-3B

VAW-11 *Early Eleven*
2 deployments with EA-1F on USS *Kearsarge* and *Yorktown* between Jun 1964 and May 1965. 22 deployments with E-1B on USS *Bennington, Bon Homme Richard, Constellation, Coral Sea, Enterprise, Hancock, Hornet, Kearsarge, Midway, Oriskany, Ranger, Ticonderoga* and *Yorktown* between Jan 1964 and Apr 1967. 6 deployments with E-2A on USS *Constellation, Coral Sea, Enterprise, Kitty Hawk* and *Ranger* between Oct 1965 and Apr 1967.
Aircraft: E-1B, E-2A, EA-1F   Code: RR   Aircraft lost: 1 EA-1F

VAW-12 *Bats*
2 deployments on USS *Independence* and *Franklin D Roosevelt* between May 1965 and Feb 1967.
Aircraft: E-1B   Code: AB, AG   Aircraft lost: 2

VAW-13 *Zappers*
9 deployments with EA-1F on USS *Bon Homme Richard, Constellation, Coral Sea, Enterprise, Independence, Kitty Hawk* and *Midway* between Mar 1965 and Jun 1968.
7 deployments with EKA-3B on USS *America, Bon Homme Richard, Constellation, Coral Sea, Enterprise, Hancock* and *Ranger* between Nov 1967 and Sep 1968.
Aircraft: EA-1F, EKA-3B   Code: VR (EA-1F), various (EKA-3B)
Aircraft lost: 4 EA-1F

VAW-33 *Knighthawks*
1 deployment on USS *Intrepid* between May and Dec 1967.
Aircraft: EA-1F   Code: AK   Aircraft lost: 0

VAW-111 *Hunters*
29 deployments on USS *Bennington, Bon Homme Richard, Coral Sea, Hancock, Hornet, Kearsarge, Oriskany, Ranger, Ticonderoga* and *Yorktown* between Apr 1967 and Jan 1974.
Aircraft: E-1B   Code: various   Aircraft lost: 1

VAW-112 *Golden Hawks*
3 deployments on USS *Enterprise* between Apr 1967 and Jul 1969.
Aircraft: E-2A   Code: NG, RR   Aircraft lost: 0

VAW-113 *Black Eagles*
4 deployments on USS *Constellation* and *Enterprise* between Apr 1967 and Jun 1973.
Aircraft: E-2A/B   Code: NK   Aircraft lost: 0

VAW-114 *Hornet Hawgs*
5 deployments on USS *Kitty Hawk* between Apr 1967 and Nov 1972.   Aircraft: E-2A/B   Code: NH, RR   Aircraft lost: 0

VAW-115 *Liberty Bells*
5 deployments on USS *Midway* and *Ranger* between Nov 1967 and Mar 1973.
Aircraft: E-2A/B   Code: NE, NF   Aircraft lost: 1 E-2B

VAW-116 *Sun Kings*
5 deployments on USS *Constellation* and *Coral Sea* between Jul 1967 and Oct 1973.
Aircraft: E-2A/B   Code: NG, NL   Aircraft lost: 1 E-2A

VAW-121 *Griffons*
3 deployments on USS *Intrepid* and *Shangri-La* between May 1967 and Dec 1970.
Aircraft: E-1B   Code: AJ, AK   Aircraft lost: 0

VAW-122 *Hummer Gators*
1 deployment on USS *America* between Apr and Dec 1968.
Aircraft: E-2A   Code: AE   Aircraft lost: 0

VAW-123 *Screwtops*
2 deployments on USS *Forrestal* and *Saratoga* between Jun 1967 and May 1973.
Aircraft: E-2A/B   Code: AA, AC   Aircraft lost: 0

VAW-124 *Bullseyes*
2 deployments on USS *America* between Apr 1968 and Mar 1973.
Aircraft: E-2A/B   Code: AJ, NG   Aircraft lost: 0

VF-11 *Red Rippers*
1 deployment on USS *Forrestal* between Jun and Sep 1967.
Aircraft: F-4B   Code: AA   Aircraft lost: 0

VF-14 *Tophatters*
1 deployment on USS *Franklin D Roosevelt* between Jun 1966 and Feb 1967. Aircraft: F-4B   Code: AB   Aircraft lost: 1

263

VF-21 *Freelancers*
7 deployments on USS *Coral Sea, Midway* and *Ranger* between Mar 1965 and June 1973.
Aircraft: F-4B/J   Code: NE   Aircraft lost: 5 F-4B, 7 F-4J

VF-24 *Checkertails*
8 deployments on USS *Bon Homme Richard* and *Hancock* between Oct 1964 and Jan 1974. Aircraft: F-8C/H/J
Code: NP   Aircraft lost: 8 F-8C, 4 F-8H, 3 F-8J

VF-31 *Tomcatters*
1 deployment on USS *Saratoga* between Apr 1972 and Feb 1973.
Aircraft: F-4J   Code: AC   Aircraft lost: 0

VF-32 *Swordsmen*
1 deployment on USS *Franklin D Roosevelt* between Jun 1966 and Feb 1967. Aircraft: F-4B   Code: AB   Aircraft lost: 0

VF-33 *Tarsiers*
1 deployment on USS *America* between Apr and Dec 1968.
Aircraft: F-4J   Code: AE   Aircraft lost: 3

VF-41 *Black Aces*
1 deployment on USS *Independence* between May and Dec 1965.
Aircraft: F-4B   Code: AG   Aircraft lost: 2

VF-51 *Screaming Eagles*
6 deployments with F-8 on USS *Bon Homme Richard, Hancock* and *Ticonderoga* Apr 1964 - Nov 1970,
2 deployments with F-4 on USS *Coral Sea* Nov 1971 - Nov 1973.
Aircraft: F-8E/H/J, F-4B   Code: NF (F-8), NL (F-4)
Aircraft lost: 4 F-8E, 1 F-8H, 2 F-8J, 2 F-4B

VF-53 *Iron Angels*
6 deployments on USS *Bon Homme Richard, Hancock* and *Ticonderoga* between Apr 1964 and Nov 1970.
Aircraft: F-8E/J   Code: NF   Aircraft lost: 7 F-8E, 6 F-8J

VF-74 *Be-devilers*
2 deployments on USS *America* and *Forrestal* between Jun 1967 and Mar 1973.
Aircraft: F-4B/J   Code: AA, AJ   Aircraft lost: 1 F-4J

VF-84 *Jolly Rogers*
1 deployment on USS *Independence* between May and Dec 1965.
Aircraft: F-4B   Code: AG   Aircraft lost: 3

VF-92 *Silver Kings*
8 deployments on USS *America, Constellation, Enterprise* and *Ranger* between Aug 1964 and Oct 1973.
Aircraft: F-4B/J   Code: NG   Aircraft lost: 9 F-4B, 4 F-4J

VF-96 *Fighting Falcons*
8 deployments on USS *America, Constellation, Enterprise* and *Ranger* between Aug 1964 and Oct 1973.
Aircraft: F-4B/J   Code: NG   Aircraft lost: 10 F-4B, 1 F-4J

VF-102 *Diamondbacks*
1 deployment on USS *America* between Apr and Dec 1968.
Aircraft: F-4J   Code: AE   Aircraft lost: 2

VF-103 *Sluggers*
1 deployment on USS *Saratoga* between Apr 1972 and Feb 1973.
Aircraft: F-4J   Code: AC   Aircraft lost: 3

VF-111 *Sundowners*
7 deployments with F-8 on USS *Intrepid, Midway, Oriskany, Shangri-La* and *Ticonderoga* between Mar 1965 and Dec 1970.
2 deployments with F-4 on USS *Coral Sea* between Nov 1971 and Nov 1973. Aircraft: F-8C/D/E/H/J, F-4B
Code: AH, AJ, AK, NE (F-8), NL (F-4)
Aircraft lost: 7 F-8C, 5 F-8D, 4 F-8E, 1 F-8H, 1 F-4B

VF-114 *Aardvarks*
6 deployments on USS *Kitty Hawk* between Oct 1965 and Nov 1972. Aircraft: F-4B/J   Code: NH   Aircraft lost: 18 F-4B, 2 F-4J

VF-142 *Ghostriders*
7 deployments on USS *Constellation, Enterprise* and *Ranger* between May 1964 and Jun 1973.
Aircraft: F-4B/J   Code: NK   Aircraft lost: 6 F-4B

VF-143 *Pukin Dogs*
7 deployments on USS *Constellation, Enterprise* and *Ranger* between May 1964 and Jun 1973.
Aircraft: F-4B/J   Code: NK   Aircraft lost: 6 F-4B, 2 F-4J

VF-151 *Vigilantes*
7 deployments on USS *Constellation, Coral Sea* and *Midway* between Dec 1964 and Mar 1973.
Aircraft: F-4B   Code: NF, NL   Aircraft lost: 11

VF-154 *Black Knights*
1 deployment with F-8 on USS *Coral Sea* between Dec 1964 and Nov 1965. 6 deployments with F-4 on USS *Coral Sea* and *Ranger* between Jul 1966 and Jun 1973.Aircraft: F-8D, F-4B/J
Code: NL (F-8), NE (F-4)   Aircraft lost: 6 F-8D, 8 F-4B, 1 F-4J

VF-161 *Chargers*
6 deployments on USS *Constellation, Coral Sea* and *Midway* between May 1966 and Mar 1973.
Aircraft: F-4B   Code: NL   Aircraft lost: 7

VF-162 *Hunters*
5 deployments on USS *Oriskany, Shangri-La* and *Ticonderoga* between Apr 1965 and Dec 1970. Aircraft: F-8E/H/J
Code: AH, AJ   Aircraft lost: 13 F-8E, 3 F-8H, 1 F-8J

VF-191 *Satan's Kittens*
8 deployments on USS *Bon Homme Richard, Oriskany* and *Ticonderoga* between Jan 1964 and Mar 1973.
Aircraft: F-8E/J   Code: NM   Aircraft lost: 10 F-8E, 3 F-8J

VF-194 *Red Lightnings*
8 deployments on USS *Bon Homme Richard, Oriskany* and *Ticonderoga* between Jan 1964 and Mar 1973.
Aircraft: F-8C/E/J   Code: NM   Aircraft lost: 8 F-8E, 4 F-8J

VF-211 *Checkmates*
8 deployments on USS *Bon Homme Richard* and *Hancock* between Oct 1964 and Jan 1974. Aircraft: F-8E/H/J
Code: NP   Aircraft lost: 10 F-8E, 2 F-8H, 4 F-8J

VF-213 *Black Lions*
6 deployments on USS *Kitty Hawk* between Oct 1965 and Nov 1972.
Aircraft: F-4B/G/J   Code: NH   Aircraft lost: 3 F-4B, 1 F-4G, 1 F-4J

VFP-62 *Fighting Photos*
1 deployment on USS *Franklin D Roosevelt* between Jun 1966 and Feb 1967. Aircraft: RF-8G   Code: AB   Aircraft lost: 1

VFP-63 *Eyes of the Fleet*
41 deployments on USS *Bon Homme Richard, Constellation, Coral Sea, Hancock, Intrepid, Midway, Oriskany, Ranger, Shangri-La* and *Ticonderoga* between Jan 1964 and Jan 1974.
Aircraft: RF-8A/G   Code: PP until 1967 then various.
Aircraft lost: 14 RF-8A, 16 RF-8G

VS-21 *Fighting Redtails*
4 deployments on USS *Kearsarge* between Jun 1964 and Sep 1969.
Aircraft: S-2E/F   Code: NS   Aircraft lost: 2 S-2E

VS-23 *Black Cats*
3 deployments on USS *Yorktown* between Oct 1964 and Jul 1968.
Aircraft: S-2E   Code: NU   Aircraft lost: 1

VS-25 *Golden Eagles*
3 deployments on USS *Yorktown* between Oct 1964 and Jul 1968.
Aircraft: S-2E   Code: NU   Aircraft lost: 0

VS-29 *Tromboners/Yellowtails*
4 deployments on USS *Kearsarge* between Jun 1964 and Sep 1969.
Aircraft: S-2E/F   Code: NS   Aircraft lost: 0

VS-33 *Screwbirds*
3 deployments on USS *Bennington* between Mar 1965 and Nov 1968. Aircraft: S-2E   Code: NT   Aircraft lost: 0

VS-35 *Boomerangs*
3 deployments on USS *Hornet* between Aug 1965 and May 1969.
Aircraft: S-2D/E   Code: NV   Aircraft lost: 1 S-2D

VS-37 *Sawbucks*
3 deployments on USS *Hornet* between Aug 1965 and Nov 1968.
Aircraft: S-2E   Code: NV   Aircraft lost: 0

VS-38 *Red Griffons*
3 deployments on USS *Bennington* between Mar 1965 and Nov 1968. Aircraft: S-2E   Code: NT   Aircraft lost: 0

VSF-3 *Chessmen*
1 deployment on USS *Intrepid* between May and Dec 1967.
Aircraft: A-4B   Code: AK   Aircraft lost: 3

US Navy Patrol Squadron Detachments to South Vietnam and Thailand

VP-1 *Fleet's Finest*
Home port: NAS Whidbey Island, Wash.
Tan Son Nhut, 7 Oct 1964-1 Apr 1965 and 13 Feb-27 May 1966; Cam Ranh Bay, 12 May-12 Nov 1967 and 15 Aug 1968-25 Feb 1969; U-Tapao RTAB, 1 Feb-15 Apr 1970; Tan Son Nhut, 1 May-27 Jul 1970; Cam Ranh Bay, 1 Apr-1 Oct 1971; U-Tapao, 1 Nov 1972-30 Apr 1973. Aircraft: SP-2H to July 1969 then P-3B   Code: YB   Aircraft lost: 0

VP-2 *Neptunes*
Home port: NAS Whidbey Island, Wash.
Tan Son Nhut, 15 Mar-1 May 1965, 25 May-30 Sep 1966 and 1-15 Oct 1967; Cam Ranh Bay, 15 Oct 1967-1 Apr 1968.
Aircraft: SP-2H   Code: YC   Aircraft lost: 0

VP-4 *Skinny Dragons*
Home port: NAS Barbers Point, Hawaii.
Cam Ranh Bay, 15 Aug 1968-10 Jan 1969 and Feb-Jul 1971; U-Tapao RTAB, 1 May-1 Nov 1972.
Aircraft: P-3A   Code: YD   Aircraft lost: 0

VP-6 *Blue Sharks*
Home port: NAS Barbers Point, Hawaii.
Cam Ranh Bay, 13 May-7 Jun 1968; U-Tapao RTAB, 27 May-15 Nov 1969; Cam Ranh Bay, 21 Sep-2 Dec 1971; U-Tapao, 20 Dec 1972-1 Feb 1973.
Aircraft: P-3A   Code: PC   Aircraft lost: 0

VP-9 *Golden Eagles*
Home port: NAS Moffett Field, Calif.
Cam Ranh Bay, 1 Apr-1 Oct 1969; U-Tapao RTAB, Dec 1971-11 Feb 1972.
Aircraft: P-3B   Code: PD   Aircraft lost: 0

VP-11 *Lovin' Eleven*
Home port: NAS Brunswick, Maine.
U-Tapao RTAB, 23 Jul-8 Nov 1972.
Aircraft: P-3B   Code: LE   Aircraft lost: 0

VP-16 *Eagles*
Home port: NAS Jacksonville, Fla.
U-Tapao RTAB, 18 Jan-18 Feb 1967.
Aircraft: P-3A   Code: LF   Aircraft lost: 0

VP-17 *White Lightnings*
Home port: NAS Whidbey Island, Wash until 1 Dec 1968 then NAS Barbers Point, Hawaii.
Tan Son Nhut, 9 Jul 1965-1 Feb 1966 and 5 Dec 1966-1 Apr 1967; Cam Ranh Bay, 9 Nov 1967-29 Apr 1968, 9 Aug-11 Sep 1969, 3-15 Nov 1969 and 15-22 Dec 1969; U-Tapao RTAB, 29 Oct 1970-29 Apr 1971. Aircraft: SP-2H to Dec 1968 then P-3A
Code: ZE   Aircraft lost: 0

VP-19 *Big Red*
Home port: NAS Moffett Field, Calif.
U-Tapao RTAB, 1-14 Apr 1968; Cam Ranh Bay, 15 Jun-15 Jul 1968 and 10 Oct 1970-30 Jan 1971; U-Tapao, 1 Nov 1971-29 Apr 1972. Aircraft: P-3B   Code: PE   Aircraft lost: 0

VP-22 *Blue Geese Squadron*
Home port: NAS Barbers Point, Hawaii.
Cam Ranh Bay, Apr 1965-Jan 1966, 16 Jul-10 Dec 1968; U-Tapao RTAB, 30 Nov 1969-29 Apr 1970; Cam Ranh Bay, 25 Jan-2 Feb 1971; U-Tapao, 27 Mar-3 Apr 1971.
Aircraft: P-3A   Code: QA   Aircraft lost: 0

VP-26 *Tridents*
Home port: NAS Brunswick, Maine.
U-Tapao RTAB, 16 Dec 1967-2 Jun 1968.
Aircraft: P-3B   Code LK   Aircraft lost: 2

VP-28 *Hawaiian Warriors*
Home port: NAS Barbers Point, Hawaii.
Cam Ranh Bay, 17 Jan-11 Feb 1969, 29 Apr-15 May 1969 and 13 Jun-18 Jul 1969. Aircraft: P-3A   Code: QC   Aircraft lost: 0

Four squadrons deployed the SP-2 Neptune to Southeast Asia to take part in the Market Time surveillance campaign to reduce infiltration in to South Vietnam by sea. VP-1 sent four detachments to Tan Son Nhut and Cam Ranh Bay between October 1964 and February 1969 but the only Neptune lost during the war was a VP-42 aircraft. USN

VP-40 *Fighting Marlins*
Home port: NAS North Island, Calif, to 15 Nov 1967 then NAS Moffett Field, Calif.
Da Nang, 29 May-3 Aug 1965; Cam Ranh Bay, 1 Mar-30 Apr 1967 and 1 Feb-1 Aug 1969; U-Tapao RTAB, 29 Apr-30 Oct 1970 and 16 Nov-20 Dec 1972. Aircraft: SP-5B to Nov 1967 then P-3B   Code: QE   Aircraft lost: 0

VP-42 *Sea Demons*
Home port: NAS Whidbey Island, Wash.
Tan Son Nhut, 18-19 Sep 1964, Oct 1964-Feb 1965 and 8 Oct 1965-13 Feb 1966; Cam Ranh Bay, 2 Apr-1 Dec 1967; Tan Son Nhut, 31 Mar-30 Sep 1967; Cam Ranh Bay, 10 Mar-3 Sep 1968. Aircraft: SP-2E/H   Code: RB   Aircraft lost: 1 SP-2E

VP-45 *Red Darters*
Home port: NAS Jacksonville, Fla.
U-Tapao RTAB, 16 Dec 1968-30 May 1969; Cam Ranh Bay, 18 Apr-28 May 1969. Aircraft: P-3A   Code: LN   Aircraft lost: 0

VP-46 *Grey Knights*
Home port: NAS Moffett Field, Calif.
U-Tapao RTAB, 18 Feb-30 Jun 1967; Cam Ranh Bay, 2 Oct 1969-31 Mar 1970. Aircraft: P-3B   Code: RC   Aircraft lost: 0

VP-47 *Golden Swordsmen*
Home port: NAS Moffett Field, Calif.
U-Tapao RTAB, 1 Jul 1967-4 Jan 1968; Cam Ranh Bay, 1 Nov 1968-31 Mar 1969 and 16 Jan-8 May 1970; U-Tapao, 9 May-13 Jul 1970. Aircraft: P-3B   Code: RD   Aircraft lost: 0

VP-48 *Boomerangers*
Home port: NAS North Island, Calif, to 15 Feb 1967 then NAS Moffett Field, Calif.
Cam Ranh Bay, 1 Oct 1965-27 Sep 1966 and 1 Apr-1 Oct 1970; U-Tapao RTAB, 1 May-30 Sep 1971.
Aircraft: SP-5B to Jan 1967 then P-3A to Feb 1968 then P-3B
Code: SF   Aircraft lost: 0

VP-49 *Woodpeckers*
Home port: NAS Patuxent River, Md.
U-Tapao RTAB, 15 Jun-14 Dec 1968.
Aircraft: P-3A   Code: LP   Aircraft lost: 0

VP-50 *Blue Dragons*
Home port: NAS North Island, Calif, to 1 July 1967 then NAS Moffett Field, Calif.
Cam Ranh Bay, 26 Aug 1965-14 Mar 1966, 23 Aug 1966-6 Feb 1967, 1 May-2 Nov 1968, 15 Jul 1969-15 Jan 1970 and 29 Sep 1970-31 Mar 1971. Aircraft: SP-5B to Jul 1967 then P-3A to 1970 then P-3B   Code: SG   Aircraft lost: 0

Other US Navy Land-based Squadrons

VAH-21
Activated at NAS Sangley Point, Philippines with a detachment at Cam Ranh Bay, 1 Sep 1968; inactivated, 16 Jun 1969.
Aircraft: AP-2H   Code: SL   Aircraft lost: 0

VAL-4 *Black Ponies*
Activated at NAS North Island, Calif, 3 Jan 1969; deployed to Binh Thuy with a detachment at Vung Tau, 23 Mar 1969; inactivated, 10 Apr 1972. Aircraft: OV-10A, YOV-10D
Code: UM   Aircraft lost: 7 OV-10A

VAP-61 *World Famous*
Home port: NAS Agana, Guam with detachments on board aircraft carriers and at Da Nang, Don Muang and U-Tapao RTAB from 17 May 1964; inactivated, 1 Jul 1971.
Aircraft: EA-3B, KA-3B, RA-3B   Code: SS   Aircraft lost: 5 RA-3B

VAP-62 *Tigers*
Home port: NAS Jacksonville, Fla, with detachments on board aircraft carriers and at Da Nang to supplement VAP-61 from 31 Oct 1966. Inactivated, 15 Oct 1969.
Aircraft: EA-3B, EA-3B   Code GB   Aircraft lost: 0

VC-5 *Checkertails*
Home port: NAS Atsugi, Japan with a detachment at Da Nang from 1965 to 31 Dec 1969.
Aircraft: A-4B/C, C-1A, DF-8D, TA-4F, US-2C   Code: UE
Aircraft lost: 2 US-2C

VO-67
Activated at NAS Alameda, Calif, 15 Feb 1967; deployed to Nakhon Phanom RTAB, 15 Nov 1967; inactivated, 1 Jul 1968.
Aircraft: OP-2E   Code: MR   Aircraft lost: 3

VQ-1 *Worldwatchers*
Home port: NAS Atsugi, Japan with detachments at Da Nang, Cubi Point and Don Muang from 1 Oct 1964 to 17 Feb 1973; home port moved to NAS Agana, Guam, June 1971.
Aircraft: C-121J, EA-3B, EC-121M, ERA-3B, EP-3B
Code: PR   Aircraft lost: 1 EC-121M

VQ-2 *Batmen*
Home port: NAS Rota, Spain with detachments at Da Nang and Cubi Point from 1 Dec 1965 to 30 Sep 1969.
Aircraft: EA-3B, EC-121M   Code: JQ   Aircraft lost: 0

VR-30 *Stagecoach West*
Home port: NAS Alameda, Calif with a detachment to Da Nang from 11 Jan 1969 to 1 Feb 1973.
Aircraft: C-1A   Code: RW   Aircraft lost: 0

VRC-50 *Foo Dogs*
Home port: NAS Atsugi, Japan with a detachment to NAS Cubi Point, Philippines from 1 Oct 1966 and a forward operating location at Da Nang from 1 Feb 1970 to 2 Jan 1971 and 15 Dec 1971 to 19 Feb 1973; moved to NAS North Island, Calif, Feb 1971 but maintained the detachments at Cubi Point and Da Nang; moved to Cubi Point, Jul 1972.
Aircraft: C-1A, C-2A, CT-39E, KC-130F   Code: RG
Aircraft lost: 3 C-2A

VW-1 *Typhoon Trackers*
Home port: NAS Agana, Guam with a detachment at NAS Sangley Point, Philippines and forward operating locations at Chu Lai and Da Nang from 1 Oct 1964 to 1 Jul 1971.
Aircraft: EC-121K/P, WC-121N   Code: TE   Aircraft lost: 0

VX-8 *Blue Eagles*
Home port: NAS Patuxent River, MD with detachments at Tan Son Nhut and Da Nang from Oct 1965 to 1 Dec 1970; activated as Oceanographic Air Survey Unit,1 Jul 1965, redesignated VX-8, 1 Jul 1967; redesignated VXN-8, 1 Jan 1969.
Aircraft: NC-121J   Code: JB   Aircraft lost: 0

United States Marine Corps Aviation Order of Battle

USMC Squadrons

VMCJ-1 *Golden Hawks*
Assigned to MAG-16, Da Nang from MCAS Iwakuni, Japan, 16 Apr 1965; reassigned to MAG-11, Da Nang, 14 Jul 1965; reassigned to MAG-15, Iwakuni, 14 Jul 1970; detachment of EA-6As to Da Nang, Mar-May 1971; detachment of EA-6As to NAS Cubi Point, Philippines, 3 Apr 1972-Jan 1973.
Aircraft: EA-6A, EF-10B, RF-4B, RF-8A   Code: RM
Aircraft lost: 1 EA-6A, 4 RF-4B, 1 RF-8A, 5 EF-10B

VMCJ-2 Detachment X *Playboys*
Deployments to NAS Cubi Point, Philippines, 3 Apr 1972 and USS *Saratoga*, May 1972; returned to 2 MAW, MCAS Cherry Point, NC, Feb 1973. Aircraft: EA-6A   Code: CY   Aircraft lost: 1

VMO-2
Deployed to Marble Mountain with MAG-16, 3 May 1965 with detachments at Dong Ha and Khe Sanh; reassigned to MAG-11, Da Nang, 31 Jan 1970; reassigned to 3 MAW, MCAS Camp Pendleton, Calif, 31 Mar 1971.
Aircraft: O-1B/C/G, OV-10A, UH-1E   Code: VS
Aircraft lost: 2 O-1B, 6 OV-10A

VMO-6
Deployed to Chu Lai with MAG-36, 1 Sep 1965 with detachments at Da Nang, Ky Ha, Phu Bai and Quang Tri; reassigned to Provisional MAG-39, Quang Tri, 16 Apr 1968; reassigned to MAG-15, MCAS Futenma, Okinawa, 12 Oct 1969.
Aircraft: O-1C/G, OV-10A, UH-1E   Code: WB
Aircraft lost: 2 O-1G, 3 OV-10A

H&MS-11
Deployed to Da Nang with MAG-11, 7 Jul 1965; reassigned to 3 MAW, MCAS El Toro, Calif, 1 Jun 1971.
Aircraft: C-117D, OV-10A, TA-4F, TF-9J   Code: TM
Aircraft lost: 1 C-117D, 1 OV-10A, 7 TA-4F

H&MS-12
Deployed to Chu Lai with MAG-12, 25 May 1965; reassigned with MAG-12 to MCAS Iwakuni, Japan, 25 Feb 1970; deployed to Bien Hoa with MAG-12, 17 May 1972-30 Jan 1973.
Aircraft: C-117D, TA-4F   Code: WA   Aircraft lost: 1 TA-4F

H&MS-13
Deployed to Chu Lai with MAG-13, 25 Sep 1966; reassigned to 3 MAW, MCAS El Toro, Calif, 30 Sep 1970.
Aircraft: C-117D, TA-4F, TF-9J   Code: YU
Aircraft lost: 1 C-117D, 1 TA-4F, 1 TF-9J

H&MS-15 Detachment N
Deployed on board USS *Hornet*, 12 Aug 1965-23 Mar 1966.
Aircraft: A-4C   Code: YV   Aircraft lost: 0

H&MS-15 Detachment
Deployed to Da Nang with MAG-15 from MCAS Iwakuni, Japan, 16 Apr-20 Jun 1972.
Aircraft: TA-4F   Code: YV   Aircraft lost: 1 TA-4F

H&MS-16
Deployed to Marble Mountain with MAG-16, 6 May 1965; reassigned with MAG-16 to MCAS Santa Ana, Calif, 20 Jun 1971
Aircraft: O-1C/G, TA-4F   Code: WW   Aircraft lost: 3 O-1C

H&MS-36
Deployed to Chu Lai with MAG-36, 1 Sep 1965; reassigned with MAG-36 to MCAS Futenma, Okinawa, 7 Nov 1969.
Aircraft: C-117D, CH-46D, UH-34D   Code: WX   Aircraft lost: 0

VMFA-115 *Silver Eagles*
Assigned to MAG-11, Da Nang, 15 Oct 1965; reassigned to MAG-13, MCAS Iwakuni, Japan, 13 Jan 1966; reassigned to MAG-11, Da Nang, 11 Apr 1966; reassigned to MAG-15, Iwakuni, 15 Feb 1967; reassigned to MAG-13, Chu Lai, 14 May 1967; reassigned to MAG-11, Da Nang, 24 Aug 1970; reassigned to MAG-15, Iwakuni, 1 Mar 1971; deployed to Da Nang with MAG-15, 6 Apr 1972; moved to Nam Phong, 16 Jun 1972; deployed to Naha AB, Okinawa with MAG-15, 31 Aug 1973.
Aircraft: F-4B   Code: VE   Aircraft lost: 23

VMA-121 *Green Knights*
Assigned to MAG-12, Chu Lai, 1 Dec 1966; reassigned to MAG-15, MCAS Iwakuni, Japan, 3 Jun 1967; reassigned to MAG-12, Chu Lai, 5 Sep 1967; reassigned to 2 MAW, MCAS Cherry Point, NC, 14 Feb 1969; converted to A-6A and redesignated VMA(AW)-121.
Aircraft: A-4C/E   Code: VK   Aircraft lost: 12 A-4E

VMFA-122 *Crusaders*
Assigned to MAG-11, Da Nang, 1 Sep 1967; reassigned to MAG-15, MCAS Iwakuni, Japan, 30 Aug 1968; reassigned to MAG-13, Chu Lai, 5 Sep 1969; reassigned to MCAS Kaneohe Bay, Hawaii, 8 Sep 1970.
Aircraft: F-4B   Code: DC   Aircraft lost: 13

VMGR-152
Based at MCAS Futenma, Okinawa, with MAG-13 and MAG-15 with a detachment at Da Nang, 1965-1971 and Nam Phong, Jun-Sep 1973. Aircraft: KC-130F   Code: QD   Aircraft lost: 4

VMA-211 *Avengers*
Assigned to MAG-12, Chu Lai, 11 Oct 1965; reassigned to MAG-13, MCAS Iwakuni, Japan, 14 Jul 1966; reassigned to MAG-12, Chu Lai, 1 Oct 1966; reassigned to MAG-15, Iwakuni, 3 Sep 1967; reassigned to MAG-12, Chu Lai, 1 Dec 1967; reassigned to MAG-15, Iwakuni, 25 Feb 1970; deployed to Bien Hoa with MAG-12, 17 May 1972; returned to Iwakuni with MAG-12, 30 Jan 1973. Aircraft: A-4E   Code: CF   Aircraft lost: 23

VMFA-212 *Lancers*
Deployed to Da Nang with MAG-15, 14 Apr 1972; returned to MCAS Kaneohe Bay, Hawaii, 20 Jun 1972.
Aircraft: F-4J   Code: WD   Aircraft lost: 2

VMF(AW)-212 *Lancers*
Deployed on board USS *Oriskany*, 5 Apr 1965; returned to MCAS Kaneohe Bay, Hawaii, 16 Dec 1965.
Aircraft: F-8E   Code: WD   Aircraft lost: 4

VMA-214 *Black Sheep*
Assigned to MAG-12, Chu Lai, 21 Jun 1965; reassigned to MAG-13, MCAS Iwakuni, Japan, 16 Feb 1966; reassigned to MAG-12, Chu Lai, 30 Apr 1966; reassigned to 3 MAW, MCAS El Toro, Calif, 3 Apr 1967.
Aircraft: A-4C   Code: WE   Aircraft lost: 2

VMA-223 *Bulldogs*
Detachment T deployed on board USS *Yorktown*, 23 Oct 1964-16 May 1965; assigned to MAG-12, Chu Lai, 15 Dec 1965; reassigned to MAG-15, MCAS Iwakuni, Japan, 1 Dec 1966; reassigned to MAG-12, Chu Lai, 2 Mar 1967; reassigned to MAG-15, Iwakuni, 3 Dec 1967; reassigned to MAG-12, Chu Lai, 23 Apr 1968; reassigned to MAG-33, MCAS El Toro, Calif, 28 Jan 1970.
Aircraft: A-4C/E   Code: WP   Aircraft lost: 4 A-4C, 10 A-4E

VMFA-115 was the first Marine Corps Phantom squadron to sustain casualties in Vietnam. Two of the Squadron's aircraft crashed into Monkey Mountain near Da Nang in poor visibility on 26 October 1965 killing all four crewmen. USMC

Photograph on the opposite page:
Phantoms of VMFA-115 and VMFA-323 are seen on the pan at Da Nang, probably in late 1965 when the two squadrons served together with MAG-11. Between them these two Marine Corps squadrons lost a total of 34 Phantoms. USMC

VMA-224 *Bengals*
Assigned to MAG-12, Chu Lai, 4 Oct 1965; reassigned to MAG-13,
MCAS Iwakuni, Japan, 1 May 1966; reassigned to MAG-12, Chu
Lai, 14 Jul 1966; reassigned to 2 MAW, MCAS Cherry Point, NC,
1 Nov 1966; converted to A-6A and redesignated VMA(AW)-224.
Aircraft: A-4E   Code: WK   Aircraft lost: 5

VMA(AW)-224
Deployed on board USS *Coral Sea*, 12 Nov 1971-17 Jul 1972.
Aircraft: A-6A/B, KA-6D   Code: NL   Aircraft lost: 4 A-6A

VMA-225
Assigned to MAG-12, Chu Lai, 1 Jun 1965;
reassigned to 2 MAW, MCAS Cherry Point, NC, 30 Sep 1965.
Aircraft: A-4C   Code: CE   Aircraft lost: 0

VMA(AW)-225 *Vikings*
Assigned to MAG-11, Da Nang, 5 Feb 1969;
reassigned to 3 MAW, MCAS El Toro, Calif, 30 Apr 1971.
Aircraft: A-6A   Code: CE   Aircraft lost: 2

VMFA-232 *Red Devils*
Assigned to MAG-13, Chu Lai, 21 Mar 1969; reassigned
to MAG-15, MCAS Iwakuni, Japan, 7 Sep 1969; deployed to
Da Nang with MAG-15, 6 Apr 1972; moved to Nam Phong,
20 Jun 1972; deployed to NAS Cubi Point, Philippines, 1 Sep 1973.
Aircraft: F-4J   Code: WT   Aircraft lost: 5

VMF(AW)-232 *Red Devils*
Assigned to MAG-11, Da Nang, 15 Nov 1966;
reassigned to MAG-33, MCAS El Toro, Calif, 1 Sep 1967.
Aircraft: F-8E   Code: WT   Aircraft lost: 7

VMF(AW)-235 *Death Angels*
Assigned to MAG-11, Da Nang, 1 Feb 1966;
reassigned to MAG-15, MCAS Iwakuni, Japan, 15 Nov 1966;
reassigned to MAG-11, Da Nang, 15 Feb 1967;
reassigned to MAG-15, Iwakuni, 10 May 1968.
Aircraft: F-8E   Code: DB   Aircraft lost: 11

VMA(AW)-242 *Batmen*
Assigned to MAG-11, Da Nang, 1 Nov 1966;
reassigned to 3 MAW, MCAS El Toro, Calif, 11 Sep 1970.
Aircraft: A-6A   Code: DT   Aircraft lost: 9

VMA-311 *Tomcats*
Assigned to MAG-12, Chu Lai, 1 Jun 1965; reassigned to MAG-13,
MCAS Iwakuni, Japan, 16 Dec 1965; reassigned to MAG-12,
Chu Lai, 15 Feb 1966; reassigned to MAG-15, Iwakuni,
2 Mar 1967; reassigned to MAG-12, Chu Lai, 4 Jun 1967;
reassigned to MAG-13, Chu Lai, 12 Feb 1970; reassigned to
MAG-11, Da Nang, 15 Apr 1971; reassigned to MAG-12,
Iwakuni, 12 May 1971; deployed to Bien Hoa with MAG-12,
17 May 1972; returned to Iwakuni with MAG-12, 30 Jan 1973.
Aircraft: A-4C/E   Code: WL   Aircraft lost: 4 A-4C, 21 A-4E

VMF(AW)-312 *Checkerboards*
Assigned to MAG-11, Da Nang, 19 Dec 1965;
reassigned to MAG-32, MCAS Beaufort, SC, 2 Feb 1966.
Aircraft: F-8E   Code: DR   Aircraft lost: 0

VMFA-314 *Black Knights*
Assigned to MAG-11, Da Nang, 15 Jan 1966; reassigned to
MAG-13, MCAS Iwakuni, Japan, 14 Apr 1966; reassigned to
MAG-11, Da Nang, 1 Aug 1966; reassigned to MAG-13, Chu Lai,
25 Sep 1966; reassigned to MAG-15, Iwakuni, 16 Aug 1967;
reassigned to MAG-13, Chu Lai, 16 Nov 1967; reassigned
to 3 MAW, MCAS El Toro, Calif, 12 Sep 1970.
Aircraft: F-4B   Code: VW   Aircraft lost: 24

VMFA-323 *Death Rattlers*
Assigned to MAG-11, Da Nang, 1 Dec 1965; deployed on TDY to
Tainan AB, Taiwan, 1 Mar 1966; reassigned to MAG-15, MCAS
Iwakuni, Japan, 24 Jun 1966; reassigned to MAG-11, Da Nang,
5 Jul 1966; reassigned to MAG-13, Chu Lai, 6 Oct 1966;
reassigned to MAG-15, Iwakuni, 15 May 1967; reassigned to
MAG-13, Chu Lai, 16 Aug 1967; reassigned to MAG-33, MCAS
El Toro, Calif, 25 Mar 1969.
Aircraft: F-4B   Code: WS   Aircraft lost: 11

VMFA-333 *Shamrocks*
Deployed on board USS *America*, 5 Jun 1972-24 Mar 1973.
Aircraft: F-4J   Code: DN changed to AJ for carrier deployment
Aircraft lost: 3

VMFA-334 *Falcons*
Assigned to MAG-11, Da Nang, 30 Aug 1968;
reassigned to MAG-13, Chu Lai, 24 Jan 1969;
reassigned to MAG-15, MCAS Iwakuni, Japan, 30 Aug 1969.
Aircraft: F-4J   Code: WU   Aircraft lost: 5

VMFA-513 *Flying Nightmares*
Assigned to MAG-16, Da Nang, 15 Jun 1965;
reassigned to MAG-11, Da Nang, 14 Jul 1965;
reassigned to MCAS Cherry Point, NC, 14 Oct 1965.
Aircraft: F-4B   Code: WF   Aircraft lost: 0

VMFA-531 *Gray Ghosts*
Assigned to MAG-16, Da Nang from NAS Atsugi, Japan, 10 Apr
1965; reassigned to MCAS Cherry Point, NC, 15 Jun 1965.
Aircraft: F-4B   Code: EC   Aircraft lost: 0

VMA(AW)-533 *Nighthawks*
Assigned to MAG-12, Chu Lai, 1 Apr 1967; reassigned to MAG-15,
MCAS Iwakuni, Japan, 7 Oct 1969; deployed to Nam Phong
with MAG-15, 20 Jun 1972; returned to Iwakuni, 31 Aug 1973.
Aircraft: A-6A   Code: ED   Aircraft lost: 10

VMFA-542 *Bengals*
Assigned to MAG-16, Da Nang, 10 Jul 1965;
reassigned to MAG-11, Da Nang, 14 Jul 1965;
reassigned to MAG-13, MCAS Iwakuni, Japan, 3 Dec 1965;
reassigned to MAG-11, Da Nang, 1 Mar 1966;
reassigned to MAG-13, Iwakuni, 1 Aug 1966;
reassigned to MAG-15, Iwakuni, 15 Aug 1966;
reassigned to MAG-13, Chu Lai, 10 Oct 1966;
reassigned to MAG-15, Iwakuni, 15 Nov 1967;
reassigned to MAG-11, Da Nang, 10 May 1968;
reassigned to 3 MAW, MCAS El Toro, Calif, 31 Jan 1970.
Aircraft: F-4B   Code: WH   Aircraft lost: 12

Statistical Summary of Air Losses

General Statistics – Aircraft Losses by Year

United States Air Force

Year	Aircraft	Fatalities	POWs
1961	1	7	1
1962	9	19	0
1963	16	37	0
1964	40	40	2
1965	225	220	32
1966	376	350	65
1967	411	426	103
1968	384	506	31
1969	275	274	1
1970	161	291	0
1971	86	66	8
1972	195	195	98
1973	18	18	0
Totals	2197	2449	341

United States Navy

Year	Aircraft	Fatalities	POWs
1964	17	13	2
1965	134	59	18
1966	169	93	26
1967	185	124	55
1968	113	101	17
1969	62	53	1
1970	50	59	0
1971	24	22	2
1972	91	41	22
1973	9	10	1
Totals	854	575	144

United States Marine Corps

Year	Aircraft	Fatalities	POWs
1964	2	0	0
1965	16	68	3
1966	35	31	1
1967	59	34	5
1968	72	45	0
1969	41	34	0
1970	23	10	0
1971	1	2	0
1972	22	17	3
Totals	271	241	12

Total for all services

Year	Aircraft	Fatalities	POWs
1961	1	7	1
1962	9	19	0
1963	16	37	0
1964	59	53	4
1965	375	347	53
1966	580	474	92
1967	655	584	163
1968	569	652	48
1969	378	361	2
1970	234	360	0
1971	111	90	10
1972	308	253	123
1973	27	28	1
Totals	3322	3265	497

Aircraft Type Summary

United States Air Force

A-1 Skyraider
Total number of aircraft lost: 201 Fatalities: 107; POWs: 4.
Aircraft lost by year: 1964 (9), 1965 (30), 1966 (42), 1967 (16), 1968 (36), 1969 (29), 1970 (21), 1971 (10), 1972 (8).
Aircraft lost by region: South Vietnam (78), North Vietnam (18), Southern Laos (51), Northern Laos (39), Other regions (15).

A-7 Corsair
Total number of aircraft lost: 6 Fatalities: 2; POWs: 0.
Aircraft lost by year: 1972 (2), 1973 (4).
Aircraft lost by region: Southern Laos (1), Northern Laos (2), Cambodia (2), Other regions (1).

A-26/B-26 Invader
Total number of aircraft lost: 22 Fatalities: 51; POWs: 0.
Aircraft lost by year: 1962 (1), 1963 (7), 1964 (2), 1966 (3), 1967 (5), 1968 (1), 1969 (3).
Aircraft lost by region: South Vietnam (10), Southern Laos (7), Northern Laos (1), Other regions (4).

A-37 Dragonfly
Total number of aircraft lost: 22 Fatalities: 13; POWs: 0.
Aircraft lost by year: 1967 (2), 1968 (6), 1969 (2), 1970 (1), 1971 (4), 1972 (7).
Aircraft lost by region: South Vietnam (16), Cambodia (5), Other regions (1).

AC-47 Gunship I
Total number of aircraft lost: 19 Fatalities: 92; POWs: 0.
Aircraft lost by year: 1965 (2), 1966 (4), 1967 (6), 1968 (6), 1969 (1).
Aircraft lost by region: South Vietnam (16), Southern Laos (3).

AC-119 Gunship III
Total number of aircraft lost: 5 Fatalities: 16; POWs: 0.
Aircraft lost by year: 1969 (1), 1970 (3), 1971 (1).
Aircraft lost by region: South Vietnam (5).

AC-130 Gunship II
Total number of aircraft lost: 6 Fatalities: 52; POWs: 0.
Aircraft lost by year: 1969 (1), 1970 (1), 1972 (4).
Aircraft lost by region: Southern Laos (6).

B-52 Stratofortress
Total number of aircraft lost: 31 Fatalities: 73; POWs: 33.
Aircraft lost by year: 1965 (2), 1967 (3), 1968 (2), 1969 (3), 1972 (19), 1973 (2).
Aircraft lost by region: South Vietnam (1), North Vietnam (18), Other regions (12).

B-57 Canberra
Total number of aircraft lost: 58 Fatalities: 37; POWs: 2.
Aircraft lost by year: 1964 (7), 1965 (21), 1966 (13), 1967 (6), 1968 (6), 1969 (4), 1970 (1).
Aircraft lost by region: South Vietnam (41), North Vietnam (5), Southern Laos (11), Northern Laos (1).

C-7 Caribou
Total number of aircraft lost: 20 Fatalities: 63; POWs: 0.
Aircraft lost by year: 1967 (3), 1968 (7), 1969 (5), 1970 (4), 1971 (1). Aircraft lost by region: South Vietnam (20).

C-47 Skytrain (not including AC-47)
Total number of aircraft lost: 21 Fatalities: 139; POWs: 1.
Aircraft lost by year: 1961 (1), 1962 (1), 1966 (3), 1967 (3), 1968 (3), 1969 (4), 1970 (3), 1972 (2), 1973 (1).
Aircraft lost by region: South Vietnam (14), Southern Laos (4), Northern Laos (2), Other regions (1).

C-123 Provider
Total number of aircraft lost: 54 Fatalities: 403; POWs: 0.
Aircraft lost by year: 1962 (4), 1963 (3),1964 (2), 1965 (8), 1966 (11), 1967 (7), 1968 (10), 1969 (3), 1970 (4), 1971 (2).
Aircraft lost by region: South Vietnam (48), Southern Laos (3), Cambodia (1), Other regions (2).

C-130 Hercules (not including AC-130)
Total number of aircraft lost: 60 Fatalities: 395; POWs: 0.
Aircraft lost by year: 1965 (6), 1966 (8), 1967 (14), 1968 (16), 1969 (8), 1970 (1), 1971 (1), 1972 (6).
Aircraft lost by region: South Vietnam (51), North Vietnam (2), Southern Laos (2), Other regions (5).

C-141 Starlifter
Total number of aircraft lost: 2 Fatalities: 11; POWs: 0.
Aircraft lost by year: 1967 (2).
Aircraft lost by region: South Vietnam (2).

EB-66 Destroyer
Total number of aircraft lost: 14 Fatalities: 28; POWs: 12.
Aircraft lost by year: 1965 (1), 1966 (2), 1967 (3), 1968 (3), 1969 (1), 1970 (1), 1971 (1), 1972 (2).
Aircraft lost by region: South Vietnam (2), North Vietnam (4), Other regions (8).

EC-121R Bat Cat
Total number of aircraft lost: 2 Fatalities: 22; POWs: 0.
Aircraft lost by year: 1969 (2).
Aircraft lost by region: Other regions (2).

F-4 Phantom (not including RF-4C)
Total number of aircraft lost: 445 Fatalities: 321; POWs: 135.
Aircraft lost by year: 1965 (13), 1966 (56), 1967 (97), 1968 (63), 1969 (65), 1970 (33), 1971 (29), 1972 (83), 1973 (6).
Aircraft lost by region: South Vietnam (97), North Vietnam (193), Southern Laos (88), Northern Laos (23), Cambodia (8), Other regions (36).

F-5 Freedom Fighter
Total number of aircraft lost: 9 Fatalities: 6; POWs: 0.
Aircraft lost by year: 1965 (1), 1966 (7), 1967 (1).
Aircraft lost by region: South Vietnam (9).

F-100 Super Sabre
Total number of aircraft lost: 242   Fatalities: 87; POWs: 6.
Aircraft lost by year: 1964 (2), 1965 (26), 1966 (26),
1967 (36), 1968 (62), 1969 (54), 1970 (26), 1971 (10).
Aircraft lost by region: South Vietnam (189), North Vietnam
(16), Southern Laos (25), Northern Laos (3), Cambodia (6),
Other regions (3).

F-102 Delta Dagger
Total number of aircraft lost: 14   Fatalities: 2; POWs: 0.
Aircraft lost by year: 1964 (1), 1965 (4), 1966 (2),
1967 (3), 1968 (3), 1969 (1).
Aircraft lost by region: South Vietnam (6), Northern Laos (1),
Other regions (7).

F-104 Starfighter
Total number of aircraft lost: 14   Fatalities: 4; POWs: 2.
Aircraft lost by year: 1965 (5), 1966 (5), 1967 (4).
Aircraft lost by region: South Vietnam (2), North Vietnam (4),
Northern Laos (2), Other regions (6).

F-105 Thunderchief
Total number of aircraft lost: 397   Fatalities: 150; POWs: 103.
Aircraft lost by year: 1964 (1), 1965 (68), 1966 (126), 1967
(113), 1968 (47), 1969 (22), 1970 (10), 1971 (1), 1972 (9).
Aircraft lost by region: South Vietnam (2), North Vietnam (274),
Southern Laos (29), Northern Laos (30), Other regions (62).

F-111A
Total number of aircraft lost: 11   Fatalities: 14; POWs: 2.
Aircraft lost by year: 1968 (3), 1972 (6), 1973 (2).
Aircraft lost by region: North Vietnam (6), Southern Laos (2),
Cambodia (1), Other regions (2).

HU-16B Albatross
Total number of aircraft lost: 2   Fatalities: 9; POWs: 0.
Aircraft lost by year: 1966 (2).
Aircraft lost by region: North Vietnam (1), Other regions (1).

KB-50 Superfortress
Total number of aircraft lost: 1   Fatalities: 0; POWs: 0.
Aircraft lost by year: 1964 (1).
Aircraft lost by region: Other regions (1).

KC-135A Stratotanker
Total number of aircraft lost: 3   Fatalities: 14; POWs: 0.
Aircraft lost by year: 1968 (2), 1969 (1).
Aircraft lost by region: Other regions (3).

O-1 Bird Dog
Total number of aircraft lost: 178   Fatalities: 93; POWs: 1.
Aircraft lost by year: 1963 (2), 1964 (3), 1965 (28), 1966 (38),
1967 (40), 1968 (40), 1969 (15), 1970 (7), 1971 (3), 1972 (2).
Aircraft lost by region: South Vietnam (159), North Vietnam (4),
Southern Laos (11), Cambodia (2), Other regions (2).

O-2
Total number of aircraft lost: 104   Fatalities: 84; POWs: 2.
Aircraft lost by year: 1967 (7), 1968 (35), 1969 (24),
1970 (16), 1971 (8), 1972 (14).
Aircraft lost by region: South Vietnam (73), North Vietnam (5),
Southern Laos (19), Cambodia (6), Other regions (1).

OV-10A Bronco
Total number of aircraft lost: 64   Fatalities: 43; POWs: 5.
Aircraft lost by year: 1968 (2), 1969 (11), 1970 (19),
1971 (10), 1972 (19), 1973 (3).
Aircraft lost by region: South Vietnam (53), North Vietnam (1),
Southern Laos (18), Northern Laos (1), Cambodia (6),
Other regions (3).

QU-22
Total number of aircraft lost: 9   Fatalities: 2; POWs: 0.
Aircraft lost by year: 1969 (2), 1971 (2), 1972 (5).
Aircraft lost by region: Other regions (9).

RF-4C Phantom
Total number of aircraft lost: 83   Fatalities: 65; POWs: 22.
Aircraft lost by year: 1966 (7), 1967 (23), 1968 (25),
1969 (10), 1970 (9), 1971 (3), 1972 (6).
Aircraft lost by region: South Vietnam (17), North Vietnam (39),
Southern Laos (16), Northern Laos (6), Cambodia (2),
Other regions (3).

RF-101C Voodoo
Total number of aircraft lost: 38   Fatalities: 11; POWs: 11.
Aircraft lost by year: 1964 (1), 1965 (9), 1966 (16),
1967 (10), 1968 (2).
Aircraft lost by region: South Vietnam (4), North Vietnam (28),
Southern Laos (2), Northern Laos (1), Other regions (3).

SR-71A
Total number of aircraft lost: 2   Fatalities: 0; POWs: 0.
Aircraft lost by year: 1970 (1), 1972 (1).
Aircraft lost by region: Other regions (2).

T-28 Trojan
Total number of aircraft lost: 23   Fatalities: 25; POWs: 0.
Aircraft lost by year: 1962 (2), 1963 (4), 1964 (10),
1966 (1), 1967 (4), 1968 (2).
Aircraft lost by region: South Vietnam (16), North Vietnam (1),
Southern Laos (5), Other regions (1).

U-2
Total number of aircraft lost: 1   Fatalities: 0; POWs: 0.
Aircraft lost by year: 1966 (1).
Aircraft lost by region: South Vietnam (1).

U-3 Blue Canoe
Total number of aircraft lost: 1   Fatalities: 0; POWs: 0.
Aircraft lost by year: 1968 (1).
Aircraft lost by region: South Vietnam (1).

U-6 Beaver
Total number of aircraft lost: 1   Fatalities: 0; POWs: 0.
Aircraft lost by year: 1966 (1).
Aircraft lost by region: Other regions (1).

U-10 Courier
Total number of aircraft lost: 12   Fatalities: 5; POWs: 0.
Aircraft lost by year: 1962, (1), 1964 (1), 1965 (1),
1966 (2), 1967 (3), 1968 (1), 1969 (3).
Aircraft lost by region: South Vietnam (11), Northern Laos (1).

United States Navy

A-1 Skyraider (not including EA-1)
Total number of aircraft lost: 65   Fatalities: 34; POWs: 3.
Aircraft lost by year: 1964 (1), 1965 (25), 1966 (27),
1967 (11), 1968 (1).
Aircraft lost by region: South Vietnam (4),
North Vietnam (41), Southern Laos (6), Other regions (14)

A-3 Skywarrior
Total number of aircraft lost: 20   Fatalities: 38; POWs: 0.
Aircraft lost by year: 1964 (1), 1965 (2), 1966 (4),
1967 (6), 1968 (1), 1969 (2), 1970 (2), 1971 (1), 1973 (1).
Aircraft lost by region: North Vietnam (5), Other regions (15).

A-4 Skyhawk
Total number of aircraft lost: 271   Fatalities: 98; POWs: 48.
Aircraft lost by year: 1964 (7), 1965 (42), 1966 (77),
1967 (77), 1968 (32), 1969 (16), 1970 (12), 1971 (1), 1972 (7).
Aircraft lost by region: South Vietnam (7), North Vietnam (177),
Southern Laos (17), Northern Laos (1), Other regions (69).

A-6 Intruder
Total number of aircraft lost: 59   Fatalities: 64; POWs: 18.
Aircraft lost by year: 1965 (5), 1966 (8), 1967 (9),
1968 (16), 1969 (4), 1970 (3), 1971 (4), 1972 (8), 1973 (2).
Aircraft lost by region: South Vietnam (1), North Vietnam (39),
Southern Laos (8), Northern Laos (1), Other regions (10).

A-7 Corsair
Total number of aircraft lost: 99   Fatalities: 30; POWs: 7.
Aircraft lost by year: 1967 (1), 1968 (14), 1969 (14),
1970 (14), 1971 (7), 1972 (47), 1973 (2).
Aircraft lost by region: South Vietnam (5), North Vietnam (39),
Southern Laos (12), Other regions (43).

C-1A Trader
Total number of aircraft lost: 4   Fatalities: 4; POWs: 0.
Aircraft lost by year: 1965 (2), 1967 (1), 1968 (1).
Aircraft lost by region: South Vietnam (1), Other regions (3).

C-2A Greyhound
Total number of aircraft lost: 3   Fatalities: 39; POWs: 0.
Aircraft lost by year: 1969 (1), 1970 (1), 1971 (1).
Aircraft lost by region: Other regions (3).

C-47 Skytrain
Total number of aircraft lost: 1   Fatalities: 25; POWs: 0.
Aircraft lost by year: 1967 (1).
Aircraft lost by region: South Vietnam (1).

E-1B Tracer
Total number of aircraft lost: 3   Fatalities: 8; POWs: 0.
Aircraft lost by year: 1965 (1), 1966 (1), 1967 (1).
Aircraft lost by region: South Vietnam (1), Other regions (2).

E-2 Hawkeye
Total number of aircraft lost: 2   Fatalities: 10; POWs: 0.
Aircraft lost by year: 1970 (1), 1971 (1).
Aircraft lost by region: Other regions (2).

EA-1 Skyraider
Total number of aircraft lost: 5   Fatalities: 5; POWs: 0.
Aircraft lost by year: 1965 (2), 1966 (2), 1967 (1).
Aircraft lost by region: North Vietnam (1), Other regions (4).

EC-121 Warning Star
Total number of aircraft lost: 1   Fatalities: 23; POWs: 0.
Aircraft lost by year: 1970 (1).
Aircraft lost by region: South Vietnam (1).

F-4 Phantom
Total number of aircraft lost: 128   Fatalities: 65; POWs: 42.
Aircraft lost by year: 1964 (1), 1965 (14), 1966 (19), 1967 (37),
1968 (21), 1969 (6), 1970 (7), 1971 (3), 1972 (16), 1973 (4).
Aircraft lost by region: South Vietnam (4), North Vietnam (60),
Southern Laos (8), Other regions (56).

F-8 Crusader (not including RF-8)
Total number of aircraft lost: 117   Fatalities: 32; POWs: 14.
Aircraft lost by year: 1964 (3), 1965 (28), 1966 (18),
1967 (26), 1968 (14), 1969 (14), 1970 (5), 1971 (3), 1972 (6).
Aircraft lost by region: South Vietnam (5), North Vietnam (54),
Northern Laos (1), Other regions (57).

OV-10A Bronco
Total number of aircraft lost: 7   Fatalities: 6; POWs: 0.
Aircraft lost by year: 1969 (2), 1970 (3), 1971 (2).
Aircraft lost by region: South Vietnam (7).

P-2 Neptune
Total number of aircraft lost: 4   Fatalities: 25; POWs: 0.
Aircraft lost by year: 1964 (1), 1968 (3).
Aircraft lost by region: Southern Laos (3), Other regions (1).

P-3 Orion
Total number of aircraft lost: 2   Fatalities: 24; POWs: 0.
Aircraft lost by year: 1968 (2).
Aircraft lost by region: Other regions (2).

RA-5C Vigilante
Total number of aircraft lost: 26   Fatalities: 25; POWs: 12.
Aircraft lost by year: 1964 (1), 1965 (5), 1966 (4),
1967 (8), 1968 (3), 1969 (1), 1971 (1), 1972 (3).
Aircraft lost by region: South Vietnam (1), North Vietnam (17),
Southern Laos (1), Other regions (7).

RF-8 Crusader
Total number of aircraft lost: 31   Fatalities: 12; POWs: 6.
Aircraft lost by year: 1964 (1), 1965 (8), 1966 (7),
1967 (3), 1968 (4), 1969 (2), 1970 (1), 1972 (4).
Aircraft lost by region: South Vietnam (1), North Vietnam (20),
Southern Laos (1), Northern Laos (1), Other regions (8).

S-2 Tracker
Total number of aircraft lost: 6   Fatalities: 16; POWs: 0.
Aircraft lost by year: 1966 (2), 1967 (3), 1968 (1).
Aircraft lost by region: Other regions (6).

United States Marine Corps

A-4 Skyhawk (not including TA-4F)
Total number of aircraft lost: 81 Fatalities: 29; POWs: 1.
Aircraft lost by year: 1964 (1), 1965 (5), 1966 (14), 1967 (22), 1968 (23), 1969 (7), 1970 (6), 1972 (3).
Aircraft lost by region: South Vietnam (70), North Vietnam (8), Southern Laos (2), Other regions (1).

A-6 Intruder (not including EA-6)
Total number of aircraft lost: 25 Fatalities: 26; POWs: 5.
Aircraft lost by year: 1967 (5), 1968 (8), 1969 (5), 1972 (7).
Aircraft lost by region: South Vietnam (7), North Vietnam (14), Southern Laos (4).

C-117 Skytrain
Total number of aircraft lost: 2 Fatalities: 11; POWs: 0.
Aircraft lost by year: 1966 (1), 1969 (1).
Aircraft lost by region: South Vietnam (2).

EA-6A Intruder
Total number of aircraft lost: 2 Fatalities: 2; POWs: 0.
Aircraft lost by year: 1972 (2).
Aircraft lost by region: North Vietnam (1), Other regions (1).

EF-10B Skynight
Total number of aircraft lost: 5 Fatalities: 10; POWs: 0.
Aircraft lost by year: 1965 (1), 1966 (1), 1967 (1), 1968 (2).
Aircraft lost by region: South Vietnam (2), North Vietnam (3).

F-4 Phantom (not including RF-4B)
Total number of aircraft lost: 98 Fatalities: 55; POWs: 4.
Aircraft lost by year: 1965 (3), 1966 (12), 1967 (16), 1968 (25), 1969 (19), 1970 (14), 1972 (9).
Aircraft lost by region: South Vietnam (67), North Vietnam (16), Southern Laos (12), Northern Laos (1), Other regions (2).

F-8 Crusader (not including RF-8A)
Total number of aircraft lost: 21 Fatalities: 5; POWs: 2.
Aircraft lost by year: 1965 (4), 1966 (5), 1967 (9), 1968 (3).
Aircraft lost by region: South Vietnam (12), North Vietnam (5), Southern Laos (1), Other regions (3).

KC-130F Hercules
Total number of aircraft lost: 4 Fatalities: 79; POWs: 0.
Aircraft lost by year: 1965 (1), 1966 (1), 1968 (1), 1969 (1).
Aircraft lost by region: South Vietnam (2), North Vietnam (1), Other regions (1).

O-1 Bird Dog
Total number of aircraft lost: 7 Fatalities: 6; POWs: 0.
Aircraft lost by year: 1964 (1), 1965 (1), 1966 (1), 1967 (2), 1968 (1), 1969 (1).
Aircraft lost by region: South Vietnam (7).

OV-10A Bronco
Total number of aircraft lost: 10 Fatalities: 12; POWs: 0.
Aircraft lost by year: 1968 (3), 1969 (5), 1970 (1), 1971 (1).
Aircraft lost by region: South Vietnam (9), Southern Laos (1).

RF-4B Phantom
Total number of aircraft lost: 4 Fatalities: 3; POWs: 0.
Aircraft lost by year: 1967 (2), 1968 (2).
Aircraft lost by region: South Vietnam (3), North Vietnam (1).

RF-8A Crusader
Total number of aircraft lost: 1 Fatalities: 0; POWs: 0.
Aircraft lost by year: 1965 (1).
Aircraft lost by region: South Vietnam (1).

TA-4F Skyhawk
Total number of aircraft lost: 10 Fatalities: 3; POWs: 0.
Aircraft lost by year: 1967 (1), 1968 (4), 1969 (2), 1970 (2), 1972 (1).
Aircraft lost by region: South Vietnam (7), Southern Laos (3).

TF-9J Cougar
Total number of aircraft lost: 1 Fatalities: 0; POWs: 0
Aircraft lost by year: 1967 (1).
Aircraft lost by region: South Vietnam (1).

US Fixed-Wing Losses To Surface-to-Air Missiles

All losses are to SA-2 except those marked with an asterisk, which were shot down by SA-7s. The information is presented in the order: date, aircraft type, unit, altitude of hit (where known), day or night, fatalities, role of mission (ie AR armed reconnaissance, CAP combat air patrol, CAS close air support, ESC escort, EW electronic warfare, FAC forward air control, FLAK flak suppression, IH Iron Hand, REC reconnaissance, SAR search and rescue, ST strike)

24 Jul 1965	F-4C	47 TFS	23,000ft	day	1 KIA	CAP
11 Aug 1965	A-4E	VA-23	9,000ft	night	1 KIA	AR
24 Aug 1965	F-4B	VF-21	11,000ft	day	0 KIA	CAP
30 Sep 1965	F-105D	334 TFS	18,000ft	day	1 KIA	AR
5 Oct 1965	F-8E	VF-162	30,000ft	day	0 KIA	CAP
16 Oct 1965	RA-5C	RVAH-1	1,500ft	day	0 KIA	REC
27 Oct 1965	F-8E	VF-191	33,000ft	day	0 KIA	CAP
5 Nov 1965	F-105D	357 TFS	6,500ft	day	1 KIA	IH
16 Nov 1965	F-105D	469 TFS	4,000ft	day	1 KIA	IH
7 Dec 1965	F-4B	VMFA-323	?	night	0 KIA	CAP
19 Dec 1965	F-4C	433 TFS	20,000ft	day	0 KIA	CAP
21 Dec 1965	A-6A	VA-85	4,000ft	night	2 KIA	ST
22 Dec 1965	RA-5C	RVAH-13	3,200ft	day	1 KIA	REC
9 Feb 1966	A-4C	VA-144	5,500ft	day	0 KIA	AR
18 Feb 1966	F-4B	VF-92	25,000ft	day	1 KIA	CAP
25 Feb 1966	RB-66C	41 TRS	30,000ft	day	1 KIA	EW
7 Mar 1966	RF-101C	45 TRS	?	day	1 KIA	REC
7 Mar 1966	RF-101C	45 TRS	?	day	1 KIA	REC
17 Mar 1966	A-4C	VA-94	6,000ft	day	0 KIA	ST
18 Mar 1966	EF-10B	VMCJ-1	?	day	2 KIA	EW
13 Apr 1966	A-1H	VA-52	7,500ft	day	1 KIA	AR
24 Apr 1966	F-105D	469 TFS	6,000ft	day	1 KIA	AR
19 Jul 1966	F-8E	VF-162	12,000ft	day	1 KIA	CAP
20 Jul 1966	EB-66C	41 TRS	29,000ft	day	0 KIA	EW
23 Jul 1966	F-105F	354 TFS	10,000ft	day	2 KIA	IH
28 Jul 1966	A-4E	VA-164	12,000ft	day	0 KIA	IH
1 Aug 1966	F-104C	435 TFS	4,000ft	day	1 KIA	CAP
1 Aug 1966	F-104C	435 TFS	5,000ft	day	1 KIA	CAP
7 Aug 1966	F-105D	333 TFS	10,000ft	day	0 KIA	ST
7 Aug 1966	F-105F	354 TFS	13,000ft	day	0 KIA	IH
4 Sep 1966	F-4C	555 TFS	4,800ft	day	1 KIA	ST
10 Sep 1966	F-4C	433 TFS	4,500ft	night	0 KIA	ST
14 Sep 1966	A-1H	VA-25	1,000ft	day	1 KIA	AR
19 Sep 1966	F-4B	VF-154	4,000ft	night	2 KIA	AR
2 Oct 1966	F-104C	435 TFS	10,000ft	day	0 KIA	AR
12 Oct 1966	A-4E	VA-164	4,000ft	night	1 KIA	AR
22 Oct 1966	RA-5C	RVAH-6	3,000ft	day	2 KIA	REC
4 Nov 1966	RF-101C	45 TRS	7,000ft	day	0 KIA	REC
22 Nov 1966	F-4C	480 TFS	14,000ft	day	1 KIA	ST
2 Dec 1966	A-4C	VA-172	?	night	1 KIA	AR
2 Dec 1966	A-4C	VA-172	?	night	1 KIA	AR
2 Dec 1966	F-4C	389 TFS	19,000ft	day	0 KIA	ST
2 Dec 1966	F-4C	480 TFS	18,000ft	day	0 KIA	CAP
3 Dec 1966	F-4C	559 TFS	?	day	0 KIA	CAP
13 Dec 1966	F-105D	421 TFS	16,000ft	day	1 KIA	FLAK
13 Dec 1966	A-4C	VA-195	?	day	0 KIA	IH
14 Dec 1966	A-4C	VA-72	5,000ft	day	1 KIA	IH
14 Dec 1966	F-8E	VF-194	6,000ft	day	1 KIA	CAP
16 Jan 1967	RF-4C	11 TRS	?	day	1 KIA	REC
19 Jan 1967	F-4C	390 TFS	14,000ft	day	0 KIA	ESC
21 Jan 1967	F-105D	354 TFS	11,000ft	day	1 KIA	FLAK
23 Jan 1967	F-4C	497 TFS	14,000ft	day	0 KIA	CAP
4 Feb 1967	EB-66C	41 TRS	30,000ft	day	0 KIA	EW
18 Feb 1967	F-105F	13 TFS	12,000ft	day	0 KIA	IH
11 Mar 1967	A-4E	VA-192	14,000ft	day	0 KIA	IH
26 Mar 1967	F-4C	433 TFS	16,000ft	day	0 KIA	ST
25 Apr 1967	A-4E	VA-192	8,000ft	day	0 KIA	IH
25 Apr 1967	A-4E	VA-212	8,000ft	day	0 KIA	IH
26 Apr 1967	A-4E	VA-192	12,000ft	day	1 KIA	IH
26 Apr 1967	F-105F	333 TFS	6,000ft	day	1 KIA	IH
5 May 1967	F-105D	469 TFS	?	day	0 KIA	ST
10 May 1967	A-4C	VA-94	8,000ft	day	1 KIA	FLAK
10 May 1967	A-4E	VMA-223	17,000ft	night	1 KIA	CAS
19 May 1967	F-4B	VF-114	3,000ft	day	0 KIA	CAP
19 May 1967	A-6A	VA-35	12,000ft	day	0 KIA	ST
19 May 1967	F-4B	VF-96	1,500ft	day	1 KIA	CAP
19 May 1967	F-8E	VF-211	1,500ft	day	0 KIA	CAP
22 May 1967	O-1E	20 TASS	8,000ft	day	1 KIA	REC
27 May 1967	F-105D	333 TFS	10,000ft	day	1 KIA	ST
30 May 1967	A-4E	VA-93	16,500ft	day	0 KIA	IH
10 Jun 1967	A-4C	VA-56	?	day	1 KIA	IH
21 Jun 1967	RF-101C	20 TRS	30,000ft	day	0 KIA	REC
6 Jul 1967	A-4E	VMA-311	12,000ft	night	0 KIA	IH
9 Jul 1967	A-4C	VA-146	12,500ft	day	1 KIA	ST
9 Jul 1967	A-4C	VA-34	10,000ft	day	0 KIA	ST
14 Jul 1967	A-4C	VA-76	9,000ft	day	0 KIA	ST
16 Jul 1967	F-8E	VF-162	5,000ft	day	0 KIA	FLAK
31 Jul 1967	F-8C	VF-111	11,000ft	day	0 KIA	IH
1 Aug 1967	RF-101C	20 TRS	18,000ft	day	1 KIA	REC
4 Aug 1967	A-4E	VA-165	10,500ft	day	1 KIA	ST
12 Aug 1967	RF-4C	11 TRS	18,000ft	day	0 KIA	REC
21 Aug 1967	A-6A	VA-196	7,500ft	day	0 KIA	ST
23 Aug 1967	F-4B	VF-142	8,000ft	day	2 KIA	FLAK
31 Aug 1967	A-4E	VA-163	12,000ft	day	0 KIA	ST
31 Aug 1967	A-4E	VA-163	16,000ft	day	0 KIA	ST
31 Aug 1967	A-4E	VA-164	13,000ft	day	1 KIA	ST
18 Sep 1967	A-4C	VA-34	3,000ft	day	0 KIA	FLAK
3 Oct 1967	F-105D	469 TFS	16,000ft	day	0 KIA	ST
7 Oct 1967	A-4E	VA-164	11,000ft	day	1 KIA	IH
7 Oct 1967	F-4D	555 TFS	18,000ft	day	1 KIA	ESC
24 Oct 1967	F-4B	VF-151	14,000ft	day	1 KIA	CAP
24 Oct 1967	F-4B	VF-151	10,000ft	day	0 KIA	CAP
26 Oct 1967	A-4E	VA-15	9,000ft	day	0 KIA	ST
26 Oct 1967	A-4E	VA-163	9,000ft	day	0 KIA	ST
26 Oct 1967	F-8E	VF-162	15,500ft	day	0 KIA	FLAK
27 Oct 1967	F-105D	469 TFS	15,000ft	day	0 KIA	ST
27 Oct 1967	F-105D	357 TFS	12,000ft	day	0 KIA	ST
6 Nov 1967	F-105D	469 TFS	19,000ft	day	1 KIA	ST
16 Nov 1967	F-4B	VF-151	12,000ft	day	0 KIA	FLAK
17 Nov 1967	A-4C	VA-34	1,200ft	day	0 KIA	ST
17 Nov 1967	F-105D	354 TFS	14,000ft	day	1 KIA	IH
17 Nov 1967	RF-4C	11 TRS	24,000ft	day	0 KIA	REC
18 Nov 1967	F-105D	469 TFS	16,500ft	day	1 KIA	ST
18 Nov 1967	F-105D	34 TFS	18,000ft	day	1 KIA	ST
19 Nov 1967	F-105F	333 TFS	9,000ft	day	0 KIA	IH
19 Nov 1967	RF-4C	11 TRS	15,000ft	day	0 KIA	REC
19 Nov 1967	F-105D	34 TFS	16,000ft	day	0 KIA	ST
19 Nov 1967	F-105D	469 TFS	10,000ft	day	1 KIA	ST
22 Dec 1967	A-7A	VA-147	15,000ft	day	0 KIA	IH
31 Dec 1967	A-6A	VA-75	3,500ft	day	2 KIA	ST
3 Jan 1968	A-4C	VA-112	11,000ft	day	0 KIA	IH
4 Jan 1968	F-8E	VF-162	15,000ft	day	1 KIA	CAP
10 Jan 1968	F-4D	13 TFS	20,000ft	day	1 KIA	CAP
25 Jan 1968	A-4E	VA-153	12,000ft	day	0 KIA	ST
14 Feb 1968	F-8E	VF-194	5,000ft	day	1 KIA	ESC
14 Feb 1968	F-105D	34 TFS	8,000ft	day	1 KIA	IH
24 Feb 1968	A-6A	VMA(AW)-533	?	night	0 KIA	ST
29 Feb 1968	F-105F	44 TFS	12,000ft	day	2 KIA	IH
19 Jun 1968	F-4J	VF-33	2,600ft	night	0 KIA	AR
28 Aug 1968	A-6B	VA-85	15,000ft	night	2 KIA	FLAK
30 Sep 1968	A-6A	VA-196	5,000ft	night	2 KIA	AR
6 Oct 1968	A-7A	VA-27	10,000ft	night	0 KIA	FLAK
20 Nov 1970	F-105G	6010 WWS	?	night	0 KIA	IH
22 Mar 1971	F-4D	13 TFS	?	day	0 KIA	ESC
26 Apr 1971	O-2A	23 TASS	7,000ft	night	0 KIA	FAC
10 Dec 1971	F-105G	17 WWS	18,000ft	day	1 KIA	IH
17 Dec 1971	F-4E	4 TFS	?	night	0 KIA	ESC
26 Dec 1971	F-4D	433 TFS	?	day	2 KIA	ST
30 Dec 1971	F-4B	VF-111	20,000ft	day	0 KIA	ST
30 Dec 1971	A-6A	VA-165	12,000ft	day	1 KIA	ST
16 Feb 1972	F-4D	25 TFS	?	day	0 KIA	ST
17 Feb 1972	F-105G	17 WWS	?	day	0 KIA	IH
28 Mar 1972	AC-130A	16 SOS	8,500ft	night	14 KIA	AR
2 Apr 1972	EB-66C	42 TEWS	24,000ft	day	5 KIA	EW
3 Apr 1972	OV-10A	23 TASS	5,000ft	day	0 KIA	FAC
6 Apr 1972	A-7E	VA-195	12,000ft	day	0 KIA	AR

6 Apr 1972	A-7E	VA-22	?	day	1 KIA	AR
7 Apr 1972	OV-10A	20 TASS	?	day	2 KIA	FAC
15 Apr 1972	F-4E	421 TFS	8,000ft	day	1 KIA	AR
15 Apr 1972	F-105G	17 WWS	?	day	2 KIA	IH
20 Apr 1972	RF-4C	14 TRS	6,000ft	day	0 KIA	REC
21 Apr 1972	F-4E	334 TFS	20,500ft	day	0 KIA	ST
23 Apr 1972	F-4E	390 TFS	?	day	0 KIA	ST
1 May 1972	O-2A	20 TASS	?	day	0 KIA	FAC*
1 May 1972	A-1H	1 SOS	3,500ft	day	0 KIA	SAR*
1 May 1972	A-7E	VA-94	14,000ft	day	0 KIA	ST
2 May 1972	A-1E	1 SOS	5,500ft	day	0 KIA	SAR*
2 May 1972	A-1G	1 SOS	6,500ft	day	0 KIA	SAR*
6 May 1972	A-7E	VA-22	1,000ft	day	0 KIA	AR
10 May 1972	F-4J	VF-96	12,000ft	day	0 KIA	FLAK
14 May 1972	O-1	? unit	4,000ft	day	0 KIA	FAC*
23 May 1972	A-7B	VA-93	16,000ft	day	1 KIA	IH
24 May 1972	A-7E	VA-94	?	day	0 KIA	IH
24 May 1972	F-8J	VF-24	11,000ft	day	0 KIA	CAP
25 May 1972	OV-10A	20 TASS	5,000ft	day	0 KIA	FAC
26 May 1972	TA-4F	H&MS-15	4,500ft	day	0 KIA	REC
1 Jun 1972	F-4E	308 TFS	11,000ft	day	0 KIA	ESC
6 Jun 1972	F-4D	13 TFS	15,000ft	day	2 KIA	CAP
7 Jun 1972	RA-5C	RVAH-1	3,000ft	day	0 KIA	REC
13 Jun 1972	A-7A	VA-37	5,000ft	night	1 KIA	AR
17 Jun 1972	A-7E	VA-192	14,000ft	day	0 KIA	ST
18 Jun 1972	AC-130A	16 SOS	?	night	12 KIA	AR*
27 Jun 1972	F-4E	308 TFS	17,700ft	day	1 KIA	ST
29 Jun 1972	OV-10A	20 TASS	6,500ft	day	1 KIA	FAC*
1 Jul 1972	F-4E	34 TFS	19,000ft	day	0 KIA	CAP
2 Jul 1972	O-1	? unit	?	day	0 KIA	FAC*
5 Jul 1972	F-4D	433 TFS	21,000ft	day	0 KIA	ST
30 Jul 1972	F-4D	435 TFS	?	day	0 KIA	ST
6 Aug 1972	A-7B	VA-56	8,000ft	day	0 KIA	IH
16 Aug 1972	F-4J	VF-114	?	night	2 KIA	CAP
17 Aug 1972	A-7A	VA-37	13,500ft	day	0 KIA	IH
19 Aug 1972	RF-4C	14 TRS	13,000ft	day	1 KIA	REC
25 Aug 1972	F-4B	VF-161	3,500ft	day	0 KIA	CAP
27 Aug 1972	F-4B	VF-151	5,000ft	day	0 KIA	ESC
6 Sep 1972	A-6A	VA-75	13,000ft	day	1 KIA	ST
10 Sep 1972	A-7C	VA-82	8,000ft	day	1 KIA	IH
11 Sep 1972	F-4J	VMFA-333	15,000ft	day	0 KIA	CAP
17 Sep 1972	F-105G	17 WWS	11,000ft	day	2 KIA	IH
6 Oct 1972	F-4E	25 TFS	16,500ft	day	1 KIA	ST
27 Oct 1972	A-7C	VA-86	13,000ft	night	1 KIA	IH
16 Nov 1972	F-105G	561 TFS	19,000ft	night	0 KIA	IH
20 Nov 1972	F-4J	VF-103	17,000ft	night	0 KIA	CAP
22 Nov 1972	B-52D	307 SW	25,000ft	night	0 KIA	ST
23 Nov 1972	O-2A	21 TASS	?	day	0 KIA	FAC
9 Dec 1972	RF-4C	14 TRS	?	day	1 KIA	REC
18 Dec 1972	B-52G	72 SW	34,000ft	night	3 KIA	ST
18 Dec 1972	B-52G	72 SW	38,500ft	night	0 KIA	ST
18 Dec 1972	B-52D	307 SW	38,000ft	night	2 KIA	ST
19 Dec 1972	OV-10A	20 TASS	?	day	1 KIA	FAC*
19 Dec 1972	A-7C	VA-82	19,000ft	night	0 KIA	IH
20 Dec 1972	B-52G	72 SW	35,000ft	night	2 KIA	ST
20 Dec 1972	B-52G	72 SW	35,500ft	night	0 KIA	ST
20 Dec 1972	B-52D	307 SW	35,500ft	night	4 KIA	ST
20 Dec 1972	B-52D	43 SW	?	night	1 KIA	ST
20 Dec 1972	B-52G	72 SW	35,000ft	night	4 KIA	ST
20 Dec 1972	B-52G	72 SW	35,000ft	night	5 KIA	ST
21 Dec 1972	B-52D	307 SW	?	night	3 KIA	ST
21 Dec 1972	B-52D	307 SW	34,000ft	night	0 KIA	ST
26 Dec 1972	B-52D	307 SW	?	night	2 KIA	ST
26 Dec 1972	B-52D	307 SW	?	night	4 KIA	ST
27 Dec 1972	B-52D	307 SW	35,500ft	night	0 KIA	ST
27 Dec 1972	B-52D	43 SW	25,000ft	night	2 KIA	ST
3 Jan 1973	B-52D	307 SW	?	night	0 KIA	ST
9 Jan 1973	A-6A	VA-115	?	night	2 KIA	ST
27 Jan 1973	OV-10A	23 TASS	6,000ft	day	2 KIA	FAC*

Summary

Aircraft losses by year

1965(13), 1966 (35), 1967 (62), 1968 (12), 1969 (0), 1970 (1), 1971 (7), 1972 (72), 1973 (3).

Aircraft losses by type

A-1 (5), A-4 (32), A-6 (10), A-7 (15), AC-130 (2), B-52 (17), EB-66 (4), EF-10B (1), F-4 (45), F-8 (11), F-104 (3), F-105 (31), O-1 (3), O-2 (3), OV-10 (6), RA-5C (4), RF-101C (5), RF-4C (7), TA-4F (1).

US Fixed-Wing Losses to MiGs

The information is presented in the order: date, aircraft type, unit, fatalities, type of MiG.

4 Apr 1965	F-105D	354 TFS	1 KIA	MiG-17
4 Apr 1965	F-105D	354 TFS	1 KIA	MiG-17
9 Apr 1965	F-4B	VF-96	2 KIA	Chinese MiGs
20 Jun 1965	F-4C	45 TFS	0 KIA	MiG-17
20 Sep 1965	F-104C	436 TFS	0 KIA	Chinese MiGs
12 Apr 1966	KA-3B	VAH-4	4 KIA	Chinese MiGs
29 Apr 1966	A-1E	602 ACS	1 KIA	MiG-17
21 Jun 1966	F-8E	VF-211	0 KIA	MiG-17
11 Jul 1966	F-105D	355 TFW	0 KIA	MiG-17
14 Jul 1966	F-8E	VF-162	0 KIA	MiG-17
19 Jul 1966	F-105D	354 TFS	1 KIA	MiG-17
29 Jul 1966	RC-47D	606 ACS	8 KIA	MiG-17
5 Sep 1966	F-8E	VF-111	0 KIA	MiG-17
16 Sep 1966	F-4C	555 TFS	1 KIA	MiG-17
21 Sep 1966	F-4C	433 TFS	0 KIA	MiG-17
5 Oct 1966	F-4C	433 TFS	1 KIA	MiG-21
5 Dec 1966	F-105D	421 TFS	1 KIA	MiG-17
8 Dec 1966	F-105D	354 TFS	1 KIA	MiG-17
14 Dec 1966	F-105D	357 TFS	0 KIA	MiG-21
19 Apr 1967	F-105F	357 TFS	0 KIA	MiG-17
19 Apr 1967	A-1E	602 ACS	1 KIA	MiG-17
25 Apr 1967	A-4C	VA-76	0 KIA	MiG-17
28 Apr 1967	F-105D	44 TFS	1 KIA	MiG-21
30 Apr 1967	F-105F	357 TFS	0 KIA	MiG-21
30 Apr 1967	F-105D	333 TFS	0 KIA	MiG-21
30 Apr 1967	F-105D	354 TFS	0 KIA	MiG-21
12 May 1967	F-4C	390 TFS	1 KIA	MiG-17
20 May 1967	F-4C	433 TFS	0 KIA	MiG-17
26 Jun 1967	F-4C	390 TFS	0 KIA	Chinese MiGs
21 Aug 1967	A-6A	VA-196	2 KIA	Chinese MiGs
21 Aug 1967	A-6A	VA-196	1 KIA	Chinese MiGs
23 Aug 1967	F-4D	555 TFS	1 KIA	MiG-21
23 Aug 1967	F-4D	555 TFS	1 KIA	MiG-21
16 Sep 1967	RF-101C	20 TRS	0 KIA	MiG-21
3 Oct 1967	F-4D	435 TFS	0 KIA	MiG-21
7 Oct 1967	F-105F	13 TFS	0 KIA	MiG-21
9 Oct 1967	F-105D	34 TFS	0 KIA	MiG-21
8 Nov 1967	F-4D	555 TFS	0 KIA	MiG-21
18 Nov 1967	F-105F	34 TFS	2 KIA	MiG-21
18 Nov 1967	F-105D	469 TFS	0 KIA	MiG-21
19 Nov 1967	F-4B	VF-151	1 KIA	MiG-21
19 Nov 1967	F-4B	VF-151	1 KIA	MiG-21
20 Nov 1967	F-105D	469 TFS	0 KIA	MiG-21
16 Dec 1967	F-4D	555 TFS	0 KIA	MiG-21
17 Dec 1967	F-4D	497 TFS	0 KIA	MiG-17
17 Dec 1967	F-105D	469 TFS	0 KIA	MiG-21
3 Jan 1968	F-105D	469 TFS	0 KIA	MiG-21
5 Jan 1968	F-105F	357 TFS	2 KIA	MiG-17
14 Jan 1968	F-105D	469 TFS	1 KIA	MiG-21
14 Jan 1968	EB-66C	41 TEWS	0 KIA	MiG-21
18 Jan 1968	F-4D	435 TFS	0 KIA	MiG-17
18 Jan 1968	F-4D	435 TFS	0 KIA	MiG-17
3 Feb 1968	F-102A	509 FIS	1 KIA	MiG-21
4 Feb 1968	F-105D	34 TFS	0 KIA	MiG-21
14 Feb 1968	A-1H	VA-25	1 KIA	Chinese MiGs
23 Feb 1968	F-4D	497 TFS	0 KIA	MiG-21
7 May 1968	F-4B	VF-92	0 KIA	MiG-21
16 Jun 1968	F-4J	VF-102	1 KIA	MiG-21
18 Dec 1971	F-4D	555 TFS	0 KIA	MiG-21
18 Dec 1971	F-4D	13 TFS	0 KIA	MiG-21
27 Apr 1972	F-4B	VF-51	0 KIA	MiG-21
10 May 1972	F-4D	555 TFS	1 KIA	MiG-19
10 May 1972	F-4E	58 TFS	2 KIA	MiG-19
11 May 1972	F-105G	17 WWS	0 KIA	MiG-21
11 May 1972	F-4D	555 TFS	0 KIA	MiG-21
18 May 1972	F-4D	421 TFS	2 KIA	MiG-19
20 May 1972	F-4D	555 TFS	0 KIA	MiG-21
13 Jun 1972	F-4E	308 TFS	0 KIA	MiG-21
21 Jun 1972	F-4E	334 TFS	0 KIA	MiG-21
24 Jun 1972	F-4E	421 TFS	0 KIA	MiG-21
24 Jun 1792	F-4D	25 TFS	1 KIA	MiG-21
27 Jun 1972	F-4E	308 TFS	0 KIA	MiG-21
27 Jun 1972	F-4E	366 TFW	0 KIA	MiG-21
27 Jun 1972	F-4E	366 TFW	0 KIA	MiG-21
5 Jul 1972	F-4E	34 TFS	0 KIA	MiG-21
5 Jul 1972	F-4E	34 TFS	0 KIA	MiG-21
8 Jul 1972	F-4E	4 TFS	0 KIA	MiG-21
10 Jul 1972	F-4J	VF-103	0 KIA	MiG-17
24 Jul 1972	F-4E	421 TFS	0 KIA	MiG-21
29 Jul 1972	F-4E	4 TFS	0 KIA	MiG-21
30 Jul 1972	F-4D	523 TFS	0 KIA	MiG-21
26 Aug 1972	F-4J	VMFA-232	1 KIA	MiG-21
11 Sep 1972	F-4E	335 TFS	0 KIA	MiG-21
12 Sep 1972	F-4E	336 TFS	0 KIA	MiG-21
5 Oct 1972	F-4D	335 TFS	0 KIA	MiG-21
6 Oct 1972	F-4E	307 TFS	0 KIA	MiG-21
12 Oct 1972	F-4E	469 TFS	0 KIA	MiG-21
27 Dec 1972	F-4E	13 TFS	0 KIA	MiG-21
27 Dec 1972	F-4E	4 TFS	0 KIA	MiG-21
28 Dec 1972	RA-5C	RVAH-13	1 KIA	MiG-21

Summary

Aircraft losses by year

1965(5), 1966 (14), 1967 (27), 1968 (12), 1971 (2), 1972 (30).

Aircraft losses by type

A-1 (3), A-3 (1), A-4 (1), A-6 (2), EB-66 (1), F-4 (51), F-8 (3), F-102 (1), F-104(1), F-105(23), RA-5C (1), RC-47D (1), RF-101C (1).

Take-off by a Type 94 MiG-21PFM in Vietnam.
Yefim Gordon archive

Index of Personnel

Bogiages, C C (2 Mar 1969)
Bogoslofski, B J (5 Nov 1969)
Bohlig, J R (19 Aug 1969)
Bohrer, L P (9 Mar 1967)
Bois, C R A (25 Aug 1967)
Bokern, R (27 Apr 1970)
Boles, R H (31 Aug 1968)
Boles, W W (18 Jan 1968)
Boli, F C (16 Sep 1971, 2 Apr 1972)
Bolling, E N (30 Mar 1972)
Bollinger, A R (4/5 Feb 1973)
Bollinger, W H (31 Aug 1965)
Bolstad, R E (6 Nov 1965)
Bolte, W L (2 Apr 1972)
Boltze, B E (26 May 1972, 6 Oct 1972)
Bomar, J W (4 Feb 1967)
Bond, R D (11 Mar 1968)
Bond, R L (30 Sep 1971)
Bonebright, R A (18 May 1969)
Bonner, L M (19 Dec 1969)
Booker, A N (25 Apr 1969)
Boorer, R B (21 Feb 1967)
Booth, H W (15 Oct 1962)
Booth, J E (23 Jun 1968)
Booth, R E (25 Jul 1968)
Boothby, L (19 Sep 1967)
Booze, D G (24 Jan 1966)
Borah, D V (24 Sep 1972)
Borden, M L (13 Oct 1966)
Borders, D L (26 Aug 1972)
Bordone, R P (24 Jul 1965, 8 Sep 1972)
Boretsky, S L (18 Mar 1972)
Borling, J L (1 Jun 1966)
Bors, J C (28 Apr 1968)
Borst, J R (30 Oct 1967)
Bosilijevac, M J (29 Sep 1972)
Bosnick, W (2 Oct 1970)
Bossio, G F (29 Jul 1966)
Boston, L S (29 Apr 1966)
Bottesch, J R (19 Jul 1966)
Bouchard, M L (19/20 Dec 1968)
Boucher, R E (30 Oct 1968)
Bougartz, T E (12 Jun 1967)
Boughner, L R (23 Apr 1972)
Boulet, D A (1 Dec 1970)
Bourque, V W (24 Oct 1964)
Bower, J E (3 Aug 1965)
Bowie, D A (17 Nov 1969)
Bowles, D P (3 Nov 1965)
Bowling, D B (26 Dec 1969)
Bowling, R H (17 Nov 1965)
Bowman, J E (4/5 May 1968)
Bowman, W P (20 Oct 1968)
Bowman, W S (25 Jul 1966)
Boyd, C G (26 Feb 1966, 22 Apr 1966)
Boyer, T L (17 Dec 1967)
Boyle, R F (10 Dec 1969)
Bracey, L (3 May 1972)
Bradburn, G F (16 Nov 1966)
Bradford, E S (11 Oct 1969)
Bradley, J H (12 Oct 1966)
Bradshaw, J J (17 Dec 1968)
Bradshaw, R S (12 Feb 1970)
Brady, A C (19 Jan 1967)
Brady, F T (12 Jul 1969)
Brady, J W (11 Sep 1972)
Branch, J A (4 Sep 1965)
Brand, J W (17 Aug 1966)
Brandenburg, D (4/5 Feb 1973)
Brandenstein, D C (20 Aug 1968)
Brandom, T M (25 Apr 1969)
Brandon, D F (22 Jan 1968)
Brandt, P A (19 Feb 1968)
Brandt, R (5 Apr 1969)
Branum, M H (8 Sep 1968)
Brashear, W J (8 May 1969)
Brattain, T L (28 Nov 1968)
Bratton, R D (4 Aug 1969)
Brauner, H P (28 Mar 1972)
Braybrooke, C (8 Oct 1967)
Brazelton, M L (7 Aug 1966)
Brazik, R (26 Jul 1967)
Brazil, E L (13 Mar 1969)
Breault, G K (14 Feb 1969)
Breckenridge, L (20 Oct 1966)
Breckner, W J (30 Jul 1972)
Breeding, M H (12 Feb 1970)
Bremner, B B (13 May 1968)
Brenn, H M (13 Apr 1967)
Brennan, H O (15 Jul 1967, 26 Nov 1967)
Brenneman, R C (8 Nov 1967)
Brenner, D G (13 Jun 1968)
Brenning, R D (26 Jul 1969)
Brenton, P F (9 Mar 1967)
Breskman, D G (18 Mar 1972)
Brett, C (17 Dec 1967)
Brett, R A (28 Sep 1972)
Breuer, D C (20 Nov 1972)
Brewer, G (14 Sep 1967)
Brewer, J D (23 May 1970)
Brice, E P (4 Jun 1968)
Bridger, B B (23 Jan 1967)
Briggs, C H (20 Jun 1965)
Briggs, F H (19 Oct 1969)
Brim, J L (28/29 Mar 1967)
Brinckmann, R E (4 Nov 1966)
Brinkman, J M (1 Apr 1968)
Britt, A F (25 Oct 1967)
Broadhead, L I (10 May 1969)
Brodak, J W (14 Aug 1966)
Brodman, R F (23 Jul 1968)
Broms, E J (1 Aug 1968)
Brooks, D L (23 Nov 1970)
Brooks, G B (30 Jul 1972)
Brooks, N G (2 Jan 1970)
Brooks, W C (1 Jul 1972)
Brooks, W L (22 Apr 1970)
Broom, P W (3 Nov 1967)
Brougher, W S (26 Dec 1965)
Broughton, J (30 Apr 1967, 2 Sep 1967)
Brown, B L (4/5 May 1968)
Brown, C A (18/19 Dec 1972)
Brown, C W (28 Jan 1968)
Brown, D A (29/30 Jul 1970)
Brown, D F (19 Jan 1970)
Brown, D H (11 Aug 1965)
Brown, D P (21 Apr 1972)
Brown, E C (24 Nov 1969)
Brown, E D (29 Jul 1965)
Brown, F M (19 Sep 1966)
Brown, G R (24 Oct 1963)
Brown, G W (8 Jul 1967)
Brown, H L (15 Jan 1965)
Brown, J G (9 Mar 1966)
Brown, J O (19 Apr 1966)
Brown, K R (2 May 1972)
Brown, M B (29 Jun 1972)
Brown, M E (13 Apr 1967)
Brown, O R (14 Jan 1973)
Brown, P G (25 Jul 1968)
Brown, R (11 Jan 1969)
Brown, R C (2 Aug 1968)
Brown, R D (14 Aug 1969)
Brown, R K (2 Jan 1971)
Brown, R M (7 Nov 1972)
Brown, T E (29 Apr 1966)
Brown, W (24 Feb 1968)
Brown, W E (30 Mar 1970)
Brown, W G (17 Jul 1972)
Brown, W K (14 Jul 1968)
Brown, W L (29 Apr 1970)
Brown, W R (3 Feb 1966)
Browne, L (2 Oct 1967)
Browning, D G (17 Sep 1966)
Browning, R T (8 Jul 1966)
Brownlee, C R (24 Dec 1968)
Brownlee, R F (19 Nov 1967, 6 Jan 1968)
Brubaker, R E (6 Jul 1967)
Bruce, G K (4 Apr 1970)
Bruch, D W (29 Apr 1966)
Brucher, J M (18 Feb 1969)
Bruck, D W (20 Oct 1968)
Brudno, E A (18 Oct 1965)
Bruhn, P C (19 Sep 1966)
Brumet, R N (9 Apr 1964)
Brungard, G J (28/29 Mar 1967)
Brunhaver, R M (24 Aug 1965)
Bruning, R (9 Apr 1965)
Brunner, G E (23 Jun 1969)
Brunson, C H (12 Oct 1972)
Brunson, R W (11 Oct 1970)
Brunstrom, A L (22 Apr 1966)
Bryan, R E (23 Oct 1968, 12 Jan 1969)
Bryant, L C (14 Mar 1966)
Buchanan, H E (16 Sep 1966)
Buchanan, J W (13 Nov 1968)
Bucher, B L (12 May 1968)
Buck, A C (11 Jan 1968)
Buckley, F R (17 Dec 1965)
Buckley, J L (21 Aug 1967)
Buckley, V P (16 Dec 1969)
Budka, R W (25 Dec 1967)
Buell, K R (16 Sep 1972)
Buerk, W C (11 Apr 1971)
Buffington, J C (9 Apr 1969)
Buffkin, B D (29 Jun 1971)
Buice, W A (9 Jul 1968)
Bull, R G (26 Aug 1968)
Bullard, W H (25 Aug 1966)
Bullock, G F (10 Oct 1966)
Bunch, W L (28 Dec 1969)
Bundy, N L (6 Sep 1966)
Bundy, W L (3 Oct 1968)
Burd, D G (1 Aug 1969)
Burdett, E B (18 Nov 1967)
Burer, A W (21 Mar 1966)
Burge, T J (27 Jan 1969)
Burgener, G E (20 Oct 1968)
Burkart, C W (12 Jun 1966)
Burke, W F (5 Feb 1969)
Burkett, S M (8 Oct 1967)
Burkett, W O (16 Apr 1969)
Burkholder, R W (27 Mar 1969)
Burnes, R W (5 Jan 1970)
Burnett, D F (5/6 Feb 1968)
Burnham, M I (19/20 Apr 1972)
Burns, D R (2 Dec 1966)
Burns, J A (19/20 Jun 1968)
Burns, J D (4 Oct 1966)
Burns, J L (20 Jul 1972)
Burns, J R (4 Aug 1966)
Burns, M T (5 Jul 1968)
Burns, P (28 Feb 1968)
Burnside, D W (1 Apr 1968)
Burr, M W (22 Oct 1965)
Burrell, C F (10 Oct 1969)
Burroughs, W D (31 Jul 1966)
Burton, C W (30 Dec 1971)
Burton, J L (6 Sep 1965)
Busch, D (18 Oct 1971)
Busch, E H (8 Jun 1967)
Busch, J T (8 Jun 1967)
Busch, P M (21 Sep 1969)
Buschette, E (12 Dec 1970)
Bush, D K (20 Jul 1972)
Bush, J R (24 Jul 1968)
Bush, J T (8 Jun 1967)
Bush, M J (18 May 1969)
Bush, P A (21 Apr 1966)
Bush, R E (24 Mar 1966)
Bush, R I (25 May 1966, 9 Jun 1966)
Bushnell, B L (8 Apr 1970)
Busico, R P (6 Aug 1969)
Bustle, L E (11 Sep 1968)
Butcher, J M (24 Mar 1971)
Butera, (21 Dec 1965)
Butler, G J (18 Jun 1968)
Butler, G L (5 Apr 1968)
Butler, J M (24 Jul 1970)
Butler, P N (20 Apr 1965)
Butler, W W (20 Nov 1967)
Butt, R L (11 Nov 1966)
Butterfield, D H (5 Jun 1967)
Butterfield, J (26 Mar 1966)
Butterfield, R A (24 Apr 1965)
Buzby, J S (30 Apr 1966)
Buzze, F C (16 Feb 1967)
Bynum, A G (23 Mar 1967)
Bynum, N S (25 Oct 1969)
Byrne, J H (13 Mar 1968)
Byrne, R E (29 Aug 1965)
Byrns, W G (23 May 1972)
Cabana, J B (28/29 Mar 1967)
Cabral, J J (16 Jun 1972)
Caffarelli, C J (20 Nov 1972)
Cahaskie, C S (29 Sep 1967)
Cain, J W (26 Apr 1967)
Cain, L N (16 Aug 1968)
Cairns, R A (17 Jun 1966)
Call, J H (2 Apr 1972)
Callaghan, D F (23 Sep 1968)
Callaghan, P A (21 Jun 1972)
Callahan, R (13 Dec 1967)
Callanan, J V (10 Mar 1969)
Callanan, R J (6 Jan 1966)
Callies, T L (1 Aug 1969)
Calvert, D R (8 Oct 1967)
Cameron, J I (2 Feb 1966)
Cameron, K R (18 May 1967)
Cameron, M F (2 May 1967)
Cameron, R J (27 Jan 1969)
Cameron, V K (29 Jul 1966)
Camerota, P P (21/22 Dec 1972)
Campaigne, J A (8 Apr 1963)
Campbell, (7 Jan 1970)
Campbell, C W (1 Mar 1969)
Campbell, D B (27 Jul 1968)
Campbell, D S (21 Feb 1967)
Campbell, I J (22 Nov 1968)
Campbell, J W (12 May 1968)
Campbell, T (6 Nov 1965)
Campbell, W E (29 Jan 1969)
Campbell, W H (21 Mar 1965)
Campbell, B W (1 Jul 1966)
Caniford, J K (28 Mar 1972)
Canter, R M (8 Dec 1965)
Canterbury, H D (22 Aug 1967)
Canup, W D (17 Feb 1968, 6 Apr 1968)
Capling, E R (19 Sep 1968)
Cappel, J J (7 Sep 1967)
Cappelli, C E (17 Nov 1967)
Caras, F A (28 Apr 1967)
Cardy, B (6 Oct 1969)
Carey, D J (31 Aug 1967)
Carey, R E (29 Sep 1967)
Carey, W G (6 Nov 1966)
Carlock, R L (4 Mar 1967)
Carlson, J W (7 Dec 1966)
Carlson, P V (12 Feb 1967)
Carlton, J E (17 Apr 1967)
Carn, R M (29 Aug 1965)
Carnes, J R (8 Jun 1965)
Carney, R A (3 Dec 1968)
Caroters, (28 Feb 1968)
Carpenter, A R (21 Aug 1966, 1 Nov 1966)
Carpenter, J V (15 Feb 1968)
Carpenter, N M (24 Jun 1968)
Carpenter, R L (31 Mar 1969)
Carr, D G (5/6 Jul 1971)
Carr, D S (2 Sep 1968)
Carr, H S (23 Dec 1972)
Carrier, D L (2 Jun 1967)
Carrier, T F (11 Feb 1967)
Carrigan, L E (23 Aug 1967)
Carroll, D I (29 Oct 1967, 2 Aug 1968)
Carroll, J (27 Feb 1971)
Carroll, P A (2 Jun 1968)
Carroll, P H (1 Nov 1969)
Carroll, R W (21 Sep 1972)
Carroll, R W (28 Jun 1966)
Carson, M (16 May 1967)
Carter, C W (19 Sep 1967)
Carter, F J (5 Nov 1969)
Carter, J L (3 Feb 1966)
Carter, R B (26 Oct 1966)
Carter, W T (10 Nov 1966)
Carter, Z A (3 Aug 1967)
Cartwright, B J (21 Dec 1965)
Cary, L E (25 Aug 1967)
Case, T E (16 Mar 1970)
Case, T F (31 May/1 Jun 1966)
Casey, D F (23 Jun 1968)
Casey, J R (9 Apr 1972)
Cash, R (18 Jun 1972)
Caskey, J B (8 Sep 1967)
Caskey, J L (9 Jun 1966)
Casper, J H (26 Jun 1969)
Casper, J R (8 Aug 1966, 14 Sep 1966)
Caspole, R W (3 Jun 1966)
Cassaro. R F (12 Jan 1969)
Cassell, R B (15 Jul 1967)
Cassell, R M (26 Jul 1967)
Castillo, R (28 Mar 1972)
Castle, R W (28 Dec 1970)
Castonguay, J J (7 May 1972)
Catchings, D S (20 Dec 1969)
Cathey, M R (8 Apr 1969)
Causey, J B (25 Feb 1966)
Cavalli, A F (28 Jun 1966)
Cavallin, L M (1 Sep 1969)
Cecka, RK (4 Apr 1970)
Cellar, C (2 Oct 1966)
Cerak, J P (27 Jun 1972)
Cerrato, F M (7 Dec 1967)
Certain, R G (18/19 Dec 1972)
Cestaric, J A (17 Dec 1965)
Chaffer, W R (25 Mar 1969)
Chaimson, R C (17 Nov 1965)
Chambers, B L (16 Oct 1962)
Chambers, C D (7 Aug 1967)
Chambers, J L (22 May 1968)
Chambers, S P (29 Jun 1965)
Chancy, E J (2 May 1966)
Chancy, G (21 Jun 1966, 11 Sep 1967)
Chandler, A (27 Apr 1970)
Chaney, D (16 Apr 1967)
Chaney, D L (17 Jan 1968)
Chapa, A (5/6 Feb 1968)
Chapman, C L (10 Mar 1967)
Chapman, H P (5 Nov 1965)
Chapman, P H (2 Apr 1972)
Chapman, R M (17 Feb 1969)
Chappell, J M (17 Dec 1965)
Charles, N A (30 Dec 1971, 20 Apr 1972)
Charvet, P C (21 Mar 1967)
Chase, O C (22 Jul 1965)
Chastain, D K (3 Dec 1968)
Chastant, R R (22 Oct 1968)
Chauncey, A R (31 May 1967)
Chavez, G A (29/30 Jul 1970)
Cheney, K J (1 Jul 1972)
Chenis, M C (17 Oct 1968)
Cherney, P F (2 Feb 1968)
Cherry, A S (9 Aug 1967)
Cherry, F V (22 Oct 1965)
Chesley, L J (16 Apr 1966)
Chesnutt, C M (30 Sep 1965)
Chessman, S R (7 Apr 1967)
Chew, R S (17 Nov 1965)
Chiarello, V A (29 Jul 1966)
Chipman, R J (27/28 Dec 1972)
Chomyk, W (21 Apr 1968)
Chorlins, R D (11 Jan 1970)
Chrisman, K L (13 Dec 1967)
Christensen, D E (2 Apr 1970)
Christensen, E E (23 Jun 1968)
Christensen, E S (7 May 1968)
Christensen, W M (1 Mar 1966)
Christensend, G H (1 May 1968)
Christian, D M (2 Jun 1965)
Christian, M D (24 Apr 1967)
Christiano, J (24 Dec 1965)
Christiansen, J M (12 Apr 1972)
Christiansen, V R (5 Jul 1972)
Christianson, P B (3 Apr 1969)
Christopherson, K A (21 Jan 1973)
Christy, R N (17 Feb 1972)
Chumley, S G (31 Jan 1966)
Church, J C (7 Sep 1968)
Churchill, C R (3 May 1970)
Chwan, M D (30 Sep 1965)
Ciarfeo, G T (1 Jun 1968)
Ciminero, J (20 Nov 1967)
Ciriello, B L (20 Oct 1968)
Claflin, R A (26 Jul 1967)
Clanton, L J (23 Mar 1968)
Clapper, G P (28/29 Dec 1967)
Clapper, J K (24 Oct 1969)
Clark, C A (18 Aug 1964, 16 Nov 1972)
Clark, C C (6 Aug 1967)
Clark, D E (23 Mar 1966)
Clark, D V (2 Oct 1966)
Clark, E S (20 Apr 1972)
Clark, J C (5 Dec 1969)
Clark, J T (6 Sep 1965)
Clark, J W (12 Mar 1967)
Clark, L (18 Oct 1966)
Clark, M (2 Apr 1972)
Clark, M N (3 Apr 1972)
Clark, P S (24 Dec 1972)
Clark, R A (9 Jan 1973)
Clark, R C (24 Oct 1967)
Clark, R D (26 Jul 1966)
Clark, R W (8 Oct 1966)
Clark, S C (14 Feb 1969)
Clark, S W (3 May 1968)
Clark, T E (8 Feb 1969)
Clark, W J (30 Nov 1967)
Clarke, C A (22 Jan 1969)
Clarke, C W (18 Mar 1967)
Clarke, F L (13 Dec 1968)
Clarke, G W (15/16 Oct 1967)
Clarton, P L (20 Jun 1966)
Claxton, C P (28/29 Dec 1967)
Clay, R F (9 Mar 1970)
Clay, W C (12 Apr 1967)
Clayton, B J (2 Oct 1966)
Clayton, J F (28 Feb 1967)
Cleary, P M (10 Oct 1972)
Cleaver, D G (3 Oct 1968)
Cleeland, D (25 Jul 1966)
Clem, T D (2 May 1968)
Clemens, R O (19 Sep 1968)
Clement, J W (11 Mar 1970)
Clement, R W (24 Jan 1969)

Clements, J A (9 Oct 1967)
Clever, L J (5 Feb 1969)
Clifton, C (20 Nov 1967)
Clingaman, R L (9 Jun 1970)
Clouser, G L (10 May 1966, 12 Oct 1972)
Clower, C D (19 Nov 1967)
Clydesdale, C F (15 Mar 1965)
Coady, R F (18 Jan 1969)
Coady, T J (29 Jul 1972)
Coakley, W F (12 Sep 1966)
Coates, D L (1 Feb 1966)
Coates, H J (4 Nov 1969)
Cobb, (31 Mar 1967)
Cobb, M J (10 Nov 1972)
Cobbs, R B (17 Jun 1966)
Cobeil, E G (5 Nov 1967)
Coburn, R W (28/29 Dec 1967)
Cochran, J K (23 Dec 1972)
Cody, H R (24 Nov 1963)
Cofer, A W (10 Mar 1969)
Coffee, G L (3 Feb 1966)
Cogdell, W K (17 Jan 1967)
Coghill, J W (13 May 1967)
Cogill, M B (2 Feb 1962)
Cohen, H (19 Jul 1969)
Coker, (8 Feb 1970)
Coker, G T (27 Aug 1966)
Colasuonno, V (12 Feb 1969)
Cole, L O (30 Jun 1967)
Cole, P M (26 Sep 1967)
Cole, R (29 Jun 1965)
Cole, R M (18 Jun 1972)
Cole, V J (27 Oct 1968)
Coleman, J R (25 Feb 1966)
Coley, B J (20 Dec 1963)
Collamore, A P (4 Feb 1967)
Collette, C D (17 Jun 1966)
Collins, G F (13 Mar 1968)
Collins, J Q (2 Sep 1965)
Collins, R D (26 Feb 1971)
Collins, R F (22 Nov 1969)
Collins, T E (18 Oct 1965)
Collins, W E (22 Jan 1969)
Collins, W M (9 Mar 1966)
Coltman, W C (28 Sep 1972)
Colton, C A (8 Jun 1967)
Coltrin, C B (25 Jun 1968)
Colwell, W K (24 Dec 1965)
Colyar, R W (19/20 Dec 1968)
Combs, D R (10 Mar 1972)
Compton, F R (21 Mar 1966)
Compton, J R (17 Sep 1968)
Compton, J R (2 Sep 1971)
Comstock, R W (5 May 1972)
Conaway, L Y (3 May 1970)
Condit, D C (26 Nov 1967)
Condit, W H (23 Jun 1969)
Condon, J C (27/28 Dec 1972)
Cone, F (23 Mar 1967)
Cone, R A (8 Mar 1969)
Confer, G R (13 Jul 1968)
Confer, M S (10 Oct 1966)
Conklin, B (29 Jul 1966)
Conlee, W W (21/22 Dec 1972)
Conley, E O (21 Jan 1967)
Conley, R F (21 Sep 1968)
Conlin, J F (6 Mar 1968)
Conlon, J F (4 Mar 1966)
Connally, J (11 May 1972)
Connell, J J (15 Jul 1966)
Conner, E R (16 May 1970)
Conner, L (27 Oct 1967)
Conner, M R (22 Apr 1970)
Connolly, V J (4 Nov 1966)
Connor, C R (28 Oct 1968)
Connor, H (18/19 Dec 1972)
Connor, J K (3 Oct 1968)
Connor, K (18/19 Dec 1972)
Conroy, R L (3 Oct 1968)
Consolvo, J W (7 May 1972)
Conway, D R (6 Aug 1967)
Cook, D P (6 Apr 1966)
Cook, D W (21 Sep 1972)
Cook, E J (16 Jan 1966)
Cook, G R (21 Oct 1969)
Cook, H C (4 Sep 1967)
Cook, J R (26/27 Dec 1972)
Cook, K E (19 Apr 1968)
Cook, K F (10 Nov 1967)
Cook, R F (4 May 1968)
Cook, W L (29 Nov 1968)

Cook, W P (22 Dec 1967)
Cook, W R (28 Apr 1968)
Cooke, C C (25/26 Apr 1972)
Cooley, D L (22 Apr 1968)
Cooley, O D (16 Jan 1968)
Cooley, R B (14 Dec 1966)
Coon, D B (10 May 1968)
Coon, J C (8 Feb 1970)
Coonon, D J (4 Jul 1968, 8 Oct 1968)
Coons, C L (17 Feb 1968)
Coons, H A (28 Feb 1968)
Cooper, D D (4 Feb 1972)
Cooper, G G (21 Jan 1967)
Cooper, R W, USAF (18/19 Dec 1972)
Cooper, R W, USN (28 Oct 1965)
Cooper, W E (24 Apr 1966)
Copack, J B (21/22 Dec 1972)
Copeland, H C (17 Jul 1967)
Corbett, C (2 May 1972)
Corbett, I (6 Oct 1969)
Corbin, K J (11 Mar 1968)
Corbitt, G W (26 Jul 1967)
Corder, J A (8 Feb 1968)
Cordero, W E (19 Jun 1965)
Cordes, D L (20 Nov 1972)
Cordier, K W (3 Dec 1966)
Cordova, S G (2 Aug 1972, 26 Aug 1972)
Core, B R (27 Jan 1968)
Cormier, A (6 Nov 1965)
Cornelius, J C (26 Jun 1968)
Cornelius, S B (16 Jun 1973)
Cornwell, L J (10 Sep 1971)
Coskey, K L (6 Sep 1968)
Costello, J F (25 May 1973)
Cote, B C (1 Apr 1968)
Cotner, M A (28 Apr 1967)
Cotterill, M J (25 Apr 1969)
Cotton, L W (9 Mar 1970)
Cotton, R C (16 Nov 1969)
Couch, D B (19 Feb 1967)
Coughlin, A R (2 Oct 1967)
Couillard, B A (20 Mar 1968)
Coulter, (9 Jan 1966)
Courtney, P H (1 Aug 1969)
Courtney, T F (2 May 1972)
Cowell, R J (9 Mar 1970)
Cox, B N (8 Dec 1969)
Cox, H B (11 Aug 1967)
Cox, J (26 May 1973)
Cox, J A (18 May 1969)
Cox, O T (16 Dec 1967)
Cox, R (22/23 May 1968)
Cox, S G (17/18 May 1966)
Cox, W R (16 Feb 1971)
Coy, J A (11 Jun 1965)
Coyman, P R (24 Apr 1965)
Crabb, M L (31 May 1966)
Craddock, R J (20/21 Dec 1972)
Cradeur, D J (4/5 May 1968)
Craig, K G (22 Aug 1966)
Craig, P C (4 Jul 1967)
Craig, T L (12 Jan 1965)
Crain, C O (8 Mar 1967)
Crane, D A (30 Jul 1972)
Crane, J R (6 Jul 1966)
Craner, R R (9 Nov 1967, 20 Dec 1967)
Craw, P R (14 Apr 1967)
Crawford, C A (19 May 1970)
Crayton, R (7 Feb 1966)
Creal, S M (8 Aug 1968)
Crebo, A R (25 Apr 1967)
Crecca, J (22 Nov 1966)
Creed, B S (13 Mar 1971)
Cressey, D C (12 May 1972)
Cressman, P R (4/5 Feb 1973)
Creswell, B L (3 Oct 1966)
Crew, J A (10 Nov 1967)
Crews, J H (22 May 1968)
Crismon, F S (30 Dec 1964)
Crisp, W H (20 Dec 1965)
Crist, K L (1 Apr 1968)
Crist, K R (17 Dec 1968)
Crist, R C (5 Aug 1965)
Crockett, W J (22 Aug 1972)
Cronin, B J (9 Dec 1964)
Cronin, M P (13 Jan 1967)
Cronkite, C L (20 Jun 1967)
Croom, W D (26 May 1970)
Cropper, C H (5 Apr 1970)
Crosby, F P (1 Jun 1965)
Cross, A L (17 Jul 1968)

Crossman, G J (25 Apr 1968)
Crosson, G J (16 May 1968)
Crotwell, B H (13 Jan 1966)
Crow, F A (26 Mar 1967)
Crowell, J E (23 May 1968)
Crumley, H R (25 Jan 1966)
Crumm, W J (7 Jul 1967)
Crumpler, C B (5 Jul 1968)
Cruz, C R (29 Dec 1967)
Cruz, R (2 Sep 1963)
Cubberly, R L (22 Mar 1971)
Cullen, J A (2 Mar 1965)
Cumiskey, J L (13 Jun 1967)
Cummings, J D (11 Sep 1972)
Cunliffe, F R (16 Sep 1972)
Cunningham, C A (2 Aug 1967)
Cunningham, G M (24 Sep 1968)
Cunningham, L J (14 Jul 1967, 9 Oct 1967)
Cunningham, N N (24 Sep 1968)
Cunningham, R H (10 May 1972)
Curran, P R (29 Sep 1969)
Curry, K R W (8 Jan 1971)
Curry, W (6 Oct 1969)
Curtis, R E (13 Mar 1968)
Curtis, T J (20 Sep 1965)
Cusack, C R (8 Aug 1968)
Cushman, C E (25 Sep 1966)
Cusimano, S B (27/28 Dec 1972)
Cuthbert, B G (23 Nov 1968)
Cuthbert, S H (3 Jul 1972)
Cutrer, F C (5/6 Aug 1964)
Cutter, J D (17 Feb 1972)
Cutting, W S (1 Apr 1968)
D'Adamo, J (10 Feb 1968)
D'Amico, D R (19 Oct 1968)
D'Angelo, G A (31 Aug 1968)
D'Angelo, S E (2 Mar 1969)
Daffron, T C (18 Feb 1970)
Dahart, R E (27 May 1970)
Dahl, F W (6 Aug 1967)
Daigle, G H (22 Dec 1965)
Daigle, B (18 Sep 1965)
Dailey, D V (13 Dec 1968)
Dalecky, W J (9 Sep 1972)
Daley, W R (20 Dec 1969)
Dallas, B B (19/20 Jun 1968)
Daly, P E (2 Mar 1969, 12 May 1969)
Dambekaln, A (24 Jul 1968)
Damon, R E (5 Aug 1965)
Dander, V (2 Aug 1968)
Daniel, E L (8 Aug 1969)
Daniels, M T (31 May 1967)
Daniels, V W (26 Oct 1967)
Danielson, B F (5 Dec 1969)
Danielson, M G (18 Jun 1972)
Dansby, C M (24 Apr 1965)
Darcy, E J (28/29 Dec 1967)
Dardeau, A T (22 Jun 1967)
Dardeau, O M (18 Nov 1967)
Darr, C E (20/21 Dec 1972)
Daughtrey, R N (2 Aug 1965)
Dauten, F W (4 Apr 1970)
Davenport, R D (28 Mar 1969)
Davidson, H M (16 Jan 1966)
Davie, T E (31 Oct 1966)
Davies, E F (17 Sep 1968)
Davies, J D (19 Mar 1970)
Davies, J E (18/19 May 1968)
Davies, J O (4 Feb 1967)
Davies, T (28 Mar 1968)
Davis, B E (18 Mar 1966)
Davis, C B (22 Apr 1970)
Davis, C J (20 Jan 1972)
Davis, D V (25 Jul 1967)
Davis, E A (26 Aug 1965)
Davis, E A (5 Mar 1969)
Davis, F E (21 Jan 1969)
Davis, F F (30 Jun 1968)
Davis, F J (13 Jun 1972)
Davis, G E (13 Mar 1966)
Davis, H M (6 Jul 1972)
Davis, J C (25 Apr 1969)
Davis, J T (8 Jul 1967)
Davis, J W (20 Jun 1972)
Davis, L L (16 Nov 1969)
Davis, R C (22 Mar 1969)
Davis, R W (26 Apr 1967)
Davis, W K (19 Jul 1969)
Davis, W S (19 Sep 1966)
Davis, W W (2 May 1970)
Davis, Y R (19 Nov 1968)

Davison, D M (5 Dec 1969)
Davison, N R (6 Dec 1963)
Dawson, C D (23 Mar 1966)
Dawson, F A (17 Feb 1968)
Dawson, J V (16 Jul 1969)
Dawson, P G (11 Jun 1965)
Day, G E (26 Aug 1967)
De la Houssaye, A (30/31 Jan 1968)
De Long, M (16 Apr 1972)
De Sousa, M A (15 Mar 1969)
Dean, M F (30 Jun 1970)
Deans, W R (11 Jun 1969)
Deas, C M (10 Feb 1971)
Deatrick, E R (13 Sep 1966)
DeBellevue, C (10 May 1972, 9 Sep 1972)
DeBlasio, R V (18 Jun 1971)
DeBock, J A (3 Aug 1967)
Deel, H B (10 May 1969)
Deforrest, R C (25 Apr 1969)
Delaney, W C (25 Apr 1969)
Deleidi, R A (7 Feb 1969)
Delgado-Marin, A (23 Nov 1967)
Delmore, J R (12 May 1968)
Delphin, B R (19 Mar 1967)
Delzangaro, F (8 Dec 1965)
Demarque, C B (23 Aug 1967)
Dempsey, J I (17 Jun 1966)
Denalt, J L (29 Jan 1970)
Dengler, D (20 Sep 1965, 1 Feb 1966)
Dennany, R L (11 Nov 1969)
Dennison, J R (1 Jan 1968)
Dennison, T A (19 Jul 1966)
Denton, G T (16 Mar 1970)
Denton, J A (18 Jul 1965)
Denton, J R (7 Sep 1968)
Derby, P D (17 Nov 1968)
Deremer, R G (2 Nov 1972)
Derrickson, T G (12 Oct 1967)
Desoto, E L (12 Apr 1969)
Despiegler, G A (15 Apr 1972)
Detar, D E (25 Apr 1970)
Dethlefsen, M H (10 Mar 1967, 8 Dec 1969)
Dethman, I (27 Mar 1968)
Detwiler, R C (22 Apr 1969)
Deuter, R C (22 Nov 1969)
Devere, R P (25 Jul 1969)
Devik, D R (10 Feb 1968)
Deville, E (18 Sep 1965)
Devlin, J J (20 Nov 1968)
Devoss, J L (16 Jun 1969)
DeWispelaere, R J (24 Nov 1969)
Dewitt, H D (15 Dec 1965)
Dewitt, W (20 Dec 1965)
Di Tommaso, R J (29 Jul 1969)
Diamond, S W (19 Jul 1966)
Dice, C R (8 Dec 1969)
Dickens, D E (21/22 Dec 1972)
Dickens, F D (16 Oct 1968)
Dickens, J L (1 Jun 1969)
Dickens, T L (4 May 1973)
Dickey, R S (15 Jul 1969)
Dickson, E A (7 Feb 1965)
Diefenbach, B (26/27 Dec 1972)
Diehl, W C (7 Nov 1967)
Dilger, H H (2 Oct 1969)
Dilger, R G (26 Jun 1967, 11 Aug 1967)
Dimond, A J (11 Jun 1965)
Dinan, D T (17 Mar 1969)
Dingee, D B (1 Jun 1972, 27 Jun 1972)
Dingee, S (27 Jun 1972)
Dion, L N (17 Aug 1967)
Disbrow, D E (23 Nov 1966)
Dives, T L (2 Aug 1969)
Dixon, L C (6 Jan 1966)
Dixon, W M (14/15 Feb 1968)
Dobbs, H R (28 Jan 1969)
Dobbs, T D (5 Sep 1966)
Dobson, E (30 Apr 1967)
Dobson, T W (10 Feb 1972)
Doby, H (4 Feb 1967)
Dobyns, R E (11 Mar 1968)
Dodge, E R (31 Dec 1964)
Dodge, R W (17 May 1967)
Dodge, W K (5 Jul 1967)
Dodson, J (22 Aug 1965)
Dole, J M (25 Oct 1967)
Dollarhide, D (20 Jul 1967)
Donahue, J W (3 Jan 1966)
Donahue, M J (13 Dec 1968)
Donald, M L 23 Feb 1968)
Donato, P N (17 Feb 1968)

Donis, J N (14 Jul 1967)
Donnelly, V G (16 Sep 1972)
Donnelly, W N (29 Mar 1965)
Donovan, M L (30 Sep 1971)
Dooley, J E (22 Oct 1967)
Doran, J T (29 Mar 1968)
Doremus, R H (24 Aug 1965)
Dorman, G S (4 Aug 1969)
Dorn, C E (3 Sep 1969)
Dorsett, T G (31 Aug 1968)
Dorsett, T K (8 Feb 1968)
Dorsey, J V (5 Feb 1969)
Doss, D W (16/17 Mar 1968)
Dotson, J S (9 Aug 1969)
Dotson, R S (18 Feb 1970, 21 Apr 1971)
Dougherty, J M (31 Oct 1966)
Doughtie, C L (10 Jun 1965)
Doughty, D J (2 Apr 1966)
Douglas, N E (17 Dec 1970)
Douglass, J A (21 May 1968)
Dove, J P (12 Jul 1967)
Dover, G R (19 Jun 1969)
Dowd, J F (29 Dec 1967)
Dowell, R S (29 Oct 1962)
Downing, B G (21 Jan 1968)
Downing, D W (5 Sep 1967)
Doyle, B F (17 Apr 1969)
Doyle, R E (12 Apr 1963)
Draeger, W F (4 Apr 1965)
Drage, R L (11 Nov 1969)
Draggett, R G (21 May 1972)
Drake, C W (18 Jun 1970)
Dramesi, J A (2 Apr 1967, 12 Aug 1967)
Dresser, G D (15 Dec 1965)
Drewry, H J (13 Dec 1968)
Driscoll, F M (29 Feb 1968)
Driscoll, J D (24 Apr 1966)
Driscoll, S J (24 May 1968)
Driscoll, W P (10 May 1972)
Drummond, D I (21/22 Dec 1972)
Duart, D H (18 Feb 1967)
Ducat, B C (2 Dec 1966)
Ducharme, E J (3 Nov 1966)
Duck, W W (2 Oct 1967)
Duckett, T A (12 Dec 1970)
Dudash, J E (26 Apr 1967)
Dudek, R (22 Oct 1968)
Dudley, A S (11 Sep 1972)
Dudley, C G (28 Jun 1966)
Duensing, J A (30 Jun 1973)
Duffin, R L (17 Nov 1967)
Duffy, D C (25 Sep 1965)
Duffy, J E (4 Apr 1970)
Duffy, T K (27 Apr 1972)
Dugan, M J (18 Mar 1967)
Dugan, T W (13 Dec 1968)
Duggan, W Y (10 Feb 1965, 31 Dec 1971)
Duke, G G (24 Jul 1966)
Duncan, N H (26 Dec 1968)
Duncan, R R (28 Aug 1968)
Dunlop, T E (6 Apr 1972)
Dunn, C P (5 Jun 1972)
Dunn, D L (10 Feb 1971)
Dunn, J H (7 Dec 1965)
Dunn, J P (14 Feb 1968)
Dunn, M E (26 Jun 1968)
Dunn, R E (25/26 Apr 1972)
Dunne, M E (8 Oct 1965)
Dunnegan, C P (28 Apr 1967)
Durham, J C (14 Feb 1966)
Duthie, L J (18 Jul 1967)
Dutton, R A (5 Nov 1967)
Duvall, D A (13 Mar 1966)
Dwyer, G T (1 Apr 1968, 21 May 1968)
Dwyer, T J (13 Sep 1966)
Dyczkowski, R R (23 Apr 1966)
Dyer, D (7 Aug 1966)
Dyer, E B (17 Sep 1972)
Dyer, G D (26 Oct 1964)
Dyer, J M (21 Apr 1970)
Dyer, R (5 Oct 1968)
Dyke, T W (6 Dec 1966)
Dziedic, D F (27 Apr 1972)
Eagan, (1 Jul 1968, 20 Dec 1968, 24 Jan 1969)
Eakin, B S (1 Feb 1966)
Earle, J S (22 Jun 1970)
Earll, D J (21 Oct 1966)
Earnest, C M (28 Nov 1972)
Eason, E R (19 Nov 1964)
East, J B (26 Apr 1969)
Eastman, L C (21 Jun 1966)

Eaton, C A (14 Aug 1966)
Eaton, D R (14 Jul 1965)
Eaton, N D (13 Jan 1969)
Eaves, S (10 May 1972)
Ebdon, T J (18 Mar 1969)
Echanis, J Y (5 Nov 1969)
Eckley, W A (28/29 Dec 1967)
Eddy, G E (1 Oct 1970)
Eddy, J L (23 Oct 1967)
Edens, R J (7 Jun 1968)
Edgar, R J (4 Feb 1968)
Edlen, K D (10 Sep 1968)
Edmondson, W R (31 May/1 Jun 1966)
Edmunds, R C (27 Oct 1968)
Edwards, H S (20 Oct 1966)
Edwards, K G (19 Jul 1972)
Edwards, R L (23 Oct 1968)
Egan, F X (19 Dec 1972)
Egan, W P (29 Apr 1966)
Egea, L R (21 Mar 1967)
Egelston, D P (8 Jul 1970)
Egge, A G (6 Oct 1972)
Egger, J C (3 Nov 1967)
Ehle, B (2 Oct 1970)
Ehrlich, D M (19 Jan 1967)
Eidsmoe, N E (26 Jan 1968)
Eikel, H A (30 Aug 1968, 24 May 1972)
Eilers, D L (24 Dec 1965)
Eisenbeisz, R A (11 Feb 1971)
Eisenbrey, D R (2 Sep 1972)
Ekman, L C (31 May 1966)
Elander, W J (5 Jul 1972)
Eldridge, T F (29 Dec 1965)
Elias, E K (30 Dec 1971, 20 Apr 1972)
Elkins, F C (12 Oct 1966)
Elkins, J (27 Aug 1965)
Ellard, J S (4 Jul 1968)
Ellinger, J (20/21 Dec 1972)
Elliot, R J (21 Aug 1967)
Elliot, R M (14 Feb 1968)
Elliott, M C (21/22 Oct 1965)
Elliott, O G (24 Jul 1968)
Elliott, R T (21/22 Dec 1972)
Ellis, B R (24 Feb 1966)
Ellis, G L (27 Sep 1967)
Ellis, J T (17 Dec 1967)
Ellis, L F (7 Nov 1967)
Ellis, M R (14 Oct 1966)
Ellison, J C (15 May 1966, 24 Mar 1967)
Elmer, D A (4 Nov 1966)
Emrich, R G (17 Nov 1967)
Encinas, E M (17 Jun 1972)
Engelhard, E C (22 Jun 1969)
Engelhardt, A A (16 Mar 1968)
England, T L (20 Mar 1967)
English, W C (4 Jun 1970)
Enriquez, J (25 Jul 1968)
Ericksen, G G (25 Oct 1965)
Erickson, D J (15 Mar 1970)
Erickson, R P (21 Sep 1968)
Ernst, A A (16 Nov 1969)
Erwin, D E (2 Oct 1968)
Escalera, D (25 Dec 1967)
Espenshield, J L (21 Oct 1969)
Estabrooks, W E (22 Apr 1967)
Estep, E B (2 Oct 1968)
Estes, E D (3 Jan 1968)
Estes, M E (11 Jun 1965)
Estes, R (22 Nov 1972)
Estes, W O (19 Nov 1967)
Estocin, M J (26 Apr 1967)
Etzel, G (2 Jul 1967)
Evans, D C (1 May 1968)
Evans, D M (18 May 1969)
Evans, J J (2 Apr 1965)
Evans, R E (2 May 1967)
Evenson, J (19 Mar 1970)
Everett, D A (27 Aug 1972)
Everett, L R (17 Oct 1971)
Everson, D (10 Mar 1967)
Evert, L G (8 Nov 1967)
Ewing, R C (25 Feb 1967)
Ewoldt, D (29 Jul 1966)
Ezell, D D (24 Apr 1965)
Faas, M J (26 Mar 1969, 18 Mar 1972)
Fabian, W H (14 Nov 1968)
Fage, R F (27 Apr 1970)
Fagg, J W (20 Jul 1972)
Fahey, J M (11 Feb 1962)
Fairchild, C R (3 Mar 1966)
Fairlamb, R C (15 Mar 1968)
Fales, P B (16 Nov 1969)
Fallert, D (24 Jul 1972)
Fannemel, W R (6 Dec 1966)
Fanning, H M (30 Oct 1967)
Fanning, J P (13 Dec 1968)
Fant, R S (25 Jul 1968)
Fantle, S (5 Jan 1968)
Fardy, J T (13 May 1968)
Farmer, J (20/21 Dec 1972)
Farnsworth, E L (19 Jan 1970, 19 Mar 1970)
Farnsworth, J F (15 Apr 1968)
Farr, J G (27 Jul 1965)
Farrell, G J (25 Jul 1966)
Farris, W F (5/6 Feb 1968)
Farrow, D A (13 May 1966)
Faulk, P (25 Apr 1969)
Faulkner, S (6 Jan 1969)
Fearno, J B (21 Mar 1966)
Featherston, F W (30 Dec 1969)
Fegan, J R (17 Jan 1969)
Fegan, R J (9 Apr 1965)
Fehrenbach, T C (6 Apr 1970)
Feinstein, J S (25 Aug 1972, 20 Nov 1972)
Feldhaus, J A (8 Oct 1966)
Fellenz, C R (24 Nov 1969)
Fellowes, J H (27 Aug 1966)
Fellows, A E (20 Mar 1968)
Feneley, F J (11 May 1966)
Fenn, F B (20 Dec 1968)
Fenter, C F (21/22 Dec 1972)
Fenzl, G J (8 Mar 1972)
Fer, J (4 Feb 1967)
Ferguson, C L (13 Jan 1965)
Ferguson, D D (30 Dec 1969)
Ferguson, S C (17 Jul 1968)
Ferguson, W A (16 Jun 1968)
Ferguson, W L (18/19 Dec 1972)
Fernandez, L (19 Jul 1967)
Fernandez, W M (19 Feb 1971)
Fernando, A (18/19 Dec 1972)
Ferracane, L J (29 May 1972)
Ferren, J W (10 Feb 1968)
Ferron, F R (10 Mar 1967)
Fickler, E J (17 Jan 1969)
Fidelibus, W T (12 Aug 1965)
Fields, B M (17 Feb 1968)
Fields, E (22 Apr 1970)
Fields, J L (28/29 Mar 1967)
Fields, K W (31 May 1968)
Fields, M R (1 Jun 1965)
Fieszel, C W (30 Sep 1968)
Files, A C (25 Mar 1967)
Filmore, L R (28 Feb 1968)
Fincher, D B (14 Mar 1970)
Findlay, C W (14 Sep 1966)
Findlay, R F (5 Jun 1969)
Findley, J H (8 Sep 1972)
Finlay, J S (28 Apr 1968)
Finn, W R (24 Dec 1971)
Finney, A T (1 Aug 1966)
Finney, C E (17 Mar 1969)
Finzer, B B (11 Aug 1966, 13 Sep 1966)
Fiorelli, J V (2 Aug 1967)
Fischer, J R (8 Sep 1966)
Fisher, B F (21 Mar 1965, 10 Mar 1966)
Fisher, D E (28/29 Dec 1967)
Fisher, D G (22 Apr 1970)
Fisher, K (7 Nov 1967)
Fitton, C J (29 Feb 1968)
Fitzgerald, D J (19 Sep 1966)
Fitzgerald, R E (2 Sep 1971)
Fitzgerald, W M (24 Oct 1963)
Fitzmaurice, J F (15 May 1970)
Fitzsimmons, W (28 Jul 1965)
Flanagan, B E (25 Feb 1968)
Flanagan, S E (21 Jul 1968)
Flanigan, J N (19 Aug 1969)
Fleenor, K R (17 Dec 1967)
Fleming, G J (26 Apr 1971)
Fleming, R A (10 Jan 1968)
Flesher, H K (2 Dec 1966)
Flinn, J L (2 Jul 1969)
Flint, G K (29 Dec 1967)
Flom, F R (8 Aug 1966)
Floyd, F J (14 Jul 1969)
Floyd, H G (24 Feb 1967)
Flynn, G E (23 Sep 1964)
Flynn, J P (27 Oct 1967)
Flynn, R J (21 Aug 1967)
Fobair, R H (24 Jul 1965)
Fodaro, T A (13 Jan 1966)
Fogleman, R R (12 Sep 1968)
Foley, B P (23/24 Nov 1967)
Foley, P A (22 Nov 1972)
Forbes, W H (20 Mar 1967)
Forby, W E (20 Sep 1965)
Ford, D E (19 Nov 1967)
Ford, M W (11 Feb 1971)
Ford, P W (30 Mar 1970, 29 Sep 1970)
Ford, R W (10 Jun 1968)
Ford, W A (24 May 1968)
Forman, R E (17 Apr 1971)
Forman, W S (21/22 Jan 1966)
Forrester, R W (27/28 Dec 1972)
Fors, G H (22 Dec 1967)
Forsgren, D H (28 Dec 1965)
Fortner, F J (17 Oct 1967)
Foss, E L (24 Jul 1966)
Foster, B E (22 Apr 1970)
Foster, B S (24 Aug 1968)
Foster, C G (2 Apr 1969)
Foster, E E (20 Jul 1967)
Foster, P L (29 Dec 1967)
Foster, R E (9 Mar 1966)
Foster, W (17 Nov 1965)
Foster, W F (23 Jul 1966)
Foulks, R A (24 Oct 1967)
Foulks, R E (5 Jan 1968)
Fowler, G E (15 Nov 1966)
Fowler, H P (26 Mar 1967)
Fowler, J A (6 Jun 1972)
Fowler, K W (25 Apr 1969)
Fowler, R M (22/23 May 1970)
Fowler, W M (30 Sep 1966)
Fox, A O (23 Apr 1968)
Foxx, R L (15 Oct 1962)
Frahman, L J (2 Jul 1966)
Frakes, D G (24 Feb 1965)
Francis, R L (27 Jun 1972)
Francisco, M C (28 Apr 1972)
Francisco. S D (25 Nov 1968)
Franco, C S (7 Jun 1966)
Franger, E M (28 Dec 1969)
Frank, T P (1 Nov 1971)
Franke, F A (24 Aug 1965)
Franklin, C E (14 Aug 1966)
Franks, R D (8 Jun 1967)
Franz. O (3 Aug 1966)
Fraser, K J (17 Feb 1972)
Frawley, W D (1 Mar 1966)
Frazer, E R (6 Feb 1970)
Frazier, F M (11 Feb 1962)
Frederick, J W (7 Dec 1965)
Frederick, P J (15 Mar 1967)
Frederick, W V (5 Jul 1967)
Freeborn, G H (21 Aug 1967)
Freeman, I D (9 Mar 1967)
Freng, S J (17 Jun 1966)
Frenyea, E H (21/22 Jan 1966)
Frey, L T (11 Apr 1968)
Friese, L V (24 Feb 1968)
Friestad, D E (22 Apr 1970, 4 Mar 1970)
Frink, J W (2 Apr 1972)
Frisbie, N E (29 Dec 1969)
Frishman, R F (24 Oct 1967, 28 Apr 1968)
Fritsch, B O (15 Jul 1966)
Fritschi, G W (25 Dec 1967)
Fritz, L D (24 Dec 1969)
Frizell, W H (1 Nov 1968)
Fromm, R E (29 Apr 1969)
Frosio, R C (12 Nov 1966)
Frost, C F (7 Jun 1966)
Fryar, B C (2 Jan 1970)
Frye, D P (18 Jul 1967)
Fryer, B L (27/28 Dec 1972)
Fryer, C W (7 Aug 1966)
Fulcher, M C (31 May 1967)
Fulghom, G G (16 Jun 1969)
Fulgram, V D (12 Jun 1967)
Fulk, J W (12 Aug 1972)
Fulk, W O (30 Mar 1972)
Fullam, W E (7 Oct 1967)
Fuller, B (30 Apr 1967)
Fuller, J L (6 Oct 1967)
Fuller, R B (14 Jul 1967)
Fuller, R T (21/22 Dec 1972)
Fuller, W O (25 Aug 1967)
Fullerton, F E (26 Jul 1968)
Fulton, R J (13 Jun 1972)
Funck, A (23 Mar 1967)
Fyan, R R (26 Apr 1968)
Fye, C R (14 Jan 1967)
Gaddis, N C (12 May 1967)
Gagan, J A (16 Jan 1966)
Gaither, R E (17 Oct 1965)
Galanti, P E (17 Jun 1966)
Galati, R W (16 Feb 1972)
Galbraith, R D (12 Dec 1968)
Galbraith, W (24 Feb 1971)
Gallager, J (24 Sep 1965)
Gallagher, D L (5/6 Feb 1968)
Gallagher, J H (12 Nov 1966)
Gallagher, J J (17 Feb 1973)
Gallanger, C L (3 Dec 1968)
Gallarco, E F (13 Jun 1965)
Gallup, R D (16 Jun 1965)
Galvani, W W (7 Oct 1970)
Galvin, R E (8 Mar 1967)
Gambino, J (7 Apr 1973)
Ganci, S J (11 Jun 1965)
Ganley, R O (24 Nov 1969)
Gannaway, C B (14 Nov 1968)
Gapp, A W (7 Jun 1967)
Gardiner, L E (30 Aug 1967)
Gardner, (7 Nov 1966)
Gareiss, K W (24 Feb 1965)
Garland, E W (5 Oct 1966)
Garrett, P E (8 Mar 1969)
Garside, F T (23 Mar 1961)
Gartley, M L (17 Aug 1968, 30 Dec 1971, 20 Apr 1972)
Garzik, J S (28 Apr 1969)
Gassman, J O (5 Sep 1967)
Gates, F H (19 Aug 1967)
Gatwood, R F (2 Apr 1972)
Gauley, J P (10 Jan 1967)
Gauntt, W A (13 Aug 1972)
Gay, T (5 Apr 1965)
Gaylord, G M (6 Apr 1970)
Gearheart, J R (31 Jan 1966)
Gee, P S (16 Jan 1968)
Gehrig, J M (18 Jun 1965)
Geiger, C (31 May 1966)
Geiger, F E (22 Jul 1965)
Geller, J B (30 Mar 1967)
Geloneck, T M (20/21 Dec 1972)
Gendebien, W R (26 Oct 1965)
George, S W (20 Jul 1966)
Gerard, R W (25 Aug 1967)
Gerhard, T (19 Nov 1967)
Gerndt, G L (23 Aug 1967)
Gerry, J L (24 Aug 1965)
Gerstel, D A (7 Sep 1972)
Getchel, P E (13 Jan 1969)
Getman, G L (9 Jun 1965)
Giannangeli, A R (2 Apr 1972)
Gibson, R E (30 Apr 1969)
Gideon, W S (7 Aug 1966)
Gieleghem, R A (1 Oct 1969)
Gierak, G G (13 Jun 1966)
Giere, B D (16 Sep 1966)
Gilbert, P F (18 Jun 1972)
Gilchrist, A (25 Feb 1970)
Gilchrist, R M (6 Oct 1966)
Gilfry, M C (6 Apr 1972)
Gill, T O (24 Jul 1968)
Gillen, T E (18 Feb 1970)
Gillespie, A (18 May 1969)
Gillespie, C R (24 Oct 1967)
Gilmore, J R (2 Jun 1969)
Gilmore, K E (25 Mar 1969)
Gilmore, P J (6 Aug 1967)
Gilroy, K A (7 Aug 1966)
Ginart, D F (3 Jun 1969)
Giroux, P J (21/22 Dec 1972)
Gist, T E (18 May 1968)
Givens, B R (25 Apr 1968)
Glandon, G A (26 May 1966)
Glanville, J T (13 Jun 1966)
Glasson, W A (12 Apr 1966)
Glenn, D E (21 Dec 1966)
Glenn, J H (15 Nov 1967)
Glidden, A (9 Nov 1966)
Glover, C G (22 May 1968)
Glover, D (16 Apr 1967)
Glover, J E (29 Sep 1966)
Glynn, L J (25 Aug 1967)
Godfrey, J H (11 Jan 1966)
Goeden, G W (17 Mar 1967)
Goeglein, J W (30 Jun 1970)
Golberg, L H (8 Aug 1966)
Gold, E F (21 Dec 1965)
Gollahon, G R (12 Aug 1965)
Golz, J B (22 Apr 1970)
Gomez, R A (23 Apr 1970)
Goodenough, R E (21 Apr 1966)
Goodermote, W K (13 Aug 1967)
Goodman, J D (8/9 Jan 1967)
Goodman, R C (20 Feb 1967)
Goodrich, E R (12 Mar 1967)
Goodwin, C B (7 Sep 1965)
Gordon, C W (7 Jan 1964)
Gordon, G A (30 Apr 1969)
Gordon, J A (16 Jul 1967)
Gordon, O (19 Nov 1964)
Gordon, W S (8 Nov 1967, 1 Oct 1969)
Gore, C (23 Feb 1967)
Gorton, T F (6 Dec 1963)
Gosen, L D (23 Jul 1968)
Goss, B J (23 Apr 1966)
Goss, R D (29 Aug 1964)
Gotner, N A (3 Feb 1971)
Gott, R H (5 Feb 1969)
Goucher, E L (4 Sep 1967)
Goudy, R L (9 Aug 1965)
Gough, J W (27/28 Dec 1972)
Gould, F A (20/21 Dec 1972)
Gould, W L (19 Sep 1966)
Gourlet, L L (9 Aug 1969)
Govan, R A (1 Apr 1967)
Gower, W R (29 Jul 1966)
Goyette, R T (22 Oct 1968)
Graber, S D (5 Apr 1968)
Grable, M R (25 Jul 1966)
Grace, J W (14 Jun 1969)
Graf, A S (29 Aug 1969)
Graf, C M (24 Jan 1973)
Graff, J H (2 Oct 1966)
Graham, A (21 Nov 1965)
Graham, A U (16/17 Oct 1972)
Graham, D L (28 Mar 1968)
Graham, J S (4 May 1967)
Grainger, P L (20/21 Dec 1972)
Granitto, D F (11 Jul 1966)
Grant, D B (24 Jun 1972)
Grant, U S (1 Oct 1968)
Grathwol, J M (22 Jan 1969)
Grauert, H H (3 Nov 1967)
Graustein, R S (21/22 Dec 1972)
Graves, R C (25 May 1967)
Gravis, J D (24 Sep 1965)
Gravitte, C M (17 Jun 1966)
Gravrock, S H (23 Jul 1972)
Gray, C A (23 Apr 1966)
Gray, C H, USA (30 Aug 1970)
Gray, C H, USAF (22 Feb 1969)
Gray, D F (23 Jan 1967)
Gray, H E (7 Aug 1965)
Gray, J A (4 Apr 1970)
Gray, J T (24 Apr 1965)
Gray, R A (9 Jun 1967)
Gray, R T (5 Jun 1973)
Graybill, (10 Sep 1965)
Grayson, W R (1 Apr 1966)
Greco, L A (6 Dec 1966)
Greeff, T H (30 Jan 1969)
Green, D G (16 Nov 1965)
Green, F C (9 Jul 1972)
Green, G (12 Sep 1965)
Green, G M (18 Aug 1968)
Green, M P (24 Jan 1969)
Green, N M (9 Jan 1968)
Green, R O (19 Feb 1966)
Greene, B B (13 Dec 1968)
Greene, C E (11 Mar 1967)
Greenhalgh, T L (22 Dec 1968)
Greenleaf, J G (14 Apr 1972)
Greenlee, S J (2 May 1970)
Greenley, J A (6 Jan 1966)
Greenwood, F R (21 Sep 1965)
Greenwood, J S (20 Mar 1966)
Greenwood, R R (2 Sep 1972)
Greer, R P (18 Mar 1968)
Greer, W A (5 Nov 1969)
Greer, W E (9 Apr 1965)
Gregory, C R (4 May 1968)
Gregory, P A (25 Jul 1970)
Gregory, R R (2 Dec 1966)
Greiling, D S (24 Jul 1968)
Greinke, N N (11 Sep 1969)
Grenoble, (17 Nov 1968)
Grenzebach, E W (12 May 1967)
Greshel, J T (14 Apr 1966)
Greskowiak, R (15 May 1965)

Grewell, C J (14 Mar 1969)
Grewell, L I (24 Nov 1969)
Griffey, T H (26 May 1966)
Griffin, C F (13 Dec 1968)
Griffin, J L (19 May 1967)
Griffith, J G (12 Mar 1968)
Griffith, W C (11 Nov 1967)
Griffiths, (18 May 1969)
Griffiths, R L (28 Jul 1965)
Griner, J A (9 Feb 1970)
Grippen, S (26/27 Dec 1972)
Gronquist, C E (20 Jul 1965)
Groves, F C (2 Feb 1962)
Groves, W J (6 Jan 1967)
Grubb, P A (16 Sep 1967)
Grubb, W N (26 Jan 1966)
Grud, T A (25 Dec 1967)
Gruters, G D (8 Nov 1967,
9 Nov 1967, 20 Dec 1967)
Gruters, T (27/28 Dec 1972)
Guarino, L N (14 Jun 1965)
Gudmunson, C E (26 Mar 1965)
Guenther, L E (26 Dec 1971)
Guerra, S R A (8 Oct 1967)
Guess, M N (5 Mar 1966)
Guillermin, L F (30 Apr 1968) (30 Apr 1968)
Guillet, A R (18 May 1966)
Guise, A L (16 Nov 1969, 21 Dec 1969)
Gulbrandson, S B (3 Oct 1967)
Gunster, D J (6 Jun 1968)
Gushwa, P E (25 Jan 1969)
Gust, R E (27 Dec 1966)
Gustafson, G C (19 Nov 1967, 6 Jan 1968)
Guttersen, L (17 Dec 1967, 23 Feb 1968)
Guy, T W (22 Mar 1968)
Guzman, M A (6 May 1968)
Haas, L F (17 Jul 1972)
Habermacher, D I (1 Oct 1968)
Hackett, C K (25 Apr 1970)
Hackett, H B (24 Jul 1968)
Hackford, R H (22 May 1966)
Hackney, D (6 Feb 1967)
Haeffner, F A (20 Nov 1967)
Hagaman, H T (22 Jan 1968)
Hagan, J R (6 May 1969)
Hagerman, R W (6 Nov 1967)
Hagman, R H (17 May 1972)
Hahn, G P (6 Jul 1969)
Haifley, M F (28 Dec 1972)
Haight, L D (17 Apr 1965)
Hail, W W (2 Aug 1965)
Haines, C H (5 Jun 1967)
Halblower, H K (2 Jan 1966)
Hale, H L (23 Mar 1967)
Hall, C (23 Apr 1972)
Hall, D J (6 Feb 1967)
Hall, D L (6 Mar 1972)
Hall, E L (8 Oct 1969)
Hall, F (19 Jun 1970)
Hall, F M (12 Apr 1969)
Hall, G H (27 Feb 1966)
Hall, G R (27 Sep 1965)
Hall, H H (27 Jan 1973)
Hall, J S (29 Jul 1966)
Hall, J W (27 Oct 1972)
Hall, K N (10 Jan 1968)
Hall, T R (6 Jun 1967, 10 Jun 1967)
Hall, W (14 Mar 1966)
Hallenbeck, D M (8 Jul 1968)
Hallmark, K V (13 Sep 1966)
Halpin, R C (28 Mar 1972)
Halvorson, E J (24 Oct 1964)
Halyburton, P A (17 Oct 1965)
Haman, K W (23 Jul 1969)
Hamann, W C (6 Sep 1965)
Hambleton, I E (2 Apr 1972)
Hamby, C L (15 Jul 1966)
Hamilton, D A (4 Jul 1968)
Hamilton, E D (31 Jan 1966)
Hamilton, G B (16 Oct 1968)
Hamilton, G T (20 Oct 1965)
Hamilton, J S (19 Apr 1967)
Hamilton, M P (7 Apr 1970)
Hamilton, R C (22 Jul 1969)
Hamm, J E (14 Mar 1968)
Hampton, F J (6 Mar 1968)
Hamrick, K J (14 Aug 1969)
Hancock, S R (25 Apr 1970)
Hand, F E (1 Apr 1968)
Handly, E C (25 Jan 1966)
Haney, D J (3 Nov 1966)
Hanks, J D (7 Jun 1970)
Hanley, L J (4 Nov 1969)
Hanley, T H (1 Jan 1968)
Hanna, R K (13/14 Jul 1968)
Hanson, C W (10 Feb 1971)
Hanson, G O (13 Jun 1972)
Hanson, R T (3 Feb 1966)
Hanson, T P (4 Sep 1967)
Hanton, T J (27 Jun 1972)
Hapgood, J (20 May 1970)
Harbison, P W (12 May 1970)
Harden, K M (5 Jul 1972)
Hardie, C D (28 Jul 1967)
Harding, J C (9 Apr 1972, 2 May 1972)
Harding, W K (12 Jun 1967)
Hardman, W M (21 Aug 1967)
Hardy, A H (14 Mar 1972)
Hardy, J C (3 Apr 1968)
Hardy, J K (12 Oct 1967)
Hardy, P B (5 Jul 1968)
Hare, J J (29 Oct 1967)
Hargett, R M (23 Apr 1969, 10 Jul 1969)
Hargrave, R W (21 Sep 1969)
Hargrove, J A (27 Jan 1967)
Hargrove, W S (20 Nov 1972)
Harley, L D (18 May 1966)
Harlow, G D (6 Aug 1968)
Harnage, D N (17 Apr 1966)
Harrington, F H (28 Nov 1965)
Harris, Carlyle S (4 Apr 1965)
Harris, Cleveland S (29 Feb 1968)
Harris, J C (1 Feb 1971)
Harris, J H (29 Mar 1965)
Harris, J L (10 May 1972)
Harris, J R (20 Sep 1965)
Harris, L E (4/5 May 1968)
Harris, R B (12 Apr 1966)
Harris, R I (2 Feb 1966)
Harris, S W (22 Apr 1970)
Harris, W G (26 Sep 1964)
Harrison, J T (22 Nov 1969)
Harrison, R (5 Sep 1972)
Harrison, R H (18 Jun 1972)
Harrold, P K (5 Dec 1969)
Hart, J L (25 Feb 1967)
Hart, T L (10 Jan 1968)
Hart, T T (21/22 Dec 1972)
Hart, V P (25 Feb 1968)
Hartenhoff, D L (18 May 1969)
Hartman, E W (6 Sep 1968)
Hartman, R D (18 Jul 1967)
Hartness, G (26 Nov 1968)
Hartney, J C (5 Jan 1968)
Hartson, S G (11 Feb 1962)
Hartzheim, J F (27 Feb 1968)
Harvey, J R (28 Nov 1972)
Harwood, (13 Dec 1968)
Harworth, E E (31 May/1 Jun 1966)
Haselton, J H (11 May 1972)
Haskell, W A (9 Aug 1972)
Hassenger, A K (24 Dec 1965)
Hastings, C W (24 Dec 1965)
Hastings, R W (30 Nov 1965)
Hatch, C E (21 Apr 1970)
Hatch, F A (25 Jun 1968)
Hatcher, D B (30 May 1966)
Hatfield, S H (24 Jan 1973)
Hathaway, C E (7 Apr 1967)
Hathaway, J H V (11 Oct 1969)
Hatlestad, R L (12 Apr 1963)
Hatton, W N (5 Feb 1969)
Hauck, J C (15 Apr 1971)
Hauer, L J (18 Nov 1967)
Hauer, R D (5 Sep 1970)
Hauschildt, J C (5 Oct 1965)
Haviland, R E (30 Jan 1973)
Hawking, T H (16 Sep 1966)
Hawkins, B W (26 Jul 1969)
Hawkins, C J (17 Apr 1966)
Hawkins, E L (20 Sep 1965)
Hawkins, G L (15 Jan 1967)
Hawkins, J P (21 Mar 1965)
Hawkins, S H (18 Sep 1967)
Hawks, E T (19 Aug 1966)
Hawks, G W (1 Jun 1972)
Hawley, D R (17 Dec 1965)
Hawley, E A (17 Feb 1972)
Hawthorne, R W (11 Sep 1967)
Hay, C E (16 May 1967)
Hayden, G M (17 Feb 1968)
Hayden, N W (18 May 1969)
Hayes, H G (7 May 1968)
Hayes, J J (22 Oct 1968)
Hayes, P J (1 Dec 1969)
Hayes, R (6 Oct 1969)
Hays, J M (4 Jan 1967)
Heathcote, C S (3 Sep 1966)
Hedditch, (25 Feb 1971)
Heenan, M E (22 Feb 1969)
Heep, W A (24 Aug 1968)
Heeren, J D (11 Sep 1972)
Hegdahl, D B (24 Oct 1967, 28 Apr 1968)
Heggen, K R (20/21 Dec 1972)
Hegstrom, R A (17 Sep 1966)
Heilig, J (5 May 1966)
Heiliger, D L (15 May 1967)
Heiskell, L L (6 Feb 1967)
Heister, R E (2 Jun 1965)
Helber, L N (24 Jan 1966)
Held, J W (17 Apr 1968)
Helgeson, E E (6 Mar 1968)
Hellbach, H J (19 May 1967)
Heller, E E (25 Apr 1969)
Helmich, G R (12 Nov 1969)
Helwig, R D (11 Sep 1969)
Hemmel, C J (21 Oct 1967)
Hemvree, R E (31 Oct 1966)
Henderson, A H (17 Mar 1967)
Henderson, H K (2 Aug 1969)
Henderson, W J (3 Apr 1972)
Hendrick, A G (3 Aug 1969)
Hendricks, (30 Aug 1965)
Hendricks, E W (20 Oct 1968)
Hendrickson, A E (3 Aug 1967)
Hendrickson, M F (25 Jul 1968)
Henke, G (28 Feb 1968)
Henneman, D E (17 Sep 1972)
Hennigar, H J (31 Mar 1967)
Henninger, H W (13 Mar 1966)
Henriquez, J S (10 Aug 1966)
Henry, D A (19 Sep 1966)
Hensley, R L (22 Apr 1970)
Hensley, T T (17 Mar 1968)
Hepler, F M (12 May 1968)
Hepler, W H (15 Feb 1967)
Herber, J A (21 Mar 1968)
Hergert, T M (8 Mar 1964)
Herman, R F (23 May 1965)
Hernandez, D E (16 Dec 1967, 28 Apr 1968)
Hernandez, H R (15 Aug 1969)
Herndon, R L (9 Jun 1967)
Herndon, T H (15 Jul 1967)
Herrick, J W (27 Oct 1969)
Herrin, H H (1 Jan 1968)
Herring, T (2 May 1970)
Herrold, N R (31 May/1 Jun 1966)
Herron, K G (24 Mar 1969)
Hersey, C F (18 May 1969)
Hersman, W C (12 Oct 1966)
Hesford, P D (21 Mar 1968)
Hess, F W (29 Mar 1969)
Hess, G K (17 Jun 1966)
Hess, J C (24 Aug 1967)
Hess, R D (8 Jul 1968)
Hessom, R C (5 Mar 1966)
Hester, D V (6 Sep 1964)
Hester, L C (10 Mar 1967)
Hestle, R (6 Jul 1966)
Hetherington, C W (21 Mar 1967)
Hetrick, R H (24 Feb 1966)
Hezel, K D (17 Nov 1967)
Hibbs, H W (8 Sep 1968)
Hickerson, J M (22 Dec 1967)
Hickman, V J (14 Jan 1964)
Hicks, T D (15 Aug 1968)
Hickson, D L (29 Apr 1969)
Hiebert, E G (11 Feb 1965)
Hiebert, F C (25 Jul 1966)
Higdon, K H (20/21 Dec 1972)
Hilbrick, B W (9 Jun 1970)
Hildebrand, L L (18 Dec 1971)
Hill, A E (23 Nov 1966)
Hill, A S (28 Dec 1965)
Hill, B F (5 Jul 1968)
Hill, G C (30 Jun 1970)
Hill, H J (16 Dec 1967)
Hill, R A (23 Mar 1966)
Hill, R D (6 Dec 1963)
Hill, R J (2 Oct 1969)
Hill, R L (18 Oct 1966)
Hills, J R (14 Feb 1966)
Hilton, R L (14 Mar 1966)
Hincewicz, E J (13 Jan 1966)
Hinckley, R B (18 Jan 1968)
Hinson, R L (17 Dec 1965)
Hirsch, T M (26 Mar 1967)
Hise, J H (25 Mar 1967)
Hiteshew, J E (11 Mar 1967)
Hitt, G C (28 Jul 1970)
Hiu, H (9 Jul 1969)
Hivner, J O (5 Oct 1965)
Hoag, J D (19 Jun 1969)
Hobbs, F L (17 Nov 1967)
Hockridge, J A (16/17 Oct 1972)
Hodges, D L (7 Oct 1967)
Hodges, J A (9 May 1965)
Hodges, J W (30 Mar 1968)
Hodges, T L (3 Aug 1966)
Hodnett, S A (24 Jul 1972)
Hoenninger, J (31 Jan 1971)
Hoff, M G (7 Jan 1970)
Hoff, S D (29 Aug 1966)
Hoffman, D W (25 Feb 1967, 30 Dec 1971)
Hoffman, H P (3 Apr 1970)
Hoffman, I L (13 Jan 1966)
Hoffman, K J (25 Jul 1968)
Hoffman, L A (22 Jul 1968)
Hoffman, R E (22 Dec 1968)
Hoffson, A T (17 Aug 1968)
Hogan, J F (20 Jan 1967)
Hogeman, C G (26 Nov 1966)
Hoggatt, R (11 Nov 1967)
Holben, N E (4 Jul 1966)
Holdeman, R E (25 Nov 1967)
Holden, E L (9 Jun 1968)
Holland, L T (12 Jun 1965)
Hollenfeld, D C (24 Sep 1965)
Holler, J E (21 May 1967)
Holley, J C (8 Jun 1966)
Holley, T S (20 Jan 1968)
Hollingsworth, H T (16 Jan 1966)
Hollis, C R (16 Nov 1968)
Holman, A H (7 Nov 1964)
Holman, G A (14 Dec 1966)
Holmes, D H (15 Mar 1966)
Holmes, F L (30 Dec 1971)
Holmes, L E (22 May 1967)
Holmes, S H (29 Sep 1965)
Holmquist, J D (23 Apr 1970)
Holoviak, N J (22 Sep 1972)
Holt, M M (2 Mar 1966)
Holt, R A (19 Sep 1968)
Holton, R E (29 Jan 1969)
Holtzclaw, J W (19/20 Jun 1968)
Holzapple, H E (20 Oct 1965)
Hom, C D (17 Aug 1967)
Honeycutt, C J (10 Nov 1967)
Hood, D R (2 Oct 1965)
Hopper, E P (10 Jan 1968)
Hopper, J C (3 May 1972)
Hopper, R W (25 Mar 1968)
Hopps, G D (10 Feb 1966)
Horacek, L J (6 Aug 1965, 17 Apr 1966)
Horchar, A A (8 Apr 1970)
Horinek, R A (25 Oct 1967)
Hornaday, R J (26 Mar 1968)
Horne, S H (14 Jan 1968)
Horsky, R M (11 Dec 1965)
Hosea, W H (28/29 Mar 1967)
Hoskins, C L (16 Feb 1971)
Hoskins, D R (25/26 Apr 1972)
Hoskinson, R E (29 Jul 1966)
Hottenroth, J R (15 Oct 1967)
Hough, V G (17 Apr 1966)
Houghton, R W (10 Mar 1967)
Houlditch, J C (6 Sep 1969)
Houser, J G (2 May 1972)
Hovston, C M (25 Jun 1972)
Howard, E R (8 Jul 1968)
Howard, F D (2 May 1967)
Howard, J D (7 Oct 1967)
Howarth, A R (14 Dec 1966)
Howell, C A (6 Mar 1972)
Howell, M (6 Nov 1965)
Howie, L G (15 May 1970)
Hoyler, J G (11 Nov 1969)
Hrdlicka, D L (18 May 1965)
Huard, J L (12 Jul 1972)
Hubbard, E L (20 Jul 1966)
Hubbard, R G (21 May 1967)
Hubbard, W A (26 May 1973)
Hubbs, D R (17 Mar 1968)
Huberth, E J (13 May 1970)
Hubler, G L (23 Feb 1968)
Hubler, P E (15 Mar 1968)
Hudelson, J E (30 Jul 1972)
Hudgens, E M (21 Mar 1970)
Hudson, D B (24 Feb 1967)
Hudson, J L (9 Jan 1970)
Hudson, L P (19 Nov 1964)
Hudson, R M (26/27 Dec 1972)
Huey, F A (21 Apr 1966)
Huggins, B G (4 Jun 1970)
Huggins, N T (1 Nov 1965)
Hughes, B A (16 Mar 1970)
Hughes, J L (5 May 1967)
Hughes, K R (11 Aug 1967)
Hughey, K R (6 Jul 1967)
Huillier, J A L (25 Jul 1968)
Hull, G D (20 Jan 1967)
Hull, G E (15 Feb 1970)
Hull, J L (19 Feb 1971)
Hume, K E (29 Mar 1965)
Humphrey, G F (1 Feb 1966)
Humphrey, J R (26 Nov 1966)
Hunsaker, I F (1 May 1968)
Hunt, J D (13 Oct 1968)
Hunt, L A (18 Jun 1972)
Hunter, H P (19 Jul 1967)
Hunter, R G (25 May 1966)
Hunter, R P (10 Feb 1966)
Hunter, R W (15 Mar 1970)
Hurst, G B (21 Feb 1970)
Hurst, J C (13 Jul 1968)
Huskey, R L (5 Nov 1969)
Huss, R A (5/6 Feb 1968)
Hutto, J L (5 Mar 1966)
Hutton, J L (16 Oct 1965)
Huwe, J F (18 Apr 1973)
Hyatt, L G (13 Aug 1967)
Hyde, M L (8 Dec 1966)
Hyland, R J (13 Aug 1965)
Hymel, R (26/27 Dec 1972)
Hynds, W G (2 Aug 1967)
Ilg, R P (3 Jun 1965)
Iman, D (2 May 1972)
Imaye, S M (8 Jul 1972, 27 Dec 1972)
Ingalls, J M (1 May 1966)
Ingvalson, R D (28 May 1968)
Innes, R B (27 Dec 1967)
Irelan, D A (2 Aug 1969)
Ireland, R N (22 Apr 1970)
Irsch, W C (9 Jan 1968)
Irving, L K (20 Nov 1968)
Irwin, R H (17 Feb 1972)
Irwin, T (13 Jan 1965)
Isaacks, R (17 Sep 1968)
Isenhour, W J (7 Jul 1966)
Israel, J W (8 Mar 1969)
Ivan, A (10 Sep 1971)
Jackman, G R (2 May 1970)
Jacks, G G (19 Oct 1967)
Jackson, C (14 Mar 1966)
Jackson, C A (24 Jun 1972)
Jackson, C E (27 Jun 1965)
Jackson, G L (28 Nov 1972)
Jackson, J (29 Apr 1970)
Jackson, J M (12 May 1968)
Jackson, J T (23 Mar 1972)
Jackson, P V (24 Dec 1972)
Jackson, W B (18 Jul 1967)
Jaco, A N (6 Sep 1969)
Jacobs, E J (25 Aug 1967)
Jacobs, J C (7 Jun 1966)
Jacobs, M J (9 Apr 1972)
Jacobs, N A (8 Oct 1969)
Jacobsen, D L (7 Nov 1966)
Jaeger, J B (4 Jul 1968)
Jaeger, J P (6 Apr 1970)
Jajtner, R C (17/18 May 1966)
James, C N (18 May 1968)
James, G D (15 Jul 1968)
James, J D (20 Jan 1969)
James, N E (27 Jan 1970)
James, S L (18 Apr 1973)
Jankowski, W L (1 May 1972)
Janssen, W L (16 Jun 1967)
Jarvis, C H (12 Feb 1967)
Jarvis, J M (26 Jun 1967, 24 Jul 1967)
Jasperson, R H (12 Oct 1972)
Jayroe, J S (19 Jan 1967)
Jeffcoat, C H (27 Dec 1972)
Jefferson, J M (12 May 1967)
Jeffords, D B (24 Dec 1965)

Jeffrey, R D (20 Dec 1965)
Jeffs, C G (12 Mar 1971)
Jenkins, H T (13 Nov 1965)
Jenkins, J J (6 Sep 1969)
Jenkins, P L (30 Jun 1970)
Jenkinson, J J (10 Dec 1968)
Jennings, H R (10 Jul 1968)
Jennings, J W (13 Oct 1965)
Jenny, D W (5 Jul 1968)
Jensen, B A (26 Aug 1967)
Jensen, D B (18 Apr 1972)
Jensen, G W (15 May 1966)
Jensen, J R (18 Feb 1967)
Jensen, T K (1 Jul 1965)
Jerome, S M (17 Feb 1969)
Jessen, D R (15 Nov 1969)
Jeszeck, J C (27 Apr 1970)
Jett, W S (2 Sep 1966)
Jewell, E M (4 Sep 1965)
Jewell, R M (28 Dec 1965)
Johns, C L (22 Aug 1966)
Johns, P F (28 Jun 1968)
Johnson, A K (8 Jul 1967)
Johnson, A L (27/28 Dec 1972)
Johnson, Don (17 Jan 1969)
Johnson, Deverl (20/21 Dec 1972)
Johnson, D A (27 Oct 1966)
Johnson, E H (20/21 Dec 1972)
Johnson, E K (5 Jul 1972)
Johnson, E S (26 Jun 1964)
Johnson, F W (6 Aug 1965)
Johnson, G D (20 Dec 1965)
Johnson, H C (29 Mar 1968)
Johnson, H E (19 Apr 1967, 30 Apr 1967)
Johnson, H N (19 Jul 1967)
Johnson, J E (6 Feb 1963)
Johnson, K L (26 Apr 1968)
Johnson, K R (18 Dec 1971)
Johnson, L C (10 Oct 1969)
Johnson, L D (8 Jun 1972)
Johnson, R C (3 Aug 1966)
Johnson, R E (18/19 Dec 1972)
Johnson, S R (16 Apr 1966)
Johnson, T (17 Nov 1967)
Johnson, T E (3 Oct 1968)
Johnston, J W (21 Oct 1968)
Johnston, S B (4 Jan 1973)
Jones, B M (28 Nov 1972)
Jones, C R, USAF (21 Nov 1965)
Jones, C R, USN (4 Apr 1967)
Jones, E D (7 Apr 1968)
Jones, G E (7 Jul 1967)
Jones, J G (12 Nov 1966)
Jones, J L (6 Sep 1969)
Jones, J W (8 Oct 1968)
Jones, L A (10 Oct 1969)
Jones, L F (29 Nov 1967)
Jones, M N (29 Jun 1966)
Jones, M S (25 Jun 1968)
Jones, O C (16 Apr 1972)
Jones, O D (12 May 1968)
Jones, P T (20 Mar 1967)
Jones, R B (27 Oct 1972)
Jones, R C (18 Jan 1968)
Jones, R W (27 Jun 1971)
Jones, T P (5/6 Feb 1968)
Jones, W A (31 Aug 1968, 28 Sep 1972)
Jones, W E (5 Jan 1968)
Jordan, L M (12 Apr 1966)
Jordan, S B (14 Jan 1966)
Jourdenais, G H (1 Apr 1967)
Joyner, D A (26/27 Dec 1972)
Joyner, J P (14 Dec 1965)
Jozefowski, T J (26 Jun 1972)
Julian, H L (18 Apr 1967)
Justice, W A (3 Jul 1970)
Justice, W P (28 Mar 1969)
Kahl, J C (27 Feb 1966)
Kahler, H (14 Jun 1969)
Kain, J E (18 Jun 1972)
Kaiser, H W (13 Sep 1966)
Kamenicky, G W (30 Sep 1971)
Kan, R S (19 Dec 1965)
Kanaar, L K (9 Nov 1965)
Kanach, J (3 Jun 1965)
Kane, J (17 May 1970)
Kane, R R (11 Sep 1967)
Kangas, W A (16 Sep 1972)
Kannel, D (16 Apr 1967)
Karas, W J (14 Jun 1969)
Kardell, D A (9 May 1965)

Karger, B E (14 May 1968)
Kari, P A (20 Jun 1965)
Karins, J J (11 Mar 1967)
Karp, R E (28 Feb 1970)
Karr, C L (4 Nov 1969)
Karst, C F (16 Nov 1968)
Kasch, F M (2 Jul 1967)
Kasler, J H (29 Jun 1966,
    8 Aug 1966, 2 Apr 1967)
Kaster, L L (5/6 Aug 1964)
Katterhenry, T F (20 Dec 1965)
Kauttu, P A (31 Aug 1968)
Kawamura, R K (14/15 Feb 1968)
Kearby, J A (23 Jun 1969)
Kearns, J T, USAF (3 Jun 1967)
Kearns, J T, USN (14 Sep 1965)
Keeler, H B (29 Jan 1969)
Keenan, T P (3 Mar 1966)
Keeter, C D (9 Jun 1965)
Keglovits, E J (30 Mar 1967)
Keirn, R P (24 Jul 1965)
Keith, R M (7 Jun 1966)
Kelch, M J (10 Aug 1965)
Kellems, R G (21 Sep 1966)
Keller, G H (18 Apr 1967)
Keller, G R (27 May 1970)
Keller, J E (21 Apr 1966)
Keller, W R (1 Mar 1969)
Kelley, D R (8/9 Jan 1967)
Kelley, J L (16 Jan 1968)
Kelley, V K (4 Sep 1967)
Kellum, D A (5 May 1970)
Kelly, M (21 Nov 1965)
Kelly, P J (15 Jun 1966)
Kemmerer, D R (6 Aug 1967)
Kennedy, J W (16 Aug 1971)
Kennedy, L (5 Oct 1966, 20 Oct 1966)
Kennedy, R E (15 Jul 1969)
Kenny, D G (31 Aug 1968)
Kent, N (4/5 May 1968)
Kent, R D (24 Dec 1968)
Kernan, J E (7 May 1972)
Kerr, E O (12 Jun 1966)
Kerr, J C G (21 Aug 1967)
Kerr, M S (16 Jan 1967)
Kerr, R A (30/31 Jan 1968)
Kerr, R G (14 Nov 1966)
Kertesz, G J (5 Mar 1969)
Kesler, H (20 Oct 1970)
Ketchie, S D (9 Apr 1972)
Ketchum, J (7 Jul 1967)
Ketterer, J A (20 Jan 1968)
Key, W D (17 Nov 1967)
Key, W N (21 May 1972)
Kibbey, R A (6 Feb 1967)
Kidd, G R (25 Apr 1969)
Kiefel, E P (10 Feb 1966)
Kiefer, H E (20 Jan 1971)
Kieffer, W L (11 Feb 1970)
Kientzler, P A (27 Jan 1973)
Kieswetter, G M (25 Jul 1966)
Kilcullen, T M (25 Aug 1967)
Kilgus, D W (4 Apr 1965, 20/21 Nov 1970)
Killebrew, F E (29 Dec 1972)
Killen, C W (11 Nov 1969)
Killian, J E (30 May 1968)
Killian, M J (30 Sep 1965)
Kilpatrick, L R (17 Jun 1972)
Kimball, F T (20 Nov 1968)
Kimmel, E W (22 Oct 1968)
Kimminau, P F (12 Feb 1968)
Kincaid, T F (26 May 1972)
Kindel, J C (14 Dec 1965)
King, C D (24 Dec 1968)
King, D L (13 May 1966)
King, H G (10 Mar 1966)
King, R R (3 Oct 1967)
King, W J (16 Dec 1971)
Kinkade, W L (31 Aug 1968)
Kinser, G A (13 May 1967)
Kippenham, C N (26 Aug 1967)
Kirby, B A (20/21 Dec 1972)
Kirby, E F (18 Sep 1965)
Kirby, J (7 Nov 1965)
Kirk, T H (28 Oct 1967)
Kirk, W L (25 Jan 1969)
Kirkpatrick, E E (6 Jun 1968)
Kirkpatrick, J H (12 Jul 1967)
Kissam, E K (11 Feb 1962)
Kittinger, J W (11 May 1972)
Klein, D D (21 Sep 1968)

Klein, R L (4 Apr 1970)
Klemm, D M (11 Jun 1967)
Klenda, D A (17 Sep 1965)
Klenert, W B (22 Oct 1966)
Klinck, H H (19 Nov 1967)
Kline, R E (27 Oct 1966, 2 Nov 1966)
Klingner, M L (6 Apr 1970)
Klinke, D H (18 Jun 1972)
Klomann, T J (20/21 Dec 1972)
Kluck, (2 Nov 1965)
Klug, P F (11 Mar 1970)
Klugg, J R (14 Nov 1970)
Klumpp, W F (31 Jan 1966)
Klusmann, C F (6 Jun 1964)
Klute, K E (14 Mar 1966)
Knabb, K K (21 Oct 1968)
Knaggs, J C (29 Oct 1964)
Knapic, B R (11 Oct 1969)
Knapp, F W (2 Nov 1967)
Knapp, H L (24 Apr 1967)
Knebel, T E (22 May 1968)
Knee, F (19 Mar 1972)
Knickerbocker, S (8 Apr 1966)
Knight, L C (8 Apr 1970)
Knight, L D (7 Oct 1966)
Knight, P G (31 Oct 1966)
Knight, R A (19 May 1967)
Knight, R H (8 Oct 1969)
Knoch, H J (28 Nov 1965, 16 Sep 1966)
Knochel, C A (22 Sep 1966)
Knott, D L (26 Dec 1969)
Knowles, B (16 May 1965)
Knowles, C M (27 Apr 1970)
Knudsen, H E (14 Sep 1966)
Knutson, R A (17 Oct 1965)
Koebberling, J B (9 Dec 1968)
Koenig, E L (14 Dec 1966)
Kohler, T (12 Aug 1972)
Kohlrusch, W F (1 Apr 1966)
Kohn, R A (21 Nov 1972)
Kollman, G E (12 Mar 1968)
Kollmorgen, L S (23 Jan 1968)
Kolstad, T C (22 Oct 1966)
Kommendant, A (8 Aug 1966)
Kondracki, J G (5 Apr 1968)
Konow, M J (4 Jun 1972)
Koonce, T T (25 Dec 1967)
Koons, D F (26 Dec 1971)
Koontz, N R (17 Aug 1968)
Kopfman, T F (15 Jun 1966)
Kopp, R A (12 Sep 1967)
Kosko, W B (5 Jun 1965, 27 Jul 1965)
Kosky, W H (26 Dec 1969)
Koss, F M (6 Jul 1972)
Koster, C R (5 Apr 1969)
Kott, S J (30 Oct 1967)
Kough, C J (4 Jun 1967)
Kovaleski, V T (14 Jan 1973)
Kowalczyk, E S (14 Aug 1966)
Kramer, G D (19 Jan 1967)
Kramer, J D (25 May 1966)
Kramer, W A (7 May 1968)
Kravitz, J S (17 Feb 1968)
Krawczyk, E C (4/5 May 1968)
Krebs, M A (7 Nov 1967)
Krech, M T (1 Apr 1966)
Kroboth, A J (7 Jul 1972)
Kroboth, S N (21/22 Dec 1972)
Krogman, A R (17 Jan 1967)
Krommenhoek, J M (25 Oct 1967)
Krouse, J C (2 Oct 1967)
Krueger, D W (26 Mar 1971)
Krueger, S P (15 Mar 1967)
Krukowski, E S (24 Oct 1964)
Krupa, R D (29 Aug 1969)
Krusi, P H (3 Nov 1967)
Kryszak, T E (3 Jun 1966)
Krzynowek, P S (6 Dec 1967)
Kubley, R R (31 Jan 1967)
Kuhl, R W (20 Jul 1967)
Kuhlman, R J (17 Jan 1969)
Kuhlmann, C F (22 Sep 1968)
Kuiper, R L (24 Dec 1965)
Kula, J D (29 Jul 1972)
Kulacz, D E (1 Apr 1968)
Kulick, T P (2 May 1967)
Kulland, B K (2 Apr 1972)
Kulzer, P G (5 May 1972)
Kunz, L G (7 Jun 1972)
Kuster, R L (30 Jun 1967)
Kwortnik, J C (1 Aug 1966)

La Haye, J D (8 May 1965)
LaBeau, M H (26/27 Dec 1972)
Lacasse, J W (2 Oct 1966)
Ladewig, M E (24 Aug 1968)
Lafever, W D (27 Jan 1968)
Lagerwall, H R (21/22 Dec 1972)
LaGrand, W J (5 Sep 1965)
Lagrange, L (2 Jul 1968)
Laib, R J (18 Jun 1972)
Laing, J H (24 Apr 1967, 21 May 1967)
Lamar, J L (6 May 1966)
Lambert, R E (7 May 1965)
Lambertson, W R (16 Sep 1968)
Lambrides, P D (17 Mar 1968)
Lambton, B R (13 Jun 1966)
Lamers, R O (2 Aug 1972)
Lamp, A W (12 Apr 1969)
Land, C D (9 Mar 1967)
Landringham, R G (29 Jun 1965)
Landry, P J (5 Nov 1970)
Lane, C (23 Aug 1967)
Lane, M C (3 Dec 1966)
Lane, M S (4 Jan 1969)
Lane, R J (6 Sep 1965)
Laney, R H (11 Jul 1966)
Lang, A E (28 Jan 1969)
Lang, B G (28 Apr 1971)
Lang, J F (28 Apr 1968)
Lang, P M (9 Aug 1969)
Langhorne, L G (3 Feb 1971)
Langston, (8 Feb 1970)
Lankford, B E (25 Dec 1967)
Lankford, C B (24 Oct 1963)
Lanning, M (17 Sep 1966)
Lannom, R C (1 Mar 1968)
Lapham, R G (8 Feb 1968)
Lapierre, E A (12 Jun 1967)
Lappin, R P (17 Jul 1968)
Larson, E (7 Aug 1966)
Larson, G A (5 May 1967)
Larson, R D (2 Feb 1962)
Larue, E U (21 Nov 1968)
Lashlee, G K (22 Dec 1967)
Lasiter, C W (4 Feb 1968)
Laskowski, M J (2 Aug 1968)
Lassen, C E (19/20 Jun 1968)
Lasseter, L T (11 Sep 1972, 23 Dec 1972)
Latella, G F (6 Oct 1972)
Latendresse, T B (27 May 1972)
Latham, J D (5 Oct 1972)
Latham, W (23 Nov 1972)
Latimer, R E (2 Dec 1968)
Lattin, G R (16 Nov 1969)
Lavender, R E (19 Sep 1969)
Lavoo, J R (19 Sep 1968)
Lawrence, B E (5 Jul 1968)
Lawrence, D A (8 May 1968)
Lawrence, D L (1 Apr 1968)
Lawrence, W P (28 Jun 1967)
Laws, R L (3 Apr 1966)
Lawson, C G (25 Jul 1968)
Lawson, J D (1 Sep 1970)
Lawson, W E (10 May 1970)
Lay, B (28 Dec 1970)
Layton, R D (4 Apr 1969)
Le Tourneau, J D (11 Feb 1962)
Leach, G P (27 Jul 1969)
Leach, R D (6 Oct 1966)
Leach, T (13 Nov 1969)
Leaphart, J L (10 Apr 1970)
Lebert, R M (14 Jan 1968)
LeBlanc, L E (21/22 Dec 1972)
Leblanc, R D (15 Jan 1970)
Lede, R L (4/5 May 1968)
Lee, C R (9 Jul 1967)
Lee, G H N (27 May 1970)
Lee, J R (24 Aug 1968)
Lee, L M (27 Dec 1967)
Lee, P B (28 Jul 1970)
Lee, R G (14/15 Feb 1968)
Leeser, L C (28 Jan 1970)
Leet, D L (12 Apr 1972)
Leetun, D D (17 Sep 1968)
Lefever, D P (5 Nov 1969)
Leftwich, R F (9 Mar 1967)
Lehecka, J A (10 Jan 1970)
Lehnhoff, E W (18 Nov 1967)
Lehrke, S L (18 Jan 1973)
Lemmond, W V (19 Sep 1969)
Lemoine, L J (29 Nov 1967)
Lemon, J C (24 Apr 1971)

Lengyel, L R (9 Aug 1967)
Lennon, F J (10 Jul 1966)
Lenski, A (30 Apr 1967, 8 May 1967)
Lentz, G A (22 Sep 1972)
Leonard, E W (18 Mar 1968, 31 May 1968)
Leonard, J B (8 Feb 1970)
Leonard, L E (23 Mar 1967)
Leonor, L C (10 Oct 1972)
Lerner, I S (20/21 Dec 1972)
Lerseth, R G (6 Sep 1972)
Lesesne, H D (11 Jul 1972)
Lesh, V E (20 Nov 1972)
Lesieur, J C (3 Aug 1966)
Lester, D W (31 Jul 1966)
Lester, R B (19 Aug 1972)
Lester, R R (4 Nov 1967)
Letter, T L (26 Oct 1969)
Leuffen, K W (23 May 1966)
Levin, H N (21 Jul 1969)
Levis, C A (2 Apr 1972)
Levy, N S (13 Aug 1966)
Lewis, C C (28 Apr 1966)
Lewis, C E (16 Jan 1968)
Lewis, C P (17 May 1972)
Lewis, E G (24 Oct 1967)
Lewis, F D (27/28 Dec 1972)
Lewis, J K (14 Feb 1968)
Lewis, J W (7 Apr 1965)
Lewis, K H (5 Oct 1972)
Lewis, L G (27 Feb 1971)
Lewis, M R (20 Jul 1966)
Lewis, R E (27 Dec 1969)
Lewnes, C L (19 Jun 1967)
Libey, G S (1 Nov 1968)
Lielmanis, A K (24 Nov 1963)
Light, C B (8 Jun 1968)
Ligon, V P (19 Nov 1967)
Liles, R L (21/22 Dec 1972)
Lillund, W A (4 Oct 1967)
Lilly, W R (6 Nov 1965)
Lindahl, J C (6 Jan 1973)
Lindberg, D C (30 Mar 1967, 21 May 1967)
Lindgren, G (13 Nov 1969)
Lindland, D F (6 Sep 1972)
Lindsey, A M (28 Oct 1965)
Lindsey, M N (29 Jun 1965)
Lindstrom, K D (21 May 1967)
Lineberger, H B (28 Jan 1971)
Lineberry, R B (27 Sep 1972)
Lint, D M (22 Apr 1970)
Liscum, R E (28 Dec 1969)
Litvin, F D (8 Oct 1966)
Livingston, D W (27 Jan 1970)
Livingstone, R A (2 Oct 1969)
Lloyd, J R (6 Aug 1972, 28 Nov 1972)
Loar, K E (17 Jun 1970)
Locher, R C (10 May 1972)
Lockard, N R (2 Oct 1966)
Locker, J D (9 Jun 1968)
Lockhart, G B (20/21 Dec 1972)
Lockhart, H J (2 Mar 1965)
Lodge, R C (10 May 1972)
Loeschner, T R (24 Apr 1965)
Loftus, R T (24 May 1968)
Loftus, W E (23 Jan 1968)
Logan, D K (5 Jul 1972)
Logan, J D (2 Dec 1965)
Logan, R C (29 Mar 1966)
Logeman, J D (30 Jul 1972)
Loheed, H B (1 Feb 1966)
Loken, R F (2 Nov 1966)
Lollar, J L (20/21 Dec 1972)
Lomax, A L (3 Feb 1968)
Long, C E (20 Dec 1969)
Long, G W (12 May 1968)
Long, J H S (18 Oct 1966)
Long, M H (2 Mar 1972)
Long, R L (22 Dec 1967)
Long, S G (28 Feb 1969)
Long, W L (8 Mar 1969)
Lono, L A (29 Sep 1969)
Looper, M (28 Feb 1968)
Lorenzo, D W (9 Jan 1968)
Lortscher, D J (28 Apr 1968)
Lotsberg, W P (10 Nov 1972)
Lott, D J (11 Mar 1968)
Louis, W K (19 Dec 1970)
Lovelace, C K (19 Jul 1965)
Low, J F (16 Dec 1967)
Lowe, G (21 Jan 1967)
Lowry, C T (20/21 Nov 1970)

Lowry, T G (18 Jun 1965)
Loyd, O H (6 Apr 1970)
Lubbers, T L (27 Apr 1970)
Luck, G E (10 Mar 1970)
Lucki, A E (23 Apr 1970)
Ludden, C H (9 Sep 1965)
Lukasik, B F (19 Feb 1964)
Lukenbach, M D (22 Dec 1965)
Luker, R B (1 Feb 1966)
Lum, D A (20 Dec 1966)
Luna, C P (10 Mar 1969)
Luna, D A (1 Feb 1969)
Luna, J D (10 Mar 1967)
Lund, E P (30 Oct 1967)
Lund, R J (6 Sep 1968)
Lundell, A J (22 Jun 1967)
Lundy, A L (24 Dec 1970)
Lundy, M E (10 May 1969)
Lunnie, L (6 Sep 1966)
Lunsford, H L (24 Jul 1967)
Lunsford, P R (25 Apr 1969)
Lurie, A P (13 Jun 1966)
Luster, D A (26 Sep 1968)
Lustfield, S L (5 Oct 1968)
Lute, J R (6 Jan 1966)
Lutz, R E (9 Feb 1972)
Lutz, W E (2 Jun 1965)
Lynch, W A (26 Nov 1966)
Lynn, D W (7 Jun 1964, 27 May 1965)
Lynn, H M (5 Feb 1969)
Lynn, R R (20/21 Dec 1972)
Lyon, D L (22 Mar 1968)
Lytle, R W (1 Nov 1969)
Maahs, M G (21 Jan 1969)
MacCann, H E (28 Mar 1968)
Maccio, D J (27 Jul 1969)
MacDonald, G D (21/22 Dec 1972)
Macdougall, T R (30 May 1967)
MacEwen, T C (24 Feb 1965)
MacGeary, F E (19 Oct 1967)
Machowski, J A (24 May 1966)
Macko, C (22 Feb 1969)
MacLaughlin, D C (2 Jan 1966)
Macnab, J V (8 Oct 1967)
Madden, J (9 Sep 1972)
Madden, R (20/21 Dec 1972)
Maddox, N G (20 May 1967)
Maddox, V (18 May 1969)
Madison, T M (19 Apr 1967)
Madison, W L (15 May 1966)
Madsen, M E (18 Jan 1967)
Magee, F H (25 Jun 1966)
Magee, R W (23 Mar 1961)
Magnusson, J A (4 Apr 1965)
Magsig, C W (9 Aug 1969)
Mahaffey, L C (18 Nov 1965)
Mahan, D F (20 Apr 1970)
Mahone, W B (4 Sep 1967)
Mahrt, M H (10 May 1966)
Mahy, H E (13 Apr 1967)
Maier, N (16 Nov 1972)
Mailhes, L S (10 Aug 1965)
Major, S R (21 Sep 1968)
Majors, W T (11 Feb 1965)
Makowski, L F (6 Oct 1966)
Malagarie, F M (16 Jan 1966)
Mallon, R J (28 Jan 1970)
Maloy, R W (15 Oct 1967)
Mamiya, J M (29 Jul 1966)
Mancini, R M (11 Jan 1968)
Mangels, J C (3 Dec 1969)
Manlove, D (12 Aug 1969)
Mann, R L (22 Oct 1965)
Manners, R W (26 Aug 1968)
Manning, P A (13 Aug 1965)
Mansell, M E (28 Apr 1969)
Mansfield, R H (1 May 1966)
Manske, C J (24 May 1969)
Mape, J C (13 Apr 1966)
Marano, F A (1 May 1972)
Marchbank, L O (16 Mar 1970)
Marenka, S (19 Nov 1967)
Margle, T J (14/15 Feb 1968)
Marik, C W (25 Jun 1966)
Marit, D F (8 Sep 1964)
Markle, J D (10 May 1972, 20 May 1972)
Marks, G M (8 May 1970)
Marks, S R (11 Mar 1968)
Marlowe, G W (23 Sep 1965)
Marquandt, A A (30 Mar 1968)
Marr, H (6 Oct 1966)
Marsh, J A (25 Apr 1969)
Marshall, J A (18 Jun 1965)
Marshall, L J (26/27 Dec 1972)
Marshall, M A (3 Jul 1972)
Marshall, M D (2 Jun 1966)
Marshall, R C (5 Sep 1965)
Martin, A C (8 Mar 1969)
Martin, A G (19 Jul 1969)
Martin, B A (2 Jul 1967)
Martin, D (20 Sep 1965)
Martin, D E (4 Apr 1967)
Martin, D K (18 Apr 1973)
Martin, E H (9 Jul 1967)
Martin, G F (2 Dec 1965)
Martin, H C (16 Mar 1970)
Martin, J B (6 Oct 1970)
Martin, J E (17 Feb 1968)
Martin, J M (20 Nov 1967)
Martin, L E (15 Jul 1968)
Martin, L N (6 Jan 1967)
Martin, M D (6 Mar 1969)
Martin, P R (24 Dec 1969)
Martin, R D (3 Jun 1966)
Martin, S A (27 Dec 1967)
Martin, W R (18 Nov 1964)
Martinez, G (10 May 1970)
Martini, M R (20/21 Dec 1972)
Marvel, J W (24 Feb 1968)
Marvin, R C (14 Feb 1967)
Mascari, P L (2 May 1969)
Masin, M H (12 Aug 1972)
Mason, A F (2 Oct 1968)
Mason, L (14 Dec 1965)
Mason, W H (22 May 1968)
Massari, R D (12 Jun 1970)
Massey, F L (28 Apr 1969)
Massucci, M J (1 Oct 1965)
Masters, J M (16 Mar 1970)
Masterson, F J (10 Jul 1972)
Masterson, M J (13 Oct 1968)
Mastin, R L (16 Jan 1967)
Mateja, A P (16 Apr 1972)
Matejov, J A (4/5 Feb 1973)
Matheny, D P (5 Oct 1967)
Mather, A E (4 Jun 1970)
Mathews, C W 17 Dec 1965)
Mathews, P T (10 Aug 1972)
Mathison, B J (1 Apr 1968)
Matsui, M K (29 Jul 1972)
Matteis, R (27 Mar 1968)
Mattern, C E (12 Apr 1969)
Matteson, G (23 Mar 1961)
Matthes, P R (24 Nov 1969)
Matthews, J R (6 Apr 1970)
Mattis, W C (11 Mar 1965)
Mattox, D E (10 Aug 1970)
Mattox, J T (17 May 1968)
Matula, V G (20 Jul 1965)
Matzko, D H (12 May 1969)
Mauterer, O (15 Feb 1966)
Maxson, E R (14 Dec 1966)
Maxwell, J W (7 Feb 1969)
Maxwell, S C (12 Sep 1968)
May, W H (23 Sep 1964)
Mayall, W T (21/22 Dec 1972)
Mayer, I (2 Oct 1970)
Mayer, R L (17 Oct 1965)
Mayercik, R M (23/24 Nov 1967)
Mayfield, M G (26 Jul 1966)
Mayhew, W J (17 Aug 1968)
Mayo, J R (4 Sep 1967)
Mays, R C (28 Feb 1967)
McAdams, J M (30 Jul 1972)
McAteer, T J (10 Nov 1966)
McBride, A C (1 Sep 1969)
McBride, E P (22 Oct 1966)
McCain, J S (26 Oct 1967)
McCall, C P (17 Jun 1966)
McCall, J K (12 May 1968)
McCallum, P V (5 Mar 1966)
McCann, E D (17 Sep 1966)
McCann, R I (9 Dec 1968)
McCarthy, J F (13 Feb 1972)
McCarthy, M (11 Jul 1966)
McCarty, J L (24 Jun 1972)
McCarty, T H (23 Jul 1969)
McCaw, R H (14 Apr 1966)
McClean, J H (16 Aug 1963)
McCleary, G C (5 Nov 1965)
McClellan, P T (14 Nov 1965)
McClelland, W J (24 Jul 1965)
McClelland, W L (11 Jul 1966)
McClendon, W R (7 Jun 1968)
McClennan, D K (28 Dec 1969)
McCluskey, J L (21 Feb 1967)
McConnell, R P (16 Jun 1973)
McCormick, C O (6 Oct 1972)
McCormick, J V (1 Dec 1965)
McCormick, M T (9 Jan 1973)
McCormick, T R (10 May 1969)
McCormick, W C (25 Apr 1969)
McCoy, F E (30 Jul 1972)
McCoy, M O (15 Dec 1970)
McCracken, D J (20 Mar 1966)
McCrary, J (28/29 Dec 1967)
McCready, R L (15 Apr 1968)
McCubbon, G D (18/19 May 1968)
McCuistion, M K (8 May 1967)
McCurdy, J A (15 Apr 1966)
McDaniel, E B (19 May 1967)
McDaniel, J L (26 Apr 1968)
McDaniel, M L (4/5 Oct 1967)
McDaniel, N A (20 Jul 1966)
McDonald, B W (23 Jun 1969)
McDonald, E R (31 May/1 Jun 1966)
McDonald, J W (3 May 1972)
McDonald, K C (31 Dec 1964)
McDonald, W (17 Nov 1967)
McDonough, J R (20 Jun 1966)
McDow, R H (27 Jun 1972)
McElhanon, M O (16 Aug 1968)
McElroy, J L (12 May 1968)
McElvain, J R (18/19 Dec 1972)
McEwen, J A (22 Oct 1965)
McFall, A D (14 Jul 1967)
McGarvey, J M (17 Apr 1967)
McGerty, M J (30 Aug 1970)
McGhee, B W (5/6 Feb 1968)
McGlohn, R H (21 Aug 1967)
McGouldrick, F J (13 Dec 1968)
McGovern, M D (11 Feb 1971)
McGrane, D P (18 Jul 1967)
McGrath, C D (27 Jun 1972)
McGrath, D A (10 Sep 1968)
McGrath, J M (30 Jun 1967)
McGrath, W D (17 Nov 1967)
McGuigan, W M (22/23 May 1968)
McHale, J B (26 Oct 1965)
McHugo, D L (25 Mar 1968)
McIlrath, J M (21 Aug 1967)
McIntyre, S W (10 Dec 1971)
McIver, A (3 May 1972)
McKamey, J B (2 Jun 1965)
McKay, H E (5/6 Feb 1968)
McKee, R G (6 Sep 1968)
McKendrick, G R (25 Jul 1968)
McKenna, F J (25 Jun 1968)
McKenney, K D (15 May 1966)
McKeown, R E (25 Aug 1972)
McKinley, G W (31 Mar 1965)
McKinney, C (14 Apr 1972)
McKinney, E P (23 Mar 1968)
McKinney, G H (16 Feb 1972)
McKinney, N B (2 Sep 1963)
McKinstry, J J (26 Apr 1968)
McKnight, G G (6 Nov 1965)
McKnight, G P (11 Dec 1965)
McLamb, H L (18 Jun 1970)
McLaughlin, A V (20/21 Dec 1972)
McLaughlin, O B (7 Jul 1967)
McLaughlin, T (25 Feb 1971)
McLean, R W (23 Oct 1967)
McLeish, C E (21 Aug 1970)
McLellan, S M (1 Apr 1968)
McMahan, R C (14 Feb 1968)
McMahon, J P (2 Apr 1969)
McMahon, J S (12 Aug 1971)
McManus, K J (14 Jun 1967)
McMican, M D (2 Jun 1965)
McMurray, F C (12 Sep 1972)
McNally, E F (16 May 1970)
McNeil, C H (9 Apr 1965)
McNeill, C L (5 Feb 1969)
McNish, T M (4 Sep 1966)
McNulty, M K (31 Jul 1965)
McPhail, W T (22 May 1968)
McPherson, E A (18 Mar 1966)
McPherson, F L (28 Jan 1966)
McPherson, T L (24 Aug 1968, 16 Sep 1968)
McPhillips, H A (14 May 1972)
McRae, D E (2 Dec 1966)
McSwain, G P (28 Jul 1966)
McTernan, M (3/4 Jan 1973)
McWhorter, H S (29 Aug 1965)
Meacham, R W (22 May 1970)
Meade, J A (17 Dec 1965)
Meadows, E T (13 Oct 1966)
Meadows, H J (23 Aug 1966, 5 Dec 1967)
Meadows, R (2 Oct 1968)
Means, W H (20 Jul 1966)
Mearns, A S (11 Nov 1966)
Mechenbier, E J (14 Jun 1967)
Mecleary, R B (26 May 1967)
Meder, P O (21/22 Dec 1972)
Medina, R (8/9 Jan 1967)
Meehan, J F (14 Feb 1969)
Meek, E C (10 Sep 1963)
Meek, J L (9 Mar 1966)
Meeks, R E (7 Aug 1967)
Meglio, R F (5/6 Feb 1968)
Mehl, J P (30 May 1967)
Mehr, L (2 Jul 1967)
Meiggs, W B (1 Aug 1963)
Meiners, P A (2 Mar 1966)
Mekkers, W L (23 Apr 1967)
Melecosky, T (3 Oct 1967)
Mellor, F M (13 Aug 1965)
Mellor, G L (26 Apr 1971)
Melnick, S B (17 Aug 1970)
Melton, L L (30 Mar 1970)
Melton, T M (4/5 Feb 1973)
Menges, G B (2 Jan 1967)
Mercer, J E (18 Jun 1972)
Mercer, P H (14 Jan 1968)
Merchant, P G (9 Nov 1965)
Meroney, V K (1 Mar 1969)
Merrick, J E (20 Oct 1966)
Merrick, J L (3 Oct 1968)
Merrihew, G F (11 Feb 1962)
Merrill, J L (18 Jan 1970)
Merrit, R J (16 Sep 1965)
Merry, D L (4/5 May 1968)
Messing, M (25 Apr 1969)
Metcalfe, M (16 Aug 1968)
Metz, J H (15 Apr 1968)
Metzger, W J (19 May 1967)
Metzler, C D (21 Jun 1971)
Meyer, A B (26 Apr 1967)
Meyer, G J (18 Dec 1968)
Meyer, W K (19 Feb 1970)
Meyer, W M (26 Apr 1967)
Meyers, R A (8 Feb 1969)
Meyers, R B (6 Jan 1969)
Mickelsen, W E (10 Aug 1969)
Middlebrooks, R N (13 Jan 1966)
Midnight, F B (22 Aug 1967)
Miecznikowski, R S (9 Apr 1969)
Milbrath, R K (5 Nov 1970)
Miles, T (19 Jul 1969)
Milikin, R M (19 Aug 1966)
Milius, P L (27 Feb 1968)
Miller, (5 Oct 1968)
Miller, A D (20 Mar 1969)
Miller, C P (5 Jan 1971)
Miller, Carl D (4 Sep 1967)
Miller, Charles D (18 Nov 1968)
Miller, Curtis D (28 Mar 1972)
Miller, D M (2 Oct 1967)
Miller, E F (22 May 1968)
Miller, E W (13 Oct 1967)
Miller, H (21 Apr 1971)
Miller, H E (13 Apr 1967)
Miller, H W (27 Dec 1967)
Miller, J R (11 Jun 1967)
Miller, L S (23 May 1966)
Miller, M A (28 Mar 1969)
Miller, R C (27 Jun 1972)
Miller, R J (2 Dec 1965)
Miller, R L (7 Mar 1967)
Miller, W N (12 Nov 1965)
Millhollon, J B (23 Apr 1967
Milligan, J E (20 May 1967)
Milliman, D W (10 Nov 1966)
Mills, J B (20 Sep 1966)
Mills, J D (29 Jan 1968)
Mills, W W (11 Jul 1970)
Mims, G I (20 Dec 1965)
Minahan, DJ (22 Jan 1969)
Minnich, R W (4 Jan 1968)
Minnick, A L (1 Sep 1966)
Minor, J M (17 Mar 1972)
Minton, B L (4 Jul 1966)
Minutoli, J R (6 Apr 1967)
Mirrer, R H (17 Jan 1971)
Miskowski, E A (27 Jul 1969)
Mitchell, Albert C (25 Apr 1968)
Mitchell, Andrew C (8 Apr 1963)
Mitchell, C B (14 Jan 1964)
Mitchell, G (19 Jun 1970)
Mitchell, G L (6 Mar 1968)
Mitchell, J R (27 Jul 1966)
Mitchell, L N (10 Jan 1968)
Mitchell, T B (22 May 1968)
Mitchell, W (20 Dec 1965)
Mitchell, W A (12 Sep 1965)
Mitzel, L L (8/9 Jan 1967)
Miyazaki, R K (31 Jan 1967)
Mize, J (27/28 Dec 1972)
Mobley, B M (21 Jul 1968)
Mobley, J S (24 Jun 1968)
Mock, R K (20 Jan 1972)
Modica, J (1 Jul 1968)
Moe, H J (26 Sep 1967)
Moe, T N (16 Jan 1968)
Moffett, P F (24 Jul 1965)
Moffitt, R E (5 May 1970)
Mohrpardt, R A (19 Apr 1966)
Molinare, A R (27 Apr 1972)
Mollicone, D A (20 Dec 1963)
Monette, N E (10 Mar 1969)
Mongilardi, P (29 Mar 1965, 25 Jun 1965)
Monlux, H D (11 Nov 1966)
Monroe, V D (18 May 1968)
Monsees, J H (8 Nov 1967, 1 Oct 1969)
Moody, J D (18 May 1969)
Moorberg, M L (2 Dec 1966)
Moore, A (24 Dec 1972)
Moore, A L (11 Oct 1969)
Moore, A M (27 May 1969)
Moore, A W (29 Nov 1971)
Moore, C L (12 Jul 1967)
Moore, D A (27 Oct 1965)
Moore, D R (2 Oct 1969)
Moore, E M (11 Mar 1967)
Moore, G H (2 Nov 1965)
Moore, H W (3 Sep 1967)
Moore, James D (25 Apr 1969)
Moore, Joseph D (3 Oct 1967, 16 Feb 1972)
Moore, J L (21 Feb 1966)
Moore, K T (3 Mar 1972)
Moore, L A (6 Dec 1967)
Moore, P M (11 Oct 1965)
Moore, R B (17 Mar 1967)
Moore, R W (20 Jan 1968)
Moore, T D (30 Nov 1967)
Moore, W J (17/18 May 1966)
Moore, W R (13 Nov 1964)
Moose, D B (16 Nov 1966)
Moran, D H (15 Jan 1967)
Moran, J L (19 Dec 1965)
Moran, R A (7 Aug 1966)
Morehouse, S H (24 Jul 1969)
Moreland, S C (12 May 1968)
Moreland, W D (16 Jan 1968)
Morgan, B H (21 Aug 1967)
Morgan, C E (6 Jul 1966)
Morgan, E E (13 Mar 1966)
Morgan, G L (21/22 Dec 1972)
Morgan, H S (3 Apr 1965)
Morgan, J R (29 May 1969)
Morgan, J S (10 Nov 1967)
Morgan, O C (28 Jul 1970)
Morgan, T R (26 Jan 1967)
Moriarty, PG (22 Mar 1971)
Moriarty, R J (29 May 1969)
Morin, R G (24 Dec 1968)
Morley, C F (18 Feb 1970)
Morley, R J (2 Mar 1968)
Morningstar, G L (16 Mar 1970)
Moroney, R J (14 Dec 1965)
Morphew, E P (16 Nov 1969)
Morre, R C (25 Jul 1966)
Morrell, D W (28 Feb 1969)
Morrill, B F (10 Aug 1970)
Morrill, D W (18 Mar 1967)
Morrill, M L (21 Aug 1967)
Morris, B R (20 Oct 1968)
Morris, G W (27 Jan 1973)
Morris, K S (16 Dec 1971)
Morris, L J (17 Jan 1969)
Morris, R A (4 Jan 1967)
Morris, R J (26/27 Dec 1972)
Morris, W K (24 Oct 1963)
Morrisey, R T (19 Aug 1969)

Morrison, G R (26 Oct 1966)
Morrison, J C (25 Nov 1968)
Morrison, P W (8 Jun 1967)
Morrissey, R D (7 Nov 1972)
Morrissey, R T (10 Jan 1966)
Morrow, R D (2 Nov 1967)
Morton, J E (3 Aug 1969)
Moruzzi, F D (17 Jul 1966)
Moser, L (3 Jun 1965)
Moser, M M (14 Oct 1967)
Moser, P K (2 Oct 1969)
Mosley, C W (8 Jul 1968)
Mosley, E (15 Oct 1967)
Moss, D L (16 Apr 1972)
Moss, R P (28 Jan 1969)
Mossman, H S (19 Aug 1972)
Mossman, J R (13 Sep 1965)
Mostello, A H (30 Jun 1970)
Mott, D P (19 May 1972)
Moulton, J (23 Nov 1972)
Mower, J W (25 Mar 1967)
Mowrey, R L (14 Dec 1966)
Moxon, A L (20 Jun 1971)
Moy, D M (5 Jun 1969)
Moyer, C G (29 Nov 1970)
Mravak, T A (3 Feb 1971)
Mueller, S A (18 Jan 1970)
Muellner, G K (17 Apr 1969)
Mulhauser, H (31 Jan 1967)
Mullen, R D (6 Jan 1967)
Mullen, W F (29 Apr 1966)
Muller, A D (24 Oct 1969)
Muller, J D (24 Jan 1969)
Mulligan, J A (20 Mar 1966)
Mullins, H E (3 Jun 1966)
Mullowney, P E (1 Oct 1969)
Mundis, G B (31 Dec 1964)
Mundt, H G (8 May 1969)
Munsch, A E (15 Sep 1967)
Murphey, D W (19 Dec 1969)
Murphy, H F (29 Jul 1972)
Murphy, J P (24 Mar 1967)
Murphy, J S (10 Feb 1972, 8 Jun 1972)
Murphy, Terence M (9 Apr 1965)
Murphy, Terry M (9 Sep 1972)
Murray, J V (18 Feb 1966)
Murray, M H (17 Dec 1971)
Murray, P P (18 Jan 1968)
Murtaugh, B W (8 Mar 1969)
Muscara, C (28 Apr 1967)
Musgrove, W (22 Jul 1971)
Muskat, M S (18 Feb 1968)
Musselman, S O (10 Sep 1972)
Myers, A (18/19 Dec 1972)
Myers, A J (1 Jun 1966)
Myers, D W (10 Mar 1966)
Myers, G L (9 Aug 1967)
Myers, W M (13 Nov 1964)
Mynar, J D (26 Sep 1967)
Nabors, J C (26 Jan 1967)
Nagahiro, J Y (20/21 Dec 1972)
Nagel, R A (26 Nov 1966)
Nakagawa, G R (20/21 Dec 1972)
Nalls, J L (18 May 1969)
Naschek, M J (21 Nov 1968)
Nash, J A (24 Jan 1969)
Nash, P (19 Sep 1968)
Nasipak, R M (22 Apr 1970)
Nasmyth, J H (4 Sep 1966)
Natter, W H (27 Nov 1966)
Naughton, R J (18 May 1967)
Naugle, B E (6 Nov 1965)
Neal, B (26 Apr 1967)
Neal, W A (20 Aug 1968)
Neal, W D (28 Jun 1969)
Needham, W F (17 Jan 1969)
Neel, C B (8 Nov 1967)
Neeld, B G (4 Jan 1969)
Neff, F R (27 Nov 1970)
Neill, J M (27 Jan 1971)
Neislar, D P (20 Feb 1969)
Nellans, W L (16 Sep 1967)
Nelson, C C (19 Nov 1967)
Nelson, D (20 Jul 1969)
Nelson, G F (8 Jun 1965)
Nelson, J (23 May 1970)
Nelson, J H (11 Apr 1970)
Nelson, M (20 May 1967)
Nelson, M W (23 Apr 1970)
Nelson, R C (6 Mar 1968)
Nelson, W H (20 Jul 1966)

Nenninger, G L (29 Oct 1967)
Ness, P L (23 Aug 1967)
Neth, F A (16 Jan 1966)
Netherland, R M (10 May 1967)
Neuens, M J (12 Aug 1966)
Neville, W E (18 Jun 1965)
Newberry, G H (29 Nov 1970)
Newberry, W E (29 Sep 1968)
Newborn, W D (8 Sep 1964)
Newcomb, W G (3 Aug 1967)
Newell, M T (14 Dec 1966)
Newendorp, J V (1 Oct 1971)
Newhouse, J W (23 Sep 1970)
Newman, J C (5/6 Feb 1968)
Newman, L J (18 Jun 1972)
Newman, T A (30 May 1968)
Newman, W E (13 Aug 1965)
Newon, D F (11 Apr 1968)
Newsom, B B (23 Jul 1966)
Newsome, G K (9 Jul 1970)
Newton, W J (23 Oct 1966)
Newville, V H (2 Oct 1967)
Nichols, A A (19 May 1972)
Nichols, H C (1 Sep 1966)
Nichols, J B (26 Apr 1967)
Nichols, J R (21 Jan 1969)
Nichols, M (17 Nov 1967)
Nichols, S E (11 May 1972)
Nicholson, J E (6 Oct 1967)
Nickerson, W B (22 Apr 1966)
Niedecken, W C (14 Feb 1969)
Nierste, R K (30 Jun 1966)
Niggle, H T (5 Feb 1969)
Nightingale, R J (17 Mar 1968)
Niski, L E (10 May 1967)
Nix, C G (1 Oct 1966)
Nolen, W E (24 Sep 1965)
Norbert, C R (20 Jul 1966)
Nordahl, L E (20 Dec 1965)
Nordin, G L (10 Dec 1967)
Norman, T W (12 Sep 1969)
Norrington, G R (5 May 1968)
Norris, B (12 Aug 1967)
Norris, T (2 Apr 1972)
Norris, T E (12 Aug 1967)
Norris, T O (29 Nov 1965)
North, K W (1 Aug 1966)
North, W (27/28 Dec 1972)
Northern, S M (25 Jul 1968)
Norton, F P (19 May 1970)
Norton, G H (13 Aug 1965)
Norton, R L (3 Dec 1968)
Nugent, J A (16 Dec 1968)
Nullis, M M (21 Dec 1970)
Nunez, G B (7 Jan 1973)
Nunn, J W (20 Jul 1967)
Nunn, R L (6 Jun 1968)
Nutting, F A (6 Apr 1967)
Nyhof, R E (18 Jun 1972)
Nyman, L F (23 Jun 1966)
Nystrom, B A (2 Dec 1966)
O'Brien, J L (10 Nov 1966)
O'Brien, L (18 Dec, 1971, 1 Feb 1972)
O'Connor, D J (26 Apr 1968)
O'Connor, T H (8 Dec 1968)
O'Connor, W J (2 May 1969)
O'Donnell, S (12 Jul 1972)
O'Grady, J F (10 Apr 1967)
O'Keefe, R W (10 Feb 1971)
O'Kieff, W B (27 Nov 1970)
O'Mara, O (5 Oct 1966)
O'Neil, J W (29 Sep 1972)
O'Neill, J E (29 Dec 1968)
O'Neill, J R (6 Feb 1963)
O'Rourke, (25 May 1967)
Oaks, R C (30 Mar 1966)
Obar, (21 May 1969)
Obenland, R R (18 May 1968)
Oberdier, L D (5 May 1968)
Ochab, J (7 Jan 1970)
Ochoa, J (6 Sep 1968)
Odell, D E (17 Oct 1967)
Oden, K J (13 Mar 1969)
Offutt, G P (1 Oct 1965)
Ogle, C R (2 Jun 1966)
Oldermann, W (30 Mar 1968)
Olds, E A (11 Mar 1968)
Olds, R (20 May 1967,
    20 Nov 1967, 27 Jan 1968)
Olmstead, F S (11 May 1972)
Olmstead, S E (17 Oct 1965)

Olsen, G E (13 Mar 1966)
Olsen, T R (1 Jul 1967)
Olson, D A (11 Jan 1968)
Olson, R E (5 Feb 1969)
Olsson, J M (19 Dec 1969)
Orell, Q R (13 Oct 1968)
Orf, P E (13 Sep 1965)
Orlowski, J M (8 Apr 1969)
Orr, T B (7 Jan 1969)
Orr, W R (12 May 1968)
Orrell, B D (9 Apr 1972, 20 Jun 1972)
Orth, J R (6 Sep 1969)
Ortiz, J H (29 Apr 1970)
Osbolt, E S S (17 May 1966)
Osborn, G H (24 Sep 1965)
Osborne, C D (13 Jul 1967)
Osborne, D H (23 Sep 1968)
Osborne, E N (28/29 Dec 1967)
Ostermeyer, W H (12 May 1972)
Ostrozny, N J (22 Nov 1972)
Otis, P W (23 May 1969)
Ott, P L (2/3 Oct 1967)
Ott, W A (8 Oct 1970)
Otto, N J (7 Aug 1967)
Overland, R M (13 Apr 1966)
Overlock, J F (16 Aug 1968)
Overly, N M (10 Sep 1967, 5 Oct 1967)
Overman, H (20 Apr 1962)
Owen, C C (15 Dec 1970)
Owens, D D (17 Jun 1972)
Owens, J L (6 Jun 1967)
Oxley, J E (22 Apr 1967)
Ozbolt, J Q (27 Mar 1966)
Pabst, E M (6 Oct 1966)
Packard, D B (10 Jun 1966)
Packard, R L (30 Jul 1967)
Padgett, J P (11 May 1972)
Page, A L (6 Aug 1967)
Page, L S (5 Mar 1966)
Page, L (17 Nov 1967)
Paige, E C (14 Mar 1966)
Paige, F O (22 Nov 1969)
Paige, G C (22 Jul 1972)
Paine, P W (7 May 1968)
Painter, J R (18 Jun 1971)
Palank, W G (1 Jun 1968)
Palenscar, A J (27 Mar 1967)
Palka, F (7 Jun 1970)
Palmer, G S (27 Feb 1968)
Palmer, K C (29 Sep 1967)
Palmgren, E D (22 Apr 1968)
Panas, G W (2 Mar 1965)
Panek, R J (28 Jan 1970)
Pappas, G T (14 Sep 1968)
Pappas, R L (25 Feb 1966)
Parcels, R L (9 Mar 1970)
Pardo, J R (10 Mar 1967)
Parish, C C (25 Jul 1968)
Parker, C L (21 Jan 1973)
Parker, F C (28/29 Dec 1967)
Parker, J E (30 Jun 1965)
Parker, J J (3 Mar 1970)
Parker, J T (21 Jul 1965)
Parker, M C (18 Mar 1967)
Parker, W W (24 Apr 1968)
Parkhurst, V (16 Apr 1972)
Parlatore, C P (3 Sep 1968)
Parr, W D (21 Apr 1968)
Parra, L (17 Jul 1968)
Parrot, T V (12 Aug 1967)
Parsley, E M (3 Feb 1966)
Parsons, D B (19 Sep 1966)
Parten, G L (19 Aug 1966)
Partridge, J (18 Oct 1971)
Paschall, R P (2 Apr 1972)
Pascoe, R M (10 Mar 1967)
Pasekoff, R E (13 Mar 1966)
Patch, D C (2 Oct 1965)
Pate, G (22 May 1968)
Patee, J (2 Jan 1968)
Patterson, B M (28 Jul 1967)
Patterson, J K (19 May 1967)
Patterson, R E (21 Jun 1967, 16 Sep 1967)
Patterson, R J (26 Nov 1967)
Patterson, W B (18 Jun 1972)
Pattillo, R N (16 Feb 1971)
Paul, C A (20/21 Dec 1972)
Paul, H W (28 Feb 1970)
Paul, L L (17 Sep 1968)
Paul, W S (15 Oct 1967)
Pauley, M I (13 Mar 1966)

Paulsen, J G (26 Sep 1966)
Paulsen, N M (24 Sep 1968)
Paulson, M L (28 Mar 1972)
Pawlish, G F (8 Mar 1967)
Paxton, D E (22 Feb 1969)
Payne, E (12 Jun 1970)
Payne, I S (30 Apr 1968)
Peacock, G H (1 Jun 1966)
Peacock, J R (11 Oct 1972)
Peacock, P (20 Feb 1971)
Pear, W F (6 Sep 1972)
Pearce, E J (28 Mar 1972)
Pearce, J D (31 Dec 1967)
Pearce, R A (16 Mar 1970)
Pearson, A J (19 Oct 1968)
Pearson, R H (11 Jun 1967)
Pearson, W E (22 Feb 1969)
Pearson, W R (2 Apr 1972)
Peck, F E (6 Mar 1968)
Pedroli, P (14 Jan 1968)
Peek, D L (9 Jan 1970)
Peel, R D (31 May 1965)
Peerson, J M (14 Mar 1966)
Peffley, R (17 Nov 1967)
Peil, G E (17 Nov 1965)
Pemberton, G T (23 Jul 1966)
Pender, O J (16 Aug 1972)
Pendergraft, R D (2 Jul 1967)
Penn, M G (6 Aug 1972)
Penn, P L (11 Aug 1966)
Pennington, R W (25 Jul 1970)
Pepper, W T (7 Jun 1970)
Perisho, G S (31 Dec 1967)
Perkins, A D (3 Oct 1967)
Perkins, G W (20 Jul 1966)
Perrine, E L (22 May 1967)
Perry, G (16 Jun 1973)
Perry, G E (10 Jan 1966)
Perry, J L (25 Oct 1965)
Perry, R A (20/21 Dec 1972)
Perry, R C (31 Aug 1967)
Perry, R D (20/21 Dec 1972)
Personnet, J A (16 Sep 1972)
Peters, C H (1 Jul 1966)
Peters, F C (2 May 1970)
Peters, G C (23 Jun 1969)
Peters, L W (21 Apr 1972)
Peters, M J (21 Feb 1966)
Petersen, F E (10 Sep 1968)
Petersen, G D (10 Sep 1967)
Peterson, C A (27 May 1969)
Peterson, C E (10 Feb 1968)
Peterson, D B (10 Sep 1966)
Peterson, D R (9 Mar 1966)
Peterson, D W (18 Jul 1967)
Peterson, K L (28 Mar 1968)
Peterson, K S (2 Apr 1968)
Peterson, L D (27 Jan 1967, 31 Mar 1967)
Peterson, M A (27 Jan 1973)
Petkunas, D W (30 Jul 1972)
Petty, J R (26 Oct 1965)
Pfaffmann, C B (8 Apr 1970)
Pfluger, F W (21 Jul 1968)
Phelps, W (23 Nov 1971)
Phenegar, W R (13 Aug 1967)
Phillips, (10 Feb 1970)
Phillips, D J (3 Jul 1966)
Phillips, J N (2 May 1970)
Phillips, J V (16 Sep 1970)
Phillips, N P (30 May 1968)
Phillips, P E (27 Dec 1969)
Phillips, R W (27 Jan 1968)
Phillips, T B (24 Oct 1964)
Phillips, W C (16 Nov 1969)
Piccoli, J P (3 Nov 1966)
Pichard, D M (2 Jul 1967)
Pick, D W (26 Aug 1968)
Picking, F W (23 Jul 1969)
Piehl, G H (24 May 1969)
Pielin, R D (3 Jun 1966)
Pierce, J W (24 Feb 1966)
Pierce, L J (16 Apr 1969)
Pierce, R G (24 Jul 1968)
Piersanti, A J (15 Dec 1970)
Piet, J M (23 Aug 1967)
Pietsch, R E (30 Apr 1968)
Pigott, C W (18 May 1969)
Pike, D S (23 Mar 1972)
Pike, P X (12 Jul 1969)
Pile, R E (5 Mar 1966)
Pilkington, T H (19 Sep 1966)

Pineau, R P (8 Oct 1967)
Piner, J T (14 Jul 1968)
Pinneker, J L (20 Mar 1966)
Pirie, J G (22 Jun 1967)
Pirrucello, J S (8 Dec 1968)
Pishvanov, N A (18 Oct 1967)
Piskula, R (27 Jul 1969)
Pitches, J S (1 Sep 1969)
Pitchford, J J (20 Dec 1965)
Pitman, P P (12 May 1967)
Pitt, A (24 Jan 1966)
Pitt, P R (12 Dec 1970)
Pittman, A D (16 Nov 1966)
Pitts, R W (5 Oct 1965)
Pitzen, J R (16 Aug 1972)
Pizzino, E (8 Mar 1969)
Pizzo, E T (5 Jan 1968)
Plank, T (12 Jul 1967)
Plants, T L (2 Jun 1965)
Plassmeyer, B H (11 Sep 1970)
Platt, F R (31 Jan 1971)
Platt, R L (10 May 1969)
Plautz, D H (14 Jan 1973)
Pleiman, J E (1 Nov 1965, 14 Mar 1966)
Plotz, L R (19 Aug 1968)
Plowman, J E (24 Mar 1967)
Plumb, J C (19 May 1967, 1 Sep 1968)
Podell, R W (9 Jun 1967)
Podhajsky, N A (29 Nov 1970)
Poestel, R E (21 Nov 1965)
Pogreba, D (22 Aug 1965, 5 Oct 1965)
Polenski, E C (18 May 1969)
Polfer, C R (7 May 1972)
Poling, R L (16 Sep 1972)
Polites, J J (18 Jan 1968)
Pollack, M (6 Jul 1967)
Pollak, J E (4 Jan 1968)
Pollard, B M (15 May 1967)
Pollin, G J (29 Apr 1967)
Polster, H (16 Jun 1969, 15 Jul 1969)
Pomeroy, J H (22 Sep 1972)
Pommerenk, A C (17 Dec 1970)
Pomphrey, M (10 Jul 1972)
Poole, C S (18/19 Dec 1972)
Poole, W S (23 May 1968)
Poor, R A (4 Feb 1967)
Pope, T (17 Jan 1969)
Popendorf, W J (29 Mar 1969)
Porter, F H (8 Dec 1966)
Porter, G H (11 Nov 1969)
Porterfield, C W (24 Mar 1968)
Post, G L (16 Mar 1968)
Potter, G G (24 Jan 1969)
Potter, T J (2 Dec 1965)
Potter, W J (29 Dec 1967)
Potter, W T (4 Feb 1968)
Potts, L F (7 Apr 1972)
Powell, J P (13 Aug 1970)
Powell, L K (21 Aug 1967)
Powell, W E (17 Aug 1968)
Powers, T R (31 Oct 1965)
Poynor, D R (19 Dec 1971)
Prater, R D (2 Apr 1972)
Pratt, L R (18 Apr 1972)
Preaux, T A (26 Apr 1967)
Prendergast, F S (9 Mar 1967)
Pressler, C E (16 Mar 1970)
Preston, J A (15 May 1966)
Preston, J F (17 Jul 1966)
Prevost, A M (1 Feb 1966)
Price, D (14 Mar 1966)
Price, D J (30 Jul 1972)
Price, L D (30 Jul 1972)
Price, W M (11 Oct 1972)
Priest, R D (22 Mar 1971)
Primm, S J (4/5 Feb 1973)
Pringle, D (14 Apr 1968)
Pritchard, W H (8 Jul 1967)
Proctor, J W (22/23 May 1968)
Profilet, L T (22 Jan 1968)
Profilet, R C (2 Oct 1968)
Profitt, G (13 Feb 1972)
Prudhomme, J D (22 Dec 1965)
Pruett, W D (5 Jul 1972)
Pugh, D G (19 Mar 1970)
Pugh, K W (12 Apr 1966)
Purcell, H P (2 Sep 1963)
Purcell, M J (1 Apr 1968)
Purcell, R B (27 Jul 1965)
Purhum, R S (16 Mar 1970)
Purrington, F R (20 Oct 1966)

Putman, C L (9 Mar 1967)
Putton, D H (28 Jul 1971)
Pyle, D E (13 Jun 1966)
Pyle, H E (16 Jul 1967)
Pyle, J W (11 May 1970)
Pyle, T S (7 Aug 1966)
Pyles, H B (18 Oct 1965)
Quill, E B (14/15 Feb 1968)
Quinn, J A (2 Oct 1969)
Quinn, M E (22 Nov 1969)
Quisenberry, J N (10 Sep 1968)
Quist, J W (18 Oct 1968)
Rabeni, J J (17 Nov 1969)
Rackley, I W (18 Oct 1966)
Rademacher, H (8 Jun 1965)
Rader, F M (27 Nov 1970)
Raebel, D V (17 Aug 1972)
Ragland, D W (31 May/1 Jun 1966)
Ragusa, F R (9 Jun 1967)
Raines, F L (19 Jun 1967)
Rainwater, J A (12 Jul 1967)
Raleigh, L R (26 Dec 1965)
Ralston, F D (13 May 1966)
Ramsbottom, W E (26 May 1972)
Ramsden, G L (23 Jan 1968)
Ramsey, D L (17 Aug 1970)
Ramskill, C R (1 May 1967)
Ramsower, I B (28 Mar 1972)
Randall, J E P (13 Oct 1965)
Randall, R I (10 Jul 1972)
Randolph, R E (25 May 1967)
Rankin, T S (14 Sep 1969)
Ransom, B R (8 Oct 1969)
Rash, M D (22 May 1968)
Rash, W A (19 Mar 1970)
Rasmussen, R T (11 Jul 1970)
Raspberry, E T (12 Jun 1967)
Ratcliff, L L (8 Feb 1971)
Ratzel, W D (18 May 1972)
Ratzlaff, B M (11 Sep 1972)
Ratzlaff, R R (20 Mar 1966)
Rausch, J F (11 Jun 1967)
Rausch, R E (16 Apr 1970)
Rawlings, G L (11 Aug 1967, 4 Nov 1967)
Rawsthorne, E A (28 Dec 1965)
Ray, J E (8 May 1966)
Ray, R B (7 Dec 1967)
Raymond, P D (5 Sep 1967)
Read, C H W (24 Aug 1968)
Reaid, R K (21/22 Dec 1972)
Reasor, T W (30 Jul 1972)
Redden, E G (3 Apr 1969)
Reddick, R R (10 Dec 1967)
Redman, S W (8 Oct 1969)
Redmond, D D (14 Mar 1966)
Reed, (12 Oct 1967)
Reed, J W (24 Jul 1970)
Reed, L L (9 May 1965)
Reed, M E (23 Oct 1968)
Reed, T M (23 Jun 1969)
Reed, W N (18 Nov 1967)
Reeder, F D (13 Dec 1968)
Reeder, W H (16 Jan 1968)
Reese, D C (9 Mar 1967)
Reese, E P (6 Feb 1970)
Reese, J R (2 Dec 1968)
Rehling, G H (6 Sep 1969)
Rehm, T M (8 Oct 1967)
Rehmann, D G (2 Dec 1966)
Reich, T A (17 Nov 1968)
Reich, W J (11 May 1972)
Reid, J E (30 Jan 1973)
Reid, R (18 Jun 1972)
Reilly, J N (19 Nov 1968)
Reilly, L G (15 May 1966)
Reinhart, (24 Dec 1968)
Reitmann, T E (1 Dec 1965)
Renelt, W A (20 Nov 1969)
Repeta, H J (23 Dec 1972)
Retterbush, G L (12 Oct 1972)
Rex, R A (8 Dec 1968)
Rex, R F (9 Mar 1969)
Rexroad, L F (17 Apr 1970)
Rexroad, R R (3 Apr 1968)
Reynes, J (20 Sep 1965)
Reynolds, D J (8 Jul 1967)
Reynolds, J A (28 Nov 1965)
Rhodes, M P (1 Jun 1968)
Rhymes, C C (25 May 1967)
Ricci, J F (3 Apr 1969)
Rice, C D (26 Oct 1967)
Rice, D W (12 Oct 1965)
Rice, H C (28/29 Mar 1967)
Rice, J J (11 Oct 1969)
Rice, M P (13 Sep 1972)
Rich, R (19 May 1967)
Richards, D C (2 Mar 1968)
Richards, J P (8 May 1970)
Richards, L D (23 Aug 1968)
Richards, L W (22 Nov 1969)
Richardson, C H (8 Oct 1968)
Richardson, D L (24 Oct 1968)
Richardson, E (24 Oct 1964)
Richardson, F W (3 Mar 1967)
Richardson, R (18 Aug 1969)
Richardson, R B (20 Oct 1968)
Richardson, R F (9 Mar 1967)
Richardson, S G (30 Nov 1965)
Richardson, W L (2 Apr 1966)
Richmond, J A (21 Mar 1970)
Richter, K W (28 Feb 1967, 28 Jul 1967)
Rickel, D J (16 May 1968)
Ricker, W E (28 Oct 1968)
Ricketts, J E (8 Apr 1969)
Ricks, W R (29 Jun 1971)
Riddle, C (11 Sep 1969)
Rider, P E (2 Oct 1969)
Rieddle, (18 Mar 1969)
Riese, G W (14 Apr 1966)
Riess, C F (24 Dec 1972)
Rigel, R L (25 Jul 1970)
Riggins, R P (21 Apr 1968)
Rindt, B A (11 Jun 1970)
Ringsdorf, H B (11 Nov 1966)
Ringwood, P (16 Jun 1972)
Rinne, L (5 Jan 1971)
Riopelle, M A (18 Mar 1969)
Riordan, J M (10 Nov 1966)
Rios, N L (6 Mar 1968)
Ripple, C W (9 Jun 1970)
Rippy, G D (6 Oct 1966)
Risher, D H (6 Sep 1968)
Risner, J R (22 Mar 1965, 3 Apr 1965, 4 Apr 1965, 16 Sep 1965, 27 Oct 1967)
Risse, W J (16 Mar 1970)
Rissel, R C (15 May 1970)
Rissi, D L (18/19 Dec 1972)
Ritchey, S L (24 May 1969)
Ritchie, H H (13 Jan 1966)
Ritchie, J R (8 Apr 1967)
Ritchie, S (10 May 1972)
Rittichier, J C (9 Jun 1968)
Rivera-Balaguer, R L (9 Jun 1967)
Rivers, W B (10 Sep 1965)
Roark, W M (7 Apr 1965)
Robb, W A (19 Sep 1972)
Robbins, R J (19 Apr 1966)
Roberge, F D (11 Aug 1965)
Roberts, C P (12 Aug 1972)
Roberts, G R (2 Dec 1965)
Roberts, H J (18 Jun 1965)
Roberts, H W (18 Dec 1968)
Roberts, K B (18 May 1969)
Roberts, M L (11 Jan 1968)
Robertson, C W (8/9 Jan 1967)
Robertson, J C (18 Jun 1965)
Robertson, J L (16 Sep 1966)
Robertson, L (7 Jul 1972)
Robinson, J (1 Dec 1970)
Robinson, K D (29 Aug 1966)
Robinson, L M (4 Jun 1967)
Robinson, L W (5 Jan 1970)
Robinson, P K (1 Jul 1972)
Robinson, R E (13 May 1967)
Robinson, W (27/28 Dec 1972)
Robinson, W A (20 Sep 1965)
Roby, C D (3 Mar 1967)
Rockett, A C (2 Jun 1967)
Rocky, R E (17 Sep 1966)
Rodenbach, W T (5 Jan 1968)
Rodriguez, A E (11 Mar 1968)
Roedeman, K P (1 Dec 1964)
Roehrich, R (18 Jan 1968)
Rogers, A V (4 Aug 1966)
Rogers, C E (3 May 1967)
Rogers, J H (8 Feb 1967)
Roggow, N L (8 Oct 1967)
Rogiers, C J (2 Oct 1967)
Rokes, D G (27 Mar 1966, 17 May 1966)
Rollins, D J (14 May 1967)
Romano, G M (2 Jun 1965)
Romano, G R (11 May 1967)
Romero, V (19 Mar 1968)
Romig, E L (17 Jun 1966)
Ronca, R F (19 Feb 1965)
Roper, J M (29 Nov 1966)
Rosato, J F (2 Jun 1966)
Rose, G A (21 Jun 1972)
Rose, G E (14 Apr 1968)
Rose, L L (3 Jun 1966)
Rose, P N (13 Dec 1968)
Rosecrans, R P (11 Nov 1966)
Rosen, M E (8 Oct 1969)
Rosenbach, R P (4 Mar 1970)
Ross, B R (20 Jun 1971)
Ross, C B (11 Sep 1969)
Ross, J S (1 Aug 1968)
Ross, R E (21 May 1972, 8 Jul 1972)
Ross, R F (17 Nov 1967)
Roth, B L (27 Jun 1965)
Roth, R C (22 Feb 1969)
Rotz, D H (19 Dec 1970)
Rough, J L (4 Apr 1967)
Rowe, B R (18 Feb 1972)
Rowley, C S (22 Apr 1970)
Royal, C L (20 Oct 1968)
Royer, R H (25 May 1966)
Rubus, G M (25 May 1970)
Rucker, E (23 May 1968)
Rudloff, S A (10 May 1972)
Rudolph, R D (8 Sep 1965)
Ruffin, J T (18 Feb 1966)
Ruffo, J S (20 Dec 1965)
Ruhling, M J (23 Nov 1968)
Rumble, W L (24 Oct 1967, 28 Apr 1968)
Runyan, A E (29 Apr 1966)
Ruonavaara, R E (28/29 Mar 1967)
Rupinski, B F (16 Jun 1968)
Rusch, S A (6 Mar 1972)
Rush, A F (21 Dec 1970)
Rush, T A (22 Apr 1970)
Russ, R D (24 Jan 1969)
Russell, D M (5 Dec 1967, 17 Jul 1969)
Russell, K (19 May 1967)
Russell, P F (19 Jul 1969)
Russell, Richard Lee (23 Jun 1968)
Russell, Richard Lee (25/26 Apr 1972)
Russell, Robert L (11 Jun 1967)
Russell, R R (31 Dec 1969)
Russo, V (20/21 Dec 1972)
Rutan, R G (17 Aug 1968)
Ruth, A E (30 May 1970)
Rutherford, A K (6 Aug 1966, 17 Sep 1966)
Rutherford, W H (29 May 1970)
Rutledge, H E (28 Nov 1965)
Rutledge, J T (29 Nov 1965)
Rutyna, A P (10 Mar 1969)
Ruyf, R P (8 Oct 1967)
Ruzicka, J L (30 Jul 1972)
Ryan, M K (9 Jul 1968)
Ryan, R E (30 Oct 1971)
Ryan, T K (2 Aug 1969)
Ryan, T P (11 Jan 1970)
Ryan, W C (12 Jan 1969, 11 May 1969)
Rybak, R J (24 Jan 1969)
Ryder, J L (9 Jun 1970)
Rydlewicz, J M (12 Aug 1971)
Ryon, J W (21 Nov 1972)
Saavedra, R (27 Apr 1968)
Sadler, M O (30 Jun 1970)
Saffell, J A (26 Apr 1968)
Sage, L C C (22 Jun 1969)
Sakahara, W T (13 Dec 1967)
Sala, J D (7 Dec 1965)
Sale, H R (6 Jun 1967)
Salinas, M P (11 Dec 1965)
Salzarulo, R P (4 Sep 1969)
Sampson, H (21 May 1972)
Sampson, L V (23 Mar 1961)
Sandberg, J A (20 Dec 1969)
Sander, R L (7 Jun 1966)
Sanders, S R (25 Aug 1969)
Sanders, T A (7 Jul 1965)
Sanders, W S (30 Jun 1970)
Sandvick, R J (7 Aug 1966)
Sanifer, R W (3 Nov 1967)
Santos, J C (13 Nov 1968)
Sarnecky, J (15 Apr 1968)
Sasser, G F (23 Dec 1972)
Sather, R C (5 Aug 1964)
Saucier, R A (1 Jul 1967)
Saukaitis, J S (16 Mar 1970)
Saunders, E F (15 Nov 1967)
Savage, W G (24 Jun 1968)
Savoy, M J (17 Jun 1966)
Sawhill, R R (23 Aug 1967)
Saxby, J F (29 Nov 1970)
Sayer, A F (7 Sep 1967)
Sayers, D L (17 Apr 1966)
Scanlan, T A (6 Mar 1969)
Scarborough, G E (12 May 1968)
Schaefer, J S (16 Mar 1970)
Schaffer, R W (3 Nov 1966)
Schaneberg, L C (30 Jun 1970)
Schanzenbach, D T (18 Oct 1968)
Scharf, C J (1 Oct 1965)
Scheu, R D (15 Dec 1965)
Scheurich, T E (1 Mar 1968)
Schiavone, R (3 Oct 1968)
Schierman, W D (28 Aug 1965)
Schiltz, R A (28 Apr 1966)
Schimmels, E R (17 Feb 1969)
Schindelar, G F (1 Jan 1968)
Schlick, C M (29 Dec 1965)
Schmidt, C W (2 Dec 1965)
Schmidt, H E (23 May 1968)
Schmidt, N (1 Sep 1966)
Schmidt, W R (9 Jun 1968)
Schober, J E (29 Aug 1969)
Schoderer, E J (10 Nov 1966)
Schoeffel, P V (4 Oct 1967)
Schoenbaum, C R (9 Jun 1967)
Schoeppner, L J (9 Mar 1970)
Scholtz, J C (20 Nov 1967)
Schoonover, C D (16 Jan 1966)
Schranz, P A (14 Mar 1970)
Schroeffel, T A (18 Feb 1966)
Schrupp, W C (30 May 1967)
Schufeldt, V (13 Nov 1965)
Schuler, R H (14 Oct 1965)
Schuler, W E (8 Dec 1966)
Schultz, H D (25 Apr 1968)
Schultz, J (5 Sep 1972)
Schultz, W L (8 Oct 1966)
Schulz, P H (16 Nov 1967)
Schumacher, F A (8 Apr 1967)
Schuyler, P (29 May 1972)
Schwartze, C J (5 Apr 1968)
Schwehm, W H (24 May 1969)
Schweitzer, R J (5 Jan 1968)
Schwertfeger, W R (16 Feb 1972)
Scott, B (8 May 1967)
Scott, D V (21 Aug 1967)
Scott, G O (20 Oct 1968)
Scott, H D (18 Jan 1970)
Scott, I E (9 Jun 1967)
Scott, L M (8 Jun 1969)
Scott, M D (24 Oct 1967)
Scott, M R (15 Mar 1966)
Scott, P R (15 Nov 1968)
Scott, R M (25 Jun 1968)
Scott, R R (27 Jan 1970)
Scott, T B (13 Dec 1972)
Scott, V C (22 Apr 1969)
Scovill, D (6 Sep 1966)
Scoville, W W (2 Oct 1967)
Screws, D R (2 May 1972)
Scrivener, S R (16 Mar 1971)
Scruggs, L M (21 Feb 1967)
Scruggs, S J (16 Mar 1970)
Scungio, V A (4 Nov 1966)
Seagroves, M A (22 Jun 1969)
Searby, B M (16 Mar 1970)
Searfus, W H (25 Nov 1967)
Sears, J F (20 Jan 1968)
Seaton, J E (6 May 1971)
Seaver, M E (10 Jul 1967)
Secanti, R M (19 Aug 1967)
Seeber, B G (5 Oct 1965)
Seek, B J (5 Jul 1972)
Seeley, D M (16 Mar 1971)
Segars, R L (29 Oct 1971)
Sehorn, J E (14 Dec 1967)
Seibert, F W (1 Dec 1969)
Seiler, C (27 Mar 1969)
Seiler, P J (19 Feb 1968)
Seitz, W J (1 May 1972)
Selaniko, L (6 Sep 1968)
Sellers, J A (25 Dec 1967)
Sellers, R (22 Nov 1972)
Sells, J D (18 May 1969)
Sells, W H (7 Feb 1965)
Sennett, R R (21/22 Jan 1966)
Serex, H M (2 Apr 1972)
Setterquist, F L (23 Aug 1968)
Seuell, J W (6 Jun 1972)
Severson, L J (25 Feb 1968)
Seybold, G C (28 Apr 1971)
Seyer, D J (14 Dec 1966)
Shaheen, C A (17 Aug 1968)
Shain, E R (28 Jul 1968)
Shamblee, G L (7 Oct 1967)
Shanahan, J F (15 Aug 1968)
Shank, E G (24 Mar 1964)
Shank, G L (23 Jul 1972)
Shankel, W L (23 Dec 1965)
Shanks, J L (23 May 1968)
Shannon, G (21 Aug 1967)
Shapiro, R D (22/23 Dec 1972)
Sharkey, J E (6 Feb 1970)
Sharp, B L (3 Dec 1969, 10 Jul 1972)
Sharp, W D (18 Nov 1965)
Sharpe, L (2 Oct 1966)
Shattuck, F W (17 Jul 1969)
Shattuck, G W (10 Apr 1967)
Shattuck, L W (1 Jul 1966, 11 Jul 1966)
Shaughnessy, J F (3 Feb 1963)
Shaw, E B (4 Sep 1965)
Shaw, J (11 Sep 1967)
Shaw, J W (25 May 1972)
Shay, D E (8 Oct 1970)
Shea, J P (19/20 Apr 1965)
Sheets, R (6 May 1972)
Shelton, C E (29 Apr 1965, 18 May 1965)
Shelton, J E (12 May 1970)
Shepard, G D (27 Dec 1966)
Shepard, H C (10 Oct 1969)
Shepherd, A S (26 Nov 1968)
Sherburn, H L (5 Feb 1969)
Sherman, J B (25 Mar 1966)
Sherman, P W (10 Jun 1967)
Shimp, A H (9 Jun 1967)
Shine, A C (2 Dec 1972)
Shine, J C (2 Dec 1972)
Shingaki, T (19 Aug 1972)
Shingledecker, A D (31 May/1 Jun 1966)
Shinn, W (6 Sep 1966)
Shinn, W C (28 Jan 1970)
Shipman, (5 Dec 1969, 18 Feb 1970)
Shiraishi, P N (21 Nov 1968)
Shively, J R (5 May 1967)
Sholl, R L (21 Feb 1967)
Shoneck, J R (18 Oct 1966)
Shook, S L (5 Jul 1969)
Shugart, K L (26 Mar 1965)
Shults, R E (13 Apr 1967)
Shumaker, R H (11 Feb 1965)
Shuman, E A (16/17 Mar 1968)
Shumock, R H (9 Apr 1969)
Shumway, G R (25 Jun 1972)
Sibson, D A (30 Dec 1967)
Siderius, J D (17 Jan 1971)
Siebert, W (12 Oct 1967)
Siegwarth, D E (17 Jun 1966)
Sienicki, T S (3 May 1972)
Sierra, E P (2 Jun 1968)
Sigafoos, W H (24 Apr 1971)
Sigler, G R (29 Apr 1967)
Sigler, J J (1 Oct 1971)
Sijan, L P (9 Nov 1967, 20 Dec 1967)
Sikkink, R D (19 Jul 1969)
Silliman, J (9 Sep 1967)
Silva, A M (22 Aug 1967)
Silva, C A (29 Jan 1967)
Silva, W E (17 Feb 1972)
Silver, (28 Feb 1969)
Silver, E R (5 Jul 1968)
Silver, L J (12 Jun 1967)
Sima, T W (14 Oct 1965)
Simmonds, D D (16 Feb 1972)
Simmons, A D (16 Mar 1970)
Simmons, R E (28 Mar 1972)
Simmons, W A (4 Jun 1968)
Simmons, W P (3 Sep 1966)
Simon, P J (14 Dec 1965)
Simonet, K A (18 Jan 1968)
Simonin, K C (28 Feb 1967)
Simpson, R L (28 Aug 1962)
Simpson, R T (18/19 Dec 1972)
Singer, D M (17 Aug 1966)
Singleton, D E (25 Jan 1969)
Singleton, J (6 Nov 1965)
Siow, G R (11 Jan 1968)
Sipes, J L (10 May 1969)
Sipos, W G (6 Apr 1967)

Sissell, C D (26 Feb 1968, 6 Mar 1968)
Sisson, W W (18 Oct 1965)
Sitek, T W (23 Aug 1967)
Sittner, R N (23 Aug 1967)
Sizemore, J E (8 Jul 1969)
Sjogren, H E (21 Feb 1966)
Skaar, W A (17 May 1968)
Skaret, G J (25 Nov 1969)
Skeels, R (16 Jun 1973)
Skeen, R R (16 May 1970)
Skinner, O G (12 Dec 1970)
Skoro, J P(13 Sep 1966)
Skowron, E R (3 Sep 1966)
Slagle, D R (2 May 1972)
Slapikas, M G (12 Jun 1967)
Slater, F L (3 May 1972)
Sledzinski, S (2 May 1972)
Sleeper, D F (26 Aug 1968)
Sloan, C P (16 Nov 1969, 21 Dec 1969)
Sloan, T N (17 Dec 1965)
Small, V J (31 Jul 1965)
Smallwood, J J (16 Jun 1973)
Smiley, A D (25 Dec 1967)
Smiley, F E (26 Aug 1967)
Smiley, S K (20 Jul 1969)
Smith, (25 Mar 1969)
Smith, B D (21 Apr 1971)
Smith, B E (25 Mar 1966)
Smith, C A (16 Nov 1966)
Smith, C D, USAF (29 Feb 1968)
Smith, C D, USMC (15 Jul 1966)
Smith, C H (7 Jun 1972)
Smith, Charles D, USAF (28 Jul 1967)
Smith, Clyde D, USMC (9 Apr 1972, 2 May 1972)
Smith, D (15 Mar 1967)
Smith, D D (7 Dec 1966)
Smith, D G (24 Oct 1969)
Smith, D L (2 Jun 1967)
Smith, David C (6 Sep 1969)
Smith, Donald C (20 Dec 1965)
Smith, E A (29 Oct 1971)
Smith, E D (28 Mar 1972)
Smith, F W (1 Sep 1969)
Smith, G A (27 Jun 1966)
Smith, G C (3 Apr 1965)
Smith, G H (28 Aug 1966)
Smith, G L (8 Jan 1971)
Smith, G M (28 Jan 1969)
Smith, Herbert E (29 Jul 1966)
Smith, Harding E (3 Jun 1966)
Smith, H H (30 Sep 1968)
Smith, H Lewis (16 May 1966)
Smith, Homer L (20 May 1967)
Smith, H V (5 Mar 1966)
Smith, Hallie W (7/8 Jan 1968)
Smith, Harry W (11 Nov 1969)
Smith, J C (17 Nov 1967)
Smith, J J (2 Oct 1966)
Smith, J L (28 Dec 1970)
Smith, J S (4 Apr 1971)
Smith, L B (12 Jan 1966)
Smith, L L (28 Sep 1972)
Smith, L P (30 May 1968)
Smith, M F (17 Dec 1967)
Smith, N R (6 Sep 1967)
Smith, N W (26 Apr 1966)
Smith, P E (20 Sep 1965)
Smith, R D (30 Oct 1968)
Smith, R E (25 Oct 1967)
Smith, R N, USMC (19 Aug 1969)
Smith, R N, USN (21 Feb 1965)
Smith, R V (23 Feb 1968)
Smith, R W (17 Apr 1970)
Smith, Richard D (11 Mar 1965)
Smith, V A (17 Jan 1969)
Smith, W D (3 Nov 1969)
Smith, W O (18 Jan 1968)
Smith, W P (22 Jun 1966)
Smith, W T (6 Aug 1967)
Smith, W W (23 Jul 1966)
Smits, H (5 Jul 1968)
Smotherman, P R (12 May 1968)
Smyly, D P (19 Nov 1967)
Snead, D L (28 Dec 1969)
Snow, R G (8 May 1969)
Snyder, D (30 Dec 1967)
Snyder, J H (15 Oct 1967)
Snyder, J L (9 Feb 1966)
Snyder, R L (10 May 1967)
Sobolik, K D (26 Nov 1966)
Sobotta, G L (6 Sep 1969)
Somers, R K (25 Feb 1971)
Sommers, C N (18 May 1966)
Sommers, C W (9 May 1966)
Sorensen, J I (31 Dec 1967)
Sornberger, J T (25 May 1970)
Souder, J B (27 Apr 1972)
Southwick, C E (24 Apr 1967, 14 May 1967, 21 May 1967)
Southworth, H B (17 Oct 1965)
Souzon, J P (16 Mar 1970)
Sox, S P (17 Dec 1967)
Spagnola, K L (2 Mar 1965)
Spaith, J A (1 Oct 1968)
Sparks, B R (5 Nov 1967)
Sparks, C P (24 Oct 1964)
Sparks, N (16 Jul 1967)
Spear, P H (24 Dec 1965)
Spearman, D G (2 Jul 1967)
Spelius, W C (17 Jul 1966)
Spence, D E (18 Feb 1972)
Spencer, L H (18 Feb 1966)
Spencer, W A (5 Jul 1972)
Spencer, W R (20/21 Dec 1972)
Spillers, J C (26 Mar 1967)
Spillers, W R (17 Dec 1969)
Spilman, D A (26 Sep 1966)
Spinelli, D A (30 Sep 1968)
Spinler, D J (21 Jun 1967)
Spitz, G R (4/5 Feb 1973)
Sponeybarger, R D (22/23 Dec 1972)
Spoon, D R (21 Jan 1967)
Sprague, S G (12 Sep 1966)
Sprick, D R (24 Jan 1966)
Springston, T (3 Jun 1967)
Sprott, A R (10 Jan 1969)
Squire, B E (12 Jul 1967)
St Pierre, D P (22 May 1968)
Stacey, J S (2 Aug 1969)
Stackhouse, C D (25 Apr 1967)
Stackhouse, J E (13 Sep 1966)
Stafford, H A (31 Aug 1967)
Stafford, R A (29 Mar 1969)
Stafford, R D (20 Nov 1972)
Stair, W T (25 Jan 1967)
Staley, R E (9 May 1968)
Stamm, E A (25 Nov 1968)
Stamm, J (17 Nov 1967)
Standerfer, R G (1 Apr 1969)
Standerwick, R L (3 Feb 1971)
Stanfield, D N (3 Sep 1969)
Stanford, D G (25 May 1969)
Stanford, E L (6 Jul 1966)
Stanley, J T (21 Feb 1966)
Stanley, R W (1 Apr 1967)
Stanley, W T (18 Dec 1971)
Stark, H D (10 Aug 1972)
Stark, W R (19 May 1967)
Starkel, M P (23 Mar 1967)
Starkweather, J F (9 Jun 1967)
Starnes, C G (29 Sep 1967)
Stavast, J E (17 Sep 1967)
Steadman, J E (25/26 Nov 1971)
Stearns, A J (20 Jul 1967)
Stearns, R H (11 Sep 1969)
Steeley, M M (25 Apr 1969)
Steen, M W (31 May 1966)
Steere, R E (19 Jul 1966)
Steffen, A R (26 Nov 1966)
Stegelin, F (18/19 Dec 1972)
Stegemann, W G (26 Jul 1969)
Stegman, T (28 Feb 1968)
Steimer, T J (8 May 1967)
Steinbrunner, D T (20 Jul 1967)
Steincamp, E E (30 Jun 1972)
Steinhauss, A W (12 Sep 1969)
Stell, J R (11 Jan 1966)
Stelter, R (2 Oct 1970)
Stennes, L R (11 Mar 1968)
Stephens, M J (26 Apr 1967)
Stephenson, H D (28 Mar 1972)
Stephenson, M L (29 Apr 1967)
Stephenson, R C (5 Feb 1970)
Stepp, W D (25 Apr 1969)
Sterling, T J (19 Apr 1967)
Stevens, C E (21/22 Dec 1972)
Stevens, J B (8 Oct 1968)
Stevens, L J (14 Feb 1969)
Stevens, P P (11 Jan 1968)
Stevenson, C O (17 Jun 1966)
Stevenson, D L (8 Oct 1969)
Stewart, C E (6 Feb 1970)
Stewart, D D (11 Dec 1965)
Stewart, F E (30 Apr 1969)
Stewart, J W (6 Apr 1971)
Stewart, L J (8 Oct 1966)
Stewart, P J (15 Mar 1966)
Stewart, R A (12 May 1967)
Stewart, V G (17 May 1969)
Stickney, P J (31 May/1 Jun 1966)
Stiglich, M L (8 Oct 1969)
Stiles, J L (20 Jan 1972)
Stine, J M (26 Sep 1966)
Stineman, J N (31 Jan 1966)
Stirling, J B (19 Jan 1967)
Stirm, R L (27 Oct 1967)
Stischer, W M (13 Apr 1968)
Stockdale, J B (9 Sep 1965, 27 Oct 1967)
Stockman, H S (11 Jun 1967)
Stocks, B (19 Nov 1967)
Stoddard, C W (14 Sep 1966)
Stokes, J C (25 Jul 1969)
Stokes, P A (17 Oct 1971)
Stolz, L G (26 Dec 1971)
Stone, C H (2 Feb 1972)
Stone, J B (28 Apr 1967)
Stone, J L (8 Apr 1969)
Stone, M E (2 Oct 1969)
Stone, R E (2 Jul 1967)
Stone, R H (2 May 1970)
Stonebraker, K A (27/28 Oct 1968)
Storey, T G (16 Jan 1967)
Storey, W D (5 Aug 1964)
Stouder, K (18 Feb 1968)
Stovall, D E (10 May 1972)
Stovin, S B (16 Jan 1968)
Stow, L R (26 Apr 1968)
Stowers, A E (21 Mar 1968)
Strahm, J F (4 Jul 1968)
Strahm, P D (14 Jan 1968)
Strasswimmer, R J (26 Mar 1967)
Stratton, C W (3 Jan 1971)
Stratton, R A (5 Jan 1967)
Street, R D (28 Nov 1965)
Stripe, A C (3 Aug 1969)
Strong, H H (25 May 1972)
Strout, R H (17 Dec 1968)
Stroven, W H (27/28 Oct 1968)
Stuart, J F (20/21 Dec 1972)
Stubberfield, R A (6 May 1965)
Stuermver, J F (10 Jul 1971, 22 Jul 1971)
Stutz, L W (2 Dec 1966)
Sullivan, D E (17 Oct 1967)
Sullivan, F J (27 Jun 1972)
Sullivan, J B (21 Jun 1966)
Sullivan, J E (29 Oct 1972)
Sullivan, J V (21 Dec 1965)
Sullivan, M J (12 Feb 1967)
Sullivan, T B (16 Nov 1967)
Sullivan, W K (18 May 1966)
Summers, C M (13 Nov 1965)
Sumpter, T W (14 Jan 1968)
Suprenant, C E (2 Apr 1970)
Surdyk, M G (1 May 1972)
Surwald, M E (17 Sep 1966)
Sutor, J K (15 Dec 1965)
Sutter, F J (31 Dec 1971)
Sutton, W C (28 Jan 1970)
Svanoe, K E (1 Jun 1969)
Swain, J N (12 May 1968)
Swanson, J W (15 Jun 1967)
Swanson, W E (11 Apr 1965)
Sweat, N (6 Oct 1969)
Sweeting, T G (7 May 1970)
Swift, R C (22 Nov 1968)
Swigart, P E (17 Sep 1968, 4 Feb 1969)
Swindle, O G (11 Nov 1966)
Swope, C F (9 Nov 1966)
Swords, S M (30 Dec 1967)
Szeyeller, E P (4 Apr 1967)
Szlapa, J F (15 Dec 1970)
Tabler, R T (26/27 Dec 1972)
Tacke, R L (8 Mar 1969)
Taft, G (8 Jul 1972)
Taft, T E (27 Dec 1972)
Talbot, S S (25 Jun 1969)
Taliaferro, J U (17 May 1965)
Taliferro, G J (2 Aug 1971)
Talken, G F (1 Aug 1969)
Talley, B L (10 Sep 1966)
Talley, J E (1 Jul 1968)
Talley, J S (25 Feb 1971)
Talley, W H (11 May 1972)
Tangeman, R G (5 May 1968)
Tanimoto, M T (24 Jul 1966)
Tannehill, R E (12 Aug 1972)
Tanner, C N (9 Oct 1966)
Tapman, T F (7 Apr 1968)
Tapp, J B (23 Mar 1966)
Tapp, M L (15 May 1966)
Tarre, (6 Aug 1966)
Tasaki, T M (6 Sep 1969)
Tashioglou, (2 May 1972)
Tate, D H (10 Feb 1971)
Tate, L B (29 Mar 1966)
Tatnall, T (12 Oct 1966)
Tatum, L B (10 Sep 1966)
Tavenner, J L (17 Mar 1968)
Taylor, C (24 May 1969)
Taylor, C M (2 Jan 1968)
Taylor, C O (13 Dec 1966)
Taylor, E D (29 Aug 1965)
Taylor, J (27 Sep 1969)
Taylor, J J (17 Nov 1965)
Taylor, M L (7 May 1970)
Taylor, N B (14 Sep 1965)
Taylor, R, USAF (11 Nov 1967)
Taylor, R, USN (23 Mar 1972)
Taylor, R P (14 Oct 1966)
Teague, C (11 Aug 1968)
Teague, F S (31 Aug 1966, 12 Aug 1967)
Teague, J E (19 Nov 1967)
Tebault, B L (4 Jun 1972)
Tebow, W J (26 Oct 1965)
Teeter, R L (28 Dec 1970)
Telshaw, B R (10 May 1968)
Temperley, R E (27 Oct 1967)
Templin, E B (21/22 Jan 1966)
Terhune, J A (9 May 1965, 14 Oct 1965)
Terla, L G T (9 Mar 1970)
Terrell, I D (14 Jan 1968)
Terrill, T (5 Apr 1970)
Terry, C H (27 Jun 1963)
Terry, R R (9 Oct 1966)
Terry, W B (8 Mar 1969)
Tersoly, J B (6 Sep 1969)
Teter, (17 Nov 1967)
Thaete, D K (1 Sep 1968)
Theate, K (16 Nov 1972)
Thies, M (26 Jun 1967)
Thoennes, M W (30 May 1967)
Thomas, A R (18 Aug 1968)
Thomas, C A (11 Jun 1969)
Thomas, D J (14 Oct 1966)
Thomas, D W (5/6 Jul 1971)
Thomas, H E (25 Jun 1965, 13 Aug 1965)
Thomas, J C (8 Sep 1964)
Thomas, J D (20 Oct 1968)
Thomas, J W (21 Sep 1966)
Thomas, K D (23 Mar 1966, (5 May 1966)
Thomas, L T (19 Dec 1971)
Thomas, R (2 Oct 1970)
Thomas, R J (18/19 Dec 1972)
Thomas, R S (22 May 1968)
Thomas, T A (6 Sep 1969)
Thomas, W E (19 May 1972)
Thompson, (14 Jan 1968)
Thompson, B (30 Apr 1967)
Thompson, C T (8/9 Jan 1967)
Thompson, D D (6 Sep 1969)
Thompson, D E (4 Feb 1967)
Thompson, D M (12 Aug 1972)
Thompson, F J (26 Mar 1964)
Thompson, F N (20 Mar 1968)
Thompson, G W (15 May 1966)
Thompson, J K (19 Aug 1966)
Thompson, M C (5/6 Feb 1968)
Thompson, V H (15 Mar 1967)
Thompson, W J (16 Jan 1968, 1 Aug 1968)
Thompson, W M (11 Jan 1969)
Thoresen, D N (11 Jan 1968)
Thorn, J A (10 Jan 1968)
Thornell, E F (10 Sep 1966)
Thornhill, D W (1 Aug 1967)
Thornton, G L (20 Feb 1967)
Thornton, L C (24 Dec 1965)
Thornton, M (2 Apr 1972)
Thorpe, D A (2 Oct 1966)
Thorsness, L K (19 Apr 1967, 30 Apr 1967)
Thum, R C (25 Nov 1968)
Thurman, C F (17 Feb 1968)
Thurman, W E (30 Jan 1967)
Thurn, J J (23 Aug 1968)
Tibbett, C B (20 Nov 1972)
Tibbetts, C E (27 Jul 1969)
Tice, FR (18 Sep 1965)
Tiddy, E (15 Mar 1969)
Tiderman, J M (21 Mar 1966)
Tiffin, R (21 Jul 1966)
Tigner, L M (22 Aug 1972)
Tillotson, T L (3 Apr 1968)
Timm, D (10 May 1972)
Tinker, C (14 Jul 1966)
Tinsley, R E (24 Jul 1966)
Tipping, H A (2 Jul 1968)
Titus, T R (11 Jun 1965)
Todd, L R (26 Apr 1968)
Todd, W A (28 Mar 1972)
Tofferi, C E (20 Oct 1966)
Tolbert, C O (23 Jul 1972, 5 Nov 1972)
Tollett, E G (12 Jan 1966)
Tolliver, T J (18 Sep 1965)
Tomchesson, T J (4/5 May 1968)
Tomes, J H (7 Jul 1966)
Tomlinson, W V (6 Mar 1968)
Toon, J W (13 Aug 1965)
Torkleson, L H (29 Apr 1967)
Tosh, B (14/15 Feb 1968)
Towle, J C (22 Apr 1970)
Townley, E F (4 May 1967)
Townsend, D P (20 Mar 1970)
Townsend, F W (13 Aug 1972)
Townsend, G R (28 Jul 1965)
Townsley, W E (18 Jan 1969)
Tracy, F (21 Jan 1967)
Train, S W (2 Apr 1970)
Tramel, J (18/19 Dec 1972)
Tramel, W O (18 Sep 1965)
Trapp, L E (26 Sep 1971)
Trautman, K W (5 Oct 1967)
Travis, L M (5/6 Feb 1968)
Treece, J A (7 Oct 1966)
Trembley, F G (21 Aug 1967)
Tremper, W F (23 Oct 1967)
Trent, A R (13 May 1970)
Tresemer, G L (14 Mar 1968)
Tribble, D M (14 Sep 1968)
Trickey, J H (26 Nov 1966)
Triebel, T W (27 Aug 1972)
Trier, R D (20 Dec 1965)
Trimble, J R (27 Dec 1972)
Trimble, L A (15 Apr 1972)
Tripp, A L (25 Jul 1968)
Trisco, W H (14 Jan 1968)
Troglen, J W (24 May 1969)
Tromp W L (17 Apr 1966)
Trowbridge, D C (26 Dec 1969)
Troyer, J M (6 Dec 1966)
Truesdale, S E (12 Apr 1963)
Tschudy, W M (18 Jul 1965)
Tucci, R L (11 Nov 1969)
Tucker, E B (24 Apr 1967)
Tucker, J H (25 Apr 1966)
Tucker, T A (31 Aug 1966)
Tucker, T M (24 Dec 1971)
Tuft, M L (6 Apr 1967, 8 May 1967)
Tullo, F J (27 Jul 1965)
Tully, W B (5 Nov 1962)
Tunnell, J W (20 Jun 1966)
Turley, M D (13 Jan 1967)
Turner, A A (25 May 1968)
Turner, E O (22 Oct 1966)
Turner, J (9 Mar 1966)
Turner, J M (26/27 Dec 1972)
Turner, M D (4 Sep 1967)
Turner, S (18/19 Dec 1972)
Turner, T M (13 Dec 1968)
Turose, M S (17 Sep 1972)
Tushek, G K (17 Jul 1972)
Tutor, R D (15 Nov 1969)
Twaddell, J W (25 May 1972)
Tye, D M (25 Nov 1969)
Tye, M J (2 Oct 1969)
Tyler, C R (23 Aug 1967)
Tyler, G E (24 Oct 1968)
Tyree, W E (9 Jun 1967)
Tyrell, L D (9 May 1968)
Tyszkiewicz, A K (14 Jan 1967)
Uffley, R D (10 Sep 1968)
Uhls, W G (29 Jan 1970)
Ulicsni, M J (8 Sep 1964)
Unckrich, W F (10 Oct 1969)
Underwood, P G (16 Mar 1966)
Unger, D L (3 May 1972)

Utly, R K (25 Jan 1969)
Uyeyama, T J (18 May 1968)
Vadyak, A (25 Jun 1969)
Vampatella, P (21 Jun 1966, 18 Aug 1966)
Van Buren, G G (28/29 Dec 1967)
Van Cleave, W S (22 Apr 1969)
Van Loan, J L (20 May 1967)
Van Orden, E W (19 Nov 1967)
Van Renselaar, L J (30 Sep 1968)
Van Vliet, H E (20 Oct 1968)
Vanbrunt, R S (6 Apr 1970)
Vance, J D (12 Aug 1972)
Vandeventer, J W (23 Apr 1967)
Vandyke, R H (11 Sep 1968)
Vangelisti, J (27 Apr 1970)
Vanhorn, S L (16 Dec 1967)
Vanhorne, D W (19 Feb 1970)
Vanpelt, A M (4 Jan 1967)
Vanwagenen, M D (5 Jul 1972)
Vaquera, R A (2 Aug 1969)
Vasiliadis, C C (3 May 1967)
Vasser, N C (21 Apr 1968)
Vaughan, J L (8 Jul 1972)
Vaughan, R R (14 Oct 1967)
Vaughan, S R (18 Dec 1971)
Vavroch, D P (26/27 Dec 1972)
Veach, C L (1 Apr 1969)
Venables, R K (20 Jan 1972)
Venanzi, G S (17 Sep 1967)
Vendevelde, K (20 Sep 1965)
Verhees, D L (13 Apr 1968)
Verich, D A (18 Aug 1966, 16 Jul 1967)
Vermilya, R S (31 Aug 1966)
Vermilyea, D W (15 Jun 1966)
Vescelius, M J (21 Sep 1967)
Vette, A R (12 Feb 1967)
Vettergren, E H (23 Mar 1967)
Vickers, E J (6 Sep 1969)
Vickers, G (18/19 Dec 1972)
Villeponteaux, J H (11 May 1966)
Vinapuu, J W (27 Sep 1968)
Vincent, H R (30 Sep 1971)
Vincent, R W (1 Jul 1972)
Vinson, B G (24 Apr 1968)
Viscasillas, P A (8 Oct 1966)
Vissotzky, R W (19 Nov 1967)
Vizcarra, V (6 Nov 1969)
Vlahakos, P G (1 Feb 1966)
Vlisides, G F (27 Jan 1965)
Vogel, H R (14 Jun 1968)
Vogel, R D (22 May 1967)
Vogt, J (10 May 1972)
Vogt, L F (17 Sep 1965)
Vohden, R A (3 Apr 1965)
Voigts, R S (24 May 1972)
Vollmer, A C (13 Jan 1965, 17 Aug 1967)
Volloy, G R (11 May 1972)
Voris, R E (24 Jun 1970)
Vrablick, M S (1 Oct 1970)
Wack, C G (7 Nov 1965)
Wackerfuss, R W (4/5 May 1968)
Waddell, D W (5 Jul 1967)
Wade, B S (12 Aug 1971)
Wade, Barton S (21/22 Dec 1972)
Wadsworth, D A (8 Oct 1963)
Wagener, D R (20 Oct 1966)
Waggoner, R F (12 Sep 1966)
Wagner, D L (17 May 1972)
Walbridge, J S (28 Feb 1967)
Waldron, K M (14/15 Feb 1968)
Waldrop, D (23 Aug 1967, 14 May 1968)
Walker, B C (7Apr 1972)
Walker, H (5 Nov 1967)
Walker, H C (14 Jan 1968)
Walker, K E (2 Oct 1964)
Walker, L F (31 Jan 1967)
Walker, M S (15 Jul 1969)
Walker, P N (21 Oct 1968)
Walker, R M (6 Dec 1968)
Walker, R P (25 Feb 1966)
Walker, S F (13 Dec 1968)
Walker, T T (7 Apr 1966)
Walkup, R E (5 Oct 1968)
Wall, G M (22 Apr 1970)
Wall, J M (17/18 May 1966)
Wallace, C F (28 Aug 1967)
Wallace, H M (18 Jan 1968)
Wallace, M W (28 Mar 1968)
Waller, T M (3 Feb 1966)
Wallerstedt, J R (4 Jan 1973)
Walling, C M (8 Aug 1966)

Walling, L M (11 Feb 1962)
Walmsley, R A (20 Jul 1966)
Walsh, B (27 Feb 1968)
Walsh, F A (21/22 Dec 1972)
Walsh, J P (26 Sep 1972)
Walsh, R A (15 Feb 1969)
Walsh, T C (10 Sep 1966)
Walsh, T H (27 Aug 1966)
Walster, T G (9 Apr 1966)
Walters, D K (20/21 Dec 1972)
Walters, G E (18 Sep 1965)
Walters, J (19 May 1967)
Walters, T L (9 Mar 1969)
Waltman, D G (19 Sep 1966)
Waltz, B L (21 Nov 1964)
Wangeman, C E (26 Mar 1965)
Wanless, D M (23 Aug 1969)
Wanner, C J (18 May 1969)
Wanzel, C J (28 Mar 1972)
Ward, B H (27/28 Dec 1972)
Ward, N C (12 Jun 1969)
Ward, R J (18/19 Dec 1972)
Ward, T J (12 Aug 1972)
Wardlaw, R W (17 May 1968)
Warner, D A (20 Jan 1971)
Warner, J H (13 Oct 1967)
Warrell, G W (28 Nov 1969)
Warren, A L (5 Dec 1966)
Warren, E (3 Jun 1966)
Warren, G D (25 Oct 1969)
Warren, T R (15 Jan 1970)
Washburn, L E (17 Jun 1966)
Waters, D D (24 Feb 1971)
Waters, S E (13 Dec 1966)
Watson, D D (31 Jul 1965)
Watson, F P (18 Jun 1965)
Watson, H A (29 Nov 1970)
Watts, J G (22 Sep 1972)
Waugh, G R (10 Aug 1970)
Wax, D J (20 Dec 1965)
Waxman, S (29 Sep 1966)
Wayne, S A (10 Mar 1967, (25 Jan 1969)
Weatherby, J W (29 Jul 1965)
Weaver, D J (17 Feb 1969)
Weaver, E G (8 Oct 1967)
Weaver, J H (16 Jan 1969)
Webb, R J (11 Jun 1967)
Webb, T R (19 Dec 1969)
Weber, J (12 Mar 1968, 24 Jun 1968)
Weber, R M (25 Jun 1966)
Webster, C R (21 Apr 1968)
Wecker, H H (1 Sep 1969)
Weedon, R E (30 Jun 1965)
Weeks, T P (10 Jul 1966)
Weger, J (22 Oct 1965)
Weichman, D R (11 Jan 1968)
Weimorts, R F (22 Apr 1966)
Weinal, T R (3 Jul 1969)
Weisman, K F (25/26 Apr 1972)
Weissmueller, C E (12 Feb 1967)
Weitkamp, E W (23 Mar 1961)
Welch, (17 Nov 1968)
Welch, E J (26 Dec 1969)
Welch, H G (20 Apr 1966)
Welch, R J (16 Jan 1967)
Welch, R M (2 Oct 1968)
Weller, G E (26 Nov 1972)
Wellman, D A (21 Oct 1968)
Wellons, P R (17 Aug 1970)
Wells, G (2 Aug 1969)
Wells, H G (27 Feb 1968)
Wells, K R (18 Dec 1971)
Wells, N E (10 Mar 1967)
Wells, N L (21 Aug 1966, 29 Aug 1966)
Welshan, J T (3 Mar 1968)
Wenaas, G J (28/29 Dec 1967)
Wendell, J H (7 Aug 1966)
Wensinger, R R (19 Oct 1968)
Werner, W C (6 Sep 1969)
Weskamp, R L (25 Apr 1967)
West, D (19/20 Jun 1968)
West, J B (29 Jul 1967)
West, J T (2 Jan 1970)
Westbrook, D E (13 Mar 1968)
Westenbarger, D P (1 Nov 1965, 14 Mar 1966)
Westerman, J P (30 Mar 1970)
Westerman, W R (27 Apr 1966)
Western, R W (12 Jun 1967)
Westfall, G H (3 Mar 1972)
Westfall, R L (11 Feb 1962)
Westin, B E (27 Apr 1966)

Weston, O B (23 Mar 1961)
Westphal, C D (20 Nov 1972)
Westwood, N P (17 May 1970)
Wetzel, W (20 Sep 1965)
Weyandt, I G (20 Jul 1967)
Whalen, P E (27/28 Dec 1972)
Wheat, B V (1 Nov 1965)
Wheat, D R (17 Oct 1965)
Wheeler, E L (21 Apr 1970)
Wheeler, G L (8 Mar 1969)
Wheeler, H C (22 Nov 1969)
Wheeler, J A (18 Apr 1965)
Wheeler, J B (10 Jan 1969)
Wheeler, R C (10 Jul 1971)
Wheeler, R L (2 Oct 1966)
Whellern, K R (21 Nov 1965)
Whinery, C E (21 Apr 1970)
Whipple, J D (2 Jun 1966)
Whitcomb, D (29 Jun 1972)
White, D E (31 Mar 1969)
White, E (24 Nov 1969)
White, J B (24 Nov 1969)
White, J D (3 Aug 1969)
White, J P (6 Oct 1972)
White, L F (6 Jan 1966)
White, M F (22 Oct 1968)
White, R E (10 Feb 1968)
Whitehill, D H (23 May 1968)
Whitesides, (23 Nov 1966)
Whitesides, R L (26 Mar 1964)
Whitford, L W (1 Nov 1969)
Whitt, J E (23 Mar 1972)
Whitteker, R L (27 Mar 1968)
Whittemore, F H (20 Jul 1967, 11 Apr 1968)
Wichman, R E (9 Nov 1968)
Wicker, C E (25 Jul 1968)
Wickham, D W (17 Dec 1965)
Wickline, G (3/4 Jan 1973)
Widdis, J W (22 Mar 1969)
Wideman, R E (6 May 1967)
Widerquist, T C (3 May 1972)
Widon, K H (11 Jan 1968)
Wiechert, R C (16 Nov 1968)
Wiehr, R D (21 Jan 1973)
Wieland, C T (18/19 Dec 1972)
Wieland, D E (8 Oct 1967)
Wier, H D (2 Jan 1971, 19 Jul 1972)
Wiesneth, R P (11 Sep 1969)
Wiggins, W L (3 Feb 1968)
Wilbanks, H A (24 Feb 1967)
Wilber, W E (13 Oct 1967, 16 Jun 1968)
Wilbrecht, K M (7 Jun 1970)
Wilburn, S F (26 Aug 1968, 19 Oct 1968)
Wilburn, W H (4 Feb 1967)
Wildfang, H (10 Feb 1968)
Wiles, C J (5 Mar 1969)
Wiles, M B C (6 May 1972)
Wiles, T (7 Jan 1973)
Wiley, F D (4 Mar 1967)
Wiley, J D (3 Aug 1967)
Wiley, P J (6 Sep 1969)
Wilhelm, F (11 Sep 1969)
Wilke, R F (17 Jan 1968)
Wilkensen, L R (8 Dec 1966)
Wilkes, S B (27 Apr 1965)
Wilkins, G H (10 Jul 1966)
Wilkinson, D E (10 May 1972)
Wilkinson, J E (8/9 Jan 1968)
Wilkinson, T R (17 May 1972, 29 Jan 1973)
Willard, J (25 Jun 1968)
Willett, D A (9 Jun 1968)
Willett, R V (16 Apr 1969)
Williams, B J (9 Dec 1972)
Williams, B R (18 Mar 1968)
Williams, Bruce R (26 Apr 1967)
Williams, C E (23 Jul 1968)
Williams, C N (24/25 Nov 1966)
Williams, D B (3 May 1972)
Williams, D R (1 Apr 1967)
Williams, D S (23 Aug 1967)
Williams, H K (18 Mar 1968)
Williams, J E (15 May 1966)
Williams, J N (31 Jan 1969)
Williams, J R (28/29 Dec 1967)
Williams, J V (7 Oct 1970)
Williams, J W (20 May 1972)
Williams, L (25 Jan 1966)
Williams, L I (29 Mar 1968)
Williams, N C (11 Jun 1965)
Williams, R (21/22 Dec 1972)
Williams, Ray C (1 Sep 1969)

Williams, Robert C (1 Jul 1966)
Williamson, D I (6 Jul 1965)
Williamson, J C (18 May 1969)
Williamson, R (20 May 1970)
Williford, J V (9 May 1969)
Wilson, A D (18 Apr 1966)
Wilson, A R (17/18 May 1966)
Wilson, C D (14 Dec 1966)
Wilson, D (23 Mar 1967)
Wilson, D W (16 Mar 1970)
Wilson, F (2 Oct 1970)
Wilson, G H (7 Aug 1967)
Wilson, G R (14 May 1967)
Wilson, G S (22 Nov 1966)
Wilson, H K (18/19 Dec 1972)
Wilson, J G (14 Jan 1969)
Wilson, J R (31 Aug 1968)
Wilson, L E (11 Aug 1965)
Wilson, R A (18 Jun 1972)
Wilson, R E (11 Jun 1972)
Wilson, R W (23 Jun 1965)
Wilson, W B (8 May 1965)
Wilson, W W (22/23 Dec 1972)
Wimbrow, N J (26/27 Dec 1972)
Winborn, S R (14 May 1967)
Windle, P R (30 Jun 1965)
Windsor, D W (28 Apr 1971)
Wingert, C J (27 Aug 1969)
Winkels, D W (16 Apr 1969)
Winn, D W (15 Apr 1968, 9 Aug 1968)
Winningham, J Q (21/22 Dec 1972)
Winstead, E R (20 Jun 1966)
Winston, C C (1 Aug 1967)
Winters, D G (19 Jul 1966)
Winters, J C (25 Jul 1966)
Wise, J C (23 Dec 1965)
Wisely, H D (24 Apr 1967, 21 May 1967)
Wistrand, R C (9 May 1965)
Witt, M B (13 Apr 1967)
Witte, R E (18 Jun 1971)
Wittenberg, R R (28 Feb 1970)
Witterman, B H (2 Jun 1966)
Wittkopp, V G (14 Apr 1966)
Wohrer, J F (26 Jul 1969)
Wolf, (18 Aug 1969)
Wolfe, D F (8 Oct 1967)
Wolfe, T H (28 Jun 1966)
Wolff, A E (31 May 1967)
Wolfkeil, W B (9 Aug 1968)
Woloszyk, D J (1 Mar 1966)
Wonn, J C (17 Feb 1968)
Wood, B T (18 Jul 1967)
Wood, C H (14 Aug 1967)
Wood, D C (16 Jan 1966)
Wood, D F (1 Apr 1968)
Wood, J W (17 Aug 1970)
Wood, P H (6 Feb 1967)
Wood, R S (2 Jun 1967)
Wood, W A (3 Nov 1966)
Wood, W C (2 Sep 1972)
Wood, W E (21 Apr 1971)
Wood, W S (2 May 1966)
Woodcock, G E (11 Dec 1966)
Woods, B (23 Sep 1968)
Woods, B D (17 Sep 1968)
Woods, C J (28 Sep 1965)
Woods, J C (19 Oct 1969)
Woods, L (24 Oct 1964)
Woods, R D (12 Oct 1966)
Woods, R F (26 Jun 1968)
Woodson, R E (1 Aug 1967)
Woodworth, S A (17 Apr 1965)
Woolcock, T E (25 Jan 1968)
Worcester, J B (19 Oct 1965)
Workman, A L (2 Oct 1966)
Worley, R F (23 Jul 1968)
Worrell, P L (2 Dec 1966)
Worst, K E (2 Mar 1966)
Wortham, M L (30 Dec 1967)
Wozniak, F J (17 Jan 1967)
Wranosky, R W (7 Dec 1965)
Wright, D I (13 Nov 1970)
Wright, D J (28 Sep 1968)
Wright, D L (24 Nov 1969)
Wright, D P (7 Jan 1968)
Wright, F W (10 Nov 1972)
Wright, G G (17 Jan 1967)
Wright, G T (19 Dec 1969)
Wright, H V (27 Mar 1969)
Wright, J A (5 Mar 1966)
Wright, J J (2 Nov 1967)

Wright, J L (8 Apr 1970)
Wright, J M (15 Jun 1968)
Wright, L P (22 Nov 1969)
Wright, M (12 Aug 1970, 20 Jun 1972)
Wright, T T (27 Feb 1968)
Wright, W C (2 Oct 1967)
Writer, L D (15 Feb 1968)
Wrye, B C (12 Aug 1966)
Wyatt, E W (27 Jul 1969)
Wyatt, W R (21 Jan 1967)
Wycoff, W J (16 Mar 1970)
Wyman, D (14 Jul 1966)
Wynder, E O (1 Apr 1968)
Wynne, P E (8 Aug 1966)
Xavier, A M (9 Mar 1966)
Yahanda, A M (14 May 1969)
Yarborough, W P (19 Jan 1967)
Yates, D L (7 May 1970)
Yates, M (12 Sep 1969)
Yeend, R C (9 Jun 1968)
Yeingst, P J (12 Feb 1967)
Yoakum, D K (26 Jun 1972)
Yonke, W D (7 Jul 1972)
York, G (18 Jul 1967)
Yost, D A (10 Jan 1968)
Young, B B (28 Mar 1972)
Young, J F (6 Jun 1968)
Young, J K (8 Dec 1966)
Young, M A (12 Oct 1972)
Young, S N (7 Mar 1967)
Young, T (25 Feb 1970)
Youngblood, (20 Oct 1966)
Youngs, J M (6 Dec 1967)
Youtsey, R D (25 Jan 1966)
Yoximer, A G (1 Apr 1968)
Yuill, J H (21/22 Dec 1972)
Yurewicz, S J (30 Nov 1967)
Zahm, J E (4 Jun 1970)
Zavocky, J J (25 Aug 1967)
Zesinger, G R (1 Oct 1969)
Ziaseker, A R (18 Jul 1968)
Ziegler, G L (23 Feb 1967)
Ziehe, G D (20 Oct 1968)
Zimmer, J A (29 Aug 1969)
Zissu, A G (8 Oct 1967)
Zock, R (3 Apr 1968)
Zook, D H (4 Oct 1967)
Zook, H J (31 May/1 Jun 1966)
Zorn, T O (17 Sep 1972)
Zuberbuhler, R V (12 Sep 1972)
Zucker, L C (20 Mar 1968)
Zuhoski, C P (31 Jul 1967)
Zukowski, R J (11 Feb 1969)
Zumbrun, J H (10 Jan 1970)

Bibliography

Books and Monographs

The 388th Tactical Fighter Wing at Korat Royal Thai Air Force Base 1972: Don Logan; Schiffer Publishing, Atglen, PA, 1995.

Aces and Aerial Victories - The United States Air Force in Southeast Asia 1965-1973: R Frank Futrell et al; Office of Air Force History, Washington, DC, 1976.

Air Base Defense in the Republic of Vietnam 1961-1973: Roger P Fox; Office of Air Force History, Washington, DC, 1979.

Air Force Bases Volume I - Active Air Forces Bases Within the United States of America on 17 September 1982: Robert Mueller; Office of Air Force History, Washington, DC, 1989.

Air Force Combat Wings - Lineage and Honors Histories 1947-1977: Charles A Ravenstein; Office of Air Force History, Washington, DC, 1984.

Air Force Heroes in Vietnam - USAF Southeast Asia Monograph Series Volume VII, Monograph 9: Maj Donald K Schneider; Air War College, Maxwell AFB, AL, 1979.

Airpower and the Airlift Evacuation of Kham Duc - USAF Southeast Asia Monograph Series Volume V, Monograph 7: Lt Col Alan L Gropman; Office of Air Force History, Washington, DC, 1985.

Air Power and the Fight for Khe Sanh: Bernard C Nalty; Office of Air Force History, Washington, DC, 1973.

Airpower and the 1972 Spring Invasion: Office of Air Force History, Washington, DC, date unknown.

Air War Hanoi: Robert F Dorr; Blandford Press, London, 1988.

Air War in Vietnam: Phil Chinnery; Bison Books/Hamlyn, London, 1987.

Air War Over North Vietnam – The Vietnamese Peoples' Air Force 1949-1977: Istvan Toperczer; Squadron/Signal Publications, Carrollton, Tex, 1998.

Alpha Strike Vietnam - The Navy's Air War, 1964 to 1973: Jeffrey L Levinson; Presidio Press, Novato, CA, 1989.

And Kill MiGs - Air to Air Combat from Vietnam to the Gulf War: Lou Drendel; Squadron/Signal Publications, Carrollton, Tex, 1997.

Apollo's Warriors - US Air Force Special Operations During the Cold War: Col Michael E Haas; Air University Press, Maxwell AFB, AL, 1997.

Archie, Flak, AAA and SAM - A Short Operational History of Ground-based Air Defense: Kenneth P Werrell; Air University Press, Maxwell AFB, AL, 1988.

Barrel Roll 1968-73 - An Air Campaign in Support of National Policy: Col Perry L Lamy; Air University Press, Maxwell AFB, AL, 1996.

Boeing B-52 Stratofortress: Peter E Davies and Tony Thornborough; Crowood Press, Marlborough, 1998.

The Boeing C-135 Series: Stratotanker, Stratolifter and Other Variants: Don Logan; Schiffer Publishing, Atglen, PA, 1998.

Boeing KC-135 Stratotanker - More Than Just a Tanker: Robert S Hopkins; Midland Publishing, Earl Shilton, 1997.

Boeing's Cold War Warrior - B-52 Stratofortress: Robert F Dorr and Lindsay Peacock; Osprey Aerospace, London, 1995.

The C-130 Hercules - Tactical Airlift Missions 1956-1975: Sam McGowan; TAB Books, Blue Ridge Summit, PA, 1988.

Captain Hook - A Pilot's Tragedy and Triumph in the Vietnam War: Capt Wynn F Foster; Naval Institute Press, Annapolis, MD, 1992.

Carrier Air Group Commanders – The Men and their Machines: Robert L Lawson; Schiffer Publishing, Atglen, PA, 2000.

Check Six - A Fighter Pilot Looks Back: Major General F C Blesse; Champlin Fighter Museum Press, Mesa, AZ, 1987.

Clashes - Air Combat Over North Vietnam 1965-1972: Marshall L Michel; Naval Institute Press, Annapolis, MD, 1997.

Code Name Bright Light - The Untold Story of US POW Rescue Efforts During the Vietnam War: George J Veith; Free Press, New York, 1988.

Code of Honor: Lt Col John A Dramesi; W W Norton, New York, 1975.

A Code to Keep: Ernie Brace; St Martin's Press, New York, NY, 1988.

Convair F-102 Delta Dagger - A Photo Chronicle: Wayne Mutza; Schiffer Publishing, Atglen, PA, 1999.

The Cold War and Beyond - Chronology of the United States Air Force, 1947-1997: Frederick J Shaw and Timothy Warnock; Air Force History and Museums Program, Washington, DC, 1997.

Crusader! - Last of the Gunfighters: Rear Admiral Paul T Gillchrist; Schiffer Publishing, Atglen, PA, 1995.

Development and Employment of Fixed-wing Gunships 1962-1972 – The United States Air Force in Southeast Asia: Jack S Ballard; Office of Air Force History, Washington, DC, 1982.

Dictionary of American Naval Aviation Squadrons, Volume 1 – The History of VA, VAH, VAK, VAL, VAP and VFA Squadrons: Roy A Grossnick; Naval Historical Centre, Department of the Navy, Washington, DC, 1995.

Dictionary of American Naval Aviation Squadrons, Volume 2 - The History of VP, VPB, VP(HL) and VP(AM) Squadrons: Roy A Grossnick; Naval Historical Centre, Department of the Navy, Washington, DC, 1999.

Douglas A-1 Skyraider: Robert F Dorr; Osprey Publishing, London, 1989.

Douglas A-3 Skywarrior (Aerograph 5): Rene Francillon and Edward Heinemann; Aerofax, Arlington, Tex, 1987.

Douglas A-4 Skyhawk: Peter Kilduff; Osprey Publishing, London, 1983.

The Douglas DC-3 and its Predecessors: J M G Gradidge; Air-Britain, Tonbridge, 1984.

F-8 Crusader Units of the Vietnam War (Osprey Combat Aircraft 12): Peter Mersky; Osprey Publishing, London, 1998.

F-111 Aardvark: Peter E Davies and Anthony M Thornborough; Crowood Press, Marlborough, 1997.

Fast Movers - America's Jet Pilots and the Vietnam Experience: John Darrell Sherwood; Free Press, New York, NY, 1999.

Foreign Invaders - The Douglas Invader in Foreign Military and US Clandestine Service: Don Hagedorn and Leif Hellstrom; Midland Publishing, Earl Shilton, 1994.

Fox Two - The Story of America's First Ace in Vietnam: Randy Cunningham and Jeff Ethell; Champlin Fighter Museum, Mesa, AZ, 1984.

Going Downtown - The War Against Hanoi and Washington: Jack Broughton; Orion Books, New York, 1988.

Gold Wings, Blue Sea - A Naval Aviator's Story: Capt Rosario Rausa; Naval Institute Press, Annapolis, MD, 1980.

Gray Ghosts – US Navy and Marine Corps Phantoms: Peter E Davies; Schiffer Publishing, Atglen, PA, 2000.

Great Naval Disasters - US Naval Accidents in the 20th Century: Kit Bonner and Carolyn Bonner; MBI Publishing, Osceola, WI, 1998.

Grumman A-6 Intruder: Robert F Dorr; Osprey Publishing, London, 1987.

Grumman A-6 Intruder/Prowler (Modern Combat Aircraft 26): Anthony M Thornborough & Peter E Davies; Ian Allan, Shepperton, 1987.

Grumman Albatross - A History of the Legendary Seaplane: Wayne Mutza; Schiffer Publishing, Atglen, PA, 1996.

Herbicidal Warfare - The Ranch Hand Project in Vietnam: Pail Frederick Cecil; Praeger, New York, NY, 1986.

A History of Marine Attack Squadron 223: 1Lt Brett A Jones; History and Museums Division, HQ US Marine Corps, Washington, DC, 1978.

A History of Marine Attack Squadron 311: Maj William J Sambito; History and Museums Division, HQ US Marine Corps, Washington, DC, 1978.

A History of Marine Fighter Attack Squadron 115: Capt John C Chapin; History and Museums Division, HQ US Marine Corps, Washington, DC, 1988.

A History of Marine Fighter Attack Squadron 232: Maj William J Sambito; History and Museums Division, HQ US Marine Corps, Washington, DC, 1978.

A History of Marine Fighter Attack Squadron 312: Maj William J Sambito; History and Museums Division, HQ US Marine Corps, Washington, DC, 1978.

A History of Marine Fighter Attack Squadron 323: Col Gerald R Pitzl; History and Museums Division, HQ US Marine Corps, Washington, DC, 1987.

A History of Marine Medium Helicopter Squadron 161: Lt Col Gary W Parker; History and Museums Division, HQ US Marine Corps, Washington, DC, 1978.

A History of Marine Observation Squadron 6: Lt Col Gary W Parker and Maj Frank M Batha; History and Museums Division, HQ US Marine Corps, Washington, DC, 1982.

Hit my smoke! Forward Air Controllers in Southeast Asia: Jan Churchill; Sunflower University Press, Manhattan, KS, 1997.

Honor Bound - The History of American Prisoners of War in Southeast Asia, 1961-1973: Stuart I Rochester and Frederick Kiley; Office of the Secretary of Defense, Washington, DC, 1998.

Interdiction in Southern Laos 1960-1968 - The United States Air Force in Southeast Asia: Jacob Van Staaveren; Center for Air Force History, Washington, DC, 1993.

Jane's Land-based Air Defence 1997-1998: Tony Cullen and Christopher F Foss; Jane's Information Group, Coulsdon, 1997.

Kaman H-43 - An Illustrated History: Wayne Mutza; Schiffer Publishing, Atglen, PA, 1998.

Life on the Line - Stories of Vietnam Air Combat: Philip D Chinnery; Blandford Press, London, 1988.

Linebacker II - A Strategic and Tactical Case Study: Lt Col Leonard D G Teixeira; Air War College Research Report, USAF Air University, Maxwell AFB, AL, 1990.

Linebacker II - A View from the Rock - USAF Southeast Asia Monograph Series Volume VI, Monograph 8: Brig Gen James R McCarthy and Col Robert E Rayfield; Office of Air Force History, Washington, DC, 1985.

The Linebacker Raids – The Bombing of North Vietnam, 1972: John T Smith; Cassell, London, 2000.

The Lockheed Constellation Series: Peter J Marson; Air-Britain (Historians), Tonbridge, 1982.

Lockheed SR-71 - The Secret Missions Exposed: Paul F Crickmore; Osprey Aerospace, London, 1997.

The Lovable One-iner - A Complete History of the Cessna L-19 Birddog: Minard D Thompson; Turner Publishing, Paducah, KY, 1998.

Magic 100 - An F-105 Fighter Pilot's 100 Combat Missions in Vietnam: Brig Gen Al Lenski; Turner Publishing, Paducah, KY, 1995.

Martin B-57 Canberra - The Complete Record: Robert C Mikesh; Schiffer Publishing, Atglen, PA, 1995.

McDonnell F-101 Voodoo: Robert F Dorr; Osprey Publishing, London, 1987.

Military Aviation Disasters - Significant Losses Since 1908: David Gero; Patrick Stephens, Sparkford, 1999.

Mosquitoes to Wolves - The Evolution of the Airborne Forward Air Controller: Gary Robert Lester; Air University Press, Maxwell AFB, AL, 1997.

The Naval Air War in Vietnam: Peter B Mersky and Norman Polmar; Nautical and Aviation Publishing Company, Annapolis, MD, 1981.

North American F-100 Super Sabre: David A Anderton; Osprey Publishing, London, 1987.

On Yankee Station - The Naval Air War over Vietnam: Cdr John B Nichols; United States Naval Institute Press, Annapolis, MD, 1987.

Once a Fighter Pilot...: Brig Gen Jerry W Cook; McGraw-Hill, New York, NY, 1996.

One Day too Long - Top Secret Site 85 and the Bombing of North Vietnam: Timothy N Castle; Columbia University Press, New York, 1999.

100 Missions North: Kenneth H Bell; Brassey's (US), McLean, VA, 1993.

One Day in a Long War: May 10, 1972 Air War, North Vietnam: Jeffrey Ethell and Alfred Price; Guild Publishing, London, 1990.

Operation Ranch Hand - The Air Force and Herbicides in Southeast Asia 1961-1971: William A Buckingham; Office of Air Force History, Washington, DC, 1982.

Over the Beach - The Air War in Vietnam: Zalin Grant; W W Norton, New York, NY, 1986.

Pak Six - A Story of the War in the Skies of North Vietnam: Gene I Basel; Jove Publications, New York, NY, 1987.

The Phantom Story: Anthony M Thornborough and Peter E Davies; Arms and Armour Press, London, 1994.

Planting the Seeds of SEAD - The Wild Weasel in Vietnam: Maj William A Hewitt; Air University Press, Maxwell AFB, AL, 1993.

Prisoner of War – Six Years in Hanoi: John M McGrath; Naval Institute Press, Annapolis, MD, 1975.

The Raid: Benjamin F Schemmer; Harper and Row, New York, NY, 1976.

Republic F-105 Thunderchief: David Anderton; Osprey Publishing, London, 1983.

The Rescue of Bat 21: Darrel D Whitcomb; Naval Institute Press, Annapolis, MD, 1998.

RF-8 Crusader Units over Cuba and Vietnam (Osprey Combat Aircraft 12): Peter Mersky; Osprey Publishing, London, 1999.

River Rats - Red River Valley Fighter Pilots: Gardner Hatch and Patti Sheridan (editors); Turner Publishing, Paducah, KY, 1989.

Roll Call: Thud - A Photographic Record of the F-105 Thunderchief: John M Campbell and Michael Hill; Schiffer Publishing, Atglen, PA, 1996.

Rolling Thunder: John T Smith; Air Research Publications, Walton on Thames, 1994.

SAC Tanker Operations in the Southeast Asia War: Charles K Hopkins; Office of the Historian, Headquarters Strategic Air Command, Offutt AFB, NB, 1979.

Search and Rescue in Southeast Asia: Earl H Tilford; Center for Air Force History, Washington, DC, 1992.

The Secret Vietnam War - The United States Air Force in Thailand, 1961-1975: Jeffrey D Glasser; McFarland and Co, Jefferson, NC, 1995.

Sir James Martin - The Authorised Biography of the Martin-Baker Ejection Seat Pioneer: Sarah Sharman; Patrick Stephens, Sparkford, 1996 (An appendix lists ejections from US aircraft in Southeast Asia using Martin-Baker seats).

Six Years in Hell - A Returned Vietnam POW Views Captivity, Country and the Future: Lt Col Jay R Jensen; POW, Orcutt, CA, 1974.

Snakes in the Eagle's Nest - A History of Ground Attacks on Air Bases: Alan Vick; RAND Corporation, Santa Monica, CA, 1995.

Spies and Commandos – How America Lost the Secret War in North Vietnam: Kenneth Conboy and Dale Andrade; University Press of Kansas, Lawrence, KS, 2000.

Tactical Airlift - The United States Air Force in Southeast Asia: Ray L Bowers; Office of Air Force History, Washington, DC, 1983.

Tail Code - The Complete History of USAF Tactical Aircraft Tail Code Markings: Patrick Martin; Schiffer Publishing, Atglen, PA, 1994.

The Tale of Two Bridges and the Battle for the Skies over North Vietnam - USAF Southeast Asia Monograph Series Volume I, Monographs 1 and 2: Maj A J C Lavalle (ed); Office of Air Force History, Washington, DC, 1985.

Tonkin Gulf Yacht Club – US Carrier Operations off Vietnam: Rene J Francillon; Conway Maritime Press, London, 1988.

The United States Air Force in Southeast Asia - The Advisory Years to 1965: Robert F Futrell and Martin Blumenson; Office of Air Force History, Washington, DC, 1981.

US Marines in Vietnam - The Advisory and Combat Assistance Era 1954-1964: Capt Robert H Whitlow; History and Museums Division, HQ US Marine Corps, Washington, DC, 1977.

US Marines in Vietnam - The Landing and the Build-up 1965: Jack Shulimson and Maj Charles M Johnson; History and Museums Division, HQ US Marine Corps, Washington, DC, 1978.

US Marines in Vietnam - An Expanding War 1966: Jack Shulimson; History and Museums Division, HQ US Marine Corps, Washington, DC, 1982.

US Marines in Vietnam - Fighting the North Vietnamese 1967: Maj Gary L Telfer, Lt Col Lane Rogers and V Keith Fleming; History and Museums Division, HQ US Marine Corps, Washington, DC, 1984.

US Marines in Vietnam - The Defining Year 1968: Jack Shulimson, Lt Col Leonard A Blasiol, Charles R Smith and Capt David A Dawson; History and Museums Division, HQ US Marine Corps, Washington, DC, 1997.

US Marines in Vietnam - High Mobility and Standdown 1969: Charles R Smith; History and Museums Division, HQ US Marine Corps, Washington, DC, 1988.

US Marines in Vietnam - Vietnamization and Redeployment 1970-1971: Graham A Cosmas and Lt Col Terrence P Murray; History and Museums Division, HQ US Marine Corps, Washington, DC, 1986.

US Marines in Vietnam - The War that Would Not End 1971-1973: Maj Charles D Melson and Lt Col Curtis G Arnold; History and Museums Division, HQ US Marine Corps, Washington, DC, 1991.

US Military Aircraft Designations and Serials Since 1909: John M Andrade; Midland Counties Publications, Earl Shilton, 1979.

Vietnam - When Will we get a Full Accounting?: Hearing before the Committee on International Relations, House of Representatives 104th Congress: First Session, 12 July 1995; USGPO, Washington, DC, 1995.

Vietnam Air War Debrief: Robert F Dorr and Chris Bishop; Aerospace Publishing, London, 1996.

Vought F-8 Crusader: Peter Mersky; Osprey Publishing, London, 1989.

The War in South Vietnam - The Years of the Offensive 1965-1968: the United States Air Force in Southeast Asia: John Schlight; Office of Air Force History, Washington, DC, 1988.

A War Too Long - The History of the USAF in Southeast Asia 1961-1975: John Schlight; Air Force History and Museums Program, Washington, DC, 1996.

Wild Weasel - The SAM Suppression Story: Larry Davis; Squadron/Signal Publications, Carrollton, Tex, 1993.

Wolfpack - Hunting MiGs Over Vietnam: Jerry Scutts; Airlife, Shrewsbury, 1987.

Periodical Articles

The 481st TFS in Vietnam - A Personal Account: Thomas E Lowe; Journal American Aviation Historical Society, Summer 1975, pages 78-88.

A-1E in SEA: Robert F Dorr; Aviation News, 24 July-6 August 1987, pages 202-203.

A-6 Intruders in Vietnam: Jesse Randall; Air Forces Monthly, September 1988, pages 35-37.

Air Commandos 1961-1966 - The Early Years: Philip D Chinnery; Wings of Fame, Volume 6, 1997, pages 104-117.

Air Rescue in Southeast Asia - Right from Hanoi's Own Backyard: Edgar Ulsamer; Air Force Magazine, October 1972, pages 30-34.

Air Rescue in Vietnam - 'That Others May Live': Harold Brown; Air Force/Space Digest, March 1967, pages 86-90.

Air War in Vietnam - The Statistical Side: Air Force/Space Digest, March 1967, pages 85.

Airpower at Khe Sanh: Walter J Boyne; Air Force Magazine, August 1998, pages 82-88.

Always with Valor: John L Frisbee; Air Force Magazine, August 1992, page 77.

American Military Airlift During the Laotian Civil War, 1958-1963: Robert L Kerby; Aerospace Historian, Spring (March) 1977, pages 1-10.

And We Remember - Frederick W Hess, Jr: Col Richard D Duckworth; Air Power History, Winter 1999, pages 64-65.

As if We Had Never Been There: Kerry S Hart; US Naval Institute Proceedings, January 1991, pages 52-56.

The Assam Dragons: Albert C Piccirillo; Journal American Aviation Historical Society, Summer 1971, pages 131-138.

The Awesome Power of Air Force Gunships: Walter J Boyne; Air Force Magazine, April 1999, pages 78-84.

Back to Hanoi: Capt Ned Shuman; US Naval Institute Proceedings, October 1992, pages 81-85.

Of Bears, Weasels, Ferrets and Eagles: Col Harold E Johnson; Air University Review, January-February 1982, pages 86-93.

The Black Ponies: Lt Cdr Daniel B Sheehan; US Naval Institute Proceedings, April 1988, pages 84-88.

Blind Bat: Sam McGowan; Air Force Magazine, July 1989, pages 82-85.

Boeing B-52s in Battle - The US Eighth Air Force's 11-day War in Vietnam: Roger A Freeman; Air Pictorial, March 1987, pages 102-108.

A Bridge Downtown: John L Frisbee; Air Force Magazine, January 1992, page 90.

The Brushfire Burns Hot - Vietnam: Air Force/Space Digest, September 1967, pages 121-130.

The C-123 Provider: Kent A Mitchell; Journal of the American Aviation Historical Society, Fall 1992, pages 162-186.

Clementine and the Big Mothers: Frank Colucci; Air Enthusiast, No 20, 1982, pages 47-56.

Combat rescue - North Vietnam: Robert F Dorr; Aviation News, 18 April-1 May 1986, pages 1224-1227.

Crosses and stripes: Wendy Alexis Peddrick; Air Force Magazine, April 1998, pages 59-65.

Destroyer: Mick Coombes; Airframe, September 1990, pages 55-61.

Did USAF Technology Fail in Vietnam? - Three Case Studies: Kenneth P Werrell; Airpower Journal, Spring 1998, pages 87-99.

A Distinguished First: John L Frisbee; Air Force Magazine, November 1990, page 103.

A Different Breed of Cats - The Air National Guard and the 1968 Reserve Mobilizations: Dr Charles J Gross; Air University Review, January-February 1983, pages 92-99.

Down in the Delta: John L Frisbee; Air Force Magazine, July 1992, page 82.

Duel Over the Dragon's Jaw: Michael O'Connor; Journal of the American Aviation Historical Society, Winter 1980, pages 273-276.

The Eagle in the Hilton: Col Jon A Reynolds; Air Force Magazine, February 1983, pages 82-85.

The Easter Halt: Walter J Boyne; Air Force Magazine, September 1998, pages 60-65.

Escape in Vietnam: Col George E Day; Air Force Magazine, September 1976, pages 84-89.

Everything That Can be Done... Combat Search and Rescue During the Vietnam War: John T Smith; Air Enthusiast, No 67, January/February 1997, pages 8-13.

FACs - Forward Air Control in Southeast Asia: Robert F Dorr; Wings of Fame, Volume 10, 1998, pages 100-115.

Fast-movers and Herbicidal Spraying in Southeast Asia: Richard D Duckworth; Air Power History, Spring 1998, pages 4-15.

First in... Wrong Way Out - A Wild Weasel Saga: Mike Gilroy; Journal of Electronic Defense, October 1999, pages 35-41, and 82.

Fishbed Hit and Run - North Vietnamese MiG-21s Versus the USAF, August 1967-February 1968: Robert L Young; Air Power History, Winter 1995, pages 57-68.

The Flight of the Blind Bat: Lt Col Richard E Hansen; Air University Review, Maj-June 1982, pages 40-47.

'Get Out, Jack! You're Burning!': Glenn B Infield; Air Force Magazine, February 1971, pages 92-95.

A Gift of Life: John L Frisbee; Air Force Magazine, August 1998, page 10.

A Good Thought to Sleep On - The Rescue of Roger Locher Did More Than Set a Couple of Vietnam War Records: John L Frisbee; Air Force Magazine, March 1992, page 79.

The Hanoi POL Strike: Col James H Kasler; Air University Review, November-December 1974, pages 19-28.

How the A-7D Rewrote the Book in SEA: John L Frisbee; Air Force Magazine, August 1973, pages 31-36.

'Huns' Over Vietnam - The F-100 Super Sabre in Southeast Asia: Robert F Dorr; Wings of Fame, Volume 3, 1996, pages 4-25.

Kaman HH-43 Huskie in Vietnam: Robert F Dorr; Aviation News, 9-22 November 1990, pages 596-599, 619.

Lance Sijan's Incredible Journey: John L Frisbee; Air Force Magazine, December 1986, page 116.

Life on Hold: Art Giberson; Vietnam Magazine, October 1994.

The Lifesavers - SEA's Air Rescuemen: Maj Carroll S Shershun; Air Force/Space Digest, June 1969, pages 39-44.

Linebacker II - A First Hand View: Charles K Hopkins; Aerospace Historian, September 1976, pages 128-135.

Linebacker II - A Pilot's Perspective: Capt Robert E Wolff; Air Force Magazine, September 1979, pages 86-91.

The Long Road to Freedom: John L Frisbee; Air Force Magazine, January 1999, page 69.

To Major Bernard F Fisher, USAF - The Medal of Honor: Laurence W Zoeller; Air Force/Space Digest, March 1967, pages 42-44.

Man on the Run: Jeffrey Ethell and Alfred Price; Air Power History, Fall 1989, pages 40-49.

Marine Aviation in Vietnam, 1962-1970: Lt Gen Keith B McCutcheon; United States Naval Institute Proceedings, May 1971, pages 123-155.

MiG-17 Over Vietnam: Dr Zoltan Buza; Wings of Fame, Volume 8, 1997, pages 100-117.

MiG-19 in the Vietnam War: Dr Zoltan Buza and Dr Istvan Toperczer; Wings of Fame, Volume 11, 1998, pages 110-113.

The MiGs' Kills: Rene J Francillon; Journal of Military Aviation, January-February 1992, pages 5-10.

Miracle at U Tapao: John L Frisbee; Air Force Magazine, August 1999, page 67.

Mission to Hanoi: Robert F Dorr; Aviation News, 29 November-12 December 1985, pages 706-708.

Mission - Troops in Contact: John L Frisbee; Air Force Magazine, October 1972, pages 35-38.

Navy Phantoms in Vietnam: Robert F Dorr; Wings of Fame, Volume 1, 1995, pages 116-139.

One Magic Moment: John L Frisbee; Air Force Magazine, June 1998, page 72.

On-scene Commander: John L Frisbee; Air Force Magazine, May 1995, page 124.

On Your Wing: Cdr John B Nichols; United States Naval Institute Proceedings, September 1994, pages 64-68.

The Other Jammer: August R Seefluth; Air Force Magazine, March 1992, pages 74-77.

Overkill: Rene J Francillon; Air Forces Monthly, September 1998, pages 39-45.

A Place Called the Doumer Bridge: John L Frisbee; Air Force Magazine, February 1988, page 100.

Rescue at a Place Called Kham Duc: Flint DuPre; Air Force Magazine, March 1969, pages 98-100.

Rescue at Ban Phanop: Capt Earl H Tilford; Air Enthusiast, No 14, pages 68-72.

Rescue Concepts Before and After: J L Butera; Aerospace Historian, March 1974, pages 8-11.

Rescue From the Gulf of Tonkin: Capt James P Coyne; Air Force Magazine, September 1972, pages 156-160.

Rescue in the Gulf of Tonkin: John L Frisbee; Air Force Magazine, August 1988, page 105.

The Rescue of Bengal 505 Alpha: Capt Dale E Stovall; Air Force Magazine, September 1974, pages 129-137.

RF-101s in Southeast Asia: Paul D Stephens; Journal American Aviation Historical Society, Winter 1969, pages 282-288.

Route Pack 6: Walter J Boyne; Air Force Magazine, November 1999, pages 56-61.

Sandy Superb: John L Frisbee; Air Force Magazine, May 1988, page 216.

Search and Rescue in Southeast Asia 1961-1975: Capt Earl H Tilford; Air University Review, January-February 1980, pages 60-74.

Search and Save!: Capt Robert L Hiett; Air Force Magazine, December 1970, pages 40-43.

The Seventh Man: John L Frisbee; Air Force Magazine, Feb 1990, page 55.

Sijan! My Name is Lance Peter Sijan!: Lt Col Fred A Meurer; Airman, June 1977.

Skoshi Tiger - The Northrop F-5 in Vietnam: Warren Thompson; Wings of Fame, Volume 5, 1996, pages 4-23.

Southeast Asia Political-military Chronology 1948-1967: Jacob Van Staaveren and Herman S Wolk; Air Force/Space Digest, March 1967, pages 137-142.

Spooky - The Story of the AC-47 Dragonship: Arthur Pearcy; Aviation News, 21 December 1979-3 January 1980, pages 4-6.

A Tale of Two Crosses - Leland Kennedy Salvaged Two Combat Rescue Attempts that Seemed Doomed to Failure: John L Frisbee; Air Force Magazine, February 1992, page 61.

Task Force 77 in Action Off Vietnam: Vice Admiral Malcolm W Cagle; United States Naval Institute Proceedings, May 1972, pages 66-109.

'That Others May Live': Lt Col Clyde Smith; US Naval Institute Proceedings, April 1996, pages 82-88.

Those Gung Ho Guardsmen in Vietnam: Lt Col W D McGlasson; Air Force/Space Digest, November 1968, pages 47-51.

'Thuds and Weasels' – The F-105 Thunderchief in SEA, 1964-1974: Larry Davis; Wings of Fame, Volume 18, 2000, pages 16-37.

Tonnage and Technology - Air Power on the Ho Chi Minh Trail: Darrel D Whitcomb; Air Power Historian, Spring 1999, pages 5-17.

Valiant Volunteer (Capt Jack Weatherby): John L Frisbee; Air Force Magazine, April 1998, page 81.

Valor in Two Dimensions: John L Frisbee; Air Force Magazine, January 1988, page 116.

The Valley of Death: John L Frisbee; Air Force Magazine, July 1998, page 39.

Veterans Day, 1967: John L Frisbee; Air Force Magazine, December 1991, page 80.

Vietnam Veterans: AC-47 'Spooky': Philip Chinnery; Flypast, September 1989, pages 36-38.

VMCJ-1 - Aerial Imagery is Available for the Asking to any Marine Corps Tactical Unit: Lt Col P A Manning; Marine Corps Gazette, October 1972, pages 40-43.

Voodoo Over Vietnam: Robert F Dorr; Aviation News, 3-16 April 1987, pages 1134-1136.

Voodoo Reconnaissance in the Vietnam War, 1966-1967: Col John Bull Stirling; Air Power History, Winter 1996, pages 15-27.

Were we Sitting Ducks?: Spence M Armstrong; Air Power History, Spring 1996, pages 54-59.

'When We'd Only Just Begun…' - An Early Rescue Attempt, 1963: Earl H Tilford; Journal American Aviation Historical Society, Fall 1977, pages 188-192.

Who Were Those Guys? - The Playboys?: Col J L Adkinson; Marine Corps Gazette, May 1986, pages 96-102.

The Wild Weasel Legacy - The Early Days: Tom Wilson; Defense Electronics, September 1988, pages 52-61.

Wild, Wild Weasel: John L Frisbee; Air Force Magazine, April 1985, page 138.

The Young Tigers and Their Friends: Walter J Boyne; Air Force Magazine, June 1998, pages 74-79.

Zoomie in Combat: Robert F Dorr; Aviation News, volume 17, no 22, 17-30 March 1989, pages 1010-1012.

Internet Sites

306th Bomb Wing Association at *http://www.306tbbw.org/*

355th TFW Honor Roll by Gene Carlson via the 355th Tactical Fighter Wing: Unofficial page of the 355th Wing at *http://www.geocities.com/Pentagon/1979/*

505th TCG: Tactical Air Control in Vietnam and Thailand, 1962-1975 at *http://www.squawk-flash.org/505th_tcg/*

A-1 Combat Journal by Byron E Hukee at *http://skyraider.org/book/*

A-1 Skyraider Association at *http://209.39.156.3/skyraider/skyassn/*

A-37 Association at *http://www.a-37.org/index.htm*

Air America Association at *http://www.air-america.org/*

Air Force Library Biographies via the Air Force News at *http://www.af.mil/news/biographies/*

All F-111 Tail Numbers via F-111.net F-111 Aardvark at *http://f-111.net/*

Arlington National Cemetery at *http://www.arlingtoncemetery.com/*

An Attack on Phan Rang by Craig Lord via Vietnam Dog Handlers Association at *http://www.vdhaonline.org/*

Autobiography of Gordon Albert Larson at *http://www.geocities.com/Pentagon/9760/swede.html*

B-57 Canberra Night Intruder at *http://home1.gte/witmark/index.htm*

B-57 Canberra, Phan Rang Air Base, '67: 13th strike by Mark Witt via Vietnam Veteran's war stories at *http://www.war-stories.com/ThirteenthStrike.htm*

B Company, 227th Assault Helicopter Battalion, 1st Air Cavalry at *http://toad.net/~n3tef/*

Batcat: The United States Air Force 553rd Reconnaissance Wing Korat Royal Thai Air Force Base and their Lockheed EC-121R Aircraft at *http://smartlink.net/~westin/batcat0.html*

Biographies on Prisoners of War and Missing in Action from the Vietnam Conflict at *http://www.asde.com/~pownet/bios.htm#top*

'Black Ponies' Web Page by AME Bob Peetz at *http://www.blackpony.org/*

Brave Jolly Green by Col Darrell D Whicomb at *http://www.thehistorynet.com/Vietnam/articles/1997/0697_text.htm*

The C-7 Caribou Association at *http://www.c-7acaribou.com/*

C-130 Hercules Headquarters at *http://.spectrumwd.com/c130/*

Defense Prisoner of War/Missing Personnel Office at *http://www.dtic.mil/dpmo/*

First Flight Across the Fence! By Berkley E Naugle via the Jolly Green Association at *http://www.jollygreen.org/Stories/BerkleyNaugle/*

Frank Vaughan's Unofficial USAF Gunship Site at *http://www.geocities.com/CapeCanaveral/8758/*

History of the Search for Capt Robert L Simpson, USAF by Eugene D Rossel via the Air Commando Association at *http://home.earthlink.net/~aircommando1/SIMPHIST.html*

Internet Home of the Mighty Bronco at *http://www.ov-10bronco.net/*

The Jack Gurner Galleries at *http://www.sky.net/~rjw/takhli/gurner*

Joe Baugher's American Military Aircraft Encyclopedia at *http://www.csd.uwo.ca/~pettypi/elevon/baugher_us/*

The Jolly Green Association at *http://www.jollygreen.org/Stories/BerkleyNaugle/*

Khe Sanh Veterans Home Page at *http://www.geocities.com/~khesanh/*

A Long, Long Night by Col Charles W Brown via the Air Commando Association at *http://home.earthlink.net/~aircommando1/cbrown.html*

Phu Cat Air Base History at *http://www.fgi.net/~rdoughty/phuhist.htm*

PJs in Vietnam: The Story of Air Rescue in Vietnam as Seen From the Eyes of its Pararescueman at *http://home.gcinet/~rlapointe/*

Profile in Courage: Remembrance Past: Capt Paul R 'Windy' Windle by Gene Rossel via the Air Commando Association at *http://home.earthlink.net/~aircommando1/windle2.html*

Spectre Association AC-130 Gunship at *http://www.spectre-association.org/spectreorg/*

The Takhli Royal Thai Air Force Base at *http://www.sky.net/~rjw/takhli/*

Tullo and the Giant by Robert A Hanson via the Airspace Magazine at *http://www.airspacemag.com/*

The U-2 Page at *http://www.blackbirds.net/u2index.html*

USAF AC-119 Gunships at *http://www.ac-119gunships.com/*

USMC/Vietnam Helicopter Association at *http://www.popasmoke.com/index.html*

Vietnam Veterans Memorial Wall Page at *http://thewall-usa.com/links/index.htm*

VMO-2 Marine Observation Two by Capt Alan H Barbour at *http://www.angelfire.com/va/cherrydeuce/*

VP-42 Crew: In Memoriam via the VP Navy home page at *http://www.vpnavy.com/vp42mem1.html*

VRC-50 Squadron History via the VRC-50 Association at *http://www.vrc-50.org/*

VSF-3 Chessmen Website via The A-4 Skyhawk Association at *http://www.skyhawk.org/*

The Willie Victor Roster at *http://personal.riverusers.com/~elmccaul*

Glossary of Operation Names, Code Names and Project Names

Able Mable
RF-101C photographic reconnaissance detachments based in Thailand and South Vietnam for operations over Laos.

Arc Light
SAC tactical B-52 operations in Southeast Asia prior to Linebacker II.

Barrel Roll
Air interdiction campaign in northern and central Laos in support of Royal Lao operations against Pathet Lao and NVA forces.

Bat Cat
EC-121R ELINT aircraft.

Bell Tone
USAF air defence detachment at Don Muang RTAB commencing 1961.

Big Eye
USAF EC-121 airborne warning and control aircraft (later called College Eye).

Black Spot
Modified C-123K with sensors and weapons for night interdiction missions over the Ho Chi Minh trail.

Blindbat
USAF C-130 flareship operations.

Blue Tree
US photo reconnaissance operations over North Vietnam.

Brown Cradle
Electronic warfare modification package for EB-66 aircraft.

Candlestick
C-123 and C-130 flareship operations.

Carolina Moon
Operation by a special C-130 detachment to bomb the Thanh Hoa bridge by using a special shaped mine in May/June 1966.

College Eye
USAF EC-121 airborne warning and control aircraft (renamed from Big Eye).

Combat Lancer
Initial deployment of the F-111A to Thailand in March 1968.

Combat Skyspot
MSQ-77 radar-controlled bombing system and missions.

Combat Talon
C-130 aircraft modified for use in Special Operations.

Combat Tree
APX-80 IFF detection system.

Commando Club
TPQ-81 and TACAN radar site at Lima Site 85 in northern Laos.

Commando Hunt
Interdiction campaigns against infiltration routes on the Ho Chi Minh Trail in Laos.

Commando Sabre
USAF F-100F fast FAC operations in high-threat areas.

Constant Guard
Deployment of tactical aircraft to Southeast Asia in 1972 as a result of the North Vietnamese Spring Invasion.

Covey
Radio call sign of FACs of the 20th TASS when operating over North Vietnam and Laos.

Crown
Airborne rescue command post.

Dixie Station
Position in South China Sea for US aircraft carrier operations over South Vietnam.

Eagle Pull
Evacuation of US and other personnel from Phnom Penh in April 1975.

Fan Song
Fire control radar for the SA-2 SAM system.

Farm Gate
Initially Detachment 2A, 4400 CCTS but subsequently applied to other early air commando units in South Vietnam.

Flaming Dart
US air raids on North Vietnam on 7 and 11 February 1965 in response to VC attacks on American bases in South Vietnam.

Freedom Train
Limited air campaign against North Vietnam starting 5 April 1972 in response to the Spring Invasion.

Frequent Wind
Evacuation of US and other personnel from Saigon, April 1975.

Giant Dragon
SAC U-2 reconnaissance operations in Southeast Asia.

Giant Scale
SR-71A reconnaissance operations in Southeast Asia.

Glowing Heat
Deployment of SR-71A to and from Kadena AB from the USA.

Green Python
RF-101C photographic reconnaissance detachment at Udorn RTAB.

Habu
Nickname for the SR-71, also used to describe SR-71A operational flights over Southeast Asia.

Hawkeye
Experimental USAF RC-47 RDF operations.

Hillsboro
USAF C-130 airborne command post operating over the Steel Tiger area.

Hilo Hattie
Experimental USAF RDF, photographic and infra-red reconnaissance operations using an HC-54.

Ho Chi Minh Trail
Network of roads, trails and tracks stretching from North Vietnam through Laos and Cambodia to South Vietnam and used for infiltration and resupply by the North Vietnamese.

Homecoming
Repatriation of US POWs from Hanoi and South Vietnam in February and March 1973.

Igloo White
Electronic surveillance system to detect movement on the Ho Chi Minh Trail in Laos.

Iron Hand
Suppression of enemy air defence operations, particularly AAA and SAMs.

Jolly Green Giant
Radio call sign and nickname for the USAF HH-3 and HH-53 SAR helicopters.

Jungle Jim
Early code name for the Air Commando's 4400th CTS based at Eglin AFB, Fla.

King
USAF HC-130P airborne rescue command post (previously Crown).

Lima Site
Temporary landing site or airstrip in Laos, used primarily by SAR forces, Ravens, Air America or Special Forces.

Linebacker I
Air campaign against North Vietnam, April to October 1972.

Linebacker II
Air campaign against North Vietnam in December 1972.

Lucky Dragon
SAC U-2 reconnaissance operations in Southeast Asia.

Market Time
USN air and surface vessel patrols along the coast of South Vietnam intended to interdict the resupply of VC units.

Misty
Radio call sign of Commando Sabre F-100F fast FAC aircraft.

Mule Train
Initial USAF C-123 detachment to South Vietnam in January 1962.

Nail
Radio call sign of FACs of the 23rd TASS operating over South Vietnam and Laos.

Niagara
USAF strike operations in support of the defence of Khe Sanh, January to March 1968.

Night Owl
Radio call sign and operations by the 8th TFW using F-4s to conduct night FAC and interdiction operations over the Ho Chi Minh Trail.

Patricia Lynn
USAF RB-57E reconnaissance aircraft and operations using advanced day and night infra-red sensors and cameras.

Pave Aegis
Refit programme of AC-130 aircraft with a 105mm howitzer.

Pave Eagle
Beech QU-22 electronic reconnaissance aircraft used to relay data collected by the Igloo White sensor system.

Pave Nail
Night observation system used by some USAF OV-10As in 1972.

Pave Pronto
AC-130A Gunship II programme.

Pave Spectre
AC-130E Gunship II programme.

Pave Way
Laser, electro-optical or infra-red guidance system for bombs.

Pedro
Radio call sign and nickname of HH-43 base rescue helicopter.

Phyllis Ann
USAF RC-47/EC-47 RDF operations.

Pierce Arrow
USN retaliatory strike against North Vietnam on 5 August 1964 following the Gulf of Tonkin Incident.

Pipe Stem
RF-101C photographic reconnaissance detachment at Tan Son Nhut in 1961.

Prairie Fire
Clandestine cross-border ground reconnaissance into Laos and North Vietnam by US Special Forces for strike control and BDA purposes (renamed from Shining Brass).

Pocket Money
Aerial mining operations against North Vietnamese harbours commencing May 1972.

Proud Deep
Protective reaction strikes against North Vietnam in December 1971 in response to build-up of SAMs near the DMZ.

Ranch Hand
USAF C-123 defoliation and herbicide unit and its operations.

Raven
USAF FAC pilots operating clandestinely in Laos.

Red Crown
Early warning and air control ship stationed in the northern Gulf of Tonkin to provide support to air operations over North Vietnam.

Rolling Thunder
US air campaign against North Vietnam between March 1965 and October 1968.

Route Packages
Numbered geographical areas of North Vietnam designated by CINCPAC to facilitate Rolling Thunder bombing operations.

Rustic
Radio call sign of FACs when operating over Cambodia.

Sandy
Radio call sign of A-1 rescue escort operations.

Senior Crown
USAF SR-71A high-altitude, high-speed reconnaissance aircraft programme.

Shadow
Radio call sign and nickname for AC-119G gunship aircraft.

Shining Brass
Clandestine cross-border ground reconnaissance into Laos and North Vietnam by US Special Forces for strike control and BDA purposes (renamed Prairie Fire).

Shufly
Early USMC helicopter detachment to South Vietnam.

Skoshi Tiger
USAF operational test and evaluation programme for the F-5 in South Vietnam.

Spad
Radio call sign and nickname for A-1 aircraft.

Spectre
Radio call sign and nickname for AC-130 gunship aircraft.

Spooky
Radio call sign and nickname for AC-47 gunship aircraft.

Steel Tiger
Designated geographic area of southern Laos and interdiction operations on the Ho Chi Minh Trail in that area.

Stinger
Radio call sign and nickname for AC-119K gunship aircraft.

Tally Ho
Air interdiction operations in Route Package I of North Vietnam.

Tiger Hound
Air interdiction operations in southeastern Laos as part of the Steel Tiger campaign.

Trojan Horse
SAC U-2 reconnaissance operations.

Tropic Moon III
B-57 fitted with LLTV and other sensors for night attacks on infiltration routes.

Water Glass
F-102 air defence detachments in South Vietnam in 1962 and 1963.

Water Pump
Detachment 6, 1st ACW deployed to Udorn to train Thai and Laotian pilots in 1964 and later applied to Detachment 1, 56th SOW at Udorn.

Wild Weasel
USAF F-100F and F-105G aircraft and operations dedicated to locating and destroying SAM sites.

Yankee Station
Position in Gulf of Tonkin for US aircraft carrier operations over North Vietnam and Laos.

Yankee Team
Early US air reconnaissance operations in northern Laos.

We hope you enjoyed this book . . .

Aerofax and Midland Publishing titles are edited and designed by an experienced and enthusiastic trans-Atlantic team of specialists.

Further titles are in preparation but we always welcome ideas from authors or readers for books they would like to see published.

In addition, our associate company, Midland Counties Publications, offers an exceptionally wide range of aviation, spaceflight, astronomy, military, naval and transport books and videos for sale by mail-order around the world.

For a copy of the appropriate catalogue, or to order further copies of this book, and any of the selected titles mentioned on this page, either write, telephone, fax, e-mail to, or order online from:

Midland Counties Publications
4 Watling Drive, Hinckley,
Leics, LE10 3EY, England

Tel: (+44) 01455 254 450
Fax: (+44) 01455 233 737
E-mail: midlandbooks@compuserve.com
www.midlandcountiessuperstore.com

US distribution by Specialty Press – see page 2.

Aerofax
MiG-21 'FISHBED'
Most widely used Supersonic Fighter

Yefim Gordon and Bill Gunston

The ubiquitous MiG-21 is unquestion-ably one of the greatest fighters of the post-Second World War era. It was Russia's first operational Mach 2-capable interceptor, and a stepping stone for many nations to enter the age of supersonic air combat. Access to the files of the MiG design bureau and other previously inaccessible sources reveal the secrets of the fighter that has flown and fought in more countries than any other supersonic jet.

Softback, 280 x 216 mm, 144 pages
335 b/w and 46 col illusts, plus colour artwork and scale plans.
1 85780 042 7 **£17.95/US $27.95**

Aerofax
BOEING KC-135
More Than Just a Tanker

Robert S Hoskins III

This book, written by a former USAF RC-135 crew commander, follows the development and service use of this globe-trotting aircraft and its many and varied tasks. Every variant, and sub-variant is charted, the histories of each and every aircraft are to be found within; details of the hundreds of units, past and present, that have flown the Stratotanker are given. This profusely illustrated work will interest those who have flown and serviced them as well as the historian and enthusiast community.

Softback, 280 x 216 mm, 224 pages
210 b/w and 46 colour photos
1 85780 069 9 **£24.95/US $39.95**

US AIR FORCE
The New Century

Bob Archer

Covers current active duty flying wings and autonomous groups, with full details of formation and changes of designation, home stations, aircraft types, years assigned, and a history of each unit with its emblem in colour.

Almost 50 aircraft types currently in service or planned for the USAF are detailed including development, unit assignments, serial batches and an explanation of the role of each variant. Bases are examined, and a list of current tail codes is presented.

Softback, 280 x 216mm, 176 pages
190 colour photos,127 unit emblems
1 85780 102 4 **£18.95/US $29.95**

List of Abbreviations

1Lt	First Lieutenant	DMZ	Demilitarized Zone
2Lt	Second Lieutenant	DPMO	Defense Prisoner of War Missing Personnel Office
A1C	Airman First Class	ECM	Electronic Counter-measures
A2C	Airman Second Class	ELINT	Electronic Intelligence
AAA	Anti-aircraft Artillery	Ens	Ensign
AB	Air Base	EWO	Electronic Warfare Officer
ABCCC	Airborne Battlefield Command and Control Centre	FAC	Forward Air Control or Controller
ABS	Air Base Squadron	FCS	Fighter Commando Squadron
ABW	Air Base Wing	FG	Fighter Group
ACCS	Airborne Command and Control Squadron	FIS	Fighter Interceptor Squadron
		FIW	Fighter Interceptor Wing
ACG	Air Commando Group	FLIR	Forward-looking Infra-red
ACS	Air Commando Squadron	FS	Fighter Squadron
ACW	Air Commando Wing	FTW	Flying Training Wing
AD	Air Division	FW	Fighter Wing
ADF	Automatic Direction Finder	GCA	Ground Controlled Approach
AEW	Airborne Early Warning	GCI	Ground Controlled Interception
AEW&C	Airborne Early Warning and Control	GRADS	Ground Radar Aerial Delivery System
AFB	Air Force Base	H&MS	Marine Headquarters and Maintenance Squadron
AFC	Air Force Cross		
ANG	Air National Guard	HC	Navy Helicopter Combat Support Squadron
ARM	Anti-radiation Missile		
ARRG	Air Rescue and Recovery Group	HU	Navy Helicopter Utility Squadron
ARRS	Air Rescue and Recovery Squadron	IFF	Identification, Friend or Foe
ARRW	Air Rescue and Recovery Wing	JATO	Jet Assisted Take Off
ARS	Air Refuelling Squadron	JCS	Joint Chiefs of Staff
ARS	Air Rescue Squadron	JPRC	Joint Personnel Recovery Center
ARVN	Army of the Republic of Vietnam	JTF	Joint Task Force
AS	Attack Squadron	JTF-FA	Joint Task Force – Full Accounting
ASW	Anti-submarine Warfare	KIA	Killed in Action
AWADS	Adverse Weather Aerial Delivery System	KWF	Killed While Flying
		LAPES	Low-altitude Parachute Extraction System
BARCAP	Barrier Combat Air Patrol		
BDA	Bomb Damage Assessment	LGB	Laser-guided Bomb
BS	Bombardment Squadron	LLTV	Low-light Level Television
BS(P)	Bombardment Squadron (Provisional)	LNRS	Limited Night Recovery System
		LORAN	Long-range Aid to Navigation
BW	Bombardment Wing	LS	Landing Site
BW(P)	Bombardment Wing (Provisional)	LSO	Landing Signal Officer
CAG	Commander Air Group	Lt	Lieutenant
CAP	Combat Air Patrol	Lt(jg)	Lieutenant (Junior Grade)
Capt	Captain	Lt Cdr	Lieutenant Commander
CBU	Cluster Bomb Units	Lt Col	Lieutenant Colonel
CCK	Ching Chuan Kang AB	LZ	Landing Zone
CCTS	Combat Crew Training Squadron	MAC	Military Airlift Command
CCTW	Combat Crew Training Wing	MACVSOG	Military Assistance Command Vietnam, Studies and Observations Group
Cdr	Commander		
CDS	Container Delivery System		
CIA	Central Intelligence Agency	MAG	Marine Aircraft Group
CILH	Central Identification Laboratory in Hawaii	MATS	Military Air Transport Service
		MAW	Marine Aircraft Wing
CINCPAC	Commander-in-Chief Pacific	MCAS	Marine Corps Air Station
CMSgt	Chief Master Sergeant	MIA	Missing in Action
CO	Commanding Officer	MiGCAP	MiG Combat Air Patrol
COD	Carrier On-board Delivery	MSgt	Master Sergeant
Col	Colonel	MTU	Marine Task Unit
CSG	Combat Support Group	NAS	Naval Air Station
CVSG	Anti-submarine Carrier Air Group	NFO	Naval Flight Officer (navigator)
CVW	Carrier Air Wing	NKP	Nakhon Phanom RTAB
Det	Detachment	NORAD	North American Air Defense Command
DFC	Distinguished Flying Cross		

NVA	North Vietnamese Army	TSgt	Technical Sergeant
OG	Operations Group	USAAC	United States Army Air Corps
OL	Operating Location	USAAF	United States Army Air Force
PACAF	Pacific Air Force	USAF	United States Air Force
PCS	Permanent Change of Station	USAFE	United States Air Force in Europe
PJ	Pararescue Jumper	USMC	United States Marine Corps
POL	Petroleum, Oil, and Lubricants	USN	United States Navy
POW	Prisoner of War	USS	United States Ship
RAF	Royal Air Force	VA	Navy Attack Squadron
RDF	Radio Direction Finding	VAL	Navy Light Attack Squadron
RESCAP	Rescue Combat Air Patrol	VC	Viet Cong
RHAW	Radar Homing and Warning	VF	Navy Fighter Squadron
RS	Reconnaissance Squadron	VFP	Navy Light Photographic Squadron
RTAB	Royal Thai Air Base	VFR	Visual Flight Rules
RVAH	Navy Heavy Reconnaissance Attack Squadron	VMA	Marine Attack Squadron
		VMA(AW)	Marine All-weather Attack Squadron
RW	Reconnaissance Wing	VMCJ	Marine Composite Reconnaissance Squadron
SAC	Strategic Air Command		
SAM	Surface-to-air Missile	VMF(AW)	Marine All-weather Fighter Squadron
SAR	Search and Rescue		
SATS	Short Airfield for Tactical Support	VMFA	Marine Fighter Attack Squadron
SEA	Southeast Asia	VMGR	Marine Aerial Refueller Transport Squadron
SEAL	Sea, Air, Land (commando)		
SEATO	Southeast Asia Treaty Organisation	VMO	Marine Observation Squadron
SFC	Sergeant First Class (Army)	VNAF	Vietnamese Air Force (S Vietnam)
Sgt	Sergeant	VP	Navy Patrol Squadron
SIGINT	Signals Intelligence	VPAF	Vietnamese People's Air Force (North Vietnam)
SMSgt	Senior Master Sergeant		
SOS	Special Operations Squadron	VQ	Navy Fleet Air Reconnaissance Squadron
SOW	Special Operations Wing		
SRS	Strategic Reconnaissance Squadron	VR	Navy Fleet Logistics Support Squadron
SRW	Strategic Reconnaissance Wing		
SSgt	Staff Sergeant	VRC	Navy Tactical Support Squadron
STOL	Short Take Off and Landing	VSF	Navy Anti-submarine Fighter Squadron
SW	Strategic Wing		
TAC	Tactical Air Command	VW	Navy Fleet Early Warning Squadron
TAC(A)	Tactical Air Controller (Airborne)	WO1	Warrant Officer 1st Class
TACG	Tactical Air Control Group	WSO	Weapons Systems Officer (navigator)
TARCAP	Target Combat Air Patrol	WWS	Wild Weasel Squadron
TAS	Tactical Airlift Squadron		
TASG	Tactical Air Support Group		
TASS	Tactical Air Support Squadron		
TAW	Tactical Airlift Wing		
TBG	Tactical Bombardment Group		
TBS	Tactical Bombardment Squadron		
TCG	Troop Carrier Group or Tactical Control Group		
TCS	Troop Carrier Squadron		
TCW	Troop Carrier Wing or Tactical Control Wing		
TDY	Temporary Duty		
TEWS	Tactical Electronic Warfare Squadron		
TF	Task Force		
TFR	Terrain-following Radar		
TFG	Tactical Fighter Group		
TFS	Tactical Fighter Squadron		
TFW	Tactical Fighter Wing		
TG	Tactical Group		
TRIM	Trails, Roads, Interdiction Multisensor		
TRS	Tactical Reconnaissance Squadron		
TRW	Tactical Reconnaissance Wing		